BOOKS BY CLAY BLAIR

NONFICTION

The Atomic Submarine and Admiral Rickover
The Hydrogen Bomb, with James R. Shepley
Beyond Courage
Valley of the Shadow, for Ward M. Millar
Nautilus 90 North, with William R. Anderson
Diving for Pleasure and Treasure
Always Another Dawn, with A. Scott Crossfield
The Voyage of Nina II, for Robert Marx
The Strange Case of James Earl Ray
Survive!
Silent Victory: The U.S. Submarine War Against Japan
The Search for JFK, with Joan Blair
MacArthur
Combat Patrol
Return From the River Kwai, with Joan Blair
A General's Life, with Omar N. Bradley
Ridgway's Paratroopers
The Forgotten War: America in Korea 1950–1953

FICTION

The Board Room
The Archbishop
Pentagon Country
Scuba!, with Joan Blair
Mission Tokyo Bay, with Joan Blair
Swordray's First Three Patrols, with Joan Blair

HITLER'S
U-BOAT WAR

HITLER'S U-BOAT WAR

THE HUNTERS

1939–1942

★

CLAY BLAIR

RANDOM HOUSE
NEW YORK

Library of Congress Cataloging-in-Publication Data

Blair, Clay.
    Hitler's U-boat war / Clay Blair.
        p. cm.
   Includes index.
   Contents: v. 1. The hunters, 1939–1942.
    ISBN 0-394-58839-8
    1. World War, 1939–1945—Naval operations—Submarine. 2. World War, 1939–1945—Naval operations, German. I. Title.
D781.B53   1996
940.54'51—dc20   96-2275

2   4   6   8   9   7   5   3

First Edition

This book is dedicated to the late Time-Life Washington bureau chief James R. (Jim) Shepley, founding father of the "Shepley School of Journalism," which in 1950–1951 had one student (me); to the peerless book editor, Marc Jaffe, who first suggested and sponsored my pursuit of serious history; to my agents, Jack Scovil and Russ Galen, who found the wherewithal; and to my wife, Joan, my collaborator in the fullest sense of the word on this book, as on many others.

FOREWORD

On a chilly day in the late fall of 1945, our submarine, the U.S.S. *Guardfish,* proudly flying battle pennants, nosed into the Submarine Base, New London, Connecticut, joining scores of mass-produced sister ships, all "home from the sea."

Collectively we submariners were known as the "Silent Service," and proud we were of that distinction. Unknown to the public, we had played a decisive role in the defeat of Japan. In forty-two months of secret warfare in the Pacific Ocean area, 250 of our submarines, mounting 1,682 war patrols, had savaged Japanese maritime assets, sinking 1,314 ships of 5.3 million gross tons, including twenty major warships: eight aircraft carriers, a battleship, and eleven cruisers. For almost three years *Guardfish,* a fine boat, had played a prominent role in that war, sending nineteen confirmed ships to the bottom (including two fleet destroyers and a patrol boat) during twelve long and arduous war patrols in Japanese-controlled waters.

After we had moored at a pier where we were to "mothball" *Guardfish,* we were startled to see a strangely different submarine close by. Painted jet black, she looked exceptionally sleek and sinister. We soon learned that she was a German U-boat that had surrendered shortly after VE-Day. She was manned by an American crew that was evaluating her on behalf of naval authorities in Washington.

This U-boat was very hush-hush and off-limits to ordinary souls. However, when she shifted her berth to "our" pier (and nicked us in the process), we became friendly with the American crew and gradually talked our way on board for a look-see. We learned that she was *U-2513,* a brand new Type XXI "electro boat," one of two such craft allotted to the U.S. Navy as war prizes. Commissioned and commanded by one of Germany's most famous U-boat "aces," Erich Topp, she and her mass-produced sister ships had been completed too late to participate in the war.

In our superficial examination of *U-2513,* we were quite impressed with some of her features, especially her top speed submerged. She had six sets of storage batteries, comprising a total of 372 cells (hence "electro boat"), which enabled her to quietly sprint submerged at about 16 knots for about one hour. This was twice the sprint speed of our submarines and sufficient to escape from almost any existing antisubmarine warship. Alternately, the large battery capacity enabled her to cruise submerged at slower speeds for a great many hours, whether stalking prey or escaping.

The next most impressive feature to us was her *Schnorchel,* or as we anglicized the German, snorkel. This was a sophisticated "breathing tube" or mast with air intake and exhaust ducts, which enabled *U-2513* to run her two diesel engines while submerged. By rigging one diesel (or both) to charge the batteries while submerged, she could in theory remain underwater for prolonged periods, thereby greatly diminishing the chances of detection by enemy eyes or radar.

Nor was that all. Her periscope optics and passive sonar for underwater looking and listening were much superior to ours. Her ingenious hydraulically operated torpedo-handling gear could automatically reload her six bow torpedo tubes in merely five minutes. A third reload could be accomplished in another twenty minutes. The thickness and strength of her pressure hull was said to give her a safe diving depth limit of about 1,200 feet, twice our safe depth limit and sufficient to get well beneath most existing Allied depth charges. She even had an "automatic pilot" for precise depth-keeping at high speeds.

Much later, when some of these details and others about the Type XXI "electro boat" leaked out, they caused an utter sensation in naval circles. Prominent experts gushed that the Type XXI represented a giant leap in submarine technology, bringing mankind very close to a "true submersible." Some naval historians asserted that if the Germans had produced the Type XXI submarine one year earlier they almost certainly could have won the "Battle of the Atlantic" and thereby indefinitely delayed Overlord, the Allied invasion of Occupied France.

The American evaluators on *U-2513* were not so sure about these claims. In the classified report they sent to the Chief of Naval Operations, dated July 1946, they wrote that while the Type XXI had many desirable features that should be exploited (big battery, snorkel, streamlining, etc.), it also had many grave design and manufacturing faults. The clear implication was that owing to these faults, the XXI could not have made a big difference in the Battle of the Atlantic. Among the major faults the Americans enumerated:

•   **POOR STRUCTURAL INTEGRITY.**   Hurriedly prefabricated in thirty-two different factories that had little or no experience in submarine building, the eight major hull sections of the Type XXI were crudely made and did not fit together properly. Therefore the pressure hull was weak and not capable of withstanding sea pressure at great depths or the explosions of close depth charges. The Germans reported that in their structural tests the hull failed at a simulated depth of 900 feet. The British reported failure at 800 feet, less than the failure depth of the conventional German U-boats.

- **UNDERPOWERED DIESEL ENGINES.** The new model, six-cylinder diesels were fitted with superchargers to generate the required horsepower. The system was so poorly designed and manufactured that the superchargers could not be used. This failure reduced the generated horsepower by almost half: from 2,000 to 1,200, leaving the Type XXI ruinously underpowered. Consequently, the maximum surface speed was only 15.6 knots, less than any oceangoing U-boat built during the war and slightly slower than the corvette convoy-escort vessel. The reduction in horsepower also substantially increased the time required to carry out a full battery charge.

- **IMPRACTICAL HYDRAULIC SYSTEM.** The main lines, accumulators, cylinders, and pistons of the hydraulic gear for operating the diving planes, rudders, torpedo tube outer doors, and antiaircraft gun turrets on the bridge were too complex and delicate and located *outside* the pressure hull. This gear was therefore subject to saltwater leakage, corrosion, and enemy weaponry. It could not be repaired from inside the pressure hull.

- **IMPERFECT AND HAZARDOUS SNORKEL.** Even in moderate seas the mast dunked often, automatically closing the air intake and exhaust ports. Even so, salt water poured into the ship's bilges and had to be discharged overboard continuously with noisy pumps. Moreover, during these shutdowns, the diesels dangerously sucked air from inside the boat and deadly exhaust gas (carbon monoxide) backed up, causing not only headaches and eye discomfort but also serious respiratory illnesses. Snorkeling in the Type XXI was therefore a nightmarish experience, to be minimized to the greatest extent possible.

The U.S. Navy did in fact adopt some of the features of the Type XXI "electro boat" for its new submarine designs in the immediate postwar years. However, by that time the Navy was firmly committed to the development of a nuclear-powered submarine, a "true submersible" that did not depend on batteries or snorkels for propulsion and concealment. These marvels of science and engineering, which came along in the 1950s, 1960s, and later, were so technically sophisticated as to render the best ideas of German submarine technology hopelessly archaic and to assure the United States of a commanding lead in this field well into the next century.

This little story about the Type XXI "electro boat" is a perfect example of a curious naval mythology that has arisen in this century. The myth goes something like this: The Germans invented the submarine (or U-boat) and have consistently built the best submarines in the world. Endowed with a canny gift for exploiting this marvelously complex and lethal weapon system, valorous (or, alternately, murderous) German submariners dominated the seas in both world wars and very nearly defeated the Allies in each case. In a perceptive study,* Canadian naval historian Michael L. Hadley writes: "During both wars and during the inter-war years as well, the U-boat was mythologized more than any other weapon of war."

The myth assumed an especially formidable aspect in World War II and after-

---

* *Count Not the Dead: The Popular Image of the German Submarine* (1995).

wards. During the war, the well-oiled propaganda machinery of the Third Reich glorified and exaggerated the "successes" of German submariners to a fare-thee-well in the various Axis media. At the same time, Allied propagandists found it advantageous to exaggerate the peril of the U-boats for various reasons. The end result was a wildly distorted picture of the so-called Battle of the Atlantic.

After the war, Washington, London, and Ottawa clamped a tight embargo on the captured German U-boat records to conceal the secrets of codebreaking, which had played an important role in the Battle of the Atlantic. As a result, the first "histories" of the U-boat war were produced by Third Reich propagandists such as Wolfgang Frank, Hans Jochem Brennecke, and Harald Busch, and by Karl Dönitz, wartime commander of the U-boat force, later commander of the *Kriegsmarine,* and, finally, Hitler's successor as *Führer* of the Third Reich. These "histories," of course, did nothing to diminish the mythology. Hampered by the security embargo on the U-boat and codebreaking records and by an apparent unfamiliarity with the technology and the tactical limitations of submarines, the official and semiofficial Allied naval historians, Stephen Wentworth Roskill and Samuel Eliot Morison, were unable or unwilling to write authoritatively about German U-boats in the Battle of the Atlantic. Hence for decade after decade no complete and reliable history of the Battle of the Atlantic appeared, and the German mythology prevailed.

My wartime service on *Guardfish* kindled a deep and abiding interest in submarine warfare. As a Washington-based journalist with *Time, Life,* and the *Saturday Evening Post,* I kept abreast of American submarine developments during the postwar years, riding the new boats at sea, compiling accounts of the noteworthy advancements—and politics—in articles and books.* In 1975 I published a work of love, *Silent Victory: The U.S. Submarine War Against Japan,* the first, full, uncensored history of the "Silent Service" in that very secret war.

The publication of *Silent Victory* triggered suggestions that I undertake a similar history of the German U-boat war. However, owing to the embargo on the U-boat and codebreaking records, still in force after thirty years, this was not possible at that time, but the idea took root. While I was engaged in other military histories over the next dozen years, Washington, London, and Ottawa gradually released the U-boat and codebreaking records. During the same period German naval scholars, notably Jürgen Rohwer, mined the German U-boat records and produced quite valuable and objective technical studies and accounts of some combat actions and related matters.

By 1987 I was able to undertake a U-boat history. Happily, Random House shared my enthusiasm for the project and provided the necessary financial resources. My wife, Joan, and I camped in Washington, London, and Germany for many months, culling and copying tens of thousands of pages of documents and microfilms at various military archives and collecting published works on the Battle of the Atlantic and codebreaking. While in Germany we made contact with the U-boat veterans association and interviewed former U-boat force commanders, skippers, and crewmen. Subsequently we kept abreast of the spate of scholarly and

---

* *The Atomic Submarine and Admiral Rickover* (1954), *Nautilus 90 North* (1958), etc.

popular U-boat books and articles about phases or aspects of the war that appeared in the late 1980s and 1990s, much of it first-rate.*

The result of this research is this new and complete history, which, owing to its length, is published in two volumes. I view the U-boat war quite differently from other historians and popular writers. As I see it, there were three separate and distinct phases: the U-boat war against the British Empire, the U-boat war against the Americas, and the U-boat war against both the British Empire and the Americas. Together with an introductory section, "Background for War," the first two phases of the war are dealt with in this volume, *The Hunters;* the third phase in Volume II, *The Hunted.* Each volume contains appropriate maps, photos, plates, appendices, and an index.

As the reader has doubtless concluded, my assessment of the U-boat peril—and war—is also quite different from that of most other historians and popular writers. In a word, the U-boat peril in World War II was and has been vastly overblown: threat inflation on a classically grand scale. The Germans were not supermen; the U-boats and torpedoes were not technical marvels but rather inferior craft and weapons unsuited for the Battle of the Atlantic. In contrast to the strategic success of our submarine force versus Japan, the German force failed versus the Allies in the Atlantic. The main contribution the U-boat force made in the war was to present a terror weapon, a sort of "threat in being," which forced the Allies to convoy, delaying the arrival of goods and supplies, and to deploy extensive anti-submarine counterforces. The myths notwithstanding, only a tiny percentage of Allied merchant ships actually fell victim to U-boats. Ninety-nine percent of all Allied merchant ships in the transatlantic convoys reached assigned destinations.

This is not to say that the Battle of the Atlantic was a cakewalk for the Allies, or for that matter, an easy threat for the Germans to mount. On the contrary, it was a bitter, painful struggle for both sides, the most prolonged and arduous naval campaign in all history. It deserves a history by one familiar with submarines of that era, with access to all the official records, uninfluenced by propaganda and stripped of mythology.

CLAY BLAIR

Washington, D.C., London, Hamburg, and
Washington Island, Wisconsin
1987–1996

---

* For a list of all sources, see Bibliography.

CONTENTS

THREE

FOUR

FIVE

SIX

BOOK TWO

THE U-BOAT WAR AGAINST THE AMERICAS
DECEMBER 1941–AUGUST 1942

SEVEN

LIST OF MAPS

Faeroes

Norwegian
Sea

Shetlands

ATLANTIC
OCEAN

Orkneys
Scapa Flow

Hebrides

The Minches

Loch Ewe
Cromarty Firth
Moray Firth

Firth of Forth

Glasgow

North Sea

Londonderry

North Channel

Firth of Clyde

NORTHERN
IRELAND

Barrow-
in-Furness

Hartlepool

Irish Sea

Galway
Bay

Liverpool

IRELAND

St. George's Channel

GREAT
BRITAIN

Lowes

Harwich

Milford
Haven

London

Bristol Channel

Folkestone
Dover

Lands End

Portsmouth

Calais

Scillies

Plymouth

Portland

English Channel

Dieppe

FRANCE

The British Isles and Northern Germany

0   100   200   300   400

NAUTICAL MILES

Gulf of Bothnia

NORWAY

en

Oslo

Stockholm

Horten

anger

Christiansand

Skagerrak

Kattegat

SWEDEN

Baltic Sea

Copenhagen

DENMARK

Gdynia

Danzig

Kiel

Helgoland

Kiel Canal

Brunsbüttel

Hamburg

Wilhelmshaven

Bremen

Berlin

POLAND

ETHER-
LANDS

GERMANY

IUM

CZECHO-
SLOVAKIA

LUX.

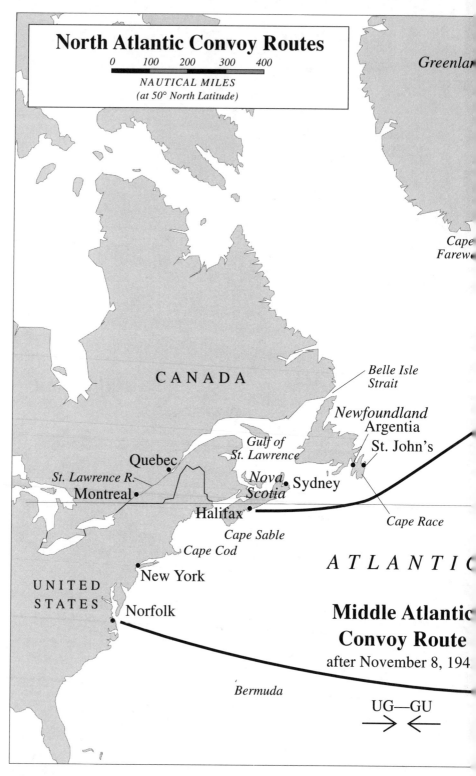

North Atlantic Convoy Routes

0   100   200   300   400

NAUTICAL MILES
(at 50° North Latitude)

Greenla

Cape
Farew

CANADA

Belle Isle
Strait

Newfoundland
Argentia
St. John's

Gulf of
St. Lawrence

Quebec

Nova
Scotia Sydney

St. Lawrence R.
Montreal

Halifax

Cape Race

Cape Sable

Cape Cod

ATLANTIC

New York

UNITED
STATES

Norfolk

Middle Atlantic
Convoy Route

after November 8, 194

Bermuda

UG—GU
→ ←

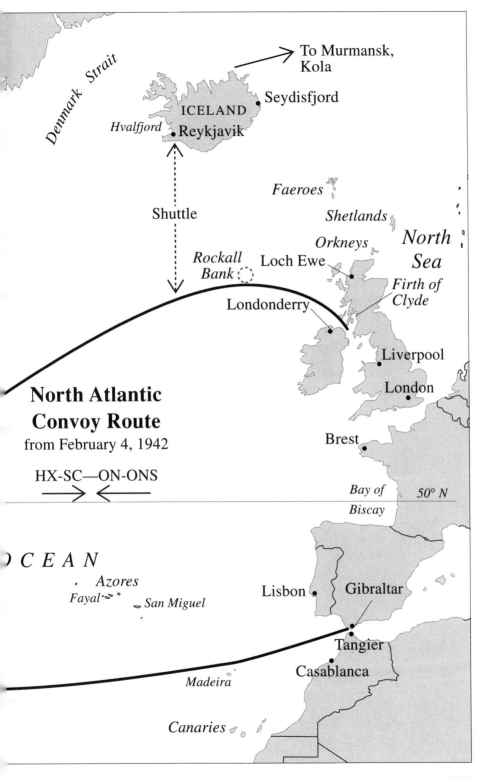

Denmark Strait

To Murmansk, Kola

ICELAND

Seydisfjord

Hvalfjord Reykjavik

Faeroes

Shuttle

Shetlands

Orkneys

North Sea

Rockall Bank Loch Ewe

Firth of Clyde

Londonderry

Liverpool

London

North Atlantic Convoy Route

from February 4, 1942

Brest

HX-SC—ON-ONS

→→ ←—

Bay of Biscay

50° N

O C E A N

Azores

Fayal *San Miguel*

Lisbon

Gibraltar

Tangier

Casablanca

Madeira

Canaries

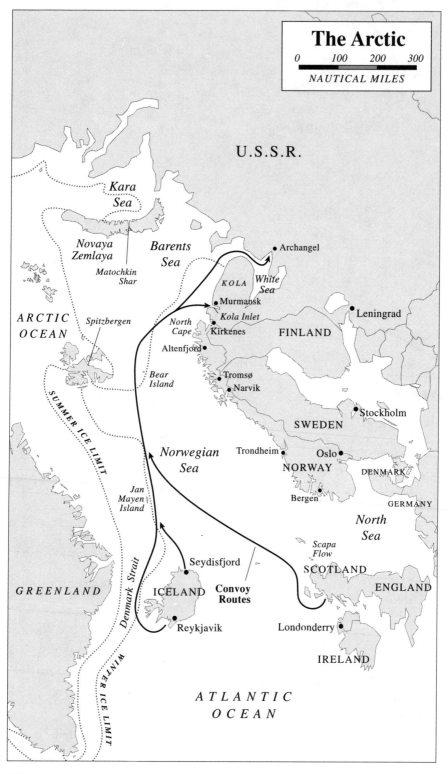

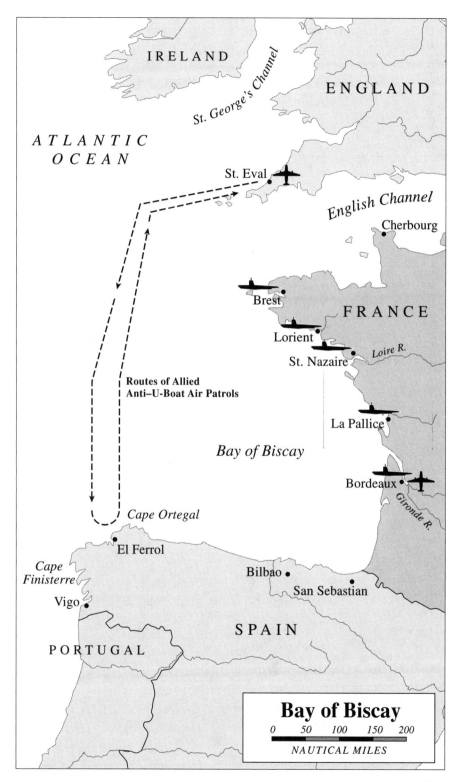

IRELAND

ENGLAND

ATLANTIC OCEAN

St. George's Channel

St. Eval

English Channel

Cherbourg

Brest

FRANCE

Lorient

St. Nazaire

Loire R.

**Routes of Allied
Anti–U-Boat Air Patrols**

La Pallice

Bay of Biscay

Bordeaux

Gironde R.

Cape Ortegal

El Ferrol

*Cape
Finisterre*

Bilbao

Vigo

San Sebastian

SPAIN

PORTUGAL

Bay of Biscay

0   50   100   150   200

NAUTICAL MILES

IRELAND

GREAT
BRITAIN

DENMA

GERMA

FRANCE

La Spezia Po

Marseilles

Toulon

PORTUGAL

SPAIN

Corsica

Rome

Sardinia

I T

Si

Gibraltar

Tangier

SP. MOROCCO

Oran

Algiers

Tunis

MOROCCO

TUNISIA

ALGERIA

Tri

The Mediterranean

0   100   200   300   400

NAUTICAL MILES

POLAND

SOVIET UNION

ECHOSLOVAKIA

HUNGARY

ROMANIA

YUGOSLAVIA

BULGARIA

ALBANIA

les

TURKEY

GREECE

Athens

Salamis

CYPRUS

SYRIA

Crete

Beirut

Haifa

LTA

PALESTINE

Mediterranean Sea

Port Said

Benghazi

Tobruk

Alexandria

El Alamein

LIBYA

EGYPT

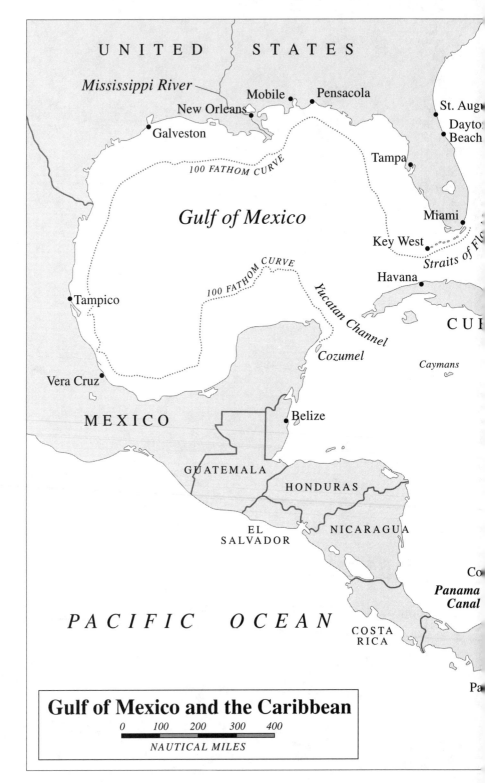

Gulf of Mexico and the Caribbean

NAUTICAL MILES

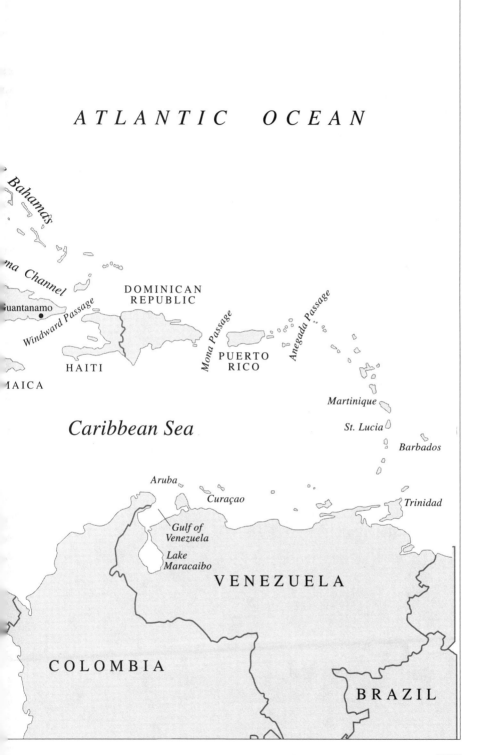

ATLANTIC OCEAN

Bahamas

na Channel

Guantanamo

Windward Passage

DOMINICAN
REPUBLIC

Mona Passage

Anegada Passage

HAITI

PUERTO
RICO

JAICA

Martinique

St. Lucia

Caribbean Sea

Barbados

Aruba

Curaçao

Trinidad

Gulf of
Venezuela

Lake
Maracaibo

VENEZUELA

COLOMBIA

BRAZIL

United States East Coast

0   100   200   300

NAUTICAL MILES

CANADA

CANADA

Portland •
Casco Bay

Halifax •

Boston •

Cape Cod

UNITED STATES

Long Island

Philadelphia •

New York •

Washington, D.C. •

Delaware Bay

Chesapeake Bay

Norfolk •

Bermuda ⟶

Cape Hatteras

Cape Lookout

Cape Fear

100 FATHOM CURVE

Charleston •

Savannah •

ATLANTIC

OCEAN

Jacksonville •

Miami •

The Bahamas

LIST OF PLATES

Cutaway illustrations of Type VIIC and Type IXC U-boats appear on pages 60 and 61.

HITLER'S
U-BOAT WAR

PROLOGUE

BACKGROUND
FOR WAR

Early Developments

For centuries, militarists recognized that a submarine's invisibility provided it with two distinct advantages: surprise in the attack and the ability to withdraw with impunity. From earliest recorded times, inventors attempted to build combatant submarines. They mastered watertightness and ballasting but could not devise a practical means for propelling the submerged submarine in a controlled direction in the face of tides and currents.

The development of an efficient coal-fired steam engine in the 1800s offered a possible solution to submerged propulsion. Steam could be "stored" under pressure for a limited time. Inventors designed submarines that were to travel on the surface to the combat zone powered by steam engines, then submerge for the attack and withdrawal, powered by stored steam. But steam-powered submarines proved to be less than satisfactory. The engines generated nearly unbearable heat inside the small hulls. The furnaces emitted sooty exhaust that could be seen for miles at sea, robbing the submarine of stealth, one of its chief assets. Moreover, the smokestack had to be disassembled and stored before diving, a cumbersome and time-consuming procedure.

Far better solutions to submerged propulsion became apparent about 1880 with the nearly simultaneous development of the internal combustion engine, the electric motor, and the storage battery. Most inventors designed submarines that were to be powered by gasoline engines on the surface and battery-driven motors while submerged. Others designed submarines powered entirely by battery-driven motors. Still others, combining old and new technology, designed submarines powered by steam engines for surface travel and battery-driven motors for submerged travel. All early versions had drawbacks: Gasoline engines were difficult to start and unreliable in operation, and emitted dangerous fumes. Batteries were bulky, heavy, and weak. Steam engines still generated too much heat.

These propulsion experiments gave promise of a practical submarine. But a breakthrough in weaponry was also needed. The existing weaponry was limited and hazardous: time-fused mines (or bombs), which had to be screwed to the bottom of enemy ships, or spar-mounted contact mines, which had to be rammed against the side of the enemy ship. Both weapons required close—near suicidal—contact with the enemy.

The solution to the weaponry was provided by an English engineer, Robert Whitehead, who lived in Fiume, Austria. In about 1866 he introduced what military historians today would describe as a "stand-off weapon": an automotive or self-propelled mine or torpedo. The Whitehead torpedo was powered by compressed air stored in a large flask. When released, the air turned pistons, which spun a propeller. The first model was primitive: fourteen feet long and fourteen inches in diameter, weighing about 300 pounds. It had a range of 700 yards at 6 knots. The experimental "warhead" in the nose, which was set off by a contact "pistol" when it hit the side of a ship, was puny: eighteen pounds of dynamite. But it worked.

The Whitehead torpedo did not create an immediate sensation in naval circles. But Whitehead soon increased its size, power, range, and the lethality of the warhead. An Austrian, Ludwig Obry, adapted the gyroscope to the torpedo, giving it directional control. With each improvement, naval authorities paid greater interest. Before long the idea took root that Whitehead torpedoes, fired from cheap, small, speedy vessels, might be employed effectively to attack expensive big ships of the line. In due course this concept evolved into the torpedo boat, then into the torpedo-firing destroyer, which were embraced first by weaker naval powers and ultimately by all navies.

The Whitehead torpedo had not been envisioned as a submarine weapon, but by happenstance it was just what submarine proponents had been looking for. With its ability to sneak up on the quarry submerged, unseen and undetected, shoot, then retire submerged with relative impunity, the submarine could be a superior torpedo launcher to the torpedo boat or destroyer.

Soon all submarine designers were recasting plans to incorporate the Whitehead torpedo. This breakthrough stimulated considerable interest among the weaker naval powers, but introduced new levels of complexity. The weapon system required a torpedo tube in the bow of the submarine's pressure hull and a compressed air system for "charging" the torpedo and for booting it from the tube. The tube had to have interlocking inner and outer doors that could be flooded for firing and drained for reloading a second or third projectile. Since the latest torpedoes were very heavy—and getting heavier as the warhead increased in size and lethality—a compensating ballast system had to be devised to offset the sudden loss of weight upon firing and the shifting about of reloads. Otherwise the delicately balanced submarine would go out of control, popping to the surface or plunging to the bottom.

Submarines employed compressed air for blowing main ballast tanks and for other purposes, stored in steel bottles under very high pressure. The incorporation of gasoline and steam engines and battery-powered motors provided the submarine with a power source to operate onboard air compressors. Hence submariners had the equipment and know-how for providing the considerable compressed air required for charging the torpedo flasks and for ejecting the torpedo from the tube.

These technological breakthroughs launched a submarine arms race. By 1890 torpedo-firing submarines utilizing a variety of propulsion systems (all steam; all electric; steam-electric; gas-electric) were under construction worldwide. The stronger naval powers—Great Britain, Germany, the United States—showed little interest in the submarine, but the weaker naval powers—France, Russia, others—embraced it with a passion. Unwilling to compete in the Anglo-German naval race, France became the first nation in the world to place substantial state resources behind submarine development. By 1906 the French navy had nearly ninety submarines in commission or under construction.

Of the submarine designers, an Irish immigrant to the United States, John P. Holland, was the most inventive and able. His boat, *Holland,* equipped to fire the Whitehead torpedo, was the engineering marvel of the 1890s, superior to all submarines in the world. For surface operations she employed a four-cylinder, 160-horsepower gasoline engine, which gave her a cruising speed of $7\frac{1}{2}$ knots. For submerged cruising she had a sixty-cell battery, supplying electrical power to a 70-horsepower motor, which gave her a top speed of about $6\frac{1}{2}$ knots for about three hours and twice that endurance at slower speed. The propulsion system was versatile and flexible. The gasoline engine could be used for surface propulsion, for turning a generator to charge batteries, or for operating the air compressor. The electric motor could be used for either surface or submerged propulsion or for starting the balky gasoline engine. The battery also supplied power for the many smaller motors throughout the boat (periscope hoist, bilge pump, trim, tank pumps, etc.) and for internal lighting.

Holland founded the Electric Boat Company in New London, Connecticut, and sold submarines to any and all comers. The U.S. Navy was his first customer. In 1900 it bought the prototype *Holland* and christened it U.S.S. *Holland* (Submarine Number 1). After rigid trials, the navy bought six more *Holland*s for "coastal defense purposes" and later, a dozen more improved models. Alarmed by France's large—and swelling—submarine force, Great Britain's Royal Navy bought five *Holland*s in 1901 for evaluation purposes. Astonished by the efficient performance of these little craft, the British embarked on a substantial submarine buildup in 1905. That same year Holland sold submarines to the belligerents Russia and Japan, producing the seeds for the submarine forces of both those nations.

The gas-electric boat was superior to all others, but it was dangerous. Notwithstanding all efforts to prevent it, gasoline seeped into bilges, emitting explosive fumes. Deadly carbon monoxide leaked from the exhaust pipes. Several gas-electric boats in the United States and British navies blew up; some crewmen were killed by exhaust fumes. These continuing dangers led submarine designers to explore two less volatile and toxic internal combustion fuels: paraffin (akin to kerosene) and "heavy" or "diesel" oil, named for the German inventor Rudolph Diesel, who in 1895 had demonstrated the first "heavy oil" or, as it came to be known, diesel engine.

Engineers in Germany slowly brought the paraffin and diesel engines forward. Owing to the difficulty of producing a reliable diesel engine that was compact and light enough to fit inside a submarine hull, the paraffin engine led by several years. The German arms conglomerate, Krupp A.G., was first to build a paraffin submarine—a tiny prototype, christened *Forelle* (*Trout*), which was launched in 1902. German industry was then in good position to exploit submarine technology but it made little headway. The reason was the unyielding opposition of Grand Admiral Alfred von Tirpitz, State Secretary of the Navy. He had persuaded Kaiser Wilhelm II to embark on a massive big-ship building program, designed to outgun the big but aging Royal Navy. Singlemindedly pursuing this ambitious undertaking, von Tirpitz refused funds for unrelated, experimental, unproven weapons and discouraged all discussions of "cheap" alternatives to his big-ship navy, such as submarines.

Sensing a new and profitable market, the Krupp firm pursued the submarine in spite of von Tirpitz's indifference. In 1904 Krupp sold the Russians the paraffin *Forelle* and then obtained orders for three larger paraffin boats, known as the *Karp* class. In subsequent years it negotiated sales agreements with numerous nations (Italy, Austria-Hungary, Norway) for larger, more sophisticated paraffin boats. At the same time Krupp mounted intense pressure on German engineers to bring the diesel engine to a practical stage for submarines.

Although the staff of the German Imperial Navy concurred with von Tirpitz's big-ship program, it fretted about the submarine arms race, which was being fueled in part by German industry. It seemed imprudent to export this important military technology, which, in the wrong hands, could cause the big-ship Imperial Navy immense grief. At the least, the staff argued, the Imperial Navy should acquire a submarine for evaluation. Yielding to these pressures, von Tirpitz finally authorized Krupp to build one submarine, or *Unterseeboot* (abbreviated as *U-boot,* or in English, U-boat). What emerged was a slightly larger and improved copy of the paraffin-powered *Karp* class, designated *U-1.* Upon her commissioning in December 1906, it was noted that Germany was not the first but rather the last major naval power to adopt submarines, and these were indebted to American technology.

Having introduced the paraffin engine and other innovations, including superb periscope optics, Krupp submarine engineers were determined to further outdo submarines of competing naval powers. Over the next several years they proposed ever larger, longer-ranged, faster, better-armed models. Still not fully persuaded that the submarine had a place in the Imperial Navy, von Tirpitz only grudgingly released funds for new construction, and in their efforts to move ahead quickly, the engineers encountered many technical setbacks. As a result, the embryonic German submarine force grew haltingly.

The German designers, meanwhile, had been pressing ahead with grander ideas. The ambitious goal was to produce, in a single, catch-up leap, a reliable oceangoing paraffin boat about 185 feet long and with a displacement of about 500 tons. It was to be armed with four torpedo tubes (two forward, two aft), with storage space for one reload in each torpedo compartment. The designers succeeded, producing several such submarines. In the years 1908 to 1910 the Imperial Navy ordered fourteen big paraffin boats, the nucleus of the emerging German submarine force. The paraffin engine was safer than gasoline and more efficient than steam, but it had one enormous military drawback: It emitted dense white exhaust, which was visible for miles at sea. For that reason submarine designers anxiously awaited a reliable diesel engine. But it came on very slowly. The French—not the Germans—were first to fit a diesel engine in a submarine. Then the Russians. The British were next. Other nations, including Italy and the United States, turned to this new technology, but German designers, demanding higher performance and reliability, held off. However, in 1910 Germany finally curtailed construction of paraffin boats and shifted to diesel, the last major power to do so. In the period 1910–1912 the Imperial Navy ordered twenty-three diesel-electric boats.

By the summer of 1914, on the eve of World War I, the submarine arms race, scarcely a dozen years old, had produced an astounding number of boats worldwide: about 400. Many of these were "old technology" gasoline- or steam-propelled submarines of limited or no military value, but a fourth of the boats were modern oceangoing diesel-electrics, armed with four or five torpedo tubes. Great Britain—not Germany—had the largest submarine fleet: seventy-six, with another twenty on the building ways. France ranked second, with seventy boats (many steam-electric) and twenty-three under construction. Czarist Russia came third with forty-one boats, most of them obsolescent. The United States ranked fourth with thirty-one, and eight more under construction. Germany held fifth place with twenty-six commissioned boats and fifteen under construction.

Undefined as yet was the role submarines were to play in war. Originally conceived as small, short-legged "coast" and "harbor" defensive weapons to thwart or counter enemy raids and blockades, they had grown into offensive oceangoing craft with substantial durability and firepower. They were believed to be capable of waging war against enemy battle fleets, acting alone or as part of a group. They were also capable of hit-and-run attacks on an enemy's maritime commerce in a *guerre de course*. Mounted systematically and with great intensity, a submarine *guerre de course* could produce a new kind of blockade, to which the "island" nation of Great Britain would be peculiarly vulnerable.

However, a submarine *guerre de course,* or war on commerce, would impose numerous legal, moral, and practical difficulties. Over the centuries civilized nations had evolved rules and regulations known as "prize laws" with respect to commerce raiding and had pledged in various international treaties to abide strictly by them. No merchant vessel of any kind was to be sunk at first sight without warning. Specific procedures were to be followed. The interceptor was required first to stop the merchant ship by signal or, if necessary, "a shot across the bow."

The interceptor was then required to establish by a ritualized procedure (known as "visit and search") whether the accosted ship was friend, foe, or neutral. If found to be a friend or a neutral transporting innocent or innocuous cargo, the ship was allowed to proceed unmolested. If found to be a foe, or a foe disguised as a neutral, or a neutral transporting "contraband" (i.e., war matériel or other prohibited cargo) to the enemy, the interceptor was permitted to capture (or sink) a foe and to capture an offending neutral. A captured ship was to be manned by a "prize crew" and sailed to a friendly or neutral port and turned over to a legal tribunal. Judges would then decide whether or not the capture had been legally correct and if the neutral's cargo was indeed contraband. If the tribunal condemned the neutral for transporting contraband, both ship and cargo could be sold at auction and the proceeds distributed to the interceptor or its sponsoring government. If, on the contrary, the tribunal found the interceptor to have incorrectly interpreted the cargo as contraband, the interceptor and/or its sponsoring government was subject to fines and damages.*

Beyond that there had evolved a strict, humane code of the sea with respect to the crews of merchant vessels. In various international treaties† it had been agreed that merchant ship crews—and passengers—were "noncombatants" and were not to be harmed or abandoned. If the interceptor found it necessary to sink the merchant vessel for whatever reason, it was required to take aboard the crewmen and passengers and land them ashore or to place them (and the ship's papers) in sound lifeboats, well supplied with provisions, sails, and navigational equipment, and give them specific directions and courses to the nearest land, or, if known, the nearest neutral ship thereabouts. Any violation of this code would be considered inhumane and barbarous and subject to severe punishment.

Submarines waging a *guerre de course* could not conveniently or safely abide by all these complicated rules. To do so would surrender the submarine's greatest asset: surprise in the attack. Stopping a ship by signal or a shot across the bow on the high seas for the ritualized "visit and search" would be an extremely difficult undertaking. The submarine would have to come to the surface, where it was most vulnerable. Many merchant ships could simply bend on more steam and outrun even the most modern submarines, which could make only 12 to 15 knots. A bold merchant ship captain might even attempt to ram the submarine.

Assuming the ship did stop on signal, the "visit and search" ritual presented other difficulties. Submarines did not carry enough manpower or small boats to board a merchant ship for a proper inspection. A small boarding party that went over on a rubber raft could be captured and held hostage, leaving the submarine captain to face the unwelcome choice of letting the ship (and his captured men) proceed or torpedoing it with the probable loss of his men. Should these difficul-

---

    *   The Admiralty law entailed was very complex and much influenced by the practice of privateering, which had been abolished by the Declaration of Paris in 1856.

    †   The codes had been legally defined and adopted by the major naval powers at the International Peace Conference at The Hague in 1899, and reaffirmed at the second such Hague conference in 1907. Hence the codes were known as "The Hague Conventions."

ties be surmounted and the ship found to be a neutral with a contraband cargo, with the limited manpower available, it would be exceedingly difficult to capture the ship, man it with a "prize crew," and sail it to a friendly or neutral port for legal adjudication. If the ship was to be sunk for whatever reason, the submarine could not take the crew aboard and land it ashore or otherwise provide much meaningful assistance. It would be necessary for the submarine to wait for the crew to provision its lifeboats, abandon ship, and stand well clear of torpedoes or gunfire, a tedious, high-risk process that would expose the submarine to constant danger of sudden counterattack from enemy naval forces.

These considerations were much discussed behind closed doors in naval establishments and in professional journals. Some navalists, including Britain's foremost submarine advocate John (Jacky) Fisher, concluded that if submarines engaged in a *guerre de course,* the prize laws could in no way be adhered to. "However inhuman and barbarous it may appear," Fisher wrote in a prescient, prewar paper, "there is nothing else the submarine can do except sink her captives." In response, Winston S. Churchill, First Lord of the Admiralty* in 1911, spoke for many British naval officers: "I do not believe this would ever be done by a civilized Power." Hence on the eve of World War I, the gentlemanly and naive assumption that submarines would only attack enemy warships was the prevailing view.

U-boats in World War I

When World War I commenced in early August 1914, the German Imperial Navy had not completed its big-ship buildup. The High Seas Fleet was therefore not strong enough to sail out and confront Britain's powerful Grand Fleet in a single, decisive battle. Nor was the Royal Navy capable of mounting a decisive attack on the Imperial Navy in its home waters. Hence a big-ship standoff ensued, during which the opposing admirals schemed ways to entrap the other's fleet in the confined waters of the North Sea by guile and deception. The naval war between these two great maritime powers thus proceeded in a curious, cautious, and unforeseen manner. There was only a single major surface-ship battle—Jutland—and it was brief and inconclusive.

Early in the war both Germany and Great Britain deployed submarines on offensive missions. The initial forays were remarkable. German U-boats sank three British heavy cruisers (*Aboukir, Hague,* and *Cressy*) and two light cruisers (*Pathfinder, Hawke*) with the loss of over 2,000 men. British submarines sank the German light cruiser *Hela.* Both navies were thus compelled to view the submarine as a grave new threat and they reacted accordingly. The British Grand Fleet withdrew temporarily from its North Sea base in Scapa Flow to safer waters in

---

* The "First Lord" of the Admiralty, a civilian, was a political appointee, comparable to the Secretary of the Navy in the United States. The "First Sea Lord," an admiral, was the uniformed naval chief.

north Ireland. The German High Seas Fleet sharply curtailed operations in its home waters, the Helgoland Bight.

The British imposed a naval blockade against Germany with the aim of shutting off the flow of war matériel. The British did not strictly observe the prize laws; even neutral ships loaded merely with food were harassed, blocked, or turned back. In retaliation, the German Naval Staff authorized German U-boats to harass Allied merchant shipping. On October 20, 1914, a U-boat, observing the prize laws, stopped, searched, and scuttled the 866-ton British freighter *Glitra* off Norway. A week later another U-boat, operating in the English Channel, torpedoed without warning a French steamer, *Admiral Ganteaume,* which was believed to be laden with troops and therefore fair game under the prize laws. In fact the ship was jammed with 2,400 Belgian refugees, including many women and children. Fortunately, it did not sink.

These two U-boat attacks on unarmed merchant ships carried profound implications for the island nation of Great Britain, entirely dependent upon her vast mercantile fleet for survival. An organized U-boat *guerre de course* might be ruinous. Accordingly, the British government denounced the attacks as illegal, treacherous, piratical, and immoral. Ship owners, merchants, and insurance carriers the world over joined the chorus of denunciation.

The Central Powers, composed of Germany and the Austro-Hungarian Empire, had planned to defeat France in a quick campaign, then turn about and crush czarist Russia. But the plan went awry. The armies in France bogged down in bloody trench warfare; Russia attacked from the east, creating a two-front war. Not having anticipated a long war, the Central Powers had not stockpiled large supplies of war matériel. As a result of the British blockade, by early 1915 the Central Powers were running out of iron ore and oil and other war essentials as well as food.

To this point U-boats, strictly observing the prize rules, had sunk ten British merchant ships for about 20,000 tons. Owing to the shortage of torpedoes—they were still virtually handmade—most of these sinkings had been achieved by gunfire or forced scuttling. The surprising ease of these successes had led the senior German admirals to conclude that if the prize rules were relaxed, even the small number of U-boats available for distant operations could impose an effective counterblockade on the British Isles. The mere appearance of a single U-boat, manned by only two dozen men, whether successful in the attack or not, caused great psychological alarm, compelling the enemy to devote a hugely disproportionate share of his manpower and resources to neutralize the threat. All this would severely impair Britain's ability to carry on the war, the advocates postulated, and might result in a tit-for-tat deal in which Britain agreed to lift its blockade of Germany.

Neither the Kaiser nor his Chancellor was keen on the proposal. Germany had already incurred heavy criticism from many quarters for sinking merely ten merchant ships. A relaxation of the prize rules would doubtless draw even harsher criticism, especially from neutral nations such as the United States, which had a substantial financial interest in sea commerce and might retaliate by entering the war. Moreover, the number of U-boats available for blockading the British Isles seemed too slight. To announce a blockade and fail abjectly would be worse than no attempt at all.

And yet the proposal would not die. Its advocates argued, not without justification, that the moral arguments were no longer relevant. In its ruthless blockade of Germany, they insisted, Britain had repeatedly violated the prize rules and other traditions protecting sea commerce, most notably in refusing the passage of neutral ships carrying only food. This line of reasoning, and other arguments, finally persuaded the Kaiser and his Chancellor to authorize a U-boat blockade of Great Britain.

The stage was carefully set. The Kaiser publicly declared that from February 18, 1915, onward, the waters around the British Isles were to be considered a "war zone." Prize rules would no longer be strictly observed. British and French merchant vessels would be sunk without warning or exceptional measures to provide for the safety of the crews. Care would be taken to spare neutrals not carrying contraband, but all neutrals would sail the waters at their own peril. U-boat skippers, the Kaiser further declared, would not be held responsible if "mistakes should be made."

So was launched history's first systematized submarine *guerre de course*. The initial results were less than impressive. In the month of February 1915, the twenty-nine U-boats of the German submarine force sank 60,000 tons of merchant shipping; in March, 80,000 tons. The weakness of the blockade lay in the small number of U-boats available. Owing to the time spent going to and from German bases and in refit, after the initial deployment it was difficult to establish organized U-boat patrol cycles that kept more than six or seven U-boats in British waters at any given time. Notwithstanding the fear and confusion and diversion of resources it precipitated, the first U-boat blockade did not achieve its main goal. First Lord Churchill declared the blockade a failure; British imports in 1915 exceeded those of 1913. The British government refused to entertain any suggestion of lifting the blockade of Germany.

With each merchant ship sinking, the cries of moral indignation intensified. Three sinkings in particular outraged the Americans: the 32,500-ton Cunard liner *Lusitania* on May 7, with the loss of 1,198 passengers (128 Americans) and crew; the 16,000-ton White Star liner *Arabic* on August 19, with the loss of 40 passengers (3 Americans); and the liner *Hesperian* on September 9. So violent was the reaction in the United States (U-boat crews make war "like savages drunk with blood" declared *The New York Times*), that in early September 1915 the Kaiser called off the blockade of Great Britain and sent many more U-boats to the Mediterranean Sea, where the hunting was less controversial and no less lucrative and there were few Americans.

With victory no closer for the Central Powers, at the beginning of 1916 the chief of the German naval staff, Admiral Henning von Holzendorff, and his Army counterpart urged the Kaiser to authorize a renewal of the British blockade. The Navy now had almost twice as many U-boats in commission (fifty-four versus twenty-nine in 1915) and ever more U-boats were coming off the slipways. The Kaiser was tempted, but the Chancellor and Foreign Minister objected, fearful of another *Lusitania,* which would almost certainly bring America into the war. After days of vacillation, the Kaiser sided with the Navy, but he imposed complicated restrictions. No passenger liners of any nationality were to be attacked anywhere. No cargo ships or tankers except those unmistakably armed could be attacked outside the war zone.

The renewed blockade commenced in February 1916. Notwithstanding the restrictions and complexity of the rules, all went well for the U-boats for two months: 117,000 tons sunk in February, 167,000 tons in March. Then came another costly error. On March 24 a U-boat mistook the 1,350-ton English Channel passenger ferry *Sussex* for a troopship and torpedoed it. The *Sussex* did not sink, but about eighty people were killed in the explosion, including twenty-five Americans. In response to the renewed cries of indignation and a blistering note from Washington threatening to sever diplomatic relations, the Kaiser backed down once more and, on April 24, ordered U-boats in waters of the British Isles again to adhere strictly to the prize rules. As a result, merchant ship tonnage sunk by U-boats in British waters fell sharply for the next four months.

The German submarine force had grown to substantial size by September 1916: a total of 120 boats of all types, many with larger 105mm (4.1") deck guns. Again the military staffs urged the Kaiser to exploit this force to the fullest. Again the Kaiser vacillated, and finally yielded, but with yet a new set of rules. Skippers were to conduct only restricted submarine warfare (by prize rules) in waters of the British Isles, where there were numerous American and other neutral ships, but they were permitted to wage unrestricted submarine warfare in the Mediterranean. This third and most intense phase of the restricted U-boat war, October 6, 1916, to February 1, 1917, was highly productive for the Germans. The U-boats sank about 500 British merchant vessels for about 1.1 million tons, raising the total bag for 1916 to about 2.3 million tons, most of that of British registry.

By early 1917 the ground war had become a brutal and fruitless bloodletting for the Central Powers and there was deep and widespread unrest at home. The German military staffs urged the Kaiser to authorize unrestricted submarine warfare in all oceans and seas. Using the results achieved in the fall of 1916, the larger number of U-boats available, plus nearly ninety new boats that were to be commissioned in 1917, the naval staff calculated that with an unrestricted U-boat campaign, nearly half of Britain's still large merchant fleet could be wiped out within five or six months, rendering her not only incapable of prosecuting the war on the continent but also leaving her population in a condition of starvation and rebellion. America be damned, the naval staff said. If she came into the war, Germany would have enough U-boats (about seventy ready for operations in the British Isles alone) to sink all her troop and supply ships before they reached Europe. By that time, too, there was no shortage of German submarine torpedoes; U-boat skippers did not have to rely so heavily on deck guns.

Turning aside peace feelers from President Wilson and others, the Kaiser approved this proposal. He announced to the world that commencing February 1, 1917, U-boats would sink on sight every merchant ship found in British territorial waters. At the same time, he assured the German military staffs that there would be no more pussyfooting or backing down, and he promulgated a radical role reversal for the surface ships of the Imperial Navy: Henceforth they were to support U-boats, rather than the other way around. "To us," he said, "every U-boat is of such importance that it is worth using the whole available fleet to afford it assistance and support."

Germany launched this all-out submarine *guerre de course* in the British Isles with multiple attacks conducted simultaneously with "utmost energy" by about sixty U-boats. To minimize detection by Allied aircraft and submarines, and counterfire from merchant ships, and to take advantage of higher speed for escape, U-boat skippers attacked at night while on the surface. The results were spectacular: 540,000 tons sunk in February, 594,000 tons in March, and an appalling 881,000 tons in April. During April alone—the grimmest month of the U-boat war—the Germans sank 423 merchant ships, of which 350 were British.* Moreover, as anticipated, the campaign scared off most of the many neutral ships trading with Great Britain.

Reflecting the growing anger and outrage in America, President Wilson reacted firmly and militantly to this all-out U-boat campaign. On the third day, February 3, 1917, he broke off diplomatic relations with Germany. At his request, on April 6 the Congress declared war on the Central Powers.

At the beginning of the war the Royal Navy possessed no special countermeasures to fight submarines. Naval tacticians wrongly assumed that since submarines would of necessity spend most of the time on the surface, they would be easy prey for gunfire and ramming. This wrong view was reinforced when the British cruiser *Birmingham* rammed and sank *U-15,* the first U-boat to be lost. But in the five months of warfare in 1914, the Royal Navy positively sank only one other U-boat, *U-18.* Three other U-boats were lost in 1914 (for a total of five) to unknown causes, probably mines.

Beginning in 1915, when shipping losses to U-boats began to climb significantly, the Admiralty diverted a substantial portion of its existing resources to anti-submarine warfare (A/S in Britain, ASW in America) and asked scientists, engineers, academics, and others to help develop ways to destroy U-boats. In the belief that the best defense was a strong offense, the chief ASW weapons to emerge in World War I were these:

• **SURFACE HUNTERS.** The Admiralty sent scores, then hundreds, then thousands of surface ships out offensively scouring the oceans for U-boats. These vessels included destroyers, frigates, sloops, trawlers, yachts, and heavily armed raiders (Q-ships) disguised as tramp steamers. Some vessels were fitted with crude hydrophones—passive underwater listening devices—which could detect the engine noise of a surfaced U-boat, but only if the hunting vessels were not moving.

In 1916 many of these offensive ASW ships were armed with a new weapon

---

* Total figures vary by source. Generally speaking, in this period the U-boats sank about 1,000 ships for about 2 million gross tons.

called the depth charge. The best of these underwater bombs, derived from mines, contained 300 pounds of TNT or Amatol and were fitted with hydrostatic fuses which could be set to detonate the charges at 40 and 80 feet, and later 50 to 200 feet. Since early depth charges were rolled from stern tracks (or racks) and exploded at shallow depth, the attacking vessel had to put on maximum speed or risk severe damage to its stern. Therefore, slower vessels could not use the 300-pound depth charges until fuses with deeper settings had been developed. In all of 1916, British naval forces sank only two U-boats by depth charge. In 1917 and 1918, when depth charges had been improved and were much more plentiful, the kill rate by this weapon increased significantly.

• AIRBORNE HUNTERS.   When the war commenced, the aviation age was merely a dozen years old. The Royal Navy had acquired about fifty seaplanes and seven nonrigid airships, called "blimps," to scout for enemy naval forces. Some of these aircraft were diverted to U-boat hunting but, owing to the unreliability of engines, slow speed, limited fuel capacity, tiny bomb loads, and other factors, they were useless against U-boats. It became apparent, however, that when an aircraft appeared near a U-boat, it dived and became essentially immobile. Hence air patrols were useful for forcing U-boats under, thus enabling ships to skirt the danger area and avoid attack. In 1915 the Royal Navy acquired much improved seaplanes (the American-designed Curtiss American) and blimps in greater numbers. These were armed with impact-fused 100- or 520-pound bombs or 230-pound ASW bombs with delayed-action fuses that exploded at a water depth of seventy feet, but the U-boat kill rate by aircraft remained essentially zero.

• SUBMERGED HUNTERS.   On the theory that it was wise to "send a thief to catch a thief," the Royal Navy saturated German home waters with submarines equipped with hydrophones. The early patrols produced no confirmed kills, but the presence of British submarines in German waters, including the Baltic Sea, where German submariners trained, caused great anxiety and disrupted routines. Beginning in 1915, British submarines began to torpedo U-boats in significant numbers. The Admiralty designed and produced a small submarine (R class) specifically for U-boat hunting but it came too late. Had British torpedoes been more reliable, the submarines doubtless would have sunk many more U-boats.

• MINES.   From the first days of the war both sides employed moored contact mines, planted in shallow water, usually defensively but often offensively. Defensive minefields were sown to prevent enemy forces from penetrating one's coastal waters for shore bombardment, interdiction of shipping, or invasion. Such minefields were charted and planted with great care, leaving secret safe lanes for friendly shipping and naval forces. In order to attack British shipping, U-boats often had to negotiate the periphery or heart of defensive minefields, a hazardous undertaking. Many U-boats strayed into British minefields or hit live mines that had drifted their moorings or had broken loose. Offensive mining was more complicated and often hit-or-miss. Surface vessels, operating under cover of darkness in great haste, planted mines in likely spots such as sea-lanes or sometimes even in the safe lanes of the defensive minefields, to catch opposing naval vessels or merchant ships by surprise. Later in the war, both sides employed submarines for minelaying, combining two much-feared naval weapons.

To prevent U-boats from reaching the Atlantic via the English Channel, the British sowed lines of mines across it from Dover, England, to Cape Gris-Nez, France. However, in 1915 and 1916, British contact mines were defective, and not until the Admiralty copied and mass-produced the standard German contact mine could the Dover "field" be depended upon to block the passage of U-boats. When the Dover field was finally effective, it forced U-boats destined for the Atlantic to go northabout Scotland, adding about 1,400 miles (and about seven days) to the voyage.

After the United States entered the war and offered the Royal Navy a secret mine with a magnetic fuse, the Allies put in motion a grandiose scheme to plant 200,000 such mines across the top of the North Sea from the Orkney Islands to Norway. Although American and British forces planted about 80,000 mines in this so-called Northern Barrage, most of these mines were also defective and, other than frayed nerves, caused the Germans small harm. Even so, Allied mines in all areas ranked high as U-boat killers.

• RADIO INTELLIGENCE. When the war began, radio transmission or wireless telegraphy (W/T) was a new military technology at which the British excelled. Taking advantage of a lucky capture of German naval codebooks, as well as an appalling lack of sophistication in German radio procedures and security, the British thoroughly penetrated German naval communications. The British first perfected Radio Direction Finding (RDF) to pinpoint and identify German shore- and sea-based transmitters. Utilizing the captured codebooks, they "read" on a current basis most German naval transmissions. This priceless intelligence enabled the Admiralty's secret signals-intelligence branch (known as Room 40) to track U-boat operations to a remarkable extent. A British historian wrote that by "early 1915, Room 40 knew the total strength of the U-boat fleet, the rate at which it was growing . . . the composition of each flotilla . . . the number of U-boats at sea or in port, and when and if it put to sea . . . losses, as evidenced by the failure of a U-boat to return, and in most cases, the size of the [U-boat] threat in any particular area."

Still, these many and varied ASW measures were absurdly inadequate. In all of 1915 the Germans lost merely nineteen U-boats while adding fifty-two boats to the force. In 1916 the Germans lost twenty-two boats while adding 108 boats. Notwithstanding a massive British antisubmarine effort, during the first four months of 1917, the Germans lost only eleven U-boats. To then, the average monthly U-boat loss rate had been only 1.7, a continuing losing battle for Britain because the Germans were producing seven or eight new boats per month.

In the wake of the spectacular shipping losses in April 1917, Britain's new Prime Minister, David Lloyd George, urged the Admiralty to organize British shipping into convoys, escorted by destroyers, frigates, sloops, and other ASW craft. This was hardly a new idea; defense of sea commerce by convoy was as old as the sail and, as the British naval historian John Winton put it, "as natural and as obvious a tactic as, say, gaining and keeping the weather gauge."

The Royal Navy had opposed the formation of convoys for numerous reasons. The principal reason, Winton wrote, was that Royal Navy officers had forgotten their history—that the main purpose of the Royal Navy was to protect Britain's sea trade. Imbued with the aggressive doctrines of the American naval theorist Alfred Thayer Mahan (and kindred souls), who postulated that control of the seas could most effectively be insured by husbanding naval assets for a single, decisive, offensive naval battle with the enemy, they opposed the diversion of naval resources to convoying, which they viewed as mundane and defensive and which, if adopted, would be an admission that Britain had, in effect, lost control of the seas to an inferior naval power.

There were other reasons. First, notwithstanding huge losses of merchant ships on their very doorstep, the Royal Navy continued to grossly underestimate the overall effectiveness of the U-boat campaign on British maritime assets. Second, the admirals insisted convoys were enormously inefficient, compelling faster ships to reduce speeds to those of slower ships, overwhelming seaport facilities during loading and unloading periods, and posing difficult organizational problems in distant, neutral ports. Third, the Admiralty doubted the ability or desire of merchant-ship captains to accept or to follow orders or to station-keep in the required tight zigzagging formations at night or in inclement weather. Fourth, the admirals held, the concentration of merchant ships into a single large body presented U-boat skippers with richer targets, which they were not likely to miss, even with poorly aimed or errant torpedoes.

With the assistance of American naval power, the Admiralty finally—and reluctantly—agreed to a test of inbound convoying in the Atlantic. The first convoy, consisting of sixteen ships, sailed from Gibraltar to the British Isles on May 10, 1917; the second of twelve ships from Norfolk, Virginia,* on May 24. The Gibraltar convoy arrived in good time without the loss of a ship. The Norfolk convoy, escorted by the British cruiser *Roxburgh* and six American destroyers, ran into minor difficulties. Two of the dozen ships could not maintain the convoy's 9-knot average speed and fell out. One of these was torpedoed going into Halifax, Nova Scotia. However, the other ten ships crossed the Atlantic in foggy weather, maintaining tight formation, zigzagging all the way, and arrived safely in the British Isles.

With the results of these tests and other data in hand, in August 1917—the beginning of the fourth year of the war—the Admiralty finally adopted the convoy system. It was a smashing success. By October over 1,500 merchant ships in about 100 convoys had reached the British Isles. Only ten ships were lost to U-boats while sailing in these convoys: one ship out of 150. By comparison, the loss rate for ships sailing independently (inbound and otherwise) was one in ten. By the end of 1917, almost all of the blue-water traffic was convoyed. These convoys had been instituted in the nick of time; U-boats sank nearly 3,000 ships for 6.2 million tons in 1917, most of them sailing independently. The historian Winton wrote: "Convoying did not win the war in 1917. But it did prevent the war from being lost in 1917."

---

* Strictly speaking, the convoy sailed from Hampton Roads, Virginia, an expansive anchorage at Norfolk. Here and below, "Norfolk" is used freely to designate Hampton Roads.

A U-boat skipper remembered the impact of convoying on the German submarine force. Convoying, he wrote, "robbed it of its opportunity to become a decisive
factor." He continued: "The oceans at once became bare and empty; for long periods at a time the U-boats, operating individually, would see nothing at all; and then
suddenly up would loom a huge concourse of ships, thirty or fifty or more of them,
surrounded by a strong escort of warships of all types." The solitary U-boat, he
went on, which "had most probably sighted the convoy purely by chance," would
attempt to attack again and again, "if the commander had strong nerves" and sta-
mina. "The lone U-boat might sink one or two of the ships," he concluded, "or
even several; but that was a poor percentage of the whole. The convoy would
steam on."

During the final twelve months of the war, convoying became the rule rather
than the exception. The British and American navies established large organizations
to administer convoys and provided surface and, where feasible (close to land), aircraft escorts, armed with new and improved aerial bombs. In many instances, intelligence from Room 40, accurately identifying U-boat positions, enabled the
authorities to divert convoys away from U-boats. After the full convoy system was
in place (outbound from the British Isles as well as inbound) in 1918, total shipping
losses fell by two-thirds from 1917: 1,133 sunk. Of these, 999 sailed independently.
In the ten months of naval war in 1918, only 134 ships were lost in convoy.

The United States Navy had entered the war itching for a grand, Mahan-like decisive naval battle. Like the Royal Navy, it soon discovered that was out of the question. In due course, its main efforts were directed at helping the British fight the
U-boat. It provided scores of destroyers and other small vessels for ASW hunter-
killer groups and convoy escort as well as minelayers for the Northern Barrage. It
also sent submarines (twenty-three in all) to conduct ASW patrols in the Azores
and British Isles, but neither the boats nor the crews were up to the task, and none
had any success. However, the infusion of U.S. Navy surface forces during the second half of 1917 enabled the British to convoy on a large scale and contributed to a
doubling of the U-boat loss rate in 1917: forty-three U-boats lost, compared with
the twenty lost in the first six months.

The sharply rising U-boat loss rate and the difficulties presented by Allied convoying were merely two of many severe problems confronting the Germans in late
1917. The resources of the entire nation and those of its allies had been spent in
three years of bloody, indecisive warfare. The winds of the worker-peasant revolution in Russia had carried seeds to Germany; Bolshevism (or communism) was
taking root in the ranks of Germany's exhausted and disgruntled military forces
and arms workers. German soldiers were deserting by the tens of thousands; there
were sporadic but ominous mutinies on Imperial Navy vessels in Wilhelmshaven,
where the crews were bored with the prosaic job of escorting U-boats in and out of
port. Many U-boat craftsmen in the shipyards of Kiel and Hamburg, stirred up by
Red agitators, were striking or otherwise slowing construction schedules.

There was yet another problem for the U-boat force. Despite Germany's reputation for efficiency and centralization, the numerous U-boat flotillas, based in Germany, Flanders, the Mediterranean, and elsewhere, were controlled by the fleet commanders in those areas. Thus there was no overall coordination and control of U-boat operations; no centralized authority for collecting experiences and information, and making recommendations for increasing efficiency and decreasing risks. Moreover, the fleet commanders were free to recommend U-boat design types to the naval staff. The result was that German shipyards were engaged in building far too many submarine types (large, medium, and small torpedo shooters; large, medium, and small minelayers; huge U-cruisers, etc.). Given the disparity in design and conflicting priorities, the acute shortages of building materials, coal, food, and skilled shipyard workers (too many drafted into the Army), the severe winter weather, and the ideological unrest, the naval staff could not meet U-boat production rates, let alone assure that the rates could be doubled or tripled in 1918 and 1919, as was envisioned.

And yet the U-boat force fought on with all its might and main. During the first eight months of 1918, U-boats sank an average of about 300,000 tons of Allied shipping per month, almost all of the victims sailing alone. U-boat losses rose slightly over 1917 (sixty-nine in ten months, compared with sixty-three in the twelve months of 1917), but the losses were offset by seventy new boats that came into service. Morale remained high.

By October 1918 the German war machine and economy were exhausted, and the nation was torn by riots and rebellion. With minor exceptions, the will to fight on had dissipated; a million or more men had deserted the German Army. One notable exception was the U-boat arm. It was still strong (about 180 boats afloat; numerous others in various stages of construction in the building yards); morale remained high, and its loyalty to the government was undiminished. However, in view of the deteriorating conditions at home, there was no longer any hope that the U-boat force alone could deliver a knockout blow to the Allies. As one condition of the preliminary peace negotiations, Germany recalled the entire U-boat force on October 21. The boats returned home to find the Imperial Navy crippled by widespread mutinies. In a final irony, some U-boats were directed to train their torpedo tubes on German battleships to help put down the mutinies. None, however, was ordered to shoot.

After the Central Powers surrendered and the Armistice became effective, November 11, 1918, Allied naval authorities gained access to German records and were able to compile a balance sheet on the German U-boat war. Germany had operated 351 U-boats of all types. These had sunk more than 5,000 Allied ships of all kinds (including ten battleships and eighteen heavy and light cruisers) for about 12 million tons. A total of 178 U-boats had been lost; about 5,000 officers and men had been killed, wounded, or captured. At war's end there were 179 U-boats ready or nearly ready for operations, 224 on the building ways, and another 200 projected. Had the war continued into 1919 or beyond, and the 224 boats under construction been placed in commission, deducting the probable U-boat loss rate, the Allies would have faced a total force of about 300 U-boats in 1919 and an even larger force in 1920.

BUSINESS REPLY MAIL

FIRST-CLASS MAIL   PERMIT NO. 1243   BOULDER CO

POSTAGE WILL BE PAID BY ADDRESSEE

Consumer
Reports

SUBSCRIPTION DEPARTMENT

PO BOX 51166

BOULDER CO 80323-1166

It had required an enormous Allied effort to deal with the U-boat: 3,330 surface hunter-killer ships and escorts of all kinds full- or part-time, nearly 500 aircraft, 75 blimps, scores of submarines, countless tens of thousands of mines. U-boat losses:

Surface warships	55 *
Probable mines	48
Submarines	18
Q-ships	11
Merchant ships	7 (five by ramming)
Aircraft	1
Known accidents	19 †
Unknown causes	19
Total	178

Most of the surviving operational U-boats were distributed among the victors: 105 to Britain, 46 to France, 10 to Italy, 2 to Belgium. It was agreed that after the U-boats had been evaluated and stripped of useful gear, all except 10 of the 46 allotted to France were to be destroyed. The U-boats on the building ways were also destroyed. And so died the German U-boat force.

The submarine, conceived initially as a coastal vessel of limited defensive capability, then employed offensively in distant waters to wage a *guerre de course,* had a profound impact on naval strategy. In the future, any nation desiring absolute command of the seas not only would have to deploy a surface fleet superior to that of all other nations or likely combinations of nations, but also have at hand sufficient antisubmarine resources to protect that surface fleet, and its merchant fleet as well, from submarine attack. Conversely, it would be well advised to maintain a force of submarines to assist in the subjugation or destruction of opposing naval forces and merchant fleets.

During the war, German propagandists and pulp-fiction writers and others created a U-boat mythology. It postulated that German submarines were technical marvels, unsurpassed in the world; that German submarine captains and crews were supermen, brilliant, heroic, and invincible; that the German submarine force, loyal to the Kaiser to the bitter end, had come within an ace of bringing Great Britain to her knees and thereby defeating the Allies. German pulp-fiction writers and serious historians alike enriched the mythology in the 1920s and 1930s.

Distinguished personages in the Allied camp also contributed to the U-boat mythology. Merely to neutralize the U-boat, the British naval historian Sir Julian Corbett wrote, had demanded "the greatest sea fight in history." Onetime First Lord of the Admiralty Winston Churchill wrote (in *The World Crisis*) that the U-boat "rapidly undermined" the life of the British Isles and "foundations of Allied strength" and that by 1918 the danger of an Allied collapse "began to look black

---

* Ramming, gunfire, depth charges, etc.

† Stranding, German mines, own U-boats, etc.

PLATE I

GERMAN SUBMARINE FORCE 1914–1918

	1914	1915	1916	1917	1918
On hand	24	29	54	133	142
Gains	10	52	108	87	70
Battle losses	5	19	22	63	69
Other losses[1]		8	7	15	9
Year end	29	54	133	142	134

Total operational boats:	351
Total sunk in combat (50%):	178
Other losses (11%):	39
Completed after Armistice:	45
Surrendered to Allies:	179

1. Sunk accidentally, interned, transferred to Austria-Hungary, to schoolboat status, etc.

PLATE 2

ALLIED AND NEUTRAL TONNAGE SUNK BY SUBMARINES IN WORLD WAR I[1]

MONTH	1914	1915	1916	1917	1918
January		47,981	81,259	368,521	306,658
February		59,921	117,547	540,006[3]	318,957
March		80,775	167,097	593,841	342,597
April		55,725	191,667	881,027	278,719
May		120,058	129,175	596,629	295,520
June		131,428	108,855	687,507	255,587
July		109,640	118,215	557,988	260,967
August	62,767[2]	185,866	162,744	511,730	283,815
September	98,378	151,884	230,460	351,748[4]	187,881
October	87,917	88,534	353,660	458,558	118,559
November	19,413	153,043	311,508	289,212	17,682[5]
December	44,197	123,141	355,139	399,111	
Totals:	312,672	1,307,996	2,327,326	6,235,878	2,666,942

Grand total tonnage: 12,850,814 gross tons   British total: 7,759,090 gross tons

1. Source: Fayle, C. Ernest, *Seaborne Trade,* Vol. 3, p. 465, Table I[a]; London: John Murray, 1924. Over the decades these figures have been refined. See, for example, Tarrant (1989), pp. 148–159. He puts the totals from German sources at 12,284,757 gross tons and from British sources at 12,026,324 gross tons.
2. World War I began.
3. Germans began unrestricted submarine warfare.
4. British began full-scale convoying.
5. War ended.

and imminent." The American Ambassador in London, Walter Hines Page, wrote that "[t]he submarine menace of 1917 threatened us with absolute and irremediable disaster" and that "[t]he submarine is the most formidable thing the war has produced—by far." The senior American naval officer in London, William S. Sims, wrote: "Could Germany have kept fifty submarines at work on the great shipping routes in the winter and spring of 1917, nothing could have prevented her from winning the war."

What made the U-boat seem so formidable in World War I was principally the blindness and obtuseness of the British Admiralty. In the run-up to the war, it refused to accept the possibility of a submarine *guerre de course* and made no real preparations for one. When the war came, the Admiralty was scandalously slow in mobilizing antisubmarine technology and putting in place major weaponry, such as the patrol aircraft, the escort destroyer, the antisubmarine submarine, a gun for merchant ships, depth charges, and reliable mines and torpedoes.

A close analysis of U-boat successes shows that they sank the overwhelming majority of Allied ships not by torpedo but by deck gun in British coastal waters and in the Mediterranean Sea where maritime traffic was dense. Most of these deck guns in the early years were 88mm (3.4"). Inasmuch as the U-boat was seldom an efficient or stable gun platform and the hull was extremely vulnerable to counterfire, had the Admiralty promptly armed British merchant ships with slightly more powerful 4" guns manned by trained gun crews, only the bravest of the U-boat skippers would have sought a one-on-one gun contest, and Allied merchant ship losses doubtlessly would have diminished significantly. Several merchant ships so armed sailing in concert would have rendered a U-boat attack by deck gun virtually suicidal, forcing the Germans to attack submerged with scarce, virtually handmade torpedoes from relatively stationary positions, which were easy to evade or outrun. At the start of 1916, only about 800 British merchant ships had guns.

The most grievous British sin, of course, was the failure to promptly adopt large-scale convoying. By the time ocean convoying was fully in place, September 1917, U-boats had already sunk about 8 million of the total 12 million tons bagged in the war. Had convoying begun much earlier, British ships could have resorted to an "evasion strategy" to avoid known U-boat positions detected by British code-breakers and other intelligence, a procedure that became almost routine in late 1917 and 1918. Moreover, if most British merchant ships sailing in these convoys had been armed with guns promptly, it is unlikely that a U-boat would have attacked so formidable an opponent by gun. A rock-bottom minimum convoy escort of one destroyer or comparable vessel with gunfire superior to the U-boat would have sufficed for defense against the few that operated singly in open ocean waters. Since U-boats invariably dived on sighting aircraft and became virtually immobilized, primitive planes—even unarmed planes—would have been highly effective in escorting coastal convoys close to shore. But the Admiralty did not adopt coastal convoys until June of 1918.

The Germans were also blind and obtuse. On the strategic level, the U-boat campaign was the chief factor in bringing the United States into the war, assuring the ultimate defeat of the Central Powers. Moreover, the Germans made the mistake of launching unrestricted submarine warfare before they had anywhere near sufficient U-boats to carry it off. This resulted in an undesirable piecemeal commitment of naval power, which the Allies were able to whittle down bit by bit. On the tactical level, the Germans failed to develop promptly an anticonvoy doctrine, such as group (or "wolf pack") night surface attacks, massing force against force at the decisive point.

Importantly, the German high command relied completely on the U-boat to interdict the flow of fresh American troops from the States to French Atlantic ports. The U-boats utterly failed in this task. In a quite awesome naval triumph which is usually overlooked, Allied maritime forces transported about 2 million soldiers from the States to France, with the loss of merely fifty-six men due to U-boats. These deaths occurred when a torpedo hit and damaged the 9,500-ton troopship *Moldavia*. U-boats sank two other troopships (*Covington, President Lincoln*), but both were returning to the States empty. As is well known, the American troops reaching France played a pivotal role in the final defeat of German armies.

The reality of the German U-boat campaign in World War I is that it failed. It caused much damage and hardship and created no little terror. However, contrary to the mythology, the campaign did not really come close to bringing Great Britain to her knees, thereby precipitating an Allied defeat. When the U-boat threat peaked in 1917, the Allies countered with massive merchant-ship building programs and convoying. As the British historian Arthur J. Marder observed,* there was never at any time in the war "widespread privation in Britain" as a result of the U-boats.

TREATIES, DISARMAMENT, AND SUBMARINES

The cost of World War I, "the war to end all wars," was ghastly: an estimated 9 million dead, 20 million wounded, countless billions of dollars squandered. The revolution in Russia, a by-product of the war, cost millions more lives. To prevent another such slaughter, the Allies vowed to disarm, dismember, and punish the Central Powers and to establish a network of treaties and alliances to insure a permanent peace and to disarm themselves.

The search for everlasting peace began at the Paris Peace Conference in January 1919, where President Wilson played a leading role. The outcome was the Treaty of Versailles, which contained a covenant establishing the League of Nations, a forum for settling international disputes. Ironically, the U.S. Senate, fearing that participation in the League of Nations might draw America into another European war, refused to ratify the treaty. Thus it fell to the other major wartime Allies—Great Britain, France, Italy, and Japan—to enforce the terms of the Versailles Treaty, to launch the League of Nations, and to lead the search for peace.

---

*   Quoted in Tarrant (1989).

At the insistence of France, which had suffered most in the war, the terms of the Versailles Treaty were harsh. The crumbling Austro-Hungarian Empire was legally dismembered. From it emerged the new, independent nations of Austria, Hungary, and Czechoslovakia, and the embryo of Yugoslavia. Germany was likewise carved up. The provinces of Alsace and Lorraine were returned to France. Large areas of eastern Germany were transferred back to the newly reestablished nation of Poland, which was also granted a corridor to the Baltic Sea, terminating in the free city of Danzig. The Rhineland and Saar were occupied by Allied troops. Germany's colonies in Africa and the Pacific were stripped away. In addition, Germany was required to pay huge reparations to the Allies—upwards of $100 billion, with the down payment, $5 billion in gold, due and payable by May 1921.

Beyond that, Germany was demilitarized. The German general staff and navy high commands were abolished. The German Army was limited to a constabulary force of 100,000 men; the navy to merely 15,000 men. Military conscription was abolished. Voluntary military enlistments had to be long-term: twenty-five years for officers, twelve years for enlisted men; no one could retire before age forty-five; no one could enlist in another service after retirement. Neither the Army nor the Navy was permitted a reserve. German industry was prohibited from building submarines, military aircraft, heavy artillery, tanks, and other weaponry.

When these terms were revealed to the Germans, they were shocked and outraged. At first Friedrich Ebert, President of the newly formed German government, the Weimar Republic, refused to sign the treaty. He did so only after the Allies threatened to invade and occupy all of Germany and to prolong indefinitely the naval blockade. Already under severe attack by militant leftists, the hapless Ebert returned to Germany to find himself a target of militant rightists, who vilified him for betraying Germany.

One of the chief Allied prizes of the war was the Imperial Navy's High Seas Fleet. At the surrender, its main force, seventy-four ships, had been interned at the British naval base, Scapa Flow. In protest of the Versailles Treaty, on June 21, 1919, German caretaker crews scuttled or attempted to scuttle the fleet. Allied sailors beached twenty-two of the seventy-four exploding and burning ships, but the other fifty-two sank, denying Allied navies ten battleships, five battle cruisers, five light cruisers, and thirty-two destroyers.

Ravaged by disease, famine, and economic chaos, postwar Germany became a political battleground. Armed bands of leftists and rightists fought pitched battles in the streets and attempted to seize by force local and national governments. The rightists were more successful. One extremist band, the Nazis, led by Adolf Hitler and composed of murderous, greedy thugs and criminals and quack ideologues who preached hatred of the Versailles Treaty and the Jews, gradually rose to dominate the street fighting.

The Allies posted a Control Commission in Germany to ensure that the prohibition against remilitarization was observed. But the resentful German militarists had not the slightest intention of observing the Versailles Treaty. With the tacit approval of Ebert and his successor in 1925, Paul von Hindenburg, the chief of the Army (*Reichswehr*), General Hans von Seeckt, and successive chiefs of the Navy

(*Reichsmarine*), admirals Adolph von Trotha, Paul Behncke, and Hans Zenker, in connivance with Gustav Krupp, head of the arms conglomerate, and other German industrialists, pursued military research and development by devious subterfuges. After the Treaty of Rapallo (1922), which reestablished relations between Germany and the Soviet Union, von Seeckt set up secret German infantry, tank, and aviation schools and factories to manufacture military aircraft, artillery shells, and poison gas in Russia. Krupp gained a controlling interest in the Swedish arms firm Bofors, which turned out Krupp-designed artillery and antiaircraft guns. Admirals von Trotha, Behncke, and Zenker maintained Germany's lead in U-boat technology by creating a Krupp front, IVS, in Holland, which sold submarines or submarine plans to Japan (a would-be enforcer of the Versailles Treaty!), Spain, Turkey, Finland, and other nations.

The victorious Allies, meanwhile, pursued the chimera of an everlasting peace. Initially the League of Nations, headquartered in Geneva, served as the main forum, but the absence of the United States and an unwillingness of the other major powers to surrender national sovereignty undermined its effectiveness. As a result, the major powers pursued other diplomatic avenues. One seemingly promising achievement was the Locarno Pact (1925). Joining with the major powers for the first time since the war, Germany appeared to accept the terms of the Versailles Treaty. It agreed to a permanent demilitarized strip along the Rhine River and swore not to make war with France or Belgium, in return for which Germany was admitted to the League of Nations. Still distrustful of Germany, France entered into separate alliances with Poland and Czechoslovakia, in which France guaranteed to protect those nations from German incursions.

The pursuit of peace reached the high-water mark in 1928 with the Pact of Paris (or Kellogg-Briand Pact). In that treaty, fifteen major powers, including Germany, renounced war as an instrument of national policy. Ultimately sixty-two nations signed the document, including the United States. The pact, outlawing war, was hailed as a diplomatic triumph, as indeed it was. But this noble document contained no provisions for enforcement; it was merely a declaration.

Beginning at the Paris Peace Conference in 1919, the major powers had declared their intention to disarm. But the talk was mostly pious hot air. Those nations bordering on Germany—France, Poland, Czechoslovakia—raised and maintained large, well-equipped armies, as did Italy, which in 1922 came under control of the fascist dictator Benito Mussolini. However, the major powers did enter into a series of naval disarmament treaties that are remarkable in retrospect and that profoundly influenced the course of naval warfare.

The impetus for naval disarmament came from Great Britain. Her motive was to halt the buildup of the United States and Japanese navies, against which Great Britain was no longer able or willing to compete. The idea appealed to President Wilson's successor, Warren G. Harding, who took office in 1921, committed to reducing naval armaments and to curbing Japanese expansionism in the Far East. At Harding's invitation, diplomats and navalists from Great Britain, the United States,

Japan, France, and Italy formally convened amid great pomp and hoopla on November 12, 1921, in Washington, D.C.

Before the Washington Naval Conference convened, the Harding Administration had made the decision—over strenuous objections of the U.S. Navy—to propose a worldwide naval disarmament scheme of drastic and unprecedented dimensions. Speaking first, Secretary of State Charles Evans Hughes laid out the proposal. He suggested that first, the United States, Great Britain, and Japan should immediately halt building all approved or projected capital ships* and not build any more for ten years. Second, that the three powers should reduce standing naval forces by scrapping in aggregate nearly two million tons of capital ships. Third, that the three major naval powers should aim to achieve by 1942 a capital ship ration of 500,000 tons for the United States and Great Britain, 300,000 tons for Japan, and 175,000 tons each for France and Italy (5:5:3:1.75:1.75) and that auxiliaries (cruisers, destroyers, etc.) should be restricted proportionately.

The conferees—and the world—were stunned. In modern-day terms it was as though the United States had proposed, without prior notice, that the major powers dismantle and scrap half or more of their strategic nuclear forces. Specifically, it meant:

• The United States, making by far the largest concessions, was to scrap or cancel thirty capital ships of about 850,000 tons: fifteen older battleships and fifteen battleships or battle cruisers under construction, including two already launched, and several at 80 percent completion. The retained force was to be eighteen capital ships of 500,000 tons.

• Great Britain was to scrap or cancel twenty-three capital ships of about 590,000 tons: nineteen older battleships and four planned *Hood*-class super dreadnoughts. The retained force was to be twenty-two capital ships of 600,000 tons.†

• Japan was to scrap or cancel twenty-five capital ships of about 450,000 tons: ten older battleships, seven battleships or battle cruisers under construction, and eight planned. The retained force was to be ten capital ships of 300,000 tons.

The complete proposal was very complicated and it led to weeks of tedious, technical haggling. The conferees could not agree on formulas for cruiser limitations, so that class of vessel was exempt, except for a stipulation limiting cruisers to 10,000 tons and 8" guns.‡ The aim of a 5:5:3 ratio among the three major naval powers survived the debates and the treaty was signed in February 1922, to have effect until December 31, 1936.

The Republican Party hailed the collective treaties as "the greatest peace document ever drawn." It may not have been exactly that, but it was astonishing and significant. The massive naval arms race launched in World War I had been stopped in its tracks. It was believed, moreover, that the treaty would curb Japan-

---

* Any vessel of 10,000 tons or more armed with guns larger than 8".

† Britain was allowed an extra 100,000 tons to compensate for the age and certain shortcomings in her capital ships.

‡ Any cruiser larger or more heavily gunned was to be considered a capital ship.

ese expansionism. In return for a pledge from the United States not to fortify the Pacific islands of Midway, Wake, and Guam, Japan promised to keep hands off Siberia and withdraw ground forces from China's Shantung Peninsula.

The failure to reach agreement on cruiser ratios caused a boiling controversy between the United States and Great Britain and led to proposals for yet another naval disarmament conference. This was held in Geneva in June 1927. Japan attended, but France and Italy, committed to building cruisers, boycotted the conference. It was just as well. After weeks of haggling, the conferees again failed to reach agreement.

The unresolved cruiser issue and other factors led President Herbert C. Hoover and Britain's Prime Minister Ramsay MacDonald to convene yet another naval disarmament conference in London in January 1930. By then the Wall Street "crash" of October 1929 had created worldwide economic instability; the Great Depression was just over the horizon. These dark economic prospects added a sense of urgency to the deliberations and to a determination to put a stop to extravagant expenditures for naval forces.

The five major naval powers attended: the United States, Great Britain, Japan, France, and Italy. The conferees began negotiations from scratch, erecting a sweeping new naval treaty on the foundation of the 1922 Washington treaty. The outcome was a further dramatic reduction in naval forces of the three major naval powers:

•   CAPITAL SHIPS.   The ratio of 5:5:3 was reaffirmed; the "holiday" on new construction extended from 1932 to December 31, 1936, when the treaty was to expire. The United States was to scrap three more battleships, retaining a total of fifteen. Great Britain was to scrap five more battleships, retaining fifteen. Japan was to scrap one battleship, retaining nine. France was permitted to build three new 23,000-ton battle cruisers. Insisting on parity with France, Italy was granted the same right.

•   CRUISERS.   That troublesome issue was finally settled, with Great Britain the winner. The Royal Navy would expand to fifty cruisers (fifteen 10,000-ton "treaty" cruisers and thirty-five light cruisers). The United States would build to thirty-seven cruisers in a mix it did not prefer (eighteen 10,000-ton "treaty" cruisers and nineteen light cruisers). Japan would retain her twelve cruisers in being (eight 10,000-ton "treaty" cruisers and four light cruisers with 8" guns), provided the United States stretched out the completion of three "treaty" cruisers on a certain schedule. France and Italy retained ten new cruisers each.

•   DESTROYERS.   All three powers were to freeze destroyers at existing levels by tonnages. Assuming 1,500 tons per destroyer, the United States and Great Britain would retain 100 each; Japan, seventy. France was allowed forty-eight destroyers; Italy, forty-two.*

Throughout these naval disarmament talks, submarines figured prominently. At the Washington conference in 1921, Great Britain, which had suffered most from U-

---

* For greater detail on American and British destroyer programs, see appendices 9 and 12.

boats, urged that all submarines be outlawed, like poison gas, and abolished. However, the other major powers—France in particular—opposed abolition. Seeking a compromise, the United States proposed limitations on submarines: 90,000 tons, or about 100 submarines, for the United States and Great Britain; 45,000 tons, or about 45 submarines, for France, Italy, and Japan. But this proposal satisfied no one.

During the submarine debate, an American of towering prestige appeared with sweeping proposals. He was Elihu Root, a former Secretary of War and Secretary of State and U.S. senator, and winner of the Nobel Prize for his tireless peacemaking efforts in various international organizations. Root formally introduced three "resolutions," the intent of which was to outlaw the submarine as a commerce destroyer, to restore the prize laws in full, and to establish legal procedures to punish any submarine skipper who violated them. The British delegates warmly welcomed the resolutions; the French vigorously opposed them. Privately the United States also opposed the resolutions, but given the reprehensible reputation of the submarine and the high moral ground from which Root spoke, the American delegation found it difficult to publicly oppose Root, and did not.

The Root resolutions provoked a heated and prolonged debate between the British and French delegates. For a time the debate on submarine limitations and the Root resolutions threatened to wreck the Washington conference. To forestall that possibility, the delegates decided to eliminate submarine limitations from the agenda entirely and to deal with the Root resolutions in a separate protocol. Therefore no agreement on submarine limitations was achieved. All five major naval powers were left free to develop any number of submarines as they saw fit. The separate protocol incorporating the Root resolutions was approved in principle, but since it was never ratified by the French government, it had no legal force.

At the Geneva conference in 1927, called to resolve the cruiser issue, the question of submarines again arose. The British again proposed that submarines be outlawed and abolished, but neither the United States nor Japan was willing. In any case, with France and Italy absent, discussions of submarine abolition or limitations were meaningless. Nonetheless, some general ideas about submarine limitations were agreed to that, although not binding, would influence future naval arms limitation treaties: new "ocean" submarines should be limited to a maximum size of about 1,600–2,000 tons, coastal submarines to about 600 tons; no submarine should mount guns larger than 5.1"; should tonnage limitations ever be agreed to, the replacement life of a submarine should be fixed at thirteen years.

At the 1930 London Naval Conference, submarines again figured prominently. In his opening remarks, the First Lord of the Admiralty, Albert V. Alexander, urged that the submarine be abolished on humanitarian grounds, or if the delegates could not agree on abolition, that submarines be restricted to purely defensive roles, that the number and size be severely limited, and that operational restrictions similar to the Root resolutions be adopted. Reversing its position at the Washington conference, the United States, in the person of Secretary of State Henry L. Stimson, resoundingly endorsed the British position. The Italians also supported abolition, provided all five powers agreed, but since the French and Japanese adamantly opposed abolition, the conferees were forced to abandon that goal and concentrate on limitations.

After much horse trading, the three major naval powers finally agreed for the first time to submarine limitations. They were to restrict submarine forces to 52,700 tons each, to build no submarines larger than 2,000 tons or mount deck guns on submarines larger than 5.1"; the replacement life of submarines was fixed at thirteen years. The 52,700-ton limit forced all three navies to scrap submarines: the United States 16,000 tons; Great Britain 10,624 tons; Japan 25,142 tons.*

To no one's surprise, France refused to sign the submarine tonnage or type limitations. She then had about sixty 1920s-vintage submarines and was still intent on a buildup to about 100 boats by 1936. Italy, which was vainly attempting to maintain submarine parity with France and then had about thirty 1920s-vintage submarines, also refused to sign.†

A watered-down version of the Root resolutions was incorporated into Part IV of the London Treaty as Article 22. Signed by all five major powers,‡ it stated:

> *(1) In their action with regard to merchant ships, submarines must conform to the rules of International Law to which surface vessels are subject.*
>
> *(2) In particular, except in the case of persistent refusal to stop on being duly summoned, or of active resistance to visit or search, a warship, whether surface vessel or submarine, may not sink or render incapable of navigation a merchant vessel without having first placed passengers, crew and ship's papers in a place of safety. For this purpose the ship's boats are not regarded as a place of safety unless the safety of the passengers and crew is assured, in the existing sea and weather conditions, by proximity of land or the presence of another vessel which is in a position to take them on board.*

The London Naval Treaty, which took effect in 1930, twelve years after the conclusion of World War I and at the onset of the Great Depression, finally established honest naval parity between the United States and Great Britain at minimal force levels for each, and, for the first time, placed a limit on submarines of the three major naval powers. In the final negotiations Japan improved her position slightly over the 5:5:3 ratio in cruisers and destroyers, and achieved "parity" in submarine tonnage. Since the prohibition on fortifying United States naval bases west of Hawaii (Midway, Wake, Guam) remained in force, and Japan was believed

---

*   The United States scrapped thirty-two ineffective prewar or wartime boats, reducing its total force to about eighty submarines, the majority (fifty-one) of these the inferior S class. Great Britain retained about fifty submarines in commission, twenty of them fairly new. Japan retained about sixty boats, about twenty of them fairly new. The treaty contained a special exemption to the 2,000-ton and 5.1" gun limitations in order that the United States could keep three new 2,800-ton boats: *Narwhal, Nautilus,* and *Argonaut,* mounting 6" guns. A similar exemption allowed Britain to keep its *X-1,* with 5.2" guns and France to keep the 3,000-ton *Surcouf,* with 8" guns.

†   In the years 1930–1932, France ordered twenty new submarines, for a total of about eighty; Italy, twenty-six, for a total of about fifty-six.

‡   And later by ten other nations: Germany, Belgium, Russia, Haiti, Nepal, Sweden, Finland, Panama, Bulgaria, and Albania.

to be fortifying Pacific islands acquired from Germany in the Versailles Treaty, in the view of many American navalists, the London Treaty gave the Japanese Imperial Navy a decided advantage over the U.S. Navy should war occur.

A final effort to achieve lasting world peace and disarmament took place in Geneva in early 1932. Delegates from sixty of the sixty-four countries of the League of Nations, including Germany, convened for the League's Conference for the Reduction and Limitation of Armaments, or as it was hopefully known, the "World Disarmament Conference." Although the United States was not a member of the League, President Herbert Hoover proposed to the group that all powers slash existing ground and naval forces by about one-third and eliminate most offensive weapons, such as tanks, large mobile guns, and bombers. He also urged that chemical and bacteriological warfare be abolished and that submarines be severely limited.* The British government submitted equally drastic proposals, including one (the MacDonald Plan) that would establish rough parity in ground forces between Germany and France at a greatly reduced level. But by that time the paramilitary Nazis were the dominant political party in Germany—on the threshold of seizing absolute control—and Japan had arrogantly invaded Manchuria. France therefore rejected any form of disarmament and thus the conference foundered.

THE REBIRTH OF THE GERMAN NAVY

The Versailles Treaty virtually abolished the German Navy. It was permitted only 1,500 officers and 13,500 enlisted men and a motley collection of training vessels: six old battleships, six old cruisers, twelve destroyers, and twelve torpedo boats.† The Germans were allowed to replace ships greater than fifteen years old, but the new ships were to be severely limited in size: a maximum of 10,000 tons for battleships, 6,000 tons for cruisers, 800 tons for destroyers.

In the teething years of the Weimar Republic, the German Navy was not held in high esteem. Ridiculed for its huge prewar and wartime expenditures for a High Seas Fleet, which had appeared to shrink from a decisive engagement with the Royal Navy, and blamed for being the seedbed of the tumultuous 1918 revolutions, which had undermined the Army and the monarchy, it was also accused of attempting to subvert the democratic Weimar government. Moreover, to its critics, the German Navy's chief claims to distinction were at best dubious: the unrestricted U-boat campaign, which many viewed as one of the chief factors in the harsh retribution demanded by the Allies at Versailles, and the impulsive scuttling of the High Seas Fleet, which many viewed as one of the greatest wastes of assets in all

---

* Hoover's proposed cutback in naval power was to include 33 percent in capital ships (fifteen to ten for Great Britain and the United States); 25 percent in tonnages of aircraft carriers, cruisers, and destroyers, and 33 percent in submarine tonnage—no submarine force to exceed 35,000 tons. By one estimate, if Hoover's plan had been approved, the United States would have scrapped a total of 300,000 tons in naval vessels, over 1,000 heavy artillery pieces, nearly 1,000 tanks, and 300 bombers.

† Plus two old battleships, two old cruisers, four destroyers, and four torpedo boats in layup.

naval history. For these reasons, and others, demands arose throughout the Weimar Republic that the Navy be abolished. Navy morale hit rock bottom; skilled officers and enlisted men resigned in droves to pursue civilian careers.

Commencing in the summer of 1921, the Navy underwent a rebirth with a new name: *Reichsmarine* (State Navy). Its guiding philosophy, in the words of one rising star, was "complete abstinence from every type of party politics" and "unconditional loyalty to state and to the government chosen by its people." Accordingly, it purged its ranks of political extremists and other undesirables. It abolished the rank of warrant officer, deemed a breeding ground of leftist revolutionaries. The new volunteers were rigidly screened to prevent political or criminal infiltration. Only those men with the highest qualifications, character, intelligence, and loyalty to the Weimar Republic were retained or accepted.

Among the rising stars in the new Navy was Erich Raeder, an austere, straight-arrow, apolitical, devout Christian officer, whose influence in all ranks was to be profound. Born in Hamburg April 24, 1876, Raeder was the grandson and son of scholars and teachers. As a student, Raeder had ideas of becoming a physician, but in 1894, at age eighteen, he changed his mind and joined the Imperial Navy. During the war he had served four uninterrupted years in cruisers with the High Seas Fleet. After the war, among other tasks, he was assigned to write a two-volume official history of cruiser operations. In 1920, having served twenty-five years in the Navy and believing he would soon be retired, he began the study of political science and law at the University of Berlin, in preparation for a second career as a teacher. However, Raeder had already been marked for higher naval responsibilities, and in 1922 he was promoted to rear admiral and designated Inspector of Naval Education. As such Raeder served, in effect, as the schoolmaster of the new Navy, responsible for screening, selecting, and educating its officers and enlisted personnel. In every respect the *Reichsmarine* was to bear his personal stamp.

Given its minuscule size and antiquated equipment, the *Reichsmarine* was hard put to define a realistic mission for itself. The Soviet Union, still torn apart by revolution, posed no real naval threat to Germany. A more likely threat was Poland. She might gobble up isolated East Prussia, expanding her frontier on the Baltic. In such an event, the antiquated ships of the German Navy might render effective service as a counterforce to the third-rate Polish Navy. But that scenario posed a larger problem: France was almost certain to ally with Poland and establish a blockade of the German coast on the North Sea and possibly send strong naval forces into the Baltic. Therefore, the Poland scenario was discouraging.

Those concerned with the long-term naval strategy postulated more optimistic plans. Based on the recent economic and political history of Europe, it was not unreasonable to assume that Germany would in due course regain its dominant industrial and financial position, and that the harsh restrictions of the Versailles Treaty would be relaxed gradually, and ultimately rescinded. The challenge was to formulate future naval strategies and plan a Navy to fit the strategies within the existing restrictions of the Versailles Treaty, assuming at the same time that the restrictions were likely to diminish with the passage of years.

In drafting long-term scenarios, the strategists categorically and absolutely ruled out another naval war with Great Britain. The distinguished German naval historian Friedrich Ruge wrote: "The 1914–18 war with Britain was considered by every [German] naval officer a tragic mistake which should never be repeated lest the consequences become far more terrible to either side. Therefore it was strictly forbidden to play with this kind of fire even in war games."

The long-range planners assumed that the most likely and formidable opponent in another war would be France, either as an ally of Poland in a dispute arising over the "Polish Corridor" or for other reasons. In event of war with France, the planners proposed the German Navy should wage another *guerre de course.* Owing to the ban on building U-boats, the planners of this commerce war recommended a new, fast, long-range surface raider powerful enough to force the French Navy to fragment and disperse its men-of-war to escort its convoys. The dispersion of French warships would deny France sufficient naval power for a blockade of the German coast or assistance to Poland in the Baltic, or interdiction of German maritime trade in the North Sea or elsewhere. Should Germany ultimately be permitted to build U-boats, they would neatly augment this strategy. Or should Great Britain ally with Germany in a war against France, the German commerce raiders would neatly augment the Royal Navy.

These strategic concepts directly influenced the design of the *Reichsmarine*'s first "replacement" battleship, the *Deutschland.* She was an extraordinary, 10,000-ton, state-of-the-art vessel. Powered by diesel engines, which gave her a top speed of 26 knots, and armed with six 11" guns, she had a cruising range of 10,000 nautical miles. As historian Ruge put it, the *Deutschland* was "faster than almost any heavier ship in existence, more heavily armed than any faster vessel, with a cruising range vastly exceeding that of any cruiser or capital ship." Hence she appeared to be the ideal "hit-and-run" commerce raider. Because of her small size (to meet Versailles Treaty restrictions) she was nicknamed a "pocket" battleship. But when the *Reichsmarine* requested funds from the *Reichstag* for the costly *Deutschland,* it met strenuous opposition and initially had to settle for four new "replacement" light cruisers of 6,000 tons, useful mainly for training purposes: *Emden* (1925), *Königsberg* (1929), *Karlsruhe* (1929), and *Köln* (1930).

Meanwhile, in violation of the Versailles Treaty, the *Reichsmarine* continued U-boat research and development through the Krupp front, IVS, in Holland. The IVS encouraged—and financed—three submarine prototypes: one small (250 tons), one medium (500 tons), and one large (750 tons). Three 250-ton boats (*Vesikkos*) and three 500-ton boats (*Vetehinens*) were built in Finland. One 750-ton boat (*E-1*) was built in Spain. The IVS also financed a plant for building torpedo tubes and torpedoes in Spain. German sailors in mufti were assigned to conduct the trials of the submarine prototypes in Finland and Spain. Other *Reichsmarine* personnel established a submarine school in Turkey to train Turkish submariners to man three submarines IVS had sold to Turkey. The school also trained German submariners.

The clandestine German research and development on U-boats and other weaponry was a poorly kept secret. French and British newspapers repeatedly exposed the subterfuge. Nor was the Allied Control Commission, withdrawn after

Germany entered into the Locarno Pact and the League of Nations, fooled. In its final report, the Commission stated: "Germany had never disarmed, had never had the intention of disarming, and for seven years had done everything in her power to deceive and 'countercontrol' the Commission appointed to control her disarmament."

Not everyone in Germany approved of these secret military activities. In 1926 and 1927 some German politicians and newspapers attacked and exposed the subterfuges. One result was that the Hindenburg government was compelled to sack the Defense Minister, Otto Gessler; the *Reichswehr* chief, Hans von Seeckt; and the *Reichsmarine* chief, Hans Zenker.

In the shakeup, the prim, apolitical Erich Raeder rose to command the *Reichsmarine,* effective October 1, 1928. He took office, he wrote in his memoirs, determined to "travel the road of absolute correctness, in an absolutely loyal and well-defined relationship to the State and its government." He demanded that all *Reichsmarine* personnel emulate his example. In the words of one German naval historian, the *Reichsmarine* became Raeder, and Raeder, the *Reichsmarine.*

At first Raeder had his hands full. The new Defense Minister, Wilhelm Groener, a former Army general, repeatedly expressed doubt in public about the need for a Navy, a sentiment shared by many Germans, including Adolf Hitler, who had savagely denounced the Imperial Navy in his book, *Mein Kampf,* and who ridiculed the *Reichsmarine*'s battleship replacement policy in a published article. But by gaining support from Hindenburg and by deft maneuvering in the *Reichstag,* Raeder succeeded in obtaining not only funds for the *Deutschland* (launched May 19, 1931) but also funds to lay the keels for two sister ships, *Admiral Graf Spee* and *Admiral Scheer.** In addition, Raeder secretly resumed support and funding for the small, medium, and large U-boat prototypes in Finland and Spain.

By 1932 Hitler and the Nazis held a majority of seats in the *Reichstag* and Hitler was scheming to unseat and replace the aged, ineffectual, but revered German president, Hindenburg. Encouraged in part by the Nazis, in part by the British proposals at the World Disarmament Conference in Geneva for German "equality" or military parity with France, behind the scenes a succession of German chancellors and defense ministers secretly authorized vast expansions of the *Wehrmacht* and *Reichsmarine.*

Raeder supervised the plans for the expansion (*Umbau*) of the *Reichsmarine,* which was approved November 15, 1932. The plan envisioned six capital ships (battleships and "pocket" battleships), an aircraft carrier, six new heavy cruisers, six squadrons of destroyers, three squadrons of minesweepers and three of motor torpedo boats, numerous auxiliaries, and—in blatant defiance of the Versailles Treaty—a substantial naval air arm and a submarine force of three (half) flotillas, comprising a total of sixteen U-boats. A submarine school, disguised as an *anti*submarine school, was to be established in secrecy on the Naval Academy grounds at Mürwik, a town near the city of Flensburg.

---

* In violation of the Versailles Treaty, these "pocket" battleships actually displaced 12,000 tons, rather than 10,000 tons.

When Hitler came to power as Chancellor of Germany on January 31, 1933, Raeder was wary and concerned. Hitler drew much of his power from the Army, not the small, apolitical Navy, which Hitler had often and freely criticized. But Raeder was soon reassured. Pledged to throw off the "shackles" of the Versailles Treaty and restore Germany to a position of military greatness, Hitler's plans included a strong German Navy.

Hitler's strategic vision for Germany—most of which was spelled out in *Mein Kampf*—was to reunite all German-speaking peoples into a single nation and then expand eastward to gain *Lebensraum* or "living space." In effect, this meant the reclamation of the Rhineland and Saar; the annexation of Austria and the Sudetenland area of Czechoslovakia; the conquest of the rest of Czechoslovakia and of Poland and Memelland, Lithuania; an alliance with or subjugation of Hungary, Romania, and Bulgaria, and, ultimately, the conquest of the Soviet Union.

Hitler believed he could successfully carry out these conquests notwithstanding the League of Nations, the Locarno and Kellogg-Briand pacts, and the various existing mutual defense treaties. France was rotten and corrupt; it would not fight. Or if it fought, it could easily be defeated. Mussolini's Italy and possibly Japan could be drawn into the Nazi orbit. By its pro-German stand for German military "equality" at Geneva and other signals, the British government appeared to endorse Hitler's plans to rearm and expand eastward.

The British attitude toward Hitler and the Germans sprang from a dense tangle of psychological, political, economic, and military factors. Many upper-class Britons who controlled the government and other institutions had vowed never to become embroiled in another slaughter on the continent. A vast majority of Britons, ravaged by the Depression, vigorously opposed expenditures for armaments of any kind. Many Britons were related to and sympathetic toward the Germans and loathed the French. These Britons believed the terms of the Versailles Treaty, insisted upon by the French, had been much too harsh and that the Germans had been punished enough. Many Britons deeply feared Joseph Stalin and the Communists and viewed a strong Germany as the most effective bulwark against the spread of communism or even an instrument for the destruction of communism.

One part of Hitler's strategy was to encourage the pro-German, antiwar attitude in Britain to the fullest possible extent. Hitler did not want a war with Great Britain "under any circumstances." Therefore the buildup of the *Reichsmarine* must not threaten the British people or the Royal Navy. Hitler planned to negotiate a bilateral naval agreement with Great Britain, fixing Anglo-German navies at a nonprovocative 3:1 ratio in capital ships. Thus the *Reichsmarine* should promote friendly relations with the Royal Navy. But until the agreement had been negotiated, the *Reichsmarine* buildup, especially the U-boat force, must be conducted with utmost secrecy and deception.

Over the next two years, 1933–1935, while Hitler and his cronies seized dictatorial powers in Germany, Raeder quietly directed the expansion of the *Reichsmarine* and cultivated friendly relations with the Royal Navy. Assuming that a bilateral Anglo-German naval treaty would be reached and that the Versailles Treaty restrictions would be rescinded, he authorized secret planning for two large battle cruisers, *Gneisenau* and *Scharnhorst,* two super-battleships, *Bismarck* and *Tirpitz,* numerous armed merchant ship raiders, and a submarine force to be composed initially of twenty-four small (250-ton), ten medium (500-ton), and two large (750-ton) U-boats.

Having consolidated his grip on Germany and rekindled its martial spirit, in the spring of 1935 Hitler, in effect, repudiated the Versailles Treaty. Berlin revealed that Germany was to initiate conscription to build the *Wehrmacht* to 300,000 men (thirty-six divisions) and that Germany was to create an air force, the *Luftwaffe.* At the same time Hitler signaled a desire to commence negotiations with the British government for an Anglo-German naval agreement. Determined to appease Hitler, the British government warmly welcomed the signals.

The negotiations commenced in earnest on June 3, 1935, in London. The British team was led by one of the chief appeasers, Foreign Secretary Samuel J. G. Hoare. The German team was led by Hitler's new Foreign Minister, Joachim von Ribbentrop. There was little debate. The Germans offered a 100:35 capital ship ratio and the British accepted eagerly. The agreement allowed the Germans to build about 183,000 tons in capital ships. Deducting the three new "pocket" battleships, comprising a total of about 36,000 tons, this left Germany with a capital ship building allowance of about 147,000 tons, which was just sufficient to build the big battle cruisers *Gneisenau* and *Scharnhorst* and the super-battleships *Bismarck* and *Tirpitz.**

The last item on the agenda was submarines. Germany insisted on parity with Great Britain (about 52,700 tons) but assured Britain it would build only to 45 percent of parity (about 24,000 tons) unless "outside considerations" compelled a larger program. In any event, Germany would not exceed 45 percent of British submarine tonnage without further negotiations. The British acceded to the German demands, provided Germany would adopt the 1930 London Treaty Submarine Protocol (Article 22) barring unrestricted submarine warfare against merchant ships. The Germans readily agreed to this stipulation.

The Anglo-German Naval Treaty was signed on June 18 and announced three days later. Hitler viewed it as one of his greatest diplomatic coups, "the happiest day of my life." The treaty constituted Germany's first *legal* release from the restrictions of the Versailles Treaty, and as such, it tended to confer the stamp of legitimacy on all German rearmament.

Most British were pleased. The Foreign Secretary, Samuel Hoare, who was named First Lord of the Admiralty in 1936, praised his own statesmanship. The treaty, he said, was "safe" and was "in the interests of peace," which "is the main objective of the British government." Among the chief benefits attained in the

---

* The initial agreement specified a limit of 35,000 tons on capital ships to conform to the limits imposed on the major naval powers by the 1930 London Naval Treaty, but the limit was later raised to 45,000 tons. In their final configuration, *Gneisenau* and *Scharnhorst* displaced 32,000 tons; *Bismarck* and *Tirpitz,* 42,000 tons.

treaty, he went on, was Germany's pledge not to engage in "unrestricted use of submarines against merchant ships." Britain's most distinguished navalist, David Beatty, former Admiral of the Grand Fleet (1916–1919) and First Sea Lord (1919–1927), told the House of Lords: "We owe thanks to the Germans. They came to us with outstretched hands and voluntarily proposed to accept a thirty-five to one hundred ratio in fleet strength. If they had made different proposals, we would not have been able to stop them. That we do not have an armament race with one nation in the world at least is something for which we must be thankful." Among the very few British critics was Winston Churchill, then out of the government and an outspoken opponent of appeasement. He denounced the treaty in his customary pungent language. That the British government would believe that Germany would abide by the submarine protocol, he said, was "the acme of gullibility."

Prior to and during the negotiations, the *Reichsmarine* had built, in utmost secrecy, six duplicates of the 250-ton U-boat prototype *Vesikko* in German shipyards. On June 29, 1935, one week after the treaty was announced, the *Reichsmarine* (State Navy), appropriately renamed the *Kriegsmarine* (Combat Navy), commissioned the first boat, *U-1*, in a public ceremony. The news came as a profound shock to the world. Out of nowhere, it seemed, the dreaded, evil, long-illegal U-boat was back.

A DRAMATIC RECONVERSION

Long in gestation and birth but as yet unformed, the new German submarine force required a skilled leader. Raeder, as he wrote, had not a shadow of doubt about the man for the job. His choice was Karl Dönitz, a forty-eight-year-old junior captain who epitomized Raeder's efforts to create a loyal, dedicated, responsible, professional naval officer corps.

The younger of two sons of Emil Dönitz, an engineer with the Zeiss optical firm, Karl Dönitz was born September 16, 1891, in Grünau, a suburb of Berlin. His mother, Anna (nee Beyer), died before he was four years old. His father, who never remarried, raised the two boys, Friedrich and Karl, in Grünau and in Jena, near the city of Weimar. They lived in middle-class comfort in an all-male environment; the boys received a classical education in private schools. Although there was no maritime tradition in the family, Friedrich joined the merchant marine and on April 1, 1910, at age eighteen, Karl joined the Imperial Navy. The father died two years later; the brothers drifted apart and ultimately became estranged. For Karl, the Navy was to be both family and career.

The career went well. After a mandatory year at sea as a cadet on the training cruiser *Hertha,* and a year at the Imperial Naval Academy in Mürwik, Dönitz won a commission and in 1912 was assigned to the new light cruiser *Breslau,* operating in the Mediterranean and Black seas. Upon the outbreak of the war in 1914, the Kaiser turned over the *Breslau* and an older battleship, *Goeben,* to Turkey as *quid pro quo* for entering the war on the side of the Central Powers. Sailing with mixed

German-Turkish crews, the two ships conducted cat-and-mouse operations against the Czarist fleet in the Black Sea. During *Breslau's* refits, Dönitz qualified as an aircraft observer, married Ingebord Weber (May 27, 1916), daughter of a German general stationed in Turkey, fathered a daughter, Ursula (1917), and published a stirring book about his shipboard adventures, *The Voyages of the Breslau in the Black Sea.*

When, in 1916, the Imperial Navy shifted its main emphasis to U-boats, Dönitz volunteered. After a three-month training course in Germany, he returned to the Mediterranean in early 1917 to serve as a watch officer on *U-39,* commanded by Walter Forstmann, Germany's second-ranking U-boat "ace." From February to October 1917, Dönitz made four war patrols on *U-39,* during which Forstmann sank thirty-two ships. Promoted to command *UC-25,* a small, old minelayer, Dönitz made two more war patrols in the Mediterranean, during which he laid two minefields and torpedoed five ships—and won a high decoration for bravery, the Knight's Cross of the House of Holhenzollern.

In the closing days of the war, September 1918, Dönitz was promoted to command a larger attack submarine, *UB-68.* On October 4, while on his first patrol in the Mediterranean, he attacked a convoy and sank a ship. But in the ensuing action, the U-boat went out of control and popped to the surface. Under heavy fire from the convoy escorts and unable to dive, Dönitz was compelled to scuttle. The British fished Dönitz and twenty-nine others from the water and took them to England, where they remained imprisoned until July 1919.

When Dönitz rejoined his wife and daughter in chaotic postwar Germany, he elected to remain in the *Reichsmarine.* For the ensuing four years, 1920–1924, he commanded a destroyer, *T-157,* at the naval base Swinemünde, on the Baltic, where the Dönitz family expanded with the birth of two sons, Klaus (1920) and Peter (1922). Following that tour, Dönitz, promoted to lieutenant commander, was assigned to the naval staff in Berlin, where he served under Rear Admiral Erich Raeder.

Raeder was favorably impressed. In one official assessment, he wrote that Dönitz was a "smart, industrious, ambitious officer" who possessed "excellent professional knowledge" and expressed "clear judgment in questions of naval war leadership" and had "good military as well as technical gifts." From 1928 onward, Raeder guided Dönitz to ever higher rungs on the career ladder: promotion to full commander and command of a destroyer (half) flotilla, 1928–1930; First Staff Officer of the North Sea High Command, 1930–1934; promotion to junior captain and to the coveted job of commander of the light cruiser *Emden,* 1934–1935.

Karl Dönitz was not pleased with his assignment to U-boats. The emphasis in the *Kriegsmarine* was the buildup of a big-ship surface navy. Submarines were clearly secondary and restricted by the terms of the Anglo-German Naval Treaty. He felt he had been "pushed into a backwater" and that his promising naval career had possibly reached a dead end.

But a dramatic reconversion occurred. After plunging into his new job with "all the energy at my command," as he put it in his memoirs, "body and soul I was once more a submariner." The reconversion led to a single-minded conviction: that notwithstanding Hitler's grand strategy, war with Great Britain was inevitable and that Germany should be building not big surface ships but submarines—hundreds of submarines.

This conviction derived from a close study of German U-boat records, official and unofficial naval histories of World War I, and his own U-boat experiences. In his view, the small, primitive Imperial Navy U-boat force had come very close to imposing a war-winning maritime blockade against Great Britain. Had Germany built large numbers of U-boats rather than big ships for the High Seas Fleet, and had the Kaiser authorized unrestricted U-boat warfare in the first year of the war, Dönitz concluded, Germany could have achieved an early and decisive naval victory over the Allies. With proper organization and planning and modern submarines and new tactics, he believed victory could be realized in the war he saw coming.

To be sure, there would be difficulties and hazards. First, convoys. Convoying saved the Allies from defeat at sea in World War I. This time around the Allies were certain to form convoys in the early days of the war. Second, sonar. The *Reichsmarine* knew the Royal Navy had developed an active electronic underwater detection device, which the British believed to be 80 percent effective at locating submarines. Third, aircraft. Reliable, fast, modern airplanes could search huge ocean areas and carry a greater payload of improved ASW bombs and depth charges.

Even so, Dönitz believed the submarine could win. This conviction was based on the significant technological advances German engineers and other specialists had achieved in submarine construction, torpedoes, and communications, and on a new tactical doctrine German submariners conceived for attacking convoys.

The new U-boat prototypes were far superior to the U-boats of World War I. Built of a new steel alloy, which was welded rather than riveted, they were tougher and more maneuverable, and dived much faster and deeper. The new medium (500-ton) boat had twice the diesel and electric horsepower of its predecessor, giving it 3 knots greater surface speed (16 versus 13) and the ability to accelerate rapidly to full speed when submerged. The surface cruising range of the new boats could be greatly extended by an ingenious fuel-conservation technique, wherein one of the two diesels could be rigged to turn both propeller shafts.

German engineers had produced what were believed to be marvelous improvements in submarine torpedoes. The warheads were nearly double the size of the World War I model (612 pounds of explosives versus 352 pounds). In addition to the "air"-propelled torpedoes, the Germans had perfected a torpedo propelled by electricity (from storage batteries), which left no telltale wake pointing to the submarine. As another measure to conceal the position of the submarine, the submarine torpedo tubes had been redesigned to absorb the bubbles created by the compressed air used to eject the torpedo. All torpedoes could be fitted with a "magnetic" pistol (or fuse) that was activated by the magnetic field of the target. Designed to explode *beneath* the keels of the targets rather than against the sides, magnetic torpedoes were deemed to be much more lethal than torpedoes with impact pistols. It was possible that only one magnetic torpedo would be required to sink an enemy ship.

Radio technology had also greatly improved since the last war. The new U-boat prototypes were equipped with a superb array of receivers and long- and shortwave transmitters. Hence a force commander could maintain clear and continuous contact with all U-boats at sea, and the boats could communicate with one another. This communications linkage enabled a force commander to receive and relay reports on enemy positions, to receive current reports from U-boats on damage inflicted on the enemy or damage sustained and the type and extent of enemy ASW measures, to know the amount of fuel and torpedoes remaining on board each boat at any given time, and to know the current weather and sea conditions in the assigned operating area.

In World War I, U-boats had failed against enemy convoys because they could seldom find them and when a U-boat did find one, it usually had to attack alone. Dönitz believed that enemy convoys could now be located by a more sophisticated deployment of U-boats on likely convoy routes, by *Luftwaffe* aerial reconnaissance, and by intelligence on enemy convoy routing derived from codebreaking, spies, and other sources. Upon receiving information on the composition, course, and speed of a convoy, Dönitz postulated, a force commander could in theory shift the available U-boats by radio to positions to intercept the convoy for a massed or group attack, which the confused escorts would be virtually powerless to prevent.

The group (or "wolf pack") attacks could be carried out either in daytime while submerged or at night while on the surface. To minimize detection in submerged daylight attacks, the U-boats were to employ only wakeless battery-powered ("electric") torpedoes, with magnetic pistols in the warheads. In night surface attacks, when torpedo wakes were harder to see, the faster, longer-range "air" torpedoes with magnetic pistols were to be used.

Dönitz thought the new ASW weapons, namely sonar and aircraft, were greatly overrated. The most advanced sonar still had serious technical weaknesses, a range of one to one and a half miles at most, and—most important—it could not detect a submarine on the surface. The electric torpedoes had a greater range (three miles) than sonar. Hence, in the initial daylight submerged attack, a U-boat could "stand off" and shoot before there was any possibility of being detected by enemy sonar. Should a hunting escort make sonar contact with the submerged U-boat after the attack, the U-boat could evade and escape with its rapid acceleration and deep diving. Aircraft could not usually see a submerged submarine or its periscope in most waters and thus posed small to no danger to a U-boat using wakeless torpedoes during a submerged daylight attack. Aircraft did not yet patrol at night; hence none would be present during a night surface attack. The principal danger posed by an aircraft was its ability to detect a submarine traveling on the surface in daylight. But aircraft were still relatively slow. A keenly alert U-boat bridge watch, Dönitz believed, could see or hear the aircraft before it saw the U-boat. With its ability to dive quickly (thirty seconds) and deep, a properly alert modern U-boat could avoid attack by any known aircraft.

To win the commerce war, Dönitz calculated, Germany would require a force of about 300 medium (500-ton) U-boats. Counting time lost going to and from the combat zone and time lost in refit and overhaul, this number would enable Germany to keep about 100 U-boats in the convoy hunting grounds. Based on the results achieved by the U-boats of World War I, Dönitz calculated, a force of modern boats could doubtless sink a million tons of British shipping a month. The British merchant marine of the late 1930s comprised about 3,000 ships of 17.5 million tons, including tankers. Thus, in a mere six months, U-boats could destroy almost one-third of it, and within a year, almost two-thirds. It therefore appeared reasonable to Dönitz that a modern German U-boat force could throttle the British in a year or a year and a half.

Early in his new job, Dönitz informally submitted these ideas to Raeder and to the Berlin naval staff, the *Oberkommando der Kriegsmarine* (OKM). He was sternly rebuffed. Hitler had assured Raeder, time and again, that war with Great Britain was unthinkable. As historian Ruge wrote, war games with Great Britain as the enemy were prohibited. The Anglo-German Naval Treaty—Hitler's great diplomatic triumph—had just been signed. Under the terms of that agreement Germany was restricted, except in unusual circumstances that required renegotiations, to about 24,000 tons of submarines. By then most of the permitted tonnage had already been allocated. Even if it had not been, the entire allowance would produce merely forty-eight medium (500-ton) boats. Besides that, Germany had agreed to sign the Submarine Protocol, which barred surprise attacks on almost all merchant ships. Moreover, many senior officers at the OKM were unshakably convinced that sonar and modern aircraft had ruled out the possibility of submarine warfare in the hunting grounds close to the British Isles. They had proposed larger submarines for operations in distant waters where enemy ASW measures were less intense. These boats were to raid enemy (i.e., French) maritime assets, in a manner similar to the "pocket" battleships and armed merchant cruisers, adhering to the "cruiser rules" and the Submarine Protocol.

Dönitz was neither discouraged nor dissuaded. He remained absolutely convinced that sooner or later Hitler would provoke war with Great Britain; that it was a grave mistake for the *Kriegsmarine* to build big surface ships; that the Anglo-German Naval Treaty, the submarine tonnage limitations, and the Submarine Protocol would be abrogated; and that Germany would be compelled for the second time to turn to U-boats for waging war at sea. He therefore did everything in his power to shape the training, weaponry, and operational planning of the new U-boat force to fit his convictions.

To the Eve of War

In 1936, when the five-power London Naval Treaty expired, there was no chance of a renewal. Japan had walked out of the League of Nations, occupied Manchuria, and had already embarked on a naval buildup in excess of treaty limits. Italy had occupied Abyssinia (Ethiopia), intervened in the Spanish Civil War on the side of fascist general Francisco Franco, and had made plans for a substantial naval buildup, which had provoked the French to follow suit. Although Great Britain and the United States agreed in principle to certain naval limitations, they were not binding, and each nation went its own way. Thus the remarkable era of naval arms limitation among the major naval powers expired.

That same year, 1936, the Führer of the Third Reich, Adolf Hitler, commenced military operations. Goose-stepping *Wehrmacht* forces reclaimed the Rhineland in March. Later in the year Hitler joined Mussolini in support of Franco, sending *Luftwaffe* and tank (*panzer*) units to Spain. But Hitler continued to seek amicable relations with the appeasing British government. As a consequence, the *Kriegsmarine* strictly adhered to the terms of the Anglo-German Naval Treaty and courted the Royal Navy by ceremonial ship visits, sailing regattas, and other means.

The treaty allowed the Germans to build 24,000 tons of submarines. In 1935 the OKM expended half that allowance (12,500 tons) to order thirty-six U-boats based on the IVS Finnish and Spanish prototypes.* Since the plans had already been drawn and the prototypes tested in Finland and Spain, and some matériel preassembled, these thirty-six boats were built quickly and commissioned in 1935 and 1936, except one Type VII, *U-32,* which was delayed to 1937.

A bitter dispute arose over how to expend the remaining 11,500 tons allowed by the treaty. In support of his conviction that war with Great Britain was inevitable and that groups, or wolf packs, of U-boats would be required to defeat the convoy system, Dönitz urged that the full 11,500 tons be allocated for the construction of twenty-three improved Type VII medium (500-ton) boats, so that he could war-game his ideas and train his men. In opposition, the OKM proposed twenty-three boats of a different mix: eight more improved small Type IIs, eight more large, long-range submarines (improved versions of the Type I, designated Type IX), and seven improved Type VII mediums. After months of procrastination, Raeder sided with the OKM.

This decision was a major setback for Dönitz and his fledgling U-boat arm. Berlin had rejected his convictions and theories about war with Great Britain. The procrastination entailed in reaching the decision and the emphasis on the large Type IXs, which took much longer to construct, delayed the buildup of the U-boat arm. No U-boats of the second order were to be commissioned in 1937 and only nine in 1938 and twelve in the first eight months of 1939. That he had failed to persuade Raeder and the OKM to adopt his theories and concepts—and submarine types—was to haunt Dönitz for the rest of his life.

The first small Type II U-boats, *U-1* to *U-12,* were commissioned in the summer of 1935. The first six of these were assigned to the submarine school in Kiel for basic training. The second six, improved Type IIBs of greater range, formed the nucleus of an organized flotilla for advanced training, also based in Kiel. Commanded by Dönitz, the flotilla was named in honor of a renowned submarine hero of the Impe-

---

* Twenty-four small (250-ton) Type II (*U-1* to *U-24*); two large (750-ton) Type I (*U-25* and *U-26*); and ten medium (500-ton) Type VII (*U-27* to *U-36*).

rial Navy, Otto Weddigen, who had sunk four British cruisers before being killed in action. Dönitz formally commissioned the Weddigen Flotilla on September 25, 1935.

The skippers of the Weddigen Flotilla were handpicked senior lieutenants averaging about twenty-eight years in age with about ten years' service in the German Navy.* Some had trained on the secret IVS prototypes in Finland and Spain; some had trained on the IVS boats in Turkey. All were recent graduates of or instructors from the submarine school. It was a small, tight group, a navy within a navy. Everyone knew everybody intimately. Two skippers, Hans-Günther Looff (*U-9*) and Hans-Rudolf Rösing (*U-11*), were married to sisters. All the men shared Dönitz's convictions that war with Great Britain was inevitable and that U-boats were to bear the burden of waging the naval war.

The Weddigen Flotilla commenced sea training on October 1, 1935, flying the new flag of the *Kriegsmarine,* the black and red swastika. Six more Type IIBs—which the Germans half-jokingly called "dugout canoes" or "ducks"—joined the flotilla over the next three months, making a total of twelve. Under the direction of Dönitz and his flotilla engineer and right arm, Otto ("Pappa") Thedsen, a fifty-year-old salt who had risen from the enlisted ranks of the Imperial Navy, the crews trained with a sense of urgency. The OKM had decreed that the flotilla must be "war ready" by March 1936, to support Hitler's reoccupation of the Rhineland, possibly provoking a war with France, which had allied not only with Poland but also with the Soviet Union, posing the possibility of a two-front naval war in the Baltic Sea.

Dönitz went to sea daily on one duck or the other. He was a demanding but fair and forgiving instructor. In contrast to customs in the Imperial Navy, he encouraged camaraderie between officers and enlisted men, a "democratic" navy, where one and all shared the same food, work, hazards, and hardships. Confined inside the little boats every day, Dönitz got to know his men well and they him. He was a charismatic leader. The men, who called him "The Lion," idolized him for his obvious competence and for the respect and concern he showed for them.

Dönitz put the ducks through a variety of drills but the main emphasis was on torpedo shooting. Every duck in the flotilla was required to carry out sixty-six daylight submerged and sixty-six night surface attacks, in which "water slugs" (shots of compressed air) were fired in place of training torpedoes. These drills were tough on all hands, but especially so on the captains. They had to plan and conduct the approaches on the target ships by day and night, taking into account winds, seas, currents, visibility, water depth, phases of the moon, and other factors, meanwhile estimating the target course and speed and calculating the proper interception course and speed for the U-boat. They were encouraged to develop a kind of sixth sense about whether or not they could be—or had been—spotted by aircraft or surface ships and therefore when to surface or submerge, when to use and when

---

* Normally, Germans entered the Navy at age eighteen, straight out of high school. Like recruits in the Imperial Navy, all spent the first year at sea crewing a full-rigged sailing ship. Hence the year of entry into the Navy was known as "crew" year, the equivalent of "class" year in other navies. The Weddigen Flotilla skippers came from the crews of 1924 to 1927.

PLATE 3

GERMAN U-BOAT TYPES

JUNE 1935–SEPTEMBER 1939

	SMALL			MEDIUM		LARGE	
TYPE	II	IIB	IIC	VII	VIIB	I	IX
Treaty size (tons)	250	250	250	500	500	750	750
War load (tons)	254	280	291	626	753	826	1,032
Length (feet)	134	140	144	212	218	237	251
Diesel H.P.	700	700	700	2,320	2,800	3,080	4,400
Fuel (tons)	12	21	23	67	108	96	154
Top speed (knots)	13.0	13.0	12.0	16.0	17.25	17.8	18.2
Range at 12 knots	1,050	1,800	1,900	4,300	6,500	6,700	8,100
Torpedo tubes	3	3	3	4/1 *	4/1 **	4/2 ***	4/2 ***
Torpedoes (total)	6	6	6	11	14	14	22
Internal torpedoes	6	6	6	10	12	14	12
Mine load	18	18	18	33	39	42	66
Max. depth (feet)	500	500	500	650	650	650	650
Crew	25	25	25	44	44	43	48
Commissioned (57):	6	18	6	10	8	2	7

* Stern tube external
** Stern tube internal
*** Four forward, two aft

not to use the periscope, and the most effective tactics for evading pursuers submerged. After these 132 simulated attacks, the boats graduated to fire real torpedoes with dummy warheads, set to run deep beneath the target ships.

During these torpedo drills, Dönitz developed new shooting procedures which were to become standard on all U-boats. In submerged daylight attacks the captain, who had sole access to the attack periscope, conducted the approach, assisted by the first watch officer at a plotting board, then aimed and fired the torpedoes. In the night surface attack, the captain conducted the approach at the plotting board in the control room, but he did not fire the torpedoes. That task was delegated to the first watch officer on the bridge, using high-power Zeiss binoculars mounted on a gyroscope compass repeater. It was a more efficient system, but not many captains willingly delegated the torpedo firing to the first watch officer. No other navy adopted this technique.

The little boats were at sea five days a week, twenty-four hours a day. The routine was exhausting. Some days they conducted as many as eight submerged daylight attacks and six night surface attacks. As one skipper remembered, fourteen attacks in twenty-four hours was "the upper limit of our physical and nervous capacity."

The ducks had strong, welded steel hulls, capable (on paper) of withstanding sea pressure to a maximum depth of about 500 feet. One way to outfox enemy

PLATE 4

THE PREWAR GERMAN U-BOAT BUILDUP

JUNE 1935–SEPTEMBER 1939

	1935	1936	1937	1938	1939
January	—	U-14,U-18, U-19,U-20	—	—	—
February	—	—	—	—	U-40,U-52, U-58
March	—	U-15	—	—	U-59
April	—	U-25	U-32	—	U-41,U-48
May	—	U-16,U-26	—	—	—
June	U-1	—	—	U-45	U-53
July	U-2,U-7	U-33	—	—	U-42,U-60
August	U-3,U-4, U-5,U-8, U-9	U-21,U-22, U-27	—	U-51,U-37	U-49,U-43 U-61
September	U-6,U-10, U-11,U-12	U-23,U-28, U-34,U-24, U-30	—	—	
October	—	—	—	U-38	
November	U-13	U-29,U-35	—	U-46,U-39, U-56,U-57	
December	U-17	U-31,U-36	—	U-47	
Totals:	14	21	1	10	11

U-1 to U-6	Type II (Duck)
U-7 to U-24	Type IIB (Duck)
U-25 and U-26	Type I
U-27 to U-36	Type VII
U-37 to U-44	Type IX
U-45 to U-55	Type VIIB
U-56 to U-61	Type IIC (Duck)

sonar was to shut down all unnecessary machinery and dive to maximum depth ("run silent, run deep"). Dönitz encouraged deep-diving drills, but a near-disaster on *U-12,* commanded by Werner von Schmidt, put a damper on these maneuvers. At 341 feet, an internal angle-bar joint failed, the hull cracked, and the boat flooded dangerously. The boat was saved and the hull was later reinforced, as were the hulls of the other ducks, but as a result of the accident, the OKM restricted all U-boats to a maximum diving depth of 150 feet. Inasmuch as Dönitz believed deep diving would be a necessary routine in wartime and should be rehearsed to the extent that it caused no anxiety, he pleaded for cancellation of the order, but his arguments were rejected. In his memoir, he commented bitterly: "For the lessons which one fails to learn in peace, one pays a high price in war."

When the *Wehrmacht* marched into the Rhineland on March 7, 1936, twelve boats of the Weddigen Flotilla—as well as the six Type IIs at the submarine school—deployed for possible naval war with Poland, France, or the Soviet Union in the North and Baltic seas. In a sense, the war deployment constituted a "graduation" exercise for the flotilla. All boats "passed" with high marks. Dönitz drew a rave review from a superior: "Through indefatigable work and personal instruction he has demanded so much from the 'U-Flotilla Weddigen' in planned training that already . . . they are ready for employment on war tasks."

Later in the year 1936, the other six ducks and the bigger boats were commissioned: the two large, 750-ton Type 1s, *U-25* and *U-26*, and nine of the ten 500-ton Type VII mediums, *U-27* to *U-36*. Notwithstanding all the work in Spain on the IVS prototype, *E-1*, the large boats, *U-25* and *U-26*, turned out to have many design flaws. They were dangerously unstable, slow in diving, difficult to maneuver, and easy to detect and hold on sonar. Both were therefore declared unsuitable for combat and relegated to experimental status or used for propaganda purposes, such as showing the swastika in Spanish waters in company with other *Kriegsmarine* warships. The nine Type VII mediums, which also had serious design and mechanical flaws and proved to be voracious fuel hogs, were organized into a second combat flotilla, named in honor of another Imperial Navy submarine hero, Reinhold Salzwedel. The Salzwedel skippers—from the crews of 1924 to 1926— were former skippers or senior watch officers on the ducks of the Weddigen Flotilla.

With all these new boats, the OKM reorganized the U-boat force. The eighteen ducks were divided into two flotillas, Weddigen and a new one, named in honor of another Imperial Navy submarine hero, Johannes Lohs. Promoted to *Führer des U-boote* (Commander, U-boats, abbreviated as FdU), Dönitz commanded all three flotillas, which comprised twenty-eight production boats (eighteen ducks, ten Type VIIs), as well as the experimental showboats *U-25* and *U-26*. The FdU senior staff was kept small: Dönitz; his chief engineer, "Pappa" Thedsen; a smart, newly recruited planner and tactician, Eberhard Godt, from the crew of 1918; and a few others.

After the Salzwedel boats had completed workup and torpedo training, Dönitz initiated the first experiments with coordinated group (or "wolf pack") attacks against simulated "enemy" convoys in the Baltic Sea. He directed these exercises from a command ship equipped with a superb array of radio transmitters and receivers. He formed the boats into "patrol lines" to intercept convoys. When a boat found and reported the convoy, he directed the others to mass and attack. Although these war games were rigged to favor the U-boats, Dönitz was well satisfied with the outcome and more than ever convinced he was on the right track.

There were many difficulties to be worked out. The most urgent was to find a way to add fuel-storage capacity, or bunkerage, to the Type VII. The engineer Thedsen, Dönitz remembered, provided the solution. He designed external "saddle" tanks that could be wrapped around the hulls amidships. These tanks increased the fuel storage capacity of the Type VII (from 67 tons to 108 tons). Nothing could be done about the first ten Type VIIs, but the extra tanks were incorporated in the seven Type VIIs of the second order (*U-45* to *U-51*), which were designated Type VIIB.

In midsummer 1937, Great Britain, in conformance with the terms of the Anglo-German Naval Treaty, notified Germany that it intended to increase its submarine force by 17,300 tons—from 52,700 tons to 70,000 tons. Still adhering strictly to the treaty, which limited Germany to 45 percent of the British submarine tonnage, the increase allowed Germany to increase its U-boat force by 7,785 tons. This dividend provoked another bitter dispute between Dönitz and the OKM. Dönitz again urged that all the new tonnage go for improved 500-ton mediums (Type VIIBs). The OKM again urged that the tonnage go for improved 750-ton large boats, the Type IXB. Raeder again ruled against Dönitz. He split the tonnage almost evenly between medium and large boats, ordering eight Type VIIBs (of 4,000 tons) and five IXBs (of 3,750 tons). Including this third order, after all the boats had been commissioned, the U-boat force was to be comprised of seventy-two boats aggregating 31,750 tons: thirty-two ducks, twenty-five medium Type VIIs, thirteen large Type IXs, plus the two large duds, *U-25* and *U-26*.

When Hitler commenced the rape of Europe in 1938, the embryonic U-boat arm deployed for war on three occasions: during the annexation (*Anschluss*) of Austria in March; the abortive attempt to absorb the Sudetenland area of Czechoslovakia in May; and the Munich Crisis of September, when Hitler gained the Sudetenland by diplomacy. On all three occasions, all thirty-six commissioned boats—including the six ducks at the submarine school—loaded war stores and sailed to predesignated stations in the North and Baltic seas, under Dönitz's command, to fight a naval war with an array of potential enemies: France, Poland, the Soviet Union, and possibly even Great Britain. It was realistic training for the crews, but the exercises left no doubt that the U-boat arm was absurdly inadequate, both in size and weaponry, for the tasks envisioned.

In late May of 1938, after Hitler had been rebuffed and humiliated in his first attempt to absorb the Sudetenland, he summoned Raeder to the Reichs Chancellery and presented him with astounding news. Reversing all previous directives, Hitler informed Raeder that the *Kriegsmarine* must now consider "the possibility" of Great Britain as a naval opponent. Hitler would continue to court the appeasing British government, seeking to cement the friendship, but at the same time, he wanted Raeder to lay firm plans for a huge naval buildup, to include "big warships" for "political purposes"—that is, "symbols of power" that were to "influence England not to join the other side in case of any political difficulties arising between us and any other nation." Hitler also wanted more U-boats. He would invoke the escape clause in the Anglo-German Naval Treaty, which, under certain circumstances, allowed Germany parity with Great Britain in submarines—a planned 70,000 tons.

Raeder assumed that Hitler intended to promptly invoke the submarine escape clause, but owing to the tense political situation that developed in the Munich Crisis, Hitler deferred naval negotiations. Nonetheless Raeder—in technical violation of the treaty—proceeded with plans to order thirty-six more U-boats, comprising

25,250 tons. Again Dönitz and the OKM locked horns over tonnage allocation, and again Raeder ruled against Dönitz. The final order included nine Type IXs (for 6,750 tons), two very large Type XB minelayers (for 3,600 tons), two huge Type XI "U-cruisers" mounting four 5" guns in two turrets (for 6,000 tons), and seventeen Type VIIs (for 8,500 tons). The Type VIIs, which Dönitz urgently needed, comprised only 34 percent of the total new tonnage.

That year—1938—Dönitz received nine newly commissioned boats. These included the first of the Type VIIBs with the "saddle" fuel tanks, *U-45;* the first of the large Type IXs, *U-37;* and the first of the improved ducks, *U-56* and *U-57,* designated Type IIC. These, and the sister ships to come, were assigned to three new flotillas, named for Imperial Navy submarine heroes: Bernhardt Wegener, Paul Hundius, and Hans Joachim Emsmann. The VIIBs were to form the Wegener Flotilla, the IXs the Hundius Flotilla, and the IICs the Emsmann Flotilla.

Meanwhile, in the last days of 1938, the OKM finalized plans for expansion of the *Kriegsmarine.* Known as the *Ziel* (Target) Plan, or Z Plan, it was an admiral's dream. It recommended a surface ship force of seventeen capital vessels (six super-battleships of 72,000 tons each, four large battleships, four aircraft carriers, three battle cruisers), three "pocket" battleships, five heavy cruisers, forty-eight light cruisers, sixty-eight destroyers, ninety motor torpedo boats, numerous minelayers and minesweepers, and a host of auxiliaries and small craft. When completed in 1948, the *Kriegsmarine* was to comprise over one million tons of surface warships.

The Z Plan also included a plentitude of U-boats—a total of 249, comprising about 200,000 tons. But the proposed mix was another sharp defeat for Dönitz, who had not been consulted. The OKM recommended sixty small Type IIs, twenty-seven huge "U-cruisers" and minelayers, sixty-two large Type IXs, but only 100 medium Type VIIs. If this mix was approved, it meant that 75 percent of the submarine force (150,000 tons) would be composed of U-boats Dönitz did not deem desirable, leaving only 25 percent (50,000 tons) for the 500-ton medium Type VIIs he considered to be most effective for his evolving doctrine.

Dönitz did his utmost to modify the Z Plan to fit his concepts. He wrote a monograph, *Die U-bootswaffe (The U-boat Arm),* propagandizing for U-boats. For security reasons he did not describe his "wolf pack" concept, but he advocated a "trade war" by U-boats and stressed the advantages of the night surface attack, doubtless to counter the views at the OKM that U-boats were highly vulnerable to sonar and aircraft attacks and were therefore of limited utility and value in British waters.* He also enlisted the political help of the biggest gun at hand: fleet commander Hermann Boehm, who advised the OKM that in a naval war with Great Britain he would rank U-boats and mines at the top of a list of desirable weapons. When Raeder presented the Z Plan to Hitler, the Führer approved it without change, but with one stipulation. Hitler demanded that the force envisioned be

---

* The monograph was published in 1939, but British intelligence apparently missed it. The Admiralty finally came by a copy in 1942, but by that time the insights it contained, foreshadowing the trade war and U-boat tactics, were of no value.

completed not by 1948 but by 1945. To assure that this deadline could be met, Hitler guaranteed Raeder that the *Kriegsmarine* was to have "priority over programs of the other services."

The adoption of the Z Plan was a flagrant violation of the spirit and terms of the Anglo-German Naval Treaty. It was to be kept secret until Hitler could devise a politically expedient way to abrogate the treaty and blame the break on the British. Meanwhile, Berlin would pretend to adhere to the treaty. As a part of that pretense, on December 12, 1938, the Foreign Minister, Joachim von Ribbentrop, belatedly invoked the submarine escape clause, which legally permitted Germany to build to parity with Great Britain, or 70,000 tons of U-boats. This move came as a nasty shock to the Admiralty, but the British government accepted the declaration without objection.

A month later, in January 1939, Raeder ordered another sixteen new U-boats, comprising about 13,000 tons. These additions were to bring the U-boat arm to parity with the British by 1942—118 boats comprising 70,000 tons. Again Dönitz lost the debate on type allocation. Raeder directed that about half the new tonnage (6,500 tons) be assigned to build another very large Type XB minelayer and two more huge Type XI U-cruisers. The other half of the tonnage was assigned for Type VIIs. This was the last U-boat order placed in compliance with the submarine tonnage limits of the Anglo-German Naval Treaty. When these orders had been fulfilled in 1942, the U-boat arm was to consist of the following types and tonnages:

32	small Type II	8,000	tons
55	medium Type VII	27,500	tons
2	large Type 1 (*U-25, U-26*)	1,500	tons
22	large Type IX	16,500	tons
3	large Type XB minelayers	5,400	tons
4	huge Type XI U-cruisers	12,000	tons
118	total boats	70,900	total tons

This mix was, of course, far from satisfactory to Dönitz. The Type VII, which he desired above all others, still comprised only 39 percent of the total tonnage. Moreover, the total number of VIIs—fifty-five—to be completed by 1942 was less than one-fifth the number he deemed necessary for a decisive attack on the British merchant marine.

Abrogating the agreements reached with Great Britain and France at Munich, in March 1939, Hitler occupied the rest of Czechoslovakia by bluff and political intrigue and rode triumphantly into Prague. That outrage overshadowed another Nazi conquest a week later when the *Kriegsmarine* reclaimed Memel, Lithuania, for Germany in another bloodless operation. As Hitler had correctly foreseen, neither France nor Great Britain lifted a finger to assist Czechoslovakia.

Having flanked Poland, Hitler intended to absorb that nation by bluff and intrigue as well. Should those methods fail, he advised his military chiefs, the

Wehrmacht, Luftwaffe, and *Kriegsmarine* should be prepared to seize Poland by military force, no later than September 1, 1939.

The Nazi rape of Czechoslovakia produced an unexpected reaction among the citizens of Great Britain. They rose up in fury and demanded that the chief appeaser, Prime Minister Neville Chamberlain, draw a line on Hitler's aggression. Confronted with this public outrage and the possibility of his ouster, Chamberlain was compelled to declare that should France honor its long-standing mutual defense treaty with Poland, Great Britain would support France.

Hitler seized upon the Anglo-French guarantees to Poland as a pretext for abrogating the Anglo-German Naval Treaty. He did so publicly, in a sarcastic speech to the *Reichstag* on April 28. Soon thereafter the *Kriegsmarine* laid the keels for the two super-battleships, *Bismarck* and *Tirpitz.* Despite these provocations and the public indignation and the stepped-up military preparations in Great Britain, Hitler continued to assert to his Nazi cohorts that neither Great Britain nor France would fight for Poland. Believing Hitler would pull another political rabbit out of his hat, Raeder naively—and irresponsibly—assured the *Kriegsmarine* that there would be no war with Great Britain.

Dönitz was more convinced than ever that the opposite was the case. He believed that the "high state of tension" which Hitler had created between Great Britain and Germany could explode "into actual hostilities at any moment." He therefore pleaded with Raeder and the OKM to approve a rapid increase in U-boat orders, with a major emphasis on Type VIIs, and to authorize theretofore prohibited U-boat exercises in the Atlantic Ocean. He got nowhere with his pleas for an increase in U-boat orders—the available shipyards were already jammed—but Raeder did permit the Atlantic exercises.

These exercises culminated in May 1939 with group or "wolf pack" attacks against a simulated convoy, composed of some *Kriegsmarine* vessels assigned to the annual fleet cruise to Lisbon and the western Mediterranean. A total of fifteen VIIs and IXs from the Salzwedel, Wegener, and Hundius flotillas participated. The "convoy" consisted of four German surface ships: a tanker, a freighter, Dönitz's "command ship," *Erwin Wassner,* and the Flotilla Salzwedel tender, *Saar*—the latter two vessels alternating as targets and defending escorts.

The fifteen U-boats deployed in five packs of three boats along a patrol line several hundred miles long. One pack quickly "found" the "convoy" and radioed a contact report to the other boats. In spite of clever evasive and defensive measures by the convoy—and extremely foul weather—the other boats converged on the target and attacked it relentlessly for over forty-eight hours, May 12 to 14. At the end of the exercise, thirteen of the fifteen boats converged for the final "kill."

The exercise was wholly artificial and weighted to favor the U-boats. There were serious lapses in communications and tracking and gross errors in position reporting. Nonetheless, Dönitz could not have been more pleased. In a lengthy after-action critique, he concluded that the "principle of fighting a convoy of several steamers with several U-boats" was "correct" and that "the convoy would have been destroyed." His group or "wolf pack" concept was therefore a sound one for defeating Great Britain; he renewed his pleas to Raeder for a step-up in the construction of Type VIIs.

Absorbed in the grandiose Z Plan, the OKM emphatically disagreed with Dönitz. The senior submarine planner at the OKM, Werner Fürbringer, a rear admiral and an assistant to Raeder's chief of staff, Otto Schniewind, framed the response. "At the present moment," Fürbringer wrote, "U-boat blockade of England has very little prospect of success for Germany. Any contradictory opinion, which takes comfort in the large number of our U-boats or in the idea that the English U-boat defense will not be effective far out in the Atlantic, can be dismissed as misleading" and, furthermore, it would be "irresponsible to commit the valuable U-boat crews" to such a war. "It can be taken as proven," Fürbringer went on, "that every English convoy, no matter whether it operates along the coast or on the high seas, will be secured by defensive forces, fully capable of destroying with certainty any attacking U-boat, even under the surface." In support of his argument, Fürbringer stressed the effectiveness of British sonar and predicted that the British would again resort to defensive minefields, which had been so deadly effective against U-boats in World War I. Until U-boats could be made "sonar-immune," it was pointless to even consider starting a U-boat campaign against British commerce.

The Fürbringer paper dismayed and enraged Dönitz. In response he drafted a reply for Fürbringer's superior, Otto Schniewind, vigorously rebutting Fürbringer's arguments point by point. Going a step beyond—a large and career-risking step—he communicated his arguments directly and emphatically to Raeder, and asked that Raeder in turn place his views "before Hitler." Hitler's response, relayed to Dönitz through Raeder, was, as Dönitz remembered it, that "he would ensure that in no circumstances would war with Great Britain come about. For that would mean *finis Germaniae*. The officers of the U-boat arm had no cause to worry."

BOOK ONE

THE U-BOAT WAR AGAINST THE BRITISH EMPIRE

SEPTEMBER 1939–DECEMBER 1941

ONE

On August 15, 1939, Grand Admiral Erich Raeder, chief of the *Kriegsmarine,* directed his staff, the OKM, to send a war alert to Karl Dönitz, commander of the German submarine force. The message stated that all senior submarine staff officers and U-boat commanders were to report for a "reunion" on August 19 at Dönitz's headquarters on the submarine tender *Hecht,* moored at a naval pier in Kiel. The word "reunion" was a coded order to deploy the German submarine force for war—merely four days hence.

Dönitz rushed back from leave the following day. Others concerned reported on board *Hecht* that day or the next in high excitement. When all had gathered, Dönitz outlined the complicated geopolitical situation that had developed, the perils entailed, and the submarine war plans.

The Führer, Adolf Hitler, had definitely made up his mind to invade Poland. The date had been moved forward from September 1 to August 26. Great Britain and France had pledged to come to Poland's aid. Although Hitler did not believe the British or French would fight, Dönitz thought otherwise: War with those nations was not only possible, but probable. There was a further complication. To avoid the prospect of a two-front war, Hitler was attempting to negotiate a nonaggression pact with the Soviet Union. But, so far, Joseph Stalin was foot-dragging. Conceivably, Moscow might reject Hitler's overtures and align with London and Paris and pledge support for Warsaw. The *Kriegsmarine* therefore had to be prepared for numerous, dizzying contingencies: war with Poland alone; war with Poland assisted by Great Britain and France; war with Poland assisted by Great

Britain, France, and the Soviet Union; war with Poland assisted only by the Soviet Union.

The *Kriegsmarine* was by no means prepared for a naval war with Great Britain and France. Notwithstanding the naval arms-limitations treaties of the 1920s and 1930s, those nations combined had an awesome array of surface ships: twenty-two battleships and battle cruisers, seven aircraft carriers, eighty-three cruisers, and countless destroyers, plus seven new battleships and eight carriers under construction. Against that the *Kriegsmarine* had two battleships (*Bismarck, Tirpitz*), and one carrier (*Graf Zeppelin*) under construction, two battle cruisers (*Gneisenau, Scharnhorst*) in commission but not combat-ready, three "pocket" battleships (*Deutschland, Admiral Graf Spee, Admiral Scheer*), of which only two were combat-ready, eight conventional cruisers, and about twenty destroyers in various stages of readiness. Altogether the Allies enjoyed a superiority of ten-to-one in surface ships.

Great Britain and France likewise enjoyed a superiority in numbers of ocean-going submarines. Great Britain had about fifty in commission, France about seventy, for a total of about 120. Against that the *Kriegsmarine* had twenty-seven. Not all the Allied submarines were of good quality or combat-ready, but the same was true of the German submarines. Of the twenty-seven oceangoing German boats in commission, two large ones, *U-25* and *U-26,* were experimental and not really suitable for combat and five were brand new or in shipyards for extended refit or overhaul, leaving only twenty fully (or nearly) ready for war on August 19.

In addition, the Germans had commissioned thirty pint-sized, 250-ton submarines—the so-called ducks. The ducks were used principally for basic or advanced training purposes, but they had three torpedo tubes and could carry six torpedoes or nine mines. Therefore all but one duck (*U-11*), which had been permanently detached for experimental work, could be assigned to limited combat roles in the North Sea or Baltic Sea. About eighteen of the twenty-nine ducks were fully (or nearly) ready for combat on August 19.

The *Kriegsmarine* war plan was designed to make the best of the several contingencies. The two combat-ready "pocket" battleships, *Admiral Graf Spee* and *Deutschland,* each with one supply ship, were to slip secretly to sea and take up waiting positions in the North and South Atlantic. Sixteen of the twenty combat-ready oceangoing submarines were to occupy waiting positions off the Atlantic coasts of Great Britain and France and off the Strait of Gibraltar. Seven ducks were to take up waiting positions in the North Sea. Should Great Britain and France declare war, the "pocket" battleships and submarines in the Atlantic were to operate offensively against the maritime forces of those nations; the submarines in the North Sea, offensively and defensively. The remaining combat-ready naval forces, including four oceangoing submarines and eleven ducks, were to operate offensively in the Baltic Sea against the tiny Polish Navy (five submarines, four destroyers, several minelayers) or, if necessary, the more formidable Soviet Navy.

That was the plan. Should Great Britain and France declare war, Raeder had no illusions about the outcome. The best that the men of the *Kriegsmarine* could do, he wrote in his memoir, was to "go down fighting" and "show that they knew how to die gallantly."

The "pocket" battleships and submarines deployed in secrecy per plan, August 19 to August 23. The *Admiral Graf Spee,* her supply ship *Altmark,* and fourteen oceangoing U-boats loaded with torpedoes sailed on the night of the 19th. Two other oceangoing U-boats, delayed in the shipyards, sailed on the nights of August 22 and 23. The *Deutschland* and her supply ship *Westerwald* sailed on the night of the 23rd. That same night the North Sea U-boat force (seven ducks) and the Baltic Sea U-boat force (three oceangoing boats and eleven ducks) sailed to waiting positions. In total, thirty-four of the fifty-seven commissioned U-boats (65 percent) deployed: sixteen to the Atlantic, seven to the North Sea, and eleven to the Baltic Sea.

Hitler's negotiations with Stalin, meanwhile, proceeded at a maddeningly slow pace. On August 20 Stalin agreed to a preliminary trade agreement, but this hardly satisfied Hitler. That day Hitler intervened directly, cabling Stalin to suggest that he receive the German Foreign Minister von Ribbentrop, who would have full powers to sign a treaty on behalf of Germany. Stalin agreed to see von Ribbentrop on August 23 and that same night, to Hitler's immense relief, Stalin signed the pact. The published treaty (binding for twenty years) specified that neither Germany nor Russia would attack the other or support a third party, or a coalition, in an attack on one or the other. The unpublished protocols and agreements doomed Poland and the Baltic States. Germany and the Soviet Union would invade Poland and divide that nation roughly in half at the Vistula River. The Soviet Union was to exercise "influence" over Finland, Estonia, and Latvia, while Germany was to exercise "influence" over Lithuania.

D day for the invasion of Poland remained fixed for August 26. But on the day before, Hitler received several pieces of news that gave him pause. The British announced ratification of a formal mutual assistance pact with Poland, which iterated in no uncertain terms Britain's determination to fight for Poland. The French ambassador called on Hitler to make it crystal clear that France would do likewise. A letter arrived from Italian dictator Benito Mussolini, stating that Italy was not prepared for war and could not immediately go to war against Great Britain and France unless Hitler provided Italy with enormous quantities of military supplies. As a result of these developments, Hitler postponed the invasion from August 26 to its original date, September 1, gaining time for another attempt to negotiate Great Britain and France into neutrality.

The frantic diplomacy and the postponement of D day prompted the OKM to realign the U-boat deployment. The pact with Stalin reduced naval requirements in the Baltic Sea; the belligerent statements from London and Paris made it prudent to deploy more U-boat strength to the west. Accordingly, between August 23 and 28 Dönitz shifted four oceangoing U-boats and ten ducks from the Baltic Sea to the North Sea. One oceangoing boat, *U-36,* sailed to backstop the ducks in the North Sea; the other three were held in reserve.

By August 28, two other oceangoing U-boats had completed refits. The first was the big, unsteady Type I, *U-26.* The OKM directed Dönitz to load her with mines and six torpedoes. In event of war, *U-26* was to lay mines off Portland, a British naval base facing the English Channel. Although the boat was not really suitable for combat, after laying the mines she was to attack Allied shipping with her six torpedoes. The second boat was a new Type VIIB, *U-53,* flagship of the Wegener Flotilla. She sailed last (with flotilla commander Ernst Sobe on board), raising the number of boats for the Atlantic, including the minelayer *U-26,* to eighteen.*

The deployment of the Atlantic boats was dictated by their fuel capacity—or range. Six medium-range Type VIIs of the Salzwedel Flotilla were to patrol individually in a semicircle off the Atlantic side of the British Isles. Six new VIIBs of the Wegener Flotilla, with twice the fuel capacity, were to patrol individually on a similar arc, but farther out—or westward—and southward to the Bay of Biscay. Five big long-range IXs of the Hundius Flotilla, with flotilla commander Werner Hartmann embarked in *U-37,* were to patrol a southern area off the Iberian Peninsula and the Strait of Gibraltar. The minelayer, *U-26,* was to wait for final orders off the west end of the English Channel.

To minimize the possibility of detection, the eighteen Atlantic-bound U-boats did not use the convenient English Channel. They went the much longer way, around the north end of the British Isles, remaining submerged in daytime, avoiding all contact with shipping. It was a slow, tedious, fuel-consuming journey during which all boats maintained absolute radio silence.† None was detected. Nor were the two "pocket" battleships. Upon reaching the Atlantic, the U-boats took up preassigned waiting stations.

The North Sea U-boat force was composed, finally, of seventeen ducks and the oceangoing Type VII, *U-36.* In event of war, five ducks were to lay mines in English and French ports. Two ducks were to patrol offensively off the northeast coast of Scotland, in hopes of mounting surprise torpedo attacks on British men-of-war. The other ten ducks and the *U-36* were deployed in defensive patrol lines in the North Sea to warn of and thwart attempts by the Royal Navy to counterattack toward Germany.

While the U-boats were taking up positions, Raeder met with fleet commander Hermann Boehm and Dönitz in Kiel. Believing that a naval war with the west was inevitable, Boehm and Dönitz urged Raeder to scrap the big ships of the grandiose Z Plan and approve an "emergency" plan to build with all possible speed 300 U-boats, to include at least 200 improved Type VII mediums. Dönitz remembered later that Raeder verbally "approved" the proposal and directed Dönitz to submit his ideas in writing to the OKM through channels. A few days later, the OKM

---

    * The U-boats and skippers are described in appendices 1 and 2.

    † Northabout the British Isles, it is about 1,400 sea miles from Wilhelmshaven to the western mouth of the English Channel.

scrapped the Z Plan and adopted the Dönitz plan to build hundreds of U-boats. But this drastic—and historic—change in direction required Hitler's approval and he was too busy with Poland to deal with naval matters.

The Germans invaded Poland on September 1. Per plan, the *Kriegsmarine* supported the *Wehrmacht* and *Luftwaffe* by attacking the Polish Navy and bombarding shore installations. Three Type II ducks, basing from Memel, joined the attacks. Two ducks claimed to have sunk Polish submarines, but in fact, all five Polish submarines (big French-built minelayers) got away. Three ran to internment in neutral Sweden. Two, *Wilke* and *Orzel,* eventually escaped from the Baltic Sea and joined the Royal Navy, as did three of the four Polish destroyers.

On September 3, the British and French declared war on Germany. But the Allies were powerless to help Poland. The Soviet Union invaded Poland from the east on September 17. Caught between the Germans and Russians, Polish forces fought heroically, but were overwhelmed and surrendered on September 27. On that day Poland ceased to exist.

THE BOAT

The medium, 500-ton Type VII oceangoing boat *U-30* patrolled a waiting station, designated U, about 150 miles west of Scotland. To the south of her, five identical sister ships of the Salzwedel Flotilla occupied waiting areas west of the British Isles. These six Type VIIs represented one-third of the German submarine force deployed in the Atlantic.

The *U-30* was one of ten Type VIIs that had been commissioned in the prewar years. A forerunner for the improved mediums in being or under construction (Types VIIB and VIIC), she was three years old and was commanded by a twenty-six-year-old lieutenant, Fritz-Julius Lemp. Born in China on the eve of World War I, the son of a German Army officer, in 1931, at age eighteen, Lemp had joined the *Reichsmarine* and had served on continuous active duty for eight years. In his fifth year, 1936, he had joined the embryonic U-boat arm. After submarine school and a tour as a watch officer on the Type VII *U-28* and further schooling to qualify for a captaincy, in November 1938 Lemp had been promoted to command *U-30*. In a recent peacetime drill *U-30* had survived a near-fatal collision with her sister ship, *U-35*. Lemp had demonstrated remarkable coolness and control in that crisis, earning the praise not only of Dönitz and Salzwedel Flotilla commander Hans Ibbeken, but also his crew—three other officers and forty enlisted men.

With the improvements incorporated in the later models, *U-30* was the submarine type Dönitz favored most. Overall she measured 211 feet and had a beam of 19 feet. Inside her cigar-shaped pressure hull, which was divided into six fore-to-aft compartments of nearly equal size, she was much smaller: about 142 feet long and about 10 feet wide in most areas. She was exceedingly cramped—a claustrophobe's worst nightmare.

The bow compartment contained *U-30*'s main firing battery: four torpedo tubes, the standard armament of all oceangoing U-boats in commission or under construction. The *U-30* carried ten torpedoes in this space, four in the tubes and six reloads—two stored above the deck plates and four in the bilges. The compartment also served as living quarters for the chief torpedoman and for about twenty-four of the lowest-ranking seamen and mechanics (stokers or firemen). They shared twelve collapsible bunks, built in along the bulkheads, and four hammocks slung in the overhead. They ate meals on small, collapsible wooden tables, while sitting on the lower bunks. The space was so densely packed with torpedoes, gear, and men that it was impossible to stand erect and there was scarcely room to move. Some submariners half jokingly called it "the cave." A more fitting description might be "snake pit." As in all ships, the bow compartment took the worst pounding in a heavy sea. The one advantage to living all the way forward was that there was no "through" traffic.

Like all the U-boats deployed in the Atlantic, the *U-30* carried two types of torpedoes, both with 616-pound warheads: the older "air"-propelled torpedoes (G7a) and the new, top secret, battery-propelled, wakeless or "electric" torpedoes (G7e). Both types were $23\frac{1}{2}$ feet long and 21 inches in diameter and weighed about 4,000 pounds, or two tons. The air torpedoes were fitted with pistols that could be set for either impact or magnetic detonations; the electrics only with magnetic pistols. Both types had to be thoroughly checked every three or four days to make certain the complicated propulsion, steering, and depth-setting mechanisms were in proper working order, especially that the batteries of the electrics were warm and fully charged. The torpedo maintenance disrupted sleeping and eating routines. The bunks had to be trussed up and the eating tables stored away to make room to pull the torpedoes partway from the tubes for servicing and to take up the deck plates to get at the reloads in the bilges. Those who lived in the compartment prayed for action; with the firing of each torpedo, they gained slightly more living space.

The next compartment aft was less forbidding. Below the deck it contained one-half (sixty-two large cells) of the boat's batteries. Above the deck were sleeping and eating accommodations for nine men: the captain, the three officers, and five other senior petty officers, midshipmen, or apprentice engineering officers. The captain's bunk, which could be sealed off by a sliding curtain, was on the port side aft. Directly across the passageway from his bunk were the sonar and radio rooms. The other eight men slept in built-in bunks along the port and starboard bulkheads. The captain and the officers ate on a small folding table in the aisle, sitting on facing lower bunks, making way for traffic to and from the bow compartment. To soften the atmosphere of the compartment—and perhaps to add a touch of elegance—the lockers and closets were faced with a veneer of varnished wood.

Toilet facilities on *U-30* were primitive. There were two heads, or toilet bowls, placed in closets about the size of a telephone booth. One was located on the starboard side, forward in the officers' compartment; the other aft, adjacent to the galley. However, inasmuch as the boat had limited food-storage space, the aft toilet closet had been taken over for that purpose. The toilet in the officers' compartment thus served all forty-four men. Since the fresh-water supply was also limited, no one was permitted to bathe with fresh-water and beards were encouraged. Body odors were masked with sweet-smelling lotions.

The next compartment aft—the control room—was located almost exactly amidships. This was the working headquarters of the boat, somewhat comparable to the bridge of a surface ship. Merely twenty feet in length, it was crammed with machinery for operating the boat, surfaced or submerged: controls for the rudder and diving planes, engine-order telegraph, gyro compass, blow and vent valves for the ballast and other tanks, navigational plotting desk, the business end of one of the two periscopes. A six-foot man could stand erect, but just barely. Dials and gauges of every description occupied every square inch of the curved bulkheads and the low overhead. To the nonsubmariner, the control room was an unbelievably cramped space with an incomprehensible array of gear, but to the submariner, every dial, gauge, and valve was well understood—and vital to his well-being and safety.

The center of the control room was dominated by the lower skirt of a large cylindrical tube, with a ladder inside, leading to the conning tower. That small, misnamed* place was a miniature combat center. It contained a duplicate helm station, gyro-compass repeater, engine-order telegraph, the business end of the slim attack periscope (which generated less wake), and the torpedo angle and depth-setting solver. During submerged attacks, the captain manned this periscope. He orally passed data (target size, estimated speed and range, angle on the bow, etc.) to the officer manning the torpedo data solver and gave steering orders to the helmsman and depth-control instructions to those in the control room below.

The conning tower was also part of the emergency escape system. The main challenge of escaping from a disabled sunken submarine was to get a hatch open against the massive outside sea pressure. To escape from a Type VII boat, the men followed this procedure. First, all hands gathered in the control room, sealed its fore and aft watertight doors, and strapped on oxygen-breathing apparatus. Next they flooded the control room with seawater to a level above the skirt on the tube leading to the conning tower. Then they bled high-pressure air into the compartment from overhead outlets. The pressurized air pushed downward on the seawater, forcing it up through the skirt into the conning tower. The men then gradually increased air pressure on the water, compressing it until the inside water pressure equalized with the outside water pressure. When that equilibrium was established, the hatch in the conning tower, leading to the bridge, would open freely. The men escaped by ducking under the skirt, going up through the flooded tube to the flooded conning tower, thence to the bridge and onward to the surface.†

The compartment aft of the control room was less austere. Below, it contained the other half (sixty-two large cells) of the boat's batteries. Above the deck plates, there were eight built-in bunks for the petty officers and thirty-six small wood-faced lockers, each measuring about one cubic foot, where the enlisted men stored

---

* Early submarines had glass portholes in the conning tower, enabling the boat to be steered, or conned, on the surface from this elevated space. But glass portholes could not withstand depth-charge explosions and had been eliminated. While traveling on the surface, the boat was actually conned from the bridge above the conning tower.

† Submarine candidates practiced escape procedures ashore in control-room mockups built into the bottom of water towers. Not surprisingly, many candidates failed this scary test.

Medium Type VII C

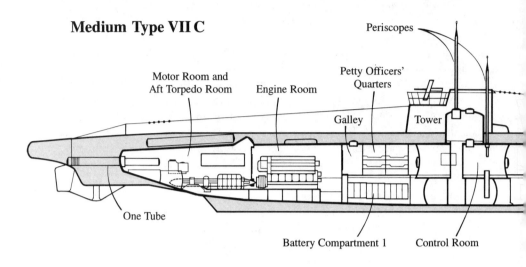

Periscopes

Motor Room and
Aft Torpedo Room

Petty Officers'
Quarters

Engine Room

Galley

Tower

One Tube

Battery Compartment 1

Control Room

(Note: Tower, bridge, and antiaircraft gun
configurations were often altered during the war.)

Large Type IX C

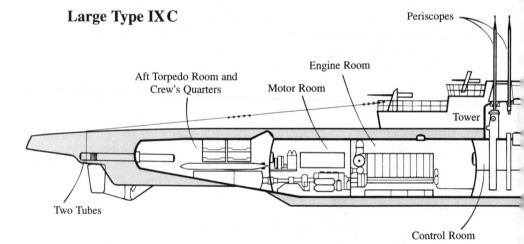

Periscopes

Aft Torpedo Room and
Crew's Quarters

Engine Room

Motor Room

Tower

Two Tubes

Control Room

Principal German Attack
Submarines of World War II

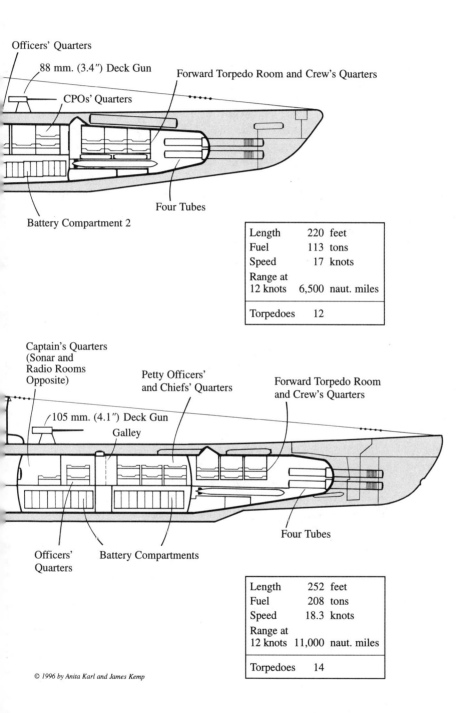

Officers' Quarters

88 mm. (3.4") Deck Gun

Forward Torpedo Room and Crew's Quarters

CPOs' Quarters

Four Tubes

Battery Compartment 2

Length	220	feet
Fuel	113	tons
Speed	17	knots
Range at 12 knots	6,500	naut. miles
Torpedoes	12	

Captain's Quarters (Sonar and Radio Rooms Opposite)

Petty Officers' and Chiefs' Quarters

Forward Torpedo Room and Crew's Quarters

105 mm. (4.1") Deck Gun

Galley

Officers' Quarters

Battery Compartments

Four Tubes

Length	252	feet
Fuel	208	tons
Speed	18.3	knots
Range at 12 knots	11,000	naut. miles
Torpedoes	14	

personal valuables, such as money, official papers, pictures, and cigarettes. The men who lived in this compartment also ate on wooden tables in the aisle, sitting on lower bunks and giving way to traffic, which was usually heavier in this area. The ship's galley, where food for all forty-four men on the boat was prepared, was located in the after port side of this compartment. The galley consisted of a miniature three-burner electric range with hood, two small ovens, and a platter-size sink. The cooks had to carry the food from the galley to the bow compartment and to the officers' compartment, then collect the dirty pots and plates.

The food on *U-30*, like the other VIIs, was considered to be excellent, but the diet was limited by the lack of storage space and refrigeration. Every nook and cranny of the boat had been utilized for storing potatoes, cheese (in several varieties), and countless cans of coffee, tea, milk, fruits, and sweets. Hard-crusted black bread was stored in mesh-net hammocks in the overheads. In addition, *U-30* carried a stock of canned bread, which, it was believed, would not mold. Scores of large sausages and smoked meats of every kind hung from the overhead all through the boat, giving the effect of a German butcher's shop.

The next compartment aft—the fifth from the bow—was the diesel-engine room. It contained two large, noisy 1,160-horsepower engines, one to port, one to starboard. Air for the engines was supplied by a large pipe—the main induction—running outside the pressure hull up into the bridge structure, with the intake at maximum possible elevation above sea level. The engine exhaust was piped overboard mixed with seawater to minimize smoke. The engine room also contained the main air compressor for charging the compressed-air storage bottles, and a small distiller for making fresh water from seawater. The output of the distiller was used mainly to refill the 124 battery cells, which ran hot and therefore evaporated water at a fairly high rate.

The last, or stern, compartment was known as the electrical room. It contained two 375-horsepower electric motors, or more precisely, motor-generators. The main driveshafts of the diesel engines ran through the core of the motor-generators. When the diesels were operating, either or both motor-generators could be clutched onto the turning driveshafts to serve as generators to charge the batteries. Or, as a fuel-saving (and range-extending) measure, the power produced by one motor-generator, operated by one diesel engine, could be routed to the other motor-generator to turn the other shaft.* Upon diving, when both diesels were shut down, the motor-generators were clutched to the driveshafts, drawing power from the batteries.

The *U-30* and her nine Type VII sister ships were equipped with a stern torpedo tube, but it was located inconveniently outside the pressure hull and had to be fired by remote controls in the stern room. The tube was loaded in port with an air torpedo, which required less care and warmth than an electric. The tube could not be reloaded at sea. This inconvenience had been corrected in the next generation of mediums (VIIB, VIIC) by locating the tube inside the stern compartment and providing space for one reload under the deck plates.

---

*   So rigged, the maximum cruising speed was a leisurely 6 knots.

Finally, there was the bridge, located atop the conning tower. During travel on the surface, when the boat was most vulnerable to detection by aircraft, four men were stationed on the bridge: the watch officer and three lookouts. Each man was supplied a pair of superb 7 x 50 Zeiss binoculars for searching the air and the horizon, which were divided into four 90-degree segments. Not an iota of slackness was tolerated; the safety of the boat depended upon the bridge watch's ability to spot a plane or enemy warship in time to dive and evade. Failure to spot a threat to the boat could result in a formal investigation and harsh disciplinary measures.

In pleasant weather a bridge watch was a welcome diversion from the crowded, smelly life belowdecks. It was also the only place where smokers were allowed to light up. But in heavy seas and cold weather, the bridge was miserable and dangerous and a poor place to smoke. Huge seas regularly smashed over the bridge, tearing at the men, who were tethered with safety harnesses, and soaking them to the skin. They came off watch wet and freezing, and often bruised and battered.

During a night surface attack, the bridge was a battle station. While the captain remained below at a plotting board to size up the big picture, the first watch officer manned the firing binoculars, called the UZO, mounted over a gyro-compass repeater. He chose and lined up the targets in the UZO and, upon receiving authorization from the captain, gave the orders to shoot torpedoes at his targets. The three—or four—lookouts on the bridge during attacks were the most able on the ship, those with exceptional night vision. During the attacks they were not permitted to watch the action. They kept their binoculars glued on their 90-degree segment of the sky and horizon, to report whatever might appear.

All oceangoing submarines of the world's navies were equipped with a big topside gun. As in World War I, these were to be used to sink unarmed or lightly armed merchant ships and for special tasks and emergency defense. Like all Type VIIs, the *U-30* mounted an 88mm (3.4") fast-firing, good-quality, but unshielded naval gun. The ammunition for it was stored belowdecks and passed up hand-to-hand during a gun action. A specially trained supervising officer and a team of gunners conducted gun actions, seldom an easy task on the narrow, open, rolling and pitching deck, which was often awash with seawater.

To an outsider, life on board *U-30* was simply appalling. The crew had no extra clothing. What they wore was soon filthy. Their hair and beards were soon matted with diesel oil and brine. The boat stank of diesel oil and sweat and cooked food and sickening sweet lotions. Except when submerged, the boat plunged, rolled, and shook wildly. Seldom could one stand or walk without a handhold. Unless properly secured, crockery and other gear flew in all directions. Cold seawater washed down the conning-tower hatch into the control room. There was always a line—sometimes a very long line—at the single toilet, which gave off its own repugnant odors. The heating and ventilation systems were not adequate. The boat was either too cold or too hot—and always damp and clammy. The food, including the canned bread, rotted and molded. Much of the vital machinery, especially the high-performance diesels, constantly broke down, it seemed.

But the young crew of *U-30* took this discomfort and the danger in stride. The boat was a fighting machine, not a permanent home. A voyage was not forever, merely several weeks. When *U-30* returned to port, the crew—like submariners everywhere—would be granted an extended rest period. The men could find comfort and cleanliness and room to stretch and unwind and, if desired, solitude and privacy on board the submarine tender or in barracks ashore or at home on leave. The men of the crew considered themselves a special breed—elite volunteers within the elite *Kriegsmarine*—and were proud of that distinction. And proud of *U-30* and her nervy Captain Lemp, distinguished from the other men by his clean white cap. Not many men on *U-30* would trade this arduous billet for any other duty.

COMPLICATED RULES

Believing that he might yet talk Great Britain and France out of going to war, before the invasion of Poland, Hitler imposed severe limitations on the two "pocket" battleships and the U-boats deployed for combat in the Atlantic and North Sea. The "pocket" battleships were not to commence any operations against Allied shipping or naval forces without Hitler's specific approval. And, as Raeder remembered it, the U-boats "were likewise hedged with severe restrictions."

One of the first and most important rules Hitler laid down was that the U-boats were not to be concentrated, offensively, against enemy naval formations. The reasons were both political and practical. First, as Raeder put it, Hitler did not want to further antagonize the Allies by sinking a prestigious man-of-war. Second, as Dönitz put it, "U-boat operations against naval forces promised little hope of success."

On the eve of war, Britain's Navy was dispersed and holed up in numerous heavily fortified bases, including Scapa Flow, Firth of Forth, Firth of Clyde, Portland, and Portsmouth. Even if the big ships put to sea, it would be very difficult for a U-boat to sink a major man-of-war, such as a battleship. There were not enough U-boats to cover the British bases in depth. The major ships were certain to be heavily escorted by aircraft and sonar-equipped destroyers and cruising at high speed (25 knots)—too fast for a U-boat to overhaul them and get into position to shoot torpedoes. A hit would be a matter of luck: the off chance that a U-boat lay almost directly on the path of an oncoming enemy man-of-war.

For these reasons, Hitler had ruled that in the initial offensive U-boats were to concentrate primarily against merchant shipping. But, again for political reasons, that pressure was to be applied with utmost finesse. All U-boats were to adhere strictly to the 1930 Submarine Protocol, which Germany had signed in 1936. That protocol (Article 22) specified that with certain exceptions, ships were not to be sunk without warning. They were to be stopped and inspected, or "visited and searched." If found to be an enemy ship or a neutral ship with contraband, inbound to an Allied port, they could be sunk, but only after the safety of the crew had been absolutely assured.

The exceptions—ships that could be sunk without warning, in the German view—were:

- Troopships, i.e., vessels known from intelligence sources or actually observed to be carrying troops and war matériel.
- Vessels in convoy, or any vessel escorted by warships or aircraft.
- Vessels taking part in enemy actions or acting in direct support of enemy operations, including intelligence gathering.

There were not enough U-boats to make any appreciable dent in the enormous Allied merchant fleet in the first offensive. Furthermore, most of the Atlantic boats had sailed on August 19 and were already low on fuel and provisions and would have to be recalled soon. Since there was no reserve to replace them, a "lull" or "gap" of several weeks would occur in U-boat operations. Therefore the initial U-boat offensive was shaped to achieve maximum psychological impact. The goal was to sink as many enemy ships in as many different locations as possible, giving the impression that U-boats were "everywhere," thereby sowing confusion and panic and reviving memories of the costly World War I U-boat siege of England. So pressured, Hitler believed, the Allies might be less willing to continue combat in behalf of Poland.

The decision to adhere strictly to the Submarine Protocol added great risk to the submarines' tasks and reduced the odds of inflicting a dramatic first blow. The biggest risk was that during the visit and search procedure, when the U-boat was exposed on the surface, it might be surprised by an enemy warship or aircraft. To minimize the possibility of surprise by aircraft, the Atlantic boats were positioned well offshore—a hundred miles or more. This put them well to sea of the "choke points" in the British Isles, where shipping converged and congregated and thus made the job of locating ships much more difficult, especially in inclement weather.

The restriction also virtually ruled out any chance that the ducks in the North Sea could contribute to the intended psychological impact by torpedo attack. The ducks were too small and underarmed (one dismountable machine gun on deck, which could be manned only in calm water) to stop, visit, and search a merchant ship. Moreover, it was believed, British aircraft patrolled all areas of the North Sea almost continuously in daylight, posing extreme dangers to those pint-sized boats. The best that could be expected of the ducks was a lucky torpedo hit on a British convoy, warship, or submarine and/or kills from the minefields some were to lay.

Even so, there was a great deal riding on this first U-boat offensive. If Hitler's political intuition was right, a smashing U-boat success might discourage the Allies from continuing the war, and Poland would have been gained at small cost to Germany. For those who did not believe the Allies would back away from war—and those included Raeder and Dönitz—it presented an opportunity to wrest Hitler's attention away from the land war and focus it on naval warfare and to impress upon him the grave peril posed by the Allied naval powers. A successful U-boat opening blow could persuade Hitler to give the tiny U-boat arm the full backing it desperately needed to wage a credible naval war.

•   •   •

On the day Great Britain and France declared a state of war with Germany, September 3 at 1256 hours Berlin time, the OKM sent an urgent, encoded message to all *Kriegsmarine* ships, U-boats, and shore stations: "Hostilities with England effective immediately." A little over an hour later, at 1400, the OKM sent another urgent message: "U-boats to make war on merchant shipping in accordance with operations order," meaning they were to observe strictly the Submarine Protocol or prize rules. Because theretofore the U-boats had been instructed not to attack any ships except in self-defense, Dönitz felt a clarification was required. From his shore headquarters in Wilhelmshaven, at 1550 German time, he radioed all U-boats: "Open hostilities against England immediately. Do not wait to be attacked first."

England, yes, but what about France? Believing that France might be even more easily dissuaded from war than Great Britain, Hitler had reached the drastic decision that U-boats should not attack any French ships of any kind. At 1752 that same afternoon, the Berlin naval staff addressed that matter with yet another message: "Boats are to take no hostile action against [French] merchant ships for the present, except in self-defense."

Another complication—and added danger! U-boats could not assume a ship was French merely because it flew a French flag or insignia. British ships or neutral ships with contraband might hoist French flags. Therefore all ships flying French flags would have to be stopped, visited, and searched to be certain they were French. If positively identified as French, they were to be allowed to sail on unmolested. This procedure could result in a great waste of time, during which the U-boat would be exposed to attack by enemy ships and aircraft.

The limitations virtually ruled out all U-boat attacks at night. In darkness it would be difficult, if not impossible, to positively distinguish a blacked-out French merchant ship from a British merchant ship. Hence no U-boat commander could confidently attack *any* convoy at night, lest a French ship be sunk by mistake.

At 1630 local time that day, Fritz-Julius Lemp in *U-30* was cruising northwest of Ireland on the surface in the extreme northern sector of his patrol area. This put him about sixty miles south of Rockall, a barren sixty-three-foot rock projecting upwards from the sea. Until then, for purposes of concealment, Lemp had been keeping well off the normal sea-lanes. About that time, the bridge watch sighted a ship on the horizon, coming from the direction of the British Isles on a northwesterly course that was taking her unusually close to Rockall. Lemp hauled around on the surface to get on her track and dived for a closer periscope inspection.

The two vessels closed at about 1900 (7 P.M.), by which time the daylight was fading. Through the periscope Lemp could see that she was a very large ship. She was blacked out and zigzagging and appeared to be armed with deck guns. On the basis of this hurried, overeager look, and her unusual track near Rockall, Lemp concluded the vessel must be a British armed merchant or auxiliary cruiser* on pa-

---

* A large, fast commercial vessel fitted with 5" or 6" guns, hence, a warship.

trol and therefore fair game for an attack without warning. He sent his crew to battle stations and ordered two torpedoes made ready.

At 1940 (7:40 P.M.) Lemp initiated the Atlantic U-boat war, firing the two torpedoes. The first ran true and struck the target squarely. The second malfunctioned and ran wild. Believing it might circle back and blow up *U-30,* Lemp dived deep to evade. When the danger had passed, he surfaced in the evening twilight and examined the listing target from the bridge through binoculars, edging ever closer, taking care to keep *U-30* down-moon in the shadows. Since the ship did not appear to be sinking, Lemp fired a third torpedo, but it, too, malfunctioned or missed.

Moving up quietly and close to the target, soon Lemp could clearly see its silhouette. He went below and checked the boat's copy of *Lloyd's Register* of merchant ships. He saw then that he had made an inexcusable and horrendous error. She was not an auxiliary cruiser, but rather S.S. *Athenia,* a well-known, sixteen-year-old, 13,580-ton British ocean liner of the Donaldson line. She was bound for Canada, jammed with 1,103 men, women, and children, including 311 Americans who were fleeing the war. If there was any doubt in Lemp's mind about the identity of the ship it was shortly removed. *Athenia's* radio operator repeatedly telegraphed a plain language distress signal, giving her position and the three-letter code, *SSS,* meaning she had been attacked by a submarine. All this was clearly audible on *U-30's* radio receiver.

Lemp then compounded the error. He had been ordered to maintain radio silence to conceal his presence, but the distress signal—and *SSS*—from *Athenia* had already given him away. He would not have unduly jeopardized the safety of his boat by breaking radio silence to inform Berlin or Dönitz of this egregious error, thereby giving the German government timely notice of a public storm certain to arise. Possibly fearing that he might be recalled and relieved—or perhaps harshly punished by the Nazi government—Lemp sent no message, thereby leaving Berlin and Dönitz completely in the dark.

Nor did Lemp make any effort to render assistance to *Athenia's* passengers and crew. Fortunately the seas were calm and the weather was good, and *Athenia* remained afloat until the following morning, enabling passengers and crew to abandon ship in an orderly manner. Three merchant ships and three British destroyers raced to the rescue and, as a result, the loss of life on *Athenia* was not calamitous: 118, including twenty eight Americans, some deaths being caused when one of the rescue ships, the Norwegian freighter *Knut Nelson,* clumsily churned up a lifeboat with her propellers.*

The hue and cry arising from this first U-boat sinking of the war was thunderous. Although the casualties had not been heavy, the incident evoked the horror of the 1915 *Lusitania* sinking in which 1,198 people, including 128 Americans, had perished. The Admiralty hurried to inform the media that *Athenia* had been sunk

---

*   The American ambassador to Great Britain, Joseph P. Kennedy, sent an official embassy delegation to Ireland to assist the American survivors and investigate the incident. One member of the party was his second-oldest son, John F. Kennedy, a Harvard student, winding up a summer of travel in Europe.

by a torpedo from a U-boat, which had been seen by some passengers. The obvious implication was that Germany had abrogated the Submarine Protocol and had launched World War II with a barbarous and inhumane campaign of unrestricted submarine warfare.

Berlin and Dönitz first learned of the *Athenia* sinking from radio news broadcasts. It came as a rude shock. Such was the care that had been exercised, both in oral and written orders, to avoid a violation of the Submarine Protocol, that it seemed inconceivable that the very first British ship—a passenger liner at that—had been sunk illegally. It was a terrible blot on the honor of the *Kriegsmarine*. It was certain to undermine—and perhaps even collapse—Hitler's attempts to negotiate Great Britain out of the war, and it would also seriously antagonize the United States.

Such was the gravity of this matter that early on September 4, Raeder flew to Wilhelmshaven to confer with Dönitz. Together they reviewed the operational orders and patrol areas of the U-boats. Although both later stated otherwise, there is little doubt that they knew that morning that Lemp in *U-30* had sunk *Athenia*. Owing to radio silence and his freedom to move about his assigned area, Lemp's position was not precisely known. But *Athenia* definitely had been sunk within the boundaries of Lemp's patrol zone, Area U.

Hitler's greatest concern was that the British would balloon the *Athenia* sinking into another *Lusitania* and generate sufficient outrage to pull the United States into the war. Before Raeder returned to Berlin, Hitler issued orders that Germany should categorically deny that a U-boat sank *Athenia* and characterize any charge that one did so as a false "British atrocity report." The German Foreign Ministry issued the official denial at noon on September 4. The spokesman asserted that no U-boat could have sunk *Athenia* inasmuch as the northern boundary of the patrol zone of the nearest U-boat lay "seventy miles to the south." The Germans claimed *Athenia* must have been sunk by a British mine or submarine.

Hitler's decision to lie about *Athenia* set in motion a complicated cover-up in which Raeder and Dönitz participated. Four days later, Raeder sent a telegram to a newspaper reporter (which was leaked to foreign naval attaches in Berlin) in which he stated that the British claim that *Athenia* had been torpedoed by a U-boat was an "abominable lie" because the nearest U-boat was "170 sea miles away" and, furthermore, the *Kriegsmarine* strictly adhered to international law, the prize rules in particular. Still later, with the full knowledge that *U-30* had sunk *Athenia*, Hitler's Propaganda Minister, Joseph Goebbels, published a preposterous article in Germany charging that the Admiralty had deliberately ordered the destruction of *Athenia* to curry favor with neutral nations and bring America into the war.

The *Athenia* sinking led directly to further complications—and risks—for U-boat skippers. Insisting that there be no repetition of this politically disastrous sinking, Hitler imposed yet another restriction. On September 4, the OKM radioed Atlantic forces, including the "pocket" battleships and all U-boats: "By order of the Führer: No hostile action is to be taken for the present against passenger ships, even in convoy."

Although the order was no doubt meant to apply mainly to large ocean liners, it did not define "passenger ships." Many ships, including tramp steamers, carried passengers. Were U-boat skippers to allow a tramp steamer with ten or twenty passengers to pass unmolested? If not, what was to be the cutoff point? Were "passenger ships" obviously transporting troops (and therefore "troopships" by the Submarine Protocol) likewise to be spared? Were convoys that included "passenger ships" to be unmolested out of fear that a stray torpedo might hit one? Unable to answer these questions or to clarify the order in any way, Dönitz was powerless to help his skippers.

"WINSTON IS BACK"

On the evening of September 3, while Lemp was torpedoing *Athenia,* Prime Minister Neville Chamberlain invited the sixty-five-year-old hawk and political exile Winston Churchill back into the government. The job: First Lord of the Admiralty, a post Churchill had held from 1911 to 1915. The Admiralty signaled his arrival with a message to all forces: "Winston is back."

Churchill's appointment came as a tonic to the British. The Admiralty was in need of vigorous leadership. The senior admiral, First Sea Lord A. Dudley P. R. Pound, appointed the previous June, was not physically fit and not viewed as an inspiring leader. He suffered painfully from arthritis of the left hip. The official naval historian Stephen Roskill wrote, he had "no intellectual interest or social graces," was "too addicted to extreme centralization," and "loved schedules and Courts of Inquiry." A senior Army general noted in his diary that during meetings of the chiefs of staff, Pound was "asleep 90 percent of the time" and "the remaining 10 percent" was "none too sure of what he is arguing about." However, Churchill liked Pound and had confidence in him. Pound was a good balance wheel.

Back in government harness and confronting Hitler, Churchill was a phenomenon: a tireless, pugnacious, mesmerizing genius with immense knowledge of military affairs. Working man-killing hours, he shook the staid Admiralty from top to bottom. From his office gushed a torrent of ideas (some of them harebrained) and memos stamped prominently "Action This Day." He demanded prompt, incisive reports on every conceivable aspect of the Royal Navy. Nothing, it seemed, escaped his notice. His memos, which usually began, "Pray tell me . . . ," were facetiously called "The Lord's Prayers."

Restricted for fifteen years by naval treaties, pinch-penny budgets, and the antiwar mood in England, the Royal Navy Churchill inherited was far superior to the *Kriegsmarine* but a pale reflection of its former self. Its main striking power consisted of twelve battleships, three battle cruisers, and six aircraft carriers. Ten of the battleships and two of the battle cruisers were of World War I vintage; two battleships (*Rodney, Nelson*) dated from 1927. The other battle cruiser (*Hood,* a huge 42,000 tons) dated from 1920. Three battleships (*Queen Elizabeth, Warspite, Valiant*) and two battle cruisers (*Renown, Repulse*) had been extensively modernized in 1936–1939. But *Queen Elizabeth, Valiant,* and *Renown* were back in the yards for major refits. Only one of the six carriers, *Ark Royal,* commissioned in

1938, had been built as such from the keel up; the other five were conversions dating from the 1920s.*

The capital ships of the Royal Navy were divided between two fleets: Home and Mediterranean. The Home Fleet, commanded by Charles M. Forbes, consisted of seven battleships, two battle cruisers, and four aircraft carriers. The Mediterranean Fleet, commanded by Andrew B. Cunningham, based in Gibraltar and Alexandria, Egypt, consisted of three battleships and one aircraft carrier. The Home Fleet was supported by about twenty heavy and light cruisers; the Mediterranean Fleet by about six. Other heavy and light cruiser squadrons were scattered all over the globe. All forces were further reinforced by scores of fleet destroyers.

The Home Fleet had three principal missions. The first and overriding task was to contain, neutralize, and destroy the surface forces of the *Kriegsmarine* and thereby deny it an opportunity to raid British shipping or attack England by shore bombardment. That task was to be accomplished in a replication of World War I naval strategy, by bottling up the *Kriegsmarine* in the North Sea—blocking a sortie into the Atlantic—and by whittling it down if it dared leave its home bases and offer battle. The main obstacle to carrying out this mission was the *Luftwaffe*. Its perceived threat to the Home Fleet precluded an offensive naval strike at the *Kriegsmarine* in the lower North Sea and compelled the main British naval strength to base in Scapa Flow, believed to be beyond German bomber range, but also ideally located to blockade the North Sea.

The second task was to impose a maritime or economic blockade of Germany, another replication of World War I strategy. Because of the presence of the *Luftwaffe* the blockade could not be mounted in the lower North Sea as in World War I, but had to be much farther north. The blockade line ran west from the Orkney Islands to Iceland and east from the Orkneys to Norway. To enforce the blockade between the Orkneys and Iceland, the Admiralty had established a Northern Patrol, composed initially of eight aging light cruisers. Ships of the blockade were to observe "cruiser rules," a stop-and-search procedure similar to the Submarine Protocol, allowing neutrals not carrying contraband to pass.

Few believed the maritime blockade would have any appreciable impact on Germany. The blockade of World War I had been deadly effective in part because Czarist Russia had been Germany's enemy. Now the Soviet Union was Germany's military ally and trading partner. Whatever food, oil, and other imports Germany required could be brought by rail and truck overland from Russia. Germany's high-grade iron ore for weaponry came from neutral Sweden. In mild weather it was sent by ships in the Baltic Sea directly to Germany. In cold weather, when the Baltic was frozen, it was sent by rail to Narvik, Norway, then by ship in Norwegian waters through the Skagerrak and Kattegat to Germany. The Royal Navy was not able to force its way into the Baltic Sea; it could not legally impose a blockade in neutral Norwegian waters. Hence the maritime "blockade" of Germany was to amount to little more than psychological harassment.

---

* Eleven new capital ships were under construction: five *King George V*-class battleships and six *Illustrious*-class aircraft carriers.

The third task of the Home Fleet was to protect British maritime assets from German submarines. Inasmuch as Germany had no submarine force until 1935, the Admiralty had not pursued ASW vigorously. Not until December 1938, when the Germans advised Great Britain that they would build to submarine parity, did the Admiralty begin serious planning for the possibility of U-boat war. All ASW plans were influenced by the belief that British sonar, developed in the last days of World War I and improved in the 1920s and 1930s, had virtually rendered submarines obsolete. Sonar, Churchill (for one) judged, was a "remarkable" device. With sonar, Churchill wrote, two destroyers were as effective as ten destroyers in World War I.

The Admiralty plans for confronting the U-boat threat derived from the experience of World War I. The Admiralty assumed that unlike the case in World War I, Germany would wage unrestricted submarine war from the first day. The Royal Navy was to combat U-boats by the following measures:

- **MINES.** It was not forgotten that mines were the greatest killer of U-boats in World War I. Defensive minefields were to be planted along the east coast of the British Isles and in the English Channel, to close off that passage. Offensive minefields were to be planted in the lower North Sea, west of Helgoland. A plan to recreate the North Sea Barrage between the Orkneys and Norway was in hand, but more serious consideration was given to planting fields between the Orkney and Faeroe islands, between the Faeroes and Iceland, and between Iceland and Greenland.

- **HUNTER-KILLER GROUPS.** Offensive patrolling by surface ships had produced small returns in World War I. However, since that time the aircraft carrier had come into service. It was believed that a carrier, escorted by a flotilla of six or eight modern, sonar-equipped destroyers, would be a formidable ASW weapons system. The carrier aircraft could patrol an enormous area in a day's time. Upon spotting a U-boat, aircraft were to attack and, if possible, sink the U-boat or at least drive it under and hold it down until the destroyers could be brought up to attack.

There were several weaknesses in this concept. The Royal Navy had only four carriers in the Home Fleet and just one of these (*Ark Royal*) was first-rate. Navy carrier pilots, trained to attack big enemy capital ships, had not drilled in searching for small U-boats. Moreover, Britain had slighted development of carrier aircraft and weaponry, giving priority to the Royal Air Force (RAF) Bomber and Fighter commands. In September 1939, the Royal Navy had only 175 carrier aircraft: 150 old wire-and-fabric biplanes (Swordfish) and 25 new monoplanes (Skuas); the former for torpedo launching, the latter for dive bombing. The aviators believed that the few planes available should be husbanded for attacks on German capital ships, not be worn out on ASW patrols.

Alternate ideas for sea-basing ASW aircraft at less cost had been proposed. One scheme was to build a number of what the Americans were to call "jeep carriers," capable of handling about a dozen aircraft. These miniature aircraft carriers could be created quickly, it was believed, by mounting a flight deck and a catapult on existing tankers or other suitable merchant-ship hulls of about 12,000 tons. The Admiralty had approved an experimental conversion of the seaplane tender *Pega-*

sus to explore this concept. Another scheme was to equip ordinary merchant ships with catapults (like those on cruisers and battleships) that could launch a recoverable seaplane or wheeled aircraft, which could land ashore.

• **LAND-BASED AIR PATROL.** The RAF had established a Coastal Command to support the Royal Navy. Its primary mission was to provide the Navy reconnaissance on German capital ship movements in the North Sea and elsewhere. Although land-based aircraft had positively sunk only one U-boat in all of World War I, it was believed that Coastal Command could serve effectively in an ASW role. But Coastal Command pilots had not drilled in submarine spotting, and the hardware had also been neglected. In September 1939, Coastal Command had 300 aircraft in its inventory, most of them obsolete, and only about half the pilots were fully trained. Only three squadrons were equipped with modern aircraft: two with long-range four-engine flying boats (Sunderlands); one with medium-range twin-engine American-designed, British-built wheeled aircraft (Hudsons). The Hudsons (replacing obsolete Ansons) were not yet fully operational.

• **CONVOYS.** This time around there was to be no agonizing debate over convoying. With the onset of war, all British merchant ships were to be placed under operational control of the British government. All Commonwealth* vessels except those which could exceed 15 knots or were slower than 9 knots were to travel by escorted convoy. In preparation for this massive undertaking, the government had created on paper a convoy control organization and had indoctrinated thousands of merchant marine officers in convoy tactics and procedure, such as station keeping, zigzagging, and communications. A list of retired Royal Navy officers who were to be recalled to serve in the convoy control organization, and at sea as convoy commanders, was on file.

The weakness—a big weakness—in the convoy plan was the acute shortage of escort vessels. Great Britain had about 175 fleet destroyers worldwide, of which about 100 were modern (1926–1939), the rest World War I vintage.† Fifteen of the latter (*V* and *W* class) had been designated convoy "escort destroyers." In addition, there were about thirty so-called sloops—smaller, slower warships, yet in some ways (range, habitability) superior vessels to destroyers for convoy escort. Most of the modern destroyers were required as screens for capital ships, for scouting, port protection, and other tasks. That left only a very few for ocean-convoy escort: the old destroyers and sloops. The old destroyers earmarked for that task required constant maintenance, and only a few were equipped with sonar.‡ For inshore, or coastal, escort in the British Isles, the Navy had some 170-foot coal-burning trawlers, fitted with 3" guns and depth charges. Some had older sonar sets, but the trawlers were too slow (11 knots) to chase a U-boat.

To help fill the gap, the Royal Navy had developed two new vessels: a *Hunt*-class, small (280 feet; 900 tons), fast (26 knots), heavily armed (four 4" guns) de-

---

   * From 1931, the British Empire or British Dominions became the British Commonwealth of Nations.

   † For more detailed information on the British destroyer situation, see Appendix 9.

   ‡ At the outbreak of the war, a total of 185 British ships had sonar: 100 modern destroyers, forty-five sloops and old destroyers, and forty trawlers.

PLATE 5

ROYAL NAVY OCEAN-ESCORT VESSELS OTHER THAN DESTROYERS 1939-1945[1]

TYPE		CLASS	BUILT/ GOT	LENGTH (FEET)	TONS
Patrol	(PCE)	*Kil*	15 (got)[2]	180	800
Corvette	(PE)	*Flower*	100[3]	205	950–1,000
Corvette	(PE)	*Flower #2*	7 (got)[4]	208	1,000
Corvette	(PE)	*Castle*	31[5]	252	1,000–1,100
Sloop	(PS)	1928-1935	22	266	1,000
Sloop	(PS)	*Bittern, Egret*	6	282–292	1,200
Sloop	(PS)	*Black Swan*	12	299	1,250–1,300
Sloop	(PS)	*Black Swan #2*	24	299	1,350
Destroyer	(DE)	*Hunt*	75	280–296	1,000
Frigate	(PF)	*Captain*	78 (got)[6]	289	1,000–1,300
Frigate	(PF)	*River*	51	301	1,400
Frigate	(PF)	*River*	8 (got)[7]	301	1,400
Frigate	(PF)	*Bay*	25	301	1,300–1,500
Frigate	(PF)	*Colony*	21 (got)[8]	304	1,300–1,500
Frigate	(PF)	*Loch*	26	307	1,430

Total ships commissioned: 501 (129 got)

1. Source: Elliott, Lenton, Tucker, etc.
2. From the United States.
3. Plus 33 more: 10 for U.S.N.; 23 to other Allied navies. (Total built: 133.)
4. From Canada.
5. Five served as convoy rescue ships. Twelve others built for Canada and one for Norway. Total built: 44.
6. From the United States.
7. From Canada.
8. From the United States.

stroyer for ocean escort, and a *Flower*-class corvette to augment the trawlers for inshore escort. The 205-foot, diesel-powered, single-screw corvette, based on a whale catcher design built for Norway, was slow (16 knots) and miserably wet, but it was a hardy sea boat that could be built cheaply and quickly. The February 1939 ship-building program of the Royal Navy included twenty *Hunt*-class destroyers, and fifty-six *Flower*-class corvettes (as well as twenty *Tree*-class trawlers), but in September 1939, these vessels were a long way from completion.*

   • **SHIP DEFENSE.** Since it was assumed the Germans would not observe the Submarine Protocol—that any and all British merchant ships were to be sunk without warning—the Admiralty had drawn plans to arm British merchant ships for self-defense as rapidly as possible after the commencement of hostilities. For

---

   * Four *Hunts* were commissioned in December 1939, the other sixteen between February and September 1940.

this purpose, the Admiralty had stockpiled hundreds of guns and thousands of shells. It also had plans to equip some merchant ships with depth charges. These were to be rolled over the side to deter (rather than to kill) U-boats. The Admiralty had indoctrinated thousands of merchant-ship captains and officers in gunnery and depth-charge use, and had encouraged the captains to ram U-boats whenever the opportunity presented itself. Without exception, all British merchant ships were to report immediately all contacts of any kind with a U-boat (*SSS*), another means of gathering intelligence on U-boat positions.

• **SUBMARINES.**   In World War I, British submarines had proved to be efficient U-boat killers. Since it was assumed that the British blockade would empty the seas of German merchant ships and that the *Kriegsmarine* would not often venture from its home bases, the Admiralty planned to commit most of the British submarine force to ASW.

Commanded by Bertram C. Watson (Rear Admiral, Submarines) from headquarters on the Firth of Forth, the Royal Navy submarine force was a deplorable hodgepodge. Long the victim of an indifferent and frequently hostile Admiralty, it consisted of fifty-eight boats of ten different types. More than half (thirty-three) were old and dangerous duds: eighteen big *O-, P-,* and *R*-class ocean boats; twelve small World War I *H-* and *L*-class boats; three huge *River*-class fleet boats. Only twenty-four of the fifty-eight boats could be ranked as first-rate: twelve relatively new medium (700-ton) *Swordfish-* or *S*-class attack boats; six large (1,800-ton) minelayers; three new large (1,300-ton) *Triton-* or *T*-class attack boats; and three new small (600-ton) *Unity-* or *U*-class attack boats, ideal for North Sea or Mediterranean operations.*

In late August 1939, there were forty-five British submarines ready for war: eighteen were based at North Sea ports, nine at Malta, two in the South Atlantic, and sixteen in the Far East. In the tense last week of August, Watson had sent eleven of the eighteen home-based boats on patrol in the North Sea to scout *Kriegsmarine* capital ships. These boats got off to a wobbly start. British aircraft mistakenly bombed *Sturgeon* and *Seahorse. Sturgeon* fired torpedoes at *Swordfish* in error, but fortunately, they all missed. The new *Triton* fired torpedoes at the old *Oxley* in error, but unfortunately, *Triton's* missiles hit. There were two survivors. *Oxley* was the first submarine to be sunk by any of the belligerents in the war. Her loss to a sister ship cast a pall in the British submarine force and raised questions in the Admiralty about competence.

The French had invested heavily in submarines. When the war commenced, the French Navy had seventy-seven submarines: thirty-eight large (1,300- to 1,500-ton) ocean boats; thirty-two medium (600-ton) boats; six minelayers (750-ton); and the monstrous (3,000-ton) white elephant *Surcouf.* About twenty of the large and medium boats, dating from the 1920s, had been modernized in the late 1930s. Nonetheless, only forty-one of the seventy-seven boats could be ranked as first-rate: twenty-nine 1,500-ton ocean boats, all built in the 1930s; six *Saphir*-class minelayers; and six new mediums of the *Minerve* class.

---

*   A substantial number of the superior *S-, T-,* and *U*-class submarines were under construction.

French submariners took great pride in their heritage as European submarine pioneers. Morale in the force was high and much was expected. But there existed serious organizational and technical weaknesses. There was no centralized, single submarine commander; most of the submarines were scattered between Atlantic and Mediterranean bases, assigned to operate with subordinate fleet commands. Some of the technical weaknesses were daunting. Owing to unreliable gyros, French torpedoes could not be fired at sharp angles. To compensate for this deficiency, many boats were fitted with complicated, ungainly torpedo-tube arrangements, such as multiple traversing external mounts of the type found on destroyers. Some boats carried torpedoes of two different sizes (21" and 15"), which led to logistical headaches.

Since Italy had not entered the war and Germany offered few targets for French submarines, it would have been advantageous had French submarines merged with British submarines in a joint ASW mission. A combined force of about 120 British and French submarines, directed by a single commander—à la Dönitz—from a centralized submarine headquarters, doubtless would have posed a formidable counterforce to the fifty-six combat-capable German U-boats. But no merger was attempted and the French submarine force was to be wasted in a variety of nonproductive missions, such as escorting convoys.

• RADIO INTELLIGENCE. In World War I, Great Britain had thoroughly penetrated German naval communications by establishing a network of direction-finding (DF) stations and by breaking codes. Between the wars, the Germans had learned about these electronic intelligence coups and had taken vigorous steps to prevent a repetition. The *Kriegsmarine* had prescribed certain radio procedures to minimize the effectiveness of enemy DFing (silence or encoded "short signals") and utilized an interior code in messages for position reporting to eliminate frequently used, possibly recognizable latitudes and longitudes.* Like the *Wehrmacht* and *Luftwaffe,* the *Kriegsmarine* had also adopted an ingenious encoding machine, Enigma, which was believed to be unbreakable.

German naval Enigma was more complicated than *Wehrmacht* or *Luftwaffe* Enigma. Moreover, *Kriegsmarine* signals security was tighter and the traffic less dense. For these reasons many British codebreakers—including some senior holdovers from the famous Room 40 of World War I—were not too hopeful of penetrating naval Enigma. Nonetheless, the assistance of some brilliant Polish codebreakers (discussed in chapter 2), a special team of British codebreakers, located in a remote countryside mansion, Bletchley Park, had tackled the job and believed it might be done, especially if the keys and other material for naval Enigma could somehow be captured.

---

* Called the "grid" system: north-to-south latitudes and west-to-east longitudes were defined alphabetically, A to Z. The large area where the alphabetized designators intersected was denoted by a "bigram." For example, the general area where *U-30* sank *Athenia* was AM. The large bigram areas, such as AM, were further subdivided into a system of numerical squares, which in turn were further subdivided. By the German grid system, *Athenia* was sunk in AM 1631, a substitute for latitude 56 degrees, 44 minutes north and longitude 14 degrees, 5 minutes west.

In the meantime, the British focused on three other avenues of radio intelligence:

• **DIRECTION FINDING (DFing).** From the opening days of the war, the British sought to improve this method of detecting enemy radio transmissions at sea. They established a new network of sophisticated land-based listening posts in the British Isles and in Canada, Bermuda, and the British West Indies. These posts were linked by a special communication system to London and manned by technicians who soon began to master this difficult technology. When, as Dönitz required, a U-boat made a "passage" report upon entering the Atlantic proper and a sinking and situation report upon leaving its patrol area, the British DFed this traffic from a growing number of widely spaced listening posts with far greater accuracy than the Germans credited.

• **TRAFFIC ANALYSIS (TA).** The U-boat radio traffic, like the *Wehrmacht* or *Luftwaffe* Enigma traffic, was stylized. Therefore after study, British radio intelligence technicians were able to distinguish U-boat traffic (Dönitz or a flotilla commander to a U-boat or vice versa) by its often repeated, unique characteristics or by the prefatory call-ups to "short signals," such as a "passage report."

• **RADIO FINGERPRINTING (RFP) and TINA.** Radio technicians had long known that every radio transmitter gave off a unique electronic "signature" and that individual telegraphers likewise had a unique "style" or "fist." It was soon possible to record the "electronic signature" of individual U-boats on strips of photographic paper, a process known as "radio fingerprinting" or RFP. Then as now, an experienced listener could distinguish the "fist" of a particular telegrapher, but the British enhanced this identifying process, TINA, with tapes and mathematical analysis. The aim was to track the comings and goings of particular U-boats and identify them again and again by these methods, but the effort was only marginally successful.

When the British technicians combined the results of DFing, TA, RFP, and TINA, and the reported U-boat sinkings and sightings from all sources, it became possible to formulate a fair picture of U-boat activity and predict probable threatened areas without the benefit of codebreaking. Hence, as in World War I, the British were able to route convoys away from known or probable U-boat positions with considerable success, thus reducing shipping losses.

• **RADAR.** The British had been last after the United States, France, and Germany, to develop radar—a technique of sending out and receiving controlled radio pulses to determine the range to an object in the air or on the sea. But fear of the growing power of the *Luftwaffe* spurred the Air Ministry and British scientists into high gear in the mid-1930s. By September 1939 Great Britain led the world in radar technology. It had girded the east and south coasts of the British Isles (facing Germany) with an elaborate overlapping network of radar stations (called Chain Home) to give early warning of German bombers. The British had also developed a small, crude radar set that could be fitted in aircraft, and a no less crude set for warships, to provide gunners accurate ranges in inclement weather and at night.

The Admiralty believed that airborne radar (known as Air to Surface Vessel, or ASV) and shipborne radar had potential to be wondrous ASW weapons. When brought to a practical stage, radar in aircraft and ships would enable the British to detect U-boats on the surface at night and in foul weather. But in September 1939, airborne and shipborne radar was virtually useless because it was not powerful or reliable enough to consistently and accurately pinpoint a small target, such as a U-boat conning tower. A scientific breakthrough of some kind was required—but nobody knew what kind. Meanwhile, the highest priority was given to perfecting an airborne set for night fighters so that the RAF Fighter Command could find and shoot down the anticipated waves of *Luftwaffe* bombers in the dark.

Winston Churchill knew full well that the naval threat to Great Britain was to be posed not by *Kriegsmarine* surface ships but by U-boats. Shortly after taking office, he told Neville Chamberlain and the War Cabinet that within nine months—by the summer of 1940—Britain "may have to face an attack by 200 or 300 U-boats." Perhaps Churchill believed that to be so or perhaps he deliberately inflated the threat to spur the War Cabinet and Admiralty into greater ASW measures. Whatever the case, his numbers were wildly off the mark. There was not to be that number of U-boats in combat-ready status for at least three years.

Meanwhile, in view of the very small number of oceangoing U-boats in the Atlantic, the inexperience of the crews, and the complicated rules of engagement imposed by Hitler, the decision of the British to initiate convoying in the Atlantic in September may well have been premature. Convoying in the Atlantic brought much vital British trade to a temporary standstill and in the months ahead, reduced imports (in Churchill's estimate) by "about one-third." Most official and unofficial British naval historians argue that it was correct to rush to convoying, but the arguments are not based on scientific analysis of U-boat weaknesses and limitations (fuel, torpedoes) or numbers, positions, weather, and so on. A case can be made that had convoying not been initiated so precipitously, British imports would not have decreased by "one-third" in these first critical months and the hard wear and tear on the convoy escorts (battleships, carriers, cruisers, destroyers, etc.), which led to extended yard upkeep and overhauls, could have been avoided.

The First Lord did, in fact, have second thoughts about the wisdom of convoying, according to Churchill's biographer, Martin Gilbert. He reports that at the end of ten weeks of war, November 9, Churchill was "deeply disturbed" by the "immense slowing down of trade" which convoying caused. After convening a high-level meeting on this subject, Churchill drafted a memo in which he advocated that Britain "secretly loosen up the convoy system (while boasting about it publicly), especially on the outer routes" and he commissioned two of his prewar advisers, Frederick Lindemann and Desmond Morton, to make an intricate study of the shipping problem. Gilbert did not, however, record the results of the study.

On one issue Churchill was absolutely correct in his judgment. As in World War I, he believed that Great Britain would require enormous and unstinting help from the United States to defeat Germany. He therefore welcomed an invitation from President Franklin D. Roosevelt, which arrived only a few days after Churchill returned to the Admiralty, to carry on a private correspondence. This secret correspondence provided Churchill with an unprecedented avenue for encouraging Roosevelt to support Great Britain and for enticing Roosevelt ever closer to war. Churchill was to use this avenue to the fullest.

His first thoughts, of course, turned to how Roosevelt might help the Royal Navy. In particular, Churchill thought Roosevelt might be persuaded to sell Britain fleet destroyers to fill the urgent need for open-ocean escorts for convoys. Owing to the decision to build five *King George V*–class battleships and half a dozen fleet carriers as well as *Hunt*-class destroyers and many corvettes, British shipyards were programmed to produce only nine fleet destroyers in the first eighteen months of the war. The idea of buying destroyers from America gradually gained momentum in the Admiralty but owing to the unfavorable political climate in America and to Roosevelt's insistence that the United States get full value in return, a full year was to elapse before a mutually satisfactory destroyer deal could be struck.

HITS AND MISSES

The six new Type VIIBs of the Wegener Flotilla, comprising another third of the German U-boats in the Atlantic, patrolled a larger arc west of the British Isles, reaching around to the Bay of Biscay. To the untutored eye, the VIIBs looked identical to the Type VIIs of the Salzwedel Flotilla, but, in fact, they incorporated significant technical improvements: greater length (218 feet versus 211), more powerful diesel engines (2,800 horsepower versus 2,320), greater surface speed (17.2 knots versus 16 knots), much larger fuel capacity (108 tons versus 67), heavier armament (fourteen torpedoes versus eleven),* and a single stern torpedo tube located internally.

The Type VIIB *U-47* patrolled Area I, 300 miles west of Bordeaux, France. Barely nine months old, *U-47* was commanded by thirty-one-year-old Günther Prien, who was destined to become the most famous submariner of all time. Prien was one of hundreds of German merchant marine officers who had been recruited into the rapidly expanding *Reichsmarine*. His background was typical of that group, upon which Dönitz had drawn for U-boat skippers.

Born in 1908 in the Baltic seaport of Lübeck, Prien was one of three children of a judge. He obtained a basic education at the *Katharineum* prep school. When his parents divorced, his mother moved with the children to Leipzig. By 1923, when Prien was fifteen, the economic chaos in Germany had reduced his mother to pauperhood. To help ease her burden—and fulfill a boyhood longing—Prien abandoned his education and left home to join the merchant marine, spending a last few hoarded marks on a three-month course at the Seaman's College in Finkenwärder.

Prien's career in the German merchant marine spanned eight years. Beginning as a lowly cabin boy on a full-rigged sailing ship, he was a good seaman, a staunch

---

* Ten torpedoes in the bow compartment, like the VIIs; two torpedoes for the stern tube; and two spare torpedoes carried in watertight canisters in the superstructure, which, in calm sea conditions, could be lowered below.

ally in forecastle and barroom brawls, and an apt pupil. Cruising to every corner of the world on a variety of merchant ships, he learned telegraphy, navigation, laws of the sea, ship handling, and the art of leadership. Rising steadily through the ranks, by 1931 he was a first mate and qualified for captain's school. But when he graduated from there in January 1932 with his master's certificate, the German merchant marine was in the grip of the Great Depression and there were no jobs for aspiring captains.

Unwillingly beached at this climactic moment in his chosen career, Prien had a tough year in 1932. He worked at odd jobs ashore, but when those ran out, he was forced to join the Labor Service (a German precursor of Roosevelt's Civilian Conservation Corps), digging ditches and draining fields. Upon learning that the expanding *Reichsmarine* had opened its officer-candidate program to merchant marine officers, Prien jumped at this opportunity and in January 1933, age twenty-five, he joined the Navy. He thus became a member of the crew of 1933, but in age and maritime experience he was the equal of the men in the crew of 1926.

After an apprenticeship especially tailored for experienced merchant marine officers, he was commissioned and moved ahead at an accelerated pace, married, had a daughter, and volunteered for U-boat duty. Upon graduation from the submarine school in 1935, he served as a watch officer on the big experimental Type I boat, *U-26,* making the showboat voyages to Spain. Rated as one of the half-dozen best U-boat officers in the force, Prien became the third and most junior officer (by crew) selected to command a new VIIB. In the Atlantic war games of May 1939, he had been the most aggressive, had "shot" from the closest range, and had "scored" highest.

For days Prien had been dodging and hiding from all ships and aircraft. On the first day of the war, September 3, he saw no ships. On September 4 he received the news of the *Athenia* sinking over radio broadcasts. Later that day came the direct order from the Führer barring attacks on passenger vessels of any kind. Still later that day a pointed reminder to observe the Submarine Protocol arrived from Dönitz: "Operation orders Para VIa remain in force for the war against merchant shipping." Prien responded accordingly. He stopped a Greek neutral and let her pass unmolested. He closed on two other ships, a Swede and a Norwegian, but when he saw their markings and flags, he did not even bother to stop them.

Near daybreak on September 5, the first watch officer of *U-47,* Engelbert Endrass, age twenty-eight, who like Prien was a onetime merchant marine officer, spotted a darkened ship that was zigzagging. Prien dived and sent the gun crew to battle stations. When he closed the track, Prien surfaced and fired a shot from his 88 mm (3.4") deck gun. Instead of stopping, the ship put on steam and turned tail, radioing the U-boat alarm, *SSS,* the position, and its name: *Bosnia.* She was a small British freighter of 2,407 tons, with a cargo of sulphur. Upon hearing the radio signals, Prien fired four more rounds from the deck gun directly at the ship. Three hit. The crew abandoned ship in panic, capsizing a lifeboat. Survivors floundered in the water.

Prien cruised among the panicky survivors, hauling them on board *U-47.* His men righted the overturned lifeboat and bailed it out. In the midst of the rescue, a

Norwegian ship came up and stopped. Prien instructed the Norwegians to assist. In response, they lowered a boat and, in due course, collected all the British survivors. After the Norwegian ship was well out of the way, Prien fired one torpedo at *Bosnia.* The ship buckled and sank in seconds. She was the second British ship to be torpedoed after *Athenia*—and the first freighter.

At dawn the next day, September 6, Prien found another British freighter, *Rio Claro,* 4,086 tons, outbound from London with a mixed cargo. Prien surfaced, gun manned. The ship stopped but began radioing the U-boat alarm, *SSS.* Prien fired a shot, but when this failed to silence the radio, he put three shells on the bridge. The radio went dead; the crew abandoned ship in lifeboats. Prien sank the ship with a torpedo, then inspected the lifeboats. All had food, water, compasses, sails, and signal flares. While he was debating whether or not to fetch a neutral ship to take the survivors on board, an aircraft appeared—perhaps in response to the *SSS*—and he dived. That apparent hostile act decided it for him: The survivors were on their own.

In the early afternoon of the next day, September 7, Prien came upon another small British freighter, *Gartavon,* 1,777 tons, carrying a cargo of iron ore. When she sighted *U-47,* she signaled *SSS* and tried to run off. A lucky hit from the deck gun brought down a goalpost mast and the radio antenna, and the ship hove to. Prien watched as the crew lowered a single boat, which pulled off in a hurry. Then, suddenly, the unmanned ship got under way and headed directly for *U-47.* Before abandoning ship, the crew had somehow rigged the ship to ram *U-47.* Prien put on emergency speed—gun blazing—and maneuvered out of the way just in time, passing so close to *Gartavon* that her wash slewed *U-47* half around.

Prien left the abandoned ship circling and approached the single, crowded lifeboat. He was chagrined at having been tricked, but nonetheless he offered the captain an opportunity to return to his ship to launch a second lifeboat. When that offer was refused, Prien made certain the one lifeboat was adequately provisioned. He told the captain that he would send a neutral to help if he came across one, but in view of the hostile act taken against *U-47* he would not radio for help. He then returned to *Gartavon* and fired a single torpedo, but it malfunctioned—zigging wildly off course. Deciding to husband his torpedoes, Prien sank the ship with the deck gun.

Due west of Prien, Herbert Schultze, age thirty, another former merchant marine officer, patrolled Area H in *U-48,* a sister ship of *U-47.* On September 5, Schultze ran across a big freighter inbound to the British Isles, but a shot from his deck gun failed to stop her. She bent on steam and hauled off, emitting clouds of soot, radioing *SSS.* In an attempt to silence the radio, Schultze directed gun fire at the bridge. The ship stopped and all the crew—save the radio operator—took to the lifeboats. While they did so, Schultze withheld fire, even though the *SSS* signals continued. After the crew had pulled off, Schultze closed on the ship and took off the radio operator. Then he fired a single torpedo, which ran true. Down went *Royal Sceptre,* a British ship of 4,853 tons, loaded with grain.

Approaching the lifeboats, Schultze asked if there were any wounded. There were none. All else was in order. He handed the radio operator over to a lifeboat, saluting his courage, then told the survivors to stand by. He had seen smoke on the horizon—an unidentified freighter coming up. Schultze made a beeline for the other ship, which turned out to be another big British freighter, S.S. *Browning*, 5,332 tons, outbound to Latin America. Schultze fired his deck gun to stop her, intending to direct her captain to rescue *Royal Sceptre*'s crew. But before he could make known his intent, the freighter crew lowered boats and abandoned ship in a panic.

Exasperated, Schultze closed on the lifeboats. He instructed the crew to return to *Browning* and to go pick up the *Royal Sceptre*'s crew. Naturally leery, the Britishers made no move to comply. Angrily waving his arms, Schultze finally got his point across. The crew returned to the ship, steamed off and picked up the *Royal Sceptre*'s crew, and carried the men on to the ship's destination in Brazil.* Over the next two days, September 6 and 7, Schultze stopped and searched several more neutrals and let them pass unmolested. Early in the morning of September 8, he found a 5,000-ton British freighter, *Winkleigh*. After the crew had abandoned ship, Schultze sank her with a torpedo.

The five large, long-range Type IX boats of the Hundius Flotilla, *U-37* to *U-41*, patrolled the most distant waters: the coast of the Iberian Peninsula and the western approaches to the Strait of Gibraltar.

Designed for extended cruising, the Type IXs were a bit roomier and less uncomfortable than the Type VIIs. Measuring 251 feet overall, the IXs were 40 feet longer than the VIIs and 33 feet longer than the VIIBs. The compartmentation inside the pressure hull of the IXs was similar to that of the VIIs except that the petty-officer quarters and galley, inconveniently located on the VIIs between the control room and engine room, had been eliminated. The eight bunks in that compartment were relocated aft, in a greatly enlarged stern room, which had two internal torpedo tubes; the galley was moved forward to the officers' compartment. The motor-generators, located in the stern room of the VIIs, were moved forward into the diesel-engine compartment. The five resulting fore-to-aft compartments were thus larger than the six compartments of the VIIs, as was the conning tower and bridge above.

All the numbers of the Type IXs were substantially greater than those of the Types VII and VIIB. Diesel horsepower: 4,000 versus 2,320 to 2,800. Motor-generators: 1,000 horsepower versus 750. Surface speed: 18.2 knots versus 16 to 17.2. Fuel storage: 154 tons versus 67 to 108. Range (at 12 knots): 8,000 versus 4,300 to 6,500. Torpedo capacity: 22† versus 11 and 14. Deck gun 105mm (4.1") versus 88mm (3.4"). Crew: 48 versus 44.

The Type IX was not the boat Dönitz preferred. His reasons were several. He

---

* Unaware of this rescue, Churchill wrongly assumed that "40 or 50" of the crew had died in the lifeboats. He likened that to "murder" and demanded that London publicize this "outrage" to the fullest. It should be characterized, he urged, as "an odious act of bestial piracy on the high seas."

† Ten in the bow compartment like the VIIs, four in the stern compartment (two in the tubes; two reloads in the bilges), and up to eight air or G7a torpedoes stored in topside canisters.

envisioned a U-boat war fought primarily close in to the British Isles, where all torpedoes were to be expended quickly, and therefore the endurance (or range) advantage of the IX was more or less superfluous. The added torpedo capacity of the IX—twenty-two versus fourteen for the VIIB—was not all it appeared to be. Eight of the twenty-two torpedoes, all air propelled, were stored topside, where they could not be serviced and could only be brought below in calm weather. What counted most with Dönitz was the *internal* torpedo capacity. The Type IX had fourteen internal torpedoes, versus twelve on the VIIB, not sufficiently advantageous to justify the threefold investment in time and matériel for the larger boat. Moreover, the IXs were slow in diving, had a greater turning circle, were clumsy submerged, lacked the rapid submerged acceleration of the VIIs, and presented the enemy a larger sonar target.

Dönitz had hopes that the five Type IXs in southern waters might operate as a pack against a convoy, tactically directed by Flotilla Commander Werner Hartmann, on board *U-37.* But for various reasons, the boats were unable to operate as a group. All patrolled independently over widely spaced areas that appeared to be virtually empty of shipping.

Heinrich Liebe, a thirty-one-year-old lieutenant, commanded *U-38.* Like Lemp in *U-30,* Liebe was the son of an Army officer. Like Lemp, Liebe had joined the *Reichsmarine* at age eighteen. After submarine school and command of the duck *U-2,* Liebe had commissioned *U-38* in December 1938.

Liebe patrolled close off the coast of Lisbon, Portugal, where traffic was densest. On September 5 he sighted a freighter, surfaced, and forced her to heave to for inspection. Awkwardly, she turned out to be the French vessel *Pluvoise.* After examining her papers, Liebe let her pass, but her captain broadcast a submarine alarm, which was picked up in Berlin. This prompted a rebuke and further tightening of the U-boat rules: "Merchantmen identified as being French are not to be stopped. Incidents with France are to be avoided at all costs."

The next day, September 6, still off Lisbon, Liebe put a warning shot across the bow of the 7,242-ton British freighter S.S. *Manaar* with his 4.1" deck gun. As it turned out, *Manaar* was armed with a gun almost as large (3.94") mounted on the stern. As *U-38* approached, *Manaar*'s gun crew opened fire. Stunned by this unexpected and hot reception—*Manaar* was the first British merchantman to fire a gun at a U-boat—Liebe dived and without further ado, sank *Manaar* with torpedoes. In view of *Manaar*'s hostile military action against him, Liebe judged *Manaar* to be excluded from the protection of the Submarine Protocol and made no effort to assist her survivors.

Liebe hauled out of the area and that night broke radio silence to give Dönitz an account of this battle and to warn other U-boats of similar dangers. In Berlin, the naval staff released the details to foreign naval attaches and to the media, stressing that *Manaar* had fired at *U-38 on sight.* Dönitz was incensed. It seemed completely unfair that his crews should be required to adhere strictly to the Submarine Protocol in the face of an enemy that was arming its merchant ships, in effect, turning them into warships. But, given the "political situation," as he put it, he could do nothing more than to warn all U-boats to exercise extreme caution.

• • •

The U-boat assigned to the most hazardous mission in the Atlantic, the unsteady *U-26,* was loaded with mines. She was commanded by a reliable and conservative skipper, thirty-two-year-old Klaus Ewerth. He was a star graduate of the first class (1933) at the secret submarine school, had commissioned the first duck, *U-1,* in 1935, and had commanded the Type VII, *U-35* for two years. In peacetime drills, he had mastered the art of minelaying.

The *U-26* mission had been conceived by the OKM. The objective was to foul the British naval base at Portland to prevent the embarkation of British Army troops to France across the English Channel. From its inception, Dönitz had opposed the mission. Sonar-equipped ASW forces were certain to be patrolling the channel approaches to Portland. It was also the home base of the Royal Navy's sonar school! They could hardly miss big, clumsy *U-26.*

Ewerth commenced a careful submerged run-in on September 4. As expected, he encountered intense ASW patrols. After playing hide-and-seek for several hours, he aborted the first attempt and returned to deep water. A second attempt also failed. Finally, on the third run-in, Ewerth reached a likely spot off the Portland harbor, the Shambles, undetected, on the night of September 8.

During the years between the wars, the German Navy had developed in secrecy a wide array of mines, vastly superior to those employed in World War I. The *U-26* was loaded with one type, the TMB, designed especially to be laid by submarines. The TMB was an untethered "seabed" (or "ground") mine, with a magnetic pistol, to be laid on the bottom in fairly shallow water (about sixty-five feet). It was 7½ feet long and had a 1,276-pound warhead (twice the explosive power of a German torpedo). When a big ship passed overhead, its magnetic field would actuate the mine's pistol, exploding the mine directly beneath the keel of the ship with devastating force.

Submarine minelaying was a tedious, exacting, and hazardous business. The mines had to be laid precisely in the selected sea channel, otherwise they would be useless. This required positioning the boat within a few *feet* of the selected site. Furthermore, by international law, minefields had to be exactly charted so they could be swept after hostilities. The charting was useful as well to the Germans. Should they decide to augment the field, they would know exactly where the first mines had been planted and these could be avoided.

The *U-26* carried her mines in the four forward and two stern torpedo tubes, with others stored in the bow and stern compartments. One by one Ewerth booted the mines out of the tubes with compressed air, charting the exact location by means of the navigational lights burning on shore and in the channel. There was no danger to the boat; the mines had delayed-action arming devices, which would not actuate until *U-26* was well clear. When all the mines had been laid—and charted—Ewerth eased away submerged to deep water and put the boat on the bottom. After the crew rested, the torpedomen loaded all six tubes with torpedoes, manhandled from the storage spaces below the deck plates.

Submariners of all nations disliked minelaying. It had to be done close to shore in shallow water where if detected, the boat became dangerously exposed to enemy attack. Putting the mines overboard and then reloading the tubes with torpedoes was dangerous and hard physical work. There was no immediate damage to shipping (as in firing torpedoes), and thus no satisfaction and seldom any credit. Besides that, many regarded minelaying as sneaky and underhanded—somehow not quite fair.

While withdrawing westward from the English Channel, the *U-26* was again detected by British ASW forces and compelled to engage in prolonged evasion. That and the long delays in planting the field put Ewerth days behind schedule and he was unable to report to Dönitz. When, on September 8, the Admiralty announced that British naval forces had sunk a U-boat that was attempting to lay mines in the English Channel, Dönitz assumed that it was *U-26*. As a check he radioed Ewerth to report his position. Receiving no reply, Dönitz was convinced *U-26* was gone.

Apart from all else, the probable loss of *U-26* caused a tremendous flap at the OKM. She had a naval Enigma and documents for it on board. If, as was assumed, *U-26* went down in shallow water, the British might salvage her or send down divers and recover the Enigma with its operating instructions and current keys. As a result, the OKM ordered that Enigma settings throughout the entire *Kriegsmarine* be changed and that henceforth no minelaying U-boat should carry an Enigma. It was a useless precaution; *U-26* was safe and sound and finally spoke up after Ewerth shook his pursuers and reached the open Atlantic.

Much later it was learned the *U-26* minefield paid off. The Admiralty announced that three big "neutral" freighters (a Greek, a Dutch, and a Belgian) triggered mines and sank. These ships displaced a total of 17,414 tons. One of the new British corvettes, *Kittiwake,* triggered another and was badly damaged, but that mishap was concealed from the Germans.

ENCOUNTERS WITH *ARK ROYAL*

Merely five days into the war, on September 8, Dönitz ordered a sweeping redeployment of the Atlantic U-boats. The main reason for the change was to amass oceangoing boats at home to deploy in a "second wave" in October, so there would be no lull or gap in the U-boat offensive. Accordingly, he ordered ten of the eighteen boats in the Atlantic (five of the six VIIBs and all five IXs) to return to Germany. The unsteady *U-26,* which found no targets for her six torpedoes, developed mechanical problems and soon joined the homeward trek, leaving only seven of the original group, all Type VIIs of the Salzwedel Flotilla, to carry on the war. To augment these, Dönitz committed the reserve force of three Type VIIs. One, *U-32,* was to go northabout the British Isles and lay a TMB minefield off the British naval base at Portsmouth, in the English Channel east of Portland. In order to save time, the other two, *U-31* and *U-35,* loaded with torpedoes, were to go directly to the Atlantic via the English Channel. The *U-31* made it through the channel safely, but *U-35,* attacked by aircraft and the British submarine *Ursula,* was forced to abort the channel passage and go northabout like *U-32.*

The ten boats recalled to Germany stayed well to the westward of the British Isles, where the remaining U-boats were patrolling. It was not a happy homebound procession. The five IXs of the Hundius Flotilla had sunk one ship—the *Manaar* by Liebe in *U-38*. The five VIIBs of the Wegener Flotilla had sunk only five ships—three by Prien in *U-47* and two by Herbert Schultze in *U-48*. However, Liebe and Schultze had further success on the way home. On September 11, Liebe torpedoed the fully loaded 9,456-ton British tanker *Inverliffey,* which blew up in a fireball. At considerable risk to *U-38,* Liebe saved the crew by towing the lifeboats from the blazing inferno. Further north that same day, Schultze sank the 4,869-ton British freighter *Firby* with his deck gun and a torpedo. Schultze provided medical care for several wounded *Firby* crewmen, provisioned the lifeboats, then radioed in the clear: "TRANSMIT TO MR. CHURCHILL. I HAVE SUNK THE BRITISH STEAMER FIRBY. POSIT FIFTY-NINE DEGREES FORTY MINUTES NORTH, THIRTEEN DEGREES FIFTY MINUTES WEST. SAVE THE CREW IF YOU PLEASE. GERMAN SUBMARINE."

The returning boats passed near Rockall, where Lemp in *U-30* was patrolling. But not happily. Since sinking *Athenia* on September 3, the *U-30* had been dogged by foul weather and a dearth of traffic. He had found and sunk by gunfire only one other ship: the 4,500-ton British freighter *Blairlogie.* Adhering strictly to the rules, Lemp gave the survivors whisky and cigarettes and stood by the lifeboats until a neutral ship rescued them.

Near Rockall on the morning of September 14, Lemp found another British freighter, the 5,200-ton *Fanad Head.* He stopped her with his deck gun, but not before she had radioed SSS and her position. After the crew had abandoned ship, Lemp decided to send a two-man team across in a rubber dinghy and blow her up with a demolition charge. This would save torpedoes, which were in short supply. The demolition team, led by Adolph Schmidt, could also ransack *Fanad Head* for fresh bread and other booty.

British shore stations and ships picked up *Fanad Head*'s distress call. The ships included the Royal Navy's newest and most formidable carrier, *Ark Royal,* which was about 180 miles to the northeast on ASW patrol, escorted by six destroyers. Three of the destroyers peeled off and proceeded southwest to *Fanad Head* at top speed. Shortly afterward *Ark Royal* launched three Skua monoplanes armed with ASW bombs.* The planes arrived at the scene in the midst of *U-30*'s demolition operation, forcing Lemp to break off and dive, leaving Schmidt and his

---

* Three sizes of aircraft bombs had been developed for ASW: 100-pound, 250-pound, and 500-pound—half the weight composed of explosives. The fuse was armed by a little propeller protruding from the nose. To kill a U-boat, extreme accuracy was required. For example, the 500-pound bomb (with 250 pounds of explosives) had to explode within eight feet of the U-boat hull to inflict fatal damage. Aircraft could also be fitted to drop the standard ashcan-shaped depth charge, but lacking a conical nose and tailfins, it tended to tumble in the air and thus follow an erratic path. Since they were not strongly constructed, depth charges also tended to break apart when they hit the water. Hence pilots preferred bombs to depth charges.

assistant stranded on *Fanad Head.* In the rush to get under, Lemp's men forgot to cut the line to the dinghy, which, unknown to Lemp, trailed over *U-30* like a marker buoy.

The three Skua pilots saw a "black object" (the dinghy) and attacked it with bombs, some of which rattled *U-30.* Unfortunately, the British pilots did not know the bombs were scandalously ill designed. Some bombs struck the water and "skipped" back into the air. The impact triggered the fuses, exploding the bombs, spewing fragments into the path of the oncoming aircraft. Severely damaged by the bomb fragments, two of the Skuas were forced to ditch. Looking on in amazement, Adolph Schmidt and his assistant on *Fanad Head* swam out and rescued both British pilots, one of whom was badly burned. Although one plane was still overhead, Lemp surfaced to recover Schmidt, his assistant—and the two British pilots—and to cut loose the dinghy. During the recovery, the surviving aircraft raked *U-30* with machine-gun fire, wounding Schmidt, who was helping the injured British pilot get below.

While *U-30*'s medic attended to Schmidt and the British pilots, Lemp set up and fired four bow torpedoes at *Fanad Head.* All malfunctioned or missed. A fifth torpedo from the external stern tube struck home and the ship blew up and sank. At that moment—it was now 1830—a second wave of *Ark Royal* aircraft comprised of six older Swordfish biplanes, each armed with six 100-pound bombs, arrived over the scene. The pilots could clearly see the submerged shadow of *U-30.* They attacked, dropping a total of eleven bombs, some of which exploded very close to the boat. Lemp went deep to evade.

Later the three fleet destroyers arrived, having traveled the 180 miles in about seven hours. All were equipped with the latest sonar manned by skilled operators. One destroyer went in search of the *Fanad Head* crew, the other two hunted—and found—*U-30.* Sonar conditions were good; the operators knew exactly what to do.

Working as a team, the two destroyers fixed *U-30* and delivered a series of devastating depth-charge attacks.* The explosions shattered glass dials—and men's nerves—damaged two torpedo bow caps, and cracked open a valve in the engine room, partially flooding that space. Before the crew could stop the leak and organize a bucket brigade to shift the water to the control-room bilges, where it could be pumped overboard, *U-30* sank to a greater depth than any U-boat had ever gone—472 feet. Throughout this punishing ordeal, Lemp remained absolute master of his boat—"even-tempered, very determined, and possessed of unshakable calm." After six hours, Lemp eluded his pursuers, surfaced, and escaped in the darkness.

Lemp broke radio silence to report the fight and his damage and to request permission to land the wounded Schmidt and the two *Ark Royal* pilots in neutral Iceland for medical care. Dönitz authorized the diversion, after which Lemp was to

---

*   Depth charges had not been much improved since World War I. The standard British depth charge, with an adjustable hydrostatic fuse, weighed 450 pounds and contained 300 pounds of Amatol explosives. It could be preset to explode at fifty-foot intervals from depths of fifty to 500 feet.

return directly to Germany. Monitoring this radio exchange, the OKM gained the impression that *U-30* had shot down the two aircraft and on the following day, Berlin propagandists gloatingly announced a "victory" over *Ark Royal.*

That day, September 14, while *Ark Royal* was launching its first flight of aircraft to attack *U-30,* one of the homebound IXs of the Hundius Flotilla, *U-39,* commanded by Gerhard Glattes, age thirty, happened upon the carrier. The view from *U-39*'s periscope was a submariner's dream: the majestic *Ark Royal* steaming alone. She had turned into the wind to launch the Skuas and, as a result, she had fallen four miles astern of the three remaining destroyers of her screen, *Faulkner, Foxhound,* and *Firedrake.*

The excitement on *U-39* could not have been greater. After twenty-six days of luckless patrolling, Glattes now had the pride of the Royal Navy in his crosshairs. Carefully, competently, coolly, Glattes ordered the bow tubes made ready and the outer doors opened. Then, at 1507, he fired a fan of three electric torpedoes with magnetic pistols. Timing the torpedo runs with a stopwatch, the crew tensely waited. Then, finally, explosions! A hit!

Or so it seemed. Actually, the torpedoes had been misaimed or had malfunctioned. None hit *Ark Royal.* Men on one of the destroyers saw *Ark Royal* swing rapidly to port, then a "high white splash" on her port side, followed by "a flash and black smoke to starboard." The British believed Glattes had underestimated *Ark Royal*'s speed (20 knots versus actual speed of 26 knots). They reported that the torpedoes had exploded harmlessly "in the wake." In his postwar memoir, Dönitz wrote that the magnetic pistols of the torpedoes had not worked properly and that all had "exploded prematurely underwater, close to the ship, but before they had reached a position below her."

Upon receiving a signal from *Ark Royal* reporting a submarine attack, the three destroyers reversed course and launched a hunt, line abreast, making 15 knots and maintaining a distance of one mile between them. Sonar conditions were good; the operators were among the best in the fleet. Within eighteen minutes, both *Foxhound* and *Faulkner* had sonar contact. *Foxhound* attacked immediately, dropping two depth charges, one set for 250 feet, one for 300 feet. *Faulkner* followed with five more depth charges set for 100 and 150 feet. In the noise of exploding depth charges, both of these destroyers lost contact, but *Firedrake* did not, and she moved in to drop five more charges set for 250 feet and 500 feet.

These twelve depth charges exploded close and rocked *U-39* violently. The first batch caused arcing flames in the battery and knocked out all lighting. Glattes took *U-39* "deep" (to about 230 feet) but the second salvo caught her and cracked sea valves and flanges. Salt water flooded into the battery, generating deadly chlorine gas. Then the electric motors shut down and *U-39,* unable to maneuver submerged, went out of control.

No one on *U-39* had ever experienced noise and terror on this scale. After twenty minutes of it, a shaken Glattes concluded the boat was fatally damaged, and he commanded the crew to prepare to abandon ship and blew all main ballast tanks. At 1546—thirty-nine minutes after firing the torpedoes—*U-39* broke surface, bow up, in broad daylight, surrounded by the three destroyers. All three vessels opened fire with guns, but when it was seen that the *U-39* crew was jumping overboard, the destroyers checked fire. Glattes's men had set a scuttling charge and opened the forward torpedo-room hatch. The charge exploded as designed and *U-39*, fatally holed, went down bow first—the first U-boat to be lost in the war. The three destroyers launched boats and fished forty-three bearded, shocked *U-39* survivors from the water. There were no casualties.

The *Ark Royal* hunter-killer group had good reason to celebrate. Until Berlin announced the capture of the two *Ark Royal* pilots and they appeared in Iceland, the group believed it had sunk two U-boats in a single day with the loss of only two Skuas. Wrongly believing that *U-39* had earlier sunk *Firby*—and sent the personal message to Churchill to pick up her survivors—Churchill boasted in a public speech that the culprit had been captured. Offsetting these supposed successes, however, was *U-39*'s near hit on *Ark Royal*. That chilling experience provided a telling argument for those who opposed using fleet carriers—and wearing out precious aircraft—in an ASW role.

Nine of the ten recalled boats reached Germany September 15 to 17. Inbound in the North Sea, one of the IXs, *U-41*, commanded by Gustav-Adolf Mügler, age twenty-six, captured two small (1,000-ton) Finnish freighters deemed to be transporting contraband and escorted them into Germany. Discounting these insignificant "prizes," the ten boats of the Wegener and Hundius flotillas had sunk only eight ships—three each by Prien and Schultze, two by Liebe. Seven of the ten skippers had sunk no ships. Moreover, one of these ten boats, *U-39*, was missing. It was not an auspicious beginning.

"A WONDERFUL SUCCESS"

The recall of the ten boats of the Wegener and Hundius flotillas, the abort of *U-26*, and the diversion of the damaged *U-30* to Iceland to land the wounded, left nine Type VIIs of the Salzwedel Flotilla to carry on the war against British shipping. Of these, five were low on fuel. Three Type VIIs of the reserve were newly arrived, but one of these, *U-32*, had been assigned to a minelaying mission* and carried only a few torpedoes.

Seven of the nine boats were deployed in abutting patrol zones due west of the English Channel, an area the British called the Western Approaches. The sea-lanes to and from the British Isles converged there and the area was dense with shipping of all kinds. To provide all these ships some protection, the Admiralty had de-

---

* Changed from Portsmouth to Bristol because of intense British ASW measures in the English Channel and because she sailed with an Enigma before the OKM prohibited Enigmas in minelaying boats.

ployed the old aircraft carrier *Courageous** with a destroyer screen to mount ASW patrols.

Three Salzwedel boats in the Western Approaches had achieved successes against British shipping in the early days of the war. On September 7, Hans-Wilhelm von Dresky, age thirty-one, in *U-33* had sunk a 4,000-ton freighter. That day and the next, Wilhelm Rollmann, age thirty-two, in *U-34* had sunk a 5,500-ton freighter and wrecked a 5,500-ton tanker, *Kennebec,* put down by British warships. Otto Schuhart, age thirty, in *U-29* got the biggest and most important ship, the 10,000-ton tanker *Regent Tiger,* sunk on September 8. Then a lull had set in, broken only by Schuhart's sinking of an 800-ton seagoing tugboat on September 13.

The killing picked up again on September 14, the day Lemp and Glattes tangled with *Ark Royal* farther north. Günter Kuhnke, age twenty-seven, in *U-28* patrolling into the mouth of St. George's Channel, sank a 5,000-ton freighter. To the west, Schuhart in *U-29* found and attacked another big tanker, the spanking-new *British Influence,* 8,500 tons.

During his attack on the *British Influence,* Schuhart had a bizarre and troubling experience, similar to that of Glattes when he shot at *Ark Royal.* Schuhart's first two torpedoes, fitted with magnetic pistols, spontaneously "prematured," or blew up before reaching the target, shaking the boat and forcing him to shoot again. Believing that something might be drastically wrong with the magnetic pistols, Schuhart later broke radio silence to report these "prematures." When Dönitz, in turn, reported the malfunctions to the Torpedo Directorate, the experts there were also deeply puzzled. Pending further investigation, the experts recommended that the magnetic pistols be set back or down "two zones" to "reduce sensitivity," an order Dönitz relayed to all boats. The reduced-sensitivity settings meant that to sink a ship of 3,000 tons or less, which had a weaker magnetic field, only contact (or impact) pistols were to be used, imposing on the skippers the need to ascertain target tonnage of medium-sized ships with a high degree of accuracy.

On September 15, *U-31,* commanded by Johannes Habekost, age thirty-two, a reserve boat which had just completed the hazardous voyage through the English Channel, picked up an outbound convoy. Per prior instructions, Habekost broke radio silence to report its course and speed to Dönitz. This was the first "clear" contact with a convoy by any U-boat in British waters and it caused tremendous excitement. Dönitz ordered all boats in the Western Approaches, including Schuhart in *U-29* and Ernst-Gunther Heinicke, age thirty-one, in the late-sailing VIIB *U-53,* to converge on the convoy. During the night Habekost in *U-31* hauled around the convoy and gained position to shoot early on the morning of September 16. He thought he sank two big ships, but apparently he also experienced torpedo malfunctions. Only one ship, the 4,000-ton British freighter *Aviemore,* went down.

Both Heinicke in *U-53* and Schuhart in *U-29* responded to the contact. Hunting

---

* *Courageous* and her sister ships, *Furious* and *Glorious,* 22,500 tons, were originally battle cruisers, laid down in 1916 and converted to aircraft carriers in the 1920s. Each carried about twenty-four Swordfish biplanes and had a crew of about 1,200.

for the convoy on September 17, Heinicke ran across a 5,000-ton inbound British freighter, *Kafiristan,* and put her under with gunfire and torpedoes. While he was attempting to assist the panicky survivors, a flight of Swordfish biplanes from *Courageous* attacked *U-53* with bombs and machine-gun fire, forcing Heinicke to crash dive—and to leave some gunners topside. They perished in the sea.

To the east of *U-53,* that same day, while he was running submerged, Schuhart in *U-29* saw a Swordfish biplane. A Swordfish 300 miles west of England over open water meant that an aircraft carrier had to be close by. Schuhart remained submerged, keeping a sharp periscope watch. At about 1800, the watch sighted a puff of smoke on the horizon. It was the carrier *Courageous!* Schuhart adjusted his own course to improve his position and went to battle stations. During quick periscope observations, he saw aircraft circling the carrier but only two fleet destroyers. The other two destroyers of her screen had gone west to the scene of the *Kafiristan* sinking to hunt Heinicke's *U-53.*

Try as he might, Schuhart could not close the range to *Courageous.* Later he wrote in his log: "At the time it looked like a hopeless operation. Because of the aircraft I could not surface and my underwater speed was less than 8 knots while the carrier could do 26. But we were told during our training to always stay close and that is exactly what I did, following him submerged. . . ."

Schuhart hung on doggedly for an hour and a half. Then suddenly, at 1930, *Courageous* abruptly altered course, turning into the wind to take on aircraft. The turn brought her directly toward *U-29.* Schuhart gave orders to open the bow caps on three forward torpedo tubes. He had to shoot by guesswork because, as he wrote in his log, "the vast size of the target upset all normal calculations and in any case I was looking straight into the sun."

At 1940, Schuhart fired a fan of three torpedoes at a range of 3,000 yards. While they were running, one of the destroyers, still unaware of *U-29,* passed by at 500 yards. To avoid detection, Schuhart took the boat deep. Going down, the crew heard and felt two hits. "The explosions were so heavy," Schuhart wrote, "that I thought the boat had been damaged. There was jubilation among the crew, although we were all wondering what would happen to us next." He leveled the boat at 180 feet—deeper by thirty feet than he had ever dived—then cautiously eased deeper.

Two torpedoes hit *Courageous.* As it happened, a Dutch passenger liner, *Veendamn,* was passing nearby. The passengers saw a huge white cloud engulf *Courageous.* At first they believed the cloud was a smoke screen, but seconds later they heard two tremendous explosions and saw flames shooting through the cloud, then pieces of steel and dismembered aircraft hurtling skyward. They watched in horror as *Courageous* rolled slowly to port and sank, fifteen minutes after the torpedoes struck. Of her 1,260-man crew, 519 perished. *Veendamn* and a British freighter, *Collingworth,* which responded to the distress call, rescued the survivors from the oily waters.

The two destroyers found *U-29* on sonar and attacked with a vengeance. The U-boat reeled under the impact of the depth charges. During one attack, Schuhart remembered, he thought the conning tower would implode. But it held. The inter-

mittent pounding went on for four hours—to 2340—until both destroyers had expended all depth charges. Easing away silently, *U-29* surfaced and Schuhart radioed Dönitz: "*Courageous* destroyed. *U-29* homebound."

By the morning of September 18, the news of Schuhart's victory had been
broadcast worldwide. The Admiralty promptly withdrew the remaining three
Home Fleet carriers from ASW missions. Although Hitler (as Raeder remembered)
had not wished to humiliate the British by sinking a capital ship, no specific order
had been issued to U-boats prohibiting attacks on such ships. In fact, the *Kriegsmarine* was ecstatic, as was Karl Dönitz. Schuhart's feat was the crowning blow of
the psychological impact Dönitz had hoped to achieve in the first U-boat offensive.
"A wonderful success," he noted gleefully in his headquarters diary. Raeder directed Dönitz to award Schuhart the Iron Cross First Class, and every member of
the *U-29* crew the Iron Cross Second Class.

Running low on fuel, food, and torpedoes, six of the nine Type VIIs of the
Salzwedel Flotilla, including the *U-30* setting out from Iceland, soon commenced
the homeward voyage to Germany. The exodus left four boats to carry on the naval
war in British waters: the newly arrived Type VII boats of the Salzwedel reserve,
U-31, U-32, and *U-35,* plus Heinicke's VIIB, *U-53,* which still had a good supply
of fuel and torpedoes. After laying a minefield in Bristol Channel during the night
of September 17, the *U-32,* commanded by Paul Büchel, age thirty-two, joined the
other three boats for torpedo attacks. But, following the sinking of a 4,900-ton
freighter on September 18, Büchel had a mechanical breakdown and *U-32* was
forced to abort the patrol, leaving only two VIIs of the Salzwedel Flotilla and *U-53*
in British waters.

Of the seven homebound Type VII Salzwedel boats, only one, *U-27,* commanded by Johannes Franz, age thirty-two, had not torpedoed and sunk a ship. It
was not from want of trying. Deployed to an area near the mouth of North Channel, separating Scotland and Ireland, Franz had conducted a relentlessly aggressive
patrol. He had stopped a total of eleven big freighters, fired torpedoes at two
freighters, and sunk two trawlers, one by gunfire, one by demolition. On September 18, he saw the inbound *Ark Royal,* recalled from ASW missions, but she was
too far off to attack. Like Glattes and Schuhart, Franz had experienced battling—
and scary—torpedo problems. On September 17, two of the torpedoes he fired at a
British freighter had "prematured" after a run of merely 273 yards, badly shaking
and damaging the boat. Like Schuhart, Franz had broken radio silence to report the
mishap to Dönitz. His report had led to another modification in torpedo-firing procedure.

Homebound on the night of September 19, a few minutes before midnight *U-
27*'s bridge watch sighted "six shapes" on the horizon and urgently summoned
Franz to the bridge. Believing the ships to be cruisers, Franz could scarcely credit
his luck. He ordered battle stations, night surface, and unhesitatingly maneuvered
to attack. Setting three torpedoes with magnetic pistols to run at a depth of twelve
to thirteen feet, Franz fired at the overlapping line of ships, hoping to sink at least

three cruisers with this one salvo, thereby duplicating the legendary feat of Otto Weddigen in World War I.

In actuality, Franz had fired at a line of seven destroyers. Two of the three torpedoes exploded prematurely about thirty seconds after leaving the tube; the third missed. Alerted by the two explosions, the destroyer *Fortune* sighted *U-27* and instantly turned toward her to attack. Shaken by the premature torpedo explosions and seeing the oncoming *Fortune*—now correctly identified as a destroyer—Franz crash-dived and went deep. *Fortune* flung out five depth charges "by eye," but they were very wide of the mark. Settling down for a proper attack, *Fortune* gained sonar contact and moved in slowly for another run, dropping five more charges set for 100 and 150 feet. These exploded close to *U-27,* bending a propeller shaft and causing a serious leak in the packing gland of the shaft.

In the noise of exploding depth charges, *Fortune* lost sonar contact. All seven destroyers then reformed line abreast for a meticulous search. Meanwhile, Franz came to periscope depth for a look at his attackers. Seeing four destroyers, all close, sweeping the seas with searchlights, Franz went very deep—to 393 feet— and ordered silent running.

The destroyers pressed the hunt. At 0127, *Forester* got a sonar contact and attacked, dropping depth charges set for 100 and 150 feet. These shallow charges caused no damage and *Forester* lost contact in the noise. For a time Franz believed he might escape, but at 0212, *Fortune* regained sonar contact and mounted two consecutive, punishing attacks with depth charges set to explode between 100 and 250 feet. Some of these went off very close to *U-27,* causing severe flooding. Assessing the damage, Franz decided to surface, hoping to escape in the dark. At 0241, three hours and forty-eight minutes after launching her torpedo attack, *U-27* came up in the vicinity of seven destroyers, some burning searchlights. Franz put on emergency speed and ran.

Fortune saw the surfaced U-boat first. She turned to ram and opened fire with her guns. In the face of this fire, Franz, two officers, the quartermaster, and sixteen others dived over the side of the fast-moving boat. They were later fished out by *Faulkner.* Seeing them jump and other men clustered on the deck, *Fortune* ceased firing after four rounds and swerved to avoid ramming, now planning to capture the men and boat intact. When *U-27* finally halted her futile attempt to escape on the surface, *Fortune* sent over a salvage party. But by then *U-27*'s engineer had set scuttling procedures in motion and the boat was sinking. *Fortune*'s engineer courageously went inside the boat in an attempt to close the sea cocks and ballast-tank vents (and grab whatever papers he could find), but it was too late. The boat was flooding fast and full of chlorine gas. She sank stern first and vertically at 0350. *Fortune* rescued the remaining eighteen men of the *U-27* crew. There were no casualties.

The remaining six Type VIIs of the Salzwedel Flotilla in the homebound procession escaped detection. Büchel in *U-32* added a minor scalp to his belt by sinking an 875-ton Norwegian ship with demolitions, as did von Dresky in *U-33,* who sank a trawler with his gun. Rollmann in *U-34* captured a 2,500-ton Estonian freighter in the North Sea and escorted it to Germany. The six boats reached Wilhelmshaven between September 26 and 30, five with barely more than cupsful of fuel left in the tanks.

Fritz-Julius Lemp in *U-30* arrived from Iceland on September 27. The boat was in terrible condition. One diesel was out, the other barely turning over. Dönitz sent out a minesweeper to tow her in, but Lemp proudly refused help and *U-30* limped into the Jade under her own power. Parading on deck with the begrimed, bearded crew was a live turkey, Alfonso, bought in Iceland to augment rations but adopted as a mascot.

Dönitz—indeed, the whole U-boat arm—knew, of course, that Lemp had sunk *Athenia*. Berlin was still denying that a U-boat had done it, so Lemp and the *U-30* crew (as well as the whole U-boat force) had to be enjoined to keep the secret, and the *U-30* logbook was altered to hide any hint of the sinking. But one worry remained: The wounded crewman, Adolph Schmidt, who had been landed in Iceland, might reveal the truth. Lemp assured Dönitz that Schmidt was completely dependable.*

Legend has it that Lemp was in hot water for sinking *Athenia* and that the OKM threatened him with a court-martial, but this is unlikely. Although the *Athenia* sinking had been a mistake, it had done a great deal to sow terror, the psychological blow Dönitz and the *Kriegsmarine* had sought. Moreover, Lemp had conducted an outstanding patrol. He had sunk three ships (including *Athenia*) in a marginal patrol area and foul weather, "shot down" (the propaganda version) two aircraft from the *Ark Royal,* demonstrated commendable chivalry and humanity by rescuing the British pilots and taking them to Iceland for medical care, survived the worst depth charging of any of the Atlantic boats with "unshakable calm," dived *U-30* to an unprecedented depth of 472 feet, and brought his boat home in spite of severe battle damage and engine defects. To have court-martialed Lemp would have sent a wrong signal to the U-boat force (punishing brash aggressiveness) and run the risk of the proceedings leaking to the Allies, thereby exposing Berlin's lies.

The scores of the first seven Salzwedel Flotilla Type VII boats, including the lost *U-27,* were otherwise disappointing. In about seventeen days of combat in the Atlantic—September 3 to September 20—they had sunk only fourteen ships and three trawlers by torpedo, gun, and demolition, and captured one prize. Discounting the trawlers, the statistical return was only two ships sunk per boat, or one ship per eight patrol days. Moreover, *U-32*'s minefield was not productive. It damaged two big freighters—and forced the British to close Bristol temporarily—but it produced no sinkings.

Even so, the skippers and crews returned to a hero's welcome. Hitler and Raeder paid brief visits to Wilhelmshaven to hand out praise and medals. The man of the hour was Otto Schuhart in *U-29,* who had accounted for four of the fourteen sinkings, including *Courageous* and two important tankers. In tonnage sunk, his

---

* So he was. When British forces occupied Iceland in 1940, Schmidt became a prisoner of war and was interrogated repeatedly. He did not reveal the *Athenia* sinking.

total was 41,905, a record for a single patrol that was to stand for a long time. The runner-up was Lemp in *U-30*, with three ships for 23,206 tons, but since *Athenia* could not even be mentioned, let alone credited, second place went to Wilhelm Rollmann in *U-34*, who had sunk two ships for 11,400 tons and had taken a 2,500-ton prize. Büchel in *U-32* sank two ships and von Dresky in *U-33* sank three, but their individual tonnage scores were only about half that of Rollmann. Kuhnke in *U-28* sank one ship.

Three boats of the first wave were still in the Atlantic: the Salzwedel reserve *U-31* and *U-35*, and the VIIB of the Wegener Flotilla, *U-53*. The last returned first. Having sunk two ships—a freighter and the 8,826-ton tanker *Cheyenne*—*U-53* raised the total score of the six Wegener Flotilla boats to eight. The reserve *U-31* sank two ships, and the reserve *U-35* sank four ships. Including the three trawlers, these six kills raised the total sinkings of the nine Salzwedel boats deployed to the Atlantic to twenty-four, and the average of sinkings per boat per patrol from 2 to 2.6.

The aggregate confirmed kills by all twenty-one oceangoing boats of the first wave were thus as follows:

Forces		Ships	Tonnage
Salzwedel Flotilla	(9 Type VII)	24	112,689
Wegener Flotilla	(6 Type VIIB)	8	37,065
Hundius Flotilla	(5 Type IX)	4	18,870
U-26 minefield	(1 Type I)	3	17,414
Total:		39	186,038

NORTH SEA PATROLS

When hostilities commenced on September 3, there were seventeen ducks and one Type VII oceangoing boat, *U-36*, deployed in the North Sea for offensive and defensive operations. After the surrender of Poland, three ducks basing at Memel, and others in the eastern Baltic Sea, redeployed to the North Sea, so that in all, twenty-three of the thirty commissioned ducks patrolled the North Sea in the first month of the war.

Five ducks were assigned to lay minefields in four British ports and one French port. When Hitler barred attacks on French shipping, the mining mission to France was canceled. Four ducks laid a total of thirty-six TMB magnetic mines in four ports on the British east coast and in the English Channel. Two of the fields (Dover and Hartlepool) failed to produce. The field at Ordfordness, planted by Karl Daublebsky von Eichhain in *U-13*, produced handsomely: three ships for 27,203 tons sunk. The field at Flamborough Head, planted by Heinz Buchholz in *U-15*, sank two medium freighters for 4,274 tons.

The other ducks and the Type VII *U-36* patrolled offensively and defensively in every nook and cranny of the confined waters of the North Sea. Two ducks, *U-9* and *U-19*, hunted British warships off northeast Scotland. Several ducks reconnoitered the east end of the English Channel. One duck, *U-14*, patrolled the British naval base at Scapa Flow. Another, *U-20*, patrolled all the way north to Narvik, Norway, above the Arctic Circle. Others cruised the Kattegat and Skagerrak.

Owing to fuel limitations, the ducks could not stay out for more than about eighteen days. Many patrols, however, were shorter. Some ducks sailed from Wilhelmshaven and returned directly there. Others went on to Kiel via the Kiel Canal. Still others sailed from Kiel to the North Sea via the Kattegat and Skagerrak and returned to Kiel via that route. Most ducks required a week or more of repairs in the shipyards between patrols. In the interval, the crews were granted liberty and leave. Only a few ducks were able to mount two patrols in September.

The North Sea was aswarm with commercial traffic: British ships, neutral ships of Norway, Denmark, Sweden, Finland, Estonia, Latvia, Lithuania, and other nations. Many neutrals were transporting "contraband" (ore, chemicals, food, weapons, timber, etc.) to the British Isles. But the ducks were too small, too slow (13 knots maximum speed), and underarmed to stop and "visit and search" shipping in conformance with the Submarine Protocol. Moreover, for political reasons, Hitler had decreed that clearly marked neutrals in the North Sea were not to be stopped. As a result, ducks were compelled to limit attacks to targets they were permitted to sink "on sight" by surprise attack: British warships and submarines and British shipping unequivocally under escort.

On the rare occasions when permissible targets appeared, the duck skippers attacked boldly. Both Fritz Frauenheim in *U-21* and Udo Behrens in *U-24* shot at British destroyers off northeast Scotland. Frauenheim claimed—and was credited with—a kill, but neither attack was successful. Horst Wellner in *U-14* and Werner Winter in *U-22* both were wrongly credited with sinking Polish submarines. They subsequently attacked British submarines and both were again wrongly credited with kills. No duck sank—or even damaged—a British warship in September.

A few skippers found escorted or unescorted British merchant ships. Otto Kretschmer in *U-23* fired a full-bow salvo of three torpedoes and one reload at an old 2,000-ton coaster under escort, but all four torpedoes malfunctioned or missed. Wilhelm Frölich in the Type VII *U-36* stopped, searched, and then sank the unescorted 1,000-ton British coaster *Truro*, after the crew abandoned ship. Werner Heidel in *U-7* also stopped and sank an unescorted British freighter, the 2,700-ton *Akenside*. These were the only two ships sunk by all the U-boats in the North Sea to September 22.

The vast flow of contraband in neutral ships in the North Sea infuriated Raeder and Dönitz. On September 23, Raeder met with Hitler in Danzig to urge relaxations in the U-boat rules, which not only would free the ducks to stop (i.e., attack) neutrals in the North Sea but would also reduce the risk and increase opportunities for the next wave of Atlantic boats. Having conquered Poland and despairing of persuading France and Great Britain to back out of the war, Hitler was then drawing plans to turn about and attack westward into France. He foresaw an early collapse of France. After that, he believed, Great Britain would seek peace.

A relaxation in the U-boat rules therefore fit Hitler's plan to maintain pressure on the West. He approved tightening the screws on neutral traffic in the North Sea and other measures favoring the U-boats, which the OKM passed to Dönitz on the following day, September 24. These were:

• Restrictions on French shipping, including the mining of French ports, were lifted. "French ships are to be treated in the same way as British ships."

• U-boats were authorized to use "armed force" against any Allied merchant ship which broadcast the submarine alarm, *SSS*. Such ships, without exception, were subject to "seizure and sinking." However, "rescue of crews is to be attempted."

• Allied "passenger" ships carrying 120 people or less (and hence presumed to be mainly cargo ships) could be sunk in accordance with the Submarine Protocol or prize rules. However, under no circumstances were "passenger" ships carrying more than 120 people to be sunk.*

The U-boat force cheered the relaxation of these rules. The authorization to sink French ships greatly reduced risks, opened the way for night surface attacks on Allied convoys, and increased the number of legal merchant-ship targets by about 500 ships of about 2.7 million gross tons. Inasmuch as all British ships were under orders to broadcast *SSS* upon sighting a submarine, the authorization to sink Allied ships making such a broadcast also greatly reduced risks by eliminating the requirement to search such ships before sinking them.

The relaxations were not all that was desired. Even though Allied ships broadcasting *SSS* could now be sunk without search, U-boat skippers still had to at least attempt to rescue the crews, a risky process at best. The prohibition against sinking a passenger ship carrying more than 120 people imposed on the skippers the difficult task of judging (by counting lifeboats, etc.) how many people might be on board. A request to sink on sight all armed ships and all blacked-out ships sailing close to the British Isles had not been approved.

Upon receiving the relaxed rules for the North Sea, the ducks fell upon neutral shipping in those waters with boldness and vigor. Heidel in *U-7* sank two Norwegians. Harro von Klot-Heydenfeldt in *U-4* sank two Finns and a Swede. Hannes Weingärtner in *U-16* sank a Swede. Joachim Schepke in *U-3* sank a Dane and a Swede. Frölich, in the Type VII *U-36,* sank one Swede and captured another, which he escorted to Germany, concluding a month-long patrol. In all, the North Sea U-boats sank or captured ten neutrals for 13,000 tons in one week.†

The hue and cry from Oslo, Stockholm, Copenhagen, and Helsinki was so deafening that Hitler was compelled to back down. On September 30 he reimposed restrictions on the ducks which brought the attack on neutrals in the North Sea to a halt. Thereafter the ducks were restricted to offensive patrolling or minelaying in British waters.

British submarines patrolling in the North Sea hunted U-boats. *Seahorse* fired three torpedoes at *U-36* and claimed a kill, but it was not so. Another British sub-

---

* The relaxations also applied to the "pocket" battleships *Deutschland* and *Admiral Graf Spee,* which were authorized to commence raiding on September 25.

† To which should be added the work of the homebound Atlantic boats, which, as related, had sunk one Norwegian and captured one Estonian and two Finns for a total of 5,400 tons.

marine (unidentified) shot at Otto Kretschmer in *U-23* in the Kattegat but also missed. Several other ducks had close encounters with British submarines, but all evaded the attacks.

One duck was lost. She was *U-12,* commanded by Dietrich von der Ropp, age thirty. On September 22 Dönitz sent her into the English Channel to attack British troopships. On the basis of the earlier reconnaissance by ducks, Dönitz did not believe the British had mined the channel. But he was wrong. Between September 11 and 17, the British and French planted 3,000 floating (or anchored) mines on a line between Dover and Cape Gris-Nez. On September 25 they commenced augmenting the barrier with another 3,636 mines, which were controlled electrically from shore stations and monitored with banks of underwater hydrophones. On October 8 *U-12* hit a mine and blew up with the loss of all hands. She was the first U-boat lost from which there were no survivors. Still disbelieving the Allies had planted a minefield in the channel, Dönitz incorrectly attributed her loss to ASW surface forces.

Had it not been for the two productive minefields planted by *U-13* and *U-15,* the returns from the North Sea ducks and the Type VII *U-36* would have been deeply disappointing. The twenty-three ducks (some making two patrols) and *U-36* sank by torpedo or demolitions, or captured, only thirteen small ships for 16,751 tons: two British and eleven neutrals. However, the two minefields added five sinkings for 15,575 tons, raising the total kills or captures by all ducks and *U-36* in the North Sea to a not inconsequential eighteen ships for 32,326 tons. But the greatest value of the North Sea patrolling was not in numbers. It provoked terror and convoying, and it was a perfect training ground for U-boat officers and men. Almost all the duck skippers—Kretschmer, Schepke, others—would soon "graduate" to Atlantic boats.

POISED FOR A NAVAL RACE

The bemedaled U-boat sailors had good reasons to swagger in the bars of Wilhelmshaven and Kiel. For political ends, Hitler had forbidden *Luftwaffe* attacks on Great Britain and the Royal Navy. Only German submariners had carried the war to England in the first month of hostilities.* Although the statistical returns (sinkings per boat) had been disappointing, in aggregate U-boats had landed stinging psychological and physical blows. The first wave had sunk thirty-nine British ships, including the carrier *Courageous* and five important tankers,† against the loss of two U-boats and eighty-one men—all captured. They had created panic and confusion at sea and prompted the British decision to initiate convoying, which, as Churchill estimated, was to reduce imports by about one-third, and to wear down

---

* The "pocket" battleships *Deutschland* and *Admiral Graf Spee* did not get into action until October.

† See appendices 2 and 17.

hundreds of aircraft and ships on ASW missions, and to divert scores of other vessels to minelaying and minesweeping.

Besides that, and of transcendent importance, during September, while the U-boat sailors were at sea, Hitler had approved a switch from the Z Plan to the construction of a massive U-boat arm. The main emphasis was to be on the improved mediums (VIIBs, VIICs), which Dönitz had been urging for three years. Sixteen shipyards were to tool up for U-boat construction, thirteen for the mediums and three for improved Type IXs (IXB, IXC).* In approving the switch, Hitler assured Raeder that U-boat construction was to take priority over most Third Reich military programs, including the *Luftwaffe*'s improved JU-88 (Stuka) dive bomber, and that skilled shipwrights who had been drafted into the *Wehrmacht* were to be released. The program envisioned a buildup to a production rate of twenty to thirty U-boats per month. Long the impoverished stepchild of the *Kriegsmarine,* the U-boat force was to become its dominant arm, as it had in World War I.

It would take time—much time—to tool up and build all these U-boats. No one was exactly certain how much time; that would depend upon a number of factors, including the sincerity of Hitler's promises of priorities for materials and the release of skilled shipyard labor from the *Wehrmacht.* At the very least, Dönitz estimated, it would be nearly two years—the late summer of 1941—before U-boats began to join the force in significant numbers. In the meantime, owing to the current glacial pace of U-boat construction, which could barely keep pace with actual and predicted battle losses, the "U-boat war" could be little more than psychological warfare, a reign of terror.

The extent of the daunting challenge facing the U-boat force bears repeating. Not counting coasters and other vessels of 1,600 tons or less, the merchant fleet of the British Commonwealth comprised about 3,000 ships of about 17.5 million gross tons. Of these ships, about 450 were tankers of about 3.2 million gross tons. By way of comparison, the United States merchant marine was only about half that size: about 1,400 ships of about 8.5 million gross tons, including about 390 tankers of about 2.8 million gross tons, plus another sixty-four tankers registered in Panama. Excluding those of Italy and Japan, the third-ranking merchant marine fleet was that of Norway, with about 800 ships of about 4.2 million gross tons, including 268 tankers of 2.1 million gross tons.†

To offset the loss of shipping—and imports—caused by U-boats and convoying, and to wage effective warfare, Churchill concluded that the Commonwealth was to require about 3 million gross tons of new merchant ships annually. At his urging the War Cabinet approved an emergency program to build ever greater numbers of cargo ships and tankers. However, British shipyards, already jammed with orders for new warships and hobbled by antiquated construction methods and

---

* The VIIs and IXs were to be built at a three-to-one ratio. In addition, construction of four big Type XB minelayers and four big Type XIV tankers was continued, as well as construction of sixteen improved ducks, Type IID. But the four 3,000-ton U-cruisers were canceled.

† France and the Netherlands ranked next, each with about 500 ships of 2.7 million gross tons. Greece, with about 400 ships of about 1.7 million gross tons, came next.

PLATE 6

BRITISH-CONTROLLED MERCHANT SHIPPING 1939-1941[1]

NUMBERS OF SHIPS OVER 1,600 GRT

	BRITISH CARGO	BRITISH TANKER	BRITISH TOTAL	FOREIGN CARGO	FOREIGN TANKER	FOREIGN TOTAL	GRAND TOTAL
9/3/39	2,520	445	2,965	——	34	34	2,999
9/30/40	2,611	442	3,053	526	178	704	3,757
9/30/41	2,358	427	2,785	592	231	823	3,608
12/31/41	2,360	427	2,787	602	227	829	3,616
Change	(-)160	(-)18	(-)178	(+)602	(+)193	(+)795	(+)617

GRT OF SHIPS OVER 1,600 GRT

(IN THOUSAND GROSS TONS)

	BRITISH CARGO	BRITISH TANKER	BRITISH TOTAL	FOREIGN CARGO	FOREIGN TANKER	FOREIGN TOTAL	GRAND TOTAL
9/3/39	14,352	3,172	17,524	——	260	260	17,784
9/30/40	14,512	3,078	17,590	2,398	1,398	3,783	21,373
9/30/41	13,221	2,944	16,165	2,704	1,683	4,387	20,552
12/31/41	13,329	2,955	16,284	2,754	1,655	4,409	20,693
Change	(-)1,023	(-)217	(-)1,240	(+)2,754	(+)1,395	(+)4,149	(+)2,909

---

1. Source: Hancock, ed. (1975), Tables 151 and 152, pp. 173–74.

labor problems, could produce less than half the wartime need: about 1.2 million gross tons per year.

There were several ways to make up the predicted shortfall. The first and cheapest way was to seize German merchant ships at sea. Another way was to purchase "laid up" ships from the United States.* Yet another way, a very expensive one, was to charter merchant ships from Norway, Greece, and the Netherlands. In the first eight months of war the British brought under control about 100 ships of about a half million gross tons from these sources.

Apart from the sale of a few "laid up" ships, the United States could not provide Britain any meaningful assistance. That was because of the 1935 Neutrality Act. This act strictly forbade American merchant ships from entering declared war zones to trade with "belligerents" and, as one enforcement measure, forbade the arming of American merchant ships. The act was modified November 11, 1939, to allow the British to purchase armaments from United States firms on a "cash and

---

* In 1939 the United States had about 1 million gross tons of merchant shipping in "laid up" status, most of it not worth activating.

carry" basis, but the restrictions on American shipping remained in force and the British had to transport the armaments in Commonwealth vessels.

The American merchant-ship construction industry was only just emerging from a deep sleep. The slow awakening had been prompted by the U.S. Maritime Commission, which Roosevelt had established in 1936 to help upgrade America's aged dry-cargo fleet.* Under the chairmanship of a feisty retired rear admiral, Emory S. ("Jerry") Land, in prewar days the commission had embarked on a ten-year program to build fifty new ships a year. In pursuit of that objective, the commission had designed and ordered several prototypes of big, fast, modern tankers and dry-cargo ships. In the year 1939, the commission delivered the first ships of the new program (twenty-eight for 242,000 gross tons), all to the United States merchant marine fleet.

Upon the outbreak of war in Europe, Roosevelt directed Jerry Land to draw up contingency plans for a massive expansion of the American shipbuilding industry. Land produced these plans—and the specifications required to carry them out—promptly. Thus the stage was set for a maritime race of unprecedented scale. On the one hand, the Germans were poised to build hundreds of U-boats. On the other hand, the Allies were poised to build hundreds of merchant ships. The outcome of this maritime race was to profoundly influence the entire course of World War II.

Dönitz later suggested—and others have echoed him—that if Hitler and Raeder had listened to him and had built 300 U-boats in the prewar years, the U-boat arm alone could have won the naval battle promptly. This is nonsense. A peacetime U-boat construction program of that size would have been exceptionally provocative. It would have forced Hitler to abrogate his prized 1935 naval treaty with Britain almost as soon as it was signed, introducing a complex new geopolitical climate. In that era of intensely competing naval powers and renewed naval construction, it is unlikely that the British Admiralty would have sat on its hands and not proceeded to build U-boat counterforces, such as large fleets of destroyers and modern ASW aircraft. Moreover, a massive U-boat construction program would almost certainly have triggered the construction of a counterforce by the United States Navy, which, as one contingency, had to plan against a German defeat of the Royal Navy and the possibility of German naval aggression in the western hemisphere.

---

* In contrast, the oil companies, which were in stiff competition with foreign carriers, were compelled to keep the American tanker fleet in first-rate condition.

TWO

B y early October 1939, the bulk of the *Wehrmacht* and *Luftwaffe* had redeployed from Poland to attack France. Hitler made a final appeal to the British and French to call off the war, but to no avail. He then ordered the Germans to launch the offensive against France, but the German generals were not ready and the action had to be postponed. The delays went on week after week until, finally, the coldest winter in memory set in and the offensive had to be put off until spring. The interval of inaction was called the "Phony War" or *Sitzkrieg* or *Drôle de guerre*.

During that fall Admiral Raeder urged Hitler to seize neutral Norway by political subversion or military force. His reasons were several. The *Kriegsmarine* believed that the British and French planned to occupy Norway to shut off the winter flow of high-grade iron ore from Narvik to Germany and to gain bases from which to launch air attacks on Germany and *Kriegsmarine* forces and bases in the Baltic Sea. There was also a possibility that Germany's erstwhile ally, the Soviet Union, which had ruthlessly invaded Finland, might overrun all of Scandinavia, dangerously flanking Germany to the north. A German occupation of Norway would not only defeat those possibilities but also gain naval bases for the *Kriegsmarine* outside the North Sea, from which even the short-legged ducks could reach British shipping lanes.

Hitler grasped the strategic advantages of this proposal. He therefore commenced an attempt to subvert the Norwegian government through a Norwegian traitor, Vidkun Quisling. At the same time he directed his military chiefs to draw plans for taking Norway—and Denmark as well—by force, should subversion fail. The *Kriegsmarine* was to play the dominant role in the conquest, employing all the power it could muster, including every available U-boat. In the revised grand strategy, the conquest of Norway and Denmark was to precede the attack on France by about a month.

Pending the launching of these enterprises, Karl Dönitz, promoted to rear admiral, was to continue the U-boat war against Great Britain and France. In planning operations for the fall and winter of 1939–1940, Dönitz was beset by three major problems.

The overriding problem was the acute shortage of oceangoing U-boats.

Although Raeder and Hitler had canceled the Z Plan, work continued on numerous surface ships: the two super-battleships *Bismarck* and *Tirpitz;* an aircraft carrier, *Graf Zeppelin;* three heavy cruisers, *Prinz Eugen, Lützow,* and *Seydlitz* (being converted to an aircraft carrier); and scads of destroyers, motor torpedo boats, minelayers, and minesweepers. As one consequence, it was not possible to initiate action to speed the completion of the U-boats under construction. During the first six months of the war, September 1939 to March 1940, only six new oceangoing boats were to be commissioned: three VIIBs, one IX, and two improved models of the latter, designated IXB. If the September loss rate (two oceangoing boats) continued, by March 1940 there was to be a net loss of six oceangoing boats, down from twenty-seven to twenty-one.

Moreover, the hard Atlantic patrolling and combat had uncovered some severe design flaws and weaknesses in the existing oceangoing boats. The engine casings of the Type VIIs were not strong enough. All the VIIs had to go into the shipyards for new engines. The engine-exhaust valves on the VIIs, which closed *against* (rather than with) sea pressure, leaked dangerously at deep depths, a flaw that had not been discovered earlier owing to the OKM's order to limit peacetime diving to 150 feet. Until these (and other) flaws were corrected, the nine surviving boats of the Salzwedel Flotilla, comprising one-third of the Atlantic force, were unsafe for combat. Owing to the jam-up in the shipyards, the flaws could not be immediately corrected. In the interim, those boats could only be used sparingly.

To bolster the Atlantic force, Dönitz was compelled to resort to two fairly desperate measures. First, he made the decision to continue patrolling with the two big experimental boats, *U-25* and *U-26,* regardless of the risks entailed. Second, he confiscated a big U-cruiser, *Batiray,* which Krupp was completing for Turkey. However, before this boat (designated *U-A*) could safely patrol the Atlantic, it had to have extensive modifications in the shipyards.

The second problem confronting Dönitz was the spreading belief that the submarine torpedoes were defective.

This was not an easy matter to prove. Torpedoes and torpedo pistols were very complicated. The line officers of the *Kriegsmarine* commanding U-boats, as well as Dönitz and his staffers, were not trained engineers or scientists. Few had even attended a college. They had to rely on the experts at the Torpedo Directorate for technical judgments. At first the experts insisted, not without some justification, that most of the reported torpedo failures, malfunctions, and misses were the fault of poor torpedo maintenance and mistakes in shooting by green captains and crews.

From the beginning of this disputation, Dönitz took the position that while some failures and misses were doubtless the fault of the crews, not all could be so attributed. No less than thirteen skippers had reported erratic or malfunctioning torpedoes while on patrol in September. These included the analytical-minded Otto Kretschmer in the duck *U-23,* who had achieved a nearly perfect shooting score in peacetime, but had unaccountably missed a slow-moving tramp steamer off northeast Scotland with four torpedoes. Two skippers, Glattes in *U-27* and Schuhart in *U-29,* had experienced and reported dangerous "premature" explosions with magnetic pistols after runs of less than 300 yards.*

After compiling a detailed and damning analysis of the torpedo performance by the September boats, Dönitz persuaded Raeder and the OKM to order the Torpedo Directorate to conduct an exhaustive technical investigation. Almost immediately the Directorate conceded two flaws that might be adversely affecting the magnetic pistols: a poorly designed cable layout in the electrics, and some kind of mechanical flaw, not yet isolated, in the air torpedoes. The Directorate recommended a rearrangement of the cables in the electrics, which was certain to cure the problem in those, but pending further investigation, the skippers should use only contact (or impact) pistols in the air torpedoes.

Dönitz had deepest misgivings about the results of this "investigation." He and many of his skippers—including Otto Kretschmer—believed the main problem was that the torpedoes were running deeper than set. The Directorate had not even addressed this possibility. Nonetheless, Dönitz had no choice but to rely on the technicians. Accordingly, he issued the advisories and new instructions for the boats preparing to sail in October.

The third major problem besetting Dönitz during the winter of 1939–1940 was a continuous demand from Raeder and the OKM to provide U-boats for special missions.

From the earliest days of hostilities, Raeder and the OKM intended to foul British seaports with magnetic mines. The main planting was to be carried out by destroyers, which were to dash across the North Sea and back in winter under cover of darkness. But the destroyers could only reach the lower east coast ports of the British Isles. Those ports beyond reach of the destroyers—in the western English Channel, the west coast of the British Isles, and the northeast coast of Scotland—were to be mined by aircraft and submarine. In addition, Raeder intended to employ submarines to mine the British naval base at Gibraltar and, provided Hitler approved, the port of Halifax, Nova Scotia, where the convoys from North America formed up.

When presented with this elaborate submarine mining plan, Dönitz objected. If

---

* Dönitz had no way of knowing it, but torpedo failures had led to the detection and destruction of both *U-27* and *U-39* of the September group.

carried to its fullest, the plan would require the diversion of virtually every avail-able combat-ready U-boat. Dönitz believed it was imperative to continue the tor-pedo war against shipping for its psychological impact, to hone the skills of the skippers and crews under combat conditions, and to continue the elusive hunt for the torpedo defects. Besides that, many skippers and crews were not qualified in minelaying.

The upshot was a compromise. During the new-moon periods of the winter months, when nights were black and long and thus ideal for minelaying, Dönitz was to employ about one-third of the oceangoing U-boat force to lay about four-teen minefields in the west coast ports of the British Isles and Gibraltar. The North Sea ducks were to lay about a dozen fields in east coast and English Channel ports, backstopping the destroyers and aircraft.

In addition to these mining missions, Raeder and the OKM proposed other spe-cial tasks for the oceangoing submarines. Dönitz deflected most of these proposals, but Berlin insisted on three. The first was to send several boats into the Mediter-ranean Sea to attack Allied shipping. The second was to send several boats to the Arctic, where they were to secretly base in Murmansk and prey on Allied shipping engaged in transporting timber (for mine props) from Scandinavia to Great Britain. The third was to land *Abwehr* (German intelligence) spies in neutral Ireland, who were to inflame anti-British sentiments.

The shortage of combat-capable oceangoing boats, the infuriating and inexcus-able torpedo defects, and the demand for boats to carry out special missions signif-icantly reduced the ability of the U-boat arm to inflict any serious damage on Allied maritime assets during the winter of 1939–1940. Nonetheless, Dönitz and his loyal, dedicated submariners were determined to give their utmost.

PRIEN IN SCAPA FLOW

During the first month of the war, Dönitz had conceived a plan to deal the Royal Navy another stinging blow. Close reconnaissance of the British naval base at Scapa Flow by ducks and *Luftwaffe* aircraft had revealed a possible flaw in its de-fenses: Kirk Sound, one of a half-dozen channels leading into the base, was not solidly closed by blockships.* Dönitz became convinced that a U-boat could slip through the gap in the channel under cover of darkness and attack the Home Fleet in its anchorage. If so, the boat might sink one or more capital ships and drive the fleet from Scapa Flow, thus weakening the British blockade and making it less haz-ardous for *Kriegsmarine* surface raiders to slip in and out of the North Sea.

Dönitz chose Günther Prien, a daring skipper and skilled seaman, to attempt this hazardous mission. Prien turned in his Enigma and all secret papers and sailed *U-47* in secrecy from Kiel on October 8, going via the Kiel Canal and Wil-helmshaven. Not until he was well out to sea did Prien brief his crew. Although the

---

* Weighted hulks, which were sunk to the bottom and held in place by cables anchored on land.

mission was fraught with danger and the risk of death or capture was great, all hands were enthusiastic.

That same day, the *Kriegsmarine*'s new battle cruiser *Gneisenau,* escorted by the light cruiser *Köln,* set sail from Kiel on a brief sortie into the North Sea. There were several reasons for this short voyage: to exercise the ships and crews in a limited combat environment; to pose a threat to North Sea merchant ships, forcing the Allies to form convoys, which were legitimate duck targets; to lure Home Fleet units from their bases into range of *Luftwaffe* aircraft; and to assuage Hitler, who had demanded to know why these expensive vessels were not being employed.

The *Gneisenau* and *Köln* went out through the Kattegat and Skagerrak. As intended, the Admiralty got wind of the sortie and Coastal Command dispatched reconnaissance aircraft to the North Sea. Early in the afternoon of October 8, one of them spotted the German ships close to the south coast of Norway. Believing *Gneisenau* was headed for a long voyage into the North Atlantic to raid Allied convoys, Admiral Forbes ordered most of the major ships in his Home Fleet to intercept her.* But *Gneisenau* easily eluded the trap. She reversed course that night and reached her berth in Kiel in the early hours of October 10. As planned, the *Luftwaffe* found and attacked the Home Fleet units in the North Sea on October 9, but not one of the hundred-odd bombs the pilots dropped hit a British ship.

Unaware that *Gneisenau* had returned to port, the Home Fleet units from Scapa Flow continued the hunt for her north and northwest of the Orkneys. Finding no trace of the Germans, Forbes finally ordered the fleet to break off the search and return to bases. The battleships *Nelson* and *Rodney,* the battle cruisers *Hood* and *Repulse,* and the carrier *Furious,* which had sailed from Scapa Flow, put in to Loch Ewe in northwest Scotland. Only the old (1916–1917) 30,000-ton battleship *Royal Oak,* which to then had been employed on convoy escort, returned to Scapa Flow. Thus the sortie of *Gneisenau* had the effect of emptying Scapa Flow of the major Home Fleet capital ships. On October 12, the *Luftwaffe,* which was also apparently unaware of Prien's mission, flew a low-level reconnaissance over Scapa Flow. Some British interpreted this as a prelude to a major bombing attack, so the big ships were retained at Loch Ewe.

Meanwhile, Prien in *U-47* inched cautiously northward in the shallow North Sea, avoiding all ships and lying doggo on the bottom during daytime. On the night of Friday, October 13, at 1915, he surfaced to begin a slow, four-hour approach to Scapa Flow, timed to bring *U-47* to Kirk Channel when the tide was highest.

Going to the bridge, Prien found the sky clear but "disgustingly" bright, lit by an undulating aurora borealis—the northern lights. Despite this unexpected and inconvenient phenomenon, Prien pressed on, planning, if necessary, to carry out the

---

* The Home Fleet aircraft carriers *Ark Royal* and the old *Hermes,* together with the battleship *Renown,* had been detached for convoy escort or to chase down the "pocket" battleship *Admiral Graf Spee* in the South Atlantic, leaving only one aircraft carrier, the *Furious,* sister ship of the *Courageous,* in the Home Fleet.

attack submerged, by periscope. At 2200, on schedule, the Orkney navigational lights came on for thirty minutes, enabling Prien to precisely fix *U-47*'s position. Approaching a jut of land, Rose Ness, at 2307, the bridge watch saw a merchant ship plodding along. Prien dived to avoid the vessel and, as a test, tried to put it squarely in his periscope crosshairs. Despite the northern lights, he could not see the ship. The lack of periscope visibility ruled out a submerged attack inside Scapa Flow. They would stay on the surface.

Prien surfaced at 2331, got his bearings, and ran due west on the flood tide. The visibility was not as good as it seemed. By mistake, he headed for the wrong channel, Kerry, separating Lamb Holm and Burray islands. He detected the mistake just in time. "By altering course hard to starboard, the imminent danger is averted," he logged.

Realigning the boat for the passage through Kirk Sound, Prien made the decision not to go south of the two blockships in the channel, the course Dönitz had suggested. Instead, he aimed for a gap between the center and northernmost blockships, clearing the northernmost blockship "with 45 feet to spare." Borne along by the swift flood tide, the penetration was made "with unbelievable speed," Prien logged. But it was nerve-rattling. During the passage, the current slewed the boat sharply to starboard, directly into a cable anchoring one of the blockships. "Port engine stopped," Prien wrote, "starboard engine slow ahead and rudder hard to port, the boat slowly touches bottom. The stern still touches the cable, the boat becomes free, it is pulled around to port, and brought onto course again with difficult rapid maneuvering. . . . But . . . we are in Scapa Flow." It was twenty-seven minutes past midnight.

Enhanced by the undulating northern lights, visibility in the wide bowl of the anchorage improved. Prien, his first watch officer, Engelbert Endrass, and the lookouts hungrily scanned the waters with binoculars. They could see no big ships in the usual anchorage between Burray and Cava islands. It seemed impossible. Was Scapa Flow empty?

Circling north, Prien scouted deeper into the basin. Then suddenly he sighted "two battleships," identified as *Royal Oak* and *Repulse,* lying at anchor, unusually close to the rugged north shore, about one and a half miles apart. Actually, the ships were the *Royal Oak* and the old 6,900-ton seaplane transport *Pegasus,* which was scheduled to be fitted with an experimental aircraft catapult for convoy escort.

Closing to a position about 3,500 yards equidistant from both ships, Prien made ready all four bow tubes. At 0055 he fired two of the electrics with magnetic pistols at "*Repulse*" and two at *Royal Oak.* The torpedo in tube number 4, intended for "*Repulse,*" misfired—did not go. The other three ran out silently and wakeless at about 30 miles per hour. The one aimed at "*Repulse*" missed and probably ran ashore. About three and a half minutes after firing, one of the two torpedoes fired at *Royal Oak* struck her on the starboard bow; the other missed. The hit blew a huge hole in the stem and keel of *Royal Oak* near the paint and anchor-chain lockers. But the noise was not sufficient to cause undue alarm elsewhere in the big ship and *Royal Oak*'s captain, roused from his bunk, attributed the explosion to some internal cause and took no special precautions.

In the darkness and confusion it was difficult for Prien to know what had happened. Wrongly believing he had damaged *"Repulse"* with one hit, and had missed *Royal Oak,* Prien mounted another attack. While the torpedomen reloaded bow tubes number 1 and 2, and readjusted the balky number 4, he swung ship and fired his stern torpedo at *Royal Oak.* No explosion. This torpedo also missed and probably ran ashore.* Therefore, when number 1, 2, and 4 bow tubes were ready, Prien swung back around and fired all three at *Royal Oak,* which he mistakenly believed to be unharmed.

All three of the torpedoes struck *Royal Oak* on her starboard side. The hits blew a huge hole in the engine room and two other holes amidships, and set off a raging fire in a magazine, hurling debris into the sky. The ship shook violently, the lights and P.A. system went out, and flames spread rapidly. Taking on a flood of water through the holes, *Royal Oak* almost immediately listed 45 degrees to starboard. Thirteen minutes after the last three hits, the old battleship rolled over and sank, with the loss of 833 of her 1,200-man crew.

Believing he had been seen, and that destroyers were after him, Prien turned about at 0128 and headed at high speed for the Kirk Sound escape route. Actually, he had not been seen, and no destroyers were after him. All British hands were either engaged in rescue efforts at *Royal Oak* or frozen in shock. Prien could have reloaded his five remaining torpedoes for a second attack on *"Repulse"* without fear of enemy counterattack. But even if the torpedoes ran true, a second attack would only have bagged inconsequential *Pegasus.* Hence his instinctive decision to get out was correct, but for the wrong reasons.

About two and a half hours after entering Scapa Flow, Prien reached the west end of Kirk Sound and began the exit. This time he went south of the blockships, in the "gap" Dönitz had recommended. "Things are again difficult," he logged. Making constant changes in speed and helm, he passed the southern blockship "with nothing to spare." Free of the blockships and their anchor cables, Prien just barely avoided a mole, then, clear of all obstructions, he bent on flank speed in Holm Sound. At 0215, he logged, "we are once more outside," adding that it was "a pity that only one [ship] was destroyed."

The next day, October 14, the Admiralty released the sad and humiliating news that *Royal Oak* had been sunk in Scapa Flow with a great loss of life. Berlin first heard the news from a radio report, but it withheld a celebration or public comment pending a report from Prien. Home Fleet commander Forbes immediately barred all Royal Navy ships from Scapa Flow. Until the defenses had been improved† the Home Fleet was to base in Loch Ewe, the cruisers of the Northern Patrol at Sullom Voe in the Shetlands, even though the defenses there were skimpy and the facilities primitive.

Southbound on the surface, in the early hours of October 16, Prien got off an encoded radio report to Dönitz: *Royal Oak* sunk; *"Repulse"* damaged. The Ger-

---

* The British recovered one or more of these intact electrics with magnetic pistols.

† Upon investigation, it was learned that another blockship to close the gap in Kirk Sound had been delayed. It arrived in Scapa Flow the next day, October 15.

mans were ecstatic. "A glorious success," the OKM gloated. It logged in its war diary that the loss of *Royal Oak* and damage to *"Repulse"* were "hard blows" that "greatly impairs British prestige," "enhances respect" for the *Kriegsmarine,* and "awakens affection" for the "young submarine arm" that had amply demonstrated its "outstanding operational efficiency."

Believing the damaged *"Repulse"* had limped to a shipyard in Rosyth in the Firth of Forth, Berlin mounted a *Luftwaffe* attack on Rosyth on October 16—the first German air attack on a Royal Navy base. *Luftwaffe* pilots confirmed (erroneously) that *"Repulse"* was in the shipyard. The planes hit the cruiser *Southampton* with one bomb, but it failed to explode. The only notable result of the attack was slight damage to a destroyer. Still quite unharmed at Loch Ewe, *Repulse* sailed from there with the carrier *Furious* for convoy duty.

By this time it was customary for returning U-boats to paint the names of enemy "kills" on the conning towers in white. The first watch officer, Engelbert Endrass, personally carried out this pleasurable task. Believing that merely the name *Royal Oak* was insufficient to convey the full drama of the kill, Endrass, who had fired the torpedoes for Prien, embellished the conning tower with a crude portrait of a massive bull charging with lowered horns and steaming nostrils. Later, a refined version of the "Bull of Scapa Flow" was to become the official insignia of the Wegener Flotilla.

By the time *U-47* entered Wilhelmshaven on the morning of October 17, its great feat of arms was known throughout Germany. Admirals Raeder and Dönitz were standing on the pier to greet Prien and his men. When the lines were secured, the admirals crossed the brow to shake hands with every man in the crew and to confer on Prien the Iron Cross First Class and to all others the Iron Cross Second Class, and to announce that Adolf Hitler was sending his personal plane to fly the crew to Berlin.

The drama and daring of the Scapa Flow deed personified the image of military courage and ingenuity Hitler was seeking to project. He directed Propaganda Minister Goebbels to give Prien and his crew the full treatment. German radios trumpeted heroic and exaggerated bulletins (including the supposed damage to *Repulse*). By the time the *U-47* crew arrived at Berlin's Templehof Airport, the German people had been whipped to a frenzy of enthusiasm. Thousands turned out at the airport and along the motorcade route and at the Kaiserhof Hotel to present flowers, candy, and other gifts, or merely to catch a glimpse of the naval heroes. It was the greatest and most exhilarating celebration in the history of submarine warfare, and it would never be equaled again in Germany or elsewhere. The reigning U-boat hero, Otto Schuhart, who had actually outdone Prien by sinking the far more versatile and valuable capital ship *Courageous,* was all but forgotten.*

The celebration and ceremonies continued for several days. Hitler invited the crew to the Reichs Chancellery for lunch and presented Prien a new and exalted

---

* Nonetheless, Schuhart's 41,950 tons sunk in a single patrol still stood as the record to beat. *Royal Oak,* at 30,000 tons, did not do it, but it elevated Prien's total for two brief patrols to four ships for 38,000 tons.

medal, the Knight's Cross of the Iron Cross, or *Ritterkreuz,* as the submariners called it. Afterward Hitler's publicist, Dr. Otto Dietrich, introduced Prien to the German and foreign press. (The American radio journalist, William L. Shirer, noted in his diary that Prien was "a clean-cut, cocky, fanatical Nazi, and obviously very capable.") That night the crew were guests of Goebbels at the Wintergarten Theater, where a fawning audience forced Prien to make a speech. Still later the crew was entertained at a night club.

The Prien hoopla gave Dönitz and the U-boat force a tremendous boost. There was no instant return; no immediate increase in U-boat production. But the feat at Scapa Flow had certainly got Hitler's attention and firmly planted the idea in his and all German minds that a single cheap U-boat manned by merely forty-four men could sink a huge battleship manned by 1,200 men. From that it was not diffi- cult to imagine what carnage a vast fleet of U-boats could inflict on Great Britain's thinly armed merchant marine. Thus the idea that Germany might, after all, defeat Great Britain at sea with U-boats gained credibility. The long-term impact of Scapa Flow was therefore immeasurably beneficial for the U-boat arm.

THE FIRST WOLF PACK

By the time Dönitz was ready to launch the second wave of U-boats to the Atlantic in early October, the Allies had organized most merchant shipping into convoys. Composed of thirty to forty ships, the majority of the convoys arrived and departed the British Isles through the Western Approaches. The heaviest convoy traffic ran across the North Atlantic between the British Isles and the strategically situated British colony of Newfoundland and its neighbor, the Canadian maritime province of Nova Scotia.*

By October 1939, the North Atlantic convoy system was fully in place. On the western end, the port of Halifax, Nova Scotia, was the gathering place. All ships bound for the British Isles that cruised between 9 and 15 knots had to join con- voys. There were two types of convoys: Halifax Fast (designated HX-F), com- posed of ships that cruised at 12 to 15 knots; and Halifax Slow (HX), composed of ships that cruised at 9 to 12 knots. Ships that cruised at speeds over 15 knots (con- sidered too fast to be vulnerable to U-boats) were allowed to proceed alone, as were ships that cruised at less than 9 knots (considered too slow and not valuable enough to warrant the holdup of faster ships).

On the eastern end, the British Isles, departing convoys were categorized as Outbound. Those convoys bound for Halifax or elsewhere in the western hemi- sphere (the reverse of the Halifax convoys), composed mostly of ships in ballast, were designated Outbound B or OB. Some ships in OB convoys peeled away after some days of travel and went due south down the mid-Atlantic to ports in West Africa. Ships outbound from the British Isles that cruised faster than 15 knots or

---

* Newfoundland rejected incorporation into the Canadian confederation in 1869. Not until 1948 did it become a Canadian province.

slower than 9 knots were also exempt from convoys.* Most North Atlantic convoys were escorted only during part of the voyage. The inexperienced and small Royal Canadian Navy (six destroyers) and the Royal Canadian Air Force (RCAF) provided escort on the western end, going east several hundred miles with eastbound convoys and returning with westbound convoys. British and French surface ships and aircraft provided escort on the eastern end for Outbound convoys in a similar manner for a like distance. The important Halifax Fast convoys were escorted all the way across to the British Isles by Royal Navy capital ships (battleships, carriers) and their destroyer screens, or by cruisers. But only reluctantly. The long transatlantic voyage was very hard on these warships. The old destroyers assigned to this task (V and W class) could not cross the Atlantic without refueling, and the Royal Navy had not fully mastered ocean refueling. The modern destroyers could just barely make it across in heavy weather, which was the usual condition. Convoy escort was "defensive," tedious, and boring for sailors trained to attack big German ships in complex fleet actions.

The Germans possessed a fairly accurate picture of Allied maritime traffic. During the 1935 crisis in the Mediterranean, when Italy invaded Abyssinia (Ethiopia), the *Kriegsmarine* codebreaking unit, *B-dienst,* directed by Heinz Bonatz, had broken the Royal Navy's old-fashioned (nonmachine) operational codes and, later, the nonsecure British merchant marine code. From the outset of the war, *B-dienst* codebreakers had supplied the OKM with current information on the movements of most British capital ships and other naval formations as well as convoy routing and rendezvous points for the convoy escorts.

In the initial U-boat offensive the OKM had deployed the Atlantic boats to individual patrol zones before the convoys had formed. Almost all of the merchant ships they sank had been sailing alone. Now that convoying was in full swing, Dönitz believed the time was ripe to initiate his group (or "wolf pack") tactics. The packs were to capitalize on convoy information provided by the codebreakers in *B-dienst.*

Dönitz planned to deploy two packs in October, composed of the ten boats he had recalled earlier: five Type VIIBs of the Wegener Flotilla and five Type IXs of the Hundius Flotilla. But that plan went awry. Five of the ten boats were unavailable: *U-47* (assigned to the Scapa Flow mission) and *U-52* (undergoing major repairs), *U-38* (assigned to a special mission to Murmansk), *U-39* (lost), and *U-41* (undergoing major repairs).

The upshot was that Dönitz could mount only one pack, composed of six boats of an unwieldy mixture of types, from two different flotillas, which had not before exercised as a group: three VIIBs, *U-45, U-46, U-48,* and three IXs, *U-37, U-40,* and the *U-42,* the latter brand-new and rushed into service before completing a full workup. The senior officer, Hundius Flotilla commander Werner Hartmann, age thirty-seven, who had taken command of *U-37,* was to tactically direct the pack at sea.

---

* Outbound convoys designated OA and OG sailed directly to West African ports and Gibraltar, respectively. Convoys bound to the British Isles from ports in West Africa gathered at Freetown, Sierra Leone, and were designated SL. Those bound to the British Isles (or "Home") from Gibraltar were designated Home Gibraltar or HG.

Five of the six boats sailed independently into stormy, cold North Sea weather in the first week of October, going northabout the British Isles. Wrongly believing the Allies had not yet mined the English Channel, Dönitz ordered the last boat, *U-40,* a Type IX making its second patrol, with a new skipper, Wolfgang Barten, age thirty, to go by way of the channel to save time and catch up with the others.

While these boats were en route to the Atlantic, Hitler, poised to attack France (or so he thought), removed another important restriction on the U-boats. Commencing October 4, U-boats were permitted to sink on sight and without warning *any* blacked-out ship (including a neutral ship) sailing close to the British Isles in the Atlantic or North Sea and the French Atlantic coast. Dönitz and his skippers cheered this news, but to minimize charges of barbarism and inhumanity, Hitler had added a caveat: U-boats were still required to "save the crew" of any ship they sank if that could be done "without endangering" the U-boat.

Rushing to catch up with the other boats, *U-40* ran at full speed through the English Channel on the surface. In the early hours of October 13, she hit a mine in the Dover–Cape Gris-Nez field. The boat blew up and sank immediately in 115 feet of water. Presumably, all hands on the bridge and in the forward compartments were killed instantly. But the watertight door in the stern room had been closed and as a result, nine enlisted men in that compartment survived the explosion and sinking. When they recovered from shock and ascertained what had occurred, the senior man, Otto Winkler, age twenty-one, organized an escape through the after deck hatch, which had a skirt for that purpose. After eating some biscuits, the men strapped on oxygen apparatus and flooded the compartment. When the water pressure in the compartment equalized with outside sea pressure, the hatch opened freely and the nine men—the first to escape a sunken U-boat—ascended.

Winkler was the last to leave the compartment. When he reached the surface he saw the eight other men swimming around in a cluster. It was dark—a new moon—and the channel water was frigid. Winkler thought he saw a lighthouse and began swimming toward it. Along the way he became nauseous and then he passed out. The next morning, two British destroyers (*Brazen* and *Boreas*) fished Winkler and two other survivors and five bodies from the water. All were wearing escape apparatus, labeled "*U-40.*" No trace was ever found of the remaining forty-six crew. Rushed to a hospital, Winkler and the other two lived to become prisoners. The next day, October 14, *Boreas* found an emergency telephone-equipped buoy, which had torn loose from *U-40* in the explosion. Inscribed on a brass plate were these instructions: "U-boat 40 is sunk here. Do not raise buoy. Telegraph the situation to the nearest German naval command."*

Unaware of this loss, the other five boats of the "pack" headed for the Western Approaches one by one. First to arrive was the new, undertrained Type IX, U-42,

---

   * In peacetime such tethered emergency buoys were standard equipment on submarines of all nations. The British were impressed with the quality of the buoy but surprised that the Germans had not removed it and the labels from the escape apparatus in order to conceal the identity of the U-boat.

commanded by Rolf Dau, age thirty-three. On the same day U-40 was lost, Dau found a 5,000-ton British freighter, Stonepool, which had separated from a convoy. Husbanding his torpedoes for pack operations, Dau attacked Stonepool with his 4.1" deck gun, but the freighter was armed, shot back, and radioed the SSS alarm. Two British destroyers, Imogen and Ilex, responding to the alarm, rushed up and attacked U-42 with guns, driving the boat under.

Attempting to evade, Dau took U-42 to 361 feet. But the destroyers fixed the boat on sonar and delivered an accurate and brutal depth-charge attack. One charge that exploded close over U-42's stern ruptured the after-ballast tanks and lifted the bow to a 45-degree angle. In a desperate attempt to avoid sliding to crush depth stern first, Dau blew all ballast tanks. The U-42 shot to the surface like a giant cork, into the waiting arms of the destroyers, which instantly opened fire, scoring hits in the bow room. Holed fore and aft, U-42 began to sink. Ilex ran in at full speed to ram, but seeing that U-42 was doomed and sinking, she backed full astern to avoid damage to herself, and merely grazed the boat abaft the conning tower. Dau and sixteen men got out of the sinking boat through the conning tower hatch; the other thirty-two men were lost. Imogen fished the dazed German survivors from the sea.

By that time Dönitz had good information from the codebreakers of B-dienst on a special French-British convoy, KJF 3, inbound directly from Kingston, Jamaica, escorted by the monster French submarine Surcouf (two 8" deck guns). Assuming all six boats had reached positions in the Western Approaches, Dönitz ordered Hartmann to lead the pack in the attack. But two of the six boats had been lost and Hartmann, having sunk two neutral ships (a Swede and a Greek) en route, was behind schedule and too far away to take tactical command of the other boats.

Two VIIBs of the pack, operating independently, found the convoy and attacked. Herbert Schultze in U-48 sank two French ships from the convoy: the 14,000-ton tanker Emile-Miguet and the 7,000-ton freighter Louisiane, plus two British freighters, apparently stragglers from other convoys. Alexander Gelhaar in U-45 also sank two ships from the convoy: the 9,200-ton British freighter Lochavon and a prohibited vessel, the 10,000-ton French passenger liner Bretagne, which was running blacked out and therefore inviting trouble. While she slowly sank, British ships rescued 300 passengers.

Gelhaar in U-45 did not have to answer for this mistake. While he was pursuing another ship of the now-dispersing convoy, four British destroyers, Icarus, Inglefield, Intrepid, and Ivanhoe, which had responded to the SSS alarms, found U-45 and attacked. Nothing more was ever heard from U-45. She was the first VIIB and the first Atlantic boat to disappear without survivors.*

The other two boats of the pack, U-37 and U-46, arrived too late to engage in a coordinated attack. However, on the morning of October 15, Hartmann in U-37 lucked into a straggler of the convoy, the 5,200-ton French freighter Vermont, and

---

* The sinking of U-45 was erroneously credited to the French destroyer Sirocco.

sank her with demolitions. But Herbert Sohler in *U-46* never found the convoy at all. His sole contribution to the action was the interception of *U-45*'s last radio transmission (not received in Germany), which helped sort out Gelhaar's first—and last—sinkings.

After the convoy dispersed, Dönitz, who was following the action by radio and by reports of distress calls and British movements provided by *B-dienst,* ordered the six boats (or so he thought) to move south to attack another convoy, HG 3, inbound from Gibraltar to the British Isles and to report results to date. Schultze in *U-48* radioed four ships sunk for 29,000 tons; Hartmann in *U-37,* three ships sunk for 11,000 tons; Sohler in *U-46,* none. Wrongly believing Schultze and Hartmann had sunk a total of seven ships from the Caribbean convoy, Dönitz added all those to Gelhaar's two and concluded that the first pack to attack an Allied convoy had sunk nine ships, an outstanding "success" that absolutely validated his pack doctrine. In reality, the first pack was so far a disaster: three of its six U-boats sunk; only four ships of the Caribbean convoy positively sunk, one of them a prohibited passenger liner!

While the boats were southbound on October 17, Hitler, still poised to attack France (as he thought), authorized a further relaxation in the rules. Henceforth U-boats could attack any "enemy" merchant ship (i.e., British or French) except big passenger liners, anywhere, without observance of the Submarine Protocol. In other words, U-boats were excused or exempted from the requirement to insure the safety of merchant-ship crews. This important relaxation allowed U-boats to wage unrestricted submarine warfare on all British and French shipping, except big passenger liners.*

The luckless Sohler in *U-46* was first to find convoy Homebound Gibraltar 3, which was heavily escorted by British destroyers transferring from the Mediterranean to home waters. He tracked the ships through the night, radioed a contact report, then submerged for a daylight attack. One of his first electric torpedoes prematured. In all, Sohler experienced seven torpedo malfunctions, but even so, he sank the 7,200-ton British freighter *City of Mandalay.* Brought into contact by Sohler's report, Hartmann in *U-37* sank the 10,000-ton British freighter *Yorkshire* and Schultze in *U-48* got his fifth ship in as many days, the 7,250-ton British freighter *Clan Chisholm.*

Following this attack, Sohler broke radio silence to report the premature torpedo detonation and other torpedo problems. Shocked—and angry—Dönitz declared that the magnetic pistol was *"not safe"* under any circumstances and without consulting the OKM or the Torpedo Directorate, he ordered all boats to use only contact (or impact) pistols. Hence the more powerful effect of the magnetic pistol—exploding the torpedo *beneath* the ship—was lost. "We're back to where we were in 1914–1918," Dönitz noted bitterly in his war diary.

---

* The Submarine Protocol remained in force for neutral shipping that was not in convoy or not blacked out. If deemed to be carrying contraband, neutrals could be sunk, but the safety of the crew had to be assured. Ships of Germany's friends or allies—Italy, Japan, Spain, Ireland, Russia—and the United States were not to be molested.

Upon learning that Dönitz had prohibited any and all use of the magnetic pistol, two days later, October 20, the Torpedo Directorate confessed to another defect. The torpedoes were indeed running deeper than set—6½ feet deeper. The Directorate technicians had known this all along, but did not report it to Dönitz because they did not believe it made that much difference when using magnetic pistols. But it did make a difference when using contact pistols. Dönitz hastened to relay this new discovery to his skippers, advising them to deduct 6½ feet from the usual depth settings for impact firing. The order introduced yet another complication. Since a depth setting of less than 13 feet was impractical when shooting in heavy seas, skippers were not to fire at any targets drawing less than 13 feet, such as destroyers.

Operations of the first wolf pack were terminated after the attack on the Gibraltar convoy. The two surviving VIIBs, *U-46* and *U-48,* low on fuel and low on, or out of, torpedoes, returned to Germany, Herbert Schultze to rave reviews. In two patrols Schultze had sunk eight ships for 52,000 tons, elevating him to first place in total tonnage sunk. Extending his patrol to the approaches of Gibraltar, Hartmann in *U-37* sank three more ships by gun and torpedo, establishing a new sinking record for a single patrol: eight ships sunk for 35,300 tons.

A careful after-action analysis of the first wolf pack deflated the earlier euphoria. In reality the attack on the Caribbean convoy was an uncoordinated free-for-all. Thanks to Sohler's contact report, the attack on the Gibraltar convoy was slightly better coordinated. However, the boats had sunk only four ships from the Caribbean convoy and three from the Gibraltar convoy. Half the pack (three of six boats) had been lost to the enemy, two boats to convoy escorts. In a significant and far-reaching report, Hartmann, who had sunk only one ship from each convoy and who had found it impossible to "tactically coordinate" the other boats of the pack, recommended that the concept of flotillas and "local pack control" (at sea) be abandoned, and that all boats should be controlled individually from Dönitz's headquarters.

Dönitz had three reasons for the failure to destroy the Caribbean convoy. First, the attack had been mounted too late—after the convoy was well into the Western Approaches and had been reinforced by local ASW vessels and had only a relatively short run to reach the safety of land. Second, in the confusion of combat, the boats making contact, *U-45* and *U-48,* had not been able to transmit accurate data on the position, course, and speed of the convoy; hence help from *U-46* had been lost. Third, there were too few boats in the initial attack—only two, actually—hence the escorts were able to concentrate on those two, sinking one, *U-45.*

The analysis led to three conclusions. First, convoys inbound to the British Isles from any direction had to be attacked as far out as possible in order to give the boats sufficient sea room for repeated attacks over several days and before the enemy added local ASW measures. Second, the boat first making contact with a convoy should not immediately attack, but instead should "shadow" it, transmitting "beacon" signals to "home" in other boats of the pack. Third, after the other boats arrived, all were to attack simultaneously in a single massive blow, which would scatter the convoy and overwhelm the escorts, maximizing opportunities for repeated attacks and minimizing counterattacks.

These tactics could be tested in Baltic training exercises, but not in Atlantic combat. There were not to be enough oceangoing boats to mount another full-scale wolf pack for months to come.

ATLANTIC U-BOAT OPERATIONS: OCTOBER–DECEMBER 1939

Apart from the first wolf pack, only four boats sailed to the Atlantic in October. One was a Type VII of the Salzwedel Flotilla, *U-34*, which despite the design flaws and other problems of the VIIs, was believed to be capable of an Atlantic patrol. The other three formed a special (but loosely organized) task force that, in response to Raeder's demand, was to lay a minefield at the British naval base at Gibraltar, then attack Allied shipping in the Mediterranean.

Commanded by Wilhelm Rollmann, age thirty-two, the *U-34* was the only boat to make a completely independent patrol in October. While going northabout the British Isles to the Western Approaches, Rollmann bagged two small freighters (one Swedish, one British). Hunting in the Western Approaches, he found an inbound convoy, Halifax 5, and despite repeated torpedo failures, he sank an 8,000-ton British freighter, *Malabar,* and so damaged another, *Bronte,* that it had to be sunk by British destroyers. But *U-34* was not combat-ready. An internal tank cracked and Rollmann was forced to abort. En route home, he captured the 3,200-ton Norwegian freighter *Snar*—his second prize in as many patrols—raising his score for two patrols to an impressive eight ships for 33,600 tons. But the *U-34*'s mechanical failure reinforced the view that until the VIIs were extensively modified, they were not safe for torpedo patrolling. Pending the modifications, no more VIIs were to be sent on torpedo patrol.

The three-boat Mediterranean task force was composed of the clumsy Type I sister ships *U-25* (finally out of overhaul) and *U-26,* and the VIIB, *U-53.* The plan was for Klaus Ewerth in *U-26,* who had laid the fruitful minefield at Portland, to precede the other boats by several days and lay delayed-action TMB mines at Gibraltar. On his signal that the field was laid, the other two boats, waiting outside in the Atlantic, were to slip through the Strait of Gibraltar into the Mediterranean, where all three boats were to attack shipping with torpedoes.

Everything that could go wrong did. Ewerth in *U-26* ran into intense ASW patrols and bad weather and was forced to abort the mine mission and did not make a second try. When he returned to Germany, he was assigned to other duty. While awaiting the go-ahead signal, the clumsy sister ship, *U-25,* commanded by Viktor Schütze, age thirty-three, attacked two ships which came his way. In the first attack Schütze experienced four contact-pistol failures under perfect conditions (stationary target, calm sea, short ranges, careful aiming) and finally sank the ship. In his second attack, by gun, the recoil cracked the torpedo-loading hatch and Schütze was forced to abort and return to Germany. Ernst-Gunther Heinicke in *U-53* refused to penetrate the heavily patrolled Strait of Gibraltar and flailed around for days out of touch.

The Mediterranean task force was thus a failure.

Schütze in *U-25* broke radio silence to report the malfunction of the four contact pistols. His report ignited an absolute furor at the OKM and Dönitz's head-quarters. Raeder demanded yet another exhaustive investigation. Meanwhile, on November 10, Dönitz ordered all boats to revert to magnetic pistols, which the Torpedo Directorate assured him had been improved. It was a calculated risk, but he reasoned that a half-baked, improved magnetic pistol was better than an impact pistol that apparently did not work at all.

Dönitz was furious. The torpedo technicians, he wrote in his war diary, did "not understand the matter." At least "30% of all torpedoes are duds." They "either do not detonate at all or they detonate in the wrong place." The skippers were "los-ing confidence" in their torpedoes, he went on. "In the end their fighting spirit will suffer. The torpedo failure problem is at present the most urgent of all the problems of U-boat warfare." But the Directorate seemed unable to correct the flaws.

In the month of November, the Atlantic U-boat campaign was disrupted by yet an-other special operation. The "pocket" battleship *Deutschland,* operating in the North Atlantic (with meager results), had incurred engine trouble and was aborting to Germany. At about the same time, the battle cruisers *Gneisenau* and *Scharn-horst* were to make a sortie into the Atlantic. Believing these movements might provoke capital ships of the Royal Navy into action, which could be tracked by *B-dienst,* the OKM directed that several U-boat traps be laid in the North Sea, utiliz-ing both oceangoing boats and ducks.

Dönitz chose four oceangoing boats for the main trap: the VIIBs *U-47* (Prien) and *U-48* (Schultze) and, reluctantly, two patched-up Type VIIs, *U-31* (Habekost) and *U-35* (Lott). He laid the trap on a line east of the Shetlands. As expected, the Royal Navy picked up the movements of *Gneisenau* and *Scharnhorst* and de-ployed to search and attack, and *B-dienst* provided the OKM with current data on the British movements. But the operations of all ships, both German and British, were hampered by hideous weather.

Patrolling on the surface in huge seas on November 28, Lott in *U-35,* sixty miles east of Shetland Island, saw a heavy cruiser (*Norfolk*) and broke radio si-lence to report her. Twelve miles northeast of *U-35,* Prien in *U-47* picked up Lott's message and plotted a course to intercept.

Despite the mountainous seas, the interception was perfect. Sighting *Norfolk's* top hamper, Prien submerged and closed to about 1,000 yards. He fired a single torpedo with the improved magnetic pistol. He then made ready a second tube, but the heavy seas slewed the boat around and Prien lost sight of *Norfolk* in the periscope. Eighty-six seconds after firing, the men on *U-47* clearly heard a detona-tion and cheered.

Prien surfaced in the turbulent seas to assess the damage. Closing the cruiser, unseen, he observed that "the upper deck [was] slightly buckled and piping [was] hanging over the starboard side." The ship's reconnaissance aircraft was "tilted on its tail." He saw black smoke at the point of torpedo impact—beneath *Norfolk's* starboard torpedo rack.

The cruiser hauled away and disappeared in rain squalls. Prien attempted to pursue for a second attack, but the heavy seas defeated him. He broke radio silence to report: "Have torpedoed one *London*-class cruiser. One hit. Wind strength 10." He did not claim a sinking then or later, merely that one hit was "highly probable." Leaping to the conclusion that *Norfolk* was sunk, the OKM was ecstatic, gloatingly logging the attack as "a magnificent success." Over Dönitz's objections, Berlin propagandists claimed that a U-boat had sunk a "*London*-class" heavy cruiser and named Prien—the "Bull of Scapa Flow"—as the U-boat skipper who had done the job.

Churchill and First Sea Lord Pound first got the news from Berlin radio. In response to an Admiralty query, *Norfolk* reported herself undamaged. She had seen an explosion in her wake but had assumed it to be an aircraft bomb. She had not sighted *U-47*. The improved magnetic pistol on the torpedo Prien fired had apparently malfunctioned. The BBC denied the sinking, but Berlin radio persisted in the claim, elevating Prien to ever greater celebrity.

At dawn on the day following Prien's unsuccessful attack on *Norfolk,* Lott in *U-35* was cruising on the surface near the Shetland Islands. Lott's radio report of his sighting of *Norfolk,* which had enabled Prien to find her, and Prien's radio report of the attack may have been DFed by the British. In any event, the British destroyer *Icarus* saw *U-35* and turned to attack, with the rising sun behind her.

Blinded by the sun, Lott's bridge watch failed to see *Icarus* approaching. Caught by surprise, Lott crash-dived and went deep—to 229 feet—and steered evasive courses. But *Icarus* got her on sonar and dropped depth charges set for 250 feet. Two other destroyers, *Kingston* and *Kashmir,* responded to *Icarus*'s alert. Directed by *Icarus* to the likely spot, *Kingston* made two depth-charge attacks, which jammed the *U-35*'s diving planes and put her at a sharp up angle. In an attempt to bring the bow down and regain control of the boat, Lott rushed all available men to the forward torpedo room and put on full speed. All in vain. The depth charges had also ruptured fuel and ballast tanks aft and no amount of weight forward could level the boat.

Believing the boat to be doomed, Lott blew all ballast tanks and surfaced. He manned his deck gun to shoot it out, but when he saw three destroyers close by and when one of them, *Kashmir,* fired at *U-35,* Lott gave up and ordered the boat scuttled. As *U-35* slowly flooded and settled, the gun crew raised their arms in surrender. *Kashmir* fished four officers and twenty-seven men from the icy water; *Kingston* picked up Lott and eleven others, who were last to leave the boat. All forty-three men of *U-35* were rescued.

Owing to the diversion of *U-47* and *U-48* to the North Sea submarine trap, only three oceangoing boats were available to mount the U-boat campaign in the Atlantic in November. These were the brand-new VIIB, *U-49,* and two IXs, *U-41* and *U-43,* the latter also brand-new. Carrying improved magnetic pistols, they sailed into the cold, mountainous, and forbidding seas.

These boats, and others, were the beneficiaries of yet another relaxation in the U-boat rules. On November 12 Hitler authorized the on-sight sinkings of any and all enemy passenger vessels of whatever size, known (or seen) to be armed, and any and all tankers, including those of neutral nations (but not American or friends or allies of Germany), which were "beyond all doubt" going to or from the British Isles or France. This relaxation meant that any tanker in British waters could be sunk without warning or without assuring the safety of the crew.

Rounding the British Isles in terrible weather, Gustav-Adolf Mügler in *U-41* sank a British trawler with his 4.1" deck gun on November 12. Taking pity on the survivors, he fished about half the surviving crew from the icy seas, intending to put them on board another trawler. Before he could do so, Mügler ran across the 11,000-ton Norwegian tanker *Arne Kjöde,* which, under the relaxed rules, appeared to be fair game for attack. While the British trawler survivors looked on in horrified fascination, Mügler sank the tanker with a single electric torpedo fitted with an improved magnetic pistol. He made no effort to rescue the tanker crew (five died). Later in the day he found another trawler and off-loaded the British.*

The weather off the British Isles turned from terrible to hideous. Accordingly, Dönitz directed the three Atlantic boats to patrol farther to the south off the Iberian Peninsula. While passing southbound through the Western Approaches, all three boats found targets. Mügler in *U-41* attacked a British freighter, *Hope Star,* but three torpedoes missed or malfunctioned. Wilhelm Ambrosius, age thirty-six, in the new IX *U-43,* sank a 5,000-ton British freighter, *Arlington Court.* Curt von Gossler, age thirty-four, commanding the new VIIB *U-49,* fired four torpedoes at the 7,000-ton British freighter *Rothesay Castle,* but without success. Two destroyers, *Echo* and *Wanderer,* pounced on *U-49* and delivered a punishing depth-charge attack, during which von Gossler was driven to the unprecedented depth of 557 feet.

Finally escaping, that night von Gossler hauled to the west to get off an important report to Dönitz. He had nothing but bad news: three G7a (air) torpedoes with improved magnetic pistols had prematured, two of them after a run of only 656 feet. One G7e (electric) with a magnetic pistol had failed to fire. This report, Dönitz wrote, was "a bitter disappointment." All "our best hopes" for the "improved" magnetic pistol "were dashed in one blow." Dönitz fumed on: "The torpedo can in no way be regarded as a front line weapon of any use."

This latest torpedo disaster—and the near loss of von Gossler's *U-49*—so infuriated Raeder that he resorted to a drastic measure. He reached outside the *Kriegsmarine* and brought in a civilian scientist, Dr. E. A. Cornelius, and named him "Torpedo Dictator." Cornelius was to have "wide powers" not only to correct the faults of the torpedoes (pistols, depth keeping, etc.) but also to take measures to increase torpedo production, which was badly lagging. The appointment was "of

---

* Helped by this rare eyewitness testimony from the trawler survivors, the prosecutors at Nuremberg cited the *Arne Kjöde* as one example of a U-boat "atrocity." Perhaps forgetting that Hitler had specifically loosened the rules on sinking neutral tankers, or not wishing to mention it, Dönitz, in his defense, stated the sinking had been "a mistake," that Mügler had "confused" (i.e., misidentified) the ship as a British tanker inbound to England. "If one or two instances of mistakes are found in the course of five and one-half years of clean submarine warfare," Dönitz testified, "it proves nothing." Mügler's rescue of the British trawler survivors, all on the same day, was entered in Dönitz's defense, effectively offsetting this alleged "atrocity."

major importance to the U-boat arm," Dönitz noted. "It is hoped he will be completely successful."

With all four bow torpedo tubes and a periscope out with unrepairable damage, von Gossler in *U-49* was compelled to abort. He limped into Wilhelmshaven after only twenty days at sea, feeling very lucky to have survived. His descent to the astounding depth of 557 feet proved to be a valuable experience. Until then it was believed that the Type VIIB would implode or "crush" at such depths. The discovery meant that the Type VIIBs could safely descend to at least fifty-seven feet below the maximum depth setting (500 feet) of British depth charges. Hence an important new avenue of escape from depth charges had opened up.

Heinicke in *U-53*, a legacy of the abortive Mediterranean task force, was still patrolling cautiously off the Iberian Peninsula. Finding a convoy, he reported it and shadowed. On instruction from Dönitz, Heinicke transmitted a "beacon" signal to home in the southbound IXs, *U-41* and *U-43*. By this means an impromptu three-boat pack developed, loosely directed by Dönitz. Mügler in *U-41*, who paused to sink a small British tramp en route, made contact with the convoy, Sierra Leone 7, taking over as the shadower from *U-53*, which had been driven off by the escorts. All three boats, operating independently, shot at ships of the convoy, but only Ambrosius in *U-43* sank one. British and French destroyers pounced on *U-41* and *U-43*. They held *U-41* down for an unprecedented twenty hours* and severely damaged *U-43*, which finally shook loose and escaped west, where Ambrosius sank a lone 2,500-ton British freighter before aborting the patrol due to battle damage, and heading for Germany.

The results of the November operations in the Atlantic were meager. Mügler in *U-41*, who reported nine torpedo failures in eleven shots, was credited with four ships for 12,914 tons, including two trawlers, but only one of the sinkings, the Norwegian tanker *Arne Kjöde*, was worth the trip. Ambrosius in *U-43*, severely damaged, was credited with four ships for 16,000 tons. Von Gossler in *U-49*, also severely damaged, sank none. Heinicke in *U-53*, who had balked at entering the Mediterranean, sank no ships, returned to Germany with eleven of his fourteen torpedoes, and went to other duty. The repairs to *U-43* and *U-49* were to keep both boats out of service until March 1940.

The operations plan for December was more encouraging. Dönitz believed he might get six boats to the Atlantic: *U-47* (Prien) and *U-48* (Schultze), released from the submarine trap in the North Sea, and four other boats, including the

---

* Far beyond normal air capacity. However, the air inside a U-boat could be crudely purified by blowing it through CO_2 scrubbing devices employing caustic potash cartridges, located in each compartment. In addition, the boats were supplied with individual CO_2-absorbing respirators with five-pound canisters of soda lime, which the men could wear like gas masks. To conserve the air supply, men not on duty were required to lie in their bunks.

VIIBs *U-51* and *U-52,* returning to service after months of repairs and modifications. But the plan was not realized, owing to what Dönitz characterized as an act of "sabotage." The crews found sand in the lubricating oil of *U-25, U-51,* and *U-52.* The *U-25* was repaired and sailed, only to abort in the North Sea with an unrelated oil leak, but *U-51* and *U-52* could not sail in December. The *U-52* was so badly damaged, Dönitz noted in his diary, that she was to be out of action "until further notice." The sailing of the other boat, *U-46,* was delayed for other reasons.

Thus, not six but only two boats, Prien's *U-47* and Schultze's *U-48,* were available to mount the Atlantic U-boat campaign in early December, and both of these were low on fuel. Taking advantage of the relaxed rules, on the way to the Shetlands Schultze sank the 6,300-ton Swedish tanker *Gustaf E. Reuter.* Both boats confronted brutally cold weather and mountainous seas, which flung ice water at the bridge watches, and pitched, rolled, and yawed the boats to alarming angles.

Prien arrived in the Western Approaches so low on fuel he had to limit his Atlantic patrol to about five days. During that brief period he sank three big and important ships: the 8,800-ton British freighter *Navasota,* the 6,200-ton Norwegian tanker *Britta,* and the 8,150-ton Dutch freighter *Tajandoen.* In the attack on *Navasota,* British destroyers counterattacked *U-47,* and for the first time in the war Prien and his men felt the impact of depth charges. But the counterattack was desultory and Prien evaded and headed home. En route he shot his last torpedoes at two ships, but the torpedoes missed or malfunctioned.

When Prien arrived in Wilhelmshaven, he was again accorded a hero's welcome. In spite of indignant denials from London, Berlin persisted in crediting him with sinking the cruiser *Norfolk,* inflating his total sinkings in three patrols to 72,000 tons. In reality he had sunk three ships for 23,168 tons on this patrol, elevating his total confirmed sinkings to 61,500 tons, which, however, put him in first place. He reported that eight of twelve electric torpedoes (with improved magnetic pistols) had missed or malfunctioned. Having completed the necessary three war patrols to qualify, all hands were awarded a new and coveted decoration: the *Kriegsabzeichen,* or U-boat badge.

Left alone in the Western Approaches in appalling weather, Schultze in *U-48* patrolled for only seven days. In that time he, too, accounted for three important ships: a 5,000-ton Greek freighter, the 6,700-ton British freighter *Brandon,* and the 7,400-ton British tanker *San Alberto,* which was so badly damaged she had to be sunk by a British destroyer. After Schultze left the Atlantic on December 19, for a period of five days there were no U-boats in those waters.

On arrival in Wilhelmshaven from this third patrol, Schultze found himself on the way to becoming a national hero, like Prien and Schuhart. He had sunk four more ships for 25,618 tons, bringing his total to twelve ships for 77,500 tons. That was almost twice the number of confirmed ships Prien had sunk and substantially greater tonnage. Inflating Schultze's kills to an even "80,000 tons," Berlin propagandists gave Schultze and his crew the full publicity treatment. The crew was awarded medals and the U-boat badge, but Schultze did not get a *Ritterkreuz.* Dönitz had decreed that to earn that high award a skipper had to sink 100,000 tons of enemy shipping or perform a feat of exceptional daring, such as Prien's penetration of Scapa Flow.

Owing to the sabotage of *U-51* and *U-52*, and the abort of *U-25*, only one boat sailed from Germany in December to make a torpedo patrol. This was the VIIB *U-46*, commanded by Herbert Sohler. Outbound in the North Sea, Sohler sank a 1,000-ton Norwegian freighter and earned the dubious distinction of being the only U-boat in the Atlantic on Christmas Day. Sohler found plenty of shipping in the Western Approaches and attacked aggressively, but he achieved no other sinkings. Two weeks into the patrol, one diesel engine broke down, forcing Sohler to abort. Reviewing the boat's shooting record for three patrols during which merely two ships for 8,000 tons had been sunk, Dönitz concluded that the fire-control party needed further training and sent the boat back to "school," a humiliation for this veteran but unlucky crew, and yet another unforeseen deduction from the dwindling Atlantic force.

Counting the first (abortive) wolf pack and the Mediterranean task force, Dönitz mounted only sixteen torpedo patrols to the Atlantic during the three-month period October–December 1939, five less than the initial deployment in September. Three of these sixteen (*U-40, U-42, U-45*) had been lost, plus *U-35* of the North Sea submarine trap.* Two, *U-43* and *U-49*, had incurred severe battle damage. *U-51* and *U-52* had been sabotaged and *U-46* had been sent to retraining. The sixteen Atlantic patrols had resulted in thirty-five ship sinkings or prizes, an average of 2.2 ships sunk or captured per boat per patrol, about the same as the September averages and thus a disappointment. The five leading skippers in tonnage sunk were Schultze, Prien, Schuhart, Hartmann, and Rollmann.

Admiralty statisticians calculated that as of December 31, 1939, a total of 5,756 ships had sailed in British convoys, most of them in home waters or the North Sea. Of these, the Admiralty boasted, only four had been sunk by U-boats. That was an understatement, but the general thrust was true. According to the meticulous work of the German U-boat historian Jürgen Rohwer, in that four months of the so-called Phony War in 1939, all U-boats, including the North Sea ducks, sank 123 merchant ships of 500 gross tons or more. Excluding the French convoy KJF 3, only fourteen of the 123 ships sunk by U-boats were sailing in convoy, three inbound from Halifax, two inbound from Sierra Leone, three inbound from Gibraltar, and the rest outbound in ballast.†

MINELAYING

In support of Hitler's planned attack on France in November 1939, Admiral Raeder and the OKM had ordered German surface ships, aircraft, and submarines to mine British seaports. The primary aim of the mining campaign was to shut off

---

*   As well as the Type VII, *U-36*, with the loss of all hands, on her second patrol in the North Sea. She was sunk by the British submarine *Salmon*, commanded by E. O. Bickford, who went on to severely damage the German light cruisers *Leipzig* and *Nürnberg*.

†   For numbers of principal inbound convoys and losses, see Plate 10 (p. 424). For a list of confirmed sinkings by ducks, see Appendix 7.

the flow of British troops and supplies to the continent. A secondary aim was to disrupt or shut down British merchant shipping, sowing terror and panic.

Restricted by a shortage of magnetic mines, which had not been mass-produced in peacetime, the campaign got off to a halting start. In October four ducks laid, or attempted to lay, minefields, each consisting of nine delayed-action TMB magnetic mines. Two fields were flops. That of Horst Wellner in *U-16,* off Dover, sank one small tugboat. Moreover, after laying the field, Wellner hit an Allied mine in the Dover–Cape Gris-Nez field on October 24, and *U-16* was lost with all hands. That of Harald Jeppener-Haltenhoff in *U-24,* at Hartlepool, sank only one 1,000-ton coaster.* Two fields produced handsomely. That of Hans Meckel in *U-19,* off Hartlepool, sank three freighters for 12,344 tons. That of Fritz Frauenheim in *U-21,* courageously planted off the British naval base in the Firth of Forth, wrecked the new British heavy cruiser *Belfast,* a spectacular victory for the ducks.

The oceangoing boats were to foul British west coast ports, which were beyond reach of the ducks or German aircraft. Dönitz assigned these missions to the available Type VIIs of the Salzwedel Flotilla, which, pending modification, had been declared unsafe for torpedo patrols. The first, most important, and dangerous mission went to Paul Büchel in *U-32,* who had planted a (nonproductive) minefield in the Bristol Channel in September. Büchel's destination was Loch Ewe, in northwest Scotland, where the Home Fleet based after Prien's raid in Scapa Flow. But *U-32* was not seaworthy and the *U-31,* commanded by Johannes Habekost, substituted.

Habekost crammed eighteen TMB mines into *U-31.* Off Loch Ewe he tangled the boat in a torpedo net—a harrowing episode—but he finally broke free, laid the mines in the outer channel, and returned home after ten days, the shortest patrol on record. The field produced no immediate results and was therefore believed to be a failure. But thirty-seven days later, on December 4, the Home Fleet flagship, the battleship *Nelson,* triggered one of the mines, incurring such heavy damage she had to be dry-docked for four months. The British concealed this disaster from the Germans.

The *U-33,* commanded by Hans-Wilhelm von Dresky, drew the next mission: Bristol Channel, where Büchel in *U-32* had apparently mislaid his field in September. Since it had to be assumed that the British were aware of the submarine minelaying and therefore the boats could not sail utterly defenseless, von Dresky carried twelve TMB mines and six torpedoes. Outbound in the North Sea, a crewman remembered, both diesels broke down and *U-33* had to lie on the bottom for three days while the engineers made repairs. "The boat was not really seaworthy," the crewman explained. "The crew was very nervous. Many [men] were reluctant to go back to sea in this boat." However, the field was highly productive: three big ships, for 25,600 tons sunk, including the British tanker *Inverdargle,* forcing the British to close Bristol for the second time.

After laying the field, von Dresky sought gun and torpedo targets. Off North

---

* The sinking of these two small ships—the 57-ton tugboat in particular—were further indications that the mine settings were overly sensitive, but the Germans remained unaware.

Ireland he stopped five British trawlers and, after permitting the crews to abandon ship, he sank them all by gun. Homebound in the Orkneys, in miserable weather, he destroyed by gun and torpedo the 3,700-ton German freighter *Borkum,* which British warships had seized as a prize. Unwittingly, von Dresky's gunfire killed four German crewmen. When the boat limped into Germany, Dönitz commended von Dresky for a "well-conducted" patrol, but *U-33* had to be sent back to the shipyards for extensive repairs.

The mining campaign built up a full head of steam in November. Finally getting into action, German surface ships and aircraft, operating under cover of the long nights, assailed British east coast and channel ports. Dashing across the North Sea and back, the surface ships laid over 500 mines. In separate missions over three nights the *Luftwaffe* parachuted forty-one mines in the mouth of the Thames River, off the Humber, and at Harwich. One of the *Luftwaffe* mines was misdropped onto mudflats at Shoeburyness. The British recovered it intact, quickly learned the secrets of the magnetic mine, and initiated a crash R&D program to produce countermeasures.

The surface-ship mine offensive was highly effective. It forced the British to close down numerous east coast and channel ports and brought shipping to a standstill. The psychological impact was as great as—or greater than—the sinkings caused by the U-boats. Seeking to calm the shocked British population and to chastise Hitler for employing a sinister and barbaric weapon, the Chamberlain government immediately revealed the secrets of the magnetic mine ("An amazing new invention," said one British official) but promised that "science and intelligence" would deal with it as effectively as it had dealt with the U-boat menace.

In the stepped-up offensive, seven ducks sailed to lay minefields in November. Two were flops: that of Otto Kretschmer's *U-23* off the British naval base in Cromarty Forth (Invergordon) and that of Herbert Kuppisch's *U-58* off Lowestoft. The other five, at Lowestoft, Ordfordness, Yarmouth, and Newcastle, produced six sinkings for 15,000 tons and damage to one freighter for 4,434 tons.

Three of these seven sinkings by the ducks were small ships of 209, 258, and 496 tons, which became known to the Germans. This revelation led Dönitz to question the reliability of the TMB magnetic mine with the same intensity he had questioned the reliability of the torpedoes. In response, the Mine Directorate conducted "live" tests of the TMB in the Baltic Sea. The results confirmed Dönitz's suspicions. The mines, the Directorate conceded, were not "positively lethal" when laid on the bottom at ninety-eight feet (thirty meters) per instructions, but rather only at eighty-two feet (twenty-five meters). Moreover, the tests revealed, the pistols were overly sensitive. As a consequence, Dönitz directed the submarine crews to lay TMB mines sixteen feet shallower than designed and to "coarsen" (or desensitize) the magnetic pistols.

Dönitz had another complaint. He did not believe the 1,200-pound warhead of the TMB was sufficiently powerful for use against big, heavily armored capital ships. He requested a mine with twice the power of the TMB. In striking contrast to the torpedo technicians, the mine technicians responded willingly and enthusiastically. They quickly converted a big submarine floating mine, the TMA, then going into production, to a ground mine. Redesignated the TMC, it had a huge warhead of 2,200 pounds and was believed to be lethal up to a depth of 118 feet (36 meters).

Two Type VIIs of the Salzwedel Flotilla, which had been in the shipyards for weeks, drew Atlantic minelaying assignments in November. These were Günter Kuhnke's *U-28* and Otto Schuhart's *U-29*. Both loaded twelve TMB mines and six torpedoes to continue the campaign in the Bristol Channel.

En route to Bristol, Kuhnke sank two ships with torpedoes. The first was the 5,000-ton Dutch tanker *Sliedrecht,* fair game under the newly relaxed rules regarding neutral tankers. After the crew abandoned ship, Kuhnke fired a single torpedo, which demolished the ship in a "terrific flash." He left the survivors to fend for themselves and only five lived. The second kill was the 5,100-ton British freighter *Royston Grange,* sunk in the Western Approaches after the crew had abandoned ship.

Kuhnke laid his field at Swansea and returned to Germany. Since it produced no immediate results, it too was believed to be a failure. The *U-28* went back into the shipyards for more weeks of repairs and modifications. About sixty days later one of the mines triggered and sank an important ship: the 9,600-ton British freighter *Protesilaus.*

The hero Otto Schuhart in *U-29,* who had sunk the carrier *Courageous,* was directed to lay his field at Milford Haven. But he broke radio silence to say that foul weather and a bright moon had forced him to abort the mission. Dönitz directed Schuhart to attempt an alternate location, but apparently Schuhart's heart was not in the task and he returned to Germany with a full load of twelve mines and six torpedoes. Furious at the failure, Dönitz criticized Schuhart for being "too cautious," but in view of Schuhart's outstanding first patrol, Dönitz decided he would give Schuhart a second chance. The opportunity for redemption did not come soon; *U-29* also went back to the shipyard for more weeks of modifications.

Five ducks laid or attempted to lay minefields in December. All five fields bore fruit, sinking a total of eight small ships for 13,200 tons. The field of Karl-Heinrich Jenisch in *U-22,* laid at Newcastle, was the most productive: four small freighters for 4,978 tons. Jürgen Oesten attempted to lay a second field in the dangerous waters of the Firth of Forth, but ASW forces drove him off before he could finish. The mines he planted bagged one small coaster. The largest ship, a 4,373-ton freighter, was sunk by the mines of Georg Schewe's *U-60,* at Lowestoft.

Two Type VIIs mounted the Atlantic minelaying campaign in December: Lemp's *U-30* and Büchel's *U-32.* Lemp was to plant a dozen TMBs in Liverpool, closing that important port. Büchel was to lay eight of the new, powerful TMC mines off the British naval base in the dangerous waters of the Firth of Clyde, where it was hoped the TMCs would bag a capital ship.

Lemp's *U-30* had been in the shipyards for seventy days undergoing battle-damage repair and modification. He believed the boat to be seaworthy, but while outbound near the Shetlands an engine failed and he had to return to Germany. He resailed, finally, on December 23, four days behind Sohler's *U-46,* which was outbound to the Atlantic for torpedo patrol. Reapproaching the Shetlands on Christmas Eve, Lemp received a message from Raeder addressed to "all U-boats" at sea: "A Merry Christmas. Good wishes for successful operations." Since all the ducks and the other oceangoing boats were in port, the greeting applied only to Lemp and Sohler.

Rounding the British Isles, Lemp reached the Butt of Lewis on the north end of the Hebrides in the early morning of December 28. There he came upon a British trawler. Believing his crew needed sharpening, Lemp battle-surfaced. After the British abandoned the trawler, he sank her with his deck gun. As it happened, that very day the 2,500-ton British freighter *Stanholme* hit one of the mines von Dresky had planted earlier in the Bristol Channel. London indignantly claimed *Stanholme* had been torpedoed without warning by a U-boat. Hearing the news in Berlin, the OKM wrongly attributed the sinking to Lemp. Perhaps mindful of the furor Lemp had caused by sinking *Athenia,* the OKM virtuously chastised Lemp for providing the British with an opportunity to condemn Germans for waging submarine warfare "during Christmas."

To reinforce the depleted Home Fleet, the Admiralty had brought home two old (1915–1916) battleships: *Warspite* (which had been modernized in the late 1930s) and *Barham.* In addition, the old battle cruiser *Repulse* and the carrier *Furious* had arrived from Canada on convoy duty. Late in the afternoon of this same day—December 28—the *Barham* and *Repulse,* escorted by five destroyers, cruised off the Butt of Lewis, to backstop the cruisers of the Northern Patrol in case *Gneisenau* and *Scharnhorst* came out again.

Resuming his voyage south, Lemp sighted the top hampers of *Repulse* and *Barham* late that afternoon. He submerged on a closing course and coolly made ready the four electric torpedoes (with magnetic pistols) in his bow tubes. Boldly maneuvering under the destroyer screen, Lemp fired two torpedoes each at *Barham* and *Repulse.* Lemp and his men heard one of the four torpedoes hit *Barham,* and cheered. It struck forward, causing considerable damage and flooding in the ammunition lockers. The other three torpedoes malfunctioned or missed.

In the excitement and confusion that ensued, the British botched the submarine hunt and Lemp withdrew without undergoing counterattack. That night he galvanized Dönitz and Berlin with this message: "Attacked two *Repulse* class, escorted by destroyers . . . one hit probable." *B-dienst* intercepted and decoded *Barham's* damage report and the instructions to her from the Admiralty to put into Liverpool for repairs because the Firth of Clyde was too crowded. Repaired in a Liverpool shipyard, *Barham* was out of action for three months.

Liverpool was also Lemp's destination. Approaching with utmost caution, he arrived there and laid his twelve TMB mines. This well-planted field paid off handsomely. Within the next thirty days one tanker and three big British freighters for 22,472 tons blew up and sank, and a 5,600-ton freighter, *Gracia,* was severely damaged. As a result, the British were compelled to close Liverpool.

Dönitz had high praise for Lemp. The minelaying, Dönitz commented in his diary, was well carried out and required "a lot of dash, thought, ability and determination." If Lemp had been under a cloud for sinking *Athenia,* his hit on *Barham* and the Liverpool minefield removed it. Including *Athenia* and the victims of his mines, Lemp's confirmed sinkings totaled eight ships for 45,678 tons, ranking him first in the Salzwedel Flotilla and third in the entire U-boat arm in tonnage sunk after Herbert Schultze and Günther Prien.

Büchel in *U-32* finally sailed in late December after eighty-nine days in and out of the shipyards. Rounding the British Isles, like Lemp he paused to sink a ship (a 1,000-ton Norwegian) to sharpen the crew. Continuing southward, he entered North Channel and proceeded with due caution to the Firth of Clyde, which was heavily patrolled and protected by antitorpedo nets. Daunted by the intense ASW measures, Büchel balked at planting the mines in midchannel where Dönitz had specified, and dropped them in a less promising location in deeper water. When Büchel returned to Germany, Dönitz sacked him, angrily noting in his diary that the job had been "too difficult for this commanding officer." None of the TMCs exploded. Thus the first use of this extremely powerful weapon failed.

The ducks and oceangoing boats mounted a total of twenty-two minelaying missions in British home waters between October and December, 1939, planting 218 mines. One oceangoing boat (*U-29*) with twelve mines aborted at Bristol; one duck (*U-61*) was driven off before it finished laying its field in the Firth of Forth. Several fields were mislaid, most notably *U-32*'s TMCs in the Firth of Clyde. Two duck fields, probably mislaid, produced no sinkings; two others sank but two very small ships. The five minefields (sixty-two mines) sown by oceangoing boats sank ten ships for about 58,000 tons; the sixteen minefields (about 140 mines) sown by the ducks sank twenty ships for 46,400 tons. The combined campaigns produced thirty ships sunk* for 104,400 tons, a statistical average of 1.4 ships per boat per patrol and one ship of 3,500 tons sunk for every seven mines planted. One duck, *U-16,* had been lost on a mine mission.

The Admiralty estimated that during the period October–December, 1939, seventy-one merchant ships were lost to enemy mines in British waters. The mines planted by U-boat accounted for almost one-half (42 percent) of these losses, plus the severe damage to the cruiser *Belfast* and moderate damage to the battleship *Nelson.* Even so, Dönitz did not share the enthusiasm of Raeder and the OKM for submarine minelaying. It was tedious, time-consuming, and very dangerous. The observed or known returns per minefield appeared to be quite meager. He distrusted the TMB mines. Minelaying diverted a great many duck skippers from torpedo shooting which, in view of the greatly relaxed U-boat rules, offered many more opportunities for success as well as valuable combat training. German aircraft and surface ships could mine almost all the ports the ducks could reach.

Dönitz urged Raeder and the OKM to release submarines from minelaying, but he won only a partial victory. All further duck minelaying was suspended, except for two missions to Cromarty Forth. However, the Atlantic boats were to continue the campaign against ports on the west coast of Britain.

---

*   Including all ships sunk in later months.

U-BOAT COUNTERMEASURES

From some garrulous German U-boat POWs and the recovery of Prien's unexploded torpedoes in Scapa Flow, Churchill and the Admiralty learned almost all there was to know about the organization and size of the U-boat arm, the characteristics, armament, and limitations of the three main classes of boats (Types II, VII, IX), the usual patrol routes and zones, the torpedo and boat defects, and the U-boat production rates. This wealth of information, together with the sharp decline in merchant-shipping losses from October to December 1939, and an absurdly optimistic estimate of U-boat kills, convinced Churchill and Pound—indeed, the entire Admiralty—that the U-boat menace had been checked, at least for the present.

But Churchill continued to fret about the future, the several hundred U-boats certain to appear in due course to savage British shipping. He therefore continued to push for ever larger numbers of convoy escorts, including "jeep" carriers, ASW surface vessels such as the *Hunt*-class small destroyers, and aircraft, as well as new merchant ships to be built at home and abroad, and to encourage R&D for improved sonar and radar, ASW bombs, and depth charges.

Of the British antisubmarine R&D programs, the three most technically difficult but promising—and urgent—were minesweeping, radar, and codebreaking. By happy coincidence for the British, all three programs began to pay the first dividends in the early weeks of 1940.

• MINESWEEPING.   Immediately after the recovery of the misdropped German magnetic mine at Shoeburyness, a team of British scientists, engineers, and mine technicians commenced a crash program to develop ways to "sweep" (i.e., explode) these mines.

The team pursued several approaches, but that which proved most practical and efficient was called the "Double Longitude," or "Double L," method. Two wooden minesweepers, sailing on a parallel course about 300 yards apart, each dragged two buoyant electrical cables, one long, one short. One cable constituted a negative electric pole, the other a positive pole. When the pairs of cables of both ships were energized in precise synchronization by five-second pulses of DC current from shipboard batteries, the salt water completed the electrical circuit, creating an intense magnetic field almost ten acres in size.

The first full sea-trial of the Double L system was conducted on the day after Christmas, merely thirty-six days after the recovery of the German mine. The trial was not completely satisfactory, but by the end of January the defects in the system had been corrected. During February 1940, a total of seventy-four sweeps were performed, resulting in the explosion of dozens of magnetic mines and the clearing of numerous fouled areas. Developed in about ninety days, the British Double L method thoroughly defeated the first generation of German magnetic mines.

Parallel with the "sweeping," the British initiated procedures for "degaussing" (neutralizing the magnetic fields) of ships to reduce their vulnerability to both magnetic mines and magnetic pistols in torpedoes. At first this was done by clamping a big, permanent, heavy electrical cable around the ship's hull and continuously energizing the cable with shipboard DC current. Later it was discovered that the same effect could be achieved by laying the energized cables on the ship's deck, or—better yet—placing them in steel tubes inside the ship's hull. Still later, it was discovered that a ship could be satisfactorily degaussed for about three months by passing a very powerful charged electric cable along the length of the hull while the ship was still in port. Although this degaussing technique (called "wiping") was temporary, it was preferred to all others because the permanent cables on shipboard were a nuisance.

• **RADAR.** The main British radar R&D was aimed at improving the reliability and accuracy of the extensive Chain Home network to give early warning of *Luftwaffe* bombers. However, work continued on miniaturized radar sets, which could be fitted in aircraft and small surface ships, such as convoy escorts. By the close of 1939, an Air Ministry research team, led by Edward G. ("Taffy") Bowen, had made some progress toward miniaturized radar for aircraft (the ASV for U-boat detection and A-I for night bomber interception), but field tests of these laboratory-built sets merely served to emphasize that a scientific breakthrough of some kind was required.

The Air Ministry's Robert Watson-Watt, who was supervising all British radar development, concluded that because of limitations imposed by the basic laws of physics, the avenues of miniaturization being pursued by Bowen's team and others would never bear practical fruit. He therefore recommended that a separate group of scientists tackle the problem independently of Bowen, with the aim of finding a solution along theretofore untried avenues. For this purpose, Watson-Watt created a new committee, chaired by the scientist Fredrick Brundrett. Seeking a fresh research team, Brundrett gave the task to the physics department at the University of Birmingham, headed by the Australian—and Cambridge graduate—Mark Oliphant.

Oliphant, with a senior assistant, John Randall, and a graduate student, Henry Boot, approached the assignment with a sense of urgency. Simply stated, the aim was to invent from scratch an entirely new "electronic valve" that was capable of generating high-frequency radio waves with sufficient power to find objects as small as bombers and submarines. That is, a powerful electronic "booster" of a new kind which could sharply focus radio waves.

The initial research of Randall and Boot led them to some obscure scientific papers published by an American physicist, Albert W. Hull. While working at the General Electric Research Laboratory in Schenectady, New York, to develop an alternative to the radio vacuum tube in the 1920s and 1930s, Hull had invented what he called the magnetron, in which the flow of electrons was controlled magnetically, rather than electrostatically. For various reasons, General Electric did not pursue the magnetron commercially, but Hull continued to work on the physics of it for the next ten years, publishing several papers that were of no interest to anyone outside of the tiny handful of specialists in that arcane science.

The magnetron per se was not the answer Randall and Boot sought, but a cursory study of Hull's papers led to an idea that was to make the practical miniaturization of radar possible and open the way to its installation on aircraft and ships.

The idea, called a "cavity magnetron," is quite simple to a scientist but difficult for the layman to understand. Radar historian David Fisher explained it this way:

The basic concept of the magnetron is to use a magnetic field to herd the electrons along, to guide them where you want them to go. Randall and Boot combined this with a totally different concept—the concept of a penny whistle.

A whistle consists of a loose, hard object in a cavity into which you blow. The force of your blowing makes the object inside rattle around in the cavity, generating sound waves which reverberate inside and then escape. The frequency with which they bounce around inside governs the frequency of the sound emitted, and that frequency is in turn decided by the dimensions of the cavity, so that a large whistle emits a long-wave, low-pitched hoot while a tiny whistle gives out a high-pitched scream. Ergo, the cavity magnetron.

Randall and Boot constructed a small solid block of copper, which would conduct their variable magnetic field. In this they carefully scooped out a precisely measured cavity. When an electric current was made to flow through the copper and a magnetic field was applied, electrons were caught in the cavity—which served as an anode—and were made to bounce around in there by the magnetic field. As they bounced back and forth, resonating, they emitted electromagnetic waves just as the bouncing ball in a whistle emits sound waves. The size of the cavity was constructed so that the electrons moved only a few centimeters between bounces and therefore produced electromagnetic waves just a few centimeters long. It was brilliant and it worked.

Randall and Boot conducted the first test of the cavity magnetron on February 21, 1940. Having no idea what the power output would be, they hooked it up to a set of automobile headlights, hoping they might at least get a dim illumination. Such was the power output, it blew out the headlights and then the bigger headlights of a truck. Finally, they wired it up to a set of neon floodlights. These held, enabling Randall and Boot to measure the wavelength and power output. As expected, the wavelength was 9.8 centimeters (usually described as "ten centimeters"); the power output of this experimental little gadget was an awesome 400 watts, or nearly half a kilowatt, four times the power output of the existing airborne radar sets. Moreover, it was an easy step to increase the power a hundredfold. A prototype, generating 50 kilowatts, picked up the *periscope* of a submerged submarine at a range of more than seven miles!

The cavity magnetron, which made possible practical radar miniaturization, was one of the greatest scientific breakthroughs of World War II—*the* greatest in general utility. The British author Brian Johnson aptly wrote in 1978: "It is impossible to exaggerate the importance of Randall and Boot's work. It lifted radar from an electronic stone age to the present day."

• **CODEBREAKING.**   The German Enigma encoding machine, employed by all military and paramilitary organizations in the Third Reich, was conceived by a Dutchman, Hugo Alexander Koch, in the years immediately following World War I. The patents for it were acquired by a German engineer, Arthur Scherbius, who attempted, unsuccessfully, to market it in the 1920s. Subsequently, two German firms (Heimsoth & Rinke and Konski & Kroger) obtained the rights and marketed the machine for commercial use (cost: $144 plus postage). By 1930 military codebreakers of all major nations had acquired the "commercial" version of Enigma for study. All professional codebreakers understood Enigma's basic principles.

The Enigma was a small, portable, battery-operated machine about the size of a typewriter. It was compactly housed in a varnished oak box with a hinged lid. It looked something like a typewriter. It had a three-tiered typewriter keyboard of twenty-six letters—but no numerals or punctuation marks. In place of the platen and typewriter keys, there was a flat panel with the twenty-six letters of the alphabet repeated in the same order. Each of the letters on the panel had a tiny light bulb behind it. To encode a message, the sender pecked out the message, one letter at a time, on the keyboard. The machine automatically scrambled—or enciphered—that letter into another that appeared, lighted up, on the panel. In a reverse process, the receiver, operating an identical Enigma, pecked out the encoded message on his keyboard, one letter at a time, and the deciphered letters lit up on the panel.

The scrambling—or encoding—mechanisms inside the machine were fiendishly clever. The basic idea was to route the electrical impulses from the keyboard to the light panel by as devious and complicated a route as possible. The heart of the mixing system was a row of three turning drums or rotors, about three inches in diameter. Each rotor was fitted on both sides with twenty-six electrical contact points, which interconnected with the other rotors by means of spring-loaded and flush contact points. When the operator struck a letter on the keyboard, the first, or right-hand, rotor revolved one notch (or 1/26th of a revolution), like an automobile odometer. With this movement the setup of the contact points with the other rotors completely changed, routing the electrical impulse on entirely new entry and exit paths. The second letter struck moved the first rotor another notch (or 1/26th of a revolution), creating yet another entry and exit path for the impulses. After twenty-six letters had been struck, the second, or middle, rotor clicked in, extending the process with its twenty-six contact points. Then, finally, the third, or left-hand, rotor with its twenty-six contact points clicked in. Altogether the three rotors had 17,576 positions (26 x 26 x 26). Another complicated feature, known as a "reflector," bounced all the electrical impulses back through the maze of rotor contact points, further scrambling them (in effect, creating the equivalent of six rotors) before they lit up the letter bulbs.

Nor was that all. The rotors were removable. They could be rearranged on the shaft or axle in six different combinations (1-2-3, 1-3-2, 2-3-1, etc.). These variables increased the possible rotor positions to 105,456 (17,576 x 6). Moreover, the rotors were fitted with ratchets on the outer rims, so that they could be set individually to start revolving from any one of the twenty-six different positions. The twenty-six optional rim-settings for each rotor, multiplied by the total 105,456 possible rotor positions, increased the possible electrical contact points available to astronomical levels.

Encoding and decoding messages on identical Enigmas was a fairly simple process for the operators, but it had to be done exactly according to a prearranged and distributed menu, which established what came to be called the "keys." First, both sender and receiver had to insert the three rotors on the axles in the identical left-to-right order (1-2-3 or 1-3-2, etc.). Second, both had to set the rotors to identical rim numbers. Third, both had to turn the three rotors until identical letters embossed on the outer faces of the rotor appeared in tiny peepholes above the rotors.

Assuming all three steps had been done correctly on identically wired Enigmas according to the prearranged "keys," the encoder and decoder were then ready to communicate.

Sitting before his typewriter keyboard, the sender commenced the automatic encoding process. As he pecked out the letters of the message, one at a time, the electrical impulses traveled through the maze of circuits, switches, and contact points, automatically scrambling or encoding the letters and lighting the bulbs behind the encoded letters on the panel. ("A" might light up as "R," for example.) An assistant copied down the encoded letters as they lit up on the panel. When the message was completely encoded, the sender gave it to a radio operator, who telegraphed it to the receiver in five-letter groups. In a reverse process, the receiver typed out the encoded message, one letter at a time on his keyboard. The machine automatically unscrambled the encoded letters, one at a time, lighting up letters on his panel in plain text. (The encoded "R" in the example would light up on the receiving machine as an "A.")

Cryptologists quite rightly believed at first that messages properly encrypted by Enigma were unbreakable. The total of the permutations offered as a result of the many variables was mind-boggling: six thousand trillion by one calculation. Such huge possibilities ruled out known codebreaking techniques, such as statistical analysis (e.g., letter frequency), and appeared to defy solutions by higher mathematics. Possession of an Enigma wired exactly like that of the enemy was only half the battle. One also had to know the three easily changeable "keys": left-to-right rotor order, rotor-rim settings, and rotor-peephole settings.

The German military was enchanted with Enigma. It was compact, easy to operate, rugged, cheap, and seemingly foolproof. Even if the enemy captured an Enigma, it would not do great harm; the keys could be changed at will. Accordingly, it was adopted by the *Reichsmarine* in 1926 and the *Reichswehr* in 1929. To increase its security beyond the "commercial" Enigma available to all, the Germans altered the wiring of the "military" version and added yet another layer of encryption: a "plugboard" on the front below the keyboard. This consisted of twenty-six holes, lettered A to Z (or, alternately, 1 to 26). When one (or more) combination of these letters was paired by cables, plugged in like an old-fashioned telephone switchboard, it rerouted the electrical impulses through yet another maze, raising encryption possibilities to figures almost beyond mathematical reckoning. To break this military version thus required knowledge not only of the three rotor keys but also of the plugboard cable arrangement.

Enigma was wondrously flexible. It enabled various Third Reich organizations to establish individual and completely different encoding setups. This was achieved in a simple way by distributing different rotor and plugboard keys (to be in force for a specific and limited time) or, in a more complicated way, by altering the internal wiring schemes, or by adding one or more rotors. Thus it was to transpire that the Enigma of the *Reichsmarine* and *Reichswehr* and the *Luftwaffe* evolved along different paths and none could read the other's transmissions without obtaining identically wired machines and the keys.

A team of Polish codebreakers, led by Marian Rejewski and including Jerzy

Rózycki and Henryk Zygalski, commenced an attack on German military Enigma in December 1932. Their tools were not inconsiderable: a "commercial" Enigma, acquired earlier; espionage materials (old keys, plugboard settings, etc.), obtained from a money-hungry German traitor, Hans-Thilo Schmidt (codenamed "Asche"), cultivated and exploited by the chief of the French codebreakers, Gustave Bertrand; and a wealth of Enigma messages intercepted by Polish stations.

The Poles were soon thoroughly familiar with German procedure for transmitting Enigma. They noted with special interest one procedural feature. After having set the four keys of their Enigmas according to the predistributed menu, the sender and receiver then engaged in yet another procedural step designed to enhance Enigma security. The sender embedded at the head of the message a three-letter encrypted key, selected at random, for that message only and repeated it twice to be certain the receiver got it, even in poor radio-transmission conditions.

The Germans believed that by instructing the sender to choose the three-letter message key at random, another level of security had been added to Enigma. But they were wrong. German Enigma operators were human and therefore predictable. At first all too many operators lazily—and predictably—chose *AAA* or *ABC* or a three-letter diagonal on the Enigma keyboard, such as *QSC* or *ESY*. Moreover, the standing instructions to repeat the message key (to insure reception in poor conditions) revealed to codebreakers vital information: the first and fourth, second and fifth, and third and sixth letters at the head of every message (the message key repeated) would always be identical. This known constant, together with the fact that no encrypted Enigma letter ever replicated itself ("R" never lit up as "R"), made Enigma vulnerable to penetration by certain very complicated higher mathematical processes.

Enigma was also vulnerable in another way. German military traffic was rigid and stylized, composed of military addresses, titles, salutations, and words often repeated. A close student of these messages could sometimes correctly guess a word or a phrase ("division," "regiment," "operation," or "nothing to report"). Correct guesses from these official messages, or from idle "test" chitchat between operators, or from lapses were known in the codebreaking trade as "cribs." In the early days, before the Germans became skilled at communications security, Enigma yielded numerous cribs.

Astonishingly, the Polish team broke German Enigma in a few weeks and were able to duplicate the machines without ever having seen the German version. Although the Germans tightened security procedures and made refinements to Enigma, for the next six years—to 1938—the Poles broke German Enigma at will and read it consistently and currently. To simplify and speed up the breaks, they developed a "cyclometer" (two sets of Enigma rotors, linked in a certain way) and an immense card file, listing possible keys and other data. In a two-week "test" in January 1938, the ten-man Polish team decoded 75 percent of German Enigma messages received and calculated that with more personnel it might have decoded 90 percent.

During the Munich Crisis of September 1938, and again in December 1938, the Germans delivered the Polish team two stunning setbacks. On September 15, the Germans abolished the procedure of distributing preset peephole settings for starting the message transmissions. Instead, Enigma operators were instructed to choose any three letters at random for the initial peephole settings and to transmit these unenciphered, or in the clear, to the receiver before transmitting the enciphered and repeated three-letter settings for the message itself. Beyond that, on December 15, the Germans distributed two additional rotors to all Enigma operators, making a total of five rotors from which to select three for insertion in the machine. The change in peephole-setting procedure—the random selection of the start position—rendered all the decoding work of the Poles to that time useless. The addition of two more rotors raised the encription possibilities, mathematically, to yet more mind-boggling levels.

The Poles were dismayed, but not discouraged. To attack the increased complexities introduced by the procedural change, they conceived two techniques. One, offered by Rejewski, was an ingenious automated machine, a sort of supercyclometer, which the Poles called a "bomba."* Its heart was comprised of three linked rotor sets from six Enigmas (eighteen rotors). When prompted in a certain way, the machine "tried out" various combinations of encrypted letters until the embedded message code was found. A total of six bombas (108 rotors) was required to conduct a full range of searching. The other technique, offered by Rejewski's associate Zygalski, made use of large, perforated, heavy paper sheets with horizontal and vertical columns of letters, which when laid one atop the other on a light table in a certain way revealed the message keys by admitting light through the holes. Each sheet had about 1,000 holes. A total of 156 separate sheets (six series of twenty-six sheets), comprising about 156,000 holes, each hand-cut with a razor blade, was required for a full range of search on a three-rotor Enigma.

The addition of the two extra rotors in December 1938 posed even greater problems for the Poles. First they had to figure out the wiring arrangement of each of the new rotors. They were able to do so because of another careless communication lapse on the part of the Germans. The Nazi S.S. and S.D. nets adopted the five-rotor option but, inexplicably and foolishly, retained the old system of predistributed initial peephole settings, which the Poles had mastered earlier. By exploiting that lapse and by intuition, the Poles, in yet another astounding cryptanalysis achievement, were able to replicate the wiring of the new rotors. By January 1, 1939, the Poles could read five-rotor S.S. and S.D. traffic accurately and consistently.

However, the solving of the five-rotor military Enigma employing random initial peephole settings, as well as random-encrypted peephole settings for individual messages, defeated the Poles. Rejewski calculated that to search by automated means, each of the six bombas in operation would have to be fitted with thirty-six of the two new rotors (for a grand total of 1,080 rotors) and be operated twenty-

---

* The origin of the name *bomba* is obscure. Some Poles say it was adopted because the idea for the machine occurred when Rejewski was eating an ice cream dessert: *bomba* loosely translates as ice cream. Others say it was adopted because the machine made a noise somewhat like the ticking of a bomb.

four hours a day. Alternately, the laborious perforated-sheet method would require 1,560 different sheets (sixty series of twenty-six sheets) with a grand total of 1,560,000 hand-cut holes. It could be done, of course, but the Poles lacked the resources for so massive an undertaking.

That was where matters stood in August 1939, a few days before the outbreak of war, when the Poles turned over to the British and French copies of all their research materials and the Polish-built German military Enigmas.

The British codebreaking unit, GCHQ, located at Bletchley Park, was directed and staffed by many veterans of the Admiralty's famous Room 40 of World War I. These included the director, Alastair Denniston, his deputy Edward Travis, and the codebreakers A. Dillwyn Knox, William F. Clarke, and others. All were quite familiar with Enigma principles—the British had bought a "commercial" Enigma in the 1920s—but they had made only cursory attempts to break German Enigma and had had no success. The Polish "gift" was therefore immensely valuable and saved the British many months of tedious work.

Before the war, GCHQ had recruited and vetted a "reserve" force, drawing heavily on academics at Cambridge and Oxford universities. When war came, the reserve was called up to Bletchley Park and divided between the codebreaking and the specialized army, air force, and naval sections, which were located in temporary one-story outbuildings misnamed "huts." Among the first call-ups were three brilliant Cambridge mathematicians: Gordon Welchman, Alan Turing, and John R. F. Jeffreys.

These three mathematicians were assigned different tasks. Alan Turing, who was fascinated by machines, set about designing a bomba which was to be more powerful and "general" in nature than the Polish one and theoretically capable of coping with whatever new complexities the Germans might add to Enigma. John Jeffreys was put in charge of manufacturing the huge numbers of perforated sheets required to solve five-rotor Enigma. Gordon Welchman was directed to study German call signs and to identify various Enigma nets.

The intellectual challenge presented by Enigma enthralled Gordon Welchman. Although GCHQ was strictly compartmentalized for security reasons, Welchman refused to be limited to a study of call signs. In a flash of brilliance, entirely on his own, he reinvented the perforated-sheet method and presented it to Dillwyn Knox, only to learn that it was already being vigorously pursued. Again straying from his limited area, Welchman offered a suggestion for Turing's bomba. This idea, as Turing's biographer put it, was so "spectacular" that Turing was "incredulous." Incorporated into Turing's design, the suggestion gave Turing's proposed machine "an almost uncanny elegance and power."

By December 1939, Jeffreys and his aides had completed two sets of perforated sheets, each set containing about one and a half million punched holes. One set was sent to Paris for the French and Polish codebreakers. Employing the British-made sheets, the Poles found the daily keys of a five-rotor Enigma net for October 28 and broke the net (called "Green" by the Allies) messages for that day only. This was the first Allied break into the five-rotor Enigma. The excitement that ensued was tempered by the fear that on January 1, 1940, the Germans would make changes in the keys or procedures, which would negate this achievement.

But the Germans made no changes on January 1. As a result, the codebreakers at Bletchley Park, employing the sheet-stacking method, broke into the *Luftwaffe* Enigma net (called "Red" by the Allies) of January 6. This was the first "all-British" codebreaking triumph over the Germans. Owing to the generally lax Enigma procedure and communications security in the *Luftwaffe,* which yielded cribs, and to cribs intuitively arrived at, thereafter British codebreakers read the *Luftwaffe* Red with fair reliability. The British also sporadically broke into the *Wehrmacht* Green and a *Luftwaffe* training code, Blue, and some other German nets that still employed three-rotor Enigma.

From January 1940 onward, the British at Bletchley Park played the dominant role in breaking Enigma. The Poles and French continued to make contributions, but the importance of their work diminished. Pending the building of the Turing bomba, incorporating Welchman's "spectacular" improvement, the British relied on the sheet-stacking method. It was a tedious and work-intensive process, requiring ever greater numbers of clerks. Nor was it a sure thing. Often as not, the British failed to recover the daily keys.

No progress whatsoever was made in breaking *Kriegsmarine* traffic. Naval Enigma employed eight rotors rather than the five rotors of *Luftwaffe* and *Wehrmacht* Enigma, ruling out the sheet-stacking method. There was scant traffic to intercept—too little grist for the codebreakers' mill. *Kriegsmarine* radio operators continued to exercise strict transmission discipline, offering no cribs. Attempts to break naval Enigma before Turing's bomba was completed were bound to fail. And so they did.

To the technical achievements at Bletchley Park must be added another, no less important. That was the superb management of the information flow. The leaders centralized the gathering, storage, and distribution of all codebreaking intelligence, however trivial. They barred the "interservice rivalry," the jealous withholding of bits and pieces to favor one military service or the other. All hands shared equally in all phases of the operation, from translators to analysts to librarians in the hugely growing data bank to the distributors of the information. And, moreover, they did so without a single leak, so far as was known in 1996.

ATLANTIC OPERATIONS: JANUARY AND FEBRUARY 1940

The winter of 1939–1940 was the coldest in forty years. In early January the Baltic Sea, the Kiel Canal, the Elbe River, and the Jade froze solid. The bitter cold and the thick ice drastically impeded U-boat construction, repairs, training, and movements. The Germans pressed every spare surface vessel into service to break ice, including the old battleship *Schleswig-Holstein,* and fitted the U-boats with wooden casings to protect the bow torpedo doors. But numerous U-boats incurred ice damage and some were locked fast to Baltic piers, unable to move.

To escape the ice, Dönitz was compelled to forward base the U-boats at the island of Helgoland, in the warmer, ice-free North Sea. German submariners passionately hated this bleak, desolate, windswept, bitterly cold outpost. All facilities for men and ships were primitive. It was difficult to get fuel oil and spare parts through the ice to the island. British submarines prowled the nearby ice-free areas designated for sea trials and training. RAF bombers made occasional raids.

In January 1940, five boats sailed from Helgoland for torpedo patrols in the Atlantic. These included the cranky and clumsy Type I, *U-25,* which had twice aborted in December; two new VIIBs, *U-51* and *U-55;* and two Type IXs, the veteran *U-41* and a new one, *U-44.* These boats carried submarine torpedoes in which no one had the slightest confidence. Dönitz summarized the torpedo situation in his war diary:

> The fact that its main weapon, the torpedo, has to a large extent, proved useless in operations has been the greatest difficulty with which the U-boat arm has had to contend since the beginning of the war and it has had a most serious effect on results. At least 25 percent of all shots fired have been torpedo failures. According to statistics covering all shots up to 6 January, 40.9 percent of unsuccessful shots were torpedo failures. . . . The commanding officers' and crews' confidence in the torpedo is very much shaken. Again and again the boats have tried in the face of strong enemy activity to fire their torpedoes under the best possible conditions and often when they have made a daring attack they have been rewarded with failures and even danger to themselves. . . . It is very bitter for commanding officers and the executive control to find that the U-boat arm cannot achieve the success expected of it, in spite of thorough peacetime training, because of torpedo failures. I will continue to do all I can to keep up the fighting spirits of the U-boats in the face of all the setbacks.

However, there was then reason for optimism. Raeder had sacked the hidebound chief of the Torpedo Directorate, Oskar Wehr, and appointed a new chief, Oskar Kummetz, and had named the scientist Dr. E. A. Cornelius "Torpedo Dictator." Kummetz was a contemporary of Dönitz's and an officer of "great energy." The new men, Dönitz believed, were "unprejudiced" and both brought fresh, inquiring minds to bear on the technical problems. After merely a few days on the job, Kummetz had telephoned Dönitz to say that he and Cornelius had conducted new tests, which had proved beyond doubt that the torpedoes were defective in several ways. This was an impressive bureaucratic victory for Dönitz, but the task of correcting the defects remained.

Because of the cold, the ice, and other factors, crews of the two new VIIBs, *U-51* and *U-55,* embarking on maiden war patrols, were not fully trained. Dönitz therefore directed both skippers to patrol in low-intensity ASW areas west of Ireland, to gain further experience before attacking enemy shipping. But neither skipper was keen on conducting a training patrol.

On the day he reached the Atlantic, Dietrich Knorr, age twenty-seven, commanding *U-51,* took the boat straight into action. He sank a 1,600-ton Swedish freighter, then went directly to the Western Approaches, where he sank a 1,500-ton

Norwegian freighter, from which he rescued two survivors. But *U-51* developed a problem in her bow torpedo tubes and Knorr was forced to abort and return to Germany.

The brand-new *U-55,* commanded by Werner Heidel, age thirty, who had done well in the duck *U-7,* also went directly into action. Rounding the British Isles, Heidel sank two small neutrals (a Dane and a Swede), then proceeded to the Western Approaches. On the tenth day of the patrol, January 29, Dönitz alerted Heidel to a convoy, which had been detected by *B-dienst.* Heidel responded by sinking the 5,000-ton British tanker *Vaclite* and a 5,000-ton Greek freighter.

One of the convoy escorts, the sloop *Fowey,* left the convoy and pursued *U-55* in foggy seas. Fixing the boat on sonar, *Fowey* attacked with depth charges, driving Heidel to 328 feet. *Fowey* dropped five charges, three set for 500 feet by mistake, two for 350 feet. The two set at 350 feet exploded very close to *U-55,* causing severe flooding and panic. Heidel temporarily contained the damage and panic and slipped away, but *Fowey* continued to hunt aggressively through the fog and called for help. Two British destroyers, *Whitshed* and *Ardent,* and a French destroyer, *Valmy,* responded, as did a four-engine Sunderland flying boat of Coastal Command Squadron 228, piloted by Edward J. Brooks.

The four ships and the aircraft hunted the damaged *U-55* relentlessly. *Whitshed* got sonar contact and attacked with depth charges. By that time the *U-55* crew could no longer contain the flooding. Believing he might escape in the fog, Heidel gave orders to surface and man the deck gun. *Fowey* sighted *U-55* making off in the fog and opened fire. *Valmy* and the Sunderland joined. The Sunderland dropped a bomb and, helpfully, a smoke float and then made a strafing run. Heidel returned the fire—until the breechblock of the gun jammed.

Gunless, unable to dive, Heidel was left no choice but to scuttle. The first watch officer and chief engineer volunteered to help Heidel open the vents. When the boat started under for the last time, there was no sign of Heidel. The survivors believed he chose to go down with the boat. The other forty-one men of the crew launched a rubber life raft, jumped into the icy water, and were picked up by *Fowey* and *Whitshed.*

The loss of *U-55* was known immediately to Dönitz. Eager to give a lift to the Coastal Command aviators who had patrolled the seas endlessly for months with no confirmed success, the RAF publicly claimed credit for the kill on January 31. The surface forces grudgingly conceded that the Sunderland may have helped—but not all that much. However, a British assessment committee gave Coastal Command partial credit for the kill along with *Fowey* and *Whitshed.* Doubtless some fault for the loss lay in Dönitz's decision to send *U-55* against an escorted convoy before she was adequately trained.

The three large boats, *U-25, U-41,* and *U-44,* were directed to patrol off the Iberian Peninsula. Arrangements had been made for any or all of these boats to secretly refuel and replenish from a German ship, *Thalia,* which had been left in the Spanish port of Cadiz for that purpose.

The clumsy and cranky *U-25* and the brand-new Type IX *U-44* led the way. En route, both boats found good hunting in the Shetlands area. Viktor Schütze in *U-25* sank three freighters (one Swede, one Norwegian, and one British) for 13,000 tons. While passing southbound through the Western Approaches, Ludwig Mathes, age thirty-one, commanding *U-44,* also sank three freighters (one Norwegian, one Greek, and one Dutch) for 14,000 tons.

After reaching the Iberian Peninsula, Mathes came across several convoys. Operating alone and shooting torpedoes that worked to perfection, in a period of ten days Mathes sank five more ships (two French, two Greek, and one Danish) for 15,500 tons. Distrustful of the proposed secret refueling in Cadiz, Mathes exercised a skipper's option and returned to Germany, where he was showered with ecstatic praise. Overcrediting him by 8,000 tons and perhaps forgetting that Hartmann in *U-37* had also sunk eight ships in one patrol (for greater tonnage), Dönitz declared the *U-44* patrol to have been "perfectly executed" and the "most successful" to date against merchant shipping.

Passing southbound through the Western Approaches, Viktor Schütze in *U-25* sank his fourth ship. Since the OKM was anxious to test the secret Cadiz base and *U-44* had declined the opportunity, Dönitz directed Schütze to refuel from *Thalia.* Schütze sneaked *U-25* into Cadiz on the night of January 30, took on food, oil, and other supplies, and returned immediately to sea. There Schütze promptly sank his fifth ship, a 6,800-ton British freighter.

At that time, ten German merchant ships in Vigo, Spain, were preparing to run through the British blockade to Germany. In order to provide them some protection, the OKM directed Dönitz to assign *U-25* as an escort. Dönitz protested. Submarines were useless in an escort role. They could not keep up submerged; while traveling on the surface they were highly vulnerable to air attack. Nonetheless the OKM insisted. However, owing to yet another mechanical breakdown, Schütze had to abort the patrol and was thus unable to comply with the order. Limping home, in the Shetlands he sank his sixth ship, the 5,200-ton Danish tanker *Chastine Maersk,* giving him a grand total of 27,335 tons, a remarkable achievement for this unsafe and unreliable boat.

The OKM insisted that Dönitz provide the German ships in Vigo an escort. Accordingly, Dönitz assigned the chore to the other Type IX, *U-41,* commanded by Gustav-Adolf Mügler, making his second Atlantic patrol. While en route to Vigo, Mügler ran into a convoy in the Western Approaches. Pausing to attack, Mügler severely damaged the 8,000-ton Dutch tanker *Ceronia* and sank the 9,875-ton British freighter *Beaverburn.* The lone convoy escort, the destroyer *Antelope,* pounced on *U-41,* fixed her on sonar, and dropped depth charges. Nothing more was ever heard from *U-41.* She was the fourth of the eight Type IXs of the Hundius Flotilla to be lost, the third to be sunk by depth-charge attack.

Dönitz planned four minelaying missions for January, but only two Type VIIs, *U-31* (Habekost) and *U-34* (Rollmann), were seaworthy. As a result, one mission was scrubbed and another was assigned to the leading torpedo shooter, Herbert Schultze in the VIIB *U-48.* The three boats were to lay eight new, powerful TMC mines and carry six torpedoes. Neither Rollmann nor Schultze had laid a minefield; Habekost had laid the field in Loch Ewe that had damaged the battleship *Nelson,* a success still unknown to the Germans.

The two Type VIIs sailed first. On the way, Rollmann in *U-34* attacked a 15,000-ton armed merchant ship with torpedoes, but they missed or malfunctioned. He then laid his mines in Falmouth. Habekost in *U-31* returned to the dangerous waters of Loch Ewe. Either these two fields comprising sixteen mines were mislaid or the mines malfunctioned. They produced one sinking: the 7,800-ton British tanker *Caroni River* in Rollmann's field at Falmouth.

After laying these fields, both boats patrolled the Western Approaches with torpedoes. Rollmann sank a 5,600-ton Greek freighter, but Habekost experienced repeated torpedo failures and sank nothing. Homebound, Habekost came upon two British battleships and a heavy cruiser, but he was out of torpedoes.

Sailing on the last day of January, Herbert Schultze in *U-48* was assigned to lay his mines in the dangerous waters off the British naval base at Portland, in the English Channel. Schultze believed he laid all eight TMC mines in the correct place, but they produced no sinkings. He withdrew to the Western Approaches to hunt ships with his six torpedoes and promptly sank a 6,900-ton Dutch freighter.

Five boats sailed from Helgoland in February to conduct torpedo patrols in the Atlantic. These were the clumsy and cranky Type I, *U-26,* three Type VIIBs, and the now-famous Type IX, *U-37,* still commanded by the Hundius Flotilla chief Werner Hartmann, who preferred the sea, however cold and miserable, to a desk and who hungered to sink ships and win a *Ritterkreuz.*

Before going on to regular patrolling, Hartmann had to carry out a dangerous special mission. The task was to land in Ireland two *Abwehr* agents* who were to intensify anti-British sentiments. While passing outbound in the Orkneys and Shetlands, Hartmann got the patrol off to a promising start by sinking two ships (one British, one Norwegian) for 5,700 tons. Continuing south, on the night of February 8, he eased *U-37* into Dingle Bay on the southwest coast of Ireland and put the two agents ashore. But all for naught. Within a few days, intelligence or police officers detected and arrested both agents.

That done, Hartmann received orders from Dönitz to carry out another special mission. *B-dienst* had developed information that the carrier *Ark Royal* and battle cruiser *Renown* were en route from the south Atlantic to Portsmouth, England, escorting the cruiser *Exeter,* which had been damaged in an engagement with the "pocket" battleship *Admiral Graf Spee.*† The OKM directed Dönitz to lay a submarine trap at the west end of the English Channel, using *U-37* and Herbert Schultze's *U-48* and any and all other available boats.

Hartmann moved into a likely interception position, but Schultze ran across an outbound convoy and chased it 350 miles to the west. The chase netted Schultze three ships for 24,700 tons, including a 9,000-ton Dutch tanker, *Den Haag,* and the 12,300-ton British refrigerator ship *Sultan Star,* but he had no torpedoes left and he

---

*   Ernst Weber-Drohl, a sixty-one-year-old former acrobat, and Wilhelm Preetz, a former ship's steward.

†   Which took refuge in Montevideo, Uruguay, and was scuttled on December 17.

had no desire to return to the submarine trap merely to serve as a lookout for Hart-mann. When Schultze returned to Germany, Dönitz first berated him for going too far west and leaving the trap, then praised him to high heavens. Schultze had not only planted a TMC minefield, but also had sunk four ships for 31,526 tons, raising his total confirmed score to sixteen ships for 109,200 tons. Schultze thus became the first skipper to sink 100,000 tons of enemy shipping. That feat earned him the coveted *Ritterkreuz*—the second such award after Prien's.

The *U-26*, commanded by a new skipper, Heinz Scheringer, age thirty-two, from the duck *U-13*, attempted to join Hartmann in the submarine trap, but he was slowed by heavy seas and arrived too late. Neither *U-37* nor *U-26* found the task force. After being released from the trap, both boats sank two ships in the Western Approaches, then proceeded to their original destination off the Iberian Peninsula. Hartmann arrived there, but the *U-26* incurred a mechanical breakdown and Scheringer was forced to abort. On the way home he sank a third ship, bringing his total to three ships for 10,500 tons.

The three VIIBs sailed from Helgoland last. Two of these, *U-50* and *U-54*, were brand-new boats, rushed into service undertrained. The *U-50*, commanded by Max-Hermann Bauer, age twenty-seven, son of the famous World War I sub-mariner and historian Hermann Bauer, from the duck *U-18*, was compelled by an oil leak to abort in the North Sea, but resailed a few days later. The *U-54*, com-manded by Günter Kutschmann, age twenty-nine, disappeared without trace. It is thought that shortly after leaving Helgoland Kutschmann strayed off course and hit a German or a British mine in Helgoland Bight.* The *U-53*, commanded by a new skipper, Harald Grosse, age thirty-three (replacing Heinicke), was delayed by a leaky conning-tower hatch.

Bauer's *U-50* and Grosse's *U-53* finally proceeded to the Atlantic. Rounding the British Isles, Bauer sank a 1,900-ton Swede in the Orkneys, then a 5,000-ton Dutch vessel west of Ireland. At about the same time, northwest of Scotland, Grosse sank four ships (two Swedes, a Norwegian and a Dane) for 11,500 tons and believed he had sunk a fifth, the 8,000-ton British tanker *Imperial Transport,* but she limped into port. Eager to restore *U-53*'s lost honor, Grosse broke radio silence to boast that he had sunk five ships for 30,000 tons. Then both he and Bauer con-tinued south to the Iberian Peninsula by independent routes.

By mid-February Dönitz believed that six boats were near or in "southern" waters. This number of boats offered another opportunity to attempt a pack attack on a convoy that *B-dienst* had reported. He therefore directed the senior captain, Hartmann in *U-37*, to assume tactical command. But unknown to either Dönitz or Hartmann, two boats had been lost (*U-41* and *U-54*) and one (*U-26*) had aborted, leaving only three in those waters: Hartmann's *U-37*, Bauer's *U-50*, and Grosse's *U-53*.

In an almost exact replication of the first wolf pack, which had been reduced from six boats to three, two of the three boats found the convoy and mounted a

---

* Dönitz wrongly believed *U-54* had reached the Atlantic and that she was sunk by the French destroyer *Simoun.*

loosely coordinated attack. Hartmann in *U-37* sank three freighters (one Greek, one French, one British) for 16,000 tons; Grosse shot at a French tanker, but his torpedoes prematured. By mistake, Grosse sank a prohibited neutral not in the convoy, the 2,140-ton Spanish freighter *Banderas,* unwisely sailing blacked out. Having expended all torpedoes, Hartmann in *U-37* and Grosse in *U-53* headed home.

Bauer in *U-50* did not find the convoy. However, while patrolling alone off Lisbon, he found another. He sank two ships—a Dutch freighter and the 4,600-ton tanker *British Endeavor*—and pursued, but during the chase one of his diesels broke down. Unable to make repairs at sea, Bauer was forced to abort and head home in the wakes of *U-37* and *U-53.*

While these three boats were inbound, news of the sinking of the prohibited Spanish vessel reached Berlin and Dönitz. The Spanish professed to be furious. The sinking strained relations between Berlin and Madrid and jeopardized future clandestine refueling operations in Spanish ports. In his eagerness to restore *U-53*'s lost honor, ironically Grosse had again besmirched the boat.

The *U-53* did not have to answer for this latest sin. In the early hours of February 24, while rounding the British Isles, she was lost. A lone British destroyer, *Gurkha,* picked her up in the moonlight shortly after midnight. *Gurkha* immediately turned to ram, but *U-53,* which was on an opposite course inside *Gurkha*'s turning circle, dived. *Gurkha* threw over a depth charge "to keep her down," then obtained a "good" sonar contact and prepared for a proper attack. *Gurkha* made three passes over *U-53,* dropping thirteen depth charges set at 150 and 250 feet. While reloading for a fourth pass, *Gurkha* noted that the sonar echo "gradually faded away and was never heard again." The *U-53* disappeared without trace in water 1,800 feet deep. She was the fourth of the VIIBs of the Wegener Flotilla to fall and the third to leave no survivors. The loss of sister ships *U-53, U-54,* and *U-55* within a period of four weeks—two on maiden patrols and all commanded by skippers making first patrols in VIIBs—did not go unremarked.

Werner Hartmann in *U-37* again came home to rave reviews. He had successfully landed two agents in Ireland, dutifully set up the futile submarine trap for *Ark Royal,* and duplicated his score on his prior patrol by sinking eight ships (including a trawler) for a total of sixteen. This tied Herbert Schultze's record for numbers of ships sunk, but not tonnage. Hartmann claimed 43,000 tons for this patrol, giving him 78,300 tons, but the true figure for the patrol was 24,539 tons, reducing his (confirmed) total to about 60,000 tons. Accepting Hartmann's claims ("80,000 tons in two patrols"), Admiral Raeder sent him and his crew a telegram of congratulations.

Bauer in *U-50* also received rave reviews for his maiden—but aborted—first patrol. He claimed sinking six ships for 36,000 tons. He either greatly exaggerated the tonnage or had torpedo failures. His confirmed sinkings were four ships for 16,000 tons.

Dönitz mounted four minelaying missions in February, all by Type VIIs of the Salzwedel Flotilla, finally out of the shipyards. Günter Kuhnke in *U-28* laid eight TMC mines off the British naval base at Portsmouth and afterward sank two ships by torpedo (one Dutch and one Greek) for 11,200 tons. Otto Schuhart in *U-29,* granted a "second chance," laid twelve TMBs in Bristol Channel and claimed sinking three British ships for 25,000 tons by torpedo on the way home. (Only two ships for 9,800 tons were confirmed in the postwar records.) This was success enough not only to warrant retaining his command but also to draw praise from the OKM. The *U-32,* with a new skipper, Hans Jenisch, age twenty-six (replacing Hans Büchel), who had sunk seven ships for 8,400 tons, including the destroyer *Exmouth* while commanding *U-22,* planted twelve TMBs in Liverpool. On the way to and from Liverpool, Jenisch attacked three ships, firing seven torpedoes. Five torpedoes malfunctioned and two missed, but he sank a 2,800-ton Swede with his deck gun.

These three minefields, planted at great risk, produced scant returns. Kuhnke's TMCs off Portsmouth resulted in no sinkings.* Schuhart's TMBs in Bristol Channel bagged only a small (710-ton) coaster, which should not have triggered a mine. Jenisch's TMBs at Liverpool sank the only important ship: the 5,000-ton British freighter *Counsellor.*

The fourth—and riskiest—mine mission was assigned to von Dresky's *U-33.* He was to plant eight TMC mines at the British naval base in the Firth of Clyde, where Büchel in *U-32* had failed earlier. Von Dresky nosed submerged into the Firth of Clyde in the early hours of February 12. Moments later, an ASW patrol boat, the minesweeper *Gleaner,* detected *U-33* by hydrophone. Seeing *Gleaner's* searchlight sweeping the water, von Dresky mistook her for a heavy cruiser. Believing the "cruiser" might pass out to sea, he laid *U-33* on the bottom at 183 feet to wait. *Gleaner* fixed *U-33* on sonar and dropped six depth charges set for 150 feet, four of which exploded directly over *U-33,* pounding the boat and causing severe leaking.

The attack caught von Dresky by complete surprise. Believing the attacker to be a destroyer, his men urged him to get *U-33* off the bottom and evade to sea, but von Dresky appeared to be paralyzed. Another five charges from *Gleaner,* which exploded close and increased the flooding, brought him to life. Believing the boat to be doomed, he ordered his men to surface, scuttle, and abandon ship. Since *U-33* carried an Enigma† and could be salvaged, he distributed the Enigma rotors among the officers, instructing them to swim well away from the boat and discard them.

When *U-33* surfaced, *Gleaner* spotted her at once, opened fire with her 4" gun, and turned to ram. However, when *Gleaner's* captain saw the *U-33* crew come on deck, arms raised in surrender, he checked fire after five rounds and lay to alongside *U-33.* Meanwhile, von Dresky ordered the engineer to set in motion the scuttling procedures. The first attempt failed but the second succeeded—trapping the engineer below. The *U-33* plunged down by the bow, and the crew jumped into the frigid water. Von Dresky exhorted the men to keep together. Many, including von

---

* A total of five TMC fields, comprising forty mines, were laid by *U-28, U-31, U-32, U-34,* and *U-48.* Only one sinking—by *U-34's* field at Falmouth—resulted. The mines were mislaid or planted too deep, or the pistols were faulty.

† The OKM had forbidden minelayers to carry Enigma. Why one was on board *U-33* is not known.

Dresky, died quickly of shock, exposure, or hypothermia. From a total crew of forty-two, only seventeen men, including three officers, lived to become POWs. The British recovered three Enigma rotors from the officers of *U-33*. These were helpful to the codebreakers at Bletchley Park but not sufficiently so to penetrate naval Enigma.

Dönitz knew at once that *U-33* was lost and the minelaying at the Firth of Clyde had failed for the second time. His source was *B-dienst,* which, remarkably, intercepted three signals from *Gleaner.* The first was an alarm at 0525, reporting *U-33* to be on the surface; the second, at 0530, was a notice stating that the *U-33* crew was surrendering; and the third, at 0545, was a request for assistance in rescuing the crew.

Counting the seven mining missions, Dönitz had mounted eighteen patrols to the Atlantic in the months of January and February, 1940. Five of the eighteen boats had been lost (*U-33, U-41, U-53, U-54, U-55*). Three (*U-25, U-50, U-51*) had aborted with mechanical defects. Yet in spite of torpedo and mine problems and unfavorable weather conditions, the eighteen boats had sunk by torpedo or mine fifty-eight ships for 233,496 tons, almost all of them sailing alone. This was an average of 3.2 ships sunk per boat per patrol, a significant improvement over the averages for the earlier months. On March 1, the six leading skippers in tonnage sunk were Schultze, Prien, Hartmann, Schuhart, Rollmann, and Lemp.

When the surviving February boats returned from the Atlantic, Dönitz had galvanizing news. Hitler had ordered the military conquest of Norway (and Denmark), to take place anytime after March 10. All available U-boats, including ducks, were to participate. Commencing March 1, the U-boat war against shipping in the Atlantic was suspended indefinitely.

The withdrawal of the Atlantic U-boats for operations in Norway provides a convenient milepost for assessing the results of the U-boat campaign in the first seven months of the war, to April 1, 1940. That assessment can best be made by a careful study of a host of statistics that challenge some and exasperate others, then as now. In brief:

• All U-boats (oceangoing and ducks) in all areas sank by torpedo, gun, mine, and demolition a total of 277 ships for about 974,000 tons, including twenty-six trawlers, almost all of them sailing alone or out of convoy.* In addition, the oceangoing boats captured four prizes. The North Sea ducks sank 41 percent of all the ships (113) and about 25 percent of the tonnage (238,000).

• Of the 277 ships sunk, 118 (43 percent) were British, including the twenty-six trawlers. The loss of ninety-two British ships other than trawlers in seven months amounted to about 3 percent of the 3,000 vessels of the oceangoing British merchant fleet. In the same seven months, the British captured, bought, or chartered ninety-two ships from foreign sources, offsetting the British losses to U-

---

* Owing to the acute shortage of escorts, and other factors, on February 12, the Admiralty discontinued "Fast" Halifax convoys (HX-F) and standardized the speed of Halifax convoys at 9 knots.

boats. Moreover, in the same period, British shipyards produced about 700,000 tons of new shipping, much of it for the merchant marine. Thus, in the first seven months of war, the British merchant marine *grew,* rather than shrank.

• Of the 277 ships sunk by U-boats, surprisingly few were tankers: only twenty-three of about 170,000 tons. Of these, fourteen for about 100,000 tons were British-owned. The other nine were French, Norwegian, Danish, Swedish, or Dutch. The British tanker losses were more than offset by captures or seizures, by new construction, and by purchase and charter of foreign vessels. Thus there was a net *gain* in the British-controlled tanker fleet.*

• Notwithstanding the growth of the merchant fleet in these seven months, British imports fell 25 percent, from a rate of about 60 million tons a year to about 45 million tons a year. The drop was caused by convoying. It was not a drop of one-third, as Churchill predicted it would be, but about one-quarter. The drop was inconvenient and led to belt-tightening and scattered deprivation, but it was nowhere near a threat to Britain's survival.

• In the same seven months, U-boat losses were heavy, a total of seventeen (30 percent of the force) to all causes: four ducks, eight VIIs and five IXs, manned by about 650 submariners. The loss of oceangoing boats was offset in part by new construction: eight boats, of which four were VIIs and four were IXs. Thus the total number of oceangoing U-boats of the Atlantic force decreased from twenty-seven to twenty-two, of which two, *U-25* and *U-26,* were marginal and several others were out of action for extended repairs. The addition of the marginal Turkish boat, *U-A,* raised the Atlantic force to twenty-three oceangoing boats by the end of March 1940.

To this point in the U-boat war, both London and Berlin claimed "victory." However, the figures suggest something like a draw. In any case, the U-boats had yet to pose a serious threat to British maritime assets. The real U-boat peril—if it ever fully materialized—lay not in the summer of 1940 as Churchill projected but in the far distant future, 1942 and beyond. Moreover, contrary to Churchill's assertions, U-boat crews had not waged war barbarically or murderously or with callous disregard for the safety of enemy mariners. For the most part, the Germans had conducted submarine warfare in a fair—and at times even chivalrous—manner. As Dönitz was to stress again and again, he ran "a clean firm" and he intended it to stay that way.

One important factor in this naval war was the increasingly anti-German, pro-British attitude of President Roosevelt. It was he who had engineered the relaxation of the Neutrality Act, which enabled American firms to sell arms to the British and French. He had also turned a blind eye to the transfer of American tankers to "Panamanian" registry, so that they could transport oil directly into the declared war zones. In addition, Roosevelt had masterminded the "Declaration of Panama" (October 2, 1939), a conference at which twenty-one American republics (not including Argentina) established a Western Hemisphere "Security Zone" that barred belligerents from "conducting warlike operations." Moreover, Roosevelt

---

* See Appendix 17.

had directed the U.S. Navy to put in place a "Neutrality Patrol" to enforce the declaration. Not least, Roosevelt, anticipating the forthcoming need for merchant shipping, had again urged Jerry Land at the Maritime Commission to increase significantly America's cargo and tanker shipbuilding capacity.

THE U-BOAT FAILURE IN NORWAY

Winston Churchill urged the Allied governments to occupy Norway to shut off the wintertime flow of Swedish iron ore from Narvik to Germany, to gain air and naval bases to attack Germany and bottle up the *Kriegsmarine* in the North Sea, and to deny this strategic area to Germany and/or the Soviet Union. After March 12, when the gallant Finns were finally crushed by Soviet forces, Neville Chamberlain and the new French Prime Minister, Paul Reynaud, approved a plan to occupy Norway, and by way of preparation, the Royal Navy's Home Fleet returned to Scapa Flow.

By that time Hitler had completed *his* plan for the occupation of Norway. It was daring and intricate. Small groups of airborne and seaborne shock troops were to simultaneously seize five key Norwegian seaports in a surprise assault. The *Kriegsmarine* was to play the major role in the campaign. Its ships were to dash out under cover of darkness, deliver the seaborne troops, then dash back to Germany before the superior Home Fleet or the RAF had time to react.

The Germans were aware of the Allied plans to occupy Norway and therefore realized they were engaged in a race. But owing to the heavy ice in the Baltic Sea, and Raeder's insistence that the operation be carried out when the moon was "new" (or dimmest) and to other factors, D day had to be put off to April 9. Meanwhile, to thwart an Allied occupation of Norway before the Germans could get there, Hitler directed the *Luftwaffe* to mount an all-out attack on the Home Fleet at Scapa Flow and the U-boat arm to patrol the North Sea, both offensively and defensively, concentrating its power against Allied warships and troopships.

This was the first time in history that an entire submarine force (however small) had been called upon to participate in a major military campaign involving close cooperation with air, sea, and ground forces. It was to be a radical—and risky—change in roles. Theretofore U-boats for the most part had patrolled alone in distant, deep, open seas with a fair degree of freedom, attacking mostly lone merchant ships with stealth and surprise and evading escorts and U-boat killers. During the Norway operation, they were to operate under very tight control in the confined waters of the North and Norwegian seas, aswarm with enemy aircraft and submarines, attacking Allied warships and troopships, which were certain to be on fullest alert for U-boats.

First and above all else, the U-boat arm had to thwart an Allied amphibious invasion of Norway. Receiving *B-dienst* intercepts indicating that such an invasion was imminent, on March 11 the OKM directed Dönitz to immediately deploy ten oceangoing boats off Norway and twelve ducks in the lower North Sea to repel the supposed invasion.

In the early stages of this deployment, two of the ten oceangoing boats were lost. On March 11, an RAF Blenheim bomber spotted the Type VII *U-31*, commanded by Johannes Habekost, on the surface, in home waters, near Wilhelmshaven. Skillfully using cloud cover, pilot Miles Villiers Delap eased in over *U-31* and dropped four improved 250-pound bombs. The *U-31* blew up and sank instantly in 102 feet of water, killing her entire crew as well as ten diesel-engine specialists and shipyard workers. She was the first U-boat to be sunk by an aircraft, but she was raised and salvaged. About two days later, probably on March 13, the outbound Type IX *U-44*, commanded by the promising new skipper, Ludwig Mathes, struck a mine in the Helgoland Bight and also went down instantly with all hands. Dönitz substituted another boat for *U-31*, but he was unaware of the loss of *U-44* for many days.

The ten oceangoing boats were directed to patrol defensively off three major Norwegian ports:

Narvik, 1,000 miles distant. Four Type VIIBs were sent there: *U-46* (Sohler), from retraining in torpedo shooting; *U-47* (Prien), from ninety days in refit; *U-49* (von Gossler), from ninety days of battle-damage repair; and *U-51* (Knorr), which had made one prior (aborted) patrol to the Atlantic in January.

Trondheim, 750 miles distant. Two Type VIIs were sent there: *U-30* (Lemp) and *U-34* (Rollmann), both from refit following Atlantic minelaying missions.

Bergen, 450 miles distant. Four boats were sent there: one Type VIIB, the *U-52,* commanded by Otto Salmann, which had been sabotaged in December and, except for a brief, barren patrol in September under another skipper, had not seen any action, and three Type IXs: *U-38* (Liebe), which had made a long, interesting but largely fruitless patrol to Murmansk; *U-43* (Ambrosius), from ninety days of battle-damage repairs; and *U-44* (Mathes), which, unknown to Dönitz, was already lost.

While these boats were moving into position, on the night of March 16 the *Luftwaffe* struck Scapa Flow. The raid was carried out by twenty-nine JU-88s and HE-111s, many dropping huge (2,200-pound) bombs. The *Luftwaffe* pilots reported great success: two direct hits on a battleship, one hit on another battleship or battle cruiser, one hit on a battle cruiser, one hit on a heavy cruiser, and near hits on other battleships. In fact, only the cruiser *Norfolk* was damaged.

Believing that all these supposedly damaged capital ships would limp to home ports for repairs, or that the entire Home Fleet might again abandon Scapa Flow, the OKM ordered Dönitz to form an "attack group" of oceangoing boats to intercept them. Accordingly, Dönitz diverted five such boats bound for Norway (including the lost *U-44*) to positions west of the Orkneys. The other five boats continued to Norway.

To avoid another *Luftwaffe* attack, the Home Fleet did in fact leave Scapa Flow on March 19. At dawn that day, Prien in *U-47* spotted three battleships, escorted by destroyers. Prien was submerged; the battleships were about five miles off, running at high speed. Since the ships were beyond torpedo range, there was nothing Prien could do. Owing to the heavy enemy air patrols in the Orkneys, he could not surface to report until dark. No other U-boats of the attack group saw these ships.

Dönitz held the attack group in the Orkneys for about ten days. Two of the four boats found targets. Liebe in *U-38* sank three Danish ships for 10,300 tons; Prien in *U-47* sank a Dane for 1,146 tons. All the boats encountered foul weather and intense ASW measures—air patrols and destroyer hunter-killer groups. For the second time *U-47* was depth charged, but she incurred no serious damage.

Believing the attack group was a "waste of time," Dönitz urged the OKM to replace it with ducks. The OKM agreed to that but insisted that some oceangoing boats remain in the Orkneys area until the ducks arrived. Accordingly, Dönitz reshuffled the oceangoing boats. He recalled (the lost) *U-44* (Mathes), *U-47* (Prien), and *U-49* (von Gossler) to Wilhelmshaven to replenish for Norway, left *U-38* (Liebe) and *U-43* (Ambrosius) in place, and brought *U-52* (Salmann) from Bergen. Liebe sank a Norwegian freighter, but neither *U-43* or *U-52* found targets. When the ducks arrived on about April 1, Dönitz recalled these three oceangoing boats to Wilhelmshaven.

The four boats assigned to patrol defensively off Norway were restricted to sinking enemy warships, submarines, and troopships. Off Trondheim, Lemp in *U-30* found and attacked a British submarine, but his torpedoes missed or malfunctioned. None of the other boats found any permissible targets. Dönitz left *U-46* (Sohler) and *U-51* (Knorr) off Norway but recalled *U-30* and *U-34* for replenishment. The *U-46* remained at Narvik; the *U-51* went south to replace *U-30* and *U-34* at Trondheim. Inbound, *U-30* (Lemp) rescued a *Luftwaffe* air crew that had ditched. The two recalled boats were hurriedly made ready to help repel the invasion.

Fourteen ducks deployed into the North Sea in March. Two of these, replacing the oceangoing attack group in the Orkneys, found targets. Joachim Schepke in *U-19* sank four small Danish freighters for 5,500 tons. Claus Korth in *U-57* sank two ships for 7,000 tons, including the 5,700-ton British tanker *Daghestan,* which had been damaged by the *Luftwaffe.* No other ducks sank ships. Two ducks were lost: *U-21,* commanded by Wolf Stiebler, which ran aground off Norway and was later salvaged, and *U-22,* commanded by Karl-Heinrich Jenisch, which disappeared off northeast Scotland with the loss of all hands, probably the victim of a British mine. The twelve surviving ducks returned to Germany to prepare for the invasion.

In total, twenty-four U-boats had deployed in March to thwart the supposed Allied invasion. But it was all a waste of time. For various political and military reasons, the Allies had also been forced to postpone Norway operations. Liebe, Prien, Schepke, and Korth had sunk twelve small freighters for 28,000 tons. Against that inconsequential score, four boats had been lost: the oceangoing *U-31* (salvaged) and *U-44,* and two ducks, *U-21* (salvaged) and *U-22.* The crews of the other twenty boats, poised for the greatest challenge the U-boat arm had yet faced, were exhausted from these nerve-racking patrols, but they had no time to rest and recuperate.

On the eve of the German invasion of Norway, April 1, the U-boat arm had shrunk to forty-eight commissioned boats, nine fewer than the day the war began. Dönitz deployed thirty-two of the forty-eight for the invasion: fourteen of the twenty-two oceangoing boats and eighteen of the twenty-six ducks. At the insistence of the OKM, two of the fourteen oceangoing boats first had to carry out special missions: temporary escort service for the outbound merchant-ship "raiders," *Atlantis* and *Orion.** The other twelve oceangoing boats, including the VIIBs *U-46* and *U-52,* still on patrol, were assigned to waiting positions in the most distant waters, north of Bergen. The eighteen ducks were assigned to waiting positions south of Bergen and in the lower North Sea.

The Germans invaded Norway and Denmark on the morning of April 9. By nightfall, German forces held all the key cities in both nations. Outwitted, the Allies were shocked by the swiftness and efficiency of the operation. They hastily geared up for air, sea, and land counterattacks in Norway.

The *Kriegsmarine* incurred grievous losses. British naval forces trapped ten fleet destroyers at Narvik. Norwegian shore batteries sank the heavy cruiser *Blücher* at Oslo. British aircraft, flying from the Orkneys, sank the light cruiser *Königsberg* at Bergen. A British submarine, *Truant,* fatally holed the light cruiser *Karlsruhe* at Kristiansand. British submarines and the Polish submarine *Orzel* sank six or more merchant ships in the supply train. British and/or Norwegian forces slightly damaged the *Gneisenau* and *Scharnhorst,* the "pocket" battleship *Deutschland* (renamed *Lützow*), the new heavy cruiser *Hipper,* the light cruiser *Emden,* and an old training cruiser, *Bremse.*

The gravest setback for the Germans on D day occurred in Narvik, where British naval forces trapped the ten fleet destroyers. A picture-postcard town nestled at the foot of majestic snow-covered mountains, Narvik is about 120 miles north of the Arctic Circle on the latitude of northernmost Alaska, yet owing to the warm sea wash from the Gulf Stream, it is ice-free year around. To mariners it is both spellbinding and challenging. To reach it they must transit nearly sixty miles of twisting narrow fjords, first Vest, then Ofot, mindful of the 11½-foot tidal changes that occur four times daily, creating swift, swirling currents.

Dönitz had deployed three oceangoing boats in Vest Fjord, the outer approach to Narvik: Sohler's *U-46,* Knorr's *U-51,* and the unsteady, big *U-25* (Schütze). The VIIBs *U-46* and *U-51* had been on patrol since March 11, almost a full month. Both boats were low on fuel; the crews were tired and tense. The *U-25* was fresh from Germany.

Narvik was a difficult area for submarines. The Arctic "nights" in April were only four or five hours long. To remain concealed, the boats had to run submerged for nineteen or twenty hours a day. This prolonged submergence badly fouled the

---

*   These ships were the first of many German merchant raiders to sail. Each was powerfully armed with six 5.9″ guns and four to six torpedo tubes, and each carried a supply of magnetic mines. Their mission was similar to that of *Admiral Graf Spee:* to raid enemy shipping in the South Atlantic, drawing off warships of the Royal Navy. The Type IX *U-37* escorted *Atlantis;* the first of the new Type IXBs, *U-64,* escorted *Orion.*

interior air, made breathing difficult, dulled alertness, and drained the storage batteries. The "nights" were barely long enough to fully charge the batteries. To do so the boats either had to make a long, time-consuming, and risky run to open water, hide in a snowstorm or fog, or creep into small, uncharted fjords branching off the main fjords. The water in the fjords was shallow in places and there was little room to evade and escape a depth-charge attack.

On D day the Admiralty ordered five destroyers to investigate rumors of a German landing at Narvik. Patrolling the outer Vest Fjord, Knorr in *U-51* saw the inbound destroyers. He mounted two separate attacks, but scored no hits. Later he surfaced and flashed a warning report intended for the German destroyers in Narvik, but his message was ambiguous and when the British destroyers reached Narvik, the Germans were not prepared. In the savage battle that ensued, the British destroyers sank two German destroyers and severely damaged four others; the Germans rallied to sink two British destroyers and damage a third.

The three U-boats in Vest Fjord were waiting to intercept the three withdrawing British destroyers. The *U-46* (Sohler) did not see them but *U-25* (Schütze) and *U-51* (Knorr) did, and each attacked with electric torpedoes with magnetic pistols. But something went drastically wrong. Schütze, who fired two torpedoes, reported no observed results. Knorr, who fired four torpedoes at close range, reported two premature explosions and two misses.

Fearing a disastrous reversal at Narvik, Hitler directed every available oceangoing U-boat to converge there, both to repel follow-up Royal Navy attacks and to transport supplies to the 2,000 German shock troops that had landed there. In response, Dönitz ordered six more oceangoing boats to Narvik, including the *Atlantis* escort, *U-37*. However, owing to a shortage of lube oil, Hartmann in *U-37* could not comply. Upon learning that, Dönitz directed Hartmann to substitute for *U-64*, which was escorting *Orion*, and although the brand-new *U-64* was merely a few days into its first patrol, he sent it to Narvik in place of *U-37*, along with her equally green sister ship, *U-65*. At the same time, Dönitz directed four boats in German ports to load army supplies and take them to Narvik: *U-26* (Scheringer), *U-29* (Schuhart), *U-43* (Ambrosius), and the duck *U-61* (Oesten). These orders committed twelve oceangoing boats to Narvik: nine in attack roles, three in supply roles.

Rushing to Narvik on April 11, Herbert Schultze in *U-48* ran across big ships of the Home Fleet that were out looking for *Gneisenau* and *Scharnhorst:* three battleships, several heavy cruisers, a light cruiser and five destroyers. He boldly mounted two separate submerged attacks against three heavy cruisers, firing a total of six torpedoes with magnetic pistols. Four of the six torpedoes prematured; none hit. Later Schultze surfaced to report the task force and the torpedo failures.

Dönitz was gravely concerned. Three boats (*U-25, U-48, U-51*) had shot a total of twelve torpedoes, and six to eight torpedoes had prematured or malfunctioned, a failure rate of 50 to 66 percent. What was causing this latest torpedo calamity? The weakening of the earth's magnetic field in extreme northern latitudes? The iron content in the Norwegian mountains? Something else?

The new chief of the Torpedo Directorate, Oskar Kummetz, was away on detached duty, commanding the Oslo invasion forces. In his absence, Dönitz conferred by telephone with the "Torpedo Dictator," Dr. Cornelius, and other technicians. They expressed doubt that the earth's magnetic field or the iron ore in Norwegian soil could be causing the failures, but they could offer no help or advice.

What to do? Dönitz believed that he should order all boats to deactivate magnetic pistols and rely only on impact (or contact) pistols. However, owing to the deep-running defect (not yet fixed), this order would rule out shooting at shallow-draft ships, such as destroyers, an unthinkable restriction. It was finally decided—and ordered—that boats operating north of 62 degrees latitude were to adopt a mixture of magnetic and impact pistols. They were to load the four forward tubes with three torpedoes fitted with impact pistols and one with a magnetic pistol. When shooting at deep-draft ships (cruisers and larger), only contact pistols were to be used. When shooting at shallow-draft ships (destroyers, etc.), two torpedoes were to be fired, one with an impact pistol and the other with a magnetic pistol. To avoid the possibility that a premature in the magnetic pistol might detonate the torpedo with the contact pistol, an interval of eight seconds between torpedoes was to be observed.

By April 12, there were nine oceangoing attack boats in or converging on Narvik. These included four big, unwieldy boats, entirely unsuitable for these confined waters: the Type I *U-25*, the Type IX *U-38*, and two brand-new Type IXBs, *U-64* and *U-65*. Some of these boats refueled from the disabled German destroyers or merchant ships at Narvik. Even though operating in very shallow and dangerous waters, all boats carried Enigmas with naval rotors in order to keep in touch with Dönitz and one another.

There were two important Enigma messages from Dönitz that day. The first contained the new—and very complicated—orders for torpedo shooting: impact pistols only against large ships, a combination of impact and magnetic pistols against destroyers. The second message ordered a redeployment. Based on *B-dienst* intercepts, an Allied landing was expected at the next large fjord to the north, Vaags. Four of the nine Atlantic boats assigned to Narvik—*U-38* (Liebe), *U-47* (Prien), *U-49* (von Gossler), and the IXB *U-65*—were to shift north to Vaags Fjord to interdict the landing. The five boats left at Narvik were positioned as follows: *U-25* (Schütze) and *U-51* (Knorr) in the outer Vest Fjord; *U-46* (Sohler), *U-48* (Schultze), and IXB *U-64* in the inner Ofot Fjord.

To soften up Narvik for the Allied landing and to wipe out the remaining German destroyers, on the morning of April 13 the Admiralty sent the old but modernized battleship *Warspite* and nine destroyers into Vest and Ofot fjords.

En route to Vaags Fjord, the new *U-65*, commanded by Hans-Gerrit von Stockhausen, age thirty-two, ran across this task force, which was reported as "ten destroyers." Although *U-65* had not completed her workups and torpedo practices, and had been at sea merely five days on her first war patrol, von Stockhausen unhesitatingly attacked two destroyers. As prescribed, he fired two torpedoes (one magnetic pistol, one contact pistol) spaced at eight-second intervals at each destroyer. The destroyers pounced on *U-65*, hurling depth charges, which damaged the boat. In the noise, von Stockhausen was not able to tell if his torpedoes hit or not. None did.

Unharmed, the British task force entered Vest Fjord, where the *U-25* (Schütze) and *U-51* (Knorr) patrolled. Schütze in *U-25* saw the task force coming in and closed to attack. Like von Stockhausen, he chose two near destroyers for his targets, firing the prescribed mixture of torpedoes with magnetic and contact pistols. Nothing happened. No hits. As the British task force nosed deeper into the fjords, the commander catapulted an aged Swordfish floatplane from *Warspite* to scout ahead. The air crew radioed back valuable information on German destroyer dispositions. Then, astonishingly, the airmen reported a U-boat on the surface at anchor in the north end of Herjangs Fjord, a tributary of Ofot Fjord, close to the town of Narvik.

This was the other newly arrived IXB, *U-64*, commanded by Georg-Wilhelm Schulz, age thirty-four, from the duck *U-10*. Commissioned in December 1939, the *U-64* had been icebound at a pier in Kiel and, like her sister ship *U-65*, had not completed workup. Schulz, like Prien, was a onetime merchant marine captain and a crack seaman, but the Swordfish caught Schulz unalert and unprepared.

The Swordfish dived at *U-64* and dropped two 100-pound ASW bombs. One hit *U-64*'s bow, opening a great gash in the hull. *U-64* sank almost instantly in 114 feet of water—the second U-boat (after *U-31*) to be sunk by an aircraft. Unassisted by surface ships, Schulz and about a dozen others who were topside floundered into the icy water. Another thirty-odd men got out of the sunken boat using the often rehearsed escape procedures. German soldiers putting out from shore in small boats rescued the shocked and freezing survivors, all of whom eventually returned to Germany by train and ship. Eight men of *U-64* died in the sinking.

The battleship *Warspite* and nine destroyers reached Ofot Fjord in the early afternoon of April 13, supported by ten Swordfish from the carrier *Furious,* standing well offshore. Warned by the Swordfish that had sunk *U-64* to expect other U-boats, the destroyers were on full alert and itching for kills.

Yet another close and savage naval battle erupted in the tight confines of Ofot Fjord that afternoon. The powerful British force confronting eight German destroyers in various stages of readiness inflicted a perfect slaughter, sinking all. Outmanned and outgunned, the Germans fought valiantly to the bitter end. They severely damaged three British destroyers but the three escaped to fight again.

Two VIIBs patrolled inside Ofot Fjord that afternoon: *U-46* (Sohler) and *U-48* (Schultze). With nine destroyers in the narrow fjords and what appeared to be an endless stream of aircraft overhead, it was a nightmarish time. Sohler in *U-46* maneuvered beneath the destroyer screen and set up on *Warspite*. As he was ready to shoot, the boat hit and rode up on an uncharted rock, exposing the entire length of the bow. Fortunately for Sohler and his men, all the British ships were intent on sinking the German destroyers and did not see this mishap. Later in the day, however, the destroyers found and depth charged *U-46* so severely that Sohler believed the boat could not survive and he ordered that the Enigma and all secret papers be destroyed. Schultze in *U-48* surfaced to exchange information with what he believed to be a German destroyer but which turned out to be British. He crash-dived to escape, but the destroyer pounded *U-48* with thirteen depth charges, all close. In the narrow fjord the explosions seemed to be magnified; they were deafening and nerve-shattering, but not fatal.

The *U-48* closed on *Warspite* and at point-blank range shot a full bow salvo—three torpedoes with impact pistols, one with a magnetic pistol. Nothing happened. Schultze then mounted attacks on two destroyers. No hits. A crewman in *U-48*, Horst Hofman, remembered these times as "unmitigated hell." He went on:

> Every day and every hour of every day we were attacking destroyers or finding ourselves trapped in the destroyers' clutches. Day in, day out, night after night . . . we scurried up and down and round and round the fjord, submerged. And the nights were short, far too short to allow us to charge our batteries and to maintain the boat ready for action. Sleep was out of the question—we hardly found time to get something to eat. . . . We used up the air in our oxygen flasks to the very last drop. . . . One after another we fired all our magnetic [sic] torpedoes. Not one of them exploded. . . . Try as we would all our efforts remained completely fruitless. . . .

The British force withdrew through Vest Fjord, where *U-25* (Schütze) and *U-51* (Knorr) were patrolling. Schütze got in two attacks, one on *Warspite,* one on a destroyer. Nothing happened. There were no hits in either attack.

At the Admiralty, First Lord Churchill urged that the Allied invasion force land directly at shattered Narvik on the evening of April 13. But as *B-dienst* had learned, the British Army commander preferred an indirect attack, to be staged from Vaags Fjord, the next inlet north of Narvik.

On the morning of April 15, the main British assault force for Narvik approached Vaags Fjord. That morning four boats were off Vaags Fjord: *U-38* (Liebe), *U-47* (Prien), *U-49* (von Gossler), and *U-65* (von Stockhausen). Liebe, Prien, and von Gossler had not yet fired any torpedoes.

The Type IX boats, *U-38* and the damaged, green *U-65,* positioned at the entrance to the fjord, got in the first licks. Liebe in *U-38* boldly attacked the battleship *Valiant* and the cruiser *Southampton.* Not one of Liebe's torpedoes hit. Next in line, von Stockhausen in *U-65,* attacked a big Polish liner, *Batory,* which had been pressed into service as a troopship. No hits.

Two VIIBs, *U-47* (Prien) and *U-49* (von Gossler), were inside Vaags Fjord, submerged. Earlier in the day some Norwegians had seen *U-49* on the surface just north of the island of Andorja and reported the sighting to the British. When the convoy entered Vaags Fjord, the British sent two destroyers, *Fearless* and *Brazen,* directly to the reported position of *U-49. Fearless* got a good sonar contact and attacked, dropping five depth charges set for 150, 250, and 350 feet. One charge exploded close to the conning tower, causing the boat to "leap." The lights went out; the boat began to flood. One other charge exploded close on the stern.

The previous November *U-49* had sustained one of the worst depth-charge attacks of the war and escaped. Perhaps the memories of that terrible experience still haunted her captain. According to a British after-action report, von Gossler "seemed to have lost his head." He apparently panicked and blew ballast tanks. Almost instantly after the first salvo of depth charges, the *U-49* popped to the surface, close to *Fearless* and *Brazen*. German crewmen ran on deck apparently to man the gun, but *Fearless* and *Brazen* discouraged this by firing a "few rounds," one of which hit the conning tower. Von Gossler gave orders to scuttle and all of *U-49*'s crew except von Gossler and a petty officer leaped into the calm but frigid water, "screaming wildly and crying for help," the British reported.

Still on the bridge of the scuttled boat, von Gossler and the petty officer were feverishly stuffing confidential papers into a bag. Seeing this, *Fearless* opened fire with machine guns, driving both Germans into the water, where they lost the bag, which had not yet been weighted. By then, both *Fearless* and *Brazen* had launched boats to fish out the survivors. British sailors in one of the boats grabbed the bag before it sank. Others pulled forty-one of forty-two survivors from the water, including one wounded, then finally the body of one man who had been killed by gunfire. The bag contained German secret grid charts showing the deployment of the U-boats assigned to Norway and other documents, but to the great disappointment of the naval codebreakers at Bletchley Park, who were still struggling fruitlessly with naval Enigma, there was nothing in the bag to help them.

Prien in *U-47* was nearby in Vaags Fjord when *U-49* was sunk. Recently Dönitz had notified him that his wife had had a second daughter.* Probing the waterways that evening, he ventured stealthily into a tributary, Bygden Fjord, leading to the town of Elvenes, the objective of the main British ground forces. There he saw a heart-stopping sight: "Three large transports, each of 30,000 tons and three more, slightly smaller, escorted by two cruisers." All eight ships were lying at anchor in the narrow south end of Bygden Fjord, disembarking troops into fishing boats. The ships, Prien logged, were "just clear of each other and in some cases, slightly overlapping."

Here was an opportunity for Prien to eclipse his triumph at Scapa Flow: sink in a single blow at least 150,000 tons of enemy shipping, including two heavy cruisers, and thwart the British counterattack on Narvik. He and his first watch officer, Engelbert Endrass, huddled to plan the attack with exacting care. They decided to fire four bow torpedoes (as prescribed by Dönitz, three with impact pistols, one with a magnetic pistol) from a submerged position at four different ships, reload the forward tubes during the ensuing chaos, surface so they could escape at maximum speed, then fire the four bow tubes again at the other four ships.

---

* Dönitz playfully radioed: "*Ein U-boot ohne sohgrohrist heute angekomman.*" Roughly, "A submarine without a periscope arrived today."

At 2242 Prien, manning the periscope, commenced the attack. The stationary enemy ships, he logged, "stretched in a solid wall before me." He fired the four bow torpedoes at eight-second intervals, set to run at twelve and fifteen feet. The chosen targets, left to right, were: cruiser, large transport, large transport, cruiser. The ranges were short: 750 to 1,500 yards. The crew waited tensely, counting off the seconds. But nothing happened. No explosions. The torpedoes had either run under the targets or the pistols had failed. "Result nil," Prien logged bitterly.

Fortunately for Prien, there was no indication that the enemy had been alerted. Therefore a second attack was possible. Prien ordered the four bow tubes reloaded. Per instructions, three torpedoes were fitted with contact pistols, one with a magnetic pistol. Prien, Endrass, and the torpedomen carefully checked all the torpedoes; Prien and Endrass reviewed the firing data. Just after midnight Prien surfaced, prepared to shoot again and run.

In the second attack, Prien shot the four bow tubes at the same stationary targets (cruiser-transport-transport-cruiser) with the same depth settings and at the same ranges. But again there were no results—no hits on the targets. One torpedo swerved off course, struck a distant cliff and exploded. Prien thought that explosion would alert the enemy and bring a counterattack, but there was no reaction.

Prien and his crew were dismayed and outraged. Eight torpedoes (six contact, two magnetic) had failed against sitting ducks. He still had one torpedo in his stern tube and prepared to fire it as they commenced a run on the surface. But this plan could not be carried out. Heading toward Vaags Fjord at full speed, *U-47* ran aground and stuck fast on an uncharted sand bar well within range of the cruisers' guns.

All efforts were then directed toward refloating *U-47*. Prien backed the diesel engines at emergency turns and blew the forward ballast tanks dry. When that failed to get the boat off the bar, he ordered all available men topside to "sally ship." They ran madly back and forth on the deck, rocking the boat. Finally *U-47* broke free. But at that instant, the starboard diesel cracked from the strain of emergency turns. Shifting that shaft to electric power, Prien sent the men below and raced toward Vaags Fjord. When he reached deep water he dived and crept out to sea. Later that night he surfaced and got off a brief report to Dönitz on the torpedo failures and the engine failure. The engine could not be repaired; Prien was compelled to abort the patrol.

Upon receiving Prien's report, Dönitz was also dismayed and outraged. "To have missed these ships, lying motionless and overlapping each other, would have been quite impossible," he wrote. "Either, therefore, the torpedoes must have been [running] at a far greater depth than that anticipated by the technical personnel, or the pistols had failed to function. And so we found ourselves with a torpedo which refused to function in northern waters either with contact or with magnetic pistols. . . . To all intents and purposes, then, the U-boats were without a weapon."

That same day—April 16—Dönitz put through an urgent telephone call to Admiral Raeder. The submarine torpedo situation, Dönitz declaimed, was scandalous.

There could be no question of crew failure. The top aces and *Ritterkreuz* holders, Prien and Schultze, shooting in highly favorable conditions, had been denied major targets (a battleship, heavy cruisers, large transports). The torpedoes obviously did not work at all in northern latitudes and they failed too often in southern latitudes. It was criminal—or worse—to send U-boats to sea with these torpedoes. Emergency measures were required to correct the faults. Raeder hastened to agree. He would again appoint a technical committee to reexamine the torpedoes from top to bottom.

Notwithstanding an order from Hitler to fight to the death for Narvik, Dönitz insisted that all U-boats be withdrawn from Vest, Ofot, and Vaags fjords. Raeder agreed to that as well. Accordingly, that night Dönitz ordered the four Narvik boats to withdraw. *U-46* (Sohler), and *U-51* (Knorr), on patrol since March 11, and *U-48* (Schultze), out of torpedoes, were to return to Germany. The *U-25* (Schütze), which still had ample fuel and torpedoes, was to patrol well offshore. Three boats were to remain off the entrance to Vaags Fjord: *U-38* (Liebe), *U-49* (von Gossler), and *U-65* (von Stockhausen). But unknown to Dönitz, *U-49* was lost, leaving only two boats at Vaags Fjord.

Relying on magnetic pistols, the boats in the Narvik area experienced further torpedo failures on April 18 and 19. Von Stockhausen in *U-65* fired three torpedoes at a light cruiser coming out of Vaags Fjord. The torpedoes prematured after a run of twenty-two seconds. Liebe in *U-38* shot at a light cruiser. No success. Knorr in *U-51* fired at a heavy cruiser. No hits. Homebound, Prien in *U-47* came upon the battleship *Warspite*, escorted by two destroyers. He shot two torpedoes with magnetic pistols at *Warspite* from 900 yards. Neither hit. One exploded at the end of its run, alerting the destroyers, which pounced on *U-47*, Prien logged, "from all directions," creating an "awkward predicament."

Still homebound, April 19, Prien came upon a big convoy composed of ten transports and numerous destroyers. He still had four torpedoes left, but he had so little faith in them that he refused to attack. Later, explaining his refusal, he told Dönitz that he "could hardly be expected to fight with a dummy rifle." Notwithstanding his engine problem, Prien doggedly and expertly shadowed the convoy, radioing position reports. The three boats in the area responded to Prien's signals: *U-25* (Schütze), *U-38* (Liebe), and *U-65* (von Stockhausen). All attacked the convoy in heavy weather. None got a hit. Unable to keep up with only one engine, Prien broke off and headed home, as did Liebe in *U-38*, who was low on lube oil.

These departures left but two boats in far northern waters: *U-25* (Schütze) and *U-65* (von Stockhausen). Believing their remaining torpedoes might function in more southerly latitudes and to remove them from the intense Allied ASW measures in Norway, Dönitz directed both boats to patrol west of the Shetlands and Orkneys. The *U-65* (von Stockhausen) encountered a battleship and heavy cruiser but she was not able to gain a shooting position. The *U-25* (Schütze) found no targets. In due course, both returned to Germany, *U-25* unexpectedly early with yet more mechanical problems. The four U-boats en route to Narvik with supplies were diverted to other Norwegian ports.

The nine attack boats deployed to Narvik had in no way alleviated the crisis. Not one boat sank any enemy ship of any kind. Two of the nine boats (*U-49, U-64*) were lost. The British forces, staging from Vaags Fjord, slogged south in hip-deep snow and, in due course, forced the German troops, reinforced by the *Kriegsmarine* destroyer survivors, out of Narvik; but the victory was only temporary.

Farther south, Allied forces landed north and south of Trondheim, intending to envelop the Germans at Trondheim in a pincer. Dönitz deployed four oceangoing boats to interdict the Allied landings: *U-30* (Lemp) and *U-50* (Bauer) in Namsos Fjord, north of Trondheim; *U-34* (Rollmann) and *U-52* (Salmann) in Romsdals Fjord, south of Trondheim. En route to Namsos Fjord on April 10, Bauer's *U-50* was found and sunk by the British destroyer *Hero,* with the loss of all hands, leaving only Lemp in *U-30* to repel the Allies. All three boats at Namsos and Romsdals fjords found targets and attacked, but ASW measures were intense and the torpedoes malfunctioned. Only one boat got a hit: Rollmann in *U-34,* who torpedoed the beached Norwegian minelayer *Fröya.*

Dönitz ordered two homebound boats, *U-46* (Sohler) and *U-51* (Knorr), to temporarily reinforce the boats at Namsos and Romsdals fjords. Sohler shot at the French super-destroyer *Albatros.* No hits. Knorr attacked a British heavy cruiser. No hits. Rollmann in *U-34* attacked a destroyer and a cruiser. No hits. Upon learning of these torpedo failures, Dönitz withdrew all the boats from the Trondheim area as well, ordering *U-46* and *U-51* home and *U-30, U-34,* and *U-52* to patrol the Orkneys and Shetlands.* There Rollmann intercepted the 20,000-ton ocean liner *Franconia,* but he again experienced torpedo failure.

Thereafter, Dönitz restricted the oceangoing U-boats to resupply missions. The first three supply boats (*U-26, U-29,* and *U-43*), which set out for Narvik, diverted to Trondheim (and the duck *U-61* to Bergen). Three other oceangoing boats rushed aviation gasoline to Trondheim: the U-cruiser *U-A,* the *U-32,* and the brand-new VIIB, *U-101.*† En route, leaking gasoline fumes very nearly incapacitated the crew of *U-32.* As a result, Dönitz canceled plans for any more "gasoline" missions. On the return trip to Germany, *U-26* (Scheringer) torpedoed and sank the 5,200-ton British freighter *Cedarbank,* loaded with supplies for British troops in Romsdals Fjord. *Cedarbank* was the only Allied ship sunk by any of the thirteen‡ oceangoing boats committed to the Norwegian invasion.

Four additional ducks were committed to Norway operations, bringing the total number engaged to twenty-two. Most patrolled in the waters of southern Norway

---

    * On May 3, Lemp in *U-30* aborted his patrol to rescue thirteen survivors of the Swedish neutral *Hagar,* which had hit a British mine. While she was approaching Trondheim, the heavy cruiser *Hipper* mistakenly shelled *U-30.*

    † *U-101* was originally numbered *U-71.* Her number (and those of sister ships) was inflated as part of a German scheme to disguise the glacial U-boat production rate.

    ‡ The other boat in the initial deployment, *U-37* (Hartmann), assigned first to escort *Atlantis,* then *Orion,* did not get into Norway operations. After completing the escort service near the Faeroes and Shetlands, Hartmann missed a British heavy cruiser but sank three ships for 18,715 tons, including the 9,100-ton Swedish tanker *Sveaborg.* The shortage of lube oil forced Hartmann to abort.

or the lower North Sea, but some patrolled off northeast Scotland and the Orkneys. The twenty-two ducks sank three enemy vessels for 8,100 tons. One of these was the 1,100-ton British submarine *Thistle,* sunk with the loss of all hands off Stavanger by *U-4,* commanded by Hans-Peter Hinsch, age twenty-five. *Thistle* was the first Allied submarine confirmed as sunk by a U-boat and the only enemy warship sunk by U-boats during the Norwegian campaign. One duck was lost with all hands: *U-1,* commanded by Jürgen Deecke, age twenty-seven. Initially the kill was credited to the British submarine *Porpoise,* but after further analysis, the Admiralty concluded *U-1* hit a mine.

On April 26, while the land battles still raged near Narvik and Trondheim, the OKM released the U-boat arm from Norway operations owing to the torpedo failures. Including the six supply missions, twenty of the twenty-three commissioned oceangoing boats had participated* and twenty-two of the twenty-six commissioned ducks. The forty-two U-boats sank, in total, eight ships for 32,522 tons in April—over half the tonnage by Hartmann in *U-37,* who was well out of the invasion zones. Against that meager return, another four boats had been lost: two VIIBs, *U-49* and *U-50,* the IXB *U-64,* and the duck *U-1.* Thus the first commitment of an entire submarine force to a major combined air-sea-land operation was an utter failure.

Dönitz and his submariners angrily blamed the U-boat failure on defective torpedoes. They had ample justification to do so, but the furor over the torpedo failures obscured a larger doctrinal point. The role change from merchant-ship killer to warship killer had not worked. Submarines were not very effective against heavily armored and armed warships, escorted by aircraft and sonar-equipped destroyers, primed to expect submarine attacks. This was especially true in the case of submarines operating in confined and shallow waters and in Arctic latitudes in the months when the nights were short. The decision to halt the war on commerce in order to commit the U-boat arm to support the conquest of Norway was thus a mistake, but since it was partially obscured by the torpedo furor, it was not fully grasped in Berlin and it was to be repeated.

---

* The Type VIIs *U-28* and *U-31* were in overhaul, and the Type IXB *U-122,* commissioned March 30, did not sail.

THREE

RETURN TO THE NORTH ATLANTIC

While the fighting in Norway was still in progress, on May 10 Hitler launched the long-postponed offensive against the West. The German blitzkrieg smashed through Belgium and northern France, splitting the Allied ground forces. The Chamberlain government fell; Winston Churchill moved up to the post of Prime Minister. Churchill attempted to reinforce and to rally the dispirited and defeatist French, but it was a lost cause. France was doomed.

Having been badly roughed up in Norway, the *Kriegsmarine* was not in shape to contribute much to the offensive in France. Owing to the loss of five ocean-going U-boats in the Norway operation and the need to refit the others and to give the combat-weary crews a rest, Dönitz deployed none during the early stages of the blitzkrieg. Submarine support was restricted to patrols by eight ducks in the North Sea. Three ducks sank six ships for 17,400 tons, including the French submarine *Doris* and the British destroyer *Grafton*, the latter while evacuating British troops at Dunkirk. The British sloop *Weston* trapped one duck, *U-13*, commanded by Max Schulte, age twenty-four, forced it to scuttle, and captured its crew.*

---

* The British salvaged *U-13* and recovered a set of "standing orders" issued by Dönitz in which he explicitly prohibited the rescue of enemy survivors in the waters of the British Isles. ("Do not rescue any men; do not take them along; and do not take care of any boats of the ship.") The prosecutors at Nuremberg introduced these orders to buttress the charge that Dönitz waged inhumane and illegal submarine warfare. Dönitz rebutted that this forceful and drastic order was necessary because too many of his skippers were wont to carry out humane rescues, which, in the heavily patrolled waters of the British Isles, risked "suicide for the U-boat."

In truth, the U-boat arm had not much heart to resume the fight. "Faith in the torpedo had been completely lost," Dönitz wrote. "I do not believe that ever in the history of war men have been sent against the enemy with such a useless weapon. These brave, enterprising [U-boat] crews, who had proved their worth during the previous months of the war, had been plunged into a state of dismal depression . . . a slough of despond."

In the days immediately following Norway, Dönitz collected and meticulously analyzed the torpedo-firing data. The skippers had carried out a total of thirty-eight attacks: four against battleships, fourteen against cruisers, ten against destroyers, and ten against transports. Discounting marginal attacks from long range at high-speed targets in poor light or other unfavorable conditions, Dönitz concluded that had the torpedoes not failed, "certain hits" (and probably sinkings or severe damage) would have occurred in one of the attacks on the battleships, seven on the cruisers, seven on the destroyers, and five on the transports. In summary, he calculated that about twenty enemy warships and transports had escaped almost certain destruction because of torpedo failures.

Dönitz used this damning data to mobilize internal political pressures against the torpedo bureaucrats, and he won over Admiral Raeder and the OKM. Upon receipt of Dönitz's "shattering summary," the OKM diarist commented that the "continual failure of the torpedoes, resulting from catastrophic technical deficiencies, must be regarded as a calamity . . . a failure of historical significance in German naval warfare at a time which is of decisive importance. . . ." Admiral Raeder declared that the correction of submarine torpedo defects was the Navy's "*most urgent problem*" and hastened to assure Dönitz and his men that "the defects are known and being put right" with the highest possible priority.

Dönitz devoted a large share of his working hours to seeking a solution to the torpedo defects—but not happily. "It is monstrous," he wrote in his log, "that I should have to be burdened with lengthy discussions and investigations of the causes of torpedo failures and their remedy. This is the business of the technical directorates and departments. But as long as these authorities are slow to do what is necessary, I am forced to take action myself."

By this time Dönitz had lost all confidence in the magnetic pistol. It was too complicated and too sensitive. Furthermore, he (rightly) believed that the British had perfected a way of reducing the magnetic fields of their ships—probably by degaussing, he thought—rendering the magnetic pistol less effective. He therefore urged that highest priority be assigned to correcting the depth-keeping defect and other suspected defects in the impact pistol.

With the return of good weather to the Baltic, the "Torpedo Dictator," Dr. Cornelius, had been carrying out intensive tests of the impact pistol. The results, presented about May 1, were "staggering" and "criminal," as Dönitz put it in his diary. Cornelius reported "a high rate of failure" owing to a poor, overly complex, and "clumsy" design. The weakness had not been detected theretofore because the torpedo technicians had not tested the pistol adequately in peacetime.

A few days after Cornelius revealed these test results, on May 5, the Germans captured the British submarine *Seal,* a 1,500-ton minelayer. When the Germans towed *Seal* to Germany, it was found that she carried twelve torpedoes (six in the tubes, six reloads) fitted with contact pistols. After Dönitz and his staffers had closely examined the pistols, Dönitz declared them to be "very sound" and "efficient" and he insisted that they be "copied." Cornelius concurred, and by this means the Germans were able to produce a reliable contact pistol in a very short time.

Meanwhile, Cornelius had some encouraging news. On May 11 he pronounced that the depth-keeping defect had been fixed. Torpedoes could be relied upon to run within a foot and a half of the depth setting. Furthermore, he asserted, "improved firing" of the magnetic pistol had been achieved.

The depth-keeping defect had not, in fact, been completely fixed. Nor would it be for another two years. There was another as-yet-undetected fault. The rudder shaft of the torpedo passed through the balance chamber, where the hydrostatic valve controlling the depth setting was located. The chamber was not airtight. As a result, when the boats ran submerged for prolonged periods (as in Norway) and the internal air pressure rose, the air pressure in the balance chamber likewise rose. This confused the hydrostatic valve, which was designed to operate at sea (or atmospheric) level, and caused it to set the torpedoes to run deeper. Since the latest testing had been carried out at sea level from surface craft or U-boats that had not remained submerged for very long, the leak in the balance chamber had no adverse effects on the hydrostatic valve, and so this flaw remained undetected.

Dönitz and his staff agonized over what to do: resume the U-boat war in the Atlantic or wait for improved torpedoes? His chief of staff, Eberhard Godt, Dönitz remembered, was of the "emphatic opinion" that the U-boat arm should not be committed to battle until all the torpedo defects had been eliminated. But Dönitz believed that any delay would do "incalculable harm" to the morale and efficiency of his men. Notwithstanding prematures and other failures, the Atlantic boats, employing magnetic pistols, had achieved considerable success in February. Dr. Cornelius had pronounced the depth-keeping defect fixed and some "improvement" in the magnetic pistol. As long as there was "even a slender prospect of success," Dönitz believed, the U-boat war in the Atlantic should be resumed.

Before that could happen, the men had to be reassured and encouraged. Admiral Raeder did his part with cheer-up visits and by awarding a *Ritterkreuz* to Dönitz. Dönitz, in turn, secured a *Ritterkreuz* for Werner Hartmann, who had sunk nineteen ships to exceed the leading ace Herbert Schultze, and one for Otto Schuhart, who had sunk the carrier *Courageous* in the early days of the war.* Dönitz personally visited every flotilla staff and U-boat to exhort his men.

Dönitz also made some important command and staff changes. He relieved

---

* Hartmann's claimed sinkings had reached the requisite 100,000 tons for a *Ritterkreuz*. His confirmed tonnage was 78,500. Schuhart claimed about 65,000 tons, including *Courageous*. His confirmed score was seven ships for 53,300 tons. However, Schuhart's record 41,905 tons sunk in a single patrol had not been topped.

three skippers: Hundius Flotilla commander Werner Hartmann in *U-37*, Herbert Sohler in *U-46*, who had returned from Norway in a state of "nervous exhaustion," and Herbert Schultze in *U-48*, who was ill and had to be hospitalized with a serious stomach or kidney disorder. Dönitz named Hartmann to be his first staff officer, replacing Viktor Oehrn, age thirty-two, who replaced Hartmann in *U-37*. He named Sohler commanding officer of the Wegener Flotilla, replacing Hans-Rudolf Rösing, who replaced Schultze in *U-48*. Prien's able first watch officer, Engelbert Endrass, age twenty-nine, replaced Sohler in *U-46*.

In resuming the U-boat war in the Atlantic, Dönitz planned to replicate the opening assault of September 1939: a maximum commitment of force across the broadest possible front. But this plan was frustrated by Hitler and by the jam-up in the shipyards. The Führer insisted that the U-boat arm continue hauling supplies to the beleaguered German ground forces in Norway. In response, the OKM directed Dönitz to assign one-third of the oceangoing force (seven boats) to these supply missions. On appeal, Dönitz was able to reduce the supply missions to merely two (*U-26, U-122*), but the reconversion of the other five boats from supply back to attack configuration delayed their availability. The jam-up in the shipyards delayed the refits of other boats. As a consequence, Dönitz was compelled to postpone the opening blow—the maximum commitment of force—to June.

Six oceangoing boats sailed in May to reopen the Atlantic U-boat war. Infuriatingly, mechanical problems compelled two boats, *U-28* (Kuhnke) and *U-48* (Rösing), to abort while still in the North Sea. The other four, *U-29* (Schuhart), *U-37* (Oehrn), *U-43* (Ambrosius), and the new VIIB *U-101*, commanded by Fritz Frauenheim, age twenty-eight, from the duck *U-21*, reached the Atlantic. To enhance their chances for success, Dönitz had obtained from Hitler another relaxation in the rules, which, in effect, permitted unrestricted submarine warfare in British and French waters. Commencing May 24, U-boats were allowed to sink without warning *any* ship, including unescorted neutrals and passenger ships.

Viktor Oehrn, new skipper of the famous *U-37*, led the way. Oehrn was very much aware that for internal political reasons and for rebuilding morale in the U-boat arm it was vital for *U-37* to achieve a smashing success. He got off to a promising start, sinking a 5,000-ton Swede and severely damaging a 9,500-ton British freighter with his deck gun.

While in the Western Approaches on May 23, however, a calamity occurred. Oehrn fired five torpedoes—all with the improved magnetic pistols—and all five failed. Oehrn broke radio silence to report the failures: two prematures, two nondetonators, and one erratic runner.

Dönitz was dismayed and furious. He immediately barred use of magnetic pistols and refused again to authorize their use until they had been fixed beyond any shadow of doubt. He ordered Oehrn and all other skippers to switch to impact pistols, which had recently been improved. At the same time, he demanded that work on copying the British impact pistol recovered from the captured *Seal* be carried forward with utmost urgency.

The switch to the improved impact pistols produced immediate returns for Oehrn. In the days following, he sank three ships by torpedo, including the 10,500-

ton French freighter *Brazza.* He went on to sink another five ships and a trawler: one by demolition, four by gun, and one by a combination of gun and torpedo. His victims included the 7,400-ton British tanker *Telena.*

One of the sinkings was to become controversial: the 5,000-ton British freighter *Sheaf Mead,* sunk in the afternoon of May 27, off Cape Finisterre, with the loss of thirty-one men. Before shooting, Oehrn observed that the freighter was armed and painted warship gray: Several guns were on the stern and perhaps another concealed under a canvas structure amidships. Having been warned by Dönitz to expect armed British auxiliary cruisers in this area (off Vigo, Spain), Oehrn convinced himself that *Sheaf Mead* was one, and therefore, when he surfaced, he made no attempt to help the survivors. He logged:

> A large heap of wreckage floats up. We approach it to identify the name. The crews have saved themselves on wreckage and capsized boats. We fish out a buoy. No name on it. I ask a man on the raft. He says, hardly turning his head, "Nix-name." A young boy in the water calls, "Help, help, please." The others are very composed; they look damp and somewhat tired and have a look of cold hatred on their faces. Then on to the old course.*

Having exhausted his torpedoes and ammo, Oehrn returned *U-37* to Wilhelmshaven after a mere twenty-six days at sea. Dönitz was ecstatic. Oehrn had achieved the objective, reopening the Atlantic U-boat war with resounding successes. In all, Oehrn put down ten confirmed ships for 41,207 tons. This was a record first patrol in numbers of ships sunk and only 700 tons shy of Schuhart's record 41,905 tons sunk in a single patrol.

The other three boats followed *U-37* into the hunting area by about a week. Neither *U-29* (Schuhart) nor *U-43* (Ambrosius) had any luck. But Fritz Frauenheim, making his first Atlantic patrol in the VIIB *U-101,* sank three British freighters for 14,200 tons in the Western Approaches. Thereafter the boats patrolled Iberian waters where, if necessary, they could clandestinely refuel in Spanish ports.

Near Lisbon on June 6, Frauenheim in *U-101* came upon a magnificent target, identified as a huge Greek passenger liner. Frauenheim surfaced, approached, and ordered the captain to abandon ship within ten minutes. The ship was not a Greek, but rather the 24,000-ton United States passenger liner *Washington,* bound from Lisbon to Galway, Ireland, jammed with American men, women, and children fleeing the war zone. On close inspection, Frauenheim discovered his error and shouted to the captain: "Sorry. Mistake. Proceed." No harm was done, but what

---

* The prosecutors at the Nuremberg trials cited Oehrn's refusal to assist the survivors of *Sheaf Mead* as another example of Nazi brutality at sea, charging that Oehrn behaved "in an exceptionally callous manner." In rebuttal, Dönitz argued that *Sheaf Mead* was "probably no merchant ship but [rather] a submarine trap," that in any case the ship was "heavily" armed, and that since Oehrn was under the impression that she was, at the least, an (armed) auxiliary cruiser, the sinking on sight was completely justified. Dönitz did not, however, condone Oehrn's indifference to the survivors. Inasmuch as there was no apparent danger to the boat, Oehrn should have "helped," he conceded.

was perceived as a very close call caused a great public uproar. Berlin at first attempted to cover up, charging (à la *Athenia*) that the submarine was British, but finally conceded that the submarine was German and that it had stopped *Washington* in error.*

GREAT BRITAIN AT RISK

France ingloriously collapsed. On June 10, as German forces closed on Paris, Hitler's ally, Benito Mussolini, seeking easy spoils, declared war on France and Great Britain. A doddery, eighty-four-year-old French military hero, Marshal Henri Pétain, who replaced Paul Reynaud as chief of state, entered into armistice negotiations with Hitler. The terms of the treaty left France divided: the northern half occupied by Germany; the southern half, or "Vichy France," unoccupied. Fiercely loyal Frenchmen who escaped to England rallied to General Charles de Gaulle, who proclaimed himself head of Free French forces.

The surrender of France and the entry of Italy into the war posed grave new naval threats to Great Britain. Under one clause of the treaty, Germany gained uncontested access to all French naval bases and seaports on the English Channel and on the Atlantic coastline (Bay of Biscay) as far south as Bordeaux, flanking the British Isles as well as her sea-lanes from the Mediterranean. Under another clause, Hitler gave his solemn word that the French fleet, neutralized in nonoccupied (or "Free Zone") bases in France and North Africa, would not be seized by Germany. But Churchill judged Hitler's word to be worthless. At any time the Führer might order the Vichy government to launch the entire French fleet against Britain. Moreover, in the absence of France as an ally, the hostile Italian fleet in the Mediterranean had to be met by a substantial diversion of British naval power to that theater.

The commander of the French Navy, Admiral François Darlan, assured Churchill privately that the French Navy would never fall into Hitler's hands; Darlan had, in fact, secretly issued orders to all French naval commanders that should Hitler go back on his word and attempt to seize the Navy, all French ships were to be instantly scuttled. But Churchill did not trust Darlan any more than he trusted Hitler: Darlan had all too eagerly joined the traitorous Vichy government in the high post of Minister of Marine. If Hitler so decreed, Darlan might well order the French fleet to attack the Royal Navy and/or to reinforce the *Kriegsmarine* for what was assumed to be Hitler's next step, an invasion of the British Isles.

Churchill therefore insisted to the War Cabinet that the French fleet had to be destroyed. It was the most "hateful" and "unnatural and painful" course of action he had ever recommended, he wrote later. The War Cabinet approved and the Admiralty issued orders for a surprise strike to be carried out on the morning of July

---

* The Berlin-based American radio journalist William Shirer, and others, speculated that the Germans had intended to sink *Washington* clandestinely and blame it on a British submarine in order to poison Anglo-American relations. No documents have come to light supporting this improbable scenario.

3. The senior British admirals entrusted with the task greeted the orders with a mixture of disbelief, dismay, and distaste. Nonetheless, they complied. At the French anchorage Mers-el-Kebir near Oran, Algeria, British naval forces sank the old French battleship *Bretagne* and severely damaged another old battleship, *Provence,* as well as the modern battle cruiser *Dunkerque* and a super-destroyer, killing a total of 1,297 French sailors. At the British naval base in Alexandria, Egypt, British naval forces disarmed and immobilized the old battleship *Lorraine,* four cruisers, and three destroyers without a fight. At the French naval base at Dakar, British forces damaged the gunned but uncompleted battleship *Richelieu.* In the British Isles, Royal Marines and other infantry boarded and captured about 200 French ships, including two old battleships, *Paris* and *Courbet,* eight destroyers, the monster-submarine *Surcouf,* and six other submarines, then "interned" about 12,000 French sailors in miserable concentration camps.

French naval personnel were justifiably outraged and embittered. As a consequence, the Free French Navy (*Forces Navales Françaises Libres*), which was formed in the British Isles, grew only slowly. Many of the French sailors seized by the British were eventually repatriated and reported to the Vichy French Navy (the damaged battle cruiser *Dunkerque,* her undamaged sister ship *Strasbourg,* numerous cruisers, destroyers, and submarines), which had escaped to Toulon, in southern France.

With the French Navy gutted and/or neutralized in Toulon, the Royal Navy still had to confront the Italian Navy. It consisted of four small (23,000-ton) older battleships, nineteen cruisers, fifty-nine destroyers, and 115 submarines. Only two of the four battleships, *Cavour* and *Cesare,* were war-ready; the other two were undergoing modernization.*

On paper, the Italian submarine force, consisting of 115 commissioned boats, represented a great threat to the Royal Navy. It was then twice the size of the German U-boat arm. Of the 115 boats, thirty-nine were big "oceangoing" boats (900 to 1,500 tons), and sixty-nine were "Mediterranean boats" (600 to 900 tons). When Italy declared war, about eighty-four of the boats were war-ready; fifty-four of these deployed to war stations in the Atlantic and Indian oceans and Mediterranean and Red seas.

This first combat sortie of the Italian submarine force was a fiasco. Within three days over half (twenty-eight) of the fifty-four boats were forced to abort. *Fieramosca* suffered a battery explosion. *Guglielmotti* and *Macalle* ran aground; the former was salvaged, the latter scuttled. The engines on *Ferraris* failed. British air and surface forces promptly sank seven boats (*Diamante, Liuzzi, Uebi Scebeli, Rubino, Argonauta, Torricelli, Galvani*) and captured another, *Galileo,* which yielded valuable intelligence documents. The Free French sloop *Curieuse* sank another, *Provana.*

---

* Four new and formidable 35,000-ton battleships were under construction. Two, *Littorio* and *Vittorio Veneto,* were nearly finished.

Italian submariners returned to their bases thoroughly shaken. In all, ten of the fifty-four submarines and about 400 men were lost in the first twenty days of operations. Part of the loss could be attributed to the poor design and quality of Italian submarines; part to unrealistic peacetime training; part to reckless bravado. These heavy losses induced a caution in the Italian submarine force which, with few exceptions, was to characterize all its future operations.

The submarine disaster led in part to a decision in Rome to change the naval codes. On July 5 and July 17, respectively, the Italians introduced entirely new submarine and surface-ship codes. These changes, together with previously directed changes in the Italian Army and Air Force codes, came as a "great shock" to British codebreakers at Bletchley Park, who, until then, had been reading Italian military codes currently and fluently. Thereafter, except for a brief period in 1941, the British were unable to break Italian naval codes.

The sudden and inglorious collapse of France plus Italy's entry into the war, leaving Britain standing alone, stunned most Americans. Notwithstanding Churchill's stirring rhetoric and the strength of the RAF and Royal Navy, the defeat of Great Britain seemed inevitable and unavoidable. A widespread fear arose that Hitler's next step after the assumed invasion and conquest of the British Isles would be the conquest of Latin America by diplomacy, trickery, or force of arms, posing a dire strategic threat to the United States. The defense of the Western Hemisphere thus became an overriding concern in Washington.

That concern, as much as the fate of Great Britain, spurred a drive for increased military mobilization in the United States in the early summer of 1940. As the Roosevelt administration viewed the situation, the most urgent military requirement was to accumulate massive new naval and air power. Should Great Britain go the way of France—oust Churchill and other hawks and reappoint an appeasing and pro-German government—the Royal Navy, like the French Navy, might fall under Hitler's control. A combined and refurbished German, Italian, French, and British Navy* would give Hitler incontestable mastery of the oceans. Against that superiority in sea power, the United States would be hard-pressed to prevent a military occupation of Latin America or, later, an invasion of its own shores.

A further complication and grave threat to America's strategic interests was posed by Japan. More aggressively expansionist than ever and rapidly growing in naval strength, with the connivance of the new Vichy government Japan had established a military foothold in French Indochina. This bold and arrogant thrust flanked and imperiled the Philippine Islands, a key United States military base in the Far East, which was an essential asset in the Navy's plan to defeat Japan in the event of war. To help deter further Japanese expansion, President Roosevelt had

---

* Reinforced by the forthcoming German super-battleships *Bismarck* and *Tirpitz,* the five new *King George V*–class British battleships and the six British carriers under construction, the four new 35,000-ton Italian battleships, and the new French battleships *Jean Bart* and *Richelieu.*

based the bulk of the Navy's fleet at Pearl Harbor, Hawaii, leaving the Atlantic area very weak in naval power.

Upon the expiration of the London Naval Treaty in 1937, the U.S. Navy had embarked upon a substantial buildup (660,000 new tons) in capital ships, cruisers, destroyers, submarines, and other vessels. When the war in Europe erupted, Roosevelt had proposed an increase of 25 percent in carrier, cruiser, and submarine tonnage. On the day Paris fell, June 14, Congress approved this increase. However, in view of the possible naval threat Hitler could pose to the Americas and that posed by Japan in the Far East, and a further threat posed by a possible alliance of German-controlled and Japanese naval forces, on June 17 Roosevelt proposed that Congress approve a $4 billion appropriation for the purpose of creating a "Two Ocean Navy," an increase in naval construction by 1,325,000 tons over that already approved. Congress passed the bill with scant debate and Roosevelt signed it into law, launching the United States on a warship-building program of awesome scope.

At this time, domestic politics dominated Washington. The big question was whether President Roosevelt would seek an unprecedented third term, running against the Republican favorite, Wendell L. Willkie. The answer, which came at the Democratic Party's Chicago convention in July 1940, was yes. Partly to undermine Willkie's growing support and partly to infuse his cabinet with internationalists who favored support for the British, Roosevelt named two distinguished Republicans to head America's military forces. Millionaire newspaper publisher Frank Knox (Alf Landon's running mate in 1936) replaced the inventor's son, Charles Edison, as Secretary of the Navy; Henry L. Stimson replaced Henry H. Woodring as Secretary of War.

The growing concern over hemispheric defense led Roosevelt to reconsider a long-standing request from Churchill for the "loan" of "forty or fifty old destroyers." Roosevelt secretly wrote Churchill that he would attempt to gain public and congressional approval for this transaction, provided Churchill would guarantee that no part of the Royal Navy would ever be turned over to Germany or scuttled; and that Britain would sell or lease to the United States for 99 years military base rights in Newfoundland, Bermuda, the Bahamas, Jamaica, St. Lucia, Trinidad, and British Guiana (Guyana), to be used to deter "an attack on the American hemisphere by any non-American nation."

"HAPPY TIME": THE JUNE SLAUGHTER

In the chaotic days of June 1940, during the collapse of France and the Allied counterinvasion of Norway, the Royal Navy was stretched to the breaking point. It had to simultaneously evacuate Allied forces from France and Norway, gear up for the attack on the French Navy in North African bases, confront the Italian Navy in the Mediterranean and Red seas and the Indian Ocean, pursue the German merchant ship raiders *Atlantis* and *Orion* in the south Atlantic, and prepare for a probable invasion of the British Isles. Because of these commitments—and the loss of fifteen destroyers sunk and twenty-seven damaged during the Norway operation and Dunkirk evacuation—the escort of convoys and other ASW measures in home waters had to be cut to the bone.

As it happened, the reduction of British convoy escort and ASW forces coincided with the implementation of Dönitz's plan to reopen the Atlantic U-boat war with a maximum commitment of force over a wide area, a plan that had been unavoidably delayed from May to June. Moreover, the U-boat crews were well rested from the ordeal in Norway. Faith in the torpedoes had been restored by the successes of Oehrn in *U-37* and Frauenheim in *U-101,* employing impact pistols only.

On June 1 there were twenty-four oceangoing boats in commission, including the ex-Turk *U-A*—three less than the day the war began. Two (the VIIB *U-100* and the IXB *U-123*) were brand-new and still in workup. One, *U-37,* was inbound from patrol. Three, *U-29, U-43,* and *U-101,* were still on patrol in Iberian waters. The other eighteen sailed from Germany in June, bringing the total deployed to twenty-one boats, the largest number committed to the North Atlantic at one time since September 1939.

Raeder and the OKM directed an all-out effort to trap and destroy the Allied forces withdrawing from Norway. In early June *Gneisenau* and *Scharnhorst* sailed for that purpose. They found—and sank—the old carrier *Glorious* and her two destroyer escorts, but in this action, one of the British destroyers, *Acasta,* hit *Scharnhorst* with one torpedo, inflicting damage sufficient to force *Gneisenau* and *Scharnhorst* to break off further operations and run into Trondheim.

At the request of the OKM, Dönitz diverted five outgoing U-boats to form a trap in the Orkneys to intercept other Allied ships retreating from Norway. One of the five, *U-65,* was forced to abort to Bergen with mechanical problems; the other four, *U-A, U-25, U-51,* and *U-52,* had no luck. When released from the trap, *U-A,* commanded by Hans Cohausz, age thirty-two, went on to the Faeroes-Iceland area to attack the line of British auxiliary cruisers of the Northern Patrol and sank one, the 14,000-ton *Andania.* The other boats, including *U-65,* which resailed from Bergen, went to the Western Approaches. En route, the cranky *U-25,* commanded by a new skipper, Heinz Beduhn, age thirty-two, from the duck *U-23,* missed a battle cruiser (*Renown* or *Repulse*) but hit and sank the 17,000-ton auxiliary cruiser *Scotstoun* (ex-*Caledonia*).

Nine boats converged in the lightly defended Western Approaches. These included Prien in *U-47,* who had rescued three downed *Luftwaffe* crewmen in the Orkneys, and Liebe in *U-38,* who had diverted to Dingle Bay, Ireland, to land another *Abwehr* agent.* In a matter of a few days these nine boats, employing torpedoes with impact pistols, inflicted an amazing slaughter. In all, eight of the nine boats in the Western Approaches sank thirty-one ships for about 162,500 tons.

• Prien in *U-47* sank seven ships for 36,000 tons, including the 13,000-ton British tanker *San Fernando* and the 2,580-ton Dutch tanker *Leticia.*

• Liebe in *U-38* sank six for 30,400 tons, including the 10,000-ton Norwegian tanker *Italia.*

---

* Walter Simon, who was caught and arrested within hours.

- Hans Jenisch in *U-32* sank five for 16,000 tons, including the 9,000-ton Norwegian tanker *Eli Knudsen.*
- Dietrich Knorr in *U-51* sank three for 22,200 tons, including the 12,000-ton British tanker *Saranac.*
- Günter Kuhnke in *U-28* sank three for 10,300 tons.
- Otto Salmann in *U-52* sank three for 9,400 tons.
- Von Stockhausen in *U-65* sank two for 29,300 tons, including the big 28,124-ton French liner *Champlain,* damaged by the *Luftwaffe.*
- Fritz-Julius Lemp in *U-30* sank two for 8,900 tons.
- Beduhn in the clumsy *U-25* made a submerged attack on a tanker, but a following ship rammed the boat and forced her to abort with bent periscopes and a damaged conning tower.

After exhausting their torpedoes, six of these nine boats followed the crippled *U-25* back to Germany. While passing North Channel submerged in the early hours of July 2, Prien, who had one supposedly "defective" torpedo left, encountered the 15,500-ton British ocean liner *Arandora Star,* outbound to Canada. When she zigzagged toward *U-47,* Prien saw guns on her bow and stern and deemed her to be fair game. He shot the supposedly defective torpedo at a range of one mile. It hit directly amidships—a perfect bull's-eye. Since it was daylight, Prien did not stick around to see the outcome.

Unknown to Prien, the *Arandora Star* was jam-packed with 1,299 male Germans and Italians who were being shipped to detention camps in Canada. There were 565 Germans, of which eighty-six were military POWs of "bad character" and 479 "civilian internees," deemed a threat to internal security. The 734 Italians were all civilian internees. The Germans and Italians were guarded by 200 British Army personnel. Including the *Arandora Star*'s crew of 174, there were 1,673 people on the ship. She was not marked with a red cross or other signs to indicate her special category nor had the Admiralty requested "free passage" for her.

Fatally holed and flooding, the *Arandora Star* remained afloat about one hour. During that time the ship got off an *SOS* and launched ten lifeboats and scads of rafts. The prisoners and guards—all mixed together—and lastly the crew abandoned ship but, the official Admiralty reports stated, many Italians refused to leave. In response to the *SOS,* a Sunderland appeared overhead and dropped packets of emergency supplies, and the Canadian destroyer *St. Laurent,* which was eighty-four miles away screening the battleship *Nelson,* raced to the rescue.

Guided by the Sunderland, the *St. Laurent* reached the scene in early afternoon. She rescued the hundreds of survivors from the ten lifeboats, then sent the lifeboats and her own boats to collect other survivors from the rafts and wreckage. Rushing the rescue so that she herself would not become a victim of the U-boat, within a mere thirty-five minutes the crews had fished every survivor in sight from the sea. When a British destroyer, *Walker,* arrived to assist, she scoured the area but could find no sign of life—or of the U-boat.

In this remarkable operation, *St. Laurent* rescued over half of those on board *Arandora Star* when Prien's torpedoes struck. Those saved included 322 Germans, 243 Italians, 163 military guards, and 119 crew. A total of 826 perished, including

713 Germans and Italians. It was by far the greatest loss of life in a noncombatant-ship sinking thus far in the war.

When *U-47* reached Wilhelmshaven, Dönitz, as yet unaware of the *Arandora Star* tragedy, praised Prien to the high heavens. He was credited with sinking ten ships for 68,587 tons, far and away the best performance by any skipper in the war. In the postwar accounting, the sinkings were to be reduced to eight ships for 51,483 tons. Even so, it was the best single patrol in confirmed tonnage sunk to that time. The fact that his torpedoes killed 713 Germans and Italians on *Arandora Star* was concealed from the Axis public.

The VIIBs *U-46* and *U-48* were under orders to join the three boats already in Iberian waters (*U-29, U-43, U-101*) to form a pack off Cape Finisterre. The pack, to be controlled by Hans Rösing, the new skipper of the famous *U-48*, was to intercept an inbound troop convoy that included the giant ocean liners *Queen Mary* (81,000 tons) and *Mauritania* (36,000 tons), bringing 25,000 Australian soldiers to the British Isles.

Southbound to the rendezvous, both Rösing and the new skipper of *U-46*, Englebert Endrass, ran across innumerable ships. Rösing in *U-48* sank three and damaged another. Endrass in *U-46* sank four, including the 20,277-ton British auxiliary cruiser *Carinthia*, and severely damaged an 8,700-ton British tanker. Both boats arrived at the rendezvous low on torpedoes.

While proceeding to the rendezvous, Frauenheim in *U-101*, who had already sunk three ships, sank three more (one British, two Greek), the last on June 14, to the west of Cape Finisterre, on the day before the scheduled rendezvous. This sinking may have alerted the *Queen Mary* convoy and caused it to veer well out to sea. Whatever the case, the pack rendezvous proved to be fruitless. None of the five boats spotted the convoy.

When this failure was realized, Dönitz released the five boats for independent patrol. With his last torpedoes Frauenheim sank the 13,200-ton British steamer *Wellington Star* and went home to high praise. His total bag—seven ships for 42,022 tons—slightly topped that of Otto Schuhart, making it the second best patrol in confirmed tonnage sunk after Prien's. Rösing in *U-48* sank four more ships, including the 7,500-ton Dutch tanker *Moerdrecht*, bringing his confirmed total on this first patrol to seven ships for 31,500 tons sunk. Endrass in *U-46* fired three torpedoes at the carrier *Ark Royal*, en route to join British forces for the attack on the French Navy, but he missed. Before returning home he sank one more ship, bringing his confirmed total for his first patrol as skipper to five ships for 35,300 tons. Berlin propagandists gave Frauenheim, Rösing, and Endrass the full publicity treatment, inflating the tonnages sunk (that of Endrass to 54,000 tons).

The return of the seven boats from the Western Approaches and the three from Iberian waters, and a decision to send *U-A* on a pioneer cruise to the African coast, left only four boats (*U-29, U-30, U-43, U-52*) to carry on the Atlantic war, pending the arrival of the last five boats outbound from Germany. Inasmuch as all four boats still had plenty of torpedoes (neither *U-29* nor *U-43* had yet sunk a ship),

Dönitz ordered all four to refuel in Spanish ports. Schuhart in *U-29,* Ambrosius in *U-43,* and Lemp in *U-30* sneaked into Vigo on June 19, 21, and 25, respectively, to refuel from the German freighter *Bessel;* Salmann in *U-52* put into El Ferrol on July 2 to refuel from the *Max Albrecht.*

After refueling, these four boats patrolled independently. Schuhart in *U-29* sank four ships for 25,000 tons, including the 9,000-ton British tanker *Athellaird,* but his attack periscope broke and he was forced to abort to Germany. Ambrosius in *U-43* also sank four ships (for 29,000 tons), including the 13,400-ton British liner *Avelona Star* and the 8,600-ton British tanker *Yarraville.* Ambrosius then returned to Germany, arriving after ten weeks at sea, a new endurance record. Lemp in *U-30* was credited four more ships for 17,500 tons, bringing his total for the patrol to six. Salmann in *U-52* sank one more, making his total four.

Meanwhile, the last five boats to sail from Germany in June arrived in the Atlantic. These were the clumsy *U-26,* the VII *U-34,* two new Type VIIBs on first patrols, *U-99* and *U-102,* and the new Type IXB, *U-122,* which had made one supply trip to Norway. The *U-26,* commanded by Heinz Scheringer, reached the Western Approaches in late June with serious engine problems. Despite the deficiencies, Scheringer patrolled aggressively, sinking three freighters* and damaging another, the British *Zarian,* in convoy. One of the convoy escorts, the new *Flower*-class corvette *Gladiolus,* pounced on *U-26* in favorable sonar conditions, dropping thirty-six of her forty-one depth charges set at 350 to 500 feet.

The charges badly pounded *U-26,* causing leaks but not fatal damage. In the early hours of July 1, Scheringer surfaced to charge his depleted batteries and to escape in the fog. By that time, the British sloop *Rochester* and a Sunderland of Coastal Command's Australian Squadron 10, piloted by W. M. ("Hoot") Gibson, had come on the scene in response to *Gladiolus*'s alert. Seeing *U-26* surface, *Rochester* commenced a high-speed run to ram. Had the *U-26*'s diesels and motors been working properly and had Scheringer been able to charge batteries, the boat might have escaped. But with *Rochester* (believed to be a "destroyer") bearing down firing her forward gun and the Sunderland overhead, he was forced under again.

The Sunderland saw the "swirl," or disturbed water, where *U-26* had submerged and ran in for an attack. Hoot Gibson dropped four 250-pound antisubmarine bombs, which exploded very close and rocked the boat. The bombs did no real damage, but Scheringer had no battery charge left and the boat was still leaking in the stern as a result of the depth-charge attack from *Gladiolus.* Fearing *U-26* would be fatally damaged by the apporaching "destroyer," Scheringer surfaced, intending to scuttle. When the boat appeared, the Sunderland dropped four more bombs, but by then *U-26*'s chief engineer had set in motion scuttling procedures and the crew was leaping into the water.

The *U-26* went down quickly with all hatches open. *Rochester* came up with guns trained. After allowing the survivors to swim a while in order to scare them

---

* A 6,700-ton Greek, the Estonian *Merkur,* and the Norwegian *Belmoira,* the latter two wrongly accredited to *U-102.*

into talking more freely, *Rochester* fished all forty-eight men from the water. There were no casualties, but the scare tactic did not work. The *U-26* crew was one of the most reticent to be captured, British intelligence reported.

That same day, July 1, the brand-new VIIB, *U-102,* commanded by Harro von Klot-Heydenfeldt, age twenty-nine, from the duck *U-20,* was only a few miles away, lying in wait for a convoy inbound from Freetown, Sierra Leone. Von Klot-Heydenfeldt found a straggler from the convoy, the coal-burning 5,219-ton British freighter *Clearton,* loaded with wheat, and he sank her with two torpedoes.* The blast killed eight of her crew; the other twenty-six abandoned in lifeboats.

In response to *Clearton*'s distress signal, the British destroyer *Vansittart,* on patrol in the area, raced to the scene. An hour later *Vansittart* got a good sonar return on *U-102* and made two runs, dropping eleven depth charges set for 350–500 feet. After that, *Vansittart* could not regain contact. She recovered the *Clearton* survivors and returned to the scene, where she found a huge oil slick. She remained in the area, hunting, until evening of the following day, July 2, noting a continuous rising of oil. From that evidence *Vansittart* concluded she had sunk the U-boat, but this was not sufficiently convincing to confirm a kill. However, in postwar years, when both German and British records could be compared, Admiralty historians concluded that *Vansittart* had indeed sunk the *U-102* with the loss of all hands, merely nine days out on her first patrol.

The new IXB, *U-122,* commanded by onetime Weddigen Flotilla chief Hans Günther Looff (Rösing's brother-in-law), age thirty-four, sank one 5,100-ton ship on June 20 and, the next day, broadcast a weather report for the benefit of the *Luftwaffe.* Nothing further was ever heard from the boat. Unable to match her loss with any Allied attack, Admiralty authorities for years listed the cause of her demise as "unknown." After a reinvestigation in recent years, Admiralty historians concluded the loss was due to an "accident"—perhaps an error committed by one of her green crewmen. She was about sixteen days out on her first patrol.

Dönitz soon learned through the Red Cross that *U-26* was lost and that all hands had been rescued. The loss of this onetime flagship of the U-boat arm was a sentimental wrench, but no surprise; her sister ship, *U-25,* had been rammed and nearly lost in the same waters only three weeks earlier. Neither of these unsafe, unreliable boats should have been sent to operate in the Western Approaches. However, far worse in terms of military effectiveness was the disappearance without trace of the new boats *U-102* and *U-122.*

The last two boats to sail from Germany in June were the old Type VII *U-34,* commanded by Wilhelm Rollmann, and the new VIIB *U-99,* commanded by Otto Kretschmer, age twenty-eight, from the duck *U-23,* who had sunk six and a half confirmed ships for 22,500 tons, including the British destroyer *Daring.* For good luck, Kretschmer had welded horseshoes on both sides of the conning tower, but he got off to an unlucky start. Outbound, one of his men fell ill and had to be landed in Bergen. This diversion took *U-99* into the path of the damaged *Scharnhorst,* homebound from Trondheim. Mistaking *U-99* for a British submarine, one

---

    * *Clearton* was wrongly credited to Lemp's *U-30.*

of *Scharnhorst*'s scout planes bombed her and forced Kretschmer to return to Germany for repairs.

The *U-34* and *U-99* reached the Western Approaches in early July. Over the next ten days both skippers found good hunting. Rollmann in *U-34* sank an impressive eight ships for 22,400 tons, including the British destroyer *Whirlwind* and the 2,600-ton Dutch tanker *Lucretia*. Kretschmer in *U-99* sank four confirmed ships for 13,800 tons and claimed another (which could not be verified) for 3,600 tons. He also took a prize, the 2,100-ton Estonian *Merisaar*, which, however, was sunk by the *Luftwaffe* en route to Bordeaux. During one of these attacks, British escorts found *U-99* and delivered a punishing depth-charge attack (Kretschmer counted 127 explosions) that kept the boat down for eighteen grueling hours and forced it to the unprecedented and terrifying depth of 700 feet.

The loss of *U-26*, *U-102*, and *U-122* left only four oceangoing boats in the Atlantic in early July: Lemp in *U-30* and Salmann in *U-52*, who had refueled in Spain, Rollmann in *U-34* and Kretschmer in *U-99*, who was out of or low on torpedoes. But these four boats were the first to benefit from an astonishingly swift and efficient move on Dönitz's part to capitalize on the German occupation of northern France.

Mere hours after the Franco-German armistice had been signed, Dönitz flew to western France to scout locations for U-boat bases on the French Atlantic coast. He chose five sites: Brest, Lorient, St. Nazaire, La Pallice (abutting La Rochelle), and Bordeaux. Meanwhile, his staff loaded a special train with torpedoes, spare parts, and other gear and sent it to Paris. From there the train was routed to Lorient, where an advance party of staff and technicians established the first U-boat base.

Lorient had been a French naval base. Undamaged by the war, it was, in the words of one of the German staffers, "a typically unlovely provincial Breton town." The better homes were hidden behind high walls shaded by palm trees; all the rest were "huddled together in dirty, narrow, gray streets" and "badly in need of repair." The staff set up operational headquarters and an officers' mess in the French Naval Préfecture. Arrangements were made to billet U-boat officers in the Hotel Pigeon Blanc, the enlisted men in the Hotel Bleu Sejour, each of which provided laundry service. Being a navy town, Lorient had numerous cafés and bars and a red-light district.

The four boats left in the Atlantic were directed to put into Lorient. Lemp in *U-30* arrived first, on July 7. Salmann in *U-52* arrived next. Then Rollmann in *U-34*, on July 18, and Kretschmer in *U-99* on July 21. They were followed by two ducks, *U-56* and *U-58*, which had patrolled over from Bergen.

These U-boat crews preferred basing in Germany, close to families and friends and familiar haunts in Kiel and Wilhelmshaven, but they quickly adjusted to the new life in a foreign country. They gorged themselves on French food and alcoholic beverages (wine, champagne, cognac) and enjoyed the company of young French women, many of whom willingly consorted with their conquerors. They traded their reeking heavy winter clothing and oilskins for clean British khakis, which the evacuating Tommies had left behind. Meanwhile, Dönitz arranged for special, luxury railway cars to transport U-boat crews to and from Germany, which were to be available when the facilities in Occupied France were ready to carry out major refits or overhauls.

Counting the four oceangoing boats that reached the Atlantic in May and the sixteen in June, these twenty boats sank ninety-one confirmed ships for about 477,409 tons, including ten tankers. This was an overall average of about 4.3 ships and about 23,000 tons per boat per patrol, far and away the best results in the war to date, the beginning of a brief period the German submariners called "Happy Time."

Dönitz could be very well pleased with the results of the resumption of the U-boat war in the North Atlantic. Three boats had been lost, but only two of those (the new *U-102* and *U-122*) were militarily significant. For each boat lost, about thirty Allied ships had been sunk, an "exchange" rate comparable to the best months of World War I.

The all-out commitment of the U-boat force in June, however, left Dönitz with no oceangoing boats to sail in July except the four at Lorient, two of which, *U-30* and *U-52,* had reported major engine problems. He was therefore compelled to rely to an unprecedented extent on Bergen-based ducks to patrol the Atlantic approaches to the British Isles.

The May–June slaughter deeply shocked American naval officers in London who were closely observing the U-boat war. Although the overwhelming majority of the merchant ships sunk were sailing alone—unescorted—the Americans, who were unaware of this fact at that time, concluded that to sail merchant ships in thinly escorted convoys was unwise or even foolish. As the U-boat slaughter in the Western Approaches continued into the fall of 1940, the American observers became ever more convinced of this conclusion, a view that was concurred in by the Navy Department in Washington.

Even though these U-boat successes clearly established a need for large numbers of convoy escorts in the event America entered the war, Washington failed to respond to this particular naval challenge. President Roosevelt and the new Secretary of the Navy, Frank Knox, rejected specific proposals from the Chief of Naval Operations, Harold R. Stark, for a force of suitable escort vessels—even the construction of a prototype. Roosevelt and Knox believed, mistakenly, that when the need actually arose, American industry could quickly mass-produce small, cheap convoy escorts on demand.

FIRST PATROLS FROM LORIENT

The swift collapse of France had caught Hitler and his military advisers by surprise. Contrary to the general belief, they had no master plan and had made no provisions for an invasion of the British Isles. Still believing that Great Britain could be pressured into an accommodation, Hitler, in fact, was looking the other way—east, toward the Soviet Union. In Hitler's view, Stalin had exceeded the spirit of the Russo-German pact by a military occupation of the Baltic states of Lithuania, Latvia, and Estonia, and the Balkan provinces of Bessarabia and North Bukovina, which greatly strengthened Stalin's hold on the east Baltic and placed Soviet forces perilously close to the rich Rumanian oil fields, Germany's chief energy source.

In his meetings with Hitler, Admiral Raeder sought to deflect the Führer's growing concern over Soviet moves and to stress the perils posed by the Royal Navy. It would be a grave mistake, Raeder insisted, to turn about and attack the Soviet Union before Great Britain had been neutralized by treaty or thoroughly defeated. That would replicate the Kaiser's great mistake of 1914 and create the worst of all possible situations: a two-front war. Rather than go east, Raeder suggested, Germany should go south to the Mediterranean and with Spain's connivance, capture the British naval base at Gibraltar. That would effectively put an end to British naval dominance in the Mediterranean and decisively assist Mussolini's forces, which were attacking out of Libya toward Egypt to seize Cairo, the Suez Canal, and the other big British naval base at Alexandria. Absolute Axis control of the Mediterranean Basin would place Germany in a favorable position to exploit the oil reserves of the Middle East as well as the limitless raw materials of Africa.

As Hitler viewed it, the situation was not analogous to 1914. The main continental enemy, France, was already beaten and occupied. Norway was occupied as well. Great Britain was flanked on the east and south—isolated and just barely hanging on. She had no foothold on the continent nor any hope of obtaining one. The British naval blockade of Germany was no longer a factor: Germany controlled Norway and the entire French Atlantic coast from the channel to Bordeaux. This time Italy and Japan were allies, not enemies.* Japan posed a threat to the Soviet Union in the Far East, which would freeze significant Soviet forces in that sphere. The Soviet Army and Air Force were nothing—a collection of ill-equipped rabble. The *Wehrmacht* and *Luftwaffe* could utterly crush the Soviet Union in a matter of six to eight weeks.

No master plan emerged from these discussions. After the fall of France, Hitler more or less improvised German operations week to week. The *Luftwaffe* and all available forces of the *Kriegsmarine* were to mount maximum pressure against British air and maritime assets, with the aim of forcing Great Britain to the negotiating table. If psychological pressure failed to get the job done, as a last resort the *Wehrmacht* might consider an invasion of the British Isles. Meanwhile, Hitler secretly drew plans for the conquest of the Soviet Union to take place in the spring of 1941.

Raeder and the OKM adamantly opposed a *Wehrmacht* invasion of the British Isles. The *Kriegsmarine* was in no position to mount a major amphibious assault. Most of its big surface forces had been sunk, damaged, or worn out in the Norway operation. Only one heavy cruiser, *Hipper,* was combat-ready. Besides that, the

---

* On September 27, 1940, Japan was to be formally welded into the Axis by the Tripartite Pact.

Navy had no landing craft, no means of transporting troops, tanks, artillery, trucks, ammo, and other impedimenta across the channel. Nonetheless, the OKM drew up a contingency plan (Operation Sea Lion), which envisioned the use of hundreds of European river barges for landing craft.

There was one—and only one—possible way to assure a successful invasion of England. That was to first commit the *Luftwaffe* to the destruction of the RAF and the Royal Navy. When the *Luftwaffe* achieved absolute mastery of the air and seas, the barges—and even big passenger ships such as *Bremen*—could cross the North Sea and English Channel with confidence. The channel could be sealed at both ends by minefields and cordons of U-boats to block Allied submarine attacks—or surface ship attacks at night by remnants of the Royal Navy. But an invasion, Raeder continued to insist, should only be attempted "as a last resort."

The *Luftwaffe* chief, Hermann Göring, was not keen on an invasion either. But he welcomed the opportunity to mount a full-scale air war against the RAF and Great Britain. He believed the *Luftwaffe* could wipe out the RAF in about three weeks and that denied this last line of defense, Britain would capitulate and sue for peace. He accordingly mobilized virtually the entire resources of the *Luftwaffe* for the task. Air Fleet 2 occupied bases in the Low Countries; Air Fleet 3 occupied bases in northern France; and Air Fleet 5 occupied bases in Norway and Denmark. Total resources: about 2,800 aircraft, of which about 1,600 were bombers or dive bombers and about 1,200 were fighters and reconnaissance planes.

Hitler made a final attempt to persuade the British people to lay down their arms in a speech to the *Reichstag* on July 19. Ridiculing Churchill's defiant oratory, he said: "I feel it to be my duty before my own conscience to appeal once more to reason and common sense in Great Britain as much as elsewhere. I consider myself in a position to make this appeal since I am not the vanquished begging favor, but the victor speaking in the name of reason. I can see no reason why this war must go on." Within one hour the answer was transmitted by BBC in London: Great Britain would not negotiate and it would never surrender.

The *Luftwaffe* air assault against the British Isles—the "Battle of Britain"—began on July 10. That day the RAF had about 2,000 aircraft in its inventory, of which about 1,200 were assigned to Bomber Command and Coastal Command and about 800 to Fighter Command. Since the *Luftwaffe* bombers and dive bombers were vulnerable and required escorting fighters, what counted most were the 700-odd Spitfires and Hurricanes of Fighter Command. The future of Britain depended upon the ability of these planes and pilots to knock out the 1,100-odd *Luftwaffe* fighters and get at the bombers.

Although Fighter Command had fewer fighters, it had the advantage of the Chain Home radar network and a highly efficient command-and-control organization. Thus the Hurricanes and Spitfires could be husbanded and shifted about to meet the greatest threat of the moment. Göring was aware of the British radar network, but having overwhelmed a similar French radar network with ease, he did not regard the British network as a serious threat nor did he even inform his pilots of its existence. Göring's failure to knock out the British radar net—and the RAF command-and-control stations—was to be a fatal error.

The British had another intelligence advantage: Enigma codebreaking. Due to a procedural change on May 10 when Germany invaded France, the codebreakers lost *Luftwaffe* Red. However, in an amazing intelligence feat, within twelve days—by May 22—Bletchley Park had recovered Red and could read it consistently and currently. *Luftwaffe* Red yielded substantial—and valuable—strategic intelligence, such as the organization and administration of the *Luftwaffe*. It did not, however, provide what was needed most: tactical intelligence, such as how many German aircraft were to strike where and when.

The chief tactical items obtained from Red Enigma were to be occasional references to "*Knickebein*" ("Dog leg" or "Crooked leg") and "*X-Gerät*" ("X-Apparatus"). The brilliant young RAF chief of scientific intelligence, R. V. Jones, correctly guessed these were radio-beam navigational systems for night or foul-weather bombing. Put on the scent by Red Enigma and helped by POW interrogations and the recovery of hardware from a downed German plane, Jones confirmed this deduction. In due course he and RAF electronic technicians were able to predict probable targets from the beam settings recovered from Enigma and to devise clever methods of "jamming" (or "bending") these beams, leading some German bombers to wrong and harmless targets. But that came later.

The *Luftwaffe* commenced the Battle of Britain with intense bombing attacks on British merchant-ship convoys in the Western Approaches and the English Channel. The main purpose of these attacks was to draw Fighter Command aircraft into combat and whittle them down in circumstances which favored the Germans. In the process, during July the German pilots sank thirty-three ships for about 70,000 tons. These losses and the threat of even greater shipping losses to German air attack led the Admiralty to divert convoys to more northerly routes into the British Isles, in effect closing down the Western and Southwestern approaches and complicating the task of the U-boats.

The new U-boat base at Lorient was ideally situated for attacks on British shipping, but Dönitz was unable to contribute significantly to the pressures on Great Britain in the month of July. Most of the oceangoing boats had returned to Germany for refits; only four oceangoing boats could sail from Lorient in July.

About the time the first of these, *U-30,* arrived at Lorient, *B-dienst* provided Dönitz with information about the attack by the Royal Navy on the French Navy at Oran and Dakar. Believing that further specific information from *B-dienst* might enable U-boats to intercept some of the British capital ships, Dönitz ordered Lemp to sail *U-30* south to the vicinity of the Strait of Gibraltar, and the U-cruiser *U-A,* which was patrolling off the African coast, to close on Dakar.

Although *U-30* and *U-A* had reported engine malfunctions, both attempted to carry out the missions. Lemp sailed from Lorient on July 13—the first U-boat into Lorient and the first to leave from there on patrol—but he was dogged by further engine trouble. After sinking a small ship—his seventh credited sinking since leaving Germany—Lemp was forced by engine malfunction to abort and return to Lorient. Northbound to Dakar from Freetown, Sierra Leone, Hans Cohausz in *U-A* sank his third ship, a 5,800-ton Norwegian freighter, but he, too, reported an engine breakdown and requested permission to abort and come home. Dönitz refused Cohausz permission, directing him to rendezvous with the German merchant raider *Pinguin* for repairs, refueling, and joint operations.

Meanwhile, *B-dienst* had provided Dönitz new information on North Atlantic convoys. Two significant changes in procedure had occurred: the shift to the northerly routes in reaction to the *Luftwaffe* attacks and creation of U-boat bases in France, and an extension of surface and air escort to 17 degrees west longitude, a line nearly 360 miles west of the British Isles. This put the likely rendezvous area northwest or west of Rockall Bank, which, with safe Atlantic routing, was about equidistant (about 1,000 miles) from Wilhelmshaven or Lorient. Hence, the advantages of mounting patrols against North Atlantic convoys from Lorient had been substantially reduced. The chief remaining advantage of Lorient over Wilhelmshaven in the war against North Atlantic convoys was the elimination of the slow, tedious voyage in and out of the confined, mined waters of the North Sea, which required running submerged in daytime to avoid enemy air and submarine patrols.

The extension of convoy escort to 17 degrees west longitude presented Dönitz with two major problems. First, in order to repeatedly attack an inbound convoy before it picked up its escort or an outbound convoy after it left its escort, U-boats had to operate well west of 17 degrees west longitude. Since this was beyond "British waters" where the unrestricted U-boat rules applied, Dönitz had to petition Hitler through Raeder and the OKM for a further relaxation of the rules. Second, operations so far to the west imposed restrictions on the use of Type VII boats, which had only half the fuel capacity of the VIIBs. In a prolonged convoy battle requiring high-speed running, even the VIIBs would be stretched. Hence fuel availability was to become a critical factor in most convoy battles.

With this new information in hand, Dönitz flew to Lorient on July 22 to confer with the skippers of the four oceangoing boats: Lemp (*U-30*), Rollmann (*U-34*), Salmann (*U-52*), and Kretschmer (*U-99*). After inspections and conferences, it was clear that *U-30, U-34,* and *U-52*—all plagued with mechanical difficulties—would have to be used with the greatest care. Only Kretschmer's new VIIB, *U-99*, was in good enough condition to mount a patrol from Lorient and return to Lorient. The other three would have to patrol home to Germany, perhaps to sail no more to the Atlantic.

Rollmann in *U-34* left first, on July 23. Capitalizing on *B-dienst* information, he intercepted inbound convoy Halifax 58 near Rockall Bank. Although some torpedoes malfunctioned or missed, he sank four ships for 29,300 tons, including the 10,400-ton British tanker *Thiara* and the 9,300-ton British freighter *Accra.* Homebound to Germany, he sank the 700-ton British submarine *Spearfish* off Norway with his last torpedo, and recovered one lucky survivor from the wreckage.

Dönitz was ecstatic. Those five sinkings, added to the eight on the outbound leg of *U-34*'s patrol in June, gave Rollmann a total bag of thirteen ships for (it was believed) 74,300 tons. Including prior successes, Rollmann had sunk twenty-four ships for 121,900 tons, elevating him to number-one U-boat "ace" in ships and tonnage. This achievement earned Rollmann a *Ritterkreuz* (the fifth such award to German submariners) and the full Berlin propaganda treatment. But it was the end for *U-34*. Hopelessly plagued with mechanical problems, *U-34* was sent to the Baltic under a school skipper. Rollmann joined the training command.

Otto Kretschmer in *U-99* sailed next. Hugging the coast of the British Isles, Kretschmer went up to North Channel and over a three-day period he sank four ships for 32,300 tons, including the 13,200-ton liner *Auckland Star.* In return, Kretschmer received another terrific pasting (fifty close depth charges) from escorts. Undamaged—and undeterred—he got on the trail of an outbound convoy and attacked three large tankers in ballast, firing one torpedo at each. Kretschmer claimed all three tankers had sunk—reporting seven ships sunk for 56,000 tons in a mere six days—but the tankers were only damaged. Although Dönitz knew from *B-dienst* that the claims were exaggerated, he liked Kretschmer's aggressive style and, perhaps for propaganda purposes, upped Kretschmer's bag to 65,137 tons, which gave him a total of 100,000 tons, qualifying him for a *Ritterkreuz.* When Kretschmer pulled into Lorient after a patrol of but twelve days—the shortest torpedo patrol on record—Raeder and Dönitz were standing on the dock to present the medal.*

Lemp in *U-30* and Salmann in *U-52* sailed last from Lorient. Homebound, Lemp sank two ships for 12,400 tons, but engine problems forced him to abort and go directly to Germany. Lemp's confirmed bag, including *Athenia,* was sixteen sinkings for 80,232 tons—plus damage to the battleship *Barham*—deemed sufficient for a *Ritterkreuz,* which was awarded while *U-30* was still at sea. Upon arrival in Germany, the boat was retired to the Baltic; Lemp and many of the *U-30* crew were assigned to commission a new IXB. Homebound, Salmann in *U-52* sank three British freighters for 17,100 tons and incurred heavy battle damage from a depth-charge attack, which kept the boat in the yards for the next four months.

By this time the eighteen surviving Type II and IIB ducks had been assigned to full-time duty at the burgeoning submarine school. The seven surviving Type IIC ducks of the Emsmann Flotilla (*U-56* to *U-62*), basing in Bergen, patrolled in the Atlantic, terminating the short voyages in Bergen or Lorient. In nine patrols mounted in July off the heavily defended North Channel, the ducks sank twelve ships for 64,600 tons, including the 7,000-ton British tanker *Scottish Minstrel.* Otto Harms in *U-56* sank the biggest vessel: the 17,000-ton British auxiliary cruiser *Transylvania.*

These duck patrols were useful for indoctrinating skippers and crews to combat, for diverting the enemy's slim ASW forces away from the oceangoing boats, for spotting outbound convoys, and for creating fear and confusion by the occasional sinking in British home waters. But, owing to the crush of students at the submarine school, the OKM ruled that commencing on October 1, the ducks of the Emsmann Flotilla (*U-56* to *U-62*) were to be assigned to the training command, together with

---

* According to postwar analysis, Kretschmer's confirmed sinkings on the duck *U-23* and *U-99* to then were fifteen and a half ships for 70,740 tons.

most of the sixteen brand-new Type IID ducks (*U-137* to *U-152*) and two Type IIBs (*U-120, U-121*) originally intended for export. These diversions were to virtually close down duck patrols in British home waters.

THE AUGUST SLAUGHTER

While the RAF and *Luftwaffe* fought the air Battle of Britain in August 1940, thirteen oceangoing boats sailed from Germany to continue the U-boat campaign in the Atlantic. These included two new boats, the VIIB *U-100*, commanded by Joachim Schepke, age twenty-eight, who had sunk eleven ships for 18,000 tons while commanding the ducks *U-3* and *U-19*, and the IXB *U-124*, commanded by Georg-Wilhelm Schulz and manned by other survivors of his *U-64*, sunk in the fjord at Narvik. All thirteen boats were to patrol the northerly hunting grounds near Rockall Bank, then put into Lorient. One IXB, *U-65* (von Stockhausen), was to first land two *Abwehr* agents in Ireland.

Since the British were transfixed by the air battle or preparing for the supposed German invasion, Dönitz anticipated another low-risk slaughter like that of June. In response to his petition, Hitler had authorized unrestricted submarine warfare to 20 degrees west longitude as of August 17.* Moreover, *B-dienst* was operating at peak efficiency, providing Dönitz a wealth of specific information on convoy routing and escort rendezvous, which offered the possibility of a resumption of pack attacks.

But a number of things went wrong in the initial foray of these nine boats. Sailing from Wilhelmshaven on August 1, the big, cranky *U-25*, commanded by Heinz Beduhn, blundered into a minefield and was lost with all hands. British air patrols caught and bombed Viktor Oehrn in *U-37* and Dietrich Knorr in *U-51*, inflicting so much damage that both boats had to abort to Lorient. The hit on *U-51* was credited to a Sunderland of Coastal Command Squadron 210, piloted by Ernest Reginald Baker. As *U-51* was approaching Lorient in the early hours of August 20, the British minelaying submarine *Cachalot*, commanded by David Luce,† torpedoed and sank her with the loss of all hands. Von Stockhausen in *U-65* was compelled to abort the landing of the two *Abwehr* agents in Ireland owing to the death of the senior agent.‡ Thereafter, *U-65* incurred a mechanical breakdown and limped into Brest, seeking repairs.

These misadventures left only five boats from Germany to patrol the convoy hunting grounds near Rockall Bank in early August. For the first ten days, all were

---

* Berlin termed the relaxed U-boat rules to 20 degrees west longitude a "counterblockade" of Great Britain in reprisal for the British blockade of Germany.

† Later, First Sea Lord.

‡ General Sean Russell, Chief of Staff of the Irish Republican Army, who, von Stockhausen reported, died of a bleeding ulcer. Russell was buried at sea. The other agent, Frank Ryan, remained with the boat.

beset by unseasonably stormy weather (as were the aircraft in the Battle of Britain). Nonetheless, Heinrich Liebe in *U-38* sank two ships for 12,500 tons, including the 7,500-ton Egyptian liner *Mohammed Ali-Kebir,* carrying 860 British troops to Gibraltar. About 320 troops perished, but about 540 were rescued by a British destroyer. These two sinkings raised Liebe's confirmed bag to eighteen ships for 87,000 tons. Counting two overclaims for 13,000 tons, he qualified for a *Ritterkreuz,* which was awarded while he was still on patrol.

With clearing weather, the five boats near Rockall Bank had somewhat better luck.

• Engelbert Endrass in *U-46* severely damaged two ships, a Dutch and a Greek.

• Hans Rösing in *U-48* sank two ships, a Swede and a Belgian, for 9,900 tons.

• Joachim Schepke in the new VIIB *U-100* sank a 5,000-ton British freighter.

• Fritz Frauenheim in *U-101* sank a 4,500-ton British freighter.

These were better returns, but until August 23, the results of the nine boats sailing from Germany were considered disappointing: merely eight ships sunk and two damaged.*

At this time *B-dienst* went "blind" or "deaf." After one full year of war, the British realized that Royal Navy codes were compromised and on August 20 they changed all the naval encoding systems. The OKM diarist commented: "This is the most serious blow to our radio intelligence since the outbreak of the war. . . . It is remarkable that it had not been done before now. . . ." *B-dienst* was hopeful that the new British codes could be broken "in six weeks or so," the diarist noted. But that hope was not to be realized.

The loss of British naval codes may not have been the most serious blow for the U-boat force. During the first year of operations Dönitz had laid numerous submarine traps for British naval formations, important troop convoys, and merchant-ship convoys, but owing to inclement weather, errors in navigation by the U-boats or the British, wrong or late information from *B-dienst,* and other factors, almost none of the traps had paid off and a great deal of U-boat patrol time had been wasted. The sailing cycles on most convoy routes had been well established; lax exhaust-smoke control and communications security in convoys was expected to continue. The only really serious setback was the loss of intelligence on positions and operations of British submarines conducting ASW.

In spite of the lost intelligence, the U-boats performed extremely well in the last week of August.

Having repaired his battle damage in Lorient, Viktor Oehrn in *U-37* returned to the hunting grounds to sink a record seven confirmed ships for 24,400 tons in merely four days, including the 1,000-ton British sloop *Penzance,* misidentified and credited as a "destroyer." Hit by air and surface escorts, Oehrn was compelled to abort to Lorient for the second time.

---

* Including Liebe's two sinkings and one ship each sunk by the aborting *U-37* and *U-51,* inbound to Lorient. *U-51*'s victim was the 5,700-ton British tanker *Sylvafield.*

- Joachim Schepke in *U-100* sank five more ships for 21,000 tons, and damaged a sixth.
- Endrass in *U-46* sank four ships for 29,800 tons, including the 15,000-ton auxiliary cruiser *Dunvegan Castle*.
- Rösing in *U-48* sank three more ships for 19,200 tons, including two British tankers, the 6,800-ton *Athelcrest* and 6,700-ton *La Brea*.
- Hans Jenisch in the Type VII *U-32*, who sailed from Germany August 15, sank three ships for 13,000 tons and damaged the British light cruiser *Fiji*.
- Fritz Frauenheim in *U-101* sank or fatally damaged two more ships (a Greek and a Finn) for 7,700 tons.
- Günter Kuhnke, in the Type VII *U-28*, sank two ships for 5,500 tons.

Perhaps influenced by Göring's generous award of the *Ritterkreuz* to *Luftwaffe* pilots for unverified and exaggerated kills in the Battle of Britain, and/or for internal and external propaganda purposes, Dönitz became less stringent in assessing U-boat claims. Berlin continued to trumpet exaggerated U-boat kills: Hans Jenisch in *U-32*, who sank 13,000 confirmed tons, was credited 40,000 tons; Joachim Schepke in *U-100*, who sank 25,800 tons, was given 43,000 tons. Dönitz more freely awarded *Ritterkreuzes*. Three other favored skippers who had made but two Atlantic patrols benefited from the relaxation: Engelbert Endrass in *U-46* (credit 105,000 tons, actual 65,347 tons); Hans Rösing in *U-48* (credit 88,600 tons, actual 60,702 tons)*; and Fritz Frauenheim in *U-101*. Frauenheim had sunk but 54,300 confirmed tons on *U-101*, but when his earlier sinkings on the duck *U-21*, including the minefield that savaged the 11,500-ton heavy cruiser *Belfast*, were added, his total was 72,300 tons.

Among the last boats to sail from Germany in August was Georg-Wilhelm Schulz's new IXB *U-124*. In honor of the German Alpine troops who had saved them when their former boat, *U-64*, had been sunk in Narvik, the *U-124* crewmen had adopted the Alpine forces insignia, the mountain flower edelweiss, and had emblazoned an enlarged version of it on the conning tower.

On the night of August 25 Schulz found convoy Halifax 65A close to the north end of the Hebrides in heavily patrolled, shallow waters and attacked on the surface. As he was threading in through the escorts, he impulsively fired his two stern tubes at a "destroyer." Both missed and the unsuspecting "destroyer" cruised on. When Schulz had brought *U-124* to firing position, he chose four freighters and fired one torpedo at each, spacing the torpedoes one minute apart. All four torpedoes were seen to hit and explode. The salvo appeared to be the most astonishing of the war: four ships of 30,000 tons sunk by four torpedoes in five minutes! But the claim was incorrect. Only two of the four ships sank. A third, the 4,000-ton *Stakesby*, was damaged but survived. The fourth torpedo must have missed.

There was no time to celebrate the supposed victory. One of the destroyers

---

* In five patrols under Herbert Schultze, including Norway, and two under Rösing, the *U-48* had sunk thirty confirmed ships for 169,823 tons, putting her far ahead of all other boats.

caught *U-124* in its searchlight and pounced, forcing Schulz to crash dive and go deep. At 295 feet the boat hit an outcrop of rock and jarred to a stop. That terrifying moment was followed by another: a rain of close depth charges. Schulz got the boat off the rock, eased deeper, and bottomed at 328 feet. The destroyer made one more desultory depth-charge run, but then gave up the hunt.

Later, after hauling well out to sea, Schulz sent a diver down to inspect the bow for damage incurred when the boat hit the rock. It proved to be serious: Three of the four bow caps had been damaged; only one was fully functional. Upon learning this, Dönitz ordered Schulz to leave the hunting grounds and go west to latitude 20 degrees, where he was to broadcast weather reports, which were urgently needed by the *Luftwaffe*. While doing so, one of the men carelessly half-flooded the stern torpedo room, causing a temporary emergency that evoked chilling memories of Narvik.

The thirteenth and last boat to sail from Germany in August was Prien's *U-47*, which put out from Kiel August 27. By then six of the surviving ten Atlantic boats that preceded him in August were in or headed to Lorient for refit, replenishment, rest, and rewards. The other four remained in the hunting grounds: Kuhnke in *U-28*, von Stockhausen in *U-65*, who had resailed from Brest, Frauenheim in *U-101*, and Schulz in *U-124* (with three damaged bow caps) on weather-reporting station.

Prien entered the hunting grounds on September 2, and that afternoon his periscope watch detected an unusual cloud of black smoke on the horizon. It turned out to be the 7,500-ton Belgian freighter *Ville de Mons,* inbound from New York with no escort and badly in need of a boiler cleaning. Prien hit her with one torpedo and saw the crew abandon in three lifeboats. When the ship showed no signs of sinking, Prien surfaced to polish her off with his deck gun, but changed his mind and put her under with another torpedo. One crewman died of exposure, but the others were rescued.

The codebreakers at *B-dienst* provided Dönitz with further information on North Atlantic convoys, deduced from lapses in Allied radio security and other sources. The information included the important news that to reduce the shipping congestion in Halifax, Nova Scotia, and to sail more merchant ships in the favorable late summer and early fall weather, the British on August 15 had initiated a second convoy system on the North Atlantic run. These new convoys departed from the more northerly Canadian port of Sydney, on Cape Breton Island, a part of Nova Scotia, which, owing to ice, closed in winter. They were designated SC to indicate the geographic location (Sydney–Cape Breton, much as HX indicated Halifax), but because they traveled at only 7½ to 9 knots, the SC became corrupted to mean "Slow Convoy," as opposed to the faster HXs.*

On September 2, *B-dienst* alerted Dönitz to inbound Slow Convoy 2, composed of fifty-three ships. Dönitz directed Prien to intercept the convoy at a designated location near 20 degrees west on September 6, before it picked up its escort. Dönitz planned that three other boats would join Prien for the attack: *U-65* (von

---

* From February 12, 1940, HX convoys sailed from Halifax every four days at a fixed speed of 9 knots. Faster ships (15 knots plus) sailed alone. SC convoys sailed from Sydney every eight days.

Stockhausen), *U-101* (Frauenheim), which had only six torpedoes left, and possibly *U-124* (Schulz), despite her three damaged bow caps. The other boat, the Type VII *U-28* (Kuhnke), could not operate so far west because of fuel limitations. However, an appeal to Berlin to release *U-124* from weather reporting was rejected, leaving only three boats (*U-47, U-65, U-101*) to attack the convoy.

En route to the designated area on the evening of September 3, Prien in *U-47* unexpectedly ran across another convoy, Outbound 207. Husbanding his torpedoes, he picked out two targets and carried out a night surface attack. He sank the big 9,000-ton British freighter *Titan* and claimed damage to another of 4,000 tons, but the latter could not be identified in postwar records.

By the morning of September 4, the three boats, *U-47, U-65,* and *U-101,* had formed a north-south scouting line along longitude 20 degrees west. The weather was miserable: gale-force winds, towering seas. On September 5 Prien lost a man overboard. Early the next day von Stockhausen in *U-65* reported contact with the convoy, but the weather and visibility were so bad he was not able to shoot. He shadowed, attempting to bring in the other boats. However, *U-101* reported serious "engine defects," forcing Frauenheim to abort to Lorient. That left only *U-47* and *U-65* to attack the convoy, which had picked up its local escorts: two destroyers, two corvettes, and three trawlers.

That same evening, September 6, in heavy seas, Prien made contact with Slow Convoy 2 and tracked. Later that night he attacked on the surface and sank three of the fifty-three ships: two British freighters, *Neptunian,* 5,200 tons, and *Jose de Larrinaga,* 5,300 tons, and the Norwegian freighter *Gro,* 4,211 tons. Owing to the weather and other factors, von Stockhausen in *U-65* was unable to get into a favorable shooting position and could not attack.

As the convoy steamed eastward toward the North Channel, Prien doggedly tracked and radioed positions. Late on the morning of September 9, south of the Hebrides, he sank a fourth ship, the Greek freighter *Poseidon,* 3,800 tons. Responding to Prien's reports a few hours later, Kuhnke in *U-28* came up and sank one ship, the 2,400-ton British freighter *Mardinian.* The bulk of Slow Convoy 2—forty-eight ships and the seven escorts—reached North Channel without further damage.

Prien, having sunk a total of six ships and, he believed, damaged one, had only one torpedo left. Since he had been on patrol only fourteen days and still had an ample supply of fuel, Dönitz directed him to go west to 20 degrees and replace the damaged *U-124* (Schulz) on the weather-reporting station. Doubtless Prien found this assignment unappealing—the boat had yet to experience the delights of Lorient—but he carried it out without complaint. When relieved on station, the *U-124* headed for Lorient. On September 10, Berlin gloatingly announced Prien's claims: six ships for 40,000 tons sunk, one damaged.

Günter Kuhnke in the VII *U-28,* low on fuel, found and tracked another convoy, Outbound 210. In the early hours of September 11 he attacked on the surface, firing at what he believed to be two tankers and a freighter. He claimed the damaging of one 10,000-ton tanker and the sinking of two freighters for 13,000 tons. Postwar analysis credited him with damage to a 4,700-ton British freighter and sinking a 2,000-ton Dutch freighter. Critically low on fuel, Kuhnke headed for Lorient, claiming a total of five ships for 30,000 tons sunk on this patrol. With these and past overclaims, Kuhnke qualified for a *Ritterkreuz* under the relaxed criteria and it was awarded when he reached Lorient. His confirmed score at this time—all on *U-28*—was thirteen ships for 56,272 tons.

Kuhnke's return left two of the August Atlantic boats in the hunting grounds: *U-47* (Prien) on weather station with one torpedo, and *U-65* (von Stockhausen). The latter had sailed from Germany on August 8, canceled the special mission to land agents in Ireland and aborted to Brest with mechanical defects, refueled in Brest and resailed, and found convoy SC 2, but had not yet fired a torpedo.

To this point—September 15—the thirteen Atlantic boats sailing from Germany in August had sunk a total of forty-four confirmed ships for about 230,000 tons, a decline to an average of 3.4 ships per boat per patrol, but still impressive. Five skippers—Oehrn, Prien, Schepke, Endrass, and Rösing—had accounted for two-thirds of the sinkings (twenty-nine). Two boats sailing in August had been lost: *U-25* (Beduhn) and *U-51* (Knorr). The base at Lorient had enabled Oehrn in *U-37* to remount his aborted patrol to good effect, but otherwise it had yet to make any substantial impact on the U-boat war.

During August the ducks of the Emsmann Flotilla mounted six patrols to the Atlantic from Germany, Norway, or Lorient. They sank a total of seven ships for 32,000 tons. One duck, *U-57*, commanded by Erich Topp, age twenty-six, sank three of the seven ships (for 24,000 tons), but was herself rammed and sunk by the Norwegian tramp *Rona* on September 3, while entering a lock in the Kiel Canal. Six men died in this mishap but *U-57* was salvaged, and Topp and the rest of the crew were assigned to commission a new VIIB. On August 31, the duck *U-60*, commanded by Adalbert Schnee, age twenty-six, torpedoed the 15,300-ton Dutch liner *Volendam*, which was transporting 321 British children to Canada, but the damaged ship was towed to port and all the children were saved.

British tanker losses remained worrisome. During the months of July and August, the oceangoing U-boats had sunk six for about 44,000 tons, the duck *U-61* one. The duck *U-57* had accounted for another, the 7,500-ton British *Pecten*. In addition, the Italian submarine *Malaspina* sank the 8,400-ton tanker *British Fame* near the Azores, and the *U-A*, on patrol off West Africa, sank yet another, the 5,800-ton Norwegian *Sarita*.* Total Allied tanker losses in July–August: ten.

STRATEGIES, SECRETS, AND DEALS

During the air Battle of Britain, Churchill made a bold and far-reaching decision, one that was to profoundly influence the course of World War II. Great Britain was to fight no less defiantly to deny the Axis control of the Mediterranean Sea, the continent of Africa, and the Middle East. After Britain had gathered sufficient military power, she was to employ the Mediterranean Basin as a staging area to coun-

---

* The *U-A* sank six other vessels for a total bag of seven for 40,706 tons.

terattack the Axis, first crushing Italy, then Germany, by attacking Germany's "soft underbelly" through Italy and the Balkans.

It was a complicated and controversial strategy, fraught with immense risk. In Africa, Benito Mussolini's forces controlled Libya, Ethiopia, and Eritrea. Striking out from Ethiopia in several directions during July and August, Italian troops had punched into the Anglo-Egyptian Sudan and the British colony of Kenya, and had overrun the whole of British Somaliland on the Gulf of Aden. Mussolini was then poised in eastern Libya to attack Egypt and he appeared to be massing troops in Albania for an attack on Greece. With the addition of two new 35,000-ton battleships, *Littorio* and *Vittorio Veneto,* and the older, smaller but modernized battleship *Dulio,* the Italian Navy had dramatically increased in strength: five battleships, plus numerous modern heavy and light cruisers and destroyers.

Almost unnoticed during the toughest days of the Battle of Britain, the British proceeded to implement the Mediterranean strategy. In August the Admiralty powerfully reinforced its two naval squadrons, Force H at Gibraltar and the Mediterranean Fleet at Alexandria, and drew plans to reinforce the island of Malta. The War Office beefed up the slim British ground force in Egypt, grandiosely named "The Army of the Nile." In collaboration with Free French leader Charles de Gaulle, Churchill designed schemes to persuade the French leaders of Vichy colonies in Africa and the Middle East to come over to the Allied side.

The Italian Army in Libya, comprised of 200,000 men, launched its offensive against Egypt on September 13. The Army of the Nile, merely 63,000 men, was unable to hold and it fell back sixty miles to Sidi Barrani, fighting a well-executed rear-guard action. With one added surge the Italians might have pushed on to Cairo, Alexandria, and the Suez Canal, but they ran out of steam and sat down.

Since the Italian Navy and Italian land-based air posed a formidable threat in the central Mediterranean, the British were hard-pressed to reinforce and resupply the Army of the Nile. Everything from England had to be sent by convoy the long way around the southern tip of Africa (the Cape of Good Hope), thence north into the Indian Ocean to the Red Sea, a tedious and inefficient route. In order to eliminate the Italian threat and open the Mediterranean to British convoys, the commander of the Mediterranean Fleet, Andrew Cunningham, repeatedly sought to lure the Italian Navy into battle, but the Italian admirals shrewdly prolonged the naval threat by avoiding a major confrontation.

Meanwhile, Churchill and de Gaulle pressed ahead with their schemes to persuade the Vichy French in Africa to come over to the Allied side. The first of these (Operation Menace) was directed at the Vichy colony of Senegal, on the African west coast. The hope was that if a joint Anglo-Free French expedition made a show of force off Senegal's chief seaport, Dakar, where the gunned but unfinished battleship *Richelieu* had taken refuge, the Vichy French would rally to de Gaulle and deliver not only Senegal, which could provide a staging base for mounting further intrigue in Vichy French West Africa, but also *Richelieu.*

A substantial British naval force was committed to this scheme: the carrier *Ark Royal* and the battleship *Resolution* from Force H, the battleship *Barham* and several cruisers, including *Fiji,* torpedoed by Jenisch in *U-32* while leaving England.

Contrary to the hope, the British warships met a hot reception at Dakar: heavy gun-fire from Vichy shore batteries, the *Richelieu,* and some Vichy French cruisers and super-destroyers, which had raced down from Toulon. During the exchange of fire, the Dakar-based Vichy submarine *Beveziers* torpedoed the *Resolution,* causing "serious damage." Chastened, the British were compelled to withdraw and cancel that scheme, but it was not a total failure. The show of force emboldened the leader of Vichy Cameroon, Jacques Philippe Leclerc, to come over to the Allied side, creating a domino effect in the Vichy colonies of Chad and French Congo. On October 12, French forces of those three colonies, together with some defecting Senegalese troops, invaded and occupied Vichy Gabon.

Not entirely unexpectedly, an Italian Army, staging from Albania, invaded Greece on October 28. Since Greece was an ally of Britain and an Italian conquest of Greece would flank Egypt on the north, imperiling the Army of the Nile and the British naval base at Alexandria, Churchill and the War Cabinet took immediate steps to assist the Greeks. British ground forces from Egypt occupied the islands of Crete and Lemnos. RAF fighter and bomber squadrons moved up to bases near Athens to support the Greek Army.

With the sudden expansion of British responsibilities and operations in the eastern Mediterranean, it became imperative that British naval forces open a direct convoy route from Gibraltar to Alexandria. Toward that end, on November 11, Cunningham staged a surprise attack on the Italian fleet anchorage at Taranto, located in the "heel" of Italy. Flying off the new carrier *Illustrious,* twenty-one old Swordfish biplanes torpedoed three of the five Italian battleships: the big, new *Littorio* and the smaller, but modernized *Dulio* and *Cavour. Littorio* and *Dulio* were knocked out of action for five and seven months, respectively; *Cavour,* severely damaged and beached, did not return to active service. The two undamaged battleships, *Vittorio Veneto* and *Cesare,* hurriedly withdrew to Naples.

This victory opened a British convoy route in the Mediterranean, but only temporarily. Humiliated, Mussolini requested help from Berlin. In response, Hitler sent about 400 *Luftwaffe* planes to the island of Sicily to assist the Italians in attacking the British convoys and the covering naval forces. Although the *Luftwaffe* wrought absolute havoc on the convoys, it was soon clear to Hitler that he would have to send additional ground and air forces to the Mediterranean Basin to reinforce the lackluster Italian armies, which bogged down in both Egypt and Greece.

The decision to fight to the utmost in the Mediterranean, Africa, and the Middle East placed immense demands on British military assets. The Admiralty committed a large portion of the Royal Navy to the Mediterranean: the carriers *Illustrious, Ark Royal,* and *Eagle;* the battleships *Warspite, Royal Sovereign, Malaya, Ramillies, Valiant, Barham,* and *Renown;* numerous cruisers; scores of destroyers and auxiliaries; and nearly two dozen submarines.* Countless other

---

* These unwisely included a dozen old *O-, P-,* and *R-* class fleet submarines, and minelayers, which because of their age and size were entirely unsuited for Mediterranean operations. Ill-equipped, ill-trained Italian ASW forces promptly sank seven of them, with heavy loss of life. In return, one British submarine, *Parthian,* sank the Italian submarine *Diamante.*

warships were pressed into service to escort the convoys which went the long way to Egypt via the Cape of Good Hope and Indian Ocean.

Washington never fully understood or approved of this diversion of resources to the Mediterranean Basin. As Washington viewed it, the British strategy amounted to wasteful and inefficient "pecking at the periphery." Washington believed that the full resources and military power of Britain should have been brought directly to bear on Germany itself.

The British decision to fight vigorously for the Mediterranean Basin, at a time when it appeared that the Germans might invade the British Isles, in effect embroiled the Royal Navy in a "two-front war." Owing to the loss of or severe damage to destroyers in the Norway operations and Dunkirk, and to the decision to deploy a large number of destroyers in ports on the English Channel to counter a possible invasion, and to the transfer of numerous destroyers to the Mediterranean, there were only a few left for convoy escort in the North Atlantic and Northwest Approaches, and most of these were old ships in need of upgrading and requiring much upkeep.

Adding to the Admiralty's problems, the first of the twenty new 280-foot, 1,000-ton *Hunt*-class destroyers, designed specifically for open-ocean convoy escort, failed to meet Royal Navy standards for that role. Hurriedly designed, they were top-heavy, dangerously unstable in heavy seas, overgunned for the size (four 4"), lacked fuel capacity for extended voyages, and despite the elimination of torpedo tubes, did not have space topside to carry more than fifty depth charges, not really enough for convoy escorting. As a consequence of that and the loss and shortage of other destroyers, the Admiralty had to send the corvettes, which had been selected for inshore escort, to blue-water escort duties. By and large the *Hunt*s had to be relegated to missions on short-legged routes in home waters and the Mediterranean Sea, a terrible setback.

In those darkest of days, Churchill intensified his secret pleas to Roosevelt for help in supplying destroyers. The President was willing but the renewed requests came at a politically awkward time. He was engaged in a tough run for an unprecedented third term against the popular Republican candidate, Wendell Willkie. He had pledged to keep the United States out of the war in Europe; he dared not alienate the large bloc of isolationist voters.

Pending the election, Roosevelt walked a tightrope. He publicly pushed through the transfer of fifty "flush-deck," or "four-stack," destroyers to Great Britain in early September, justifying that measure as a good deal for the United States since the rights to British bases obtained in the exchange enhanced the security of the Western Hemisphere.

The fifty destroyers for Great Britain came from a fleet of 273 American vessels that had been built in the latter years of World War I. Originally named after American naval heroes, most were renamed for towns common to Britain and the United States (e.g., Annapolis, Georgetown, Richmond, etc.); hence they were known as *Town*-class vessels. They were 315 feet in length, displaced 1,200 tons, and had a top speed of about 29 knots. The main armament consisted of four 4" guns, one 3" gun, and twelve torpedo tubes. Forty-three of these ships went to the

Royal Navy and seven to the Royal Canadian Navy, named for Canadian rivers. The Royal Navy manned three vessels (*Bath, Lincoln, Mansfield*) with Norwegian crews; one ship, *Cameron,* was damaged in an air raid on Portland and never became operational.*

Much nonsense has been written about these vessels, such as dubbing them "fifty ships that saved the world." In fact, these ships required a great deal of work, modification, and upgrading. About four months passed before most of the ships reached England and by the time they were fully operational, the dire emergencies that prompted their acquisition had passed. While the symbolic value of the transfer was great for the British, the *Town*-class historian, Arnold Hague, wrote, "The tactical effect of the ships themselves was, however, small . . ." and they "passed quite quickly from the operational scene."

Privately and secretly Roosevelt did much more to assist the British. Among his most important steps was to send a military mission, headed by Rear Admiral Robert L. Ghormley, to London in August, ostensibly to assess British chances for survival, but in reality to begin long-term, Anglo-American joint planning for the defeat of the Axis.

In reaction to the U-boat slaughter of British-controlled shipping, at about this same time (August 1940), Roosevelt approved a proposal from Admiral Jerry Land of the U.S. Maritime Commission to greatly increase construction of merchant ships. Since the half-dozen major shipyards in the United States were already burdened with contracts for the huge expansion of the Navy, Land established seven new shipyards (three on the Gulf Coast, four on the West Coast) to build the new merchant ships. The modified Maritime Commission program envisioned letting contracts for two hundred new ships by July 1941, but that was merely a small, first step in what was to grow into the greatest merchant-ship building program in the history of the world.†

Seeking new sources for merchant ships, Churchill sent a secret mission to Washington and Ottawa. The mission members brought along blueprints for what was wanted: a simple, welded, 440-foot coal-burning cargo vessel of 10,000 gross tons, capable of cruising at 11 knots on a single shaft. Although the Maritime Commission was already overburdened, Washington agreed to build sixty such ships for the British. Ottawa, in turn, agreed to build twenty-six more, relying mostly on riveted construction rather than welding. The British designated those sixty ships *Ocean*-class; the twenty-six Canadian versions, *Fort*-class.‡

Provided some refinements were incorporated, the Maritime Commission decreed that the British *Ocean*-class cargo vessel should be adopted for the 200 cargo vessels already on order. The chief change was in propulsion: oil-fired boilers

---

* See Appendix 9.

† In 1940, the Maritime Commission produced fifty-four new ships, including sixteen tankers. Forty-one of these ships went to the Army and Navy and thirteen to the private sector.

‡ Henry J. Kaiser's Todd-California company in Richmond, California, built thirty ships; his Todd-Maine company built the other thirty in Portland, Maine. The first American-built ship, *Ocean Vanguard,* was launched ten months later, August 17, 1941.

rather than the coal-fired "Scotch boilers" in the British ships. The Americans designated this type of vessel the *EC-2* Emergency Cargo Ship, but they became popularly known as the "Liberty" ships, or facetiously, "The Ugly Duckling."*

As the web of friendship between Great Britain and the United States knitted ever tighter, Churchill and the War Cabinet decided to share Britain's most closely held scientific and technical achievements with the United States. Led by the scientist Henry Tizard, another secret mission, which included the radar expert Taffy Bowen, left for Washington in late August on the liner *Duchess of Richmond*. The mission carried along a 450-pound Mark VII aerial depth charge and plans and specifications for the Mark VIII 250-pound aerial depth charge; the formula for RDX, an explosive 50 percent more powerful than TNT, to be produced in America as Torpex; a Rolls-Royce Merlin aircraft engine; a Swedish-built Bofors automatic antiaircraft cannon; a proximity fuse for large-caliber antiaircraft guns; a power-driven gun turret for heavy bombers; the latest model of British sonar; plans and specifications for an ahead-throwing antisubmarine mortar called the Hedgehog; plans and specifications for a miniaturized shipborne high frequency direction finder (HF/DF or Huff Duff); plans and specifications for an "escort," or "jeep," aircraft carrier; plans and specifications of the Chain Home British antiaircraft radar net, together with data on the latest models of airborne radar, the antibomber A-I and antiship ASV; and three models of the latest version of the Randall and Boot cavity magnetron, much improved since the first test in February.

All of these items were of intense interest to the American military and the scientists and engineers, and some of them were of great value. But none excited the scientists and engineers more than the Randall and Boot cavity magnetron. It was, an American scientist later wrote, "the most valuable treasure ever brought to these shores." Somewhat chagrined to discover it had been inspired by a forgotten American invention (Hull's magnetron), Washington assigned the task of its full development to the Radiation Laboratory at the Massachusetts Institute of Technology, which in turn farmed out various technical chores to laboratories at General Electric, Westinghouse, the Radio Corporation of America, and Bell Telephone.

At this time, Great Britain and the United States also entered into an agreement to exchange codebreaking information. Both nations had a great deal to share: Sensational new breakthroughs had occurred. In Washington, Army and Navy codebreaking teams, working independently, cracked through difficult Japanese codes in September 1940. The Army team, led by William F. Friedman, broke the Japanese diplomatic machine code, Purple, which had been introduced eighteen months earlier, in February 1939. Within the same week, the Navy team, led by Laurence F. Safford and Agnes Driscoll, broke the Japanese naval code, JN-25, which had been introduced in June 1939.

Friedman's Purple machine, which utilized stepping switches rather than ro-

---

* The first American-built Liberty ship, *Patrick Henry,* was launched on September 27, 1941. She could carry 2,800 jeeps or 300 freight cars.

tors, enabled American codebreakers to "read," on a continuous basis, all high-level diplomatic traffic between Tokyo and Japanese embassies in Washington, London, Berlin, and elsewhere around the globe. Laurence Safford later characterized Friedman's break into Purple as "the masterpiece of cryptanalysis in the war era." The Navy team's break into JN-25 gave it complete and current access to the Japanese Imperial Navy's operational traffic, but it required compilation, by hand, of huge "code books," together with thousands of English translations, a tedious task that took the Navy team another year to complete.

At about this same time, September 1940, the British Tabulating Machine Company delivered the first two prototypes of the Turing-Welchman bombes to Bletchley Park. These wondrous machines, in effect, automated the hunt for five-rotor Enigma keys. The bombes were not a panacea. They had to be prompted with cribs; without cribs they were useless. But after a full year of intense work on various German Enigma nets, Bletchley Park had plenty of cribs on file and its personnel had developed an uncanny sense for spotting new cribs.

Fed a daily dose of cribs, the bombes enabled Welchman and his codebreaking group to break *Luftwaffe* Red—but no other Enigma nets—consistently, currently, and accurately. A distinguished British scholar-historian at Bletchley Park, Peter Calvocoressi, remembered: "We were never again to lose Red. It became the constant staple . . . it was broken daily, usually on the day in question and early in the day."

The military historian Bradley F. Smith has documented the background of the Anglo-American cryptographic agreement.* He wrote that the initial proposal came from a U.S. Army representative in London, Brigadier General George Strong, and that thereafter senior American officials pressed for an exchange, apparently with President Roosevelt's blessing. On the other hand, British and American codebreakers, traditionally suspicious and secretive, were actively opposed to the agreement and delayed it as long as possible. Largely at the urging of Secretary of War Henry Stimson, the deal was finally struck in mid-December 1940, in a one-page document that has not yet been released to the public.

MORE HAPPY TIMES

Facing the second year of the war and fully aware of the tightening bond between the United States and Great Britain, Dönitz was a frustrated warrior. He had not once wavered from his belief that Great Britain could only be defeated by a massive U-boat assault. He viewed the preparations for a possible invasion of the British Isles—and rumors of secret preparations for an attack on the Soviet Union—as ludicrous diversions of resources from the main task.

Hitler had promised U-boats—hundreds of U-boats—but Hitler had not delivered. When push came to shove for steel and other materials, the *Wehrmacht* and

---

*   In *The Ultra-Magic Deals* (1993).

Luftwaffe consistently took precedence. Moreover, preparations for the invasion of Britain (conversion of river barges to landing craft, etc.) had diverted labor and matériel from the U-boat construction program. Dönitz complained to Raeder and the OKM that twenty-three oceangoing boats had been delayed four to six months because of a shortage of torpedo tubes. As a result of this bottleneck—and others—the modest production schedule of U-boats for 1940 had fallen behind by thirty-seven boats. Besides that, Dönitz warned, unless emergency steps were taken, the U-boat arm would run out of torpedoes in October.

Under intense pressure from Dönitz, Admiral Raeder had a showdown meeting with Hitler. Perhaps by that time Hitler realized the *Luftwaffe* was losing the Battle of Britain, that an invasion was out of the question, and that the war with Britain could not be won without massive numbers of U-boats. Whatever the case (documentation is lacking), Hitler at last emphatically and explicitly granted highest possible priority ("Special Stage," replacing the overused "First Priority") to U-boat and submarine torpedo construction, and to U-boat maintenance and repair and training.

Hitler also raised the possibility of stopgap assistance from an ally. Benito Mussolini had offered to send thirty oceangoing submarines to operate in the Atlantic, provided Hitler would permit them to base in German-occupied Bordeaux. Dönitz was skeptical. Word of the Italian submarine fiasco in June—especially the craven surrender of *Galileo* to a British trawler—had reached the U-boat arm. Nonetheless the offer could hardly be refused.

Dönitz had to be encouraged by news of the Hitler-approved U-boat construction program, to be carried out with "Special Stage" priority. It envisioned a production rate of twenty-five U-boats a month by December 1941, merely fifteen months away. If those numbers were realized, it seemed possible that the naval war with Great Britain could be won in 1943. But Dönitz had no knowledge of the fabulous cavity magnetron, nor of the Turing-Welchman bombes, nor of the miniaturization of radar and HF/DF (Huff Duff) to fit on small vessels, nor had he any inkling of the ability of the U.S. Maritime Commission to mobilize merchant-ship construction on a truly immense scale.

The turning point in the Battle of Britain occurred on September 15,* when RAF Fighter Command decisively repulsed a massive *Luftwaffe* attack, claiming 183 kills. The confirmed kill was only about one-third that number, but the blow was a crushing setback for the exhausted and riddled *Luftwaffe*. Two days later, Hitler officially postponed the invasion of England (Sea Lion) and intensified secret planning for the invasion of the Soviet Union (Barbarossa) in the spring of 1941.

Through the winter of 1940 the war against Great Britain was waged by the *Luftwaffe* and *Kriegsmarine*. The *Luftwaffe* shifted to night bombing of British cities ("The Blitz"). The *Kriegsmarine* continued the campaign against British shipping by U-boats, a few warship and merchant-ship raiders, torpedo boats, and

---

* Commemorated as "Battle of Britain Day."

surface-ship minelayers. The oceangoing U-boat force continued to bear the burden of the naval war.

In preparation for the invasion, Dönitz had moved U-boat headquarters to a spartan building in Paris, linked to a superb radio net. When the invasion was canceled, he directed the staff to prepare to move onward to Lorient. But the move was delayed until adequate communications facilities could be established in Lorient. In the interim, Dönitz—promoted to vice admiral—directed the boats from his Paris headquarters and conferred at length, either in Paris or Lorient, with every skipper within hours of his return from war patrol.

Dönitz commenced the second year of submarine warfare with twenty-four commissioned oceangoing boats, three fewer than the day the war began, and only about half of that number fully combat-ready. The other half included four brandnew boats in workup and unavailable for combat; two trained but green boats which had not yet made war patrols; the *U-A,* returned from her long—but very successful—voyage to West Africa in need of drastic modifications; the Type VII *U-31,* salvaged and recommissioned but an unknown quantity; three marginal Type VIIs; three aging Type IXs; and the VIIB *U-52* in the shipyard for overhaul.

It was not much of a force to wage a submarine war. But Dönitz had some factors working in his favor. The bases at Lorient and St. Nazaire were fully staffed and capable of providing fast refits. The torpedoes (with British-type impact pistols) were more dependable; the shortage of torpedoes was being overcome by emergency measures. Most of the constricting rules of warfare had been rescinded. The first group of big Italian oceangoing submarines had arrived in Bordeaux.* The codebreakers at *B-dienst* had established the general pattern of the inbound and outbound North Atlantic convoys. The convoys were thinly escorted and other ASW measures had been reduced to a minimum.

Although the inbound and outbound North Atlantic convoys sailed on predictable schedules through a relatively restricted area in the Northwest Approaches, the experience of August had shown that those convoys were not all that easy to find. The British varied the sailing routes, going north or south of Rockall Bank, and diverted around locations where convoys were under attack or where a U-boat had been seen or DFed. With so few boats to patrol, Dönitz could cover only a few of the possible routes and still keep the boats close enough to one another to mount pack attacks. Since the boats could not "see" or "hear" for more than a few miles, and less in unfavorable weather, many convoys had slipped by undetected.

To assist in convoy spotting, Dönitz had appealed to the *Luftwaffe* for aerial reconnaissance near Rockall Bank. Two "naval" air *gruppes,* basing in France, were designated for that purpose. However, the *Luftwaffe,* fully committed to the Blitz, to air-dropping newly produced "acoustic" mines† in British seaports, and to other

---

* See Appendix 8.

† Developed between the wars, German acoustic mines were laid on the bottom in shallow water, like magnetic mines, but actuated by the "noise" of a ship's propeller, rather than its magnetic field. They were immune to magnetic sweepers and could be set to "sleep" for many days, or to allow several ships to pass before exploding.

Grand Admiral Karl Dönitz, Commander in Chief U-boats from September 28, 1935, to January 30, 1943, and of the German Navy from January 30, 1943, to May 1, 1945, when he succeeded Adolf Hitler as chief of state.

Grand Admiral Erich Raeder, Commander in Chief of the German Navy from October 1, 1928, to January 30, 1943.

Winston S. Churchill, First Lord of the Admiralty from September 3, 1939, to May 10, 1940, thereafter Prime Minister, and Alfred Dudley Pickman Rogers Pound, First Sea Lord from June 12, 1939, to his death in office on October 15, 1943.

Admiral Percy L. H. Noble, Commander in Chief Western Approaches from February 17, 1941, to November 19, 1942.

(National Archives, 306NT291a14)

Surprise unveiling of the reborn U-boat arm in 1935. These small U-boats are new Type II "Ducks," used mostly as school boats.

(Imperial War Museum, A28893)

A nest of U-boats showing clearly the difference in size of the Type VII and the larger Type IX, one of which is moored outboard in the front row. For additional information, see the contrasting cutaways on pages 60 and 61.

Preparing for a war patrol, a German sub-mariner finds a cramped writing nook in the bow torpedo room, which is festooned with sausages, cheese, bread, and other food.

Loading a torpedo into the bow room. Standard German torpedoes were 23½ feet long, 21 inches in diameter, and weighed 3,383 pounds. Including four missiles in the torpedo tubes, the usual war load forward in the Type VII and Type IX was ten.

The Commander in Chief U-boats and the boats at sea kept in touch by means of radio transmissions, encoded and decoded on a naval Enigma machine. This is a "four-rotor" naval Enigma, on display at the Smithsonian Institution.

Ready and eager for action in the Atlantic, the Type VII *U-564* sails for a war cruise.

The British Home Fleet at Scapa Flow, where Günther Prien in *U-47* sank the battleship *Royal Oak*.

Günther Prien, Germany's most celebrated U-boat skipper. He sank 189,156 tons of Allied shipping to rank third in tonnage among all skippers. Killed in action March 1941.

Otto Schuhart in *U-29* hit the British aircraft carrier *Courageous,* shown here mere moments before she sank

A Type VII in the rough waters of the North Atlantic, seeking victims.

(Bundesarchiv, MW422019a)

Herbert Schultze, skipper of *U-48,* who sank 183,432 tons, to rank fifth.

(U.S. Naval Institute, 99741)

oachim Schepke, skipper of *U-100,* who sank 155,882 tons to ank thirteenth. Killed in action March 1941.

Otto Kretschmer, the "Tonnage King," who sank forty-five ships for 269,872 tons to rank number one among all German skippers. Captured by the British from his sinking boat, *U-99,* in March 1941, he spent the rest of the war in a POW camp.

Hit by a U-boat torpedo, an unidentified Allied tanker sinks beneath the waves.

Heinrich Lehmann-Willenbrock, skipper of *U-96,* who sank 183,223 tons to rank sixth. He was depicted, fictionally, in Lothar-Günther Buchheim's novel, TV miniseries, and feature film *Das Boot.*

Reinhard Suhren, fabled executive officer of *U-48* and later skipper of *U-564.* The skippers of *U-48* credited Suhren with aiming and firing the torpedoes that accounted for over 200,000 tons of Allied shipping.

Adalbert Schnee, skipper of *U-201,* won fame and high decorations for bold attacks on Allied convoys. He sank twenty ships and damaged several others.

Jürgen Oesten, skipper of the Type IXB *U-106,* sank ten ships and damaged the British battleship *Malaya.*

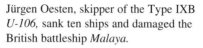

Eitel-Friedrich Kentrat, skipper of *U-74,* returning to base after a successful cruise.

The unlucky Type IXC *U-154,* homebound from a patrol in tropical waters, floats over spare torpedoes to the lucky *U-564.*

A German Focke-Wulf 200 Condor, military version of a prewar airliner. Based in France to scout out Allied convoys for the benefit of the U-boats, the Condors were much feared by the Allies but, in reality, achieved little.

British warships capture the Type IXB *U-110,* May 9, 1941. The attempt to tow her to port failed and she sank, but not before an Allied boarding party got her naval Enigma machine, codebooks, and other priceless intelligence booty.

The Type IXB *U-109* returning from a war cruise.

Safely berthed in the massive U-boat pens at St. Nazaire, Occupied France, two Type VIIs undergo refits.

missions, had not yet provided assistance. "Despite all my endeavors," Dönitz complained in his diary, the *Luftwaffe* "reported no forces available for this task."

When Hitler indefinitely postponed the invasion of England in mid-September, two oceangoing boats of the August group were still on patrol: *U-47* (Prien) on weather-reporting station at 20 degrees west longitude, and *U-65* (von Stockhausen). Ready or not for combat, twelve oceangoing boats sailed in September: five from Germany and seven from Lorient. All were assigned to interdict North Atlantic convoys in the Northwest Approaches, attacking whenever possible at night on the surface to avoid being pinned down by escorts and, at the same time, radioing contact reports and beacon signals to bring in other boats.

The *Ritterkreuz* holder Otto Kretschmer in *U-99* was the first to sail from Lorient. To help indoctrinate Italian submarine skippers in Atlantic warfare, Kretschmer took along Primo Longobardo, skipper of the *Torelli*. Near Rockall Bank Kretschmer promptly sank two medium-size freighters, one British, one Norwegian. Alerted by von Stockhausen in *U-65*, who had found an inbound convoy, Halifax 71, and had sunk two ships from it, *Hird* and *Tregenna*, Kretschmer closed on the scattering convoy and picked off another medium-size British freighter, *Crown Arun*.

The famous, record-holding *U-48* left Lorient behind Kretschmer. She had yet another new skipper, her third in a year. He was Heinrich Bleichrodt, age thirty, replacing *Ritterkreuz* holder Hans-Rudolf Rösing, whom Dönitz had sent to Bordeaux to work with the Italian submarine command. On September 15, near Rockall Bank, Bleichrodt intercepted an inbound convoy, SC 3. In his first attack as skipper, Bleichrodt assured *U-48*'s first-place standing by sinking four ships for 12,500 tons, including one of the escorts, the sloop *Dundee*, but no other boats made contact.

Proceeding westward, beyond the escort "chop line" at 17 degrees west longitude, on the morning of September 18 Bleichrodt found an unescorted outbound convoy. He tracked the ships during the daylight hours and attacked in bright moonlight on the surface. For his first target he chose a large "passenger ship" in the center of the convoy. He fired two torpedoes at her, but both were poorly aimed and missed. In a second attack, he fired one torpedo at the "passenger ship" and one at a 5,000-ton freighter. Both torpedoes hit and both ships sank.

The "passenger ship" was the convoy flagship, the 11,000-ton British liner *City of Benares*, crowded with 400 passengers. Among these were ninety English children who were being resettled in Canada to escape the Blitz. In the rush to abandon the sinking ship in darkness and heavy seas, the crew let go some lifeboats haphazardly. These crashed down upon others, killing or throwing passengers or crew into the icy waters, and holing some boats. Some lifeboats drifted for many days before they were found. Altogether about 300 passengers—including seventy-seven of the ninety children—died in the sinking.

Although the *City of Benares* was unmarked and darkened, and the Admiralty had not requested safe passage for her, the cries of outrage ("Hitler's foulest deed") from London for this sinking exceeded those evoked by the sinking of *Athenia* a year earlier. The impact was heightened by the release of the grim lifeboat stories of the thirteen surviving children. As a result of this tragedy and the near-disaster on the liner *Volendam* three weeks earlier, the British government canceled the Children's Overseas Resettlement Scheme. Having no idea of the pain and suffering he had caused, Bleichrodt went on to sink yet another British freighter the following night, bringing his total bag to seven confirmed ships for 31,800 tons sunk within four days, another new record for *U-48*.

Still at his weather-reporting station, on September 20 Günther Prien in *U-47* was nearly run down by the forty-ship convoy, Halifax 72. Having only one torpedo left, Prien broadcast an alert to Dönitz and abandoned his weather station to track the convoy. Upon receiving the alert, Dönitz directed five other boats—all from Lorient—to converge on Prien's beacon signals. The five boats found Prien on the night of September 21, forming a pack of six, the largest number of U-boats ever concentrated against a convoy.

The boats attacked doggedly over a period of about twenty-six hours. Bleichrodt in *U-48* went in first. Firing his last torpedoes, he sank a 4,400-ton British freighter and damaged another. He then replaced Prien as the convoy "shadower," radioing beacon signals and position reports. Kretschmer in *U-99* attacked next, damaging *Elmbank* and sinking two British ships, the 9,200-ton tanker *Invershannon* and the 3,700-ton freighter *Baron Blythswood*.* Prien came up to fire his one remaining torpedo, but it malfunctioned or missed. He then joined Kretschmer for a joint gun attack to sink the damaged *Elmbank*. On the second night, Joachim Schepke in *U-100* boldly maneuvered on the surface into the center of the convoy. In one of the most astonishing and fruitful U-boat attacks of the war, Schepke sank seven confirmed ships for 50,300 tons, in a mere four hours. His victims included the 10,000-ton British tankers *Torinia* and *Frederick S. Fales*. Hans Jenisch in *U-32* damaged a 7,900-ton freighter, but von Stockhausen's attack failed.

Based on reports from the boats and *B-dienst* intercepts, Dönitz believed the pack had sunk thirteen ships of the convoy, thus for the first time emphatically validating his tactical theories. The confirmed score was not far off: eleven ships for 72,700 tons sunk and two damaged for 13,000 tons.

While five of the six boats of the pack were inbound to Lorient, Dönitz and Berlin propagandists hastened to gloat over the victory and shower fulsome praise and awards on the skippers. Dönitz credited Prien in *U-47* with sinking 43,130 tons on this patrol, bringing his credited total to twenty-four ships for 151,400 tons. That tied Rollmann in numbers of ships credited, but put Prien ahead of Rollmann by about 25,000 in tonnage. Overcredited with one sinking, for a total of eight ships for 61,300 tons on this patrol, counting past claims, Joachim Schepke in *U-100* qualified for a *Ritterkreuz*. Also overcredited with one sinking, for a total of nine ships for 61,300 tons, Bleichrodt in *U-48* received unstinting praise.

---

* Kretschmer rescued from a sinking raft a single survivor of the freighter, Joseph Byrne. After giving him food and medical assistance, Kretschmner turned him over to a lifeboat under sail. Since Kretschmer and Longobardo had chosen English as their common language, Byrne thought he had been rescued by a British submarine!

Otto Kretschmer in *U-99* was accurately credited six and a half ships for 22,600 tons.*

The first three boats to sail from Germany in September were aging clunkers: the VII *U-29*, commanded by *Ritterkreuz* holder Otto Schuhart; the salvaged and recommissioned VII *U-31*, commanded by Wilfred Prellberg, age twenty-seven; and the IX *U-43*, commanded by the old hand Wilhelm Ambrosius, returning to the Atlantic after three months of battle-damage repairs. Outbound, two of the three boats were compelled to abort temporarily to Bergen: *U-29* with periscope problems, *U-43* with leaks.

After reaching the Atlantic, Schuhart in *U-29* came upon convoy Outbound 217. He gave the alarm and tracked, bringing up the nearby *U-31* (Prellberg) and *U-43* (Ambrosius). Schuhart and Ambrosius sank one British freighter each, but Prellberg's torpedoes malfunctioned or missed. Thereafter, Schuhart in *U-29* had an engine malfunction and was forced to abort to Lorient. Several days later, Prellberg in *U-31* found another outbound convoy, from which he sank a ship, but a second attack was thwarted by an Allied submarine escorting the convoy, which drove off *U-31* with a salvo of torpedoes. Also forced to abort with mechanical problems, while approaching Lorient Prellberg was attacked by another Allied submarine (*Trident*) and very nearly sunk. Ambrosius in *U-43* conducted what Dönitz characterized as an "unsatisfactory" patrol, and upon arrival in Lorient he was sent to command a training flotilla in the Baltic.

Responding to Schuhart's report of the outbound convoy, a Lorient boat, *U-32* (Jenisch), which had just sunk a ship traveling alone, found convoy Outbound 217 on September 26. Jenisch torpedoed the 6,900-ton British freighter *Corrientes,* and doggedly clung to the convoy, going ever westward. The abandoned *Corrientes* did not sink, but two days later another Lorient boat, Oehrn's *U-37*, found the hulk and put it under with gunfire and a torpedo. Pursuing the convoy far to the west, Jenisch sank two more ships from it near 25 degrees west longitude, as well as four more ships on his return leg to Lorient. Crediting Jenisch with sinking eight ships for 42,644 tons on this patrol, Dönitz awarded him a *Ritterkreuz.*†

After polishing off the hulk *Corrientes,* Oehrn in *U-37* sank five other ships for 23,200 tons, including the 7,000-ton tanker *British General,* giving him a confirmed score of twenty-three and a half ships for 101,414 tons, for which he was

---

* Counting one half credit for the *Elmbank,* Prien's confirmed score on this patrol was six and a half ships for 37,585 tons, bringing his confirmed total to twenty-two and a half ships for 151,652 tons. Schepke's confirmed score for this patrol was seven ships for 50,300 tons, bringing his confirmed total to twenty-four ships (tying Rollmann) for 94,175 tons. Bleichrodt's confirmed score for this patrol was eight ships for 34,588 tons. Kretschmer's total confirmed score, counting one half credit for the *Elmbank,* was twenty-two ships for 110,683 tons.

† Counting one half credit for *Corrientes,* Jenisch had sunk seven and a half confirmed ships for 39,250 tons in seven days. Over credited with sinking 82,644 tons on this and his prior patrol, Jenisch now had a total credited score of 104,818 tons. His confirmed score was seventeen and a half ships for 76,290 tons.

awarded a *Ritterkreuz*. Upon his return to Lorient, Oehrn relinquished command of
U-37 and resumed his former job as first staff officer to Dönitz, replacing Werner
Hartmann, who was itching to return to sea with a new boat.*

THE OCTOBER SLAUGHTER

Still in Paris, on the first day of October 1940, Dönitz had eighteen oceangoing
boats under his direct command,† ten of them captained by *Ritterkreuz* holders.
But that modest force was to be pared by one-third during the month. Four aged
and unreliable Type VIIs were to be withdrawn from combat to the training command, and two VIIBs were to patrol home for extended overhaul and modification.
On orders of the OKM, one IXB, *U-65,* was to make an extended cruise to Freetown, Sierra Leone, replicating *U-A*'s impressive lone voyage to that area.

To help fill the gap created by these diversions, the OKM directed that most of
the Italian boats arriving at Bordeaux were to patrol northward into the zones
theretofore reserved for the German boats. Dönitz greeted this decision with skepticism. At Hitler's personal order, the Italian boats were to remain under operational command of the Italian U-boat chief, Vice Admiral Angelo Perona, in
Bordeaux.‡ No Italian boat had ever operated in the cold, rugged North Atlantic;
none had trained for the difficult tasks of convoy tracking and pack attacks. Dönitz
believed the Italian boats might prove useful for reconnaissance—convoy spotting—but until the skippers and crews had received intensive training under German supervision, he doubted they would make any significant contribution. His
skepticism was to be borne out.

Two new boats which had sailed from Germany in late September reached the
hunting grounds in early October. One was the VIIB *U-103,* commanded by Viktor
Schütze, who had made several Atlantic patrols in old *U-25.* The other was the
IXB *U-123,* commanded by Karl-Heinz Moehle, age thirty, from the duck
U-20. Both boats were first assigned to weather-reporting duty at 26 degrees west,
to indoctrinate the green crews to the Atlantic and to satisfy the demands of the
Luftwaffe. On October 6, Schütze in *U-103* sank the 7,000-ton Norwegian tanker
Nina Borthen; Moehle in *U-123* sank a 6,000-ton freighter.

Two days later Dönitz ordered the *U-124* (Schulz), outbound from Lorient on

---

* While commanding *U-37,* Hartmann and Oehrn had sunk forty-two and a half confirmed ships
for 180,000 tons. This ranked the boat first in total number of ships sunk. But since total tonnage sunk
counted for more, the *U-48,* which had sunk thirty-six confirmed ships for 204,411 tons under three
skippers, was still regarded as the top boat, about 53,000 tons ahead of Prien's *U-47.*

† Seven boats at sea; ten in Lorient or St. Nazaire undergoing refits; the new Type VIIC *U-93*
preparing to sail from Germany.

‡ Hitler was concerned that if Dönitz took direct control of the Italian submarines, the Italians
might demand direct control of the *Luftwaffe* squadrons that had been sent to North Africa to support
the Italian Army's attack on Egypt.

his second patrol, to relieve *U-103* and *U-123* on weather duty. The latter two boats were to form a patrol line west of Rockall Bank with two other boats from Lorient, Liebe's *U-38*, which had sunk the 14,100-ton British steamer *Highland Patriot*, and Bleichrodt's *U-48*. Bucking foul, heavy weather, Schütze in *U-103* found inbound Slow Convoy 6, from which he sank two ships and damaged another, the 3,700-ton *Graigwen*. Bedeviled by the mountainous seas and fog, Moehle in *U-123* could not find the convoy, but he came across the damaged *Graigwen* and sank her with a torpedo. Nor could *U-38* or *U-48* find the convoy.

While searching for Schütze's convoy, Bleichrodt in *U-48* ran straight into another big inbound convoy, Halifax 77. He radioed an alert and beacon signals. Then, in his third well-executed night surface attack in a month, Bleichrodt sank three ships for 21,900 tons, including the 10,000-ton British steamer *Port Gisborne* and the 7,100-ton Norwegian tanker *Davanger*. In response to Bleichrodt's alert, Fritz Frauenheim in *U-101*, coming up from Lorient, found a straggler from the convoy and sank it.

Farther north, the brand-new *U-93*, commanded by Claus Korth, age twenty-nine, entered the operating area. Commissioned merely two months earlier, July 30, 1940, the *U-93* was the first of the new Type VIICs to reach the Atlantic. The VIICs were nearly identical to the VIIBs, but they were two feet longer and incorporated some internal design and mechanical refinements. The VIIC was to become the standard "production line" medium U-boat.

Korth found convoy Outbound 227 on October 14. He gave the alarm, drawing *U-103* (Schütze) and others into the chase. In his attack, Korth in *U-93* missed his targeted ships, but hit and sank the 9,300-ton British freighter *Hurunui*. Coming up, Schütze in *U-103* picked off one 4,700-ton ship from this convoy with his last torpedoes, then turned about for Lorient. Korth lost that convoy but found yet another outbound convoy. In two attacks on the night of October 16–17, he again missed his targeted ships but hit and sank two others.

To the south of Korth, Georg-Wilhelm Schulz in *U-124* encountered and sank a (1,813-ton) lone British freighter, *Trevisa*, in the early hours of October 16. Schulz did not know it, but that ship had become separated from Slow Convoy 7, escorted by a single warship, the sloop *Scarborough*, which was looking for a local escort group comprised of sloops *Fowey* and *Leith* and two corvettes. Twenty-four hours later, Bleichrodt in *U-48* sighted SC 7, flashed an alert to Dönitz, and immediately attacked, sinking the 9,500-ton British tanker *Languedoc*, a 3,800-ton British freighter, *Scoresby*, and damaging a 4,700-ton British freighter. A few hours later, Liebe in *U-38* sank by gun and torpedo another ship that had separated from SC 7, the 3,600-ton Greek *Aenos*. Upon receiving Bleichrodt's contact report, Dönitz ordered five other boats to converge on the probable course of the convoy. Meanwhile, Bleichrodt in *U-48* ran across a westbound British freighter which had separated from an outbound convoy. He chased and sank her, but that action took him too far west to again attack SC 7. Liebe in *U-38*, believed to be too far north of the convoy, was actually the next to find it, in the early morning hours of October 18. He reported the contact and attacked, damaging the 3,700-ton British freighter *Carsbreck*.

Based on Liebe's report, the five boats Dönitz had ordered to attack SC 7 raced to the northeast. On the evening of October 18, all five made contact with SC 7, which had been reinforced by its local escort. That night all U-boats attacked in calm seas by the light of a full "hunter's moon." It was a chaotic and confusing battle. Kretschmer in *U-99* captured its drama from the U-boat point of view in his log of October 18–19, a legendary document:

1745: Wind, southeast, force 3; sea 3; moderate cloud. *U-101* [Frauenheim] which is 2 or 3 miles north, signals by searchlight: 'Enemy in sight to port.'

1749: A warship is sighted, bearing 030, steering east. Soon afterwards, smoke to left of her. Finally the convoy. While hauling ahead to attack, we sight a steamship in the southeast, apparently on a westerly course.

1928: Submerge for attack.

1950: Surface, as the ship is making off slowly to the east. Haul further ahead: at 2000 [hours] pass within a few hundred meters of a U-boat on the surface, apparently *U-101* again.

2024: Another U-boat has torpedoed the ship. Shortly afterwards, exchange recognition signals with *U-123* [Moehle]. Convoy again in sight. I am ahead of it, so allow my boat to drop back, avoiding the leading destroyer.* The destroyers are constantly firing starshells. From outside, I attack the right flank of the first formation.

2202: Weather: visibility moderate, bright moonlight. Fire bow torpedo by director. Miss.

2206: Fire stern torpedo by director. At 700 meters, hit forward of amidships. Vessel of some 6,500 tons sinks within 20 seconds. I now proceed head on into the convoy. All ships are zigzagging independently.

2230: Fire bow torpedo by director. Miss because of error in calculation of gyro-angle. I therefore decide to fire the rest of the torpedoes without the director, especially as the installation has still not been accepted and adjusted by the Torpedo Testing Department. Boat is soon sighted by a ship which fires a white star and turns towards us at full speed, continuing even after we alter course. I have to make off with engines all out. Eventually the ship turns off, fires one of her guns and again takes her place in the convoy. I now attack the right flank of the last formation but one.

2330: Fire a bow torpedo at a large freighter. As the ship turns towards us, the torpedo passes ahead of her and hits an even larger ship after a run of 1,740 meters. This ship of some 7,000 tons is hit abreast the foremast, and the bow quickly sinks below the surface, as two holds are apparently flooded.

2355: Fire a bow torpedo at a large freighter of some 6,000 tons, at a range of 750 meters. Hit abreast foremast. Immediately after the torpedo explosion, there is another explosion with a high column of flame from the bow to the bridge. The smoke rises some 200 meters. Bow apparently shattered. Ship continues to burn with a green flame.

0015: Three destroyers approach the ship and search the area in line abreast. I

---

* In the confusion of night actions, U-boat skippers often misidentified sloops, frigates, and corvettes as "destroyers." For a British account of the battle see Lund and Ludlam, *Night of the U-boats* (1973).

make off at full speed to the southwest and again make contact with the convoy. Torpedoes from the other boats are constantly heard exploding. The destroyers do not know how to help and occupy themselves by constantly firing starshells, which are of little effect in the bright moonlight. I now start to attack the convoy from astern.

0138:   Fire bow torpedoes at large heavily-laden freighter of about 6,000 tons, range 945 meters. Hit abreast foremast. The explosion sinks the ship.

0155:   Fire bow torpedo at the next large vessel of some 7,000 tons. Range 975 meters. Hit abreast foremast. Ship sinks within 40 seconds.

0240:   Miss through aiming error, with torpedo fired at one of the largest vessels of the convoy, a ship of the *Glenapp* class 9,500 tons.

0255:   Again miss the same target from a range of about 800 meters. No explanation, as the fire control data were absolutely correct. Presume it to be a gyro failure, as we hear an explosion on the other side of the convoy some seven minutes later.

0302:   Third attempt at the same target from a range of 720 meters. Hit forward of the bridge. Bow sinks rapidly level with the water.

0356:   Fire at and miss a rather small, unladen ship, which had lost contact with the convoy. We had fired just as the steamer turned towards us.

0358:   Turn off and fire a stern torpedo from a range of 690 meters. Hit aft of amidships. Ship drops astern, somewhat lower in the water. As torpedoes have been expended, I wait to see if she will sink further before I settle her by gunfire.

0504:   Ship is sunk by another vessel by gunfire. I suppose it to be a British destroyer, but it later transpires that it was *U-123* [Moehle]. Some of her shells land very close, so that I have to leave the area quickly. The ship was *Clintonia,* 3,106 tons.

No one could ever precisely sort out who sank what from SC 7 that night. Some boats obviously torpedoed—and claimed—the same ships. When Dönitz asked for reports, some boats included ships sunk in earlier actions, adding to the confusion. Based on flash reports while the boats were still at sea, Dönitz concluded that the six boats he believed to have engaged SC 7 had sunk thirty ships for 196,000 tons. In the postwar years, German U-boat scholar Jürgen Rohwer, working in collaboration with the Admiralty, determined that the U-boats had sunk considerably less: twenty ships for 79,646 tons. The comparison:

		Dönitz		*Rohwer*	
U-38	(Liebe)		None	1	3,554 tons
U-46	(Endrass)	4	21,000 tons	3	8,453
U-48	(Bleichrodt)	3	21,000	2	13,355
U-99	(Kretschmer)	7	45,000	6 ½	28,949
U-100	(Schepke)	3	14,600		None
U-101	(Frauenheim)	8	51,000	3	8,837
U-123	(Moehle)	5	44,500	3 ½	14,685
U-124	(Schulz)		None	1	1,813
	Total:	30	197,100	20	79,646

Four boats in the Atlantic that were out of torpedoes or low on fuel headed for Lorient. Kretschmer in *U-99* arrived on October 23, having been out but nine days—the shortest war patrol on record. Frauenheim in *U-101* came in the next day, having been out only twenty days. Kretschmer got a new load of torpedoes, topped off his fuel tanks, and resailed a week later, October 30, the fastest turn-around time yet recorded at Lorient. Apparently exhausted, *Ritterkreuz* holder Fritz Frauenheim, who had overclaimed by five ships for 42,200 tons, left *U-101* and went to the training command.

Günther Prien in *U-47,* who had sailed from Lorient too late to engage in the action with SC 7, arrived in the hunting grounds on October 19. Within mere hours he found the large, heavily escorted inbound convoy Halifax 79. In response to his alert, Dönitz directed four other boats to converge on Prien and attack.

A second savage convoy battle ensued on the night of October 19–20. All five boats tore into the formation, shooting left, right, and center, also hitting ships hit by others. Fresh from Lorient with a full load of torpedoes and fuel, Prien was the most aggressive shooter, claiming eight ships for 50,500 tons. Based on flash reports, Dönitz concluded that the other four boats sank an additional nine ships for a grand total of seventeen ships for 113,100 tons. The confirmed total was also much less. Again, it was difficult to establish who had sunk what. Dönitz's credits and Rohwer's postwar analysis:

		Dönitz		*Rohwer*	
U-38	(Liebe)	2	13,000	2	12,619
U-46	(Endrass)	3	23,000	2 1/2	16,987
U-47	(Prien)	8	50,500	4	22,552*
U-48	(Bleichrodt)	1	7,000	1/2	3,011
U-100	(Schepke)	3	19,600	3	19,894
	Total:	17	113,100	12	75,063

Dönitz and the Berlin propagandists groped for adjectives to gloat over these successes. Combining the attacks on SC 7 and Halifax 79 into one prolonged battle ("The Night of the Long Knives"), Dönitz logged that eight U-boats, manned by about 300 men, had sunk forty-seven ships for 310,000 tons, "a colossal success." The propagandists credited Prien with his claim of 50,500 tons, elevating his credited total to 200,000 tons, a new milestone for a single skipper, which drew a telegram of congratulations from Hitler and yet another exalted award: a cluster of Oak Leaves to his *Ritterkreuz*. Credited with sinking 105,396 tons in two brief patrols on *U-48* (plus the sloop *Dundee*), Bleichrodt earned a *Ritterkreuz*. Frauenheim in *U-101* was credited with 51,000 tons; Kretschmer in *U-99* with 45,000 tons; Moehle in *U-123* with 44,500 tons; and Schepke in *U-100* with 34,200 tons.†

---

*   Shared credit for two ships with *U-46* and *U-48*.

†   Prien's confirmed total was twenty-six and a half ships for 173,552 tons. Bleichrodt's score for the patrol was six and a half ships for 40,000 tons, raising his confirmed total to fourteen and a half ships for 74,682 tons.

When Bleichrodt in *U-48* was awarded the *Ritterkreuz,* an unusual problem arose. He refused to wear the medal unless a *Ritterkreuz* was also presented to Reinhard Suhren, age twenty-four, who had been the first watch officer on *U-48* since the beginning of the war. The *U-48*'s total bag then stood at a record 42½ ships for 244,411 tons. Bleichrodt insisted that Suhren was deserving of the medal because he had fired torpedoes from the bridge that had accounted for at least 200,000 of the tons. Bleichrodt's case was strengthened by the fact that Viktor Oehrn in *U-37* had recently obtained a *Ritterkreuz* for another nonskipper, Suhren's older brother Gerd, the engineer on the *U-37,* who had kept the boat running in spite of numerous defects. Dönitz agreed with Bleichrodt, and Reinhard Suhren got his medal.*

The numbers pouring out of Berlin were dizzying and inflated. Nonetheless, there was no denying that SC 7 and Halifax 79 had been savaged. The nine boats engaged in those actions had sunk a total of thirty-three confirmed ships for 154,709 tons. The Allied losses included five big, valuable, fully loaded tankers: the British *Longuedoc, Shirak, Caprella,* and *Sitala,* and the Swede *Janus.* In addition, Prien had severely damaged another big British tanker.

Three of the five boats engaged in the attack on Halifax 79 returned to Lorient: *U-38* (Liebe), *U-47* (Prien), merely eight days out, and *U-100* (Schepke), merely eleven days out. The other two, *U-46* (Endrass) and *U-48* (Bleichrodt), proceeded to Germany for scheduled yard overhauls and modifications. While passing near the coast of Norway on October 25, Endrass in *U-46* was caught on the surface by three Hudson aircraft of Coastal Command Squadron 233. One aircraft, piloted by Arthur T. Maudsley and a Canadian, Everett Baudoux, was riddled by *U-46* gunners but dropped ten 100-pound bombs; another, flown by Pilot Officer Winnicott, dropped two 250-pound bombs; the bombs of the third plane, commanded by Pilot Officer Walsh, failed to release. The bombs fell close, inflicting severe damage on *U-46* and fatally injuring one crewman. Unable to dive, Endrass limped into Kristiansand, Norway, escorted by the German minesweeper *M-18.* From there he went on to Germany with an air and surface escort. The high-scoring *U-46* and *U-48* were to remain in German shipyards for the next three months.†

Relieved of weather reporting, Georg-Wilhelm Schulz in *U-124* was directed to patrol against shipping. On October 20, he intercepted convoy Outbound 229 and sank two big freighters for 11,000 tons. In return, the escorts pounded *U-124* with a prolonged and dogged depth-charge attack, the second for the boat in as many patrols. When the cook pointed out that both depth-charge attacks had occurred on the day he served chocolate pudding, Schulz banned that dessert on *U-124.* Cruising east to fill the void northwest of Rockall Bank, Schulz expended the rest of his torpedoes to sink two more lone ships, then headed for Lorient, having

---

* Kretschmer in *U-99* argued similarly and successfully that his quartermaster, Heinrich Petersen, deserved a *Ritterkreuz.* Although the *Ritterkreuz* was normally awarded only to officers, Dönitz made an exception in this case.

† Pilot Maudsley was killed later in the war. Baudoux rose to the rank of wing commander in the RCAF.

put down a total of five confirmed ships for 20,000 tons, in what Dönitz praised as a "well-executed" patrol.

The four old Type VIIs in Lorient, crammed with French goodies for families and friends, sailed home to the training command in October. Outbound from Lorient the *U-31* (Prellberg) was attacked for the third time by an enemy submarine, but evaded. The *U-29* (Schuhart), plagued with engine problems, was diverted to the Bay of Biscay to escort the inbound German merchant-ship raider *Widder* (which had sunk or captured ten ships for 58,645 tons) into Brest, and resailed later. The *U-28, U-31,* and *U-32* patrolled homeward through British waters in heavy, foul weather.

On October 26 a *Luftwaffe* plane attacked and set on fire the huge 42,348-ton British ocean liner *Empress of Britain* off the northwest coast of Ireland. Upon learning of the attack—and that the ship was being salvaged—Dönitz directed *U-28, U-31,* and *U-32* to find and sink her.

Prellberg in *U-31* was most ideally positioned to intercept the *Empress,* but *Ritterkreuz* holder Hans Jenisch in *U-32* poached into Prellberg's area in the early hours of October 28 and found her first. Two seagoing tugs had the *Empress* in tow; two destroyers provided escort. Jenisch lay doggo on the surface in the dark, allowing the destroyers and tugs to pass, then coolly fired a fan of three torpedoes at *Empress* from a point-blank range of 656 yards. Two hit, and the *Empress* went down—the largest ship sunk in the war to then. Berlin propagandists released the news that same day, glorifying Jenisch as the shooter and crediting him with a grand total of 146,816 tons.*

Two days later, on October 30, in rainy and foggy weather, Jenisch found a lone British freighter, *Balzac,* and attacked submerged, firing one torpedo, which prematured close aboard. Believing she was being shelled, *Balzac* broadcast an alarm, which brought up two British destroyers, *Harvester* and *Highlander.* Unaware of the destroyers, Jenisch attempted a second submerged attack on *Balzac. Harvester* spotted *U-32*'s periscope and turned to ram, but when Jenisch saw the destroyer, he broke off the attack and went deep. Fixing *U-32* on sonar, *Harvester* ran in and dropped six depth charges, all wide. *Highlander* followed with a salvo of fourteen.

Some of *Highlander*'s charges exploded close to *U-32,* knocking out the electric motors and rupturing the stern ballast tank and high-pressure air lines. After assessing the damage, Jenisch rushed all hands to the bow compartment to take the up angle off the boat and surfaced on diesel power, hoping to escape in the rain and darkness. But *Harvester* and *Highlander* spotted the boat with searchlights and opened fire at point-blank range with 4.7" guns and machine guns. Upon learning that all high-pressure air lines were ruptured and the boat could not dive, Jenisch gave orders to abandon ship and scuttle. *Harvester* and *Highlander* fished thirty-three survivors from the icy waters, including Jenisch. Nine of the crew perished.

---

* His confirmed total was eighteen and a half ships for 118,638 tons.

The British were glad to have captured Jenisch and most of his crew, the first U-boat POWs to be recovered after those of *U-26,* four months earlier. British propagandists hastened to boast of capturing a U-boat "ace" (or *Ritterkreuz* holder), stressing that Jenisch had sunk the *Empress of Britain.* In a vain attempt to undercut the British—and perhaps to reassure the German public—Berlin propagandists promptly and vehemently denied the claim. To buttress their denial, the Germans resorted to the bizarre step of broadcasting a fictional account of Jenisch's "victorious homecoming," including a detailed firsthand report from "Jenisch," describing his sinking of the *Empress.*

Resuming his voyage home, Prellberg in *U-31* found an outbound convoy and chased it westward. At that time there were four Italian boats patrolling near the path of the convoy and three more approaching the area. Dönitz relayed word to the seven Italian boats through his liaison in Bordeaux, Hans-Rudolf Rösing, but none of the Italian boats found the convoy and Prellberg soon lost it in the foul weather. Breaking off the chase, Prellberg came upon the abandoned hulk of the 5,400-ton British freighter *Matina,* torpedoed earlier by Kuhnke's homebound *U-28.* Prellberg shot five torpedoes at the drifting hulk; three missed, but two hit and she went down.

On the morning of November 2 Prellberg spotted a British destroyer and crash-dived. Intending to attack the destroyer, Prellberg went to battle stations and commenced tracking, but the seas were too heavy to fire torpedoes. His would-be victim was *Antelope,* which had single-handedly sunk *U-41* in February and was then maintaining an alert watch.

Picking up *U-31* on sonar, *Antelope* immediately carried out a "pounce attack," firing a full pattern of six depth charges. At the same time, she broadcast an alert, which brought up the destroyer *Achates,* but the sonar set on *Achates* failed. Carrying on alone, *Antelope* conducted a second attack, dropping another six depth charges which severely jarred the boat, but did no serious damage. Prellberg skillfully evaded *Antelope* for the next two hours, but the destroyer found him again and carried out another carefully organized attack, dropping another pattern of six depth charges, followed immediately by three more.

Antelope's third and fourth attacks fatally damaged *U-31.* The charges ruptured the stern ballast tanks, flooded the after tube and main induction, leaving the boat with a steep up-angle. In an attempt to regain the trim, Prellberg packed every available man into the bow compartment, but this had no effect and *U-31* slid down by the stern to 311 feet. The boat's engineer believed he could overcome the damage but, as Prellberg later told the British, he believed "a hero's death to be an overrated gesture" and ordered the engineer to surface and scuttle.

When *Antelope* saw *U-31,* she opened fire and lowered away a whaleboat, intending to board and capture secret documents. But *U-31,* with sea cocks open, was making speed on her electric motors and the whaleboat could not catch up. While Prellberg and his men were diving over the side into the heavy seas, *Antelope* resumed gunfire and attempted to come alongside *U-31* in order to board. But the flooding and unmanned *U-31* suddenly turned sharply to port and rammed *Antelope,* holing two fuel tanks and a boiler room and causing other damage. The collision, however, pushed *U-31* over. Flooding through the conning-tower hatch, she sank like a stone.

The *Antelope* whaleboat fished Prellberg and forty-three others of the forty-five-man crew from the water. One panicked *U-31* crewman, who "had used [up] his energy by continually screaming," the British diagnosed, fell into a coma and died aboard *Antelope*. During subsequent interrogation of the survivors, the British learned that *U-31* had been sunk earlier off Wilhelmshaven by a British aircraft and salvaged. She had earned the dubious distinction of being the only U-boat in the war to be "sunk twice."

Only one of the four old Type VIIs that had set off for Germany in October got there on schedule: Kuhnke's *U-28*. Under his command, the *U-28* had sunk a total of thirteen and a half confirmed ships for 59,000 tons. *Ritterkreuz* holder Kuhnke turned the boat over to the training command and went on to commission a new boat. The other homebound Type VII, Schuhart's *U-29*—the last Type VII to serve in the combat zone—finally got home in early December, after a stint at weather reporting. Under *Ritterkreuz* holder Schuhart, *U-29* had sunk twelve confirmed ships for 84,588 tons, including the carrier *Courageous,* but none on her final patrol. Schuhart went to a job in the training command. Partly as a result of their many defects, the ten Type VIIs had lasted only about one year in the Atlantic.

During September and October, four Emsmann Flotilla ducks patrolled home via North Channel to join the training command. Two of the four, *U-58* and *U-59,* sank three ships for 17,500 tons; the others had no luck. Two of the new Type IID ducks patrolled from Germany to Lorient via North Channel to temporarily replace the withdrawing ducks. Both had great success. Outbound to Lorient, the *U-137,* commanded by Herbert Wohlfarth, age twenty-five, from the old duck *U-14* (on which he had sunk nine confirmed ships), sank three ships for 12,000 tons, including the 4,753-ton British tanker *Stratford,* and damaged a 5,000-ton freighter. On a second patrol from Lorient, Wohlfarth hit the 10,500-ton auxiliary cruiser *Cheshire,* putting her out of action for six months. Outbound to Lorient, the *U-138,* commanded by Wolfgang Lüth, from the duck *U-9* (on which he had sunk or captured eight confirmed ships), sank four ships for 34,600 tons, including the 13,900-ton British tanker *New Sevilla,* during a single and remarkable three-hour night surface action. On a second patrol from Lorient, Lüth sank a 5,300-ton British freighter and damaged a 7,000-ton British tanker. Believing the latter had sunk, Dönitz credited Lüth with a total score (on *U-9* and *U-138*) of 87,236 tons,* plus the French submarine *Doris,* and awarded him a *Ritterkreuz*—the only commander of a duck to be so honored—and promoted him to command the lackluster Type IX *U-43,* in Lorient.

The four Bordeaux-based Italian boats that pioneered the way into the rugged North Atlantic performed poorly, as expected. One, *Malaspina,* reported and attacked a convoy, but her skipper, Mario Leoni, missed and—worse—failed to radio the convoy's course and speed. As a result, Dönitz was not able to direct other Italian or German boats to the scene. Moreover, it was discovered that Italian opera-

---

* Lüth's confirmed score was thirteen ships for 57,192 tons.

tions were restricted by a design flaw in the boats. They were not equipped with external main air-induction pipes for the diesel engines. The air for the diesels was drawn through the conning-tower hatch, which had to be open at all times when the boat was on the surface. In the rough Atlantic, torrents of seawater spilled down the hatch, flooding poorly located electrical panels in the control room.*

SERIOUS BRITISH LAPSES

In early November Dönitz commenced the relocation of U-boat headquarters from Paris to Lorient. The official opening date was not without significance: November 11, Armistice Day. He established living and working quarters in a large château in adjacent Kerneval, overlooking the Scorff River, the main waterway into Lorient. His personal staff remained unusually small: Eberhard Godt, chief of staff; Viktor Oehrn, first staff officer; Hans Meckel, from the duck *U-19,* communications officer; and a few others—so few that visitors from Berlin invariably expressed astonishment.

At about this same time the Todt Organization, which had built Germany's *autobahns,* commenced work on massive submarine "bunkers" or "pens" at Brest, Lorient, St. Nazaire, and La Pallice. Designed to provide a bombproof shelter for refitting and overhauling the U-boats, those huge structures were built of steel-reinforced concrete, and had walls and roofs twelve feet thick. The four pens could accommodate a total of about eighty U-boats. Some of the slips in the bunkers had locks so they could be pumped out, to provide dry-docking.

RAF reconnaissance aircraft took photographs of the foundations of the first bunkers at Lorient and La Pallice. Thus the British had fair warning, but they did not take advantage of the knowledge. RAF Bomber Command gave priority to targets in Germany. The U-boat bunkers were never high on the RAF target list in 1940 and 1941 and the construction proceeded with only sporadic and ineffective interference from Bomber Command, a serious lapse the British were to regret and one the Americans could never fathom.

By November, Dönitz had every reason to expect increased assistance from the *Luftwaffe* in locating convoys. But it was not forthcoming. The *Luftwaffe* air *gruppes* in France designated for this purpose were still scandalously ill-equipped. On November 16 Dönitz logged that one *gruppe* could provide no help because "*one* aircraft crashed." Another *gruppe* reported that all planes were grounded for two months with "mechanical defects." A *gruppe* based in Bordeaux, equipped with the long-range, four-engine Focke-Wulf 200 Condor, the military version of a civilian airliner, which flew between France and Norway, could provide only one aircraft daily. But the few Condor crews were no help. On the rare occasions when

---

* British air and surface forces had sunk another six Italian submarines in the Mediterranean area since June: *Iride, Gondar, Berillo, Foca, Durbo,* and *Lafolé.* Another, *Gemma,* was mistakenly sunk by another Italian submarine. A British boarding party recovered valuable intelligence documents from *Durbo* before she sank. Total Italian submarine losses in the first five months of combat: seventeen.

they spotted a convoy, they invariably gave erroneous position reports and attacked the convoys, forcing them to divert to new courses (or even scatter) before Dönitz could assemble the available boats for a pack attack.

Fourteen oceangoing U-boats sailed to attack the North Atlantic convoy routes in November, four from Germany, ten from France. The Italians added nine boats from Bordeaux. All Axis submarine operations during the month were hampered by foul, cold weather and by the temporary suspension of Allied convoys caused by the Atlantic sortie of the "pocket" battleship *Admiral Scheer,* which sailed from Kiel undetected by the British in late October.

The heroes Otto Kretschmer in *U-99* and Günther Prien in *U-47* were the first two skippers to leave from France. Both carried journalists (or propagandists) whose job it was to glorify the skippers and crews—and the U-boat arm—in words and pictures in order to stimulate a flow of volunteers to the submarine school. Prien welcomed his passenger, Wolfgang Frank*; Kretschmer, who disdained publicity (he was known as "Silent Otto"), did not.

Going up the west side of Ireland to North Channel on the afternoon of November 3, Kretschmer sighted the smoke of a lone inbound, zigzagging British freighter, the 5,400-ton *Casanare*. After dark he closed on the surface and sank her with a single torpedo. During the attack Kretschmer spotted another lone ship which turned out to be the 18,700-ton British liner *Laurentic,* converted to an armed merchant cruiser for the Northern Patrol. Swinging around, Kretschmer fired a single torpedo at *Laurentic*. It hit with a solid thwack, but the ship did not sink. Closing to point-blank range (580 meters), Kretschmer fired another torpedo, which missed, and yet another, which hit, but, Kretschmer logged, the third torpedo had "no particular effect."

In the midst of this attack, yet another big ship appeared on the scene: the 11,300-ton armed merchant cruiser *Patroclus*. She had unwisely come up to rescue survivors of *Casanare* and *Laurentic*. Closing her, Kretschmer fired two torpedoes from 1,200 meters. Both hit but with "no particular effect." Easing in to 850 meters, Kretschmer fired a third torpedo, then, to save torpedoes, attacked *Patroclus* with his deck gun. But when *Patroclus* fired back "with accurate time-fuse shells," Kretschmer hauled out of range and shot yet another torpedo, which hit, but again "with no particular effect."

Although both *Laurentic* and *Patroclus* were badly holed and doomed, Kretschmer was determined to hasten their end. While the torpedomen reloaded the tubes, he cruised about until a Sunderland appeared and drove him down. An hour and a half later he surfaced to resume the shooting, only to find two fleet destroyers, *Achates* and *Hesperus,* racing into the area. Dodging them, Kretschmer hit *Laurentic* with one torpedo and *Patroclus* with two. Both ships then sank quickly.

---

* In addition to his articles, Frank published a propaganda book in 1942 about Prien's war patrols, *Prien Attacks*. In the 1950s, Frank also published an anecdotal history of the U-boat war, translated as *The Sea Wolves,* as well as other works.

Hauling off into the darkness, Kretschmer broke radio silence to accurately report sinking three ships for 35,414 tons and three internal torpedoes remaining. An exultant Dönitz ("another great success") ordered Kretschmer to return to Lorient. Since Kretschmer's credited score totaled 217,198 tons—the second skipper after Prien to be credited 200,000 tons or more—Hitler awarded Kretschmer Oak Leaves to his *Ritterkreuz* and Berlin propagandists rushed out the news. En route to Lorient on November 5, Kretschmer ran across convoy Halifax 83 and sank the 7,000-ton British tanker *Scottish Maiden* with his last torpedoes, elevating his total for the patrol to four ships for 42,400 tons.* Hitler invited Kretschmer to Berlin for presentation of the Oak Leaves and asked him to stay for lunch at the Reichs Chancellery. When the Führer asked what he could do to help the U-boat arm, Kretschmer was blunt: Give us many more U-boats and *Luftwaffe* reconnaissance.

Kretschmer had scarcely got off his radio report to Dönitz on November 5 when the "pocket" battleship *Admiral Scheer,* passing unseen in the Denmark Strait between Iceland and Greenland, found and attacked the thirty-eight-ship convoy Halifax 84 near 32 degrees west longitude. This was the first time in fourteen months of war that any German surface warship had found and attacked a North Atlantic convoy. *Admiral Scheer* sank the lone convoy escort, the 14,000-ton armed merchant cruiser *Jervis Bay,* then five other ships, for a total of 47,300 tons, and damaged two others.

Caught utterly unawares by this attack, the Admiralty went to full battle stations. The Home Fleet (*Nelson, Rodney, Repulse, Hood,* etc.) deployed into the Atlantic to intercept *Admiral Scheer,* should she turn about for Germany or head for a French Atlantic port. All in vain; *Scheer* slipped away to the South Atlantic. In the meantime, the Admiralty aborted three inbound convoys from Halifax; the normal convoy cycle did not resume until November 17, with the sailing of Halifax 89. "The loss of imports," the Admiralty historian wrote, "caused to this country by the pocket-battleship's sudden appearance on our principal convoy route was, therefore, far greater than the cargoes actually sunk by her."

The suspension of North Atlantic convoys during the period November 5 to about November 17 frustrated the U-boats. None sank a ship between November 5 and November 21, the longest "dry spell" of the war to then. During it, only a duck returning to Germany via North Channel and two Italian boats had any luck. In a well-executed night surface attack against a homebound Gibraltar convoy, Herbert Wohlfarth in the duck *U-137* sank four ships for 13,300 tons.† The Italian boat *Marconi* sank a 2,700-ton ship from Halifax 84, *Vingaland,* which had been damaged by a Condor after *Scheer's* attack. The *Baracca* sank a 4,900-ton British freighter.

---

* Making his confirmed total score thirty-two and a half ships for 182,032 tons.

† Berlin propagandists crowed that Wohlfarth had sunk a grand total of 61,500 tons in "small submarines" (the ducks *U-14* and *U-137*). His confirmed total was a duck record of sixteen ships sunk, plus severe damage to the auxiliary cruiser *Cheshire* and another ship, but the total confirmed tonnage sunk was only 36,800.

• • •

Prien, the Bull of Scapa Flow, had a frustrating patrol. He stopped a small Portuguese neutral with his deck gun, the propagandist Wolfgang Frank wrote, and
after inspecting her papers, he let her pass. For the next ten days he saw not a single ship. Unaware that *Admiral Scheer* had caused a temporary halt to the convoys,
Prien and his first watch officer, Amelung von Varendorff, age twenty-six, concluded that the Admiralty had rerouted convoys away from the Rockall Bank area.
Prien thought the convoys were going far to the north; von Varendorff thought they
were going far to the south. "Our tempers were getting frayed," Frank wrote.

When the Admiralty resumed convoys on November 18, Wohlfarth in the homebound duck *U-137* spotted Outbound 244 near North Channel. In response to Wohlfarth's alarm, Dönitz directed five Lorient boats to converge on *U-137*. Prien found
the convoy and attacked, firing five torpedoes. None hit the target: three missed, one
misfired and "ran hot" in the torpedo tube, and one broached. Viktor Schütze in *U-
103* sank two ships for 10,900 tons. When one ship turned to ram *U-103*, Schütze
fired a "down the throat" shot at her, but the torpedo glanced off the ship's side and
did not explode. Maneuvering wildly, Schütze barely managed to escape.

Coming up last, Karl-Heinz Moehle in the IXB *U-123* made contact with the
convoy in the early hours of November 22. In a remarkably dogged and aggressive
series of attacks over the next thirty hours, Moehle sank six ships for 28,000 tons.
In the last action, while firing a finishing shot submerged, Moehle collided with "an
unknown object," damaging the conning tower and both periscopes, and was forced
to abort to Lorient after merely fifteen days at sea. It was to take fifty days to repair
U-123; the crew returned to Germany for leave, which extended through Christmas.

In vain pursuit of the convoy Outbound 244, on November 23 Joachim
Schepke in *U-100* happened upon inbound Slow Convoy 11. He gave the alarm,
which brought up Klaus Korth in the VIIC *U-93*. Korth had no luck, but Schepke
pursued and attacked relentlessly over twenty hours, reporting seven ships sunk for
41,400 tons, equaling his dazzling performance on his prior patrol. Postwar analysis confirmed seven ships sunk but reduced the tonnage to 24,601.

A knotty problem arose over Schepke's sinking claims. According to his reckoning, he had sunk eleven ships for 36,372 tons on the ducks *U-3* and *U-19*, and
twenty-six ships for 176,938 tons on *U-100*, for a total of thirty-seven ships for
213,310 tons. If true, that made Schepke the third skipper to sink over 200,000
tons and to qualify for Oak Leaves to his *Ritterkreuz*. But Dönitz knew from
B-dienst and other sources that Schepke was a notorious tonnage overclaimer; in
fact, his claims were ridiculed throughout the U-boat arm as "Schepke-tonnage."
And yet there was no denying that Schepke had positively sunk thirty-four ships—
twenty-three of them in a mere ninety days on *U-100*—to rank first in *number* of
ships sunk, a feat deserving of an extraordinary award. Accordingly, Dönitz recommended Schepke for Oak Leaves to his *Ritterkreuz* even though, by Dönitz's
count, he had not yet sunk 200,000 tons.

Far to the south, off Freetown, von Stockhausen in the IXB *U-65* conducted a one-
boat submarine war. His primary task was to interdict cargo ships taking supplies

via the Cape of Good Hope to the Army of the Nile in Egypt. On November 11, he reported to Dönitz that he had refueled from the *Nordmark* (serving as a supply ship for *Admiral Scheer*), but in the twenty-eight days since leaving Lorient he had not yet sunk a ship.

This negative news was keenly disappointing. It led Dönitz to again protest to the OKM the "diversion" of U-boats to South Atlantic waters. But the OKM insisted on sending yet another boat to that area. Reluctantly, Dönitz assigned the mission to the aging Type IX *U-37,* commanded by a new skipper, Nikolaus Clausen, age twenty-nine, from the duck *U-142.* He sailed on November 28 and was to refuel from a German supply ship in the Spanish Canary Islands.

Dönitz was on the point of recalling *U-65* when von Stockhausen spoke up to report "heavy traffic" and the sinking of four independent ships for 21,000 tons between November 15 and 18. These included two tankers, the 7,600-ton Norwegian *Havbör* and the 5,000-ton British *Congonian.* This promising report persuaded Dönitz to leave *U-65* in the Freetown area, refueling from *Nordmark* a second time later in the month. But the British, who were aware of *U-65*'s presence from the sinkings and from DFing, gave her a wide berth and intensified the air patrols. Von Stockhausen carried out the second refueling on November 28 (handing over a survivor of one sinking) and yet another on December 7, but he sighted no enemy ships for four full weeks, leading Dönitz to again doubt the wisdom of sending boats to this distant area.

In the waning days of November, four boats from Lorient remained on patrol in the stormy, forbidding North Atlantic: the old IX *U-43,* with a new skipper, Wolfgang Lüth, who had twice aborted with mechanical difficulties before reaching the hunting grounds; the *U-47* (Prien); the *U-93* (Korth); and the IXB *U-103* (Schütze). Only one of the four had any luck: Viktor Schütze in *U-103,* who sank three ships for 13,000 tons. Korth in the first VIIC to reach combat, *U-93,* who had burned up a lot of fuel to no purpose, was forced to return to France prematurely, earning the dubious distinction of being the first boat to return to Lorient without having sunk a single ship. Adding another dubious first, *U-93* was hit at dockside by a rarely seen RAF bomber. The damage was slight, but it delayed *U-93*'s readiness to January 1941.

Seven other U-boats sailed in November, raising the number in the hunting grounds to ten. Five came from Germany; two from Lorient. Three of the boats from Germany were new. Almost immediately upon entering the combat zone, two of them, *U-95* and *U-104,* tangled with enemy ships, both sinking one and damaging one. Thereafter, the IXB *U-104,* commanded by Harald Jürst, age twenty-seven, from the duck *U-59,* disappeared without a trace, perhaps the victim of crew error.* The duck *U-140,* commanded by Hans-Peter Hinsch, age twenty-six, sank three ships for 13,200 tons in North Channel and returned to the submarine school.

On the last day of November, eight oceangoing boats remained in the hunting

---

* After *U-102,* she was the second new IXB to disappear without a trace on her first patrol.

grounds, including Prien, who was low on fuel—and patience—and had set a course for Lorient. One boat, the VIIB *U-101,* fresh from Lorient with a new skipper, Ernst Mengersen, age twenty-eight, from the duck *U-18,* sank a ship; all others reported "no traffic."

Believing the British had shifted convoy routes to the south, Dönitz ordered about half of the boats, including Prien's homebound *U-47,* to search in that direction. It was a shrewd guess. Just after dark on December 1, Mengersen in *U-101* spoke up to report contact with a big inbound convoy, Halifax 90.

Dönitz ordered Mengersen to shadow the convoy and delay any attack until other boats could converge. Mengersen tracked and broadcast beacon signals but could not resist the temptation to shoot, and he tore into the convoy, firing all twelve of his torpedoes. He claimed sinking four ships for 33,000 tons and damaging two for 11,000 tons. His confirmed victims included the 8,800-ton British tanker *Appalachee.* Prien in *U-47* attacked next, in the early hours of December 2, claiming one ship of 10,000 tons sunk and damage to the 8,400-ton British tanker *Conch.* He then attacked an unidentified ship with his deck gun until escorts chased him off. Otto Kretschmer in *U-99,* fresh from Lorient, arrived next and shot five torpedoes to sink the 16,400-ton auxiliary cruiser *Forfar,* which was in the process of shifting over to escort convoy Outbound 251. *Forfar* was the third big auxiliary cruiser to be sunk by Kretschmer within a month.

One of the new boats from Germany, the VIIC *U-95,* commanded by Gerd Schreiber, age twenty-eight, from the duck *U-3,* came up and found the tanker *Conch,* which Prien had damaged. Schreiber fired three torpedoes at her. Two glanced off with only slight effect, but one hit solidly. Believing *Conch* was going under, Schreiber broke off the attack to seek other victims. But the *Conch* stubbornly refused to sink.

Two other boats hurried to the scene: the *U-52* (Salmann), returning to the Atlantic after overhaul in Germany, and the cranky *U-43* (Lüth) from Lorient. On the morning of December 2, Salmann sank two British freighters for 7,000 tons and damaged another. Lüth's approach course took him right into the path of convoy Outbound 251. He attacked and sank two ships for 19,400 tons, including the 12,200-ton British tanker *Victor Ross.*

Two destroyers, the Canadian *St. Laurent* and the British *Viscount,* responded to the convoy distress calls. When daylight came they spotted a U-boat on the surface and drove it under. *St. Laurent* obtained a sonar contact and commenced attacking with depth charges. *Viscount* soon joined. In all, the two destroyers made thirteen separate attacks over four hours, dropping a total of eighty-one depth charges variously set at 150, 250, 350, and 500 feet. They did not sink a U-boat (as believed), but their presence—and attacks—held all the boats down and the convoy slipped away.

When Dönitz learned that the convoy was getting away, he fumed and fretted. Never enough boats! Too little time to concentrate for a mass attack! No help from the *Luftwaffe!* He plotted the probable course of the convoy, exhorted the boats to pursue, and called on the *Luftwaffe* for assistance. It dispatched three aircraft—a record, all-out effort—but none of the planes found the convoy.

Later that afternoon, December 2, the *U-94,* another new VIIC from Germany, commanded by Herbert Kuppisch, age thirty-one, from the duck *U-58,* overtook and reported the convoy. When he received the contact report, Dönitz directed all skippers, including Mengersen in *U-101,* who had no torpedoes, to close the enemy formation. Still tracking, after dark that day Kuppisch moved in on the surface and attacked, sinking two British freighters for 12,700 tons. Attempting to rejoin, Kretschmer in *U-99* torpedoed and sank a 4,300-ton Norwegian straggler and, later, the abandoned British tanker *Conch.* No other boats found the convoy on the second day.

Upon receiving flash reports from the six boats that had attacked the convoy, Dönitz believed they had achieved another sensational victory. He calculated that the boats had sunk a total of eighteen ships for 120,698 tons, not counting unreported tonnage from Salmann in *U-52.* Jürgen Rohwer's postwar analysis reduced the victory considerably. The comparison:

			Dönitz		*Rohwer*
U-47	(Prien)	2	17,000 tons	1 1/3 *	10,347 tons*
U-52	(Salmann)	3	?	2	7,034
U-94	(Kuppisch)	3	21,000	2	12,747
U-95	(Schreiber)	2	12,000	1/3	2,792
U-99	(Kretschmer)	3	29,698	2 1/3	23,470
U-101	(Mengersen)	5	41,000	3	17,105
	Total:	18	120,698	11	73,495

After an analysis of the flash reports and other data, Dönitz reduced the total U-boat sinkings in Halifax 90 from eighteen to sixteen. Eager to exploit the victory, on December 3 Berlin propagandists lumped in Lüth's two kills in Outbound Convoy 251 and boasted that U-boats had sunk eighteen ships for 148,000 tons within the previous twenty-four hours. Including *Conch,* not sunk until December 3, the confirmed figures from the two convoys were thirteen ships for 92,855 tons. Ernst Mengersen, who had first spotted Halifax 90 and pulled in the other five boats, was cited by name and credited with sinking five ships for 41,000 tons.

Three of the six boats in these actions returned to Lorient. Prien and his crew and the propagandist Wolfgang Frank in *U-47* were not a happy lot. In thirty-four days of patrolling in foul weather, they had sunk but one confirmed ship, the 7,555-ton Belgian freighter *Ville d'Arlon* (plus damage to the tanker *Conch*). But Dönitz offered good news: *U-47* was to be overhauled at Lorient; all hands were granted home leave extending through Christmas.

Assigned to weather reporting, Otto Kretschmer in *U-99* sank one 5,200-ton freighter, then aborted to Lorient with an engine breakdown. Crediting Kretschmer with sinking four ships for 34,935 tons on this sixteen-day patrol, Berlin propagandists gleefully pronounced that having sunk a total of 252,100 tons, Kretschmer was the new king of the U-boat aces, as indeed he was.† Berlin urged Kretschmer

---

*   Shared credit for tanker *Conch* with *U-95* and *U-99.*

†   Kretschmer's confirmed total was thirty-five and a fraction ships for 191,515 tons.

to write a propaganda book (as had Prien and Werner Hartmann), but "Silent Otto" refused. When Dönitz granted him and his crew home leave extending through Christmas, Kretschmer took the whole crew on a skiing holiday.

Of the Lorient boats remaining on patrol, only Viktor Schütze in the IXB *U-103* had any luck. He sank two more ships, then returned to Lorient, also having been out for thirty-four grueling days. Credited with sinking eight ships for 46,000 tons on this patrol, his total claims (on *U-25* and *U-103*) were twenty ships for 109,317 tons.* He was awarded a *Ritterkreuz* and home leave extending through Christmas.

Close by the scene of the battle with Halifax 90, on December 1 the Italian submarine *Argo,* commanded by Alberto Crepas, came upon another inbound convoy, Home Gibraltar 47. As Crepas shot torpedoes, the Canadian destroyer *Saguenay,* commanded by F. H. Davidson, spotted *Argo* and turned to ram. A torpedo hit *Saguenay* on the port side forward, blowing off sixty feet of her bow and killing twenty-one men. The British destroyer *Highlander* raced up to assist *Saguenay* and took off ninety men, including eighteen wounded. Remarkably, a skeleton crew of Canadians put out fires and saved *Saguenay,* which was towed into England by British tugs. Credited with preventing attacks on the merchant ships of Homebound Gibraltar 47, *Saguenay* remained under repair for many months.

This near-fatal attack on an enemy destroyer was the highlight of the Italian submarine effort in the fall of 1940. To then, nine of the twenty-seven Italian boats had sunk twelve ships, including five (!) neutrals.† In return, one Italian boat, *Faá di Bruno,* had been lost. This first kill of an Italian boat in the Atlantic was the result of a dogged twenty-hour hunt on November 6/7 by the Canadian destroyer *Ottawa,* commanded by Edmond R. Mainguy, and the British destroyer *Harvester,* commanded by M. Thornton. There were no survivors.‡

During December, five of the Italian submarines, including *Argo,* sank five more Allied freighters, two of them stragglers from Slow Convoy 15 and two stragglers from convoys Outbound 252 and 260. In return, a second Italian boat was lost. She was the *Tarantini,* torpedoed off Bordeaux by the British submarine *Thunderbolt.* There were no survivors of this boat either.

In the three-month period September 2 to December 2, 1940, the second phase of the "Happy Time," German U-boats inflicted yet another appalling slaughter on British-controlled shipping. The twenty-four oceangoing boats sailing to the North Atlantic in this period sank 140 ships for about 760,000 tons. In eleven patrols (three from Germany or Norway; eight from Lorient) the ducks sank another seventeen ships (including two tankers) for about 89,000 tons, making the total 157 ships for about 847,000 tons, of which seventeen for about 140,000 tons were

---

* Schütze's confirmed score for the patrol was seven ships for 38,465 tons; his confirmed total, nineteen and a half ships for 93,801 tons.
† Two Spanish, one Yugoslav, one Swede, and a Greek.
‡ At this time the Admiralty wrongly credited the British destroyer *Havelock* for this kill.

tankers.* Remarkably, in the same period only three U-boats (the marginal VIIs *U-31* and *U-32*, and the new IXB *U-104*) had been lost, making the "exchange rate" of lost ships to lost U-boats about fifty to one!

Numerous factors had contributed to the slaughter: intelligent and intuitive deployment of the few U-boats available, leading to the pack attacks on seven different convoys; boldness, skill, and confidence on the part of two dozen skippers; excellent torpedo performance in night surface attacks; inadequate and inept convoy-escort and ASW measures; and, lastly, not a little luck. "In all cases," Dönitz logged, "first contact" with the convoys "was a matter of *chance.* The convoy approached a U-boat."

The British had reason for concern. In the six months of "Happy Time," mid-May 1940, when the U-boats returned to the Atlantic, to December 2, they had sunk an impressive total of 298 ships for more than 1.6 million tons, almost all of them in the Northwest Approaches. The total included thirty-seven tankers, of which twenty-seven were British-owned.

Eighteen U-boat skippers were mainly responsible for the slaughter in this "Happy Time." All were enshrined forever in the pantheon of German naval heroes. Their confirmed successes:

Skipper	Boat	Ships	Tons
Otto Kretschmer	*U-99*	30 1/3	175,804
Joachim Schepke	*U-100*	23 1/2	121,712
Viktor Oehrn	*U-37*	23 1/2	101,415
Günther Prien	*U-47*	20 1/3	124,470
Engelbert Endrass	*U-46*	17	95,658
Heinrich Bleichrodt	*U-48*	14 1/2	76,292
Fritz Frauenheim	*U-101*	14	68,949+
Hans Jenisch	*U-32*	15 1/2	68,404
Viktor Schütze	*U-103*	12 1/2	60,592
Hans-Rudolf Rösing	*U-48*	12	60,702
Heinrich Liebe	*U-38*	12	73,191
Wilhelm Rollmann	*U-34*	13	52,424
Karl-Heinz Moehle	*U-123*	9 1/2	43,854
Fritz-Julius Lemp	*U-30*	8	38,736
Otto Salmann	*U-52*	9	37,678
Günter Kuhnke	*U-28*	7 1/2	22,942+
Wolfgang Lüth	*U-138*,† *U-43*	7	59,331
Herbert Wohlfarth	*U-137*	7	25,444
Total		255+	1,307,598+

The Americans continued to observe the slaughter of this "Happy Time" with awe and concealed contempt. The U-boat successes in the pitched convoy battles of the fall reinforced their belief that a poorly escorted convoy was worse than no

---

* Does not include two tankers and two freighters sunk by *U-65*, patrolling in West African waters.

† *U-137* and *U-138* were Type IID ducks.

convoy at all, inasmuch as it presented the German packs a convenient mass of targets—too many eggs in one very vulnerable basket. The absence of surface-ship escorts to protect the convoys also reinforced the American view that Churchill's Mediterranean strategy, which drained off substantial British naval assets from the home waters, was a foolish diversion at a most critical time. Above all, the Americans faulted the British authorities for failing to direct Bomber Command to mount a maximum effort to prevent the construction of the U-boat pens in the French Atlantic ports.

Prime Minister Churchill was keenly alive to the looming shipping crisis. He wrote in his war memoir:

> Amid the torrent of violent events, one anxiety reigned supreme. Battles might be won or lost, enterprises might succeed or miscarry, territories might be gained or quitted, but dominating all our power to carry on the war, or even keep ourselves alive, lay our mastery of the ocean routes and the free approach and entry to our ports. . . . How willingly would I have exchanged a full-scale [German] attempt at invasion [of the British Isles] for this shapeless, measureless [U-boat] peril, expressed in charts, curves and statistics. . . .

Apart from the measures taken in late 1940 to obtain new merchant ships in the United States and Canada, Churchill directed the Admiralty to drastically improve its handling of convoys and fast independent ships. As one measure, the Admiralty rerouted all transatlantic convoys farther northward to outdistance the supposedly efficient German convoy-spotter planes. As another, it released ships that could cruise at 13 knots or faster from the obligation to sail in convoy.*

In addition, the British took steps to beef up the protection of the poorly escorted transatlantic convoys. With the threat of a German invasion reduced to nil by the victory of the RAF over the *Luftwaffe* and the onset of foul winter weather, the Admiralty released a number of fleet and other destroyers from anti-invasion duties and assigned them to convoy escort. Even so, there remained an acute shortage of escort destroyers, caused in part by the heavy destroyer battle losses and damage, and by the failure of the first twenty-three new, small *Hunt*-class vessels to measure up for duty in the North Atlantic, and by the delays in the arrival or readiness of the fifty four-stack destroyers from the U.S. Navy. In November, Churchill vented his frustrations in a memo to the Admiralty:

> *Action This Day.* What is disconcerting is that out of 151 destroyers, only 84 are available for service and out of 60 for [convoy escort and ASW in] Northwest Approaches only 33 [are available]. More than a month ago, the Admiral [at North-

---

* Theretofore only ships that could cruise at 15 knots or faster were permitted to sail outside the 9-knot Halifax convoys. The new and riskier procedure allowed scores of newer, faster, armed merchant ships such as tankers to sail alone, reducing the travel time.

west Approaches] was found with only 24 available. . . . I cannot understand why such an immense proportion of destroyers are laid up from one cause or another.

In order to increase the availability of convoy escorts, the Admiralty initiated several other changes. On the western end, the transatlantic convoy sailings from America were "opened out" or delayed. Rather than every four days, about half of the important Halifax convoys sailed every six days. Rather than every eight days, all the Sydney (or Slow) convoys sailed (from Halifax after ice closed Sydney) every ten days. On the eastern end, the Admiralty shifted convoy destroyer bases from Bristol and Liverpool to Loch Ewe in North Scotland and Belfast in Northern Ireland. These changes enabled more escorts to remain with the convoys farther out to sea on both ends of the routes.

By this time the 205-foot British and Canadian-built single-screw *Flower*-class corvettes had begun to enter service in substantial numbers.* Although they were intended originally only for inshore coastal-convoy duty, out of dire necessity the Admiralty was forced to employ them on both ends of the transatlantic routes. An Admiralty naval architect, David K. Brown, wrote recently:

> The *Flower*-class . . . had many drawbacks in ocean work. They were short so that pitch and heave motions were severe, which led to a high incidence of [sea] sickness and, in all probability, of poor decision-making, while their standard of habitability was low. Inadequate bilge keels led to heavy rolling, and they were too slow either to keep up with a surfaced submarine or to return quickly to station. . . . The *Flowers* were not a good design. . . . The early short-forecastle *Flowers* were the worst. They had bunks in the forecastle, where the motion was worst. To reach the bridge or engine room meant crossing the open well deck, inevitably getting wet in bad weather. Worse still, the galley was aft and food had to be brought along the open upper deck to the mess, getting cold, if not spilt on the way.

Coastal Command, led by Frederick Bowhill, had matured considerably since the beginning of the war, but it was still a poor stepchild of the RAF. Its daylight aircraft patrols with Sunderlands and Hudsons had been useful in forcing down U-boats, but no aircraft of Coastal Command had yet sunk a German U-boat unassisted by a surface craft. From July 1940, when the U-boats shifted to night surface attacks, these Coastal Command air patrols had been virtually useless inasmuch as it was almost impossible to spot a U-boat at night by eye.

What was needed was ASW radar. At the beginning of 1940, the Air Ministry had provided a few 1.5-meter-wavelength ASV (airborne radar sets) for a handful of Coastal Command and Navy aircraft types (Hudson, Swordfish, Walrus) to be used to track big enemy surface ships. However, since these sets were not capable of detecting U-boats, Coastal Command and the Royal Navy had requested the

---

* The first British-built *Flower*-class corvette, *Gladiolus,* was launched January 24, 1940. By the end of 1940, British yards had launched seventy-six. The first Canadian-built corvette, *Dunvegan,* was launched February 11, 1940. By the end of 1940, Canadian yards had launched forty-five. Total corvettes completed by the end of 1940: 121.

"crash" production of 4,000 improved 1.5-meter-wavelength sets (ASV-II). "Unfortunately," Admiralty historian J. David Brown wrote recently, "the Air Ministry bureaucracy failed to recognize the importance of the program" and pigeonholed the request, giving priority to Fighter Command for Air Interception (A-I) radar to help find enemy bombers. The upshot was that by the end of 1940, only forty-nine Coastal Command aircraft and a few experimental Navy Swordfish biplanes had the improved ASV-II radar sets, an appalling lapse second only to the British failure to prevent the building of U-boat pens in French Atlantic ports.

Even when properly calibrated and working at peak efficiency, the improved 1.5-meter-wavelength Mark II ASV radar in these Coastal Command aircraft was almost useless for killing a U-boat at night. For complicated electronic reasons apart from ground or sea "clutter," the radar went "blind" when the aircraft got within a mile of the U-boat. An alert U-boat watch thus had time to maneuver left or right off the flight path of the "blind" aircraft, avoiding its bombs or depth charges.

What the aircrews needed was some means of "seeing" during that last mile to the U-boat. In late October 1940, an officer in Coastal Command headquarters, Humphrey de Verde Leigh, proposed one possible solution: a very powerful, steerable searchlight, mounted on a retractable bed in the underside of the fuselage. Bowhill enthusiastically endorsed the proposal and detached Leigh to work on it full time. But owing to technical problems, bureaucratic inertia, and indifference, it was to take Leigh a full eighteen months to work out the bugs, to gain full approval from the Air Ministry, and to get the searchlight into combat, yet another serious British lapse.

Radar for British escort ships was similarly slow in coming. It was not until June 19, 1940, that a British destroyer put to sea with a test ASW radar. She was *Verity,* fitted with a 1.5-meter-wavelength set, designated Type 286M. It had a "fixed" antenna, which could only "look ahead." In order to search a wider path in the seas, it was necessary to swing the ship to port and to starboard. British engineers were at work on a rotating antenna and a cathode-ray display tube (Planned Position Indicator, or PPI), which presented the host vessel at the center and other vessels as "lingering blips" on a flat screen.

The 286M was useful for stationkeeping in convoys, but to detect U-boats the ships—no less than the aircraft—required a more powerful radar based on the Randall and Boot cavity magnetron. This was coming, but also slowly. On August 12, 1940, at Swanage Bay, British scientists carried out the first successful test of a 10-centimeter-wavelength radar against a submarine. However, as with the improved 1.5-meter-wavelength ASV-II radar, the Air Ministry gave highest priority for centimetric radar to Fighter Command to facilitate bomber interception. Six months passed before a naval vessel put to sea to test a (fixed-antenna) shipboard 10-centimeter radar designated Type 271M.

On the other side of the hill, it soon became apparent that the handful of German U-boats could not sustain the slaughter of the "Happy Time." The captains and crews, worked to exhaustion, had to have R&R, and their vessels required refits and overhauls. The winter weather was ever more forbidding. It and the short winter days drastically reduced visibility and therefore the chance of spotting ex-haust smoke from ships in convoy. Notwithstanding British beliefs to the contrary, meaningful assistance in convoy spotting from the *Luftwaffe* was still virtually nonexistent. Moreover, the shortage of U-boats had become even worse. All the old Type VIIs and all the ducks had been lost or withdrawn from the Atlantic to the Training Command. Several other oceangoing boats had returned to Germany for overhaul and upgrading. Many of the new U-boats in Baltic workup incurred de-lays owing to mechanical failures. The big Italian submarines at Bordeaux were less than useless.

Hard times lay ahead.

FOUR

A Brutal Winter

A dolf Hitler, the continentalist, was irrevocably committed to an invasion of the Soviet Union in the spring of 1941. On December 18, 1940, he issued preparatory orders for that undertaking, Operation Barbarossa.

Planning for Barbarossa was complicated by Mussolini's failures in North Africa and Greece. Before he invaded the Soviet Union, Hitler had first to rescue Mussolini and protect Germany's strategic position in the Balkans by sending ground forces—the *Afrika Korps*—to North Africa as soon as possible, and by invading and occupying Greece (Operation Marita) in March. For these reasons, "The Army must be sufficiently strong," Hitler said. "After that everything can be concentrated on the needs of the Air Force and the Navy."

The need to supply these far-flung projects with manpower and matériel slowed U-boat construction. On December 27, ten days after Hitler issued the preparatory orders for Barbarossa, Admiral Raeder conferred with him to make the strongest possible case against Barbarossa. His remarks to Hitler were preserved in abbreviated form by a stenographer:

> It is absolutely necessary to recognize that the greatest task of the hour is concentration of all our power against Britain. In other words, the means necessary for the defeat of Britain must be produced with energy and speed. All demands not absolutely essential for warfare against Britain must deliberately be set aside. There are serious doubts as to the advisability of Operation Barbarossa before the overthrow of Britain. The fight against Britain is carried on primarily by the Air Force

and the Navy. There is therefore the greatest need to produce the weapons used by these two services and to concentrate these weapons on the British supply lines, which are taking on increased significance in view of the fact that the entire armament industry, particularly aircraft and ship construction, is being shifted to America. Britain's ability to maintain her supply lines is definitely the decisive factor for the outcome of the war. . . . The Naval Staff is firmly convinced that German submarines, as in the World War, are the decisive weapons against Britain.

Hitler was unmoved. The war against Great Britain was to take second or third priority until Mussolini had been rescued, the Balkans had been secured, and the Soviet Union had been conquered. Although these operations were to be carried out primarily by the *Wehrmacht* and *Luftwaffe,* the *Kriegsmarine* was to have many important responsibilities, such as blocking the Soviet Navy in the Baltic and Black seas and in Arctic waters, defending Norway and Greece against possible British amphibious invasions, and arranging naval transports for the shipment of the *Afrika Korps* and its impedimenta from Italy to North Africa and a supply line to support that force.

Raeder wrote later that Hitler's decision to leave Great Britain undefeated and unoccupied in favor of an attack on the Soviet Union was "sheer madness." Nonetheless, he accepted that decision like a good soldier and put the OKM to work on the various plans.

The naval war in the Atlantic was to be pressed to the fullest possible extent throughout 1941. The U-boats were to bear the main burden but they were to be augmented by the numerous merchant-ship raiders, the heavy cruisers *Hipper* and *Prinz Eugen,* the "pocket" battleships *Admiral Scheer* and *Lützow,* the battle cruisers *Gneisenau* and *Scharnhorst,* and finally, the super-battleships *Bismarck* and *Tirpitz.*

The problem—the perennial problem—was the acute shortage of oceangoing U-boats. Thirteen new oceangoing boats had been commissioned between September 1 and December 1, 1940, but three oceangoing boats (*U-31, U-32, U-104*) had been lost in that period and two (*U-28* and *U-29*) had been retired to the Training Command. This worked out to a net gain of eight oceangoing boats, for a total of thirty-one commissioned boats, including *U-A.* However, many new boats were still in workup. Even assuming that Baltic ice did not unduly delay them, it was to be March or April before most of the new boats could reach the Atlantic.*

In view of the paucity of U-boats and the absence of reliable tactical information from *B-dienst* and the *Luftwaffe,* Dönitz urgently needed intelligence on British convoy movements. He therefore insisted to Raeder that something be done to compel the *Luftwaffe* to provide the long-promised, much-needed aerial reconnaissance. Since the reconnaissance would help the planned antishipping raids of the German surface warships as well, Raeder agreed, but he had no influence with the *Luftwaffe* chief, *Reichsmarshal* Göring. Raeder and Göring were scarcely on speaking terms.

---

* The normal workup period at that time for a new boat was about four months.

The course of action taken entailed political risk: Raeder went over Göring's head and sent Dönitz to make his case directly to one of Hitler's close staff officers, General Alfred Jodl. The interview, Dönitz wrote, "was very satisfactory and Jodl was convinced." The outcome was that Hitler personally directed that *Luftwaffe Gruppe* 40, commanded by a former naval officer, Martin Harlinghausen, be placed under Dönitz's operational control. Although the *gruppe* had only a few Condors—and the pilots had much to learn—Dönitz optimistically wrote in his diary that Hitler's order was "a great step forward."

Göring was furious that Hitler had given Dönitz command of *Luftwaffe Gruppe* 40 without consulting him. Later, when Göring came to France in his private train, he invited Dönitz to visit. "This was the first time I had ever seen him," Dönitz wrote later. "He did his most to persuade me to agree to a cancellation of the Führer's order, but this I refused to do. He then asked me to stay to dinner, but I declined the invitation, and we parted bad friends."

By December 1940, the oceangoing boats available for patrol had shrunk to six, the lowest number of any month in 1940. Four sailed from Lorient and two, the VIIC *U-96* and the IXB *U-105,* embarked from Germany on maiden patrols.

These six boats, as well as the November boats still on patrol, confronted raging westerly gales, the onset of a brutal and frigid winter, which was to be even worse than that of 1939–1940. The parade of gales churned up awesome grey seas which lifted the boats to giddy crests, then dropped them into terrifying troughs. The boats pitched and shuddered, slewing wildly to port and starboard and rolling to impossible angles. The winds flung biting cold spray—or hail and sleet—at the men on the bridge. From time to time huge waves broke over the bridge, submerging the men and bashing them about, putting human lungs and safety belts to the test. More often than not, visibility was nil. Conditions below were pure hell, like living inside a tumbling, wet barrel. It was not possible to cook or serve meals. Few cared. Even the oldest salts felt queasy and disoriented.

The boats also confronted the possibility of another disruption in the convoy cycles. The heavy cruiser *Hipper* was en route to the North Atlantic, with specific orders to attack Halifax convoys. The purpose of *Hipper*'s mission was twofold: to destroy valuable cargoes and to draw heavy elements of the Home Fleet to the western Atlantic so that the battle cruisers *Gneisenau* and *Scharnhorst* and their supply ships could slip unchallenged through the North Sea into the Atlantic later in the month. If *Hipper* succeeded in finding a Halifax convoy, it was probable that the British would again suspend Halifax convoys until the threat had been eliminated.

Joachim Schepke in *U-100* was the first to sail from Lorient. By then, Berlin had decreed that two boats were to be assigned to weather reporting at all times to assist in the *Luftwaffe*'s Blitz of England. The *U-100* was to relieve one of the two weather boats, broadcasting "short signals" three times a day from about 20 degrees west longitude.

This assignment was not welcomed. Gathering the weather data and encrypting the messages for transmission was tedious. Because of atmospheric disturbances, it was often necessary to transmit a signal several times. Repeated broadcasts increased the chances that the British could obtain a DF fix on the boat. Although the broadcast position was beyond the range of most British ASW aircraft, there was always the possibility that the British would send out a destroyer group to hunt down the boat. At the least, the Admiralty would divert merchant ships from the area of the DF fix, decreasing the chances that a weather boat would find targets of opportunity.

En route to his station on December 5, Schepke ran head-on into a raging winter storm. The winds and seas were so hostile that for the next two days he averaged only seventy-two miles westward, more than half of that while running submerged. When he finally reached his station, he received a message from Dönitz to all boats to temporarily maintain radio silence except when attacking. *B-dienst* had informed Dönitz that the British had definitely DFed the previous weather boat.

Schepke had been awarded Oak Leaves to his *Ritterkreuz* but curiously, the Berlin propagandists had not publicized the award. Possibly Dönitz had withheld an announcement until Schepke had sunk several more ships to compensate for his well-known overclaims. If so (the record is not clear), Schepke had good reason to hunt relentlessly in spite of the ghastly weather.

Schepke had two opportunities to run up his score on December 8, but both failed. In the early, dark hours, the bridge watch spotted a "large steamer," but an "inexperienced helmsman," Schepke wrote, turned the boat the "wrong way" and the watch lost sight of the ship and could not find it again. Later, in daylight, the bridge watch spotted another ship. Schepke submerged to attack, firing two torpedoes from very close range. When both torpedoes missed—probably because of the mountainous seas—Schepke broke off, intending to attack again after dark on the surface. But when darkness fell, Schepke and the watch lost sight of the ship and it, too, got away. The failures left Schepke and his crew angry and dispirited.

The new VIIC *U-96*, commanded by Heinrich Lehmann-Willenbrock, age twenty-nine, from the ducks *U-5* and *U-8*, was the next boat to sail from Germany. On the afternoon of his eighth day at sea, December 11, while en route to a weather-reporting station, Lehmann-Willenbrock stumbled into the midst of the big inbound convoy, Halifax 92. Attacking submerged, he sank the 10,900-ton British freighter *Rotorua*. Pursuing the convoy after dark on the surface in huge seas, Lehmann-Willenbrock got ahead and sank three more ships for 15,200 tons.

To the west of *U-96*, Schepke in *U-100*, finally authorized to broadcast weather reports three times a day, had a change in luck. On December 14 the watch spotted two separate ships sailing unescorted. Schepke sank both in surface attacks, but in the rough seas it took five torpedoes to put them under. The first ship was the 3,670-ton British freighter *Kyleglen*, overclaimed at 4,573 tons. The second was accurately claimed at 3,380 tons. The expenditure of five torpedoes to sink these two modest ships further depressed Schepke, leaving him with a "heavy heart," as he logged.

That same day Lehmann-Willenbrock in *U-96,* patrolling about 100 miles to the northeast of Schepke, also had good luck. He sank an 11,000-ton British steamer and damaged a 5,100-ton freighter. The sinking raised Lehmann-Willenbrock's score to five confirmed ships for 37,000 tons, an outstanding debut, especially in view of the foul weather and the almost complete absence of convoy contacts from the Condors and the other U-boats.

On December 15, Schepke reported that a "hurricane" struck the hunting grounds. It raged for the next forty-eight hours, forcing all the boats to run submerged most of that time, surfacing only to freshen the air supply and to charge batteries. Despite the difficulties, Schepke dutifully broadcast weather reports three times a day.

The terrible weather in the North Atlantic prompted the OKM and Kerneval to consider the possibility of concentrating boats in the southern Atlantic waters, as Dönitz had done the winter before. The shift would doubtless please Rome. On December 9 the modest British Army of the Nile had counterattacked and pushed the bloated, inept Italian Army back into Libya. Concentrated U-boat attacks against the convoys taking supplies to the British ground forces in Egypt via Gibraltar, Freetown, and the Cape of Good Hope would not only help the reeling Italians but also force the British to intensify ASW measures in the South Atlantic, thinning out the Mediterranean naval forces.

Dönitz opposed a concentration of U-boats in the south for several reasons.

First, he still believed the decisive battleground was the North Atlantic, that U-boat operations elsewhere constituted an unwise diversion of his meager resources. Although U-boat successes in the North Atlantic were declining sharply, the presence of even a few U-boats compelled the British to maintain convoying, which of itself reduced imports to the British Isles significantly.

Second, the returns from the two IXs in southern waters appeared to be even poorer than those in the inhospitable North Atlantic. The *U-65* (von Stockhausen) patrolling off Freetown had reported no further successes since November 19. The other, *U-37* (Clausen), had sunk seven ships, but all were small, aggregating merely 11,000 tons.*

Third, facilities for refueling boats in southern waters were iffy. *Nordmark,* the supply ship for the "pocket" battleship *Admiral Scheer,* had gone far south, beyond the Cape of Good Hope. The presence of British naval forces in the Canary Islands had twice forced Clausen in *U-37* to abort planned refuelings there and he had to return to Lorient prematurely.

The upshot of those deliberations was a decision to shift not German but Italian submarines from the North Atlantic to the South Atlantic. Dönitz was not unhappy with this solution. Italian submarine operations in the North Atlantic had failed utterly. Dönitz put it this way in his diary: "They do not serve any practical purpose. . . . I have not received one single enemy report from them on which I could take action. . . . I am not at all sure that their presence in the operations area of

---

* Three of the sinkings were awkward "mistakes": a Spanish trawler, the 2,800-ton Vichy tanker *Rhone,* and—worst of all—the 1,400-ton Vichy submarine *Sfax.*

German boats . . . does not do more harm than good." He did not think the Italians were "sufficiently hard and determined" or flexible enough for submarine warfare in the North Atlantic. They were "inadequately disciplined" and were unable to "keep calm in the face of the enemy." They had not the faintest idea of how to shadow a convoy, or accurately report its position and course, or how to attack at night. Their attacks were "clumsy," and they let themselves be seen too often.

After the "hurricane" blew through the North Atlantic, on December 18 Lehmann-Willenbrock in *U-96* continued his outstanding first patrol by detecting and attacking convoy Outbound 259 with his last torpedoes. He damaged but could not sink a 10,000-ton British tanker that was sailing in ballast. He shadowed the convoy and radioed a report to Dönitz, who directed Schepke in *U-100* and Salmann in *U-52* to close and attack, but neither boat could reach the convoy.

En route to find the damaged tanker, Schepke came across a lone, outbound 10,100-ton British freighter, *Napier Star.* He tracked the ship during daylight hours, surfaced after dark, and attacked, firing three torpedoes. One missed but two hit, and she went down. Upon receiving word of this sinking—Schepke's third on this patrol—Dönitz logged happily that Schepke had become the "third skipper to pass 200,000 tons." He gave this news—and the award of the Oak Leaves to Schepke's *Ritterkreuz*—to Berlin propagandists, who released it on December 21, crediting Schepke with sinking forty ships for 208,975 tons.*

Schepke still had two torpedoes and was determined to sink at least one more big ship. In the early dark hours of December 22, the watch spotted a likely possibility: a 10,000-ton vessel sailing alone, possibly an armed merchant cruiser. Schepke bent on full speed for a surface attack, but as he was preparing to shoot, both diesels broke down. Exasperated, he submerged to finish the attack on electric motors, but at the climactic moment in the approach, the periscope malfunctioned. When the engineer reported the diesels were back in commission, Schepke surfaced in very heavy seas and continued the chase, pulling around and getting ahead in the dark. While he was closing for a third attack, the ship sighted *U-100* and "maneuvered wildly," denying Schepke a good shooting angle. Believing it to be "now or never," as he described the situation, Schepke fired his last two torpedoes, but both missed.

These failures, Schepke logged on his twenty-first day at sea, caused morale on *U-100* to fall "pretty low." Having sunk "only" three ships for 18,000 tons, Schepke wrote in self-flagellation, they had been out all that time "for nothing." Moreover, Christmas was merely three days away. Seeking some means of lifting morale, Schepke hit on the idea of requesting permission to go to Kiel rather than Lorient for *U-100*'s scheduled overhaul. Perhaps sensing that the *U-100* crew needed cheer—or feeling they deserved it—Dönitz approved the request. Schepke's return to Germany (to huge acclaim) left only one of the eighteen "aces"

---

* His confirmed score was thirty-seven ships for 155,882 tons.

(or *Ritterkreuz* holders) in the Atlantic: Heinrich Liebe in *U-38,* who relieved Schepke as weather reporter.*

On Christmas Day 1940, there were eight U-boats in the Atlantic: six in northern waters and the Type IXs *U-65* and *U-37* returning to Lorient from African waters. All celebrated the holiday by decorating the boats with miniature Christmas trees, gorging on special meals and sweets, and, on some of the boats, enjoying tots of alcoholic beverages.

The hunting in the North Atlantic during the last week of the year remained poor. The four U-boats fresh to the area sank only three ships. The only *Ritterkreuz* holder at sea, Heinrich Liebe in *U-38,* sank two, generously sharing credit for one with the Italian boat *Tazzoli.* Gerd Schreiber in *U-95* sank the other, a 12,800-ton British freighter.

The poor hunting during most of December was not the fault of the cruiser *Hipper.* She had entered the Atlantic convoy lanes on December 9, but she had not found a Halifax convoy or any other target. After ten days of futile searching, she had suffered an engine malfunction, forcing her to abort to France. Inbound to Brest on Christmas Day, she came across a military convoy outbound for Egypt, escorted by several cruisers and the carriers *Furious* and *Argus,* which were ferrying aircraft. *Hipper* mounted an ineffective, glancing attack, then ran in to Brest. As intended, her sudden appearance drew Home Fleet units into the Atlantic, enabling *Gneisenau* and *Scharnhorst* to sortie undetected. But all for naught. *Gneisenau* incurred wave damage off Norway and both ships aborted to Kiel, another humiliating setback for the *Kriegsmarine.*

Returning from African waters, von Stockhausen in *U-65* had a run of luck, sinking four unescorted ships for about 27,000 tons, including two tankers, the 9,000-ton Panamanian *Charles Pratt* and the 5,900-ton *British Premier.* This raised his total claims for this ninety-day patrol to Freetown—the longest cruise on record to then—to eight ships (four tankers) for 52,800 tons, confirmed in Allied records as eight sinkings (four tankers) for 47,785 tons. Adding past overclaims, including generous credit for sinking the 28,000-ton French liner *Champlain,* which had been wrecked by the *Luftwaffe,* von Stockhausen's total bag reached 100,000 tons and he qualified for a *Ritterkreuz.* After extended home leave while *U-65* was in overhaul, he went to a job in the Training Command.†

The return of *U-65* raised anew the issue of sending German U-boats to African waters, provided the resupply problem could be solved. To some staffers at the OKM and Kerneval, the total score for *U-65*'s patrol—eight ships—was impres-

---

* Remarkably, all eighteen skippers who had won the *Ritterkreuz* to then were still alive: Prien, Kretschmer, Lüth, and Schütze on leave from their boats in Lorient; Schepke and Endrass on leave from their boats in Germany; Rollmann, Schuhart, Frauenheim, Rösing, Kuhnke, and Oehrn in staff or training jobs; Hartmann, Lemp, and Bleichrodt fitting out new boats in Germany; Jenisch in a British POW camp. Herbert Schultze, hospitalized after Norway, had returned to command of *U-48,* which was undergoing overhaul in Germany.

† His confirmed total, including *Champlain,* was twelve ships for 87,278 tons.

sive. Besides that, the presence of the boat in southern waters had drawn some convoy escorts and warships from the Mediterranean and North Atlantic and compelled the British to mount extensive ASW air and surface patrols off Freetown. But Dönitz was still not persuaded. The sinking of eight ships in a ninety-day patrol—an average of one ship every eleven days—was a "barely acceptable" return, he logged. Counting prepatrol preparations, the patrol itself, and the postpatrol overhaul, the total investment in time for *U-65*'s African foray was about six months. In that time she might have conducted several patrols in the North Atlantic, possibly sinking double the number of ships, as well as spotting convoys for other boats.

The results achieved by U-boats in December were predictably disappointing. In the six patrols in the North Atlantic, the oceangoing U-boats sank thirteen and one-half ships for about 90,000 tons, a further decline to about 2.3 ships for 15,000 tons per boat per patrol.

There was little hope for improvement of merchant-ship sinkings in the immediate future. Only four U-boats were left in the hunting grounds on December 31, 1940, two of these assigned to weather reporting and all attempting to cope with the worst winds and seas anyone had ever experienced. Owing to the delays in the refits and the overhauls and the readiness dates of new boats, only ten boats were to be available to replace those four in January. Moreover, Germany was in the grip of a winter even more frigid than the last, again raising the probability of thick ice in the Baltic, Kiel Canal, the Elbe, and the Jade, which would severely curtail or prevent submarine-school training and delay the workups of the newly commissioned boats.

KNITTING ANGLO-AMERICAN RELATIONS

By New Year's Day 1941, Winston Churchill had made good progress on what he viewed as the most important measure necessary to defeat the Germans: to draw the United States, spiritually and physically, deeper into the war on Britain's side.

After winning election to an unprecedented third term in November 1940, President Roosevelt declared that the United States must become an "Arsenal of Democracy," guaranteeing freedom of speech and worship, and freedom from fear and want, to all peoples. In response to Roosevelt's request, and to another from Churchill ("Give us the tools and we will finish the job"), Congress debated, then overwhelmingly approved a radical scheme called "Lend-Lease." In effect, the Lend-Lease Act rescinded the "Cash and Carry" policy of the amended Neutrality Act and gave Roosevelt sweeping powers to "transfer title to, exchange, lease or lend or otherwise dispose of" military supplies to any nation whose "defense was vital to the defense of the United States."*

---

* Lend-Lease was signed into law on March 11, 1941. Designed primarily to help Great Britain, which had run out of gold and credits, by war's end American outlays for Lend-Lease totaled $50.6 billion, of which $31 billion went to Britain.

In public Roosevelt continued to insist the United States would not go to war. The "Destroyer Deal," Lend-Lease, and other measures were merely helping hands to a friend—like lending a fire hose to a neighbor whose house was burning down—or prudent defensive measures to insure the security of the United States. Behind the scenes, however, Roosevelt was nudging the United States ever closer to direct military intervention. During a visit to the British Isles in January 1941, Roosevelt's most trusted and influential White House advisor, Harry L. Hopkins, told Churchill: "The President is determined that we shall win the war together." The top-secret joint military war planning begun in August 1940 by the Ghormley Mission in London resumed in earnest in Washington in February 1941, resulting in a detailed joint plan (ABC-1) for waging war against the Axis, which, with the signing of the Tripartite Pact on September 27, 1940, included Japan.

In essence, ABC-1 specified that should the United States be drawn into the war, the Allies were to defeat Germany and Italy first, Japan second. In the meantime, or "short of war," the United States was to assume as soon as practicable certain large military responsibilities in the Atlantic Ocean area, the most important of which was convoy escort between Canada and Iceland, which the British had occupied after the fall of Denmark and were developing into a halfway station for surface-ship escorts and a base for Coastal Command aircraft. In preparation for taking on that and other tasks, on February 1, 1941, Roosevelt established the Atlantic Fleet, commanded by Ernest J. King; authorized construction of a naval base at Argentia, Newfoundland, and several in the British Isles; and approved the transfer to the Atlantic Fleet of three battleships (*Idaho, Mississippi, New Mexico*), a carrier (*Yorktown*), four light cruisers, and Destroyer Squadrons 8 and 9 from the Pacific Fleet, which was still based at Pearl Harbor, Hawaii, to deter Japanese aggression in the Pacific.

The Chief of Naval Operations, Harold Stark, and the Commander-in-Chief of the Atlantic Fleet, Ernest King, chose the best and the brightest of the young officers to formulate plans for the escorting of Atlantic convoys. These officers included three who became heads of the uniformed Navy in the postwar years: Robert B. Carney, Louis E. Denfeld, and Forrest P. Sherman. On February 15, 1941, Stark approved the plans and named one of the most competent of the senior naval officers, Arthur Leroy Bristol, Jr., to command the convoy organization they had proposed: Support Force, Atlantic Fleet,* which reported to King.

Soon after the creation of the Support Force, President Roosevelt ruled that American naval vessels should not escort eastbound North Atlantic convoys from United States soil nor should they go beyond Iceland. Accordingly, Bristol established his headquarters on the magnificent new 16,500-ton destroyer tender *Prairie* and moved her to Argentia, in Placentia Bay, Newfoundland, where, under terms of the "Destroyer Deal," hundreds of American workers were feverishly building ship and aircraft bases for the U.S. Navy. Soon thereafter, Washington executed a deal with the exiled Danish government in which the Americans agreed to protect

---

* The main element of the Support Force was Task Force 4, later redesignated Task Force 24.

Greenland and Iceland from Axis forces. In return, the Danes gave the Americans the right to develop air and ship bases on Greenland and Iceland, the eastern terminus of the proposed new convoy-escort scheme.

Stark and King assigned substantial combat forces to Bristol's support force. These included, in addition to the tender *Prairie,* a destroyer flotilla (twenty-seven ships), a patrol wing (forty-eight Catalina flying boats*), a submarine squadron (fifteen *R*-class boats), two new 8,700-ton seaplane tenders (*Albemarle, Curtiss*), and two destroyers that had been converted to seaplane tenders (*Belknap, George E. Badger*). Bristol also controlled the American naval vessels assigned to the Northern Patrol off Greenland waters. Most of his forces were based at the new facilities at Argentia, but some ventured to Iceland to begin the development of an Anglo-American anchorage at Hvalfjord, near Reykjavik in the Denmark Strait.

From the beginning of the war, the Prime Minister of Canada, W. L. Mackenzie King, had willingly placed Canada's seven British-built destroyers under absolute control of the British Royal Navy. The Canadian destroyers had served as convoy escorts and with the anti-invasion naval forces. By the end of 1940, Canada had also placed at the disposal of the Royal Navy her seven ex-American *Town*-class four-stack destroyers and the sixteen Canadian-built *Flower*-class corvettes which had been commissioned by that time. In all, thirty Canadian ships (fourteen destroyers) were placed under the command of the Royal Navy.†

Although Canada was a vibrantly growing nation of the Commonwealth, the British ruling establishment continued to view Canadians as crude "country cousins" in a Third World nation. This was especially the case in the high circles of the Royal Navy. When Anglo-American war planners secretly convened in early 1941 to work out war plan ABC-1, no one bothered to include the chief of the Canadian Navy, Percy W. Nelles. Under terms of the ABC-1 agreement, the Atlantic Ocean was divided into two spheres of responsibility, a British one in the east and an American one in the west. The British, who regarded the Canadian Navy as merely another subordinate command of the Royal Navy (and not a very good one at that), casually pledged that when America came into the war, covertly or overtly, Canadian naval forces would automatically come under American command.

The failure of the war planners to even consult the Canadians outraged Percy Nelles and other Canadian naval authorities. When Bristol and staff actually arrived in Argentia on *Prairie* to take over North Atlantic convoy escort in the western zone, the Canadians quietly boiled. Bristol added insult to injury by assuming emperor-like status in Newfoundland, even "relocating" about two hundred families from the Argentia area. Inasmuch as Newfoundland had not yet formally joined the Canadian government and the British had leased it to the Americans for bases in the "Destroyer Deal," Bristol was perfectly within his rights and he exercised them as he saw fit, apparently without due regard for Canadian sensitivities.

---

* The PBY Catalina was a twin-engine flying boat, designated Patrol Bomber (PB), built by Consolidated (Y). Combat radius: 600 miles at 103 knots. Bomb load: 4,000 pounds.

† See Appendix 10.

PLATE 7

ROYAL CANADIAN NAVY OCEAN-ESCORT VESSELS OTHER
THAN DESTROYERS 1939–1945[1]

TYPE		CLASS	BUILT/ GOT	LENGTH/ FEET	TONS
Corvette	(PE)	Flower	69	205	950–1,000
Corvette	(PE)	Flower #2	4 (got)	208	1,000
Corvette	(PE)	Flower #2	37[2]	208	1,000
Corvette	(PE)	Castle	12 (got)	252	1,000–1,100
Frigate	(PF)	River	7 (got)	301	1,400
Frigate	(PF)	River	61[3]	301	1,400
Frigate	(PF)	Loch	3 (got)	307	1,400

Total ships built in Canada:	167
Total ships got (all ex-RN):	26
Total ships commissioned:	193

1. Sources: Tucker (pps. 502-522), Elliott, Lenton, etc.
2. Plus eight for the U.S.N. and seven for the R.N. Total built: 52.
3. Plus two for the U.S.N. (*Asheville, Natchez*). Total built: 63.

For various reasons the American convoy-escort service to be provided by Bristol and staff was delayed from April to September 1941. When it finally came into being, the Americans presented the Canadians with a *fait accompli* and took virtual command of most Canadian naval elements in the western Atlantic, in accordance with the terms the British had offered. Seniors in the swelling Canadian Navy were naturally furious at this blatant and arrogant assumption of authority in their home waters and launched a bureaucratic campaign to right what they saw as an egregious wrong. However, they failed, and this command inequity remained in place for a long time to come.

In due course, the slowly maturing Canadian Navy was to play a vital role in the Battle of the Atlantic, contributing scores of warships and escorting about half of all the convoys on the North Atlantic run. Most histories of this naval struggle fail to stress the important Canadian role; some do not mention it at all; a few even ridicule the Canadians.*

From this planning and activity, it can be seen that the Americans well understood that convoying was a vital measure in countering the U-boat threat and by early 1941 had placed convoying requirements at the very top of Atlantic Fleet priorities. However, as will be seen, the "loan" (gift) of fifty four-stack destroyers to the British and Canadians gutted the available American escort forces severely

---

* Beginning in the 1980s, a crop of Canadian military and naval historians has worked diligently—and successfully—to correct the record. See Bibliography: Douglas, Hadley, Lund, Milner, Sarty, Steury, et al.

in the Atlantic—so severely that for the next two years (1941–1942) in return for their generosity, the Americans were to pay a heavy price in lost seamen and ships.

That was only the beginning of President Roosevelt's generosity to the British on the Atlantic naval front. The increasingly sympathetic attitude in America for the British, who were enduring the horrors of The Blitz in the winter of 1940–1941, and the enactment of Lend-Lease relaxed many political constraints on the President. In the early weeks of 1941, he further assisted the British in the following specific ways:

•   The transfer of ten *Lake*-class United States Coast Guard cutters to the Royal Navy. Commissioned in the years 1928–1932, these beamy, long-range vessels were 250 feet in length, displaced about 2,000 tons, and had a top speed of 17 knots, about the same as that of a Type VII U-boat and slightly faster than a corvette. At the time of transfer, the main armament consisted of two 3" guns and depth-charge throwers and tracks. Most of these Coast Guard vessels were in good condition. The British designated them sloops and put them into immediate service as convoy escorts on the routes between Sierra Leone and the British Isles. The gift of these warships was also to be costly to the Americans.

•   The allotment of about fifty first-class American tankers to the British maritime "shuttle," which transported oil and petroleum products from the Caribbean to ports on America's East Coast for onward shipment to the British Isles in armed British tankers. This measure freed up a like number of British tankers which were used for the Atlantic crossing. In effect, this Lend-Lease gift made good the forty-two British tanker losses to U-boats since the onset of war. To replace the American tankers, a few weeks later Congress authorized Roosevelt to "requisition" (i.e., seize) "refugee tankers" of French, Danish, and other flags that were in American ports.

•   The gradual transfer to British charter of about seventy-five Norwegian and Panamanian tankers then under charter by oil companies in the Americas. Counting the "shuttle" and these chartered vessels, the British tanker fleet in effect exceeded its size at the beginning of the war. Washington paid the whole of the charter costs in Lend-Lease dollars, a currency the Norwegians prized above all others.

•   Construction of a 13,000-ton "escort" aircraft carrier, *Archer,* for the Royal Navy. Conceived originally to provide convoys air cover against enemy aircraft, the "escort" or "jeep" carriers had a flight deck about 500 feet long and could carry fifteen to twenty fighter aircraft. Prodded by President Roosevelt, in early 1941 the Maritime Commission converted two new sister ships of the Moore Macormack line to prototype "jeep" carriers, H.M.S. *Archer* for the British and U.S.S. *Long Island* for the U.S. Navy.*

---

*   Simultaneously, British yards were in process of converting a 467-foot, 5,600-ton German-built prize, *Hannover,* into the "jeep" carrier H.M.S. *Audacity,* which could carry six fighters. *Long Island* and *Audacity* were commissioned in June; *Archer* in November 1941.

• In an especially broad interpretation of the Lend-Lease Act, President Roosevelt authorized British warships to put into American naval shipyards for repairs and upgrading. This gesture helped ease the pressures in British naval shipyards, already jammed with ships awaiting attention. The British battleships *Malaya* and *Resolution,* which incurred battle damage, were the first capital ships to take advantage of this gift.

• In addition to all kinds of aircraft and ships and weaponry, President Roosevelt promised the British that among the "tools" to be provided in quantity by the Arsenal of Democracy was centimetric-wavelength radar for aircraft and ships. In anticipation, some quarters of the vast American electronics industry were retooling.

Scientists at the M.I.T. Radiation Laboratory were vigorously pushing R&D on all radar but especially centimetric-wavelength radar, employing the Randall and Boot cavity magnetron, paralleling the work of British scientists. By January 1941, the lab and its many subcontractors had produced an experimental model for ships with a revolving antenna and a single cathode-ray display screen (PPI), which produced lingering "blips." By March 1941, when the British mounted the first experimental centimetric-wavelength radar in a Fighter Command Beaufighter night interceptor, American engineers mounted a similar experimental version in a B-18 bomber. When the first British warship, the corvette *Orchis,* put to sea with Type 271M centimetric radar in March 1941, the American destroyer *Semmes* was similarly fitted with an American-made model, Type SG.*

In addition to the foregoing, Roosevelt directed the Maritime Commission to provide the British with a substantial number of newly built tankers in addition to the sixty *Ocean*-class dry-cargo ships already under construction for the British. Jerry Land estimated that he could deliver to the British about twenty-one new tankers in 1941, most of them toward the end of the year. The need to provide these tankers as well as the sixty *Ocean*-class ships as soon as possible infused the Maritime Commission with a sense of urgency that was to benefit not only the British but also the Americans.

Furthermore, in late winter and early spring of 1941, Land proposed two new merchant-ship building programs, which President Roosevelt promptly approved. Under the first, of March 1941, in addition to the sixty *Ocean*-class ships and twenty-one tankers earmarked for Britain and 200 Liberty ships in the works for the American merchant marine, Land added 200 more ships for the American merchant marine, half of them Liberty ships. Under the second program, of April 1941, Land added yet another 306 merchant ships, bringing the total of approved new merchant-ship orders to about 800. This was over and above the 2,000 ships under contract for the U.S. Navy and other American military forces.

---

* In tests, *Orchis* picked up a surfaced submarine at 5,000 yards, a trimmed-down submarine at 2,800 yards, and—remarkably—an eight-foot-high submarine periscope at 1,300 yards (two thirds of a nautical mile).

UNHAPPY TIMES

While Dönitz took leave in the month of January 1941, his chief of staff, Eberhard Godt, directed the U-boat war.

At the beginning of the year, four December boats were still on patrol, two on weather-reporting station. These four were joined by five others: two new IXBs, *U-105* and *U-106*, which sailed from Germany, and three boats from Lorient. All were handicapped by winter darkness and by a seemingly endless parade of brutal storms. The only *Ritterkreuz* holder on patrol, Heinrich Liebe in the aging Type IX *U-38*, who had sunk two ships in December (sharing one with *Tazzoli*), incurred "heavy" depth-charge damage and was forced to abort to Lorient. At mid-month there were seven U-boats in the North Atlantic and a number of Italian boats, including *Torelli*, commanded by Primo Longobardo, who had trained in combat under Otto Kretschmer in *U-99*.

The hunting continued to be very poor. The glancing attack by *Hipper* on the military convoy on Christmas Day and the hideous weather had led the British to delay again the sailing of Halifax convoys. For example, when convoy Halifax 103 was ready to put to sea, the bad weather forced thirty-one ships to abort the voyage. In the whole month of January, only 243 ships crossed from Canada to the British Isles in convoys, 170 of them in Halifax convoys, seventy-three in Slow Convoys.

In the first half of January, Axis submarines in the North Atlantic sank only six ships, all sailing alone or stragglers from storm-tossed convoys. Primo Longobardo in *Torelli* accounted for three of the sinkings for 12,291 tons, the most successful patrol by an Italian submarine to then. The new Type IXB *U-105*, commanded by Georg Schewe, age thirty-one, from the duck *U-60*, sank the 4,800-ton British freighter *Bassano*. The new IXB *U-106*, commanded by Jürgen Oesten, age twenty-eight, from the duck *U-61*, sank the 10,600-ton British freighter *Zealandic*. The promising new skipper, Georg-Wilhelm Schulz in *U-124*, sank the 6,000-ton British freighter *Empire Thunder*, an exasperating and near-fatal victory requiring the expenditure of five torpedoes. The first two missed, the third hit, and the fourth missed and circled back, missing *U-124* by "a few meters."* The fifth hit and finally sank the ship. After thirty-eight miserable days at sea, Schulz returned to Lorient in ill humor.

At this time, a third Italian boat was lost in the North Atlantic. She was the *Nani*, commanded by Gioacchino Polizzi. She was sunk on January 7 by depth charges from the British corvette *Anemone*. There were no survivors from this boat either.

One of the new VIICs, *U-96*, commanded by Heinrich Lehmann-Willenbrock who had sunk five ships on his first patrol, sailed from Lorient on January 9, after merely twelve days in port. He arrived off Rockall Bank on January 16, and that

---

* Circular torpedo runs, caused by a malfunctioning gyro or stuck rudder, were experienced by submarines of all navies. It is believed that many submarines that disappeared on patrol for "unknown" reasons were the victims of their own torpedoes.

day and the next *U-96* found and attacked two big British freighters, which were sailing unescorted: one for 14,118 tons and one for 15,000 tons.

Lehmann-Willenbrock expended all twelve torpedoes to sink these ships and returned to Lorient on January 22, having been out only fourteen days. His score of 29,000 tons sunk was far and away the best performance by any U-boat in the month of January.

In conformance with Hitler's personal order, *Luftwaffe Gruppe* 40, based in Bordeaux, commenced convoy-spotting in January. An average of two Condors per day patrolled the area near Rockall Bank. The airmen found convoys on January 11, 16, and 20, but owing to the unfavorable weather, the scarcity of U-boats, and the incorrect position reports from the Condors, Godt was not able to put a single boat in contact with any of the convoys. When it was discovered that the position reporting from the Condors could not be relied upon, the airmen were directed to shadow the convoys and send beacon signals to home in the U-boats.

Another six boats sailed in the second half of January: four from Lorient, including the IXB *U-103*, commanded by *Ritterkreuz* holder Viktor Schütze, and two from Germany. The latter were the record-holding VIIB, *U-48*, once more under command of *Ritterkreuz* holder Herbert Schultze, and the new IXB *U-107*. The last was commanded by Dönitz's son-in-law Günter Hessler, age thirty-one, who had married Ursula Dönitz in November 1937 and had joined the U-boat arm in April 1940. These boats, too, found poor hunting. The Condors spotted convoys on January 26, 28, and 30, but owing to failures in communications and other factors, none of the U-boats could be brought into play.

In the waning days of this frustrating month, on January 29, a Lorient VIIC, *U-93,* commanded by Claus Korth, ran into the heavily escorted inbound Slow Convoy 19. Upon receiving Korth's report, Godt ordered all boats in the vicinity—and the Condors—to home and close on beacon signals from *U-93*. Meanwhile, Korth attacked, sinking three ships for 21,300 tons, including the 10,500-ton British tanker *W. B. Walker.* Herbert Kuppisch in *U-94* came up and sank two straggling freighters. Oesten in *U-106* sank another straggler. An escort, the crack British destroyer *Antelope,* which had sunk *U-31* and *U-41,* mistook an empty life raft for the U-boat and rammed it, botching the counterattack.

Dönitz returned from leave February 1. By then the active "aces" were prepared to resume the Battle of the Atlantic. Herbert Schultze in *U-48* and Viktor Schütze in *U-103* were already in the hunting grounds. Günther Prien, Otto Kretschmer, and Wolfgang Lüth were in Lorient, preparing their boats for combat. Fritz-Julius Lemp, Joachim Schepke, and Engelbert Endrass were in Germany, also preparing their boats for combat. If all went well, by the end of the month all eight "aces" who still commanded U-boats were to be back in action.

All did not go well, however. In Lorient on February 4, Wolfgang Lüth's *U-43* mysteriously flooded and sank at dockside, knocking the boat out of action for three months. A court of inquiry found that a ballast-tank vent valve had been left open by mistake. The court blamed the first and second watch officers, Hinrich-

Oskar Bernbeck and Erwin Witte, and ordered them to pay for the repairs out of savings and salaries(!). In Germany, the intense cold and a sudden onset of heavy Baltic ice delayed the overhaul of Schepke's *U-100* and the workup of Lemp's new boat, the IXB *U-110.**

Counting six new boats that were to sail from Germany, Dönitz had eighteen boats to deploy in February. Notwithstanding the terrible weather and the paltry returns of January, he insisted that the bulk of the boats should operate in the North Atlantic in cooperation with the Condors employing so-called improved communications procedures. But he also agreed to remount German patrols to West African waters, one by Clausen's *U-37*, replicating its voyage of December, and another by the *U-A*, which was entirely unsuitable for anticonvoy operations in the North Atlantic.

Two factors had led Dönitz to view patrols to West African waters more favorably. First, the *Afrika Korps,* commanded by Erwin Rommel, was en route to North Africa to rescue the reeling Italian Army, half of which (130,000 men) had surrendered to the still small but adept British Army of the Nile. The Italian submarines in West African waters had failed to make any significant dent in the British convoys rounding the Cape of Good Hope to support the Army of the Nile. Any U-boat successes against those convoys would amount to direct German support for Rommel. Second, the battle cruisers *Gneisenau* and *Scharnhorst* had finally broken out of the North Sea. The heavy cruiser *Hipper,* sailing from Brest, was to join them for raids against the British convoys in the South Atlantic. The supply ships supporting *Gneisenau* and *Scharnhorst* could also supply the U-boats.

In the North Atlantic, Dönitz's son-in-law Günter Hessler in the new IXB *U-107* found convoy Outbound 279 on February 3. After flashing an alert, Hessler attacked, sinking a 4,700-ton freighter, then shadowed during the day. Dönitz relayed the report and ordered six other boats to converge on the convoy. Still shadowing, on the following evening Hessler sank a second ship of 5,000 tons. No other boats found the convoy, but while searching for it, Salmann in *U-52* and Moehle in *U-123* came across the inbound Slow Convoy 20, from which they sank one ship each, as did Hessler in *U-107,* responding to their reports. Korth in *U-93* polished off another ship from this convoy with his deck gun, a 2,700-tonner which had been damaged by a Condor.

The Admiralty got wind of the breakout of *Gneisenau* and *Scharnhorst* from the North Sea and positioned powerful Home Fleet forces (*Nelson, Rodney, Repulse,* etc.) south of Iceland to intercept them. A British cruiser, *Naiad,* got a fleeting glimpse of the German vessels southbound in the Denmark Strait, but the British disbelieved—or discounted—the report. Equipped with primitive radar,

---

* Endrass's *U-46* and five new boats rushed from Kiel to Helgoland to escape the Baltic ice. Several new oceangoing boats and a number of school ducks were trapped by ice, frozen at dockside until late March.

Gneisenau and *Scharnhorst* evaded *Naiad* at high speed and withdrew northward into the strait to prepare for a second try on February 3–4.

The *Gneisenau* and *Scharnhorst* had orders to attack Halifax convoys in the area west of Iceland. Assuming the attack would again draw out the Home Fleet, the OKM directed Dönitz to lay a submarine trap south of Iceland to ambush its ships. On February 8, *Gneisenau* and *Scharnhorst* intercepted convoy Halifax 106, but upon seeing that the convoy was escorted by the battleship *Ramillies,** the Germans, who were under orders to avoid battles with capital ships, broke off the attack. As anticipated, the Home Fleet sailed west in pursuit of *Gneisenau* and *Scharnhorst.* Dönitz, meanwhile, had positioned eight German U-boats to the submarine trap south of Iceland. One of these, Herbert Schultze in *U-48,* sighted—and reported—a "battle cruiser and a light cruiser," but he was unable to get into shooting position. On February 10, a Whitley of Coastal Command Squadron 502, piloted by J. A. Walker, caught Korth in *U-93* on the surface and bombed the boat, hastening her return to Lorient. The repairs to *U-93* were to take three months. No other boats intercepted Home Fleet units. The submarine trap was thus a failure.

Dönitz was not displeased by this diversion. He believed the Condor reconnaissance flights near Rockall Bank had forced the British to divert convoys well to the north to avoid aerial detection. Later, when the OKM released the boats of the submarine trap, he left six boats on patrol lines due south of Iceland. Since this area was beyond range of the Bordeaux-based Condors, Dönitz requested that Condor flights be staged to that area from Norway.

Southbound to African waters, on the morning of February 9, Nikolaus Clausen in *U-37* ran into convoy Home Gibraltar 53. Comprised of twenty-one ships, the convoy was thinly escorted by one destroyer and one sloop. Clausen gave the alarm, then attacked, claiming three ships for 13,500 tons sunk, but again he inflated the tonnage. His confirmed score was two ships for 3,300 tons.

There were no other German U-boats in Iberian waters, but the heavy cruiser *Hipper,* southbound from Brest to join *Gneisenau* and *Scharnhorst,* was within easy reach, as were the Condors basing at Bordeaux. Sensing a "historic" opportunity to mount a combined U-boat, aircraft, and surface-ship attack on the same convoy, Dönitz directed Clausen to shadow the convoy and to send beacon signals. Meanwhile, Dönitz instructed *Gruppe* 40 to fly as many Condors as possible to the scene and invited the OKM to bring up *Hipper.* Five Condors took off. The OKM initially refused to commit *Hipper* but, on second thought, did so.

Homing on *U-37*'s beacon signals, audible at 150 miles, the Condors reached the convoy late in the afternoon of February 9. In this first successful joint aircraft/submarine operation, the Condor pilots reported damage to nine ships for 45,000 tons. The confirmed score was five ships sunk. One Condor was damaged

---

* Following *Hipper*'s convoy attack on Christmas Day, the Admiralty had again assigned battleships and submarines to escort these important ocean convoys: the British tender *Forth* and eight submarines, based at Halifax for this arduous duty, joined by the Free French monster submarine *Surcouf.*

and crash-landed in Spain, but the crew survived and eventually returned to Bordeaux.

Still shadowing the shattered convoy for *Hipper*'s benefit, in the early hours of February 10, Clausen in *U-37* struck again. His targets this time were two "big tankers." His six torpedoes missed the tankers but, Clausen believed, struck and sank two ships behind the tankers for 7,500 tons. Actually, he hit only one ship, a 1,473-ton freighter, which sank, making his total confirmed score three ships sunk for 4,773 tons.*

The riddled convoy Home Gibraltar 53 was scheduled to merge with an inbound unescorted convoy of nineteen ships from Sierra Leone. Racing up from the southwest, *Hipper* came upon this convoy on February 12 and sank seven ships for 32,800 tons, her first clear success in the Atlantic. She then found another freighter which had separated from the Gibraltar convoy. She took off the crew and sank the freighter, but was then compelled to abort to Brest with engine problems for the second time. Condors escorted her into port.

Dönitz was enormously pleased with this unique operation. The combined German forces had savaged two convoys, sinking sixteen confirmed ships: eight by *Hipper,* five by the Condors, three by *U-37.* Foreseeing the possibility of combined submarine and surface-ship operations with *Gneisenau* and *Scharnhorst,* he directed that three IXBs (*U-105, U-106, U-124*) prepare for departure to West African waters to be followed by the *U-A,* which was sailing from Germany. Having expended all torpedoes, Clausen in *U-37* aborted his trip to Africa and returned to Lorient, where he received unstinting praise and the news that the famous but weary *U-37* was to patrol home for retirement to the Training Command.

The diversion of Condors to the *U-37–Hipper* operation and a decision to put Condor crews through a crash course in navigation and communications delayed the staging of these aircraft from Norway. Hence the boats hunting south of Iceland had no help from the Condors for many days. They found no convoys, but several of them picked off lone ships and convoy stragglers in heavy weather. Lehmann-Willenbrock in *U-96* sank the 8,100-ton British tanker *Clea* and a freighter, and teamed up with Viktor Schütze in *U-103* to sink the 10,500-ton British tanker *A. F. Corwin.* Schütze went on to sink three other ships for 23,000 tons, including another 10,500-ton British tanker, *E. R. Brown.* A new VIIC from Germany, *U-69,* commanded by Jost Metzler, age thirty-two, another former merchant marine officer, sank two unescorted ships for 14,100 tons. Herbert Schultze in *U-48,* Otto Salmann in *U-52,* and Ernst Mengersen in *U-101* also sank two ships each. Karl-Heinz Moehle in *U-123,* on weather-reporting duty, sank one.

Finally, on the afternoon of February 19, a lone Condor staging from Norway found a convoy, Outbound 287. Dönitz ordered five boats to converge on the position and *Gruppe* 40 to send out more Condors at first light the following morning.

---

* These three kills brought Clausen's total confirmed sinkings on *U-37* to ten ships for 16,000 tons in about two months. All the ships were small, averaging 1,600 tons.

But the operation was a failure. Three Condors reached the area, but all gave different positions, leading to the belief that a second or perhaps even a third convoy had been detected. Adding further confusion, *B-dienst* picked up distress calls from a ship reporting a Condor attack in yet another position. One boat, Lehmann-Willenbrock's *U-96*, homed on a Condor beacon signal, came upon the convoy in foul weather, and sank a straggler, the 7,000-ton British tanker *Scottish Standard*. But no other boats could find the convoy.

Several days later, on February 22, a Norway-based Condor reported a convoy near the Orkneys. Dönitz directed two boats, outbound from Germany in the North Sea, to the scene: the VIIB *U-46*, commanded by Engelbert Endrass, returning from a long overhaul, and a new VIIC, *U-552*, commanded by Erich Topp, whose duck, *U-57*, had been rammed and sunk in the Elbe. But, many hours later, the airmen corrected the contact report: The convoy was not near the Orkneys but two hundred miles or more west of the Orkneys, en route to Halifax. It was Outbound 288.

Upon receiving the corrected position report, Dönitz ordered four boats to intercept the convoy and, if possible, three additional, including the weather boat, Moehle's *U-123*. The operation was temporarily thrown into confusion when *B-dienst* reported another distress call from a ship being attacked by a Condor in a position that in no way corresponded to the "corrected" position report. Dönitz rightly dismissed this last report, logging in his diary that *B-dienst* reports could no longer be relied upon.

A new VIIB from Germany, *U-73*, commanded by Helmut Rosenbaum, age twenty-seven, from the duck *U-2*, made contact with the convoy Outbound 288 and flashed a report. Dönitz instructed Rosenbaum to radio beacon signals and hang on "at all costs" while the other boats—and more Condors—attempted to converge. During the night of February 23–24, five German boats and the Italian *Bianchi* attacked. Lehmann-Willenbrock in *U-96* sank three ships for 18,400 tons, including the 11,000-ton auxiliary cruiser *Huntingdon*. Gerd Schreiber in the VIIC *U-95* sank three ships for 13,900 tons. Moehle in *U-123* sank one, as did Metzler in *U-69*, Rosenbaum in *U-73*, and Adalberto Giovannini in *Bianchi*. In retaliation, a Sunderland and three corvettes delivered a determined depth-charge attack on the green *U-69*, but the damage was not serious.

During this melee, the Italian submarine *Marcello*, commanded by Carlo Alberto Teppati, arrived on the scene. One of the convoy escorts, the ex-American four-stack destroyer *Montgomery*, merely a month out of her overhaul and upgrade, spotted *Marcello* and attacked with guns and depth charges. The attack was successful; *Marcello* sank with all hands. She was the first Axis submarine to fall victim to one of the American warships transferred to the Royal Navy in the "Destroyer Deal."*

Having exhausted all torpedoes, most of the U-boats headed for Lorient. Based on flash reports, Dönitz calculated that the German boats had sunk ten ships for

---

* Originally the Admiralty credited a Sunderland of Coastal Command Squadron 210 with the kill on *Marcello* on January 6, 1941. In a postwar reassessment, credit went to *Montgomery*.

77,000 tons from convoy Outbound 288. In actuality, the U-boats sank eight ships for 42,282 tons. Claiming seven ships for 55,600 tons sunk on this patrol, Lehmann-Willenbrock qualified for a *Ritterkreuz*. As a result of sinking four more ships on his patrol, Karl-Heinz Moehle also qualified for a *Ritterkreuz*.* The new skippers, Günter Hessler in *U-107* and Jost Metzler in *U-69*, having sunk four and three ships, respectively, on their maiden patrols from Germany, received warm praise.

South of Iceland on February 24, Erich Topp in the new VIIC *U-552*, who had sunk six ships for 37,000 tons on the duck *U-57*, found the next convoy, Outbound 289. Dönitz ordered three boats to join Topp, including two other new boats from Germany: the VIIC *U-97*, commanded by Udo Heilmann, age twenty-seven, from the duck *U-24*, and the new IXB *U-108*, commanded by Klaus Scholtz, age thirty-two. Topp shadowed tenaciously, then attacked, firing all five torpedoes in his bow and stern tubes. All missed. Before he could reload and attack again, an aircraft drove the boat under and the convoy got away.

When Topp surfaced after dark with all tubes reloaded, he saw a big ship coming up unescorted. He set up quickly and fired a fan of three torpedoes, estimating the range at about 1,600 yards. All missed. As the ship approached *U-552*, Topp saw that he had vastly underestimated her size and therefore the range; it was the huge 43,000-ton French luxury liner (in Allied service) *Ile de France*. Topp quickly fired his remaining bow torpedo at this fast-moving behemoth, but it too missed. That shot made nine torpedoes fired for nine misses; only three torpedoes remained.

Meanwhile, Udo Heilmann in the new boat *U-97* came up in response to Topp's reports and found Outbound 289. Perhaps wrongly assuming that Topp was in contact, or wishing to have the convoy all to himself, Heilmann attacked it in the early hours of February 24, without broadcasting a contact report. In five hours he sank a 6,900-ton tanker, *British Gunner*, and two freighters and damaged a 9,700-ton tanker in ballast. When he reported the result, Dönitz was angry at Heilmann for not sending beacon signals and attempted to bring Topp in again, as well as Gerd Schreiber in *U-95*. Topp regained contact with the convoy off Iceland in a raging gale, but the weather defeated him and Schreiber as well.

The ranking tonnage "aces" of the U-boat arm, Günther Prien in *U-47* and Otto Kretschmer in *U-99*, sailed from Lorient on February 20 and 22, respectively. Prien had been in port seventy-six days; Kretschmer for seventy-two. There had been a substantial turnover in the crews on these two famous boats. The first watch officers on both had left for commanding officers school; other officers had been promoted and assigned to new boats. Owing to British mines and submarines and sporadic air attacks on Lorient, there had not been much opportunity to drill the

---

* Lehmann-Willenbrock's confirmed score for the patrol was six and a half ships for 44,232 tons, raising his total confirmed score to thirteen and a half ships for 110,322 tons. Including his sinkings on the duck *U-20*, Moehle's confirmed score was eighteen and a half ships for 77,310 tons.

crew replacements. Both skippers had refused repeated suggestions from Dönitz to take safe jobs in the Training Command.

While Prien was en route to the hunting grounds on February 22, the *Gneisenau* and *Scharnhorst* reappeared off Newfoundland. The two battle cruisers attacked a westbound convoy which was approaching the dispersal point in Canadian waters. Between them they sank five ships for 25,784 tons, their first kills since entering the Atlantic on February 4. The battle cruisers then proceeded to the South Atlantic to attack convoys off Sierra Leone. Their appearance off Newfoundland caused great consternation in Ottawa, London, and Washington and yet another disruption and further delays in the convoys departing Halifax. For Admiral Bristol and other Americans in the Support Force who were preparing to escort North Atlantic convoys, this attack by two battle cruisers in what was soon to be the American area of responsibility was a sobering reminder that U-boats were not the only threat and gave rise to the idea of basing some of the old and the new American battleships* at Argentia and at Hvalfjord, Iceland, on the Denmark Strait.

Prien in *U-47* sailed directly up the west coast of Ireland. On the afternoon of February 25 he ran into convoy Outbound 290, composed of thirty-nine ships and seven escorts. Prien reported, shadowed, and broadcast beacon signals. Dönitz ordered Kretschmer in *U-99* and two boats on first patrols to join: Heilmann in *U-97*, who was out of torpedoes en route to Lorient, and Rosenbaum in *U-73*, who was on weather station. He alerted *Gruppe* 40 to fly Condors on the following day.

Shortly after midnight on February 26, Prien attacked the convoy alone. There was no moon, but the northern lights provided excellent visibility. His first salvo sank a 5,300-ton Belgian freighter and damaged an 8,100-ton British tanker in ballast. After reloading his tubes, he came in and fired a second salvo, sinking two more freighters, a 3,200-ton Swede and a 3,600-ton Norwegian. While again reloading his tubes he continued to track and send beacon signals, adding that he had sunk 20,000 tons. But no other U-boat came up that night.

Later that day, February 26, guided by Prien's beacon signals, the Condors found and attacked the convoy. One Condor appeared at noon; five in late afternoon. Astonishingly, they sank seven ships for 36,250 tons and damaged another one of 20,755 tons. All the while Prien doggedly and bravely tracked and sent beacon signals. In his last message of the day, Prien reported that he had been "beaten off" by Allied aircraft and had been depth-charged by escorts. He revised his sinking report upward slightly to 22,000 tons. In actuality, Prien had sunk 12,000 tons.

Heilmann in *U-97*, who had no torpedoes, made contact with the convoy that evening and took over as shadower. He attempted to bring up Rosenbaum in *U-73* and Kretschmer in *U-99*, but the attempt failed and the convoy dispersed. Dönitz

---

* The "old" battleships (1917–1919) capable of carrying out this task were the three on transfer from the Pacific Fleet (*Idaho, Mississippi, New Mexico*). The new 35,000-ton Treaty battleships, *North Carolina* and *Washington,* were commissioned April 9 and May 15, respectively. Two aircraft carriers, *Ranger* (1934) and *Yorktown* (1937), could provide additional scouting and firepower. The new carrier *Hornet* was commissioned on October 20, 1941.

ordered Prien, Kretschmer, and Rosenbaum to rake the ocean westward. Prien sank a lone 4,200-ton British freighter, but neither Rosenbaum nor Kretschmer had any luck. Adalberto Giovannini in *Bianchi* found two stragglers from the convoy and positively sank one.* Altogether Prien and Giovannini sank four confirmed ships from Outbound 290 and Prien also damaged a tanker in ballast.

The devastating storms in the North Atlantic raged all through the month of February. A "hurricane" hit convoy Halifax 106, sinking two ships and disabling numerous others. Even so, a total of 307 ships crossed from Canada to the British Isles in convoys. During the month, Axis submarines in the North Atlantic sank eleven loaded eastbound vessels, all stragglers from convoys Halifax 106 and 107 and Slow Convoys 20 and 21.

ATTACKING NAVAL *ENIGMA*

The original plan for the Americans to provide convoy escort on the Canada-Iceland leg of the North Atlantic run starting in April 1941 raised anew the issue of exchanges of intelligence information between the British and Americans. In particular the Americans wanted all available information on German and Italian naval operations in the Atlantic Ocean area. In addition to the growing number of U-boats, which were patrolling ever westward toward Canada, four powerful German warships and five merchant-ship raiders plus twenty-three Italian submarines posed a serious threat to American convoy-escort operations.† Moreover, an even greater menace was in the offing: the super-battleships *Bismarck* and *Tirpitz*.

As related, the senior civilian officials of the British and American governments had agreed (in writing, December 1940) to exchange data on breaking Axis codes. What the Americans needed most at that time were the fruits of British successes in breaking German and Italian naval codes. In return, the Americans were to share the fruits of their successes in breaking Japanese codes, in particular the recent sensational cryptographic triumph of duplicating the Purple code machine.

Not all Allied codebreakers on both sides of the Atlantic were keen on the proposed exchange. By nature codebreakers are an obsessively secretive lot, loath to divulge technology to those outside of their respective circles. Each side had misgivings about the trustworthiness of the other, and not without reason. After World War I, the British had indiscreetly and boastfully revealed the secrets of Room 40. Codebreaker Herbert Yardley had indiscreetly and boastfully revealed the secrets of American cryptography. Moreover, each side had been breaking codes of the other for years, an activity justified as spying on a potential "enemy."

---

* *Bianchi* claimed sinking four ships for 26,800 tons on this patrol, plus a possible hit on another of 7,800 tons. This was an Italian record that stood for some time—and is still credited in some Italian accounts of the war. Jürgen Rohwer credits Giovannini with three ships for 14,705 tons.

† Heavy cruiser *Hipper;* "pocket" battleship *Admiral Scheer;* battle cruisers *Gneisenau* and *Scharnhorst;* merchant-ship raiders *Atlantis, Kormoran, Orion, Penquin, Thor* (each with six 5.9" guns and four torpedo tubes), plus a possible hit on the 5,400-ton British "boarding vessel" *Manistee,* sunk by Hessler in *U-102*.

That said, it is also probable that some American codebreakers were quite eager to foster the exchange. Most Americans believed the British Isles were still at great risk, that the Germans might invade in the spring of 1941. They thought it was possible that during the winter Blitz, or the intense preinvasion bombing, or the invasion itself, the British codebreaking establishment could be wiped out or compromised. Others believed that based on the success with the Purple machine codes, the Americans could more effectively exploit existing Enigma technology than the British could, especially by bringing into play appropriate sectors of the vast American electronics and calculating-machine industries.

Whatever the case, the Americans initiated the first step in the Anglo-American codebreaking exchange in early 1941. In Chesapeake Bay on January 25, four Americans—two Army, two Navy*—boarded the new British battleship, *King George V,* which had just brought the new British Ambassador, Edward F.L.W. Halifax, to America. These Americans had with them a Purple machine (or perhaps two machines; sources conflict) and other important materials relating to the decoding of Japanese diplomatic and naval transmissions.

The *King George V* cautiously crossed the Atlantic during the sortie of *Gneisenau* and *Scharnhorst* into those waters. She arrived at Scapa Flow in a snowstorm on February 6. A British brigadier, John H. Tiltman, an expert on nonmachine ciphers who had been designated escort for the Americans, transferred them to a cruiser which took them to the Thames Estuary. From there the deputy director of the Government Code and Cipher School, Edward W. Travis, accompanied the party by automobile to the British codebreaking facility at Bletchley Park. Its commander, Alastair Denniston, welcomed the Americans warmly and courteously.

The American party remained in England about five weeks. Historians of Allied codebreaking still dispute exactly what transpired. Beyond doubt, the Americans turned over the Purple machine (or two of them) and instructed the British in its use. It is what the Americans got in return for this extraordinary gift that is disputed. Some historians say the British disclosed all they knew about Enigma and Italian codes; others say that the British did not—that they were secretive, told little, and kept the Americans at arm's length. The most astute of these historians, Bradley Smith,† leans to the view that the British withheld too much and thereby shortchanged the Americans. What is not in dispute is the fact that the Americans got no Enigma machine or a clone of one in exchange for the Purple machine.

The Purple machine helped the British enormously. With it they read high-grade Japanese diplomatic traffic for the rest of the war. Of particular benefit to the British (and, of course, the Americans) was the Purple traffic between the Japanese Ambassador in Berlin, Baron Hiroshi Ōshima, and Tokyo. In a previous tour of duty in Berlin, Ōshima had gained the confidence of Hitler, Göring, von Ribbentrop, and other leaders in the Third Reich. The Germans again talked freely of their

---

* The Army's Abraham Sinkov and Leo Rosen; the Navy's Prescott H. Currier and Robert H. Weeks. The Army's legendary codebreaker William F. Friedman was scheduled to head up the party, but after his successful attack on Purple, he had suffered a nervous collapse.

† *The Ultra-Magic Deals* (1993).

military plans and weaponry. Ōshima frequently relayed the gist of these talks to Tokyo in Purple code, providing the British—and the Americans—a sort of peep-hole into Hitler's mind as well as much specific information on German weaponry.

At this time the British did not have a whole lot of Enigma technology to give the Americans, especially in the naval field. With the assistance of the Turing-Welchman bombas and cribs from various sources, the British were able to read *Luftwaffe* Red consistently, but even that was a tense daily struggle. As has been revealed by numerous British codebreakers,* little to no progress had been made on breaking naval Enigma. Some did not think naval Enigma could ever be broken without the capture of the daily key settings and other aids.

At the time the Americans arrived in England, the British in fact had afoot an elaborate plan to capture naval Enigma materials. This proposed theft was a high-risk proposition not favored by all concerned. If the Germans became aware of or even got a hint of the theft, they might tighten Enigma security and/or increase its complexity, causing the British to lose—and never regain—*Luftwaffe* Red. How-ever, the depredations of *Hipper, Gneisenau,* and *Scharnhorst* and the merchant-ship raiders, the prospect of a sharp increase in the number of U-boats, the looming threat of *Bismarck* and *Tirpitz,* and perhaps pressures from Washington for naval intelligence persuaded the British to go ahead with the theft.

The Germans had thinly occupied the Lofoten Islands off Narvik to exploit the local cod and herring fisheries. Advocates of the theft were persuaded that a strong and well-organized commando raid on the islands might result in the capture of *Kriegsmarine* Enigma and other codes. The operation, Claymore, was staged from Scapa Flow on March 1, 1941. The commando force was substantial: 600 men in two channel steamers, escorted by five big *Tribal*-class destroyers, which were covered by two cruisers and, more distantly, by stronger elements of the Home Fleet.

Landing in the early hours of March 4, the commandos caught the Germans by complete surprise. To cover the real purpose of the raid, the British blew up the fisheries. In the brisk, brief battle, they captured 213 German prisoners, but disap-pointingly, they found no Enigmas. The five *Tribal* destroyers attacked German shipping in the fjords, sinking a 9,800-ton fish factory ship, *Hamburg,* and several coasters. One German armed trawler, *Krebs,* bravely fought back. Her skipper, Hans Kupfinger, and thirteen other men were killed in the one-sided fight. Board-ing the wrecked vessel, three British officers from the destroyer *Somali* discovered that Kupfinger had thrown his Enigma machine overboard, but he had died before he could destroy all the Enigma documents, two extra rotors, and some German naval hand ciphers.

The British got a priceless haul from Claymore: Enigma key tables and ring and plugboard settings for February 1941. Utilizing this material, in less than a week (by March 10) the codebreakers at Bletchley Park were able to read the whole of *Kriegsmarine* home waters code, *Heimisch,* or as the British called it,

---

* See writings of Clarke, Denniston, Hinsley, Morris, Welchman, as well as numerous secondary sources.

Dolphin, for the month of February. That month-old traffic was of no immediate tactical value, but since 95 percent of all *Kriegsmarine* traffic was encoded in *Heimisch* (Dolphin), it provided insights into past *Kriegsmarine* operations and administration and encoding procedures, as well as much specific information on U-boats.

At about this same time the British made an important break into a German naval hand cipher, *Werftschlüssel* (literally, Dockyard Key) or *Werft*. This was a "pencil and paper" cipher used by all minor naval vessels and port facilities in German and Norwegian waters. An unglamorous section at Bletchley Park, known as "Cinderella," had been attacking this hand cipher (and others) cryptanalytically with only slight success. However, as Christopher Morris, one of those in the section, has revealed, from "March 1941" the British read *Werft* traffic "as a rule currently" for the rest of the war. In all, the Cinderella section decoded 33,000 *Werft* messages over forty-seven months, an average of about twenty-three signals a day.

Inasmuch as many *Kriegsmarine* messages had to be transmitted in both Enigma and *Werft* in order to reach the less important ships and the shore stations, the two systems provided cribs into one another. "Indeed," Morris wrote, "the 'cross-ruffing' between the two was for some time the prize exhibit which Naval Section could display to distinguished visitors, such as Winston Churchill. . . . " Transmissions in *Werft* from big ships to port authorities or to little ships, such as tugs, or from U-boats in Baltic workup to dockyards or to target ships or tugs, enabled Morris and his fellow codebreakers to pinpoint the locations of the big ships and to identify and track newly commissioned U-boats. When there was a dearth of cribs for Enigma and *Werft,* the British resorted to "gardening," or planting mines in specific zones of known German-swept channels. This invariably provided a spate of warning traffic and/or instructions to minesweepers in Enigma and *Werft,* which could be "cross-ruffed," providing a new source of cribs, which the British called "Kisses."

When the four Americans departed Bletchley Park in late March 1941, they were probably aware of the British Enigma thefts in the Lofotens and the solid break into *Werft.* They did not return entirely empty-handed. One of the Navy delegates, Robert Weeks, has revealed that the British gave them a "paper" Enigma machine (i.e., a detailed drawing) with "all the rotor[s] and *umkehrwaltz* [reflectors] laid out" and some Enigma keys. According to the American codebreaking historian David Kahn,* the two Army delegates, Sinkov and Rosen, wrote in their official report (of April 1941) that "we were invited to ask questions about anything we saw, no doors were closed to us and copies were furnished of any material which we considered of possible assistance to the United States."

On the other hand, based on independent interviews with Sinkov, two American codebreaking historians stress the point that the British did not—repeat not—reveal how they actually *broke* Enigma. In his book,† Thomas Parrish, referring to his interview of Sinkov in February 1984, wrote that on "one or two occasions,"

---

*   *Seizing the Enigma* (1991).

†   *The Ultra Americans* (1986).

the British discussed some "cryptanalytic details" of Enigma with the Americans, but this type of presentation was "essentially an account of some British achievements." Sinkov said, "It was far from enough to enable us to get into the actual process of producing information." Based on a review of Sinkov's papers and an interview with him in October 1990, the aforementioned Bradley Smith wrote that the American party was told only "in a general way" about British decryption processes. "They were not allowed to see a bombe or even told of its existence." Smith concluded: "The American team therefore had no hard evidence to prove the importance of analytic-machine methods in the British cryptanalytic effort, even though they suspected that some machine-calculation method was being used at Bletchley."

Among those in Washington who felt the British had betrayed the Americans was the U.S. Navy's senior codebreaker, Laurence Safford. In view of the Navy's growing responsibilities—and war risks—in the Atlantic at this time, doubtless Safford was under intense pressure to produce information on German and Italian naval operations in that area. He was bitter toward the British and remained so for the rest of his life, later giving vent to his feelings in several published articles and papers.

As a consequence of this "broken deal," as Bradley Smith characterized this first cryptography "exchange," American codebreakers had to face the possibility of breaking Enigma on their own. This added a huge new burden to Safford's work already in progress, such as solutions to the Japanese naval codes. At that time, the Navy's entire communications-intelligence organization, including radio-intercept stations in the Atlantic and Pacific areas, had only about 550 staffers, of whom only forty-four were commissioned officers.

Safford therefore sought outside help. Chief among those he leaned upon was a thirty-eight-year-old naval reservist, Howard Theodore Engstrom. Although the codebreaking historians have largely overlooked Engstrom, he was to play the key role in the American attack on naval Enigma, an enterprise of vital importance, which in the rush to give all credit to the Poles and British has likewise been neglected.

Engstrom was the middle of three sons of Scandinavian immigrants—a Swedish father and Norwegian mother. His father, a lifeguard in Plymouth and Manomet, Massachusetts, died when he was ten, leaving his mother, a laundress, to raise the boys, the youngest of whom died at age eleven. A brilliant student, Howard graduated from Plymouth High School in 1918, at age sixteen, and from Northeastern University in 1922, age twenty, with a degree in chemical engineering.

Adept at foreign languages and mathematics, Engstrom chose an academic career. He got a master's degree in mathematics from the University of Maine (1925) and a doctorate in mathematics from Yale (1929). For the next two years (1930–1931) he was a National and International Research Fellow at the California Institute of Technology and in Göttingen, Germany, where he became fluent in German. From 1932, he was an assistant, then associate professor of mathematics at Yale University. In 1935, he married a Finnish-born woman, Karin Ekblom, who had obtained a bachelor of nursing degree from Yale the year before.

In response to a recruiting drive by the Navy's Radio Intelligence Organization, which Safford commanded from May 6, 1936, Engstrom accepted a reserve commission as a lieutenant, junior grade. From 1936 to 1940, while on active tours of duty in the summers, he had worked sporadically with Safford. On his stint in the summer of 1940 in Washington, specializing in machine ciphers, he had put in "ten hours a day, seven days a week," he wrote his older brother, Walder, a bank president in Plymouth.

While still at Yale in the early months of 1941, at Safford's request Engstrom began some preliminary theoretical work on naval Enigma, it is believed. Several months later, in July 1941, he was called to full-time active duty in Safford's outfit, with the rank of lieutenant. As will be seen, he rose swiftly to higher rank and responsibilities. His codebreaking achievements, for which both the American and British governments decorated him,* produced results on a par with those of the British mathematicians Alan Turing and Gordon Welchman.

"The Battle of the Atlantic"

In early March, Churchill met with First Sea Lord Dudley Pound to discuss merchant-shipping losses in the Atlantic. In order to "concentrate all minds and all departments concerned" on the U-boat war, Churchill told Pound he was going to proclaim a "Battle of the Atlantic," just as he had proclaimed the "Battle of Britain" during the *Luftwaffe* assault the previous August.

Forthwith Churchill established a Battle of the Atlantic Committee and named himself (in his capacity as Minister of Defense) chairman. Composed of ministers and "high functionaires concerned," the body met once a week for several hours or more. On March 6, Churchill distributed a Directive for the Committee, which listed thirteen steps he believed were necessary to win the Battle of the Atlantic. In part:

• Hunt and kill U-boats and Condors at sea. Bomb U-boats in building yards and naval bases and Condors on *Luftwaffe* airfields.

• Give "extreme priority" to fitting out 200 merchant ships (later reduced to 35) with catapults to launch fighters against Condors, so that every convoy could sail with four such ships.†

• Concentrate the bulk of the air strength of Coastal Command over the main convoy routes in the Northwest Approaches.

• On a trial basis, allow all merchant ships that could make 12 knots or faster (rather than 13 knots or faster) to sail unescorted—outside the convoys.

---

* From the President, a coveted Distinguished Service Medal, stressing his "brilliant skill and initiative . . . his outstanding professional judgment, astute planning and uncompromising devotion to the fulfillment of an exacting assignment." From British ambassador Halifax on behalf of King George VI, an Order of the British Empire, praising Engstrom's "exceptional character and genius."

† In addition, the aircraft tender *Pegasus,* which Prien missed in Scapa Flow, and four other warships fitted with catapults patrolled as hunter-killer vessels in the Condor zones of operations.

• Give "first claim" (priority) to arming merchant ships with short-range antiaircraft guns to ward off Condors.

• Provide British seaports (e.g., Mersey, Clyde, Bristol Channel) with "maximum" antiaircraft defense to counter the ongoing *Luftwaffe* Blitz, which had reached as far as the Liverpool docks.

• Within four months, reduce by at least 400,000 gross tons the 2.6 million gross tons of merchant shipping idled in British ports with storm, battle, or other damage, even at the expense of new construction.*

• Speed up by every conceivable means the "terrible slowness" of the turnaround time of merchant ships in British ports and ports abroad.

An important factor underlying Churchill's resounding proclamation was the abysmal (but concealed) failure of the British military to kill U-boats. In all of 1940, British forces had positively destroyed only twelve oceangoing German submarines. In the six months between September 1, 1940, and March 1, 1941, British forces had sunk only three confirmed German U-boats—none at all in December, January, and February. Given that poor performance, U-boat production was far outpacing U-boat losses.

Under the impetus provided by the Battle of the Atlantic Committee, the British took several further important measures to increase the U-boat kill rate. These were:

First, improvements in U-boat tracking by exploiting secret intelligence from old—and new—sources.

Up to the outbreak of the war, the Naval Intelligence Division (NID) of the Royal Navy had atrophied. Since then a newcomer to the job—and the arcane world of intelligence as well—John H. Godfrey, had revived the branch by dint of his own innate talent and by an infusion of outside help from academe, the legal profession, and Fleet Street. One of his reserve lieutenants, Patrick Beesly, wrote† that Godfrey was "a man of wide interests, great energy and determination, an innovator and original thinker" as well as "a practical and successful seaman."

Inasmuch as the Admiralty was an operating command as well as a policy-making, administrative, and procurement agency, like RAF Fighter and Bomber Commands, it had a central "war room." It was located in a new, low-ceilinged, bombproofed concrete structure, jokingly called "Lenin's Tomb" or "The Citadel," but officially, the Operational Intelligence Center (OIC). It was manned twenty-four hours a day by personnel of Godfrey's intelligence division, under the leadership of a called-up admiral, J. W. (Jock) Clayton, described by Beesly as "a man of

---

* The 2.6 million gross tons translates to about 520 ships of 5,000 gross tons. Remarkably, British shipyards more than doubled the goal, sending 975,000 gross tons (the equivalent of 195 ships of 5,000 gross tons) back to sea by July 31, reducing the idled, damaged shipping to about 1.6 million gross tons.

† *Very Special Intelligence* (1977) and *Very Special Admiral: The Life of J. H. Godfrey* (1980).

unruffled calmness, impossible to rattle and with very shrewd judgment" and close friends in high places.

One of the main tasks of the OIC was to keep track of Axis naval forces. For this purpose there were four sections: German Surface Ship Plot (Patrick Barrow-Green); Italian-Japanese Surface Ship Plot (Norman Denning, later vice admiral); Axis Submarine Plot; all supported by the DF Section (Peter Kemp, a journalist, later a popular naval historian).

Of these sections, the Axis Submarine Plot, or U-boat Tracking Room, was the busiest. At the outset of the war it was commanded by an old hand from Room 40, Ernest W. C. Thring, a regular naval officer. He was fortunate early on to have gained the services of a thirty-seven-year-old lawyer, Rodger Winn, a called-up reservist. Crippled as a young boy by poliomyelitis, Winn was left with a twisted back and a limp, but by a "tremendous triumph of willpower," as Beesly put it, he had overcome these physical disabilities and created a successful legal practice. In OIC he demonstrated an uncanny—even eerie—ability to read German minds and predict the behavior of U-boats.

After observing Winn at close quarters for a year, the commander of OIC, Jock Clayton, recommended to John Godfrey that Winn replace Thring as head of the U-boat Tracking Room. Clayton's recommendation to appoint a "civilian" rather than a career officer to lead this vital section was so "revolutionary" and "unprecedented," Beesly remembered, it had to be bucked all the way up to First Sea Lord Dudley Pound. He approved the recommendation and at the beginning of 1941 Winn assumed the post, "a stroke of singular good fortune," Beesly judged.

Soon after Winn took over the U-boat Tracking Room, the British captured Enigma materials from the trawler *Krebs* and broke the hand cipher *Werft*. David Kahn wrote that on March 12, Bletchley Park teletyped the first ten decrypted naval Enigma messages to Winn, the next day thirty-four, and subsequently many more. Indeed, there was soon a virtual flood. These first decrypts were dated and of no immediate tactical value to Winn, but they greatly enhanced his knowledge of the U-boat arm, its strategy, and its tactics.

The next important measure to increase U-boat kills was the shift of Western Approaches Command from Plymouth to Derby House in Liverpool. This took place on February 7, 1941, at which time a new commander, Percy Noble, age fifty, replaced Martin Dunbar-Nasmith, who remained at Plymouth.

Noble and his chief of staff, J. M. Mansfield, soon built up a naval contingent at Derby House of about one thousand men and women. They created a huge "war room" with a wall map of the North Atlantic Ocean over two stories high. This operations center was linked twenty-four hours a day by secure teletype and telephone to the OIC in London, so that at all times the former was as up-to-the-minute on enemy naval operations as the latter.

At this same time, in response to Churchill's directive, RAF Coastal Command concentrated its main air strength in the Northwest Approaches. Its 15 Group, commanded by J. M. Robb (later by Leonard H. Slatter), also moved from Plymouth to Derby House, Liverpool. There its staff virtually merged with that of

Western Approaches and utilized the same "war room," insuring the closest possible air-navy coordination and cooperation. In his memoir,* the RAF's John C. Slessor, then serving in Bomber Command, wrote that as a further result of Churchill's March 6 directive, no less than seventeen squadrons of aircraft were transferred from Bomber Command to Coastal Command in 1941 and 1942, and that a "critical proportion of the effort of Bomber Command itself was devoted to the war at sea."

The notorious neglect of Coastal Command had led to a proposal that it be transferred from the Air Ministry to the Admiralty. Churchill was not in favor of this drastic proposal, but he had ordered a full investigation which brought to light in shocking detail the shortcomings of the command. The upshot was a far-reaching decision (to take effect April 15, 1941) to leave Coastal Command in the Air Ministry for administrative purposes, but to transfer operational control of the organization to the Admiralty. Thereafter naval requirements—U-boat hunting in particular—were to take precedence over all other missions.

One of Percy Noble's first and most vigorous initiatives was to provide unstinting support for the training of convoy escorts. This important activity had been concentrated at Tobermory on the island of Mull in the Inner Hebrides the previous July. The headquarters ashore, like other British naval schools, was named as though it were a ship—in this case, H.M.S. *Western Isles*. The school was commanded by a notoriously tough and smart called-up vice admiral, G. O. Stephenson. Every new escort vessel had to spend a month under Stephenson's lash, an ordeal well depicted by Nicholas Monsarrat in his famous novel† of life aboard the fictional wartime corvette *Compass Rose*.

Up to this time, British and Canadian convoy escorts had been assigned to duty in a helter-skelter fashion, based on availability and combat readiness. With the influx of new destroyers, sloops, and corvettes, and the sixty ex-American destroyers and sloops in early 1941, it became possible to commence a long-sought goal: the formation of British and Canadian "Escort Groups." These groups were to be composed of ships, more or less permanently teamed up and assigned as a single entity to convoys. The Admiralty believed that when so permanently organized and trained, the groups could better protect convoys—and kill U-boats—than randomly assigned single vessels. Fostered by Percy Noble and trained by Stephenson, there were soon a dozen such groups, each consisting on paper of ten destroyers, sloops, or corvettes, of which six to eight were maintained at readiness to sail. The performance of the groups, manned almost solely by wartime conscripts or volunteers, was ragged at first and never perfect, but gradually became quite proficient.

All Americans who visited British military agencies in 1941 were impressed by the degree of unification that had been achieved in the Battle of the Atlantic. From the War Cabinet to the Battle of the Atlantic Committee to the Admiralty and the Air Ministry, to Bletchley Park and the OIC and Derby House, all hands

---

* *The Central Blue* (1956).
† *The Cruel Sea* (1951).

worked with an extraordinary singleness of purpose. The tight control and the canalization of the growing body of intelligence on U-boat operations and the shrewd exploitation of that intelligence at all levels were in a sense unheralded and unquatifiable weapons of the highest order, and they were to make a very big difference in the naval war.

THE LOSS OF PRIEN

Ironically, at the time Churchill proclaimed the "Battle of the Atlantic," the U-boat force was in the worst shape since the beginning of the war. On March 1, 1941, there were only eight German U-boats in the North Atlantic, including a new Type IID duck, *U-147*. Five U-boats, including *U-147*, patrolled between Iceland and Scotland. Two others patrolled near Rockall Bank: Prien in *U-47* and Kretschmer in *U-99*. The eighth U-boat, Heilmann in *U-97*, was out of torpedoes and assigned to weather reporting.

There was no help on March 1 from the Condors, but after dark, Erich Topp in the VIIC *U-552* ran into the inbound convoy Halifax 109, which was approaching the coast of Scotland, leaving little sea room. Topp broadcast an alarm and with his last three internal torpedoes sank a 12,000-ton British tanker, *Cadillac*, his first success in *U-552*. A new VIIC, *U-70*, commanded by Joachim Matz, age twenty-seven, from the duck *U-59*, merely eight days out of Helgoland, arrived and set up on the *Cadillac*, only to see Topp blow it up in his face. Gerd Schreiber came up in the VIIC *U-95* and sank two ships for 11,100 tons. Reinhard Hardegen in the duck *U-147* sank a 4,800-ton Norwegian freighter, then returned to Germany.

One of two Condors staging from Norway reported an outbound convoy and attacked on the morning of March 2. Dönitz directed six of the seven oceangoing boats in the hunting grounds to form a north-south patrol line west of Rockall Bank. While the boats were moving into position through a dense fog on March 3, Condors scoured the probable course of the convoy but saw nothing. Nor did the near-blind boats.

After a hurried analysis of this failed operation, Dönitz ordered a drastic—and "lamentable"—change in Condor operations. Concluding that when Condors openly attacked a convoy they forced it to make a drastic alteration in course to avoid the converging U-boats, Dönitz barred Condors from attacking convoys. Henceforth they were only to spot and report convoys and make every possible effort to remain undetected, restrictions that hardly pleased the Condor crews.

The next day, March 4, a Condor reported another outbound convoy. It was not clear from the position report whether this was the same outbound convoy or a new one or if the position report was accurate. Nonetheless, Dönitz redeployed the six boats in a patrol line farther west, adding to it the *U-A*, commanded by Hans Eckermann, en route from Germany to Lorient to stage to West African waters. After the line was in place, on March 5, Gerd Schreiber in *U-95*, in the center of the line, inexplicably broke radio silence to report his accumulated sinkings. Assuming the British had DFed *U-95*'s report and would alter the convoy's course to avoid him—as well as the whole patrol line—Dönitz logged that Schreiber had made "an extremely clumsy mistake." Dönitz may have been correct; the convoy got away.

The failure to intercept either of these two outbound convoys led to a more detailed analysis of Condor/U-boat operations. The study revealed that in two months the U-boats had benefited only once (February 19–20) from Condor convoy reports. Almost without exception, Condor reports were incorrect as to the positions and courses of the convoys. Besides that, it took too long to redeploy the boats. By the time they reached the most likely interception line based on the reported convoy course (whether accurate or not), the report was twenty-four hours old and not reliable. Dönitz therefore directed that until better means of submarine/aircraft position reporting and cooperation could be found, "no more U-boat operations" were to be "undertaken on aircraft reports." Condors were to continue patrolling and reporting convoys for the benefit of all German forces and they were again allowed to attack convoys on sight.

On March 6, Dönitz redeployed the boats. Five VIIs formed a north-south patrol line west of Rockall Bank, and the *U-A* went west to relieve *U-97* as the weather reporter. The patrol line had only just formed when Prien in *U-47* encountered and reported an outbound convoy. He shadowed and broadcast beacon signals to bring up the other boats. Dönitz directed three other boats of the patrol line—*U-37* (Clausen), *U-70* (Matz), *U-99* (Kretschmer)—and also the westbound *U-A* to converge on Prien's signals. This was convoy Outbound 293, escorted by two destroyers, *Wolverine* and *Verity,* and two corvettes, *Arbutus* and *Camellia.*

Prien in *U-47* and Kretschmer in *U-99* met in moderate, misty seas at 6:00 P.M. Talking by megaphone across the water, they planned a joint attack on the convoy. As they were talking, the two destroyers—both with Type 286M radar—loomed out of the mist: *Wolverine,* commanded by James M. Rowland, and *Verity.* Patrolling ahead of the convoy, the destroyers caught Prien and Kretschmer by surprise, forcing both U-boats to crash-dive. The destroyers found Prien and worked him over with depth charges. Kretschmer went deep and slipped away. Later in the night, both boats surfaced.

Meanwhile, Joachim Matz in the new *U-70* arrived, taking up position in the dark ahead of the convoy. Matz had been in the Atlantic all of two weeks and had yet to fire a torpedo. At 0430 hours on March 7, he attacked, firing all four bow torpedoes at four different ships. He later claimed that he had hit and sunk all four (for 35,500 tons) but in reality, he had hit but only damaged the 6,400-ton British freighter *Delilian* and possibly the 6,600-ton British tanker *Athelbeach.* Ten minutes later, Prien, who was low on torpedoes, radioed Dönitz an updated position report, then attacked, choosing the largest ship in the convoy, the 20,640-ton Norwegian whale-factory ship, *Terje Viken,* converted to a tanker. Prien hit her with two torpedoes, but she was in ballast and thus very hard to sink. Although damaged, she sailed on.

Having reloaded his four bow tubes, at 0600 Matz came in for a second attack. He saw the damaged *Terje Viken* and fired three torpedoes at her, but all three missed. He was on the point of firing his fourth bow tube when another boat hit the factory ship with one torpedo. That shot came from Kretschmer in *U-99*. Kretschmer then fired one torpedo at another ship, but missed. Swinging about, he shot three torpedoes at the possibly damaged tanker *Athelbeach,* which hit but did not sink her. To save torpedoes, Kretschmer went after the crippled *Athelbeach* with his deck gun, but the gunners were not successful and he was forced to expend another torpedo, which finally put the tanker under.

The four escorts, under tactical command of James Rowland in the destroyer *Wolverine,* reacted aggressively. While the convoy was making a sharp evasive turn to port, they lit up the area with star shells and commenced hunting *U-47, U-70,* and *U-99,* all of which were in close proximity. The corvette *Arbutus* got the first sonar contact at 0448 hours and dropped depth charges, calling up the other corvette, *Camellia.* The destroyers *Wolverine* and *Verity* spotted U-boats and drove them under, dropping depth charges.

Matz, who still had one torpedo in a bow tube, closed submerged on the 7,500-ton Dutch tanker *Mijdrecht.* He hit and damaged the ship, but the Dutch captain saw *U-70*'s periscope ahead and turned at it to ram. His aim was good; *Mijdrecht*'s bow cleaved into *U-70*'s conning tower, smashing the bridge and periscopes and throwing the boat down and under as though it had been hit by a huge wave. *Mijdrecht* was not seriously damaged; her crew repaired the hole made by the torpedo and sailed on.

The collision caused leaks in *U-70*'s conning tower but no serious damage to the pressure hull. Matz hauled off into the mist to surface and assess the topside damage. At 0815 hours, the corvette *Camellia* spotted *U-70* about four miles ahead and charged, forcing Matz to crash-dive. *Camellia* radioed an alarm, which brought up the other corvette, *Arbutus. Camellia*'s sonar failed, but she fired a salvo of six depth charges "by eye." At 0925, *Arbutus* arrived, got a firm sonar contact, and in two quick successive attacks, fired twelve depth charges. Acting on *Arbutus*'s sonar information, *Camellia* also attacked again, firing another six charges, but lacking sonar, *Camellia* was of little help and she was ordered off to protect the damaged ships and to rescue survivors.

Arbutus doggedly pursued *U-70,* firing five more salvos of six charges over the next three hours. In all, *U-70* took fifty-four charges from *Arbutus* and *Camellia.* The last three attacks by *Arbutus* fatally wrecked *U-70.* She flooded aft and went out of control, assuming a 45-degree up-angle. Matz crammed all available men into the bow compartment, but to no avail. The boat slipped down by the stern to 656 feet. Unable to regain control, Matz blew all ballast tanks with his last bit of high-pressure air and surfaced to scuttle. Seeing her, *Arbutus* came in to ram, firing her 4" deck gun and other weapons.

When Matz opened the conning-tower hatch, the pressure inside the boat was so great that it blew him and five other men straight up into the smashed bridge. Seeing the *U-70* crew jumping into the water, *Arbutus* veered off and dropped two life rafts. With hatches and sea cocks open, the *U-70* plunged down by the bow and sank. *Arbutus* fished Matz and twenty-five other men from the water. Twenty Germans died in the sinking.

The movements of Prien's *U-47* and Kretschmer's *U-99* that day are not certain. The destroyers *Wolverine* and *Verity* apparently made sonar contact and repeatedly attacked both boats. Kretschmer reported later that an "old type" destroyer drove him under and held him down for about nine hours, delivering fifty-one depth charges. It is possible that Prien in *U-47* was caught in the same barrage and was destroyed.

Nothing more was ever heard from Prien. That night Prien—as well as Matz—failed to respond to requests from Dönitz for position and sinking reports.

Later that same evening, March 7, at 10:00 P.M., Hans Eckermann in *U-A* made contact with the convoy farther west and radioed a position report. Nikolaus Clausen in *U-37*, who had not yet found the convoy, requested beacon signals. Eckermann broadcast another position report a half hour after midnight, March 8. Soon after that, he closed the convoy and attacked, firing two torpedoes at the lead ship in the starboard column. Eckermann believed both torpedoes had hit, but only one did, causing slight damage to the 5,300-ton British freighter *Dunaff Head.*

At that time the destroyers *Wolverine* and *Verity* were steaming on the starboard side of the convoy. The *U-A* lay directly in the path of *Wolverine.* Hoping to catch the U-boat by surprise and ram her, *Wolverine*'s captain, James Rowland, refrained from firing star shells or speeding up or changing course. Thirteen minutes later Rowland saw "smoke resembling diesel exhaust" dead ahead and his sonar operator reported a contact. Three minutes later *Wolverine* spotted a wake, then the U-boat itself "zigzagging wildly at high speed." Rowland rang up full speed but withheld gunfire, still hoping to ram. But *Verity* spoiled the plan, firing star shells, which lit up the area and forced the U-boat to crash-dive about three-quarters of a mile ahead of *Wolverine.*

Rowland reduced speed but was unable to make sonar contact or estimate where the boat had dived. He and *Verity* reversed course. Seven minutes later *Wolverine* and *Verity* obtained "firm" sonar contacts. Rowland ran in and fired two separate salvos, comprising eighteen depth charges. He followed up with three more modified salvos, a total of six depth charges, and dropped a flare to mark the U-boat's position. There was no apparent result from these twenty-four depth charges, but Rowland's engineer reported that he had "unmistakably seen and smelt shale oil," indicating possible damage to the U-boat's fuel tanks.

In an analysis of this attack, the British, unaware that *U-A* had torpedoed *Dunaff Head,* were to claim that the U-boat *Wolverine* and *Verity* attacked was Prien's *U-47,* which they sank. No positive evidence ever developed to support this claim. Possibly it was true. Possibly Prien chased the convoy westward during that evening. But it does not seem likely. He had already attacked five ships by torpedo on this patrol (four on February 26); he could not have had enough torpedoes left to justify pursuit and another attack. He made no contact reports that night; if his radio was out of commission, there would have been no point in chasing the convoy, unless Prien thought the radio might be repaired in time to be of use. Significantly, Otto Kretschmer, who had an ample supply of torpedoes, did not chase the convoy westward that night.

Eckermann in *U-A* later reported that immediately after firing his torpedoes (at *Dunaff Head*) the boat was subjected to a brutal depth-charge attack. This was doubtless delivered by *Wolverine* and *Verity*. The *U-A*'s first watch officer, Carl Emmermann, remembered: "We got away and surfaced in the dark close by the destroyers. Eckermann wanted to run off at high speed on the diesels, but I persuaded him to creep away quietly on the electric motors, so we wouldn't make smoke or noise. We escaped by the skin of our teeth." Later, when he was well clear, Eckermann radioed Dönitz that *U-A* had suffered "heavy" depth-charge damage and that he was compelled to abort to Lorient.

Wolverine continued the hunt tenaciously. Rowland wrote that at about 0410 *Wolverine* picked up the noise of a U-boat on the surface and commenced a chase at 20 knots, slowing occasionally to 8 knots to listen on sonar in order to reestablish the U-boat's bearing. After one hour—a twenty-mile chase—*Wolverine* spotted the U-boat dead ahead and Rowland prepared to ram at full speed. But the U-boat crash-dived "200–300 yards" ahead. Passing over the spot, Rowland saw a V-shaped "rush of bubbles" intensified by "phosphorescence." Based on six years of prior duty in submarines, Rowland was positive the bubbles were caused by air from venting ballast tanks and that he had a U-boat at shallow depth, directly under his keel. He turned hard to port, and at four-second intervals he fired ten depth charges set for 100 feet.

Unless Rowland had been chasing a phantom or a whale or a school of porpoises, his depth-charge salvo should have blown the U-boat to smithereens, releasing wreckage and bodies. But to Rowland's "great disappointment," no wreckage of any kind rose to the surface. Rowland saw a mysterious "faint orange light" for "about ten seconds" near the spot where the depth charges exploded, but he could not pause to investigate because sonar still had "firm contact" on the target. He circled around, maintaining the sonar contact, and continued dropping single depth charges sporadically until 0755, but ceased further attacks when "porpoises were sighted in the vicinity at daylight."

So many false claims of U-boat sinkings had been made that the Admiralty had established strict criteria for crediting a positive kill. *Wolverine*'s evidence was not sufficient to meet the criteria. However, when it discovered from Matz and others captured from *U-70*, and from other sources, that Prien had been in the vicinity and had not returned from this patrol, the Admiralty's Assessment Committee accepted this "circumstantial evidence" and ruled that *Wolverine* "probably sunk . . . *U-47*, commanded by Prien." Doubtless another factor that entered into this weak and uncertain assessment was the propaganda benefit to be gained by crediting a British captain and crew with destroying Germany's most famous U-boat ace. It is more likely that Prien was lost on March 7 by depth-charge attack, by a circular-running torpedo, by a crew error, or by a catastrophic structural failure in *U-47*. It is also possible that *U-47* was lost by unknown causes (mine, crew error, etc.) en route to Lorient with a defective radio.

Whatever the case, the four escorts of convoy Outbound 293 deserved highest praise and awards. Their aggressive U-boat attacks had not only fended off Germany's two foremost U-boat aces with slight losses in ships* but also had sunk one of them, as well as the *U-70,* and had nearly sunk *U-A.* No other escort team had ever done as well. Moreover, *U-47* and *U-70* were the first confirmed U-boat kills by British forces since the loss of *U-31* on November 2, ending a humiliating dry spell of more than four months.

Dönitz felt "great anxiety" when *U-47* and *U-70* failed to respond to inquiries. But he could not permit himself to believe that both boats—the invincible Prien in particular—had been lost. He consoled himself with the possibility that Prien and Matz had radio failures, that any day Prien would appear off Lorient with new battle pennants flying from his raised periscope. And yet . . .

There was better news from southern waters. Very, very good news, in fact. The three Type IXB boats en route to Freetown, Sierra Leone, *U-105, U-106,* and *U-124,* had refueled March 4 to March 6 from the German tanker *Corrientes,* in the Spanish Canaries, then continued southward. On March 6 the lead boat, *U-124,* commanded by Georg-Wilhelm Schulz, met *Gneisenau* and *Scharnhorst* off the African coast. The next day, the battle cruisers found inbound convoy Sierra Leone 67, escorted by the British battleship *Malaya* and other vessels. Inasmuch as the German ships were still under orders not to engage British capital ships, they pulled off and *U-124* was alerted. The plan that evolved was for *U-124* and *U-105* to close the convoy and sink *Malaya,* so that *Gneisenau* and *Scharnhorst* could return and attack the merchant ships. If any ships survived this combined assault and slipped by, the *U-106,* which was trailing the other boats by several days, might intercept them farther north.

The plan did not work out, but the U-boats nonetheless had great success. Attacking first in the early hours of March 8, Georg Schewe in *U-105* sank a 5,200-ton British freighter. Sailing into the middle of the panicked convoy, Schulz in *U-124* fired all six tubes (four forward, two aft) over a period of twenty-one minutes, at six different ships. He claimed sinking five of them for 33,000 tons and leaving another of 6,000 tons "in sinking condition." Postwar analysis credited him with sinking four British freighters for 23,300 tons, a remarkable salvo. Later, Jürgen Oesten in *U-106* arrived at the same place and sank a 7,500-ton British freighter. Total confirmed results: six ships sunk for 36,000 tons.

The *Malaya* was not touched, therefore *Gneisenau* and *Scharnhorst* could not attack the convoy. They refueled from their supply ships and set a course northwestward to attack Halifax convoys. The *U-124* cruised west to meet the merchant-ship raider *Kormoran* to obtain torpedoes and fuel, and to await a ren-

---

* The four boats that attacked the convoy sank but one ship, the tanker *Athelbeach*—by Kretschmer—in ballast. Prien and Kretschmer torpedoed and wrecked the whale-factory ship *Terje Viken,* also in ballast, but the hulk was finally sunk on March 14 by gunfire from two British destroyers and a corvette. Matz damaged *Delilian* and *Mijdrecht* but they reached port, as did *Dunaff Head,* torpedoed by Eckermann in *U-A.*

dezvous with the Germany-bound "pocket" battleship *Admiral Scheer,* to deliver her a spare part for her primitive radar. The *U-105* and *U-106* proceeded directly to Freetown.

THE LOSS OF SCHEPKE AND KRETSCHMER

Still pressing the case for intensified warfare against Britain, Admiral Raeder persuaded Hitler to mount *Luftwaffe* mass bombing raids on the British seaports of Portsmouth, Bristol, Liverpool, and the Firth of Clyde. In preparation for this heavy assault, to take place between March 10 and 20, *Luftwaffe* planners demanded detailed U-boat weather reporting between those dates. When this demand reached Dönitz on March 9, he had only four U-boats in the North Atlantic and one of them, *U-95,* had no torpedoes. He assigned a Germany-bound boat, Clausen in *U-37,* to a "north" weather station and Schreiber in *U-95* to a "south" weather station. That left only two boats to wage the North Atlantic convoy war: Otto Kretschmer's *U-99* and a brand-new VIIC, *U-74,* commanded by Eitel-Friedrich Kentrat, age thirty-four, from the duck *U-8.* It was a "fantastic situation," Dönitz complained in his diary.

But reinforcements were on the way. On March 11 Fritz-Julius Lemp sailed from Germany in the new IXB *U-110,* manned by many seasoned veterans of Lemp's *U-30.* Lemp had been absent from the Atlantic for six months; the *U-110* had been caught temporarily in Baltic ice and as a result, the boat had had only ten days of crew training "in freezing weather" and no torpedo, gunnery, or pack attack drills. The next day Joachim Schepke, the second-ranking tonnage ace after Kretschmer, sailed in *U-100,* having enjoyed ten weeks of home leave, vacation, and publicity tours. The ice in home waters had also prevented Schepke from conducting refresher drills.

While Lemp and Schepke were rounding the British Isles, the *Luftwaffe* commenced its devastating mass bombing raids on British seaports, and the big German surface ships in the Atlantic were on the move. Sailing far to the west into Canadian waters (near Newfoundland Bank) on March 15 and 16, the battle cruisers *Gneisenau* and *Scharnhorst* again attacked dispersing outbound convoys, sinking sixteen merchant ships for 82,000 tons, then headed for Brest. The heavy cruiser *Hipper* sailed from Brest on March 15 to join the "pocket" battleship *Admiral Scheer* for a break back to Germany through the Denmark Strait. Getting wind of some of these movements, the Admiralty deployed heavy units from the Home Fleet and from Halifax to intercept the ships, but the Germans cleverly eluded the pursuers.

Three days after reaching the Atlantic, on the afternoon of March 15, Lemp in *U-110* took up a position about 150 miles south of Iceland. Since the visibility was very poor, he submerged every four hours to listen on hydrophones for convoy propeller noises. At 10:00 that night, the sonar operator reported the heavy, slow thump-thump-thump of distant propellers. Lemp surfaced and ran down the bearing. He saw "15-to-20 steamers" and "several large tankers" and "at least two destroyers." At ten minutes past midnight, March 16, Lemp got off a contact report to Dönitz and prepared to attack.

This was convoy Halifax 112, composed of forty-one fully laden merchant ships and tankers. It was guarded by Escort Group (EG) 5, which had joined it that morning. Commanded by Donald Macintyre* in the World War I destroyer *Walker,* EG-5 was composed of four other old destroyers (*Vanoc, Volunteer, Sardonyx, Scimitar*) and two new corvettes (*Bluebell, Hydrangea*). Hastily formed in early March, EG-5 had sailed on its maiden voyage with an outbound convoy and was then on its homebound leg. It had had no tactical drills before sailing.

Lemp chose what he believed to be a 10,000-ton tanker for his first target. Actually, it was the 6,200-ton British tanker *Erodona*. He fired two bow torpedoes at her. The first broached and ran erratically; the second missed. A third torpedo from a stern tube hit, causing an immense explosion which led Lemp (and Donald Macintyre in *Walker*) to believe *Erodona* had been "blown to bits." In reality, the ship was only severely damaged and it was later towed into Iceland.

The flames lit up the area "like daylight." The destroyer *Scimitar* saw *U-110* and charged, bringing up *Walker* and *Vanoc,* the latter equipped with a nonrotating Type 286M radar. Seeing the destroyers, Lemp dived and went deep under the convoy at high speed. The destroyers dropped twenty-four depth charges where he had dived, to no effect. *Walker* rejoined the convoy, leaving *Vanoc* and *Scimitar* to "hold down" the U-boat until the convoy was safely past—or so it was thought.

An hour later, Lemp surfaced and chased the convoy. At 0410 he sent Dönitz another report, then mounted a second attack. Having reloaded his tubes, Lemp fired four bow torpedoes, two at a freighter, two at a tanker. One broached; the other three missed. A fifth torpedo, he claimed, hit an 8,000-ton tanker, but that hit could not be confirmed. EG-5 was unaware of this second attack by *U-110*.

Lemp tracked doggedly during the early morning of March 16, broadcasting positions. When Dönitz ordered all boats in the vicinity to report their positions, he heard from the north weather boat, Clausen in *U-37,* Kretschmer in *U-99,* Schepke in *U-100,* and, surprisingly, Kentrat in *U-74,* who was under orders to relieve *U-95* as the south weather boat. Dönitz ordered Lemp to send beacon signals for the benefit of the nearest boats, *U-37* and *U-99*. Lemp did so, but then a mechanical problem and later a Sunderland forced him to run submerged and he lost contact. However, at noon Clausen in *U-37* made contact and broadcast beacons which brought up Kretschmer's *U-99* and Schepke's *U-100*.

At about sunset that evening, Lemp regained contact with the convoy and broadcast a position report and beacon signals. This brought in Kentrat's *U-74,* but in the interim, Lemp lost contact again. When Kentrat came alongside to confer by megaphone, Lemp, believing the convoy had zigged sharply northeast, suggested both boats should search in that direction. This assumption took *U-74* and *U-110* off in the wrong direction. By then *U-37, U-99,* and *U-100* had made contact, but none broadcast any beacon signals to help Lemp and Kentrat.

The three boats in contact with Halifax 112 closed to attack. The original alarm from Lemp had reported "at least two destroyers" in the escort, an estimate that had not been revised. Clausen, Schepke, and Kretschmer were therefore astonished

---

* In the postwar years, a popular naval historian.

to find not two but seven escorts—five destroyers and two corvettes. One of the destroyers, *Scimitar,* sighted Schepke in *U-100* and drove him under, calling up the destroyers *Walker* and *Vanoc.* When Schepke came up an hour later, a destroyer was still present. It drove him down a second time and dropped depth charges.

Otto Kretschmer commenced his attack at about 10:00 P.M. He boldly steamed into the middle of the convoy on the surface and fired his eight remaining torpedoes. It was another remarkable performance by Kretschmer. One torpedo missed, but the other seven slammed into six different ships, four of them tankers, which exploded in searing flames. Kretschmer believed that all six ships, totaling 59,000 tons, had sunk, making this salvo the single most destructive of the war and, counting earlier sinkings, bringing his total bag on this patrol to a record-setting 86,000 tons. But he had overestimated his latest sinkings by one vessel. Five ships, including three tankers* for 34,500 tons, sank, but the sixth, the 9,300-ton British tanker *Franche Comte,* got her fires under control and survived. Hiding in the dense smoke from the burning tankers and dodging the seven escorts, Kretschmer plotted a course to take him out of the area and on to Lorient.

The other boats, meanwhile, were attempting to attack. It was not an easy setup. The flames from the burning tankers brightly lit the area. The seven escorts swarmed hither and yon, adding more light with star shells and dropping depth charges. At fifty minutes after midnight, Donald Macintyre in *Walker* spotted a U-boat close ahead and put on full speed to ram. This was probably Clausen in *U-37,* who had not yet fired torpedoes. He crash-dived *U-37* 100 yards ahead of *Walker.* Macintyre ran right over the boat and dropped ten depth charges set for 250 feet. He heard a "heavy explosion" and saw "orange flames" in his wake and believed he had sunk his first U-boat. But he had not. Clausen in *U-37* reported heavy collision damage which forced him to resume his voyage to Germany.

Headed off in the wrong direction, Lemp in *U-110* and Kentrat in *U-74* saw the flames and explosions. They turned about and ran full speed toward the battle scene. Coming up, both saw escorts everywhere firing star shells and dropping depth charges. Nonplussed by the sight of all these escorts—many more than he had reported—Lemp logged that the convoy "must have been reinforced" by other destroyers. Both boats had narrow escapes with destroyers; neither could get in.

Macintyre in *Walker* got a "firm" sonar contact at 0130, March 17. This was Schepke in *U-100,* who had not yet fired any torpedoes either. Macintyre called up the destroyer *Vanoc* and let loose a salvo of nine depth charges, set for 500 feet. When the noise subsided, Macintyre regained contact and fired off eight more depth charges with deep settings. *Vanoc* arrived, gained contact, and almost immediately fired six depth charges, set for 150, 250, and 500 feet. *Walker* then went off to rescue some survivors, but *Vanoc* continued the hunt. After she regained sonar contact, *Vanoc* fired six more depth charges with the same settings.

Some of these twenty-nine depth charges fell very close to *U-100.* The explo-

---

* The 6,600-ton and 8,100-ton Norwegians *Fern* and *Beduin* and the 5,700-ton British *Venetia.* Assigning full credit for *Terje Viken* and *Athelbeach* (probably damaged by *U-47* and *U-70*), Kretschmer sank a total of five tankers for 47,663 tons in ten days!

sions smashed instruments, knocked out the pumps, and caused heavy flooding. The boat went out of control and slid, stern first, to 750 feet—deeper than any U-boat had ever gone. Fearing that the pressure hull might implode, and believing that he could torpedo *Vanoc,* Schepke ordered the engineer to blow all ballast tanks and surface.

Schepke came up at about 0300. By then *Walker* had rejoined *Vanoc.* The technicians manning the Type 286M radar on *Vanoc* picked up a contact at 1,000 yards—the first verifiable British surface-ship radar contact on a U-boat. At about the same time, Schepke saw *Vanoc,* which was coming on at full speed to ram. To back the boat around and fire torpedoes, Schepke called for full power, but the diesels wouldn't start, nor, at first, the electric motors. When the motors finally came on the line, Schepke mistakenly ordered full speed ahead, rather than astern, on the starboard motor, ruining any chance of firing torpedoes.

Schepke thought *Vanoc* would miss astern, but he was wrong. Killing her engines to minimize damage to herself, *Vanoc* hit the *U-100* at a perfect right angle on the conning tower at 0318. Schepke shouted "Abandon ship!" They were his last words. *Vanoc's* huge sharp bow crushed him to death on the bridge. The *U-100* sank almost immediately. *Vanoc* signaled *Walker:* "Have rammed and sunk U-boat."

After picking up thirty-eight survivors of the freighter *J. B. White,* sunk by Kretschmer, *Walker* rushed up to circle *Vanoc* protectively while *Vanoc's* men fished survivors of *U-100* from the water. *Vanoc* found six, including Siegfried Flister, who was making an indoctrination cruise with Schepke before taking command of his own boat, and five enlisted men.

Close by, Kretschmer in *U-99,* was still trying to slip out of the area undetected and go home. His onetime quartermaster, Heinrich Petersen, for whom Kretschmer had obtained a *Ritterkreuz* and who had been promoted to lieutenant and second watch officer, had the bridge watch. One lookout was not alert. Glancing into the lookout's zone, Petersen saw *Walker* merely a few yards off. Believing that *U-99* must have been seen, Petersen made a serious mistake and ordered a crash dive, rather than running off in darkness at full speed.

No one on *Walker* had seen *U-99,* but while *Walker* was still circling *Vanoc,* the sonar operator picked up a contact. Macintyre disbelieved the report—a third U-boat contact in as many hours was simply too much to credit—but when the operator insisted it was a moving U-boat, Macintyre ordered an attack. *Walker* ran down the bearing and dropped six depth charges at *U-99,* which was trying to run off at about 400 feet. The charges exploded close beneath the boat, tossing it wildly and smashing air, fuel, and ballast tanks. Flooding and out of control, the *U-99* slid down to 700 feet or more. Realizing the boat could not survive submerged, Kretschmer blew all ballast tanks and the *U-99* shot to the surface. Kretschmer had no torpedoes; he hoped to escape in darkness.

Nine minutes after *Walker* dropped her depth charges, at 0352, *Vanoc* signaled *Walker:* "U-boat surfaced astern of me." *Vanoc* beamed her searchlight on *U-99* and both ships opened fire with 4" guns. Kretschmer called for full power, but neither the diesels nor electric motors would function. Moreover, the steering gear was broken. With a heavy heart, Kretschmer gave orders to scuttle and abandon ship. He got off a final, terse, confused, plain-language radio message to Dönitz: "Two destroyers. Depth charges. 53,000 tons. Capture. Kretschmer." He then notified *Walker* with his signal light: "We are sunking [sic]." *Walker* and *Vanoc* ceased fire after two minutes, having registered no hits, and prepared to capture survivors.

Walker closed the flooding *U-99* cautiously, with scramble-nets rigged. She picked up forty men, including the new, twenty-three-year-old first watch officer, Hans-Joachim von Knebel-Döberitz; the second watch officer, *Ritterkreuz* holder Heinrich Petersen; a prospective commanding officer, Horst Hesselbarth; two midshipmen on an indoctrination cruise; and, lastly, Kretschmer. The engineer, Gottfried Schroder, who had gone back to open ballast-tank vents—probably needlessly—and two enlisted men were not found.

At Kerneval, Dönitz first learned of the disaster from the crippled, Germany-bound *U-37*, which picked up and relayed Kretschmer's final, confused message. It came as a shattering blow; doubly so as nothing had been heard from Prien in *U-47* or Matz in *U-70* for ten days (since March 7) and all hope for them had been lost. Nor, ominously, was there any word from Schepke in *U-100*.

Winston Churchill helped clear the air. Even before Macintyre's EG-5 reached Liverpool to great acclaim, he announced to the House of Commons that Germany's two leading U-boat aces, Otto Kretschmer and Joachim Schepke, had been captured and killed, respectively. That announcement forced Berlin to concede the loss on March 20.* The communiqué sent a shock wave through the U-boat arm, for by then it was known that Prien had been lost as well.

British intelligence deduced from the POWs of *U-70, U-99,* and *U-100* that Prien, too, was gone, and those sources played a role in the Admiralty's decision to credit *Wolverine* with the kill. But the Admiralty did not rush to claim credit for killing Prien and *U-47.* Nor did Berlin have anything to say. Prien's biographer, Wolfgang Frank, wrote that Hitler forbade the release of news of Prien's loss, since it would "have a deleterious effect on the public morale," especially if announced close to the loss of Kretschmer and Schepke. Berlin withheld the news of Prien's loss, Frank wrote, for ten more weeks—to May 23.†

---

* The Berlin communiqué credited Kretschmer with sinking 313,611 tons, plus three destroyers, and Schepke with 233,871 tons. Dönitz had misread Kretschmer's final message to mean that he had sunk two destroyers plus 53,000 tons on the patrol. Kretschmer's final, confirmed score (on *U-23* and *U-99*) was forty-three and a half ships for 247,012 tons (half credit for the whale-factory ship cum tanker *Terje Viken*), including three auxiliary cruisers, the destroyer *Daring,* and one prize. On March 21, Kretschmer was promoted to *Korvettenkapitän* (Commander). Schepke's final confirmed score (on *U-3, U-19,* and *U-100*) was thirty-seven ships for 155,882 tons. Kretschmer's score was never equaled; he remained the "Tonnage King" of the war. Schepke was to be outgunned by many skippers, winding up in 13th place. A *Kapitänleutnant,* he was not posthumously promoted.

† Prien's total confirmed score, all on *U-47,* was thirty-two and a third ships for 202,514 tons, including the battleship *Royal Oak,* and half credit for *Terje Viken.* He stood third among all skippers in tonnage sunk. Hitler's decision to withhold news of his loss led to numerous wild—and persistent—rumors, such as that Prien and his crew had mutinied and as punishment had been sent to a labor camp on the Russian front, where all were killed. On March 19, Prien was posthumously promoted to *Korvettenkapitän.*

More Bad News

From the German viewpoint, the U-boat war in the North Atlantic in the last two weeks of March went from bad to worse. Setting off on his second patrol from Lorient in *U-69*, Jost Metzler wrote that the weather was "appalling," even worse than it was on his first patrol in February. The "elements seemed to have gone mad," he remembered. It was impossible to conduct organized reconnaissance; visibility was virtually nil.

Nonetheless the Condors, based in Norway and France, flew patrols. On March 19, they reported three convoys, two outbound and one inbound. With merely five boats in the north hunting grounds, all engulfed in raging seas, Dönitz was unable to do much about the reports. He ordered Engelbert Endrass, fresh from Lorient in *U-46*, and three other boats, including the new VIICs *U-98* and *U-551* from Germany, to intercept one outbound convoy, but none of the four boats could find it.

A day later, March 21, Metzler in *U-69* came upon a convoy inbound from Halifax. Dönitz directed Herbert Schultze in *U-48* and four Italian boats in the area to converge on Metzler's report. But during that day Metzler, tracking submerged, was detected and driven deep by two aggressive escorts. Working as a team, the two escorts depth-charged *U-69* for "several hours," throwing the boat "backwards and forwards," Metzler wrote melodramatically, in "a slow, bitter, life-and-death struggle. . . ." During the struggle, the convoy got away. The destroyers finally broke off the attack to rejoin the convoy, leaving Metzler and his crew thoroughly shaken.

Fritz-Julius Lemp in the new *U-110*, patrolling far to the west of Iceland on the night of March 23, found a 2,500-ton Norwegian freighter. He tracked her carefully and fired a torpedo at close range. It missed, as did two others, fired singly. These three misses raised Lemp's total misses on this patrol to nine, doubtless reflecting the lack of practice in the Baltic because of the ice conditions. Lemp, however, blamed not himself or his fire-control team, but the torpedoes.

Having "lost confidence" in the torpedoes, Lemp, "fighting mad," attacked the ship with his 4.1" deck gun. In the excitement of this first gun attack, "somebody" (as Lemp put it) forgot to remove the tampion (waterproof plug) from the muzzle of the gun barrel. When the crew fired the first shell, the gun "was blown to bits." No men were killed or seriously hurt, but the hurtling pieces of steel slashed through ballast-tank vents and fuel tanks, causing severe damage and heavy oil leaks which forced Lemp to abort, having sunk no ships that were confirmed in postwar records. He arrived in Lorient in an angry mood, complaining of the lack of training in the Baltic and the unreliability of the torpedoes.

The increasing number of reported torpedo failures caused grave concern at Kerneval and prompted yet another close analysis. The study revealed that six new boats sailing from Germany had experienced twenty-one torpedo failures or misses in the month of February. In spite of the restricted shooting practice in home waters and the unfavorable seas, these failures were not the fault of the skippers, Dönitz insisted, but had to be some new "unexplained" defect in the torpedoes. One possible explanation, Dönitz speculated, was that the unprecedented extreme cold in Germany was adversely affecting the inner mechanism of the torpedoes. Hence he insisted that boats sailing from Germany not be loaded with torpedoes that had been exposed to extreme cold, and furthermore, that tests of torpedo performance in extreme cold be carried out.

Farther east that same day, the new VIIC *U-551*, commanded by Karl Schrott, age thirty, from the duck *U-7*, reached her patrol area southeast of Iceland. Commissioned on November 7, the *U-551* had completed her final workup in the ice-free waters off Bergen, sailing on March 18. On this fifth day of his maiden patrol, Schrott found the lone 7,430-ton Belgian freighter *Ville de Liège*, and prepared to attack at dawn on the surface. Spotting *U-551*, *Ville de Liège* radioed an alarm.

The British armed trawler *Visenda*, which was escorting a nearby convoy, responded. Racing up at full speed (13 knots), *Visenda* saw *U-551* on the surface four miles ahead. The U-boat crash-dived, but *Visenda* closed and got sonar contact, held it, and during the next hour and a half, fired a total of eighteen depth charges. These charges destroyed *U-551*. *Visenda*—the first ASW trawler to kill a U-boat—brought back proof: a plywood locker door with German lettering, articles of clothing stenciled with six different German names, a novel in German, and "pieces" of a human body, identified by medical authorities as the heart and lung of "an adult but not an old person." German POWs identified the locker door; it came from the port side aft of the bow compartment. Based on this—and other data—the Admiralty's Assessment Committee speculated that one of *Visenda*'s depth charges must have detonated a torpedo in *U-551*'s bow compartment, demolishing the forward end of the boat and blowing the locker, clothing, and other debris to the surface.

When *U-551* failed to respond to radio queries that night, Dönitz was gravely concerned. If, as he feared, *U-551* had met with misfortune, it meant that five U-boats—about 25 percent of the Atlantic operational force—had been lost in the area south southeast of Iceland in a period of merely seventeen days: *U-47* (Prien), *U-70* (Matz), *U-99* (Kretschmer), *U-100* (Schepke), *U-551* (Schrott). Besides that, *U-37* (Clausen) had been rammed submerged and had survived only by greatest good luck, and *U-A* (Eckermann) had nearly been lost in a depth-charge attack.

The loss and near loss of seven boats in so brief a period in the North Atlantic gave rise to the suspicion that the British had developed some new means of locating U-boats. But Dönitz had no idea what it might be. Was there a spy in the *Kriegsmarine* or *Luftwaffe* with access to U-boat positions or radio traffic? Had British scientists achieved some technological breakthrough in radar that enabled them to put sets on escorts? Had British scientists developed a new and tremendously improved sonar? Or DFing gear? Or some wholly new device unknown to German science?

These suspicions prompted Dönitz to withdraw the boats from the Northwest Approaches. On March 25, he repositioned the six boats left in the hunting grounds on a 300-mile north-south line at 20 degrees west longitude. The extreme northern end of the line—closest to Iceland—was occupied by the most experienced skipper and boat: Herbert Schultze in the record-holding *U-48*. Engelbert Endrass, in *U-46*, occupied a position in the center of the line.

Schultze in *U-48* found an inbound convoy passing south of Iceland on March 29. This was Halifax 115, guarded by eight escorts. With remarkable daring, skill, and calm, Schultze attacked and fired five torpedoes which sank four ships. He claimed 24,500 tons; his confirmed score was four ships for 17,300 tons, plus one tanker damaged. In view of the heavy escort, Dönitz ruled against sending the "extremely inexperienced boats" to help Schultze. No other boats found the convoy.

That same day, farther south in the patrol line, Metzler in *U-69* found convoy Outbound 302. In response to his alarm, Schultze in *U-48* and Endrass in *U-46* attempted to intercept. Endrass found it, but was only able to sink a 1,800-ton freighter. Still tracking far to the west on March 30, Metzler sank what he claimed to be a 7,000-ton freighter, but which in reality was half that size. In this, and a previous action, Metzler reported five electric-torpedo failures, which combined with the nine misses or failures reported by Topp in *U-552* and a similar number by Lemp in *U-110,* intensified the concern at Kerneval about torpedo reliability.

Altogether in March 1941, three hundred loaded ships crossed the North Atlantic, all from Halifax.* Bedeviled by an acute shortage of U-boats, by foul weather, by increasingly aggressive surface and air convoy-escort forces (some with 1.5 meter-wavelength radar), and by the failures of the Condors and Italian submarines, the Germans in that area turned in poor results: a total of twenty-four confirmed ships sunk, half of them loaded ships (four tankers) in eastbound Halifax convoys. Almost half of these had been sunk by two *Ritterkreuz* holders: Kretschmer in *U-99* and Schultze in *U-48.* In return, British forces had sunk five U-boats, an "exchange rate" of about five British ships for each U-boat lost, a disastrous ratio for the U-boat arm.

In striking contrast to the boats in the north, the three Type IXBs enjoying better weather in the south continued to do very well. Off Freetown, on March 16, Jürgen Oesten in *U-106* made contact with another convoy, Sierra Leone 68, en route to Britain. Oesten radioed an alarm and beacon signals to bring up Georg Schewe in *U-105,* then attacked, sinking a 6,800-ton freighter. Mounting a second attack on the next night, Oesten claimed sinking three freighters for 21,000 tons and damage to another. Schewe in *U-105* made contact, and over the next three days, March 18 to March 21, the two boats chewed away at the convoy, until all fourteen internal torpedoes on each boat had been expended. Schewe sank four ships for 25,500 tons; Oesten in *U-106* claimed one "freighter" sunk, one damaged. Unknown to Oesten, the "freighter" claimed as sunk was actually the battleship *Malaya,* which was escorting the convoy. Slightly damaged, *Malaya* limped across the Atlantic to the island of Trinidad, thence to the United States, where, as related, under the provisions of Lend-Lease, she was repaired and refitted along with the battleship *Resolution,* which had been badly damaged by the Vichy French submarine *Beveziers* in the abortive Allied attack on Dakar.

---

* Because of winter ice, Sydney, Nova Scotia, was closed and Sydney, or Slow, Convoys sailed from Halifax.

Schewe and Oesten reported great success. In seven days of tenacious attacks, Schewe claimed sinking six ships for 41,000 tons, Oesten five ships for 36,000 tons—a total of eleven ships for 77,000 tons. The confirmed score was less: Schewe five ships for 27,000 tons, Oesten three ships for 17,000 tons—a total of eight ships for 44,000 tons, plus Oesten's hit on *Malaya*, which put her out of action for months.

Winston Churchill was especially shocked and enraged by the losses in this convoy. In a "rocket" to First Sea Lord Dudley Pound he expressed his displeasure and criticized the absence of destroyers in the escort, especially since *Malaya* was in the formation. Pound replied that the destroyers at hand did not have sufficient range to sail with Sierra Leone convoys, and refueling at sea was deemed to be too dangerous since the ships involved were virtually unmaneuverable during the process. To this Churchill responded: "Nonsense!" If there were four destroyers present, three could protect the other one while it refueled from a tanker in the convoy.

The third IXB in southern waters, Georg-Wilhelm Schulz's *U-124*, attempted to rejoin the others after resupplying from *Kormoran*, but she had a catastrophic failure in both engines, which left her helpless. After the engines were repaired, she closed the coast of Africa and sank a lone 3,800-ton British freighter, bringing Schulz's total credited sinkings, including substantial overclaims, to 100,117 tons, earning him a *Ritterkreuz*. While Schulz was closing on Freetown, Schewe in *U-105* and Oesten in *U-106* downloaded deck torpedoes and then hauled westward and resupplied from *Kormoran* and the supply ship *Nordmark*, respectively. En route to the rendezvous, Oesten claimed sinking a 5,000-ton freighter, bringing his total claims to about 82,000 tons. Having heard from *B-dienst* that Oesten had hit *Malaya*, Dönitz awarded him a *Ritterkreuz*.*

To then Dönitz, unshakably convinced that the decisive naval battleground lay along the convoy routes in the Northwest Approaches—between Iceland and the British Isles—had resisted to the utmost any "diversion" of U-boats from that area. But the poor returns and the loss of five boats to "obscure" (i.e., unexplained) causes (three of them commanded by his most experienced and notable skippers) led him to a profound decision: He would withdraw *all* U-boats from that rich target area for the time being and disperse them to more distant areas where British ASW was less intense, such as the waters west of Iceland and in the South Atlantic.

This little-noted decision was a milestone in the U-boat war against the British Empire: the first clear-cut defeat for the German submarines.

The principal reason for that defeat was the paucity of U-boats. Counting all gains and losses, at the end of March 1941, Dönitz still controlled only twenty-seven combat-ready oceangoing boats, the number with which he began the war nineteen months earlier. Three of these boats were temporarily unavailable be-

---

* Schulz's confirmed score—all in *U-124*—was thirteen ships for 57,683 tons. Oesten's confirmed score, including six ships for 20,754 tons in the duck *U-61*, was twelve ships for 58,723 tons, plus damage to *Malaya*.

cause of battle or other damage; three were patrolling off West Africa. That left only twenty-one boats to patrol the North Atlantic convoy routes, and half of these were new. Owing to the travel and refit time, only a third—seven boats—could be in the hunting grounds at one time. In view of the clever diversion of convoys and the ever-growing numbers of experienced, aggressive-minded surface escorts, there were simply not enough U-boats to find, track, and carry out successful pack attacks on enemy convoys in the Northwest Approaches.

The decision to disperse the U-boats to distant waters west of Iceland and to the South Atlantic entailed a severe penalty. The Type VIIBs and VIICs in the North Atlantic did not have sufficient fuel capacity for extended patrolling at long ranges, especially if required to chase one or more convoys at high speed. The fuel limitations were to reduce the number of boats available to form a pack in the more westerly North Atlantic hunting grounds. Similarly, the extreme distances involved in South Atlantic patrolling were to reduce the combat availability of the bigger boats sent to that area. Notwithstanding the prospective increase in the size of the Atlantic U-boat force, the number of boats that could be brought to bear on enemy shipping on any given day was to decline.

It was at this time—March 1941—that Lend-Lease was enacted and that President Roosevelt transferred the ten Coast Guard cutters to the Royal Navy (in addition to the fifty destroyers), and authorized other measures to provide the British cargo ships and tankers, to reinforce the British oil "shuttle" in American waters, and to repair British warships in American shipyards. Dönitz characterized these measures as "a chain of breaches of international law" and urged Hitler to lift the tight restrictions on attacking American ships. Absorbed with planning operations in the Soviet Union, the Balkans, and the Mediterranean Basin, Hitler was still wary of antagonizing the Americans and risking open warfare with them, and rejected the proposal.

DECLINING PROSPECTS

Hitler launched Operation Marita, the rescue of the Italian armies in Greece, on April 6. Attacking from Austria, Hungary, Romania, and Bulgaria, German ground and air forces simultaneously overran Yugoslavia and attacked the northeastern Greek frontier. Within three weeks, the Germans conquered most of the Hellenic Peninsula, forcing the recently arrived British ground and air forces to evacuate to the island of Crete and to North Africa, where Rommel's modest *Afrika Korps* had pushed the Army of the Nile, renamed the British Eighth Army, back into Egypt.

The U-boat war in the Atlantic proceeded in conformity to Dönitz's decision to withdraw from the Northwest Approaches. On April 1 he shifted the nine boats in the hunting ground very far to the west. They formed a north-south patrol line at 30 west longitude—about equidistant between Iceland and Greenland—where Dönitz assumed British ASW measures to be less intense. At the same time, he ordered four big boats to sail to West African waters to reinforce the three boats already patrolling that area.

Infuriatingly, the OKM insisted that the U-boat force carry out three special missions during April. Two boats were to occupy weather-reporting stations for the benefit of the *Luftwaffe* at all times. Another two boats were to conduct hunts for British auxiliary cruisers, which had been reported in the Denmark Strait. Yet another two boats (of the southern group) were to escort a German blockade runner, *Lech,* which was loaded with a "valuable cargo," from Rio de Janeiro to the Bay of Biscay. "These tasks," Dönitz complained in his diary, "will probably result in less tonnage sunk and I am bound to call attention to this fact. . . ."

Dönitz had only just established the nine-boat patrol line to the southwest of Iceland on April 1 when *U-76,* a new VIIB outbound from Germany, discovered the fifty-one-ship convoy Outbound 305 in the Northwest Approaches area, 400 miles to the east! The *U-76* was commanded by Friedrich von Hippel, age twenty-six, who had begun the war as a watch officer on Werner Hartmann's *U-37* but had been beached because of chronic stomach problems. The boat had been delayed in training by the Baltic ice and, after sailing from Kiel, had aborted to Bergen with mechanical difficulties. She had been in the Atlantic merely two days.

Because of the "strong" ASW measures in the Northwest Approaches, Dönitz was reluctant to bring the other boats back to the east. He therefore instructed von Hippel not to attack but to track the convoy 400 miles to westward, into the waiting arms of the patrol line, a challenging and risky assignment for a green skipper. The British were almost certain to DF von Hippel's position reports, go after him, and divert the convoy. Von Hippel hung on, but during that day he ran into "sailing vessels and trawlers" south of Iceland and was forced to run submerged for nine hours to evade detection. When he surfaced to report losing the convoy, Dönitz directed him to "press on" to the west and to do his "utmost" to regain contact.

Meanwhile, one of the new boats in the western patrol line, Eitel-Friedrich Kentrat's *U-74,* encountered inbound Slow Convoy 26, twenty-two ships escorted by the 11,400-ton auxiliary cruiser *Worcestershire.* When Dönitz received this contact report, he instructed Kentrat to shadow and send beacon signals and not to attack until the other boats came up. Herbert Schultze in *U-48,* who had only one torpedo left and was low on fuel, could not respond, but the other eight boats did, forming the largest pack yet.

The pack commenced attacking late in the evening of April 2. Engelbert Endrass in *U-46,* who had previously sunk two ships for 10,500 tons, including the 8,700-ton Swedish tanker *Castor,* on this patrol, led the assault. He sank another tanker, the 7,000-ton *British Reliance,* and a 4,300-ton freighter, but a torpedo that hit the 4,900-ton British freighter *Thirlby* failed to detonate and another missed the 5,400-ton British freighter *Athenic.* Eitel-Friedrich Kentrat in *U-74* attacked second, sinking a 5,400-ton Belgian freighter and a 4,300-ton Greek freighter and damaging the single escort, the auxiliary cruiser *Worcestershire.* Helmut Rosenbaum in the new *U-73* attacked third, sinking a 5,800-ton freighter and a 6,900-ton tanker, *British Viscount,* which exploded in flames, brilliantly lighting the seascape.

The British were stunned to learn of U-boats attacking so far west. On orders of the convoy commander, the surviving sixteen ships scattered, some firing guns at real or imagined U-boats. The British, meanwhile, directed other escorts to the scene. A destroyer, *Hurricane,* escorted the damaged auxiliary cruiser *Worcestershire* on to Liverpool. Two destroyers, *Havelock* and *Hesperus,* searched for survivors of the six sunken ships. Five other warships, including the destroyers *Veteran* and *Wolverine,* rounded up the other scattered ships and reformed them into a convoy.

By happenstance, the new boat, von Hippel's *U-76,* which was still westbound in search of convoy Outbound 305, ran across the tracks of the scattered ships of Slow Convoy 26. At 0630 on the morning of April 3, von Hippel fired two torpedoes at one of the ships, the 2,000-ton Finnish freighter *Daphne.* Both missed, but von Hippel tracked submerged and five hours later he sank her.

The other U-boats pursued the reforming convoy eastward. That night, April 3–4, two of the boats caught up and attacked. Herbert Kuppisch in *U-94* sank a 5,400-ton British freighter. Robert Gysae, age thirty, in the new VIIC *U-98,* on his maiden patrol, sank two other freighters. While the destroyer *Veteran* rescued survivors, the destroyer *Wolverine* counterattacked the U-boats, driving them off and holding them down, preventing further attacks.

Late in the afternoon of April 4, while running submerged, von Hippel in *U-76* sighted another ship from the convoy, the 5,400-ton British freighter *Athenic,* sailing alone. Von Hippel attacked, firing one torpedo, which hit. The crew of *Athenic* radioed an alarm and then abandoned ship. Still submerged, von Hippel came in from the other side and fired two more torpedoes. Both hit; *Athenic* blew up with a thunderous roar.

Upon hearing *Athenic*'s submarine alarm—*SSS*—four escorts that were shepherding the remnants of the convoy raced to the scene: the destroyers *Havelock* and *Wolverine* (credited with sinking Prien in *U-47*), the corvette *Arbutus* (credited with sinking Matz in *U-70*), and the sloop *Scarborough.* When they closed the area early on the morning of April 5, von Hippel in *U-76* was on the surface, charging batteries. The watch saw one of the escorts and crash-dived. *Wolverine* obtained sonar contact and notified *Arbutus* and *Scarborough.* Bedeviled by a sonar malfunction, *Wolverine* dropped only two depth charges, one at a time. *Arbutus* got sonar contact but lost it in the noise of *Wolverine*'s attack. Coming up, the sloop *Scarborough* gained a firm sonar contact and fired off eight depth charges.

The ten charges dropped on *U-76* fell close. The first single charge from *Wolverine* smashed all the instruments. The next caused a welded seam to give way, bent a stanchion, and put out all the lights. The eight charges from *Scarborough* caused severe flooding aft. Believing the boat to be doomed, at 0925, merely four minutes after *Scarborough*'s attack, von Hippel surfaced to scuttle.

In compliance with the Admiralty's standing orders, the corvette *Arbutus* boldly ran in to try to capture a U-boat. While von Hippel and his crew were leaping into the water, *Arbutus* nuzzled alongside *U-76.* The first lieutenant of *Arbutus,* Geoffrey Angus, and three seamen jumped on the forward deck of *U-76*—the first British in the war to board a German U-boat. While they raced to the bridge to enter the boat and grab the Enigma and secret papers, other hands from *Arbutus* tied cables and an 8" hawser to *U-76* in an attempt to prevent her from sinking.

When Angus reached the conning-tower hatch, he saw the boat was "half full" of seawater. The water had mixed with the battery acid, causing strong chlorine gas. Deciding it would be fatal to enter the boat, Angus slammed down and dogged shut the conning-tower hatch to stop the escape of air and to keep the boat afloat.

It was a heroic try, but *U-76* was still flooding aft and sinking rapidly. To save herself from capsizing, *Arbutus* had to let go the wires and hawser, and the boat sank. *Wolverine* picked up von Hippel and thirty-nine of his crew; *Scarborough* and *Arbutus* rescued one man each, for a total of forty-two. The British noted that a seaman on *U-76* died when saltwater leaked into the potash cartridge of his escape apparatus, producing a toxic gas that he inhaled.

Counting the survivors of *U-70*, *U-76*, *U-99*, and *U-100*, the British had captured 113 German submariners (fourteen officers, ninety-nine enlisted men) within one month. Some of these POWs talked freely (or were coerced or tricked into talking freely) and revealed many technical details about the Type VII boats, the organization of the U-boat arm, and the French bases. One of the officers even told the British about the rift that had occurred between Dönitz and Göring over command of the Condors. According to a British intelligence report, another German officer revealed the "astonishing" successes *B-dienst* had achieved in breaking British naval codes, but that was old stuff.

When Dönitz queried the boats for sinking reports on Slow Convoy 26, he calculated the pack attack had been highly successful: twelve (of twenty-two) ships sunk for 80,000 tons, plus damage to the auxiliary cruiser *Worcestershire*. He was close. Unknown to Dönitz, the lost *U-76* had sunk two ships of the convoy for 7,400 tons, which brought the confirmed total to eleven ships sunk (of twenty-two) for 54,000 tons. The other eleven ships eventually reached port.*

The retreat from the dangerous Northwest Approaches to more distant waters westward appeared to be not a defeat but a stroke of genius in the case of Slow Convoy 26. For the loss of only one (green) boat, *U-76*, the pack had sunk eleven confirmed ships inbound to the British Isles with full and valuable loads. But the discovery of and success against that convoy was really beginner's luck. The big expenditure of fuel to get to westward of Iceland severely restricted the ability of the VIIs to hunt and chase the enemy.

A number of those westerly boats had all but exhausted fuel and torpedoes. As a consequence, five boats followed *U-48* to France. The high scorer of this returning group was Herbert Schultze in the famous, record-holding *U-48*, credited with sinking six ships for 40,000 tons on this patrol (confirmed score: five ships for 27,256 tons). Next was Engelbert Endrass in *U-46*, credited with five ships for 32,000 tons (confirmed score: four ships for 21,778 tons). Two skippers making maiden patrols received high praise: Eitel-Friedrich Kentrat in *U-74*, who discovered Slow Convoy 26, sank a freighter, and damaged the auxiliary cruiser *Worcestershire*, and Robert Gysae in *U-98*, who sank four ships for 15,588 tons. Two

---

* The 4,900-ton *Thirlby* escaped the U-boats but was hit and severely damaged by a German aircraft while entering North Channel.

skippers making second patrols from France were criticized for failing to make the most of opportunities: Udo Heilmann in *U-97,* who sank three confirmed ships for 20,500 tons, including two British tankers, the 8,000-ton *Chama* and 8,100-ton *Conus,* but had failed to home other U-boats to convoy Outbound 289; and Jost Metzler in *U-69,* who sank but one confirmed ship for 3,800 tons.

The departure of these boats left only three in the North Atlantic hunting grounds. Three others sailed from France, but two of them were assigned to the OKM-ordered special mission of hunting British auxiliary cruisers in the Denmark Strait. Klaus Scholtz in *U-108* carried out this mission successfully, sinking the 16,400-ton *Rajputana.* Herbert Kuppisch in *U-94* had mixed results. On the way into Denmark Strait, he sank the 5,600-ton Norwegian tanker *Lincoln Ellsworth,* but when he shot at his principal target, an unidentified 15,000-ton auxiliary cruiser, the torpedoes malfunctioned.

The loss of eleven ships (two tankers) in Slow Convoy 26 so far to the west of Iceland speeded up a plan to base substantial British ASW forces in Iceland to extend strong convoy protection farther to the west of that island. This decision, in effect, filled a gap caused by the postponement of the U.S. Navy plan to provide convoy escort on the Iceland-Canada leg and the delays in readiness of the Canadian corvettes.

The Admiralty sent three of the newly formed Escort Groups to Iceland: B-3, B-6, and B-12. These groups were, so to speak, spliced into the center of the North Atlantic convoy run. They were to meet the escorts of westbound convoys at about 20 degrees west and relieve them. Then they were to escort those convoys to about 35 degrees west (900 miles or about five days), whereupon they were to turn about and escort eastbound convoys (Slow, Halifax) back to about 20 degrees west, where they were to hand over convoy protection to those escorts returning to the British Isles. Inasmuch as these escorts had limited range, especially in heavy weather, and had to run into Iceland to refuel, three groups were required to carry out this scheme.

In addition, the Admiralty transferred Coastal Command Sunderlands and Hudsons to Iceland. These planes, equipped with 1.5-meter-wavelength ASV II radar sets, were to provide air protection for the convoys. Although ground facilities were as yet primitive, the aircrews were able to take advantage of the improved April flying weather and the longer days (and shorter nights), which increased opportunities to sight by eye surfaced U-boats.

It should not be imagined that the British suddenly put in place a strong and reliable splice in the North Atlantic convoy run. The new system required terribly rigid convoy routing and escort scheduling. Working on an overly intricate timetable unforgiving of error, the surface and air escort, manned by green crews, often became lost and were unable to find the convoys, throwing everything into confusion. Ships and planes broke down or ran short of fuel and had to abort missions. Inclement weather and the presence of icebergs complicated the linkups. Moreover, the extreme rigidity of the scheme raised the possibility that the Germans might divine the convoy routes and rendezvous and take advantage of the weak links in the splice.

• • •

Dönitz had laid plans for a major U-boat campaign in West African waters during April, employing seven large boats, which were to replenish, as required, from the German supply ships *Nordmark* and *Egerland,* parked in mid-Atlantic. But the OKM insisted that two of the boats already in African waters, *U-105* (Schewe) and *U-106* (Oesten), be detached to escort the blockade-runner *Lech* from Brazil. Accordingly, the two boats withdrew to waiting stations near the *Nordmark,* refueling numerous times. While milling around in mid-ocean waiting for *Lech* to sail, Schewe in *U-105* encountered and sank a lone 5,200-ton British freighter, but had no further luck in April. Jürgen Oesten in *U-106* sank no ships in April. In response to repeated protests of this waste of firepower from Dönitz, the OKM finally agreed to release one boat, *U-105,* but insisted that the other, *U-106,* remain on standby for the *Lech* voyage.

The diversion of *U-105* and *U-106* left only one boat off Freetown in the first half of April: *U-124,* commanded by Georg-Wilhelm Schulz. After replenishing from *Kormoran,* Schulz closed the coast and sank three ships for 11,000 tons between April 4 and 8. The last was the 2,700-ton British freighter, *Tweed.* Coming up to investigate the wreckage, Schulz found that one of *Tweed*'s two lifeboats had capsized and that several men clinging to it were injured. Schulz fished the survivors from the water and righted the lifeboat. A doctor on *U-124,* Hubertus Göder, tended the wounded.* Schulz stocked the lifeboat with food, water, cognac, and cigarettes, gave the survivors a course to Freetown, then proceeded with the patrol, sinking three more ships for 15,000 tons off Freetown. He returned to Lorient on May 1, completing a voyage of sixty-seven days. He was credited with sinking twelve ships for about 62,000 tons. Although the confirmed sinkings were reduced to eleven ships for 52,397 tons, it remained one of the outstanding patrols of the war.

Dönitz's son-in-law, Günter Hessler in the new IXB *U-107,* led the parade of reinforcements to African waters in April. Following Hessler came Viktor Schütze in *U-103* and Heinrich Liebe in the weary IX *U-38,* then lastly Hans Eckermann in *U-A.* The *U-103* and *U-A* were forced to abort with mechanical problems. The *U-103* resailed in April, but *U-A* was delayed for weeks.

Southbound, Hessler in *U-107* encountered heavy, unescorted traffic. Between April 8 and April 21, he sank five British ships for 30,600 tons, including the 8,500-ton British tanker *Duffield.* The fifth ship was *Calchas,* a 10,300-ton freighter. Seeing the crew abandon the sinking ship, or so he believed, Hessler said later, he closed submerged to offer assistance to those in the lifeboats. But "a feeling which I could not explain," he went on, deterred him from surfacing. As he raised his periscope for a close look, "sailors who had been hiding under the guns and behind the bulwarks, jumped up, manned the guns and opened fire at the

---

* Some of the larger Type IXs sailing to African waters carried physicians, who were regarded as noncombatants. Schulz's decision to render assistance to these British survivors, he said later, was "approved" by Dönitz, and Schulz submitted an official account of it to the tribunal at Nuremberg to assist in Dönitz's defense.

periscope." Hessler pulled down the scope and went deep at full speed, leaving the British gunners an empty sea. This close call cooled Hessler's humanitarian instincts.

The British were deeply disturbed by these German successes in West African waters. At the peak of Hessler's onslaught, April 9, the War Cabinet approved a bold and risky plan (Operation Puma) to seize the Spanish Canary Islands. The purpose of the operation was both to deny the Germans use of the islands and to turn them into a British naval base, in part as a facility to counter U-boats in southern waters. The Admiralty formed a strong task force (three aircraft carriers, a battleship, three heavy cruisers, nineteen destroyers), which was to put 10,000 British troops ashore. However, Puma was postponed (and eventually canceled) in favor of tough diplomacy. Churchill demanded that Franco bar German U-boats (and other naval vessels) from the Canaries—or else. Confronted with this pressure, Franco obliged the British.

The denial of the Canaries as a clandestine refueling base did not cause Dönitz to lose sleep. He did not like sending U-boats into the Canaries. British naval forces were closely watching the islands; earlier they had twice denied Clausen in *U-37* entry. Franco was not trustworthy. In the uncertain political climate, he might at any time seize and intern any U-boat found in those waters. Dönitz preferred replenishing the boats from German supply ships in the South Atlantic.

In what was developing into a remarkable patrol, Hessler in *U-107* sank his sixth British ship, a 7,400-tonner, on April 30. He then withdrew to the mid-Atlantic to replenish from *Nordmark* and *Egerland*. Behind him to African waters came Liebe in *U-38* and Schütze in the resailed *U-103*. Schütze sank a 2,300-ton freighter on April 25.

A SLIGHT BRITISH LEAD

In mid-April there were nine U-boats in the North Atlantic hunting grounds. Six patrolled a line well southwest of Iceland. Two patrolled directly south of Iceland. A new VIIB, *U-75*, commanded by Helmuth Ringelmann, age twenty-nine, was westbound through the Northwest Approaches. Three of the eight boats were low on fuel and poised to return to France; three others, including a new VIIC, *U-553*, commanded by Karl Thurmann, age thirty-one, sailed to replace them. However, *U-553* was compelled to abort to Bergen with engine problems.

The hunting in these distant western waters was disastrously poor. In the three-week period April 4 to April 25, the boats attacked no convoys. In the two-week period April 10 to April 25, only three boats had successes: Otto Salmann in *U-52* (two ships for 14,000 tons), Helmut Rosenbaum in *U-73* (one ship for 8,600 tons), and Karl-Heinz Moehle in *U-123* (one ship for 7,300 tons).

One of the ships sunk by Salmann in *U-52* was the 6,600-ton Dutch freighter *Saleir*, an empty straggler from convoy Outbound 306. She went down on April 10 near 31 degrees west. As it happened, a new (1940) American destroyer of the Argentia-based American Support Force, *Niblack*, commanded by Edward R. Durgin, was close by on a reconnaissance patrol. Durgin rescued three boatloads of survivors and while doing so, his sonar operator reported contact on a U-boat. Durgin went to battle stations and drove off the U-boat with three depth charges. According to *Niblack*'s official history, "This bloodless battle apparently was the first action between American and German forces in World War II."*

The complete absence of convoy contacts aroused suspicion in Kerneval. Dönitz became convinced there must be a spy in the German or Italian armed forces giving away U-boat positions. He imposed drastic new restrictions on the number of people at Kerneval, Bordeaux, Berlin, and elsewhere who were authorized to know the position of U-boats, or to tune in on U-boat radio traffic. At his request, Admiral Raeder sent the following tough message to all *Kriegsmarine* commands:

> The U-boat campaign makes it necessary to restrict severely the reading of signals by unauthorized persons. Once again I forbid all authorities who have not express orders from the operations division or the admiral commanding U-boats to tune in on the operational U-boat [radio] wave. I shall in the future consider all transgressions of this order as a criminal act endangering national security.

It also occurred to Dönitz that the British had possibly improved DFing and—inconceivable as it seemed—broken the naval Enigma. He therefore ordered the boats to maintain strict radio silence, except when reporting weather or convoy contacts, and requested the OKM to introduce "a new U-boat cipher." The OKM, Dönitz logged, "approved" his request for a new cipher, but putting it into service was to take a long time.

Dönitz was correct on both counts. The British had improved DFing and, no less important, the processing of DF information. Moreover, commencing April 22, the codebreakers at Bletchley Park, utilizing the material captured from the *Krebs* in the Norway raid and "cryptanalytical methods," broke "the whole of the [Enigma] traffic of April 1941," the official historian wrote. Hence Rodger Winn in the U-boat Tracking Room of the O.I.C. was privy to *all* U-boat traffic for the months of February (previously broken) and April. That traffic, plus traffic from the hand cipher *Werft*, provided him with a complete picture of U-boat operations for those two months, including Dönitz's decision to shift the boats out of the Northwest Approaches to the waters west of Iceland.

From the February and April Enigma traffic, Bletchley Park learned for the first time that the *Kriegsmarine* maintained a fleet of eight trawlers in the Atlantic for weather reporting. At least two of the trawlers were at sea at any given time, one north of Iceland, one in mid-Atlantic. The trawlers carried naval Enigma. They broadcast weather reports in a special cipher, *Wetterkruzschlüssel,* and also carried "short signal" books. A naval officer at Bletchley Park, Harry Hinsley (later the distinguished historian of British intelligence), suggested that the Admiralty at-

---

*   This dubious distinction is often accorded the destroyer *Greer* later in the fall.

tempt to capture one of these trawlers at the earliest possible date to gain more Enigma keys and material.

The Admiralty looked upon this suggestion favorably and commenced drawing plans. This proposed capture "at sea" was not out of the ordinary. Over a year prior, the commander of the Home Fleet, Charles Forbes, had urged all light Royal Navy vessels to form a "boarding party" for the purpose of capturing a U-boat. His advisory on how to go about this was a bit ferocious and hardly in keeping with the humane customs of the sea.

The first and overriding objective was, of course, to prevent the U-boat crew from scuttling the boat by opening the ballast-tank vents or by setting demolition charges and then jumping overboard. This objective might be achieved, Forbes suggested, by trapping Germans belowdecks, thus forcing them to close the vents or defuse the charges in order to preserve their own lives. The prospective British captors, Forbes went on, should therefore come up to the surfaced U-boat at full speed and open fire with Lewis machine guns at the personnel as they came up through the conning-tower hatch and appeared on the bridge. "The object will be most effectively achieved," Forbes continued callously, "if a body gets jammed in the mouth of the hatch at an early stage." Those Germans already up and clear of the hatch and who did not appear to be taking hostile action were to be spared and captured, except those seen to be throwing papers overboard. Machine gunners should "open immediate and effective fire" on those particular Germans, Forbes said, advancing a policy that was tantamount to murder.

The next step was to put a small, armed party on the deck of the U-boat. The boarding party was to evacuate "all the officers and most of the men" from the U-boat to prevent them from diving the vessel and escaping. The party was to leave "two or three of the crew" belowdecks and keep them there "continuously" under supervision to ensure that no live demolition charges were in place and to get the boat shipshape. If all Germans had already left the boat, "one or more of the crew should be forced to reenter it" for the same purpose.

Frustrated by the lack of successes on the North Atlantic run and believing that he might have overreacted to the British ASW threat, in the waning days of April Dönitz shifted the bulk of the North Atlantic U-boat force eastward toward the British Isles. Late on the afternoon of April 27, Erich Topp in *U-552* found a big target at about 17 degrees west longitude: the 10,100-ton British freighter *Beacon Grange*, sailing alone. Topp attacked submerged, firing all four bow tubes. The ship went down; the crew broadcast the submarine alarm, *SSS*, then took to the lifeboats.

Nine hours later, April 28, Karl-Heinz Moehle in *U-123* found convoy Halifax 121 at about 17 degrees west. It was composed of forty-seven ships and was guarded by nine escorts. The convoy offered the Germans in that area the first opportunity in almost four weeks to mount another pack attack. Dönitz instructed Moehle to shadow and broadcast beacons, so the other boats in the area and Condors from France and Norway could converge.

The British DFed Moehle's shadow reports and warned the convoy commander as well as the commander of convoy Outbound 314, which was passing close
by on a westerly course. The warning helped some. The escorts attempted to drive
Moehle off for good, but he hung on tenaciously, regaining contact at dawn. The
Condors failed to locate the convoy and the escorts forced Moehle off again and he
lost contact, but three other boats made contact with it later in the day.

The convoy commander was fully aware that U-boats were converging, but he
did not expect an attack before dark. Erich Topp in *U-552,* who had submerged
ahead of the convoy, did not wait. In mid-afternoon, he let the lead escorts pass,
then fired at the 8,200-ton British tanker *Capulet.* Some torpedoes hit, wrecking
the ship, but it did not sink. Admiralty intelligence noted later that this was the first
daylight attack by a submerged U-boat on a fully escorted convoy since the summer of 1940. Later, some ASW experts speculated that in view of the strengthened
convoy escort and the coming of short nights, all the U-boats in the northern area
might revert to strictly daylight submerged attacks.

The escorts counterattacked. Two destroyers, *Maori* and *Inglefield,* found *U-
552* on sonar and delivered five depth-charge attacks. These held Topp down for
hours while the convoy proceeded and, as a result, Topp was unable to mount a
second attack. Meanwhile, three escorts from convoy Outbound 314 joined convoy Halifax 121, raising the total escorts to twelve. One of the joining escorts, the
destroyer *Douglas,* attempted to sink the wrecked tanker *Capulet* by gunfire, but
failed, then joined in the U-boat hunt.

After dark Lehmann-Willenbrock in *U-96* broadcast another position report,
then attacked on the surface. In a well-aimed salvo of four bow torpedoes, he sank
three big loaded ships: the 8,500-ton British tanker *Oilfield,* the 9,900-ton Norwegian tanker *Caledonia,* and the 8,900-ton British freighter *Port Hardy.* The *Oilfield*
burst into flames which lit up the scene and forced Lehmann-Willenbrock to dive,
losing an opportunity for a second attack. All three ships, totaling 27,300 tons,
sank.

The twelve escorts hunted relentlessly. The corvette *Gladiolus* got a sonar contact and dropped ten depth charges. Joined by two ex-American four-stack destroyers from convoy Outbound 314, *Leamington* and *Roxborough,* the three ships
carried out four further depth-charge attacks. The other newly arrived escort, the
British destroyer *Douglas,* delivered a punishing depth-charge attack on what
proved to be IXB *U-65,* under a new skipper, Joachim Hoppe, age twenty-six, who
had commanded the boat merely sixteen days and had not yet fired any torpedoes.
The attack destroyed *U-65.* There were no survivors. She was the seventh U-boat
lost in the waters of the Northwest Approaches in as many weeks.

Dönitz made every conceivable effort to mount continuing attacks on Halifax
121 by U-boat and Condor, but the British cleverly routed the convoy away from
the boats and all efforts to find it again failed. In total, four boats had made contact.
Two boats had shot torpedoes which had resulted in the sinking or destruction of
four ships, three of them loaded tankers. That was a blow, but the other forty-three
ships of convoy Halifax 121 reached port safely.

On the day after the attack, April 29, the corvette *Gladiolus* was detached from the convoy to rescue survivors of the freighter *Beacon Grange,* sunk by *U-552* two days earlier. Directed to the lifeboats by a Sunderland, *Gladiolus* picked up forty-one men. After the last man came aboard, *Gladiolus* saw a puff of smoke on the horizon. Racing toward it at full speed, *Gladiolus* spotted the conning tower of a U-boat and what was described as a "kite" flying above the boat. *Gladiolus* came up but the boat (and "kite") disappeared beneath the sea. *Gladiolus* got sonar contact and made three attacks, dropping thirty-one depth charges. These brought up a large air bubble and an inflatable life raft, which, however, sank or disappeared before it could be recovered. *Gladiolus* proudly claimed a kill, but no U-boat was lost on this day.*

During April, 307 loaded ships sailed in convoys from Halifax to the British Isles. German U-boats sank sixteen vessels (five tankers) from these convoys—eleven from Slow Convoy 26, four from convoy Halifax 121, and a small straggler from Halifax 117. Besides that, the oceangoing U-boats sank eleven other ships (one tanker) for about 70,000 tons, which were sailing alone per the new policy that allowed ships of 12 knots or faster to go it alone. Total sinkings by U-boats in the North Atlantic area in April therefore came to twenty-seven.† In return, two U-boats, *U-65* and *U-76,* had been lost. As before, the very great successes of the U-boats in the waters off West Africa tended to obscure the lean convoy hunting on the North Atlantic run.

At this time, Dönitz confronted yet another possible diminution of the Atlantic U-boat force. Berlin war planners suggested that U-boats should be sent to the eastern Mediterranean and Aegean seas to support German ground forces in Greece and North Africa. The boats were to operate against British naval and merchant shipping, which was evacuating British forces from Greece to Crete and to North Africa, and resupplying the British in those places, as well as British forces in Palestine.

Since this suggestion appealed to Hitler and his senior advisers, Admiral Raeder and Dönitz had to mount a major campaign to kill it. Meeting with Hitler on April 20, Raeder argued that the plan was not advisable because, first, it would divert U-boats from the decisive North Atlantic battleground where Dönitz had a total force of but thirty boats, of which barely eight to ten were in the hunting grounds at any given time; second, because the confined Mediterranean was a dangerous place for submarine operations and only the most experienced skippers and crews could be sent there, robbing the North Atlantic force of its most productive boats; and third, because a U-boat base would have to be created in Italy or Yugoslavia, draining scarce submarine technicians from France or Germany.

In place of German boats, Raeder suggested, Berlin should propose to Rome that the Bordeaux-based Italian boats operating unproductively in the Atlantic be

---

* The Admiralty credited *Gladiolus* with sinking Hoppe's *U-65* in this attack, but after further research in the postwar years, the credit was withdrawn and reassigned to the destroyer *Douglas.*

† In addition, the duck *U-147* in British waters and the Italian submarine *Tazzoli* near Gibraltar each sank a freighter. As related, the IXB *U-108,* on a special mission in the Denmark Strait, sank a big auxiliary cruiser.

withdrawn and sent to the eastern Mediterranean. The stenographer recorded that Hitler roundly approved this proposal: "The Führer is in complete agreement with the decision not to send German submarines into the Mediterranean, likewise with the withdrawal of Italian submarines from the Atlantic." When he heard the news, Dönitz rejoiced. But the idea of sending German U-boats to the Mediterranean in support of German ground forces was not as dead as he thought.

By then, as related, four Bordeaux-based Italian submarines had been lost in the North Atlantic, leaving a net force of twenty-three. Most of these now patrolled southward to the Azores or beyond to West African waters. Four medium boats fleeing the Red Sea (via the Cape of Good Hope) were to join the Bordeaux force in May. Under the recall plan, ten boats were to commence the return to Italy in June. In nine months of operations to May 1, 1941, all Atlantic-based Italian submarines had positively sunk thirty-three ships (including five neutrals and a ship shared with *U-38* and a ship shared with *U-107*), and had severely damaged the Canadian destroyer *Saguenay*.*

The U-boat campaign in the decisive North Atlantic area in the winter of 1940–1941 fell well short of what the Germans had expected. The U-boats sailing to that area in the five months from December 1 to May 1 sank only about 125 merchant ships for about 752,658 tons. This was an average of about 150,500 tons a month, sharply less than the monthly average attained in the "Happy Time," May through November, 1940. Patrols to the South Atlantic area raised the total sinkings substantially, disguising the declining results in the north. The patrols to the south added about sixty-five ships for about 364,215 tons, raising the total of sinkings by all U-boats sailing in that five-month period to 194 ships for about 1.1 million tons. British shipyards in that same period produced less than half that tonnage, but the total loss was more than made up by the return to service of nearly 1 million gross tons of damaged shipping that had been idled in British shipyards.

London continued to bemoan loudly the loss of tankers but in fact, the tanker losses in that five months were not overwhelming: twenty-seven ships for about 231,500 tons. Twenty-three of these tankers were lost in the North Atlantic; four in the South Atlantic. Of the total, twenty were British-owned; six were foreign ships on charter, and one was the Vichy French *Rhone,* sunk in error. Owing to the construction of new tankers in British yards,† and to various Lend-Lease measures to supply American and foreign tankers to the British, and to the participation of American ships in the Caribbean–East Coast "shuttle," the oft-predicted oil crisis in the British Isles did not yet occur, according to the official British oil historian, D. J. Payton-Smith.

---

* The Italians commenced withdrawing submarines from the North Atlantic in May. The high scorer was Primo Longobardo in *Torelli,* who sank four confirmed ships for 17,489 tons. Second was Adalberto Giovannini in *Bianchi,* with three confirmed ships for 14,705 tons. The four boats lost in the North Atlantic were *Tarantini, Marcello, Faa Di Bruno,* and *Nani.*

† Eight for 77,000 tons in the last quarter of 1940 and first quarter of 1941.

It was not yet apparent, but by the end of April 1941, the Battle of the Atlantic in northern waters had turned slightly in favor of the British, at least for the nonce. Under operational control of the Admiralty, Coastal Command had built air bases in Iceland and the Faeroes, extending daytime air escort of inbound and outbound convoys ever westward. No Coastal Command aircraft had yet sunk a U-boat unassisted, but the increased air coverage gave warning of U-boats to the convoy surface escorts, drove the U-boats off, and held them down, frustrating shadowers and the assembly of packs. The Escort Groups shuttling between the British Isles and Iceland, and those based at Iceland, likewise presented a menacing obstacle. With increasing numbers of escorts available, it was now possible to detach one or more warships to hunt and drive off the convoy shadower and to counterattack and hold down the attacking U-boats, preventing a second attack while the convoy evasively altered course. Inasmuch as U-boats avoided rather than attacked enemy air and surface escorts, with each passing month the escort crews gained more experience and skill in U-boat hunting, while the experience and skill of the U-boat crews declined, a trend that was certain to continue unless the Germans found some means of attacking the escorts.

More difficulties lay ahead for the U-boats. The British had penetrated naval Enigma. Should the Admiralty's other planned captures succeed, Bletchley Park, employing increased numbers of Turing-Welchman bombes, stood a good chance of a really decisive break into naval Enigma. The number of primitive (but useful) 1.5-meter-wavelength radar sets in Coastal Command aircraft and surface escorts was steadily increasing. New electronic devices were nearly ready for mass production: the greatly improved centimetric-wavelength radar for aircraft and surface vessels, employing the Randall and Boot cavity magnetron; miniaturized High Frequency Direction Finding (HF/DF, or Huff Duff) sets, suitable for installation on convoy vessels, enabling them to home on high-frequency radio transmissions from nearby U-boats*; and greatly improved radio gear for communications between the surface escorts (Talk Between Ships, or TBS) and between the surface escorts and air escorts, the latter an important advance usually overlooked in accounts of the U-boat war.

Week by week the United States had become more deeply involved in the Battle of the Atlantic. In addition to the measures already described, on April 18 Atlantic Fleet commander Ernest King grandly declared that the waters of the "Western Hemisphere," for which he was responsible, now extended eastward to approximately 26 degrees west longitude (a line just west of Iceland and south to the Azores) and stated in effect that any transgression of that line by the Axis powers would be viewed as "unfriendly."

---

* U-boats radioed contact and shadow reports to Kerneval using high-frequency bands. If Kerneval so ordered, the shadowers "homed" other boats to the local scene in medium frequencies. To prevent a pack attack, convoy escorts had to react to the high-frequency contact and shadow reports because the local "homing" signals came too late in the game. Inclusion of Huff Duff on escort ships presented a problem, however, because ships with surface-search radar could not accommodate both, and no ship wanted to leave radar behind. As a result, most Huff Duff was to be installed on convoy rescue ships and fighter catapult ships, and later on jeep carriers.

In response to requests (read directives) from London, the Canadians, too, were poised to enter the Battle of the Atlantic for the first time in an important way. Pending the arrival of the destroyers of the American Support Force, the Canadians were to assume responsibility for convoy escort in Atlantic home waters and out to 35 degrees west, where the spliced-in Iceland-based British escort groups took over the convoys. For this purpose, the Canadians established the Newfoundland Escort Force, some thirty-eight warships,* commanded by a Canadian, L. W. Murray, based at St. John's. It was supported by twenty-four American-built aircraft in two squadrons of the Canadian Eastern Air Command.†

Since improved British ASW measures in the Northwest Approaches made it necessary to again operate the Type VIIs ever farther westward, incurring the penalties imposed by fuel limitations, Dönitz needed far more U-boats to regain the upper hand than he or anyone had ever envisioned. Not just 300, but perhaps twice that number. U-boat production was increasing dramatically: Forty-three new boats were commissioned in the four-month period January–April 1941,‡ but owing to the usual four months required for workup, these were not to reach the Atlantic in substantial numbers until June and beyond. Even assuming modest combat losses and a maximum production rate, rising to twenty or more boats per month in the second half of 1941, by the beginning of 1942 Dönitz could expect to have no more than about 100 oceangoing boats of all types for Atlantic operations.

Given the accelerating rate of aircraft, escort, and ship production in Great Britain, Canada, and the United States, the late-starting and lagging U-boat production, and ever-declining experience levels of U-boat crews, Dönitz was to be hard-pressed to regain the upper hand in the Battle of the Atlantic by 1943 or ever. And yet there was not the slightest sense of defeat among the staff at Kerneval. Even discounting the skipper overclaims, it was clear that the small U-boat arm was causing terror and significant harm to British maritime assets and forcing a great expenditure of Allied resources to counter the threat. Convoying alone—as Churchill repeatedly lamented—had reduced Great Britain's imports by "one-third." It was not actually that bad, but bad enough.

---

* Thirteen destroyers (six Canadian, seven British), four British sloops, and twenty-one corvettes (seventeen Canadian, four British).

† Squadron 10 at Gander with fifteen Digbys, the Canadian version of the USAAF B-18 twin-engine bomber; Squadron 116 at Dartmouth, Nova Scotia, with nine ex-British Catalinas, which the Canadians called Cansos. At this time there were eighteen U.S. Navy Catalinas at Argentia and six USAF B-18s at Gander available, for reconaissance but, of course, not overt combat. The Catalinas had an effective range of 600 miles, the B-18s 350 miles.

‡ Eight boats in January, eight in February, thirteen in March, and fourteen in April. However, seven new boats were held in the Baltic for R&D or for repairs or for duty with the Training Command. So great were the demands of the Training Command that eight submarines captured from the Allies were commissioned for training purposes: H.M.S. *Seal,* the Norwegian *B-5* and *B-6,* the Dutch *O-8, O-12, O-25, O-26,* and *O-27.*

FIVE

Flower Petals of Rare Beauty

The diversion of German military power to the Balkans to rescue the Italians and for the conquest of the Hellenic Peninsula and Crete delayed Barbarossa, the German invasion of the Soviet Union, by about five weeks. Hitler set a new D day, June 22. Although it was late in the year to launch this immense military operation, he was confident that the ragtag Red Army would collapse before the onset of winter.

After that, he would deal with Great Britain. In the meantime, the *Kriegsmarine* was to continue pressure on the British, tying down naval and air forces and blocking any and all British attempts to assist the Soviets, such as another invasion of Norway. All U-boats and merchant-ship raiders were to take special pains to avoid any "incident" with the United States that might provoke Washington to open intervention during Barbarossa.

Commencing in late May 1941, newly commissioned Type VII U-boats departed the Baltic for battlefronts in ever increasing numbers: twelve in June, nine in July, twelve in August. This was a far cry from the "twenty-five to thirty" new U-boats per month envisioned in the construction programs of 1939 but double or triple the usual monthly rate of new arrivals in the Atlantic, and therefore the first significant increase in force levels since the onset of war. Owing to the slight battle losses incurred from December 1940 to May 1, 1941 (seven), and to a continuation of that modest trend through the summer months, Dönitz had the means not only to intensify the U-boat war in the "decisive" North Atlantic arena, but also to send another wave of Type IXs to the promising waters of West Africa.

Nineteen U-boats sailed to the North Atlantic in May. The first, *U-94,* a VIIC commanded by Herbert Kuppisch, reported a convoy south of Iceland on May 7. This was Outbound 318, which had sailed from the British Isles with thirty-eight ships. It was heavily guarded by Escort Group 7, commanded by I. H. Bockett-Pugh, composed of ten warships: three destroyers (including the ex-American four-stacks *Campbeltown* and *Newmarket*), five corvettes, a sloop, and an ASW trawler. Coastal Command aircraft from Iceland and Scotland provided air cover. Per plan, three ships had left the convoy earlier that day to put into Iceland. Five other ships, including the 10,000-ton liner *Ranpura,* an armed merchant cruiser, had joined, making a total of forty ships.

At the time Kuppisch detected the convoy, a complicated change-up in the escort for Outbound 318 was in progress. Escort Group 3, commanded by Addison Joe Baker-Cresswell, had sailed from Iceland to relieve Bockett-Pugh's Escort Group 7 for the middle leg of the trip. Composed of nine warships (three destroyers, three corvettes, three ASW trawlers), Escort Group 3 had in company the auxiliary cruiser *Ranpura* and four freighters that were also en route from Iceland to join Outbound 318. To assure a safe changeover of the escort groups, the sloop *Rochester* and five corvettes of Bockett-Pugh's Escort Group 7 were to remain with the convoy for an extra twenty-four hours before going to other duties. Hence there were fifteen warships in the vicinity of Outbound 318.

It was a bright moonlit night and, after broadcasting the convoy contact, Kuppisch elected to attack submerged. He let the lead escorts pass and gained a position in the middle of the convoy, "between two 10,000-ton liners," probably the British ships *Ranpura* and *Ixion.* He then fired four torpedoes into the columns of ships. He claimed sinking four vessels for 20,000 tons, but actually only two sank: the 10,300-ton *Ixion* and a 5,700-ton Norwegian freighter. The flagship of Escort Group 3, the destroyer *Bulldog,* joined by the destroyer *Amazon* and the Escort Group 7 sloop *Rochester,* pounced on *U-94* and, during four hours, dropped eighty-nine depth charges, "a severe and accurate counterattack," Kuppisch logged, "which caused considerable damage." The counterattack prevented a second attack by *U-94,* but Kuppisch repaired the damage and continued his patrol.

Acting on Kuppisch's contact report, Dönitz alerted six other boats that were patrolling west of Iceland. Two boats found the convoy in bright moonlight during the night of May 8: Fritz-Julius Lemp in *U-110,* from Lorient on its second patrol, and the new VIIC *U-201,* commanded by Adalbert ("Adi") Schnee, who began the war as first watch officer of Kretschmer's *U-23* and later commanded the ducks *U-6* and *U-60.* Lemp had been on patrol three weeks and had sunk one 2,500-ton freighter. Sailing from Bergen, Schnee had been on patrol one week. He had polished off the abandoned hulk of the tanker *Capulet* (wrecked by Topp in *U-552*) and possibly a 2,000-ton steamer.

Lemp and Schnee met on the morning of May 9, ahead of the convoy, which at that time had no air cover. Since a bright moon was expected again that night, they agreed that a surface attack would be dangerous. And since they assumed that by then the escorts had left the convoy, the two skippers (communicating by signal flags) elected to attack submerged in daylight as soon as possible, to avoid the possibility of losing the convoy. The senior man (and *Ritterkreuz* holder) Lemp was to go first; Schnee was to attack half an hour later, after the convoy had been thrown into confusion by Lemp's attack.

Lemp submerged and let the convoy come on. Surprised to see the escorts, he nonetheless decided to continue with the attack. At about noon, he hit the convoy's right flank, setting up on four different ships, three of which he believed he sank. In actuality, two British freighters, the 5,000-ton *Esmond* and the 2,600-ton *Bengore Head,* went down. The fourth torpedo misfired, but after it had been readjusted, Lemp prepared to shoot at a tanker. The convoy executed an emergency turn to port and when Schnee attacked about thirty minutes later, he shot into what was then the rear of the formation. He hit two 5,900-ton freighters, the *Gregalia,* which sank, and the *Empire Cloud,* which was severely damaged and abandoned, but later salvaged and towed to Scotland.

At the time of these attacks, the convoy was guarded by the nine warships of Baker-Cresswell's Iceland-based Escort Group 3. The flagship, the destroyer *Bulldog,* along with the ex-American four-stack destroyer *Broadway* and one of the three corvettes, *Aubrietia,* hunted *U-110,* which was still at periscope depth, preparing to shoot at the tanker. All three escorts obtained firm sonar contacts. *Broadway* attacked, dropping a single depth charge. Seeing Lemp's periscope, *Aubrietia,* commanded by V. F. Smith, attacked it twice, dropping sixteen well-placed depth charges set for 100 and 200 feet.

The depth charges from *Aubrietia* fell very close to *U-110.* The blasts smashed the diving gauges and other instruments, knocked out the electric motors, diving planes, rudder, and compass, ruptured an aft fuel or ballast tank, sheared off the high-pressure air valves in the control room, and generated chlorine gas in the forward battery. Flooding aft, the boat went out of control and slid stern first to 300 feet. Seeing that *U-110* was beyond all hope, Lemp ordered the engineer to "prepare for emergency blow," which would bring them up. But before he could give the order, Lemp and the crew felt an "unexpected rocking motion," indicating that the boat had surfaced of its own accord, perhaps owing to a rupture in a high-pressure air line, which blew the ballast tanks.

Lemp rushed to the bridge to find a terrifying sight: *Bulldog, Broadway,* and *Aubrietia* close at hand, all firing at *U-110* with every available weapon. *Bulldog* and *Broadway* were coming in at full speed to ram. Lemp shouted: "All hands abandon ship as fast as possible!" There was no time to connect the detonation charges for scuttling. The fastest way to scuttle was to open the ballast-tank vents. The first watch officer, Dietrich Loewe, who was in the control room with the engineer, Hans-Joachim Eichelborn, remembered that Lemp next shouted: "Open the vents" and that Eichelborn did so. But something went wrong. Either Eichelborn failed to carry out the order or the controls malfunctioned. The vents remained closed.

There were forty-seven men on board *U-110.* In response to the cry "abandon ship," all hands rushed pell-mell to the bridge in such haste that the radio operator did not take time to destroy or bring the Enigma and code materials with him, and a war correspondent, Helmut Ecke, left behind his still and movie cameras and film. Climbing down on deck through murderous British gunfire, the men dived over the side into the icy water. Loewe remembered that although two men had been wounded, all hands got away from the boat "alive" and that he and Lemp and Eichelborn were the last to leave the bridge. They did not do so, he said, until the water was "one meter above the base of the conning tower" and they were certain that *U-110* was going down.

Coming in to ram with all weapons blazing, the Escort Group commander, Baker-Cresswell in *Bulldog,* noted that *U-110* was down by the stern but did not appear to be sinking. Believing he might get a boarding party on her or even capture the boat, he ordered full-speed astern to cancel the ramming and in the same breath summoned the boarding party. At about the same time T. Taylor, skipper of *Broadway,* got the same idea and also canceled his ramming. To panic the German crew, hasten the evacuation of the boat, and thereby possibly prevent scuttling, Taylor came right up to *U-110*'s bow and dropped two shallow-set depth charges. In the process, however, *Broadway* fouled *U-110*'s bow plane, which cut a deep gash in the destroyer's thin side plating (flooding ten oil tanks and the forward magazine) and damaged the port propeller. The terrific blast of *Broadway*'s two depth charges may well have caused panic inside *U-110* and added momentum to an already frenzied evacuation.

Exactly what transpired in the next few minutes is a matter of lasting controversy. Loewe stated that after he and Lemp were in the water, they saw the bow and conning tower of *U-110* lift "high out of the water," indicating that she had not sunk! "Let's swim back on board ship," Lemp yelled, according to Loewe. Lemp's apparent aim was to open the vents or set off the demolition charges to assure scuttling or, perhaps, at least to throw the Enigma and coding materials over the side. But *U-110* had drifted off too far; they could not return to the boat. They turned around, Loewe said, and swam toward *Bulldog,* which was lowering a whaler manned by a heavily armed boarding party.

At this point, Lemp disappeared from the scene. Some German submarine veterans, most recently Peter Hansen, insist that the boarding party, en route to *U-110* in the whaler, spotted Lemp in the water and that one of the members of the party "promptly shot" him to prevent any interference with the mission and to conceal the fact that the British boarded *U-110.* (The correspondent, Helmut Ecke, claimed that the British shot at him while he was in the water.) Others say that Lemp threw up his arms in despair and disappeared beneath the waves, an apparent suicide. The Admiralty has said only that Lemp and fourteen enlisted men died in the sinking.*

Intent on raiding or capturing *U-110,* Baker-Cresswell in *Bulldog* and Taylor in *Broadway* made no effort to fish the Germans from the icy waters. Smith in *Aubrietia,* who had temporarily lost his sonar, hauled out of the area to make repairs. While doing so, he rescued forty-nine survivors from the lifeboats of the freighter *Esmond,* sunk by Lemp. The Germans were left to fend for themselves for

---

* Lemp was the fifth *Ritterkreuz* holder to fall in combat, after Jenisch, Prien, Schepke, and Kretschmer. Lemp's confirmed score on *U-30* and *U-110* was seventeen ships for 91,277 tons.

about two hours. Many died of wounds, hypothermia, and shock, or drifted out of sight.

The boarding party from *Bulldog,* commanded by twenty-year-old Sub-Lieutenant David E. Balme, rowed the whaler right up on the forward deck of *U-110.* Carrying rifles and pistols, the nine men jumped out and spread around the deck and bridge to shoot any Germans who might attempt to interfere with the mission. To Balme's astonishment, both the conning-tower and control-room hatches were dogged shut, not what one would expect of a scuttling U-boat. Pistol drawn, he opened the hatches, expecting to confront crewmen below. But the boat was deserted. All hands had abandoned ship. All the lights were on, burning brightly; there was no sign of flooding or any indication of chlorine gas.

After a hurried inspection, Balme signaled Baker-Cresswell on *Bulldog* that the U-boat appeared to be "seaworthy and towable" and requested that he send an engineering party to operate *U-110*'s machinery. Baker-Cresswell directed Taylor on *Broadway* to send an engineer to *U-110* via whaler, then eased *Bulldog* close to *U-110* to receive an old, rusty 2" steel cable that two of Balme's men had found in a topside locker on the U-boat.

Meanwhile, belowdecks, Balme and the other six members of his party were collecting intelligence items of incalculable value. Balme described that work in a secret report to the Admiralty. In part:

> The U-boat had obviously been abandoned in great haste as books and gear were strewn about the place. A chain of men was formed to pass up all books, charts, etc. As speed was essential owing to the possibility of the U-boat sinking (although dry throughout) I gave orders to send *all* books, except obviously reading books, so consequently a number of comparatively useless navigational books, etc., were recovered. All charts were in drawers under the chart table in the control room; there were also some signal books, log books, etc. here. . . . Meanwhile the telegraphist* went to the W/T [radio] office just forward of the control room on the starboard side. This was in perfect condition, apparently no attempt having been made to destroy any books or apparatus. Here were found C.B.s [codebooks], Signal Logs, pay books, and general correspondence, looking as if this room had been used as a ship's office. Also the coding machine [Enigma] was found here, plugged in as though in actual use when abandoned. The general appearance of this machine being that of a typewriter, the telegraphist pressed the keys and finding results peculiar, sent it up the hatch.

The convoy, meanwhile, had pressed on, guarded by the destroyer *Amazon,* two corvettes, and two ASW trawlers. *Amazon* got a sonar contact on Schnee's *U-201* and called in the corvette *Nigella* and the trawler *St. Apollo.* The three vessels fixed *U-201* on sonar and pounded her with depth charges for about four hours. Schnee and his men counted ninety-nine explosions. Some of these caused extensive damage to *U-201,* including a serious leak in an external fuel-oil tank,

---

* Alan Osborne Long.

which helped the escorts track the boat. Finally, Schnee got away—without again having seen *U-110*. That night he reported his successes and battle damage to Kerneval, adding that since he had seven torpedoes left, he would make every effort to repair the leak and continue the patrol. And he did.

Left far behind with *U-110*, Baker-Cresswell in *Bulldog* believed he had a good chance of towing the boat to Iceland. He finally got the 2" steel cable from *U-110* and attached it to his own ship. Upon boarding the boat, the engineering party from *Broadway*, led by G. E. Dodds, found her to be fully "intact," with a "negligible quantity of water in the bilges." However, there were two problems: the port shaft of *U-110* was turning over slowly, and there was a "slight bubbling noise" aft. Unable to read German, Dodds could not stop the port electric motor or start the starboard motor to equalize the forward motion. He attributed the "bubbling noise" to a leaking ballast- or fuel-tank vent, perhaps damaged by the depth charges. Unfamiliar with submarines, he could not blow that tank. If the venting continued, the tank would flood completely, taking *U-110* down by the stern.

Meanwhile, *Aubrietia* returned to the scene and commenced fishing the Germans from the water. Altogether she rescued thirty-four men, including the first watch officer, Loewe, the engineer Eichelborn, the second watch officer Ulrich Wehrhrofer, and the war correspondent Ecke. All the Germans were hurried belowdecks to distance them from the angry survivors of *Esmond* and to conceal from them the boarding of *U-110*. Two Germans died on board *Aubrietia*, leaving a net bag of thirty-two prisoners.

As *Aubrietia* was pulling the last German on board, *Bulldog* reported a firm sonar contact. Baker-Cresswell cast loose the steel towing cable and called up the damaged *Broadway* and the *Aubrietia*. The three vessels attacked the contact for an hour and a half, dropping thirty-two depth charges, and causing some anxious moments for the British boarding parties inside *U-110*. However, no evidence of a kill could be found and later this contact was classified as "doubtful." The hunt was terminated and the salvaging of *U-110* resumed. To conceal the capture of the U-boat from the survivors of *Esmond* and *U-110*, Baker-Cresswell ordered *Aubrietia* to leave the area and find the destroyer *Amazon*, and transfer all survivors and prisoners to her.

Baker-Cresswell in *Bulldog* reattached the old, rusty steel cable to *U-110*, which by then was heavily down by the stern. Having been aboard *U-110* for about five hours and having ransacked her of everything useful and interesting (including six sextants and ten pairs of Zeiss binoculars, Ecke's cameras, and Lemp's *Ritterkreuz*), Balme's boarding party—and engineer Dodds's party from *Broadway*—closed all watertight doors, dogged down all hatches, and returned to their ships. Escorted by the damaged *Broadway*, *Bulldog* headed for Iceland—400 miles distant—towing the yawing *U-110* at a speed of 6 knots. All went well for about seventeen hours—about 100 miles—but at 11:00 the following morning, March 10, *U-110* suddenly upended and sank, "her bow standing vertically out of the water." The loss, Baker-Cresswell wrote, was a "bitter blow."

In the dark of that same morning, March 10, far to the west, a new VIIC, *U-556*, commanded by Herbert Wohlfarth, from the ducks *U-14* and *U-137*, caught up with the convoy.* Wohlfarth attacked on the surface, firing two torpedoes at two different ships. He claimed both ships sank, but in fact, he had hit only one, for damage. The convoy dispersed, but Wohlfarth hung on looking for strays, and later that day, attacking submerged, he torpedoed and sank a 4,900-ton British freighter. Still later he stopped a 5,100-ton Belgian freighter with one torpedo and finished her off with his deck gun.

Based on flash reports from three of the boats and from distress calls picked up by *B-dienst,* Dönitz concluded that the four boats which had attacked convoy Outbound 318 had sunk thirteen ships for 76,248 tons. The confirmed result was about half the claim, seven ships sunk for 39,255 tons: two by Kuppisch in *U-94;* two by Lemp in *U-110;* two by Wohlfarth in *U-556;* and one by Schnee in *U-201.* As a result of these and past overclaims and credits, Kuppisch and Wohlfarth were awarded the *Ritterkreuz.†*

Baker-Cresswell in *Bulldog* reached Iceland late on March 10. He transferred the thirty-two German prisoners from *Amazon* to *Bulldog* and the next day set off for Scapa Flow, making 25 knots to avoid any possibility of a U-boat attack. En route he talked individually and cagily with the three German officers and the correspondent Ecke, to see if any of them had an inkling that *U-110* had been boarded or taken in tow. Apparently none did. Nor did any of the enlisted men, who were canvassed in a similar manner by the crewmen of *Bulldog.* Since some of the Germans had seen *Bulldog* launch the whaler with the boarding party, Baker-Cresswell and his crew put about a "cover story" that *U-110* had "sunk" before it could be boarded.‡

The intelligence haul from *U-110,* which filled "two packing crates," was eye-popping and historic: a working naval Enigma, the keys for *Heimisch* (the Home Waters or Dolphin code) for April and June,§ the keys to the double-enciphered *Offizierte* (Officers-Only) code, a book containing the *Kurzsignale* (Short Signal)

---

* En route to the Atlantic, Wohlfarth attacked by gun and sank the unarmed 166-ton Faeroe fishing schooner *Emanual.* His gunfire killed three of the eight fishermen. Later in a Berlin radio address, he described how he set the schooner ablaze: "a most beautiful sight to see." The British characterized this attack as a "revolting incident" and cold-blooded "murder" but did not introduce the affair at Dönitz's trial at Nuremberg.

† Kuppisch's confirmed sinkings on the duck *U-58* and on *U-94* were seventeen ships for 87,282 tons. Wohlfarth's confirmed sinkings on the ducks *U-14* and *U-137* and the VIIC *U-556* were nineteen ships for 47,919 tons, including the fishing schooner *Emanual.*

‡ The crews of *Bulldog, Broadway,* and *Aubrietia,* as well as the rescued crew of *Esmond* on board *Aubrietia,* who had witnessed or participated in the boarding of *U-110,* in total some 400 men, were sworn to secrecy. Remarkably, no word of the boarding leaked. An account of it was not officially released by the Admiralty until 1959, when the official naval historian Stephen Roskill published a slim book, *The Secret Capture.*

§ The current *Heimisch* keys for May, printed on water-soluble paper, had apparently been destroyed by the Germans or possibly lost or ruined during the transfer to *Bulldog.* Hence it was not possible for Bletchley Park to read *Heimisch* currently until June. Duplicate *Heimisch* keys for June were obtained when, in a well-planned action, a British naval task force captured the 300-ton German weather-reporting trawler *München* on May 7.

code, and *Kriegsmarine* grid charts, as well as special charts showing the safe routes through German minefields in the North Sea and along the French coast, decoded U-boat traffic (in *Heimisch*) for the period April 15–May 9, administrative correspondence, a complete set of technical manuals and diagrams of all the Type IXB fuel, air, hydraulic and other systems, and hundreds of mundane items, down to the citation for the award of the Iron Cross Second Class to the engineer, Eichelborn. After he had been briefed on the haul, First Sea Lord Dudley Pound telexed Baker-Cresswell, who had codenamed the boarding Operation Primrose: "Hearty congratulations. The petals of your flower are of rare beauty."

The Admiralty showered praise and awards on all those concerned with the victory over *U-110*. Pound immediately promoted Baker-Cresswell from commander to captain. In a special ceremony at Buckingham Palace, King George VI appointed Baker-Cresswell and the *Aubrietia* captain, Smith, Companions of the Distinguished Service Order (DSO). He awarded Balme, Dodds, and the captain of *Broadway,* Taylor, the Distinguished Service Cross (DSC). Three others received the Distinguished Service Medal (DSM) and fourteen officers and men were "Mentioned in Dispatches." When the King gave Dodds his DSC, the official naval historian wrote, the King told Dodds the operation "was perhaps the most important single event in the whole war at sea."

Although British intelligence officers stressed to the German prisoners the cover story that *U-110* had sunk before it could be boarded, the first watch officer, Loewe, was not fully convinced. He remembered that he had talked to six of the *U-110* crewmen on *Amazon* or *Bulldog* and that "none" had actually seen the boat sink. Loewe's suspicions were fully aroused when the British gave the engineer, Eichelborn, the citation for his Iron Cross Second Class, which, Eichelborn believed, he had possibly left "in a folder in the control room." If so, the British had certainly boarded *U-110*. Loewe remembered that he then discussed the matter with the senior German POWs, Otto Kretschmer and Hans Jenisch, and that it was decided that Loewe should inform Dönitz.

Before the war, Dönitz had adopted a coding system which officer POWs could incorporate in letters to their families. It was a duplication of a World War I submarine POW code, in which the arrangement of the first letters of certain words stood for the dots and dashes of Morse code. The families were under instructions to forward all POW mail to Dönitz, who would examine the letters for important encoded information, such as the cause of the loss of the boat, torpedo failures, and so on.

The British had broken this relatively simple code in World War I and were not surprised when it resurfaced in World War II. Hence they "read" all encoded information going back to Dönitz. From this flow of encoded mail, they gleaned inside information not otherwise revealed, some of it quite useful. They also used the mail code as a channel to funnel "disinformation" to Dönitz and for other purposes.

Very likely the British returned Eichelborn's medal citation to test if the cover story on *U-110* was working among the Germans. That is, to provoke a reaction of some kind that would indicate what the Germans really knew. Falling for this gambit, Loewe encoded a letter to his family for Dönitz, employing the prearranged designation for *U-110,* which was U-E-O. In his letter Loewe encoded the message: "Suspicion U-E-O in enemy hands." The British, of course, confiscated this letter and intensified efforts to persuade the *U-110* survivors that the boat had not been boarded.*

Unaware of what had transpired on *U-110,* Lemp died a hero in German eyes and, as was customary, Dönitz named a barracks in his honor in Lorient. But when the true story of what had happened gradually emerged in the postwar years, some German U-boat veterans were outraged. One, Peter Hansen, wrote that Lemp's "irresponsible disregard of the standing orders to destroy all secret matters is directly responsible that [sic] thousands of U-boat men died needlessly and hundreds of U-boats were destroyed also as a consequence. While the radio shack staff and officers were also partially responsible for this disaster, the principal culprit was Fritz-Julius Lemp himself. If the English did not shoot Lemp, then he should have been put up against a wall by the Germans for his irresponsibility and neglection of duty."

Harsh words, these, but the thrust is correct. Lemp had a duty to protect Enigma at all costs, including, if necessary, his life. He should not have left *U-110* until he was certain beyond any doubt that she was going down—and going down fast. In the final line of his secret report on the boarding, David Balme posed a key question with all words of it capitalized for emphasis. If *U-110* was properly rigged for scuttling, he wrote, "WHY WERE BOTH CONNING TOWER HATCHES CLOSED?"

Altogether the U-boats sank seven empty freighters for about 40,000 tons from convoy Outbound 318 and damaged two other freighters, both of which made port. But after that battle, the boats in the North Atlantic were again hard-pressed to find targets. Between May 10 and May 20, they sank only four ships. The most notable of these was the 10,500-ton auxiliary cruiser *Salopian,* by Robert Gysae in *U-98;* the least notable was a 500-ton French sailing ship gunned under by Wolfgang Lüth in the old Type IX *U-43,* which had sunk at dockside in Lorient in early February and was finally back in action. Returning to Lorient after a thirty-two-day patrol, *Ritterkreuz* holder Karl-Heinz Moehle in *U-123* reported sinking merely one

---

* The British continued to work on Loewe to an extraordinary degree. Later, in April 1942, when he was transferred to a POW camp in Canada, the British arranged that he meet another *U-110* survivor, who told him: "I know that two men saw the ship go down." This prompted another encoded letter from Loewe to Dönitz amending the first: "U-E-O was sunk. It is possible that the enemy was aboard at one time." Still later, in February 1944, the British arranged for Loewe to meet yet another *U-110* crewman, who told him that the British boarded *U-110* topside and rigged a towing hawser but did not get inside and the boat "sank vertically, stern first." This prompted another message from Loewe to Dönitz in April 1944: "Submarine sunk. Enemy did not get inside submarine." Having finally persuaded Loewe to accept the cover story by these artifices, the British let that message pass, and furthermore, they returned Loewe to Germany in a POW swap, so that he could tell Dönitz face-to-face that the *U-110* had sunk, that the British did not get inside *U-110,* and that therefore, Enigma had not been compromised.

ship (in April). Judging that Moehle had "health" problems, Dönitz relieved him of command and sent him to the Training Command.*

In search of convoys beyond reach of Iceland-based air and surface escorts, Dönitz moved the bulk of the boats ever westward. By May 19, nine patrolled a line at 41 degrees west, directly south of Greenland. Late that afternoon, Herbert Kuppisch in *U-94*—who had earlier found convoy Outbound 318 and won a *Ritterkreuz*—intercepted convoy Halifax 126, escorted by only one auxiliary cruiser. Upon receiving the report, Dönitz instructed Kuppisch to shadow and withhold attack until the other boats came up.

Commencing at 0400, May 20, the boats struck, Kuppisch first. He fired two torpedoes at one target but both missed. Speeding onward into the center of the convoy, the torpedoes hit two other ships, both of which sank. Later that afternoon Kuppisch sank a 6,100-ton Norwegian tanker, *John P. Pedersen.*

Five other boats had successes. Herbert Wohlfarth in *U-556,* still on his first patrol, sank the 8,500-ton tanker *British Security* and a 5,000-ton freighter, and damaged a 13,000-ton British tanker. Hans-Georg Fischer in a new IXB, *U-109,* sank a 7,400-ton freighter. Wilhelm Kleinschmidt in another new IXB, *U-111,* sank a 6,000-ton freighter. Robert Gysae in *U-98* sank a 5,400-ton freighter and damaged another. Claus Korth in *U-93* wrecked and set on fire the 6,200-ton tanker *Elusa.* Counting past overclaims, the sinking earned Korth a *Ritterkreuz.*†

Upon receiving the first distress call from the convoy, the Iceland-based Escort Group 12, commanded by C. D. Howard-Johnston, raced west. Consisting of eleven warships (five destroyers, four corvettes, two ASW trawlers), it arrived to find the convoy dispersed and utterly disorganized. Howard-Johnston, in the destroyer *Malcolm,* deployed the escort group to round up the scattered ships and reform them into a convoy.

One of the corvettes, *Verbena,* commanded by Denys Arthur Raynor, was ordered to tow the smoldering hulk of the tanker *Elusa* to Iceland, if at all possible. Closing on the hulk, Raynor was astonished to see a U-boat on the surface also approaching *Elusa.* Giving the alarm, *Verbena* opened fire, forcing the boat to dive. Upon reaching the site of the dive, *Verbena* dropped five depth charges, while the ex-American four-stack destroyer *Churchill* came up to assist. Both ships got a firm sonar contact and both conducted repeated depth-charge attacks. The records are not clear, but the U-boat was probably Eitel-Friedrich Kentrat's *U-74,* fresh from France. At this time Kentrat reported such "heavy" depth-charge damage that he was forced to abort to Lorient.

When Dönitz learned from one of the U-boats that "five destroyers" had come up to escort the convoy, he ordered all boats to break off the attack and reform a patrol line farther south. He left one boat in northern waters, Kleinschmidt's new *U-111,* to transmit a series of "dummy" radio messages, designed to make the British think the pack was still stalking convoy Halifax 126 eastward and trick

---

* Moehle had sunk 19½ confirmed ships for 84,301 tons on the duck *U-20* and the IXB *U-123.*

† Korth's confirmed sinkings on the duck *U-57* and the VII *U-93* were 16½ ships for 76,782 tons.

them into routing the next convoy south, into the arms of the reformed patrol line. This was the first known instance in which Dönitz employed "radio deception." While carrying out the deception on May 22, Kleinschmidt encountered and sank a 4,800-ton freighter sailing alone. Based on flash reports from the boats, Dönitz concluded that the pack had dealt convoy Halifax 126 a severe blow: nine ships sunk for 71,484 tons. He was correct. The six boats had sunk nine ships, but, as usual, the tonnage was inflated. The confirmed total was 54,451 tons sunk, including the tanker *Elusa,* which could not be salvaged, and the other two tankers, plus damage to another tanker.

"Sink the *Bismarck*"

U-boat operations in the North Atlantic were interrupted on May 22 by the most dramatic event in the naval war to that time: the Atlantic sortie of the super battleship *Bismarck.*

Accompanied by the new heavy cruiser *Prinz Eugen, Bismarck* sailed from Kiel in the early hours of May 19. Bletchley Park could not read naval Enigma on a current basis in May; thus the Admiralty had no advance warning from that source. But the British naval attaché in Stockholm learned of the sortie on the night of May 20 and alerted the Admiralty. The next day, British reconnaissance planes spotted the two ships near Bergen. Bletchley Park broke an old (April) Enigma message which stated that *Bismarck* had taken on board "five prize crews" and "appropriate charts," which led the Admiralty to believe, correctly, that *Bismarck* and *Prinz Eugen* were embarked on a convoy-raiding sortie in the North Atlantic. When he got the news, Winston Churchill gave a simple—but legendary—order: "Sink the *Bismarck!*" All available capital ships of the Home Fleet and Force H from Gibraltar put to sea.

Bismarck and *Prinz Eugen,* equipped with primitive radar, entered fog-shrouded Denmark Strait on May 23, hugging the ice pack off Greenland. Two 10,000-ton heavy cruisers, *Suffolk* and *Norfolk,* also equipped with primitive radar, were patrolling the passage. *Suffolk,* which had better radar than *Bismarck,* found the Germans late that evening and brought up *Norfolk. Bismarck* detected *Norfolk* on radar and fired her first salvos of the war. She got no hits; moreover, the shock of her 15" guns damaged her radar. As a consequence, *Prinz Eugen* moved into the van. Tracking by radar, *Suffolk* and *Norfolk* hung on tenaciously.

In response to the alert, the new commander of the Home Fleet, Admiral John Tovey, sent the big (42,000-ton) battle cruiser *Hood* and the new battleship *Prince of Wales,* with destroyer screens, to intercept the German ships in the south end of the Denmark Strait. The four converging British ships significantly outgunned the German ships. *Hood,* like *Bismarck,* had eight 15" guns; *Prince of Wales* had ten 14" guns. *Suffolk* and *Norfolk,* like *Prinz Eugen,* each had eight 8" guns. But *Hood* was ancient and thinly armored, and *Prince of Wales* was still in workup and some of her guns were not yet firing properly. *Suffolk* and *Norfolk,* also ancient, were less well-armored than *Prinz Eugen.*

In the early morning hours of May 24, the opposing naval forces met. The British made the mistake of opening the attack on a slanting course, which prevented them from bringing all guns to bear simultaneously, and which offered the Germans a better target. Mistaking *Prinz Eugen* for *Bismarck*, *Hood* opened fire on the former at a range of fourteen miles. *Bismarck* and *Prinz Eugen* responded immediately with deadly accurate fire. Taking a hit in her magazines, *Hood* blew up and sank within minutes. The British destroyer *Electra* could find only three of her 1,419-man crew. Badly damaged by two hits and bedeviled with malfunctioning guns, *Prince of Wales* disengaged and retired behind a smoke screen. But she had got two or three 14" hits in *Bismarck*'s forward fuel tanks and a fuel-transfer station, which deprived *Bismarck* of a crucial thousand tons of fuel oil.

In view of the damage to *Bismarck*, the German commander, Admiral Günther Lütjens, changed plans. The *Prinz Eugen* was to separate from *Bismarck* and raid British shipping alone. *Bismarck* was to go directly to St. Nazaire for repairs. Before the new plan could be executed, however, Lütjens had first to shake his shadowers, *Suffolk*, *Norfolk*, and the damaged *Prince of Wales*, and the destroyers. He swung *Bismarck* at the shadowers—as if to attack—and during the resulting confusion, *Prinz Eugen* slipped away, southbound into the vast Atlantic.*

When Dönitz learned that *Bismarck* had been hit, he volunteered the entire Atlantic U-boat arm to assist. Lütjens hastened to accept the offer and, as a first step, he requested that Dönitz set a submarine trap in grid square AJ-68, 360 miles due south of Greenland. The plan was that Lütjens would "lure" his shadowers into the square on the morning of May 25 so that the U-boats could attack them, causing sufficient diversion for *Bismarck* to elude them.

On the afternoon of May 24, Dönitz directed five boats to form the trap. Three of the boats were commanded by *Ritterkreuz* holders: Lüth in the old Type IX *U-43*, Endrass in the old Type VIIB *U-46*, and Kuppisch in the Type VIIC *U-94*, who had only a few torpedoes. The other two boats, fresh from Germany on maiden patrols, had not fired any torpedoes: the first Type IXC† to reach the Atlantic, *U-66*, commanded by Richard Zapp, age thirty-seven, and the VIIC *U-557*, commanded by Ottokar Paulshen, age twenty-five. Kleinschmidt's IXB *U-111* was to join the trap after refueling from one of *Bismarck*'s supply ships, *Belchen*. Two other boats, Helmut Rosenbaum's *U-73*, fresh from Lorient, and Claus Korth's *U-93*, took stations slightly to the east of the trap.

Dönitz set a second submarine trap in the Bay of Biscay, 420 miles due west of Lorient. It was comprised initially of four Type VII boats: Herbert Schultze's *U-48*, outbound from Lorient, and three inbound boats. One was Udo Heilmann in *U-97*, who had sunk three ships for 17,852 tons, including the 6,466-ton tanker *Sangro*, an ex-Italian prize. The others were Robert Gysae's *U-98*, and Herbert

---

* Undetected but bedeviled by engine problems, *Prinz Eugen* was forced to abort, reaching Brest on June 1 without having attacked any enemy ships.

† The IXC was identical in all respects to the IXB, except that the fuel tanks held forty-three more tons of oil: 208 versus 165 tons. This gave the IXC an added 2,300 miles range at 12 knots: 11,000 miles versus 8,700.

Wohlfarth's *U-556*, who had no torpedoes; they were to serve as "lookouts" for the other boats. Two other boats in Lorient which were nearly ready for patrols, Klaus Scholtz's *U-108* and Erich Topp's *U-552*, were alerted to sail on the night of May 25 to reinforce this trap, if necessary. Another boat, Kentrat's *U-74*, inbound with severe depth-charge damage, voluntarily joined the trap.

By late afternoon, May 24, Dönitz logged proudly, "all available" forces of the U-boat arm had been committed to assist *Bismarck*: a total of fifteen boats, seven in western waters, eight in the Bay of Biscay. This was the largest commitment of the U-boat force to a single task since the invasion of Norway, fourteen months earlier. Every skipper and crew involved was keenly aware of the historic nature of the mission and determined to do everything possible to support *Bismarck*.

Late that evening, May 24, *Bismarck*'s shadowers drew the new aircraft carrier *Victorious* onto her track. When *Victorious* had closed to within 120 miles of *Bismarck*, she launched nine old Swordfish biplanes, each armed with a single 18" aerial torpedo and fitted with primitive ASV radar. The Swordfish picked up a contact and prepared to attack, but the "blip" turned out to be the *Norfolk*, which by radio put the planes back on the correct course. A second "blip" proved to be three U.S. Coast Guard cutters, *Modoc*, *Northland*, and *General Greene*, on "neutrality patrol." Immediately afterward, however, the planes found *Bismarck*. Courageously flying into a wall of antiaircraft fire, the Swordfish attacked within view of the Coast Guard cutters, scoring one hit. Astonishingly, all nine Swordfish survived and returned to *Victorious*.

The single torpedo hit on *Bismarck* did no damage, but the attack had important consequences. During *Bismarck*'s violent maneuvering to avoid the torpedoes, the makeshift repairs to the damage sustained earlier in the day from *Prince of Wales* fell apart and *Bismarck* lost more oil and took on tons of water, which slowed her. This mishap led Lütjens to abandon the plan to "lure" his pursuers into a submarine trap, and he headed directly for Brest, which was closer than St. Nazaire. Accordingly, Dönitz shifted seven of the eight boats (leaving *U-111* to refuel) in western waters east toward the presumed track of *Bismarck* and moved the five boats in the Bay of Biscay trap farther to the north.

During the early hours of May 25, *Bismarck* shook her pursuers. The Germans rejoiced. If Lütjens could remain undetected and maintain speed, *Bismarck* would soon reach the Bay of Biscay U-boat patrol line and would be within range of *Luftwaffe* aircraft based in France, which could provide an aerial umbrella. The onset of nasty Atlantic storms would help *Bismarck* remain undetected. The British wept. The great prize had unaccountably slipped from their grasp. The stormy weather diminished hope that she could be found again.

Unaware of the severity of the damage to *Bismarck* and of her critical loss of fuel, the British did not know where she was going. South in the Atlantic? North back to Germany? East to France? Based on incorrect or botched plotting of DF fixes on *Bismarck*'s radio transmissions, Admiral Tovey leaned to the view that *Bismarck* was to break back to Germany via the Iceland-Faeroes passage, and wrongly deployed Home Fleet forces accordingly. At the same time, however, First Sea Lord Dudley Pound at the Admiralty directed Force H (the carrier *Ark Royal* and the battle cruiser *Renown*), coming up from Gibraltar, to deploy on the assumption that *Bismarck* was headed for France. Thus two of the three possibilities were covered, albeit thinly. But the nasty weather worked in *Bismarck*'s favor, restricting and blinding carrier- and land-based air patrols.

During the desperate but fruitless hunt for *Bismarck* on May 25, the codebreakers at Bletchley Park, who were reading the *Luftwaffe* Red Enigma currently, but not naval Enigma, picked up an important message in Red that related to *Bismarck*. In response to a query from the chief of staff of the *Luftwaffe*, who was in Athens for the German airborne assault on the island of Crete,* Berlin informed him that *Bismarck* was "making for the west coast of France." Bletchley Park rushed this vital information to the Admiralty, but by that time both the Admiralty and Admiral Tovey had intuitively concluded that *Bismarck* was headed for France and were redeploying all naval forces accordingly. Nonetheless, the information from Bletchley Park was reassuring.

In the foulest possible weather, on the morning of May 26, the First Sea Lord Pound directed Coastal Command and carrier-based air to concentrate reconnaissance along a presumed track to Brest. At 10:30—thirty-one hours after *Bismarck* had been lost—a newly arrived, American-built Coastal Command Catalina found her. Ironically, the pilot was a U.S. Navy ensign, Leonard ("Tuck") Smith, who was "on loan" to indoctrinate RAF pilots to the peculiar flying characteristics of the Catalina. While Smith zoomed into the clouds to avoid the heavy ack-ack from *Bismarck,* the British pilot, Flying Officer D. A. Briggs, got off a contact report in a simple code, which *B-dienst* quickly broke and transmitted to *Bismarck* and to Dönitz.

Bismarck was then 690 miles west of Brest—about thirty-five hours out—but Force H was only seventy-five miles to the east, blocking her way. The Force H commander, James F. Somerville, directed a radar-equipped cruiser, *Sheffield,* and a succession of ASV-radar-equipped Swordfish biplanes from *Ark Royal* to shadow *Bismarck* while he prepared to launch a flight of Swordfish with torpedoes. The first flight of fourteen Swordfish mistakenly attacked the *Sheffield,* which only escaped destruction by resorting to violent maneuvers. The second flight of Swordfish (fifteen aircraft), firmly guided by *Sheffield,* attacked *Bismarck* at 8:47 P.M., launching thirteen torpedoes. Two hit, one amidships on the armor blister to no effect, the other all the way aft, wrecking *Bismarck*'s steering gear, propellers, and rudder, leaving her unmaneuverable.

From the contact reports of British aircraft intercepted by *B-dienst* and one message from Lütjens on *Bismarck,* Dönitz was able to plot the probable track of *Bismarck* and her pursuers. He directed the Bay of Biscay submarine trap, which

---

* The Germans assaulted Crete on May 20 with 20,000 paratroopers and infantry in gliders, in 600 air transports, supported by 630 bombers and fighters. Forewarned from breaks in *Luftwaffe* Enigma, the 40,000 British defenders slaughtered the Germans, killing 4,000 men. Nonetheless, the Germans finally prevailed, killing 2,000 Commonwealth troops and capturing 12,000. During the battle and evacuation, the *Luftwaffe* inflicted devastating losses on the Royal Navy: the cruisers *Gloucester, Fiji,* and *Calcutta* and six destroyers sunk; the battleships *Warspite* and *Barham,* the carrier *Formidable,* the cruisers *Perth, Orion, Ajax, Carlisle, Naiad,* and eight destroyers damaged.

had been reinforced by Rosenbaum's *U-73* but less Topp's *U-552,* which did not sail (making a total of seven boats), to the most likely point of action and by the evening of May 26, notwithstanding the gale-whipped, raging seas, all were within a few miles of *Bismarck* and Force H. At 8:00 P.M. the carrier *Ark Royal* and the battle cruiser *Renown* of Force H, making high speed, nearly ran down one of the boats, Wohlfarth's *U-556.* But Wohlfarth, serving as a "lookout," had no torpedoes! In frustration he logged: "If only I had torpedoes now! I should not even have to approach, as I am in exactly the right position for firing. No destroyers and no zigzagging. I could get between them and finish them both off. The carrier has torpedo bombers on board. I might have been able to help *Bismarck.*" He reported the contact and shadowed, but the big ships soon outran him.

When Dönitz got word that *Bismarck* could not maneuver, he ordered all seven boats of the Biscay trap (including Gysae's *U-98,* critically low on fuel and out of torpedoes) to converge on *Bismarck* and defend her. Gysae in *U-98* and Wohlfarth in *U-556* were to continue as "lookouts" and guide other U-boats to the enemy. Homing on *Bismarck*'s beacon signals, Rosenbaum in *U-73* found her first, shortly after midnight May 27. *Bismarck* was then under torpedo attack by a flotilla of five destroyers, commanded by Philip Vian in *Cossack* (which had a Type 286 radar), responding to *Sheffield*'s shadow reports. Rosenbaum observed and reported this destroyer action, which resulted in two more torpedo hits on *Bismarck,* but he was unable to attack the wildly maneuvering destroyers or to find *Sheffield,* and soon lost contact in the foul weather.

Homing on *Bismarck*'s or *U-73*'s beacons, the "lookout" Wohlfarth in *U-556* arrived next, critically low on fuel. He logged: "What can I do for *Bismarck*? I can see her star shells and gun flashes. Sudden bursts of gunfire. It is an awful feeling to be so near, yet unable to help. I can only continue to reconnoiter and guide the U-boats that still have torpedoes." By this time the battleships *King George V* (ten 14" guns) and *Rodney* (nine 16" guns) and the heavy cruisers *Dorsetshire* and *Norfolk* were closing on *Bismarck* in raging seas. Knowing he was doomed, Lütjens sent off a message to Hitler: "We fight to the last in our belief in you my Führer and in the firm faith in Germany's victory."* The last signal from Lütjens, at 0710 (German time), was: "Send U-boat to save War Diary."

Dönitz ordered Wohlfarth in *U-556,* who appeared to be closest to *Bismarck,* to carry out the risky mission of picking up the war diary. But Wohlfarth responded that he was so low on fuel that he had to abort to Lorient then and there. The next nearest boat, Kentrat's heavily damaged *U-74,* drew the assignment. But before Kentrat could even attempt to carry it out, *King George V* and *Rodney* opened fire with big guns and the cruisers *Dorsetshire* and *Norfolk* hit *Bismarck* with one or

---

* Hitler, who was angry that Lütjens had not sunk the *Prince of Wales* the morning he sank *Hood* and returned *Bismarck* and *Prinz Eugen* directly to Germany, replied coolly: "I thank you in the name of the German people." Hitler appended a word to the *Bismarck* crew: "The whole of Germany is with you. What can still be done will be done. The performance of your duty will strengthen our people in the struggle for their existence." In response to an earlier request from Lütjens in the same series of messages, Hitler awarded *Bismarck*'s gunnery officer, Adalbert Schneider, a *Ritterkreuz* for sinking *Hood.*

more torpedoes. Fighting back with all operating guns and flags still flying, the wrecked *Bismarck* sank beneath the waves at 10:40 A.M.,* with the loss of over 2,200 men.

British ships moved in to rescue *Bismarck* survivors. They fished out 110, but further rescues were broken off when one of the ships radioed a U-boat alarm, forcing all British vessels to evacuate the area, leaving behind hundreds of German survivors in the sea. Later that evening, Kentrat in *U-74* found three survivors and hauled them aboard, prompting Dönitz to mount an organized search by six boats over the next four days. Herbert Schultze in *U-48* reported finding wreckage and "a number of floating corpses," but no survivors. A German weather-reporting trawler, *Sachsenwald,* found two other survivors, making a total of five recovered by German forces before Admiral Raeder canceled the search on May 31.

Kentrat in the severely damaged *U-74* had a very difficult time returning to Lorient with the *Bismarck*'s survivors. By the time he arrived off the coast, saltwater had leaked into the battery, creating chlorine gas. He was thus unable to dive and make the customary submerged approach to Lorient. An unidentified British submarine spotted *U-74* and fired torpedoes from dead astern, but the bridge watch was keenly alert and managed to "comb" the torpedoes. The necessary repairs kept the boat out of action until late July.

The loss of *Bismarck* marked a turning point in the German naval war. Its humiliating failure, together with the failure of the battle cruisers *Gneisenau* and *Scharnhorst* to inflict any substantial damage on British maritime assets, brought to a close the dominance of the big surface ships in the *Kriegsmarine*. Never again was one to sortie into the Atlantic. Virtually overnight the U-boat became the *Kriegsmarine*'s preferred ship, the only possibility for defeating Great Britain at sea. Admiral Raeder's influence on Hitler declined; that of Dönitz rose commensurately.

President Roosevelt seized upon the *Bismarck* sortie to nudge the United States closer to open intervention. On May 27, the day *Bismarck* went down, he legally declared a state of unlimited national emergency. "The Battle for the Atlantic," Roosevelt said somewhat expansively, "now extends from the icy waters of the North Pole to the frozen continent of the Antarctic." The blunt truth, he went on, was that the Nazis were sinking merchant ships three times faster than British and American shipyards could replace them and everything pointed to an eventual attack on the Western Hemisphere. "It would be suicide to wait until they are in our front yard," he concluded. Therefore he had ordered the Army and Navy to intensify air and surface-ship patrols in the North and South Atlantic and had directed the U.S. Maritime Commission to dramatically increase the production of merchant shipping. Two weeks later, he froze German and Italian assets in the United States and closed down all the consulates of those two nations.

---

* Coming to rest on the sea bottom, standing perfectly upright on her keel, according to photographs obtained in 1989 by a remote-control deep submergence vehicle. Her upright posture appeared to confirm the assertion of several British and German naval historians that *Bismarck*'s captain, Ernst Lindemann, scuttled her.

Behind the scenes, Roosevelt initiated even more warlike measures in the Atlantic area. He directed the Army and Navy to prepare an expeditionary force to join the British, should they decide to seize the Spanish Canaries (and the Portuguese Azores and Cape Verde Islands). When that operation was again deferred, Roosevelt volunteered another expeditionary force to relieve the British garrison in Iceland, an operation (Indigo) that was to be carried out on July 7. As agreed earlier in ABC-1, the U.S. Navy stepped up measures to provide escort of convoys on the leg between Canada and Iceland.

The *Bismarck* affair brought the U-boat war against shipping in the North Atlantic to a virtual standstill in the last ten days of May. The twenty boats in that area sank only two ships. Ottokar Paulshen in the new *U-557*, which nearly had been lost in an accident during its Baltic workup, got a 7,300-ton freighter; the Type IID duck *U-147*, commanded by Eberhard Wetjen, on an indoctrination patrol to the Atlantic, got a 2,500-ton freighter. When the new IXB *U-109*, commanded by Hans-Georg Fischer, age thirty-three, reached Lorient on May 29, having sunk only one ship on an eighteen-day patrol, Dönitz judged that Fischer was incapable of commanding a U-boat and sacked him. To replace Fischer, Dönitz brought back the *Ritterkreuz* holder Heinrich Bleichrodt, then commanding *U-67*, which was in the Baltic conducting sonar R&D work.

Altogether 347 loaded ships sailed from Halifax to the British Isles in Slow and Halifax convoys during May. The U-boats sank thirteen (or .04 percent) of these vessels—nine from convoy Halifax 126 and four stragglers from other eastbound convoys. In addition, U-boats in this area sank seven ships from the westbound convoy Outbound 318 plus six other ships that were sailing alone for 31,500 tons. The duck *U-138* sank another lone freighter near North Channel. Total sinkings in the northern area in May: thirty-one ships.*

The successful attack on convoy Halifax 126 near 41 degrees west longitude, hastened the plans of the Admiralty and Western Approaches to deploy convoy-escort groups from Halifax out to 35 degrees west, where they were to hand over to the Iceland-based British escort groups. The first such Canadian escort group (of the Newfoundland Escort Force) sailed from St. John's on June 2 to rendezvous with eastbound convoy Halifax 129. Commanded by J.S.D. (Chummy) Prentice, the group was composed of three Canadian corvettes, *Chambly, Collingwood,* and *Orillia.* Bedeviled by communications and engine problems, this pioneering Canadian force did not shine, according to the British, but all things considered, Prentice judged, his ships performed well, at least individually.

This convoy, Halifax 129, would be recorded as the first transatlantic eastbound convoy to be escorted "clear-across" or "end-to-end." That is, a Canadian escort group from St. John's to 35 degrees west; an Iceland-based British escort group from 35 degrees west to 20 degrees west; a British escort group from 20 degrees west to North Channel. Canadian and British aircraft in Newfoundland and Iceland provided limited air escort to the convoy but, as will be seen, no U-boats

---

* One Italian submarine, *Otaria,* sank the 4,700-ton British freighter *Starcross* from the northbound convoy Sierra Leone 73; another, *Marconi,* sank the 8,100-ton British tanker *Cairndale* off Spain.

were available to attack Halifax 129. In a reverse procedure, convoy Outbound 331 was recorded as the first transatlantic westbound convoy to be escorted "end-to-end." To field enough escort groups to provide this "end-to-end" transatlantic service, it was necessary to reduce the number of ships in each group, a calculated risk but one deemed worth running.

RICH TROPHIES IN WEST AFRICAN WATERS

Thinly stretched in every theater, the Royal Navy was not prepared physically or mentally to fight U-boats in equatorial West African waters. Reginald ("Bob") Whinney, a career officer who had specialized in ASW, was appalled by what he found when he arrived in Freetown to train the local escort force. The senior officer, Admiral Algernon Willis, Whinney wrote in his memoir, was "severe, unbending, and very thin, ashen, unhappy-looking, possibly operationally tired, possibly not fit. What a choice where the crying need was for driving, but essentially benign, encouraging leadership." Summing up the situation, Whinney continued:

> With few exceptions, the officers at Freetown were then the unhappiest collection I had ever met or was to meet in my whole Service career. There were several reasons for this. Certainly the climate was one of them. It was very debilitating due to the heat, the humidity and the prevalence of malaria. The living conditions were appalling; recreation was almost nil and social life did not exist. To cap this, it appeared that it was to Freetown, where the drink was duty-free—gin two pence a glass—that a number of officers who had been in recent trouble, including over drink, were sent. In many cases, these poor chaps had not enough to do. (Let it hastily be added that I was not in such a category.) Finally, Freetown was not an area of hot war and so got little priority from the Admiralty; and to cap the lot again, there was no inspiring lead from the top.

By early May five large boats patrolled in South Atlantic waters. One, Oesten's *U-106,* escorted the blockade-runner *Lech* from Brazil, a mission that took her to 50 degrees west longitude, the deepest penetration of the Western Hemisphere by any U-boat to then. At the insistence of the OKM, *U-106* remained in Brazilian waters to escort a second blockade runner, *Windhuk,* but the sailing of that ship was delayed indefinitely. When the OKM finally released *U-106* on May 7, Oesten was low on fuel and had engine problems and had to rendezvous with the supply ship *Egerland,* which had been prepositioned in the South Atlantic to support *Bismarck.*

The other four boats patrolled off the African coast, resupplying from *Egerland* and another supply ship, *Nordmark.* Schewe in *U-105* and Hessler in *U-107* were the last boats to refuel from *Nordmark.* While they were doing so, on May 3 and 4, the new arrivals, Heinrich Liebe in *U-38* and Viktor Schütze in *U-103,* patrolled off Freetown, picking off unescorted ships with little fear of ASW measures. Liebe sank two for 10,200 tons; Schütze sank six for 28,800 tons.

These four boats then switched places. After replenishing, Schewe's *U-105* and

Hessler's *U-107* closed on Freetown, while Liebe's *U-38* and Schütze's *U-103* hauled off to mid-Atlantic to find *Egerland*. Schewe sank four ships for 28,400 tons, including the 11,800-ton British freighter *Rodney Star;* Hessler sank two ships for 16,300 tons. Counting past overclaims, Schewe's victories earned a *Ritterkreuz.** While Schewe was sinking the fourth ship on May 16, a torpedo misfired and a crewman was seriously injured. On instructions from Dönitz, Schewe hauled out and transferred the injured man to *Egerland,* then refueled and set course for Lorient.

Three boats rendezvoused with *Egerland* from May 13 to May 17, then set off for Freetown waters to join Hessler in *U-107*. After they departed, on May 18, *Egerland* reported she had only six torpedoes left. Another *Bismarck* supply ship, *Gedania,* was therefore ordered to relieve *Egerland*. Two other boats sailed from Lorient for African waters in May: Eckermann's *U-A* and Jost Metzler's *U-69,* the first Type VII to attempt a very long-range cruise.

During his service in the merchant marine, Metzler had often called at West African ports, as had his leading seaman, Bade, "an old sea dog." Metzler and Bade got the idea that two ports on the African Gold Coast in the Gulf of Guinea—Takoradi and Lagos—could be mined by a medium-sized U-boat. When Metzler proposed the scheme to Dönitz, it was approved, and *U-69* sailed on May 5, crammed with sixteen TMB mines and eight torpedoes—the mines and six torpedoes below and two torpedoes in topside canisters.

To conserve fuel, Metzler inched south on one diesel, rigged to turn the other motor. It was a long, slow, monotonous trip during which they saw not a single ship worth a torpedo. When they reached the equatorial latitudes, Metzler wrote, "the moist heat was almost unbearable," even at night. Two weeks later, on May 19, Metzler rendezvoused with *Egerland*. He refueled in a mere three hours, turned over his Enigma and all secret papers (as required of boats on a mining mission), and set a course for the Gold Coast.

Inbound to Africa to lay the mines, on the evening of May 21 the watch spotted a lighted southbound ship. The lights indicated she was a neutral, but Metzler believed she might be a disguised U-boat hunter. He cautiously approached her and asked for identification by signal light. When she replied *"Robin Moor,"* Metzler's suspicions intensified because he could find no such ship in *Lloyd's Register.* Moreover, when daylight came, Metzler saw the name *Exmoor* on her stern, listed in *Lloyd's* as a 5,000-ton American ship. Was she *Robin Moor, Exmoor,* or a disguised hunter?

The captain came across to *U-69* in a whaler, bringing his ship's papers and cargo manifest. He explained that the ship had only just been bought by Americans and that as a consequence, her name had been changed from *Exmoor* to *Robin Moor.* Metzler claimed he saw "radio apparatus" and "guns" on the manifest and that the ship was therefore "a neutral carrying contraband" and thus fair game under the prize rules. Despite the explicit orders from Hitler, the OKM, and Dönitz to avoid any contact with American ships, Metzler decided to sink her. After the

---

* His confirmed score on the duck *U-60* and *U-105* was fifteen ships for 86,232 tons.

crew had abandoned ship in lifeboats, Metzler put her under with one torpedo and thirty rounds from his deck gun. *Robin Moor* was the first American ship to be sunk by a U-boat in the war.

Metzler wrote that he then extended every effort to assure the safety of the survivors, according to the prize rules. He rounded up all the lifeboats, stocked them with "food, bread, butter, brandy and medical supplies." He then towed them toward Africa "for several hours," to a "spot where in a few days they would be driven by the gentle current on to the African shore." In fact, the currents took the survivors, including a woman and a two-year-old child, the other way (toward South America). They spent about two weeks in the open boats—a terrible ordeal—before reaching shore.

By coincidence, Churchill had chosen this moment to further stir up Americans—and draw them closer to war—with another *Lusitania* or *Athenia* incident. The Admiralty announced that the Germans had sunk the Egyptian passenger liner *Zamzam*, en route from New York to Egypt, with "196 American passengers" on board, all of whom were presumed to be lost. To heighten the impact of this "atrocity," the Admiralty spokesman stressed that the lost Americans were volunteer ambulance drivers; hence, in journalese, *Zamzam* became a "mercy ship."

As intended, the story was shocking. The *New York World–Telegram* carried it with a double-bank front-page banner headline:

196 AMERICANS FEARED LOST WITH EGYPTIAN MERCY SHIP

The *Zamzam* had been sunk on April 16 by the merchant raider *Atlantis,* but only after all 340 passengers (138 Americans) and all their baggage had been brought on board *Atlantis.* Subsequently, all the passengers—and the baggage—had been transferred to the German freighter *Dresden,* which in due course landed them safely in France.* Berlin propagandists trumped London propagandists by immediately revealing the humanity and consideration shown the *Zamzam* passengers, but the news of the sinking of *Robin Moor* pushed the Berlin version of the *Zamzam* story off the front pages, leaving the casual American reader with the impression that the Germans had "killed 196" Americans on the "mercy ship" *Zamzam* and had callously sunk the *Robin Moor* as well; all within a matter of days. Thanks to Metzler, London won the propaganda battle after all.

When Dönitz heard the news of the *Robin Moor* sinking, he was furious. Metzler remembered that Dönitz sent "rocket after rocket to me, bombarding me with questions about the details and the reasons for the sinking." No explanation seemed to satisfy Dönitz. "The Admiral's tone conjured up a picture for me of a court-martial on my return," Metzler wrote.

---

* A *Life* magazine photographer and a *Fortune* magazine writer were among the passengers on *Zamzam.* After the Germans released them, they collaborated on an article for *Life,* which included some surreptitious photographs of the affair.

• • •

The hunting off Freetown remained good.

• After refueling from *Egerland,* Heinrich Liebe in *U-38* sank five ships for 29,400 tons, bringing his total to seven.

• Jost Metzler in *U-69* bravely laid his TMB mines in the harbors of Takoradi on May 27, and Lagos on May 29. Later, Metzler lightheartedly described these extremely hazardous missions as "crazy exploits," but they were successful. The British were forced to close both harbors. One mine damaged a 5,400-ton freighter in Takoradi; another sank a 2,900-ton freighter in Lagos.

• Viktor Schütze in *U-103* sank four ships for 22,500 tons, including the 6,900-ton tanker *British Grenadier,* bringing his total to eleven.

• Homebound to Lorient, Georg Schewe in *U-105* sank another ship, bringing his confirmed total to twelve for 70,500 tons.

• Jürgen Oesten in *U-106,* who had been sidetracked on escort missions for almost seven weeks, sank two ships for 13,200 tons, bringing his total to seven, plus the hit on the battleship *Malaya.*

• Günther Hessler in *U-107* sank three more ships for 14,500 tons, bringing his total to eleven, including a second tanker, the 8,000-ton Dutch *Marisa.**

• After refueling from *Egerland* on May 29, Hans Eckermann in *U-A,* conducting an exceedingly cautious patrol, sank no ships.

• The Italian submarine *Tazzoli* sank the 8,800-ton Norwegian tanker *Alfred Olsen.*

By the first day of June, Günther Hessler had sunk fifteen confirmed ships for 101,000 tons, counting the four sunk in his first patrol in the North Atlantic. That day, he came upon a lone British freighter, the 5,000-ton *Alfred Jones,* off Freetown. There was something about the way this ship looked and behaved that aroused Hessler's suspicions, leading him to conclude she might be a disguised U-boat killer. He therefore approached her with extreme caution and attacked with two torpedoes. Both hit, severely damaging the ship, and the crew appeared to abandon in lifeboats. Still wary, Hessler approached submerged, resisting the temptation to surface for a gun attack and to offer assistance to the survivors. Upon closing, he saw dozens of sailors hiding on her tilting deck, prepared to leap to a half dozen 4" to 6" guns, depth-charge chutes, and other weapons, which were camouflaged by wood crates. He pulled back and fired a third torpedo, which put her under.†

This sinking raised Hessler's score on *U-107* to sixteen ships for 106,000 tons—twelve sunk in the South Atlantic, to tie Georg Schewe's memorable patrol in *U-105.* By custom, Hessler should have received a *Ritterkreuz,* but there was no word from Kerneval. The reason, Dönitz wrote later, was that "I found it a little difficult to recommend him because he was my son-in-law." When Admiral

---

* Hessler testified in defense of Dönitz at Nuremberg that he gave the survivors of one of these ships, the Greek *Papalemos,* water and precise instructions for reaching land.

† At Dönitz's trial, he cited the *Alfred Jones* as another example of the perils confronting U-boat skippers who were tempted to offer assistance to survivors.

Raeder learned of the delay, Dönitz continued, Raeder said that "if I did not recommend Hessler at once, he would." But still Dönitz held back.

The aggregate sinkings of the boats in the South Atlantic in May were more than sufficiently impressive to justify the "diversion" of these boats from the North Atlantic. The sinkings served another purpose as well: They compelled the British to drastically curb the unescorted ship traffic in that area, to increase convoying from Freetown, and to draw a substantial number of surface escorts from the North Atlantic to the South Atlantic. Accordingly, Dönitz directed two more IXBs, *U-66* and *U-123,* to sail to West Africa in June.

Thanks to the priceless intelligence haul from Lemp's *U-110,* British codebreakers could read naval Enigma fluently and currently throughout the month of June.* The torrent of information, which the British called Most Secret Ultra (shortened to Ultra), gave a select few in the Admiralty an astounding view of the *Kriegsmarine*'s innermost secrets, including everything about U-boat operations. Rodger Winn's assistant in the U-boat Tracking Room, Patrick Beesly, remembered: "We rapidly learned the exact number of U-boats at sea, and not only the contents of their own signals but, even more important, the instructions constantly being pumped out to them by Dönitz from his headquarters in Lorient."

The radio traffic between Dönitz and his skippers also revealed to the Admiralty day-by-day positions of nearly all the U-boats. Hence the Admiralty had an opportunity to organize task forces and "pounce" these boats by surface ship and aircraft and destroy them, putting an end to the U-boat menace in one simultaneous operation. But to attack twenty-odd U-boats in diverse locations simultaneously, the Admiralty believed, would tip off the Germans that Enigma had been broken and lead them to take corrective measures, such as changing the keys, or perhaps even introducing a new code machine.

Rather than attack the U-boats frontally, the Admiralty elected to impede their operations in indirect ways. These were principally two: by routing convoys away from the known U-boat positions and by thwarting the plan to use *Bismarck*'s supply ships for refueling U-boats at sea.

The refueling scheme was to be thwarted by directly confronting the supply ships and capturing or sinking them, as if the British had come upon them as a result of comprehensive and diligent blue-water patrolling. To be sure, there was a risk of arousing German suspicion, but less so in sinking big surface ships because the surface ships were easier to detect by radar than U-boats. The Admiralty knew, from breaking Enigma dispatches from *Bismarck,* that Lütjens had informed the OKM that British surface-ship radar was amazingly effective, capable of picking up a surface ship at a range of "at least 35,000 meters," or about twenty miles.

The assault on *Bismarck*'s supply ships began on June 3 in the North Atlantic.

---

* An attempt in late May to capture Enigma keys for July from the weather-reporting trawlers *August Wriedt* and *Heinrich Freese* failed. Confronted by their attackers, the Germans jettisoned all Enigma materials.

The cruisers *Aurora* and *Kenya* attacked the 10,000-ton tanker *Belchen,* which was parked eighty miles southwest of Greenland. *Belchen* had refueled Kleinschmidt's *U-111* and Paulshen's *U-557,* and when the cruisers struck, she was in the process of refueling Korth's *U-93. Belchen* threw off the hoses and scuttled. Korth dived but he shied from attacking the cruisers.

Later that day, Korth surfaced and rescued all fifty survivors of *Belchen.* Dönitz instructed him to make for another *Bismarck* supply ship, *Friedrich Breme,* offload the survivors, refuel, and resume his patrol. But Korth demurred on the grounds that should that rendezvous fail, he did not have enough fuel to reach France. Halfway back to Lorient, on June 6, Korth spotted and reported a southbound convoy, but owing to his shortage of fuel and the presence on board of the fifty *Belchen* survivors, he did not attack or shadow it for the benefit of other boats. Although Korth had won his *Ritterkreuz* earlier on this patrol, when he arrived in Lorient, Dönitz upbraided him for not attacking and tracking the convoy, regardless of the presence of the *Belchen* survivors. Logging that Korth seemed to be losing his fighting edge, Dönitz decided to send him to West African waters on his next patrol.

The loss of *Belchen* was a stiff blow to Dönitz. She had been ideally situated to resupply the western patrol line, enabling those boats to double the time in the operating area. After Korth in *U-93,* Walter Kell, age twenty-seven, commanding the VIIC *U-204* on his maiden patrol from Germany, had been next in line to refuel from *Belchen.* So that operation, and several others as well, had to be canceled.

In the two days following the destruction of *Belchen,* June 4 and 5, British naval forces struck at four other German supply ships in the North and South Atlantic. Aircraft from *Victorious,* the battleship *Nelson,* and the cruiser *Neptune* teamed up with the armed merchant ship *Esperance Bay,* forcing the 4,000-ton *Gonzenheim* to scuttle. In the same area, the destroyer *Marsdale,* trained for boarding, captured the 9,000-ton tanker *Gedania* before she could scuttle. In southern waters, the cruiser *London* and the destroyer *Brilliant* forced the 9,900-ton tanker *Esso Hamburg* and the 9,800-ton tanker *Egerland* to scuttle.

In the capture of *Gedania,* which was en route to relieve *Egerland,* the British and Germans fought a pitched battle, during which several *Gedania* crewmen were killed. After the victory the British found numerous secret papers, including Enigma materials and the operational orders issued to *Gedania.* These orders contained a wealth of new information: instructions for conducting a rendezvous with a U-boat (coded meeting points, communications procedures, recognition signals), precise (coded) routes to be followed by supply ships and blockade runners when approaching French ports,* and, not incidentally, the location of the North Atlantic weather-reporting trawler during June.

Dönitz learned of the loss of *Egerland* from Heinrich Liebe in *U-38,* who was approaching her to replenish when she was scuttled and who then searched unsuccessfully for survivors. It was another blow. Her loss and the loss of her relief, *Gedania,* meant that the highly rewarding U-boat operations off the West African

---

* On June 6, aircraft from the carrier *Eagle* intercepted and bombed the inbound 9,200-ton blockade runner *Elbe* near the Azores, forcing her to scuttle.

coast were to be interrupted until a substitute resupply ship could be stationed in those waters. Dönitz therefore directed the five boats remaining in the Freetown area to replenish, if necessary, from another *Bismarck* supply ship, the 10,700-ton tanker *Lothringen,* which had parked farther north.

Continuing this secret campaign, the British had five more successes. On June 12 the cruiser *Sheffield* forced the 10,400-ton tanker *Friedrich Breme* to scuttle. On June 15 the carrier *Eagle* and the cruiser *Dunedin* captured the *Lothringen,* obtaining Enigma materials and wiping out the proposed resupply of the U-boats in the Freetown area. On June 21 the cruiser *London* forced the 4,400-ton *Babitonga,* a merchant-raider supply ship, to scuttle. On June 23 destroyers of the 8th Flotilla and the *Marsdale* teamed with aircraft and forced another merchant-raider supply ship, the 3,000-ton *Alstertor,* to scuttle.

Nor was that all. On June 28 the cruiser *Nigeria* and three destroyers of the Home Fleet pounced on the 136-foot, 344-ton weather-reporting trawler *Lauenburg,* commanded by fifty-eight-year-old Hinrich Gewald. A boarding party from the destroyer *Tartar,* commanded by T. Hugh P. Wilson and advised by codebreaker Allon Bacon, captured the trawler and intelligence materials of "inestimable value" (as the Admiralty later put it), including the daily Enigma ring and plugboard keys for July. These enabled Bletchley Park to continue reading naval Enigma fluently and currently through that month.

All these sinkings again aroused deepest suspicion at Kerneval. As a consequence, on June 16, Dönitz introduced a complicated new system for disguising U-boat positions from outsiders. He issued the boats a set of fixed "reference points" (Franz, Oscar, Herbert, etc.) to use in directing them to new areas. In place of ordering a boat to go to the standard *Kriegsmarine* grid square BC-64 (for example), he ordered it to go to a grid square which lay (for example) 250 degrees, 150 miles and 050 degrees, 200 miles, respectively, from reference point "Franz." To thwart British DFing, the boats were to respond to a change in position or an attack order by a simple "yes" or "no" (in Short Signal code), depending upon their ability to comply.

Both Bletchley Park and the U-boat skippers found this new system difficult to master. The official British historian wrote that the delays encountered in breaking the new system, "reduced during [the second half of] June the operational value of what was derived from reading Enigma currently," but that by July, "the problem had largely been overcome." The U-boat skippers criticized the system as "too cumbersome"; many made errors or miscalculations that took them to the wrong place.

Denied the services of the supply ships *Egerland, Gedania,* and *Lothringen,* which, as related, the British wiped out, and badly in need of refits or overhauls and rest for the crews, one by one the boats in West African waters returned to France. Georg Schewe in *U-105* and Jürgen Oesten in *U-106* arrived on June 13 and June 18, having been out for 112 and 110 days, respectively. Dönitz had high praise for both skippers. Schewe's score of twelve ships for 70,500 tons established a new record for a single patrol.

Trailing *U-105* homeward by about a week, Heinrich Liebe in *U-38* sank his eighth ship, the 7,600-ton British freighter *Kingston Hill.* This sinking put Liebe over the 200,000-ton mark and he thus became the sixth skipper to earn Oak Leaves to his *Ritterkreuz.** Having commanded *U-38* since the outbreak of war, Liebe had been in continuous Atlantic combat longer than any other skipper. When he reached Lorient, Dönitz sent him to a job in the Training Command, but the weary *U-38* was retained in the Atlantic.

While he was homebound, Günther Hessler in *U-107* sank two more ships, his thirteenth and fourteenth. The last was the 5,000-ton Greek freighter *Pandias.* Despite his earlier close call with the *Alfred Jones,* Hessler remembered that he helped the Greeks square away the lifeboats and gave them food and water and instructions for reaching the African coast.†

With the sinking of *Pandias,* Dönitz finally authorized a *Ritterkreuz* for his son-in-law. The reckoning for this patrol was the most conservative of the war: fourteen ships (including two tankers) for 90,793 tons. Postwar accounting confirmed fourteen ships for 86,699 tons, which was to stand as the best single patrol of the war by any submarine of any nation. The announcement of the award by the German propagandists was also conservative. Berlin credited Hessler with eighteen ships for 111,272 tons in two patrols, whereas his confirmed total was eighteen ships for 118,862 tons. Upon arrival in Lorient on July 2, after ninety-six days at sea, *U-107,* like the other "south boats," went into the yards for a long overhaul.

Viktor Schütze in the homebound *U-103* trailed *U-107* by a week. Schütze sank two more ships, bringing his confirmed total for this patrol to thirteen ships (one tanker) for 65,172 tons. The last sinking, on June 29, proved to be an embarrassment. She was the 6,600-ton Italian blockade-runner *Ernani,* disguised as a Dutch vessel. After sinking her, Schütze was compelled to make a secret emergency refueling stop from the German tanker *Corrientes,* moored in the Spanish Canaries. Counting his earlier sinkings on *U-25* and *U-103,* this patrol also put Schütze over the 200,000-ton mark, earning Oak Leaves to his *Ritterkreuz.*‡ Upon arrival in Lorient, July 12, Schütze was promoted to command a training flotilla in the Baltic.

Of the boats returning from West African waters, the VIIC *U-69,* commanded by Jost Metzler, had the most difficult time. By mid-June Metzler was running out of food and fuel, and confronted problems with the fresh-water distillers. To augment the thin food supply, Metzler violated a maritime superstition and killed porpoises. The cook minced the porpoise meat and made fish cakes. At first the crew was reluctant to eat porpoise, but it finally gave in, pronouncing the cakes "delicious." After *Gedania* and *Lothringen* were lost, Dönitz directed Metzler to refuel secretly from *Corrientes,* but Metzler had doubts that he could get to the Canaries before he ran out of fuel.

---

* His total confirmed score—all on *U-38*—was thirty-one ships for 168,506 tons, ranking him ninth in the war.

† This second act of assistance to survivors on this patrol was also entered by Hessler in defense of Dönitz at the Nuremberg trials.

‡ Schütze's confirmed score on *U-25* and *U-103* was 36 ships for 187,179 tons, ranking him fourth in the war.

While inching along on one diesel, late on the afternoon of June 26, *U-69* happened upon convoy Sierra Leone 76 northbound from Freetown. These were the first enemy ships *U-69* had seen in almost a month and although Metzler had little fuel, he reported the convoy to Kerneval and closed on two diesels to make a night surface attack. Sneaking into the columns of ships, Metzler fired his last four torpedoes at four different ships. He claimed two ships for 17,500 tons sunk and one of 6,000 tons probably sunk, but postwar records confirmed only two British freighters sunk for 13,000 tons, the *Empire Ability* and the *River Lugar.* In the ensuing chaos, a couple of corvettes or sloops chased and fired guns at *U-69,* but Metzler hauled away with no damage. Dönitz instructed Metzler to shadow and report for the benefit of two southbound boats, the Type IXs *U-123* and *U-66,* but owing to the lack of fuel, he could not comply.

The *U-123,* until recently under command of Karl-Heinz Moehle, was now in the hands of a new skipper, Reinhard Hardegen, age twenty-eight, from the duck *U-147,* which was sunk with the loss of all hands on June 2. A onetime naval aviator, Hardegen had incurred injuries in a plane crash (shortened right leg; bleeding stomach) that would have disqualified him from submarine duty. But he had concealed the injuries and got a berth as first watch officer on Georg-Wilhelm Schulz's *U-124,* then command of *U-147* for one indoctrination patrol to North Channel before Dönitz, unaware of his disqualifying injuries, gave Hardegen command of *U-123.*

Southbound to Freetown on June 20, Hardegen came upon what appeared to be a lone British ship and attacked submerged, firing one torpedo. It missed. After a long submerged chase, Hardegen fired again. This time the torpedo hit and the crew abandoned ship, which, however, remained afloat. Closing, Hardegen gave her a "finishing shot," a solid hit, but still the ship would not sink. Refusing to expend yet another torpedo, Hardegen surfaced for a gun action. He finally sank the ship with his 4.1" gun, but upon approaching the lifeboats, he discovered she was not a British ship, but rather the 4,333-ton Portuguese neutral *Ganda.* Later, when a diplomatic squall ensued, the Germans blamed the sinking on a British submarine and Dönitz ordered Hardegen—as he had Lemp in the *Athenia* incident—to alter his patrol report to conceal the sinking.

After secretly replenishing from the *Corrientes* in the dark, early hours of June 25, Hardegen left the Canaries and continued southbound, the crew wilting under the unfamiliar heat and humidity of the tropics. On the following day, Kerneval relayed Metzler's contact on Sierra Leone Convoy 76 to Hardegen, who plotted a course to intercept and found it in the afternoon of June 27. But the convoy was then escorted by "several destroyers" and corvettes and a Sunderland. Hardegen tracked until dark, then surfaced to report the convoy (twenty-three ships) to Dönitz, who authorized Hardegen to attack, but also to track for the benefit of the southbound *U-66.*

Hardegen launched his attack shortly before midnight, shooting three torpedoes at three different ships. Two hit the intended targets, the third missed and may have hit a ship—or may not have. Hardegen claimed sinking a 10,000-ton tanker and two 5,000-ton freighters in this salvo, but Admiralty records show that only two freighters, a 5,600-ton Britisher and a 2,000-ton Dutchman, went down. The escorts hunted and found *U-123* and attacked her with depth charges for eleven hours, but Hardegen escaped serious damage by diving to 654 feet, well below the maximum settings for British depth charges.

The next day Hardegen raced north to regain the convoy and reported his successes ("20,000 tons" sunk) to Kerneval. He made contact in the afternoon and reported, but a Sunderland drove him off. He continued pursuing northward through that night and the following day, June 29, by which time the other southbound boat, *U-66,* commanded by Richard Zapp, had made contact. That day and the next Zapp sank three stragglers, two Greeks and a Britisher, for 15,600 tons. Hardegen attacked the main body of the convoy that day, sinking the 4,000-ton British freighter *Rio Azul,* which he reported to be an auxiliary cruiser.

Upon learning that the convoy had been reinforced with air and surface escorts and that Hardegen had chased it about 400 miles to the north, on July 1 Dönitz ordered both Hardegen and Zapp to turn about and resume patrols toward Freetown. However, by the time the boats reached Freetown, the Admiralty had strengthened ASW measures and, apparently with Ultra help, had routed convoys and individual ships away from that area. As a result, Hardegen and Zapp sank only one more British freighter each before returning to Lorient. Except *U-A,* which sank no ships at all in a seventy-six-day patrol, these were the least productive patrols to Freetown that summer.

Meanwhile, Jost Metzler in the VIIC *U-69,* who had put Hardegen and Zapp onto convoy Sierra Leone 76, continued on to the Canaries to refuel from *Corrientes.* To Metzler's amazement, Berlin Radio announced—by name—his claimed successes "off the coast of Africa": 31,500 tons. That counted the results of the mining missions but not *Robin Moor,* Metzler noted. On the night of June 28–29, *U-69* nosed alongside *Corrientes,* "with her last drops of fuel." After the crew had gorged on food and the fuel tanks had been topped off, the *U-69* proceeded onward to Lorient. On the way Metzler—who had no torpedoes—boldly attacked and sank the heavily armed 3,000-ton British freighter *Robert L. Holt* with his deck gun, a running artillery duel which Metzler described as the "craziest exploit" of this long and unusual patrol.

Metzler arrived in St. Nazaire on July 8, having been continuously at sea for sixty-four days, an extraordinary record-setting voyage for a Type VIIC. By that time the furor over the *Robin Moor* had been all but forgotten, obscured by the smashing successes of the *Wehrmacht* and *Luftwaffe* in the Russian campaign. Dönitz dutifully noted that "the sinking of the American ship S.S. *Robin Moor* was contrary to the orders given," but the court-martial Metzler had feared did not materialize. To the contrary, Dönitz warmly praised Metzler for a "well-executed" patrol, citing especially the minelaying and the dogged gun attack on the *Robert L. Holt.* He credited *U-69* with sinking six ships for 36,224 tons, including the British *Sangara,* which was salvaged, but not counting *Robin Moor.* Postwar records credited Metzler with sinking six ships for 28,400 tons, including *Robin Moor* and a ship sunk by a mine, plus the damage to *Sangara.* After Dönitz had learned all the details of this unusual and arduous patrol, he awarded Metzler a *Ritterkreuz.*

Excepting *U-A,* the eight boats that patrolled African waters from March to June achieved some of the most outstanding results of the U-boat war. All seven skippers earned a *Ritterkreuz* or Oak Leaves to the *Ritterkreuz.* The confirmed totals:

		Ships	Tons
U-107	(Hessler)	14	86,699
U-105	(Schewe)	12	70,500
U-103	(Schütze)	13	65,172
U-124	(Schulz)	11	52,397
U-38	(Liebe)	8	47,279
U-106	(Oesten)	8	37,224*
U-69	(Metzler)	6	28,400
Total		72	387,671

These seventy-two sinkings, reported in May and June 1941, substantially raised the total U-boat successes for those months. The figures also tended to obscure the relatively thin hunting in the "decisive" North Atlantic area.

The depredations in the South Atlantic finally forced the Admiralty to intensify ASW measures in that area. One important step was the initiation of "end-to-end" escort for the Sierra Leone convoys. Under the new plan, approved on July 1, each Sierra Leone convoy was to be guarded from Freetown to Gibraltar waters by at least five corvettes. There the convoy was to merge with the Gibraltar convoys, inbound to the British Isles with another group of corvettes. The complete plan required sixty-six corvettes, thirty-six for the Freetown to Gibraltar leg, thirty for the Gibraltar to the British Isles leg. Since there were only ninety-nine corvettes in service,† the plan could not be fully implemented without drawing corvettes from the North Atlantic convoy routes. Hence the urgent need for the U.S. Navy to assume responsibility for escorting North Atlantic convoys from Canada to Iceland at the earliest possible time.

June Patrols to the North Atlantic

The *Bismarck* affair had disrupted the U-boat patrol cycles in the Atlantic and gutted the western patrol line south of Greenland. By June 1, the line consisted of merely four boats. However, seven of the twenty boats that sailed in June were en route to reinforce it, plus *U-557,* which had withdrawn, temporarily, to refuel from the scuttled *Bismarck* supply ship *Belchen.* At the request of the OKM, two other new VIIs sailing from Germany to join the patrol line, *U-79* and *U-559,* were tem-

---

    *   Plus damage to the battleship *Malaya.*

    †   About six to eight new corvettes were commissioned each month. The Battle of the Atlantic Committee judged this production rate "not satisfactory," especially since the first batches of corvettes were due for extensive overhauls, to be carried out under Lend-Lease in American shipyards.

porarily diverted to the Denmark Strait to assist in a proposed sortie of the "pocket" battleship *Lützow* (ex-*Deutschland*).*

Positioned beyond range of ASW aircraft based in Iceland or Newfoundland and close enough to *Belchen* for refueling, Dönitz expected great results from the western patrol line. But problems arose. *Belchen* was lost almost immediately and Korth's *U-93* took *Belchen's* survivors to Lorient. In addition, another boat, Richard Zapp's new IXB, *U-66,* lost all four of its torpedo-tube bow caps and aborted—unnecessarily soon, Dönitz logged. The remaining ten boats, thinly spread across possible convoy routes, were bedeviled by heavy fog, caused when cold Arctic air masses met the warm waters of the Gulf Stream.

From Ultra the Admiralty knew the approximate position and strength of the U-boat patrol line. Working in close harmony, Rodger Winn in the U-boat Tracking Room and officials of the Admiralty Trade Division and those at Derby House in Liverpool routed the eastbound Halifax convoys well around the line. Thus the only ships the boats encountered were the (mostly empty) unescorted westbound singles or doubles, which had dispersed from the outbound convoys west of Iceland before the "end-to-end" escort came into being.

The absence of any Halifax convoys was deeply puzzling to the Germans. Suspecting that the Admiralty might be routing them well to the north of the patrol line, along the edge of the ice pack between Newfoundland and Greenland, Dönitz obtained permission from the OKM to send Kleinschmidt's *U-111*—which had refueled from the now-scuttled *Belchen*—to explore the coast of Newfoundland from Cape Race north to Belle Isle Strait. Since this was to be the first penetration of "American" waters by a U-boat, and Hitler wanted no unnecessary provocations during Barbarossa, Kleinschmidt was barred from shooting at anything except "especially valuable ships" (cruisers or larger warships or huge liners, such as the *Queen Mary,* converted to troop transports) and was to maintain absolute radio silence during the reconnaissance.

This was a challenging assignment for a boat on its maiden patrol, doubly so because Kleinschmidt had no navigational charts of the Newfoundland area. Upon closing the coast, he encountered heavy pack ice, icebergs, and dense fog. He explored the area for a week, during which he incurred ice damage to two torpedo-tube caps, then withdrew well to the east to radio a report to Dönitz. He had seen no traffic. Because of the extensive ice pack, Kleinschmidt believed it improbable that the convoys were being routed that way. After reflecting on this report, Dönitz moved the patrol line further south—to no avail.

Although the patrol line found no Halifax convoys, the boats encountered and continued to sink a number of westbound singles and doubles. The top shooter was the *Ritterkreuz* holder Herbert Schultze, who was taking the famous but weary *U 48* home to the Training Command. In merely nine days, Schultze sank five ships for 38,462 tons, including three tankers: the 9,500-ton British *Inversuir,* the 6,000-

---

* Probably acting on Enigma intelligence, on June 13 Coastal Command launched fourteen torpedo-carrying Beauforts at *Lützow* in Norwegian waters. One plane got a hit that knocked *Lützow* out of action for the next seven months.

ton British *Wellfield,* and the 10,700-ton Dutch *Pendrecht.* This tonnage put Schultze over the 200,000-ton mark and Dönitz awarded him Oak Leaves to his *Ritterkreuz,* the fourth skipper after Prien, Kretschmer, and Schepke to earn that high honor in the North Atlantic.* Schultze left *U-48* in Germany and returned to France to command the 3d Combat Flotilla at La Pallice.

No less aggressive was the *Ritterkreuz* holder Engelbert Endrass in the equally weary VIIB *U-46.* But he was bedeviled by torpedo failures—four, he reported. On June 2 and 6, he attacked and hit a freighter and a tanker, but each time the torpedo failed to detonate. On June 8 he simultaneously attacked a tanker and a freighter. Two more torpedoes failed to detonate, but nonetheless Endrass damaged the 6,200-ton British tanker *Ensis* and sank a 5,300-ton freighter. In retaliation, *Ensis* turned on *U-46* and rammed her, knocking out the attack periscope. Endrass put *Ensis* under with a finishing shot, then aborted to France. Inbound to Lorient he sank a 5,600-ton freighter by torpedo and gun. His overclaims of 16,500 tons sunk also put Endrass beyond the 200,000-ton mark and he, too, was awarded Oak Leaves to his *Ritterkreuz.*†

Another *Ritterkreuz* holder, Wolfgang Lüth in the old but recently rehabilitated Type IX *U-43,* replaced Endrass in the patrol line. He sank two ships for 7,500 tons, but *U-43* was not really combat-worthy. When Lüth returned to Lorient, the boat went back into the yard for another overhaul, to remain there until November, having completed only two war patrols in twelve months, during which Lüth sank only five ships.

The other skippers of the patrol line—some on maiden voyages—sank another fourteen ships between June 1 and June 18. The most successful of these was Klaus Scholtz in the Type IXB *U-108,* making his third Atlantic patrol. He claimed sinking four ships for 27,300 tons, including a 14,000-ton auxiliary cruiser. In reality he sank four freighters for 17,000 tons.‡

Erich Topp in *U-552,* who had made three patrols to North Channel in the duck *U-57* and two in *U-552,* requested that dangerous area again. In view of the fact that the duck *U-141,* on indoctrination patrol, had been severely damaged there in recent days, Dönitz was hesitant, especially since the shortest nights of the year were fast approaching. Finally, Dönitz consented.

The plan was for Topp to coordinate operations, if possible, with three Type

---

* Schultze's confirmed score—all on *U-48*—was twenty-eight ships for 183,435 tons, ranking him fifth among the German aces in the war. The *U-48* remained the leading boat of the war, sinking fifty-four and a half ships for 320,429 tons under Schultze, Rösing, and Bleichrodt. Kretschmer's *U-99* ranked second.

† Endrass's confirmed score—all on *U-46*—was twenty-four ships for 134,566 tons.

‡ In defense of Dönitz at Nuremberg, Scholtz's first watch officer, Heinz-Konrad Fenn, submitted a document—and photographs—asserting that after Scholtz sank the 4,200-ton Greek freighter *Dirphys* on June 8, he gave the survivors in the lifeboats twenty loaves of bread, plenty of water, and instructions for sailing to land, and temporarily brought one of the survivors on board *U-108* for medical treatment.

IID ducks on indoctrination patrols close to the British Isles: the *U-141,* repaired in Lorient; the *U-143,* sailing from Germany; and the *U-147,* which had earlier sailed from Germany. Unknown to Dönitz, the *U-147,* commanded by Eberhard Wetjen, had been sunk on June 2 by British warships, the destroyer *Wanderer* and corvette *Periwinkle,* following Wetjen's bold solo attack on convoy Outbound 329.

Topp found the area teeming with ASW aircraft, forcing him to crash-dive up to ten times a day, a nerve-racking routine during which several of his men broke down. Nonetheless, he found and sank three ships for 24,400 tons, including the 11,000-ton British freighter *Norfolk.* These sinkings brought Topp's claims to 100,000 tons, earning him a *Ritterkreuz.** On June 18, Topp came upon an inbound convoy and attempted to attack and bring in the ducks and other boats, but the escorts drove him off. The duck *U-141* was unable to cooperate with *U-552* but she shot at two ships, sinking one.

Another duck, the *U-138,* commanded by twenty-five-year-old Franz Gramitsky, who had served in combat under Schepke and Lüth on other ducks, had arrived in Lorient from Germany for a top-secret special mission. Gramitsky was to penetrate the mined British naval base at Gibraltar for the specific purpose of sinking the battleship *Renown* or an aircraft carrier or, at the very least, a heavy cruiser. Should he succeed in sinking a capital ship—as Prien had at Scapa Flow— he was assured of a *Ritterkreuz.* Should he run into difficulty, the crew was to scuttle and swim to Spain, where it was to be assisted in making its way back to Lorient.

Gramitsky sailed from Lorient on June 12. Other than he, no one on the boat knew the purpose of the mission. Early on the morning of June 18, when *U-138* was about 100 miles west of the Strait of Gibraltar, inbound on the surface, the bridge watch spotted what was believed to be a "cruiser" and dived. Actually, the "cruiser" was the destroyer *Faulkner,* which in company with four sister ships of the 13th Destroyer Flotilla, *Fearless, Forester, Foresight,* and *Foxhound,* was conducting a sonar sweep, probably forewarned by Ultra to be on the lookout for *U-138.* The skilled sonar teams on *Faulkner* and *Forester* had helped kill the first U-boats of the war, *U-27* and *U-39.*

Faulkner obtained sonar contact on *U-138* and attacked immediately, dropping six depth charges set for 100 to 250 feet. These exploded with uncanny accuracy, wrecking and flooding the boat. Out of control, her internal spaces awash with water, she twice slid down to 650 feet before Gramitsky could blow her ballast tanks and get her to the surface. When she popped up, the entire crew jumped overboard. *Forester* saw the doomed boat on the surface and attacked with guns. She dropped six more close depth charges before she realized *U-138* was already sinking, vertically, stern first. *Faulkner* fished out the entire crew of twenty-eight men; there were no serious casualties.

---

* Topp's confirmed sinkings on the duck *U-57* and on *U-552* were fourteen and a half ships for 94,076 tons.

A REVEALING CONVOY BATTLE

To June 18, none of the boats on the distant western patrol line had seen any sign of a Halifax convoy. "The lull in traffic . . . is striking," Dönitz logged. He decided to move the line southeastward, to "mislead" the enemy, in case they "had knowledge of the patrol line." At the same time, he directed Kleinschmidt in *U-111,* the northernmost boat in the line, to return to the ice pack off Newfoundland, to see if the convoys were sailing far to the north. The shift to the southeast produced no results. On June 19, therefore, Dönitz disbanded the patrol line and scattered the twenty boats in the North Atlantic to positions within a huge rectangle, measuring roughly 1,000 by 1,800 miles. The twenty boats included the new VIICs *U-79* and *U-559,* which had been assigned to the Denmark Strait to support the aborted *Lützow* sortie, but *U-559* had bent her periscopes in the ice and was forced to head for Lorient.

While westbound to her designated station, shortly after midnight on June 20, the new VIIC, *U-203,* commanded by Rolf Mützelburg, age twenty-eight, from the duck *U-10,* sighted a battleship, escorted by a single destroyer. She was the aged *Texas,* part of a temporary United States naval task force that included the other two old battleships, *New York* and *Arkansas,* all deployed to help the British intercept the anticipated sortie of *Lützow.* Since *Texas* was then about 800 miles south-southwest of Iceland and ten miles inside a zone in which Hitler had authorized attacks on neutral warships, Mützelburg boldly went to battle stations and chased the zigzagging giant northeast, wondering if *Texas* (like the fifty destroyers and ten Coast Guard cutters) had been loaned, sold, or given to Great Britain. But *Texas* was making high speed and after a sixteen-hour pursuit that took the vessels 148 miles inside the zone, Mützelburg had to give it up, a great disappointment.

Later in the day, when Mützelburg reported his unsuccessful chase, it caused a great stir in Kerneval and Berlin. D day for Operation Barbarossa was merely forty-eight hours away; Hitler had made it clear that U-boats and merchant-ship raiders were to avoid incidents with United States vessels. And yet the appearance of *Texas* within the "German zone" was a defiant challenge. Since Dönitz and Raeder and others at the OKM believed Germany should not show weakness lest the United States transgress further, they concluded that Mützelburg had acted correctly in attempting to attack *Texas,* and Raeder so informed Hitler, who was in "complete agreement." However, since errors in navigation were more the rule than the exception, it was also agreed that no action against neutral (i.e., American) warships was to be taken within twenty miles of the German boundary line, and Dönitz so informed the boats.

Later that night, June 21–22, Hitler personally telephoned Raeder to nullify the new policy. During Barbarossa, Hitler stated, attacks on American warships anywhere in the German zone were *not* to be undertaken. "Until there is a clear development of the Barbarossa campaign," the OKM logged, Hitler "desires that all incidents with the U.S.A. be avoided." Hitler himself "will decide when attacks on U.S.A. warships are again to be permitted."

Dönitz relayed the new policy to the boats on June 21: "The Führer has ordered, for the next few weeks, avoidance of any incident with the U.S.A. Proceed accordingly in any doubtful case." As a further precaution, Hitler had ordered that the U-boats were to attack only clearly recognizable British cruisers, battleships, or aircraft carriers within and without the zone, bearing in mind that American ships in that category might be blacked out and should not be mistaken for British.

This order, Dönitz complained in his memoirs, created "a situation which was unique in the history of war." It meant that "U-boats could no longer attack their most dangerous enemies, the destroyers, frigates, and corvettes, whether British or any other nationality. . . . The British antisubmarine forces thus had a completely free hand." But this was splitting hairs. Because of the shallow torpedo settings required and the resulting erratic performance, U-boats did not customarily attack convoy escorts. They avoided and evaded escorts and when counterattacked by escorts, they went deep. And yet it rankled to be restricted from attacking escorts, and Dönitz did not hesitate to make his views known to the OKM.

Returning to his designated patrol area, on the afternoon of June 23—the second day of Barbarossa—Mützelburg in *U-203* happened upon convoy Halifax 133 at longitude 41 degrees west—400 miles due south of Greenland. His contact report galvanized Kerneval; it was the first Halifax convoy any U-boat had found in thirty-five days. Since it had a very long way to go, there was a good possibility that ten or more boats could be brought up to attack it along its track. Accordingly, Dönitz instructed Mützelburg to shadow and radio beacon signals for the benefit of the other boats, thus launching an epic chase and battle.

Initially composed of forty-nine ships laden with valuable cargos, Halifax 133 had sailed on June 21. It was the fifth eastbound transatlantic convoy to be provided "end-to-end" or "clear-across" escort and to sail at increased speed to accommodate the 12- to 15-knot ships that theretofore had been sailing outside convoys. A newly formed Canadian escort group (the destroyer *Ottawa* and four corvettes, three Canadian and one British) was to take the convoy east to 35 degrees west, where an Iceland-based British escort group was to shepherd it through the middle leg to about 20 degrees west. In a reverse process, another Canadian escort group (corvette *Wetaskiwin* and four others), sailing from Iceland, was to relieve a British escort group at 35 degrees west and shepherd convoy Outbound 336 onward to Canada.

Mützelburg in *U-203* tracked Halifax 133 throughout the afternoon and evening of June 23, sending frequent reports. All over the ocean the widely scattered boats plotted the positions by the new "reference point" system and calculated the chances of making an interception. After two other new VIICs, *U-79* and *U-371*, had made contact and reported, in the early hours of June 24 Dönitz authorized *U-203* to attack.

In his first salvo of the war, Mützelburg fired at three large ships. He claimed that two sank, but only the 4,400-ton Norwegian freighter *Solöy* was confirmed. Heinrich Driver, age twenty-eight, in the new *U-371*, attacked next, sinking the 4,800-ton Norwegian freighter *Vigrid*, which was straggling. The crew and ten

American Red Cross nurses launched four lifeboats. Two boats headed for Greenland, the other two for Ireland. Wolfgang Kaufmann, age twenty-nine, in the new *U-79* had no opportunity to shoot, but he shadowed and reported. *Ottawa,* commanded by Edmond R. Mainguy, and the four corvettes of the Canadian escort group, engaged in the "first Canadian Navy convoy battle," sped hither and yon, unable to communicate and dropping depth charges to little purpose.

At that time, two consecutive convoys, Outbound 335 and Outbound 336, were proceeding westward in this area. Noting that Outbound 336, composed of twenty-three ships and guarded by a Canadian escort group of five corvettes, was to pass close to the besieged Halifax 133, Western Approaches ordered the convoy commander to alter course to avoid that area. The convoy commander's regular radio operator was ill; his substitute, who could not decode the message, mindlessly filed it away. A similar message was sent to the flagship of the Canadian escort group, *Wetaskiwin,* but the Canadians had not yet found the convoy and the message could not be delivered. Thus Outbound 336 continued on a converging course with eastbound Halifax 133, bringing together a total of sixty-five merchant ships and two newly formed Canadian escort groups.

Later on the morning of June 24, about seven hours after his attack on Halifax 133, Mützelburg in *U-203* made contact with Outbound 336. The operational orders required that Mützelburg report the convoy so Kerneval could bring up other boats, withholding an attack until authorized. But Mützelburg impulsively assaulted the formation, sinking two freighters, the 5,000-ton British *Kinross* and the 2,000-ton Dutch *Schie.* Later that afternoon, he reported this new convoy and the upsetting news that he had already attacked it and that owing to a broken muffler valve he was aborting immediately—before any other boats could make contact. Dönitz angrily ordered Mützelburg to shadow and report, but he had lost contact and could not comply.

From Mützelburg's reports, and others, Dönitz realized that two convoys were passing "in a narrow area," and there was an opportunity for a slaughter. He therefore passed along all information and instructed the converging boats to attack whichever convoy they considered "most favorable." At the same time, Western Approaches, seeking to protect the most valuable (eastbound) ships, ordered the Canadian *Wetaskiwin* group, still searching for Outbound 336, and five of the British escorts with convoys Outbound 335 and Outbound 336, to reinforce the eastbound Halifax 133.

By the time these orders were received, the *Wetaskiwin* group had picked up the distress calls from and the position of the long-sought Outbound 336. Contrary to orders of Western Approaches, the leader of the *Wetaskiwin* group, Guy S. Windeyer, elected to divide his force so that Outbound 336 would not be completely unprotected. He sent two corvettes to Halifax 133 and attached *Wetaskiwin* and two other corvettes to Outbound 336. His disobedience of a direct order was to evoke criticism—and ridicule—of the Canadian Navy, but upon investigation at a later date, Derby House approved of the decision. However, by the time the *Wetaskiwin* group finally caught up to the convoy, it had dispersed into a dense fog and the group could not provide meaningful support.

About six U-boats elected to pursue this dispersing convoy. These included two experienced skippers, Ernst Mengersen in *U-101* and Klaus Scholtz in *U-108*. But all the U-boats were hampered by fog and fuel shortages. Only Scholtz in *U-108* sank a ship, the 4,400-ton Greek *Nicolas Pateras*.

During the daylight hours of June 24, Wolfgang Kaufmann in the new *U-79* continued to track the eastbound Halifax 133. Early that evening Peter Lohmeyer, age thirty, a merchant marine veteran who had trained on the recently sunk duck *U-138*, came up in his new VIIC *U-651* and attacked three ships. He claimed sinking all three, but only one, the 5,300-ton British freighter *Brockley Hill*, went down. The Canadian escorts counterattacked in confusion, again to no purpose. After Lohmeyer's attack, the British corvette *Gladiolus* from Outbound 335 and four other escorts from Outbound 336 arrived, raising the total escort force with Halifax 133 to ten.

Shortly after midnight, June 25, *Gladiolus* saw a U-boat speeding very close across her bow. This was Walter Flachsenberg, age thirty-two, in another new VIIC, *U-71*, boldly but unalertly maneuvering to attack the rear of the convoy. *Gladiolus* put on full speed to ram but, when it was realized on second thought that *Gladiolus* was 600 miles from land and might sink herself in the ramming, the collision was aborted, giving *U-71* time to crash dive. *Gladiolus* got a firm sonar contact and carried out five separate attacks, dropping thirty depth charges. The recently arrived British corvette *Nasturtium* joined *Gladiolus,* which was nearly out of depth charges, and dropped six. A half hour later, *U-71*, severely damaged internally, surfaced to escape in the darkness. Seeing her, *Gladiolus* opened fire, but could not use her 4" gun because *Nasturtium* was in the way. When she cleared out, *Gladiolus* brought her gun to bear and claimed a fatal "direct hit" on the conning tower. Although *Gladiolus* was criticized for not ramming the boat in the first attack, she was credited with a kill in the second attack. In fact, Flachsenberg got *U-71* away, aborting to Lorient with severe damage.* Dönitz heaped praise on Flachsenberg for extricating *U-71* from "a very difficult situation."

Surrounded by ten escorts, convoy Halifax 133 proceeded eastward on June 26. At nightfall, a half dozen U-boats moved in for the kill. Wolfgang Kaufmann, the patient shadower in the new *U-79*, hit and damaged a 10,400-ton British tanker, but she kept on going. Erich Topp in *U-552*, who had come west from the North Channel area and was low on fuel and torpedoes, hit a freighter, but the torpedo failed to detonate. Owing to his shortage of fuel, Topp was forced to return to Lorient. Another new VIIC, *U-562*, commanded by Herwig Collmann, age twenty-five, which had only just arrived in the Atlantic, tried to attack but was driven off. Yet another new VIIC, *U-564*, commanded by Reinhard Suhren, who had won a *Ritterkreuz* while serving as first watch officer on the famous *U-48*, attacked and hit three big ships in one amazing salvo: the 8,800-ton Dutch freighter *Maasdam,* the 8,700-ton British freighter *Malaya II,* and the 9,500-ton Norwegian tanker *Kongsgaard.* The *Maasdam* sank. She had on board a company of American Marines en route to the American Embassy in London. Rescue ships took the

---

* Earlier, the aggressive *Gladiolus* also had been erroneously credited with sinking *U-65.*

Marines to Iceland. The *Malaya II,* carrying a load of ammunition, blew up with a horrific blast. The *Kongsgaard* was damaged but she kept going.

Another VIIC, *U-556,* commanded by the *Ritterkreuz* holder Herbert Wohlfarth, fresh from Lorient on his second patrol, joined the attackers in the early hours of June 27. Notwithstanding a noisy coupling in his port motor, Wohlfarth decided to attack submerged during daylight and pulled ahead of the convoy and dived. Before he could shoot, the British corvette *Nasturtium* got *U-556* on sonar and fired off all her remaining twenty depth charges. Responding to her alarm, the British corvettes *Celandine* and *Gladiolus* came up, but when neither could get a sonar return, they expressed doubt about the contact. Insisting she had a good contact, *Nasturtium* guided *Celandine* to the likely spot. *Celandine* dropped twenty-four charges, to no apparent effect. Still skeptical of this "contact," both *Celandine* and *Gladiolus* repeatedly expressed doubt, but finally *Gladiolus,* too, got a contact and made a ten-charge attack, which brought up a large oil patch.

The charges from *Nasturtium, Celandine,* and *Gladiolus* had, in fact, severely damaged *U-556.* Wohlfarth shut down the noisy port motor but heavy flooding aft short-circuited the starboard motor, forcing him to restart the port motor. However, the flooding aft continued to the point that Wohlfarth lost control of the boat, which slipped down to 426 feet. Believing his only chance of survival lay in surfacing to attack the corvettes (in violation of Hitler's orders), Wohlfarth blew ballast tanks and came up almost beneath *Gladiolus,* which was in the process of firing three of her last ten depth charges. One of these actually hit the aft deck of *U-556* and bounced off.

Gladiolus, Nasturtium, and *Celandine* opened fire at point-blank range with 4" guns, scoring hits on *U-556*'s conning tower. The gunfire killed some Germans and persuaded Wohlfarth to scuttle and abandon ship. Believing there was a chance to capture *U-556, Gladiolus* launched a whaler with a boarding party, led by Lieutenant J. G. Gifford-Hull, who fished out a "German officer" to "help." However, upon entering the conning tower, the British sailors saw that the control room was flooded and smelled chlorine gas. Since *U-556* was obviously going down fast, Gifford-Hull abandoned the attempt to capture her, coming away only with a torpedo-maintenance booklet and a Very pistol.

Meanwhile, *Gladiolus* picked up Wohlfarth and thirty-nine of his crew. Four Germans died in the sinking; another died from inhaling toxic gas in his escape apparatus. Wohlfarth was the sixth *Ritterkreuz* holder to fall, the third to be captured.* British interrogators did not rate the crew highly. Except for Wohlfarth and a few capable and experienced chiefs and petty officers who had earlier served with him, the senior officers and men, the interrogators reported, were "unreliable" newcomers "of limited experience" who had been "hastily promoted." The junior men were "decidedly poor stuff."

That afternoon there was a change-up in the escorts of Halifax 133. The Canadian group (the destroyer *Ottawa,* five corvettes) peeled off and went into Iceland, where it was criticized—and even ridiculed—for "losing" five ships of the convoy

---

* His total score on the ducks *U-14* and *U-137,* and *U-556* was 20 ships for 56,389 tons.

and accomplishing nothing in return. It was replaced at sea by C. D. Howard-Johnston's British Escort Group 12, bringing the total escorts for the final leg to thirteen.

The U-boats continued to track and attack Halifax 133. In the early hours of June 29, Peter Lohmeyer in the new *U-651* caught up again after a four-day chase. Closing submerged, he fired two torpedoes and hit the 6,300-ton British freighter *Grayburn,* the convoy flagship, which was loaded with 10,000 tons of steel. It sank in four minutes. But the next ship in the column, the 8,000-ton British tanker *Anadara,* plowed into the submerged *U-651* with a heavy jolt that threw the boat out of control and weakened seams.

The more battle-wise warships of Escort Group 12 deployed in a fighting mood. As a deterrent they first dropped depth charges at random. However, two escorts, (destroyer *Scimitar,* minesweeper *Speedwell*) soon reported firm sonar contacts and they conducted deliberate attacks. Some of the depth charges fell close to *U-651,* doubtless opening seams weakened by the collision with *Anadara.* Flooding aft, *U-651* slid down to 525 feet and Lohmeyer exhausted his battery in a vain effort to regain control of the boat with the motors. In a last desperate effort to escape on the diesels, he blew all ballast tanks and surfaced.

When Lohmeyer lit off the diesels they emitted small puffs of black smoke. The destroyer *Malcolm* saw the smoke six miles off, gave the alarm, and charged in, firing her main batteries. Four other escorts, including the destroyer *Scimitar* and the corvette *Nasturtium,* came up, firing guns. In the face of the fire, Lohmeyer scuttled and abandoned ship. Rigging scramble nets, *Malcolm* picked up Lohmeyer and all forty-four of his men, but *Scimitar* closed *Malcolm* and snatched one of the Germans from the net. The Admiralty credited Escort Group 12 with the kill, but in later years, Admiralty historians withdrew the credit and bestowed it upon *Anadara,* which retroactively became the first merchant ship to be credited with sinking a U-boat.

As the convoy drew closer to the heavily patrolled Northwest Approaches, Dönitz called off the boats, directed them elsewhere, and asked for reports. He calculated that in all, about fourteen U-boats had made contact with Halifax 133, including four more new boats from Germany which joined near the end of the chase. The confirmed results were shockingly low: five U-boats sank six ships for 38,000 tons* and damaged two tankers, *Tibia* and *Kongsgaard.* In return, two boats, *U-556* and *U-651,* had been lost, and *U-71* very nearly lost, a ruinous "exchange rate" of three ships sunk for each boat lost. Two boats had sunk three ships for 11,300 tons from convoy Outbound 336. Grand total: nine ships for 49,300 tons, three of them by Mützelburg in *U-203,* who, Dönitz logged, conceded his "mistake" in launching an impulsive attack on Outbound 336 and of aborting before any other boats arrived.

---

* An assertion by Herbert A. Werner, first watch officer of the new boat *U-557,* in his 1969 best-selling book *Iron Coffins,* that the boat attacked Halifax Convoy 133 on June 24 and sank 30,000 tons of shipping from it (and was forced to abort after a brutal depth-charge attack), is not substantiated in German records.

•   •   •

The battle with Halifax 133 led to important changes in the U-boat strategy and tactics, including, most notably, a withdrawal of the boats from the Greenland area to more easterly hunting grounds. The reasons were several:

•   Although the ocean west of Iceland and south of Greenland was still devoid of ASW aircraft and experienced escorts and was therefore safer for U-boat operations, the area was simply too large for effective convoy hunting by patrol lines with the few boats then available. The *U-203* discovered convoy Halifax 133 only after Dönitz had disbanded the western patrol line and scattered the boats over a huge area. But in scattering the boats, Dönitz foreswore the ability to quickly bring them up for a pack attack—to mass maximum strength at the point of contact with the enemy.

•   Operations in this very distant area were extremely difficult for the relatively short-ranged Type VII boats. The fuel expended going out and back left little for patrolling the area for any appreciable time, or for confidently engaging in extended convoy chases. Apart from that, the expenditure of all torpedoes or a simple mechanical failure—such as *U-203*'s defective muffler valve—forced a costly termination of the patrol. Until the U-tankers, or "supply boats," which were still under construction,* became operational and the Type VIIs could be replenished and obtain medical help and spare parts at sea, thus greatly extending time on patrol station and reducing the number of aborts, operations in the Greenland area were simply not efficient.

•   The higher speed of Halifax convoys posed great difficulties for the U-boats. The Type VIIs had a maximum (engine-straining) speed of 17 knots; the Type IXs, 18 knots. Unless held down by surface or air escorts, the boats could shadow effectively, but to *overtake* even a zigzagging fast Halifax convoy to gain favorable shooting positions from ahead or the flanks required much time (as well as fuel), increasing the chances of being discovered and counterattacked by escorts and thus losing the element of surprise.

•   The weather conditions and the onset of the summer solstice were not favorable for U-boat operations in the Greenland area. Returning boats reported dense, blinding fog during half the patrol days. The fog restricted not only reconnaissance but also navigation (by sun and star sights), leaving many skippers with only a vague idea of where they were. When not fogbound, the very long days—and very short nights—in those north latitudes restricted the available hours for night surface attacks, when the boat was most effective and mobile, and compelled skippers to resort in many instances to submerged daylight attacks, when the boat was least mobile and most vulnerable to sonar detection.

---

* Six large Type XIV supply boats were under construction. The first two, *U-459* and *U-460*, were to be completed in November and December 1941, the other four in early 1942. A plan was under consideration to convert the big Type XB minelayers to supply boats. The first three of these, *U-116, U-117,* and *U-118,* were to be completed in July, October, and December of 1941. Allowing time for extensive acceptance trials, shakedowns, and workups, none of these supply boats could be expected to reach the Atlantic before the spring of 1942.

• • •

The British sailed 383 loaded ships in convoys from Halifax and Sydney to the British Isles in the month of June. The U-boats found only one convoy that month, Halifax 133, from which they sank six loaded ships of the forty-nine. No other loaded eastbound ship from Canada fell victim to the U-boats in June; hence 377 loaded ships (or about 99 percent) reached destinations. In the first two weeks of June, before convoying on the Iceland-Canada leg was fully in effect, the U-boats had better luck in sinking singles, most of them empty ships from disbursing Outbound convoys south of Greenland. They destroyed twenty-two such singles, plus two from convoy Outbound 336, a total of twenty-four empty ships for 134,754 tons. In the second two weeks, after the Iceland-Canada leg was afforded better protection by the Canadian escort groups and aircraft and the Halifax convoy speed was increased to accommodate the 12- to 15-knot vessels, the U-boats sank only five singles in that area.*

The failure of the U-boats to find eastbound convoys in the North Atlantic and to inflict greater damage on the only one they found, Halifax 133, and Dönitz's decision to withdraw the boats from the Greenland area, was a clear victory of the British defense over German offense. It was due, in part, to radio intelligence (Ultra, DFing, Traffic Analysis, RFP, TINA), which enabled the Royal Navy to sink the supply ship *Belchen* and to divert most convoys around the U-boat patrol lines; in part to the initiation of "end-to-end" surface escorts (however green the Canadians) and air escort from Newfoundland and Iceland; in part to the higher speed of the Halifax convoys, in part to the inability of the boats to operate effectively in far western areas, and in no small part to the steady decline in the experience level of the U-boat skippers and crews. Not for sixteen more months (October 1942) did the U-boats again inflict any appreciable damage on a Halifax convoy.

COASTAL COMMAND

The British attack on the U-boat force in Atlantic waters by aircraft of Coastal Command had produced virtually zero kills by June 1, 1941. Two Sunderlands had shared credit with surface ships in the destruction of two U-boats (*U-26, U-55*), but no Coastal Command aircraft flying in the Atlantic area had sunk a U-boat unassisted.†

There were numerous reasons for this abysmal showing. Chief among these was that Coastal Command remained a poor stepchild of the RAF, still in third place in weaponry, electronics, and manpower. As one consequence, Coastal Com-

---

* In addition, U-boats off North Channel sank five ships for 29,200 tons, and near the Azores, *U-553* sank two ships for 8,000 tons, including the Norwegian tanker *Ranella.* The Italian submarines in southern waters sank six ships for 24,700 tons, including the 8,000-ton British tanker *Auris.* British destroyer *Wishart* sank the Italian submarine *Glauco,* which was withdrawing from Bordeaux to Italy.

† See Plate 9. RAF aircraft in the Mediterranean had sunk two Italian submarines (*Argonauta, Rubino*) unassisted and shared credit for two others (*Gondar, Durbo*) with British surface ships.

mand was still unable to mount a credible attack on the U-boat force. An official study showed that in mid-1941 Coastal Command had only about two hundred ASW aircraft in frontline squadrons.*

The principal contribution Coastal Command had made thus far in the Battle of the Atlantic was to thwart single and pack U-boat operations in the Northwest Approaches and Icelandic waters out to about 300 miles. This was primarily the doing of the hundred American-built twin-engine Lockheed Hudsons flying on convoy escort or offensive ASW patrols. However, the Hudsons could carry only three or four 250-pound depth charges and did not have sufficient fuel to safely patrol much beyond 300 miles or to loiter for very long at that distance from home. The best they could do was to force a U-boat to submerge and hold it down. This was also true of the forty British-built twin-engine Whitleys. They could carry twice the depth-charge load of the Hudsons (six), but they could not fly on one engine, a severe handicap for over-water operations. Hence the Hudsons and Whitleys, which made up about 70 percent of Coastal Command's frontline strength, were not really satisfactory for offensive actions against U-boats.

What Coastal Command urgently needed for convoy escort and offensive ASW patrols was a long-range aircraft with a large bomb load. The twenty four-engine Sunderland flying boats partially filled that need. They could carry eight 250-pound depth charges on patrols out to about 700 miles. However, the huge Sunderland was not an efficient aircraft; its four engines required much maintenance. A Coastal Command study showed that each of the Sunderlands flew an average of only two sorties per month. The British would continue producing Sunderlands on a modest scale, but no one favored anything more than that.

Better yet was the American-built Catalina, of which Coastal Command had thirty. They could carry twice the bomb load of a Sunderland (sixteen 250-pound depth charges) out to about 900 miles. The Americans were gearing up to produce Catalinas at a high rate,† but in view of its two-ocean force deployment and large new responsibilities in the Atlantic, the U.S. Navy had first call on Catalinas and only a trickle could be diverted to the British and Canadians. At the end of 1941, Coastal Command still had only thirty-six Catalinas in four frontline squadrons (209, 210, 240, 413) based in and around the British Isles.

In June 1941, Coastal Command got a new chief, Philip Joubert de la Ferté, replacing Bowhill. He urged an expansion of Coastal Command to provide for increased emphasis on *offensive* patrolling, especially in the Bay of Biscay, a choke point through which U-boats had to transit inbound and outbound to French bases. However, Bomber Command, gearing up for the supposed war-winning strategic air assault on Germany, stoutly resisted the diversion of any aircraft to Coastal Command.

Nonetheless, for a brief time Joubert appeared to have won at least part of his case. The War Cabinet allotted Coastal Command the first nine of the new four-engine B-24 Liberator bombers arriving from America. The B-24 had about the

---

*   See Plate 8. Of these, 130 were American-built Catalinas (30) and Hudsons (100).

†   In the war, American factories built 3,290 Catalinas.

PLATE 8

COASTAL COMMAND ASW AIRCRAFT BASED IN THE
BRITISH ISLES JUNE–JULY 1941[1]

TYPE	NO.	ENGINES	LOAD BOMBS/DCS	RADIUS NAUT. MI.	SORTIES PER MONTH
Catalina	30	2	16/250-lb.	900	85
Sunderland	20	4	8/250-lb.	700	40
Wellington	20	2	12/250-lb.	550	70
Whitley	40	2	6/250-lb.	500	170
Hudson	100	2	3/250-lb.	450	570
Total	210[2]				

1. Source: Monthly Anti-Submarine Rpt. June and July 1941. ADM. 199/1245. "The Air Offensive Against U-boats," 6/1/42.

2. Does not include Blenheims, Beaufighters, and Ansons.

PLATE 9

AXIS SUBMARINES DESTROYED ALL OR IN PART BY THE
ROYAL AIR FORCE TO AUGUST 1941[1]

DATES	SUBMARINE	AIRCRAFT/ SQUADRON	PILOT	SURFACE SHIP CO-OP	AREA
1/30/40	U-55	Sunderland/228	Brooks	Yes	Atl.
3/11/40	U-31	Blenheim/82	Delap	No	Jade
6/28/40	Argonauta	Sunderland/230	Campbell	No	Med.
6/29/40	Rubino	Sunderland/230	Campbell	No	Med.
7/1/40	U-26	Sunderland/10	Gibson	Yes	Atl.
9/30/40	Gondar	Sunderland/230	Alington	Yes	Med.
10/18/40	Durbo	2 Londons/202	Hatfield/ Eagleton	Yes	Med.

1. Source: Franks (1995), Axis Submarine Losses.

same operating radius as a Catalina (900 to 1,000 miles), but it was twice as fast (205 knots versus 105 knots), could carry twice the bomb load (8,000 pounds versus 4,000 pounds), was more rugged and more heavily armed with defensive machine guns and 20mm cannons, and, of course, it was a land plane that could base at existing airfields. These nine B-24s went to a new Coastal Command squadron, 120, based at Nutt's Corner, Northern Ireland, commanded by Terence M. Bulloch, but all other B-24s arriving from America went to Bomber Command.

Joubert turned to the scientific community for assistance to improve Coastal Command's operations, especially the miserable U-boat kill rate. The Admiralty sent him a brilliant physicist, Patrick M. S. Blackett, who was to win a Nobel Prize in the postwar years. Utilizing a statistically oriented method of applied science initially devised for the RAF, which came to be called "Operations Research," Blackett and a small team analyzed thousands of U-boat contact and attack reports. Based on this analysis ("quantitative, analytic thinking with empirical checking"), the Blackett team advised that:

• Navigation in Coastal Command was appallingly bad. Aircraft crews seldom knew precisely where they were, did not actually patrol designated areas, and too often failed to meet convoys they were assigned to escort.

• The 1.5-meter-wavelength ASV II radar, installed in three quarters of Coastal Command's frontline aircraft, was not being properly exploited. Radar operators were undertrained and overworked. Radar sets were not properly maintained and calibrated.

• Aircraft were flying too high to get the most from the sets. Based on exaggerated claims of radar proponents, air crews expected too much of ASV II radar, and when it failed to perform as advertised, they denounced it.

• In the majority of U-boat contacts, the Germans saw the aircraft first and dived to safety. Aircraft spent too much time and too many assets futilely depth-charging elusive targets.

• The usual depth settings on the standard 250-pound depth charge were too deep and the explosive in the warhead was too feeble.

• A prevailing view that a monster 2,000-pound depth charge was required to compensate for aiming errors was absolutely wrong.

The Blackett reports contained many recommendations to correct the deficiencies. Among them: thorough training for navigators and radar-maintenance personnel and radar operators, and a lowering of expectations about the sets; comfortable work stations and frequent eye rest for radar operators; an altitude limit of 4,000 feet for convoy spotting and 2,000 feet for U-boat spotting when using radar; the use of beacon signals to improve convoy locating; the camouflaging of the undersides of aircraft with white paint to decrease visibility; the mounting of binoculars on pedestals for daytime searching; a twenty-five-foot fuse for depth charges; a larger "stick" of 100-pound depth charges utilizing the more powerful explosive RDX or Torpex (TNT and cyclonite, enhanced with aluminum powder).

Some of these recommendations touched off intense controversy. The most heated was the debate over depth-charge size. Most airmen refused to believe that larger numbers of small depth charges were preferable to a smaller number of one-ton "killer" depth charges. As a result, R&D on the 2,000-pound and also less powerful weaponry, as well as a depth-charge bombsight, was pursued. Meanwhile, the standard airborne ASW weapon remained the 250-pound depth charge dropped by eye. However, Blackett's recommendations that the spacing of the stick be lengthened threefold and the warhead be beefed up with Torpex, and the twenty-five-foot fuse were followed.*

In an oft-quoted assertion, Winston Churchill wrote that the only thing that really frightened him in World War II was the U-boat peril. If that were the case, the failure of the British at this time to see the potential of the B-24 as a highly effective ASW weapon and to insist that all arriving B-24s be assigned to ASW missions is all the more difficult to understand. The usual explanation is that the War Cabinet was so firmly wedded to the concept that Germany could and must be defeated by strategic bombing alone that every single big bomber had to be reserved for Bomber Command. Therefore, the War Cabinet denied Coastal Command any further four-engine bombers for a long time to come.

Numerous other important factors entered into this decision, not the least of which was the inability of Coastal Command to convince a majority in the War Cabinet that a proper aircraft such as the B-24 was potentially an effective U-boat killer. As will be seen, this decision was most unfortunate, one of the worst mistakes the British War Cabinet made in the war. A number of studies would show that a Coastal Command ASW force of merely a hundred B-24s could well have decisively crushed the U-boat peril in the summer of 1941, sparing the Allies the terrible shipping losses in the years ahead.

INDIGO

In a secret speech to the House of Commons on June 25, Prime Minister Churchill expressed satisfaction at the changing fortunes of the British in the Battle of the Atlantic. His decision to establish the Battle of the Atlantic Committee† to focus utmost attention on that struggle had paid dividends. In spite of the increase in the size of the U-boat force, merchant-ship losses in the vital North Atlantic convoys had actually declined, as had shipping losses to enemy aircraft. Moreover, British shipyards were making astonishing progress in clearing out the backlog of ships idled with damage; the German air raids on the docks at Bristol Channel, Liverpool, Firth of Clyde, and elsewhere had tapered off to nearly zero; a new organization, the Ministry of War Transport, presided over by the business tycoon

---

 * The Admiralty's minimum depth-charge setting was fifty feet, to protect the launching vessel from backblast. Commencing in the summer of 1941, Coastal Command set aerial depth charges at fifty feet, pending the development of the twenty-five-foot hydrostatic fuse. The focus on this problem revealed that the fuses on the 250-pound aerial depth charges were unreliable, doubtless a contributing factor to the low kill rate. A high-priority R&D program soon provided reliable fuses.

 † The Committee met weekly from March 19 to May 8, thereafter every fortnight, then less frequently. Altogether it held sixteen sessions in 1941, the last on October 22.

Frederick Leathers, had already developed more efficient methods of handling shipping and rail traffic.

There were two other big reasons for Churchill's optimism in his secret appraisal to the House on June 25. These were:

•   Barbarossa, the German invasion of the Soviet Union, launched three days before on June 22. Although the British believed the Germans would defeat the ragged Soviet Army within several months, the military effort put into Barbarossa appeared to preclude any German invasion of the British Isles in 1941. If indeed this proved to be the case, the destroyers and other light ships of the Home Fleet on anti-invasion duty could be reassigned to convoy escort and also, possibly, to hunter-killer groups. This added commitment of naval power to the North Atlantic would doubtless bring about the long-sought and necessary increase in U-boat kills.

•   Indigo, the American occupation of Iceland. Even as Churchill spoke to the House, a powerful American task force was about to set sail for that purpose.

President Roosevelt had set Indigo in motion on June 6. A momentous American enterprise, its main purpose was to absolutely secure air and naval bases for the American forces that were to assume responsibility for escorting convoys between Canada and Iceland, and for British escort forces working on the middle and eastern legs of the route. London also expected that the arrival of the Americans in Iceland would free up the British occupation forces there for duty in North Africa.

Admiral Stark in Washington ordered Atlantic Fleet commander Admiral King to carry out Indigo on June 16. This was the first large-scale American military operation of World War II and, of course, the first major American expeditionary force to embark for overseas duty. It was carried out with dispatch and with naval professionalism, a credit to King and all concerned. Doubtless this new feather in King's cap was a factor in his selection to lead the U.S. Navy throughout World War II.

Inasmuch as Washington and London had to guard against an angry Axis reaction to Indigo, the American amphibious force was very strong and the troops designated for occupation duty were well-trained regular U.S. Marines rather than Army draftees. Proud of the Navy's remarkably successful achievement in moving troops overseas in World War I, Admiral King was absolutely determined to repeat that success in World War II. Therefore he had ruled that whenever it fell to the Navy to move troops at sea (whether U.S. Marines, U.S. Army forces, or foreign), the troopships were to be massively guarded by American battleships, cruisers, and destroyers.

The importance and rigidity of the American troopship convoy policy cannot be overstated. Neither at the time nor later did the British appear to understand—or accept—the policy. This led to many misunderstandings between the British and American naval authorities and to unintentional—or intentional—distortions and misstatements in most British and many American accounts of the Battle of the Atlantic: for example, the outright falsehood that King was oblivious to or disdainful of the U-boat threat and therefore transferred most American destroyers to the Pacific.

The American troopship escort policy was initiated with the occupation of Iceland. In late June about four thousand Marines boarded four Navy troopships (APs). Their impedimenta filled two attack cargo ships (AKs). Admiral King directed seventeen warships to protect the force: old battleships *Arkansas* and *New York;* light cruisers *Brooklyn* and *Nashville;* and thirteen destroyers* of Squadron 7, of which nine were new (1940) and four were aged four-stacks.

Designated Task Force 19, the convoy sailed from the United States on July 1. En route, one of the new destroyers, *Charles F. Hughes,* came upon one of the two Greenland-bound lifeboats from the Norwegian freighter *Vigrid,* sunk from convoy Halifax 133 by *U-371.* The *Hughes* rescued the fourteen survivors of that boat, who included four of the ten American Red Cross nurses, who had been in the boat for twelve miserable days.†

The convoy arrived in Reykjavik harbor on the evening of July 7. Ironically, the debarking American Marines—the First Provisional Marine Brigade—were greeted by the surviving American Marines of the 12th Provisional Company who were torpedoed by *U-564* while on the Dutch freighter *Maasdam,* also in convoy Halifax 133.

The Americans promptly set about building bases on Iceland. The next important contingent to arrive, on August 6, was the U.S. Navy's Patrol Wing 7, consisting of a squadron (VP 73) of Consolidated Catalinas and a squadron (VP 74) of Martin Mariners, a newer, more powerful, and heavily armed twin-engine flying boat.‡ These three dozen aircraft were supported by two aviation destroyer tenders (AVDs), *George E. Badger* and *Goldsborough.*

At that time there were three squadrons of RAF Coastal Command aircraft based in Iceland. These squadrons flew about fifty American-built aircraft: nine Catalinas in Squadron 209, twenty-six Hudsons in the (overstrength) Squadron 269, and eighteen Northrop scout bombers in Squadron 330, manned by Norwegian pilots. In addition, the RAF had provided about ten Hurricanes to counter possible German air strikes.

Two weeks after the arrival of the Marines, Admiral King further reinforced the Iceland force by the creation of Task Force 1 and, on September 1, by the creation of the Denmark Strait Patrol. The first was composed of the old battleships *Arkansas, New York,* and *Texas;* the Denmark Patrol by the newer first-line battleships recently transferred from the Pacific fleet: *Idaho, Mississippi,* and *New Mexico,* plus Atlantic Fleet Destroyer Squadron 2, composed of nine new vessels.§ These warships moored in the anchorage at Hvalfjord or in Reykjavik. Should *Tirpitz* and/or the "pocket" battleships *Lützow* and *Scheer* or the heavy cruiser *Hipper* attempt to break into the Atlantic via the Denmark Strait, or *Prinz Eugen, Gneisenau,* and *Scharnhorst* attempt to return from Brest to Germany by that route, the

---

* *Benson, Bernadou, Buck, Charles F. Hughes, Ellis, Gleaves, Hilary P. Jones, Lansdale, Lea, Mayo, Niblack, Plunkett, Upshur.*

† A British destroyer came upon one of the two Ireland-bound lifeboats of *Vigrid* and rescued two more American nurses. The two other lifeboats were never found.

‡ With twice the engine power and twice the fuel capacity and about the same range, the Mariner could carry four times the bomb or depth-charge payload as the Catalina.

§ *Anderson, Hammann, Hughes, Morris, Mustin, O'Brien, Russell, Sims, Walke.*

American warships were to operate in a "reconnaissance" role under direction of the British Home Fleet. The presence of these big American ships in Iceland enabled the British to dilute the strength of the Home Fleet and send a big-ship force to the Far East to deter possible Japanese advances on Hong Kong, Singapore, and other British outposts.*

The unprecedented peacetime American Selective Training and Service Act, passed in September 1940, limited draftees to one year's service in the United States only. At Roosevelt's request, in August 1941, Congress revised and extended it, removing the restriction on overseas assignments and lengthening the term of service to eighteen months. Roosevelt thereupon directed the War Department to send about 5,000 Army troops to Iceland to reinforce the Marines and the British forces.

Admiral King organized a second large Navy Task Force, 15, to carry out this mission. Guarded by the battleship *Mississippi,* four light cruisers (*Quincy, Tuscaloosa, Vincennes, Wichita*), and fifteen destroyers, the twenty-one-ship convoy sailed September 5. The new carrier *Wasp* (1940) ferried the 33rd Pursuit Squadron of the Army Air Forces to Iceland. On September 25, the American Army commander assumed responsibility for the defense of Iceland, but the Marine brigade and all but a handful of the British ground forces remained for the time being.

In very short order the Americans turned Iceland into a virtually impregnable military fortress. As a base for the Denmark Patrol, for air and surface-ship escorts for convoys and, later, for offensive air and surface-ship ASW patrols, as well as a way station for transoceanic military air transports, Iceland was to become the most vital of Allied outposts in the Atlantic Ocean area.

German naval authorities were incensed. Believing this latest American move in the Atlantic was a provocation too brazen to ignore, Dönitz proposed to Admiral Raeder and the OKM that it be countered by a U-boat assault. He found willing ears in Berlin, and Raeder set off at once to petition Hitler to lift the restrictions against attacking American warships and merchant ships (and British warships smaller than cruisers) in Icelandic waters.

Raeder met with Hitler on July 9, the eighteenth day of the offensive against Russia, Barbarossa. The American occupation of Iceland, Raeder insisted, "greatly affects our U-boats as well as surface vessels in the execution of the war in the Atlantic." But Hitler refused to lift the restrictions. The stenographer recorded his views thus:

> The Führer explains that everything depends on the U.S.A.'s entry into the war being delayed another month or two. First, because the Eastern Campaign must be carried out with all the aircraft allotted for that purpose, and the Führer does not wish to deplete their numbers; secondly, because the effects of the victorious Eastern Campaign on the whole situation, even on the attitude of the U.S.A., would be tremendous. For the present, therefore, he desires that no alteration be made in the instructions, and that all incidents should be avoided.

---

* The Admiralty alerted the new battleship *Prince of Wales,* the battle cruiser *Repulse,* and the new carrier *Indomitable* (on shakedown in the Caribbean) for this task.

The American occupation of Iceland thus drew scant naval reaction from Germany.

BARBAROSSA: THE BALTIC AND THE ARCTIC

One prime objective of the German invasion of the Soviet Union was the great city of Leningrad (St. Petersburg), which is at the extreme eastern end of the Baltic on the Gulf of Finland. Army Group North struck out for Leningrad from East Prussia, angling northeast through the Russian-occupied Baltic States of Lithuania, Latvia, and Estonia. At the same time, a pro-Hitler, German-equipped Finnish Army struck at Leningrad from the northwest. The German blitzkrieg quickly overran the Baltic States, but the German-Finnish attack on Leningrad bogged down on the outskirts of the city.

The Soviet Union's Red Banner (or Baltic) Fleet was based in the Gulf of Finland, guarding the seaward approaches to Leningrad. It comprised two old (1911) but modernized battleships, three heavy cruisers, forty-seven destroyers, and about seventy submarines. Its surface force was no match for the available *Kriegsmarine* surface forces in the Baltic, but Admiral Raeder and the OKM were deeply concerned about the possible damage the powerful (but untested) Soviet submarine force could inflict, should it deploy offensively into the Baltic. On the other side, the Soviet naval chief, Commissar Nikolai G. Kuznetsov, anticipated an offensive strike by *Kriegsmarine* surface forces in the Gulf of Finland in support of Army Group North.

Neither navy, however, was called upon to provide offensive action. Assuming defensive stances, each began the war by laying massive minefields in the narrow mouth of the Gulf of Finland, to hold the opposing naval force at bay. Both navies augmented the minefields with patrolling submarines and destroyers, and other small surface craft. The *Kriegsmarine* also mounted destroyer and submarine patrols in the Danish Belts of the western Baltic and in Norwegian waters, to warn of or block a possible naval thrust by Great Britain, which had quickly formed an uneasy alliance with the Soviet Union.

On the eve of Barbarossa, the OKM had cleared the eastern Baltic waters of U-boat training activities. The workup (*Agru Front*) flotillas moved operations to distant and inconvenient Norwegian waters, basing at Horten and staging tactical exercises in Oslo Fjord. En route to Norway, the new IXC *U-128,* commanded by Ulrich Heyse, who came from the destroyer forces, ran hard aground on an uncharted rock and ripped her bottom open. The depot ship *Odin* and the light cruiser *Nürnberg* rescued the crew and towed the boat into Horten, where she was patched up and then returned to Kiel for major repairs. Ironically, Heyse, age thirty-five, a onetime merchant marine officer, was one of the most mature and experienced ship handlers in the submarine force. He survived the court of inquiry and retained command.

The Germans and pro-German Finns deployed nine submarines behind the minefields spanning the Gulf of Finland on minelaying and torpedo missions. The five German boats were Type IID ducks, temporarily detached from the Submarine School.* Three of the five sank small, coastal-type Soviet submarines. A *Shchuka*-class Soviet submarine, *307,* torpedoed and sank the duck *U-144,* commanded by Gert von Mittelstaedt, age twenty-nine, who had earlier sunk one of the Russian submarines, *M-78.* After the loss of *U-144,* the OKM withdrew the German ducks. A Latvian vessel under Soviet control hit a mine planted by the Finnish boat *Vesihiisi* and later sank. The *Vesikko* and *Vetehinen* each torpedoed and sank a Soviet freighter. German mines, aircraft, and ASW vessels—and the advancing German ground forces—destroyed a very large number of Soviet submarines, or forced the crews to scuttle. Apart from *307's* victory over *U-144,* the Soviet submarine force failed abjectly; its survivors fell back to Leningrad.

Barbarossa included a little-known German thrust from northern Norway to capture Murmansk and Archangel. As a gesture of friendship and cooperation with the Soviets, in late July the British War Cabinet sent a carrier task force (*Furious, Victorious*) to that Arctic area. Carrier-based aircraft struck at German forces in Petsamo, Kirkenes, and Trosmö, incurring heavy losses to little effect.

Ever since the British raid on the Lofoten Islands in early March 1941, Hitler had worried constantly about another British raid or a full-scale amphibious assault in Norway. This British carrier strike at the North Cape intensified his concern. He urged Admiral Raeder to fortify Norway with the *Kriegsmarine's* big surface ships, but this was not possible. The *Bismarck's* sister ship, *Tirpitz,* was still fitting out; the "pocket" battleships *Lützow* and *Admiral Scheer* were in German yards for battle-damage repairs and overhaul, respectively; the battle cruisers *Gneisenau* and *Scharnhorst,* as well as the heavy cruiser *Prinz Eugen,* were in French Atlantic ports—the *Gneisenau* and *Scharnhorst* damaged by British air raids.

The only effective German naval vessels available for reconnaissance and offensive strikes in Norwegian and Arctic waters were U-boats. Hitler and Raeder therefore reached the decision that until the big surface ships were again available, U-boats were to patrol those waters. The OKM directed Dönitz to maintain at least two ducks in the Shetlands and Orkneys to warn of a possible British sortie from Loch Ewe or Scapa Flow toward Norway and at least two oceangoing boats in the Arctic to support German forces attempting to advance on Murmansk.

Dönitz fumed. These new assignments required the diversion of about four ducks and four to six oceangoing boats. Inasmuch as the orders came directly from Hitler, however, Dönitz apparently did not challenge or appeal them.

Two new VIICs that had been rushed through workup inaugurated the Arctic patrols off Murmansk in July. These were *U-81,* commanded by Fritz Guggenberger, age twenty-six, and *U-652,* commanded by Georg-Werner Fraatz, age twenty-four. After replenishing in Trondheim, the boats reached the Kola Bay area in early August. Four other new VIIs soon followed. Handicapped by the long Arctic days and very short nights and a scarcity of traffic, these six oceangoing boats

---

* The Finnish boats included the German duck prototype *Vesikko,* the German Type VII prototype *Vetehinen,* and two others.

operating in the Murmansk area achieved almost nothing. Fraatz in *U-652* sank a 600-ton freighter. Eberhard Hoffmann, age twenty-nine, in *U-451* sank a 550-ton patrol boat. Karl-Ernst Schroeter, age twenty-eight, in *U-752* sank a 600-ton freighter. Helmut Möhlmann, age twenty-eight, in *U-571* damaged a 3,900-ton freighter, which beached herself, a total wreck. Grand total: four ships for 5,600 tons.

Barbarossa thus proved to be a costly inconvenience for the U-boat arm. It closed the east Baltic to tactical training, forcing *Agru Front* to move to Norway. It diverted about eight ducks from the submarine school for several months and several others from Atlantic patrols and sent six oceangoing boats to the Arctic, establishing a U-boat presence in that area that was to remain there for the rest of the war and to grow to substantial size.

Viewing these disruptions and diversions as a "waste," Dönitz was especially incensed over the assignment of oceangoing boats to the Arctic. "I repeatedly protested," to the OKM, he wrote, making his reasons plain:

> Concrete successes so far have been meager in the extreme and of no account, for the reason that such traffic as there is consists of little ships which cannot be attacked by torpedo with much prospect of success.
> The decisive factor in the war against Britain is the attack on her imports. The delivery of these attacks is the U-boats' principal task and one which no other branch of the armed forces can take over from them. The war with Russia will be decided on land, and in it the U-boats can play only a very minor role.

Hitler was not dissuaded. His "intuition" that the British would soon again invade Norway became an article of faith. At his specific direction, ever greater numbers of U-boats were to go there to repel this supposed invasion and, later, to take on other tasks.

JULY PATROLS TO THE NORTH ATLANTIC

Owing to the complicated new restrictions Hitler had placed on U-boats pending the success of Barbarossa, Dönitz was compelled to give Iceland and the Northwest Approaches a wide berth. Hence in July 1941, he shifted most of the twenty boats that sailed afresh to more southerly waters to attack Gibraltar and Sierra Leone convoys. In addition, Dönitz sent another wave to Freetown: four boats, all commanded by *Ritterkreuz* holders. These four were to refuel secretly from the German tanker *Corrientes* in the Spanish Canaries.

Reading naval Enigma currently and fluently, the British almost completely outwitted Dönitz in July. They reinforced the Gibraltar and Sierra Leone convoys with extra air and surface escorts and cleverly diverted the convoys, taking advantage of an unseasonably dense fog in the central Atlantic. They brought to bear such strong diplomatic pressure on Spain's dictator Francisco Franco that he closed the Canaries to German U-boats, forcing a cancellation of the special four-boat task force to Freetown. As a result, no U-boat discovered a convoy in July. All the initial convoy contacts came from Focke-Wulf Condors basing in Bordeaux, or from the Italian boats based there.

The first Condor contact came on July 1, about 600 miles due west of Lorient. Dönitz ordered five boats to operate against the convoy, including the crack *U-96*, commanded by *Ritterkreuz* holder Heinrich Lehmann-Willenbrock. The boats established the convoy's precise position by taking widely spaced bearings on the Condor's beacon signals. Late on July 2, Klaus Scholtz, inbound from the Greenland area in *U-108*, found the convoy—Gibraltar-bound, he reported. But before Scholtz could bring up the other boats or the aircraft, he lost the ships in a dense fog and put into France, completing a highly satisfactory patrol of forty-one days during which he sank seven ships for 27,000 tons.

Pursuing this contact through fog to the southwest, on the morning of July 5, Lehmann-Willenbrock in *U-96* happened upon a curious formation of five ships: a Royal Navy yacht, *Challenger*, leading a 6,000-ton freighter, *Anselm*. Three corvettes, *Petunia*, *Lavender*, and *Starwort*, were deployed to port, starboard, and astern of *Anselm* with good reason: *Anselm* was a troopship with 1,200 soldiers on board.

Braving the menace posed by this unusually heavy escort, Lehmann-Willenbrock closed submerged and fired a full bow salvo at the *Challenger* and *Anselm*. He missed *Challenger* but two torpedoes hit *Anselm*. The ship sank in twenty-two minutes, but that was time enough for the crew to launch all but one of the lifeboats. Nonetheless, 254 of the 1,200 soldiers were lost. The yacht *Challenger* pulled sixty survivors from the water.

The three corvettes immediately pounced on *U-96*. *Starwort*'s sonar was out of commission, so *Petunia* and *Lavender*, which had firm contacts, delivered the attack. *Petunia* launched six depth charges and *Lavender*, twenty. When the attack carried the corvettes close to the survivors in the water, the depth-charging had to be broken off, but it had been deadly accurate. Later in the day Lehmann-Willenbrock reported to Kerneval that he was aborting the patrol with "extreme" depth-charge damage.

The second Condor report came a week later, on July 7: another outbound convoy about 250 miles off North Channel. Dönitz alerted all boats in the vicinity, but none was able to find the convoy. Nor any other convoy. As a result, confirmed sinkings in the first three weeks of July were abysmal: Lehmann-Willenbrock's troopship, plus three other ships for 13,300 tons; one by Klaus Scholz in *U-108* and two by Robert Gysae in *U-98*.*

Dönitz was baffled and frustrated. Twice in a period of six days (July 15 to 20) he logged: "The difficult problem as ever is to *find* convoys." As usual, he blamed the lack of contacts on the shortage of U-boats. "Only when the number of boats is

---

* During the same three-week period, three Italian boats, *Malaspina*, *Morosini*, and *Torelli*, operating west of Gibraltar, sank five ships for 30,400 tons.

larger," he logged, "and there are more of them to keep a lookout, will the situation become more favorable." He shifted the boats here and there, forming temporary patrol lines, then dissolving them and reforming new lines in other areas. But the British cleverly countered these moves. Nothing seemed to work for the Germans.

The third convoy contact came from the Italian boat *Barbarigo* on July 22, west of Gibraltar. She called in *Bagnolini*. *Barbarigo* sank a confirmed ship, the 8,300-ton British tanker *Horn Shell; Bagnolini* claimed hits on two ships, but no British report confirmed her attack. Upon learning of this contact, Dönitz attempted to bring up the four boats of the canceled Freetown special task force. One of these four, the *U-109*, commanded by Heinrich Bleichrodt, could not respond. She had put into Cadiz, Spain, for emergency repairs from the German supply ship *Thalia*. Dönitz substituted Rolf Mützelburg's *U-203*, which had come south in vain pursuit of another ship, but the British took prompt evasive action and neither Mützelburg nor the other three skippers could find *Barbarigo*'s convoy.

The fourth convoy contact came from another Condor on July 25, 400 miles due west of the English Channel. This was a combined outbound Gibraltar-Sierra Leone convoy, designated Gibraltar 69. It was composed of twenty-six ships, escorted by nine corvettes and an armed trawler. Eleven widely dispersed U-boats picked up the Condor's beacon, enabling Kerneval to plot the convoy's position with fair accuracy. Beacons from a second Condor were intercepted by fifteen U-boats, which confirmed the initial position.

Dönitz detailed eight U-boats to operate against this southbound convoy. All raced to the plotted position at maximum speed. The *U-79*, commanded by Wolfgang Kaufmann, out from Lorient on its second patrol, and the IXC *U-126*, commanded by Ernst Bauer, age twenty-seven, fresh from Germany on its first patrol, reached the designated position first. Neither saw any sign of the convoy and after a megaphone conference, Bauer radioed the bad news to Dönitz, who in turn directed the eight boats to search along specific bearings to the south and southwest.

On the following morning, July 26, another Condor found the convoy. Six boats picked up its beacon signal and Kerneval plotted a new fix. Presumed to be accurate, the new fix put the convoy 215 miles from the position reported by the Condor. Seven boats were "quite close" to the reported fix and yet, inexplicably, none could find the convoy. Was the Condor's report accurate after all? Were the British transmitting deceptive beacon signals? Another Condor searched both positions later in the day, but saw nothing.

Dönitz was at the point of calling off the chase when one of the boats spoke up to report contact. She was the new IXC *U-68*, commanded by Karl-Friedrich Merten, age thirty-five, a senior officer from the crew of 1926, twenty-seven days out on his maiden patrol from Germany. Dönitz ordered Merten to shadow and send beacon signals. As he was doing so, unknown to Merten, the convoy was in the process of splitting up. Half of the ships—those bound for Sierra Leone—left unescorted, making best speed. Two of the nine corvettes left to join a Gibraltar convoy homebound to the British Isles.

At about midnight three other boats joined Merten's *U-68*: Kaufmann's *U-79*, Bauer's *U-126*, and Mützelburg's *U-203*. After they had checked in, Dönitz directed Bauer to shadow and authorized Merten to shoot at will, but his attack was thwarted by a corvette. When he lost contact, it fell to Kaufmann in *U-79* and Mützelburg in *U-203* to launch the first torpedoes. Kaufmann claimed sinking three ships for 24,000 tons and damage to two others. Mützelburg claimed sinking two ships for 14,000 tons. In fact, Kaufmann sank one confirmed ship, a 2,500-ton British freighter, and Mützelburg sank one confirmed ship, a 1,500-ton British freighter.*

Three of the seven corvettes counterattacked. *Rhododendron* fired off twenty-four depth charges, probably at Merten's *U-68*. *Sunflower* and *Pimpernel* teamed up on another U-boat. They attempted to ram, but the boat dived. They fired twenty-two depth charges. These timely and aggressive counterattacks, plus defensive action by the other four corvettes, drove the U-boats off and prevented any further attacks that night.

During the daylight hours on July 27, Bauer in *U-126* continued to shadow and send out beacon signals. These enabled Merten in *U-68*, Mützelburg in *U-203*, and two other new VIICs from Germany, *U-561*, commanded by Robert Bartels, age thirty, and *U-562*, commanded by Herwig Collmann, to regain contact. But Bartels suffered a mechanical breakdown and was forced to abort. Yet another boat, *U-371*, commanded by Heinrich Driver, making his second patrol, later found the detached, southbound Freetown section of the convoy and sank two 7,000-ton freighters.

At about dark, Dönitz authorized the shadower, Bauer in *U-126*, to attack. To him and the other boats he sent an exhortatory message: "All boats off the convoy to utilize any chances of attack. If no good chances beforehand, attempt as from 0200 to attack simultaneously. Split up escorts. Escorts probably weaker than in previous night. Continue to report contact and send beacon signals. Bring up other boats, attack yourselves. Press on!"

Bauer in *U-126* did not wait long. Shortly before midnight he closed on the surface and fired six torpedoes—four from the bow tubes and two from the stern tubes. In this, his first attack of the war, Bauer claimed sensational results: four ships for 20,000 tons sunk. In fact, he had sunk two 1,300-ton freighters, the British *Erato* (the convoy flagship) and a Norwegian. The corvettes *Rhododendron* and *Begonia* counterattacked; the convoy dispersed.

Two other boats moved in to attack the remaining ships, which were fleeing in all directions. Merten in *U-68* shot at one of the corvettes. He saw a jet of red flame at the side of the corvette and claimed a sinking. He either missed or the torpedo failed; no corvette was hit that night. Bartels in *U-561* claimed sinking two ships (one a 12,000-ton tanker) for 16,000 tons, and damage to a 5,000-ton auxiliary cruiser. But only one ship, a 1,900-ton British freighter, actually went down.

By the evening of July 28, five of the original thirteen Gibraltar-bound ships had reformed into a loose convoy, escorted by five corvettes and a Catalina. Three U-boats were still stalking the ships. Sighting the U-boats, the Catalina and two corvettes swept astern of the convoy, forcing two U-boats off.

---

* Unlike the North Atlantic convoys, ships in Gibraltar convoys were usually quite small, misleading U-boat skippers into substantial overclaims.

Mützelburg hung on doggedly and launched his second attack after dark. He claimed sinking three ships for 17,000 tons, plus a "destroyer." Actually, he sank only two small freighters for 2,800 tons, one British, one Swedish. The corvette *Rhododendron* reported that three torpedoes had been fired at her, but she evaded them by "violent maneuvers." She and the corvette *Fleur de Lys* counterattacked, each expending all depth charges except three, but Mützelburg escaped without noteworthy damage.

Misled by the overclaims from the six boats that had shot at convoy Outbound Gibraltar 69, Dönitz believed another "great convoy battle" had taken place. He calculated the skippers had sunk seventeen or eighteen ships for about 108,000 tons, plus a destroyer and a corvette, figures Berlin propagandists hastened to inflate and release.* In reality, the sinkings were half of the Dönitz calculation and the tonnage only one-quarter of the claim. Five boats had sunk seven confirmed Gibraltar-bound ships for 11,303 tons and Heinrich Driver in *U-371* had sunk two of the thirteen Freetown-bound ships for 14,000 tons. Total: nine ships for 25,300 tons. No destroyer or corvette had been sunk. Seventeen of the twenty-six merchant ships reached port.†

During the month of July, 412 loaded merchant ships sailed from Canada in Halifax and Sydney (or Slow) convoys to the British Isles. Remarkably, not one ship fell victim to a U-boat. To avoid possible angry Axis reaction to the American occupation of Iceland, Halifax 135 followed a "southerly" route. Halifax 136 included the first CAM (fighter-plane catapult) ship. At mid-month, Halifax 138 and Slow Convoy 37 sailed experimentally across the Gulf of St. Lawrence and into the Atlantic via Belle Isle Strait, thence to Cape Farewell, then north along the ice-bound east coast of Greenland. These convoys encountered heavy fog and icebergs and, as a result, a number of collisions occurred.

The heavy ship traffic in the opposite direction on the North Atlantic run also fared well. Altogether eleven outbound convoys comprising 536 vessels sailed from the British Isles. As related, Robert Gysae in *U-98* sank two empty freighters for 10,800 tons from convoy Outbound 341. A Focke-Wulf Condor damaged an empty freighter in Outbound 346.

In sum, upward of one thousand Allied ships of about 5 million gross tons sailed the North Atlantic route in east and west convoys in July, virtually unharmed by the oceangoing U-boats.

Toward the end of July, the British instituted a new system for naming these outbound convoys. After Outbound 346, all convoys bound ultimately for the West Indies, Latin America, or West Africa were named Outbound South (OS). Off North Channel on July 26, Philipp Schüler in the duck *U-141* hit two empty

---

* Berlin claimed that U-boats sank twenty-four ships for 140,500 tons, plus a destroyer and a corvette.

† Mützelburg in *U-203*, credited with sinking a total of five ships for 31,000 tons plus a "destroyer," earned a propaganda interview on Berlin radio. His confirmed score was three small merchant ships for 4,305 tons. The Italian submarine *Torelli* sank the 8,900-ton Norwegian tanker *Ida Knudsen*.

freighters in OS 1. One of them, of 5,100 tons, sank; the other limped back to port. After Outbound 349, all convoys bound for Canada or the United States East Coast were named Outbound North (ON). The odd-numbered convoys were slow, the even-numbered convoys were fast.

THE ATLANTIC CHARTER

The German invasion of the Soviet Union introduced vast new complexities for the Allies. Joseph Stalin appealed to both Britain and the United States for massive military supplies (aircraft, tanks, machine guns, rifles, etc.) and demanded that Britain relieve pressure on Russia by opening a "second front"—an invasion of Occupied France. Neither Churchill nor Roosevelt relished the idea of helping the odious and untrustworthy Stalin, but as Churchill put it colorfully, "If Hitler invaded Hell, I would make at least a favorable reference to the Devil. . . ." A "second front" in Occupied France was out of the question, but both Churchill and Roosevelt pledged to supply Stalin with arms; Churchill without charge, Roosevelt through the Lend-Lease program.

Further complications arose in the Far East. A month after the Germans invaded the Soviet Union, on July 24, Japan occupied Vichy French Indochina (Vietnam). This brazen thrust destabilized the Far East, posing a grave new threat to China, to the Philippines, and to British and Dutch possessions or dominions in Southeast Asia and in Australasia. In hawkish reaction, Roosevelt froze Japanese assets in the United States, placed an embargo on oil exports to Japan, retained the bulk of the Pacific Fleet at Pearl Harbor, and directed that the Philippines be heavily reinforced with aircraft, submarines,* and other weaponry. The British and Dutch joined in the oil embargo, reducing Japan's oil imports by 90 percent. As related, Churchill directed the Admiralty to send a Royal Navy task force (*Prince of Wales, Repulse, Indomitable,* etc.) to the Far East.

The decision to supply the Soviet Union as well as Great Britain with Lend-Lease arms and to reinforce the Philippines put a nearly unbearable strain on the American "Arsenal of Democracy." As a result, the expanding American Army and Army Air Forces could not be properly equipped; Army conscripts drilled with dummy rifles and tanks. The strain led American military leaders to criticize forcefully the British Mediterranean strategy, which they still viewed as a waste of precious military assets in a peripheral theater. Passing through London on his way back from Moscow, Roosevelt's special emissary, Harry Hopkins, conveyed these views to Churchill in no uncertain terms, emphasizing that American strategists

---

* The United States maintained a small and aged naval force in the Far East, grandiosely designated the Asiatic Fleet. For years its principal striking force—designed to defend the Philippines from a Japanese naval assault—was a flotilla of six 800-ton World War I S-class submarines. In 1939 and 1940 the flotilla had been reinforced by eleven modern fleet submarines. Roosevelt's order sent another twelve fleet submarines to Manila, increasing the total submarine force of the Asiatic Fleet to twenty-nine boats, twenty-three of them modern fleet boats. In event of hostilities, all were to be provided with super-secret magnetic torpedo pistols similar to the ill-designed German magnetic pistols.

believed that "the Battle of the Atlantic would be the final decisive battle of the war, and that everything should be concentrated on it." His message was echoed by the American military representatives in London, whose views strongly influenced Washington strategists.

Given these disputes and the shifting character of the war, Churchill and Roosevelt were persuaded that the time had arrived for a meeting between them and their senior military advisers. It was decided that the meeting was to take place secretly "at sea." Churchill and party departed Scapa Flow on the battleship *Prince of Wales;* Roosevelt and party departed the United States on Admiral King's Atlantic Fleet flagship, the heavy cruiser *Augusta.* The ships met on August 9 in the mutually convenient, well-defended, and smooth anchorage Placentia Bay, at the newly established American naval base in Argentia, Newfoundland.

Churchill and his party came more or less believing the Americans were on the verge of declaring full-scale war, or could be persuaded to do so. Accordingly, the British had prepared elaborate—and specific—joint military plans for the defeat of Germany and Italy. Churchill eloquently outlined these plans, which contained four principal elements in this chronological sequence:

• **MASTERY OF THE SEA-LANES.** With American naval assistance the Royal Navy was to vanquish the U-boats, the super-battleship *Tirpitz,* and any and all other Axis vessels that posed a threat to Allied control of the ocean commerce lanes.

• **MASTERY OF THE MEDITERRANEAN BASIN.** With American assistance—perhaps three divisions of ground troops—Britain was to gain complete and absolute control of the Mediterranean Sea, North Africa, and the Middle East, and knock Italy out of the war by relentless and heavy air bombardment.

• **STRATEGIC AIR ATTACKS ON GERMANY.** With American assistance—about 6,000 heavy, four-engine B-17 and B-24 bombers to start—Britain was to mount a relentless and punishing air bombardment of German cities and war plants from bases in the British Isles and Italy, with the aim of creating "internal convulsion or collapse" and the overthrow of Hitler and the Nazi regime.

• **INVASION.** If necessary, some time in 1943, Britain and the United States were to land "armored spearheads" in "several" occupied nations (e.g., France), which were to link up with secretly armed resistance groups to overthrow the Germans. About 15,000 tanks and about 200 oceangoing tank-landing ships (landing ship tank or LST) were to be required. Allied manpower—particularly American manpower—was to be held to a minimum; hence no large-scale American Army was necessary.

Still under pressure from strong isolationist elements in the United States, Roosevelt came to Argentia in no mood to intervene overtly in the war or to make any commitments beyond those already made in ABC-1. The American military advisers were therefore forbidden to engage in detailed discussions, and had prepared no position papers. Although they disagreed with or had grave reservations about all of Churchill's points except the first (mastery of the sea-lanes), they confined their discussions to commitments already made to the British, such as convoy escort between Canada and Iceland.

The British were deeply disappointed at the warily aloof attitude of the Americans and the outcome of the conference. However, Churchill achieved an extremely important concession, perhaps not fully grasped at the time. He persuaded Roosevelt that the British Mediterranean strategy was valid in principle, setting Roosevelt apart from his military advisers and putting an end—at least temporarily—to American criticism of British operations in that area. This concession was to have a very great impact on the course of Allied military operations for the remainder of the war.

For political and propaganda reasons, both Churchill and Roosevelt were desirous of marking the conference with a high-minded joint declaration. This emerged in the form of an unsigned press release entitled "The Atlantic Charter," given out several days after the meeting. It firmly linked the United States and Great Britain in a moral partnership to defeat the Axis and to seek disarmament and political freedom for all nations and people in the postwar world. Perhaps anxious to salvage something positive from what had been essentially a profitless conference, Churchill attached great importance to the document. "The fact alone of the United States, still technically neutral," he wrote, "joining with a belligerent Power in making such a declaration was astonishing."

AUGUST PATROLS TO THE NORTH ATLANTIC

The attack on convoy Outbound Gibraltar 69 in late July was the only noteworthy success of the U-boat force since its extended battle in late June with Halifax 133, a drought of one full month. Even so, Dönitz continued drawing the boats ever eastward and southeastward into the waters of the Southwest Approaches, the Iberian Peninsula, and the Canaries.

By August 1 the twenty-odd boats on patrol were deployed in three groups: a main group of twelve boats in areas several hundred miles west of Ireland and the English Channel, replicating the U-boat dispositions during the early days of the war; a group of four boats in areas due west of Gibraltar Strait; another group of four boats skippered by *Ritterkreuz* holders—the canceled Freetown special task force—in areas west of the Canaries. The eight boats in the Gibraltar-Canaries area were authorized to secretly put into Spanish ports (Cadiz, El Ferrol) in event of an emergency. Hans-Dietrich von Tiesenhausen, age twenty-eight, in the new *U-331*, who had burned up much fuel futilely chasing Outbound Gibraltar 69, replenished in Cadiz.

On August 2 a boat of the northernmost main group, the *U-204*, commanded by Walter Kell, reported an inbound convoy about 500 miles due west of Brest in dense fog. Kell had detected the convoy on his hydrophones, but had not made visual contact. Upon receipt of his report, Dönitz ordered Kell to shadow while he launched Focke-Wulf Condors and brought up the other eleven boats of the main group. These included *Ritterkreuz* holder Engelbert Endrass, who was taking *U-46*—the last of the original VIIBs of the Wegener Flotilla—home to the Training Command.

The convoy Kell had found was inbound Sierra Leone 81, composed of seventeen big ships. The escort, joined by a contingent from Gibraltar, was very strong: twelve warships, including the ex-American four-stack destroyers *Campbeltown* (with Type 286 meter-wavelength radar) and *St. Albans,* and the destroyer *Wanderer;* a catapult ship, *Malpin,* equipped with a Hurricane; and nine corvettes.

The Condors and the boats closed on the convoy on August 3. *Malpin* launched its Hurricane, piloted by R.H.W. Everett, a noted English jockey. He got close on the tail of a Condor and emptied his guns. The Condor came apart and crashed into the sea—the first to fall to a ship-launched fighter. Everett ditched alongside the destroyer *Wanderer,* which put over a whaler and pulled him from the sea. Honored with a DSO, Everett was killed five months later while conducting a routine aircraft-ferry mission in the British Isles.

One of the first boats to join Kell was the *U-401,* a new VIIC commanded by Gero Zimmermann, age thirty-one. Commissioned on April 10, *U-401* had completed her workup in Oslo Fjord in ninety days. She sailed from Trondheim July 9 on her first Atlantic patrol and had been at sea for twenty-six days. This, her first contact with the enemy, was brief and fatal. The destroyers *Wanderer* (which had helped sink the duck *U-147* in June) and *St. Albans* and the corvette *Hydrangea* detected *U-401* on sonar and delivered a punishing depth-charge attack. The boat disappeared with the loss of all hands.

By the evening of August 3, about ten U-boats—most of them new boats on maiden or second patrols—had converged on Sierra Leone 81. Unaware of the loss of *U-401* or of the heavy escort with this convoy, Dönitz radioed: "This night is decisive. Go in and attack! You are more numerous and stronger than the enemy." But there was a full moon and the escorts were too numerous, and none of the boats got in to shoot. Another new VIIC from Germany, *U-565,* commanded by Johann Jebsen, age twenty-five, barely escaped disaster. Crippled by a diesel-engine breakdown, Jebsen was forced to abort.

During the daylight hours of August 4, the boats and the Condors continued to track the convoy. It drew ever closer (200 miles) to the west coast of Ireland where it was well within reach of Coastal Command aircraft. During the pursuit, yet another new VIIC from Germany, *U-431,* commanded by Wilhelm Dommes, age thirty-four, lost both diesels. Dommes repaired one but could do nothing about the other, and he, too, was forced to abort.

After dark on that day, the remaining boats, including Engelbert Endrass's *U-46,* closed to attack in bright moonlight. The escorts beat off Endrass and five other boats, and only four managed to shoot that night. The first was the VIIC *U-372,* commanded by Heinz-Joachim Neumann, age thirty-two, on its maiden patrol from Germany. He claimed sinking two ships for 12,000 tons and a probable hit on another 7,000-ton vessel. In reality, his salvo sank two medium British freighters for a total of 8,300 tons. He missed the British freighter *Volturo,* which retaliated and forced Neumann under with close fire from her 4" gun and smaller weapons, and drew in the corvette *Zinnia. Zinnia* chased, firing her 4" gun, but Neumann dived and escaped.

Next to shoot was the dogged shadower, Walter Kell in *U-204.* He chose what he claimed was a 14,000-ton freighter, but which was probably the convoy flagship

Abosso, a steamer of 11,300 tons, with 274 passengers embarked. If he hit *Abosso* (or another ship), it did not sink. He then sank the 5,000-ton British freighter *Kumasian.* Next to shoot was Helmuth Ringelmann in *U-75.* He claimed sinking two British freighters for 12,000 tons, but his confirmed score was one, the British *Cape Rodney,* for 4,512 tons. Last to shoot was Eitel-Friedrich Kentrat in *U-74,* who claimed sinking one ship of 8,000 tons and damage to three others of 8,000 tons. His torpedoes actually sank the 5,400-ton British freighter *Harlingen.*

Coastal Command aircraft appeared at dawn over the convoy and encountered a blast of "friendly" antiaircraft fire from tired and itchy-fingered British gunners. One aircraft sighted a U-boat and dropped two 500-pound ASW bombs, but these inflicted no known damage. Having been drawn very close to the Irish coast, the U-boats were compelled to break off. The four boats that shot torpedoes claimed sinking six ships for 46,500 tons, but in reality they had sunk five for 23,200 tons. Based on unusually thorough information from *B-dienst,* Dönitz concluded that the boats had positively sunk four ships for 24,500 tons and probably damaged six others. Considering that most of the boats were "quite inexperienced" and the convoy escort (as it turned out) was strong, and the moonlight unfavorable, Dönitz logged that he was well satisfied with the outcome.

Several other boats of this group also returned to port. Engelbert Endrass in *U-46,* who sank no ships on this patrol, retired *U-46* to the Training Command. Like his mentor, Prien, and his peers, Kretschmer and Schepke, Endrass turned down a safe job in the Training Command in favor of combat and returned to Lorient as a replacement skipper. The *U-558,* commanded by Günther Krech, age twenty-six, onetime naval aviator and first watch officer on Schepke's *U-100,* was forced to abort when one of his midshipmen became gravely ill.

Despite the risks, after the battle with Sierra Leone 81, on August 5 Dönitz resumed U-boat warfare in the waters off Iceland and the Northwest Approaches. This decision was prompted in part by *B-dienst* codebreakers who made a tentative but useful break in the North Atlantic convoy codes; in part by the belief that since no U-boats had operated in those waters for weeks, he might catch the Allies napping; in part because fourteen more new U-boats were Atlantic-bound in August, raising the total Atlantic operational force to over sixty oceangoing boats, enough to send an unprecedented thirty-eight boats out in August and to cover several widely spaced hunting grounds simultaneously.

Accordingly, the boats at sea or sailing afresh were deployed into three loose groups: a North Group, near Iceland; a Center Group west of Scotland and Ireland; and a South Group off Gibraltar Strait. British codebreakers promptly detected this redeployment, noting especially the newly created North Group, which posed a possible threat to the *Prince of Wales,* en route to Argentia, Newfoundland, with Churchill and his party.

The North Group was established, initially, by holding two new Atlantic-bound boats near Iceland. One of these was the *U-501,* commanded by thirty-six-year-old Hugo Förster, the most senior skipper in the Atlantic, but new to submarines. Com-

missioned on April 30, the *U-501* was the first of a new type, designated IXC/40.*
Four days out of Trondheim, on August 11, Förster intercepted a slow outbound
convoy about seventy miles due south of Iceland. Heavily escorted by surface vessels and aircraft, the convoy was designated Outbound North 5. Förster's contact
report was confirmation to the Admiralty's U-boat Tracking Room that U-boats
were back in Icelandic waters.

Another new boat picked up Förster's report. She was the VIIC *U-568*, commanded by Joachim Preuss, age twenty-seven, from the duck *U-10*. Förster was
driven off by air escorts that dropped close depth charges or bombs, but in the
early hours of August 12, Preuss got in and shot at an escort (in violation of
Hitler's order) and a ship he reported as a 7,000-ton freighter. He hit an escort, the
corvette *Picotee*, which blew up and sank, but he apparently missed the freighter.
Other escorts counterattacked *U-568* and drove the boat under and held it down
while the convoy escaped. The *Picotee* was the first British warship to be sunk by
a U-boat in almost a year.

Later that same day, two other new boats of the North Group reported separate
outbound convoys passing south of Iceland. The boats were the VIIC *U-206*, commanded by Herbert Opitz, age twenty-six, and the IXC *U-129*, commanded by the
veteran Nikolaus Clausen, who had returned the famous old *U-37* to the Training
Command. Escorts drove Opitz off his convoy, but Clausen stuck with his, which
he described as "large." Dönitz directed Opitz, Förster, Preuss, and two other new
boats to home on Clausen's beacon signals and to pursue the convoy westward—
and to attack it to destruction.

The possibilities offered by convoy Outbound North 5 persuaded Dönitz to
make a large northwestward shift of the Center Group. On his orders, the entire
Center Group (twelve boats) joined the chase on August 13, speeding toward
Greenland. Thus eighteen U-boats were unknowingly heading directly toward the
track of the *Prince of Wales*, en route home from Argentia, Newfoundland, to Iceland, screened by two American destroyers, on one of which Ensign Franklin D.
Roosevelt, Jr., was embarked. Aware from Ultra of the shift of U-boats and the
danger posed to the *Prince of Wales* and her distinguished party, Admiralty officials—and perhaps those on board the battleship and destroyers—doubtless spent
a sleepless night devising evasive courses. But Churchill casually passed off the
moment in his memoirs, writing that the voyage to Iceland was "uneventful, although at one point it became necessary to alter course owing to the reported presence of U-boats near-by."

The long chase of convoy Outbound North 5 to westward by these eighteen
boats produced nothing. Clausen in *U-129* lost contact with the convoy and no
other boat could find it. None saw the *Prince of Wales*, which arrived safely in Iceland as scheduled on August 16, and departed for Scapa Flow with a British destroyer screen the following day. Outfoxed by the U-boat Tracking Room, during
the next eighteen days only one of the U-boats at sea sank an Allied ship, and it

---

* The IXC/40 was identical to the IXC except that her fuel tanks held six more tons of oil, giving
her an extra 400 miles range: 11,400 miles at 12 knots versus 11,000 miles for the IXC.

was an insignificant 1,700-ton Panamanian freighter. That U-boat was the aging Type IX *U-38,* commanded by a new skipper, Heinrich Schuch, age thirty-five. The *Prince of Wales* reached Scapa Flow undetected.

During these futile chases in the northern area, Kerneval received word from a "spy" that a big convoy had left Gibraltar for the British Isles. Dönitz alerted the South Group, sent out Condors and pulled in the four-boat group patrolling west of the Canaries. A boat of the South Group, Wolfgang Kaufmann's *U-79,* found the convoy, Homebound Gibraltar 70, on the afternoon of August 10. Dönitz ordered Kaufmann to shadow and to send beacon signals for the benefit of the other boats and the Condors, but the convoy was heavily escorted by aircraft and surface vessels, and "destroyers" drove Kaufmann under.

The group from west of the Canaries, composed of the four *Ritterkreuz* holders who had aborted the special mission to Freetown, raced in at maximum speed. On the morning of August 11 one of these skippers, Claus Korth in *U-93,* found the convoy, reporting that it had made a sharp turn north and was tightly hugging the Portuguese coast. An air escort drove Korth off and bombed him, causing so much damage that he was forced to abort to France. But Korth's report enabled Kaufmann in *U-79* to reestablish contact and another *Ritterkreuz* holder, Herbert Kuppisch in *U-94,* to find the convoy. The escorts drove off Kaufmann and Kuppisch, delivering a "heavy" depth-charge attack on Kaufmann in *U-79.* Acting on these reports, another boat of the South Group, von Tiesenhausen's *U-331,* also found the convoy. He was driven off "three times," he reported, and was finally forced to abort with a mechanical breakdown.

At that time Reinhard Hardegen in the IXB *U-123,* returning to Lorient from his long and frustrating patrol off Freetown, was passing close to the Iberian Peninsula. Dönitz ordered Hardegen to reinforce the attack on Homebound Gibraltar 70. Acting on a Condor position report, which proved to be accurate, Hardegen found the convoy late in the day on August 12. But he, too, was driven off and heavily depth-charged—126 explosions, thirty-six of them very close, he reported. The impact of the blasts temporarily disabled both diesels and caused a serious lube-oil leak, which compelled Hardegen to resume his return to Lorient, concluding a sixty-eight-day patrol.

Next to find the convoy were two *Ritterkreuz* holders in IXBs, Heinrich Bleichrodt in *U-109* and Georg-Wilhelm Schulz in *U-124.* Both were also driven off by aircraft or surface escorts. Bleichrodt in *U-109* reported "oil and bubble leaks" which forced him to abort to Lorient, returning to base for the first time with all torpedoes. Frustrated by the escorts, Schulz was unable to gain shooting position and after five sleepless days and nights, he broke off the chase. He, too, returned to Lorient with all torpedoes.

Receiving a steady stream of failure reports from the boats, most of them manned by experienced skippers, Dönitz was puzzled and disconcerted. Recounting in his log the "difficulties" the boats were experiencing in attacking this convoy, he surmised that the escorts were employing some kind of "surface location apparatus." He therefore issued a radical new order: All boats were to attack the *escorts* first, firing "fan shots" (two or more torpedoes). If possible, they were to coordinate these attacks and shoot simultaneously, sparing no torpedoes. However, no boat was able to mount an attack on any escort of Homebound Gibraltar 70.

Finally, on August 15, Dönitz called off the chase. It had been a disastrous failure. Not one of the ten boats making contact with the convoy, including the promising skipper Reinhard Hardegen in *U-123* and the four *Ritterkreuz* holders Bleichrodt, Korth, Kuppisch, and Schulz, had been able to get in and launch torpedoes. Four boats had been compelled to abort with battle damage or mechanical breakdown. Only by a miracle, it seemed, did all boats survive this brutal engagement.

Of the failures, none was more disappointing than that of the special four-boat task force, all commanded by *Ritterkreuz* holders. Forced to cancel the original mission to Freetown owing to the loss of German supply ships, they had patrolled west of the Canaries, then joined the attack on Homebound Gibraltar 70. In about five weeks of patrolling, not one of these aces had fired a torpedo! Upon reaching France, three of the four left their boats for other duty. Korth in *U-93*, "formerly considered very capable," and who gave the impression of being "rundown," Dönitz logged, was sent to a job in the Training Command. Kuppisch in *U-94*, said to have developed "a case of nerves," went to Dönitz's staff in Kerneval. Schulz in *U-124* was promoted to command the 6th Combat Flotilla at St. Nazaire.

These three veterans were replaced by three very young—but combat-experienced—officers. The *U-93* went to Horst Elfe, age twenty-four, crew of 1936, who had made seven war patrols as a watch officer on Kretschmer's *U-99*, after which he commanded the duck *U-139* for eight months. The *U-94* went to Otto Ites, age twenty-three, crew of 1936, former watch officer on the record-holding *U-48*, who had commanded the duck *U-146* for four months (and sunk a ship). Johann Hendrick Mohr, age twenty-five, crew of 1934, who had been first watch officer to Schulz on the IXB *U-124* for eight months, moved up to command of the boat.*

Mere hours after the luckless chase of Homebound Gibraltar 70 had been terminated, on August 17, a Focke-Wulf Condor reported an outbound convoy about 250 miles west of Ireland. This was Outbound Gibraltar 71, guarded by British Escort Group 5. To August 13 this area had been occupied by the Center Group, but Dönitz had sent that group northwest toward Greenland in fruitless pursuit of convoy Outbound North 5, leaving the center area thinly covered. However, Adalbert Schnee in *U-201*, three days out from Brest, made contact with the convoy and

---

* At this time nine newly arrived VIIs in the Atlantic force were also commanded by young skippers from the crews of 1934 and 1935: Horst Uphoff, age twenty-four, in *U-84;* Eberhard Greger, age twenty-five, in *U-85;* Fritz Meyer, age twenty-five, in *U-207;* Heinz-Otto Schultze, age twenty-five, in *U-432;* Hans Ey, age twenty-five, in *U-433;* Ottokar Paulshen, age twenty-five, in *U-557;* Reinhard Suhren, age twenty-five, in *U-564;* Johann Jebsen, age twenty-five, in *U-565;* Georg-Werner Fraatz, age twenty-four, in *U-652.*

sent beacon signals. The escorts drove Schnee off, but on the following day, August 18, other Condors, homing on Schnee's beacon signals, relocated the convoy and brought up the few available boats.

The latest orders from Dönitz for dealing with inbound or outbound Gibraltar convoys specified that the boats were to attack the escorts first. In the early hours of August 19, three boats closed on Outbound Gibraltar 71. Walter Kell in *U-204,* literally following the order, fired first at the Norwegian-manned, ex-American, four-stack destroyer *Bath* and blew it to smithereens. He also claimed sinking two big freighters for 16,000 tons, but these could not be verified in postwar records. Critically low on fuel, Kell was forced to put into France. The *U-559,* commanded by Hans Heidtmann, age twenty-seven, attacked next. Heidtmann claimed sinking two big freighters for 22,000 tons and damage to another of 8,000 tons, but postwar records credited only one ship sunk, a 1,600-ton British freighter. Schnee in *U-201* attacked third, claiming a tanker and two freighters for 20,000 tons, but in reality he sank two British freighters for 5,000 tons. In sum: the destroyer *Bath* and three freighters sunk, totaling 6,650 tons.

The British took emergency action to protect Outbound Gibraltar 71. The destroyers *Gurkha II* (ex-*Larne*) and *Lance* left military convoy WS 10X and joined the surface escort, adding strength plus the new radio-detecting locating device, HF/DF or Huff Duff. Gibraltar-based Catalinas and Sunderlands arrived to provide additional protection. Condors continued to distantly shadow and report the convoy, but none of the boats could penetrate the large escort screen on the night of August 19–20. *Gurkha II* and *Lance* reported a qualified success in DFing the U-boats with Huff Duff. Owing to a shortage of fuel, Heidtmann in *U-559* had to put into France.

Two boats commanded by exceptionally able and aggressive skippers hung on: Adalbert Schnee's *U-201* and Reinhard Suhren's *U-564.* They closed on the night of August 22–23. Making his second attack on Outbound Gibraltar 71, Schnee claimed sinking two freighters for 9,000 tons and damage to two others for 12,000 tons (raising his total claims on this convoy to six ships sunk for 37,000 tons plus damage). Schnee did in fact sink two freighters, but they were small: one of 800 tons, the other of 2,000 tons. Making his first attack on the convoy, Suhren fired eleven torpedoes over about five hours. He sank the corvette *Zinnia* (which went down in fifteen seconds) and claimed sinking four freighters for 20,000 tons and damage to four other freighters for 20,000 tons. Postwar records credited Suhren with no sinkings other than *Zinnia,* but damage to two freighters: the 1,200-ton *Clantara,* abandoned and sunk by a seagoing tug, and the 2,100-ton *Spind,* which was also abandoned.

Dönitz directed four other boats, including Erich Topp's *U-552,* to join the attack on Outbound Gibraltar 71. Fresh from Lorient, *Ritterkreuz* holder Topp found the hulk of *Spind* and put it under with his deck gun, but he subsequently incurred an engine breakdown and was forced to abort, returning to St. Nazaire with a full load of torpedoes. The other three boats chased the convoy, which appeared to head for Lisbon, but the strong surface and air escort drove them off.

Based on flash reports from the five boats, Dönitz believed another great convoy battle had occurred. He credited Kell, Heidtmann, Suhren, Schnee, and Topp with sinking fifteen ships for 90,000 tons, damage to five others for 29,000 tons, plus the sinking of a "destroyer" each by Kell and Suhren. In fact, the five boats had sunk the destroyer *Bath,* the corvette *Zinnia,* and eight small vessels for about 14,000 tons.

When Adalbert Schnee in *U-201* reached Lorient, Dönitz presented him a *Ritterkreuz.* According to postwar accounting, at the time of the award, Schnee had sunk (on the duck *U-60* and on *U-201*) only eight or nine ships for about 20,000 tons. Doubtless much weight was given to Schnee's dogged pursuit of Outbound Gibraltar 71 in the face of punishing enemy countermeasures, and to his substantial overclaims. Reflecting the poor returns of the summer of 1941, it was the only *Ritterkreuz* to be awarded to a German U-boat skipper in the period from August through October.

THE CAPTURE OF *U-570*

Dönitz reconstituted the Center Group near Rockall Bank on August 23. Two ducks, *U-141* and *U-143,* reconnoitered close to North Channel to alert the group to outbound convoys; seven oceangoing boats lay in wait offshore. The weather was foul; a gale had whipped up huge seas. Even so, Coastal Command aircraft were out hunting, forcing every boat to dive several times a day.

One of the boats was the VIIC *U-69,* commanded by Jost Metzler, who had won a *Ritterkreuz* in July for his long and adventurous patrol to the Gulf of Guinea. Several days into the patrol, Metzler felt "very unwell." He "refused to give in" and "stayed on the bridge day and night as usual," but finally he could "go on no longer." Struck down by a kidney infection, Metzler reported his condition to Dönitz, who ordered the boat to return at once to France. The first watch officer assumed command and took the boat into St. Nazaire. After a lengthy hospitalization—and recovery—Metzler was assigned to command a new boat under construction.

Another boat of this group was *U-557,* commanded by Ottokar Paulshen, making his second patrol. On the evening of August 26, in heavy weather, Paulshen discovered—and reported—convoy Outbound South 4, en route to Sierra Leone. It was escorted by three destroyers, a sloop, two ex-Coast Guard cutters, and two trawlers. Upon receiving Paulshen's report, Kerneval set in train a complicated movement of the U-boats. Seven boats were to join *U-557* for the attack on Outbound South 4. Seven others, patrolling in Greenland or Iceland waters, were to speed southeast and south to form a new Center Group in case another Outbound South convoy was coming behind OS 4.

All eight boats in pursuit of Outbound South 4 were experienced. The *U-95,* commanded by Gerd Schreiber, was on its fifth Atlantic patrol. The other seven were on second patrols. But the gale-whipped seas made convoy tracking difficult to impossible. In view of the weather conditions, Dönitz authorized Paulshen in *U-557* and all other boats to attack when or if they could. In the early hours of August 27, Paulshen closed and sank four big freighters for 20,400 tons and possibly damaged another of 5,000 tons. Only one other skipper got in: Günther Krech in *U-558*, who sank a 10,300-ton British freighter.

During this chase, *B-dienst* reported an inbound convoy passing close to the southern coast of Iceland. By then, Iceland was teeming with British and American air and naval forces. Coastal Command aircraft were mounting thirty to fifty missions a day. Moreover, Hitler's order prohibiting attacks in that area on warships smaller than a cruiser and American warships of any kind was still in force. Although Dönitz still regarded Icelandic waters as dangerous, he decided to mount an all-out effort to intercept this convoy.

Yet another complicated shift of the U-boats ensued. The seven boats that were headed southeast and south to reconstitute the Center Group were turned around and sent to Icelandic waters. Nine boats of the large Greenland group were detached and directed to search eastward and northeastward. These redispositions put sixteen U-boats, about half on maiden patrols, in pursuit of the convoy.

Unknown to the Germans, there were then *three* eastbound convoys comprising over 100 ships passing south of Iceland, all closely bunched. Leading the line was Halifax 144. Next came Slow Convoy 40, about 150 miles astern. Last came Halifax 145, about 150 miles behind Slow Convoy 40. Reading the decrypted Enigma signals to the U-boats, Rodger Winn in the U-boat Tracking Room advised Derby House to divert and reroute all three convoys. According to the official naval historian, Stephen Roskill, all three convoys "passed well to the south of the U-boat patrol lines."

Coastal Command mounted an all-out air escort. On August 25, a Catalina of 209 Squadron, based on Iceland, caught the new *U-452*, commanded by Jürgen March, age twenty-seven, on the surface. Commissioned on May 29, *U-452* had rushed through workup in about eighty days and had only just reached the Atlantic. Attacking "low on the deck," the Catalina accurately dropped a stick of four 450-pound depth charges set to detonate shallow, per Professor Blackett's recommendation. Two charges closely straddled *U-452*'s bow, blowing her out of the water stern first. Responding to the alarm, the armed trawler *Vascama* came up to find the Catalina strafing an exposed conning tower. *Vascama* attacked, dropping twenty depth charges, which brought up "pieces of wood." Nothing more was ever heard from *U-452*. The Admiralty gave the Catalina and *Vascama* equal credit for the kill, but doubtless the Catalina, piloted by Edward A. Jewiss, deserved the lion's share. Four months later Jewiss died in an airplane crash.

Ninety miles to the northwest another new boat, the VIIC *U-570*, hunted for the convoy. She was commanded by thirty-two-year-old Hans Rahmlow, crew of 1928, a recent recruit to the U-boat arm who had commanded the school duck *U-58* for five months before going to *U-570*. Commissioned on May 15, this boat also had been rushed through workup, completing *Agru Front* in Norway, where the boat bottomed and incurred some damage while diving to escape a British aircraft. Only four of the forty-three-man crew—the engineer, Erick Mensel, two petty officers, and one seaman—had previously made war patrols. The first watch officer, Bernhard Berndt, crew of 1935, had served in the Navy six years, but he also was new to U-boats. The second watch officer, Walter Christiansen, a former midshipman, had been commissioned in the spring.

After a rousing farewell party in Trondheim, where much beer and wine had been consumed, U-570 sailed at 0800 hours on August 24. She was not shipshape: The diesels were not properly tuned, the air compressor was on the blink, some batteries were not properly strapped down, the four spare torpedoes in the bow compartment were not securely stowed, one bow torpedo tube leaked. The hydrophones, knocked out when the boat bottomed, had not been repaired because no one in Norway knew how.

When the boat reached open seas, a large proportion of the crew became desperately seasick. Since only one or two sick men could be accommodated on the bridge at a time, and not for long, most men had to vomit in buckets belowdecks. The retching and the revolting odors inside the confined pressure hull touched off an epidemic of seasickness. Many men were not capable of standing watches; many of those who did were disoriented, unalert, and unwilling or unable to correct even the simplest deficiencies. Some of the improperly stowed bow torpedoes worked loose and rammed against the torpedo-tube inner doors; the untuned diesels labored inefficiently.

Directed to intercept the inbound convoy, on the morning of August 27, seventy-two hours out of Trondheim, U-570 took up a waiting position about eighty miles off the south coast of Iceland. Because the hydrophones were out of commission, Rahmlow had to conduct a visual search for the convoy, remaining on the surface in mounting seas in an area patrolled by Coastal Command, which that day mounted thirty-six missions from Iceland.

In order to give the seasick men a brief respite, at 0800 hours Rahmlow dived to ninety feet and remained there, virtually motionless, for about two and a half hours. At 10:50, he brought the boat to periscope depth and looked around for surface traffic, but neglected to search the skies for hostile aircraft. He surfaced, threw open the hatch, and climbed to the dripping bridge. Before the diesels lit off, Rahmlow heard the engines of an aircraft and immediately crash-dived.

The plane was a twin-engine Lockheed Hudson of Coastal Command's 269 Squadron, based at Kaldadarnes, Iceland. Piloted by thirty-one-year-old James H. Thompson, it had only just embarked on a search-and-destroy mission. When U-570 surfaced, the Hudson crew picked her up on ASV radar. Reflexively throttling back into a shallow dive, Thompson reached U-570 before she got under and dropped a stick of four 250-pound depth charges set to detonate at fifty feet, per the new procedure. The copilot and navigator, John O. Coleman, saw two charges straddle the bow.

The impact of the explosions inside U-570 was terrific. The boat heaved violently and rolled almost completely over. The lights went out. Dials and depth gauges in the control room shattered. Mindless panic swept through the green, seasick crew. A rumor spread that saltwater flooding aft had entered the battery, creating chlorine gas. All men aft rushed wildly forward to the control room. Others slammed shut the control-room hatch and closed down the ventilation system, isolating the aft half of the boat. In an attempt to dive, Rahmlow called for full speed on the electric motors and hard down-angle on the bow planes, but nothing happened. The impact of the explosion had disengaged or broken the electric busses and fuses and there was no one in the aft room to reset or fix them, a simple task.

There was now only small danger to *U-570* from above. The Hudson had dropped its full load of depth charges; it had nothing left to shoot except machine guns. An experienced, well-trained U-boat crew could have coped and escaped, but Rahmlow lost control. Assuming the rumors of chlorine gas to be true, he ordered the crew to don escape apparatus and go to the conning tower and bridge, prepared to scuttle and abandon ship.

It was one matter to abandon ship and scuttle in rough seas with a ship—even a hostile ship—nearby to offer rescue, quite another to leap into the water with nothing in sight except a circling twin-engine, land-based aircraft. As required, Rahmlow and his crew threw the Enigma and other secret papers over the side, but balked at leaping into the hostile and empty seas. Believing the crowd of Germans on the bridge had come up to man the deck gun and machine guns, Thompson made several strafing runs. On the fourth pass, to his utter astonishment, Thompson saw one of the Germans holding aloft a white shirt and another a white-painted board, obvious gestures of surrender. "Hold fire!" he shouted.

Puzzling over this unprecedented development, Thompson pulled up and circled warily. While the gunners, Fredrick J. Drake and Douglas Strode, kept their machine guns trained on *U-570*'s bridge, Thompson radioed an alarm and requested help. Another Hudson of 269 Squadron, piloted by Hugh Eccles, en route from Scotland to Iceland, heard the call and homed on Thompson, as did a Catalina of Coastal Command's 209 Squadron, piloted by Edward Jewiss, who had sunk *U-452* two days earlier. Eccles took photographs and served as a radio-relay station; Jewiss, fully armed with depth charges, circled, prepared to attack *U-570* at the slightest sign that she was diving.

Believing chlorine gas made diving impossible, Rahmlow had only one means of salvation: rescue by another U-boat after the aircraft ran low on fuel and had to leave, or after dark when they were blind. He therefore rushed off a plain-language radio message to Dönitz: "Am not able to dive. Being attacked by aircraft." He gave his position and said he was unable to receive radio transmissions. In response, Dönitz ordered any and all boats in the vicinity to render assistance. The closest was another new VIIC, *U-82,* commanded by Siegfried Rollmann, age twenty-six. He attempted to close *U-570* to rescue the crew, but was unable to do so, he told Dönitz, because of the heavy enemy air patrols.

When Derby House watch-standers received the radio reports from Coastal Command—and the interception of Rahmlow's plain-language message to Dönitz—they were electrified. Here was another opportunity to capture a U-boat intact and perhaps its Enigma and other secret gear and papers as well. Assuming personal command of the operation, Admiral Percy Noble ordered a small armada of surface vessels to race to *U-570:* two four-stack ex-American destroyers; the British *Burwell* and the Canadian *Niagara;* and four British trawlers, *Kingston Agathe, Northern Chief, Wastwater,* and *Windermere.* The nearest vessel was the trawler *Northern Chief,* about sixty miles to the southeast, an eight- or nine-hour run in the heavy seas. Derby House's orders to *Northern Chief:* "Prevent the U-boat from scuttling by any means."

Thompson circled over *U-570* in his Hudson as long as his fuel permitted, then returned to the 269 Squadron base at Kaldadarnes. As he banked around to land, he saw that the entire squadron had turned out on the field to welcome him and his crew. But the ceremony went awry. While the Hudson was on its final approach, it ran into a violent gust of wind and crashed nose-first into a swamp. Thompson and his crew were not seriously injured, but the plane was a wreck. Later, at Buckingham Palace, King George awarded Thompson and his copilot-navigator, Coleman, the Distinguished Flying Cross.

The trawler *Northern Chief,* commanded by N. L. Knight, arrived at the scene about 10:00 P.M. It was raining; darkness was falling; visibility was poor. Jewiss' Catalina and several Hudsons were circling the U-boat and firing flares to guide the trawler. In compliance with the orders from Derby House to prevent scuttling "by any means," when Knight found *U-570* he signaled the Germans by lamp, in English, to show a "small white light" and said: "If you make any attempt to scuttle, I will not save anyone and will fire on your rafts and floats." Rahmlow replied: "I cannot scuttle or abandon. Save us tomorrow please."

During the night the weather worsened; strong winds, rough seas, and heavy swells. The seasick Germans spent an unspeakably miserable night on the *U-570,* rolling and plunging. By radio signals and searchlight, the *Northern Chief* homed the trawlers *Kingston Agathe, Wastwater,* and *Windermere* and the four-stack destroyers *Burwell* and *Niagara* to the scene. Having been airborne about sixteen hours (about thirteen of them circling *U-570*), Jewiss's Catalina departed for Iceland.

The senior naval officer, S.R.J. Woods, skipper of the British destroyer *Burwell,* assumed command of all forces, weighed the situation, and formulated a plan. For reasons unknown, the *U-570* obviously could not dive or operate her diesel engines; otherwise she could have escaped from the aircraft and the trawler *Northern Chief.* Obviously, too, these Germans were not the fearless warriors of fable. They had not attempted to fight either the aircraft or *Northern Chief.* They had surrendered and they wished, above all, to be rescued. But they could not be trusted. If Woods took them off the boat they were certain to scuttle. His plan—endorsed by Derby House—was to hold the Germans hostage on *U-570* while he towed the boat to Iceland, denying them rescue and threatening harsher measures if they scuttled.

Woods put his plan into action after daybreak. While the other vessels circled, maintaining a sonar watch for other U-boats, Woods opened a dialogue with Rahmlow by signal lamp. Insisting that the boat was sinking, Rahmlow requested immediate rescue. Although *U-570* was low in the water and down by the bow, Woods disbelieved Rahmlow and said: "Send half the crew below and blow ballast tanks. Do not destroy or throw overboard any papers or books. Do not scuttle or you will not be picked up." Woods then attempted to pass a towline to the U-boat, but the seas were too rough and he got no cooperation from the Germans.

As Woods was working out his next step, a single-engine Northrop float plane suddenly appeared overhead and, notwithstanding the presence of six Allied warships, dropped two small bombs near *U-570,* then mistakenly attacked the *Northern Chief,* which returned fire. Manned by a Norwegian crew of Squadron 330 thirsting for a kill, the plane had come from Iceland. Woods, establishing contact with the Norwegians by radio, calmly explained the situation and refused their request to make a second attack on *U-570.*

The inadvertent attack by the Norwegians greatly upset the Germans. Although Rahmlow continued to insist the boat was sinking and repeatedly requested immediate rescue, he suddenly appeared to be more cooperative and agreed to assist in attaching a towline. Woods successfully passed a hemp messenger line to the Germans, but when they attempted to pull a steel cable across, the hemp line parted. Suspecting that the Germans had possibly sabotaged the line, Woods concluded that another application of force was in order and directed a machine gunner to fire a burst over the heads of the Germans. "Unfortunately," as a British after-action report put it, "owing to the laboring of the two vessels, some of the bullets hit the conning tower, wounding five of the [U-boat] crew. It did, however, have the desired effect." The Germans began to cooperate in earnest. Most of the crew went belowdecks. Rahmlow blew ballast and fuel tanks, raising the boat to maximum surface buoyancy. The fuel dumping helped diminish the fury of the seas.

Rahmlow then signaled Woods: "Would you take off my wounded?" Woods replied "Yes." He attempted to do so by twice floating a tethered raft to *U-570,* but owing to the heavy seas, both attempts failed, notwithstanding the oil from *U-570* and additional oil released by the trawlers *Wastwater* and *Windermere.* Since a trawler had superior maneuverability in heavy seas, Woods directed *Kingston Agathe,* commanded by H. O. L'Estrange, to make another attempt.

Not unimpressed with the great importance of these orders, L'Estrange turned to with a will. He assembled a four-man boarding party, led by H. B. Campbell, and maneuvered close to *U-570.* The boarding party climbed into a tethered raft and drifted across the water, hauling a hawser. With help from the Germans, the party landed on *U-570.* The Germans stressed to Campbell that the aft section of the boat was filled with chlorine gas and flooding, and that the boat was sinking. While other members of the party prepared to attach the hawser to the stern of *U-570,* Campbell rushed below to search for the Enigma and other intelligence documents. Finding nothing of value, Campbell carefully opened the aft control-room hatch. He saw water up to the floor plates in the engine room, apparently smelled chlorine gas, and, influenced by what the Germans told him, signaled L'Estrange that the boat was indeed sinking.

According to an official American intelligence report, at this point the hostage plan conceived by Woods began to unravel. *"The first persons to leave the submarine,"* the Americans wrote with underlined emphasis, *"were its officers and not the wounded."* That is: Rahmlow, the first watch officer, Bernhard Berndt, and the engineer Erick Mensel, but not the junior officer Walter Christiansen. The latter later told the British, the American report stated, that "The crew were resentful at the Commanding Officer and the other officers of the boat going on board the *Kingston Agathe* before and without them." The five wounded, the Americans wrote, went across to the trawler on the raft later. Altogether, *Kingston Agathe* took aboard twelve Germans.

It is not known why Rahmlow and the other two officers were taken off first. Perhaps a mix-up in signals occurred or *Kingston Agathe* did not understand the hostage scheme. The Americans wrote that Woods "had not planned nor did he desire to remove any of the crew other than the wounded from the submarine until he had forced them to place the ship in as stable and seaworthy a condition as possible," and that the "enthusiastic, but somewhat untimely interference" of *Kingston Agathe* "resulted in loss of control of the situation" by Woods and "very nearly resulted in the loss of the submarine" because the three men with the authority to assure the seaworthiness of *U-570* were removed from the boat.

Acting with or without orders from Woods—the records are not clear—the Canadian destroyer *Niagara,* commanded by T.P.E. Ryan, then took center stage. *Niagara* came up astern of *U-570* and shot lines to the Germans, who "very willingly" pulled a raft to the boat. Ryan signaled the Germans to commence evacuating the boat via the raft but as Ryan logged it, the Germans "did not want to come over to us as they had been previously ordered to remain on board" by Woods on *Burwell.* However, when a German-speaking chief petty officer insisted in no uncertain terms that they get on the raft, the Germans complied. Shuttling the raft back and forth, *Niagara* brought aboard the remaining thirty-one men, including the junior officer, Christiansen. The Canadians stripped the prisoners of clothing and papers, gave them dry clothing, coffee, and rum, and later a full meal, then placed them under heavy guard in a stokehold.

By that time the men of the boarding party from *Kingston Agathe* had attached the towline to *U-570,* closed the conning-tower hatches, and returned to their ship. Based on the reports of "flooding," no one believed the boat could survive the trip to Iceland. Nevertheless, the attempt had to be made. Woods released the trawlers *Wastwater* and *Windermere* for other duties, and the remaining four ships, *Burwell, Niagara, Northern Chief,* and *Kingston Agathe,* covered by Coastal Command aircraft, set off for Iceland. Several hours later, when the formation increased speed, the tow cable broke. *Northern Chief* then took over the tow; *Kingston Agathe* proceeded to Iceland with the German prisoners. Woods signaled Knight on *Northern Chief:* "If tow parts during the night, sink [*U-570*] with depth charges."

That night the weather cleared. At dawn on August 29 the *U-570* was still down by the bow, but not sinking. Knight logged: "Slight sea and swell. U-boat towing well astern at 6 knots." Since the weather looked to remain "fine and clear," Knight believed they could reach Reykjavik. But Woods was doubtful and he ordered Knight to head for the closest protected harbor, Thorlakshafn, near the town of Eyrarbakki. At about 7:00 P.M., August 29, *U-570* grounded gently on the beach, stern first, then turned sideways and settled. Two salvage tugs arrived four hours later from Reykjavik to help moor the boat firmly in place.

The capture of *U-570* had not gone according to plan and the British were lucky to get her to a safe anchorage. As reflected in the American intelligence report, her various captors did not part on the best of terms. But thanks to some impressive seamanship under difficult and trying conditions, the job got done. Since hundreds of men, including scores of Americans in Iceland, knew about the capture, and the British doubted that the Americans could keep the capture secret, and since the capture put the German submarine force in a very poor light, London not only released the news of her surrender but also made every effort to exploit the feat with newspaper stories and radio broadcasts.

Over the next several days, British salvage, intelligence, and submarine officers boarded *U-570*. They found the interior awash in a revolting mixture of vomit, excrement, fruit, bread, flour, diesel oil, and salt water. The Germans had smashed the torpedo-data computer, the gyro compass, and the hydrophone console; about one-third of the sixty-two batteries were cracked. However, except for a few minor hull and tank defects, the boat was structurally sound. The experts concluded there had never been any danger of the boat flooding and sinking and strongly doubted that chlorine gas had developed in the aft section. Following the initial attack by Thompson's Hudson, a well-trained crew could have safely dived the boat, repaired the damage, and escaped.

A British submarine captain, George R. Colvin, and a small crew went out to Iceland and assumed "command" of *U-570*. After some minor repairs had been made, Colvin took her under heavy escort to Barrow-in-Furness, on the northwest coast of England. Subsequently the British put her through a rigorous testing regime which enabled engineers to chart her performance characteristics (crash-diving time, turning circle, submerged speed, depth limits, etc.) down to the finest detail. Although there were few surprises, this exact information was quite useful to Allied ASW forces.

The British and Americans were much impressed with some features of the Type VII. The most striking one, they proclaimed, was the rotating "bicycle"-type seat on the attack periscope in the conning tower, "a submarine captain's dream."* Other laudable features: the bridge fire-control system (UZO), the hydrophones (six times more efficient than British hydrophones),† the pressure-hull thickness (7/8" amidships, 11/16" at bow and stern), and the expertness of the welding. The only real faults found were the appalling neglect of crew habitability or comfort (overcrowding, and shortage of bunks, fresh water, food storage, and eating areas, etc.) and the inadequate provisions for storing distilled water for the batteries.

Churchill sought every possible avenue for exploiting the *U-570* politically. His first thought was to send it to the United States for repairs. It would be a "peculiarly provocative thing" for the Americans to do, he wrote. The Americans were quite willing—even eager—to get their hands on *U-570,* but the Admiralty objected.‡ Churchill's second thought was to give the boat to a Yugoslavian subma-

---

 * The American technicians who examined *U-570* urged the Navy Department to copy the seat, but this was not done during the war.

 † The Type VII acoustic gear: very sensitive multi-unit hydrophones, consisting of 48 sensors arrayed on the port and starboard bow section; underwater "telephones" for communication between U-boats; shallow and deep water fathometers; experimental mine-detecting gear with a range of about 500 yards, which, however, had been "sabotaged" by the Germans. There was no "active" or "search" sonar ("pinging gear").

 ‡ The British gave the Americans one of the G7a "air" torpedoes from *U-570,* together with all technical information derived from the tests.

rine crew, which had arrived in Alexandria, Egypt, in a boat unfit for further combat service. "I rather like the idea of the Yugoslavs working a captured German U-boat," Churchill wrote. However, the Admiralty's view was that, having declined to give the boat to the Americans, it would "perhaps be undesirable for political reasons" to give her to the Yugoslavs. Finally *U-570* was commissioned in the Royal Navy as H.M.S. *Graph,* a playful allusion to the reams of charts her tests had generated. Commanded by Peter B. Marriot, she was overhauled and made ready for ASW patrols.

The capture of *U-570* provided one other highly classified ASW tool. For the purpose of instructing boarding parties in techniques for capturing other U-boats and Enigma materials, the British built three full-scale mockups of the Type VIIC control room and the wardroom and radio-room areas just forward where the Enigma and its keying materials were usually stored. The control room was equipped with a blow- and vent-valve manifold (with German and English lettering) so that the boarders could learn to thwart scuttlings by the ballast-tank flooding method.

British intelligence officers interrogated the disgruntled and dishonored crew of *U-570* in London Cage, Kensington. The British were struck by the youth, the lack of experience and training, and the general "incompetence" of the men. Many prisoners had abandoned the boat carrying diaries, letters, and other personal papers, which provided additional valuable insights into the German submarine force.

Later, the four officers were transferred to an officers' POW camp, Grizedale Hall, a country mansion in the Lake District of northwest England. Rahmlow was temporarily held in isolation, but the first watch officer, Bernhard Berndt, and the other two officers, Mensel and Christiansen, reported to the senior POW, Otto Kretschmer, who was aware from British newspapers and radio broadcasts that *U-570* had "surrendered." Kretschmer convened a "Council of Honor," composed of senior U-boat prisoners, to "try" Berndt. The Council found him and Rahmlow (*in absentia*) guilty of "cowardice." Kretschmer informed Dönitz of the proceedings and the verdicts in an encoded letter, which the British allowed to pass. The Council assumed that when the Germans had defeated and occupied England and recovered German POWs, a German military court would try Rahmlow and Berndt, find them guilty, and execute them.*

When the German POWs learned later that *U-570* had been brought into Barrow-in-Furness, which was merely thirty miles away, the "convicted" Berndt proposed an extraordinary scheme to regain his personal honor. He would escape, make his way to the boat, and destroy it. The scheme appealed to Kretschmer. After he had approved it, other POWs assisted by providing forged identity papers, maps, and clothing.

Berndt escaped, per plan, but the camp commandant, James R. Veitch, either

---

* The Council absolved the engineer, Mensel, who had no "command" responsibility, and the very junior officer, Christiansen, of any blame for the surrender.

knew of the escape in advance or discovered it at once and alerted nearby Home Guard units. Mere hours after the escape, one unit found Berndt and, while attempting to capture him, shot him dead. At Kretschmer's direction, the German POWs buried Berndt with full military honors. Veitch retained Rahmlow in isolation and later transferred him to a camp for *Luftwaffe* officers.

Dönitz first learned of the capture of *U-570* ("a depressing event") through British newspapers and radio broadcasts. He gained the impression from those sources, and perhaps from Kretschmer's letter, that Rahmlow, suffering from "gas poisoning," had been "temporarily unable to command" and that it was Berndt, temporarily commanding, who surrendered the boat. When he learned further that Berndt had been "shot while trying to escape," Dönitz logged: "Probably the full significance of his behavior did not dawn upon him until he was a prisoner, when he preferred death while trying to escape to all else."*

None of the sixteen boats deployed near Iceland found the three inbound convoys. Two boats had been lost, due principally to Coastal Command aircraft: *U-452* and *U-570.* On the day after the capture of *U-570,* August 28, another Iceland-based aircraft severely depth-charged two other boats, the new IXC/40 *U-501* (for the second time) and the veteran *U-73,* commanded by Helmut Rosenbaum. The latter was so badly damaged that Rosenbaum was compelled to abort.

The return of U-boats to Icelandic waters was thus a costly failure: one boat lost, one captured, one knocked out and another nearly so, for no enemy tonnage sunk whatsoever. Moreover, many boats had exhausted fuel in fruitless chases and had to break off patrolling and return to France. The experience of August served to reconfirm the earlier belief that Icelandic waters were simply too dangerous for U-boat operations, especially for new boats with green crews. Dönitz accordingly withdrew the boats and sent those with adequate fuel, as well as the boats sailing fresh from Germany and France, back to distant Greenland waters, beyond reach of Coastal Command aircraft based in the British Isles and Iceland.

The U-boat war in the North Atlantic was further confused and diluted on August 22. In a meeting with Admiral Raeder, Hitler expressed gravest concern over the naval situation in the Mediterranean. British aircraft and naval forces (including submarines) had inflicted substantial losses on Axis ships attempting to supply Rommel's *Afrika Korps* from Italy, imperiling the German and Italian forces in North Africa. In stark contrast, the British and Free French forces which were establishing or consolidating footholds in the Middle East were being freely resupplied by Allied shipping in the eastern Mediterranean. It had been expected that the Italian submarine force would ensure the safety of Axis shipping to North Africa and interdict Allied shipping in the eastern Mediterranean but, Hitler declared,

---

* The OKM reserved judgment. It advised Dönitz that, based on the scanty information in hand, it was inadvisable to assume that Rahmlow had become incapable of command, or that Berndt surrendered the boat, or that Berndt did not realize "the enormity of his behavior until later." Until more information was available, the OKM concluded, neither man should be condemned as "guilty."

"The Italians have achieved nothing with their submarines." It was therefore "highly desirable," Hitler stated, "to relieve [i.e., support] the *Afrika Korps* with a few German submarines." A minimum of six U-boats (three groups of two boats), Hitler directed, should be sent to the Mediterranean as soon as possible.

Raeder protested. The decisive naval battleground was the North Atlantic. Except in cases of "great emergency," he insisted, no U-boats should be diverted to the Mediterranean—or to the Arctic or to other tasks—until Dönitz had at least forty boats on patrol in the Atlantic at all times, which would require a total operational force of 120 or more oceangoing boats. But Hitler overruled Raeder. Everything possible must be done to assist Rommel as soon as possible. "The surrender of North Africa," he declared, "would mean a great loss both to us and to the Italians."

These orders caused consternation and anger at Kerneval. Berlin did not appear to understand the fundamentals of the naval war. Already Hitler had diverted U-boats to the Arctic and the OKM had assigned too many U-boats to special missions, such as escorting blockade runners in and out of France. These diversions depleted the Atlantic U-boat force, which had to fight the decisive naval battle. Six boats could not rescue Rommel, and it was not likely to end there. Further diversions to the Mediterranean could be expected.

There were other complications. The passage through the heavily defended Strait of Gibraltar was considered to be perilous, as were operations in the confined, heavily phosphorescent, and often clear waters of the Mediterranean. Only the medium Type VII boats, manned by the most experienced and dependable skippers and crews, could be detailed to the Mediterranean, robbing the Atlantic force of considerable cream. The Mediterranean boats would require bases—and a pipeline of supplies and spare parts—manned by scarce German submarine technicians. Logically, too, the Mediterranean boats should be commanded not by Kerneval but by a subordinate submarine headquarters in that theater of war.

Hitler's decision to send U-boats to the Mediterranean in support of the *Afrika Korps* was a grave error, ranking alongside his failure to fully support mass production of U-boats at an earlier date. The hard-learned lesson of Norway—that U-boats were not appropriate weapons for supporting land forces—appeared to have been forgotten. As feared at Kerneval, the commitment of U-boats to the Mediterranean was to increase, diverting large numbers from the North Atlantic convoy routes during a critical period of the naval war.

As in July 1941, upwards of one thousand Allied merchant ships of about 5 million gross tons crossed the North Atlantic in east and west convoys unharmed by the enemy in August. Of these, 568 were loaded ships sailing from Canada to the British Isles in the Halifax and Sydney (or Slow) convoys.* In addition, 414 empty ships sailed in Outbound North convoys. The only ship to be sunk by the U-boats

---

* To accommodate this massive traffic, Halifax and Slow convoys now sailed every six days. The established speed for Halifax convoys (from HX 147 onward) was 10 knots; for Slow convoys, still 7½ knots.

on the North Atlantic run in August was the corvette *Picotee,* escorting the Iceland-bound section of convoy Outbound North 5.

The U-boats fared better during August in the attacks on Gibraltar and Sierra Leone convoys. They sank eight ships and two escorts (destroyer *Bath,* corvette *Zinnia*) from convoy Outbound Gibraltar 71; five ships from convoy Outbound South 4; and five ships from convoy Sierra Leone 81, inbound to the British Isles. Total: twenty ships out of the 200 in these convoys.*

---

* The Italian submarine *Tazzoli* sank the 7,300-ton Norwegian tanker *Sildra* off Freetown. This was the seventh tanker to fall victim to the Italians in the Atlantic and the only Allied tanker lost to the enemy that month.

SIX

ALLIED NAVAL OPERATIONS

At the beginning of the third year of war, on September 3, 1941, the British Admiralty was overburdened by urgent operational tasks. Among the most important:

• The management and defense of military and merchant-ship convoys in the North and South Atlantic.

• The inauguration and defense of a new convoy system from Iceland to northern Russia ("Murmansk Convoys").

• Maintenance of an adequate force in the Home Fleet to cope with raids by big German surface ships and merchant-ship raiders.

• The continuing naval struggle for mastery of the Mediterranean Sea.

• The deployment of an Eastern Fleet to help deter Japanese aggression in the Indian Ocean and the Far East.

The most demanding and difficult of these tasks was the protection of Atlantic convoys, Britain's lifeline. Amid great secrecy in September 1941, important modifications in that mission took place.

The most significant was the assumption by the Americans of responsibility for escort of convoys on the Canada-Iceland leg of the North Atlantic run. The entry of the "neutral" Americans into this "undeclared war" also greatly affected the deployment and operations of Canadian naval forces.

When Atlantic Fleet commander Ernest King took on responsibility for this escort service in early September, he committed most of his Atlantic Fleet to the job: all six battleships, five heavy cruisers, fifty destroyers (twenty-seven new; twenty-three old), and forty-eight Catalina and Mariner patrol planes. Two of the three newer battleships and two heavy cruisers were to maintain the Denmark Strait Patrol from Hvalfjord; two of the three older battleships and two heavy cruisers, basing at Argentia, were to provide backup. In addition, two of the three aircraft carrier task forces in the Atlantic were to be kept on standby in Bermuda or Argentia.

By terms of the Anglo-American agreement, ABC-1, King's resources included the entire Atlantic-based Canadian Navy. The Canadians warmly welcomed the entry of the Americans into the war, but, as related, resented the fact that a non-belligerent or neutral nation now commanded their Atlantic naval forces. Moreover, being offensive-minded, they were not overjoyed with the strictly defensive tasks King assigned to all Canadian warships.

At this time, moreover, the Canadian Navy was all but invalided with severe growing pains. It was swamped with commissioned warships to man: three 6,000-ton *Prince*-class ocean liners that had been converted to armed merchant cruisers, thirteen destroyers from various sources,* about fifty Canadian-built corvettes, and numerous other smaller Canadian-built vessels, such as minelayers and minesweepers. Excepting a handful of career sailors, almost all of its 19,000 men and women were just off the streets of Montreal, Toronto, and Vancouver, or the farms in the "prairie provinces." There had been no time to properly train these volunteers; many men reported for duty still wet behind the ears. Moreover, even before new ships completed workups, Ottawa siphoned away up to a third of their personnel to man other new ships, such as the corvettes, which Canada was turning out at the rate of about five to six a month.

In September 1941, the 10-knot Halifax convoys and the 7½-knot Sydney (or Slow) convoys departed Canada every six days. The fastest ships and those with the most valuable cargoes, such as oil or petroleum products, sailed in Halifax convoys. The slower, smaller ships were in Sydney (or Slow) convoys. Logically the Americans with their fifty fast destroyers took over escort of Halifax convoys and delegated escort of Slow convoys to the Canadian Navy.

Initially, the Canadians were able to provide only twenty thinly trained warships to ocean-convoy escort: five destroyers and fifteen corvettes. The British contributed five ex-American four-stack destroyers and some corvettes to the Canadian contingent, but this was not sufficient naval force for proper escort of the Slow convoys. The Canadians asked the Americans for additional help, but Admiral King said no. He did not have enough destroyers to carry out his own high-priority tasks. These included escort for the Halifax convoys, escort for the Denmark Strait Patrol and its big-ship back up in Argentia, escort of the three carrier task forces, in the Atlantic fleet, plus numerous special missions, such as a force of fifteen destroyers to escort Task Force 15 (taking U.S. Army troops to Iceland) and a force of eight destroyers to escort a special British troopship convoy to Cape Town, South Africa, and beyond.

---

* Five surviving prewar vessels plus *Assiniboine* and seven ex-American four-stacks. One of the prewar vessels, *Saguenay,* had only just returned from prolonged battle-damage repairs in a British shipyard.

Furthermore, King and other Americans did not believe in and refused to countenance "mixed" naval forces: ships of different nationalities operating in a single unit, such as an escort group. Although outwardly similar in many respects, American and British-Canadian warships operated by different tactical and communications doctrines and had different sonar, radar, weapons, and machinery, such as boilers. As a result, the "mixed" naval forces suggested a high probability of collisions and other disasters in the brutal North Atlantic, and a low probability of efficient combat operations against the enemy. They required a cumbersome double pipeline for spare parts, ammunition, and other items of supply, as well as double administrative staffs to oversee housekeeping matters, such as pay, leave, medical care, disciplinary measures, etc.

The Canadian warships were not on a par with the British and American warships in detection equipment. The British had let the Canadians in on the secrets of shipboard 1.5-meter-wavelength search radar (Type 286) and the Canadian electronic firms were turning out sets slowly. However, even by the end of 1941, only fifteen of the seventy Canadian corvettes had Type 286 radar. Canadian development of the more sophisticated centimetric-wavelength radar (Type 271) lagged badly. Canadian vessels were fitted with a prewar British sonar that had none of the advanced capabilities and refinements of the latest British wartime models.

Admiral King, in consultation with the Admiralty, made substantial changes in convoy procedures in the western North Atlantic. Chief among these was to move the Mid-Ocean Meeting Point (MOMP) eastward to an area between 26 degrees and 22 degrees west, and about 300 miles south of Iceland. This enabled the Allies to eliminate the cumbersome "middle leg" escort by the three Iceland-based British escort groups (3d, 7th, 12th), which, in any case, could not base in Iceland in winter months owing to the lack of supporting facilities and to the ghastly weather. This change eliminated one North Atlantic mid-ocean convoy-escort rendezvous, difficult in fair weather, almost impossible in foul winter weather, and it enabled the Admiralty to strengthen escort forces in the South Atlantic.

After these changes, the Atlantic convoy-escort system worked as follows:

• Sailing from Argentia, the American escort groups, composed of five destroyers, accompanied the fast (10-knot) Halifax convoys from Canadian waters to the MOMP at 26-22 degrees west. After handing over to a British escort group, the Americans put into Iceland, escorting ships bound only to Iceland (if any) and ships which were to join convoys sailing to northern Russia. Following brief voyage repairs, the American group sailed back to the MOMP at 26-22 degrees west to take over escort of even-numbered (fast) Outbound North convoys to Canadian waters. Upon dispersal of the convoy at about 55 degrees west, the Americans put into Boston or Portland for repairs and R&R. Thereafter the Americans sailed back to Canadian waters to repeat the cycle. American Catalinas and Mariners based at Argentia and Iceland provided air escort.

Three American destroyer tenders supported the American groups. These were the magnificent *Prairie* at Argentia, also serving as headquarters ship for Admiral Bristol's Support Force, and two smaller tenders, the *Melville* at Argentia and the *Vulcan* at Iceland. The latter vessels also accommodated destroyer squadron headquarters.

• Sailing from St. John's, the Canadian escort groups, composed of British and Canadian destroyers and corvettes, accompanied the 7½-knot Slow convoys from Canadian waters to the same MOMP at 26-22 degrees west. After handing over to a British escort group, the Canadians, like the Americans, put into Iceland for brief voyage repairs. Thereafter they returned to the MOMP to take over escort of slow (odd-numbered) Outbound North convoys and accompanied them to a dispersal point at about 55 degrees west. Then the Canadian and British escorts put into St. John's, Newfoundland, for voyage repairs and R&R, after which they sailed to repeat the cycle. American and Canadian aircraft in Newfoundland and American and British aircraft in Iceland provided air escort.

• Sailing from the British Isles, the British escort groups accompanied the fast and slow Outbound North convoys westward to the MOMP at 26-22 degrees west. Without stopping in Iceland, after handing over to the appropriate American or Canadian escort groups, the British groups accompanied the eastbound fast Halifax and Slow convoys onward to the British Isles. Coastal Command aircraft (Catalinas, Sunderlands, Hudsons, Northrops, Whitleys, etc.) based in Iceland, North Ireland, and Scotland provided air support.

The British were equipping air and surface escorts with improved radar as fast as possible. By September 1941, about thirty escort ships of the Royal Navy had been fitted with Type 271M (fixed antenna) and/or Type 271P (rotating antenna) centimetric-wavelength sets. These vessels included twenty-four corvettes, two four-stack destroyers, and a sloop. If scheduling permitted, Western Approaches included at least one warship fitted with centimetric-wavelength radar with each convoy.

These new radar sets did not immediately provide the British with a war-decisive weapon as some writers have suggested. All radar of that era was notoriously temperamental and prone to breakdown. Most shipboard sets were out of commission half the time. In order to keep the sets running as much as possible and in proper calibration, the Admiralty had to provide the surface ships with trained radar technicians, and these were scarce. The Admiralty also had to train a corps of specialized sailors to operate radar at maximum efficiency.

On paper the new escort procedure in the North Atlantic appeared to be the most efficient use of the few available air and surface craft. In practice, it was a nightmare, especially for the Canadian escort groups. The new route required that all the convoys on the Canada-Iceland leg travel for about eleven days through notoriously frigid and dangerous winter seas, where gales and hurricanes endlessly spawned, ships iced up, and huge waves slammed them hither and yon in a reckless dance, smashing bridge windows and lifeboats, snapping off masts and other top-hamper. No man or ship could withstand this incessant pounding for long, especially the sailors manning the ex-American four-stacks and the little corvettes in British and Canadian service.

After only a few weeks of these operations, it became clear to Admiral Bristol in Argentia and to Admiral Noble in Liverpool that the surface escort forces for convoys in the North Atlantic were woefully inadequate. Bristol notified King that the American Support Force had unavoidably shrunk from fifty to forty-four destroyers and that to escort the fast convoys properly on the Canada-Iceland leg he needed at least fifty-six destroyers (for seven escort groups of six ships each, plus reserves) or, preferably, seventy-two (for nine escort groups plus reserves). Furthermore, for proper escort of the Slow convoys, the Canadians needed a minimum of sixty-three ships (for nine escort groups).

Another formidable problem lay just ahead. The forty-eight American Catalinas and Mariners at Argentia and Iceland, and the nine British Catalinas at Iceland, were nonwheeled flying boats. When the waters from which these planes operated iced up, they could no longer take off and land and had to be withdrawn to more hospitable climes. One possible solution was to replace these aircraft with an amphibious Catalina (PBY-5A), which had retractable wheels built in the hull, but there was an acute shortage of these planes.

It was important to keep aircraft patrols in Iceland. Apart from the useful escort services these aircraft provided the convoys, they served another role: "cover" for the priceless British break in naval Enigma. To preserve knowledge of that break from the Germans, the British had decreed that any "operational use" of Enigma information (Ultra), such as evasion of or an attack on a U-boat pack, had to be ostensibly the result of "discovery" of the pack by a routine air patrol.

The second most urgent and difficult responsibility of the Admiralty in the fall of 1941 was the inauguration and defense of convoys between Iceland and northern Russia.

By September 1, 1941, it appeared to Roosevelt and Churchill that the Germans were winning in the Soviet Union; indeed, that the Red Army was on the verge of collapse. Almost daily, Stalin demanded that the British open a "second front" in Occupied France to relieve German pressure on the Soviet forces. Fully committed in North Africa, the British were in no way able to open a "second front." However, in keeping with his belief that the British must do everything they could to assist the Soviets, physically and spiritually, Churchill initiated what were to become famous as the "Murmansk Convoys."

The first such convoy—a hastily assembled formation—sailed from Reykjavik on August 21. It consisted of six merchant ships and the old aircraft carrier, now an aircraft ferry, *Argus,* escorted by the fully operational fleet carrier *Victorious,* the heavy cruisers *Devonshire* and *Norfolk,* and six destroyers. The most notable military cargo was a batch of thirty-nine Hurricane fighters: twenty-four fully assembled on *Argus* and fifteen in crates on a merchant ship. Iceland-based Hudsons and Northrops, of Coastal Command Squadrons 269 and 330 provided additional air cover out to 150 miles.

The destination of this naval formation was the seaport Archangel, on the White Sea in north Russia, about 600 miles due north of Moscow. The ships went northward through the Denmark Strait, hugging the edge of the late summer ice boundary in the Greenland Sea, passing near Jan Mayen Island. From there they sailed northeastward past Bear Island (south of Spitzbergen Island; north of North Cape, Norway) into the Barents Sea, thence south into the White Sea via the

Gourlo, a sort of natural channel connecting these two bodies of water. *Argus* flew off her fighters to Murmansk; the rest of the ships put into Archangel, where the crated fighters were quickly assembled and flown to Murmansk.

This first trickle of military supplies to the Soviets was largely a propaganda play to bolster the spirits of the Russians and their will to resist the Germans. It also provided Churchill a response, of sorts, to Stalin's demands for a "second front." To further these psychological and political aims, the British unstintingly publicized the "Murmansk convoys" in articles, books and films, stressing the ever-present danger of enemy aircraft and U-boat attack, the hideous weather and icebergs, the horrible consequences in store for those shipwrecked in these frigid waters. As a result, the Murmansk convoys were to become the most famous of the war, even more so than the much more important and no less perilous North Atlantic convoys.

Churchill directed that Murmansk convoys were to sail from Iceland at ten-day intervals. For Home Fleet commander John Tovey, this new task created a demand for escorts he was not able to fill. He decreed that as a bare minimum, each convoy bound for northern Russia was to be escorted by one heavy cruiser, two destroyers, a minesweeper, and two ASW trawlers, the empty return convoy by the same heavy cruiser, a destroyer, and two minesweepers. In addition to aircraft from Iceland, a second heavy cruiser, based near Bear Island, was to provide backup during the polar transit.

The Russia-bound convoys were designated PQ, the return convoys QP. It proved to be impossible to sail these convoys on a ten-day cycle; the British had to settle on a fortnightly cycle. PQ 1 (ten merchant ships, heavy cruiser *Suffolk,* and two destroyers, etc.) sailed from Iceland to Archangel on September 28 and arrived October 11. At the same time, QP 1 (those first ships which went over in late August) sailed homeward. Neither convoy incurred losses. PQ 2 sailed October 18, PQ 3 November 9, and so on. The sailings of return QP convoys 2, 3, etc., overlapped with the sailings of the PQs.

To the end of 1941, the British escorted fifty-three loaded ships in seven PQ convoys to northern Russia and thirty-four ships in returning QP convoys. These ships delivered 800 fighter aircraft, 750 tanks, 1,400 trucks and other military vehicles, and about 100,000 tons of ammunition and other supplies. Although many were damaged by weather, no ships were lost to German forces.

The Russians had promised to keep Archangel open year-round with icebreakers. However, they failed to keep this promise after December 12, so for the rest of the winter the convoys put into Murmansk (hence "Murmansk convoys"), an ice-free port at the head of the Kola Inlet on the Barents Sea. Less developed than Archangel, Murmansk proved to be an inhospitable place for the Allied sailors to lay over; nor did the Russians go out of their way to show their appreciation. As a consequence, in spite of the extra hazardous-duty pay, Allied merchant sailors came to detest as well as fear the Murmansk convoys, even though, in reality, ship losses were not great by comparison with other convoy routes.

GERMAN NAVAL OPERATIONS

In Berlin at the start of the third year of the war, Barbarossa, the German invasion of the Soviet Union, dominated all else. Hitler personally directed the Germans from a secret hideaway, *Wolfsschanze* (Wolf's Lair), in eastern Prussia. Worried about his far-flung flanks, he rejected a recommendation of his generals for a massive blitzkrieg in the center toward Moscow and strengthened the northeastward drive on Leningrad and the southeastward drive on Kiev. These diversions delayed the drive on Moscow (Operation Typhoon) to October 1, perilously close to the onset of winter.

By comparison, the Desert War in North Africa was a puny sideshow: about 120,000 Germans and Italians pitted against a like number of British and Commonwealth forces. And yet much was at stake for Hitler in that sideshow: German prestige, the integrity and solidarity of the Pact of Steel, and, not least, control of the Mediterranean Basin, the Balkans, and the Middle East.

The Desert War was governed absolutely by logistics. On September 3, neither side had sufficient strength to crush the other. However, the British had three advantages: *Luftwaffe* Ultra, which helped them to intercept and smash the convoys supplying the Axis forces; superior naval forces in the Mediterranean Sea; and use of the less-threatened sea route to Egypt via the Cape of Good Hope. London was confident that by October or early November the British Eighth Army would be strong enough to launch an offensive (Crusader), which would crush the Italians and Erwin Rommel's *Afrika Korps* and rescue a besieged Commonwealth garrison at Tobruk, which Rommel had bypassed.

The projected large growth in the Atlantic U-boat force did not occur in the fall of 1941. There were several reasons. Problems had mounted at home. There was a shortage of shipyard workers (estimated at 20,000) and torpedo-recovery vessels in the Training Command (only 300 rather than the 1,000 needed). The shortage of shipyard workers resulted in shoddy workmanship in some yards, and many U-boats had to return for extensive and time-consuming repairs before sailing to the Atlantic. The shortage of torpedo-recovery vessels delayed the boats in workup and reduced practice shooting from forty-three to twenty-six torpedoes. The shifting of some *Agru Front* training flotillas from the eastern Baltic to Norwegian waters caused other delays and the workup period had to be lengthened from 90 days back to 120 days. As a result, many new U-boats were backing up in the Baltic and Norway, not yet fully fit for combat. In addition, eleven more new VIICs were diverted to the Arctic during the fall.

On September 3, about half the Atlantic force was at sea on combat operations in the Atlantic. Apart from the boats in refit at French bases or routinely returning from patrol, many boats were unavailable for various reasons:

- In response to orders from Hitler, six of the most experienced Type VIIs were being prepped at French bases for transfer to the Mediterranean.
- On orders from the OKM, six new VIIs were assigned to patrol the Arctic.

The first two, *U-132* and *U-576,* replaced the *U-81* and *U-652,* which transferred to the Atlantic force.

• On orders from the OKM, *Ritterkreuz* holder Jürgen Oesten's *U-106* was diverting to the Azores to escort the blockade-runner *Annaliese Essberger* into Bordeaux.*

• Three boats, commanded by veteran skippers, were aborting: Helmut Rosenbaum in *U-73* with heavy bomb damage incurred off Iceland; Ernst Mengersen in *U-101* with disabled engines; Nikolaus Clausen in the new *U-129* with a suspected case of diphtheria.

• Herbert Opitz's new *U-206* was also aborting. Opitz had rescued six British airmen who had ditched their aircraft. Although Opitz insisted otherwise, Kerneval believed this act of humanity cramped the boat's fighting ability.†

The assignment of fourteen new boats and two Arctic transfers to the Atlantic force in August enabled Dönitz to deploy an unprecedented number of U-boats to the Atlantic areas. On September 3, thirty-six boats were on patrol or proceeding to patrol in three sectors:

• A group, *Markgraf* (fourteen boats), southeast of Greenland, to attack east-bound and westbound convoys on the North Atlantic run.

• Two groups, *Bosemüller* (seven boats) and *Kurfürst* (eight boats), well to the southwest of the British Isles and west of the Bay of Biscay and the Iberian Peninsula, to attack convoys inbound to or outbound from Gibraltar and Sierra Leone.

• Seven boats, patrolling independently in the South Atlantic, to attack ship-ping off Sierra Leone and elsewhere on the West African coast.

Dönitz and his staff were hopeful that notwithstanding the decreasing level of combat experience, the boats would find convoys and turn in good results. After a full year of blindness, German codebreakers at *B-dienst* had penetrated the Royal Navy's main operational code (Number 2, *Köln* in Germany) and had made some progress in cracking a special naval code (Number 3, *München* in Germany) em-ployed jointly by Great Britain, Canada, and the United States for convoy opera-tions. Although *B-dienst* incurred the inevitable delays and failures of all codebreakers, the flow of information was deemed sufficient and timely enough to help in finding convoys. It was also hoped that the intelligence picture could be improved by the sighting and tracking reports of the Norwegian- and Bordeaux-based Condors, whose crews had become somewhat more proficient in navigation.

To ensure the secrecy of the U-boat positions from the British, Dönitz had in-troduced new and stringent measures. All U-boats were to be addressed by the sur-name of the skipper rather than by number (*U-Topp* for *U-552*). Naval grid squares were to be double-enciphered, using encoding tables which were to be closely held and changed frequently. Shore stations were forbidden to keep charts of U-boat po-

---

* The vessels met on September 3. The *U-106* escorted to September 8, when Focke-Wulf Con-dors took over off Cape Finisterre. The blockade runner reached Bordeaux safely.

† Dönitz approved of the rescue. An account of it was prepared for his defense at Nuremberg, but it was not submitted.

sitions. A new Enigma for U-boats, employing a fourth internal rotor that vastly increased possible permutations, was nearly ready.*

Lacking naval Enigma keys for September, the British codebreakers could not read *Heimisch* (Dolphin) traffic currently and fluently. But they had mastered the dockyard code, *Werft,* and some weather-reporting codes. These and other sources provided sufficient cribs to enable Bletchley Park's bombes to break back into *Heimisch* (Dolphin) with a delay of one or two days. This intelligence, combined with more sophisticated land-based HF/DF stations, Traffic Analysis, and RFP and TINA, and U-boat sightings by merchant ships, warships, and Coastal Command aircraft, and the knowledge of and insights into U-boat operations and tactics gained by complete access to Enigma traffic during the summer, enabled the Admiralty to continue evading the U-boats through the fall of 1941 with an astonishing degree of success.

THE NORTH ATLANTIC RUN

Owing to the great distance to Greenland waters, which severely limited the patrol time of the Type VII boats, to the fog on the Newfoundland Bank and other hazards to navigation, and to radio interference, Dönitz had curtailed U-boat operations in that distant area in the summer of 1941. However, the intensified British ASW measures in Icelandic waters and in the Northwest Approaches—in particular the air patrols—persuaded Dönitz to again shift the weight of North Atlantic operations westward toward Greenland, beyond reach of Iceland-based short-range Hudsons and the long-range Catalinas and Mariners.† There was another advantage. Dönitz knew that the inexperienced Canadians now escorted Sydney (or Slow) convoys between Canada and Iceland. The many green U-boat skippers and crews entering the Atlantic on maiden patrols stood a far better chance of success and survival against these convoys than others.

Beginning with group *Markgraf,* for the next seventy days—early September into early November—Dönitz attempted to maintain one or more large groups in the waters southeast of Greenland. Because of the fuel limitations of the Type VIIs, the makeup of these wolf packs changed often, the new boats from Germany or France replacing the boats that were forced to terminate patrols.

Two new boats that had pioneered Arctic patrols in the summer, *U-81* and *U-652,* sailed from Trondheim to join the *Markgraf* group. On the morning of

---

* The fourth rotor, known as the Beta Wheel, was mounted on the rotor axle and was a fixed addition inside the machine, somewhat like the reflector, although the Beta Wheel could be set in a "neutral," or nonoperating, position. The other three rotors remained interchangeable, with a total of eight rotors to choose from.

† The safer area was referred to as the "Air Gap" or "Greenland Air Gap" or "Black Hole," or by other slangy nomenclature.

September 4, an Iceland-based Coastal Command Hudson of British Squadron 269 spotted *U-652*, but her young skipper, George-Werner Fraatz, age twenty-four, crash-dived before the Hudson could mount an attack.

As it happened, there was a lone American destroyer about ten miles to the south—*Greer*, a four-stack, similar to the fifty American destroyers given to Britain. Commanded by Laurence H. Frost, *Greer* was en route to Iceland with mail and freight for the American occupation forces. Sighting *Greer*, the Hudson signaled that a U-boat lay along her track. As a precaution Frost ordered general quarters and increased speed to 22 knots. The Hudson returned to the place where *U-652* had dived and dropped four 250-pound depth charges and circled for twenty minutes to mark the location, then proceeded to Iceland.

Under the ambiguous orders then in force for American warships, *Greer* could defend herself, but she was not specifically authorized to mount an unprovoked attack on a U-boat. Coming up, *Greer* slowed to 10 knots and got *U-652* on sonar and held the contact, maneuvering to keep the U-boat on her bows. Why Frost elected to act aggressively against *U-652* is not certain; perhaps to drill his crew, perhaps to hold the U-boat in place until other British ASW forces arrived. Unable to evade and doubtless fearing the arrival of other ASW forces, after three hours of harassment Fraatz, who may have believed *Greer* was one of the fifty four-stack destroyers transferred to Britain, shot a torpedo at her. It was the first German U-boat attack on an American warship in the war.

Fully alert to a possible attack, Frost evaded the torpedo and counterattacked, dropping eight depth charges. Fraatz responded with a second torpedo, which Frost also evaded. During the evasion, Frost lost sonar contact, and Fraatz escaped, temporarily. Frost regained contact two hours later and mounted a second attack, dropping eleven more depth charges. None fell close and Fraatz again eluded *Greer*. Frost hunted for another four hours, then gave up and proceeded to Iceland. *Greer*'s failure to pursue more aggressively—and to call in other ASW forces—drew angry comments from Atlantic Fleet commander Ernest King.

To this time the United States had publicly maintained a pretense of neutrality. That pose, however, could not be sustained for long. American destroyers were preparing to escort their first fast convoy, Halifax 150, from Canada to Iceland. Partly to justify that overt intervention in the war, Roosevelt indignantly denounced *U-652*'s attack on *Greer* as unprovoked "piracy" and revealed that he had issued what the media described as orders to "shoot on sight" any Axis submarines or ships that threatened the freedom of the seas. "When you see a rattlesnake poised to strike," Roosevelt explained in a "Fireside Chat" radio broadcast, "you do not wait until he has struck you before you crush him."

Admirals Raeder and Dönitz seized upon Roosevelt's public declaration to urge Hitler to rescind the complicated restrictions on U-boats. Meeting with the Führer at his headquarters, *Wolfsschanze*, they proposed, in effect, that U-boats be permitted to wage unrestricted submarine warfare to within twenty miles of the coast of North and South America. But Hitler demurred. Impeded by rain, poor roads, and other factors, the Russian campaign was not going as rapidly as planned. However, "great decisions" were expected by the end of September,

Hitler said. Therefore, "care should be taken," he told Raeder and Dönitz, "to avoid any incidents in the war on merchant shipping before about the middle of October." Since this would leave German submariners fighting with one hand tied behind their backs, Hitler directed Dönitz to tactfully inform his men of "the reason for temporarily keeping to the old orders."

Perhaps put on the scent of a convoy by *B-dienst,* or influenced by the *Greer* incident, merely hours after the encounter between *U-652* and *Greer,* Dönitz shifted the entire *Markgraf* group (fourteen boats) 150 miles farther to the west—toward safer waters southeast of Greenland. On September 9, two of the most recent boats to join the group, *U-81* and *U-85,* patrolled close to the ice pack on the east coast of Greenland. Early that day Friedrich Guggenberger in *U-81* found and sank a lone 5,600-ton British freighter. A little to the south of Guggenberger, Eberhard Greger, age twenty-six, in *U-85* ran into a huge mass of ships. He shot at one British freighter, but missed, and got off a contact report.

The *U-81* and *U-85* had found Slow Convoy 42. Composed of sixty-five ships making about 5 knots, it was escorted by the newly formed Canadian Escort Group 24, consisting of the modern Canadian destroyer *Skeena,* commanded by the combat-experienced J. C. Hibbard, and corvettes *Alberni, Kenogami,* and *Orillia.*

Acting on Greger's contact report, Dönitz directed the entire *Markgraf* group to close and attack. Three other boats joined *U-81* and *U-85* during the night of September 9–10 and the next day. All five U-boats found good hunting.

• Guggenberger in *U-81* carried out two further attacks, expending all his torpedoes except one. He claimed sinking four more ships (for a total of five ships for 31,000 tons), but only one other of 3,300 tons went down.

• Siegfried Rollmann, age twenty-six, in the new *U-82,* sank one ship, the 7,500-ton *Empire Hudson,* equipped with a catapult and aircraft.

• Although Eberhard Greger in *U-85* reported five torpedo failures in two attacks, he claimed sinking three ships for 15,000 tons, and possibly one other, but only one for 4,700 tons could be confirmed. He sank her during a submerged periscope attack. In response, skipper Hibbard in the destroyer *Skeena* and Reginald Jackson in *Kenogami* (on her first combat cruise), aggressively pounced on *U-85,* dropping depth charges which inflicted such serious engine damage that Greger was forced to abort.

• Heinz-Otto Schultze, age twenty-six, in the new *U-432,* sank three ships for 9,500 tons and shadowed aggressively.

• Georg-Werner Fraatz in *U-652* damaged the 6,500-ton British tanker *Tahchee* and the 3,500-ton British freighter *Baron Pentland.* Owing to a mix-up in signals, the corvette *Orillia,* commanded by W.E.S. (Ted) Briggs, took the tanker *Tahchee* in tow and set off for Iceland, leaving only three escorts. The *Baron Pentland* was abandoned, but her cargo of lumber kept her afloat.

Total bag in the first assault by these five boats: seven ships for 30,600 tons sunk; two for 9,900 tons damaged.

Upon receiving the news that Slow Convoy 42 was under attack, Western Ap-

proaches ordered surface and air escorts to rush to its assistance. The first reinforcements were two Canadian corvettes, *Chambly* and *Moosejaw,* Canada's first
"Support Group."* The two corvettes caught up with some ships of the disorganized convoy at about 2200 on the night of September 10. Mere minutes after arriving on station, *Chambly,* commanded by J. D. Prentice, got a "good" sonar
contact, ran down the bearing, and attacked with four depth charges. *Moosejaw,*
commanded by F. E. Grubb, maneuvering to assist, saw a U-boat surface dead
ahead and opened fire with her 4" gun. However, the gun jammed and Grubb put
on speed to ram.

The boat was the new Type IXC/40 *U-501,* commanded by Hugo Förster, age
thirty-six, thirty-five days out from Trondheim. In that long, arduous time, Förster
had sunk one freighter, a 2,000-ton Norwegian, on September 5, expending six torpedoes and forty rounds from his deck gun to do so. *Chambly*'s depth charges
caught the boat at 131 feet, putting out lights, smashing dials and valves, and
blowing off the port diving plane. Although *U-501* was faster than the corvettes
and Förster might well have escaped in the dark, he made the decision to scuttle.

As *Moosejaw* closed *U-501* to ram, Förster put on rudder and ran parallel with
the corvette, the sides of the two vessels merely inches apart. To the astonishment
of Germans and Canadians alike, Förster suddenly leaped from the deck of *U-501*
to the deck of *Moosejaw.* "It is not clear how he did it," Grubb reported, "but he
did not get wet in the process." That Förster had given up the fight so quickly and
was first, rather than last, to leave his ship caused deep resentment among the Germans. Förster later justified his action as the first step in a process to "negotiate the
surrender of the crew," but few Canadians believed that.

Unprepared "to repel boarders," Grubb veered off before any more Germans
could leap on his ship. Abandoned by the captain, *U-501*'s first watch officer,
Werner Albring, assumed command and ordered the boat scuttled. In the ensuing
minutes, *Chambly* sent across a nine-man boarding party, led by Edward T. Simmons, to grab secret papers. Simmons found eleven Germans still on the deck of
U-501 and forced two of them at gunpoint to the bridge to help him, but it was all
for naught. Flooding swiftly by the stern, the boat literally sank beneath Simmons's feet. *Moosejaw* and *Chambly* rescued thirty-seven Germans, including all
six officers and midshipmen; about eleven German enlisted men were never accounted for. One man of the boarding party, William I. Brown, was swept away
and could not be found.

British intelligence officers noted the youth, the lack of experience and training
of *U-501*'s crew, the exceptional seniority of Förster, and his newness to the U-
boat arm. Only seven men of the forty-eight-man crew had made prior patrols in
U-boats. One enlisted man was merely seventeen years old. According to the
British author Terence Robertson, when Förster was delivered to the officers'
POW camp at Grizedale Hall, Otto Kretschmer convened the Council of Honor to

---

* As the designation makes clear, a "Support Group" was different from an "Escort Group."
Usually it was a reinforcing element for a threatened convoy. "Hunter-Killer Groups" often served in
the role of "Support Groups."

try Förster for cowardice, as he had tried Rahmlow and Berndt of *U-570.* But when camp officials got wind of the plan, they isolated Förster and sent him to another POW camp.

While *Chambly* and *Moosejaw* were sinking *U-501,* a half dozen other U-boats of group *Markgraf* commenced a second assault on the main body of Slow Convoy 42.

•   *Ritterkreuz* holder Wolfgang Lüth in the weary IX *U-43* fired a salvo of six torpedoes, but four broached and ran erratically and the other two missed.

•   Siegfried Rollmann in *U-82* carried out a second and third attack, claiming four more ships sunk for 26,000 tons. Postwar accounting credited three ships for 16,900 tons, including the 7,500-ton British tanker *Bulysses* sunk, and damage to the 2,000-ton Swedish freighter *Scania.*

•   *Ritterkreuz* holder Georg Schewe in the IXB *U-105* sank a 1,500-ton straggler, but his diesels failed, forcing him to abort.

•   Fritz Meyer, age twenty-five, in the new VIIC *U-207* sank two freighters for 9,700 tons, and possibly a small Canadian freighter.

•   Hans-Heinz Linder, age twenty-eight, in the VIIC *U-202* missed with all five torpedoes in his first attack. In a second attack he finished off the damaged *Scania* with two torpedoes and wrongly claimed sinking an escort.

•   Heinz-Otto Schultze in the new *U-432,* making his third attack, sank a 1,200-ton freighter—his third confirmed victim.

•   Hans Ey, age twenty-five, in the new *U-433* damaged a 2,200-ton freighter.

•   Hans-Peter Hinsch in the new *U-569* was forced to abort with mechanical problems before he could shoot.

Total bag in the second assault on Slow Convoy 42: eight ships for 31,300 tons sunk and possibly another for 1,500 tons; one ship for 2,200 tons damaged.

During the morning of September 11, reinforcements arrived from Iceland to assist this besieged convoy escort: Catalinas of British Squadron 209, five destroyers of British Escort Group 2 commanded by W. E. Banks in *Douglas,* the smart British corvette *Gladiolus,* the Canadian corvette *Wetaskiwin,* and two British trawlers, *Buttermere* and *Windemere.* These raised the total surface escorts for that day to twelve.

In the early afternoon, a Coastal Command aircraft reported a U-boat lying ahead of the convoy. Banks in *Douglas* sent two of his destroyers, *Leamington* and *Veteran,* to investigate. At 3:00 P.M., both destroyers saw a U-boat on the surface about seven miles dead ahead. This was Fritz Meyer's new VIIC *U-207,* merely two weeks out of Trondheim. *Leamington* and *Veteran* charged at 22 knots and Meyer crash-dived, but he was too late and both destroyers soon got *U-207* on sonar. In three deliberate, well-planned attacks, *Leamington* and *Veteran* dropped twenty-one depth charges. Having no tangible proof of a kill, *Leamington* and *Veteran* did not get credit in wartime for one, but nothing further was ever heard from *U-207* after this attack. In the postwar years, the Admiralty gave the two destroyers credit for the kill.

For the next five days, six U-boats stalked Slow Convoy 42 eastward toward Iceland and beyond. But the large force of surface escorts, including three American destroyers (*Hughes, Russell, Sims*) that came out from Iceland, and Iceland-based aircraft held the U-boats off. Late on September 16, however, as the convoy approached North Channel, Robert Gysae in *U-98* attacked and sank a 4,400-ton British freighter. Still later, Heinz-Joachim Neumann in *U-372* found the abandoned hulk of the freighter *Baron Pentland*, damaged by Fraatz in *U-652*, and sank her.

Total confirmed damage to Slow Convoy 42 in all the attacks: nineteen of the original sixty-five ships for 73,574 tons sunk (one tanker), and the 6,500-ton tanker *Tahchee*, hit but saved.

In terms of ships sunk, to then this was the second-worst convoy loss of the war after Slow Convoy 7, from which U-boats sank twenty-one ships in October 1940. It came just as the Americans took command of the Canada-Iceland convoy-escort forces and it naturally made a powerful impression on Atlantic Fleet commander King, as well as Support Force commander Bristol. It virtually cast in concrete the prevailing American view that a poorly escorted convoy was much worse than no convoy at all.

The Canadians drew a barrage of official and unofficial criticism for the performance of their Escort Group 24. They could be faulted perhaps for attempting too much too soon, mostly out of nationalistic pride, but the Admiralty was also at fault. It permitted this insufficiently equipped and trained naval force to assume large responsibilities before it was fully qualified and then routed the convoy north, directly into the arms of *Markgraf,* rather than south to avoid this menace.*
Although *Orillia* mistakenly left the convoy prematurely, the other Canadian warships performed well or even better than anyone had any right to expect, all things considered. In this battle, the Canadians sank their first U-boat, *U-501,* and so badly damaged *U-85* that she had to abort.

One final aspect of this battle should be stressed. It was much easier for U-boats to track and attack a slow convoy, whether eastbound or westbound, as opposed to a convoy that traveled two to four knots faster, such as the Halifax convoys. Although seemingly slight, the edge in speed enjoyed by "fast" convoys was just sufficient to outrun most U-boats converging on a convoy from the more distant areas of a patrol line. Moreover, the fast destroyers escorting fast convoys could drop back to drive down and hold off U-boat shadowers and still catch up with the convoy, whereas the shadower subjected to such harassment could not.

Assuming from the overclaims in the flash battle reports that group *Markgraf* had sunk well over twice the tonnage confirmed in postwar records, for the loss of two boats (both on maiden patrols), Dönitz was not unhappy with the results.

A new patrol line, group *Brandenburg,* replaced group *Markgraf.* It was composed of nine boats, some of them newly arrived from Germany or France.

One of the boats assigned to *Brandenburg* was the VIIC *U-94,* now com-

---

* The Admiralty routed the eastbound Slow Convoy 43, Halifax 148, the American Task Force 15 en route to Iceland with Army troops, and other convoys to the south of *Markgraf.*

manded by young Otto Ites, age twenty-three, who had been a watch officer on the famous *U-48* for two full years of combat. As such he had served under the boat's four *Ritterkreuz* holders: Herbert Schultze, Hans-Rudolf Rösing, Heinrich Bleichrodt, and Reinhard Suhren. Ites had orders to return *U-94* to the Baltic for a thorough yard overhaul and upgrade.

En route to the *Brandenburg* patrol area on September 15, the *U-94* came upon elements of convoy Outbound North 14 and/or other lone vessels. Making the most of this lucky find, in a series of skilled night surface attacks, Ites sank three freighters (two British, one Greek) for 16,477 tons, a notable debut for this young skipper who had obviously learned well on *U-48*. He had no luck while in *Brandenburg* but two weeks later, October 1, Ites sank the impressive 12,800-ton British tanker *San Florentino,* a straggler from the storm-scattered slow convoy Outbound North 19. This success raised his total bag to four ships for 29,300 tons, earning a warm welcome for the boat when it arrived in Kiel for overhaul.

Unknown to Dönitz, one of the *Brandenburg* boats, Eitel-Friedrich Kentrat's *U-74,* came upon Slow Convoy 44 on September 18. It consisted of sixty-six ships, thinly escorted by another Canadian escort group comprised of one destroyer and four corvettes. Kentrat got off a contact report, but Kerneval did not hear him. Other boats did and while they were converging on his beacon, Kentrat attacked the convoy twice, expending all torpedoes. He claimed sinking four large freighters for 26,000 tons, but only two ships for 8,000 tons were confirmed: a British freighter and the Canadian corvette *Levis,* commanded by C. W. Gilding. The Canadian corvettes *Mayflower* and *Agassiz* were able to rescue forty survivors of *Levis;* seventeen Canadians perished.

Other boats made contact with Slow Convoy 44 late on September 19 and attacked. The first was *Ritterkreuz* holder Erich Topp in *U-552.* He claimed sinking two tankers and two freighters for 27,000 tons. Postwar records confirmed two tankers, the 8,200-ton British *T. J. Williams* and 6,300-ton Norwegian *Barbro,* and one 4,200-ton freighter, a total of 18,700 tons. The *U-69,* commanded by Wilhelm Zahn, who had been relieved of command of the duck *U-56* earlier in the year because of nerves, found the blazing *Barbro* and gave it a finishing shot, but the torpedo failed to detonate and Zahn sank no ships. Nor did any other boat.

Total damage to Slow Convoy 44 by Kentrat and Topp: seven ships (two tankers) for 26,700 tons.

During this engagement, eastbound convoy Halifax 150 passed several hundred miles to the south. Comprised of fifty fast merchant ships of several nationalities, including the 17,000-ton British liner *Empress of Asia,* it was the first Halifax convoy to have an exclusively American escort group. The group consisted of five destroyers, the new *Ericsson* and *Eberle,* and three four-stacks: *Dallas,* Ellis,* and *Upshur.* Because the nine U-boats of group *Markgraf* had raced north to attack

---

*   American destroyers were named for people, cruisers for cities. The destroyer *Dallas* was named for a nineteenth-century naval hero. To avoid confusion, no cruiser named for the city of Dallas, Texas, was commissioned during the war.

Slow Convoy 44, Halifax 150 encountered no enemy opposition. One freighter of the convoy, *Nigaristan,* caught fire and had to be abandoned. Per plan, a British escort group composed of two destroyers and four corvettes relieved the American escort at the Mid-Ocean Meeting Point (MOMP) south of Iceland and took the convoy onward to the British Isles. The American destroyers put into Iceland to refuel and to prepare for a return voyage to Canada with a fast Outbound North convoy.

The Americans learned numerous lessons on this mission. Chief among them was what the British had found out the hard way: that owing to fuel limitations and instability, the aged American four-stack destroyers, such as *Dallas,* were not really suitable for North Atlantic convoy escort.

British codebreakers made some strides in penetrating the double-enciphered German naval grid codes and could plot or guess at the positions of many boats of group *Brandenburg* and reroute convoys around them. As a consequence, the boats of this group scoured empty seas for days. The lack of contacts convinced Dönitz and his staff, as Dönitz logged it, that the British had "information obtained by methods undiscovered by us," which enabled them to evade U-boat packs. In view of the intense measures taken recently to safeguard radio security and other factors, Dönitz doubted that the British "information" was derived from codebreaking. Moreover, on September 19, *B-dienst* assured Dönitz in writing that "a penetration of our codes does not come into the question"; it simply was not possible. Nonetheless, at Dönitz's request the chief of the *Kriegsmarine* communications service, Vice Admiral Erhard Maertens, initiated a new and intensive investigation into cipher security.

Altogether the Allies sailed nearly 1,000 ships east and west in twenty North Atlantic convoys in September. The U-boat packs mounted successful attacks on two Canadian-escorted Slow convoys, 42 and 44, sinking twenty-six merchant ships (three tankers) for about 100,000 tons and one escort, the Canadian corvette *Levis.* In return, British and Canadian escorts sank two U-boats, *U-207* and *U-501,* and Canadian escorts forced another, *U-85,* to abort with battle damage. The U-boats sank four other lone freighters for 12,800 tons in northern waters, making a total bag of twenty-eight ships for about 110,000 tons. About 970 ships in eighteen transatlantic convoys got through safely. A harsh gale scattered one convoy, Outbound North 19.

For the Germans, an ominous new trend had set in. In August and again in September, about half the U-boats on patrol returned to bases without having sunk a confirmed ship. This was due, in part, to the inexperience and lack of workup time for the skippers and crews of the many new boats; in part to the sharp reduction in Allied merchant ships sailing outside convoys; and in part to the assignment of U-boats to larger and larger groups, or "wolf packs," most of which the Allies shrewdly evaded with the help of Ultra.

On the other side, and no less ominous, British forces had not increased the rate of U-boat kills. They had carried out two sinkings and the capture of *U-570* in August and two sinkings of August-sailing boats in September. However, they sank none of the twenty-six U-boats sailing on war patrol from Germany or France in September. This lack of kills was due in part to the continuing inability of Coastal Command aircraft to sink sighted U-boats, and in part to the "evasive" convoy strategy, which drastically curtailed contacts between surface escorts and U-boats.

It was all well and good to ensure "the safe and timely" arrival of convoys in the British Isles, a strictly defensive policy, but unless the rate of U-boat kills increased sharply and soon by offensive action, the Atlantic U-boat force would grow to be a truly formidable foe.

ANOTHER FIERCE CONVOY BATTLE

By the beginning of October in the North Atlantic, the luckless *Brandenburg* pack had dissolved and a new pack, *Mordbrenner,* was in process of formation. Four new boats arriving from Germany were to serve as the cadre. They were to be augmented by four veteran boats sailing from France, including Ernst Mengersen in the VIIB *U-101,* which was to be retired to the Training Command. But Mengersen's radio failed two days out from France and he was forced to abort to Lorient.

Four boats returning to France in early October came upon single merchant ships and sank three.

• Horst Hamm in the new VIIC *U-562* found the 7,500-ton British freighter *Empire Wave,* which had been fitted with a catapult and fighter. She had sailed westward in the storm-scattered convoy Outbound North 19. Hamm hit and sank her with two torpedoes. The crew launched two fifty-foot lifeboats; the port boat held sixteen men. Fifteen days later, an Iceland-based American Catalina found the port boat and later that day a British trawler rescued the sixteen men. The starboard boat was never found.

• Günther Heydemann in the new VIIC *U-575* found a cluster of four ships, apparently stragglers from a storm-tossed convoy. He shot three torpedoes into the cluster, sinking the 4,700-ton Dutch freighter *Tuva.*

• Wilhelm Dommes in the *U-431* sank the 3,200-ton British freighter *Hatasu.*

While en route to join group *Mordbrenner* off Greenland, one of the four new boats from Germany, the IXC/40 *U-502,* commanded by Jürgen von Rosenstiel, age twenty-eight, ran into a fat target sailing alone. She was the 15,000-ton Norwegian whale-factory ship *Svend Foyn,* converted to a tanker. Massively laden with 20,000 tons of oil and ten(!) dismantled B-24 Liberator bombers on her main deck, and 220 passengers, she had sailed with convoy Halifax 152, escorted by an American group. When the convoy ran into heavy weather on October 1, *Svend Foyn*'s cargo shifted, forcing her to heave to for several hours, and during that pause the convoy proceeded without her.

When von Rosenstiel in *U-502* spotted *Svend Foyn* on the afternoon of October 7, he fired two torpedoes. One missed but the other hit the starboard side of the ship, blowing a hole in her plates seventy feet long and forty feet wide. When he surfaced *U-502* three-quarters of a mile astern to assess the damage, *Svend Foyn* opened fire with her 4" gun and machine guns, forcing the U-boat to dive and evade and forgo a second attack. Although the whale-factory ship was badly smashed up internally, the crew dumped 7,500 tons of oil and in a fine display of seamanship nursed the stricken vessel into Iceland six days later.

Upon learning that *Svend Foyn* had been torpedoed, the American escort commander commenced zigzagging the convoy, Halifax 152, toward the MOMP, where a British escort group awaited. While so maneuvering at dusk, some ships of the convoy missed turn signals. As a result, the "convoy [became] completely broken up," the escort commander wrote later. The ragtag group he turned over to the waiting British was not a pretty sight; however, all eventually reached their destinations.

At the same time, a British group likewise fouled up. It was the escort for the fast convoy Outbound North 22. Sailing in heavy gale weather, the British had not been able to get a navigational fix on stars or the sun for three days. Relying only on dead reckoning, they arrived on October 7, but they were fifteen miles north of the rendezvous and the Americans could not find them. Most ships in this convoy sailed onward and dispersed, fortunately with no losses.

In the meantime, the German group *Mordbrenner* formed up on a line in the "Air Gap," running southeasterly from Greenland. First came three of the four new boats from Germany. They were soon joined by *Ritterkreuz* holder Heinrich Bleichrodt in the IXB *U-109* from France, who had yet to sink a ship in his four months in this new command. The next boats from France assigned to the pack, Karl Thurmann in *U-553* and Joachim Preuss in *U-568,* lagged by four days. Another six boats from France, including Mengersen's resailing *U-101,* were to join *Mordbrenner* at mid-month, bringing the total to thirteen boats.

The North Atlantic was crowded with convoys: three inbound to the British Isles and two outbound. Aware from Ultra that *Mordbrenner* was forming southeasterly from Greenland, the British diverted all five convoys well to the south of the three boats of the cadre already on station. But the codebreakers at Bletchley Park "lost" naval Enigma on October 12 and 13, and the Admiralty's U-boat Tracking Room was reduced to educated guesswork about the exact positions of the lagging fourth boat from Germany, *U-502,* and the eight boats en route from France to join the pack.

In the early hours of October 15, Thurmann in *U-553* ran right into one of the five convoys. This was Slow Convoy 48, which had sailed with fifty ships and a Canadian escort group composed of the ex-American four-stack destroyer *Columbia* and seven corvettes (five Canadian, one British, one Free French). Several days after sailing, the convoy had run into a storm; about eleven merchant ships were straggling. One Canadian corvette, *Shediac,* whose radio was not properly tuned, had separated and was lost. *Columbia* and two other corvettes were attempting to round up the stragglers, leaving only four corvettes with the main body of the convoy.

Thurmann in *U-553* got off a contact report and attacked. He missed his main targets, but claimed his torpedoes sank two ships for 11,000 tons and possibly a third of 4,000 tons. He was credited in postwar records with sinking two ships for 6,000 tons. Upon receiving Thurmann's report, Dönitz directed him to shadow and brought up nine other boats—the new *U-502* from Germany and the eight veteran boats en route to Greenland from France—to expand *Mordbrenner.*

While Thurmann shadowed during October 15 and the nine other boats homed on his beacon, British codebreakers recovered naval Enigma. They saw that a major U-boat attack against Slow Convoy 48 was developing. In reaction, they launched Catalinas from Iceland and directed numerous American and British surface ships nearby—including escorts of other nonthreatened convoys—to reinforce the Canadian escort group. Meanwhile, the destroyer *Columbia* and the two corvettes with her returned to the convoy. In the late afternoon, *Columbia* saw and attacked *U-553.* Thurmann responded by shooting torpedoes at *Columbia,* but he missed.

That night several boats closed on Thurmann's beacon signals. On the way in, Günther Krech in *U-558,* a onetime *Luftwaffe* pilot who had served as first watch officer on Schepke's famous *U-100,* found and sank the 9,500-ton Canadian freighter *Vancouver Island* (ex-German *Weser*), which was sailing alone. Joachim Preuss in *U-568,* making contact with the convoy itself, sank a 6,000-ton British freighter. The crack British corvette *Gladiolus,* credited with full or part credit for three U-boat kills (*U-26, U-556,* and incorrectly so for *U-65*), counterattacked and drove Preuss off.

The surface reinforcements arrived on October 16. First came five American destroyers which had escorted Halifax 151 to the MOMP and were returning to Canada with the fast convoy Outbound North 24. Next came two British destroyers from eastbound Troop Convoy 14. Last came two of six British corvettes from the slow convoy Outbound North 25, and a Free French corvette from Iceland. Total escorts, including the scattered Canadian group: eighteen (eight destroyers, ten corvettes), by far the strongest protection ever provided a North Atlantic convoy.

The senior officer in the escort force, the American Navy captain Leo H. Thebaud, commander of Destroyer Squadron 13, assumed tactical control. He was not overly pleased with some of the American skippers and vessels in his outfit. Of the five new destroyers that had so far reported for duty, he wrote later, only one had been properly worked up, only one had ever fired her main battery, and some had not even fired machine guns. Four of his skippers had considerable seniority and rank but no destroyer experience and their "ship handling ability and confidence in command were certainly far from an inspiration to their ship's companies." These "beautiful ships," Thebaud lamented, "were being sent to sea in that condition on escort duty in the North Atlantic winter to pit their ignorance and lack of skill against enemy submarines experienced from two years of warfare."*

The gathering U-boats struck at Slow Convoy 48 again in pitch darkness on the

---

* Stark and King ruled that older destroyermen were to be transferred to other duty. The objective was to reduce the average age of squadron commanders to forty-five, division commanders to forty-three, and ship captains to forty-one, or less. Thebaud, age fifty-one, was soon relieved by John B. Heffernan, age forty-seven.

night of October 16–17. In his second attack, Thurmann in *U-553* expended all his torpedoes. He sank a 6,600-ton Panamanian freighter and claimed a "destroyer," but he missed the latter. Günther Krech in *U-558* sank the 9,600-ton British tanker *W. C. Teagle* and the 6,600-ton Norwegian tanker *Erviken,* and probably another 1,400-ton Norwegian freighter. Heinz-Otto Schultze in *U-432* sank the 9,700-ton Norwegian tanker *Barfonn* and a 5,300-ton Greek freighter but missed two others. Schultze described his hit on the Norwegian tanker *Barfonn,* which was loaded with aviation gasoline:

> A colossal flame leapt from the convoy. In a moment it resolved itself into a tremendous flame which shot upwards from the water, accompanied by a roar like the passing of an express train. The great column of fire, whose diameter might have been equal to the length of the ship from whose tanks it sprang, seemed almost to reach the cloud base. The whole convoy was lit up by its brilliance.

In this chaos, the escorts charged to and fro, hurling depth charges and firing star shells. A torpedo from Schultze's *U-432* or Krech's *U-558* hit the gallant corvette *Gladiolus,* which blew up and disappeared with the loss of all hands. Preuss in *U-568,* who had sunk the British corvette *Picotee* in August, deliberately fired at and hit a "hostile" destroyer, which had slowed to a near dead stop to avoid colliding with a corvette.

The "hostile" destroyer was the new, stoutly built American vessel *Kearny,* commanded by Anthony L. Danis, age forty-two. The torpedo hit *Kearny* on the starboard side, killing eleven men and injuring twenty-two—the first American casualties of the North Atlantic naval war—and causing immense damage. However, Danis and his chief engineer, Robert J. Esslinger, and others, were able to control the damage* and to nurse *Kearny* out of the danger zone at 10 knots. Subsequently, *Greer* escorted *Kearny* into Iceland, where technicians on the tender *Vulcan* patched her back together.

The next day, October 17, British Escort Group 3, comprised of four destroyers, several corvettes, and several trawlers, joined Slow Convoy 48 while Catalinas from Iceland provided continuous air cover. The U-boats hung on, dodging aircraft, but they were not able to penetrate the tight escort screen to mount further attacks. The British destroyer *Veronica* carried out five depth-charge attacks and claimed a success, but no U-boat was sunk at this time and place. A Catalina bombed Krech in *U-558,* inflicting damage, but Krech gamely hung on for another twenty-four hours. During the night of October 17–18, Ernst Mengersen in *U-101* hit the ex-American four-stack British destroyer *Broadwater,* inflicting such damage that she had to be abandoned and sunk.

Total damage to Slow Convoy 48: nine of fifty merchant ships for 51,000 tons definitely sunk (three tankers), plus the corvette *Gladiolus* sunk; destroyer *Broadwater* fatally damaged; and the American destroyer *Kearny* severely damaged.

---

* For saving the ship, Danis, Esslinger, and Chief Motor Machinist Mate Aucie McDaniel were awarded the Navy Cross, the highest naval award, second only to the national Medal of Honor.

President Roosevelt seized upon the *Kearny* incident to build public support for his decision to escort North Atlantic convoys and for repeal of the Neutrality Act. In a bellicose Navy Day speech on October 27, he said the United States had tried to avoid shooting but that the "shooting has started" and that "history has recorded who fired the first shot." Although Hitler had insisted that "incidents" with United States ships be avoided, Joachim Preuss in *U-568* was not criticized for the hit on *Kearny*. For past victories and for causing the loss of the destroyer *Broadwater*, Ernst Mengersen, who returned *U-101* to the Training Command, was awarded a *Ritterkreuz** and promoted to a staff job.

In the days following the attack on Slow Convoy 48, Dönitz formed the twenty boats in the North Atlantic that were already out or newly sailed into three groups:

• **MORDBRENNER.**   Never fully formed, this group of three new boats from Germany plus Bleichrodt's *U-109* from France was still in place southeast of Greenland and had achieved nothing. After the OKM obtained permission from Hitler, Dönitz sent these four boats westward toward Newfoundland to scout out and attack convoys that might be going northeastward through the Strait of Belle Isle.

This was the first U-boat group to deliberately and overtly operate in "American waters," theretofore avoided for political reasons. British codebreakers decrypted the Enigma traffic ordering the assault and the Admiralty warned the Canadians what was afoot. Thus alerted, the Canadians mounted maximum air and surface ASW patrols, but the aircraft and ships available were few, the crews inexperienced, and the weather unfavorable for flying.

• **REISSWOLF.**   Composed of the new IXC/40 *U-502* from Germany and the seven veteran boats from France, all of which had attacked Slow Convoy 48, this pack replaced group *Mordbrenner* on a line southeast of Greenland. British codebreakers also noted its formation and rerouted convoys accordingly.

• **SCHLAGETOD.**   Composed of nine veteran boats newly sailing from France, this pack was to occupy waters slightly to the southeast of the *Reisswolf* pack, extending the U-boat line another 200 miles across the supposed convoy routes.

While outbound from France on the night of October 20, Horst Uphoff in *U-84*, a boat of the *Schlagetod* group, ran into what he reported as "four fast ships" 350 miles west of Ireland. Actually it was a formation of five big, fast armed merchant cruisers, escorted by the British *Hunt*-class destroyer *Croome* and the ex-American Coast Guard cutters *Sennen* and *Totland*, northbound to the British Isles. Doubtful that the other boats of *Schlagetod* could catch these ships before they came into range of Coastal Command aircraft, Dönitz relayed Uphoff's report with instructions that no boat of the group should pursue the contact unless it had "a good chance of success."

---

* In addition to *Broadwater*, Mengersen had sunk one ship on the duck *U-18* and nine ships on *U-101*, for a total of ten confirmed ships for about 54,000 tons.

As it happened, at about that time one of the five big ships, *Ranpura,* had an engine failure and was forced to fall out of formation. The cutter *Sennen* dropped back to protect *Ranpura* and the other ships reduced speed from 14 to 11 knots. The reduction in speed enabled Uphoff in *U-84* to close and shoot a fan of two torpedoes at one of the ships. However, both torpedoes missed and exploded at the end of their runs. Hearing the explosions, the other four big ships and two escorts, *Croome* and *Totland,* increased speed to 14 knots again, leaving *Ranpura* and *Sennen* behind, and spoiling Uphoff's hopes for a second attack on the main body.

After Dönitz alerted the *Schlagetod* group to this contact, one of the boats, Reinhard Hardegen in *U-123,* was only about seventy miles to the northwest. Believing he had a "good chance of success," Hardegen belayed his voyage to Greenland, reversed course, and homed on *U-84*'s beacon at maximum speed. When the ships speeded up and left *U-84* behind, Dönitz canceled the operation, ordering all *Schlagetod* boats to resume their journey to Greenland waters. Risking a reprimand—or worse—Hardegen ignored the order and pressed on. His gamble paid off. In the early morning hours of October 21, Hardegen came upon the four fast-moving big ships and the two escorts. Maneuvering around the escorts, Hardegen set up on the third and fourth ships, intending to shoot a fan of three bow torpedoes at the third ship and a stern torpedo at the fourth ship, but an escort got in the way and he only had time to fire the bow torpedoes.

His target was the 14,000-ton Cunard White Star liner *Aurania.* One torpedo hit, causing considerable damage and confusion. When *Aurania* took on a heavy list, the crew rigged out lifeboats as a precaution, and one boat, holding six of her 250-man crew, launched prematurely and capsized. However, *Aurania* was not fatally holed; her captain got the ship under control and escaped at 8 knots, while the *Croome* and *Totland* threw out depth charges. Futilely chasing the other three big ships, Hardegen got off a contact report to Kerneval, then later returned to the scene of his attack to give *Aurania* a finishing shot. There he found nothing but a capsized lifeboat and one survivor, Bertie E. Shaw. Hardegen picked up Shaw, who cleverly misled Hardegen into believing *Aurania* had sunk so that he would not pursue her.*

Credited with sinking *Aurania,* Hardegen returned to his original westward course to Greenland. Later that day—October 21—his bridge watch spotted smoke puffs. It was inbound convoy Sierra Leone 89, consisting of twenty big freighters and tankers, escorted by three destroyers and three corvettes, as well as Coastal Command Catalinas, which had joined that day. While Hardegen was getting off a contact report, an escort, the sloop *Wellington,* spotted the boat and signaled its presence to a Catalina. The plane found and attacked *U-123,* dropping four 250-pound depth charges set for fifty feet. These exploded close to the boat, rattling Hardegen and his crew—and Shaw, the English prisoner, as well—but they did no serious damage. Three surface escorts combed the area, holding down *U-123* until the convoy was safely away.

---

* An account of Hardegen's rescue of Shaw as an example of German humanity was prepared for Dönitz's defense at Nuremberg but not submitted.

Upon receiving Hardegen's report, Dönitz ordered group *Schlagetod* to find and attack the convoy. That night Siegfried Rollmann in *U-82* and Rolf Mützelburg in *U-203* made contact. Rollmann threaded through the escorts and fired, sinking two big British freighters. One, *Treverbyn*, loaded with 6,700 tons of iron ore, disappeared instantly with no survivors. In the light of star shells, the sloop *Wellington* spotted a U-boat and ran in to shoot and ram, but her gun misfired and the boat evaded and dived. *Wellington* threw off depth charges, but none hit the mark; however, they discouraged further attacks by U-boats.

The next day, October 22, Coastal Command saturated the air over Sierra Leone 89 with Whitleys and Catalinas and one of its precious few long-range B-24 Liberators of Squadron 120. The continuous air coverage held off the *Schlagetod* boats as well as two Condors. The British aircraft carried out five attacks on U-boats, but the bombs and depth charges failed to release or misfired or fell wide of the target. In what was said to be the "first" attack by a B-24 Liberator on a U-boat, the aircraft dropped four 450-pound depth charges, set for fifty feet. One misfired but three exploded, doubtless shaking the boat, but no U-boats were sunk as a result of this or the other air attacks.

The presence of very heavy air and surface escort—and the onset of a storm—persuaded Dönitz to call off the pursuit. Having diverted for several days to chase the big, fast armed merchant ships and Sierra Leone 89 to little effect, group *Schlagetod* finally resumed its northwestward course toward Greenland. The chases had eaten up much fuel. Only Hardegen in the Type IXB *U-123* had enough left to conduct an effective patrol.

"WE ARE AT WAR"

In the last week of October, U-boats in several areas of the North Atlantic intercepted convoys. The first report came from Eitel-Friedrich Kentrat's veteran *U-74*, en route to Greenland waters. Shortly after leaving France, on the morning of October 27 Kentrat found and reported the fast Outbound North 28, about 550 miles west of Ireland. Since the convoy appeared to be headed toward the shrinking *Reisswolf* pack southeast of Greenland, Dönitz ordered Kentrat to withhold attack and to shadow, while he moved the five remaining *Reisswolf* boats into position. Dönitz, however, was not optimistic. The weather was foul and two of the five *Reisswolf* boats were very low on fuel.

The veteran Type IXB *U-106*, sailing fresh from France with plenty of fuel, joined in the chase. She had a new skipper, Hermann Rasch, age twenty-seven, replacing *Ritterkreuz* holder Jürgen Oesten, who had been promoted to command Combat Flotilla 9 at Brest. A weird and disturbing episode had occurred on *U-106* shortly after sailing. A gale had suddenly struck the boat in a following sea; a giant wave from astern had "pooped" the bridge, washing all four men on topside watch into the sea. The *U-106* had cruised blindly for nearly an hour before the mishap was discovered. Rasch had reversed course to mount a search, but had found no trace of the four men. One consequence of this mishap was that Rasch had to stand bridge watches in place of the lost watch officer, imposing a tremendous added strain on himself.

Kentrat in *U-74* mounted a remarkable 1,000-mile chase of Outbound North 28 across the North Atlantic. Based on his continuing reports and beacons, Dönitz moved the *Reisswolf* group to intercept. Four *Reisswolf* boats, including Rasch's newly joined *U-106,* made contact. However, when Dönitz finally authorized an attack, the strong escort of American destroyers drove off Kentrat and all other boats except Rasch in *U-106.*

Rasch launched his attack in the early, foggy hours of October 30, about 500 miles east of Newfoundland. He chose two big tankers in ballast and fired two bow torpedoes at each. He missed one tanker but hit the other with both torpedoes. The victim was the old (1921) 9,000-ton U.S. Navy fleet oiler *Salinas.* Rasch thought—and claimed—that she blew up and disintegrated, but that was not correct. *Salinas* was badly damaged, but her captain, Harley F. Cope, and his crew held *Salinas* together* and finally got her into Argentia, escorted by the four-stack destroyer *Du Pont.* Rasch logged that the American destroyers depth-charged *U-106* for nine hours, inflicting considerable damage and flooding aft, and thwarted another attack on the convoy.

The arduous chase of Outbound North 28 brought an end to the operations of the *Reisswolf* group. Three boats (*U-73, U-502,* and *U-568*) that were low on fuel, turned about for France. Two others, *U-77* and *U-751,* held in place southeast of Greenland to cadre a new pack, *Stosstrupp.* Kentrat in *U-74* and Rasch in *U-106* continued the chase of Outbound North 28 westward into Newfoundland waters, attempting to bring in the four boats of the *Mordbrenner* group, which had patrolled off the mouth of Belle Isle Strait, but the attempt failed. Total damage to Outbound North 28: the American tanker *Salinas* torpedoed but saved.

At about this time the nine boats of the *Schlagetod* group, which had diverted to chase the armed merchant cruisers and Sierra Leone 89, reached Canadian waters and formed a patrol line to the northeast of Newfoundland. Four of the nine were very low on fuel and could remain only a few days. One boat, Hardegen's Type IXB *U-123,* was detached and sent to keep a watch for convoys off Belle Isle Strait, replacing the *Mordbrenner* group, which had gone south in a futile effort to find Outbound North 28 in the approaches to Newfoundland. Hardegen's arrival brought the total number of boats in Newfoundland waters to seven, but three of the four boats of the *Mordbrenner* group were very low on fuel and the fourth, *Ritterkreuz* holder Bleichrodt's *U-109,* was again beset with mechanical difficulties.

The new group *Stosstrupp,* which was to patrol southeast of Greenland replacing *Reisswolf,* was to consist initially of eight boats: three on maiden patrols from Germany; two left over from the *Reisswolf* group; and three boats newly sailed from

---

* Cope; his executive officer, Ashton B. Smith; and two other men were awarded the Navy Cross for saving the ship. Admiral King complained that such high awards for merely saving one's ship—without harm to the enemy—were inappropriate, and they were accordingly curtailed.

France, all commanded by *Ritterkreuz* holders: Heinrich Lehmann-Willenbrock in *U-96,* Erich Topp in *U-552,* and the *U-567,* commanded by Engelbert Endrass, who had replaced the boat's original skipper in France.

Group *Stosstrupp,* however, was stillborn. Upon arriving at his assigned grid square in the early hours of October 31, Erich Topp in *U-552* sighted a fast, eastbound convoy. This was Halifax 156, composed of forty-four ships, escorted by five American destroyers. Topp simultaneously attacked one of the destroyers with two torpedoes and got off a contact report.

Topp's target was the four-stack destroyer *Reuben James,* commanded by Heywood L. Edwards. One of the two torpedoes hit the *"Rube"* on the port side, splitting her in half. The bow blew up and sank instantly; the stern remained afloat about five minutes. The other four American destroyers, *Benson, Hilary P. Jones, Niblack,* and *Tarbell,* rescued forty-five of the 160-man crew from the oil-covered waters, leaving 115 men of *Reuben James,* including skipper Edwards and all of his officers, unaccounted for.

The *Reuben James* was the first U.S. Navy vessel to be sunk by enemy forces in World War II. The loss caused profound shock. The Chief of Naval Operations, Harold R. Stark, said: "Whether the country knows it or not, *we are at war.*" The folksinger Woody Guthrie memorialized the sinking in a ballad. President Roosevelt seized upon the loss to build further support for his intervention in the Atlantic and his request for repeal of the Neutrality Act. The Congress responded quickly but cautiously to the proposed legislation and after a lively debate, passed several amendments to the Neutrality Act that satisfied Roosevelt.*

Topp shadowed convoy Halifax 156, but there were only two other boats close by: Lehmann-Willenbrock in *U-96* and Endrass in *U-567.* On the morning of November 1, Topp and Endrass mounted a second attack on the convoy but failed to hit their targets. That same morning a British escort group, which included the ex-American four-stack destroyer *Buxton* and the destroyer *Wolverine,* came up to take over from the Americans. *Buxton* reported that one or two U-boats fired torpedoes at her, but she evaded and launched a counterattack, dropping sixteen depth charges before losing sonar contact. Undamaged, Topp and Endrass continued to shadow and Dönitz sent out Condors, but British air and surface escorts thwarted further attacks on Halifax 156.

In the meantime, Lehmann-Willenbrock in *U-96,* responding to Topp's contact, had run into another convoy, Outbound South 10, en route to Sierra Leone. He shadowed it southward, bringing up some boats of group *Stosstrupp* in that area. With Topp, Endrass, Lehmann-Willenbrock, and other *Stosstrupp* boats chasing convoys in opposite directions, Dönitz canceled plans to form *Stosstrupp* and sent the two holdover boats from *Reisswolf, U-77* and *U-751,* to join group *Schlagetod*

---

* Reflecting the lingering isolationist sentiment, the Senate vote on November 7 was 50 to 37; the House vote on November 13 was 259 to 138. President Roosevelt signed the bill on November 17. The amendments permitted United States merchant ships to arm and to call at ports of "belligerents," meaning in this instance ports in the British Isles and the Dominions. U.S. Navy gun crews, to be known as the "Armed Guard," were to man the guns on merchant ships.

northeast of Newfoundland and—confusingly—renamed group *Schlagetod* group *Raubritter.*

By the end of October, the four-boat group *Mordbrenner,* the first pack to patrol "American waters," had achieved nothing. Groping through fog, outwitted by British codebreakers, harassed by green Canadian aircraft crews, not one of the boats had sunk a ship. In response to orders from Kerneval, the pack had moved southeast in an attempt to intercept Outbound North 28. But no *Mordbrenner* boat found that convoy. Two Type VIIs of the pack, critically low on fuel, had to break off and head for France, and *Ritterkreuz* holder Heinrich Bleichrodt in *U-109,* bedeviled by mechanical problems, had to withdraw well to sea to make repairs. Homebound, Alfred Schlieper, age twenty-six, in the new VII *U-208,* sank a 3,900-ton British freighter. When he reported that he could not fully repair *U-109,* Bleichrodt was assigned to escort blockade runners.

Only one *Mordbrenner* boat was left in Newfoundland waters by October 31. She was the new VIIC *U-374,* commanded by Unno von Fischel, age twenty-five, son of a World War I U-boat commander who was an admiral in the *Kriegsmarine.* Thirty-three days out from Kiel on his maiden patrol, von Fischel was also critically low on fuel. The luckless hunt for Outbound North 28 had drawn him about fifty miles southeast of Cape Race, Newfoundland. There, while preparing to depart for France, he found and hit a lone 5,100-ton British freighter, *King Malcolm,* which sank in thirty seconds.

Apparently this ship went down before it could radio an alarm, for only a few hours later a big eastbound convoy sailed directly into *U-374*'s path. This was Slow Convoy 52, comprised of thirty-six ships, which had sailed from Sydney, Nova Scotia, on October 29, with nine Canadian escorts. After it had cleared Cape Race—the most southeasterly point of Newfoundland—the Admiralty had diverted it due north, apparently in an effort to avoid the U-boats that had been stalking Outbound North 28. The diversion unwittingly pointed the convoy toward group *Raubritter* (ex-*Schlagetod*) and—by another happenstance—at von Fischel's *U-374.*

Upon receiving von Fischel's contact report on November 1, Dönitz directed him to shadow and withhold attack until the eight boats of group *Raubritter* and all other available boats in the Newfoundland waters could be brought up. The other boats included Kentrat's *U-74* and Rasch's *U-106,* which had chased Outbound North 28, and Hardegen's *U-123,* which had been detached from *Raubritter* to scout Belle Isle Strait. These orders put twelve boats on the trail of Slow Convoy 52, including the shadowing *U-374.* But four of the eight *Raubritter* boats and the *U-374* were so low on fuel that they could not pursue for more than a day or two.

During November 2, von Fischel in *U-374* shadowed the convoy through fog and attempted to attack. He was repulsed by the Canadian corvette *Buctouche,* which forced him off and down. *Buctouche* threw off six depth charges, which caused minor damage, but von Fischel's biggest worry was his fuel shortage. To conserve oil, he bottomed at 305 feet and lay doggo. Later he surfaced and set a course for France.

Group *Raubritter* and Hardegen in *U-123* raced south to intercept the Slow Convoy 52. Late on the afternoon of November 2, Hardegen made contact and radioed his position and shadowed for nine hours, but he did not attack, a curious and unexplained lapse for which he was later criticized. However, his reports and beacons brought several *Raubritter* boats into shooting position in the early hours of November 3. Hans-Heinz Linder in *U-202* sank two ships for 6,600 tons and Hans-Peter Hinsch in *U-569* sank one for 3,300 tons. Later that same day, Rolf Mützelburg in *U-203* sank two other ships for 10,500 tons, but a depth-charging escort prevented him from making a second attack. Fleeing U-boats in the fog, two other ships of the convoy ran aground, but they were salvaged. Total damage to Slow Convoy 52 by U-boats: five confirmed ships sunk for 20,400 tons.

When the Admiralty realized that it had erred in rerouting Slow Convoy 52 northward, it made the unprecedented decision to abort the convoy. The remaining twenty-nine disorganized and confused ships groped through fogbound Belle Isle Strait into the Gulf of St. Lawrence and returned to Sydney, Nova Scotia, to sail later with Slow Convoys 53 and 54. The nine Canadian escorts proceeded eastward, per schedule, in order to meet a preassigned westbound convoy. This was the only instance in the war that an entire convoy on the North Atlantic run was aborted.

While racing up to join the battle on November 3, Kentrat in *U-74* came upon an unidentified outbound convoy in foggy seas. This was probably a Halifax convoy eastbound at 10 knots. In response to Kentrat's report, Dönitz directed a *Raubritter* boat, Horst Uphoff's *U-84,* and the three newly arrived boats (originally assigned to the stillborn *Stosstrupp* group) to home on Kentrat's beacon. But Uphoff in *U-84* was too low on fuel to carry out these orders and the new boats could not find Kentrat in *U-74*. He, too, soon lost the convoy in the fog and having expended a great deal of fuel in his dogged chase of Outbound North 28, Kentrat set a course for France. On the way home he found and sank the 8,500-ton British steamer *Nottingham,* which was sailing alone.

After Slow Convoy 52 aborted, Dönitz withdrew all U-boats from the far distant Newfoundland waters. Four boats of group *Raubritter,* including three that had sunk ships from that convoy—Linder in *U-202,* Mützelburg in *U-203,* and Hinsch in *U-569*—headed for France on one diesel to stretch fuel. Upon reaching Brest, Mützelburg was awarded a *Ritterkreuz.**

Eight boats that still had fuel, including Rasch in the IXB *U-106* and Hardegen in the IXB *U-123,* and the three new VIIs from Germany, reconstituted group *Raubritter* on a line south of Greenland. British intelligence pinpointed the location of the group and diverted convoys. Rasch in *U-106* had fleeting contact with a convoy escort (described as a "destroyer") but he was not able to capitalize on the encounter. While en route from France to join *Raubritter,* the *U-561,* commanded by Robert Bartels, sank two stragglers for 8,500 tons from Slow Convoy 53. However, no boat of the reconstituted *Raubritter* group found a convoy. Little by little the group fell away as the boats ran low on fuel. The famous old Type IX *U-38,*

---

* In a propaganda broadcast, Berlin credited Mützelburg with sinking 50,000 tons. His confirmed score was eight ships for 26,086 tons.

commanded by Heinrich Schuch, who had sunk only one 1,700-ton ship since taking over from *Ritterkreuz* holder Heinrich Liebe four months earlier, followed *U-101* home to the Training Command.*

In the early days of November, Berlin issued orders that had the effect of shutting down the U-boat war on the North Atlantic run again. Twenty U-boats were to be diverted to special missions:

• Eight boats were to support a proposed sortie of the "pocket" battleship *Admiral Scheer* into the North Atlantic.

• Six boats were to escort incoming or outgoing prize ships, raiders, or blockade runners.

• Six more Type VIIs were to go to the western Mediterranean to thwart a rumored British amphibious landing in Algeria.

Dönitz was dismayed. The diversions to these special tasks, he logged in vast understatement, was "most injurious to our cause." They meant that the U-boat war against North Atlantic and Gibraltar convoys would "practically have to cease." He flew to Berlin to protest directly to Admiral Raeder, but he gained only a minor technical concession on the escort missions, which slightly reduced the commitment of U-boats for that purpose.

The eight boats assigned to the *Admiral Scheer* sortie consisted of four boats already on Arctic patrol, three boats newly sailed from Germany, and one boat from France. The four Arctic boats were to explore and report on the outer limits of the ice fields and broadcast weather reports. The other four boats were to patrol the Denmark Strait and the waters around Iceland to report—and attack—British and American ships of the Home Fleet attempting to intercept *Admiral Scheer.*

British codebreakers closely followed German preparations for the *Scheer* breakout. Suspecting that *Bismarck*'s sister ship, the super-battleship *Tirpitz,* might accompany *Scheer,* the Admiralty laid an intricate joint British-American trap to sink both ships, à la *Bismarck.* In early November, Home Fleet commander Admiral Tovey moved his most powerful ships† to Iceland, joining forces with the American Denmark Strait Patrol, the battleships *Idaho* and *Mississippi,* and two heavy cruisers, *Wichita* and *Tuscaloosa,* plus destroyer screens. On November 5, the Anglo-American task force sailed into the Denmark Strait to set the trap, but it was all for naught. On November 13 Hitler canceled *Scheer*'s breakout on the

---

* Her departure left only one boat of those that in 1939 had launched the war in the Atlantic: Wolfgang Lüth's Type IX, *U-43.*

† The new battleship, *King George V,* and the new fleet carrier, *Victorious.* The Admiralty had sent the other new battleship, *Prince of Wales,* and the battle cruiser *Repulse* to Singapore. The new carrier, *Indomitable,* was to reinforce the Far East Fleet, but during workup in the Caribbean, she ran aground off Jamaica and went into Norfolk for lengthy repairs, joining new British carriers *Illustrious* and *Formidable,* which were also in Norfolk for repairs, and she never got to Singapore.

grounds that her possible loss would be an unacceptable blow to German prestige and that she was needed for the defense of Norway.

After the *Scheer* breakout was canceled, the OKM released the four boats on reserve near Iceland, but not the boats in the Arctic. Two of the four released boats provided Dönitz a cadre around which to build a small (six-boat) pack, *Steuben,* for a top-secret special operation of his own: a new—possibly sensational—assault on Allied shipping in Newfoundland waters. Two *Ritterkreuz* holders in Type IXs, Wolfgang Lüth in *U-43* and Georg Schewe in *U-105,* were to go right into the convoy anchorage and iron-ore loading docks at St. John's and Conception Bay, Newfoundland, respectively, and attack shipping. Four other boats were to remain offshore to provide emergency assistance or rescue, if required, and to capitalize on the havoc and panic that seemed certain to ensue.

This last, feeble offensive U-boat thrust on the North Atlantic run in November also had to be canceled. A new order from Berlin directed Dönitz to prepare to send virtually every combat-ready Type VII of the Atlantic force to the Mediterranean to support the land warfare in North Africa. This new order was to shut down the U-boat offensive on the North Atlantic run for a considerable time.

During October, about 900 ships in twenty convoys crossed the North Atlantic east and west. The many U-boats on patrol were able to mount a telling attack on only one, Slow Convoy 48, from which they sank nine of the fifty merchant ships for 51,000 tons, caused the destruction of two British escorts (four-stack destroyer *Broadwater;* corvette *Gladiolus*), and severely damaged the new American destroyer *Kearny.* In addition, Eric Topp in *U-552* sank the American four-stack destroyer *Reuben James* from convoy Halifax 156. Five other U-boats sank five singles, bringing the total sinkings in this month in the North Atlantic to seventeen ships.

In November the U-boat campaign in the North Atlantic sputtered out almost completely. About 850 merchant ships crossed east and west. Before the withdrawal of the U-boats, the Germans sank five ships from Slow Convoy 52 and forced it to abort, and later two stragglers from Slow Convoy 53, a total of seven ships for about 29,000 tons. In addition, two U-boats sank two singles for a total of 12,400 tons. There were no further losses to enemy action in the eastbound convoys, but in convoy Halifax 161, a Norwegian freighter rammed the American destroyer *Du Pont.* She survived, but repairs in a Boston shipyard required two months. There were no casualties in the ten Outbound North convoys, but violent gales battered and scattered ships in four of those convoys. Many westbound vessels, including the Canadian destroyer *St. Laurent* (of Outbound North 33), incurred heavy damage from the howling winds and mountainous seas. On November 25, Western Approaches reported there were twenty-six stragglers from Outbound North 37.

In addition to all other urgent tasks in November, Admiral King had to provide eighteen ships of his Atlantic Fleet for a prolonged special mission in behalf of the British. This was the transport of about 20,000 Commonwealth troops to Cape

Town and beyond to the Far East. Designated WS 12X, this convoy of six U.S. Navy troopships sailed from Halifax on November 10. In keeping with King's policy of providing massive escort for troop convoys whether American or foreign, WS 12X was guarded by eleven warships: the carrier *Ranger,* the heavy cruisers *Quincy* and *Vincennes,* and eight destroyers.* The big Navy tanker *Cimarron* was included to refuel the warships at sea.

In December, the story on the North Atlantic run was much the same as in November. About 815 ships crossed the North Atlantic east and west in appalling weather. Two new Type IXCs outbound from Germany sank four loaded ships: Ernst Kals, age thirty-five, in *U-130,* got three for 15,000 tons from Slow Convoy 57, which was nearing the British Isles under British escort; Arend Baumann, age thirty-seven, in *U-131,* sank a 4,000-ton straggler from convoy Halifax 166, also under British escort. No other U-boat sank a loner. For the third month in a row, there were no casualties in Outbound North convoys. But terrible gales scattered seven of these eleven westbound convoys, severely damaging many more cargo ships and escorts.

The U-boat campaign in the North Atlantic in the last third of 1941 was thus a flop, an unheralded victory for the British and a grim setback for the Germans. During this period about eighty convoys, comprising about 3,700 ships, crossed east and west. The U-boats mounted notable attacks on only four of the 80 convoys, all Slow (or Sydney) escorted by the new, green, ill-equipped Canadian groups: 42, 44, 48, and 52. The Germans sank forty-two merchant ships for about 173,800 tons from those four convoys, plus twelve independents and stragglers for about 60,000 tons, as well as four escorts: the corvettes *Levis* and *Gladiolus,* and the destroyers *Broadwater* and *Reuben James.* The first group foray into "American waters" forced Slow Convoy 52 into an unprecedented abort, but the majority of its ships promptly resailed.

For the effort expended, this was a shockingly low return for the U-boats—a far cry from the rich harvest of Allied shipping a year earlier during the same time period by half or fewer U-boats. Moreover, the damage to the American destroyer *Kearny* and tanker *Salinas* and the sinking of the American destroyer *Reuben James* had actually worked against the Germans, making it less difficult for Roosevelt to gain the important amendments to the Neutrality Act and drawing the United States ever closer to overt war with the U-boat force.

The lack of success in the North Atlantic led strategists at the OKM and not a few planners in Kerneval to wonder if the U-boat war was any longer worth the large expenditure of manpower and resources, especially in view of the enormous drain caused by the lagging campaign in the Soviet Union. In rebuttal, Dönitz again argued that the mere presence of U-boats in the North Atlantic forced the Allies to continue convoying, which by itself significantly reduced British imports and required a large counterforce of Allied manpower and resources that might

---

* *Mayrant, McDougal, Moffett, Rhind, Rowan, Trippe, Wainwright, Winslow,* all of which were to be away until after the New Year. Counting the damaged *Kearny* and *Du Pont* and the lost *Reuben James,* Admiral Bristol's support force was reduced by eleven American destroyers in November.

otherwise be diverted to other theaters of war. Moreover, the North Atlantic patrolling provided combat experience at remarkably small cost (merely two new boats, *U-501* and *U-207,* lost in the last third of 1941) for the new generations of German submariners who were to man the scores of new U-boats coming off the production lines in 1942 to deliver Great Britain the final crushing naval blow.

PATROLS TO WEST AFRICA

Although the patrols to West African waters during the late summer of 1941 had produced scant returns and there were no German resupply ships immediately available, and British diplomatic pressure had closed the Spanish Canaries to U-boats, Dönitz believed patrols to this area should be continued. The presence of U-boats in the South Atlantic forced the British to convoy and to draw ASW forces from elsewhere, and kept pressure on the flow of British supplies to Egypt and the Middle East going via the Cape of Good Hope. Accordingly, two waves of four Type IXs sailed for the Freetown area in the early fall.

The first wave achieved very little. Believing that British ships might be taking cover in the American hemispheric defense zone, which extended to South American waters, Dönitz sent two of the four boats across the "narrow neck" of the South Atlantic to Brazil: Richard Zapp's *U-66* and Wilhelm Kleinschmidt's *U-111,* the first two U-boats to go south of the Equator.* Kleinschmidt sank two big freighters sailing alone: a 5,700-ton Dutchman bound for Egypt with a cargo of aircraft, and an 8,400-ton Britisher bound for England with a cargo of pig iron and manganese.† Zapp in *U-66* sank the 7,000-ton Panamanian tanker *I. C. White* 600 miles south of the Equator. Patrolling the once-rich hunting grounds off Freetown, Klaus Scholtz in *U-108* and *Ritterkreuz* holder Günter Kuhnke in *U-125* were outwitted by British intelligence and ASW forces. Neither boat sank a single ship.

The second wave of four boats had better luck—at first. Southbound off the coast of Africa on September 21, Dönitz's son-in-law Günter Hessler in *U-107* found a northbound convoy, Sierra Leone 87. It was composed of eleven big ships and five ill-trained, ill-equipped escorts, led by the ex-Coast Guard cutter *Gorleston.* Inexplicably, the escorts had not topped off fuel tanks in Freetown; none was fully combat-ready.

When Hessler reported the convoy, Dönitz ordered him to shadow until he could bring up the other three southbound boats of the second wave. The first to arrive was Karl Friedrich Merten in *U-68,* making his first patrol in South Atlantic waters. In the early hours of September 22, Hessler and Merten attacked the convoy. All four of Hessler's torpedoes malfunctioned or missed, after which an en-

---

*   A onetime merchant marine officer, Kleinschmidt had crossed the Equator before and was thus a "shellback." He arranged an appropriately brutal initiation ceremony—presided over by King Neptune in costume—for the "polliwogs" crossing the line for the first time.

†   Kleinschmidt wrote that he supplied the survivors of both ships with chocolate, cigarettes, matches, and brandy.

gine failed, forcing him to withdraw for repairs. Merten fired three torpedoes. He claimed sinking two ships for 14,000 tons and damage to a 7,000-ton tanker. In fact, he sank no ships, but hit and severely damaged the 5,300-ton British freighter *Silverbelle.*

The escorts fired star shells and churned around, but they mounted no organized counterattack. Three of the five, including *Gorleston,* stood by the damaged *Silverbelle,* whose crew was desperately attempting to make repairs. Falling well behind the convoy, *Gorleston* took *Silverbelle* in tow until Derby House ordered her, as well as the corvette *Gardenia,* to rejoin the convoy forthwith. Another of the escorts, the small Free French minesweeper *Commandant Duboc,* took *Silverbelle* in tow. A week later *Duboc* ran low on fuel and was forced to return to Freetown with *Silverbelle*'s crew, leaving the hulk still afloat.

Early the following night a third southbound boat caught up with the convoy. She was *U-103,* commanded by Werner Winter, age twenty-nine, making his first full Atlantic patrol as a skipper. He closed the formation after dark, fired a salvo of five torpedoes, and claimed sinking four ships for 24,000 tons and damage to another of 6,000 tons. In reality, he hit and sank two big freighters for 10,600 tons. The three escorts, including the corvette *Gardenia,* rescued survivors, but again conducted no counterattacks. Low on fuel, *Gardenia* departed when the *Gorleston* caught up, leaving a total of three escorts and eight merchant ships.

Merten in *U-68* closed that night for his second attack. He saw a damaged freighter and a damaged tanker, he reported later, but he bravely chose to attack one of the "destroyers." He set up on and fired at one "destroyer," but both torpedoes missed. It was then discovered that *U-68*'s batteries were too low to permit a dive, so Merten was forced to break off the attack, withdraw, and commence a battery charge.

The fourth and last boat to arrive was the *U-67,* commanded by Günther Müller-Stöckheim, age twenty-seven. Commissioned on January 22, 1941, under the command of *Ritterkreuz* holder Heinrich Bleichrodt (who later went to *U-109*), the *U-67* had been diverted during the spring and summer to R&D experiments.* Until now, she had not made a real war patrol and her long-suffering crew was eager for a kill.

As Müller-Stöckheim closed to attack, a valve in the main ballast-tank air manifold failed. The engineer logged in his personal diary: "I had to report to the commander that other minor defects had occurred and that the boat was not fully fit to dive." Undeterred, Müller-Stöckheim pressed the attack, firing three torpedoes at what he believed to be a 7,000-ton ship. He hit and sank a 3,800-ton British freighter, which went down so quickly that it capsized and sucked under its three lifeboats. The escorts rescued the survivors but again conducted no counterattack.

Having repaired his engines, Günter Hessler in *U-107* caught up with the convoy in the early hours of September 24. In this second attack, he claimed sinking three ships for 26,000 tons, including a 13,000-ton tanker. He actually sank three

---

* Her upper hull area was coated with rubber strips (known as "*Alberich*") to deflect sonar. The experiment was a failure.

freighters for 13,600 tons. In his report to Kerneval, Hessler stated that only one ship of the convoy remained and that it was closely guarded by escorts.

Upon receiving Hessler's report, Dönitz called off the attack, well pleased at the results. Based on reports from the four boats, he estimated they had positively sunk five ships for 41,000 tons, possibly sunk four more for 24,000 tons, and damaged two for 12,000 tons. Hence, he logged, the entire convoy, "except one ship," was "wiped out." In reality, the four U-boats had sunk only about half of the convoy: six of the eleven ships for 28,000 tons. At that time a seventh ship, *Silverbelle,* under tow by *Duboc,* was still struggling to stay afloat.

In due course the remaining four ships of Sierra Leone 87, escorted by *Gorleston* and two other escorts, reached the British Isles. The failure of the escorts to prepare properly for the mission and to carry out vigorous counterattacks drew harsh criticism from Derby House. An account of the failures was circulated to ASW forces as an example of what not to do, and Derby House took steps to ensure that the skipper of *Gorleston* did not again command an escort group.

The four boats that had attacked Sierra Leone 87 went separate ways. Winter in *U-103* and Hessler in *U-107* proceeded independently to patrol off Freetown. Also outwitted by British intelligence and ASW forces, neither boat sank another ship. Müller-Stöckheim in *U-67* and Merten in *U-68* could not immediately go further south. A man on *U-67* was ill with a venereal disease; Merten in *U-68* had fired most of his torpedoes.

When apprised of the situations on *U-67* and *U-68,* Kerneval directed the two boats to rendezvous with Kleinschmidt's *U-111,* which was en route home from the South Atlantic. The plan was that a doctor on board *U-68* was to examine the sick man on *U-67.* If the doctor could not administer a cure, the man was to return to France on *U-111.* At the same time, Merten in *U-68* was to take on torpedoes from *U-111.* In that way both *U-67* and *U-68* could resume their voyages to the South Atlantic.

Kerneval ordered the three boats to rendezvous in a remote area: Tarafal Bay, Santo Antão Island, in the Portuguese Cape Verde Islands. The British codebreakers intercepted several messages relating to the rendezvous, including an indiscreet one from Kleinschmidt in *U-111,* which mentioned Tarafal Bay by name. The Admiralty ordered the big *River*-class submarine *Clyde,* commanded by David Ingram, which was on ASW patrol in the Canary Islands, to go to Tarafal Bay and attempt to sink all three U-boats.

This order to act tactically on Enigma information was risky. Until then the Germans had not used the Cape Verde Islands for U-boat operations. Should *Clyde* fail to sink all three boats, a report of her appearance in remote Tarafal Bay at the exact moment of the first U-boat rendezvous there was certain to raise deep suspicion in Germany that Enigma had been compromised.

As scheduled, Merten in *U-68* and Kleinschmidt in *U-111* arrived in the bay on the evening of September 27. The boats anchored side by side about 200 yards offshore. While Merten and Kleinschmidt had dinner, the crews transferred four torpedoes from *U-111*'s topside canisters to *U-68.* Neither skipper felt quite at ease in those confined, unknown waters. Shortly before midnight both boats got under way and stood out to sea, intending to return the following night to meet Müller-Stöckheim in *U-67*.

At that same moment, *Clyde* nosed into Tarafal Bay on the surface. Her bridge watch saw *U-68* and Ingram turned to shoot a bow salvo. Before he could fire, however, he caught sight of *U-111*. Believing *U-111* was coming in to ram, Ingram broke off the attack on *U-68* and turned to deal with *U-111*. But when Kleinschmidt in *U-111* saw *Clyde,* he elected to crash-dive rather than ram, a decision that drew harsh criticism from his men. *Clyde* passed directly over *U-111*, with mere inches between the two hulls.

When *U-111* disappeared from view, Ingram resumed his attack on *U-68,* which was still unaware of his presence. Remaining on the surface, Ingram fired all six bow tubes at *U-68,* but Merten's alert bridge watch saw the torpedoes approaching and he turned *U-68* on a parallel course and crash-dived. The torpedoes missed, but two hit the distant shore and exploded. Confronting two alerted, submerged U-boats, Ingram dived *Clyde* to reload his torpedo tubes and search for his quarry by hydrophone.

While the three submarines were submerged in the bay, groping blindly for one another, a fourth was entering on the surface. She was Müller-Stöckheim's *U-67*. When he heard the two torpedo detonations, he was shocked and puzzled—and promptly dived. He picked up the swish of propellers on his hydrophones, but could see nothing through his periscope. Prudently he decided to surface and withdraw to open sea.

Shortly after *U-67* surfaced, Müller-Stöckheim caught sight of a "shadow" on his port bow. This was *Clyde,* which had reloaded tubes and surfaced with her deck gun manned. Ingram saw *U-67* at the same moment and turned *Clyde* to ram. Recognizing the "shadow" as a big *River*-class British submarine on a collision course, Müller-Stöckheim backed his engines emergency power and put the rudder hard over. The result was that *U-67* avoided being rammed but unintentionally hit *Clyde* a glancing blow in her stern.

The two submarines broke clear and dived. *Clyde* was not seriously damaged; *U-67* was a mess. Her bow was bent around at a 90 degree angle and three of her four bow torpedo tubes were inoperable and leaking. Since the crew could not repair the damage, she had to abort and return to France, taking the man with venereal disease who was partly responsible for this disastrous rendezvous.

During the ensuing day—September 28—the four submarines hauled out to sea and scattered. Müller-Stöckheim in *U-67* got off the first report to Kerneval: He had heard "two explosions" in the bay and had collided with a British submarine and had to abort. Fearing that *Clyde* had sunk *U-68* or *U-111* or both, Dönitz asked for position reports. Kleinschmidt spoke up to report that a British submarine had indeed fouled the rendezvous and that it had attacked and may have sunk *U-68*. Merten in *U-68* finally reported that he was *not* sunk or damaged and that he had taken on torpedoes from *U-111* and wished to continue his patrol to the South Atlantic. Since the damaged *U-67* had to return to France, Merten requested a second rendezvous with her to take off whatever fuel and torpedoes she could spare. Kerneval arranged the second meet in a remote cove on the coast of Africa in

Vichy French Mauritania. The *U-67* then limped back to France and the *U-68* proceeded to the South Atlantic.

After leaving the Cape Verde Islands, Kleinschmidt in the homebound *U-111* set a course for France. Since his track was to take him west of the Canary Islands, close to the place where the boats of the second wave had attacked Sierra Leone 87, Kerneval directed him to be on the lookout for the abandoned hulk of *Silverbelle,* wrecked by Merten in *U-68.*

While looking for the hulk on the morning of October 4, Kleinschmidt saw smoke on the horizon. Believing he had found a big freighter, he turned *U-111* to attack. The smoke was coming from a coal-burning armed trawler, *Lady Shirley,* which had come out from Gibraltar to salvage *Silverbelle* or, possibly acting on Ultra information (the records are not clear), to intercept *U-111.* As *U-111* closed, the lookout on *Lady Shirley* spotted her conning tower at a distance of about ten miles. The lookout thought it was the funnel of a merchant ship, but *Lady Shirley*'s captain, A. H. Callaway, turned toward the object on the "off chance" that it might be a U-boat. Still believing the trawler was a big freighter, Kleinschmidt dived to position *U-111* for a submerged torpedo attack. Listening to *Lady Shirley*'s screws, the hydrophone operator warned Kleinschmidt that the target was a small ship drawing very close, but Kleinschmidt stubbornly clung to his conviction that she was big and pretty far off.

Coming up pinging, *Lady Shirley* got a good sonar contact at 1,600 yards. She ran in and dropped four depth charges, two set for 150 feet, two set for 250 feet. These exploded while *U-111* was still at periscope depth—fifty feet—and did little damage. In response to this rude and shocking development, Kleinschmidt ordered a gun action. He surfaced *U-111* close to *Lady Shirley,* but both diesels malfunctioned and the engine room filled with dense choking smoke, impeding repairs and making another dive inadvisable.

Thus crippled, Kleinschmidt attempted to proceed with the gun action. But *Lady Shirley* was bearing in, firing her 4" gun and smaller weapons. Kleinschmidt got his 20mm gun on the bridge manned, but the close, accurate, and continuous fire from *Lady Shirley* prevented the Germans from running down onto the main deck to man *U-111*'s 4.1" gun.

Like two sailing ships of yore, the *Lady Shirley* and *U-111* lay side by side, pumping shells at one another from point-blank range. Having seized the initiative, Callaway in *Lady Shirley* never relinquished it, and the German gunners could not get to the big deck gun. In the exchange of fire, *Lady Shirley* incurred five casualties (one killed, four wounded) in her fourteen-man crew, but she killed seven Germans, including the 20mm gunner and all three line officers: Kleinschmidt, first watch officer Helmut Fuchs, and second watch officer Friedrich Wilhelm Rösing, younger brother of *Ritterkreuz* holder Hans-Rudolf Rösing, who was then commanding Combat Flotilla 3 in La Pallice.

Upon the death of the three officers, a prospective commanding officer, Hans Joachim Heinecke, who had been helping with the malfunctioning diesels, assumed command of *U-111* and ordered her abandoned and scuttled. The engineer opened the vents and the forty-five survivors, including five wounded, jumped overboard. Nineteen minutes after the start of the gun battle, *U-111* plunged under for the last time.

The triumphant little *Lady Shirley* fished the survivors from the water and set a course for Gibraltar. One of the wounded Germans who had lost a leg died en route and was buried at sea, leaving forty-four of the fifty-two-man crew. The survivors were shocked and humiliated that Kleinschmidt, a merchant marine veteran, had mistaken a trawler for a big freighter and that the big and powerful *U-111* had been bested by a lowly British trawler manned by fourteen men.

As in the case of *U-570* and *U-501,* from which German prisoners had been taken recently, British intelligence officers noted well the inexperience of the *U-111* crew. Kleinschmidt, who came from torpedo boats and cruisers, had been in the submarine arm only one year. The first watch officer, Fuchs, age twenty-four, had been in the Navy only four years. Normally a second watch officer, Fuchs was temporarily serving in the higher post because the regular first watch officer had injured himself ashore and did not sail. Rösing, crew of 1936, was actually a year senior to Fuchs, but he had only recently transferred from the *Luftwaffe* and had no prior experience in submarines and was therefore serving as second watch officer. Among the petty officers, only five had served in submarines before joining *U-111* but, as a British report put it, only two of the five would have been considered "experienced" by prewar standards. Some of the enlisted men had been in the Navy only ten months.

Despite repeated assurances from the OKM to the contrary, the appearance of the British submarine *Clyde* in Tarafal Bay fouling the rendezvous of *U-67, U-68,* and *U-111* convinced Dönitz that the British were reading naval Enigma. He logged on September 28: "It appears improbable that an English submarine would be in such an isolated area by *accident.* It is more likely that our cipher material is compromised or that there has been a break of security." Accordingly, an emergency modification to naval Enigma was put into effect on October 1, which blinded Bletchley Park. But within seven days British codebreakers broke back into Enigma and read it currently until October 12, when, as related, another blackout of two days occurred.

Prodded by Dönitz, the chief of *Kriegsmarine* communications, Vice Admiral Maertens, intensified his new and supposedly comprehensive investigation into Enigma security. On October 24 Maertens turned in an eighteen-page report to the OKM and Dönitz in which he reaffirmed Berlin's unshakable belief that Enigma was safe. Maertens dismissed the appearance of *Clyde* at Tarafal Bay as doubtless the result of a routine ASW patrol. Had the British planned a "trap" based on Enigma decryptions, he wrote, they would certainly have sent more than one submarine. He likewise dismissed other worrisome events that Dönitz had described, attributing them to British DFing or sightings by enemy and neutral ships and aircraft. As to the possibility that the British had recovered the Enigma from the captured *U-570,* he could not say positively one way or the other, but there was as yet no evidence they had, and in any case, *U-570* carried Enigma keys that were to expire soon.

The Maertens investigation was slipshod. The American historian Timothy Mulligan, who unearthed the Maertens report, aptly wrote in his analysis that by focusing narrowly on the Tarafal Bay incident and several others, Maertens altogether neglected the main point: the difficulty U-boats had in finding convoys on the North Atlantic run from Canada to the British Isles and vice versa.

It may well be that Maertens viewed the investigation as a waste of time—old history. Two steps were already afoot to greatly increase the security of U-boat codes:

• Commencing about October 5, U-boats were to begin using a special Enigma net, separate from the standard *Kriegsmarine* Home Waters net (*Heimisch;* Dolphin in Britain). The Germans called the new U-boat net *Triton;* the British called it Shark. Access to *Triton* (Shark) other than by operating U-boats was to be severely limited to eight naval commands and the six Atlantic U-boat combat flotillas. U-boat crewmen not on patrol were barred from listening to the circuit. No weather ships, of course, were to use the *Triton* (Shark) net, so the chance of again capturing the keys, other than from a U-boat (à la *U-110*), was remote.

• A new Enigma machine employing four rotors on the axle (rather than three) was nearly ready for distribution to U-boats for use on the *Triton* (Shark) net. The Germans believed that by employing a fourth rotor and by changing the selection and order of all four rotors frequently, the naval Enigma would be even more difficult—indeed, impossible—to break by the most sophisticated and ingenious mathematical theories. The enemy would have to capture both a four-rotor machine and the daily keys. If the keys were also changed frequently, success from captures would be at best short-lived.

British codebreakers at Bletchley Park had found clues in *Heimisch* (Dolphin) traffic that a new Enigma net for U-boats (*Triton,* or Shark) and a new machine employing four rotors were in preparation. On October 7, after intercepting some early German tests of *Triton* (Shark) traffic in four-rotor Enigma, which proved to be unbreakable, they described it as "an ominous sign of worse things to come." They warned that Shark could not be broken without a new, complex, high-speed "four-rotor" bombe, but, the official British historian wrote, they failed to stress the urgency of designing and building such a bombe. Some even doubted that a workable four-rotor bombe could be built.

In fact, Bletchley Park was neither mentally nor physically capable of confronting a new challenge of this magnitude. Its chief cryptanalysts, Gordon Welchman and Alan Turing (in Hut 6 and Hut 8), were utterly swamped with work and exhausted; the dozen "three-rotor" bombes in operation were incapable of absorbing further loads. Moreover, owing to the need for utmost secrecy, the importance of the work at Bletchley Park was not appreciated or understood by those not in the picture and, as a result, London bureaucrats had not given the codebreakers the support they required and deserved. On October 21 Welchman and Turing and two other senior cryptanalysts sent an extraordinary letter directly to Churchill, begging for help. They pointed out that owing to "shortage of staff" and "overworking," the naval team in Hut 8 had to cease night shifts, with the result that "the finding of the [Enigma] naval keys is being delayed at least twelve hours every day." A similar situation existed in Hut 6, which was working on *Luftwaffe* and *Wehrmacht* Enigma.

In response to the letter, Churchill directed that Bletchley Park be given "all they want on extreme priority." The shortages of personnel were swiftly overcome, but the difficult—perhaps impossible—four-rotor bombe was not pursued with vigor. It was not until December that anyone tackled a possible design; another month passed before a technical team could be assembled to pursue this daunting task.

IN SUPPORT OF ROMMEL

Berlin rightly worried about the Mediterranean Basin. The Italian naval and air forces had failed to gain control of this vital strategic area. Capitalizing on breaks in *Luftwaffe* Enigma, which directed German aircraft to escort specific convoys, British aircraft, surface ships, and submarines had cut heavily into the flow of supplies from Italy to German and Italian forces in North Africa. The lack of supplies had prevented Rommel's *Afrika Korps* from capturing bypassed Tobruk and had undermined the ability of Axis forces to repulse a possible British offensive. Moreover, a belief persisted in Berlin that the British were preparing an amphibious landing behind Axis forces—in Algiers and Oran—to trap Rommel between giant pincers.

To cope with this increasingly perilous situation, the OKM directed that in addition to the six U-boats ordered to the Mediterranean in September, Dönitz must do everything possible to interdict the flow of British supplies to the Mediterranean via the Strait of Gibraltar.

Dönitz was reluctant to comply. He continued to view the war in the Mediterranean as a distant second in importance to the war in the North Atlantic. Based on the small size and small number of ships in the Gibraltar convoys, he did not believe the flow of supplies from the British Isles via Gibraltar to be all that significant. The bulk of British supplies, he argued correctly, went to Egypt via Freetown, Sierra Leone, and Cape Town, South Africa. Moreover, the U-boat attacks on Gibraltar Convoys 70 and 71 in August had shown that those convoys were very heavily protected by air and surface escorts, so much so that they could almost be viewed as U-boat traps. Only the most experienced U-boat skippers had any chance of success against them and, as the attacks in August had shown, the chances were slight. Those experienced skippers were urgently needed in the North Atlantic, where the opportunities for delivering a meaningful blow at Great Britain's lifelines were greater and the risks smaller.

The upshot was a compromise. Dönitz was to continue the U-boat war against the Gibraltar convoys; however, the boats, organized into smaller groups of about eight, were to be deployed much farther offshore where British air patrols were less intense and where the U-boats might also intercept Outbound South convoys en route to Sierra Leone, inbound Sierra Leone convoys, and military convoys outbound via Cape Town to Egypt, known as Winston Specials. The packs could be temporarily reinforced, as required, by boats outbound to the North Atlantic or by those with sufficient fuel and torpedoes homebound to France. The Bordeaux-based Condors were to assist the packs in hunting and tracking convoys.

For the first three weeks of September, the hunt for Gibraltar and Sierra Leone convoys was fruitless. The boats and Condors found several, but owing to the ability of the British to read naval Enigma and thus to evade U-boat patrol lines and to miserable weather, neither of the first two packs, group *Bosemüller* (seven boats) and group *Kurfürst* (eight boats) sank a ship. As the boats departed for other tasks or to France, the remainder were regrouped into a single pack, group *Seewolf,* but it had no success either. On September 14, Coastal Command aircraft (as yet unidentified) bombed and seriously damaged two VIICs of this pack, Gerd Schreiber's veteran *U-95* and Robert Bartels's *U-561,* forcing both to abort.

Soon after group *Seewolf* dissolved, an Italian boat operating west of Gibraltar reported a northbound convoy. This was Homebound Gibraltar 73, consisting of twenty-five ships, escorted by a destroyer, two sloops, eight corvettes, and the fighter-catapult ship *Springbank.* Only three U-boats were close enough to intercept and attack this convoy, but one of these, *U-371,* commanded by Heinrich Driver, was en route to the Mediterranean under orders not to attack any ships in the Atlantic.

Driver passed close to the convoy and reported its position. His report enabled Dönitz to put the other two boats on the convoy track. Fresh from France, these boats were *U-124* under command of twenty-five-year-old Johann Mohr, the boat's former first watch officer, and *U-201,* commanded by Adalbert Schnee, who had won a *Ritterkreuz* for his dogged attack on Gibraltar 71 in August. The *U-124* was a IXB, a type that Dönitz considered to be too large, slow-diving, and too clumsy for attacks on the very heavily escorted Gibraltar convoys, but he had utmost confidence in young Mohr.

Taking up a waiting position about 600 miles west of the English Channel on the afternoon of September 20, Mohr detected smoke on the horizon. It was a convoy, but not the one he was expecting. This one was Outbound Gibraltar 74, southbound from the British Isles. Composed of twenty-seven ships, it was escorted by a sloop, five corvettes, and the "jeep" carrier *Audacity,* on her maiden voyage in convoy duty. Upon receiving Mohr's report, Dönitz directed him to shadow and send beacons to bring up the only other boat in the area, Schnee's *U-201.*

Mohr shadowed until Schnee made contact, then attacked after dark on September 20. In his first salvo, he fired three torpedoes and got three hits. He claimed sinking two freighters for 15,000 tons and damage to an 8,000-ton tanker. In reality he sank two small freighters for 4,200 tons total and did no harm to the "tanker." The merchant ships lit the sky with brilliant new star shells, called snowflakes,* and chased *U-124* off and down.

The next day, while Mohr in *U-124* and Schnee in *U-201* maneuvered to close

---

* Snowflake was a double-edged sword. On the one hand it lit the area "like day," robbing the U-boats of concealment. On the other hand it provided enough light to enable the U-boats to clearly see the targets and to make follow-up submerged night attacks by periscope.

after dark, Dönitz sent out Condors to attack the convoy. In response, *Audacity* launched her six Martlets (the British version of the American-built Grumman Wildcat). One of the Martlets shot down a Condor—the first aerial victory for a "jeep" carrier in the war—and another machine-gunned *U-124* or *U-201,* forcing one or the other to dive. However, one of the Condors bombed and sank a freighter that had fallen behind while rescuing the crews of the two ships Mohr had sunk.

Mohr and Schnee closed on the convoy after dark from opposite sides. Mohr set up on three ships, intending to fire two torpedoes at each. As he was on the point of shooting, all three ships blew up and sank. Schnee, as Mohr reported to Dönitz, had beat him to the punch. Schnee claimed sinking 14,000 tons, but the three ships totaled only 4,500 tons. Harassed by escorts and the Martlets from *Audacity,* neither boat was able to make another attack.

Total damage to Outbound Gibraltar 74 by Mohr and Schnee: five ships for 8,700 tons.

The fortuitous encounter with Outbound Gibraltar 74 was all well and good, but the main assignment for *U-124* and *U-201* was the heavily escorted, Homebound Gibraltar 73, which the Italian boats were still stalking and reporting. Astonishingly, the convoy appeared to be headed directly into the area where Mohr and Schnee had attacked Outbound Gibraltar 74. On September 24 Dönitz sent Condors out to check on the Italian reports. The aircraft confirmed the convoy's position and course, adding that the Italians had attacked it, sinking and/or damaging three ships.* Two other VIIs sailing from France, Rolf Mützelburg's *U-203* and Franz-Georg Reschke's *U-205,* were directed to reinforce Mohr and Schnee.

Homing on the Condor beacon signals, Mohr in *U-124* was first to make contact with Homebound Gibraltar 73, closing the ships in heavy seas and rain on the morning of September 25. First he shot two torpedoes at what he claimed to be a cruiser, but which was probably a destroyer. Both missed. Then he fired one torpedo at what he claimed to be a destroyer. It also missed. Finally, he fired two torpedoes at what he claimed to be a 12,000-ton tanker. Both torpedoes hit the target, but it was a 3,000-ton British freighter and it sank.

Late that night, Mützelburg in *U-203* came up to join Mohr, and both skippers attacked at about the same time. Mohr claimed sinking two more ships for 11,000 tons, but postwar records credited only two small British freighters for 2,700 tons. Mützelburg claimed sinking a freighter and a tanker for 20,000 tons. Postwar records credited three small freighters for 7,700 tons. The escorts drove Mohr and Mützelburg off and under.

During September 26, Mohr and Mützelburg doggedly clung to the convoy, bringing up Schnee in *U-201* and Reschke in *U-205.* After dark, Mohr and Schnee attacked again. Firing off his remaining torpedoes, Mohr claimed sinking a ship of 3,000 tons and possible damage to another of 5,000 tons. Postwar records credited

---

* Apparently the work of the Italian boat *Malaspina,* commanded by Giuliano Prini, but the boat was lost without trace at this time. The reported sinkings could not be confirmed in British records.

only a 1,800-ton freighter. Schnee claimed sinking a corvette and two freighters for 8,000 tons. No corvette was hit but the 5,200-ton fighter-catapult ship *Spring-bank* and another freighter of 2,500 tons went down. Still hanging on, the following night Schnee expended the last of his torpedoes, claiming two more freighters for 8,000 tons, but only one for 3,100 tons was confirmed. Mützelburg in *U-203* had no chance to attack again. An aircraft "with United States markings" caught and bombed Reschke in *U-205,* forcing him to abort to France for repairs.

When Mohr, Schnee, and Mützelburg radioed their sinking reports, Dönitz was elated. Mohr claimed a total of six ships for 41,000 tons; Schnee seven ships for 30,000 tons plus a corvette; Mützelburg two ships for 20,000 tons and possibly another. Total claims: fifteen ships for 91,000 tons plus a corvette definitely sunk; two other ships possibly sunk. By postwar accounting, Mohr had sunk six small ships for 11,700 tons, Schnee six small ships for 15,200 tons (and no corvette), and Mützelburg three small ships for 7,700 tons. Confirmed totals: fifteen ships for 34,500 tons definitely sunk—five for 8,700 tons from Outbound Gibraltar 74 and ten for 25,800 tons from Homebound Gibraltar 73.

On October 2 a Condor found a southbound convoy, Outbound Gibraltar 75, and Dönitz launched a half-dozen boats in pursuit. Hans-Werner Kraus in *U-83* and Walter Flachsenberg in *U-71* soon made contact and shadowed doggedly, sending beacon signals, but they were hampered by heavy weather and clever British evasions. Klaus Bargsten in *U-563* reestablished contact with the convoy close to the coast of Portugal, but it again evaded pursuit and reached Gibraltar on October 14 without the loss of a single merchant ship. Bravely trailing the ships right into the western approaches to the Strait of Gibraltar, Herbert Opitz in *U-206* fired at and hit what he thought was a destroyer, but proved to be the British corvette *Fleur de Lys,* which sank instantly with heavy loss of life.

The Germans had an efficient spy network in place in Algeciras, Spain, and directly across the Gibraltar Strait at Tangier, Vichy French Morocco. The spies provided Berlin with precise information on Allied ship and convoy movements at Gibraltar and in the strait. Reading the *Abwehr* Enigma net currently and fluently, the British were aware of the spy network,* but they could do nothing to thwart its operations or to disguise the ship movements.

The spies reported to Berlin that convoy Homebound Gibraltar 75 was preparing to sail at any hour. Upon learning this, Dönitz directed the boats that had unsuccessfully chased the Outbound Gibraltar 75 south to the strait, plus others organized as group *Breslau,* to prepare to attack Homebound Gibraltar 75. While waiting, two of the six boats, Walter Kell in *U-204,* which had escorted the blockade runner *Rio Grande* to the Azores, and *Ritterkreuz* holder Reinhard Suhren in *U-564,* clandestinely refueled from the German supply ship *Thalia* in Cadiz.

Aware from Enigma decrypts that six boats were lying in wait west of Gibraltar

---

* The official British historian wrote that the Admiralty "sometimes received the decrypt of the German report of an arrival at Gibraltar before it received the British notification signal."

to intercept Homebound Gibraltar 75, the British delayed its sailing for nearly a week. During the wait, Kell in *U-204* sank the 9,200-ton British tanker *Inverlee;* Opitz in *U-206* sank a 3,000-ton freighter; Hans-Werner Kraus in *U-83* attacked a naval task force consisting of the ancient British carriers *Eagle* and *Argus* (serving as aircraft ferries), the cruiser *Hermione,* and a screening destroyer. Kraus missed the carriers but he was credited, incorrectly, with sinking a destroyer. The task force escaped the gauntlet of U-boats unharmed.

The British mounted daily ASW sweeps to clear out the U-boats lying in wait west of the Gibraltar Strait. On October 19, after Kell in *U-204* sank the tanker, the sloop *Rochester* and the corvette *Mallow* found and counterattacked Kell's *U-204.* Coming up to assist, the corvettes *Bluebell* and *Carnation* found an oil slick and the air and fuel flasks of a torpedo, but this was not deemed conclusive evidence of a kill. The Admiralty rated the attack as merely "promising," but, as was discovered later, *Rochester* and *Mallow* had sunk Kell's *U-204* with the loss of all hands.

Finally on the evening of October 22, Homebound Gibraltar 75 sailed. It consisted of seventeen ships and a massive escort of thirteen warships—four destroyers, one sloop, seven corvettes—and the 6,700-ton fighter-catapult ship *Ariguani.* Ten of the thirteen escorts were equipped with radar—three of them with the powerful new Type 271 centimetric-wavelength sets. In what Dönitz logged as "excellent" work, German spies immediately reported the sailing and the exact number and types of ships in the convoy.

Dönitz relayed to group *Breslau* (five boats) information on the sailing. Several of the boats made contact on the first night, but the escorts beat off the attacks. The destroyer *Vidette* got a radar contact on a U-boat at three and a half miles and ran in at flank speed to ram, firing her main battery, but the boat crash-dived. *Vidette* mounted an attack, but her crew botched the depth-charge launching and the boat got away.

On the second night, October 23–24, three U-boats closed the convoy to attack. The corvette *Carnation* forced one boat under and held her down with depth charges, but the other two boats had better luck. Klaus Bargsten in *U-563* missed a freighter but hit the big *Tribal*-class destroyer *Cossack,* blowing off her bow. In two attacks, Reinhard Suhren in *U-564* fired all eleven internal torpedoes. He claimed hits on six ships for damage, but in reality he hit and sank three British freighters for 7,200 tons. The British tried mightily to save *Cossack* but she sank under tow.

During October 24 and 25, the boats shadowed and reported while Dönitz sent out several flights of Condors and brought up three Italian boats. A Catalina of British Squadron 202 spotted one of the Italian boats, *Ferraris,* on the surface seventeen miles ahead of the convoy. Piloted by Norman F. Eagleton, the Catalina attacked with two depth charges and machine guns, but the charges failed to explode. Seeing the Catalina circling, the destroyer *Lamerton* raced up, firing her 4" guns. Mistaking the destroyer for a corvette, *Ferraris* responded with her 3.9" gun and tried to run. But *Lamerton* easily overtook her, whereupon the Italians scuttled and surrendered.

By the night of October 25–26, when the convoy had been reduced to fourteen ships and ten escorts, three boats ran in to attack. Walter Flachsenberg in *U-71* shot four torpedoes at a "destroyer" but missed. Other escorts pounced on *U-71* and depth-charged her for seven hours, Flachsenberg reported. Kraus in *U-83* fired his last three torpedoes at three different ships, claiming all sank. In reality he hit only one ship, the fighter-catapult ship *Ariguani*, which was saved and towed back to Gibraltar. While preparing to shoot, Bargsten in *U-563* was intercepted, attacked, and driven under by the corvette *Heliotrope*, but she, too, botched her depth-charge attack. Bargsten fired two torpedoes at a "destroyer" (perhaps *Heliotrope*) from extreme range and claimed a sinking, but his torpedoes also missed.

Group *Breslau* had shrunk to two boats by the evening of October 26: Bargsten in *U-563* and Suhren in *U-564*. That night Bargsten fired five of his remaining six torpedoes at two freighters, but all missed. Having downloaded one torpedo from a deck canister, Suhren fired it at a freighter from extreme range. He claimed sinking a 3,000-ton ship, but he also missed. Using radar and intership radio to good effect, the destroyer *Duncan*, the sloop *Rochester*, and the corvette *Mallow* counterattacked both boats and held them off.

Although Bargsten and Suhren had only one torpedo between them, during October 27 both boats shadowed the Homebound Gibraltar 75 tenaciously. Their reports and several sightings by Condors enabled Dönitz to vector one other boat to the convoy. She was Heinz-Otto Schultze's *U-432*, homebound from the attack on Slow Convoy 48. Homing on Bargsten's and Suhren's beacons, in the early hours of October 28 Schultze closed and fired at two freighters. He claimed both sank, but only the 1,600-ton *Ulea*, which had bravely attempted to ram *U-432*, went down.

Based on flash reports from all the boats, Dönitz calculated that group *Breslau* had won a sensational victory over Homebound Gibraltar 75: a destroyer and seven freighters for 34,000 tons sunk by Kraus, Bargsten, and Schultze, six ships for 25,000 tons damaged by Suhren. The reality was much less, reflecting the smaller size of ships in these convoys: the destroyer *Cossack* and four freighters for 8,800 tons sunk, the fighter-catapult ship *Ariguani* damaged. Two boats were lost: Kell's *U-204* and *Ferraris*.

As related, on the night of October 31, the *U-96*, commanded by *Ritterkreuz* holder Heinrich Lehmann-Willenbrock, who was outbound to a Greenland patrol line, came upon a convoy. This was Outbound South 10, consisting of thirty-four big ships and six escorts bound for Sierra Leone. Since no other U-boats were close by, Kerneval authorized Lehmann-Willenbrock to attack the convoy alone.

There was a full moon; the sky was cloudless. In such light a surface attack was perilous, but there was not enough light for a submerged attack. Making the best of an unfavorable situation, Lehmann-Willenbrock remained on the surface and fired four torpedoes at two big ships from "considerable" range. He claimed two hits "amidships" on each ship, but postwar records confirmed only one sinking, a 6,000-ton Dutch freighter. As Lehmann-Willenbrock hauled out to get off shadow reports, one of the escorts, the ex-Coast Guard cutter *Lulworth,* spotted *U-96* at two miles and counterattacked at high speed. Her gunfire drove *U-96* under and prevented another attack. *Lulworth* threw off twenty-seven depth charges but none fell close. Lehmann-Willenbrock evaded and later surfaced and got off another shadow report.

An interested observer on *U-96* was Lothar-Günther Buchheim, a twenty-three-year-old "war artist" or propagandist. To then, artist Buchheim had depicted the U-boat war with oil paintings and charcoal sketches of returning boats and skippers from a shore billet. Equipped with Leica cameras and notebooks, he was making his first war patrol. Shot with a professional artist's eye, his photographs were remarkable—the best of the war. Many years after the war, Buchheim drew on his notes of this voyage to write a long novel, *Das Boot* (1973), which became a worldwide best-seller, the basis for a six-hour German television miniseries, and a taut and realistic 145-minute feature film of the same name, released with English dubbing as *The Boat.* Still later (1976) Buchheim published a "nonfiction" picture book, an impressionistic history of the U-boat war, using his own pictures and combining fact and fiction.

German submariners were delighted with Buchheim's wartime art, photographs, and heroic stories, but they were appalled by his postwar writings and the film. They denounced him for opening the film *Das Boot* with scenes of a wildly drunken orgy at an officers' club in Lorient; for the negative, defeatist, antimilitary tone of the book and film; and for the implied criticism of Dönitz. Two U-boat skippers, Karl-Friedrich Merten and Kurt Baberg, were so enraged by Buchheim's "nonfiction" U-boat history that in 1985 they published an entire book (*Nein! So War Das Nicht*) pointing out Buchheim's errors and/or misleading statements.

When Dönitz received Lehmann-Willenbrock's shadow report, he deployed Condors and directed ten other inbound and outbound boats to home on *U-96*'s beacons. The boats were organized into a new group, *Stoertebecker.* While they were converging, Lehmann-Willenbrock attempted a second attack on Outbound South 10 during the night of November 1–2, but the escorts, ex-American four-stack destroyer *Stanley* and ex-Coast Guard cutter *Gorleston,* and the British corvette *Verbena* drove *U-96* off with gunfire and depth charges.*

Dönitz had great hopes for the eleven boats of group *Stoertebecker.* But the group ran into a massive storm—vividly captured on film by Buchheim—which killed any chance for a coordinated attack. After two days of frustration, Dönitz canceled the chase and directed the group to intercept a reported Homebound Gibraltar convoy. When this hunt failed, Dönitz redirected the group to intercept the northbound convoy Sierra Leone 91, but that pursuit failed as well. Outwitted by British evasions and diversions and bedeviled by foul weather, fuel shortages, and mechanical problems, group *Stoertebecker* was finally dissolved. It sank no ships.

---

* Buchheim's depiction of Lehmann-Willenbrock sinking a tanker at this time was fiction, based on an attack that *U-96* had conducted earlier in the year.

These several U-boat groups patrolling the eastern Atlantic waters in September and October of 1941 to shut down the flow of British supplies to the Mediterranean via the Gibraltar Strait also turned in quite disappointing results. They had mounted attacks against four Gibraltar convoys (Outbound 74 and 75; Homebound 73 and 75) and had sunk nineteen small ships for about 43,400 tons, plus the destroyer *Cossack* and corvette *Fleur de Lys*. However, most of the damage in this arduous and risky campaign had been inflicted on the less vital Home bound convoys. To the end of November 1941, all these boats sank only five small Gibraltar-bound merchant ships totaling 8,700 tons and one ship for 6,000 tons from Outbound South 10. This was not much help to Rommel's *Afrika Korps*.

THE CRISIS IN THE MEDITERRANEAN

Of the initial wave of six U-boats that sailed from France to join Axis forces in the Mediterranean, the first, Heinrich Driver's *U-371*, entered the Gibraltar Strait on the night of September 21. It was a dangerous passage. British radar-equipped aircraft and surface ships based at Gibraltar patrolled the strait, which at its narrowest point is merely eight miles wide. To hasten the passage and to take advantage of the east-flowing current (Atlantic to the Mediterranean) Driver remained on the surface. His short signal signifying he had arrived safely in the Mediterranean evoked relief at Kerneval.

During the next two weeks the other five Mediterranean-bound boats also passed through the strait successfully. All patrolled with extreme caution, remaining fully submerged during daylight hours. None had any immediate successes, but Driver in *U-371* earned the appreciation of the Italian Navy by rescuing forty-two survivors of an Italian patrol boat, *Albatros*. Meanwhile, in the eastern Mediterranean, Italian administrative and technical personnel established a German submarine base at Salamis, Greece, an island near Athens.

The first task of the Mediterranean U-boats was to shut off the flow of supplies to Tobruk, the Commonwealth enclave on the coast of Libya that Rommel had bypassed during his drive on Egypt. This was a difficult undertaking for the U-boats, working in unfamiliar waters. The British sent supplies at night in small coastal vessels and motorized barges that were hard to find, and because of their shallow draft, almost impossible to hit with torpedoes. Moreover, to avoid the heavy concentration of aircraft (both friends and foes) in those confined waters, the boats had to run submerged for unusually long periods each day, as in the Norway operations. The prolonged submergence built up air pressure inside the hull, which entered the torpedo depth-control mechanism via the as-yet-undetected leak, fooling the mechanism and causing the torpedoes to run deeper than set.

The early reports from the Mediterranean boats were not encouraging. While attacking a small vessel with the deck gun, Driver's *U-371* was hit by counterfire and forced to abort to Salamis with wounded and damage. Hans Heidtmann in *U-559* fired seven torpedoes at small vessels and missed with all. Later he claimed sinking a "destroyer" by torpedo, but it could not be confirmed. Hans-Dietrich von Tiesenhausen in *U-331* claimed sinking a barge by gun, but it was only damaged. Wolfgang Kaufmann in *U-79* fired four torpedoes at a 600-ton British gunboat, *Gnat.* Three passed under the ship; one hit. Kaufmann claimed a sinking, but *Gnat,* too, was only damaged. During the entire month of October, the six Mediterranean boats of the first wave sank only four small ships confirmed in postwar records: two 500-ton barges by Helmuth Ringelmann in *U-75* and two coasters for 2,000 tons by Udo Heilmann in *U-97.**

A second wave of six U-boats embarked from France to join the Mediterranean force in early November. The first two of these were Friedrich Guggenberger in *U-81* and Franz-Georg Reschke in *U-205.*

While Guggenberger was passing through the Bay of Biscay on the afternoon of October 30, a Catalina of British Squadron 209, recently withdrawn from Iceland and based in southwest England, caught *U-81* on the surface. The pilot, Denis M. Ryan, circled to attack, but Guggenberger shot back and hit the Catalina. Thereupon a Hudson of British Squadron 53, also based in southwest England, arrived and attacked, dropping three depth charges. When Guggenberger crashdived, Ryan in the Catalina attacked, also dropping three depth charges. The six charges caused so much damage that *U-81* had to abort to Brest.

After hurried repairs, Guggenberger resailed for the Gibraltar Strait. During the period of new moon, November 11–12, *U-81* and Reschke's *U-205* passed through the strait undetected.

At that time the British Force H, having flown off forty-four aircraft to reinforce Malta, was returning to Gibraltar. That formation consisted of the fleet carrier *Ark Royal,* the ancient carrier *Argus* (serving as an aircraft ferry), the old battleship *Malaya,* the cruiser *Hermione,* and seven destroyers.

Italian aircraft reported the return of Force H to Gibraltar. Dönitz, in turn, directed Guggenberger in *U-81* and Reschke in *U-205* to likely positions along a track running east from Gibraltar. At dawn on November 13, Reschke in *U-205* intercepted the formation and fired a fan of three bow torpedoes at *Ark Royal.* After a run of three minutes, twenty-nine seconds, Reschke observed a flash of fire at *Ark Royal* and jubilantly assumed one hit, but he was mistaken. After a run of nearly nine minutes, Reschke *heard* two detonations and assumed a hit on a destroyer. That was also wrong. None of his three torpedoes had hit anything.

Later that afternoon Force H, thirty miles east of Gibraltar, steamed right at *U-81* at 19 knots. Carefully raising his periscope in calm seas, at 4:29 P.M., Guggenberger fired all four bow torpedoes—two at *Malaya* and two at *Ark Royal*—from a very long range. A destroyer forced Guggenberger deep, so he could not observe the torpedo runs. At six minutes, six seconds and at seven minutes, forty-three seconds, he heard detonations. He assumed probable hits on *Malaya* and an "uncertain" target.

---

* After passing through the Gibraltar Strait, the Mediterranean boats employed a different Enigma net, *Süd* (called Porpoise by the British), which Bletchley Park was unable to break. Hence the Admiralty's U-boat Tracking Room "lost" these boats and countermeasures were difficult to mount.

Guggenberger missed *Malaya* but one torpedo struck *Ark Royal* amidships on the starboard side. The explosion flooded a boiler room, killing one man. When *Ark Royal* took on a heavy list, the crew initiated emergency damage-control measures and flooded tanks on the port side to compensate. For a time it seemed that the crew had matters well in hand; nonetheless, the new destroyer *Legion* came alongside and took off all men except the damage-control parties. Two salvage tugs set out from Gibraltar to tow the wounded carrier to port.

The other destroyers of the force hunted—and found—*U-81* and mounted a punishing counterattack. Guggenberger logged 130 depth charges, but he took *U-81* deep and none fell close enough to cause serious damage. His report that night, together with that of Reschke in *U-205*, led Dönitz to believe that Guggenberger had hit *Malaya,* and that Reschke had hit *Ark Royal,* a remarkable and highly satisfactory day's work.

During the night of November 13–14, the two salvage tugs arrived and took *Ark Royal* in tow. The damage-control parties got up steam in one boiler, but suddenly an uncontrollable fire swept through the engine spaces. At 4:30 A.M., the damage control parties conceded defeat and abandoned ship. At 6:13 A.M., November 14, the famous *Ark Royal* rolled over and sank. Her loss, announced that day by the Admiralty, was a grievous blow. Although only one man had died, the Royal Navy had no fleet carrier available to replace her, leaving the British Mediterranean naval forces without sea-based air cover.

Kerneval was confused. It assumed Reschke in *U-205* had sunk *Ark Royal* and that Guggenberger in *U-81* had severely damaged *Malaya.* The confusion was not sorted out until both boats put into the Italian submarine base at La Spezia later in the month. After studying the patrol reports, Dönitz correctly credited Guggenberger with sinking *Ark Royal*—and gave him a *Ritterkreuz* for that feat—but incorrectly credited him with a hit on *Malaya.*

The destruction of the *Ark Royal* and the supposed hit on *Malaya* were sensational psychological achievements for the German submarine force. In a single blow, one U-boat operating in strange waters had delivered the Royal Navy a greater setback than had the entire Italian Navy in seventeen months of operations. But, in a larger sense, the victory was to prove disadvantageous to the German submarine force. It spawned the erroneous idea in Berlin that German U-boats could easily and cheaply gain control of the Mediterranean Sea.

Owing to the shortage of boats and to Berlin's diversions, the earlier decision to send only the most experienced skippers to the Mediterranean had been abandoned. The next two boats to attempt the passage through the Strait of Gibraltar were Hans Ey in *U-433* and Johann Jebsen in *U-565.* Young Ey had made one Atlantic patrol; young Jebsen, two. Neither skipper had sunk a ship, although Ey had damaged one freighter.

The two boats passed through the Gibraltar Strait without being detected on the night of November 15–16. Dönitz directed them to operate close to Gibraltar, in the area near Guggenberger's *U-81* and Reschke's *U-205,* to thwart the supposed

British amphibious landing in Algeria. They were named group *Arnauld,* in honor of the World War I submarine hero von Arnauld de la Périère, who was to take command of the Mediterranean U-boats at that time but was killed en route to Rome in a plane crash.

Fully aware of the mounting U-boat threat in the western Mediterranean, the British set a U-boat trap on November 16. They sailed a "dummy convoy" east from Gibraltar, composed of several empty merchant ships, escorted by two sloops and four corvettes. At least one of the corvettes, *Marigold,* was equipped with Type 271 centimetric radar.

That night, November 16, *Marigold* fell out of formation with a temporary engine defect. Later, while she was hurrying to catch up with the "convoy," Ey in *U-433* saw her sailing alone, very close to the place where *Ark Royal* had sunk. Mistaking the corvette for a light cruiser, Ey attacked her, firing four torpedoes, all of which missed. Unaware that she was under attack, *Marigold* made radar contact on *U-433* and ran in at full speed to ram, firing her 4" gun. She closed to 300 yards, but Ey crash-dived. *Marigold* hastily threw off five depth charges by eye, but these did no harm. *Marigold* then stopped and quietly lay to, attempting to find *U-433* with hydrophones.

Believing the "cruiser" had gone off, Ey came up to periscope depth to look around and surface. *Marigold* got a good sonar contact on *U-433* and attacked at once, dropping ten shallow-set depth charges. Some of these exploded directly below the U-boat, causing such terrible damage that Ey gave the order to surface, scuttle, and abandon ship. Seeing the boat come up astern, *Marigold* swung around to attempt a boarding, firing her main gun and smaller weapons. But the abandoned *U-433* ran off on one diesel, zigzagging crazily and flooding rapidly. After she sank, *Marigold* picked up Ey and thirty-seven of his men. Two other Germans, Ey reported, attempted to swim to the Spanish coast, thirty miles away. They were never found. Unaware of this loss, Dönitz assumed ten U-boats were still operating in the Mediterranean.

Marigold's destruction of *U-433* achieved fame of a sort in British naval circles. It was the first U-boat kill in which Type 271 centimetric radar played a key role.

Taking advantage of intercepted *Luftwaffe* Enigma traffic, which revealed that Rommel intended to launch an all-out attack on the bypassed Commonwealth garrison at Tobruk, on November 18 the British Eighth Army unleashed its long-planned, all-out offensive, Crusader, from Sidi Barrani, Egypt. Caught by surprise, the Germans and Italians fought stubbornly, but the weight of the British attack pushed them back. The offensive, together with the lingering belief that the British intended to make an amphibious landing behind Rommel in Algeria to trap Axis forces in a pincer, led Hitler to declare an "emergency." The *Kriegsmarine* was to make every conceivable effort to save Rommel's *Afrika Korps;* above all the German Navy was to put an end to the British attacks on Rommel's supply ships, no matter what the cost.

In response, Raeder and the OKM reached a fateful decision. As related, every available U-boat of the Atlantic operational force was to be committed to the task of saving Rommel and gaining control of the Mediterranean Basin. The five boats then on Arctic duty, based in northern Norway, were transferred to the Atlantic force, replaced by four new boats from Kiel. In all (Raeder reported to Hitler), fifty U-boats were to be assigned to support Rommel: twenty Type VIIs in the eastern Mediterranean and thirty boats in the western Mediterranean and/or just outside the Atlantic gateway to the Strait of Gibraltar.

The Admiralty saw from naval Enigma intercepts what was afoot and took countermeasures. Coastal Command intensified patrols in the Bay of Biscay with radar-equipped aircraft based in southwest England and Gibraltar. Derby House transferred numerous radar-equipped escorts from the North Atlantic run to Gibraltar. A radar-equipped Swordfish squadron formerly based on the carrier *Ark Royal* shifted to a land base in Gibraltar. The newly arrived, radar-equipped escorts and aircraft patrolled the Gibraltar Strait day and night to block the passage of U-boats.

Of the nine U-boats already inside the Mediterranean, not all were available for this emergency. The U-boat refit and repair facilities at Salamis and La Spezia were not fully operational and many delays were incurred. The first boat to sail on a second Mediterranean patrol was von Tiesenhausen in *U-331,* leaving from Salamis. His first task was to land and recover a German commando party at R'as Gibeisa, Libya, which was to blow up a British military train. Von Tiesenhausen put the commandos ashore, but the British caught them in the act.

While patrolling submerged near the British naval base at Alexandria, Egypt, on the morning of November 25, von Tiesenhausen's hydrophone operator reported heavy screws. Running down the bearing, von Tiesenhausen came to periscope depth and saw a heart-stopping sight: the battleships *Queen Elizabeth, Barham,* and *Valiant,* escorted by about eight destroyers. He set up on the *Queen Elizabeth,* but she eluded him and he was forced to turn to the next behemoth in line. This was the 31,100-ton *Barham,* but the ship so massively filled his periscope lens, he could not identify her. He fired a full salvo of four bow torpedoes and went very, very deep—to 820 feet, a record.

Barham—badly damaged by Lemp in *U-30* in December 1939—was in the process of shifting formation. Three of von Tiesenhausen's four torpedoes hit her broadside, one or more in or near a magazine. *Barham* blew up with a thunderous explosion and sank within three minutes, taking down her skipper and about half the crew; in all, 862 men died. After Prien's *Royal Oak,* she was the second battleship to be sunk by a U-boat, the first while at sea. The Admiralty withheld the news of her loss for many weeks.

Von Tiesenhausen did not see or hear the results of his attack. That night he reported to Dönitz that he had "torpedoed a battleship" but the outcome was unknown. Absent evidence of a sinking or an announcement from the Admiralty or inside information from *B-dienst,* Dönitz was restrained in his praise, logging only that the attack was "very satisfactory." However, when the British finally announced the loss of *Barham,* Dönitz awarded von Tiesenhausen a *Ritterkreuz.*

•   •   •

In the last week of November, ten more boats headed for the Mediterranean via the Gibraltar Strait. The first five got through but two of those were lost shortly thereafter.

The first loss was *U-95,* commanded by the veteran Gerd Schreiber, who had commissioned the boat in August 1940 and had commanded her ever since. After passing through the strait shortly after midnight on November 28, the bridge watch spotted an "object" in the dark. The object was a Dutch submarine in British service, *O-21,* commanded by Johannes Frans van Dulm, returning to Gibraltar from a luckless patrol off Italy.

Schreiber in *U-95* went to battle stations. Believing the other submarine might be a friendly U-boat or an Italian boat, he was hesitant to shoot. He made three undetected approaches, aborting each. On the fourth, he flashed the current German recognition signal. This strange signal galvanized *O-21.* Van Dulm went to battle stations, set up on *U-95,* and fired a stern tube. It missed, but a second stern torpedo hit *U-95* and blew her to pieces. Cautiously approaching the wreckage, van Dulm found Schreiber, three other officers, and eight men in the water. He fished them out and took them to Gibraltar.

At Gibraltar, Schreiber was incarcerated with Hans Ey, skipper of *U-433,* which had been sunk two weeks earlier. Schreiber and Ey discovered a weak link in the British security chain and escaped, intending to find sanctuary on Spanish soil. But the British recaptured both skippers and sent them on to London.

The second loss inside the Mediterranean was Ottokar Paulshen's *U-557.** After passing through the strait on the night of November 26, Paulshen was directed to patrol in the eastern Mediterranean, off Alexandria, in company with the Italian submarine *Dagabur.* On the night of December 14, *Dagabur,* commanded by Alberto Torri, found the 5,200-ton British light cruiser *Galatea,* inbound to Alexandria. Torri fired two torpedoes at the cruiser and "heard" two detonations. Whether or not he hit her was never resolved. Paulshen in *U-557* joined the attack and shot. Shortly thereafter, *Galatea* went down.

Following this victory, Paulshen set a course for the new U-boat base at Salamis. Late in the evening of December 16, while he was passing about fifteen miles west of Crete, the Italian PT boat *Orione* sighted him. Mistaking *U-557* for an Allied submarine, *Orione* came at Paulshen full speed with machine guns blazing and rammed. Badly holed, the *U-557* went down; *Orione,* also badly damaged, barely survived the encounter. When the Germans learned of the attack the next day, they correctly surmised that *Orione* had attacked *U-557* and sent air patrols from Crete to search for survivors. None was found.

The next five boats sailing to the Mediterranean in late November, during the period of a full moon, encountered the intensified British ASW measures. None of the five made it through the strait. In brief:

---

*   He had a new first watch officer replacing Herbert Werner, the author of *Iron Coffins,* who had qualified for his own command.

- After refueling in Vigo, *Ritterkreuz* holder Lehmann-Willenbrock in *U-96* was caught in the strait by one of the radar-equipped Swordfish, formerly of *Ark Royal*. The plane dropped two 450-pound depth charges from low altitude. Hit and severely damaged, and hounded by six surface craft, Lehmann-Willenbrock bottomed at 180 to 240 feet for about five hours to make repairs, then aborted to France. Still on board *U-96*, the propagandist Lothar-Günther Buchheim drew upon the retreat of *U-96* for the climax of his novel, *Das Boot*, greatly exaggerating the incident, as well as the British air threat to the U-boat pens in France. The film and miniseries did likewise.*

- Sailing from St. Nazaire on November 29, Herbert Opitz in *U-206* struck a mine on the same day and sank with the loss of all hands. The British mistakenly credited the loss of *U-206* to a Whitley of British Squadron 502 on November 30, but in a postwar assessment the credit was withdrawn. When she failed to respond to queries, Dönitz correctly assumed she had struck a mine off St. Nazaire and demanded that the OKM intensify minesweeping on the French coast.

- Sailing from Brest, Klaus Bargsten in *U-563* (who had sunk the destroyer *Cossack*) was caught by a Whitley of Squadron 502 in the Bay of Biscay. Attacking out of the sun, the pilot, W. W. Cave, dropped six depth charges which so damaged the boat that she could not dive. After its depth-charge attack, the plane strafed *U-563* five times, wounding Bargsten (two bullets in his shoulder) and two of his men.

  Bargsten radioed for help. In response, Dönitz ordered Opitz's sunk *U-206* and another Mediterranean-bound boat, Walter Flachsenberg in *U-71*, to assist *U-563*. However, Flachsenberg incurred an engine breakdown and was himself forced to abort to France. The wounded Bargsten got *U-563* into Lorient, but the boat was so smashed up that she had to return to Germany for rebuilding. Taking advantage of inclement weather, Bargsten made the voyage roundabout the British Isles on the surface without being detected. Upon reaching Germany, he and his crew were given a long Christmas leave and a new boat. Pilot Cave and his copilot, A. E. Coates, a New Zealander, were both killed later in the war.

- Sailing from Brest, Günther Krech in *U-558* attempted a passage through the strait on the night of December 1–2, in the light of a nearly full moon. Radar-equipped British aircraft detected Krech west of the strait and two of them attacked. When the aircraft called in surface vessels, the sloop *Stork* and the corvette *Samphire* responded, hurling off depth charges. The British assessed the combined air–surface ship attack as inconclusive, but in fact, *U-558* was badly damaged and Krech was forced to abort to France.

After a temporary reverse, the British Eighth Army regrouped and drove Axis forces farther west in Libya and liberated Tobruk. Fifteen more U-boats, some of them commanded by skippers on first Atlantic patrols, and some of which refueled in Vigo, headed for the Strait of Gibraltar.

---

* See Krug (1996), "Filming *Das Boot*."

• Still on his first patrol out of Germany, Jürgen Könnenkamp in *U-375* sailed directly to the strait. Trapped and depth-charged by the British ASW forces on the night of December 6, Könnenkamp was forced to retreat into the Atlantic, where he told Dönitz he would try again "on a more favorable night." Two nights later, December 9, he made it.

• Sailing from Brest December 3, on his second patrol, Alfred Schlieper in *U-208* cleared the Bay of Biscay, but was never heard from again. It was later determined that on December 7 *U-208* was detected, depth-charged, and sunk by the British destroyers *Hesperus* and *Harvester*, seventy miles west of the strait. There were no survivors.

• Sailing from St. Nazaire December 7, on his second patrol, Heinrich Heinsohn in *U-573* was forced to abort with a leaking torpedo tube. Resailing on December 11, *U-573* passed through the strait on December 18.

• Still on his first patrol out of Germany, Johannes Liebe in *U-332* received orders to refuel in Vigo, then go into the Mediterranean. While approaching the coast on December 6, *U-332* was detected and bombed by a Catalina of British Squadron 202, piloted by Hugh Garnell, who called in ASW surface ships. Liebe escaped these pursuers, but two days later, December 9, another British aircraft found and bombed or depth-charged *U-332,* inflicting such heavy damage that Liebe was forced to abort to France. Later in the war, airman Garnell was killed in the South Pacific.

• At sea on his second Atlantic patrol, Günther Heydemann in *U-575* also received orders to refuel in Vigo and proceed to the Mediterranean. While approaching the coast on December 9, he, too, was detected and depth-charged. He refueled in Vigo, per orders, on the night of December 11, but while doing so Heydemann discovered the depth-charge damage was so severe that he had to abort to France for repairs.

• Sailing from St. Nazaire on his third patrol, Hans Peter Hinsch in *U-569* attempted to transit the strait on the night of December 16, during bright moonlight. British aircraft detected Hinsch in the strait and drove him under with depth charges. The boat was so badly damaged that Hinsch was also forced to return to France for repairs.

• Sailing from Brest, Hans-Heinz Linder in *U-202* had orders to go through the strait after the full moon. He reached the western approaches to the strait during the night of December 21, but he was forced to return to France. He did not sail again until March.

• Sailing from Kiel after a refit, the ex-Arctic boat *U-451,* commanded by Eberhard Hoffmann, making his first Atlantic patrol, was ordered into Lorient for a quick refueling before going through the strait. After three days in Lorient, Hoffmann put out to sea, arriving off the strait in the early hours of December 21. As Hoffmann was preparing to enter, one of the radar-equipped Swordfish, formerly of Squadron 812 on *Ark Royal,* detected *U-451* at three and a half miles. Descending to sixty feet, the Swordfish dropped three 250-pound depth charges, all set to detonate at a depth of fifty feet.

Hoffmann crash-dived, unwittingly leaving his first watch officer, Walter Köhler, crew of 1934, topside. Alerted by flares from the Swordfish, the British corvette *Myosotis* rushed to the area of the attack. She found a thick oil slick but could get no radar or sonar contact. Hearing shouts from Köhler, the British found him and hauled him aboard *Myosotis.* Köhler did not know if *U-451* had been sunk or had escaped. Thus his rescue and capture could not be regarded as proof of a kill. But kill it had been; nothing was ever heard from *U-451* again. She was the first German U-boat to be sunk at night by an aircraft.*

• Sailing from France on his second patrol, Unno von Fischel in *U-374* passed through the strait on the night of December 10–11. Kerneval logged a desperate message from von Fischel stating that he had been detected, that he was being chased by "four destroyers," and that he required "immediate aircraft aid." The last was perhaps a garble; von Fischel well knew that German "aircraft aid" in the strait was next to impossible. Thereafter he apparently decided to attack his attackers. On December 11 he sank a 500-ton patrol vessel, *Rosabelle,* and the gallant 500-ton trawler *Lady Shirley,* which two months earlier had sunk Wilhelm Kleinschmidt's *U-111* in an open-ocean gun action. These victories enabled von Fischel to shake the other pursuers and enter the Mediterranean.

By the third week of December thirty-seven U-boats had set off for the Mediterranean via the Gibraltar Strait. Three boats had been lost approaching or attempting the passage (*U-206, U-208, U-451*); eight had turned back, six with severe battle damage and two with mechanical or other problems. Thus only twenty-six of the thirty-seven boats got inside the Mediterranean Sea and three of these, *U-95, U-433,* and *U-557,* had been lost almost immediately, leaving twenty-three.

While attempting to attack separate convoys in the eastern Mediterranean, two more U-boats were lost to British escort forces in December. On December 23 the destroyers *Hasty* and *Hotspur* depth-charged and forced Wolfgang Kaufmann in *U-79* to scuttle. Kaufmann and all forty-three other crewmen were rescued. On December 28 the destroyer *Kipling* depth-charged Helmut Ringelmann in *U-75* and forced him to scuttle. Ringelmann and about eighteen others were killed in the action; *Kipling* fished out twenty-five Germans. These two losses reduced the number of U-boats patrolling inside the Mediterranean to twenty-one.

In addition to sinking the carrier *Ark Royal,* the battleship *Barham,* and the light cruiser *Galatea,* the U-boats operating in the Mediterranean in November and December, 1941, sank two other warships (the Australian sloop *Parramatta* and the British corvette *Salvia*) and eight freighters or tankers for about 30,500 tons. These losses, together with a successful attack by Italian frogmen on the battleships *Queen Elizabeth* and *Valiant* in Alexandria harbor,† the loss of the cruiser *Neptune* and

---

* After *U-64* at Narvik, in April 1940, the second U-boat kill by a navy Swordfish, unassisted by surface ships.

† Launched by the Italian submarine *Scirè* on the night of December 18–19, the frogmen entered the harbor, riding three slow-running "human torpedoes," or "pigs," with detachable delayed-action, 485-pound warheads. The delayed explosives shattered the 32,000-ton *Queen Elizabeth* and sister ship *Valiant,* the 7,500-ton tanker *Sagona,* and the destroyer *Jervis.* Both battleships sank in the shallow water and were out of action for many months. The six Italian frogmen who carried out this amazing deed survived but were captured.

damage to the cruiser *Aurora* by Axis mines, and the transfer of German airpower (*Luftflotte* 2) from the Russian front to the Mediterranean, temporarily broke the Royal Navy's command of the Mediterranean Sea. It was unable to provide the British Eighth Army flank support, and partly as a result, the British offensive, Crusader, bogged down after the capture of Benghazi in Libya. The Axis forces dug in at El Agheila and another stalemate in the North African desert war ensued.

In the early stages of Mediterranean U-boat operations, Dönitz controlled the boats from Kerneval. He assumed that the boats were to return to the Atlantic when the military situation in North Africa turned in favor of the Axis. However, on December 7, the OKM transferred control of the boats to the German high command in Rome, headed by airman Albert Kesselring. His senior naval adviser (and "liaison" to the Italian Navy) was Eberhard Weichold. *Ritterkreuz* holder Viktor Oehrn (ex-*U-37*) temporarily held the title Führer U-boats, South. A fifty-three-year-old Italian-speaking officer, Franz Becker (crew of 1906), administratively commanded the twenty-one surviving U-boats, all assigned to the 29th Flotilla based at Salamis, La Spezia, and Pola, Yugoslavia.

Contrary to Dönitz's assumption, no U-boat sent to the Mediterranean in 1941 (or later) ever returned to the Atlantic. The Mediterranean Sea was to become a seemingly endless drain of U-boats. It was a diversion of strength from the "decisive" area of the North Atlantic run and a move that achieved little at high cost.

THE LOSS OF *KOTA PINANG*, *ATLANTIS*, AND *PYTHON*

Notwithstanding the sharp decline in U-boat successes in West African waters, Dönitz continued patrols to that area in late fall of 1941. As before, the presence of even a few U-boats accomplishing little compelled the British to convoy, drew ASW forces from the decisive North Atlantic area, and indirectly helped Rommel.

Two further "waves" set off for that distant area.

The first of two boats, Ernst Bauer in *U-126* and Nikolaus Clausen in *U-129*, sailed in late September. They—and the other boats in the South Atlantic—were to be supported by a supply ship, *Kota Pinang*, which sailed from Bordeaux at the end of September. Alerted to this scheme by Enigma decrypts, the Admiralty ordered two Gibraltar-based cruisers, *Kenya* and *Sheffield*, to intercept *Kota Pinang*. *Kenya* found her about 750 miles west of Spain in the early hours of October 4 and sank her by gunfire, leaving the survivors to fend for themselves.

Clausen in *U-129* had been assigned to rendezvous with *Kota Pinang* and provide escort. He arrived that morning in the midst of the shelling. After *Kenya* hauled out, Clausen closed the lifeboats and took aboard the 119 German survivors. He reversed course for Lorient, but upon learning of this setback, Dönitz directed Clausen to take the survivors into El Ferrol, Spain. Two days later, Clausen stood off that port, transferred the survivors to a Spanish tugboat, then returned to Lorient to replenish his greatly depleted food and fresh-water supplies. In due course the German survivors were repatriated to German-occupied France.

The loss of *Kota Pinang* was a severe blow to the South Atlantic U-boat campaign. As a result, it was necessary to start four of the five boats in South Atlantic waters on homeward voyages, leaving only Merten's *U-68,* which had resupplied from both the *U-111* and the damaged *U-67.* Homebound, Zapp in *U-66,* Winter in *U-103,* and Hessler in *U-107* were temporarily attached to the luckless group *Stoertebecker* off Gibraltar, but none had sufficient fuel or provisions to operate effectively, and they soon went on to France. Upon arrival, Hessler was promoted to the job of first staff officer to his father-in-law, replacing Viktor Oehrn, who went to the Mediterranean.

As it happened, at this time the famous German raider *Atlantis* was homebound from a long voyage in the Pacific. Dönitz made arrangements to resupply Merten's *U-68,* Bauer's *U-126,* and Clausen's *U-129* from *Atlantis,* but shortly after sailing, Clausen in *U-129* suffered an engine failure that forced him to return to France for the second time.

That left only two boats in the South Atlantic in late October: Merten in *U-68* and Bauer in *U-126.* Exploring very far into the South Atlantic to find the convoy routes, Merten reconnoitered the islands of Ascension and St. Helena. He found nothing at Ascension, but at St. Helena he boldly slipped into the harbor at Jamestown and sank the 8,100-ton British tanker *Darkdale* with a salvo of four torpedoes. He then took *U-68* east to explore the African coast at Walvis Bay, British Southwest Africa. On the way, he sank two big British freighters for 10,300 tons, which were sailing alone. Off Freetown, Bauer in *U-126* sank three lone ships for 16,900 tons, including the 7,000-ton tanker *British Mariner,* and on October 19, the 5,000-ton American freighter *Lehigh,** which was zigzagging, leading Bauer to mistake it for a British vessel, or so he claimed. Both boats then hauled out to the mid-Atlantic to rendezvous with the homebound raider *Atlantis.*

The second wave of U-boats to the South Atlantic was more ambitious. Four boats, including Bauer's *U-126,* supported first by the raider *Atlantis,* then by a supply ship, *Python,* freshly sailed from France, were to attack shipping directly off Cape Town, South Africa. The other three boats were Joachim Mohr in *U-124,* Nikolaus Clausen in the delayed *U-129,* and the *U-A,* returned to the Atlantic after months in a shipyard, still commanded by Hans Eckermann. From Enigma traffic, the Admiralty divined what was afoot and set in motion countermeasures to spoil the German operation.

As arranged, Merten in *U-68* met *Atlantis* on November 13, but the seas were too rough to carry out a resupply. The vessels remained in touch, awaiting a break in the weather. Meanwhile, the British authorized yet another "tactical use" of naval Enigma. Heavy cruisers *Devonshire* and *Dorsetshire* and the light cruiser *Dunedin* sailed independently to track down and sink *Atlantis,* the supply ship *Python,* and the five U-boats that were to rendezvous with them. On November 14,

---

*   After *Robin Moor, Lehigh* was the second American ship to be sunk by U-boats before America entered the war.

the weather abated and *U-68* came alongside *Atlantis*. Merten took on oil, food, water, soap, towels, underwear, and cigarettes, then left to patrol home by way of Freetown.

As also arranged, Bauer in *U-126* met *Atlantis* on November 22, a fine morning. Bauer had developed engine trouble that he was unable to repair and had received permission from Kerneval to abort the Cape Town mission and return to France. Hence Bauer's supply requirements were not urgent.

The skipper of *Atlantis,* Bernhard Rogge, invited Bauer and "a few" of his crew to breakfast. Believing the area to be safe from enemy attack, Bauer accepted. While Bauer was taking a bath, an *Atlantis* lookout reported masts on the horizon. This was the heavy cruiser *Devonshire,* armed with eight 8" guns. Based on Enigma decrypts, the Admiralty had directed her to the rendezvous area, ostensibly on routine patrol. Her scout plane had found *Atlantis* and *U-126.*

Devonshire opened fire at a range of about seven miles. *Atlantis* and *U-126* separated immediately, leaving Bauer and his men stranded on board *Atlantis.* Commanded by a junior watch officer, *U-126* submerged to avoid the gunfire and to attack *Devonshire* if the opportunity presented itself. Aware that *U-126* was nearby, *Devonshire* remained at extreme range and maneuvered at high speed, pumping shells at *Atlantis.* When these had wrecked *Atlantis* beyond any hope, Rogge scuttled and abandoned ship.* Seeing that *Atlantis* had sunk, *Devonshire* cleared the area to avoid an attack by *U-126.*

The *U-126* surfaced and picked up Bauer and the other submariners. Bauer got off a report of the disaster to Kerneval, then organized a rescue of the 305-man crew of *Atlantis.* He took 107 men on board *U-126:* fifty-five, including all wounded, belowdecks and fifty-two on the upper deck. The other 198 men were distributed among six lifeboats. Bauer took the lifeboats in tow and set a course for the South American coast, reporting his action to Dönitz, adding that on the return voyage, *U-126* would require refueling.

Upon learning of the disaster, the OKM and Kerneval arranged for the newly arrived supply ship *Python* to rescue the *Atlantis* survivors and return to France. But the Cape Town U-boat assault was to proceed anyway, Merten's *U-68* substituting for Bauer's *U-126,* whose engines were still unreliable. The four boats of the reconstituted Cape Town group were to replenish from *Python* before she returned to France.

Homing on the beacon signals of Bauer's *U-126, Python* came up on November 24. She took aboard the 305 *Atlantis* survivors and then replenished Bauer in *U-126.* Thereupon Bauer departed for France. *Python* steamed to a new rendezvous 1,700 miles south of the *Atlantis* sinking, in order to replenish the four Cape Town boats. Learning of these new arrangements via Enigma decrypts, the Admiralty set in motion a second trap.

En route to the rendezvous with *Python,* on the afternoon of November 24, Mohr in *U-124* sighted the top-hamper of a British warship. She was the old light

---

* *Atlantis,* the most successful of the raiders, had been at sea for 622 days, had steamed 102,000 miles, and had sunk or captured twenty-two ships for 145,698 tons.

cruiser *Dunedin,* zigzagging at high speed. Mohr hauled around to take position along the cruiser's path, then submerged for a periscope attack. Bedeviled by temporarily inoperable bow planes and a broken depth gauge, Mohr's attack was less than picture-perfect. Moreover, when he was finally ready to shoot, *Dunedin* suddenly altered course away. In desperation Mohr fired three torpedoes from the extreme range of 6,000 yards. Astonishingly, after a run of five minutes and twenty-three seconds, two of the three torpedoes hit *Dunedin.* She blew up and sank instantly, with heavy loss of life.

According to plan, two U-boats met *Python* on November 30: Merten in *U-68* and Eckermann in *U-A.* Resupplying for the fourth time on his prolonged patrol, Merten in *U-68* took on a full load of fuel. The next day, December 1, while Merten was transferring torpedoes from *Python* to *U-68,* Eckermann in *U-A* nuzzled up to take on fuel. Coached to the rendezvous by the Admiralty, the heavy cruiser *Dorsetshire,* armed with eight 8" guns, arrived in the late afternoon and launched a scout plane, which spotted the German vessels. Concerned that *Python* might have British POWs on board, *Dorsetshire* fired two "warning shots" from twelve miles, intending to force *Python* to surrender.

Caught unawares, the German vessels dispersed immediately. The defenseless *Python* ran away at flank speed, leaving the two U-boats between her and *Dorsetshire.* Merten and Eckermann dived to attack, but everything possible went wrong. Merten's torpedoes were not yet properly stowed nor had the boat been trimmed. When he dived, *U-68* went out of control, plunging steeply by the bow. The emergency action required to save the boat spoiled any chance of mounting an attack. Eckermann in *U-A* botched his attack, firing five torpedoes from excessive range with a setup which underestimated *Dorsetshire*'s speed. To avoid further U-boat attack, *Dorsetshire* hauled off and left the area, and *Python* scuttled.

After *Dorsetshire* disappeared, the two U-boats surfaced amid *Python*'s survivors. Including the crew of *Atlantis,* there were 414 Germans variously distributed in eleven lifeboats and numerous rafts. The *Atlantis* captain, Bernhard Rogge—the senior officer present—assumed command of the rescue. He put about 100 survivors on board *U-68* and another 100 on *U-A* and redistributed the remaining 200 men in the ten lifeboats. Each of the U-boats then took five lifeboats in tow. Eckermann in *U-A* reported this second disaster to Kerneval, adding that both U-boats and their trains of lifeboats had sufficient fuel to reach France, about 5,000 miles distant.

The news of this second sinking came as a terrible shock. Dönitz canceled the Cape Town foray and directed the other two boats, Mohr in *U-124* and Clausen in *U-129,* to find *U-68* and *U-A* and render all possible assistance. Racing north on the night of December 3, Mohr in *U-124* encountered a blacked-out, zigzagging freighter, which he stopped and searched. She was the 6,300-ton American vessel *Sagadahoc,* bound for Durban, South Africa. Concluding that her cargo was contraband, Mohr ordered the crew into lifeboats and then sank her, the third American merchant ship to fall victim to U-boats before the United States entered the war.

By December 5, Mohr in *U-124* and Clausen in *U-129* had arrived at the scene of the *Python* disaster. Rogge transferred the 200 survivors in the lifeboats to *U-124* and *U-129* and cast the lifeboats adrift. The four U-boats, each carrying about 104 survivors, then proceeded north at much higher speed. Half the survivors on each boat were belowdecks, the other half on the upper deck, sitting in rubber dinghies or rafts, which would float free in case the boat had to crash-dive. For the survivors topside it was a long, cold, miserable ride.

Meanwhile, Dönitz turned to the Italians for assistance. They sent four big Bordeaux-based boats racing south at maximum speed. These met the four German U-boats at separate locations near the Cape Verde Islands, December 16 to 18, gave them fuel, lube oil, and food, and took aboard 260 German survivors.* While *Torelli* was en route to France, a British destroyer or corvette caught and severely depth-charged her, but she survived. The other seven boats arrived in France without mishap.

The *Atlantis-Python* rescue operation soon became a legendary tale. Not a single German of the 414 on *Atlantis* and *Python* was lost. But the sinking within the space of sixty days of first *Kota Pinang,* then *Atlantis,* and then *Python* convinced Dönitz that resupply of submarines from surface ships was no longer feasible. Patrols to Freetown—or to Cape Town—had to be abandoned until U-boat tankers under construction became available.

The loss of *Atlantis* and *Python* raised anew the suspicion that the British had broken naval Enigma. The OKM agreed the losses were not "coincidental," but after yet another cursory investigation of communications security, it reaffirmed its faith in Enigma, citing the fact that in recent weeks three prize ships had arrived in France and two blockade runners had departed France and despite heavy radio traffic, none had been attacked. This conclusion was based in large part on the false assumption that the British would act tactically on *all* Enigma information.

In the second six months of 1941, Dönitz mounted eighteen patrols to West African waters. Four boats of the special Freetown task force had to abort owing to the loss of German surface resupply vessels. Another boat, *U-67,* rammed by the British submarine *Clyde,* was forced to abort. The other thirteen boats sank nineteen confirmed ships, an average of only 1.5 ships sunk per boat per (extended) patrol. Six boats sank no ships. One boat, *U-111,* was lost to British forces. No boats sailed to that area in November and December.

An Epic Convoy Battle

As another measure in the effort to support Rommel's *Afrika Korps,* in early December, the OKM directed Dönitz to maintain a dozen boats on continuous patrol in the Atlantic close to the western mouth of the Strait of Gibraltar. They were to continue the attacks on convoys going from the Mediterranean to the British Isles and vice versa.

---

* Merten in *U-68* transferred seventy men to *Tazzoli;* Mohr in *U-124* gave *Calvi* seventy men; Clausen in *U-129* gave *Finzi* seventy men; and Eckermann in the bigger *U-A* gave *Torelli* fifty men.

Again Dönitz demurred. Most British supplies, he iterated correctly, went to the Mediterranean via Freetown and Cape Town, not via Gibraltar. Moreover, British ASW forces in the waters immediately west of Gibraltar had been reinforced greatly, and the inbound and outbound Gibraltar convoys were certain to be more heavily escorted than ever. Owing to the heavy commitment of Type VIIs to the Mediterranean and the setbacks ten other Type VIIs had incurred attempting the passage, Dönitz did not have enough Type VIIs to attack Gibraltar convoys. If the OKM insisted on these operations, Dönitz would be forced to use some Type IXs, which were not considered to be suitable for attacks on heavily escorted convoys.

The OKM insisted.

As a first step, Dönitz redeployed the special six-boat group, *Steuben,* from Newfoundland waters to the approaches to Gibraltar. It contained two Type IXs: Wolfgang Lüth's aged *U-43* and Georg Schewe's *U-105.* While passing near the Azores in heavy weather on November 29, Lüth came upon elements of the storm-scattered convoy Outbound South 12, originally composed of fifty-two merchant ships, guarded by six escorts.

What Lüth found was about half the convoy and half the escorts. He sank two British freighters in the convoy, the 5,600-ton *Thornliebank* and the 4,900-ton *Ashby.* The first was a loaded ammo ship, which blew up with an awesome roar, throwing debris all over the place. Later, in a propaganda broadcast, Lüth asserted that a grenade hurled from *Thornliebank,* a kilometer away, hit and bruised his quartermaster, Theodor Petersen, who was topside. Two ex-Coast Guard cutters, *Totland* and *Sennen,* and another escort sighted *U-43,* drove her under, and depth-charged her for several hours, but Lüth evaded and escaped.

A day or so later, on December 2, Lüth came upon the 11,900-ton American tanker *Astral,* sailing alone from the Caribbean loaded with gasoline. Believing her to be a 12,300-ton British tanker of the *San Melito* class, or so he wrote in a wartime propaganda book,* Lüth hit and sank her with torpedoes. He described the result:

> The tanker offered a magnificent show as she burned . . . for hours afterwards thick clouds of smoke hovered so far above the location that we could see a couple of small, bright "fair weather" clouds underneath them. Over half the sky was covered with black smoke. . . .

None of the thirty-seven-man crew survived. Dönitz attempted to vector the other five boats of group *Steuben* to Outbound South 12, but all efforts failed. Since these six boats were low on fuel after this futile chase, group *Steuben* had to be disbanded. The *Ritterkreuz* holders Lüth in *U-43* and Schewe in *U-105* (who

---

* *Boot Greift Wieder An: Ritterkreuzträger Erzählen* (Boat Strikes Again: Tales of the Knight's Cross). This and other war patrols of Lüth have been described by an American biographer, Jordan Vause, in his *U-boat Ace* (Annapolis, 1990). For details of the loss of *Astral,* which remained unexplained for twenty years, Vause relied on two separate articles by Edward F. Oliver and Arthur Gordon in *U.S. Naval Institute Proceedings,* March 1961 and October 1965, respectively.

had sunk no ships on this patrol) set a course for France. Initially the other four Type VII boats were ordered to refuel at Vigo and go directly to the Mediterranean, but later some of these orders were modified.

Inbound to refuel at Vigo for transit to the Mediterranean, one of the *Steuben* boats, *U-434*, commanded by Wolfgang Heyda, age twenty-eight, on his first patrol from Germany, ran into convoy Outbound Gibraltar 77. While Heyda shadowed, Dönitz brought up Lüth in *U-43* and another Type IX, Müller-Stöckheim's *U-67*, reconditioned after her collision with the British submarine *Clyde* in the Cape Verde Islands and fresh from Lorient. Lüth found and attacked a destroyer with his last torpedoes, but he missed. Owing to a critical shortage of fuel, he had to break off and head for France, unable even to shadow. For the same reason Heyda had to break off and go into Vigo. Left alone, Müller-Stöckheim in *U-67* found the convoy and shot a bow salvo at a fast-moving "destroyer." One torpedo circled back and nearly hit *U-67;* the others missed. The "destroyer," other escorts, and British aircraft from Gibraltar thwarted a second attack.

At this time, German spies near Gibraltar reported that convoy Homebound Gibraltar 76 was on the point of sailing for the British Isles. Although he was reluctant to send Type IXs against Gibraltar convoys, the shortage of Type VIIs forced Dönitz to position Müller-Stöckheim's *U-67* to watch for the convoy.

Meanwhile, Dönitz created a new group, *Seeräuber,* to reinforce Müller-Stöckheim. It was comprised of two ex-*Steuben* group Type VII boats that had refueled in Vigo, Wolfgang Heyda's *U-434* and Dietrich Gengelbach's *U-574*, both still on first patrols, and four other Type IXs: *U-107* and *U-108,* newly sailed from France, the former commanded by a new skipper, Harald Gelhaus, age twenty-six, the latter by the old hand Klaus Scholtz; and two brand-new boats, Bruno Hansmann in *U-127* and Arend Baumann in *U-131,* both merely two weeks out of Germany. It was a less-than-satisfactory group: Five of the seven boats were Type IXs; five of the seven skippers were making first patrols.

In the afternoon and evening of December 14, fifty-eight ships departed Gibraltar for the Atlantic. First to leave was Homebound Gibraltar 76, comprised of thirty-two merchant ships and seventeen escorts. Next came a special convoy comprised of one freighter and three tankers, with five escorts, bound for Freetown and points south. Two old hands in Type VIIs, who were preparing to enter the Mediterranean via the strait, spotted the convoys: Eitel-Friedrich Kentrat in *U-74* reported Homebound Gibraltar 76; Heinrich Schonder in *U-77* reported the Freetown convoy.

Notwithstanding the urgency of getting these two boats into the Mediterranean, Dönitz directed both to attack the convoys, even if the chances of success were slim. Unable to gain position for an attack, Kentrat in *U-74* broke off and ran the strait on the night of December 15. Dodging the escorts and aircraft, Schonder in *U-77* shot at a freighter and a tanker, sinking the former, the 5,000-ton *Empire Barracuda.* He then resumed his passage to the Mediterranean, getting through on the night of December 16. A little farther west that night, one of the *Seeräuber* boats,

Scholtz's IXB *U-108,* sank the 4,800-ton freighter *Cassequel,* which was, awkwardly, a neutral Portuguese sailing alone. Scholtz then shadowed the convoy tenaciously.

German spies near Gibraltar reported the departure of Homebound Gibraltar 76. They listed the precise number of merchant ships (thirty-two) but they understated the escort, reporting "three destroyers," a "submarine," "several corvettes," and the aircraft tender *Unicorn.* Actually, the escort was massive: three destroyers, four sloops, nine corvettes, and the "jeep" carrier *Audacity* (which resembled *Unicorn*), carrying four Martlet fighters to ward off Condors.

The Homebound Gibraltar 76 guardian was Escort Group 36, commanded by forty-five-year-old Frederic J. ("Johnny") Walker in the sloop *Stork.* Son of a career naval officer, Walker was a tough, outspoken, onetime middleweight boxer with twenty-seven years of regular service. Between the wars he had specialized in ASW, rising to command the ASW school at Portland in 1937, but he had been "passed over" for promotion to captain. Rescued from a staff job, Walker had been given command of the newly formed EG-36 (two sloops, seven corvettes) in March 1941. The group had come out to Gibraltar on its first mission in late November. While waiting for Homebound Gibraltar 76 to sail, it had patrolled the western approaches to the Gibraltar Strait. One of the corvettes incorporated into the group at Gibraltar, *Marigold,* had sunk Ey's *U-433* a month earlier.

Upon receiving Kentrat's contact report, Dönitz alerted and deployed group *Seeräuber* on a north-south line west of Gibraltar and sent out Condors from Bordeaux. However, the visibility was poor on December 15 and neither the U-boats nor the Condors could find the convoy. The usually reliable German spies caused considerable confusion at Kerneval by incorrectly reporting that owing to the U-boat threat, Homebound Gibraltar 76 had aborted and returned to Gibraltar shortly after sailing.

On the night of December 15, well after the departure of Homebound Gibraltar 76, four destroyers conducted an ASW sweep thirty miles south of Cape St. Vincent in the western approaches to the Gibraltar Strait. These were the Australian *Nestor* and the British *Croome, Foxhound,* and *Gurkha II.* At about 11:00 P.M., *Nestor* sighted a U-boat on the surface about seven miles off. *Nestor* alerted the other destroyers, rang up full speed, and manned her guns. *Gurkha II* and *Foxhound* raced up, taking positions on *Nestor*'s beams. At a range of about six miles, *Nestor* opened fire on the U-boat with her main battery, firing eight rounds but achieving no hits.

Her quarry was the brand-new Type IXC *U-127.* Commanded by Bruno Hansmann, age thirty-three, she had sailed from Kiel seventeen days earlier. Assigned to group *Seeräuber,* she was holding down the southern end of the patrol line. Based on the erroneous spy report—that Homebound Gibraltar 76 had put back into Gibraltar—Hansmann was lying in wait in case it resailed that night.

Upon reaching the spot where *U-127* had dived, *Nestor* slowed to 18 knots and got an excellent sonar contact. Holding the contact, she carried out a rapid but careful attack, dropping five shallow-set depth charges. *Foxhound* also got contact and prepared to run in, but upon hearing a dull explosion deep beneath her keel, she broke off the attack. *Nestor, Gurkha II,* and *Croome* also heard the explosion. Soon afterwards the destroyers found oil and wreckage—pieces of wood, some clothing, and "human remains." It was surmised from this evidence that *Nestor*'s depth charges had ignited an "internal explosion" on the U-boat. *Nestor* was correctly credited with an unknown U-boat kill; nothing further was ever heard from *U-127.*

Condors from Bordeaux found Homebound Gibraltar 76 on the morning of December 16 and shadowed, unseen by any of the escorts. Dönitz relayed the position report to group *Seeräuber.* In the late afternoon, Klaus Scholtz in the IXB *U-108* regained contact, reported his position, and shadowed. Dönitz passed this information to the other *Seeräuber* boats, promising Condor support and urging them to converge at highest speed, to get in front of the convoy, and to attack by dawn on December 17, "without fail." Intercepting this Enigma traffic, the Admiralty alerted the convoy to the impending danger and ordered *Audacity* to mount ASW patrols, commencing at dawn.

By the early hours of December 17, four boats were in touch with the convoy: Scholtz in the IXB *U-108,* still shadowing doggedly; Gelhaus in the IXB *U-107;* Baumann in the IXC *U-131;* and Gengelbach in the VII *U-574,* fresh from refueling in Vigo. With the coming of light, a Martlet from *Audacity* took off and scouted. Shortly thereafter the pilot reported a U-boat twenty-two miles ahead of the convoy. Upon sighting the Martlet, it dived.

Hearing this report, EG-36 commander Johnny Walker in the sloop *Stork* left the convoy to carry out a U-boat hunt. On his instructions, the three destroyers *Blankney, Exmoor II,* and the ex-American four-stack *Stanley,* and the corvette *Penstemon,* joined the chase.

The destroyers raced ahead to the reported position. Arriving first, *Blankney* hurled off depth charges at a doubtful contact. When *Exmoor II* and *Stork* arrived, Walker repositioned the three ships to conduct an organized sweep, but they found nothing. Coming up last, the corvette *Penstemon,* in company with the destroyer *Stanley,* got a firm sonar contact. Shortly after 11:00 A.M., *Penstemon* carried out a deliberate attack, dropping ten depth charges set from 150 to 400 feet.

The boat was the Type IXC *U-131,* commanded by thirty-seven-year-old Arend Baumann. This very senior officer (crew of 1922) was three weeks out from Kiel on his first patrol. During its hurried workup, *U-131* had damaged its hydrophones. They had not been repaired, leaving *U-131* "deaf" when submerged and thus unable to evade properly. Some of the ten charges fell very close, causing extensive internal damage. Baumann eased away slowly and attempted repairs, but after an hour and forty-one minutes, he gave up and surfaced, getting off a frantic message to Kerneval reporting he was "unable to dive" and asking for assistance. Kerneval replied that no assistance could be provided, adding: "If there is no other way, sink your boat."

When *U-131* surfaced, the destroyer *Stanley* sighted her and gave the alarm. All five ships plus a Martlet from *Audacity* converged on the position. The closest destroyer, *Exmoor II,* opened fire with her main battery at about six miles, but achieved no hits. The Martlet pilot, George Fletcher, bravely—but unwisely— roared in and strafed *U-131,* drawing return fire from Baumann's gunners. The

German gunners hit the Martlet in the cockpit, killing or fatally wounding Fletcher, and the Martlet crashed into the sea.

When four of the five escorts brought *U-131* under heavy fire, Baumann ordered the crew to scuttle and abandon ship. At 1:21 P.M., *Exmoor II* reported, the *U-131* upended and sank stern first. *Exmoor II* rescued forty-four Germans, including Baumann. *Stanley* picked up the other four. *Stork* recovered the dead Martlet pilot, Fletcher, and buried him at sea. The Admiralty generously credited *Stork, Blankney, Exmoor II, Stanley, Penstemon,* and *Audacity* for the kill, but the Germans said it was *Penstemon*'s skilled depth-charge attack that directly led to the destruction of *U-131*.

Several U-boats clung to the convoy during the night of December 17–18. Klaus Scholtz in *U-108* reported that he torpedoed one ship, but he was mistaken. No ships were hit that night.

The next morning shortly after 9:00, December 18, the destroyer *Stanley* spotted a U-boat on the surface about six miles off. The other two destroyers, *Blankney* and *Exmoor II,* and the sloop *Deptford,* joined *Stanley* for the hunt. When *Stanley* had closed to three miles, the U-boat dived, leaving *Stanley* at a disadvantage since her sonar was temporarily out of commission. Nonetheless, she dropped nineteen single depth charges in a squarish pattern around the presumed position of the boat. Running in to help, *Blankney* got a firm sonar contact at close range and dropped six charges. She then relayed her contact to the four-stack *Stanley,* who fired off fourteen more depth charges with deep settings. For good measure, *Blankney* fired another six depth charges with medium settings.

The victim of these forty-five depth charges was the *U-434,* a Type VII commanded by Wolfgang Heyda, still on his first patrol from Germany. He had refueled in Vigo, under orders to proceed to the Mediterranean, but had been diverted to group *Seeräuber* for the attack on Homebound Gibraltar 76. Built in Danzig at a new U-boat shipyard, *U-434* had numerous serious structural defects, including unreliable gears in the ballast-tank flood and vent valves. Some of the depth charges fell close, inflicting such heavy damage and flooding that Heyda was forced to surface.

When *U-434* popped up, *Blankney* was merely 2,000 yards off. She put on flank speed to ram, firing her main battery. As *Blankney* closed, all the Germans except one officer manning a machine gun jumped overboard. At the last second *Blankney*'s captain decided to board rather than ram, but the decision came too late. *Blankney* struck the U-boat a glancing blow, which did no harm to the boat but rather damaged *Blankney*. She lowered a whaler with a boarding party, but Heyda had set demolition charges and *U-434* blew up and sank before the whaler reached her. *Blankney* rescued Heyda and forty-one others. Four Germans, including the defiant officer who had manned the machine gun, could not be found. *Blankney* and *Stanley* shared credit for the kill.

By design or by accident, the surface escort for Homebound Gibraltar 76 gradually diminished. The corvette *Carnation* was first to leave. Then the sloops *Black Swan* and *Fowey.* Then the corvette *La Malouine.* After damaging herself in the collision with *U-434,* the destroyer *Blankney,* joined by another destroyer, *Exmoor*

II, which was low on fuel, returned to Gibraltar. By the evening of December 18, the surface escort had decreased by nearly a third—to eleven ships.

The sole remaining destroyer, the ex-American four-stack *Stanley,* took up position at the stern of the convoy. In the early hours of December 19, *Stanley* saw a U-boat and gave the alarm. Johnny Walker in *Stork* ordered *Stanley* to fire a flare to indicate her position. Upon seeing the flare, Walker established visual communications with *Stanley,* but it was immediately interrupted by a frantic message from *Stanley:* "Torpedoes passed from astern." Moments later, a torpedo hit *Stanley,* and she "blew up in a sheet of flame several hundred feet high."

The shooter was Dietrich Gengelbach in the Type VII *U-574,* who had refueled in Vigo and was still on his first patrol. He did not have long to savor the victory. Walker in *Stork* led several corvettes to the scene and within nine minutes *Stork* had a good sonar contact and attacked, dropping fifteen shallow-set depth charges in two runs. Some of these fell close to *U-574,* causing such damage that Gengelbach was forced to surface, merely fifteen minutes after the first depth-charge explosion.

The boat came up 200 yards in front of *Stork.* Catching sight of her, Walker bent on flank speed to ram, firing snowflakes and his main battery. Gengelbach, too, bent on flank speed, circling to port. *Stork* pulled so close to *U-574* that the British gunners could not depress the main gun to shoot and, as Walker reported, they were reduced to "fist-shaking and roaring curses." Eleven minutes into the chase, *Stork* rammed *U-574* forward of the conning tower and rolled her over. For good measure, Walker dropped ten more depth charges set to explode at fifty feet.

A Wagnerian drama ensued on the shattered *U-574.* Gengelbach gave the order to scuttle and abandon ship, but then he and the engineer officer fell into some kind of dispute. The Germans reported later that during the dispute the engineer apparently committed suicide with his pistol. Gengelbach chose suicide as well. After all his men had jumped overboard, he threw himself into the conning tower and went down with the boat.

Having done away with *U-574,* at the cost of damage to her own bow and loss of her sonar dome, *Stork* proceeded to search for British survivors of *Stanley.* Homing on cries in the water, *Stork* picked up five Germans from *U-574* and twenty-five British sailors from *Stanley.* The corvette *Samphire* found eleven more Germans and three more men from *Stanley.* In all, *Stork* and *Samphire* rescued sixteen Germans and twenty-eight British.

All this time the *Ritterkreuz* holder Klaus Scholtz in the IXB *U-108* had been dogging the convoy with remarkable tenacity. During sixty hours of tracking and reporting, he had made several torpedo attacks, claiming, incorrectly, that he had hit at least one ship. While *Stork* and the other escorts were preoccupied with the rescue of survivors from *U-574* and *Stanley,* Scholtz attacked the formation of freighters, firing his last torpedoes at the 2,900-ton British *Ruckinge.* Scholtz reported a sinking, stressing that he was out of torpedoes, but Kerneval ordered him to keep shadowing.

The *Ruckinge* was wrecked but she did not sink. However, her thirty-nine-man crew hastily took to lifeboats, leaving behind the ship's "confidential papers." *Stork* and the freighter *Finland* recovered the survivors. When Walker learned that the captain had left secret papers behind, he ordered the corvette *Samphire* to board the hulk and recover them. After this was done, *Samphire* sank the *Ruckinge* by gunfire.

During that day, December 19, Condors patrolled from Bordeaux. En route to Homebound Gibraltar 76, they found and reported a southbound convoy. Although the southbound convoy was obviously a more valuable military target, Dönitz was not confident of the Condor position reports and clung to the bird-in-hand. He told the *Seeräuber* boats that Homebound Gibraltar 76 was "still the object of operations" but authorized an attack on the southbound convoy if any boat encountered it without deviation. Continuing on to Homebound Gibraltar 76, the Condors received a hot reception from *Audacity*'s Martlets. The British pilots shot down two Condors that day and damaged a third.

Meanwhile, Dönitz had dispatched three other Type VIIs from French bases to reinforce group *Seeräuber*. All, he logged, were manned by aggressive and "experienced" skippers, who, he was "confident," could deal with this "difficult" convoy. The skippers were Walter Flachsenberg in *U-71*, *Ritterkreuz* holder Engelbert Endrass, the reigning U-boat ace still in Atlantic combat,* in his new command, *U-567*, and Gerhard Bigalk in *U-751*. Flachsenberg and Bigalk had arrived in the Atlantic in June. Flachsenberg had sunk no confirmed ships; Bigalk had sunk one for 5,400 tons. Since taking over the *U-567* in September, Endrass had made one patrol but had sunk no ships.

Despite deteriorating weather and exhaustion, the three remaining IXs of group *Seeräuber*, *U-67*, *U-107*, and *U-108*, hung on to the convoy during December 19 to 21. Only *U-67* and *U-107* had torpedoes, but neither had any luck. Müller-Stöckheim in *U-67* fired three of his remaining nine torpedoes at a "large destroyer" but missed, he reported, "owing to a misfire in the middle tube." All three boats were harassed by Martlets from *Audacity*. One Martlet pilot claimed to have found two U-boats twenty-five miles astern of the convoy, lying side by side on the surface with a "plank" between them. The pilot said he strafed the boats and despite counterfire from both, "shot three men" off the plank. The British surmised that the boats had collided and were repairing the damage.

Homing on Scholtz's beacons, the three Type VIIs newly sailed from France made contact with the convoy on the afternoon of December 21. Perhaps needlessly, Dönitz radioed them: "Given equal firing opportunity, sink the aircraft carrier first. You'll find it easier then." Aware from Admiralty signals that six U-boats were stalking the convoy, Walker in *Stork* ordered the sloop *Deptford* and some corvettes to haul away some distance and stage a "mock battle" (star shells, gunfire) to mislead and draw off the U-boats. However, the "battle" had the opposite of the intended effect. Seeing it, several freighters in the convoy became alarmed and fired off snowflakes, giving away the game and lighting up the real convoy.

---

*   The other eight *Ritterkreuz* holders then commanding Atlantic boats were Lüth in *U-43*, Lehmann-Willenbrock in *U-96*, Schewe in *U-105*, Bleichrodt in *U-109*, Schnee in *U-201*, Mützelburg in *U-203*, Topp in *U-552*, and Suhren in *U-564*. With twenty-one confirmed ships to his credit, Lüth ranked second after Endrass.

These snowflakes served as a beacon for Engelbert Endrass in *U-567*. He ran in and torpedoed the 3,300-ton British freighter *Annavore*. Loaded with iron ore, she sank instantly; only four of her crew could be found. Upon seeing this attack, Walker in *Stork* ordered the *Deptford* group to break off the mock battle and rejoin the convoy.

At almost exactly this same moment, 11 P.M., Bigalk in *U-751* saw *Audacity* steaming unprotected, silhouetted against the light of snowflakes. He mistook the 10,000-ton "jeep" carrier for a new fleet carrier of the 23,000-ton *Formidable* class. "Good God!" he exclaimed when recounting the attack later in a Berlin radio broadcast. "What a chance!" Quickly but coolly, Bigalk set up and fired three bow torpedoes. All hit *Audacity*. Flooding heavily from three solid hits, *Audacity* (an ex-merchant ship with no hull armor) went down in ten minutes. Unaware that she had sunk, Bigalk submerged to reload his bow tubes, intending to finish her off with another salvo. But when he surfaced, there was no sign of "*Formidable*." Upon his report of the attack, Dönitz congratulated him and later, when Bigalk returned to France, he received a *Ritterkreuz*.*

A wild nighttime action ensued. Directed by Walker in *Stork*, the ten remaining escorts of Homebound Gibraltar 76 ran hither and yon, firing snowflakes, rescuing survivors of *Audacity*, and dropping depth charges. The corvettes *Samphire, Vetch,* and *Marigold* each carried out an attack on a U-boat, but no kills resulted. Spotting a U-boat on the surface, the sloop *Deptford* turned to ram. When the boat dived, *Deptford* raced up and threw off ten shallow-set depth charges "by eye." After the noise subsided, *Deptford* got a solid sonar contact and attacked with care, firing another ten depth charges. Holding the contact, *Deptford* carried out three more full-scale depth-charge attacks. The Admiralty ruled there was not sufficient evidence to credit a U-boat kill, but years later, after a painstaking study of the British and German records, British historians concluded that *Deptford* had sunk Englebert Endrass in *U-567*.†

The attack on Endrass utterly drained the crew of *Deptford*. Returning to the convoy in pitch darkness, improperly alert, *Deptford* smashed into the port side of *Stork*. Her bow, Walker logged, rode right up on *Stork*, crushing the after cabin, where the five survivors of Gengelbach's *U-574* were being held. Two of the Germans, Walker reported dispassionately, "were pulped, literally, into a bloody mess." Fortunately *Deptford* had not hit any of *Stork*'s vital machinery, and after the two sloops got untangled, both continued onward at considerably reduced speed, neither with working sonar.

During December 22, Dönitz requested reports from the *Seeräuber* boats. Nothing had been heard from Bruno Hansmann in the new Type IXC *U-127*, for days. It was wrongly assumed that escorts from Homebound Gibraltar 76 had sunk

---

* At the time of the award, Bigalk had sunk two confirmed ships for 15,370 tons, including *Audacity*. Klaus Scholtz in *U-108*, who had skillfully shadowed the convoy for seven full days and sunk one ship from it, received a *Ritterkreuz* at the same time. His confirmed score was thirteen ships for 61,760 tons.

† Endrass had sunk a total of 25 confirmed ships for 137,990 tons while commanding *U-46* and *U-567*. He ranked eighteenth in tonnage sunk in the war.

her rather than, as was the case, the destroyer hunter-killer group. It was also assumed, correctly, that the convoy escorts had sunk the new Type IXC *U-131,* as well as the two new Type VIICs that had refueled in Vigo, Heyda's *U-434* and Gengelbach's *U-574.* No one would permit himself to believe that the invincible Engelbert Endrass in the VIIC *U-567* was gone, and yet he did not reply to repeated requests for his position and status. When it was finally conceded that *U-567* was lost, Dönitz withheld the news for weeks.

After assessing the battle on December 22, Dönitz called off the chase and directed Müller-Stöckheim's *U-67,* Gelhaus's *U-107,* Scholtz's *U-108,* and Bigalk's *U-751* to return to France. Upon tabulating the results of this epic chase, Dönitz was devastated: one aircraft tender* and three (actually only two) small freighters sunk at a cost of five (as he thought) U-boats, including Endrass. It was a terrible setback for the U-boat force.

Reinforced by surface and air escorts based in the British Isles, including a B-24 Liberator of British Squadron 120, which came out 800 miles, Homebound Gibraltar 76 reached its destination on December 23. Although the loss of *Audacity* and the four-stack *Stanley* was a sharp blow, the Admiralty lavished praise and awards on escort commander Johnny Walker and his captains. In relentlessly aggressive actions, they had positively sunk three U-boats (*U-131, U-434, U-574*) within a period of three days—an unprecedented achievement—and had brought home thirty of the thirty-two merchant ships of the convoy, a timely and smashing victory.

The U-boat effort to assist Axis forces in North Africa in the fall of 1941 was thus costly: thirteen boats and about 600 men lost in combat in merely six weeks—the greatest loss rate of the war to then—and another half-dozen boats knocked out with battle damage. No less disconcerting was the complete curtailment of the U-boat war in the North Atlantic in favor of assisting the *Afrika Korps.*

Dönitz drafted a tactful plea to the OKM. He conceded the urgent need to assist Axis ground forces in North Africa by sending U-boats to the Mediterranean, but he urged that attacks on Gibraltar convoys on the Atlantic side of the strait be curtailed. It was unfair and a terrible waste of assets to pit inexperienced skippers against the heavily escorted Gibraltar convoys. Four skippers on first patrols had been lost in the chase of Homebound Gibraltar 76. It was also unwise, he insisted, to send the big, clumsy Type IX boats against heavily escorted Gibraltar convoys or to patrol them near the heavily defended Gibraltar Strait. Of the five Type IXs sent against Homebound Gibraltar 76, only Scholtz in *U-108* had managed to sink a ship. The others had had an arduous and perilous time; two IXs (*U-127, U-131*) had been lost.

---

* Kerneval privately discounted Bigalk's claim to have sunk a *Formidable* class carrier, but let the claim stand publicly. Unaware as yet that the British even had a "jeep" carrier, and based in part on erroneous information from German spies at Gibraltar, in part on a report from Müller-Stöckheim in *U-67,* who had seen and shot at *Audacity* during the chase but described her as an aircraft "mother ship," Kerneval continued to believe Bigalk had sunk the aircraft tender *Unicorn.*

The OKM agreed—reluctantly. U-boat attacks against the heavily escorted Gibraltar convoys were to be terminated, and patrols to the Atlantic area immediately west of Gibraltar cut to a bare minimum.

ASSESSMENTS

The formal entry of the United States into World War II marked the end of the twenty-eight months of U-boat warfare almost solely against the British Empire. It provides a convenient milestone to assess the outcome of the Anglo-German naval campaign. In order to draw some conclusions, it is necessary to examine closely another barrage of numbers.

In these first twenty-eight months of war, the Germans deployed 153 oceangoing attack U-boats to the various war zones.* According to the most reliable source, British author V. E. Tarrant, these boats sank 1,124 British and "neutral" ships of about 5.3 million gross tons.† The sinkings included twenty-eight warships: aircraft carriers *Courageous* and *Ark Royal;* battleships *Royal Oak* and *Barham;* the first "jeep" carrier, *Audacity;* light cruisers *Dunedin* and *Galatea;* nine destroyers (among them the American *Reuben James* and the ex-American four-stacks *Bath, Broadwater,* and *Stanley*); three sloops; six corvettes; and three submarines (British *Thistle* and *Spearfish;* French *Doris*).

The loss of 5.3 million gross tons of British and "neutral" merchant shipping to Axis submarines was undeniably a tough blow. Not the least of the considerations was the heavy loss of life in the ranks of the British merchant-ship crews. The Admiralty put that figure to December 31, 1941, at 9,267 men. Most died quickly and horribly in the explosions and sinkings, or slowly and agonizingly in lifeboats and on rafts. Although statistically the odds of a ship being hit or sunk were quite low, every voyage was a prolonged and terrifying nightmare for the crewmen.

It is seldom mentioned in accounts of the Battle of the Atlantic of the period under review but, remarkably, the British were able to make up this loss of 5.3 million gross tons of merchant shipping to Axis submarines in several ways. These included the construction of about 2 million gross tons of new (and superior) merchant shipping in British yards and the one-time confiscation, purchase, or lease of about 4 million more gross tons from Axis and Allied "neutral" sources.‡ In fact, the total British-controlled merchant marine fleet actually *increased* during this period from about 3,000 ships of 17.8 million gross tons to about 3,600 ships of 20.7 million gross tons.§

Some writers have described an "oil crisis" in the British Isles caused by the heavy loss of Allied tankers to U-boats in this period. Actually, Allied tanker losses to Axis submarines were not crippling: 117 vessels of about 936,777 gross tons, of which seventy-six of 628,110 gross tons were British-owned.¶ During the period

---

*   See appendices 1, 5, and 6.

†   See Appendix 18.

‡   This total included 180 ships from Norway, 156 from Greece, 147 from the Netherlands, and 137 "prizes" or "requisitioned" vessels.

§   See Plate 6.

¶   See Appendix 17.

under review, British shipyards made up about half of the loss of British-owned tanker tonnage by completing thirty-seven new and larger tankers of about 365,000 gross tons. Besides that, in this period the British government acquired control of about 200 tankers from Norway, the Netherlands, Belgium, and other nations. Over and above that, in 1941 the United States diverted fifty tankers to the British "oil shuttle" in American waters and authorized U.S. (and Panamanian) companies to charter tankers to the British in war zones. As a result of these gains, the size of the British-controlled tanker fleet actually *increased* substantially by the end of 1941. Owing to that and to petrol rationing and other fuel-conservation measures, the official British historian wrote, no real oil crisis occurred in the British Isles in this period.

However, total imports to the British Isles continued to fall sharply, from about 60 million tons in 1939 to about 45 million tons in 1940 to an uncomfortable and worrisome rock-bottom 31 million tons in 1941. By the end of that year, almost all consumer goods and food in the British Isles were rationed and "Victory Gardens," begun as patriotic gestures, had become virtual necessities.

In addition to U-boat sinkings of and damage to merchant ships, there were numerous other causes for the drastic loss of imports. Chief among these were the diversion of shipping for strictly military purposes and delays incurred by convoying. Other reasons: *Luftwaffe* bomb and mine damage to shipping and seaports; the loss of convoy routes in the Mediterranean Sea; inefficiencies in the British unloading and distribution systems; overcrowding in ship refit, overhaul, and damage repair facilities; labor problems;* and increased shipping accidents and collisions due to convoying and to the shutting down of navigational aids, and to other wartime restrictions.

In return for the destruction of and damage to this Allied shipping, the Atlantic U-boat force did not escape unharmed. To December 31, 1941, forty-nine ocean-going U-boats manned by about 2,150 men were lost in Atlantic combat operations to all causes.† The British rescued and imprisoned 39 percent (828) of these men; the others died terrible deaths at sea. Five other oceangoing U-boats manned by about 220 men newly arrived in the Mediterranean were lost in those waters during November and December 1941. The British rescued and imprisoned 54 percent (119) of these men. The total of fifty-four oceangoing U-boats lost in action to the end of 1941 amounted to about 35 percent of the 153 oceangoing attack boats deployed in all war zones outside the Baltic. The total of 2,400 men lost (947 captured) was the cream of the prewar submarine force.‡

---

* When the British belatedly shifted from riveted to welded construction for some vessels, the riveters went out on strike. Regardless of the hardships inflicted on the civilian population, including themselves, dockyard workers also struck from time to time for increased wages and benefits.

† During workup in the Baltic, three new VIICs, *U-560, U-580,* and *U-583,* were lost in accidental collisions. The *U-560* was raised and salvaged but relegated to a school boat.

‡ In addition, eleven Type II ducks, manned by 275 men, were lost in all waters. Two were accidentally rammed and sunk by German-controlled surface ships; four were sunk by mines, four by British warships, one by a Russian submarine. The British captured seventy-eight men from three of these ducks: *U-13, U-63,* and *U-138.*

•   •   •

To this point it would be difficult to declare a "victor" in the so-called Battle of the Atlantic. Inasmuch as the British had persuaded the Americans to provide significant help (sixty warships; North Atlantic convoy escort; occupation of Iceland; amendments liberalizing the Neutrality Act; the "oil shuttle"; and most significantly, Lend-Lease), they had assured themselves of victory over the U-boat in the long term. However, in the short term, many more difficult months lay ahead. The British had not defeated the U-boat force; rather, they had taken the necessary steps to prevent it from defeating them.

In truth, neither Germany nor Great Britain had been properly prepared for a submarine war in the Atlantic, and it showed. When that war came, neither side responded with war-decisive measures. Both sides made errors of commission and omission. A review of these helps to set the stage for the second phase of the U-boat war.

First, the British side.

• The appeasing antiwar attitude held during the prewar years by a majority of British citizens and the various governments opened the way for Hitler to abrogate the Versailles Treaty and enter into a bilateral naval agreement with the British, which allowed him to create a second U-boat force. In light of the naval experience of World War I, this has to be ranked as an egregious and unfortunate mistake, but given the dark economic situation of the 1930s and the mood of the British democracy, perhaps unavoidable and inevitable.

• Although it then became possible that the British would have to fight a U-boat force again, the London government did not take sufficiently vigorous steps in the late 1930s to prepare for that contingency. Made smug by the success of convoying in World War I and overconfident of modern sonar to detect submerged U-boats unfailingly, the Admiralty neglected men and weaponry for possible antisubmarine warfare in the wider reaches of the Atlantic.

One result was that when war came the British did not have nearly enough surface and air escorts to support convoying, or adequate ASW weaponry. When the 1,000-ton *Hunt*-class destroyers intended for Atlantic ocean escort failed to meet satisfactory standards, the British had to rely heavily on the slow corvettes, which had been earmarked for inshore escort and were not adequately armed or suited for the rough waters of the open ocean. Historically, the scandalously neglected stepchild of the RAF, Coastal Command, remained outside Admiralty control for too long and did not get the men, aircraft, electronics, and weaponry required for proper escorting of convoys and killing U-boats.

Beyond that neglect, the Admiralty squandered some of its most valuable ASW assets in ill-conceived ventures, such as hunter-killer operations in 1939 and the attempted occupations of Norway in the spring of 1940 and of Greece in 1941. Hunter-killer operations cost the Royal Navy the carrier *Courageous*. The attempted occupations of Norway and Greece cost it numerous destroyers sunk or damaged, besides those lost at Dunkirk.* Elsewhere all too many destroyers were worn down in futile hunter-killer patrolling.

_____

* See Appendix 9.

• The British had no way of foreseeing the sudden, craven collapse of France. However, when it became unequivocally clear in the summer of 1940 that the Germans were shifting the entire oceangoing U-boat operational force to bases on the Atlantic coast of occupied France, the British failed to take steps to interfere. Had the War Cabinet directed RAF Bomber Command to focus its airpower on those bases rather than on German cities, doubtless the British would have prevented the construction of the massive, bombproof U-boat pens. The failure to do so or to mount vigorous ASW air patrols over the Bay of Biscay, a "choke point" that all inbound and outbound U-boats in France had to transit, were British errors of omission in 1941 of regrettable proportions.

• The secret British break into naval Enigma in 1941 was a triumph of intelligence, literally and figuratively. However, it was a two-edged sword. While it enabled the British to evade U-boats and save ships, at the same time it had the effect of reducing the U-boat kill rate.

To the end of 1941, most U-boats were sunk or disabled while tracking or attacking convoys. The successful "evasion" strategy therefore sharply reduced contacts between U-boats and convoys with a commensurate reduction in opportunities to kill U-boats. In all of 1941, British-controlled ASW forces sank only thirty oceangoing U-boats, an average of 2.5 per month. British intelligence put new U-boat construction at an average of twenty boats per month. It was not that high in 1941, but even so, it was at least six times or more than the kill rate. Thus it was clear—at least to the Americans—that the British could not rely so completely on convoy "evasion" much longer. In addition to strengthening defensive convoy escort, they needed to hurl offensive air and submarine forces at U-boat construction yards, training areas, bases and pens, the Bay of Biscay, and elsewhere to kill U-boats at a much higher rate.

Some historians have argued that the British failure to honor the December 1940 Anglo-American Enigma deal in spirit and give the Americans complete access to Enigma-breaking secrets in 1941 was another regrettable British mistake. The British were hard-pressed to find technicians and facilities to build three-rotor bombes, let alone the anticipated new generation of four-rotor bombes. The Americans had technicians and facilities to do both. Had the British revealed Enigma-breaking machine technology to the Americans more willingly and sooner, it is likely that specialized American production know-how could have minimized the possibilities of "losing" naval Enigma for an extended time, as was soon to be the case. That same advanced codebreaking technology could also have better detected the German breaks into Anglo-American naval codes, which also occurred.

• Although it soon became clear that the land-based aircraft of Coastal Command served well in an ASW role, even if only to hold U-boats down while the convoys fled the area or surface vessels arrived, the British War Cabinet in 1941 continued to rank the ASW role of Coastal Command far below the role of Bomber Command in razing German cities. Coastal Command therefore lacked adequate numbers of suitable ASW aircraft, centimetric-wavelength ASV radar, and electronic navigation and position-finding systems. The development of stable aerial bombs and depth charges with more powerful Torpex warheads and fuses capable of actuating at shallow (25-foot) depths likewise lagged, as did the powerful Leigh Light, which was imperative for nighttime ASW operations.

•   British management of the naval assets of Canada, a chief ally in the U-boat war, left much to be desired. Where this clumsy growing child with huge new responsibilities required sensitive nourishment, it got too much abuse and contempt. Had the Royal Navy provided the Canadian Navy more vigorous and sympathetic training in convoying and ASW and with improved ships, electronics, and weaponry, sooner rather than later the Canadians in time doubtless could have done as well in the escort role as the British, or perhaps even better. Although it was not so great a factor in this period, American management of Canadian naval assets was no better.

Second, the German side.

•   Hitler erred in his assumption that he could occupy Poland with small or no military intervention by Great Britain and France. He likewise underestimated the willingness of the British to fight for home and hearth, epitomized in the person of Winston Churchill. The Führer's decision to postpone the defeat of Great Britain in favor of the conquest of the Soviet Union was another fatal miscalculation. That huge enterprise diverted men and materials from the construction of U-boats, the one weapons system that had any chance of isolating and defeating Great Britain. The failure to rush production of U-boats to the maximum after Hitler abrogated the Anglo-German naval treaty early in 1939 ceded to Great Britain valuable time in which to ward off a truly decisive U-boat blow and to coax help from the American "Arsenal of Democracy."

•   Hitler erred not only in failing to provide a vigorous increase in U-boat production but also in his insistence on diverting large numbers of U-boats to Norway, the Arctic, and the Mediterranean. At the close of 1941, about one-third (thirty) of the entire combat-ready oceangoing U-boat force was posted in those areas, leaving only sixty-four boats of that type in the Atlantic force, not nearly enough U-boats to wage anything like decisive naval warfare. To no avail, Dönitz rightly argued that the U-boat arm should be maximally deployed against the vital North Atlantic convoy run between Canada and the British Isles, not split up and sent to less important areas or assigned to support land operations or to escort surface ships or to report weather.

•   Hitler and Mussolini erred in the strategic and tactical deployment of the thirty-one oceangoing Italian submarines that had been based at Bordeaux by mid-1941.* As Dönitz suspected, neither the boats nor the crews were qualified for combat in the rough and dangerous waters of the North Atlantic. Doubtless far better successes would have been achieved had the Italian boats been assigned earlier rather than much later to patrol southward to the Azores, Canaries, and Cape Verde islands, and to West African waters. Had they been so deployed, these submarines also would have forced the British to provide substantial ASW forces in the southern area much sooner, further reducing these scarce resources in the North Atlantic area.

---

*   See Appendix 8.

• To avoid another *Lusitania* incident or a similar outrage while he sought to negotiate Great Britain and France out of the war, Hitler initiated U-boat warfare with a set of rules and restrictions so complicated that U-boat skippers had to be issued a special handheld "wheel" device to sort out what could or could not be sunk. These rules substantially reduced the effectiveness of the U-boats, increased the risks that had to be run, and led in part to the high U-boat losses in the first year of the war.

The accidental sinking of *Athenia* by Lemp in *U-30* on the first day of hostilities, rightfully denounced in London as an outrage, made a mockery of Berlin's claims to be fighting a carefully "restricted" U-boat campaign. In the face of the universal perception that Germany had launched barbarous "unrestricted" U-boat warfare, the continuation of these complicated rules and restrictions was, to say the least, an ill-advised course for Hitler to follow, and it gained him absolutely nothing, politically or otherwise.

• Dönitz erred in his insistence that the *Kriegsmarine* stake almost all on the overtouted medium Type VIIC U-boat. Conceived to attack convoys in the Northwest, Western, and Southwestern Approaches in groups or "wolf packs" on relatively brief missions, the VIIC was not suitable for longer-range operations and for hard, fuel-guzzling convoy chases in the central and western North Atlantic without means at hand to provide spare parts and to refuel and replenish torpedo, food, and water supplies. Besides that, the VIIs were much too crowded and cramped for sustained operations and lacked air conditioning for summer months and proper heating for winter months.

In view of the propensity of the high-performance diesel engines to break down under continuous strain, the VIIs would have benefited greatly by the inclusion of a third diesel engine. So fitted, when one engine broke down a Type VIIC could still keep two engines on line and maintain chase speed. The addition of a third diesel engine would have necessitated an increase in the length of the VIIC, and that in turn would have made possible an increase in its external fuel capacity and its top speed by perhaps one or two knots. The added living space inside the pressure hull certainly would have improved habitability.

• Dönitz also erred by greatly overestimating the ability of single U-boats or groups of U-boats to find, shadow, and attack convoys. As the U-boats on the North Atlantic run were forced ever westward to avoid British air and surface escorts and U-boat hunters, the ocean areas to be searched for convoys by eye and passive sonar increased almost exponentially. To overcome this handicap, Dönitz requested—then demanded—large numbers of long-range *Luftwaffe* reconnaissance aircraft specifically to locate convoys. Hitler and Göring assured Dönitz that his requests and demands were to be met, but in fact they were unable to provide anywhere near adequate and competent air reconnaissance at sea. The Condors, which were based in France and Norway in 1941, were too little and too late. Crews were insufficiently trained in navigation and communications.

In the absence of good intelligence on convoy locations, Dönitz was compelled to resort to convoy-hunting "patrol lines," the spacing of the U-boats of a group (or "wolf pack") on a straight line at precise positions about fifteen miles apart. The

PLATE 10

PRINCIPAL NORTH ATLANTIC CARGO CONVOYS INBOUND TO THE BRITISH ISLES 1939–1941

Numbers of Ships Arriving and Losses to Enemy Action[1]

DATES	HALIFAX	SYDNEY, N.S.	FREETOWN, S.L.	TOTALS
1939				
September	8	——	3	11
October	63 (3)	——	90	153
November	159	——	109 (2)	268
December	187	——	81	268
Totals:	417 (3)		283 (2)	700 (5)
1940				
January	173 (1)	——	86	259 (1)
February	162 (2)	——	89	251 (2)
March	264	——	77	341
April	287	——	79	366
May	301	——	73	374
June	336 (7)	——	101	437 (7)
July	355 (5)	——	185	540 (5)
August	489 (17)	40 (3)	206	735 (20)
September	260 (14)	130 (9)	137 (1)	527 (24)
October	319 (20)	155 (25)	152	626 (45)
November	261 (4)	94 (7)	155 (1)	510 (12)
December	218 (15)	89 (2)	161	468 (17)
Totals:	3,425 (85)	508 (46)	1,501 (2)	5,434 (133)
1941				
January	170 (1)	73 (6)	131 (1)	374 (8)
February	199 (6)	108 (5)	149 (2)	456 (13)
March	300 (13)	——	148 (12)	448 (25)
April	307 (15)	——	128	435 (15)
May[2]	347 (13)	——	164 (1)	511 (14)
June	306 (6)	77	82 (10)	465 (16)
July	297	115	56	468
August	471	97	45 (6)	613 (6)
September[3]	275	238 (24)	45 (7)	558 (31)
October	263 (1)	256 (11)	50 (2)	569 (14)
November	218	235 (7)	91	544 (7)
December	207 (1)	213 (3)	62	482 (4)
Totals:	3,360 (56)	1,412 (56)	1,151 (41)	5,923 (153)
Grand Totals:	7,202 (144)	1,920 (102)	2,935 (45)	12,057 (291)[4]

1. Source: The numbers of ships arriving in convoys are derived from British Monthly Anti-Submarine Reports, September 1939 to December 1941, and are probably accurate. The ship loss ( ) figures in those bulletins, compiled from incomplete wartime data, are not accurate. The losses shown here (including escorts) are from Röhwer, *Axis Submarine Successes*. Note well that these figures do not include the considerable independent sailings and losses.

2. Enigma captured from U-110.

3. American escort of North Atlantic convoys began.

4. Ship losses amounted to .02 percent of total.

PLATE 11

ALLIED CONVOYS THAT LOST SIX OR MORE SHIPS

SEPTEMBER 1939–DECEMBER 1941

DATE	CONVOY	SHIPS SUNK	G.R. TONS
9/21/40	Halifax 72	11	72,737
10/16/40	Slow 7	21	79,646
10/19/40	Halifax 79	12	75,063
11/23/40	Slow 11	7	24,601
12/1/40	Halifax 90	10	65,064
1/29/41	Slow 19	6	34,724
2/28/41	Outbound 288	8	42,282
3/17/41	Sierra L. 68	7	38,003
4/2/41	Slow 26	11	53,908
5/7/41	Outbound 318	7	39,255
5/20/41	Halifax 126	9	54,451
6/24/41	Halifax 133	6	38,269
7/27/41	Out-Gib. 69	9	25,300
8/19/41	Out-Gib. 71	10	15,185
9/10/41	Slow 42	19	73,574
9/19/41	Slow 44	7	26,700
9/22/41	Sierra L. 87	7	33,290
9/25/41	Home-Gib. 73	10	25,818
10/15/41	Slow 48	11	53,208
Totals:	19 convoys	187[1]	871,078

1. From inbound convoys, 153 ships; from outbound convoys, 34 ships.

organization and deployment of the U-boats in these search lines and shifting of the lines resulted in heavy radio traffic back and forth, thereby providing the British with a continuous flow of standardized and predictable messages—the necessary grist for the codebreakers' mills. Moreover, the patrol lines were of such great length (165 miles per twelve boats) that it was difficult for the boats most distant from the convoy contact to close in time to attack, especially in daytime when enemy air was present. Hence, in most instances, "convoy battles" consisted of first-night strikes carried out by a few of the boats in the patrol line. The usual depiction of a voracious "pack of wolves" circling and hungrily gnawing at a convoy over a number of days was the product of darkly imaginative propagandists on both sides.

This propaganda has left the impression that the U-boats savaged one merchant-ship convoy after another. This is not true. In the first twenty-eight months of the war, the British sailed about 900 Atlantic convoys. U-boats achieved major victories (six or more confirmed ships sunk) over only nineteen of these convoys.* The vital inbound Atlantic convoys in this period—Britain's lifeline—were com-

* See Plate 11.

prised of a total of 12,057 ships. The U-boats sank only 291 of these vessels.*
Ninety-eight percent of all the ships in these convoys reached the British Isles.

• The German technical branches failed scandalously to provide U-boats
with efficient, safe, and reliable electronics and torpedoes, essential for the success
of World War II submarine warfare. *Kriegsmarine* scientists and engineers egre-
giously neglected radar technology, especially in failing to vigorously pursue
miniaturized centimetric-wavelength radar for U-boats. The early development of
this important detection device by the Germans would have greatly enhanced the
ability of U-boats to find and attack convoys at night and in times of poor or no
visibility, to defend themselves from sudden surprise attacks by radar-fitted enemy
surface and air forces, and to navigate precisely near coastlines. The pursuit of this
electronic technology doubtless would have resulted also in a greater appreciation
at much earlier dates for and knowledge about radar detectors of various wave-
lengths to counter search radar employed by the Allies. The failure of *Kriegsmarine* engineers to test the air and electric torpedoes and pistols more thoroughly in
prewar years needs no further comment, except to say that at the end of 1941 the
torpedoes still had serious defects.

• The Germans not only underestimated the ability of the British to develop
powerful miniaturized radar, but also their ability to DF U-boat radio transmissions with a high degree of accuracy. At the end of 1941, the greatly improved
British land-based HF/DF (Huff Duff) networks provided fairly reliable information on U-boat positions, and a miniaturized HF/DF for surface ships was ready.
The Germans had scant to no HF/DF technology and scoffed at the possibility that
the British systems were effective.

• The Germans consistently underestimated not only the willingness of President Roosevelt and the American government to support the British in various
ways, but also America's ability to produce mind-boggling quantities of ships of
all kinds. Dönitz arrogantly dismissed the colossal American shipbuilding projec-
tions as so much "propaganda" and, at the same time, almost uncritically accepted
U-boat-sinking claims, which in some cases were inflated, intentionally or otherwise, by as much as 100 percent. These judgments greatly distorted the actual
progress of the naval race, exaggerating the successes of U-boats and minimizing
the ability of Great Britain and America to produce shipping. Thus the Germans always thought they were doing infinitely better than was truly the case.

What emerges from this analysis is that, contrary to the general perception at
the close of 1941, German U-boats were nowhere close to isolating and strangling
Great Britain. Although occasionally successful, group or "wolf pack" tactics were
on the whole a failure, and the Type VII as well as the Type IX U-boats were unsuitable for this kind of warfare in the Atlantic. For all the reasons laid out above,
the rate of U-boat nonperformance (no sinkings per patrol) had reached ominously
high levels in all areas, so much so that it is clear that U-boats had lost any
prospect of crushing Great Britain, let alone defeating the formidable new enemy,
the United States.

---

* See Plate 10.

Nonetheless, the myth of U-boat prowess and invincibility had taken firm root in the public mind for the second time in this century. Rightly, Churchill had proclaimed a Battle of the Atlantic to sharply focus the attention of British ASW authorities on the U-boat problem. This battle cry achieved its purpose more rapidly than is generally credited. Therefore, one is still left to puzzle over Churchill's lugubrious postwar assertion that the only thing that really worried him during the war was the U-boat peril.

BOOK TWO

THE U-BOAT WAR AGAINST THE AMERICAS

December 1941–August 1942

SEVEN

JAPAN STRIKES

At the urging of the new and bellicose Prime Minister, Hideki Tojo, on November 5, 1941, the Japanese government resolved to launch war against United States, British, and Dutch forces in the Pacific and Far East. During the ensuing days the Japanese warily and vaguely revealed the decision to Hitler, seeking a written pledge of mutual support—that is, a declaration of war against the United States. Hitler welcomed Japan's decision to launch war, but he haggled over the treaty in an attempt to persuade Japan to launch war against the Soviet Union as well. The Japanese were unwilling to include this in a formal treaty but they left Hitler with the impression that after they had consolidated their Pacific conquests, Germany could count on their support. Meanwhile, Japan would shut off the flow of American (but not Soviet) ships bringing Lend-Lease supplies to the Soviet Union via Vladivostok.

It had always been Hitler's intention to avoid overt war with the United States. In view of his growing military difficulties in the Soviet Union, there was good reason to adhere to that policy. But, as Admiral Raeder—and indirectly, Dönitz—insisted, from a naval point of view the United States was already waging war against Germany by the occupation of Iceland, by escorting North Atlantic convoys, by arming its merchant ships and allowing them to proceed into the war zone, and by supplying Great Britain and the Soviet Union with an immense flow of Lend-Lease war matériel at no cost. The entry of Japan into the war was bound to draw substantial Allied naval and air forces from the Atlantic and the Mediterranean to the Pacific and Asian waters, greatly enhancing the possibilities of decisive Axis maritime victories in the Atlantic and Mediterranean. Hence it was in Germany's best interest to welcome Japan into the war and also to join her arm-in-arm, perhaps even coordinating naval warfare in some areas, such as the Indian Ocean. Moreover, a full partnership would give Germany access to a supply of critical raw materials from the Japanese-occupied territories in Southeast Asia.

There were other considerations. The failure of the German armies to capture Moscow and Leningrad quickly, and to destroy the Soviet armies, had led to uneasiness and doubt in some German quarters. A new fighting partner and a dramatic stroke—such as a ringing declaration of war against the United States—was almost certain to raise spirits and renew energies. The *possibility* of a Japanese attack on the Soviet Union in the Far East might forestall the transfer of Soviet troops from that region to face the Germans outside Moscow and elsewhere, increasing the chance of a German victory in the Soviet Union when the warm weather returned in the spring.

So it was decided: When Japan launched war against the United States, Germany—and Italy—were to declare war in partnership. Perhaps to justify this fateful decision, which many in his inner circle opposed, Hitler commenced in private an unprecedented outpouring of bile and venom about President Roosevelt and a sinister circle of American Jews who held him captive.

Although the Japanese professed friendship and complete trust, they artfully concealed from Hitler their plan for launching the war. It was ambitious. In the opening phase, Japanese forces were to strike nearly simultaneously the United States Pacific Fleet at Pearl Harbor, the United States Asiatic Fleet and Army Air Forces at Manila, and the British fleet at Singapore (mainly the battleship *Prince of Wales* and the battle cruiser *Repulse*), and capture the American islands of Wake and Guam, the British islands of Tarawa and Maiken, and the British colony at Hong Kong. In the second phase, to follow immediately, Japanese forces were to invade and capture the Philippines, Malaya, Borneo, Sumatra, Java, Burma, and other British and Dutch possessions in Southeast Asia.

The Japanese attempted to conceal their preparations for war from Washington by pretending to carry on diplomatic negotiations through the ambassador, Admiral Kichisaburo Nomura. But Washington was not deceived. It was reading the chief Japanese diplomatic code, Purple, currently and fluently, and was fully alive to the deception and anticipated a Japanese attack at almost any hour. The problem was that the Japanese Imperial Navy had recently made a change in its main operational code (JN-25), which American codebreakers had not yet cracked. As a result, they had lost track of the Japanese battle fleet and therefore did not know in which direction the Japanese intended to strike. The prevailing guess was that the Japanese were to go south—perhaps to Malaya. The least likely target on nearly everyone's list was Pearl Harbor.

The Commander in Chief of the Japanese fleet, Admiral Isoroku Yamamoto, did not favor war. He had traveled abroad often and had the greatest respect for the industrial potential of the United States. He actively lobbied against war behind the scenes, stating that "[i]f I am told to fight regardless of the consequences, I shall run wild for the first six months or a year, but I have utterly no confidence for the second or third year." His arguments carried little weight with Tojo and other hawks, who believed that in view of its naval commitments to the Atlantic, the United States might be reluctant to fight in the far Pacific or, if it did, it would probably soon tire of the fight and enter into negotiations. If it turned out so, one year of naval wild-running was all Tojo needed.

Confronting the growing possibility of war with the United States, Yamamoto had discarded the old Japanese plan of meeting the American fleet in a climactic battle in Far Eastern waters. In its place, he designed a surprise attack on the Pacific Fleet at Pearl Harbor, to be carried out by a force of aircraft carriers and supporting vessels. Throughout most of 1941 the naval elements concerned had relentlessly rehearsed various aspects of the plan in utmost secrecy. Meanwhile, Japanese engineers produced special aerial torpedoes (with wooden fins) that would work in the shallow waters (forty feet) of the Pearl Harbor anchorage, and huge aerial bombs, fashioned from 16" armor-piercing battleship gun shells.

After assembling in secrecy at a remote island, Etorofu, in the Kuriles, the Japanese strike force (*Kido Butai*) sailed on November 26. Commanded by Admiral Chuichi Nagumo, it was composed of six fleet carriers, two battleships, two heavy cruisers, three escorting submarines, and a long train of supply ships.* To avoid being seen by commercial shipping, the force traveled far to the north and hugged unfavorable weather fronts. All ships maintained absolute radio silence. The force was preceded by twenty-five large Japanese fleet submarines, which took preassigned patrol stations in Hawaiian waters. Five of the fleet submarines carried 78-foot two-man "midget" submarines, which were to sneak into the Pearl Harbor anchorage when the boom was open and attack capital ships.

On Sunday, December 7, 1941, the *Kido Butai* launched about 350 aircraft at Pearl Harbor. Striking with complete surprise, the Japanese airmen sank four battleships (*Arizona, California, Oklahoma, West Virginia*), an old target ship (*Utah*), and a minelayer (*Oglala*). They damaged four other battleships (*Maryland, Nevada, Pennsylvania, Tennessee*), three light cruisers (*Raleigh, Honolulu, Helena*), a seaplane tender (*Curtiss*), three destroyers (*Cassin, Shaw, Downes*), and a repair ship (*Vestal*).† Two hundred and nineteen American aircraft were destroyed. Fortunately for the Americans, two carriers of the Pacific Fleet, *Lexington* and *Enterprise,* were at sea with their supporting ships and escaped damage, and a third carrier, *Saratoga,* was in California. Inexplicably, Nagumo failed to attack the shore-based fleet oil-storage tanks and the repair shops, thereby making it possible for the surviving elements of the fleet, including the three carriers, to continue basing in Pearl Harbor. The Japanese fleet submarines had no luck; all five midget submarines foundered or were sunk. Only one of the ten crewmen survived.

---

  * The fleet carriers: *Akagi, Kaga, Soryu, Hiryu, Zuikaku, Shokaku.* The battleships: *Hiei, Kirishima.* The heavy cruisers: *Tone, Chikuma.*

  † Three of the four battleships that sank were salvaged; *Arizona* was not. *Oklahoma* did not return to service, but *California* and *West Virginia* eventually did. The four damaged battleships were put back in service within several months.

Japanese aircraft hit and destroyed only one of the approximately forty American fleet submarines based in Pearl Harbor and Manila. Within mere hours of the attack on Pearl Harbor, Washington directed the others, as well as the six old *S* boats in Manila, to "wage unrestricted submarine warfare against Japan." Most left on independent patrols within a few days. Having trained for years to operate with the battle fleet, American submarine force commanders and skippers had never even considered, let alone planned for, an unrestricted war against Japanese merchant shipping, and many found it difficult to adjust to this new role. Furthermore, it gradually became apparent that there were drastic defects in the torpedoes. Like the German torpedoes, the American torpedoes ran much too deep and there were flaws in the magnetic and contact pistols. The upshot was that American submariners achieved little in the first few months of the war in the Pacific.*

The sneak attack of the *Kido Butai* on Pearl Harbor was a classic, well-executed tactical operation, indisputably a great naval victory. As intended, it crippled the Pacific Fleet, giving Japan virtually a free hand to carry out the planned conquests in Southeast Asia. And yet, strategically it may have been a mistake. The treacherous nature of the attack, which cost the lives of 2,403 American military personnel—and wounded 1,178—outraged Americans and generated hatred toward the Japanese to a degree that nullified any possibility that the Americans would ever lose interest in the Pacific war and negotiate a settlement. As the historian Ronald H. Spector put it, "Had [Japan] avoided American possessions and concentrated on the British and the Dutch, Roosevelt would have found it awkward trying to win support for a war in defense of distant European colonies in Asia, rather than leading a righteous crusade to avenge Pearl Harbor."

The loss of American warships at Pearl Harbor and the extent of the Japanese threat in the Pacific necessitated the rapid transfer of some warships from the Atlantic Fleet to the Pacific Fleet. First to shift was Task Force 17, comprised of the aircraft carrier *Yorktown* and two light cruisers (*Richmond, Trenton*), which left the Panama Canal Zone December 22. Four modern (1939–1940) destroyers, *Hughes, Russell, Sims,* and *Walke,* provided escort. Contrary to published statements implying that upwards of twenty-four American destroyers left the Atlantic Fleet for the Pacific Fleet in December 1941,† these were the only destroyers to make the shift that month.

Washington alerted other warships of the Atlantic Fleet to prepare for transfer to the Pacific Fleet in early January 1942. Chief among these were the older battleships *Idaho, Mississippi,* and *New Mexico,* which had been in the Atlantic only about six months. These were to be escorted by five modern (1939–1940) destroy-

---

* For complete details, see my *Silent Victory: The U.S. Submarine War Against Japan* (1975).

† See Gannon, *Operation Drumbeat,* p. 177. He wrote that "two squadrons of the newest, long-legged destroyers had been removed to the Pacific Theater in late December." This incorrect assertion is apparently derived from an error in the U.S. Navy's Administrative History of World War II, No. 138 (Atlantic Fleet), p. 261: "Two squadrons of the best and newest destroyers were transferred to the Pacific in late December, 1941. . . ." Normally, a destroyer squadron was composed of twelve vessels. Only Squadron 2, composed of two understrength *divisions* (3 and 4), transferred to the Pacific at this time. (For more detail, see Appendix 12.)

ers of the Atlantic Fleet: *Anderson, Hammann, Morris, Mustin,* and *O'Brien.* All these ships sailed to the Pacific in early January, as did two other modern (1938) destroyers, *Sampson* and *Warrington.* Total destroyers transferred to the Pacific in December and January: eleven, nine from Squadron 2 and two from Squadron 9.

These transfers left the Atlantic Fleet with nine capital ships: three old battleships useful only for convoy escort (*Arkansas, New York, Texas*), two new battleships in extended workup (*North Carolina, Washington*), and four carriers (*Hornet,* preparing to leave for the Pacific, *Ranger, Wasp,* and the "jeep" *Long Island*). Fourteen cruisers (five heavy; nine light) in various states of readiness made up the rest of the heavy striking power of the Atlantic Fleet, plus, of course, the destroyers, of which more later.

Lastly, Washington canceled the transfer to Argentia, Newfoundland, of a reinforced squadron of about eighteen *S*-class submarines and the new tender *Griffin.* Intended originally to augment Admiral Bristol's Support Force (a dubious assignment), two divisions comprising twelve boats and *Griffin* went to the Pacific instead. The six boats of the other division were loaned to the Royal Navy.*

The Japanese war plan unfolded with astonishing efficiency and speed. Basing on the island of Formosa, Japanese aircraft quickly destroyed American air power in the Philippines and drove out the Asiatic Fleet, setting the stage for an invasion of Luzon. On December 10, Japanese aircraft from Indochina bombed and sank the *Prince of Wales* and *Repulse* at sea, with the loss of 840 sailors out of 3,761. ("In all the war," Churchill wrote, "I never received a more direct shock."†) The Pacific islands of Wake, Guam, Tarawa, and Maiken and the British colony of Hong Kong fell. Japanese forces invaded Malaya and other forces gathered to strike at Borneo, Sumatra, and Java.

During the final days before the attack on Pearl Harbor, while they were still frantically seeking Hitler's signature on the treaty of partnership, the Japanese had continued to conceal their war plans, telling Hitler only that "war may come quicker than anyone dreams." Thus the attack on Pearl Harbor came as a complete shock to Hitler. Viewing himself as the senior partner in the Axis, he was embarrassed and angry that the Japanese had not taken him into their confidence—had, in fact, deceived him to a certain extent—and had not sought his advice or approval, or even assistance, as did the Italians. It was not only a personal slap in the face, but also a signal that Tokyo intended to fight its war as it saw fit and in its own best interest, without consultation with Berlin and Rome.

Nonetheless, Hitler swallowed his pride and fulfilled his pledge to the Japan-

---

* *S-1, S-21, S-22, S-24, S-25,* and *S-29.* The *S-25,* renamed *Jastrazab,* and manned by a Polish crew, was accidentally sunk off Norway by Allied forces on May 5, 1942.

† Including the work of the Italian frogmen in Alexandria harbor on December 19 and the Mediterranean-based U-boats, in a period of thirty-seven days the Royal Navy incurred its own "Pearl Harbor": the carrier *Ark Royal,* the battleships *Prince of Wales* and *Barham,* the battle cruiser *Repulse,* the "jeep" carrier *Audacity,* and the light cruisers *Dunedin, Neptune,* and *Galatea* sunk; the battleships *Valiant* and *Queen Elizabeth* severely damaged.

ese. He summoned his puppet legislators to the *Reichstag* on December 11 and declared war on the United States, publicly spewing bile at Roosevelt. Later that same day, Hitler, Mussolini, and Tojo jointly vowed not to lay down arms until the United States and Great Britain were crushed—and not to make a separate peace. In response, Roosevelt asked the Congress to declare war on Germany. But there were no pronouncements from Moscow; Japan and the Soviet Union remained wary nonbelligerents.

For Churchill, the Japanese attack on Pearl Harbor and Hitler's declaration of war on the United States was a mixed blessing. On the one hand, America's full-scale entry into the war assured eventual victory ("So we had won after all," he wrote). On the other hand, American fury at the Japanese raised the disturbing possibility that the Americans might reverse the agreed-upon Anglo-American strategic war plan and go after Japan first, Germany and Italy second. If so, it would prolong British losses in men and resources on far-flung battlefields and oceans, and bring deprivation, discomfort, and danger at home.

To make sure that the Americans stuck to the plan, Churchill hurried to Washington for a second round of face-to-face talks with Roosevelt. He and a large party of senior military advisers left the Firth of Clyde on December 12 on the new battleship *Duke of York*. Encountering fierce North Atlantic storms, the battleship (on its shakedown cruise) and its escorts turned south and ran through the Bay of Biscay, boldly passing within one hundred miles of Brest and crossing what Churchill described as the "stream" of U-boats entering and leaving French bases. Aware of U-boat positions from decrypted naval Enigma, the Admiralty guided the *Duke of York* through the Bay of Biscay on evasive courses. Crossing the middle Atlantic, she arrived in Norfolk, Virginia, without incident on December 22. The next day Roosevelt and Churchill and their respective military chiefs commenced a series of meetings on global strategy known as the Arcadia Conference.

A New War

When Hitler declared war against the United States, the bulk of the German submarine force was committed, directly or indirectly, to the support of Axis forces in North Africa, a task for which it was not suited and which Dönitz believed to be a wasteful diversion from the "decisive" task of shutting off the flow of imports to Great Britain in the North Atlantic.

Kerneval rejoiced over the formal declaration of war with the United States. It provided Dönitz with the strongest possible arguments for a curtailment of the dangerous and unremunerative Mediterranean/Gibraltar operations and a resumption of full-scale U-boat war in the North Atlantic without restrictions. It offered the possibility of launching a devastating attack on Allied shipping in American waters before the Americans could organize convoys or effective ASW forces, perhaps decisively disrupting the flow of war materials from the Arsenal of Democracy on its very doorstep.

The German problem—the all too familiar problem—was the acute shortage of

U-boats. Owing to battle losses and retirements, diversions to the Arctic and the Mediterranean, and the mounting delays in new production and workups, on January 1, 1942, the Atlantic U-boat force numbered only sixty-four oceangoing U-boats: nineteen Type IXs; forty-four Type VIIs; and *U-A.**

The Atlantic U-boat force was not only short of boats but also relatively green. Forty-four of the sixty-four boats (69 percent) had been in the Atlantic six months or less. Fourteen of the forty-four recent arrivals (32 percent) had only just joined the force in December 1941. Six of the Type VIIs were transfers from the Arctic force and had yet to make a full war patrol in the Atlantic.

Many authors have described a "great growth" of the U-boat peril in 1942, often put at an increase of "twenty boats per month." If this figure is meant to describe newly commissioned attack boats, it is only a slight exaggeration. In the first five months of 1942, the Germans commissioned seventy-eight new attack boats, a monthly average of 15.6. In the remaining seven months of 1942, when new commissionings actually reached and slightly exceeded twenty boats per month, the total figure was 148, or a monthly average of 21.1. For the entire year the figure was 226, a monthly average of 18.8 boats.

That, however, is merely one part of the story. Some of these new attack boats were assigned to the Submarine School or to R&D projects and never reached a war front. A few were lost to mines or in accidents in the Baltic. Owing to delays in workup or to commissioning dates late in 1942, about half of the 226 new boats commissioned in 1942 did not reach war fronts until 1943. About fifty of these were lost on first patrols from Germany or Norway, most of them having achieved nothing noteworthy, and, of course, they were only a brief "paper" addition to the war-front flotillas.

The only meaningful figure in this welter of numbers is the actual "growth" of the Atlantic U-boat force. This was nowhere near the oft-implied "twenty boats per month." Owing to the delays in the Baltic, diversions to the Arctic and the Mediterranean, and combat losses, in the first six months of 1942 the Atlantic U-boat force grew by only thirty-four attack boats, or an average of 5.6 per month. Doubtless by coincidence, the growth was divided exactly between Type VIIs and Type IXs:

	1/1	2/1	3/1	4/1	5/1	6/1	7/1	Growth
VIIs	43	49	47	48	51	52	60	+17
IXs	20	23	29	30	33	35	37	+17
Totals	63	72	76	78	84	87	97	+34

---

* Of the 64 boats of the Atlantic force, fourteen (22 percent) were not combat-ready or available. The VIICs *U-73, U-561*, and *U-572* were ordered to the Mediterranean in January to replace losses. The ex-Turk *U-A* was undergoing conversion to a provisional U-tanker. The IX *U-43*, the VIIs *U-94, U-201, U-563*, and *U-101* were homebound to or in Germany for overhaul, battle-damage repairs, or retirement. The Arctic transfer *U-752* was in Kiel for overhaul before going to the Atlantic. Four other VIIs were undergoing battle-damage repairs in French bases: *U-71, U-202, U-558*, and *U-569*.

Owing to the vast distances from France to North America—3,000 miles from Lorient to New York—only the twenty Type IXs were suitable craft for the impending campaign in those waters. One of the twenty was the older *U-43* and eight were Type IXBs with a range of only 8,700 miles at 12 knots. The other eleven were Type IXCs with a range of 11,000 miles at 12 knots.

At the time Berlin authorized the U-boat attack on North America, eight of the twenty Type IXs were not available for that purpose. The weary IX *U-43* was under orders to return to Germany for a prolonged overhaul. Four IXs (*U-68, U-124, U-126, U-129*) were returning from patrols to the South Atlantic and required long overhauls. Three IXs (*U-67, U-107, U-108*) were committed to the arduous battle with convoy Homebound Gibraltar 76 and had to return first to France to replenish fuel and torpedoes and give the crews some rest.

Only six Type IXs could be made ready for launching the U-boat war in American waters. Contrary to some published accounts, Dönitz did not handpick U-boat "aces" for the initial attack. He made do with six Type IX boats and skippers at hand in France. These were:

- Richard Zapp in the IXC *U-66*. Zapp had arrived in the Atlantic in May 1941 and had made three patrols: one in the North Atlantic, cut short by a mechanical breakdown, and two long patrols to the South Atlantic, during which he had sunk five ships.

- Heinrich Bleichrodt in the IXB *U-109*. Bleichrodt had won a *Ritterkreuz* in two patrols on the famous *U-48* in the fall of 1940, sinking fourteen and a half ships. Subsequently he had commissioned the Type IX *U-67*, which was temporarily diverted to sonar R&D. Assigned to command *U-109* in June 1941, Bleichrodt had made two Atlantic patrols, both bedeviled by mechanical problems, and had concluded the second on escort duty. He had sunk no ships on *U-67* or *U-109*.

- Reinhard Hardegen in the IXB *U-123*. The boat had come to the Atlantic in September 1940 commanded by Karl-Heinz Moehle, who won a *Ritterkreuz*. Since taking command in May 1941, Hardegen had made two patrols, one to Freetown, one to Newfoundland. He had sunk one confirmed ship on the duck *U-147* and five confirmed ships on *U-123*—none on his second patrol in *U-123*.

- Ulrich Folkers in the IXC *U-125*. The boat had reached the Atlantic in July 1941, under command of *Ritterkreuz* holder Günter Kuhnke, who took her on one luckless patrol to the South Atlantic. Promoted to command *U-125* on December 15, 1941, Folkers had not yet made a patrol or sunk a ship as skipper.

- Ernst Kals in the IXC *U-130*. Sailing from Kiel on his first patrol, Kals had run into the eastbound Slow Convoy 57 on December 10. Attacking alone, he had fired six torpedoes and sunk three freighters for 15,000 tons. Recalled from patrol to prep for the attack on America, he reached Lorient on December 16, after merely seventeen days at sea.

- Jürgen von Rosenstiel in the IXC/40 *U-502*. The boat had made one Atlantic patrol, September 29 to November 9, during which von Rosenstiel sank no ships but severely damaged the whale-factory ship *Svend Foyn*.

These six Type IXs comprised the first wave. A second wave of Type IXs sailed to United States waters about two weeks after the first. A third wave of Type IXs put out shortly after the second, to patrol the West Indies and the Caribbean Sea. Other IXs followed.

Although the first boats to American waters enjoyed the advantages of surprise and weak ASW forces, patrols to that area were not without great dangers and difficulties. Apart from the vast distances to and from the areas, the chief drawback was the extremely shallow water along much of the United States East Coast, the "continental shelf," which in the New York area extends seaward nearly 100 miles. To avoid any possibility of being trapped in these very shallow waters by ASW forces, the big clumsy IXs were advised to attack only at night, leaving time to run out to the 200-meter curve (656 feet of water) before daylight, a fuel-wasting but prudent procedure. Since it was likely that the Americans would divert all coastal shipping to these shallow waters and patrol them with aircraft, and possibly order shipping to put into the many convenient ports along the East Coast at night, the succeeding waves of U-boats, lacking the element of surprise, might face even greater difficulties.

There was one very promising spot in this otherwise hostile subsurface geography: the Outer Banks of North Carolina, whose chief feature was Cape Hatteras. At that protrusion, the continental shelf is less than thirty miles wide, merely a two-hour run to deep water at full speed on the surface. Hence, if shipping hugged the coast, as might be expected, to take advantage of air cover, Cape Hatteras offered the possibility of dense traffic with easy access to a deep-water sanctuary and probably lightships and lighthouses to provide precise navigation.

Farther to the south, off the coast of Florida, the subsurface geography was likewise favorable. From Palm Beach south to Miami the continental shelf extends seaward only about ten miles. However, the Florida coastline is a long way from Lorient and the waters are highly phosphorescent. A Type IX patrolling those waters could stay only a short time and ran the danger of its glittering wake being spotted by aircraft at nighttime.

To add physical and psychological punch to the assault on North America, Dönitz suggested that a group of Type VIIs should patrol Canadian waters near Halifax, Nova Scotia, and St. John's, Newfoundland. Apart from ships these boats might sink, their mere appearance would hold in place Allied escorts and ASW forces on the North Atlantic run and in Canadian waters, which otherwise might be transferred to United States waters. It was even possible that this group of U-boats might force the Allies to abort eastbound convoys, just as they had aborted the besieged Slow Convoy 52 in early November. If so, some ships taking supplies to the Soviet Union via Murmansk might be delayed or might not arrive at all, a setback for the Red Army at a crucial time.

Not everyone at Kerneval or the OKM approved of the commitment of the Type VIIs to Canadian waters. The weather in the North Atlantic—and the Newfoundland area—was certain to be hideous and radio-communications poor. The Type VIIs could barely reach Newfoundland in good weather at one-engine speed with enough fuel left to make a productive patrol. Under the best of circumstances, at one-engine speed, it would take each boat about two and a half weeks to reach the area and two and a half weeks to return, leaving only fuel and food enough for about ten days of patrolling in Canadian waters, and even less if a protracted convoy chase became necessary. If they encountered stormy seas en route to Canada, further delays could be expected, drastically curtailing the time available for covering patrol zones. Moreover, the continental shelf seaward of Newfoundland and Nova Scotia was no less shallow and wide than that in United States waters. The Grand Banks, with an average depth of about 250 feet, extends about 200 miles to the east of Newfoundland.

Besides that, the critics argued, was it not wiser to use the VIIs to continue the U-boat war against North Atlantic convoys closer to home? Owing to the diversion of boats to the Mediterranean (and to British evasion tactics, based on Enigma), the North Atlantic convoys had scarcely been hit in the fall of 1941. Thousands of ships loaded with weaponry, oil, and food had reached Iceland and the British Isles unmolested, some proceeding onward to Murmansk. Operating much closer to home bases, the VIIs could almost certainly be employed more efficiently and with less physical and psychological strain on the crews against these convoys.

Dönitz prevailed. The Type VIIs were to augment the Type IXs in American waters, regardless of risks and inefficiencies. By ingenious use of some of the ballast and fresh-water tankage, the VIIs could extend their range by about 1,000 miles, gaining a little more mobility in Canadian waters. The VIIs attempting to patrol the more distant hunting grounds off Cape Hatteras would have no mobility. To conserve fuel, they would have to lie doggo on the bottom most of the daylight hours and hope shipping came their way.

The upshot was that ten Type VIIs comprising a first wave were to sail to Canadian waters in December. Two were commanded by *Ritterkreuz* holders: Rolf Mützelburg in *U-203* and Erich Topp in *U-552*. However, five of the ten were new boats sailing from Germany on first patrols.* Other waves of VIIs were to follow.

On December 17, Dönitz summoned to Kerneval the six skippers of the Type IXs of the first wave, which bore the code name *Paukenschlag* (Drumbeat). It was a new war, a new opportunity to strike an unwary and untested opponent a heavy blow. In view of the depressing failures of the *Wehrmacht* in the Soviet Union and North Africa, a dramatic U-boat victory in American waters would help lift morale in Germany and rekindle Hitler's and the OKM's support for the U-boat arm, which had achieved so little in the Atlantic in the second half of 1941.†

Tactically, Drumbeat was to be a replication of the opening U-boat campaign of September 1939. The boats were to operate not in groups, or wolf packs, but in-

---

    * See Appendix 4.

    † Perhaps to counteract the U-boat failures and lift morale, at this time five skippers received high honors: Otto Kretschmer, in a British POW camp, was awarded the coveted Crossed Swords to his *Ritterkreuz;* Reinhard Suhren in *U-564,* who had won a *Ritterkreuz* as first watch officer on the famous *U-48,* was awarded Oak Leaves to his *Ritterkreuz,* as was Heinrich Lehmann-Willenbrock in *U-96.* Eitel-Friedrich Kentrat in *U-74* and Robert Gysae in *U-98* received the *Ritterkreuz.* As skipper of

dependently over a wide area, striking simultaneously on a signal from Kerneval. As in 1939, the aim was to cause the greatest possible physical and psychological jolts. The *Ritterkreuz* holder Heinrich Bleichrodt in *U-109* and the inexperienced Ernst Kals in the new *U-130* were to patrol in the Newfoundland–Nova Scotia area, backing up the ten Type VIIs. Richard Zapp in *U-66*, Reinhard Hardegen in *U-123*, Ulrich Folkers in *U-125*, and Jürgen von Rosenstiel in *U-502* were to patrol American waters between New York and Cape Hatteras. As in 1939, the skippers were to give priority to largest possible targets—preferably loaded tankers—which were sailing independently. Escorted convoys were to be avoided. To achieve maximum impact, Dönitz suggested that the skippers attempt to sink ships with two-fan shots and authorized the use of deck guns when the conditions for such action were safe.

Folkers in *U-125* and von Rosenstiel in *U-502* sailed for the United States on December 18. Outbound from the Bay of Biscay, Folkers in *U-125* encountered the besieged Gibraltar 76, but when he reported the convoy, Kerneval told him to avoid the battle and continue to America. Von Rosenstiel in *U-502* developed a heavy oil leak which left a telltale trace on the surface of the water, and he aborted and returned to Lorient on December 22. Hardegen in *U-123* sailed December 22. Zapp in *U-66* sailed on Christmas Day. Bleichrodt in *U-109* and Kals in *U-130*, who were Canada-bound, sailed on December 27, by which time all ten Type VIIs assigned to patrol to Canada were at sea. Total force of the first wave: fifteen boats, of which three Type IXs, *U-66*, *U-123*, and *U-125*, were to attack shipping in United States waters.

Some historians have asserted that British codebreakers detected the sailings of these boats and that London flashed quite specific warnings to Washington and Ottawa, which were largely ignored. These assertions are only partly true.

Based on daily information supplied by Rodger Winn in the Admiralty's U-boat Tracking Room, the naval staff in Washington issued daily U-boat position reports to the Commander in Chief, Atlantic Fleet. The reports were not very helpful. Almost all contained caveats and disclaimers:

December 24: General situation obscure and good information lacking.
December 25: Situation vague and no indicated activity in North Atlantic.
December 26: Sub situation still obscure. No indications of any great activity in North Atlantic but at least two subs are probably west of 40 degrees west. . . .
December 27: Situation in Western Atlantic is vague and obscure. There are possibly 2 or 3 west of 40 degrees west, present position unknown.

U-564, Suhren had sunk eight confirmed ships for 27,136 tons and shared credit for two other sinkings. Lehmann-Willenbrock in *U-96*, the leading ace in tonnage sunk still in active combat, had sunk a total of 18½ confirmed ships for 143,604 tons. Kentrat in *U-74* (then in the Mediterranean) had sunk five confirmed ships for 27,561 tons. Gysae in *U-98* had sunk nine confirmed ships for 46,727 tons.

In his weekly summary of December 29 for the Admiralty, Rodger Winn wrote that "There are indications of an inconclusive character that several U-boats may be moving to the Western Atlantic, possibly to operate in the Caribbean or off Halifax." There was no suggestion that any U-boat might operate off the United States East Coast.

These vague reports from London came intermingled with word of one horrific disaster after the other in the Pacific and Far East. Besides these setbacks, about ten Japanese submarines, operating close off the coasts of California and Oregon in December, sank the American tankers *Emidio* and *Montebello,* damaged five other American tankers, and damaged two American freighters. They also shelled an oil field near Santa Barbara, intensifying rumors that the Japanese were on the point of invading California.*

THE "NORWAY PARANOIA"

While the fifteen group Drumbeat boats were slowly plowing westward, the British mounted another surprise commando raid on Norway. Perhaps conceived principally to capture a four-rotor Enigma or Enigma keys and other material, the raid called for a two-pronged assault on December 26–27: a main thrust in Vest Fjord, leading into Narvik, and a secondary thrust much farther south at the island of Vaagsö in Nord Fjord near Alesund. Owing to the breakdown—and abort—of one troopship, the main assault on Vest Fjord was less than satisfactory. However, the secondary assault on Vaagsö was successful. In addition to operations ashore, British naval forces (the cruiser *Kenya,* four destroyers) sank or captured five German merchant ships, two trawlers, and a tugboat. The Admiralty has revealed that the raids netted "cryptoanalytic materials." The OKM diarist logged that a shore-based naval communications facility at Maaloe (in Nord Fjord) had been destroyed with no survivors, and that "the whereabouts of secret documents is unknown."

Amounting to no more than a pinprick, these raids resulted in profound consequences for the *Kriegsmarine* and the U-boat arm. In a first, small reaction, the OKM temporarily diverted five new Type VII boats sailing from Germany to Nord Fjord to interdict British naval forces. When informed of this, Dönitz was dismayed. He protested to the OKM that all five boats were designated for the second wave to American waters; the diversion to Norway was a useless waste of time and fuel, as well as a high-risk assignment for new crews merely a few days out from Kiel on first patrols. Moreover, he curtly refused a further OKM suggestion that nine boats be permanently assigned to the west coast of Norway to protect against further Allied attacks.

The British raids coincided with a flood of rumors reaching Berlin from vari-

---

* According to the information available up to 1996, there was no coordination between the Japanese submarine assault off the West Coast and the German U-boat assault off the East Coast. Both assaults apparently evolved independently. By pure coincidence, the assaults were mutually supporting. For example, the Japanese submarine attacks held ASW aircraft on the West Coast for weeks and compelled Pacific forces to initiate convoying, heavily escorted by Pacific Fleet destroyers.

ous sources, forecasting a full-scale Allied invasion of northern Norway. The supposed invasion was to be coordinated with a Soviet attack westward through Finland, possibly abetted by the Swedes. If the attacks developed as rumored, Germany was to be flanked on the north, cut off from vital Swedish iron ore and nickel, and vulnerable to Scandinavian-based Allied air and naval forces attacking over and across the Baltic.

Predisposed to believe the rumors, Hitler summoned Admiral Raeder to *Wolfsschanze* on December 29. "If the British go about things properly," Hitler fumed, according to the stenographer, "they will attack northern Norway at several points." This, Hitler declared, "might be of decisive importance for the outcome of the war." Therefore, he continued, the *Kriegsmarine* must use "all its forces for the defense of Norway." By that, Hitler meant *Bismarck*'s sister ship, the super battleship *Tirpitz* (then in home waters), the battle cruisers *Gneisenau* and *Scharnhorst* (in Brest, France), the "pocket" battleship *Admiral Scheer* (in home waters), and the heavy cruisers *Prinz Eugen* (in France) and *Hipper* (in home waters).

Raeder demurred. He did not believe the British raids presaged a major invasion, nor did he credit the rumors of a Soviet thrust through Finland and Sweden. By keeping *Gneisenau* and *Scharnhorst* and *Prinz Eugen* in France, the Germans would compel the British to retain a sizeable counterforce in home waters that might be used elsewhere—the Mediterranean, for example. Hence the presence of those big ships in France indirectly helped Rommel. Moreover, the ships had been in French ports so long and had been so denuded of experienced personnel that all three would require weeks of workup before they were ready for the combat they were sure to face in a dash to Norway.

Hitler flew into a rage. Perhaps influenced by the destruction at Pearl Harbor and the nearly simultaneous loss of the *Prince of Wales* and *Repulse* in the Far East, he denounced the value of battleships in the air age.* He concluded the meeting by directing Raeder to be ready to carry out his orders on his signal. *Tirpitz* was to move to Trondheim (as already scheduled) within three weeks. *Gneisenau* and *Scharnhorst* and *Prinz Eugen* were to be brought home as soon as possible—and at any risk—via the English Channel, and thence sail to Norway together with *Admiral Scheer* and *Hipper.* Appropriate air and surface and U-boat escorts were to be provided for all big-ship movements.

There was no detailed discussion of deploying U-boats for the defense of Norway. At that time four Type VII boats had been assigned to Arctic patrols to attack the Murmansk convoys,† but the OKM had concurred in Dönitz's refusal to pro-

---

* And foolishly agreed with Raeder's proposal that construction of Germany's single aircraft carrier, *Graf Zeppelin,* for which no aircraft had yet been developed, be vigorously pursued, even though there was an acute shortage of high-grade steel and shipyard workers for the U-boat production lines.

† Rudolf Schendel in *U-134,* Burkhard Hackländer in *U-454,* Joachim Deecke in *U-584,* and Bernhard Lohse in *U-585,* based in Kirkenes on the Barents Sea in extreme northern Norway. En route to Kirkenes, Schendel in *U-134* by mistake attacked and sank the 2,200-ton German freighter *Steinbek* off Tana Fjord, killing twelve men. Uninformed of German ship traffic, and defended by Dönitz, Schendel was held blameless.

vide large numbers of boats for the defense of Norway. However, Hitler had insisted that the *Kriegsmarine* use "all its forces" for the defense of Norway. The OKM interpreted this to mean every U-boat except those in the Mediterranean assisting Rommel, but deferred such a drastic U-boat redeployment pending a thorough study of the Norway situation and more specific instructions from Hitler.

Thus the opening U-boat campaign in North American waters proceeded on uncertain grounds. Should what became known as Hitler's "Norway paranoia" intensify, there was every possibility that the fifteen boats of the first wave would be recalled to thwart the supposed Allied invasion of Norway and that subsequent waves to the Americas would be canceled for the same reason. A dramatic U-boat strike was therefore absolutely essential to avoid what Dönitz viewed as another useless diversion of the U-boat force.

"ALL WE NEED IS SHIPS"

When the Arcadia Conference convened in Washington on December 23, there was a new face in the senior American group: Admiral Ernest J. King, age sixty-three, former commander of the Atlantic Fleet. In the aftermath of Pearl Harbor, Roosevelt had appointed King (effective December 30) to the newly recreated post of Commander in Chief, U.S. Fleet, a position comparable to that of the Royal Navy's First Sea Lord. King exercised operational and administrative control of the Atlantic Fleet, commanded by his successor, Royal E. Ingersoll; the Pacific Fleet, commanded by Chester W. Nimitz, replacing Husband E. Kimmel; the Asiatic Fleet, commanded by Thomas C. Hart; and the United States Coast Guard, which President Roosevelt had transferred from the Department of the Treasury to the Navy by executive order on November 1, 1941. For the time being, Admiral Harold R. Stark retained the title of Chief of Naval Operations, but his days in Washington were numbered and his responsibilities were limited to administrative matters and "long-term planning."

King was a brilliant, salty fighter, so flinty and tough, the story went, that he "shaved with a blow torch." In his forty-year professional career he had served on surface ships and submarines, had qualified as a naval pilot, and had been a pioneer in naval aviation and carrier operations. No one knew the strengths and weaknesses of the Navy—and its senior officer corps—better. No one was more offensive-minded or more eager to avenge the treachery of Pearl Harbor, which had left the Navy in shock and despair. Although King was approaching retirement age, Secretary of the Navy Frank Knox had recommended him to Roosevelt as the admiral most qualified to shake the Navy out of its post–Pearl Harbor paralysis.

King had only just arrived in Washington. He was still in the process of setting up an office and recruiting a staff. "Nothing was ready," he said later. "I had to start with nothing." However, he had participated in the meetings at the Atlantic Conference in Argentia the previous August and thus he knew most of the American and British luminaries. He said little and the British delegates, including First Sea Lord Dudley Pound, gained the impression that King's mind was focused more on the war in the Pacific than on the war in Europe and the Mediterranean.

This was only partly right. Having just left command of the Atlantic Fleet, King was as acutely aware of naval problems in the Atlantic theater of war as was any British delegate. In particular King, like the British, was deeply concerned about a possible sortie to the Atlantic by the super battleship *Tirpitz,* to be joined by the battle cruisers *Gneisenau* and *Scharnhorst,* the "pocket" battleship *Admiral Scheer,* and the heavy cruisers *Prinz Eugen* from Brest and *Hipper* from the Baltic. An Atlantic raid by those six German big ships would present a daunting challenge to the depleted British Home Fleet and the American Atlantic Fleet and would imperil troop and supply convoys. The danger would be increased if the Vichy French warships in Martinique elected to reinforce the Germans or to sail independently against Allied naval forces or the Panama Canal.

Throughout the Arcadia Conference, a flood of profoundly upsetting bulletins arrived from the Pacific and Far East, announcing one Japanese victory after another. The conferees were thus compelled to spend much time devising emergency measures to help beleaguered Allied forces in that theater. Nonetheless, they hewed to the main purpose, which was to lay out a global strategy for winning the war and to formulate war-production schedules to implement the strategy. All delegates, including most emphatically Admiral King, again affirmed the earlier agreements to crush Germany and Italy first, Japan second, but there was much uncertainty and disagreement over how this was to be done and at what point the Allies were to shift from the defensive to the offensive in the Pacific to minimize the consolidation of Japanese conquests.

Underlying all discussion was a unanimous desire to launch offensive action against Germany and Italy at the earliest possible time. Churchill proposed a plan (Gymnast) for an Allied invasion of French Northwest Africa, designed to trap Rommel and satisfy Soviet demands for a "second front." Still skeptical of Churchill's "Mediterranean strategy," and believing the Allies should strike directly for the German heartland, Army Chief of Staff George C. Marshall counterproposed an Allied invasion of Occupied France (Sledgehammer) in late summer of 1942. Admiral King enthusiastically approved Marshall's early invasion plan, in part because he believed it might result in the evacuation of German U-boat bases in France, forcing the Atlantic U-boats back to more vulnerable and inconvenient bases in Norway and Germany.

Not wishing to delay the commitment of American forces against the Germans a day longer than necessary, Roosevelt overrode Marshall and approved Gymnast, but he also authorized a buildup in the British Isles (Bolero) for Sledgehammer, or its larger alternative, Roundup, to take place in 1943. Others proposed that the Allies seize and fortify islands in the Atlantic off Africa (the Azores, the Canaries, Cape Verdes), but when King pointed out bluntly that "[w]e cannot do *all* these things," the last proposals were tabled.

In the end, the conferees settled on the following major courses of action:

• Support to the fullest extent possible the Soviet Union, which, with the assistance of the bitterly cold winter weather, had repulsed the Germans at the gates of Moscow and Leningrad. The aid for the Soviets was to go the long way via the Cape of Good Hope to the Persian Gulf and also by the shorter route to Murmansk on convoys, sailing from Iceland and fully supported by Allied naval forces, including, when and if necessary, capital ships.

•   Carry out Gymnast, the Allied invasion of French Northwest Africa, by May 25.

•   Commence immediately an American troop buildup (Bolero) in the British Isles for Sledgehammer in 1942, or if that operation proved to be unfeasible, for Roundup in 1943. Five or six American infantry and tank divisions which had completed most of their training were to embark for Northern Ireland and England as soon as possible. These forces would also serve as a deterrent to a German invasion of the British Isles, still believed to be a possibility.

•   Stop the Japanese short of Australasia. For that purpose, the Americans were to hold open a "line of communications" running from Hawaii to the Southwest Pacific islands of Samoa, Fiji, and New Caledonia and commence a military buildup in those places and in Australia for counterattacks.

•   Substitute the American Army's 5th Infantry Division for the American Marines and for the British forces in Iceland, enabling the Allies to redeploy those forces to active battlefronts.

The Arcadia decisions generated a huge demand for shipping: troopships, freighters, tankers, and large and small landing craft. Merely to meet their first and most urgent assignments, the Americans were to deploy over 100,000 men and a million tons of supplies to overseas bases in January and February alone. The later, larger-scale operations (Gymnast, Sledgehammer) were to require staggering numbers of troops, weaponry, landing craft, and tens of millions of tons of supplies. However, it soon became evident that there was nowhere near enough shipping to expeditiously carry out all these operations. The new chief of Army plans, Dwight D. Eisenhower, expressed the situation simply but forcefully in his diary: "Ships! Ships! All we need is ships! What a headache!" Churchill later put it more eloquently: "Shipping was at once the stranglehold and sole foundation of our war strategy."

As an emergency step, it was agreed to pool British- and American-controlled merchant shipping. Although the British merchant marine had suffered heavily in the twenty-eight months of war, as related, the losses had been offset to a considerable extent by new construction and acquisition of foreign shipping. Hence it was still very much a formidable force, amounting to some 20 million gross tons, but it was stretched thin to meet British commitments, and many of the ships were worn out or laid up awaiting battle-damage repairs. Sorely neglected in the prewar years, the American merchant marine numbered only about 1,500 ships of about 8 million gross tons. About a third of the ships were old and decrepit and another third were tankers unsuitable for troop and cargo movements. However, when pooled, the two merchant fleets (including tankers) amounted to almost 30 million gross tons.

Pooling assets helped, but it did not solve the acute shortage of shipping. As a result, the planners had to cancel or defer many of the courses of action agreed upon at the Arcadia Conference. One of the first casualties was Gymnast, the early invasion of French Northwest Africa. It was postponed indefinitely. The deployment of American Army troops to Iceland (Indigo) and to Northern Ireland (Magnet) had to be trimmed back and stretched out. Although the Americans continued to urge the buildup (Bolero) for a 1942 invasion of Occupied France (Sledgehammer), it, too, had to be canceled, replaced by the alternate plan, Roundup.

For the long term it was agreed at the Arcadia Conference to build merchant ships on an unprecedented scale. The U.S. Maritime Commission was ready.* Before the Arcadia Conference, Roosevelt had directed the commission to build 12 million tons of new shipping: 5 million in 1942 and 7 million in 1943.† During the Arcadia Conference on January 3, Roosevelt raised the goal to 18 million tons: 8 million in 1942 and 10 million in 1943. After the conference, on February 19, Roosevelt raised the goal yet again to 24 million tons: 9 million in 1942 (750 ships) and 15 million in 1943 (1,500 ships). When—and if—achieved, the last program was to increase the combined Anglo-American merchant fleet to nearly 50 million tons, not counting projected losses.

The early, urgent troop movements arising from the Arcadia Conference imposed a great strain on the U.S. Navy. Coming on the heels of the disasters in the Pacific and Far East, the loss of a troopship at sea would be not only another tragic setback but also an intolerable shock to the American public. King therefore continued in force the policy that all troopships were to sail in convoys and were to be very heavily escorted whenever possible by battleships and cruisers, as well as numerous destroyers, which were to maintain a continuous sonar watch and form virtually impenetrable walls of steel around the troopships.‡ The naval historian Thomas B. Buell wrote that the new commander of the Pacific Fleet, Chester Nimitz, "used almost the entire Pacific Fleet" to escort the first contingent of Marines to Samoa in mid-January.

The number and availability of American destroyers for convoy escort in the Atlantic in late 1941 and in 1942 soon became controversial issues and led to much acrimony between London and Washington and also between the American Army and Navy. Owing to the propensity of popular writers and even naval historians—especially British historians—to accept uncritically the assertions of one side or the other in these debates, an inexcusably distorted record has evolved. The facts are as follows.

---

* To January 1, 1942, the Maritime Commission had produced 185 ships (54 tankers), of which 103 (27 tankers) were built in 1941.

† Maritime Commission goals were expressed in the larger, more impressive deadweight tonnage figures. American shipyards were to produce about 85 percent of the projected tonnage. To do so was to require about 90 shipyards and 700,000 workers, a very large percentage of them women, personified—and glorified—by nicknames "Rosie the Riveter" and "Wilma the Welder."

‡ Excepting giant British ocean liners, such as *Queen Mary, Queen Elizabeth,* and *Aquitania,* which were placed at the disposal of the Americans for transporting troops to distant Australia. These ships cruised at 26 knots and were therefore too fast for sustained escorts and, in any case, deemed unlikely to be hit by a U-boat, or if hit, unlikely to sink owing to dense compartmentalization.

Since the outbreak of war in Europe, the United States had been building war-ships as fast as possible. Owing to the long lead times required, Washington as-signed highest priority to building ten new battleships, thirty-one *Essex*-class fleet carriers, and numerous heavy and light cruisers and submarines. Shortly after Pearl Harbor, partly at the urging of London, the Navy added twenty-five "jeep" carriers for convoy escort to the urgent list. High priority had also been granted for the re-pair, modernization, and refitting of British warships, for the construction of six British "jeep" carriers, and about 300 other British vessels suitable for convoy es-corts.*

As a result of these construction priorities and the transfer of the fifty four-stackers to Great Britain and Canada, when America declared war the Navy con-fronted an acute shortage of destroyers. In total it had 177, of which only about 100 were modern (post-1934). The others were four-stackers that had been in con-tinuous service since World War I or had been demothballed and recommissioned recently.† The American destroyers were divided three ways in December 1941: ninety-two in the Atlantic, seventy-two in the Pacific, and thirteen with the Asiatic Fleet.

At the time of Pearl Harbor, the ninety-two destroyers in the Atlantic were working very hard on various assignments. The hard work and rough North At-lantic seas resulted in the need for repairs, refits, and overhauls. Thus at any given time, about fourteen destroyers (15 percent) were in shipyards and not immedi-ately available. The others were engaged in various special duties in December 1941, some of which bear repeating:

• North Atlantic convoy escort between Canada and Iceland. Although the American destroyers rotated in and out of that assignment frequently, at all times about thirty were carrying out this task. About twenty-five of these made up the five American escort groups; the others were at Argentia or Iceland.

• As related, in December eight American destroyers were assigned to escort a special British troop convoy, WS 12X, from Halifax to Cape Town.‡ These ships were tied up in that operation for most of December 1941, and several required re-fits thereafter.

• As part of Task Force 19, composed of *Arkansas* and *Nashville,* six Ameri-can destroyers were assigned to escort Troop Convoy 16 (TC 16) from New York

---

* At the time of Pearl Harbor, the six British "jeep" carriers under construction were *Archer, Avenger, Biter, Dasher, Tracker,* and *Charger.* The last was retained by the U.S. Navy for training air crews, replacing its only "jeep" carrier, *Long Island,* which was sent to the Pacific. Ten of the twenty-five newly ordered "jeep" carriers were to go to the Royal Navy, raising the number of Royal Navy "jeep" carriers under construction in American yards to fifteen. Later, American shipyards produced an-other twenty-three "jeep" carriers for Great Britain, making a total of thirty-eight, two of which went to the Canadian Navy. British yards produced four.

† The Navy demothballed and recommissioned seventy-two four-stackers in Philadelphia and San Diego in the period from March 1 to June 30, 1940. Less the fifty for the British and Canadian navies, the American Navy got twenty-two. The American Navy commissioned eighteen new destroy-ers in 1940 (*DD 415* to *DD 432*) and seventeen in 1941 (*DD 433* to *DD 444, DD 453* to *DD 457,* and *DD 463*).

‡ See Appendix 16.

to Iceland. Two of three American troopships aborted with mechanical problems; three British troopships joined from Halifax.

• As related, in December four American destroyers were assigned to escort the carrier *Yorktown* and the light cruisers *Richmond* and *Trenton* to the Pacific.

• In January, five American destroyers were assigned to escort the three older battleships to the Pacific. Two other destroyers went there as well.

• Numerous American destroyers were assigned to escort the remaining battleships, carriers, and heavy cruisers of the Atlantic Fleet, some of which were on standby to intercept a sortie of the super battleship *Tirpitz* and/or other big German ships or the Vichy French warships in Martinique.

There was to be no dramatic increase of the Atlantic destroyer force in the months ahead. Construction of new destroyers was not yet in high gear. The Navy commissioned only two new destroyers in December 1941 and three in January 1942. Two more were to be commissioned in February and three in March. The new destroyers had to undergo weeks of shakedowns and workups before joining the fleet.

Worse yet, the Navy had no ships other than destroyers suitable for blue-water convoy escort. That it did not was a noteworthy and regrettable lapse. President Roosevelt and, later, naval historian Samuel Eliot Morison and others blamed the Navy.* But in his postwar memoir, King blamed Roosevelt. The official documentation of that era supports King overwhelmingly.

Early in the European war, the Navy's General Board—a group of senior admirals facing retirement, including King—recognized the need to acquire large numbers of vessels suitable for escorting convoys. As King wrote, the board agreed that fleet destroyers were "all right" for this purpose, but the board (like the Admiralty) deemed destroyers to be overpowered, overgunned, and too costly to produce in quantity for that task. Hence the General Board, King went on, sought a design "less elaborate than the destroyer." Believing it was "essential to build *something* at once," at King's urging, the board recommended, as an emergency measure, quantity production of the new and proven 327-foot *Treasury*-class Coast Guard cutter, but this proposal was rejected by the Navy and by President Roosevelt. Although they had excellent sea-keeping characteristics and crew habitability, the Navy considered them too big, too expensive, and a little too slow for convoy escort.

In London, meanwhile, the members of Admiral Ghormley's mission and the naval attaches closely analyzed British efforts to produce an ideal oceangoing convoy escort to serve in place of the Royal Navy's fleet destroyers and the inadequate corvettes. As related, the first effort—the *Hunt*-class destroyer—proved to be a flop. The second effort—a 290-foot, 1,100-ton, 21-knot "destroyer escort," or in British naval terminology, "frigate"—which was to be built in Canada and the United States under Lend-Lease, held much greater promise.

In early 1941, one of the senior assistant naval attachés in London, Edward L.

---

* Morison wrote that the Navy was "woefully unprepared materially and mentally" for U-boat warfare, in part because it had not requested ASW vessels and escorts.

Cochrane, a noted naval engineer, returned to Washington to take over the Bureau of Ships. On February 1 that year, Cochrane directed the design staff to rush blueprints for a slightly larger and improved version of the British frigate. With a length of 306 feet, a displacement of 1,400 tons, and a speed of 23.5 knots, this "destroyer escort" perfectly met the General Board's recommendation for a ship "less elaborate than the destroyer."*

When the blueprints were completed, the then Secretary of the Navy, Charles Edison (son of inventor Thomas Alva Edison), and Admiral Stark presented them to Roosevelt for approval. To their dismay, Roosevelt approved a British request to build fifty frigates, but denied authority for the Navy to produce destroyer escorts for itself. As King recalled in his memoir, when he—as Atlantic Fleet commander—asked Stark why "nothing was being done to provide adequate escort vessels," Stark replied that "presidential approval could not be obtained." Furthermore, Roosevelt continued to reject requests from Edison's successor, Frank Knox, and from Stark to build destroyer escorts right up to—and beyond—America's entry into the war.

There were several reasons behind Roosevelt's position:

First, as King put it, Roosevelt was "something short of realistic in assessing the submarine menace." Based on his experience in World War I, Roosevelt had a "predilection for small antisubmarine craft," which could be mass-produced cheaply and quickly when the need arose.† At his urging the Navy had contracted for prototypes of two such vessels: a 110-foot, 14-knot, wood-hull submarine chaser (SC) and a 173-foot, 22-knot, steel-hull patrol craft (PC). But neither was suitable for hunting modern U-boats in rough North Atlantic waters.‡ King's successor as Commander of the Atlantic Fleet, Royal Ingersoll, put it this way in his oral history:

> The submarine-chasers of which the Navy [eventually] had a lot were not very good. They were one of Mr. Roosevelt's fads: he was a small-boat seaman himself and loved to cruise on little things like the [165-foot presidential yacht] *Potomac*

---

* The British frigate and its American counterpart, the destroyer escort, were similarly armed: three 3"/50 caliber guns, two depth-charge tracks on the stern, and eight depth-charge throwers on the port and starboard quarters. The slightly larger American version incorporated three torpedo tubes. In later models, the main battery of the American version was upgraded to two 5"/38 caliber guns. Both the British and American types had extensive antiaircraft weaponry.

† During World War I, in his role as Assistant Secretary of the Navy (1913–1920), Roosevelt played an important part in the production of 440 110-foot, wood-hulled subchasers by 30 American shipyards. These little gasoline-powered, short-legged craft were suitable for relatively calm waters but not the rugged North Atlantic and, of course, they were not equipped with antiaircraft armament and ammo storage. Stark's biographer, B. Mitchell Simpson III, wrote: "... The real need was for a larger ship that could be used in all kinds of weather. When he was Chief of Naval Operations, Stark struggled unsuccessfully to convince Roosevelt of this need, because Roosevelt favored smaller patrol craft."

‡ The SC mounted one 3"/50 caliber gun and a few depth charges. The PC mounted two 3"/50 caliber guns and depth charges. The guns were no larger than the gun on the Type VII U-boat and smaller than the guns on the Type IX. Owing to the lack of space for antiaircraft weapons, neither craft could operate safely where Axis aircraft might be encountered.

and he liked small ships. But the submarine-chaser was no craft to combat the submarine on the high seas.

Second, a mindless theory had taken deep root in Washington—fostered by Jerry Land at the U.S. Maritime Commission and others—that one way to defeat the U-boat was simply to produce merchant ships at a much faster rate than U-boats could sink them. Hence, in the early days of the war, Roosevelt awarded a higher priority to building merchant ships than to any convoy escorts other than the small SCs and PCs.

Third, in his desire to pit American soldiers against the Germans at the earliest possible time (Gymnast and/or Sledgehammer) and to meet requirements in the Pacific, Roosevelt awarded a very high priority for landing craft. The estimated numbers required were prodigious: 8,000 to 20,000 (large and small) for Sledgehammer and not less than 4,000 for the Pacific. Production of these vessels in American yards also took precedence over the British frigates and American destroyer escorts throughout most of 1942.

When America entered the war, Roosevelt ordered fast, mass production of SCs and PCs. The SC program was known as "Sixty Ships in Sixty Days."* The Navy had no objection to this directive. As anticipated, the little SCs and PCs proved to be necessary school boats for the tens of thousands of reservists coming into the Navy and for convoy escort in inshore waters and in the Gulf of Mexico and Caribbean Sea. But as the official papers of Knox, King, Stark, and Ingersoll reveal, the Navy deeply resented Roosevelt's stubborn and quixotic refusal to authorize mass production of the destroyer escorts required for rougher waters where enemy aircraft might be encountered. In one angry letter to Stark on the subject, Knox aptly characterized Roosevelt's policy as "Blind Folly."†

It is abundantly clear from these and other contemporary records—and it bears repeating—that the American Navy was fully alive to the urgent need for convoy escorts and repeatedly urged President Roosevelt to authorize them. He, not the Navy, was responsible for the prolonged delay in the production of the British frigates and American destroyer escorts. Roosevelt vastly underestimated the U-boat threat in Atlantic waters and authorized only the wrong kind of ships (PCs, SCs) to deal with the threat, both unfortunate—and ultimately scandalous—miscalculations for which Roosevelt avoided any blame, then or later. Statements to the effect that Admiral King in particular failed to anticipate the need for Atlantic convoy escorts or delayed the construction of same in favor of weaponry to fight in the Pacific are gross distortions.

Although the main task of the Coast Guard in prewar years had been search and rescue, it had served ably in the hunt for seagoing bootleggers in the 1920s.

---

* See Appendix 14.

† The keels of the first two of the fifty British vessels were laid on February 28, 1942. Altogether, only ninety-two destroyer escorts were laid down in American yards in 1942, fifty for the British, forty-two for the Americans. Owing to the low priority (for a time, tenth place) none was commissioned until 1943. By prior agreement, the Americans ultimately retained forty-five of the fifty British vessels, delaying delivery of the rest until well into 1943.

Therefore its 30,000 personnel (25,000 military; 5,000 civilians) and 168 named ships one hundred feet in length or larger were a welcome addition to the Navy. Most of these larger vessels, along with several big yachts, were to be pressed into service as convoy escorts. The sixty-seven larger Coast Guard vessels based in the Atlantic and Pacific were:

Class	Number	Length	Displacement	Comm.
Treasury (PG)	7	327'	2,200 tons	1936–37
Tampa (PG)	4	240'	1,500 tons	1921–22
Northland (PG)	1	216'	1,800 tons	1927
Cutter (PG-A)	6	165'	1,000 tons	1932–35
Cutter (PC-B)	16	165'	337 tons	1931–34
Cutter (SC)	33	125'	232 tons	1927

The most formidable of these vessels was the aforementioned 327-foot *Treasury* class, named for persons who had held the post of Secretary of the Treasury.* A modification of the Navy's discontinued *Erie*-class gunboat, the *Treasury* or *Secretary* class had a top speed of 19.5 knots and a range of 7,000 miles at 13 knots cruising speed. Designed originally to accommodate a small seaplane for search and rescue purposes, the vessel was beamy (41 feet) and thus quite roomy. Some vessels were armed with two single 5"/51 caliber guns; others with three single 5"/51 caliber guns. All had depth-charge tracks; some had Y-type throwers.

A naval officer, Andrew G. Shepard, thought these seven ships made excellent convoy escorts. "They are considerably more roomy, so that they can carry a large number of survivors. They are better sea boats than destroyers, and lend themselves better to boat operations and rescues. In connection with picking up people, their hospital accommodations are superior to those of destroyers."

A NEW CONVOY PLAN

The fifteen U-boats bound for American waters encountered hideous weather: brutal cold and mountainous seas. Horst Degen in the new Type VII *U-701* reported that his first watch officer, who rashly went topside without a safety belt, was washed overboard and lost. Despite the hostile weather, Degen and two other new skippers of VIIs found—and attacked—shipping along the way. Between January 2 and 7, Degen fired eleven internal torpedoes at "a group" of ships and at two ships sailing alone. Nine torpedoes missed or failed, but two hit, sinking the 3,700-ton British freighter *Baron Erskine*. Joachim Berger in *U-87* sank the 8,200-ton British tanker *Cardita*. Peter Cremer in *U-333* fired four torpedoes at a 10,800-ton American tanker, but missed. None of the boats could down-load torpedoes from deck canisters in such weather. Degen made the entire Atlantic crossing with no in-

---

* *Bibb, Campbell, Duane, Alexander Hamilton, Ingham, Spencer, Taney.* The *Alexander Hamilton* retained her full name to distinguish her from the four-stack Navy destroyer *Hamilton*.

ternal torpedoes and was therefore compelled to evade two other ships he encountered.

On January 8 Degen, Berger, and Cremer—and other boats—ran headlong into a winter hurricane. Cremer remembered:

> The waves were as high as houses. They struck the deck like an avalanche and swept away the few things they could seize on. Fenders and lines under the outer casing disappeared, supports cracked like matchwood. The boat listed up to 60 degrees—as the pendulum in the control room showed—so that it seemed one could plunge one's bare hands in the water, then righted itself like a self-righting doll, owing to its low center of gravity, only to tip over immediately to the other side. . . . The U-boat literally climbed the mountainous seas, plunged through the wave crests, hung for a moment with its stem in the empty air and plunged down the other side into the trough of the waves. When it buried its nose, the screws in the stern seemed to be revolving in the air. The stern dropped down, the screws disappeared in the maelstrom and the exhaust broke off with a gurgle. In the hard thumps, *U-333* shuddered in every frame member like a steel spring. . . .

Degen wrote that he attempted to maintain a topside watch, but when a gigantic wave tore loose a bridge gun, which swiveled around and severely injured his second watch officer, he gave up the effort. Like Cremer, he dogged the conning-tower hatch shut and sat out the storm. For nearly a full week *U-701* ran submerged, making twenty or thirty miles a day, coming up once or twice daily for brief periods to ventilate the boat and to recharge batteries. Finally the storm abated and Degen was able to repost a bridge watch, down-load torpedoes, and obtain a celestial fix, his first in ten days.

These violent storms also caused grief in the Allied camp. They utterly scattered six westbound convoys: Outbound North 51 to 56. In the escort group of Outbound North 55, the American destroyer *Mayo* and the British destroyer *Douglas* collided, and both ships had to abort with heavy damage. Iceland reported winds of 100 miles an hour, "the worst storm in fifteen years." The high winds drove the American cruiser *Wichita* and six other vessels aground, destroyed five American Catalinas, and wrecked minefields and antisubmarine booms, DF stations, and military barracks. In addition, Iceland reported that the American "escort for [convoy] ON 56 [was] unable to sail." Storms badly damaged *Broome* and *Dickerson,* two of the five destroyers of that group.

As the U-boats of the first wave drew close to the North American coast, *B-dienst* picked up the distress call of a Greek vessel that had dropped out of a convoy 180 miles east of Newfoundland with a broken rudder. Dönitz notified Reinhard Hardegen in *U-123* and authorized him to investigate if he was no more than 150 miles away. Although Hardegen was over twice that distance from the stricken ship, he ignored the restriction and closed on the position, eager for a kill. But when he found the Greek, she was surrounded by a tug and two "destroyers," an enemy force that cooled Hardegen's ardor. He aborted the attack and resumed his slow, one-engine journey to New York, regretting this brash and useless expenditure of fuel.

As a *ruse de guerre* to conceal the westward movement of these boats, Dönitz had assigned a new Type VII from Germany, *U-653*, commanded by Gerhard Feiler, age thirty-two, to broadcast dummy radio signals, simulating a heavy concentration of U-boats in the Northwest Approaches. The British, however, were not fooled. By January 2, Rodger Winn had developed enough data to enable Washington to notify the Atlantic Fleet that "Information indicates that five or six [U-boats] are proceeding west to Newfoundland area" and that "activity [was] expected there shortly." Two days later Washington told the Atlantic Fleet: "Positions are not definite but six [U-boats] are thought to be moving west." In his weekly summary of January 5 for the Admiralty, Winn noted the deception tactics of *U-653* and speculated that her purpose was in part to conceal the "concentration" of "six U-boats off Newfoundland." The next day, January 6, Washington told the Atlantic Fleet: "The westward movement of U-boats which was suspected is now confirmed but the number operating seems to be larger than was at first suspected. There are several [U-boats] probably already in the western Atlantic in the vicinity of Newfoundland" and "seven more" westbound.

The reports from Winn remained equally vague until about January 12. In his weekly report to the Admiralty of that date, he stated:

> The general situation is now somewhat clearer and the most striking feature is a heavy concentration off the North American seaboard from New York to Cape Race.
>
> Two groups have so far been formed. One, of six boats, is already in position off Cape Race and St. John's and a second, of five boats, is apparently approaching the American coast between New York and Portland. It is known that these five U-boats will reach their attacking areas by 13th January.
>
> Five other U-boats are between 30 degrees and 50 degrees west, proceeding towards one or the other of the above areas, and may later be reinforced by another five westbound boats, making a total of twenty-one boats.

This report was nearly accurate. By January 12, the first boats had reached North American waters and were presumably to open hostilities, simultaneously, on January 13. However, not "five" but only three were headed for the "American coast between New York and Portland": Zapp in *U-66,* Hardegen in *U-123,* and Folkers in *U-125.* The other westbound boats that Winn reported (making a total of twenty-one) were the lead boats of the "second wave."

While still in Canadian waters that same day—January 12—Hardegen in *U-123* reached a point about 110 miles southeast of Cape Sable, Nova Scotia. There he came upon the 9,100-ton British freighter *Cyclops,* sailing alone. Although he was behind his scheduled arrival off New York and was not authorized to sink any ship under 10,000 tons before January 13, Hardegen could not let a tempting target such as *Cyclops* get away. He closed and fired two torpedoes, and both hit. Radioing SSS (submarine attack), *Cyclops* went down with the loss of 100 of her 181-

man crew. Without pausing to help the survivors, Hardegen resumed his course to New York, having tapped out the first beat on the drum.

The Arcadia conference in Washington was still in session when Winn's appreciation of January 12 circulated. First Sea Lord Dudley Pound expressed the deepest concern. Except for the Canada-Iceland leg of the North Atlantic run, shipping in North American waters was not organized into convoys. Ships of convoys westbound from the British Isles normally dispersed well to the east of the North American coast (at about longitude 55 degrees west), sailing onward to destinations unescorted. Ships en route from the Caribbean or the United States East Coast to join eastbound convoys in Sydney and Halifax also sailed alone. Unless immediate measures were taken, this traffic, as well as the heavy local American coastal traffic, lay wide open to U-boat attack.

Obviously all this shipping would benefit from an extension of the convoy network to the East and Gulf coasts of the United States and to the Caribbean Sea. No naval authority in the Allied camp contested that view, but the hows and whens generated enormous heat. In dealing with this issue, most historians—especially British historians—have gone badly astray, depicting the Americans as dumb and inept or even criminally neglectful country cousins. Relying consistently on biased sources, historians have wildly distorted in particular the capabilities and views of Admiral King, distortions that have been allowed to stand for all too long.

The wildest of the distortions is that Admiral King had learned nothing from the British experience in fighting U-boats, or that he was so narrowly focused on the Pacific theater that he failed to appreciate, or deliberately ignored, the extent of the U-boat threat in the Atlantic. For these reasons, it was charged, King "refused" to initiate convoying or even "opposed" convoying.

Nothing could be further from the truth. For a full year, December 1940 to December 1941, first as commander of the Atlantic Fleet and then as Commander in Chief of the U.S. Fleet, King had had closer contact with German U-boat operations than any other senior officer in the U.S. Navy. He had established the naval bases in Argentia, Bermuda, and elsewhere to fight U-boats, and directed the occupation of Iceland and the formation of the naval and air bases there. He had deployed the Atlantic destroyer force and naval-air patrol squadrons in Argentia and Iceland to escort North Atlantic convoys. One of his destroyers, *Niblack,* had been the first American warship to attack a U-boat with depth charges. Another, *Greer,* had been the first to exchange close fire with a U-boat. Yet another, *Kearny,* had been the first American warship to be hit by a U-boat torpedo and also the first to incur battle casualties. Still another, *Reuben James,* had been the first American warship to be sunk by a U-boat. From this firsthand combat experience, and from his direct contacts with the Royal Navy, and from the flood of reports from Admiral Ghormley's mission and the American naval attachés in London, King had an unusually firm grasp of the menace to merchant shipping posed by U-boats.

In his capacity as Commander in Chief, Atlantic Fleet, King not only organized and supported convoying on the North Atlantic run, but he also urged shore-based naval authorities to prepare to initiate convoying on the United States East Coast. Three weeks *before* Pearl Harbor, King wrote a high-ranking naval authority:

> It seems to me that the time is *near at hand* when we shall have to begin to make up our own convoys at Boston, New York, Hampton Roads [Norfolk]. . . . Each of these posts requires an organization to deal with the make-up of convoys, such as that now in force at Halifax and at Sydney, Nova Scotia, when ice permits.
>
> I am told that organizations of the necessary scope and size and readiness *do not exist.* May I therefore suggest that steps be taken at once—if not already under-way—to get the indicated convoy ports organized, to which end it would be well to have first-hand knowledge of how Halifax is organized—and managed.*

At this same time, King proposed to the Chief of Naval Operations, Admiral Stark, several important changes to improve the North Atlantic convoy system. These proposals were designed to eliminate the Allied dependence on Iceland as an in-terim escort layover base because the weather was so hostile, the R&R accommo-dations were so inadequate, and handovers of convoys between escort groups were so uncertain, especially in winter weather.

The King plan would also release American destroyers for convoy duty on the United States East Coast. These ships would help overcome the "weakness of our coastal defense force," King wrote, and prepare for the "imminent probability of a [Axis] submarine attack."†

It should not be necessary to stress that these documents portray King as a se-nior officer very much concerned with convoying, one doing his utmost to im-prove the existing system and urging all to prepare for convoying in United States coastal waters. And yet, in view of the lingering and absurd charges that Admiral King was ignorant of or hostile to convoying, the repetition is justified.

Inasmuch as many historians denigrate or ignore altogether the role of the Canadian Navy in the protection of Allied merchant shipping, it is also appropriate at this point to restate its substantial contribution. Of the escort vessels required to implement the King proposal, nearly 40 percent were to be Canadian. In addition, Ottawa was to manage the North Atlantic convoy escort and routing until the American Navy was in position to assume that duty.

The naval staffs in Washington and London offered several modifications to the King convoy plan, but the basic outline remained intact and was the subject of much discussion at the Arcadia conference. In these sessions, Churchill and Pound argued that there should be a single overall commander of all convoy escorts in the North Atlantic rather than three separate commands, as King proposed, and that the single commander should be the admiral at Western Approaches, Percy Noble. Under the existing plan, King commanded all American and Canadian escorts in

---

* King to Rear Admiral Adolphus Andrews, November 17, 1941, King Papers, Library of Con-gress. His italics. Andrews responded, with considerable asperity, that such port organizations were al-ready in place and reminded King that two prototype convoys had sailed from New York, one in July, one in September 1941, admittedly, however, attended by a great deal of confusion.

† King to CNO Stark, November 17, 1941, cited in Marc Milner, *North Atlantic Run,* pp. 90–93.

the western Atlantic. He did not wish to relinquish "strategic control" and put the American ships under a British commander for logistical and other reasons, among them the possibility that when established, convoys on the United States East Coast might be commanded by Canadian or British officers.

King's adamant stand on this command-and-control issue vastly irritated the British. Although it was by then obvious that the Royal Navy was wearing out and was to be massively overshadowed by the American Navy in all waters, including the Atlantic, the British did not gladly surrender naval first place to the Americans. They continued to press hard for strategic control of all North Atlantic convoy escorts. Some American historians have suggested that the British falsely, deliberately, and continuously criticized King and the American performance in ASW to strengthen the case for British control, and that British historians, wittingly or unwittingly, have passed along these calculated criticisms as fact.

The King convoy plan was the subject of further intense discussions at a "Convoy conference" in Washington on January 22, following the Arcadia conference. The British again pressed for a single North Atlantic escort commander and urged the formation of convoys on the United States East Coast. Toward that end, they confirmed an offer by the Admiralty to lend the United States "upon completion" ten Royal Navy corvettes that were "in refit" or "under construction" to speed up the formation of convoys. King continued to oppose the idea of a single commander of escorts but gladly accepted the offer of ten corvettes inasmuch as he was doing everything possible to amass sufficient escorts for a convoy system in the Eastern Seaboard.*

Within forty-eight hours—by January 24—the conferees at the Convoy conference had hammered out and agreed to and distributed a modified version of the King plan. It preserved the existing multinational command structure, eliminated Iceland as an escort base, and adopted the "straight through" Great Circle route farther southward, thereby forswearing the ability to reroute convoys on evasion courses in the extreme northern latitudes. Under the plan, 200 warships (seventy destroyers, 130 corvettes) were to participate in the escorting of Halifax, Slow, Outbound North, and Outbound North (Slow) convoys. The Americans were to provide about thirty destroyers; the British about twenty-eight destroyers and sixty-one corvettes; and the Canadians thirteen destroyers and seventy corvettes or minesweepers.

In addition to the North Atlantic convoy escort, the King plan was designed to provide about twenty-four destroyers for other important escort duty. Fourteen destroyers (ten Royal Navy, four American) were to be reserved for escorting troop convoys. The other ten destroyers (all American) were to cadre the new convoy network on the United States East Coast.

When he received a copy of the foregoing convoy escort agreement, Dudley Pound was not pleased. Five days later, January 29, he cabled Washington to say

---

* Contrary to the impression in some accounts, these ten corvettes did not arrive in American ports for months. In a sense they were quid pro quo for the ten *Lake*-class Coast Guard cutters transferred to the Royal Navy a year earlier.

he had "personally" examined the plan and had strong reservations in several areas. His grumpy comments, paraphrased:

• He was "seriously disturbed" at the length of time the plan had been under discussion and the "resulting delay in putting our combined available escort forces to the most economical use."

• There should be a convoy system on the United States Eastern Seaboard and it was "important to lose no time in finding a scheme which will release the necessary forces for this purpose."

• The present system of "divided control" of escorts was "wasteful of our resources" and he urged "most strongly" that Western Approaches should exercise "strategic direction" at "the earliest possible moment." He stressed that such "strategic direction" in no way implied "unified control of Atlantic by British."

To this time the Admiralty was under the impression—or professed to be—that the United States had committed fifty-one destroyers to escort duty on the North Atlantic run. Thus, under the new King plan, it appeared that in proposing a total contribution of about thirty American destroyers, Washington was freeing up twenty-one destroyers that the Admiralty believed could be used to cadre a convoy network on the Eastern Seaboard, not merely the ten destroyers King had promised for that purpose. Thus Pound proposed in his message to Washington a different arithmetic distribution of vessels that would make available "twenty-one destroyers" for "U.S. East Coast convoys" of which "roughly twelve U.S. destroyers" should possibly become "immediately available for work on the American seaboard."

It should be stressed that in these exchanges at no time did King agree to the British assumption (or proffered assumption) that "twenty-one" American destroyers would be released to cadre East Coast convoys. To the contrary, King repeatedly stated that only ten American destroyers were to be allocated for that purpose. Nonetheless, ensuing official Admiralty accounts of the convoy agreement stated that, in fact, only ten American destroyers became available for the East Coast and the "discrepancy" (i.e., nonappearance of eleven American destroyers) "can only be explained on the assumption that the balance were employed elsewhere."*

The upshot of these prolonged and testy discussions was a modified King plan, which included these chief features:

• That for North American waters, the Canadians were to provide six escort groups for the purpose of escorting North Atlantic convoys to and from Halifax and latitude 45 degrees west (West Ocean Meeting Point, or WESTOMP), which was about 1,100 miles one-way. To be designated the Western Local Escort Force (WLEF), this force (to supersede the Newfoundland Escort Force) was to consist of forty-seven ships: five Canadian destroyers, twelve Royal Navy destroyers "on loan," and thirty corvettes, mostly Canadian.†

---

* In British accounts, it is asserted that King deceptively sent these eleven so-called "missing" destroyers to the Pacific.

† In early 1942, the Canadian Newfoundland Escort Force could call on eighty-three Canadian warships: thirteen destroyers and seventy corvettes.

• That for waters of the British Isles, the Royal Navy was to provide a similar but smaller group to escort North Atlantic convoys to and from Northern Ireland and Scotland and 22 degrees west (East Ocean Meeting Point, or EASTOMP), eliminating the British layovers in Iceland. To be designated the Eastern Local Escort Force (ELEF), this group was to be composed of eighteen British destroyers.

• That for the long (1,800-mile) intervening space between WESTOMP and EASTOMP, the Allies were to create a multinational force, composed of fourteen close-escort groups, five American, five British, and four Canadian. To be designated Mid-Ocean Escort Force (MOEF), it was to be comprised of 143 ships: fifteen American destroyers; fifteen British destroyers; twelve Canadian destroyers, and 101 corvettes, fifty-two British, forty-nine Canadian. In addition, the Americans were to provide one Iceland-based group (five destroyers) to "shuttle" eastbound and westbound Iceland traffic (much of it bound to or from Murmansk) to and from the passing Slow Convoys and Outbound North (Slow) convoys.

The MOEF groups were to travel "straight across" the Atlantic from WESTOMP to Londonderry, Northern Ireland, and oppositely from EASTOMP to St. John's, Newfoundland. If granted the authority to go at best cruising speed (12–14 knots) from meeting points to bases and vice versa, by strictly following a Great Circle route, the MOEF forces could save sufficient fuel to make it "straight across" the ocean. American destroyers of the MOEF were to make one round-trip west-east to Londonderry and east-west to Canada, then return to Boston or Portland for maintenance and repairs and crew R&R.

After further discussions between Washington and London, and some minor modifications, King and Pound approved the King convoy plan on February 3 and 4, respectively. In his declaration of acceptance, King iterated that a single commander with "strategic control" of transatlantic convoys was "not acceptable" inasmuch as the existing setup of American control (over American and Canadian forces) in the western Atlantic was "working satisfactorily." In his declaration of acceptance, Pound expressed "considerable reluctance" on that point because "it perpetuates a system of dual control with all its proved disadvantages and delays." The British "will do all we can to make scheme work," Pound went on, "but I must be free to reopen question should I consider our [merchant-ship] trade is suffering."

As one measure to expedite the transfer of American destroyers from the North Atlantic run, at this time Admiral King directed that the six Atlantic-based 327-foot *Treasury*-class Coast Guard cutters be assigned formally and permanently to convoy-escort duty in that sector. In due course, five of these six big, roomy vessels (*Bibb, Campbell, Duane, Ingham, Spencer*) were to become workhorses on that convoy route, incomparably superior to the American, British, and Canadian four-stackers and in many ways more suitable for this task than modern American fleet destroyers.

Owing to the necessary transfer of eleven modern destroyers of the Atlantic Fleet to the Pacific Fleet in December and January and to a sudden and unforeseen heavy demand for destroyers to escort individual troopships and troopship convoys in the Atlantic, Admiral King was unable to provide the promised fifteen

American destroyers for the MOEF plus five in Iceland. In fact, little by little, almost all American destroyers on the North Atlantic run had to be withdrawn to escort troopship convoys in the Atlantic, and for other urgent tasks, including assistance to the British Home Fleet.

British and Canadian historians, displaying no knowledge or understanding of the American policy of providing massive destroyer escort for troopships, have criticized King for leaving the escort of cargo or nontroopship convoys on the North Atlantic run to the Canadians and British. Typically, Canadian historian W.D.G. Lund wrote that "[w]hen the United States entered the war, all of the American destroyers were withdrawn immediately for service in other theaters, and by February 1942 there were only two United States Coast Guard cutters available for duty as convoy escorts."*

This assertion utterly ignores the fact that the strength of the Atlantic Fleet destroyer force actually remained fairly constant in 1942 and was ever-present in that theater, engaged mostly in escort of troopships convoys and capital ships, many working in behalf of the British. The issue boils down to this: In view of the scant resources, when faced with the challenge of escorting cargo or troopships, King chose to escort the latter, reflecting the American view that military lives were more precious than military cargo. One result, the American naval historian Robert W. Love, Jr., wrote, was that "[t]he Navy's defense of American troop shipping was one of the unalloyed victories of World War II."†

BEATS ON THE DRUM

By sunset on January 13, the three Type IXs of the first wave had reached their assigned positions off the East Coast of the United States. Hardegen in *U-123* was near the eastern tip of Long Island; the new skipper Folkers in *U-125* was off New Jersey; and Zapp in *U-66* was east of Cape Hatteras. In the early, dark hours of January 14, Hardegen came upon the armed and loaded 9,600-ton Panamanian tanker *Norness.* In two surface attacks, he fired five electric torpedoes from close range. Three of the five hit and *Norness* sank in shallow water, with about 100 feet of her bow sticking out. A new American destroyer in workup, *Ellyson,* rescued twenty-four survivors the following day.

After lying on the bottom during the day to give his crew some rest and to save fuel, on the night of January 14 Hardegen approached the outer reaches of New

---

* See essay in Boutilier (1982) and appendices 12 and 16. According to the U.S. Navy's daily ship position reports, in the period February 10 to February 20, 1942, there were still five American Escort Groups (A-1 to A-5), composed of twenty destroyers, serving on the North Atlantic run, plus two *Treasury*-class cutters. These were escorting cargo convoys HX 175 and 176, ON 67 and 69, and SC 70. By mid-March, the number of American destroyers in that duty was twelve, plus one cutter. By May 1, the number was about ten destroyers plus two cutters in the five American escort groups. Canadian or British escorts increased these American MOEF groups to full strength.

† Love, *History of the U.S. Navy* (1992), vol. 2, ch. 4.

York Harbor in very shallow water, close enough to see the glow of lights in lower Manhattan. Somewhat awestruck by this sight—and the realization that the men of *U-123* were the first German warriors to see it—Hardegen invited others to the bridge, including a propagandist-photographer, Alwin Tölle. But it was too dark and the boat was too far away for photographs.*

When the sight-seeing was done, Hardegen reversed course and cruised easterly toward deeper water, keeping Long Island on his port hand. In the early hours of January 15, the watch spotted a lighted vessel coming up astern. She was the loaded 6,800-ton British tanker *Coimbra,* bound for Halifax. Hardegen closed to about 900 yards and fired two electrics. One or both hit and *Coimbra* exploded in a giant fireball. She, too, sank, bow up in shallow water. Thirty-six men died; six men, all injured, were rescued.

Had Admiral Raeder sent *Tirpitz* to attack the United States, Admiral King, from his headquarters in Washington, would have directed the Atlantic Fleet commander, Royal Ingersoll, to engage and sink her. But repelling a U-boat attack against merchant shipping close off the coast called into play entirely different naval commands, which were based ashore and charged with "local defense."

Established before the war, these commands, called "Coastal Frontiers," superseded the old Naval Districts administratively and otherwise. The Coastal Frontier commanders kept close track of naval and commercial ships sailing within their frontier. In event of hostilities the commanders were to defend the frontier, protect coastal shipping, and support the Atlantic Fleet and Army and other forces operating within the frontier.

The first, busiest, and most important of these commands was the North Atlantic Naval Coastal Frontier, soon renamed the Eastern Sea Frontier. Its area of responsibility extended north-south along the coast from the Canadian border to North Carolina and 200 miles out to sea. It was commanded by King's Naval Academy classmate (1901) sixty-three-year-old Adolphus Andrews, an able, energetic admiral and friend of the President. He had established his headquarters in the Federal Building, 90 Church Street, in downtown Manhattan, complete with an operations center, where his staff plotted all shipping on huge wall maps.

Owing to the shortage of warships, Andrews had none permanently under his command. The plan was that should the Eastern Sea Frontier come under attack by surface raider or U-boat, Andrews would call upon the Atlantic Fleet for warships. In view of that fleet's commitments to escort troop convoys and to other tasks, the prospects of help to combat U-boats were thin to nonexistent, at least until the new King convoy plan was approved. Accordingly, Andrews had mobilized and brought to war readiness what one official naval historian aptly labeled a "tatterdemalion fleet," consisting of twenty small craft: seven Coast Guard cutters (the 165-foot *Dione* and six 125-footers), four prewar 110-foot SCs, three 200-foot, World War I *Eagle*-class subchasers, two ancient (1905) gunboats, and four large (170- to

---

* Later Berlin propagandists released fabricated still and motion pictures of "the lights of New York," ostensibly photographed by Tölle. Although the fabrications were amateurish, German audiences accepted them as authentic. The stills and movie footage were still in circulation in 1996.

245-foot) converted yachts. Of these vessels, only the Norfolk-based, 16-knot, Coast Guard cutter *Dione,* which had a single 3"/50 caliber bow gun and stern depth-charge tracks, was anywhere near capable of engaging a U-boat. Moreover, only *Dione* and two other vessels were consistently reliable mechanically.

Nor did Andrews command any land-based combatant aircraft with which to fight U-boats. This situation was akin to that of the Royal Navy in 1939 when the Admiralty did not yet exercise operational control of Coastal Command. This has not been understood, apparently, by many historians of the U-boat war and thus demands explanation and clarification. From the perspective of the 1990s, the story seems quaint, even a bit preposterous.

Between the World Wars, when it became obvious that aircraft had become an important instrument of warfare, American Army and Navy leaders fell into hot disputes over strategic control of military aviation. In this bureaucratic struggle, the Army won an important victory: All land-based aircraft—notably bombers of all types—were to be assigned to the Army Air Corps (from June 20, 1941, Army Air Forces), a semiautonomous branch of the Army. Under the agreement, which had the force of law, the U.S. Navy, like the Royal Navy, was restricted to capital-ship- and carrier-based aircraft, big flying boats or seaplanes (such as Sunderlands, Catalinas, and Mariners), and rigid dirigibles and nonrigid blimps, plus a few non-combatant wheeled, executive, utility, and trainer aircraft based ashore.

On January 12, 1942, Admiral Ingersoll's Atlantic Fleet had under its control 150 aircraft other than those based on ships: about 100 Catalinas and about 50 scout and utility planes. The Catalinas—known as patrol bombers—were based in Iceland (8), Argentia (8), Newport, Rhode Island (6), Norfolk (38), San Juan, Puerto Rico (12), Coco Solo, Panama (24), and Natal, Brazil (6). Like the Sunderland force of the Royal Navy in 1939, the primary mission of the Catalina force was to seek out and warn of enemy capital ships (such as *Tirpitz*) that posed a threat to the Atlantic Fleet or to the Panama Canal or other important coastal installations. In addition, the sixteen Catalinas at Argentia and Iceland provided limited convoy escort between those places.

Owing to the deliveries of Catalinas to the British* under Lend-Lease and to the loss of Catalinas in the attack on Pearl Harbor, in early 1942 the Navy was desperately short of Catalinas and the newer seaplane patrol-bomber, the Mariner. In order to help overcome this shortage, King had to suspend the deliveries of Catalinas to the Royal Navy from January through March 1942. Although the deliveries were to resume in April (climbing to fifty aircraft per month), the temporary suspension annoyed the Admiralty and provided yet another reason to berate King, who sent most of the Catalina production in those months to the Pacific to replace the Catalina losses at Pearl Harbor and elsewhere.

In view of the acute scarcity of American Catalinas in the Atlantic Ocean area, Admiral Ingersoll was unable to provide Admiral Andrews of the Eastern Sea Frontier with these aircraft for offshore hunter-killer ASW patrols, especially since

* At this time Coastal Command had four Catalina squadrons in the British Isles: 209, 210, 240, and the Canadian 413. These had a total of thirty-six aircraft, plus reserves and trainers. The other British Catalinas were based elsewhere.

no appreciable U-boat threat had yet developed in American waters. The few Catalinas that Ingersoll did bring into play in January 1942 were used principally to provide limited escort for troopship convoys. The upshot was that for inshore air patrols Andrews could mobilize only about 100 unarmed or lightly armed naval and Coast Guard aircraft and four Navy blimps, based at Lakehurst, New Jersey.

Of these craft, only the blimps were capable of sustained overwater ASW patrols and could carry enough bombs or depth charges to mount an attack on a U-boat. In June, 1940, President Roosevelt had authorized a force of forty-eight blimps for local convoy escort and ASW patrols, but only these four were combat-ready at Lakehurst on January 1, 1942, when the Navy commissioned the first combat Squadron 12.* These blimps flew forty-five ASW patrols and six convoy escort missions in January 1942.

Although it seems grossly illogical—even preposterous—from this distance, in the immediate prewar years the Army Air Forces, like the RAF, was assigned the principal aircraft ASW role in American waters. This was owing to a hazy strategic doctrine under which the Army had responsibility for defending the coastlines as well as the continental United States. Although the British had shown that the RAF Coastal Command became a superior ASW arm after the Admiralty was granted operational control, President Roosevelt and Secretary of War Stimson had firmly resisted all efforts by the U.S. Navy to duplicate that arrangement in the American military establishment. One big reason was that if it were done, the U.S. Navy would inevitably push for the acquisition of the superior four-engine land-based aircraft (B-17s, B-24s) that were controlled solely by the U.S. Army Air Forces. If the Navy were allowed to acquire such aircraft, it would undermine the Army's absolute hold on strategic air power and aircraft.

On January 14, 1942, the U.S. Navy remounted its efforts to acquire and control land-based aircraft for the ASW role and for other purposes. This came in the form of a request from the chief of the Navy's Bureau of Aeronautics, John H. Towers, to the chief of the Army Air Forces, Henry "Hap" Arnold, for 400 long-range four-engine B-24 Liberators and 900 medium-range twin-engine B-25 Mitchells from the Army allotment. Arnold denied the request because, he wrote, he was "critically short by 1,190 planes of the barest needs to meet United States Army Air Forces requirements" and because the request raised "questions of far greater import than the possibility of diverting planes" to the Navy.

After assuming the post of Commander in Chief of the U.S. Fleet, King resubmitted this request with utmost vigor and persistence. His relentless campaign for land-based aircraft vastly irritated Secretary of War Stimson, a onetime National Guard officer, who much earlier (1911–1913) had served as Secretary of War in the Taft Administration and who fancied himself a skilled military strategist. He

---

* These four were model Ks, the "mass"- production blimp of World War II. They were 252 feet in length, armed with Mark XVII depth charges, and had carrier pigeons (!) for secure communications with Lakehurst. In June 1942 Congress authorized a total blimp strength of 200 K types or variations. Goodyear Aircraft contracted to build 134 Ks during the war plus a number of 149-foot model L trainers, duplicates of its five-ship prewar "advertising fleet," which the Navy bought soon after Pearl Harbor.

had developed an intense antipathy to the Navy, in particular to King, who could be a brusque and undiplomatic advocate, and to Frank Knox. Stimson's testy views about the Navy and King colored the views of the entire Army establishment.* His acid criticisms in his lengthy personal diaries have provided critics of King—British critics in particular—with much ammunition for decades. These critics seldom if ever suggest that Stimson was anything but objective and simon-pure in motive.

In rejecting King's campaign for land-based aircraft for ASW, Stimson, Marshall, and Arnold argued that the Army Air Forces were perfectly capable of carrying out the air ASW role. In fact, they held, the Army could do the job better than the Navy, which lacked the necessary infrastructure for and familiarity with land-based aircraft. President Roosevelt either believed this to be true or else chose to remain removed from this increasingly bitter inter-service debate. Whatever the reason, where a presidential ruling or guidance was obviously required, none was forthcoming. This was yet another failure by the President to appreciate the potential peril of the U-boat threat and provide firm leadership to meet it. On this issue as well, he has escaped all blame.

Hap Arnold delegated the air ASW mission on the American East Coast to Arnold N. Krogstad, chief of the 1st Bomber Command of the First Air Force. Like most air units of those frantic days, 1st Bomber Command was in a transitory stage, neither fully formed nor trained. Many of its most skilled pilots had been siphoned off to cadre the hugely expanding Army Air Forces or to more pressing combat assignments. What remained was a thin veneer of experienced men and a very large number of keen but green air crews that still required extensive training in air tactics, bombing, and navigation, manning about 100 multi-engine medium and large bombers at four airfields along the Eastern Seaboard. None of the planes was equipped with radar or depth charges. None of the airmen knew how to find and attack a U-boat or how difficult it was to sink one. As a result, there was not the slightest possibility that 1st Bomber Command could effectively carry out the air ASW role.

In compliance with his assigned mission to repel and destroy U-boats, the chief of 1st Bomber Command, Arnold Krogstad, established a headquarters in the Federal Building in Manhattan, down the corridor from Admiral Andrews's operations center. Carefully observing the separation of military forces, Krogstad set up an independent operations center, unlinked electronically or otherwise to the Eastern Sea Frontier operations center. Working in loose "cooperation" with Andrews, Krogstad had commenced ASW patrols.

The sinking of two tankers in the waters of the Eastern Sea Frontier by Reinhard Hardegen in *U-123* triggered a rapid and energetic response in the Federal Building. Andrews and Krogstad deployed all available aircraft, blimps, and small craft to hunt down and kill Hardegen and his cohorts. The Navy planes and blimps patrolled near the shore; the Army planes patrolled farther out to sea. Inasmuch as

---

* War-planner Eisenhower fumed in his diary that if someone shot King it might help win the war.

nobody knew how to find and kill a U-boat, this response was futile. Communications between the various shore-based commands and airfields and the forces at sea or in the air were primitive or ineffective.

King's critics have excoriated him for failing to respond more promptly and aggressively to the Drumbeat U-boat threat. The most recent and vociferous critics have been Americans: Michael Gannon and Montgomery C. Meigs.* Gannon wrote that since there were twenty-five American destroyers in East Coast ports from Maine to Virginia on January 12, the Navy was derelict—or cowardly or worse—in not deploying destroyer hunter-killer groups to confront the *U-123* and the other Drumbeat U-boats. When he later discovered that four of the twenty-five destroyers (*Dallas, Kearny, Lea, MacLeish*) were in drydock or to be used "only in an emergency," Gannon reduced the available destroyers to twenty-one in the paperback edition of his book but did not tone down his criticism of King and the Navy.

The harsh criticism Gannon leveled at the Navy on this issue is not justified. The British and American navies had long since declared the type of hunter-killer operations he proposed to be futile, wasteful, and dangerous. Most all of the twenty-one destroyers he lists were already committed to other vital tasks:

• Thirteen of the twenty-one destroyers on the Gannon list were to join the battleship *Texas,* carrier *Wasp,* and heavy cruiser *Quincy* to escort (as Task Force 15) America's first big troop convoy, AT 10, sailing from New York to Iceland and Northern Ireland on January 15. At the very last minute, that convoy was scaled back to three big troopships (*Chateau Thierry, Munargo, Strathaird*), and four of these thirteen destroyers (*Charles F. Hughes, Hilary P. Jones, Ingraham, Lansdale*) were reassigned to join the cruisers *Vincennes* and *Nashville* to escort (as Task Force 16) another troop convoy, BT 200, composed of seven troopships carrying 22,000 men, sailing from New York to the Pacific on January 22.

• Two other destroyers on the Gannon list (*Mustin, O'Brien*) were under orders to join three other destroyers (*Anderson, Morris, Hammann*) to escort the battleships *Idaho, Mississippi,* and *New Mexico,* which, as related, shifted from the Atlantic to the Pacific in January.

• Another destroyer on the list (*Gleaves*) sailed from Boston on January 15 to escort the valuable 7,000-ton destroyer tender *Melville* to Argentia for further transfer to Londonderry, where she was to establish an American destroyer base for the new "straight through" convoys. (The *Treasury*-class Coast Guard cutter *Ingham* also served in the escort.)

• Still another destroyer (*Bristol*), commissioned on October 22, 1941, was en route from New York to Casco Bay, Maine, for additional workup.

• Yet another destroyer (*Ellyson*), commissioned on November 28, 1941, and still in workup, sailed from Newport, Rhode Island, for more sea trials and, as related, on January 14, rescued survivors of the torpedoed tanker *Norness.*

Gannon wrote that there was "no pressing urgency" for the sailing of the big

---

* In books *Drumbeat* (1990) and *Slide Rules and Submarines* (1990), respectively.

troop convoy AT 10 on January 15 and that it "could easily have been delayed," so the original thirteen destroyers of its escort could hunt U-boats. This is not the way Washington saw it. Although they had been reduced in numbers at the last minute, the political and symbolic value of the troops bound for Iceland (Indigo) and Northern Ireland (Magnet) in AT 10 were very great. Those troops were to release other troops for combat, to deter a possible German invasion of the British Isles in the spring of 1942, and to prepare for Gymnast, partially satisfying Moscow's demands for a "second front." To have delayed the sailing of that troop convoy and the equally vital troop convoy BT 200 in order to hunt an unknown number of U-boats, which to then had sunk only two ships in waters of the Eastern Sea Frontier, would have not only vastly upset all convoy and warship schedules but also incurred the wrath of the American Army, which almost hourly pressed King to hurry troopship sailings. Besides that, the majority of the warships with convoy AT 10 were, in fact, sailing directly to Canadian waters, where there were by far the greatest number of Drumbeat U-boats.

FIRST ACTIONS OFF CAPE HATTERAS

Having achieved the psychological impact desired by sinking the tankers *Norness* and *Coimbra*, Hardegen in *U-123* cleared out of the shallow waters of New York. Southbound off New Jersey in the dark early hours of January 17, Hardegen claimed, he found and sank an unidentified 4,000-ton freighter with a single torpedo. Postwar German records credited him with the 2,000-ton American ship *San José*. But Gannon has established from official survivor reports that *San José* was not torpedoed. She collided with another ship, *Santa Elisa*, and sank. Gannon could not identify Hardegen's claimed victim. No other vessel in his area went down that night. Perhaps Hardegen happened upon the collision scene and believed that his torpedo had fatally hit *San José* or *Santa Elisa*, which caught fire in the collision, burned for six hours, and finally limped into New York.

Hardegen in *U-123* and Richard Zapp in *U-66* reached the Cape Hatteras area almost simultaneously on January 18–19. Wading into a throng of lighted, unescorted ships, Zapp sank the loaded 6,600-ton American tanker *Allan Jackson* and the 8,000-ton Canadian passenger-cargo vessel *Lady Hawkins*. Of the forty-eight men on the *Allan Jackson*, thirty-five died in the flaming inferno. Of the 312 crew and passengers on *Lady Hawkins*, about 250 were killed or died after horrible ordeals in lifeboats.

Hardegen, who had only five torpedoes left, was astounded at the dense ship traffic off Cape Hatteras. He logged that at one point he had in sight "no fewer than twenty steamers, some with their lights on." During the night of January 18–19, in a period of seven hours he claimed he sank four ships by torpedo and gun: another unidentified 4,000-ton freighter, the 5,300-ton American freighter *City of Atlanta*, the 3,800-ton Latvian freighter *Ciltvaira*, and the 8,200-ton American tanker *Malay*, southbound in ballast. Postwar records listed the unidentified freighter as the 4,500-ton *Brazos*, but again, Gannon's research reveals that it was not so. Like

San José, Brazos was sunk in a collision six days earlier.* The sinkings of the *City of Atlanta* and *Ciltvaira* were confirmed, but the tanker *Malay* was only damaged and limped into Norfolk.

To this point, Hardegen and Zapp had sunk three tankers and damaged another in U.S. waters. These four ships were a tiny segment of the huge and vital Allied tanker traffic on the United States East Coast. This traffic was composed of ships en route to and from the Caribbean (Aruba, Curaçao, Trinidad) and the Gulf of Mexico (Texas, Louisiana) to United States East Coast ports and to Halifax to join convoys to the British Isles. Inasmuch as attacks on this traffic were to become a prominent feature of the German U-boat campaign in American waters, further details about this traffic are appropriate.

In the early days of the American oil boom, the industry shipped oil from the rich fields in Texas and Louisiana to the East Coast refineries and consumers in railroad tank cars and to closer places by barges on the Mississippi, Ohio, and other rivers, by trucks, and by short pipelines. Experience with oil tankers in the Caribbean and elsewhere demonstrated that oil or petroleum "product" (such as gasoline) could be shipped much more economically by water than by railroad. By June 1941, 95 percent of all oil brought to the East Coast from Texas and Louisiana came by ship, 3 percent by truck, barge, or pipeline, and only 2 percent by railroad cars.

By that same time, June 1941, it had become obvious to the Roosevelt administration that the movement of oil and petroleum products was to be among the most vital of wartime enterprises. Roosevelt therefore named an "oil czar," Harold I. Ickes, Secretary of the Interior, to head what became the Petroleum Administration for War (PAW). Cutting its teeth on the British oil "shuttle" of 1941, when fifty American tankers were diverted to that task, PAW, working closely with the oil industry, developed a complete picture of oil problems to be expected in wartime and an array of plans and programs to overcome them.

The plans included ways to greatly increase the efficiency of existing oil transport by seagoing tankers to the East Coast ports and also new or fallback plans should that tanker fleet prove to be insufficient. The most important programs were:

• The construction of about 14,000 miles of pipeline, the most economical and efficient system for moving oil. The most prominent of these was the Big Inch, a stupendous network of 24" seamless steel pipe for moving crude oil, which ran from Longview, Texas, to an existing pipeline hub, Norris City, Illinois, thence to the East Coast; in all, a distance of 1,475 miles. The pipe itself held 3.8 million barrels of oil, "a perpetual reservoir of oil moving constantly eastward," as an oil historian put it, delivering about 300,000 barrels daily. Second was the only slightly less stupendous Little Big Inch, a network of 20" pipe to move finished product (100 octane aviation gasoline, etc.), which ran from Texas to the East Coast via Seymour, Indiana. The pipe itself held 2.9 million barrels of product and delivered about 235,000 barrels daily. Third was the Plantation pipeline, which ran

* *Brazos* collided with the British "jeep" carrier *Archer* in workup in the Caribbean.

from Baton Rouge via Bremen, Georgia, to Greensboro, North Carolina, and was later extended to Richmond and Norfolk. This pipeline (12" to Bremen, 10" to Greensboro) delivered about 50,000 barrels a day.*

• The rehabilitation of the railroad tank-car system. On the eve of war, there were about 145,000 oil-carrying railroad tank cars scattered around the United States, with an average capacity of 215 barrels each. About 105,000 of these were involved in transporting oil or petroleum products. When war came, most of these cars were assigned to haul crude oil or product from Texas to the East Coast in special mile-long express trains composed of up to 100 cars each, transporting an aggregate of about 22,000 barrels of oil or product. The shipment of oil by railroad cars climbed spectacularly from 141,000 barrels a day in October 1941 to 585,000 barrels a day in April 1942, to 828,000 barrels a day in September 1942, to one million barrels a day (about fifty one-hundred-car trains) in March 1943.

• Dramatic improvement of oil-barge operations on rivers, lakes, and intercoastal waterways and tanker-truck operations on highways and byways. In January 1942, United States companies had in operation 1,400 oil barges and 106,000 tanker trucks. As a result of more efficient routings and other measures, these vehicles delivered twice or more oil than theretofore. Moreover, by directing tanker trucks to take over almost all oil hauling under 200 miles on a twenty-four-hour-a-day basis in all weather, PAW freed up thousands of railroad tank cars for use in the special Texas-East Coast oil trains.

At the time of Drumbeat, when 95 percent of the oil arriving at East Coast ports came by ship, the American-registered fleet consisted of about 350 big, modern, seagoing tankers of about 3 million gross tons.† About 260 of these were engaged in moving crude from Texas to the Eastern Seaboard. The sea-lanes were also crowded with British and British-controlled tankers en route from the Caribbean and Gulf of Mexico to Halifax to join convoys.

Upon learning of the possible arrival of U-boats in United States East Coast waters in early January, Admiral Andrews had directed that these tankers and all other coastwise shipping should travel well offshore to avoid "bunching" targets for the Germans in the usual and well-known lanes. Western Approaches at first directed British-controlled shipping to put into or remain in American ports until the U-boat picture clarified, but quickly released these vessels and routed them "evasively" to Halifax or to Bermuda for onward voyages in Halifax convoys to the British Isles. As a result, U-boats sank only one more British-owned tanker in waters of the Eastern Sea Frontier in January and February.

Low on fuel and out of torpedoes, Hardegen set a course for France. When he was well clear of the American coast, he radioed Dönitz the results of his one-week

---

* The Big Inch, begun in July 1942, delivered the first crude to the Philadelphia area about a year later, in August 1943. The Little Big Inch, begun in April 1943, delivered the first product to Linden, New Jersey, in March 1944. During the war, these two lines delivered about 380 million barrels of oil and product. The Plantation, built in 1941, came into full operation in 1942.

† Excluding Panamanian-registered vessels.

foray in American waters, January 12 to January 19. It was a heavy beat on the drum: eight ships sunk for 53,060 tons, including three tankers. Counting past overclaims, Hardegen believed he had sunk "over 100,000" tons and therefore qualified for a *Ritterkreuz*. Well pleased with this drumbeat, Admiral Raeder and Dönitz replied with congratulations and the award.*

But Hardegen was not yet done. Homebound in mid-Atlantic, he found and aggressively attacked and sank two ships with his deck gun: the 3,000-ton British freighter *Culebra* on January 25, and the 9,200-ton Norwegian tanker *Pan Norway* in ballast on January 26.† Fortunately for the fifty-one survivors of the *Pan Norway*, an Italian freighter under Swiss charter (hence a "neutral") was close at hand and upon orders from Hardegen, she put about and rescued the Norwegians. Unfortunately for Hardegen, a bridge gun blew up during the attack on *Culebra*, severely wounding the propagandist Alwin Tölle. Unable to provide proper medical care, Hardegen resourcefully set up a plan with Kerneval to transfer Tölle to the inbound blockade runner *Spreewald*, which had a doctor on board.

After Hardegen had cleared out of the Cape Hatteras area, Richard Zapp in *U-66* returned. On January 22 and 23, he sank two loaded American freighters, the 2,300-ton *Norvana* (sugar) and the 8,000-ton *Venore* (iron ore), and the loaded 8,100-ton British tanker *Empire Gem*. Low on fuel and torpedoes, Zapp also called it a day and headed for France. In his radio report, he also claimed a heavy beat on the drum: five ships for 50,000 tons sunk, all off Cape Hatteras. His confirmed score was five ships for 33,456 tons. Counting overclaims on prior patrols, Zapp's total sinkings were about 75,000 tons, not enough for a *Ritterkreuz*, but his successes in American waters earned a "well done" from Dönitz and a propaganda broadcast from Berlin.

The last of the three boats to arrive in the Cape Hatteras area was the green skipper Erich Folkers in *U-125*. Having been assigned initially a patrol zone east of the New Jersey coast, he had seen no traffic and was hungry for kills. He found two victims on the afternoon and evening of January 25. The first was the American tanker *Olney*, which had grounded on a shoal. Folkers fired a total of seven torpedoes at this sitting duck, but inexplicably, he claimed, only one hit for damage. In fact, *Olney* reported (with relief) all seven torpedoes missed. Later that night, Folkers shot two torpedoes at the 5,700-ton American freighter *West Ivis*. This time the torpedoes worked and *West Ivis* sank in fourteen minutes.

Low on fuel—and frustrated—Folkers set a course for France. He stated in his report to Dönitz that he still had six torpedoes in his bow compartment, but that three of his four bow tubes were "out of order." Kerneval instructed Folkers to down-load torpedoes to his stern room in case he should find a worthwhile ship on

---

* Including one ship sunk on the duck *U-147*, Hardegen's confirmed sinkings were eleven ships for 60,787 tons. Owing to the vivid and precise description of the sinkings of the two "unidentified" ships for 8,000 tons in Hardegen's log, Gannon was persuaded to credit them. An American researcher, Edward R. Rumpf, suggests that those two ships could have been the 1,300-ton Norwegian *Octavian* and the 5,300-ton Panamanian *Olympic*, whose loss has been attributed to another U-boat.

† With these two sinkings, Hardegen's claimed score for the patrol rose to ten ships for 66,135 tons, the best patrol in recent memory. The final, confirmed score was seven ships for 46,744 tons, not counting the two "unknowns."

the way home. Folkers complied with this unusual order, but he did not find another target. His beat on the drum was faint.

The first three Type IXs of Drumbeat to enter waters of the Eastern Sea Frontier thus hit eleven ships and sank ten in that area, from January 14 through January 24. Hardegen in *U-123* sank four positively confirmed ships (two tankers); Zapp in *U-66* sank five positively confirmed ships (two tankers); Folkers in *U-125* sank one positively confirmed freighter. Other claimed sinkings remain conjectural. This damage was only slightly greater than that inflicted by the Japanese submarine skippers off California in December: nine merchant ships (seven tankers) hit; two tankers sunk. The damage inflicted by Axis submarines on both coasts was cause for serious concern, but not for panic.

THE ATTACK ON CANADA

In most accounts of the opening U-boat campaign in the Americas, the patrols of the twelve U-boats (two IXs, ten VIIs) committed to Canadian waters in January are seldom fully described. In fact, they inflicted almost twice the damage as did the first three Type IXs in United States waters during the same period.

Those twelve boats confronted appalling weather. Blinding blizzards raked the bleak land and seascapes. Thick ice encrusted the exposed superstructures, adding tons of destabilizing weight to the boats. Before diving, the bridge watch had to chip ice from the flanges of the main air-induction inlet so the valve would seat properly. There was small comfort below; most of the VIIs had no cold-weather heating systems. One boat recorded inside temperatures of 33 degrees Fahrenheit day after day. Unheated periscopes fogged up to the point of uselessness.

Warned by the Admiralty of the oncoming U-boat assault, the Canadian Navy and American air and naval forces in the Newfoundland and Nova Scotia area were on full alert. They added an escort group of nine vessels to convoy Halifax 169 and diverted it to the northeast. In spite of the unfavorable flying conditions, they mounted maximum air patrols.

Ernst Kals in the new Type IXC *U-130,* embarked on his first full-length war patrol, took position in Cabot Strait, separating Newfoundland and Cape Breton Island. On January 12, a Canadian plane found Kals on the surface and attacked with 250-pound depth charges. Fortunately for Kals and his men, the air crew botched the attack and *U-130* escaped undamaged. Remaining in the strait, in the early hours of January 13, Kals opened the U-boat campaign in Canada. In two separate attacks he fired five torpedoes, got four hits, and sank two ships: the 1,600-ton Norwegian freighter *Frisco,* and the 5,400-ton Panamanian freighter *Friar Rock.* Reporting these first successes to Dönitz, Kals complained of "heavy" air cover and "tremendous" cold.

Hounded by the stepped-up air patrols, Kals nonetheless closed on the seaport of Sydney, Cape Breton Island, where it was believed slow convoys assembled. He surfaced on the evening of January 16 twelve miles off the coast. He observed Sydney as Hardegen had observed New York City. Like New York, Sydney was brightly lighted. But no convoys emerged. Earlier, on January 9, after the departure of Slow Convoy 64, Sydney had "closed" for the winter and the assembly of all convoys had been shifted to Halifax.

Kals nearly came to grief the next day. Two "destroyers" found *U-130* on the surface. When one turned to ram, Kals crash-dived just in time. However, the ice-caked main induction did not seat properly and eight tons of ice water flooded the engine room, dragging *U-130* to the bottom at 157 feet. Perhaps because the "destroyer's" depth-charge racks were iced up, no attack ensued. After pumping out the excess water, Kals surfaced and ran out to sea. In response to a message from Dönitz giving *U-130* "freedom of action," Kals, who had a good supply of fuel, immediately departed Canadian waters for the warmer and safer waters off Cape Hatteras. On the way there he sank the 8,200-ton Norwegian tanker *Alexandra Höegh,* which was sailing alone well offshore.

The other big boat in Newfoundland waters, the Type IXB *U-109,* commanded by *Ritterkreuz* holder Heinrich Bleichrodt, experienced similar difficulties from the brutal weather and maddening torpedo problems as well. Patrolling off the south coast of Nova Scotia, Bleichrodt found a 5,000-ton freighter hove to, apparently waiting for a pilot to guide her into Yarmouth. In five separate approaches on this sitting duck, Bleichrodt fired five torpedoes from about 600 yards. All torpedoes inexplicably failed or missed, a demoralizing experience for Bleichrodt, who had not sunk a ship on *U-109* since taking command of her the previous May. In view of the "heavy" ASW measures and miserable weather in Canadian waters, and the size and clumsiness of *U-109,* doubtless Bleichrodt would have also welcomed a shift to Cape Hatteras, but the IXB *U-109* lacked the fuel capacity of the IXC *U-130* (165 tons versus 208 tons) and he had to stay put and endure the hardships. Before setting off for home, Bleichrodt sank one confirmed ship in Canadian waters, the 4,900-ton British freighter *Thirlby.**

The ten Type VIIs assigned to Canadian waters patrolled a wide section of the Newfoundland and Nova Scotia coastlines, conserving fuel to the greatest extent possible. The *Ritterkreuz* holder Erich Topp in *U-552,* who also carried a propagandist-photographer, bagged the first ship on January 15, the 4,100-ton British freighter *Dayrose,* sailing alone off Cape Race on the Avalon Peninsula, Newfoundland. But it took five torpedoes to sink her: three failed or missed, only two hit.

Cruising directly off St. John's over the next several days—his periscopes damaged by ice—Topp had more torpedo difficulties. On January 17, he attacked a freighter escorted by two "destroyers." Three more torpedoes failed or missed; a "destroyer" counterattacked and drove him off. The next day, off St. John's, he intercepted the 2,600-ton American freighter *Frances Salman.* Again it took Topp five torpedoes to sink his victim; three missed or failed, only two hit. On the night

---

* Bleichrodt was wrongly credited with sinking the 6,100-ton British freighter *Empire Kingfisher,* which ran aground.

following, Topp conducted a gun attack on what he described as a "10,000-ton Greek freighter," firing 126 rounds. He claimed she went down, but the sinking could not be confirmed in Allied records. Having shot thirteen torpedoes to sink two (confirmed) ships for 6,722 tons, Topp set a course for home, furious at the nine torpedo failures or misses and the meager return for the time and risk invested and extreme discomfort endured.

Two other Type VII boats, both on maiden patrols, departed Canadian waters at about the same time. The first was Joachim Berger in *U-87*, who had sunk a tanker en route to Canada. On January 17 Berger attacked another tanker, the 8,100-ton Norwegian *Nyholt*, with torpedoes and gun. The ship went down, but during the action *U-87* was herself, in Berger's words, badly "shot up," forcing him to abort to France. The other boat was Friedrich-Hermann Praetorius's *U-135*. He sank no ships in Canadian waters, but on his way home he got the impressive 9,600-ton Belgian freighter *Gandia*, a straggler from convoy Outbound North 54, which had been scattered by winter storms.

Of the remaining seven Type VIIs in Canadian waters, Karl Thurmann in *U-553* was the most successful. In spite of seven torpedo "misses" (he reported), he sank two big tankers for 17,366 tons: the 9,106-ton British *Diala* and the 8,260-ton Norwegian *Inneröy*. Peter Cremer in the new *U-333* ranked second in tonnage, sinking three freighters (with four torpedoes) for 14,045 tons. Third was another new skipper, Hans Oestermann in *U-754*, who sank four freighters (two British, two Greek) for 11,386 tons. Walter Schug in the new *U-86*, who also had a close call from a Canadian aircraft, sank a crippled 4,300-ton Greek freighter and severely damaged the 8,600-ton British tanker *Toorak*. On the way home he attacked another tanker, but the torpedoes failed or missed. The *Ritterkreuz* holder Rolf Mützelburg in *U-203* sank two ships, including, awkwardly, a Portuguese neutral, but in aggregate, the two came to a mere 2,000 tons. Two other skippers, Horst Uphoff in *U-84* and Horst Degen in *U-701*, who had sunk a ship en route to Canada, sank no ships in Canadian waters. When he got home, Dönitz harshly criticized Degen for his "awkward temerity," for wasting torpedoes, and for not conducting a more thorough search for his first watch officer after he was washed overboard early in the patrol.

In addition to these sinkings in Canadian waters, some of these VIIs caused American naval authorities gray hairs. The battleship *Arkansas*, the "jeep" carrier *Long Island*, the light cruiser *Philadelphia*, and the new, small seaplane tender *Barnegat*, with appropriate destroyer escort, were at Argentia, Newfoundland, preparing to sail to the States January 18. Upon learning of the sinking of the freighter *Dayrose* and trawler *Catalina* on January 15 off Cape Race, merely sixty miles from Argentia, American naval authorities sent an eight-ship hunter-killer group, consisting of four American destroyers (*Badger, Ellis, Ericsson, Greer*) and four Canadian corvettes to Cape Race to attack and drive off U-boats and assure a safe passage for the big ships. Owing to further sinkings by U-boats off Cape Race and to the inability of the Allied warships to find and to kill U-boats, the sailing of *Arkansas, Long Island*, et al., had to be postponed to January 22.

Because of fuel limitations, by January 22 all ten Type VIIs of the first wave in

Canadian waters had commenced the long, slow, arduous voyage home, as had Bleichrodt in *U-109*, who was ordered to follow a southerly course and scout the island of Bermuda. The VIIs had caused shock and not a little chaos in Canadian waters, but the prolonged travel time, miserable weather, strong ASW measures, and exceptionally large number of torpedo failures had resulted in disappointing returns. Even so, counting sinkings en route to and from Canada, the ten VIIs had bagged a total of eighteen confirmed ships for 85,400 tons. The two confirmed victories by Kals in *U-130* and one each by Bleichrodt in *U-109* and Hardegen in *U-123* brought the total sinkings in Canadian waters by all U-boats of the first wave to twenty-two.

Having come down to Cape Hatteras from Canada—and sunk a big tanker en route—Ernst Kals in the Type IXC *U-130*, was the fourth and last U-boat of the first wave to directly invade United States waters. He found good hunting. According to Allied records, on January 22 he sank the 5,300-ton Panamanian-registered tanker *Olympic*. Swinging north to the coast of New Jersey, on the night of January 25 he sank the loaded 9,300-ton Norwegian tanker *Varanger*. The explosion rattled windows ashore, thirty-five miles away. Returning to the Cape Hatteras area on January 27, he hit and blew up the 7,100-ton American tanker *Francis E. Powell*. Having exhausted all torpedoes, Kals attacked yet another 7,000-ton American tanker, *Halo*, with his deck gun, but she got away.

Homebound to France, Kals reported his claims to Dönitz: six ships for about 48,000 tons, including four tankers plus damage to a fifth tanker. Postwar accounting credited him with six confirmed sinkings (four tankers) for 37,000 tons. Disallowing Hardegen's two unidentified freighters, for which no official confirmation has yet been found, Kals—making his first full war patrol—sank more ships in North American waters than any other skipper. Counting the three ships for 15,000 tons he had sunk on his seventeen-day voyage from Kiel to Lorient in early December, his total score—nine confirmed ships for 52,000 tons—was one of the best starts by any skipper in the war. As with Hardegen and Zapp, Berlin propagandists gave Kals prominent play.

Per orders, *Ritterkreuz holder* Heinrich Bleichrodt in *U-109* scouted Bermuda on his way home, but found no targets. The diversion used more fuel than anyone anticipated, so much, Bleichrodt reported, that *U-109* could not make it back to France. In response, Kerneval directed Kals in *U-130* to rendezvous with *U-109* and transfer fuel. While waiting at the rendezvous point, Kals spotted the 8,000-ton British freighter *Tacoma Star*, but he had no torpedoes. He obligingly tracked the ship, homing in Bleichrodt in *U-109*. When Bleichrodt arrived on February 1, he sank the ship, then took on fuel from *U-130*. Thanks to Kals for tracking and for fuel, Bleichrodt was able to sink two more ships by torpedo and gun on his way back to France: the 11,300-ton Canadian tanker *Montrolite* and a 3,500-ton Panamanian freighter. With these victories, Bleichrodt claimed five ships for 33,700 tons. Postwar accounting gave him four confirmed ships for 27,700 tons on this patrol—his first sinkings in fifteen months.

• • •

Homebound to France from Canadian waters, Peter Cremer in the new Type VII *U-333,* who had sunk three ships for 14,000 tons, came upon a lone, zigzagging freighter on January 31. He submerged and closed to 400 yards to look her over. Concluding she was British, Cremer hit her with his last two torpedoes. After the first torpedo struck, the ship radioed an *SOS* in plain language, identifying herself as the British *Brittany.* She was actually the 5,100-ton German blockade runner *Spreewald,* homebound from the Far East with a cargo of 3,365 tons of rubber, 250 tons of tin, and eighty-six British prisoners of war she had received from the German merchant-ship raider *Kormoran.* *

From the open radio broadcasts, Dönitz and the OKM divined the error immediately. The OKM was furious. Given the "dire raw materials situation," the OKM's diarist fumed, the loss of *Spreewald*'s cargo "by an unforgivable error" was "extremely painful." Dönitz, too, was angry; the incident had tarnished the glorious success of Drumbeat. When he learned from Cremer that *U-333* was the shooter, Dönitz directed that upon his arrival, Cremer was to be court-martialed for "disobedience in action, manslaughter, and damage to military property."

Meanwhile Dönitz set in motion a massive sea and air rescue. Cremer in *U-333,* Hardegen in *U-123* (who was looking for *Spreewald* to transfer the wounded propagandist), and Günther Heydemann in *U-575* (who was to escort *Spreewald* into France) were first on the scene. Three other Type VIIs, inbound from Canada, arrived next. Then came two boats outbound to North America, including the Type IXB *U-105,* commanded by a new skipper, Heinrich Schuch. Lastly, five Condors from France searched a large area around the reported position. Owing to fuel shortages, the inbound boats were unable to search extensively and Hardegen in *U-123* soon proceeded onward to Lorient; the propagandist survived his injuries.

Forty-eight hours after the sinking, on the afternoon of February 2, Schuch in *U-105* found survivors in three lifeboats and three rafts: twenty-five of sixty Germans and fifty-five of the eighty-six British POWs. Another lifeboat, containing *Spreewald*'s captain and twenty other German sailors, had separated and could not be found. Schuch put the eighty survivors below and headed for France at full speed. When he reported that one German survivor was gravely injured, Dönitz sent out a Dornier seaplane to pick him up. However, while landing in the rough sea, the seaplane broke off a wing and Schuch had to rescue the airmen as well. Other outbound boats searched for the missing Germans from *Spreewald,* but they were never found.

When Cremer in *U-333* arrived in Lorient on February 9, he faced an instant court-martial. However, after all the technicalities had been entered and analyzed, Dönitz's first staff officer, Günter Hessler, rose to Cremer's defense. The sinking was indeed regrettable, but the simple fact was that the disguised *Spreewald* was

---

* Intercepted by the Australian cruiser *Sydney* in Australian waters on November 19, 1941, soon after giving *Spreewald* her prisoners, *Kormoran* sank *Sydney* with the loss of all hands. *Kormoran* herself was so badly wrecked in the engagement she had to scuttle, with the loss of eighty-five of her 400-man crew.

not where she was supposed to be. Therefore Cremer was not at fault. That Cremer had conducted an outstanding maiden patrol and showed great promise weighed heavily in his favor. The court acquitted him; everyone involved was sworn to secrecy. The *Spreewald* affair remained hushed up for years.*

Notwithstanding the disappointing returns of the VIIs and IXs in Canadian waters and the *Spreewald* incident, Dönitz—and Berlin propagandists—pronounced the first foray of U-boats into North American waters a great success, as indeed it was. Counting ships sunk en route to and from North America, the five Type IXs had sunk twenty-three for about 150,000 tons. Combined with the eighteen sinkings for about 85,000 tons by the VIIs, the total was forty-one ships for about 236,000 tons, plus damage to several others. The sinkings included thirteen tankers, eight of them British or British-controlled.†

In return, not a single U-boat had been lost; only one, Berger's *U-87,* had incurred serious damage from Allied forces.

EXPLOITING BRITISH ANTISUBMARINE TECHNOLOGY

The British continued to badger the Americans to organize convoys on the United States East Coast. Toward that end, Churchill and Pound offered Roosevelt and King, in addition to the ten corvettes, twenty-four British ASW trawlers, as well as ten motor torpedo boats under construction in Canada. King eagerly accepted the twenty-four trawlers‡ but declined the Canadian vessels because the "Sixty Ships in Sixty Days" were to be completed long before the Canadian vessels, or so it was thought.

The British War Cabinet sent several military missions to the United States. Their purpose was to give the Americans the benefit of the British experience with U-boats and find out if the Americans were "really short of escort craft on the East Coast," and if, as suspected, King was siphoning off the destroyers released from the North Atlantic run to reinforce the Pacific Fleet. Predictably, the reports of these missions were uniformly negative. The Americans had not yet learned how difficult it was to find and kill a U-boat. There was little to no coordination be-

---

* Cremer himself was first to reveal the full story in his book, *U-boat Commander* (1982).

† Some of the boats of the second wave sailing in January overlapped the December boats and sank ships in January. Some of the December boats sank ships in early February. Totals by both groups in the month of January only: forty-two ships sunk (fifteen tankers) for 230,685 tons; five ships (four tankers) damaged.

‡ Twenty-two of the twenty-four trawlers were standard 170-foot coal-burners with a top speed of 12 knots. They were equipped with a 4" bow gun, depth charges, and British sonar. One, *Northern Princess,* was believed to have foundered in heavy seas en route to Newfoundland and was lost with all hands. Actually, she was torpedoed by Otto Ites in *U-94* en route to America. The first ten trawlers did not reach New York until March 12. The others came later in the month. Many were in need of voyage repairs or refits and did not carry spare parts or metric-gauge tools and required scarce high-grade coal, but the British crews were indomitable and inspiring.

tween the air and naval forces—no single operations center. In total numbers, the air and naval ASW forces were "quite inadequate." There was as yet no single guiding hand within the U.S. Navy to formulate ASW tactical doctrine and to prescribe training methods and to coordinate R&D for new weaponry. The weaponry available was inadequate to the task. For example, American depth charges had a maximum depth setting of only 300 feet.

All this was undeniable. The reports later provided rich grist for those historians who sought to make the case that the Americans had "learned nothing" from the British experience with U-boats and/or that they—and King—had failed to grasp or were oblivious to the U-boat threat. But the reports failed to take notice of the very large number of ASW measures underway in America over and above the massive ship and aircraft building and repair programs. A great many of these ASW measures were a direct outgrowth of the British experience:

• **THE MOBILIZATION OF SCIENCE.** Emulating the British example, in June 1940, America had mobilized its huge scientific and engineering community to assist the military. President Roosevelt had established the National Defense Research Committee, chaired by Dr. Vannevar Bush. Composed of a glittering array of eminent scientists, the committee had recruited thousands of willing scientists and engineers who had fanned out through the military establishments to contribute their talent to the war effort or who pursued military projects in their own institutions and laboratories.

The Navy bureaus and the Naval Research Laboratory (NRL) did not always welcome this outside talent with open arms. Many of the civilian scientists met calculated hostility. Nonetheless, by the time America entered the war the Vannevar Bush committee or its offshoots had launched a great array of ASW projects, based upon the work of British or American scientists, engineers, and mathematicians, some of whom had adopted the new British technique of "operations research."

• **RADAR.** Based on the British cavity magnetron, American R&D on radar had grown enormously. By January 1, 1942, MIT's Radiation Laboratory had fifty different radar projects in the works. However, quantity production of centimetric-wavelength radar for naval ships and aircraft proved difficult. According to one authority,* "not a single microwave [centimetric] set was in use" on January 1, 1942. But the groundwork was well laid and the breakthroughs came quickly. On February 17, the Navy contracted for mass production of a 300-pound airborne (air to surface) centimetric-wavelength radar, Model AS-G (known colloquially as "George"), which could detect a coastline at a range of 100 miles, convoys at eighty-five miles, and surfaced U-boats at nine miles or more. Contracts for powerful long-range shipborne (surface to surface) centimetric-wavelength radar (Model S-G, also called "George") followed almost immediately.

• **HUFF DUFF.** Encouraged by the work of British and French radio engineers, as well as American specialists in that field, the NRL was pursuing with highest priority R&D on a High Frequency Direction Finder (Huff Duff) for ship-

---

* James Phinney Baxter III, in his book *Scientist Against Time* (1950).

board installation. Spearheaded by the NRL's Maxwell K. Goldstein, who worked in collaboration with engineers at International Telephone and Radio Laboratories, the R&D led to a set, designated Model DAQ. It, together with the British Model FH-3, was installed in the new destroyer *Corry* in the early months of 1942 for comparative tests.

The upshot was the development of yet another American set, DAR, which was put into "mass" production in the late summer of 1942. In Goldstein's words, the DAR was an extensively modernized version of the British FH-3. While it utilized "most of the basic components" of the FH-3, the DAR incorporated "the complete use of U.S. tubes, stabilization of the radio frequency oscillator, a new 'on course' indicator of the cathode-ray type and a new power supply (with speaker) of compact design."

The DAR (and its variations) was to become one of the most effective ASW "tools" of World War II. Parallel to its development, engineers at the NRL and at International Telephone and Radio Laboratories produced an equally effective land-based Huff Duff, Model DAJ.

• **DEPTH CHARGES.** As the British reports noted, American depth charges had an unacceptable depth limit of 300 feet. American scientists discovered other faults. The charges sank too slowly and followed an erratic underwater trajectory. The warheads were too weak. A crash R&D program was already underway to produce depth charges with 600-foot depth limits, faster sinking rates, improved trajectories, and 50 percent more explosive power, by substituting the British-developed Torpex for TNT. Two reliable standard depth charges for surface vessels were soon to emerge: the Mark VII, with a 600-pound warhead, and the Mark IX, with a 300-pound warhead. The big Mark VII could only be rolled from the stern tracks. The smaller Mark IX could be rolled from stern tracks or fired from Y guns or the improved K guns.

• **EXPENDABLE SONOBUOYS.** British scientists had proposed an ingenious device, the sonic- or sonobuoy, which was designed to be tossed from a merchant ship or escort during a suspected or actual U-boat attack. Fitted with a miniaturized hydrophone and a radio transmitter, the sonobuoy would float free to the rear of the convoy, where it could pick up the noise of a submerged submarine and send a warning signal.

The British did not pursue the sonobuoy, but the Americans, believing the device had great potential, had launched a large R&D program to produce improved sonobuoys for aircraft. Upon reaching the suspected area of a submarine or after detecting one by sight, the aircraft was to drop a pattern of sonobuoys. Since each buoy was to have a different coded signal, the aircraft would be able to follow the submerged moves of the submarine and set up an attack based on the detected movement, and/or call in surface forces to assist in the attack.

• **AIR-DROPPED WEAPONS.** By the time the United States entered the war, the British, but not the Americans, had developed an aerial depth-charge pistol with a shallow setting of about twenty-five feet for attacking surfaced or crash diving U-boats. Profiting from British technology, the Americans hastened to fit a version of this pistol to the 250-pound Mark XVII aerial depth charge. Moreover, by substituting British-developed Torpex for TNT, the Americans increased the lethality of the aerial depth charge by 50 percent.

Aware from the British experience that aircraft attacks on U-boats had not been very successful, American scientists sought a more sophisticated device for killing fast-diving U-boats. The upshot was a small, smart, acoustic airborne torpedo that, after entering the water, "homed" on the noise of the submerged U-boat.

Declared feasible in December 1941, scientists and engineers at the Harvard Underwater Sound Laboratory, the Columbia University Underwater Sound Laboratory, the Navy's David Taylor Model Basin, General Electric, and Western Electric and its subsidiary Bell Laboratories pursued this weapon with the highest priority in utmost secrecy using the cover name "Mark XXIV Mine." Informally known as "Fido," this weapon was ready for use in merely twelve months. It would prove to be one of the most effective ASW devices produced during the war, so successful that the original order for 10,000 torpedoes was cut back to 4,000.

The "Fido" was seven feet long and seventeen inches in diameter. It weighed 680 pounds and had a 92-pound Torpex warhead. It could "chase" a submerged U-boat for ten minutes at a maximum speed of 12 knots. Since a U-boat could outsmart Fido by surfacing and running away at high speed on diesels, the characteristics of Fido remained very secret throughout the war, to the point that the weapon could not be employed except on a fully submerged U-boat, and not even then if an Allied ship or another U-boat was on the surface nearby.

• **LORAN.** The British experience had demonstrated that a means of all-weather navigation was essential for reporting positions of sighted U-boats, for more effective rendezvous of convoys with air and surface escorts, for evasive maneuvers of convoys, and for other military purposes.

In October 1940, an American scientist, Alfred Loomis, proposed an electronic navigation system which was based on radio pulses emitted in a certain way by shore-based transmitters. In early 1941 a team at MIT's Radiation Laboratory, headed by Melville Eastham, pursued this proposal and by September of that year had demonstrated its feasibility. Known as Long Range Aid to Navigation (LORAN), the system proved to be capable of providing nearly precise navigational fixes up to 700 miles from the shore-based transmitters in daytime and 1,400 miles at night in any weather. Soon after America entered the war, the Army and Navy established five LORAN transmitting stations in Canada and Greenland, for the benefit of the North Atlantic convoy network. From this beginning, the LORAN system was to spread over half the globe.

• **MAGNETIC AIRBORNE DETECTOR (MAD).** American scientists had suggested before the war that the mass of metal of a submerged submarine could probably be detected from a low-flying aircraft equipped with a magnetometer. In October 1941, a Catalina equipped with primitive MAD gear verified the theory and by the time America entered the war, a very large MAD R&D program was underway to intensify the sensitivity of the magnetometer. An improved MAD had been installed in a blimp based on the East Coast and sets were being installed in other blimps.

Upon getting a MAD contact, the blimp dropped floating flares or lights to mark the course of the submerged submarine so that it or other ASW forces could set up an attack. To make the flares and lights fall vertically—and accurately—they were fired backward at a speed equal to the forward motion of the blimp. R&D was underway to reduce the weight of MAD gear so that units could be mounted on each wingtip of fixed-wing aircraft, to provide improved "directionality," and for a Magnetic Airborne Bomb Sight (MABS). The latter was to compensate for the forward speed of the aircraft and automatically fire bombs or rockets rearward which, like the flares and lights, were to fall vertically to the target.

• **SONAR AND SONAR PRESENTATION.** Apart from work underway to greatly increase the power and sophistication of sonar, American scientists had urged development of an electronic "plotter," which would simplify the difficult job of tracking and attacking submarines for the benefit of the unskilled reserves who were to man most of the Navy's ships. The answer from the laboratories was the important Antisubmarine Course Plotter. Based on electronic inputs from the sonar and from the gyro compass and the pit log of the surface vessel, it automatically displayed on a cathode-ray tube the track of the submarine and the track of the attacking surface ship.

These and many other new devices were in due course to immeasurably assist the Allies in the U-boat war, but, as the British reports noted, there remained the absence of a single guiding hand to direct the Navy's ASW effort. An important step to remedy this deficiency was taken on February 7, 1942—as the first wave of Drumbeat U-boats was arriving back in France. On that date Atlantic Fleet commander Royal Ingersoll established in Boston what was called the Atlantic Fleet ASW Unit, commanded by Wilder D. Baker, an experienced destroyerman and escort-group commander, detached from the North Atlantic convoy run.

The purpose of the Baker group was to develop and standardize tactics, weaponry, and training for killing U-boats. At King's direction or invitation, all Sea Frontiers and the Army Air Forces attached liaison officers to the unit. At Baker's invitation, ten men skilled in "operations research" from a division of the National Defense Research Committee, known as the Antisubmarine Warfare Operations Research Group (ASWORG), joined his unit. Soon after the unit was staffed, King transferred it from Boston to his headquarters in Washington, and bestowed upon it extraordinary powers.

Emulating the British example in its earliest days, the Baker group produced manuals for carrying out attacks on U-boats and also for "attack teachers." The latter were elaborate hands-on layouts to simulate battles versus U-boats. Evolved from "a few" imported British models, the American attack teachers were produced by three firms: General Electric, Sangamo, and the Submarine Signal Company. As in the Royal Navy, the U.S. Navy required that all American officers involved with ASW had to master the intricacies of the attack teacher.

At the Federal Building in downtown Manhattan, meanwhile, Admiral Andrews and General Krogstad had to improvise with the inadequate "tools" at hand. The "tatterdemalion fleet" of the Eastern Sea Frontier, augmented by a few Navy minesweepers, tugboats, and other utility craft—whatever could get to sea—patrolled close offshore, but these little ships were so busy searching for and picking up survivors of the many torpedoed ships that they had little time for hunting and fighting U-boats. The Navy and Coast Guard aircraft and blimps patrolled the inner shipping lanes. Krogstad's keen but green bomber pilots, alternating basic bomber training with ASW patrols, reconnoitered lanes further offshore. Several air crews found and attacked what they believed to be U-boats, but these contacts were doubtless products of overactive imaginations.

The British continued to pressure King to initiate convoying on the United States East Coast. However, King, Ingersoll, Andrews, and all other senior naval officers resisted this pressure because they did not believe, as the British did, that inadequately escorted cargo convoys were better than no convoys at all. The American view had been formed to a great extent by the severe British shipping losses in the thinly escorted North Atlantic convoys of the summer and fall of 1940 and on the losses in the fall of 1941 on the North Atlantic run when inadequately trained and equipped Canadian vessels served as convoy escort. The abort of the Canadian-escorted Slow Convoy 52 in Newfoundland waters in early November 1941 was still vivid in American minds and doubtless influenced King and others.

In his attack on the U.S. Navy, historian Michael Gannon argues that inasmuch as Dönitz had focused his U-boats on "America's doorstep," leaving the North Atlantic convoy run "quiet," the Allies should have immediately shifted the bulk of ASW and escort forces from North Atlantic to North American waters, both to attack U-boats and to provide escorts for an East Coast convoy network.

This argument, which appears logical and prudent, is, in fact, neither.

• The North Atlantic convoy run was definitely not "quiet," meaning unthreatened. The U-boats, en route to and from the Americas, crossed the North Atlantic along routes approximately the same as the convoys. Since the U-boats traveled alone, rather than in groups, or wolf packs, and maintained radio silence, they were very difficult to locate and evade. Any one of those U-boats could happen upon a North Atlantic convoy at any hour. If the convoy was not properly escorted, the result could be catastrophic.*

• In the initial wave of U-boats Dönitz sent to the Americas, twelve of the fifteen boats went to Canadian waters. They patrolled off Halifax, St. John's, and Sydney, where transatlantic convoys originated and dispersed. Deprived of proper escorts, these convoys could be massacred in Canadian waters by succeeding waves of U-boats.

• Owing to Hitler's "Norway paranoia," in early January Berlin ordered Dönitz to establish a defensive line of U-boats between Iceland and the Faeroes. Although some of these boats assumed positions to the north of the regular convoy

---

* In support of his argument that the North Atlantic run was "quiet" at this time and therefore a shift of ASW forces was prudent and justified, Gannon cites figures to show how few convoys were attacked and ships were lost in that area. But these figures are not convincing, as ship losses to U-boats in that area were seldom high. As related, 98 percent of the ships in North Atlantic convoys—literally thousands upon thousands of vessels—reached destinations.

routes in the Northwest Approaches, as will be seen, they posed a definite threat to inbound North Atlantic convoys as they entered and departed the British Isles. To leave those convoys unescorted could also invite catastrophe.

- The U.S. Navy was already in the process of shifting its patrol bombers and many of its destroyers from the North Atlantic run to American waters, as noted, leaving the preponderance of the escort job on the North Atlantic run to the Canadians and British. As also noted, most of these American destroyers had to be assigned to escort troopship convoys. To uproot the remaining Canadian and British escorts and also move them to East Coast waters not only would have exposed the North Atlantic convoy run to U-boat attack, but also would have placed those warships far from home bases and supply lines, decreasing their effectiveness and availability.

Meanwhile, Admiral Andrews continued to provide Allied shipping all the protection he could with "the tools at hand." He laid defensive minefields on the approaches to the main Atlantic ports: Portland, Maine; Boston; New York; Charleston; and the entrances to the Delaware and Chesapeake bays off Cape May, New Jersey, and Cape Henry, Virginia. He pulled back shipping from well offshore to newly marked inshore lanes very close to the beach in shallow water, where U-boats were less likely to be and where the few available aircraft might offer a modicum of protection. He encouraged the use of protected shortcuts, such as the Cape Cod Canal. He advised merchant ships to exercise strict smoke discipline, to lay over in port at night if possible, or to run blacked out and to zigzag and to minimize radio transmissions, which U-boats might monitor. Unaccustomed to all this rigamarole—or contemptuous of being told what to do by the Navy—the captains of many American merchant ships simply ignored the rules and did what they pleased, and not a few lost their ships.

As a result of the sinkings in the Eastern Sea Frontier, on January 24 King directed Ingersoll to make available to Andrews and to other Sea Frontier commanders Atlantic Fleet aircraft which were based within their respective areas of responsibility. This gave Andrews operational control of forty-four Catalinas, thirty-eight at Norfolk and six at Newport. Ingersoll notified "all Sea Frontier commanders" that the transfers were not permanent but rather a temporary "emergency measure." He stressed that the use of such planes for ASW patrols by Sea Frontiers "should not unduly interfere with scheduled operations of Atlantic Fleet aircraft, especially those on convoy escort."*

Shocked and bewildered by the Japanese successes in the Pacific and Far East, the American public was at first only dimly aware of the gravity of the U-boat campaign in American waters. The Navy did its utmost to keep Americans in the dark by imposing censorship, by downplaying—or lying about—the extent of

---

* Catalinas helped escort Troop Convoys AT 10 and BT 200. Others provided escort for the new British "jeep" carrier *Archer*, which, as related, collided with another vessel during workup in the Caribbean and was being towed to Charleston by the Navy tug *Cherokee*.

shipping losses, and by issuing reassuring claims of U-boat kills. A member of the Washington naval staff, Ladislas Farago, asserted in his book *The Tenth Fleet* that a Navy publicist even deliberately fabricated the legendary radio message from one Argentia-based Hudson pilot, Donald F. Mason, who erroneously claimed a kill: "Sighted Sub. Sank Same." But, in fact, as Admiral Bristol in Argentia asserted in an after-action report to Ingersoll on January 28 (copies to King and Stark), the cry of triumph from Mason was quite genuine, even though he had not actually sunk a U-boat.*

GERMAN DIVERSIONS AND DELAYS

During the first weeks of January 1942, rumors of an Allied invasion of Norway intensified in Berlin. Doubtless the British inspired many of the rumors, partly to deceive Hitler, partly to encourage the embryonic Norwegian underground to rise up and strike, and partly to raise the spirits of all Norwegians. Given the recent Allied disasters at Pearl Harbor, Manila, and elsewhere in the Pacific, as well as the grievous British naval setbacks in the Mediterranean, the rumors were incredible. And yet Hitler seized upon each new report as though it were gospel.

As the Norwegian nightmare festered in Hitler's mind, Raeder and the OKM drew plans to execute the Führer's order of December 29, 1941, specifying that "all ships" of the *Kriegsmarine* were to be deployed to defend Norway. The super-battleship *Tirpitz* shifted on January 15 from German waters to Norway. Although Raeder remained adamantly opposed to Hitler's order to redeploy the battle cruisers *Gneisenau* and *Scharnhorst* and the heavy cruiser *Prinz Eugen* from France to Norway via the English Channel and Germany, he directed the OKM to carry it out, making arrangements with the *Luftwaffe* for massive air support.

Hitler's concern over Norway reached fever pitch on January 22. During a meeting with Raeder's chief of staff, Vice Admiral Kurt Fricke, according to the stenographer, the Führer declared that Norway was the "zone of destiny" in the war. An Allied invasion of Norway appeared to be imminent. Hitler was "deeply concerned about the grave consequences which unfavorable developments in the north Norwegian area could have on the entire course of the war." Therefore, Hitler iterated, the *Kriegsmarine* must employ "every available vessel" in Norway. It must "defend the sea lanes to Norway, and must dislodge with all available forces any enemy troops which have landed, entirely forgoing all other [naval] warfare except for the Mediterranean operations." Furthermore, Hitler demanded "unconditional obedience" to all his orders and wishes concerning defense of this area and the "greatest speed and efficiency" in carrying them out.

---

* Owing to the difficulties of operating Catalina seaplanes in the freezing waters of Newfoundland, the Army had grudgingly agreed to equip the Navy's Patrol Squadron 82, based in Argentia, with "land-based" Hudsons that had been earmarked for the RAF. Bristol's message, on January 28 at 2317 hours, concluded: "Pilot D F Mason Amm 1st Class NAP whose first report was Sighted Sub Sank Same."

Fricke left this meeting with the impression that Hitler had ordered that all U-boats other than those in the Mediterranean supporting Rommel were to be deployed in defense of Norway. This implied a cancellation of the U-boat campaign against America. However, on the following day, Hitler's naval aide, Karl-Jesko von Puttkammer, telephoned Fricke to say that Hitler had noted "with satisfaction" the "mounting sinkings in American waters" and that Hitler "wanted these operations to continue." The OKM diarist logged: "This is in significant contrast to his instructions—given only yesterday—about defending Norway."

In view of Hitler's satisfaction with the U-boat campaign in the Americas, the question of exactly how many U-boats were to be diverted to the "defense" of Norway and when they were to be transferred remained unsettled. Dönitz doubted the Allies intended to invade Norway. So any diversion of boats to its defense would be a foolish waste of U-boats. Intent on maximizing the impact of the U-boat campaign in the Americas, he did not press the OKM for a decision. The upshot was a complicated and extemporized commitment, which, however, was to diminish significantly the force of the U-boat campaign against the Americas.

When these discussions began, there were four boats in extreme northern Norway, basing at Kirkenes, merely 100 air miles from Murmansk. Their mission was to warn of and to repel the supposed Allied invasion and to interdict Allied shipping between Iceland and Murmansk. Operating in difficult seas and near-total Arctic darkness, three of the boats had confirmed successes in January: Rudolf Schendel in *U-134* sank a 5,100-ton freighter from Murmansk-bound Convoy PQ 7; Joachim Deecke in *U-584* sank a 250-ton Russian submarine, *M-175;* Burkhard Hackländer in *U-454* sank the 1,900-ton British destroyer *Matabele* and damaged a 5,400-ton British freighter from PQ 8 and a 600-ton Russian trawler.

Hackländer's attack on Convoy PQ 8, an indirect hit on the Soviet Union, was a tonic to Berlin. Apart from the sinking of the destroyer *Matabele,* and damage to the freighter, Hackländer overclaimed sinking a 2,000-ton freighter, damage to another 5,000-ton freighter, and heavy damage to another "destroyer." The OKM diarist gloated that Hackländer's attack served notice that the Arctic Ocean was no longer "free" to the Allies. Inasmuch as Hackländer had incurred damage requiring yard repair in Trondheim, the OKM sent a new boat, *U-456,* direct from Kiel to Kirkenes as a replacement, bringing the commitment of boats to Norway to five, although no master deployment plan had as yet been formulated. The four operational boats at Kirkenes patrolled off Murmansk—but none had any luck.

As the invasion rumors intensified during January, to Dönitz's dismay the OKM directed that as many boats as possible be held on patrol in the area between Iceland and the British Isles. This order applied to thirteen new boats sailing from Germany, and three experienced boats returning from overhaul in Germany or Norway, a total of sixteen, most of which had been earmarked for patrols to North America. Some of these boats served as defensive scouts during the shift of *Tirpitz* to Norway; some searched, in vain, for a military convoy of "ten transports," wrongly reported to be deploying American forces from Iceland to Scotland for the supposed invasion of Norway. The diversion of these sixteen U-boats sharply reduced the impact of the opening phase of the U-boat campaign against North America.

In addition to these sixteen boats, *Ritterkreuz* holder Wolfgang Lüth in the aged Type IX *U-43* patrolled home to Germany for overhaul through the same area. Although the British were still reading naval Enigma in January and diverting convoys around the U-boats, Lüth found excellent hunting. He sank four ships for 21,300 tons, the second two from convoy Outbound North 55, disorganized by the heavy winter storms. Upon reaching Germany, Lüth, having sunk a total of twelve confirmed ships for 68,000 tons on *U-43,* relinquished command to a new skipper. Although he could have selected virtually any desk or training job in the *Kriegsmarine,* like Prien, Kretschmer, Schepke, Lemp, Endrass, and other *Ritterkreuz* holders, Lüth elected to return to combat—in a new boat.

One of the thirteen newly sailed boats, *U-213,* commanded by Amelung von Varendorff, Prien's second watch officer at Scapa Flow, was a curiosity: an improvised minelayer, designated Type VIID. Six of these boats (*U-213* to *U-218*) had been ordered after the start of the war. They were basic VIICs into which a 32-foot mine compartment had been spliced immediately aft of the control room. The compartment contained five silos, each designed to hold three vertically launched SMA anchored or moored mines, with 770-pound warheads. The addition of the mine compartment enabled the designers to incorporate more fuel saddle tanks, giving the VIIDs an extra fifty-six tons of oil, extending the range of these boats by 1,600 miles beyond that of the regular VIIC (8,100 versus 6,500). However, the SMA mine proved to be defective, and pending a redesign the OKM had barred its use, releasing the VIIDs for torpedo operations, for which they were also well equipped.

Four of the newly sailed boats patrolled close to two seaports of Iceland, Reykjavik and Seidisfjord. Off Reykjavik on January 29, Ernst Vogelsang in the *U-132,* who had made an Arctic patrol in the fall, attacked a "destroyer" which was towing a disabled freighter into port, firing all four bow torpedoes. Some hit and the "destroyer" was severely damaged. She was taken under tow by a British tug, *Frisky,* but capsized and was sunk by gunfire from the new American destroyer *Ericsson.* In reality, the ship was one of the 327-foot, 2,200-ton *Treasury*-class Coast Guard cutters, *Alexander Hamilton,* which had come across as part of the escort of convoy Halifax 170. She was the second—and largest—American warship after *Reuben James* to be sunk by a U-boat. Twenty-six of her crew perished. While an American destroyer rescued her survivors, another new destroyer, *Stack,* jumped on *U-132* and inflicted such heavy depth-charge damage that Vogelsang was forced to abort to France. Although numerous American warships had claimed kills of or damage to U-boats, *Stack* was the first American vessel to do harm to a U-boat. Repairs to the *U-132* kept her out of action for the next four months.

Most of the newly sailed boats patrolled in the Northwest Approaches or close to the Faeroes and Shetlands. This familiar territory was more perilous than ever. Apart from the saturation air coverage mounted by Coastal Command aircraft fitted with ASV radar, the British had twenty-five escort groups, comprised of 205 ships (seventy destroyers, sixty-seven corvettes, sixty-eight sloops, etc.), based in ports in the British Isles. Most of these ships were equipped with Type 286 meter-wavelength radar, and many had the superior Type 271 centimetric-wavelength radar.* Some were being fitted with High Frequency Direction Finders (Huff Duff).

None of the U-boats found any signs of the supposed Norway invasion forces, but on January 26, Alfred Manhardt von Mannstein in *U-753,* ten days out on his maiden patrol, ran into part of a convoy, Outbound North 59, which had scattered in a winter storm. He alerted Kerneval and attacked a tanker, but missed, and a "destroyer" of the escort group counterattacked *U-753.* Von Mannstein reported that the "destroyer" dropped only two depth charges but these had caused serious internal damage. Furthermore, the "destroyer" had "run over" the boat (in an apparent attempt to ram) and caused damage topside. As a result, von Mannstein reported, *U-753* was no longer "seaworthy" and he was forced to abort to France. Dönitz directed six other boats to this convoy, but none made contact. Thus the sixteen boats diverted to the "defense of Norway" in January sank only one confirmed ship, the Coast Guard cutter *Alexander Hamilton.*

One of the six boats directed to the scattered Outbound North 59 was Otto Ites in *U-94.* Newly sailed from Germany after an overhaul, the boat developed mechanical troubles, as a result of which Ites was returning to Germany. Homebound on January 30, Ites radioed Kerneval that while ventilating his electric torpedoes, he had discovered that due to an air leakage, "excessive pressure" built up in the torpedo balance chamber containing the depth-setting controls, possibly causing the controls to make the torpedoes run deeper than set. Ites's message arrived in Kerneval at the very time the staff was puzzling over the very large number of torpedo failures reported by the first wave of boats to North America. Although it was known that a great many of these failed torpedoes had not been ventilated, Dönitz logged, the leaking balance chamber might account for many. Consequently, as an interim step, he immediately forbade all boats at sea to ventilate torpedoes, and relayed news of the discovery to the Torpedo Directorate, with a demand for new and urgent tests.

As it turned out, the twenty-three-year-old Otto Ites had discovered the last major defect in the standard electric torpedo. Three weeks later the torpedo technicians confirmed the leakage and, pending a redesign of the balance chamber, recommended temporary corrective measures which would permit ventilation of torpedoes for those boats already on patrol or preparing to sail. Dönitz was simultaneously elated and furious. He and his skippers had insisted all along that the torpedoes were still running too deep, but to no avail. Now, thirty months into the war, they were vindicated, thanks to one young skipper with minimum education, a damning commentary on the state of science and engineering in Hitler's Germany.

The correction of this torpedo defect almost at the outset of the U-boat campaign against the Americas was fortuitous, to say the least. It contributed significantly to the success of U-boats everywhere, but especially to those in the second and subsequent waves patrolling North American waters.

---

* By January 1, 1942, seventy-three ships (fifty-nine corvettes, fourteen destroyers) of the Royal Navy in all waters had been fitted with Type 271 centimetric-wavelength radar.

•   •   •

Hitler himself drew the formal plan for the use of U-boats to defend Norway on February 6. Altogether, he decreed, twenty U-boats were to be deployed for that purpose at all times: eight on a patrol line between Iceland and the British Isles (to interdict the supposed oncoming American invasion forces from Iceland); six in Kirkenes (to block an invasion force and to attack PQ and QP convoys in Arctic waters); and two each at Narvik, Trondheim, and Bergen, to provide a last-ditch defense against the attacking forces. In addition, the *U-A* and three large Dutch submarines—captured early in the war and used since at the Submarine School— as well as four "small" submarines, were to be placed on standby to ferry gasoline and other supplies to Narvik and Tromsö for the *Luftwaffe*.

Hitler's order coincided with a sudden onset of brutal cold in the Baltic region. The OKM diarist logged: "Never in all its history has the German ice observation service witnessed ice conditions as bad as these." Moreover, the ice would be even worse in March, "when surface water reaches lowest temperatures." Summing up, the ice observers predicted Baltic ice to a thickness "not yet experienced in this century," a forecast that proved to be accurate.

The sudden buildup of thick Baltic ice was another severe setback for the U-boat arm. Over the winter nearly 100 boats coming off the ways or in various stages of workup were to be immobilized—frozen at dockside or otherwise delayed for three to four months. The majority of the seventy-eight boats commissioned in the months of November 1941 to February 1942, inclusive, did not leave the Baltic for seven or eight months.* The thirty-seven boats commissioned in March and April 1942 were Baltic bound, on average, six months. As a result, the flow of new boats to all war fronts in 1942 fell off sharply: thirteen in February, thirteen in March, eight in April, six in May.

Because of the prolonged delays imposed by the Baltic ice, it was all the more difficult to assign Type VIIs to the "defense of Norway." Five (including *U-454* in overhaul) were already in Norway, leaving a deficit of fifteen. The deficit was to be met by diverting three more of the new VIIs sailing from Germany in January, all seven of the new VIIs sailing from Germany in February, and seven of the ten new VIIs sailing from Germany in March, bringing the total to twenty-two boats. The overage compensated for the boats, such as *U-454,* that were in overhaul or repairing battle damage.

Inasmuch as Hitler demanded that the twenty boats for the "defense of Norway" be in place no later than February 15, and because of the Baltic ice, the order could not be met promptly with newly sailing boats, Dönitz assumed temporary responsibility for providing the eight boats for the anti-invasion patrol line between Iceland and the British Isles. He fulfilled this obligation by prolonging the patrols of some of the newly arrived January boats and by holding some of the newly sailing February boats in the area, as well as some boats outbound to and inbound

---

* Examples: Commissioned on November 22, 1941, *U-438* sailed from the Baltic on August 1, 1942. Commissioned on December 11, 1941, *U-600* sailed on July 14, 1942. Commissioned February 26, 1942, *U-611* sailed on October 1, 1942.

from the Americas (as fuel permitted), and by sending several boats to the area from France. These holds in and diversions to the Northwest Approaches were to further reduce the number of boats in the hunting grounds of Canada and the United States.

The last major step in the naval reinforcement of Norway was the shift of *Gneisenau, Scharnhorst,* and *Prinz Eugen* from France to Norway, via the English Channel and Germany. Amid the greatest secrecy, the ships sailed from Brest the night of February 11–12, heavily supported by minesweepers, torpedo boats, destroyers, *Luftwaffe* fighters, and—distantly—the U-boats on the patrol line in the Northwest Approaches. From Enigma and other intelligence sources, the British were aware of the plan and had prepared a counterplan (Fuller) to sink all three ships. However, the British early-warning network (submarines, aircraft, land-based radar, etc.) broke down and Operation Fuller failed. No less than 250 British aircraft, five destroyers, and a half-dozen torpedo boats belatedly attacked the German formation in the English Channel with torpedoes and bombs, but these forces were too little and too late, a humiliating failure.

Nonetheless, the German ships did not reach Germany unscathed. In anticipation of the channel dash, the British had sown new minefields along the predicted track of the ships. Both *Gneisenau* and *Scharnhorst* hit British mines. The damage to *Gneisenau* was slight, but after reaching the Jade, she struck a sunken wreck that damaged her bottom and put her in drydock for what the OKM predicted to be "three weeks." On the night of February 26–27, an RAF bomber hit her with a bomb that blew up a forward magazine and wrecked the ship beyond repair. The two mines *Scharnhorst* struck damaged a turret and her turbo-electric motors, delaying her transfer to Norway for what the OKM predicted to be "several months," but which stretched to a full year.

Notwithstanding the unavailability of the two battle cruisers, the OKM proceeded with plans to shift the "pocket" battleship, *Admiral Scheer,* and the undamaged heavy cruiser *Prinz Eugen* to Norway. Escorted by three destroyers, they sailed from the Jade on February 21. *Tirpitz* left Norway to join them for an attack on the Murmansk convoys, but one of four British submarines lying off Trondheim, *Trident,* commanded by G. M. Sladen, fired a salvo of three torpedoes at *Prinz Eugen* and blew off her rudder and thirty feet of her stern. Sladen's success forced the Germans to cancel the Arctic sortie and return to Norway, yet another embarrassment for the *Kriegsmarine. Prinz Eugen* limped back to Germany for eight months of repairs, after which she was converted to a training ship and did not again leave the Baltic.

These events reduced the big ships for the defense of Norway—and for attacking Murmansk convoys—to three: the super battleship *Tirpitz,* the "pocket" battleship *Admiral Scheer,* and the heavy cruiser *Hipper.*

More Failures in Gibraltar-Azores Waters

The deployment of U-boats to North America and Norway in December and January left very few to patrol southward to the areas near Gibraltar and the Azores. Furthermore, when the OKM learned that two more boats—Unno von Fischel's *U-374* and Herbert Schauenburg's *U-577*—had been lost in the Mediterranean in January,* it ordered Dönitz to send three from the Gibraltar-Azores area into the Mediterranean. Helmut Rosenbaum in *U-73* and Robert Bartels in *U-561* passed through the Gibraltar Strait on January 14 and 15, respectively, but Heinz Hirsacker in *U-572*, who had shown great promise as first watch officer on Wilhelm Georg Schulz's *U-124*, balked on January 16, reporting "bad weather and heavy defenses." Dönitz ordered Hirsacker to "try again," but a second effort, on January 19, also failed. The Mediterranean force was thus left with twenty-one boats.

These new transfers coincided with a bold new offensive by Erwin Rommel. Because of the loss of or damage to capital ships in late 1941, the Royal Navy lost control of the Mediterranean Sea. Axis convoys got through to Rommel with tanks and supplies, giving him a temporary upper hand in the war of logistics. Upon learning from a penetration of Allied codes† that the British Eighth Army was in a weakened condition, Rommel struck from El Agheila on January 21. He had recaptured Benghazi within a week and forced the British back toward Tobruk. Hirsacker's balk at this critical juncture—when Rommel most needed U-boats to interdict the coasters supplying the Eighth Army—was an embarrassment to the U-boat force. The consequences to Hirsacker were to be dire.

The transfers to the Mediterranean left but four Type VIIs in southern waters between the Azores and Gibraltar in January. One, *U-373*, commanded by Paul-Karl Loeser, was detached to escort a blockade runner, *Elsa Essberger,* into France, a mission that failed when British aircraft from Gibraltar found and attacked both vessels, forcing the German ship to flee to safety in El Ferrol, Spain. Believing the *Elsa Essberger* could make repairs and resail, Loeser hung around for days off El Ferrol, but the repairs took much longer than expected. Having wasted three weeks to little purpose, Loeser returned to France.

The other three boats in southern waters made contact with inbound convoy Sierra Leone 97. When the British learned of this contact, they ordered a new, experimental unit composed of four destroyers (*Croome, Hesperus, Laforey,* and *Wescott*) to sail from Gibraltar to attack the U-boats. Designated as a "Striking Force," it represented in miniature the favored offensive solution to the U-boat

---

* The British submarine *Unbeaten* sank *U-374* off Sicily on January 12, 1942, and recovered one survivor, a bridge lookout. British aircraft sank *U-577* off Tobruk on January 9, 1942, with the loss of all hands. The *U-331* ran hard aground off Tobruk on January 27, 1942, but in an amazing display of resourcefulness and seamanship, von Tiesenhausen saved her and returned to base.

† An Italian agent, employed in the American Embassy in Cairo, had broken into a safe and photographed the American "Black" code materials, which the military attachés used to inform Washington of British plans and operations and military strength in North Africa.

threat. Serving as "bait," the convoy had "lured" in the U-boats. Having no direct responsibility for protection of the ships in the convoy, the Striking Force was free to pursue and attack the U-boats to the limit of its endurance.

Commanded by I. H. Bockett-Pugh in *Wescott,* whose EG-7 had recovered the Enigma from Lemp's *U-110* in May 1941, this first sortie of a Striking Force was not a model of perfection. To fool and evade the U-boats, the British ordered the convoy to make a drastic alteration in course. The Striking Force failed to get this word and could not find the convoy. Then the Admiralty ordered two of the four destroyers to more urgent missions. *Croome* and *Wescott* peeled off, leaving *Laforey* and *Hesperus,* which finally found the convoy on the morning of January 14, trailed by a Condor, which was reporting its position to Kerneval. *Laforey* drove the aircraft off with gunfire, but the plane had already brought in the three boats, including young Horst Elfe's *U-93,* on her second patrol under his command.

In the early hours of January 15, *Laforey* and *Hesperus* took station about ten miles on the port beam of the convoy. Soon thereafter, *Hesperus* got a contact on her meter-wavelength radar at 3,000 yards. *Hesperus* swung around, bent on flank speed, opened fire with her main guns, and turned on her 10" searchlight. The light revealed a U-boat running away at about 17 knots. This was Elfe's *U-93. Laforey* joined in the chase, but *Hesperus,* with a clear lead, rammed *U-93* on her starboard side with a glancing blow and launched five depth charges set for 50 feet.

The blow from *Hesperus* threw Elfe and several others on the bridge into the water and jammed the conning-tower hatch shut, trapping the rest of the crew below. Saltwater leaked into the battery, forming chlorine gas. As the flooding boat filled with deadly fumes, those trapped below worked frantically to open the hatch, finally succeeding at the last possible second. *Hesperus* launched a boat to board, but *U-93* sank before it could reach her. *Hesperus* picked up Elfe and thirty-five other survivors; *Laforey,* four. Six Germans were not found. Damaged by the collision, *Hesperus* returned to Gibraltar, where she was highly commended for this aggressive attack, but also reminded of the urgent need to prevent Germans from abandoning ship and scuttling, so that "secret papers" (i.e., Enigma machines, keys, and documents) could be recovered. To prevent scuttling, boarding parties were again—and specifically—authorized to take "drastic action" with weapons to "keep the [U-boat] crew below." That is, shoot any Germans attempting to leave their sinking ships.

Although the Striking Force had botched the rendezvous with the convoy and the British had reduced it by half, it had to be judged a qualified success. Its remaining two ships accounted for the only confirmed U-boat sunk by the British in the Atlantic in January.

Outbound to North America, on January 16 Siegfried von Forstner, on his second patrol in the Type VII *U-402,* ran into a southbound "Winston Special" troop convoy due west of the Bay of Biscay. He reported that it was composed of five steamers, escorted by merely "one destroyer," but a Condor that was nearby protecting the outbound merchant-ship raider *Thor,* and which responded to the report—and boldly attacked the convoy—reported nineteen ships, escorted by five destroyers. Closing on the formation, von Forstner fired at the 12,000-ton liner *Llangibby Castle,* which had 1,000 troops on board. The hit blew off her rudder and killed twenty-six men.

Declaring this military convoy to be a "must" target, Dönitz diverted three other America-bound Type VIIs and alerted the remaining two Type VIIs in the Gibraltar-Azores area, putting six boats on the scent. The two boats near the Azores were low on fuel and had to go home; two of the four American-bound boats could not find the convoy and resumed voyages to westward. Von Forstner in *U-402* hung on, bringing up twenty-nine-year-old Werner Pfeifer in the brand-new Canada-bound Type VII *U-581.* Pfeifer could not find the convoy; however, he attacked what he believed to be a corvette, firing three torpedoes. It was not a corvette, but probably the British ASW trawler *Rosemonde,* which disappeared about this time with the loss of all hands.

Although damaged, the *Llangibby Castle* made it to the port of Horta in the Portuguese Azores, where by international law she was entitled to make battle repairs. When it became clear to Kerneval that the main body of the convoy had eluded the boats, Dönitz ordered von Forstner in *U-402* and Pfeifer in *U-581* to close on Horta, wait for the *Llangibby Castle* to resail, and then sink her in a coordinated attack.

Pfeifer in *U-581* arrived off Horta on the night of January 31. She was not a happy boat; the thirty-one-year-old engineering officer, Helmut Krummel, was a strict disciplinarian to whom Pfeifer had granted unusual authority. "Every petty officer had been punished at his hands," a British intelligence officer wrote later, and "on one occasion a chief petty officer had threatened Krummel with personal violence in the presence of other officers." As the crew saw it, according to the British report, the skipper, Werner Pfeifer, who had known Krummel before the war, had "come under the evil influence of this man."

Pfeifer was determined to carry out the mission. In an astonishing display of boldness—and a blatant violation of the neutrality laws—he submerged and cruised right into the harbor at Horta. Coming quietly to the surface merely 100 yards from shore, Pfeifer found *Llangibby Castle* moored on the other side of a stone pier, beyond reach. Had the pier been made of wood rather than stone, Pfeifer recalled, he would have fired torpedoes. Thus thwarted, he aborted the attack, withdrew to sea, and met von Forstner in *U-402.* Thereupon the two skippers worked out a plan to guard the two exits from Horta: Pfeifer in South Channel, von Forstner in North Channel.

Meanwhile, the Admiralty directed Gibraltar to provide assistance to *Llangibby Castle.* Bockett-Pugh in the destroyer *Wescott* sailed with a reduced Striking Force, that included the *Hunt*-class destroyers *Croome* and *Exmoor* and an ocean-going tug.

Wescott was the first ship of the Royal Navy to be equipped with a new, secret ASW weapon, the Hedgehog. This was a bow-mounted, multiple-barrel mortar capable of firing a salvo of twenty-four 65-pound bombs (with 30-pound warheads) into a small circular pattern about 250 yards ahead of the ship. The bombs were to be armed with the new and more powerful explosive Torpex, and had contact pistols that required no depth setting. They would not explode unless they hit a target or the ocean floor.

Hedgehog had several theoretical advantages over the conventional stern or stern-quarter launched or dropped depth charge. It eliminated the need for the attacker to run directly over the U-boat and speed up to sonar-deafening levels to avoid depth-charge damage to its own stern, and also eliminated the useless, sonar-deafening explosions of depth charges that usually missed. With Hedgehog, so the theory went, the attacker could maintain sonar contact with its quarry at all times and frustrate the usual U-boat evasions during the run-over and the depth-charge explosions.

Hedgehog also had several disadvantages. It was big and had a terrific recoil, and could therefore be mounted only on the bows of the larger escorts.* It was a "precision instrument" that was complicated to arm and fire, and it still had many "bugs." Moreover, inasmuch as a direct hit was required to detonate the bombs, there was no possibility of inflicting *damage* on a U-boat or of terrorizing the Germans with near misses. As a consequence, many escort commanders and their crews remained skeptical.

When *Llangibby Castle* sailed in the early hours of February 2 by the light of a full moon, the three destroyers of the Striking Force took station to seaward. *Wescott* and *Croome* were off the South Channel where Pfeifer in *U-581* was waiting. *Exmoor* was off the North Channel where von Forstner in *U-402* was waiting. Pfeifer saw the destroyers, dived, and boldly fired a torpedo at one of them, but it missed. Moments later, the port diesel-exhaust valve suddenly failed, flooding the engine room and dragging the boat stern first to 524 feet. To stop the descent and regain control of the boat, Pfeifer blew main ballast tanks. *Wescott* and *Croome* heard all this racket on sonar and closed to attack, just as the *U-581* popped to the surface, running hell-bent for asylum in neutral Portuguese waters.

Sighting the boat, *Wescott* put on full speed to ram, but she miscalculated the angle and missed. As the two ships passed, side by side, thirty feet apart, *Wescott* dropped ten shallow-set depth charges, which exploded all over *U-581*. Unable to fire her main batteries because *Croome* was in the way, *Wescott* hauled out and turned 180 degrees and closed *U-581* bow-to-bow for another ramming attempt. By then, Pfeifer had ordered his men to abandon ship and scuttle and most of his crew was topside, wearing lifesaving gear. As the vessels closed bow-on at nearly 50 miles per hour, the Germans leaped overboard.

Wescott struck *U-581* abaft the conning tower, riding up and over the after deck, incurring minor damage to herself. The U-boat upended and sank immediately, stern first. Ironically, *Wescott* had had no opportunity to use her Hedgehog. *Wescott* and *Croome* (merely a spectator) rescued Pfeifer and forty men, including

---

* Corvettes and the fifty British frigates under delayed construction in the United States and their American counterparts, the destroyer escorts, were to be fitted with Hedgehogs. The Americans had in the works a small version of Hedgehog, called Mousetrap, for installation on *SC*s and *PC*s. The Mousetrap was designed to forward fire eight contact bombs by means of rockets, which had no recoil.

the unpopular engineer, Krummel. Six Germans were unaccounted for. One, the second watch officer, Werner Sitek, swam to shore and was later repatriated to Germany.* British intelligence officers, who exploited the bitterness of this unhappy crew, reported that apart from the officers, "only three men" of *U-581* had had "any previous U-boat experience."

When the rudderless *Llangibby Castle* sailed out of Horta, she took the North Channel, where von Forstner in *U-402* was waiting. The destroyer *Exmoor,* joined by the destroyer *Croome,* assumed escort duties. Von Forstner fired a total of five torpedoes at one or the other of the destroyers, but all missed. Upon sighting *U-402,* the destroyers attacked with guns and depth charges, driving her off. Although he was low on fuel, von Forstner hung on to the formation until Heinz Hirsacker in *U-572,* returning from his second balk at the Gibraltar Strait, homed in on his beacons. But Hirsacker was no help; he made no attacks. To Kerneval's chagrin, the *Llangibby Castle,* closely escorted by the three-destroyer Striking Force and later by aircraft, finally reached Gibraltar with her 1,000 troops.

Thus the half-dozen U-boats patrolling in southern waters during January sank just one confirmed ship: the ASW trawler *Rosemonde.* In return, Bockett-Pugh's experimental Striking Force in two separate forays had sunk two U-boats: Elfe's *U-93* and Pfeifer's *U-581.* In view of these losses and the lack of success, and the shortage of boats for the defense of Norway and the campaign in the Americas, Dönitz convinced the OKM that patrols to the Gibraltar-Azores area should be temporarily terminated.

---

* Pfeifer filed formal, written charges against the British, asserting that while in distress, his ship was unlawfully sunk in neutral Portuguese waters. Bockett-Pugh, awarded the DSO for the sinking, rightly dismissed the charges as nonsense. The Admiralty concurred.

EIGHT

THE LOSS OF NAVAL ENIGMA

Thanks to the captures of naval Enigma materials in the spring of 1941, the British had been able to read three-rotor Enigma on the *Heimisch* network (Dolphin to the British) with little delay until the end of that year. The principal source of cribs for breaking this traffic was the short-signal book captured from *U-110,* which the U-boats used for making weather reports. The short-signal weather reports were carelessly rebroadcast by German meteorological stations in a less secure code that the British could read. Working back from the readable text of the meteorological stations, the British were usually able to puzzle out the daily key settings for U-boat Enigma with little delay and minimum usage of bombes.

By January 1942, the Germans had issued to the Atlantic and Mediterranean U-boats new four-rotor Enigma machines and a new short-signal book for use on the new U-boat Enigma net, *Triton* (Shark to the British). Had the British had a copy of the new short-signal book, very likely they could have broken back into Naval Enigma by means of the rebroadcast meteorological traffic. But absent the new short-signal books, they were stymied. They could not read four-rotor Enigma, an incalculable setback.

There were several possibilities for breaking into four-rotor Enigma in use on the *Triton* (Shark) net. The fastest way was to capture a copy of the new short-signal book. Doubtless that had been one purpose behind the British commando raid in Norway in late December, but no short-signal books had been found. Another way was to feed such cribs as could be obtained from other sources into the three-rotor bombes. But it took three-rotor bombes twenty-six times longer to find the daily settings of a four-rotor Enigma. Yet another way was to build fast, high-technology, four-rotor bombes. The British pursued the first and third possibilities, even though there was much doubt that a four-rotor bombe could be designed and produced in time to influence the outcome of the war.

The loss of Atlantic U-boat Enigma imposed a tremendous burden on Rodger Winn and his assistants in the Admiralty's U-boat Tracking Room. Although Winn could draw upon a large store of knowledge accumulated during the six months of 1941 when Bletchley Park was reading the *Heimisch* (Dolphin) network, a steadily improving land-based British HF/DF network and *Werft* traffic, POW interrogations, photo reconnaissance in the Baltic, and German propaganda in various media glorifying U-boat skippers, he could no longer provide exact and timely tactical information on Atlantic U-boat movements. After the Germans switched to four-rotor Enigma, Winn's weekly U-boat summary of February 9 was gloomy: "Since the end of January, no Special Information has been available about any U-boats other than those controlled by Admiral Norway. Inevitably the Atlantic picture is 'out of focus.' Little can be said with any confidence in estimating the present and future movements of U-boats."

The British contempt for Admiral King and America's alleged inability to cope with or its indifference to the U-boat threat has drawn stinging rebukes and silly statements from British and American historians, but none sillier than that of Francis H. Hinsley, the official historian of British intelligence in World War II. In his otherwise superlative history, he writes, in effect, that so inept were the Americans at ASW that the Allied loss of Atlantic U-boat Enigma at the very time Dönitz launched the all-out U-boat attack on the Americas did not really adversely affect the Allies. "Not even the best intelligence about their [U-boat] activities off the American coast," Hinsley wrote, "would have facilitated either an effective counterattack on them or the effective evasive routing of shipping so long as the U-boats were at liberty, in the absence of air cover, to operate close inshore and, in the absence of a convoy system, to do so against unprotected shipping."

To the contrary, had the Allies not lost naval Enigma, the story of the U-boat assault on America might have been quite different. Along with other vital bits of information, naval Enigma doubtless would have revealed that:

• The U-boat attack on the Americas was not a token gesture or feint but rather an all-out effort employing every U-boat Dönitz could lay his hands on and increasing in scale week by week.

• The U-boat campaign in United States waters was to include not only the twenty Type IXs existing on January 1, 1942, the status and movements of which were fairly well known to Allied intelligence, but also a mass of Type VIIs, which, owing to their limited range, had not been foreseen as a threat to American waters.

• Some U-tankers were to be employed to support the campaign in the Americas. They were to provide fuel, food, medical backup, and spare parts for both the Type VII and Type IX attack boats, thus increasing the range, endurance, and productivity of both. Had the Allies learned of this important new dimension in the U-boat war much earlier than was the case, they could have planned countermeasures, such as a carrier strike at a refueling rendezvous, when many U-boats were present and relatively vulnerable. As will be seen, for all too many months the British intelligence agencies refused to credit the rumors of "U-tankers."

• Owing to the close access to deep (hence safer) water, the U-boats were to concentrate attacks off the Cape Hatteras area and off the southern coast of Florida, where the continental shelf was narrowest and most favorable for submarine operations. Had this been known, the Americans could have marshalled their weak ASW forces at those places sooner than they did, especially at Cape Hatteras.

• U-boats were to operate in United States waters not in groups, or wolf packs, as was then standard practice, but singly, maintaining radio silence. Had these important tactical facts been deduced from decrypted Enigma, American naval officers from King down might have been much more willing to risk convoying in those waters despite the dearth of escorts. A single U-boat could usually sink only one or two ships in a convoy before being pinned down or evaded and, while the radio-silence rule was in force, could not summon other boats.

• The big German surface ships (*Tirpitz,* etc.) were unable for various reasons to make sorties into the Atlantic in early 1942 to attack Allied convoys. Had this been positively known from Enigma, the Americans could have earlier released their heavy naval counterforces at Iceland, Bermuda, and Argentia, and perhaps even reduced the number of destroyers in troopship convoys. If so, destroyers for use in a convoy network along the Eastern Seaboard could have been made available much sooner.

• German codebreakers at *B-dienst* had made a substantial penetration into Naval Cypher Number 3, employed by the Allies for most convoy operations. According to intelligence historian Hinsley, for about ten months in 1942 (about February 15 to December 15) *B-dienst* could read "a large proportion of the signals—sometimes as much as 80 percent." Decrypts of naval Enigma might well have revealed this grave lapse in Allied naval communications security, which in 1942 gave the Germans a decided advantage in the seesaw battle of codebreaking.

To this time there was still no free exchange of cryptographic technology between the British and the Americans. The British had provided Admiral King with Rodger Winn's estimates on probable U-boat operations in the Atlantic, derived in part from Enigma and *Werft,* but they had not fully revealed their secret techniques for breaking Enigma. With the formal entry of America into the war and the nearly simultaneous loss of naval Enigma, and the increasing ship losses in American waters, the British finally began to share their hard-earned cryptographic technology with the Americans.

This technology exchange was lent impetus by President Roosevelt and Winston Churchill. On February 25, Churchill wrote an extraordinary private note to Roosevelt, which was hand-carried to Washington in a diplomatic pouch. Churchill asked Roosevelt to "burn" the letter after reading, but the President did not, and a copy was published in 1989 by Louis Kruh.* In part:

_____

* See Kruh article in *Cryptologia,* April 1989.

One night when we talked late [during the Arcadia Conference] you spoke of the importance of our cipher people getting into close contact with yours. I shall be very ready to put any expert you care to nominate in touch with my technicians. Ciphers for our two navies have been and are continually a matter for frank discussion between our two Services. But diplomatic and military [Army and Air Forces] are of equal importance and we appear to know nothing officially of your versions of these. . . .

In fact, Churchill went on, "some time ago" British codebreakers had cracked some codes used by the American "diplomatic corps." Churchill had put a stop to that activity "from the moment when we became Allies"(!), as he put it, but he had been advised that the possibility that "our enemies" had also broken these diplomatic codes could not be dismissed.

At this time the American codebreaking agencies were in a swivet, particularly those of the U.S. Navy, which had failed to detect in advance any hint of the Japanese attack on Pearl Harbor. In the weeks following that disaster, a bureaucratic battle for control of that anomalous and vulnerable group had erupted in the Navy Department. The principal contestants had been the new Director of the Office of Naval Intelligence (ONI), Theodore S. Wilkinson, and the Director of the Office of Naval Communications (ONC), Leigh Noyes, and his deputy, Joseph R. Redman. Distrustful of ONI's ability to do anything right, Admiral King had sided with Noyes and Redman, and therefore ONC had won control of U.S. Navy codebreakers.

Among the many notable changes Noyes and Redman initiated was the bureaucratic beheading of Laurence Safford, who had commanded the Navy codebreaking unit (OP20G) brilliantly for almost six years. Inasmuch as a free exchange of cryptographic technology with the British was in the works and Safford had made no secret of his distrust of and hostility to the British (for not giving bombe technology in exchange for the Purple machine), Noyes and Redman decided to remove Safford from the mainstream. Denying Safford's appeal to keep his post, on February 14 Noyes transferred him from command of OP20G to OP20Q, an outfit concerned with the security of American (and Allied) codes and research. As one consequence, Safford did not receive a high wartime decoration and was not selected to flag rank, a scandalous injustice in the view of most of the old hands in OP20G.

This demotion naturally angered and depressed Safford. Doubtless it colored a memo he wrote on March 18 to Noyes and Redman. As Safford put it, the reason for the memo was to stress the need to safeguard the secrets of the breaking of Japanese codes by sharply limiting the dissemination of information derived from this source. However, owing to the pessimistic asides in the memo, it has attained near-legendary status among historians of American codebreaking.

Typically Safford opened his memo with a slap at the British. They had done a good job in World War I of DFing U-boats and decrypting U-boat radio traffic, he wrote, then had stupidly and egotistically bragged about it in print after the war. "Apparently it never occurred to the British that the Germans would profit by these revelations," Safford wrote accusingly.

Admiral Ernest Joseph King, Commander in Chief of the U.S. Fleet (CominCh) from December 20, 1941, and Chief of Naval Operations (CNO) from March 26, 1942. He held those posts throughout the war and retired on December 15, 1945.

President Franklin Delano Roosevelt, onetime Assistant Secretary of the Navy, demanded and got an awesome "two-ocean navy" in World War II but failed to properly prepare the U.S. Navy for the U-boat threat in the Atlantic.

Admiral Adolphus Andrews, Commander in Chief Eastern Sea Frontier, was an able leader, but in 1942 he lacked the "tools" to combat the U-boat assault on the Americas.

Admiral Royal Eason Ingersoll relieved Admiral King as Commander in Chief Atlantic Fleet in December 1941.

(National Defence Headquarters, Ottawa, R423.)

(National Archives, 242HB51609)

(National Archives, 242GAP102T3)

Admiral Percy W. Nelles, Chief of the Royal Canadian Naval Staff from 1934 to 1943.

Reinhard Hardegen, skipper of the Type IXB *U-123,* who led Drumbeat, the U-boat assault on East Coast shipping in January 1942.

Erich Topp, skipper of *U-552,* launched Drumbeat in Canadian waters. In the war, he sank thirty-four ships for 185,434 tons, to rank fourth among all skippers.

(Bundesarchiv/U.S. Naval Institute)

Peter-Erich Cremer, another Drumbeater, commanded *U-333* on two patrols to the U.S. East Coast.

The vast majority of all North Atlantic convoys got through unharmed by U-boats. Here a convoy forms up in an East Coast anchorage.

American blimps provided added convoy escort for a limited distance offshore.

The burning American tanker S.S. *Robert C. Tuttle* struck a mine off Norfolk, Virginia, planted by the Type VII *U-701*. The *Tuttle* was salvaged, but American forces sank *U-701*.

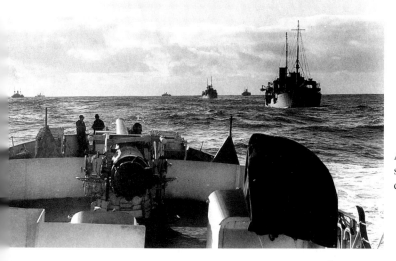

A convoy arrives safely at its destination.

The U.S.S. *Toucey,* a World War I "four-stack" destroyer, commissioned December 9, 1919. President Roosevelt "lent" the British and Canadian navies fifty such vessels in the fall of 1940 in return for base rights at sites in the Western Hemisphere. These and the other American four-stacks served as troop and cargo convoy escorts.

The *Duane,* one of six big American *Treasury*-class Coast Guard cutters that also served as convoy escorts in the North Atlantic, plows into typically heavy seas.

A corvette, the workhorse cargo convoy escort of the North Atlantic. Shown here, the Royal Canadian Navy's *Kitchener.* British and Canadian shipyards produced hundreds of corvettes. Cheaply built, miserably wet and brutally uncomfortable, the corvette nonetheless played a decisive role in the Battle of the Atlantic.

(National Archives, 80G25092)

A British-built carrier-based Swordfish torpedo bomber. When fitted with radar and depth charges, these old planes served well in the early years of the war as antisubmarine weapons systems.

(National Defence Headquarters, Ottawa, PL 102453)

The long-range Catalina patrol bomber. American and Canadian factories produced 3,290 Catalinas during the war. The Canadians called this plane the Canso, one of which is shown here. Originally designed to be a flying boat, some later versions were fitted with wheels to become amphibians.

The American-designed Lockheed Hudson, built in America and Britain. Shown here is the newer, slightly larger U.S. Navy version, the Ventura.

The British-designed and -built Sunderland flying boat, employed by RAF Coastal Command in antisubmarine operations. The British produced about seven hundred Sunderlands during the war, some of which were supplied to Commonwealth squadrons.

(National Defence Headquarters, Ottawa, TL 33248)

RE 685056)

The American-designed and -built B-24 Liberator patrol bomber, a highly effective antisubmarine weapon as well as a strategic heavy bomber.

American aircraft attack and sink the Type XB (minelayer-tanker) *U-118.*

The big *Treasury*-class Coast Guard cutter *Spencer* attacks the Type IXC *U-175* with a salvo of depth charges.

After blowing *U-175* to the surface, a *Spencer* boarding party attempts but fails to enter the boat to seize intelligence materials.

Final gasp of *U-175*. The *Spencer* closes to rescue German survivors.

A famous photograph symbolizing the defeat of the German U-boat force shows a survivor of *U-175* pleading for rescue.

Shocked survivors of *U-175* huddle on the deck of the *Spencer*.

As one consequence of the British disclosures, he went on, in World War II "German ciphers and communications procedure are such that the information obtainable by radio is substantially zero." With the exception of "weather codes" and certain other "minor systems," Safford continued, the only German naval messages that had been read had been "the result of captures."

Therefore, he concluded glumly, "our prospects of ever breaking the German 'Enigma' cipher machine are rather poor."

On their part, the British remained contemptuous of the American intelligence setup in general and codebreaking in particular. There was still no centralized intelligence agency in Washington, no place where all the bits and pieces of information on the enemy came together for analysis and dissemination. Codebreakers in the Army, Navy, Coast Guard, and FBI still toiled in nearly complete isolation, more or less competing with one another, rather than working as a unified team, à la Bletchley Park. The pressures of war—the challenge of breaking naval and other Enigmas for one—demanded closer cooperation between British and American intelligence services. It was coming, but the traditional barriers and safeguards gave way all too slowly. Not until April did the British and Americans take positive steps toward meaningful intelligence exchanges.

First Type VII Patrols to the United States

Notwithstanding the diversion of nearly fifty Type VII U-boats to duty in the Mediterranean and in the defense of Norway, as well as the delays caused by the worst ice of the century in the Baltic, Dönitz was able to send twenty-six boats to American waters in January of 1942: twelve Type IXs and fourteen Type VIIs.

The boats sailing to the Americas in January were to cover an enormous area reaching from Canada to the Caribbean. The twelve Type IXs were to patrol the more distant United States East Coast and the Caribbean. Notwithstanding the "heavy" ASW measures, "tremendous cold," and poor returns of the December VIIs, the bulk of the January VIIs were to patrol Canadian waters, although three VIIs were to venture experimentally into United States waters.

Seven of the twelve Type IXs that put out in January were to attack shipping directly in United States coastal waters. Five of these were older, shorter-range model IXBs that had carried out the attack on Freetown the previous year. Outbound from France, one, Heinrich Schuch in *U-105,* ran into convoy Sierra Leone 98 and with two torpedoes sank one of the escorts, the former Coast Guard cutter *Mendota,* redesignated as the sloop *Culver,* which was fitted not only with Type 271 centimetric-wavelength radar but also one of the most advanced British shipboard HF/DF (Huff Duff) sets. Immediately thereafter Schuch was directed to search for *Spreewald* survivors and, as related, upon finding some, aborted to France. The other four IXBs patrolled from New York to Cape Hatteras. The other two boats of this group, both new longer-range Type IXCs, patrolled farther south in Florida waters.

When the first of these six Type IXs reached United States waters in late January and early February, they found that ASW measures had not improved very much. Apart from various defensive steps in the Eastern Sea Frontier, the most important new measure was the temporary employment of Catalinas on loan from the Atlantic Fleet for ASW patrols.

The new "straight through" King convoy plan for the North Atlantic run, effective February 4, yielded, as promised, ten destroyers to cadre a convoy network on the Eastern Seaboard. Seven of these,* all modern, were "made available" to Admiral Andrews of the Eastern Sea Frontier in the period February 6 to February 8. However, the proffered British component of this network (ten corvettes, twenty-four ASW trawlers) was nowhere to be seen. In fact, none of these British vessels was to arrive for weeks. Andrews mustered a total of twenty-eight other vessels in his frontier that were capable—but only just barely—of coastwise convoying but, as he told King, he needed a minimum of twice that number of ships merely to initiate convoying.

A further complication arose. Another big troopship convoy, AT 12, was scheduled to leave New York February 10. The fact that the Admiralty had provided only two four-stack destroyers at EASTOMP to escort the first such convoy, AT 10, had infuriated King. He therefore pointedly telexed the Admiralty to ask if it could provide AT 12 proper escort from EASTOMP. The Admiralty replied that owing to the need to escort its own troopship convoy, Winston Special 16, it could not provide substantial escort for AT 12 until the end of February. It therefore became necessary to postpone the departure of AT 12 by nine days, to February 19, at which time six of the seven destroyers (less *Roe*) on temporary duty with the Eastern Sea Frontier were assigned to reinforce the escort of AT 12. To replace them, Ingersoll released four four-stacks,† which, of course, were less satisfactory both in number and quality. In all, Ingersoll was able to loan Andrews eleven different destroyers for ASW purposes in February.

Notwithstanding the obvious dearth of escorts, the British continued to pressure King to initiate convoying on the Eastern Seaboard. On February 12, King directed Andrews to submit a convoy plan. Andrews in turn queried the commanders of the naval districts within his frontier. All remained opposed to convoying until such time as sufficient escorts were available. Reminding King that each day sixty-six different northbound ships and a "like number" of southbound ships passed through his frontier (a total of 120 to 130 vessels daily), for which a minimum of sixty-eight escorts were required, Andrews recommended that "no attempt be made to protect coastwise shipping by a convoy system until an adequate number of suitable escort vessels is available."

At about this same time, February 12, the German battle cruisers *Scharnhorst* and *Gneisenau* and the heavy cruiser *Prinz Eugen* left Brest on the "channel dash" to Germany. The sudden movement of these big German ships increased the threat of an Atlantic sortie by them or *Tirpitz* and *Admiral Scheer* or by all of them, pos-

---

*   *Hilary P. Jones, Ludlow, Mayrant, Roe, Rowan, Trippe, Wainwright.*

†   *Jacob Jones* and *Dickerson* (damaged at Iceland in January) at New York; *Dallas* and *Upshur* at Norfolk. *Roe* remained until about March 3.

sibly in conjunction with the Vichy naval forces at Martinique, to attack Allied cargo and troop convoys. Because the Allies could not read naval Enigma, this possibility froze Atlantic Fleet heavy units—and attendant destroyers—at Iceland, Bermuda, Argentia, and Casco Bay, Maine.

Accidents to Atlantic Fleet destroyers continued to contribute to the shortage of that type of vessel. On February 18, the valuable 14,000-ton Navy supply ship *Pollux,* en route to Argentia, and two escorting destroyers, *Truxtun* and *Wilkes,* ran aground on the Avalon Peninsula in a wild storm. The *Pollux* and the four-stacker *Truxtun* were completely wrecked, with the loss of 212 out of 386 men in the two crews. Although damaged, *Wilkes,* a new destroyer, managed to back off and survive. She returned to service after extensive repairs.

The most successful of the six January Type IXs patrolling United States waters was Hermann Rasch in the veteran *U-106,* making his second patrol as skipper. Still under a cloud for having lost the entire bridge watch on his first patrol to Newfoundland, Rasch hunted off the coast of New York, Delaware, and Maryland. In two weeks, January 24 to February 6, he sank by torpedo and gun five ships for 42,000 tons, including the 6,800-ton American tanker *Rochester* and one of the largest and fastest passenger-cargo vessels in the world, the 15,400-ton Swede, *Amerikaland.* His patrol not only removed all doubts about his competence, but also earned a well-done from Dönitz and from Berlin propagandists.

The other three IXBs attacking from New York to Cape Hatteras had good success despite a large number of torpedo misses or failures.

• Between February 2 and February 5, Werner Winter in *U-103* (four torpedo failures or misses) sank by gun and torpedo four confirmed ships for 26,500 tons, including three American tankers: the 6,200-ton *W. L. Steed;* the 8,300-ton *India Arrow;* the 8,400-ton *China Arrow.* Winter also claimed a "destroyer" but it was not so.

• In the eleven days from February 8 to February 18, *Ritterkreuz* holder Klaus Scholtz in *U-108* (four torpedo failures or misses) sank five freighters for 20,000 tons, including *Ocean Venture,* one of the sixty Liberty ships built for Britain, embarked on her maiden voyage.

• In the period from January 31 to February 6, Harald Gelhaus in *U-107* (three torpedo misses or failures) sank two ships for 10,800 tons, including the 7,400-ton British tanker *San Arcadio,* which was sailing well offshore.

The two new longer-range IXCs which patrolled Florida waters were Ulrich Heyse, age thirty-five, in *U-128,* who had been delayed for months repairing damage incurred in a grounding en route to Norway, and Fritz Poske, age thirty-seven, in the new *U-504.* Florida, like Cape Hatteras, where the continental shelf was very narrow, proved to be a rich and relatively safe hunting ground. The deep-water sanctuary began merely ten miles offshore at the edge of the north-flowing Gulf Stream, a natural and heavily traveled sea-lane.

Both boats operated in an overlapping coastal area between Daytona Beach and Palm Beach in good warm weather and moonlight conditions, with no interference from ASW forces, despite the heavy phosphorescence of the water. In the period from February 19 to March 5, Heyse in *U-128* sank by torpedo two American tankers (*Pan Massachusetts*, 8,200 tons, and *Cities Service Empire*, 8,100 tons) and the 11,000-ton Norwegian tanker *O. A. Knudsen* by torpedo and gun east of the Bahamas. From February 22 to February 26, Poske in *U-504* sank by torpedo two American tankers (*Republic*, 5,300 tons, and *W. D. Anderson*, 10,200 tons) and the 8,200-ton Dutch tanker *Mamura*. Only one crewman survived from the *W. D. Anderson*. Poske incurred "serious damage" to his superstructure from "heavy seas," which forced him to abort. Homebound, he sank a 2,800-ton British freighter by torpedo. Both skippers took advantage of bright lights ashore to silhouette targets. In spite of the human carnage and the oil-soaked beaches, a few Florida resort owners resisted a blackout on the grounds that it would discourage winter tourism.*

These six Type IXs of the "second wave," which sailed to the United States East Coast in January, thus sank twenty-three ships for about 157,000 gross tons, including eleven tankers, ten in the Eastern Sea Frontier and one, by *U-128*, just east of the Bahamas. This almost exactly replicated the bag of the five Type IXs of the "first wave," which sailed to the Americas in December. The two "waves" comprising eleven Type IXs sank an aggregate of forty-six ships for about 307,000 tons. The claimed tonnage sunk was substantially greater.

Many merchant marine crewmen were killed or died in lifeboats, and many of the survivors suffered ghastly ordeals. In an account of the U-boat assault against the United States, author Gary Gentile† reported that of 1,631 passengers and crewmen on board twenty-nine ships sunk in January and February 1942, 999 persons died and 632 survived. The heavy fatalities included the 250 passengers and crewmen who perished in the sinking of the Canadian liner *Lady Hawkins*. Discounting that ship, the death rate of merchant marine crewmen on the other ships sunk was, by his figures, about 50 percent.

The delayed big troopship convoy AT 12 sailed from New York on February 19. It consisted of fifteen transports carrying 14,688 soldiers for Iceland (Indigo) and Northern Ireland (Magnet). It was escorted by Task Force 32, comprised of the battleship *New York*, the light cruiser *Philadelphia*, and ten American destroyers. As related, six other American destroyers on temporary ASW duty on the Eastern Seaboard reinforced the convoy. Task Force 32 put into Iceland to serve as an anti-*Tirpitz* force and later to load troops for the return to the States. At EASTOMP, six British destroyers relieved Task Force 32 to shepherd the Northern Ireland section onward. Admiral King deemed the British escort to be inadequate. The inadequacy was responsible, in part, for a forthcoming proposal for American warships to escort eastbound troopship convoys all the way across the Atlantic.

---

*   Many writers have made too much of this resistance to blackouts or dimouts. Only rarely were moon, weather, and tactical conditions such that distant shorelights were advantageous to the very few German U-boats operating in Florida waters. Most civil defense authorities and mayors all over the East Coast opposed blackouts and dimouts. They were said to increase the danger of crime and automobile and truck accidents and to decrease nighttime restaurant dining, nightclubbing, etc., causing economic hardships for a large number of people.

†   *Track of the Gray Wolf* (1988).

• • •

Thirteen VIIs of the second wave—four captained by *Ritterkreuz* holders—operated in foul, frigid Canadian waters, harassed by ASW forces. Despite five torpedo failures or misses, the ranking U-boat ace, Heinrich Lehmann-Willenbrock in *U-96,* who wore newly minted Oak Leaves on his *Ritterkreuz,* bagged an impressive five ships for 25,500 tons off Halifax, Nova Scotia, including the 9,000-ton British tanker *Kars.* Upon his return to France, Lehmann-Willenbrock was promoted to command the 9th Combat Flotilla at Brest,* replacing Jürgen Oesten, who was sent to provide technical help for the U-boats basing in Norway. The second most successful skipper was Siegfried Rollmann in *U-82,* who sank two tankers (British *Athelcrown,* 12,000 tons; Norwegian *Leiesten,* 6,100 tons) and the 1,200-ton British destroyer *Belmont,* another of the fifty American four-stackers transferred to Britain, which was escorting return troopship convoy NA 2. There were no survivors of *Belmont.* Although he reported six torpedo failures or misses, *Ritterkreuz* holder Gerhard Bigalk in *U-751* sank two ships for 11,500 tons and, in a running gun battle off Halifax, damaged an 8,100-ton Dutch tanker.

Six other VIIs of this group sank one ship each. Ludwig Forster, age twenty-six, in the new *U-654,* reported nine torpedo failures or misses (seven on a stopped target), but he hit and damaged the Free French corvette *Alysee,* which was escorting convoy Outbound North 60. The Canadian corvette *Hepatica* took *Alysee* in tow, but the latter foundered before reaching port. *Ritterkreuz* holder Robert Gysae in *U-98* sank a 5,300-ton British freighter. Upon his return to France, he left the boat to commission a new and much larger boat.† Two boats sank no ships: Günther Heydemann in *U-575,* much delayed on his outbound leg by the search for *Spreewald* survivors, and Wilhelm Zahn in *U-69.* Having made three barren patrols in *U-69,* upon his return to France Zahn went to other duty.

Homebound with only one "defective" torpedo in his stern room, Siegfried Rollmann in *U-82* found another convoy 600 miles west of Lorient. Dönitz urged caution. If it proved to be a Gibraltar convoy, he told the staff, in view of the probable heavy escort, it should be avoided. However, when Rollmann reported the escort to consist of "only corvettes," Kerneval assumed it to be an Outbound South convoy and attempted to vector in three VIIs that were en route to America. Unable to attack and low on fuel, Rollmann nonetheless shadowed dutifully, but the intercept failed. The convoy was indeed an Outbound South—Number 18—and the radar-equipped British escorts were alert and adept. On February 6, the sloop *Rochester* and the corvette *Tamarisk* trapped *U-82* and sank her with depth

---

* Credited with sinking 25 confirmed ships for 183,223 tons—all on *U-96*—Lehmann-Willenbrock, who provided the prototypical U-boat skipper for *Das Boot,* ranked sixth in the war.

† A Type IXD, the largest attack submarine built by the Germans during the war. Conceived to satisfy the advocates of the canceled U-cruisers, the IXD was 35 feet longer (287 versus 252) than the Type IXC and had double the fuel capacity (442 tons), giving it twice the range (24,000 versus 12,000 miles). Like the Type IXC, the IXD was slow-diving and clumsy and was thus unsuitable for attacking escorted convoys. The older onetime flotilla commanders Hans Ibbeken and Ernst Sobe commissioned the first two Type IXDs, *U-178* and *U-179.* Gysae and *Ritterkreuz* holder Wolfgang Lüth commissioned the next two, *U-177* and *U-181.*

charges, with the loss of all hands. The *U-82* was the first of the boats sailing to American waters to be lost.

Two of the thirteen VIIs assigned to Canadian waters probed experimentally southward into United States waters, well to seaward, opposite New York. These were Reinhard Suhren in *U-564,* also wearing new Oak Leaves on his *Ritterkreuz,* and Gerhard Feiler in the new boat *U-653.* Suhren sank the 11,400-ton Canadian tanker *Victolite* by torpedo and gun and attacked a British tanker by gun, but she escaped, only slightly damaged. Near the same area (350 miles east of New York) Feiler in *U-653* sank one ship, a 1,600-ton Norwegian freighter.

Suhren still had a good supply of torpedoes, but he was critically low on fuel. In response to his request for help, Kerneval directed Werner Winter, homebound in the IXB *U-103,* to refuel *U-564.* However, owing to bad weather and imprecise navigation, the rendezvous failed and Kerneval had to call upon Harald Gelhaus, homebound in the IXB *U-107.* During the rendezvous, on February 13, Gelhaus rammed Suhren, holing his starboard fuel tank and crushing all four of the bow tubes. The accident forced Suhren to abort and left Gelhaus so low on fuel he returned in company with Suhren, from whom, ironically, he might obtain fuel if necessary. Had the Allies been able to read naval Enigma, they might well have attacked this rendezvous and destroyed the two disabled U-boats.

While creeping east at one-engine speed, Suhren and Gelhaus ran into a group of six big westbound tankers dispersing from an Outbound North convoy. Owing to his smashed bow tubes, Suhren could not attack. Gelhaus hit the Norwegian tanker *Egda* with his last torpedo, but since she was in ballast the damage was slight. No other boats were close enough to reach this rich group of targets.

The brief probes of the Type VIIs *U-564* and *U-653* into United States waters produced small returns, but they convinced Dönitz that by following the Great Circle route and observing stringent fuel discipline, the VIIs could patrol for a week to ten days in United States waters. A February foray into these waters by another VII, the battle-tested *U-432,* commanded by Heinz-Otto Schultze, which arrived under unusual circumstances, demonstrated that if refueled at sea the VIIs could operate in those waters for even longer periods.

The voyage of *U-432* to United States waters had its roots in yet another infuriating demand by the OKM for escort duty. This time it was for the outbound minelayer-raider *Doggerbank,* which had orders to plant fields in the approaches to Cape Town, South Africa. The OKM directed Kerneval to provide one or more Type IXs as the escort. However, upon objections from Dönitz, who did not want to divert any scarce IXs from the attack on the Americas for this prolonged task, the OKM agreed that a Type VII would suffice. Furthermore, it was also agreed that the VII was to refuel from *Doggerbank* and leave her when she reached a point closest to the United States.

The escort task fell to Schultze in *U-432,* who sailed on January 21. Schultze accompanied *Doggerbank* in heavy weather until January 31, when he refueled at sea—the first refueling of a Type VII in the Americas operations—and departed for the Cape Hatteras area. Although British intelligence had detected the sailing of *Doggerbank* and suspected her destination, she went on to achieve modest success.*

Well stocked with fuel, Heinz-Otto Schultze in *U-432* reached the Cape Hatteras area February 14. Patrolling from Hatteras north to the Maryland coast and back, over the next twelve days he sank six confirmed ships for 27,900 tons, outperforming the reigning "ace," Lehmann-Willenbrock in *U-96,* to register the best Type VII patrol in American waters to then. Awkwardly, his first two victims were Brazilian "neutrals": the 5,200-ton *Buarque* and the 4,100-ton *Olinda.* The pro-American Brazilian dictator-president Getulio Vargas registered an immediate and vehement diplomatic—and public—protest. Berlin braced for "reprisal measures" against Axis assets in Brazil.

The fourteen VIIs of the second wave that sailed to the Americas in January thus sank twenty-four ships (three tankers) for about 125,000 tons. This was an average of 1.7 ships sunk per boat per patrol, the same as the averages of the ten December boats, which sank eighteen ships for about 85,000 tons, or, again, 1.7 ships per boat per patrol.† Two skippers of Type VIIs of the February group, Lehmann-Willenbrock in *U-96* and Schultze in *U-432,* accounted for almost half the total bag of the second wave: eleven ships (one tanker) for about 53,300 tons.

FIRST FORAYS TO THE WEST INDIES AND CARIBBEAN

Of the twenty-six German U-boats that sailed to the Americas in January, none generated more interest than the five Type IXCs directed to areas in the Caribbean Sea. Designated group *Neuland* (New Land), their specific mission was to interdict the flow of oil and bauxite from South America to North America. *Neuland* was backstopped by a group of five big Italian boats, which patrolled from Bordeaux to western Atlantic waters just east of the Windward Islands chain.

Most South American oil originated in two places: the rich fields under the shallow Lake Maracaibo, Venezuela, and the British West Indies island of Trinidad. The Maracaibo crude was shipped in small, shallow-draft tankers through the Gulf of Venezuela to huge refineries on the Dutch islands of Aruba‡ and Curaçao, which lay a few miles off the north coast of Venezuela and which, upon the fall of the Netherlands, had been occupied by British troops, who were in the process of being replaced by American troops. Large seagoing tankers carried the gasoline and petroleum derivatives onward. Most of the Trinidad oil was refined on that island. Strategically located close off the northeast coast of

---

* Outwitting a patrol plane, a light cruiser, and an auxiliary cruiser, *Doggerbank* laid seventy-five mines off Cape Town on the night of March 12–13. Returning to Cape Town on the night of April 16–17, she laid another eighty mines. Her 155 mines caused temporary chaos in Cape Town, sank two freighters, and damaged three other ships.

† See Plate 12.

‡ The Lagos refinery on Aruba, which produced 7 million barrels of petroleum products per month, was the largest in the world.

Venezuela, Trinidad was also a port of call for ships southbound to Latin American and African ports and for a fleet of shallow-draft ships that carried bauxite (the base mineral for aluminum) north from British Guiana and Dutch Guiana (Surinam) to Trinidad, where the bauxite was transferred to larger ships.

Group *Neuland* was composed of three veteran boats and two new boats that had made brief transit patrols from Germany to Lorient in December, but had seen no noteworthy action. Three boats sailed on January 20 to the Aruba-Curaçao area, 4,000 miles distant: Günther Müller-Stöckheim in *U-67,* Jürgen von Rosenstiel in *U-502,* and Werner Hartenstein in the new *U-156.* The other two sailed on January 25 for the Trinidad area, 3,600 miles distant: Nikolaus Clausen in *U-129* and Albrecht Achilles in the new *U-161.* All traveled southwest across the Atlantic at one-engine speed, an agonizingly slow voyage of three weeks or more. As in Drumbeat, the five boats were to launch attacks on the same day—February 16, when the moon was new.

While the boats were creeping toward the Caribbean, Dönitz and Berlin fell into sharp dispute over how to launch a key part of this operation. Berlin—Admiral Raeder himself—ordered that the three Aruba-Curaçao boats were to open the campaign with a surprise shelling of the huge refineries and tank farms on those islands, which were easily accessible from the sea. Although it was known that the islands were occupied by British and American forces and that Aruba had three big (7.5") coast-defense guns, Raeder thought a sudden night attack would catch the Allied forces by surprise, set the refineries and tank farms afire, and put them out of action for months. Believing that a surprise attack on the unarmed tankers would be more profitable—and certainly less risky and more satisfying to his submariners—Dönitz vigorously opposed the order on the grounds that the shelling might fail and would alert enemy shipping to the presence of U-boats and perhaps lead to a temporary halt in tanker traffic, resulting in failure for group *Neuland.* Admiral Raeder refused to rescind his order; nonetheless, Dönitz defied Raeder and directed the boats to open the campaign by attacking tankers, after which, if conditions permitted, they were to shell the refineries and tank farms.

In the early hours of February 16, thirty-two-year-old Werner Hartenstein in *U-156,* the newest but most senior skipper (crew of 1928) of the *Neuland* group, opened the German Caribbean campaign. He eased into the mouth of San Nicholas, the harbor of Aruba, and shot a salvo of torpedoes at three moored tankers. All hit, sinking one (the 2,400-ton British *Oranjestad*) and severely damaging the other two, including one American vessel. In due course, the two damaged tankers were repaired and returned to service.

Even though he had given away his presence, after dark that same day, Hartenstein boldly directed his crew to man the 4.1" deck gun and smaller weapons and shoot up the refinery and tank farm. But disaster ensued. The gunners forgot to remove the tampion (or bung) from the muzzle of the gun, and the first round exploded inside the barrel. The blast killed a gunner, severely wounded the gunnery officer, Dietrich-Alfred von dem Borne, son of a high-ranking *Kriegsmarine* officer, and mangled the gun muzzle. Hartenstein's medic attempted to repair von dem Borne's shattered leg—a ghastly ordeal for both doctor and patient—but it was obvious that if he were to survive, he needed sophisticated medical care. Accordingly, Hartenstein resourcefully requested permission from Dönitz to put von dem Borne ashore on the Vichy island of Martinique. After clearing the request with Berlin, Dönitz authorized the landing, even though the Vichy French on Martinique, fearing American reprisals, were reluctant.

Martinique was still under surveillance by Allied aircraft, surface vessels, and submarines to prevent the possible "escape" of the old Vichy French aircraft carrier *Béarn,* the heavy cruisers *Emile Bertin* and *Jeanne d'Arc,* and other warships to European waters or to attack—and close—the Panama Canal and/or to destroy the refineries on Aruba and Curaçao. Hartenstein therefore approached the harbor at Fort-de-France with extreme caution. Vichy French naval officers overcame their reluctance to this plan and sent out a launch and brought von dem Borne ashore. The French doctors amputated his leg; he eventually recovered from his wounds and returned to Germany. American naval observers on Martinique soon learned of the transfer, which seemed to confirm rumors (all false) that the Vichy French on Martinique were actively assisting German U-boats. In reprisal, President Roosevelt insisted that the French "immobilize" (by removing certain machinery) the Martinique-based warships "within 36 hours" or face an American bombing attack. The French immobilized the warships.

Raeder was miffed that his shelling order had not been more aggressively carried out and he gave Dönitz a new, explicit order to hit the refinery on Aruba. In response, Dönitz shifted Müller-Stöckheim in *U-67* from Curaçao to Aruba and brought in Rosenstiel in *U-502.* Aruba by that time was on full alert and blacked out. Its single Dutch motor launch cruised defensively off the harbor entrance; the three big coast-defense guns were manned and trained out. As a result, neither boat was able—or willing—to conduct an effective night gun action, and the refineries and tank farms remained untouched.*

Released from the shelling mission, the three boats concentrated on the shipping in the Aruba-Curaçao area. All had success. Returning from Martinique, Hartenstein in *U-156* sank four more ships, the last two with the deck gun, which they had made operable by using a hacksaw to cut off the mangled muzzle. These vessels included two tankers, the American *Oregon,* 7,000 tons, and the British *La Carriere,* 5,700 tons. Rosenstiel in *U-502* sank by torpedo five confirmed tankers: three small ones on the Maracaibo run, the Panamanian *Thalia,* 8,300 tons, and the Norwegian *Kongsgaard,* 9,500 tons, and claimed a sixth, plus damage to a 9,000-ton American tanker. Müller-Stöckheim in *U-67* had a run of bad luck. He reported six torpedo failures or misses on two separate ships, then, later, a crack in his pressure hull that limited his diving depth to ninety-eight feet. Despite these failures and handicaps, he sank by torpedo two tankers (the American *J. N. Pew,* 9,000 tons; the Panamanian *Penelope,* 8,400 tons) and damaged a smaller one.

These attacks paralyzed temporarily the Maracaibo-Aruba-Curaçao shallow-

---

* Dönitz's reluctance to shell the refineries and tank farms on Aruba and Curaçao—worth far more to the Axis than the tankers *U-67* or *U-502* might sink—must be regarded as a serious strategic lapse.

draft tanker traffic. The tanker crews—mostly Chinese—mutinied and refused to sail without Allied escorts. No tankers entered Aruba or Curaçao; the huge refineries were forced to shut down operations temporarily. Dutch authorities jailed the Chinese mutineers, but the traffic was not restored to normal until Admiral John H. Hoover, commander of the Caribbean Sea Frontier, sent two destroyers and some Catalinas from Puerto Rico to escort the Lake Maracaibo tanker fleet, and an American admiral to organize, command, and coordinate all Allied forces in this vital strategic area.

Of the two U-boats at Trinidad, the new *U-161*, commanded by twenty-eight-year-old Albrecht Achilles making his first patrol as skipper, had the first successes. Cruising bravely into the shallow, confined Gulf of Paria, separating Trinidad from mainland Venezuela, Achilles approached Trinidad's well-lighted principal city, Port of Spain, as though *U-161* were a cruise ship. Lying on the surface off Port of Spain just before midnight on February 18 in thirty-six feet of water, Achilles fired a bow salvo at two ships. Two of the four torpedoes failed or missed, but the other two hit a 7,000-ton British tanker and a 7,500-ton American freighter. Both ships settled to the shallow bottom, but both were later salvaged and returned to service.

Fully alive to the strategic importance of Trinidad, both as a source of oil and as a way station for shipping, Admiral Hoover was in the process of creating a powerful ASW base on the island, comparable to that on Iceland. But the work had only just begun and Achilles caught the Allied forces by surprise. Thus he was able to make the long run through the shallow waters to open seas on the surface without countermeasures. Although the results were in no way comparable, his bold penetration of the Gulf of Paria was to be compared to Prien's feat at Scapa Flow.

Thereafter Achilles cruised northward in the Windward Islands. Although the Allies temporarily shut down most shipping in those waters, over the next two weeks Achilles found and sank by gun and torpedo two tankers (British *Circe Shell*, 8,200 tons; Canadian *Uniwaleco*, 9,800 tons) and the 7,000-ton American freighter *Lihue*, which was armed and fought back spiritedly. An American submarine, *S-17*, patrolling Anegada Passage in the Windward Islands on March 4–5, reported a hairraising but luckless encounter with a U-boat that was doubtless *U-161*.

When Achilles examined the British island of St. Lucia submerged on March 9, he saw two big ships at dockside in the principal harbor, Port Castries. They were an 8,000-ton Canadian liner and an 8,200-ton British cargo-passenger ship, both of which had arrived that morning. Achilles surfaced after dark, crept silently into the harbor on electric motors, and torpedoed both ships. They sank to the shallow bottom, but were later salvaged and returned to service. As *U-161* withdrew to open water, shorebased machine gunners fired and hit her, but the bullets caused little damage.

Cruising farther north in the Windward Islands, Achilles found and sank two more ships in the following days. The first he claimed as a 5,000-ton tanker, but she was probably a 2,000-ton Canadian freighter. The second was the 1,100-ton United States Coast Guard lighthouse tender *Acacia*. Achilles sank the lightly armed *Acacia* with his deck gun, bringing his confirmed score to five ships (two tankers) for 28,000 tons, plus four ships for 30,500 tons sitting on the bottom in the harbors at Trinidad and St. Lucia. The American four-stack destroyer *Overton* rescued thirty-five crewmen of *Acacia.*

The other boat at Trinidad, the veteran *U-129,* commanded by Nikolaus Clausen, patrolled southeast of the island in the open Atlantic to intercept the bauxite traffic. In four days, February 20 to 23, Clausen torpedoed and sank four freighters for 11,700 tons. He then cruised south along the coast to British and Dutch Guiana (Surinam) to interdict the bauxite traffic at the source, but he was defeated by the shallow waters of the wide (100 miles) continental shelf at those places and an emergency hold, or diversion, of shipping. Returning to his former hunting ground near Trinidad, in seven days, February 28 to March 6, Clausen sank three more freighters for 13,900 tons, bringing his confirmed score to seven ships—all freighters—for 25,600 tons.

Having delivered a jarring physical and psychological wallop in the Caribbean, the five boats of group *Neuland* commenced the prolonged journey home. The group had failed to knock out the refineries on Aruba and Curaçao, but it had sunk twenty-four ships (twelve tankers) for 119,000 tons, and probably damaged eight ships (five tankers) for about 50,000 tons. Had they not been hit in shallow harbors, six of the damaged ships (two by Hartenstein, four by Achilles) almost certainly would have been lost forever. Had Müller-Stöckheim in *U-67* not had torpedo problems and a pressure-hull leak, the group's score doubtless would have been even greater.

While Clausen in *U-129* was homebound in the Bay of Biscay, a Coastal Command Whitley of Squadron 502, piloted by Victor D. Pope, bombed the boat in darkness. However, she survived and reached Lorient. Inasmuch as his claims exceeded 100,000 tons, Clausen was awarded a *Ritterkreuz.** Berlin propagandists crowed over his successes and also, deservedly so, those of Achilles. Detached from *U-129,* Clausen, like Gysae and Lüth, went back to Germany to commission one of the new IXD U-cruisers.†

In terms of the desired impact on the oil traffic in the Caribbean, group *Neuland* was a remarkable success: twelve tankers sunk, five damaged, and a temporary shipping paralysis at Aruba-Curaçao. But it was also expensive. Like the earlier patrols to Freetown, those of group *Neuland* were long: an average of sixty-five days. Although the new boats of the group (*U-156, U-161, U-502*) resailed after about one month of rest and refit in France, the older boats (*U-67, U-129*) would require about two months of refit. Hence, in terms of time expended per boat per patrol, including refits, the average return on investment was not all that impressive—to say nothing of the wear and tear on the crew in tropical waters. Moreover, group *Neuland* had had the advantage of surprise in virgin territory. Succeeding patrols to the

---

* At the time of the award, Clausen's confirmed score on *U-37* and *U-129* was nineteen ships for 63,855 tons, including, by error, two Vichy vessels: the submarine *Sfax* and the small tanker *Rhone.*

† His departure left eight *Ritterkreuz* holders engaged in the U-boat war against the Americas: Bigalk, Bleichrodt, Hardegen, Mützelburg, Schnee, Scholtz, Suhren, and Topp.

Caribbean, some staffers at Kerneval believed, were to confront intensified ASW measures—however green and inept—with the likelihood of decreasing returns on investment at much greater risk. Thus, those staffers regarded patrols to the Caribbean, like the patrols to Freetown, as uneconomical until a means of resupplying the boats with fuel and torpedoes in that area could be devised.

Based on past performance, Kerneval did not expect much help from the five Italian boats which patrolled just east of the Windward Islands during group *Neuland*'s foray. At best, it was believed, they might provide a diversion. But these Italian submariners—some trained by the Germans in the Baltic or on war patrols in the North Atlantic—delivered the greatest single coordinated blow of any group of Italian boats in the war.

• Carlo Fecia di Cossato in *Tazzoli* sank six ships for 29,200 tons, including the British tanker *Athelqueen,* 8,800 tons.

• Athos Fraternale in *Morosini* sank three ships for 22,000 tons, including the Dutch tanker *Oscilla,* 6,300 tons, and the British tanker *Peder Bogen,* 9,700 tons.

• Ugo Giudice in *Finzi* sank three ships for 21,500 tons, including the British tanker *Melpomene,* 7,000 tons, and the Norwegian tanker *Charles Racine,* 10,000 tons.

• Antonio de Giacomo in *Torelli* sank two ships for 16,500 tons, including the Panamanian tanker *Esso Copenhagen,* 9,200 tons.

• Luigi Longanesi-Cattani in *Da Vinci* sank one ship for 3,644 tons.

The total came to fifteen ships for about 93,000 tons, including six tankers. Although *Torelli* was caught on the surface and bombed by Allied aircraft, which killed two men, she and the other four boats returned safely to Bordeaux. When the results of group *Neuland* and those of the Italian group were combined, the total of these first nine Axis submarine attacks in the West Indies and the Caribbean were impressive indeed: thirty-nine ships (eighteen tankers) positively sunk for about 212,000 tons, plus probable severe damage to eight ships (five tankers) for about 50,000 tons.*

The twenty-five German boats of the January group that reached American waters delivered a severe blow to Allied shipping. The eleven Type IXs, including group *Neuland,* sank forty-seven confirmed ships for 276,000 tons (and damaged many others). The fourteen Type VIIs sank twenty-four confirmed ships for 125,000 tons (and damaged others). It was the most successful U-boat foray of the war: seventy-one confirmed ships sunk (twenty-three tankers) for about 401,000 tons.† In return, Allied forces sank but one U-boat, *U-82.*

---

* In the wake of the Italian group, Emilio Olivieri in *Calvi,* patrolling alone in the same area and southward to British and Dutch Guiana, sank five ships for 27,571 tons, including three tankers (the Americans *T. C. McCobb,* 7,500 tons, and *E.V.R. Thayer,* 7,100 tons, plus the Panamanian *Ben Brush,* 7,700 tons), bringing the results of the first Italian patrols to the West Indies to twenty ships (nine tankers) sunk for 120,417 tons. However, the Italians sank no more ships in the Atlantic in 1942.

† Some of the January boats sank ships in January, February, and March; some of the February boats sank ships in February. Total sinkings by all U-boats in the month of February only: fifty-nine confirmed ships sunk (twenty-three tankers) for 331,219 tons and nine ships damaged (eight tankers).

Doubtless this victory influenced Hitler's decision to continue the campaign in the Americas and to jump-promote Dönitz to four-star admiral effective March 14. When he got news of the promotion, Dönitz notified all U-boat shore stations and the boats at sea, expressing his "thanks and gratitude to you, my U-boat men."

Notwithstanding this astonishing success, Admiral Raeder and the OKM were annoyed to learn that Dönitz had not launched a second group of Type IXs to replace group *Neuland* in the Caribbean with no intervening gap. Declaring that the interdiction of Allied oil and bauxite traffic in the Caribbean was of greater importance than any other task, Admiral Raeder insisted that Dönitz patrol the Caribbean "to the fullest extent possible" and to make another attempt to shell the refineries and tank farms on Aruba and Curaçao.

UNFORESEEN AND UNPLANNED CONVOY ATTACKS

Dönitz had planned to equal or exceed the January U-boat offensive in the Americas in February with twenty-six or more boats. But owing to Hitler's "Norway paranoia" and to the delays in the buildup of the Atlantic force caused by the Baltic ice, eight Type VIIs had to be diverted, temporarily, for the Iceland-Scotland patrol line. Moreover, believing that the Freetown area, unpatrolled since the *Atlantis-Python* disaster in November 1941, might be undermanned and/or unalert, Dönitz decided to send two Type IXs to the South Atlantic. The upshot was that only eighteen boats (nine IXs, nine VIIs) put out for American waters in February. Two-thirds (six of nine) of the Type IXs and nearly half (four of nine) of the Type VIIs were new, and because of the Baltic ice most had not completed a full training cycle.

Based on the experiences of Suhren in *U-564* and Feiler in *U-653*, Dönitz had concluded that by following a Great Circle route and exercising stringent fuel discipline and limited mobility, the Type VIIs could operate in American waters for perhaps as long as ten days, or nearly as long as the VIIs in Canadian waters. He therefore directed that the difficult and less-productive patrols to Canadian waters be temporarily suspended and that all eighteen boats of the February group patrol United States and Caribbean waters.

The February boats were the first to benefit from the British inability to read four-rotor Enigma and thereby avoid known U-boat positions. While en route to the Americas on the same day, February 21, two new Type IXs, *U-154* and *U-155*, attacked big convoys in the mid-Atlantic that were sailing in opposite directions.

Acting on the report of another boat, Walther Kölle, age thirty-four, in *U-154* found the fast, strongly escorted, eastbound convoy Halifax 175. He got off the mandatory contact report, shadowed, then attacked doggedly, firing all fourteen internal torpedoes at a variety of ships, to absolutely no effect. After receiving his shooting report (ten unexplained misses, four "duds" on a tanker) Kerneval ordered Kölle to abort at high speed to Lorient. Upon his arrival it was discovered that the torpedo-data computer was out of calibration. Kölle had been bound for the Caribbean. Repairs and further training delayed his departure to March and, to Berlin's consternation, diminished the U-boat campaign in the Caribbean.

Adolf-Cornelius Piening in *U-155* found convoy Outbound North 67, which was westbound along a newly adopted, more southerly Great Circle route. Composed of thirty-five merchant ships, including many tankers in ballast, it was escorted by two old and two new American destroyers (*Nicholson* and *Lea* equipped with meter-wavelength radar) and a Canadian corvette. It was trailed by a 1,600-ton "rescue ship," the *Toward,* which had accommodations for several hundred survivors and a medical staff, as well as one of the new shipborne Huff Duff sets, to take local bearings on U-boat shadowers for the benefit of the escorts.

Among the ships in the convoy was the 8,000-ton British tanker *Empire Celt,* equipped with a new and experimental antitorpedo device known as the Admiralty Net Defense. The device consisted of huge rolls of strong steel "nets," which could be "streamed" from fifty-foot poles over the starboard and port sides in times of danger, or when sailing alone. During controlled tests, the nets had stopped British submarine torpedoes, but this voyage was the first "combat" trial of the device. Although the nets could not be streamed at speeds greater than 9 knots and they were difficult to handle and had to be replaced after each voyage, their advocates believed them capable of providing about 50 to 60 percent protection for freighters and tankers. The Admiralty Net Defense project manager, C.N.E. Currey, and a senior American submariner, George C. Crawford, were embarked on *Empire Celt* to oversee and observe the combat trial.

The rescue ship *Toward* DFed the contact reports of Piening in *U-155* and gave the alarm. The destroyer *Lea* made a desultory search down the bearing for one hour, then returned to her position in the screen. Piening in *U-155* evaded *Lea,* the three other destroyers, and the corvette, and in the early morning hours of February 22 attacked three ships with a bow salvo. His torpedoes sank the 8,000-ton British tanker *Adellen* and a 1,800-ton freighter. While the convoy continued on course, *Toward* and *Nicholson* picked up the survivors.

Inasmuch as the convoy was westbound, Dönitz directed all boats outbound to America that were near the convoy to converge. Two other new Type IXs, Erich Rostin in *U-158* and Jürgen Wattenberg in *U-162,* and four VIIs homed on Piening's beacons, and by late evening on February 23, seven America-bound U-boats were stalking convoy Outbound North 67 and maneuvering around the escorts. By sheer chance and improvisation, it became the first group attack on a North Atlantic convoy since the previous November 2, when the Germans drove Slow Convoy 52 back into Newfoundland.

The old hand Günther Krech in the Type VII *U-558* was the next boat to attack. His strike on February 24 proved to be one of the most notable of the war. In five hours he sank five confirmed ships: four big tankers in ballast for 32,600 tons* plus a 4,400-ton freighter. Having shot all of his torpedoes save one, Krech returned to France, where he received unstinting praise from Dönitz and the usual buildup from Berlin propagandists.

Next, two Type IXs closed to attack: Rostin in *U-158* and Wattenberg in *U-162.* Rostin hit and damaged a tanker. Then he and Wattenberg probably fired si-

---

* Three British, *Inverarder,* 5,600 tons; *Anadara,* 8,000 tons, which was credited in postwar years with sinking *U-651*; *Finnanger,* 9,500 tons; and the Norwegian *Eidanger,* 9,400 tons.

multaneously at the tanker *Empire Celt*, which was in the process of streaming her Admiralty Net Defense. A torpedo broke through the net and hit amidships, making a gaping hole. She fell out of the convoy and broke in half. The bow sank. A tug from Newfoundland rescued forty-five men from the stern, including Currey and Crawford, and attempted to tow it to St. John's, but the effort came to naught thirty-five miles short of the goal. The failure of the combat trial was a "grave blow" to the Admiralty Net Defense program, a British authority wrote. Nonetheless, the Admiralty fitted numerous ships of 8,000 tons or more with the device.*

The next skipper to attack was Ulrich Borcherdt in the new Type VII *U-587*. While outbound from France on February 13, Kerneval had diverted Borcherdt in *U-587* and Viktor Vogel in the new sister ship *U-588*, and Otto Ites in the veteran *U-94*, to search for survivors of a Focke-Wulf Condor that had ditched. On February 15, Borcherdt had found five survivors in a dinghy and picked them up. He had then to rendezvous with a homebound boat to hand over the survivors. The first rendezvous, with Gerhard Bigalk in *U-751*, had gone awry; the second, on February 18, with Ernst Kals in *U-130*, had succeeded. It was a fortunate outcome for the Focke-Wulf crew, but in the search and the handover, Borcherdt had burned up a great deal of precious fuel.

The expenditure of fuel prompted Dönitz to make an extraordinary entry in his daily diary. However "satisfactory" and "natural" the rescue of the aircrew may "appear," he wrote, "it is nevertheless always difficult to decide whether submarines on their outward voyage should be used to search for crews of planes that have been forced down. Under present conditions every drop of fuel is vital to the boats . . . It may well happen that a request for help will have to be refused for the sake of operational duties." Upon reading this entry, the OKM commented that such was the value of experienced aircrews engaged in naval warfare that "a *very* serious reason would have to be given if such a request were refused."

Coming up astern of the convoy to mount his attack, Borcherdt in *U-587* saw the trailing rescue-ship *Toward*. She was burning "dim" side lights and was equipped with what Borcherdt believed to be "cable-laying gear." Concluding from these observations that she might be a "decoy" or a "Q" ship, Borcherdt fired one torpedo at her. It missed or malfunctioned, leading Borcherdt and Kerneval to conclude later—and incorrectly—that the torpedo had been deflected by antitorpedo nets. Borcherdt then attacked the convoy, possibly hitting one tanker already fatally damaged by Krech. Escorts thwarted a second attack.

The U.S. Navy decorated the commanding officer of the American escort group, Albert C. Murdaugh in the destroyer *Edison*, for "particularly outstanding" work in defending the convoy. But in reality, it was a major disaster and embarrassment: eight British-owned or controlled ships (six tankers) sunk, for about 55,000 tons, and one British tanker damaged. The results, Dönitz logged, were

---

* The Allies equipped 768 merchant ships with net defense. A total of twenty-one ships fitted with nets were attacked by torpedoes during the war. The nets deflected ten attacks, but five ships were damaged and six were sunk.

"particularly satisfactory," especially in view of the number of green skippers involved. The engagement powerfully reinforced his conviction that when sufficient boats were available to find, shadow, and attack, organized group operations against convoys could be resumed with every possibility of good success.

The reports from Krech and other skippers of antitorpedo nets on *Empire Celt* caused deep concern at Kerneval. It seemed "astounding" to Dönitz that a ship could make 9 or 10 knots with streamed nets. He immediately informed the torpedo technicians of this discovery, stressing the urgent need to develop a "countermeasure." The only feasible countermeasure was a reliable magnetic pistol, which would run under the nets and explode the torpedo beneath the ship. The technicians had produced a new and improved magnetic pistol, but it was still undergoing tests. In view of the harsh punishment handed down to their predecessors for the failure of the original magnetic pistol, doubtless the technicians were reluctant to release the new pistol until it was faultless.

Altogether the U-boats had interrupted six cargo convoys on the North Atlantic run in February. These were the loaded eastbound convoys Halifax 173 and 175 and Slow Convoy 67. Three were the empty westbound convoys Outbound North (Slow) 61 and 63 and Outbound North 67. The Germans sank twelve ships from these convoys (six tankers) and three corvette escorts (*Alysee, Arbutus, Spikenard*). In addition, they damaged two tankers. This was hardly a "quiet" time, certainly no time for a wholesale transfer of escorts from the North Atlantic run to the East Coast, as suggested by Michael Gannon.

During the attack on Outbound North 67, or shortly thereafter, Wattenberg in the new Type IXC *U-162* reported a serious casualty. The caps of two bow tubes had broken loose, blocking the other two bow tubes. He later managed to clear the two blocked tubes and patch the broken ones and requested permission to proceed, but Kerneval decided not to send a new skipper in a partly disabled boat onward to America. She was diverted to escort the incoming blockade-runner *Osorno* into France, but the rendezvous failed.

The unforeseen, unplanned attacks on convoys Halifax 175 and Outbound North 67, which resulted in the return of a boat (*U-558*) and two aborts (*U-154, U-162*), diminished the strength of the February group outbound to the Americas from eighteen to fifteen boats. Moreover, owing to the high expenditure of fuel in the rescue of the Condor air crew and the attack on Outbound North 67, Borcherdt in *U-587* had to be limited to Canadian waters, reducing the group en route to United States waters to fourteen boats.

Unknown to Dönitz, the group was further reduced as the boats passed southbound through Canadian waters. On March 1 an American Navy Hudson, piloted by Ensign William Tepuni of the Argentia-based Patrol Squadron 82, spotted and attacked Ernst Kröning's new Type VII *U-656*, about sixty miles southeast of Cape Race. The boat went down with all hands. She was the first confirmed U-boat to be sunk by U.S. forces and the first to be sunk in North American waters. Two weeks later, on March 15, a Hudson of the same squadron, piloted by airman Donald F. Mason, who had earlier won a DFC and great fame ("Sighted Sub. Sank Same.") for a nonsinking, spotted and attacked Otto Gericke's new Type IXC/40 *U-503*, near the same area. She, too, went down with the loss of all hands. Both Tepuni and Mason were awarded DFCs; airman Mason was promoted to ensign.

ANOTHER HEAVY BLOW

Only thirteen of the eighteen U-boats which sailed to American waters in February actually got there. These included Ulrich Borcherdt in *U-587*, restricted by his low fuel situation to Canadian waters, and Ernst Bauer in the IXC *U-126*, assigned to the northeast coast of Cuba to attack ships entering and leaving the Caribbean via the Windward Passage, separating eastern Cuba and Haiti. The other eleven boats—five IXs and six VIIs—patrolled the United States East Coast.

Borcherdt in *U-587* had a miserable time in Canadian waters. The weather was still frigid and Allied ASW forces, which sank *U-656* and *U-503* that month, were improving. Between those two U-boat sinkings, on March 8, Borcherdt complained to Kerneval that in a period of nine days he had encountered destroyers or patrol craft ten different times. He shot at some of these and at other vessels, but he managed to sink only one 900-ton coastal freighter. Homebound, he claimed to have sunk a severely damaged and abandoned (but unidentified) tanker.

Nearing the western edge of the Bay of Biscay on March 27, Borcherdt encountered and reported a "fast" southbound convoy. This was one of the prize targets of the war: the heavily escorted Winston Special 17, composed of thirty troop transports with 60,000 British soldiers embarked.* The luckless Borcherdt had only one air torpedo left and could not attack. He shadowed for the benefit of other boats, but one of the many escorts, the destroyer *Keppel*, accurately DFed him with its new Huff Duff, and four other escorts—*Leamington, Grove, Aldenham, Volunteer*—pounced on *U-587* and sank her by depth charges with the loss of all hands. No other boats were able to respond to *U-587*'s contact report, so the tracking and loss were to no avail. She was the third of the February boats to be lost in combat and the second boat (after Rollmann's *U-82*) to be sunk homebound from the Americas.

In contrast, the old hand Ernst Bauer in the Type IX *U-126*, patrolling the Old Bahama Channel north and northeast of Cuba, enjoyed beautiful weather, weak or no ASW forces, and dense shipping near the Windward Passage. In a mere twelve days—March 2 to March 13—Bauer sank by torpedo and gun seven confirmed ships for 33,000 tons and damaged three others of 23,000 tons. His victims included the 8,200-ton Panamanian tanker *Hanseat* sunk and two other tankers damaged. In view of his past overclaims and his role in the rescue of survivors of the German merchant raider *Atlantis*, Bauer was awarded the *Ritterkreuz* and got the usual buildup from Berlin propagandists.†

---

* Some of the troops were bound for an amphibious assault (Ironclad) on the Vichy French island of Madagascar, to prevent a possible Japanese lodgement, which would pose a grave threat to British shipping in the Indian Ocean.

† At the time of the award, Bauer's confirmed score was fifteen ships sunk for 62,221 tons.

• • •

American ASW forces were still not much improved. As related, eleven different destroyers released from the North Atlantic run patrolled the Eastern Sea Frontier intermittently in February, but about half of them had been siphoned off to escort troop convoy AT 12. At the end of February, there were only five destroyers (including *Roe*) on ASW duty in the Eastern Sea Frontier.

During the month of March, Atlantic Fleet commander Ingersoll made available to Andrews on a temporary basis fourteen different destroyers.* Andrews later calculated that these warships spent a total of sixty-three days on ASW duty in his area during the month, an average of about two destroyers in service per day. The four-stack *Herbert* contributed the most: eighteen full days.

The demand for destroyers increased in all sectors. Apart from the diminishing number providing escort on the North Atlantic convoy run, among the important tasks performed in March were:

• Escort of Pacific-bound troopship convoy BT 201 from New York to Panama, March 4 to March 12, which merged with Task Force 18 (Pacific-bound carrier *Hornet* and cruisers *Nashville* and *Vincennes*). Nine American destroyers or destroyer transports or destroyer minesweepers escorted the formation: *Dickerson, Ellyson, Grayson, Gwin, Manley, Meredith, Monssen, Stansbury,* and *Sturtevant.* The *Grayson, Gwin, Meredith,* and *Monssen* accompanied *Hornet* into the Pacific for the "Doolittle raid" on Tokyo and remained in that theater, bringing the total number of destroyers transferred from the Atlantic to the Pacific to fifteen.

• Escort of two high-priority supply convoys, AS 1 and AS 2, to Ascension Island and Freetown, March 14 and March 19. The escorts consisted of the new British "jeep" carrier *Archer* (in transit), the British cruiser *Devonshire*, the American cruisers *Cincinnati* and *Memphis,* and eight American destroyers: *Cole, Du Pont, Ellis, Greer, Jouett, Somers, Upshur,* and *Winslow.*

• Escort of British troopship convoy NA 5 (two vessels) from Halifax to the British Isles, March 14 to March 22. Two new (1941) American destroyers, *Nicholson* and *Swanson,* carried out this task.

• Escort of troopship convoy TA 12, returning to the States, March 14 to March 25. This escort was Task Force 32, comprised of the battleship *New York,* the cruiser *Philadelphia,* and the ten destroyers that had escorted the eastbound troopship convoy AT 12.†

• Escort of Task Force 39 (renamed 99) consisting of the carrier *Wasp,* the new battleship *Washington,* and the heavy cruisers *Tuscaloosa* and *Wichita* from Casco Bay, Maine, to Scapa Flow, March 25 to April 4. Six modern destroyers were assigned to the task: *Lang, Madison, Plunkett, Sterett, Wainwright,* and *Wil-*

---

* *Cole, Dahlgren, Dallas, Dickerson, Du Pont, Ellis, Emmons, Greer, Hamilton, Herbert, Macomb, Roper, Tarbell, Upshur.*

† The destroyers assigned to convoys AT 12 and TA 12 were at sea on these tasks about thirty-five days, February 19 to March 25. Adding a week for refit and R&R, every destroyer assigned to escort a troop convoy to Europe was tied up about six weeks.

son. Placed under British control, this American force reinforced the British Home Fleet, which had been diluted to supply ships for Force H at Gibraltar, engaged in the British conquest of Madagascar.

Accidents to destroyers continued. During workup just prior to the trip to Scapa Flow, the carrier *Wasp* and the destroyer *Stack* collided in fog on March 17 off the Delaware Capes. Badly damaged, flooded and heeled over, *Stack* barely survived this mishap and was in repair for months. One of her crew, Frank LeR. Knight, who alertly and bravely clawed his way aft to set all of *Stack*'s depth charges on "safe" after the collision, won the Medal of Honor.

The first of the eleven February boats to reach the United States coast was the Type VII *U-578*, commanded by Ernst-August Rehwinkel, who had earlier made a patrol in the Arctic. Shortly after midnight on February 27, while cruising thirty miles off the New Jersey coast in shallow water, Rehwinkel spotted a zigzagging blacked-out, northbound tanker. She was the 7,500-ton American *R. P. Resor,* loaded with 78,720 barrels of fuel oil and newly armed with a gun manned by a nine-man Navy Armed Guard crew. Rehwinkel fired a two-fan shot from close range. Caught unawares, *Resor* blew up in a thunderous fireball. Only three of the fifty men on board survived. She burned for two days in clear view of those ashore.

That afternoon, two of the four-stacks on ASW duty in the Eastern Sea Frontier, *Dickerson* and *Jacob Jones,* sailed from New York. Recently released from North Atlantic convoy duty, *Jones* was the namesake of another World War I four-stacker which had been sunk by a U-boat in European waters on December 6, 1917. Her orders were to patrol close inshore at night and out to the 100 fathom (600 foot) curve in daylight. Near dark, she and *Dickerson* paused briefly at the smoking hulk of tanker *Resor,* which Rehwinkel in *U-578* had destroyed, to look for survivors. Finding none, the destroyers moved on to set up patrols.

At about five o'clock the following morning, February 28, while lying on the surface, Rehwinkel in *U-578* saw the *Jacob Jones* coming directly toward him, apparently oblivious to the U-boat's presence. Rehwinkel waited calmly for the range to close, then fired two bow torpedoes. Both hit and *Jacob Jones* blew apart and sank. As she went down, her armed depth charges exploded and the concussions killed many men in the water. Later in the morning, an Army aircraft spotted the wreckage and a small patrol boat rescued eleven out of her crew of about 200. No more were ever found. The loss of *Jacob Jones*—the second American destroyer after *Reuben James* to be sunk by a U-boat—underscored not only the futility but also the dangers of hunter-killer ASW destroyer patrols.*

Rehwinkel had fuel for about one week of patrolling in American waters. Heavy storms raked the East Coast during the first week of March, making it difficult for him and all other U-boat skippers to find and sink ships. On March 7, he reported, an aircraft bombed him off Cape Hatteras—the first German report of an

---

* In keeping with the Navy's policy of naming some ships after those lost in combat, the new destroyer escort program included a *Reuben James* and a *Jacob Jones.*

attack on a U-boat in United States waters—but the bombs were "small" and the attack was ineffectual. Having found no other targets, he headed home. On the way back he sank a 3,100-ton freighter that was sailing alone.

The other ten February boats (five IXs, five VIIs) arrived almost literally in Rehwinkel's wake. Piening and Rostin in the Type IXCs *U-155* and *U-158,* who had expended torpedoes and fuel on Outbound North 67, bracketed Cape Hatteras. Operating in heavy weather, Piening in *U-155* had a run of bad luck. His first watch officer was washed overboard and lost, the first German submariner to die in United States waters. Piening sank one 7,900-ton freighter, *Arabutan,* but, awkwardly, she was another "neutral" Brazilian. Rostin in *U-158* had better luck. With small difficulty, he sank by torpedo and gun two American tankers in ballast, the 7,000-ton *Ario* and the 11,600-ton *John D. Gill,* plus an American freighter, and he damaged the 11,600-ton American tanker *Olean,* also sailing in ballast. Piening in *U-155* returned to France after forty-nine days at sea and Rostin in *U-158* after fifty-eight days. Both skippers were commended for aggressive first patrols.

En route to America, young Otto Ites in the Type VIIC *U-94*—praised by Kerneval for his discovery of the leak in the torpedo balance chamber—sank a 7,000-ton British freighter and one of the twenty-four America-bound British ASW trawlers, *Northern Princess.* While patrolling off New York in heavy weather on March 7, he sank a 5,200-ton passenger-cargo ship that was blacked out and zigzagging. She turned out to be yet another Brazilian "neutral," *Caryu,* the fourth Brazilian ship sunk by U-boats within three weeks. In angry reprisal, the Brazilian president, Vargas, froze German and Japanese assets in Brazilian banks, seized other German and Japanese properties, and whipped the public into an angry mood, setting the stage for a declaration of war.

Ites sank one other ship—for a total of four for 28,300 tons—before the shortage of fuel compelled him to head for France. En route he ran into a convoy, Outbound North 77, which he reported, then attacked, firing four torpedoes at an 8,000-ton British tanker, *Imperial Transport,* in ballast. He damaged that ship and attempted to shadow the convoy, but owing to a shortage of fuel he had to break off before any other boats came up. Upon his arrival in France, Dönitz awarded Ites a *Ritterkreuz.**

Viktor Vogel in the new Type VII *U-588* ran almost parallel with Ites in American waters, from New York southward. Inbound, he sank a 4,900-ton British freighter. Off New York on March 2, he hit a 4,800-ton British tanker in ballast with one torpedo, then doggedly attacked her with his deck gun, firing an astonishing 200 rounds over a period of four hours. Vogel claimed a sinking, but although heavily damaged, the ship survived and limped into New York. Off the New Jersey coast on March 10, after the storms had abated, Vogel torpedoed the 6,700-ton American tanker *Gulftrade,* which broke into halves before sinking. After ten days in American waters, Vogel commenced the long voyage to France. He arrived on

---

* At the time of the award, Berlin propagandists declared Ites had sunk 11 ships for over 100,000 tons. His confirmed score on the duck *U-146* and *U-94* was nine ships for 47,257 tons, plus damage to the 8,000-ton tanker.

March 27, having spent forty-four days at sea—thirty-four days going to and from North America.

The son of a senior Imperial Navy officer, Otto von Bülow in the new VII *U-404* arrived next. Passing southbound near Halifax, he found a 5,100-ton American freighter stopped outside the port, apparently waiting for a pilot. Mistakenly believing she was a much larger ship underway at 10 knots, von Bülow fired "a lot" of torpedoes at her before he got a hit and sank her. He then proceeded to the New York area, where he sank two more ships in two days, a 7,600-ton American freighter and—awkwardly—the aged 1,900-ton Chilean neutral, *Tolten*. Berlin had assured the pro-German Chilean government that its ships (bringing copper to the United States) were to enjoy safe passage, provided they were not in convoy or blacked out. In compliance with American rules, *Tolten* was blacked out, so von Bülow was not held responsible. One crewman survived the sinking.

Cruising southward off the New Jersey coast, low on torpedoes and fuel, on the evening of March 16 von Bülow found the 8,100-ton British tanker *San Demetrio*. Earlier in the war the "pocket" battleship *Admiral Scheer* had severely damaged this ship with gunfire during *Scheer*'s attack on convoy Halifax 84. By heroic efforts, the crew had saved her, an action which had been romanticized in a wartime propaganda film. Von Bülow hit her with a torpedo, just forward of the bridge. "Nothing happened," he remembered. "No boat was lowered. Nothing at all. Then all at once flames engulfed the entire length of the ship. The heat from the fire was so great I had to draw back to 800 meters or more." Nineteen of the fifty-three-man crew died in the inferno.

Having exhausted fuel and torpedoes to sink four confirmed ships for 22,700 tons on his maiden patrol—a noteworthy first outing—von Bülow commenced a slow, eighteen-day return to France. On the way, on March 22, he ran into an Allied force of "two cruisers, six destroyers, and five big ships" and shot his last two torpedoes. He heard two "thuds," but no explosions, leading him to conclude both torpedo pistols had failed. No other U-boat was able to respond to this rich find.

Two veteran boats of the February group converged on Cape Hatteras.

Johannes Liebe in the Type VII *U-332* got there first, very low on fuel. Kerneval hoped to give him some fuel from Heyse's *U-128*, homebound from Florida waters, but Heyse, who was under orders to scout Bermuda, reported that owing to an acute shortage of food, he was unable to detour.* Restricted to merely six days, Liebe continued the slaughter off Cape Hatteras with the sinking of three ships: a four-masted 700-ton American sailing schooner, a 5,000-ton Yugoslavian freighter, and the 11,600-ton American tanker *Australia*.

Johann Mohr in the Type IXB *U-124* arrived next. Inbound near Bermuda, he sank the 7,200-ton tanker *British Resource*, which blew up, spewing flames 600

---

* Two American "seaplanes," probably acting on a DF fix, found and attacked Heyse off Bermuda on March 7, dropping a total of six depth charges. Two were duds; the other four fell wide of the mark.

feet into the sky. Approaching Cape Hatteras waters on the evening of March 16 in the darkness of the new moon, Mohr sank a 1,700-ton Honduran freighter.

The next day, March 17, Mohr closed submerged on Cape Hatteras in shallow water. Beginning late that afternoon, in the space of eight hours he found and attacked three ships. His torpedoes sank two—a 5,100-ton Greek freighter and the 9,600-ton American tanker *E. M. Clark*—and severely damaged the 6,900-ton American tanker *Acme*. During these attacks, the four-stack destroyer *Dickerson* and the 165-foot Coast Guard cutter *Dione* (armed with a 3" bow gun, depth-charge racks, and Y guns) were on ASW patrol near Cape Hatteras. Engrossed in rescuing survivors of the Greek and the *E. M. Clark,* neither warship conducted an attack on *U-124,* but a Navy seaplane dropped two close depth charges, which rattled the boat and convinced Mohr to head for deeper water for a day's rest.

The following night, March 18–19, Mohr returned to shallow water in pitch darkness, navigating by the Cape Hatteras lighthouse and other helpful aids. The *U-124* lay silently on the surface, waiting. Soon the bridge watch spotted two blacked-out American tankers: the southbound 6,000-ton *Papoose* in ballast, and the northbound 7,000-ton *W. E. Hutton,* loaded with 65,000 barrels of heating oil. Mohr coolly torpedoed both ships. *Hutton* exploded in a giant fireball. Fifteen of the total fifty-five crewmen on both ships perished. The survivors rowed to shore or were rescued.

The four-stack destroyer *Dickerson* raced south to the scene. En route, she came upon the northbound 7,700-ton American freighter *Liberator,* which had a 4" gun manned by a green Armed Guard crew. Mistaking *Dickerson* for a U-boat, the gun crew on *Liberator* opened fire. Remarkably, one or two rounds struck *Dickerson*'s bridge. The blast killed two sailors, fatally wounded the skipper, John K. Reybold, and wrecked the bridge. *Dickerson* returned to Norfolk for funerals and repairs, her fate, like that of *Jacob Jones,* underscoring the futility and dangers of ASW hunter-killer patrols.

Perhaps attracted by the muzzle blasts of the gun on *Liberator,* Liebe in *U-332,* who was nearby but very low on fuel, bore in to attack her. His torpedoes struck solidly and *Liberator* went down. Five crewmen died in the sinking, but a Navy tugboat rescued thirty-five survivors, including the Armed Guard, who came ashore bragging that before being themselves sunk, they had hit—and sunk—a "U-boat," actually the destroyer *Dickerson*. After expending his last three torpedoes on a tanker—all misses—Liebe commenced a protracted voyage home. He claimed four ships sunk for 22,000 tons; the postwar accounting confirmed four ships sunk but raised his tonnage to 25,000.

Mohr in *U-124* hauled out to deep water again to rest his crew and to download torpedoes from the topside canisters. He returned submerged to Cape Hatteras in the late afternoon of March 20. By then, another veteran Type VII, Walter Flachsenberg in *U-71,* who had sunk the 6,400-ton Norwegian tanker *Ranja* offshore, had entered the Cape Hatteras area. That night Flachsenberg sank a 5,800-ton American freighter, and Mohr in *U-124* damaged by torpedo and gun two more blacked-out American tankers: the 8,000-ton *Esso Nashville* and the 11,400-ton *Atlantic Sun.* Mohr claimed both ships sank, but they survived. *Esso Nashville* broke in half; *Atlantic Sun* escaped with slight damage. The destroyer-transport *McKean,* which was passing by, and two Coast Guard cutters salvaged the stern section of *Esso Nashville,* which later returned to service with a new bow.

In his eight-day patrol off Cape Hatteras, Mohr had expended eighteen of his twenty torpedoes. On the last night, March 23, he shot the other two at the loaded northbound, 5,400-ton American tanker *Naeco.* She blew up in a fireball; twenty-four of her thirty-eight-man crew perished in the flames or water. The four-stack destroyer *Roper,* the Coast Guard cutter *Dione,* the minesweeper *Osprey,* and another naval vessel raced to the scene, but by that time Mohr was homebound in deep water. The ships could only collect *Naeco*'s living and dead.

When Mohr compiled his final score, he was ecstatic: ten ships (eight tankers) sunk for 64,000 tons. He submitted his sinking report to Dönitz in the form of a ditty, which the propagandist Wolfgang Frank later rendered into English, downgrading his tonnage:

> *The new-moon night is black as ink*
> *Off Hatteras the tankers sink*
> *While sadly Roosevelt counts the score—*
> *Some 50,000 tons—by Mohr.*

Both Mohr and Frank got the figures wrong. In actuality Mohr had sunk seven ships (five tankers) for 42,048 tons and damaged three tankers for 26,167 tons. Even so, when the severe damage to *Acme* and *Esso Nashville* was figured in, Mohr's was the most productive patrol in American waters to then. Counting his overclaims and those on two prior patrols, Mohr exceeded 100,000 tons and qualified for a *Ritterkreuz.* It was awarded promptly, and Mohr got the usual buildup from Berlin propagandists.*

Flachsenberg in *U-71* remained in shallow Cape Hatteras waters. He reported that American air patrols had intensified and that the pilots "were now getting pretty slick with their bombs." Nonetheless, in the days following, Flachsenberg sank a loaded tanker and a freighter. In the wake of his attack on the tanker, the 8,000-ton *Dixie Arrow,* which blew up in a fireball, a Navy seaplane and the four-stack destroyer *Tarbell* raced to the scene. The plane dropped two close bombs; *Tarbell* carried out an aggressive depth-charge attack, but she broke it off when it was realized her charges were injuring Allied survivors in the water. *Tarbell* then rescued twenty-two of *Dixie Arrow*'s thirty-three-man crew.

Homebound on March 31, Flachsenberg encountered several ships north of Bermuda. He sank the 12,900-ton British tanker *San Gerardo.* The next day he sank a 5,800-ton British freighter with his last torpedoes. Flachsenberg's total of five ships (three tankers) for 39,000 tons was one of the two most productive patrols by the Type VIIs in American waters. He returned to France April 20 after

---

* At the time of the award, Mohr's confirmed score was fifteen ships for 64,832 tons, including the light cruiser *Dunedin,* sunk during the *Atlantis-Python* rescue.

fifty-six days at sea—another VII record in this campaign—logging that he had traveled 7,906 miles.

The last of the February boats to arrive in United States waters were two Type IXs: the new skipper Heinrich Schuch in the veteran IXB *U-105* and Georg Lassen in the new IXC *U-160*. Having apparently failed to follow a Great Circle route, Schuch ran critically low on fuel. Inbound, he sank two tankers, the 10,400-ton British *Narragansett* and the 7,600-ton Norwegian *Svenör,* north of Bermuda, then proceeded to Cape Hatteras. His fuel shortage drastically restricted his action and he sank no other ships.

Lassen in *U-160,* who had been first watch officer on Schuhart's *U-28* when the latter sank the carrier *Courageous,* had had a devastating setback during Baltic workup: an internal fire had killed seven of his crew and seriously wounded one other. Notwithstanding this reverse, and an undertrained crew, Lassen sank five ships and damaged a tanker. One of the ships was the 8,300-ton American cargo-passenger vessel *City of New York,* with 124 persons on board. The four-stacker *Roper* rescued sixty-nine survivors, including a woman who had given birth to a baby in a lifeboat. Another victim was the 14,647-ton British cargo-passenger vessel *Ulysses,* the second largest vessel after the *Amerikaland* to be sunk in American waters. En route from Australia to Halifax—thence to Britain—*Ulysses* had a crew of 195 men and carried ninety-five passengers, including sixty-one women and children, and a cargo of 11,000 tons of pig iron, rubber, wool, and other goods. All 290 crew and passengers got away safely in ten lifeboats and were soon rescued by the destroyer-transport *Manley.*

Although the Allies might have found it difficult to credit, the foray of the February group was not altogether satisfactory in German eyes, owing mainly to the disappointing returns from the Type IXs. Nine Type IXs had sailed, but two had aborted, one had been lost, and one (*U-105*) had arrived with insufficient fuel for a fully effective patrol. As a consequence, the nine Type IXs that embarked for the Americas had sunk, in total, only twenty-eight ships (thirteen tankers) for 176,630 tons, half accounted for by two skippers, Mohr in *U-124* and Bauer in *U-126.* This was a disappointing decline to an average of 3.1 confirmed ships sunk per Type IX per patrol.

In contrast, the returns from the VIIs were very good. Nine VIIs had sailed. As related, Krech in *U-558* had returned to France after his successful attack on Outbound North 67, Borcherdt in *U-587* had been held in Canadian waters, and Kröning in *U-656* had been sunk inbound to the Americas. Thus only six of the nine VIIs intended for United States waters actually got there, but the six sank twenty-two ships, including the destroyer *Jacob Jones.* When added to the sinkings of Krech and Borcherdt, sinkings by the VIIs per boat were slightly greater than those of the IXs: twenty-nine ships (ten tankers) for 167,864 tons, an average of 3.2 confirmed ships sunk per boat per patrol.

Despite the disappointing returns of the IXs, in aggregate the eighteen boats of the February group struck another heavy blow at Allied shipping: fifty-seven confirmed ships (twenty-three tankers) sunk for 344,494 tons. In return, the Allies had sunk three U-boats with the loss of all hands: *U-503, U-587,* and *U-656.*

HEATED EXCHANGES

The slaughter off Cape Hatteras by Mohr in *U-124* and the other February boats infuriated London. Where were the American destroyers which had been released from the North Atlantic run to form coastal convoys? Could not coastal convoys be initiated with the British ASW trawlers that had just arrived? Why not transfer some American destroyers from the Pacific to the Atlantic?

Most British officials apparently refused to understand the American problem: the density of the ship traffic, the immensely long coastline, the shortage of proper escorts owing to other urgent tasks. The British obtuseness and ignorance are perfectly reflected in a private diary entry of Under Secretary of State for Foreign Affairs, Alexander Cadogan, of March 16, in which he quite wrongly assumes that the ten British corvettes and twenty-four British ASW trawlers had already arrived in the United States: "Not much news, except of fearful sinkings—nearly all on American coast. Americans *do* certainly seem to be terrifyingly inefficient. And we have lent them about forty naval vessels!"*

Needlessly drawing attention to the "immense" tanker losses,† on March 12 Churchill cabled President Roosevelt's troubleshooter, Harry Hopkins, demanding "drastic action" to expand the convoy network. Unless it were done—and done quickly—Churchill insisted, the British would be compelled to halt tanker sailings and to take other drastic steps which would reduce vital British imports, already well below absolute minimum requirements.

Roosevelt replied on March 16 that under the new King escort plan for the North Atlantic run, "we had hoped that ten United States destroyers would . . . be made available for work on the Atlantic seaboard," but that "this has not worked out completely," in part because:

• The British had not yet provided a full quota of MOEF escorts and owing to that, "it has been necessary to reinforce eastbound British midocean escorts" with American vessels.

• The Canadians likewise had not yet provided a full quota of escorts for WLEF and owing to "the weakness of the Canadian western local escorts" American vessels had to stay with westbound convoys about 300 extra miles "westward of the agreed limit," WESTOMP.

• The unforeseen decision to deploy Task Force 39 (renamed 99) to Scapa Flow to reinforce the British Home Fleet was to cause a further drain of American destroyers.

• The British ASW trawlers "have only recently arrived or are approaching" and those that had arrived were undergoing "essential voyage repairs."‡

---

* No British corvettes arrived in March; only fourteen British trawlers were ready for duty on April 1.

† To March 1, 1942, all the U-boats assigned to the campaign in the Americas had sunk forty-five tankers and damaged thirteen. Eighteen of the forty-five were sunk in the waters of the Eastern Sea Frontier, eleven in the Caribbean, and sixteen elsewhere. (See Appendix 17.)

‡ Moreover, on February 26, Andrews reported to King that the trawlers were "not satisfactory escorts."

Roosevelt expressed the hope that Churchill could have a talk with First Sea Lord Dudley Pound "to see if we can't get the complete revision of the transatlantic escort working so that the ten destroyers can get on to the patrol along our Atlantic seaboard. . . ." He went on to say that "I feel sure we are going to get on top of this but it requires some help from you during the next few weeks."

In the meantime, for the "next few weeks" Roosevelt had two suggestions for Churchill which would "more effectively deal with the submarine":

• Open out the cycle of transatlantic convoys to sailings every "eight days"* until July 1, at which time "our mounting production of small escort vessels [SCs, PCs] and planes will come into full play."

• Direct Western Approaches personally to order British merchant vessels operating in the western Atlantic "to conform to routes prescribed by the [U.S.] Navy" and to douse running lights at night.

The opening out of the cargo-convoy cycle on the North Atlantic run would, of course, further reduce vital British imports. However, Roosevelt thought that preferable to the "unwise" Admiralty alternative proposal to reduce the number of escorts per North Atlantic cargo convoy. In any case, Roosevelt hastened to add, with the American merchant-shipbuilding program going so well, he was "sure" that any decline in vital British imports caused by opening out the convoy cycle could be made up "in the second half of the year."

Perhaps regretting the asperity of his March 16 communication, on March 18 Roosevelt again wrote Churchill to say, in part, that he expected by May 1 to get "a pretty good coastal patrol working from Newfoundland to Florida and through the West Indies." To do so, Roosevelt went on, he had "begged, borrowed and stolen every vessel of every description over eighty feet long. . . ." Roosevelt then took a gratuitous and wholly unjustified swipe at admirals King and Stark and others, which has been exploited by King's critics:

> My Navy has been definitely slack in preparing for this submarine war off our coast. As I need not tell you, most Naval officers have declined in the past to think in terms of any vessel of less than two thousand tons. You learned that lesson two years ago. We still have to learn it.

What Roosevelt intended to convey was that "his" Navy insisted that anything less than a fleet destroyer was inadequate to serve as a convoy escort. Of course, this was not true. As related, the Navy's General Board in 1939, on which King served, recommended the construction of a 1,200-ton destroyer escort (or British frigate) for convoy escort, and in early 1941, the Bureau of Ships had produced plans for such a vessel. In spite of repeated recommendations from Stark and Navy secretaries Edison and Knox, Roosevelt had at first disapproved this vessel, then relegated it to tenth priority while granting the inadequate little SCs and PCs highest priority. The General Board's recommendation in 1939 that the Navy acquire

---

*   Naval authorities were considering seven days, not eight.

2,200-ton *Treasury*-class Coast Guard cutters was merely an emergency measure, which the Navy itself had disapproved.*

Doubtless smarting from Roosevelt's swipe at the Navy and what could be viewed as groveling to the British, Admiral King jumped into this high-level exchange with both feet. Over Roosevelt's signature, he sent Churchill a testy and taunting cable on March 19, which Churchill thought showed "a touch of strain":

> Your interest in steps to be taken to combat the Atlantic submarine menace . . . impels me to request your particular consideration of heavy attacks on submarine bases and building and repair yards thus checking submarine activities at their source and where submarines perforce congregate.

In response, Churchill replied the next day, March 20:

> The highest importance is attached by us to bombing U-boat construction yards and bases and they will play a leading part in our spring bombing offensive. All is in readiness for this, including a vastly improved method of finding our way to the target. . . . We have been only held back by weather, which is the worst experienced for bombing purposes in fifteen years. . . . No chance will be lost. We are also studying the attack by long range aircraft upon U-boats coming from Bordeaux to the Caribbean. It is a question of competing claims.

In a communication to Roosevelt on March 29, Churchill expanded on British bombing plans. The RAF was now "emphasizing" attacks on "U-boat nests" in order to "cope with future U-boat hatchings." Two hundred and fifty RAF bombers had struck Lübeck the previous night, with "best ever" results. Coastal Command was gearing up to mount "a day and night patrol" over the Bay of Biscay to harass and delay and kill U-boats outbound from and inbound to the bases in France, thereby reducing pressure on the American seaboard. For that purpose Churchill favored an Admiralty request that four (and later six) squadrons of twin-engine Wellington and Whitley bombers be transferred from Bomber Command to Coastal Command. In recompense, Churchill pleaded for an increase in the buildup of American bomber forces in the British Isles, "even a hundred American heavy bombers" to augment Bomber Command.

In most accounts of Drumbeat and the continuing U-boat campaign in American waters, the impression is given that King would not—or could not—initiate coastal convoying until about May 15. This is not the case. On March 20, King ordered† that several coastal-convoy routes be initiated "at once" even though "escort for a time will be meager." These were:

---

* Earlier, Roosevelt wrote Churchill that "I have always held destroyers should not be used [for] coast patrol as they are all-purpose ships." Few in the Navy quarreled with that view, but King and most senior officers argued that coastal convoys required, at minimum, destroyer escorts (or frigates), which had the necessary seaworthiness, range, endurance, and firepower.

† King to Ingersoll, information to NSHQ, Ottawa, March 20 at 1305 and 1310 hours.

• A three-legged ocean network from Trinidad to a MOMP near Bermuda, thence to Halifax. The ships were to sail every fourteen days. A few American destroyers and Canadian corvettes were to serve as escorts.

• An inshore-coastal network from Boston to Halifax and vice versa.* A few American destroyers and Canadian corvettes were to serve as escorts. When this had been established, ships of Outbound North convoys were no longer to disperse offshore but were to continue in convoy to Halifax, thence in the new coastal convoys to Boston, New York, and southward.

When he received these orders, Ingersoll must have blinked. The following day, March 21, he tactfully reminded King of the many tasks to which his existing overworked destroyers had already been assigned. These still included: escort of cargo convoys on the North Atlantic run; escort of AT and NA troopship and AS high-priority cargo convoys; escort of monthly convoys from New Orleans to the Caribbean and Charleston to Bermuda. In addition, there were a number of "special tasks" right at hand or just ahead in April:

• Escort of the repaired British fleet carrier *Furious* and new "jeep" carriers *Archer* and *Avenger* (in transit) from American ports to EASTOMP.

• Escort of combined troop convoys AT 14 and NA 7, April 7 to April 18. This was comprised of seven troopships guarded by Task Force 37: the cruiser *Philadelphia* and ten American destroyers.

• Escort of Pacific-bound convoy BT 202, from East Coast ports to Panama, April 10 to April 17. This was comprised of seventeen troopships guarded by Task Force 38: the battleship *Texas,* cruiser *Brooklyn,* and eleven American destroyers.

• Escort of Task Force 36, *Ranger* on an aircraft-ferry mission to Ghana, for which five American destroyers were required.

• Deployment for an indefinite period at Argentia on April 23 of a special "heavy strike force" to counter a possible sortie of *Tirpitz,* et al., into the Atlantic. This force was to consist of one new battleship (*North Carolina,* later *South Dakota*), one fleet carrier (*Ranger,* later *Wasp*), two heavy cruisers, one light cruiser, and four or five American destroyers.†

• Escort of combined troop convoys AT 15 and NA 8, April 30 to May 12. This was comprised of thirteen troopships guarded by Task Force 38: the battleship *New York,* cruiser *Brooklyn,* and fourteen American destroyers.

To meet all these and other commitments, Ingersoll urged:

• That the layover in Londonderry of American destroyers assigned to AT and the returning TA convoys, then working on a five- to six-week cycle, be shortened.

• That the escorts to be released for other tasks by opening out the North Atlantic convoy cycle to seven days be American ships.

---

* Halifax-Boston convoys were designated XB; Boston-Halifax convoys, BX.

† Including Task Force 39 (99), comprised of the new battleship *Washington,* carrier *Wasp,* cruisers *Wichita* and *Tuscaloosa,* and six destroyers temporarily at Scapa Flow, the U.S. Navy earmarked altogether about twenty warships specifically to counter a sortie of *Tirpitz* et al.: two carriers, two new battleships, four heavy cruisers, a light cruiser, and about ten destroyers.

- That the British and Canadians provide their "agreed quota" of vessels for each of the five American MOEF groups.

At about this same time, King and Andrews also initiated an informal system of coastal convoying between Florida and Norfolk and between Norfolk and New York–Boston. Under this makeshift system, known as the "Bucket Brigade," ships zigzagged north and south in lanes very close along the coast only in daylight on prescribed legs. At night they put into ports or man-made anchorages, protected by antisubmarine nets and mines. Wherever necessary—and possible—Andrews provided local escort from his slowly growing forces, which on April 1 consisted of the following:

20	SCs, PCs, etc. (93' to 173')
60	Coast Guard cutters (75' to 165')
14	British trawlers (170')
82	Navy aircraft (14 Catalinas)*
4	blimps
89 to 100	Army aircraft

As the Bucket Brigade evolved, a northbound ship hugging the coast might travel in four daylight legs as follows:

Key West to Jacksonville, thence
Jacksonville to Charleston, thence
Charleston to Cape Fear or Cape Lookout, thence
Cape Fear or Cape Lookout to Norfolk.

Andrews deployed the bulk of his ASW forces in the dangerous Cape Hatteras area on the leg between Cape Lookout and Norfolk. Northbound ships usually gathered at Cape Lookout. From there, they sailed in informal convoys in daytime around Cape Hatteras, usually escorted by four small warships as well as aircraft. One (slow) warship led the convoy; three (fast) escorts patrolled to seaward and to the rear of the formation. Navy aircraft, such as scout planes, patrolled over the formation.

At Norfolk—or more precisely, Hampton Roads—northbound ships could choose to proceed via the safe "inland" Chesapeake Bay to Baltimore and other ports. Remaining on this inland route, those ships could go farther north yet via the nineteen-mile Chesapeake and Delaware Canal† to Delaware Bay, thence to Wilmington and Philadelphia and Camden. Alternatively, a northbound ship might take the shallow-water "outside" lanes close to shore from Norfolk to Delaware Bay and/or to New Jersey ports and New York. From New York, northbound ships

---

* Plus other Atlantic Fleet Catalinas, based at Norfolk, temporarily on loan. The 82 Navy aircraft included 15 of 70 Vought OS2U Kingfisher scout seaplanes that were diverted from delivery to the British and were manned by Coast Guard aircrews.

† The canal could accommodate ships drawing up to 25 feet and up to 500 feet in length. Most loaded northbound tankers drew too much water to use the canal, but all southbound tankers (in ballast and drawing less water) of 500 feet in length or less were required to go that way.

might cruise the "inland" route via Long Island Sound, Block Island Sound, and Rhode Island Sound to Buzzard's Bay, thence through the eight-mile Cape Cod Canal to Cape Cod Bay and Boston, Portland (Maine), and other points north.

While the American Navy was putting into place these measures to protect merchant shipping, Admiral King continued to insist that highest priority be given to the protection of troopship convoys. By April, the sailings of AT convoys from the States and NA convoys from Canada (often merged) had been regularized. However, King was still concerned over what he viewed as the inadequate protection provided AT and NA convoys by the Royal Navy from EASTOMP to the British Isles. In response to King's complaints about inadequacy, on April 4 the Admiralty suggested that the American Navy assume full responsibility for the escort of the AT and NA troopship convoys all the way across the Atlantic. On April 9, King agreed to this suggestion.* As a result, fewer American destroyers became available for coastal-convoy duty on the Eastern Seaboard than originally foreseen, further delaying the initiation of that network.

Throughout the convoy controversy in February and March, Admiral King vigorously sought to rectify the absurd policy whereby the Army Air Forces retained primary responsibility for providing land-based air patrols against U-boats. On March 26, King won a partial victory. In a dense, legalistic document, signed by Secretary of the Navy Frank Knox and Secretary of War Henry Stimson, the latter agreed to transfer temporarily operational control of the 1st Bomber Command, now commanded by Westside T. Larson, to Admiral Andrews of the Eastern Sea Frontier.† By April 1, Andrews directly controlled and coordinated 170 fixed-wing aircraft (eighty-two Navy, eighty-eight Army), based at eighteen East Coast fields, plus four blimps and a small but growing—and dedicated—volunteer Civil Air Patrol, flying unarmed spotter aircraft out of two airfields in New Jersey and Delaware.

The agreement did not, however, foreclose the Army's role in ASW. To the contrary, the Army Air Forces specifically and explicitly retained long-term overall responsibility for carrying out land-based air attacks on U-boats. Despite the British experience—the poor kill-rates of Coastal Command aircraft in hunter-killer roles—the airmen were convinced that the best way to succeed in that mission was by *offensive* air patrols. Accordingly, at Langley Field, Virginia, the airmen activated a Sea Search Attack Group, reinforced by an R&D outfit, the Search Attack Development Unit. Commanded by William C. Dolan and equipped with Douglas B-18 Bolo bombers fitted with hand-built centimetric-wavelength radar sets and other ASW devices (floating flares, sonobuoys, etc.), the Sea Search Attack Group commenced experimental offensive ASW patrols on the East Coast, independent of and overlapping the patrols of the 1st Bomber Command.

---

* Public Records Office (PRO), Kew, "Control of Shipping in West Atlantic During U-boat Campaign. January-June 1942." Document ADM 205/21, pp. 1–10.

† The same agreement gave Admiral Hoover of the Caribbean Sea Frontier operational control of the Army Air Forces's fifty-plane Antilles Air Task Force.

GLOBAL NAVAL CHALLENGES

Most accounts of the German U-boat campaign in American waters in the spring of 1942 describe that operation in isolation. This depiction leads invariably to an absurdly incomplete and even distorted picture of American counteractions.

When the U-boat campaign off the United States East Coast reached its peak in April 1942, the following major naval operations were in progress or afoot worldwide.

The Japanese in the Indian Ocean.

In the first week of April, powerful Japanese naval and amphibious forces sailed from Malaysia into the Bay of Bengal. A covering force of five carriers, four battleships, and supporting vessels challenged the newly arrived but weak British Eastern Fleet (three carriers, five old battleships) based at Ceylon. The Japanese sank the old, small carrier *Hermes,* the cruisers *Cornwall* and *Dorsetshire,* the destroyers *Tenedos* and *Vampire,* the corvette *Hollyhock,* and two fleet tankers, and forced the British Eastern Fleet to retreat 3,000 miles west to Kilindini, Kenya (near Mombasa) on the east coast of Africa. During this foray, various Japanese warships and aircraft sank in addition twenty-three British-controlled merchant ships for about 112,000 tons and damaged others. Japanese submarines sank another half dozen merchant ships. Japanese amphibious forces landed at Rangoon, Burma, and on the Andaman Islands, posing a threat to India.

Churchill sent a series of urgent appeals to Roosevelt for assistance in this theater. Among other proposals he suggested that the carrier *Ranger* and battleship *North Carolina* of the Atlantic Fleet might join the British Eastern Fleet or, alternately, that *North Carolina* join the battleship *Washington* on anti-*Tirpitz* duty in Scapa Flow, thereby releasing the battleship *Duke of York* to join the Eastern Fleet. Admiral King rejected these proposals, suggesting instead that American heavy bombers be rushed to the Indian Ocean area.

Churchill also proposed that the American Pacific Fleet consider making a threatening gesture of some kind which might draw these Japanese naval forces back from the Bay of Bengal into the Pacific. Unknown to Churchill, at that time the American carriers *Hornet* and *Enterprise,* plus support forces, were boldly approaching the Japanese home islands to launch the "Doolittle raid," which, by uncanny coincidence, was exactly the kind of naval action Churchill sought to relieve pressures in the Indian Ocean. Although the Japanese naval forces withdrew from the Bay of Bengal a few days before the Doolittle raid was carried out April 18, the raid, too often casually dismissed as a stunt, was to profoundly influence the course of the Pacific war in the two months ahead.

The British in Madagascar.

At about this same time, British naval and amphibious forces massed in Cape Town and Durban, South Africa, to invade Vichy Madagascar, thereby denying the Japanese the possibility of a collaborative occupation, à la Indochina. As related, it was this operation (Ironclad) that drew important forces from the British Force H at Gibraltar, forcing a dilution of the Home Fleet at Scapa Flow to reinforce Force H at Gibraltar and the transfer of American Task Force 39 (99) (carrier *Wasp*, battleship *Washington*, etc.) to Scapa Flow to reinforce the Home Fleet on anti-*Tirpitz* duty.

The lead ships of the British invasion force sailed from Durban to Madagascar on April 25. Elements of the British Eastern Fleet sailed from Kilindini in support. The British hoped that Vichy French forces on Madagascar would not oppose the landing, which took place on May 5, but the French mounted a spirited defense for several days before they were overwhelmed.

To speed up augmentation of Allied airpower in the Indian Ocean area, Churchill urgently requested that Roosevelt ferry fighter planes to West Africa. When Roosevelt acceded to this request, King assigned the task to the carrier *Ranger*. Loaded with sixty-eight Curtiss P-40 Warhawk aircraft, *Ranger* sailed from Rhode Island on April 22, escorted by the cruiser *Augusta* and five destroyers.* The aircraft flew off *Ranger* on May 10, landing at Accra, Ghana (on the Gold Coast). From there, they flew on to India. *Ranger* and escorts returned to the United States.

It is customary for historians—especially British historians—to portray Admiral King at this time as fixated on Pacific operations to the neglect of the U-boat war in the Atlantic. However, these same historians invariably fail to note the British fixation on Indian Ocean operations at this time and the consequent drain of Allied naval assets from the Atlantic.

Malta.

The *Luftwaffe* in the Mediterranean Basin supporting Rommel's *Afrika Korps* launched a series of brutal bombing raids on the British island of Malta at this time, viewed by many Allied war planners as a prelude to an airborne invasion. Believing Malta to be a strategic and psychological asset of incalculable value, Churchill insisted that heroic measures be made to deny it to the Germans, assuring the Maltese that "the Navy will never abandon Malta."

The defense of Malta thus became another heavy drain on Allied naval assets in the Atlantic. The *Luftwaffe* and Italian air and naval forces inflicted severe damage on British convoys attempting to fight through to the island. To reinforce the thin British air forces on Malta, Churchill asked Roosevelt on March 31 if the carrier *Wasp*, en route to Scapa Flow in Task Force 39 (99), could fly off Spitfires for Malta. Although Admiral King was not keen to risk a new fleet carrier in this graveyard of warships,† in due course he relented and *Wasp* took on forty-seven Spitfires in the Firth of Clyde and sailed to the Mediterranean on April 14.

Escorted by the battle cruiser *Renown*, cruisers *Charybdis* and *Cairo*, and a flock of destroyers, including the American *Lang* and *Madison*, *Wasp* slipped through the Gibraltar Strait unseen and launched the Spitfires on April 20. In the

---

*   *Ellyson, Emmons, Hambleton, Macomb, Rodman.*

†   Over Roosevelt's signature, King pointedly asked Churchill why the Admiralty could not use the British carrier *Furious*, departing the United States on April 3, for this purpose.

first week of May, *Wasp*, with American destroyers *Lang* and *Sterett*, made a second trip from the Clyde to the Mediterranean in company with the British carrier *Eagle* and escorts. On May 9, *Wasp* flew off another forty-seven Spitfires to Malta.

The Murmansk Run.

In response to a direct order from Hitler, *Tirpitz*, the "pocket" battleship *Admiral Scheer*, the heavy cruiser *Hipper*, supporting destroyers, and the *Luftwaffe* threatened Allied PQ and QP convoys en route from Iceland to Murmansk and return. *Tirpitz* made one sortie in March—her first combat mission—but it was a complete failure. However, owing to her presence and that of *Admiral Scheer* and *Hipper*, the British were compelled to sail heavy ships of the Home Fleet to provide cover for the Murmansk convoys.

As the periods of daylight in the Arctic became longer in April, the risk of German attacks on Murmansk convoys increased. This seasonal factor led Admiral Pound to suggest to the War Cabinet that the Murmansk convoys might not be worth the risk. But in view of the impending German spring offensive against the Red Army, Roosevelt insisted it was not only impolitic but also dangerous to suspend the Murmansk convoys. He not only refused to consider a suspension but also demanded that the Admiralty increase the size and frequency of Murmansk convoys to clear out 107 merchant ships loading or loaded for Murmansk, which were backing up in Iceland and elsewhere.

Reflecting the views of the Admiralty, Churchill parried. The Murmansk run had cost the Royal Navy the cruisers *Trinidad*, damaged, and *Edinburgh*, sunk.* Besides that, the battleship *King George V* of the Home Fleet had been damaged in a horrendous collision with the destroyer *Punjabi*, which broke in half and sank. The battleship had to have extensive repairs before she could again provide cover for a Murmansk convoy.† The best Churchill could promise was the sailing of three PQ convoys of twenty-five to thirty-five ships every two months. Based on this lukewarm projection, Roosevelt and King rightly concluded that to keep promises made to Stalin, ships of the American task force temporarily at Scapa Flow would have to be assigned to escort Murmansk convoys. Not without reason, King began to suspect that the goal of the Admiralty was to pull American naval assets ever deeper into the multifarious British naval schemes, however ill-advised those schemes (such as Madagascar and Malta) seemed to the Americans.

Sledgehammer.

Uppermost on the American list of naval operations—or possible operations—in early April was Sledgehammer, the emergency invasion of Occupied France,

---

   * En route to the British Isles with convoy QP 11, *Edinburgh* went down with close to six tons of gold in 465 ingots of twenty-six pounds each. Most of the gold (payment to the Americans for war supplies) was recovered by British divers in 1981 and split with the Soviets.

   † The commander of Task Force 99, Robert C. Giffen, wrote King that British destroyers "used bad technique" in heavy fog at 18 knots and that his battleship, *Washington*, had a "close call" in this mishap, nearly colliding with the British destroyer *Martin*. Incidents of this kind reinforced King's conviction that American and British naval forces should not be "mixed."

should the Red Army collapse under the weight of the German spring offensive. On April 8, Army Chief of Staff George Marshall and Harry Hopkins arrived by air in London to obtain British approval for Sledgehammer in 1942 and to discuss the larger alternative, Roundup, in 1943.

Owing to the impending Doolittle air raid on Japan and to cryptographic intelligence that indicated another big—perhaps even decisive—naval battle brewing in the Pacific, King remained in Washington. However, it bears repeating that King fully approved of Sledgehammer (and Roundup) in part as a means of evicting German U-boats from French bases and in part to curb what he viewed as the British peripheral operations in the Mediterranean Basin and Indian Ocean, and to keep the Admiralty focused to the greatest extent possible on operations the Americans believed to be most likely to lead to an early defeat of Germany.

The British opposed both Sledgehammer and Roundup but deliberately and deceptively gave Marshall and Hopkins the impression that they approved Roundup so that the Americans would not abandon the campaign against Germany and go all-out after Japan. In fact, what the British sought was a revival of the canceled Gymnast, the invasion of Vichy French Northwest Africa, to trap Rommel's *Afrika Korps* between Gymnast forces and the British Eighth Army.

While Marshall and Hopkins were in London, Churchill and First Sea Lord Pound repeatedly drew attention to the heavy Allied shipping losses to U-boats on the United States Eastern Seaboard, and continued to insist that the Americans initiate convoying in that area. Doubtless Marshall agreed with that line—it was the American Army line as well—and perhaps he influenced Hopkins, who on April 14 cabled President Roosevelt to urge that coastal convoying be initiated. In part, Hopkins said:

> Shipping losses in western North Atlantic during period January 12th to April 12th of United Nations tonnage are 1,200,000 gross tons. During the past week we have lost in the same area 150,000 tons of which 106,000 tons were tankers. It seems to me that the ships we are losing are in the main far more important than the cargoes. We are going to need all of these ships desperately in the next few months.
>
> British are agreeable to reducing stocks [i.e., imports] to make sure that ships are not sunk and it seems to me that we should be able to do the same thing. In other words, unless the cargoes are absolutely essential the ships should not be permitted to sail until our new [convoy] scheme comes into operation next month. I doubt very much that anything short of convoy is going to do this job and risking further ships without reasonably sure protection is the wrong policy. I should feel somewhat differently about this if every cargo was absolutely essential to the war effort during the next few weeks, but if the British can give up cargoes temporarily, I am sure we can. . . .
>
> I cannot impress upon you too strongly the concern which all here [in London] have in regard to this matter. This is only natural because this island is so dependent on imports and they realize full well the significance of these sinkings to the future of the war. I need not dwell on the importance of every possible ship to us during the coming months. I had planned to postpone a discussion of this until I could see you, but the matter seems to me to be of such urgency that I decided to take it [up] by cable.

Doubtless this provocative cable dismayed King, who was at that very time doing everything in his power to meet the other multifarious British naval requests and to initiate convoying in the Eastern Sea Frontier. Moreover, as he cabled Hopkins (for delivery to Churchill) on April 16, King had already decided to suspend tanker sailings:

> Conference of representatives of agencies concerned have reached decision to lay up tankers operating on Atlantic coast for a period, depending upon availability of more protection. Opportunity will be taken to arm ships as rapidly as possible. Action on dry cargo ships under consideration. . . .

From that day, April 16, to April 29, a period of two weeks, all tankers under American control in the Western Hemisphere remained in ports. On April 18, the British likewise suspended tanker sailings in the Gulf of Mexico and Caribbean, but after a change in routing plans resumed sailings six days later, April 23. Under the new routing plans, British-controlled tankers were to sail to Trinidad, thence due east across the Atlantic to Freetown, and from that place to the British Isles in Sierra Leone convoys.

In a separate message to Roosevelt, Churchill expressed delight and satisfaction over his meetings with Marshall, Hopkins, and others, and regret that Admiral King had not come over as well. "We have established the most intimate contacts with the United States Army and Air Force [sic] but as Harry will tell you, we are not nearly so closely linked up on the Naval side. Yet all depends on this being successfully handled in unison. I am therefore sending the First Sea Lord [Pound] back with General Marshall and Harry in order that he may discuss with you and Admiral King the whole position and make long-term plans. . . ."

The American party and First Sea Lord Pound departed the British Isles by air on April 18. Pound remained in Washington for a week, April 20 to April 26, conferring with Roosevelt, King, and others on the many naval matters on the agenda.

Pound and others in the British naval party found Admiral King and his senior aides preoccupied with the Pacific. British historians and writers depict this preoccupation as some sort of chicanery or disloyalty or, in view of the U-boat threat in the Atlantic, scandalous stupidity.

In fact, King had every justification for being preoccupied with the Pacific that week. Allied codebreakers, who had partially broken back into the latest variation of the Japanese naval code, JN 25, had picked up clues which indicated that the Japanese might be planning an amphibious attack in "late April" on Port Moresby, New Guinea, and/or the islands of New Caledonia and Fiji. The capture of Port Moresby would provide the Japanese an ideal staging base for an invasion of Australia, which had been designated as the main Allied stronghold in the southwest Pacific. The capture of New Caledonia and/or Fiji would put the Japanese in position to cut the Allied line of communication to Australia, which, under terms of the Arcadia conference, the Americans were pledged to keep open. Beyond that, on April 18, American naval codebreakers had found hints in the partially decrypted radio traffic that the Japanese might be planning another big assault on Hawaii or perhaps even California(!).

The major American naval forces in the Pacific at that time were ill-disposed to thwart Japanese moves in the southwest Pacific. The carriers *Hornet* and *Enterprise* and supporting vessels were only just beginning the return voyage from the April 18 Doolittle air raid on Japan. There was no way they could replenish in time to reinforce Allied naval forces in the southwest Pacific by "late April." If the Japanese were to be thwarted in that area, the carriers *Lexington* and *Yorktown* and supporting forces, including land-based aircraft, would have to do the job.*

There was little debate in Washington over whether or not an attempt should be made to thwart the Japanese in the southwest Pacific. Another major setback in the Pacific, such as the loss of Port Moresby or New Caledonia or Fiji or even Australia, combined with the fall of Bataan and Corregidor† would be devastating. It might topple the Churchill government and even lead to an impeachment of President Roosevelt. At the least, such a setback would again besmirch the Navy's reputation.

The situation was so fraught with danger that King insisted on a face-to-face meeting with Pacific Fleet commander Chester Nimitz at a mutually convenient site. Thus, on April 24, when First Sea Lord Pound and his party were settling in for sweeping and prolonged strategy talks, King and his senior advisers abruptly left Washington to meet with Nimitz and his senior advisers, April 25 to April 27, in San Francisco. There the principals and their staffs hammered out a plan for a precious few American capital ships to battle Japanese capital ships on the high seas for the first time in the war.

Left high and dry in Washington, it is little wonder that First Sea Lord Pound and his delegates felt snubbed by Admiral King and wrongly came away convinced that King was much too narrowly preoccupied with the Pacific. Nonetheless, Pound's conferences with Roosevelt and King's subordinates usefully cleared the air on a number of important naval issues, including the impending start-up of convoys in all waters of North America which were accessible to U-boats.

The convoy routes in American waters, to be initiated in the first two weeks of May, if possible, were:

• *Key West–Norfolk–Key West.*

This route was to be protected by forty-three warships organized into five escort groups and aircraft. The ships were to include nine American four-stack destroyers, to be permanently assigned to the Eastern Sea Frontier in April‡; five of the ten British corvettes that finally arrived in April§; twelve of the fourteen British

---

* The other carrier in the Pacific, *Saratoga,* torpedoed by a Japanese submarine on January 11, 1942, and repaired on the West Coast, was still in workup.

† Forces on Bataan surrendered April 9 and those on Corregidor, May 6.

‡ *Broome, Decatur, Dickerson, Du Pont, Herbert, MacLeish, McCormick, Roper,* and the miscellaneous auxiliary *Semmes.*

§ *Fury, Impulse, Ready, Restless,* and *Temptress.*

ASW trawlers that completed voyage repairs and came into service in April; two big gunboats (ex-yachts *Plymouth* and *St. Augustine*); nine new 173-foot PCs; four 165-foot Coast Guard cutters (*Argo, Calypso, Dione, Icarus*) and two World War I Eagle subchasers. Eight other vessels (four 165-foot Coast Guard cutters; two British trawlers; two Eagles) were to serve as a reserve force. Fifty-seven small craft along the route were to provide ASW patrols and rescue.

- *Halifax–Boston–Halifax.*

This route was to be protected by the Canadian WLEF, composed of four-stack destroyers and corvettes.

- *A direct Halifax–Caribbean–Halifax route.*

To be utilized exclusively for Canadian oil imports and protected by one Canadian group (four corvettes) withdrawn from the MOEF, this route was to commence operations May 17. Initially the convoys were to be comprised of six tankers sailing every fourteen days, but by June 8 the sailings had increased to one every ten days, directly from Aruba, bypassing Trinidad.

- *Trinidad–Aruba–Trinidad.*

This British tanker "shuttle" route, which commenced operations on May 18, was to be protected by one British escort group withdrawn from the MOEF. After reaching Trinidad, loaded British tankers were to sail independently from Trinidad east to Freetown, thence to the British Isles in Sierra Leone convoys, thereby bypassing the hazardous American Eastern Seaboard. Tankers returning to Trinidad to join the reverse convoys to Aruba were to sail in Outbound South convoys.

- *Others.*

Several other routes in the Gulf of Mexico and the Caribbean were to be established as escorts became available.

HARDEGEN'S SECOND PATROL

As in January, Dönitz sent twenty-six U-boats to the Americas in March: six Type IXs and twenty Type VIIs. It was a relatively experienced group. Two-thirds of the boats had made patrols to the Americas earlier in the year. Six boats (three IXs; three VIIs) were commanded by *Ritterkreuz* holders: Klaus Scholtz in *U-108;* Heinrich Bleichrodt in *U-109;* Reinhard Hardegen in *U-123;* Adalbert Schnee in *U-201,* returning from a long overhaul in Germany to make his first patrol to the Americas; Rolf Mützelburg in *U-203;* and Erich Topp in *U-552.*

The March boats were to be supported by two U-tankers. One, the *U-A*, commanded by Hans Cohausz and temporarily released from standby supply duty for the "defense of Norway," was to refuel three Type VIIs, then return to Germany.

The other, *U-459,* the first U-tanker designed as such,* was to sail directly from Germany to the western Atlantic, refuel fifteen boats, then return to France. The *U-A* was a temporary and less than satisfactory expedient, but *U-459,* commanded by "an old gentleman," Georg von Wilamowitz-Möllendorf, age forty-eight, a veteran of the Imperial Navy, was a timely physical and psychological backup for the U-boat campaign in American waters.

All twenty-six March boats were assigned to patrol United States and Caribbean waters, none to Canadian waters. Three short-range Type IXBs and all twenty Type VIIs were to operate from New York to points southward. Three long-range Type IXCs were to carry out a second strike in the Caribbean. At the insistence of Admiral Raeder and the OKM, one of the Caribbean boats, Ernst Kals in *U-130,* was to shell the refineries and tank farms on Curaçao.

Wearing his newly won *Ritterkreuz,* Reinhard Hardegen in *U-123* was the first of the six Type IXs to sail in March. He departed with sixteen torpedoes (fourteen internal, two in topside canisters) and another propagandist, Rudolf Meisinger. After weathering a four-day gale, in the three days following, March 22 to March 24, Hardegen came upon two big, loaded tankers in mid-Atlantic, sailing alone. He sank the first, the 7,000-ton American *Muskogee,* with a single air torpedo. The second, the 8,100-ton British *Empire Steel,* was more difficult. One torpedo misfired in the tube, a second was fired in error. The next two torpedoes hit solidly, and the ship, loaded with gasoline, exploded in flames. Hardegen manned his deck gun to polish off the flaming hulk, but the heat was so intense that he broke off the action after eight rounds. There were no survivors from either ship.

Approaching Hatteras on the afternoon of March 26, the bridge reported smoke puffs on the horizon. Upon closing this target, Hardegen was disappointed to find what appeared to be an ancient 3,000-ton tramp steamer sailing alone. Nonetheless, he tracked her and after dark fired one torpedo from close range. It hit with a solid thwack, but the detonation appeared to be weak. Hardegen again manned his deck gun to polish off his victim.

Unsuspected by Hardegen, his quarry was the *Atik* (ex-*Carolyn*), one of two old (1912) American "Q" ships engaged in a highly classified ASW patrol 250 miles off the East Coast. She was four days out from Portsmouth, New Hampshire, on her shakedown cruise. Her sister ship *Asterion* (ex-*Evelyn*), also on her shakedown cruise, was close by, but not in direct communication. As part of her ruse,

---

* The Type XIV U-tankers, affectionately known as *Milchkuhs* (Milk Cows), were indeed bovine: 220 feet in length, 31 feet shorter than a Type IX, with bulbous external saddle fuel tanks, which gave the boat a surface displacement of nearly 1,700 tons. The Milk Cow had a fuel-oil capacity of about 650 tons—about 200 tons for its own use and 450 tons for its "customers." Its crew of 53 included a doctor. It was lightly armed for defense: no torpedo tubes; antiaircraft guns on the bridge. Apart from its slow surface speed and clumsiness while submerged, the chief drawback of the Type XIV was that it had no room below to carry torpedoes for its "customers"; four were carried in deck canisters.

when the torpedo struck, *Atik* lowered away two lifeboats, as if the crew were abandoning ship.

When Hardegen closed to fire his deck gun, *Atik* suddenly came alive in a most startling and formidable fashion. Her bulwarks fell away, revealing a gun aimed directly at *U-123*. The gun blazed, but fortunately for Hardegen and his men, the shells fell wide. Then came a hail of machine-gun fire and a barrage of depth charges. Astonished and chagrined—feeling like a schoolboy, he said later—Hardegen ran off at flank speed, frantically evading the fire. Some shells and bullets hit the bridge, fatally wounding a midshipman, Rudolf Holzer.

After collecting his wits and ascertaining that the *U-123* was not seriously damaged, Hardegen dived and reapproached *Atik* for a second torpedo attack. Carefully aiming at *Atik*'s engine room from very close range, Hardegen fired one electric, which hit and detonated satisfactorily. *Atik* went down slowly but surely. Hearing her final distress calls, her sister ship *Asterion* and other warships and aircraft searched for *Atik* survivors, but none were found.

By this time—the end of March—ASW forces in the Eastern Sea Frontier had increased substantially over those of January, when Hardegen pioneered Drumbeat. Andrews had almost 100 small surface ships of all kinds and about 100 Navy and Coast Guard planes and four blimps under his direct command, plus about 100 Army Air Forces planes and Atlantic Fleet Catalinas at his beck and call. In addition, King and Ingersoll were to make available twenty-three different destroyers in April,* which were to log a total of 140 ASW patrol days.

Hardegen reached the Cape Hatteras area on March 30 in bright moonlight, having downloaded his two topside torpedoes. Although the area was teeming with air and surface patrols, over the next forty-eight hours he attacked three ships, firing one torpedo at each. All missed or malfunctioned. He mounted a second attack on the third target, the 7,100-ton American tanker *Liebre,* with his gun and set her on fire. A further attack was thwarted by a patrol boat, which drove Hardegen under in shallow water (100 feet), but failed to stalk *U-123* with persistence and vigor. Hardegen claimed *Liebre* sank, but she was sailing in ballast and was only damaged. She returned to service four months later.

In view of the heavy ASW measures, Hardegen rightly concluded that the shallow waters of Hatteras were no place for a big, clumsy Type IX. Accordingly, he cruised south to the Georgia coast, off St. Simon's Island. On the night of April 7–8, he found and attacked two big, loaded, northbound American tankers, the 9,300-ton *Oklahoma* and the 8,000-ton *Esso Baton Rouge,* firing four of his remaining seven torpedoes on the surface in water merely 43 feet deep. Both ships exploded in fireballs and Hardegen claimed they sank, but both were later salvaged and returned to service. Since no counter-attack developed, Hardegen lurked off Georgia for another day, and in the early hours of April 9 he sank the 3,400-ton American refrigerator ship *Esparta* with a single torpedo.

---

* *Bristol, Broome, Buchanan, Cole, Dallas, Dickerson, Du Pont, Edison, Ellis, Emmons, Greer, Hambleton, Hamilton, Herbert, Lea, MacLeish, Macomb, Nicholson, Noa, Roper, Semmes, Swanson, Woolsey.*

Hardegen then proceeded south to the Florida coast, where he noted the "intense" phosphorescence in the waters, which left a dangerous luminous trail astern of the boat. While cruising close off St. Augustine in forty-six feet of water, late on the evening of April 10, Hardegen found the loaded 8,100-ton American tanker *Gulfamerica,* northbound on her maiden voyage with an Armed Guard crew manning a 4"/50 caliber gun. Although the ship was more than a mile away and moving fast, Hardegen fired one of his last two torpedoes at her. It hit and *Gulfamerica* blew up in a fireball within view of those ashore. She later drifted out to sea and sank, the only tanker to be destroyed beyond repair by the Type IX boats in the Eastern Sea Frontier in April.

Almost immediately, ASW forces converged on *U-123.* These included Army and Navy aircraft from nearby bases in Jacksonville, the four-stack destroyer *Dahlgren,* and *Atik*'s sister "Q" ship *Asterion,* still on her shakedown cruise. One of the aircraft dropped a brilliant flare directly over *U-123.* Hardegen crash-dived—and hit bottom at sixty-six feet—but *Dahlgren* saw the flare, got *U-123* on sonar, and dropped six close depth charges. The boat "takes a terrible beating," Hardegen logged. "The crew members fly about, and practically everything breaks down. Machinery hisses or roars everywhere."

Trapped in shoal water and severely damaged, Hardegen was certain that *U-123* was done for and ordered the crew to prepare to abandon ship. Since the boat could be salvaged easily in such shallow water, he distributed the Enigma rotors (to be disposed of randomly) among the officers and made certain that Enigma documents (printed on water-soluble paper) were out in the open. Others set the scuttling charges and handed out escape apparatus. But *Dahlgren* did not persist in her attack. Nor did she bring up *Asterion* or other ASW forces. Her skipper concluded wrongly that he had not actually made a U-boat contact and steamed off.

Scarcely believing his good luck, Hardegen later surfaced and limped to deep water. He lay on the bottom to rest the crew and make repairs. By late evening of April 12, the boat and crew were again ready for action. They found it off Cape Canaveral: the 2,600-ton American freighter *Leslie,* northbound from Havana with a load of sugar, and the 4,600-ton British freighter *Korsholm,* loaded with phosphate. He sank *Leslie* with his last torpedo and *Korsholm* with his deck gun, and then set a course for France.

Hardegen happily calculated his sinking report for Dönitz. By his reckoning, on this patrol he had sunk ten ships (seven tankers) for 75,837 tons, substantially exceeding the tonnage sunk on his first patrol to America and—as he logged exuberantly—making *U-123* the second U-boat (after the retired *U-48*) "to pass 300,000 tons." However, both these claims were inflated (as of course were those of *U-48*). On this patrol to then, Hardegen had sunk nine confirmed ships for about 54,300 tons and damaged the tanker *Liebre.* However, two of his tanker sinkings, *Oklahoma* and *Esso Baton Rouge* for 24,300 tons, were salvaged, reducing the net bag to seven ships of about 30,000 tons. Under command of Moehle and Hardegen, *U-123* had sunk not "300,000" tons but about 172,000 tons.

Imitating Johann Mohr in *U-124,* Hardegen reported his sinkings in verse, rendered thus by historian Michael Gannon:

For seven tankers the hour has passed,
The Q-ship hull went down by the meter,
Two freighters, too, were sunk at last,
And all of them by the same Drumbeater!

Hardegen's report electrified the U-boat staff in Paris and the OKM in Berlin. But, as on his first patrol to American waters, he was not yet done. Homebound on April 16, he sank the 4,834-ton American freighter *Alcoa Guide* by gun. Reporting this victory, Hardegen raised his total claims to eleven ships for 79,649 tons, a record-breaking patrol (without torpedo resupply), which drew unstinting praise from Admiral Raeder and Dönitz. Since his total claims had reached or exceeded 200,000 tons on April 23, a message from Hitler arrived, adding Oak Leaves to Hardegen's *Ritterkreuz.* *

When *U-123* reached Lorient, Admiral Raeder and Dönitz were standing on the pier to congratulate Hardegen and all hands for "a superbly executed operation." Hardegen later flew to *Wolfsschanze* to receive his Oak Leaves—and a vegetarian dinner—from Hitler. Still later, he took *U-123* to Germany for battle-damage repairs and an extended overhaul, which kept her in Germany until December. Having acquired fame rivaling that of the past U-boat heroes Prien and Kretschmer, Hardegen left *U-123* for a job in the Training Command and did not return to combat.

The other five Type IXs of the March group turned in mixed performances, due in part to the shutdown of Allied tanker shipping in the last two weeks of April.

Richard Zapp in *U-66,* who reached Trinidad in mid-April with twenty-four torpedoes (ten in topside canisters), carried out a notable patrol. He sank six confirmed ships for about 44,000 tons—more *confirmed* tonnage sunk than Hardegen and Mohr—and damaged a 12,500-ton British tanker. Four of the six sinkings were tankers.† While still at sea on this sixty-eight-day patrol, Zapp was awarded a *Ritterkreuz*‡ and upon his return to France he left the boat to command Combat Flotilla 3.

Ernst Kals in *U-130* attacked, per orders, the refinery and tank farms on the island of Curaçao in the early hours of April 19. But after firing only twelve rounds, which did no discernible damage, counterfire from the shore batteries on Curaçao drove him off. Frustrated by the temporary shutdown of tanker shipping in the Caribbean and by some torpedo failures, Kals sank only two confirmed ships, a 5,400-ton freighter and, while homebound, the 7,700-ton American tanker

---

* Hardegen's confirmed score on the duck *U-147* and *U-123* was twenty-three ships for 132,081 tons, not counting the two unidentified ships usually credited on his first patrol to America but counting the two sunk but salvaged tankers, *Oklahoma* and *Esso Baton Rouge.*

† Panamanians *Heinrich von Riedemann,* 11,000 tons, and *H. G. Seidel,* 10,400 tons; Norwegian *Sandar,* 7,600 tons; and the Dutch *Amsterdam,* 7,300 tons.

‡ At the time of the award, April 23, Zapp's confirmed score was thirteen ships for 80,014 tons. By the end of the patrol, it stood at fifteen ships for 103,495 tons.

Esso Boston. His was a disappointing, exceedingly long and frustrating patrol of seventy-five days.

After refueling from the U-tanker *U-459* on April 20—her first "customer"—the *Ritterkreuz* holder Klaus Scholtz in the IXB *U-108* patrolled Bermuda, the Florida Straits, and the Windward Passage. While inbound and outbound, and in his assigned areas, Scholtz sank five confirmed ships for about 31,000 tons. His victims included two tankers: the 9,900-ton American *Mobiloil* and the 8,100-ton Norwegian *Norland.*

Walther Kölle in *U-154,* patrolling near Puerto Rico, reported "no traffic" and "strong" aircraft ASW patrols. As a result, Dönitz shifted him northward to the promising waters of the Windward Passage, where he sank five ships for 28,700 tons and returned to France after sixty days. His victims included three tankers: two 5,000-ton Americans, *Comol Rico* and *Catahoula,* and the 8,000-ton British *Empire Amethyst.*

Ritterkreuz holder Heinrich Bleichrodt in *U-109,* patrolling Cape Hatteras and south to Florida waters, sank two freighters for 11,500 tons and a 555-ton Nicaraguan freighter, a disappointing patrol.

In aggregate, the six IXs that sailed to the Americas during March sank twenty-nine confirmed nonsalvaged ships (thirteen tankers) for 164,100 tons, with Zapp in *U-66* and Hardegen in *U-123* accounting for nearly half the total. These successes reversed the disquieting downward trend of the IX sinkings, raising the average returns per boat per patrol slightly above those of the December IXs: 4.8 ships for 27,351 tons. The refueling of the IXB *U-108* by *U-459* enabled Scholtz to extend his patrol to seventy-one days. However, by exercising stringent fuel discipline, Bleichrodt in the IXB *U-109* patrolled for a like number of days without replenishing, although certainly not without constant concern about running out of fuel.

A SPECTACULAR FORAY

The twenty Type VIIs that sailed to the Americas in March—the largest deployment of VIIs so far—patrolled the United States East Coast from Maine to Florida. All twenty had made prior combat patrols, twelve of the twenty (60 percent) to the Americas. Only one skipper, Wilhelm Schulze in *U-98,* replacing *Ritterkreuz* holder Robert Gysae, was new but his crew was skilled and earlier had made a patrol to Canadian waters. As related, three of the VIIs were commanded by *Ritterkreuz* holders, two of whom had made prior patrols to Canada: Erich Topp in *U-552* and Rolf Mützelburg in *U-203.* Another *Ritterkreuz* holder, Adalbert Schnee in *U-201,* sailed from a long overhaul in Germany. The resupply boats *U-A* and *U-459* were to refuel eight of the twenty VIIs, six of them outbound to America, two of them homebound to France.

Eight of these VIIs sailed in the first two weeks of March for Cape Hatteras. Three refueled in mid-ocean from the *U-A:* Horst Uphoff in *U-84;* Hans-Heinz Linder in *U-202,* who had used much fuel in a failed attempt to find and escort the inbound blockade runner *Germania;* and *Ritterkreuz* holder Rolf Mützelburg in

U-203, who had also used much fuel in a fruitless chase of a convoy, Outbound North 77, found and reported by Otto Ites, who was homebound from the Americas to France in *U-94.* The other five boats sailed at one-engine speed, following the Great Circle route.

All eight VIIs inbound to Cape Hatteras found and attacked important targets, which were sailing in Canadian or American offshore waters.

Paul-Karl Loeser in *U-373* sank two freighters (one British, one Greek) for 9,900 tons.

Helmut Möhlmann in *U-571* sank the 11,000-ton British refrigerator ship *Hertford,* loaded with meat and dairy products.

Hans-Heinz Linder in *U-202* and Horst Uphoff in *U-84* each sank 5,200-ton freighters.

Hans Oestermann in *U-754* sank the 8,600-ton tanker *British Prudence.*

Ritterkreuz holder Erich Topp in *U-552* hit and burned out the 6,300-ton Dutch tanker *Ocana,* which was later sunk by Allied forces.

Heinz Hirsacker in *U-572* (still under a cloud for his balk at the Gibraltar Strait in January) conducted a lackluster small-gun attack on the 6,200-ton British tanker *Ensis,* which escaped with slight damage.

Rolf Mützelburg in *U-203* encountered an unidentified convoy while passing through Canadian waters on March 25, but his attack was thwarted by "well-aimed" depth charges from escorts.

Seven of these eight boats reached the Cape Hatteras area in late March and early April, overlapping Hardegen in *U-123.* Notwithstanding the intensified American ASW measures and a bright, full moon, three of the boats found good hunting. In a spectacular week's work, April 3 to April 10, Erich Topp in *U-552* sank six more ships (four tankers)* for about 40,000 tons, the best performance by any Type VII skipper in American waters. In the period from March 31 to April 6, Hans Oestermann in *U-754* also sank six more ships for 23,000 tons: a freighter, two tankers (American *Tiger,* 6,000 tons; Norwegian *Kollskegg,* 9,900 tons), and a tug and two of her three barges. Although his hydrophones were out of commission, "making shallow water operations difficult," Helmut Möhlmann in *U-571* sank the 10,000-ton Norwegian tanker *Koll* and two freighters. Mützelburg in *U-203* claimed sinking three tankers and a freighter for 36,000 tons, but two of the tankers escaped, only damaged, reducing his confirmed score to one freighter and the 8,100-ton British tanker *San Delfino.* Hirsacker in *U-572* sank two freighters for 9,500 tons and damaged a tanker. Arriving last, Uphoff in *U-84* sank one 3,000-ton freighter. Neither Linder in *U-202* nor Loeser in *U-373* sank a ship off Cape Hatteras.

The total bag for these first eight boats was a slaughter: twenty-six ships (ten tankers) for nearly 150,000 tons, counting Topp's tanker, *Ocana.*

It had been expected that the refueling from supply boats was to increase substantially the patrol days of the VIIs in American waters. In reality, that was not the

---

* Three Americans: *B. T. Benson,* 8,000 tons; *Atlas,* 7,100 tons; *Tamaulipas,* 7,000 tons; and the British *Splendor,* 7,100 tons.

case. The three boats that refueled from *U-A* outbound to America were at sea an average of fifty-five days. Two others homebound to France, Möhlmann's *U-571* and Hirsacker's *U-572,* refueled from the tanker *U-459,* extending their patrols to an average sixty days. Hence, the average time at sea for the five boats of the group that refueled, inbound or outbound, was fifty-seven days. The average time at sea for the three boats that did not refuel was fifty days, making the average gain for the boats of this group that refueled merely seven days.

Nor did refueling increase the ship sinkings by this group. The five of eight boats that refueled, inbound or outbound, sank ten ships—an average of two victims per boat. The three boats that did not refuel sank sixteen ships—an average of 5.3 victims per boat. Sinkings still depended upon the skill and aggressiveness of the skippers and crews, weather, opportunity, luck, and availability of torpedoes. Some skippers of this group (Topp and Mützelburg, for example) ran out of torpedoes. Replenishment and resupply could not be fully exploited until a means of providing the boats with torpedo reloads could be arranged.*

Erich Topp's claims for this and prior patrols exceeded 200,000 tons, and he therefore qualified for Oak Leaves to his *Ritterkreuz.* Hitler announced the award by radio on April 11, while Topp was homebound.† Later, the Führer presented the medal to Topp at *Wolfsschanze,* at the same time he awarded Hardegen his Oak Leaves. Although Topp had his choice of virtually any assignment, he preferred to remain in combat with *U-552.* He thus became the leading "ace" at the front.

The other twelve VIIs sailed, day by day, during the second half of March. This group included *Ritterkreuz* holder Adalbert Schnee in *U-201,* on his first patrol to the Americas, and several promising skippers, among them Peter Cremer in *U-333,* exonerated for the accidental sinking of the blockade runner *Spreewald;* Siegfried von Forstner in *U-402;* and Heinrich Zimmermann in *U-136.* Cremer had made a prior patrol to Canada. Like Schnee, von Forstner and Zimmermann were on their first patrols to American waters.

Outbound, three of the VIIs of this group of twelve refueled from *U-459:* the veteran *U-98,* commanded by the new skipper, Wilhelm Schulze, age thirty-two; Peter Cremer in *U-333;* and Werner Schulte in *U-582,* who had used much fuel attempting without success to meet and escort the blockade runner *Rio Grande* into France.

---

* To fulfill this need, in the fall of 1941 Dönitz and the OKM had ordered the conversion of four Type VIICs (*U-1059* to *U-1062*) to torpedo-supply boats, designated Type VIIF. Similar in length (254 feet) and shape to the Type VIID minelayer, the VIIF had a torpedo-storage compartment inserted between the control room and engine room that had space for twenty-four torpedoes, in addition to the boat's own internal load. Pending the arrival of the VIIFs (in 1943), two captured Dutch boats (commissioned *U-D3* and *U-D5*) were converted to torpedo-supply boats. However, the conversions were begun too late for the campaign in the Americas.

† Berlin propagandists credited Topp with sinking 31 ships for 208,000 tons, including a destroyer and an "escort." At the time of the award, his confirmed score on the duck *U-57* and *U-552* was 28 ships for about 163,000 tons, including the American destroyer *Reuben James* and the 227-ton British ASW trawler *Commander Horton.*

While Schulte in *U-582* was en route to his refueling rendezvous with *U-459* on April 16, the American submarine *R-1*, on ASW patrol, shot four torpedoes at her. Credited with a U-boat kill, the first by an American submarine, the *R-1*'s skipper, James D. Grant, was awarded the Navy Cross. But *U-582* had escaped the encounter undamaged and replenished as planned.

Refuellings were difficult. None of the VIIs had ever practiced the procedure. The crews had not even been properly briefed, the technical adviser on *U-459* wrote. To carry out a refueling, which took one and a half to five hours, the sea had to be relatively calm and the seamanship excellent. The U-tanker went ahead at 3 to 4 knots on electric motors and floated a towing hawser and oil hose back to the boat to be refueled. Usually everything went wrong, the adviser went on:

> In the case of 8 [of 15] boats, mishaps occurred causing greater or lesser delays, through hose leakages caused by poor maneuvering, by repeated passing-over of hoses, by inept handling on deck (chafing and tearing because of the lack of chafing mats . . .) or through hooks on the diving planes. While the hoses were being passed over, one boat fouled the hoses with its forward hydroplanes, tore the hawser and both hoses away and, when this was cleared, let go the whole equipment. . . . [However] the crew [of *U-459*] behaved magnificently in these operations, which were often most difficult, pushing themselves to the limit of physical endeavor. For example, the provisioning of 4 boats in a period exceeding 16 hours in one day; on another day working 8 to 10 hours with lifelines attached, with seas and breakers constantly washing over them.

The *U-459* doled out its fuel and food sparingly on a rigid schedule drawn up by U-boat headquarters. Most VIIs received about 30 cubic meters of fuel (about 30 tons) and a week to ten days' supply of food, including fresh bread baked in a special facility on board *U-459,* which could produce eight loaves per hour.

Schulte in *U-582* had spent three weeks on the abortive rendezvous with *Rio Grande,* and was very low on fuel when he reached *U-459.* He was allotted 55 cubic meters (about double the usual quota), but even this was not enough to safely carry out an aggressive patrol in United States waters. Dönitz therefore diverted him to the island of Bermuda, about 600 miles southeast of New York. There Schulte encountered heavy weather, scant shipping, and "strong" ASW measures. Hounded by aircraft and patrol boats, he shot a triple bow salvo at a "fast passenger ship" but missed. He returned to France with no sinkings to credit—an exceedingly frustrating voyage—and, of course, a refueling to little purpose.

The other eleven VIIs of this group closed on the United States coast from New York to Florida. Several went to the Cape Hatteras area to replace the VIIs that had sailed earlier in the month, arriving just ahead of or during the onset of the new moon, April 14. Among these new arrivals was Eberhard Greger in *U-85,* embarked on his fourth war patrol. Southbound off New Jersey on the night of April 10, he sank the 4,900-ton Swedish freighter *Christina Knudsen* with two torpedoes. In the evening of April 13, concealed by the darkness of the new moon, Greger lay in wait in shallow water off Bodie Island, north of Cape Hatteras.

That same day, the four-stack *Roper* sailed from Norfolk to Cape Hatteras on ASW patrol. Commanded by Hamilton W. Howe, *Roper* was armed with five 3"/50 caliber guns, six torpedo tubes, and seventy-five 300-pound depth charges, which could be rolled from her stern tracks or shot from Y and K guns. She had recently been equipped with a British-built Type 286 meter-wavelength radar.

Just after midnight, April 14, while southbound off Bodie Island, *Roper* got a radar contact at 2,700 yards. Inasmuch as these waters were teeming with smaller Navy and Coast Guard patrol boats, fishing trawlers, tugboats, and salvage craft, initially the contact caused no great excitement. *Roper* routinely turned to run down the bearing. While doing so, sonar picked up the noise of fast screws. That report caused excitement. The contact was moving too fast to be the usual patrol or fishing boat.

The radar contact was *U-85*. Trapped by a destroyer in water only 100 feet deep, Greger had two choices: to dive and possibly be pounded to pieces by depth charges, or to run at full speed on the surface to deep water. Perhaps hoping he could shake the destroyer in the darkness, Greger chose to run. But he did not know the destroyer had radar. Despite numerous indications to the contrary, Dönitz and his submariners still believed that radar was too big, bulky, and sensitive for installation on small ships.

Chasing at 20 knots, *Roper* gradually overhauled *U-85*. In a last but futile effort to rid himself of the pursuer, Greger fired his stern tube at 700 yards. The torpedo missed, running close down *Roper*'s port side. When *Roper* closed to 300 yards, and appeared to be coming in to ram, Greger gave the order to scuttle and abandon ship. To facilitate this final, desperate act and get out of *Roper*'s way, Greger abruptly turned hard to starboard.

When *U-85* turned, *Roper* switched on her 24" searchlight and opened fire at point-blank range. Seeing the Germans running on deck to abandon ship, the excited Americans, they said later, concluded they had come up to man *U-85*'s deck gun to shoot it out.* In reaction, the Americans raked the U-boat's deck with machine-gun fire, cutting down the Germans who were trying to jump over the side.

With her sea cocks open, *U-85* quickly flooded and went down by the stern in ninety-eight feet of water. As she did so, the Americans, as they said later, saw "about forty" Germans in the water or on the deck of *U-85,* many crying out in German, "please save us." *Roper* thus had the opportunity to capture U-boat prisoners for intelligence and propaganda purposes, and there was a good possibility that in such shallow water Navy divers could enter *U-85* and recover a four-rotor Enigma, the new short-signal book, and other secret materials. But the excited Americans apparently did not give these matters any consideration. *Roper* swung around, charged through the German survivors in the water, and dropped eleven depth charges set for fifty feet, directly on top of *U-85*. Those Germans who were

---

* A doubtful conclusion, probably influenced by Allied propaganda depicting German submariners as fanatical, mad-dog Nazi killers. No rational U-boat skipper would engage in a surface gun battle with a destroyer, which had the advantage in firepower, gun armor, and speed to ram, as well as the ability to call in aircraft and other ASW forces.

not cut to pieces by *Roper*'s propellers were killed by the depth charges. Not one man of the crew survived. The force of the explosions shattered *U-85* externally and internally and rolled her nearly flat in the sand on her starboard side.

Fearing other U-boats might be near—the fate of sister ship *Jacob Jones* perhaps fresh in mind—*Roper* radioed an account of her attack and hauled away. After daylight, a Catalina, a blimp, and five other aircraft appeared. The Catalina spotted the German bodies and bits of wreckage and dropped a depth charge for good measure. Other aircraft drew *Roper* back to the scene with smoke flares. *Roper*, too, dropped another depth charge, then lowered away two boats to collect the bodies and debris. In the midst of this gruesome operation, *Roper*'s sonar reported a U-boat contact—perhaps the hulk of *U-85*—and she broke off to fire four more depth charges to no purpose.

Roper's boats found thirty-one German bodies. Two of them were badly mangled. After searching the clothing of these two, *Roper*'s men callously left them in the sea. The other twenty-nine bodies were brought on board, stacked on deck, and covered with a tarpaulin. *Roper* dropped two more depth charges on *U-85*, then headed triumphantly for Norfolk. Outside the harbor, a Navy tug, *Scioto*, took off the twenty-nine bodies. After they had been searched again (two useful diaries were found), photographed, and fingerprinted, they were buried in marked graves with full military honors in the National Cemetery, Hampton, Virginia, in coffins provided by the Veteran's Administration.

The Navy immediately initiated efforts to salvage *U-85* and/or to recover her intelligence materials. Numerous small craft, including two of the twenty-two* newly arrived British ASW trawlers, *Bedfordshire* and *Saint Loman*, swarmed over *U-85*. Early in these operations, hard-hat divers found an armed but unexploded depth charge lying on the bottom alongside *U-85*. A Navy demolition team exploded the charge, no doubt further damaging the boat. Between April 15 and May 4, Navy divers made about one hundred descents to the wreck. Inasmuch as she was lying nearly flat on her starboard side, none of the divers could get inside the boat to look for her Enigma or other intelligence material. Because of the depth-charge damage to her air lines and tankage, she could not be raised—or even righted—by salvage air.

When it was finally decided that *U-85* could be raised only by "extensive" use of pontoons, the salvage effort was abandoned. The divers stripped *U-85* of much topside gear—the 20mm bridge gun, the IZO torpedo aimer, and the gyro-compass repeater—and "dismantled" the 88mm deck gun, which still had the tampion in the muzzle. But they could not pry open the storage canister and remove the topside torpedo. They reported no evidence of gun hits by *Roper* and concluded that *U-85* was "probably scuttled."†

* Several days earlier, April 11, one of the British ASW trawlers, *St. Cathan*, was accidentally rammed and sunk by a merchant ship off North Carolina, leaving twenty-two.

† Sport divers, including Homer H. Hickam, Jr., author of *Torpedo Junction*, routinely dive on *U-85*, but none has entered her. Hickam disputes the Navy's report in one instance: He found evidence that one of *Roper*'s 3"/50 caliber guns registered a hit on *U-85*, "just abaft the conning tower." Hickham also found a G7a air torpedo—probably from the topside canister—resting on the deck of *U-85*.

Several other VIIs were near Cape Hatteras when *Roper* sank *U-85*. The Bucket Brigade convoy scheme between Key West and New York was in operation by that time, and aircraft patrolled Hatteras from dawn to dusk. There was no authorized ship traffic at night. Daytime U-boat operations close to shore where the Bucket Brigade convoys sailed were hazardous.

Two of the VIIs mounted attacks. Near sunset on April 17, *Ritterkreuz* holder Adalbert Schnee in *U-201* found and damaged a 7,500-ton tanker, but—awkwardly—it turned out to be the Argentine neutral *Victoria*. American naval vessels rescued the crew and eventually confiscated the ship from the pro-German Argentines, setting in train a diplomatic uproar that ultimately drew an apology to the Argentines from Berlin. In the late afternoon of April 18, Heinrich Zimmermann in *U-136* boldly attacked an eight-ship Bucket Brigade convoy, which was escorted by the hard-working 165-foot Coast Guard cutter *Dione,* two British ASW trawlers, a small patrol boat, and several aircraft. Zimmermann fired two torpedoes at the loaded 9,000-ton American tanker *Axtell J. Byles.* One torpedo broached, alerting the escort; the other hit, blowing a hole in the tanker, but she survived and reached Norfolk. *Dione* responded with a salvo of eight depth charges and called in eight aircraft, which dropped more depth charges and bombs. However, Zimmermann escaped undamaged.

It was not yet apparent to Dönitz, but the fact was that, however thin and green, by mid-April American ASW air and surface forces, augmented by the British ASW trawlers, had rendered the Cape Hatteras area and most of the continental shelf unproductive for U-boat operations. Several VIIs of the March group dutifully remained near Cape Hatteras, but after April 20, as Dönitz noted later, none had any success and most reported "strong" ASW patrols.

Granted freedom of action, most of the VIIs hauled away from Hatteras. These and others patrolled several hundred miles offshore, beyond range of most air patrols, loosely covering the sea lanes from Massachusetts to Georgia. An exception was Siegfried von Forstner in *U-402,* who had sunk one freighter inbound but none in a frustrating week off Hatteras. At the end of his patrol, he hugged the shallow North Carolina coast south to Cape Lookout and Cape Fear. There he sank the 5,300-ton Russian tanker *Ashkabad* and a big (215-foot, 1,000-ton) but ancient (1906) yacht, *Cythera,* which the Navy, for the second time in two world wars, had acquired and converted to an escort/rescue vessel.

The Russian *Ashkabad* sank in shallow water and her skipper believed she could be salvaged. But according to the writer Gary Gentile, the destroyer *Semmes,* uninformed of this prospect, came along and destroyed her with gunfire to clear the ship channel. Hit by two torpedoes, the ancient yacht *Cythera* blew to pieces. As she sank, her armed depth charges exploded, killing all but two enlisted men of the seventy-one-man crew. Von Forstner fished both from the water and took them back to Germany—the first American naval POWs to be captured by the Germans. Both were to survive the war.

The hunting offshore was spotty:

• Ludwig Forster in *U-654,* who had sunk a 7,000-ton British freighter inbound, sank two other freighters 300 miles east of Hatteras for a total of 17,755 tons, making him the high scorer of this group.

- Second place went to *Ritterkreuz* holder Adalbert Schnee in *U-201,* who sank three freighters for 15,300 tons by torpedo and gun, 400 miles east of Georgia. Schnee also had a fleeting glimpse of the liner *Aquitania,* inbound from Australia to New York to take American troops to Northern Ireland, but she was going very fast and there was no way he could overtake her.

- Karl-Ernst Schroeter in *U-752* got wartime and postwar credit for sinking three ships for 15,500 tons by torpedo and gun, but research by Gary Gentile has disallowed one, the 4,800-ton Norwegian freighter *Reinholt,* which was only damaged by gunfire.

- After his abortive attack on the Bucket Brigade convoy, Zimmermann in *U-136* went north to New Jersey and New York waters, where he sank two freighters for 12,400 tons, the second, the Dutch *Arundo,* merely fifteen miles east of the Ambrose lightship marking the channel into New York harbor. On his way home he attacked the 300-ton Canadian sailing ship *Mildred Pauline* by gun. He reported that he had "missed," but in fact, she went down.

- Günther Heydemann in *U-575* turned in a second disappointing patrol to the Americas, sinking only one ship for 6,900 tons while inbound.

Worse yet, two VIIs sank no ships at all: Walter Schug in *U-86* and Wilhelm Schulze, the new skipper of the veteran *U-98,* who had refueled from *U-459* inbound to America. Both skippers shot at freighters, but missed. Caught by a "destroyer" in fifty-nine feet of water off Florida, Schulze in *U-98* fired four torpedoes at his assailant, but missed. In retaliation, the (as yet unidentified) "destroyer" carried out a "heavy" depth-charge attack, Schulze reported, but it was not "persistent" and thus he was able to escape.

Having suffered a two-day engine breakdown and refueled from *U-459,* Peter Cremer in *U-333* also headed for Florida waters. On the afternoon of April 30, while 300 miles east of Jacksonville, he spotted the masts of the modern 11,000-ton, double-hull tanker *British Prestige,* zigzagging at 10 knots, loaded with high-octane aviation gasoline. Cremer tracked her until dark, then fired two bow torpedoes. When both missed, he submerged, reloaded the tubes, then surfaced to pursue, hampered by a very bright moon. Hauling around, he submerged for a periscope attack, closing to point-blank range, silhouetting the big ship against the moon. As he was on the point of firing, the zigzagging *British Prestige* unwittingly rammed *U-333.* The tanker lurched to starboard, the startled skipper reported, and the crew heard a loud "rumbling crushing noise." It was obvious the ship had hit a submerged object—U-boat? whale?—but she did not pause to investigate. Unknown to the captain or crew, her outer hull was ripped open from stem to stern.

The collision severely damaged *U-333.* Her stem was "twisted to port," jamming shut the two port bow torpedo tubes. The bridge structure was mangled; the attack periscope was bent to port at a crazy angle and could not be retracted. Had Cremer aborted the patrol, no one would have reproached him, but it was his second mistake in as many patrols—sinking *Spreewald* had been the first—and there was the possibility that he might lose his command. He therefore set his crew to work with welding torches and mallets to cut and hammer *U-333* back into operable condition. Remarkably, the men succeeded, and Cremer closed the Florida coast near Fort Pierce with his "half-wrecked" boat.

Cremer lay silently on the surface in bright moonlight on May 5, fifteen miles offshore in twenty-six feet of water. At about midnight, the 8,300-ton American tanker *Java Arrow,* a straggler from a Bucket Brigade convoy, came along southbound, in ballast. Cremer fired two torpedoes by eye. Both hit and the ship "burned furiously" and sank, or so Cremer believed. Actually, she was salvaged and returned to service. Four hours later, when the 1,300-ton Dutch freighter *Amazone* appeared, Cremer fired two more torpedoes. Both hit and *Amazone* went down. Two hours later—near dawn on May 6—yet another ship loomed up, the 7,100-ton American tanker *Halsey,* northbound with a load of naphtha and fuel oil. Cremer fired two bow and one stern torpedo at her by eye. The two bow shots hit and *Halsey* exploded in a fireball and sank.

American ASW forces responded vigorously to this last sinking. First on the scene was *PC-451,* a prewar Navy prototype, manned by the Coast Guard. The force of her depth charges slammed *U-333* into the sand at sixty-six feet, froze her hydroplanes, and caused other external and internal damage. Then came sister ship *PC-450* and the 125-foot Coast Guard cutter *Vigilant,* and two other smaller Coast Guard patrol boats. But Cremer managed to outwit these attackers, clawing along the sandy bottom toward deep water—197 feet—his thrashing propeller noises drowned out by the errant depth-charge explosions.

After fifteen hours of brutal punishment and nerve-stretching tension, Cremer got away, or so he thought. An aircraft had followed *U-333*'s leaking oil trail and had brought up the four-stack *Dallas,* en route from the Navy's sonar school in Key West to Charleston. But *Dallas* was not equal to the challenge. After dropping twenty-five 300-pound depth charges, she resumed her voyage, and by what the Germans deemed "a miracle," *U-333* escaped, battered but undaunted.

Cremer was not finished. Limping home in the dark and rainy early morning hours of May 10, 500 miles east of Florida, he ran across the 5,200-ton British freighter *Clan Skene* sailing alone. He fired his last two bow torpedoes. Both hit and the ship went down. Upon hearing the full and amazing story of Cremer's patrol, Dönitz awarded him a *Ritterkreuz.* Cremer's first patrol to America had ended with a court-martial, his second in a blaze of glory and publicity.*

Hans-Dieter Heinicke in *U-576,* making his second patrol to American waters, hit and sank a 5,100-ton bauxite freighter 400 miles east of Hatteras, then headed toward Cape Cod, Massachusetts. Passing northbound off New York, he shot at the Norwegian freighter *Tropic Star.* One torpedo hit but failed to explode, and the lucky *Tropic Star* sailed on. Off Cape Cod in the early hours of April 30, Heinicke found a formation of freighters, possibly a Boston-Halifax convoy. He fired his last torpedoes at four overlapping ships, hitting the 1,300-ton Norwegian *Taborfjell,* loaded with Cuban sugar. She sank. Three of her crew survived and were rescued

---

* At the time of the award, Cremer's claimed sinkings—not counting *Spreewald*—were seven ships for 56,800 tons. His confirmed sinkings were six ships for 27,641 tons. He wrote in his book *U-boat Commander* that the tonnage requirement for the award of the *Ritterkreuz* was 50,000, indicating a cut of 50,000 tons from the earlier criterion, but that assertion is not borne out elsewhere in the German records. Doubtless Cremer's astonishing courage, resourcefulness, and aggressiveness influenced the award.

by the British submarine *P-552,* one of the nine American submarines recently loaned to the Royal Navy.*

Later that day, April 30, Heinicke spotted the most impressive group of targets yet found in American waters. It was the American troop convoy AT 15, composed of seven transports, including *Aquitania,* bound from New York to Argentia, Iceland, and Northern Ireland. Traveling at 12 knots, it was escorted by the battleship *New York,* the light cruiser *Brooklyn,* the new British "jeep" carrier *Avenger* (in transit), and fourteen destroyers, as well as air patrols. It was to join another troop convoy, NA 8, composed of four troopships sailing from Halifax on May 3, which increased the total number of troopships to eleven, with 19,000 troops embarked.

Having no torpedoes, Heinicke could only grind his teeth in frustration. After the formation had passed within firing range, he surfaced to shadow and report, but one of his diesels broke down. Consulting his plotting board, Dönitz saw that there were four VIIs inbound to America within 600 to 1,000 miles of the convoy. Although he did not believe there was much hope of an interception, he felt obliged to try, in view of the valuable targets entailed. He directed the four boats to proceed at full speed and to form a patrol line, running due south from Cape Race, Newfoundland, and urged Heinicke in *U-576* to make every possible effort to regain contact.

After getting his diesel back on line, Heinicke did, in fact, regain contact, at about the time convoys AT 15 and NA 8 merged, on May 3. However, he reported "strong" air escort forced him off and down and thereafter he "lost" the convoy again. Acting on Heinicke's latest report, Dönitz shifted the four-boat patrol line thirty miles north—closer to Cape Race—directly into the shallow fog-shrouded waters of the Grand Banks. However, none of the five boats found the convoy, and Dönitz canceled the operation.

In all, the twenty VIIs that sailed to the Americas in March sank forty-six confirmed ships (twelve tankers) for about 242,000 tons, nearly a third of the total (thirteen ships for 71,000 tons) accounted for by two skippers, Erich Topp in *U-552* (five tankers) and Hans Oestermann in *U-754* (three tankers). It was a spectacular foray—the high point for the VIIs in American waters—but a close analysis by the U-boat staff revealed a disappointing trend. The average sinkings per patrol of the March group declined sharply from those of the VIIs of the February group: down from 3.2 ships for 18,651 tons to 2.3 ships for 12,097 tons. Moreover, contrary to many accounts—and the myths arising later—the first big refueling operation of VIIs had *not* resulted in increased sinkings. The eight VIIs of the March group that replenished sank an average of only 1.6 ships for 9,396 tons per patrol. Three refueled VIIs sank no ships: Schug in *U-86,* Schulze in *U-98,* and Schulte in *U-582.*

---

* In addition to the six *S*-class submarines, the U.S. Navy in early 1942 loaned the British three *R*-class boats for use in ASW training. The Canadian minesweeper *Georgian* accidentally rammed and sank *R-19,* renamed *P-514,* off Cape Race.

Owing to the increase in average sinkings by the Type IXs, in aggregate the twenty-six boats of the March group almost exactly duplicated the aggregate sinkings of the twenty-six boats of the January group: seventy-five confirmed ships (twenty-five tankers) sunk for 406,046 tons. This was another severe blow to Allied shipping. However, when it is taken into account in this comparison that one January boat aborted, that eight others were manned by green skippers and crews, that all the January VIIs patrolled in the more heavily defended Canadian waters, that the weather was far less favorable, and that eight of the March boats refueled, it was less of a blow than might have been expected.

The failure of the more experienced boats of the March group to significantly exceed the aggregate returns of a like number of January boats was a certain indication that the provisional convoying measures and ASW in the Eastern Sea Frontier were beginning to take effect. The loss of Greger's *U-85*, the near losses of Hardegen's *U-123* and of Cremer's *U-333,* and the vigorous counterattack incurred by Zimmermann in *U-136* during his assault on a Bucket Brigade convoy, were other indications. Since a steady improvement in ASW measures in the Eastern Sea Frontier was expected, Dönitz and his staff drew plans to shift the weight of the U-boat campaign to the less well-guarded shipping lanes in the Gulf of Mexico and the Caribbean.

PATROLS TO OTHER WATERS

Had Hitler not unwisely insisted that about fifty U-boats be assigned to defend against a supposed invasion of Norway and to support Rommel's operations in North Africa, the U-boat campaign of 1942 in American waters doubtless would have been much more devastating than it was. As Dönitz predicted, the U-boats diverted to those peripheral tasks achieved little. Several were lost. These operations, in brief:

Arctic.

In compliance with Hitler's direct order to send more U-boats to the Arctic, between January and the end of March eighteen new Type VIIs went directly there from Germany, raising that force to about twenty-five boats.* Those operating in the Arctic waters were commanded by a rear admiral, Hubert Schmundt, who was advised by Jürgen Oesten. These boats based in Kirkenes and Narvik and returned often to Trondheim for refits and battle-damage repairs. Schmundt, Oesten, and other staff officers established headquarters aboard ships, first on the E-boat tender *Tanga* in Kirkenes, then on the luxury yacht *Grille* (built for Hitler) in Narvik.

The Arctic boats had no luck whatsoever in the month of February. While they patrolled in the nearly twenty-four-hour darkness of the Arctic winter, convoys PQ 9, PQ 10, and PQ 11 (in all, about fifty merchant ships) arrived in Murmansk

---

* See Appendix 5.

without any harm from U-boats. The opposite-sailing QP convoys likewise escaped attack by German forces.

When *Tirpitz* sailed March 6 on her futile first mission against convoys PQ 12 (sixteen ships) and QP 8 (fifteen ships), four U-boats based at Kirkenes deployed off Murmansk to intercept PQ ships that might escape *Tirpitz.* Two other U-boats sailed from Narvik to directly support *Tirpitz.* One, Otto Köhler's new *U-377,* was mistakenly attacked by the *Luftwaffe,* which claimed an "enemy submarine" sinking. When it was realized that the "enemy" was probably Köhler in *U-377,* the OKM, fearing the boat lost, upbraided the *Luftwaffe,* but *U-377* was not seriously damaged.

Patrolling close off Murmansk, Burkhard Hackländer in *U-454,* who had intercepted PQ 8 in January, also intercepted PQ 12. He sent beacons to call in the other three boats near Murmansk, but only Max-Martin Teichert in the new *U-456* found him. Neither boat had success, and PQ 12 arrived without loss. In a biting critique to the OKM, Dönitz pointed out that the boats had been placed too close to Murmansk; they needed much more sea room to operate against a PQ convoy.

The next Murmansk convoy, PQ 13, and its westbound counterpart, QP 9, sailed on March 20 and 21, respectively. A massive Arctic storm scattered the twenty ships of PQ 13 over thousands of square miles of ocean. As the various ships straggled into the Murmansk area, the *Luftwaffe* sank two and three of the four U-boats sank one each: Friedrich-Karl Marks in *U-376,* Siegfried Strelow in *U-435,* and Max-Martin Teichert in *U-456.*

At this time, three Norway-based U-boats commanded by older but green skippers were lost. The British minesweeper *Sharpshooter,* which was escorting the westbound convoy QP 9, came out of a snowstorm on March 24 and rammed and sank the *U-655,* commanded by Adolph Dumrese, age thirty-two, who was on his first war patrol. *Sharpshooter,* which recovered "two lifebuoys and a canvas dinghy," reported: "Submarine turned upside down and sank stern first." There were no survivors. An escort of PQ 13, the British destroyer *Fury,* was credited with sinking *U-585,* commanded by Bernhard Lohse, age twenty-nine, on March 29, but it was discovered after the war that *U-585* did not attack PQ 13. Assigned to lay TBM mines (the Bantos field) off the Rybachi Peninsula, she may have been destroyed by one of her own mines. There were no survivors. En route to Norway, a new boat, *U-702,* commanded by Wolf-Rüdigen von Rabenau, age thirty-four, struck a mine in the North Sea and sank with all hands.

The next Arctic convoys, PQ 14 and QP 10, sailed on April 8 and 10, respectively. Enlarged to twenty-four freighters, PQ 14 unexpectedly ran into drift ice which caused damage to numerous ships and forced sixteen of the twenty-four freighters and two minesweeper escorts back to Iceland. Eight freighters, including the convoy commander's flagship, the 7,000-ton British *Empire Howard,* pressed on to Murmansk. As the stragglers were approaching the Kola Inlet, Heinz-Ehlert Clausen, age thirty-two, in the new boat *U-403,* hit and sank *Empire Howard* with two torpedoes. Friedrich-Karl Marks, age twenty-seven, in another new boat, *U-376,* fired three torpedoes at "a 10,000-ton cruiser," doubtless *Edinburgh,* and claimed hits for damage. But *Edinburgh* reached Murmansk unhurt, as did the other seven freighters. *Luftwaffe* planes and U-boats hit the opposite-sailing QP 10, composed of sixteen empty freighters. The *Luftwaffe* sank two ships and severely damaged a third, the 5,800-ton Russian *Kiev*. Siegfried Strelow in *U-435* sank the *Kiev* and a 6,000-ton Panamanian freighter, bringing total losses to QP 10 to four ships, and Strelow's total sinkings (from two convoys) to three ships for 18,252 tons, making him far and away the tonnage leader among the German skippers based in Norway.

In all, during February, March, and April 1942, the Arctic U-boat force sank merely five merchant ships for about 30,600 tons, plus the 250-ton British ASW trawler *Sulla*. In return, three U-boats were lost with all hands in the same period. Of course, no Allied invasion of Norway occurred.

Northwest Approaches.

Until the Norway-based U-boat force reached a permanent strength of about twenty-five boats, Dönitz continued to maintain eight or more U-boats from the Atlantic force on patrol in the Northwest Approaches. In early February these boats, designated group *Westwall*, comprised four boats earmarked for permanent duty in Norway and four new boats en route to France to join the Atlantic force. As noted earlier, these boats attacked several convoys on the North Atlantic run.

The *U-586*, commanded by Dietrich von der Esch, age twenty-seven, who was merely three weeks into his first patrol, discovered convoy Outbound North (Slow) 63 on February 6. In response to his report, three other *Westwall* boats—all new— converged on his beacons: Heinrich Zimmermann in *U-136*, Amelung von Varen-dorff in the Type VIID (minelayer) *U-213*, and Hans-Jürgen Zetzsche, age twenty-six, in *U-591*. But Zetzsche was too low on fuel to chase, and before he could get in an attack he was forced to break off and head for Norway. Von der Esch reported that he fired a full bow salvo at a "cruiser," but the four torpedoes were "duds." He reloaded his bow tubes and then fired four more torpedoes at three escorts but, he reported, all missed.

The British escort of this convoy DFed these U-boat contact reports by Huff Duff. The ex-American four-stack destroyer *Chelsea* and the corvette *Arbutus*, equipped with Type 271 centimetric radar, peeled off to run down a bearing. *Arbutus* got a radar contact at 3,000 yards on one of the boats, Zimmermann's *U-136*. *Arbutus* drove *U-136* under and attacked with depth charges, but Zimmermann counterattacked with torpedoes and blew *Arbutus* to pieces. Temporarily disabled by jammed steering gear, *Chelsea* finally came up to assist. She saw a U-boat, probably *U-136*, and opened fire with her guns, but the boat swung around and passed close down *Chelsea*'s port side, then dived. *Chelsea* got a sonar contact and carried out four deliberate depth-charge attacks, but Zimmermann evaded and con-tinued to shadow the convoy.

Concerned that these green skippers might come to grief, Dönitz called off the attack. En route to Norway for permanent duty, von der Esch in *U-586* encoun-tered the 9,100-ton Norwegian tanker *Anna Knudsen* sailing alone. He fired his last three torpedoes at her, claiming a hit for damage, which was later confirmed. He then proceeded to Bergen, then onward to Narvik to operate against PQ convoys.

Also en route to Bergen and low on fuel, Zetzsche in *U-591* found a group of targets on February 10. It was Slow Convoy 67, composed of twenty-two ships, thinly escorted by six Canadian corvettes that were pioneering Admiral King's new "straight through" escort scheme—a nonstop voyage from St. John's, Newfoundland, to Londonderry, Northern Ireland ("Newfie to Derry" as the sailors put it). In response to Zetzsche's report—and aware of his low fuel situation—Dönitz authorized him to attack. Zetzsche shot all of his internal torpedoes at three ships; one 4,000-ton Norwegian freighter sank.

Zimmermann in *U-136* came up on Zetzsche's beacons. Shortly before midnight, he fired a bow salvo at a cargo ship and one of the escorts. He apparently missed the cargo ship, but one or more torpedoes hit the Canadian corvette *Spikenard*, which blew up and went down slowly—the second corvette (after *Arbutus*) sunk by Zimmermann within five days. No immediate effort was—or could be—mounted to look for *Spikenard* survivors. The next day at 11:00 A.M., a British corvette, *Gentian*, found eight *Spikenard* crewmen on a raft. No others were ever found. The other twenty-one ships and the five corvettes of Slow Convoy 67 reached port safely.

Continuing his patrol in the vicinity of Rockall Bank, Zimmermann in *U-136* had further success. On February 16, he sank a straggler from convoy Halifax 174, the 6,900-ton British motorship *Empire Comet*. Three days later he found the big, fast, heavily escorted convoy Halifax 175. It was his report that brought up Kölle in the new, Americas-bound Type IXC *U-154*, who, as related, shot all fourteen internal torpedoes to no effect, owing to a defective torpedo-data computer. Zimmermann also had a frustrating experience: his last two torpedoes failed or missed. Two other *Westwall* boats, von Varendorff's Type VIID (minelayer) *U-213* and Karl-Ernst Schroeter's *U-752*, also responded, but by then the convoy was nearing the British Isles and Coastal Command aircraft frustrated their attacks. Schroeter reported two hits on a big tanker—as well as two misses—but his hits could not be confirmed.

Altogether, group *Westwall* and the Americas-bound boats had come upon a half dozen east- or westbound North Atlantic convoys in February. Dönitz logged that the increasing frequency of North Atlantic convoy contacts was "surprising." Six months earlier he and others at Kerneval had suspected that the British might be reading naval Enigma and had demanded an investigation. Yet no one at Kerneval detected any relationship between the increasing convoy contacts and the changeover to four-rotor Enigma.

In order to maintain the eight boats of the *Westwall* group on station in the Northwest Approaches during March, Dönitz was compelled to provide six boats from France that had been scheduled to sail to the Americas in late February. Inasmuch as four of the six—Berger in *U-87*, Praetorius in *U-135*, Thurmann in *U-553*, and Degen in *U-701*—had patrolled to the Americas in the first wave and were familiar with that distant territory, the diversion to *Westwall* was frustrating not only to Dönitz but also to the skippers and crews.

Only four of the eight *Westwall* boats had contact with the enemy in the month of March, and the results were slight. On March 1, in foul weather, Praetorius in *U-135* found an Outbound North convoy 240 miles west of the Hebrides. He shot four torpedoes but all missed. Five other *Westwall* boats attempted to home on Praetorius's beacons, but the bad weather defeated them. A few days later von Varendorff in the Type VIID (minelayer) *U-213* came upon a large ship escorted by two destroyers, but owing to the heavy weather he was unable to attack.

Conducting an exceptionally bold patrol close to the dangerous south coast of Iceland, during a six-day period, March 6 to March 11, Degen in *U-701* attacked five different ships and patrol craft, firing seven torpedoes. He claimed sinking one cargo ship and three patrol craft for 4,100 tons, but the postwar records credited only one 272-ton fishing trawler and two 500-ton British ASW trawlers, *Notts Country* and *Stella Capella*.

Gerd Kelbling, age twenty-six, in the new *U-593*, merely ten days out from Germany, found a convoy, but owing to the freeze-up on the Baltic, the boat had had scant tactical training. Dönitz therefore ordered Kelbling to attack only in darkness and only if the circumstances were completely favorable. Air and surface escorts thwarted his attack.*

During the abortive sortie of the *Tirpitz* against the Murmansk convoy PQ 12, March 6 to 11, the OKM placed the eight boats of the *Westwall* group under control of the admiral commanding group North, to support and protect *Tirpitz*. Four experienced boats, designated group *York,* were to hunt aggressively for Home Fleet units that might sortie to intercept *Tirpitz*. The other four less experienced boats were to play supporting roles, but upon a request from Dönitz, these four were returned to Kerneval's control, and were replaced by four new boats sailing from Germany. Neither group *York* nor the four boats released to Kerneval found any targets. At Dönitz's suggestion, beginning on March 25, the four new boats from Germany commenced replacing group *York,* which also returned to Kerneval's control. The eight new boats that replaced *Westwall* were to remain permanently based in Norway.

The OKM directed that the four boats of group *York,* inbound to France, detour through the Denmark Strait to scout for Home Fleet or American capital ships. Since the *York* boats were low on fuel, Dönitz could not comply. Rather, he assigned that task to a new Type VII, *U-252,* commanded by Kai Lerchen, age thirty-one, which sailed from Germany March 26 on a special mission (Dana) to land a German agent on Iceland.† After landing the agent, Lerchen reconnoitered the Denmark Strait, where he sank a 1,400-ton Norwegian freighter. Inbound to France on April 14, he ran into a convoy and reported. Since Lerchen also had had

---

* Kelbling reported that an escort fixed his boat with a "bright red light" at a range of 4,000 yards and "accurate" gunfire followed at a range of 2,000 yards. Kerneval speculated that the light might be "infrared rays," until it was informed, to the staff's chagrin, that such rays were invisible. The matter was finally dismissed as "probably a colored searchlight," but in the flap over the light, the "accurate gunfire" at 2,000 yards in total darkness—an almost certain indication that the escorts were equipped with miniaturized, highly sensitive, and accurate radar—was overlooked. Assured by the technical services that escorts were not large enough to carry effective radar, Kerneval continued to accept that brass-bound judgment as reliable.

† The agent, who has not been identified in published sources, was put ashore on the north coast of Iceland on or about April 7. Presumably his mission was to report Allied ship sailings.

scant tactical training, Dönitz authorized him to attack only at night under favorable conditions.

The convoy was Outbound Gibraltar 82, escorted by a trimmed-down version of British Escort Group 36, commanded by the "U-boat killer" Johnny Walker in the sloop *Stork.* The Admiralty DFed Lerchen's contact report and alerted Walker, who in turn notified the four corvettes of his group. *Vetch,* equipped with Type 271 centimetric-wavelength radar, picked up *U-252* on the surface at 7,500 yards and chased for thirty minutes, firing her main battery and snowflake. In defense, Lerchen shot two torpedoes, which only barely missed *Vetch,* then dived. *Stork* joined *Vetch,* and the two vessels dropped forty-five depth charges, which destroyed *U-252* with the loss of all hands. Walker lowered a whaleboat to look for survivors, but the boatmen found only "a revolting mixture of oil, wood, blood, and guts." They fished up some small wooden pieces from the boat, a sheepskin coat, and a pair of leather trousers, which contained a penciled chit headed "*U-252,*" and "a human heart and lungs, complete but penetrated by splinters." *Stork*'s physician pickled the heart and lungs in a bottle "for the future pleasure of the Medical Branch."

When no word came from *U-252,* and her loss was presumed, Dönitz remarked on the similarity of her disappearance to that of Rollmann's *U-82* in early February. Both boats had reported "lightly escorted" convoys in nearly the same area on the western edge of the Bay of Biscay and were never heard from again. He concluded, wrongly, that the British had organized a "dummy convoy" of "special antisubmarine vessels," designed to trap U-boats going to and from France. Thus he forbade the U-boats to attack convoys in this area "for the present." Walker's success over *U-252* was, therefore, much more important than the Admiralty realized. Inbound and outbound Gibraltar convoys as well as Outbound South and inbound Sierra Leone convoys were to enjoy uncontested passage while off the coast of France and the British Isles.

In all, during the period from January to March inclusive, Dönitz mounted thirty-three patrols to the Western Approaches or other areas in the eastern Atlantic.* Except for that of von Varendorff in the VIID (minelayer) *U-213,* all the patrols were of short duration. Some were merely transfers from Germany to France. These patrols accounted for ten Allied ships for 17,600 tons, including four warships: the American Coast Guard cutter *Alexander Hamilton;* the British corvette *Arbutus;* the Canadian corvette *Spikenard;* and the British ASW trawler *Rosemonde.* In return, two boats were lost: *U-252* and *U-581.*

Mediterranean.

Counting the new arrivals and deducting losses, on February 1, 1942, twenty-one U-boats remained in the Mediterranean.† Operating from Italian-managed bases at La Spezia, Pola, and Salamis, the force had a new commander: the able destroyer expert Leo Karl Kreisch, replacing Viktor Oehrn. The main missions of the force

---

* See Appendix 2.
† See Appendix 6.

remained two: support of Rommel's North African offensive by attacking the coasters supporting the opposing British Eighth Army, and thwarting the British reinforcement of the island of Malta.

As in 1941, the U-boat patrols in the Mediterranean in 1942 were short—seldom more than three weeks—but harrowing in the extreme. The skies were filled with British, German, and Italian aircraft whose air crews could not distinguish between enemy and friendly submarines. Both Allied and Axis air and surface forces planted scores of offensive and defensive minefields. Allied shipping was closely guarded by veteran radar-equipped air and surface escorts, making attacks difficult. Allied submarines posed another hazard.

As a consequence, the Mediterranean U-boats, like the Arctic U-boats, produced thin results. In January, five U-boats recorded attacks, four against Allied destroyers. Near Alexandria, Hermann Hesse in *U-133* hit and sank the British destroyer *Gurkha II*. Off Tobruk, Heinrich Schonder in *U-77* hit but only damaged the British destroyer *Kimberley*. In the same area, Wilhelm Dommes in *U-431* sank a 300-ton patrol yacht. All other attacks failed.

In February, seven U-boats recorded attacks. Dommes in *U-431* claimed hits on a destroyer and a tanker; Helmut Rosenbaum in *U-73* claimed sinking a destroyer; Robert Bartels in *U-561* claimed a hit on a freighter; Georg-Werner Fraatz in *U-652* claimed hits on a destroyer, a sloop, and a small tanker; Hans-Werner Kraus in *U-83* claimed sinking a corvette and small freighter and hits on a destroyer and a freighter; Fritz Guggenberger in *U-81,* who had won a *Ritterkreuz* for sinking *Ark Royal,* claimed hits on a light cruiser; and Hans-Otto Heidtmann in *U-559* claimed sinking a 4,000-ton freighter. But, according to Jürgen Rohwer and postwar Allied records, not one of these ships sank and only a few of the hits for damage could be confirmed.

The deep-running defect in the electric torpedoes had been fixed by March and results improved, but only slightly. Johann Jebsen in *U-565* sank the 5,500-ton British light cruiser *Naiad.* Fraatz in *U-652* sank the British destroyer *Jaguar,* the British frigate *Heythrop,* and probably a 2,600-ton British tanker. Kraus in *U-83* damaged a small freighter. But yet another U-boat was lost. Leaving Salamis on March 14, the *U-133,* commanded by a new skipper, Eberhard Mohr, age twenty-six, blundered into a defensive minefield and blew up. There were no survivors.*

Admiral Raeder and the OKM were dismayed by the slim returns of the Mediterranean boats. Berlin pointedly logged in early March that although the Mediterranean war patrols were "brief," there were more U-boats in the shipyards undergoing refit than there were boats on patrol and demanded an explanation from the new U-boat force commander, Leo Kreisch. The latter conceded that the situation was "unfortunate" but explained that many boats returned from patrol with battle damage from aircraft, that there were "difficulties" in the supply lines

---

* Leaving twenty Type VIIs in the Mediterranean U-boat force on April 1, 1942. Between January 5 and March 18, 1942, British submarines sank five Italian submarines in the Mediterranean. *Unbeaten,* which earlier sank *U-374,* got one; *Upholder* got two; *Ultimatum* and *Thorn,* one each.

(from Germany), and that Italian shipyards were "10 percent to 15 percent slower" than German shipyards. He was doing everything possible to speed things up.

In all, during the period from January to April, the twenty-one boats of the Mediterranean force sank only six confirmed ships for about 14,500 tons. Four of the seven victims were British warships: the light cruiser *Naiad,* destroyers *Gurkha II* and *Jaguar,* and the frigate *Heythrop.* Another British warship, the destroyer *Kimberley,* was damaged. These sinkings did not materially assist Rommel, but the presence of the U-boats in the Mediterranean caused the Allies many difficulties.

West Africa.

Two Type IXs sailed to Freetown on February 11: Karl-Friedrich Merten in *U-68* and Axel-Olaf Loewe in the new Type IXC/40, *U-505.* To conserve fuel, both ran on one diesel engine. South of the Canary Islands, Loewe in *U-505* encountered a "fast" convoy, but he was forced off by the escorts, he reported, and could not shoot. Merten encountered no ships on the voyage south.

The boats reached Freetown in the early days of March. The tropical weather was a shock to the crew of *U-505,* fresh from the frigid Baltic. "The boat was heating up like a furnace in daytime," a crewman wrote. "Off watch, we went up on the bridge to get a little relief from the stifling heat down below. The uniform was tropical—no shirts after the first glaze of tan, tropical khaki shorts and pith helmets."

Four months had passed since a U-boat had invaded Freetown waters. Operating independently, Loewe and Merten found many ships sailing alone. In the first eight days of March they sank two ships each. Loewe got the 7,600-ton Norwegian tanker *Sydhav* and a 5,000-ton British freighter; Merten got two big British freighters for 14,400 tons. Merten also attacked what he believed to be a British submarine, operating with a decoy ship, but both torpedoes missed. These attacks left Merten with ten torpedoes and Loewe with fourteen.

The attacks jolted British naval authorities in the Freetown area. They held single ships in port and reorganized convoys. In the days following, Merten and Loewe reported "no traffic" and requested permission to cross the Atlantic to Brazil. Owing to the delicate political situation vis-à-vis Brazil—and to the distances and unfavorable trade winds—Dönitz denied the request, directing Loewe in *U-505* to remain off Freetown and sending Merten in *U-68* southward to Lagos, Nigeria.

Loewe patrolled slowly back and forth off Freetown. It was a trying time. "We spotted nothing—absolutely nothing," a crewman wrote. "It was disgruntling to say the least. . . . The strain was beginning to show. Looking at the same faces day in and day out, listening to the same stories, grown old after the first few weeks, and now the dismal luck on the hunt had frayed nerves here and there. It showed in little ways—sharpened remarks and glum faces, lined with fatigue that resulted from stifling, sleepless days and nights."

Southbound to Nigeria, Merten in *U-68* ran into a mass of single ships off Cape Palmas, Liberia. In a period of twenty-four hours, March 16–17, he sank by torpedo and gun four more British freighters for 19,100 tons. Although he had only three torpedoes left, he proceeded onward to Lagos per orders. On March 25 he came upon a five-ship convoy with three escorts, but an aircraft spotted him and foiled his attack. Running low on fuel, he reversed course and headed home. Rounding Cape Palmas on March 30, he encountered another five-ship convoy. With his last torpedoes, he sank a 5,900-ton British freighter, bringing his kills to seven ships for about 40,000 tons.

Upon receiving Merten's report of heavy shipping off Cape Palmas, Kerneval shifted Loewe in *U-505* to that area. He reported traffic off Cape Palmas, but now it was closely escorted. After being bombed by an aircraft and hunted and depth-charged by a surface vessel, he hauled south into open ocean, crossing the Equator with appropriate ceremonies. Finally on April 3—twenty-nine days since his last success—Loewe found ships. In two night surface attacks over a period of twenty-four hours, he sank two freighters, one American and one Dutch, each of 5,800 tons. He then cruised back to the Freetown area, where he spent another two weeks without seeing so much as a fishing boat. He returned to Lorient on May 7, having been out for eighty-six days, during which he sank four ships for 25,000 tons.

Dönitz was well pleased. The two boats had bagged eleven ships for about 65,000 tons. Moreover, doubtless they had disrupted Allied shipping in the South Atlantic and possibly held in place ASW forces that might otherwise have been shifted to the Americas. Had he had any Type IXs to spare, he would have sent them to Freetown, but all available IXs were committed to the campaign in American waters. Thus Freetown was again left in peace for the next several months.

SHARING DEEP SECRETS

The British and the Americans in early April finally began to freely discuss technology for breaking naval Enigma. The breakthrough came at an Allied conference in Washington, from April 6 to April 17. The primary purpose of that conference was to unify and integrate the collection and distribution of raw Axis intercepts and the Allied HF/DF networks in the Atlantic and Pacific, but the conferees went far beyond that.

The chief of the British delegation was the old Naval Intelligence Division hand Humphrey R. Sandwith, a captain in the Royal Navy. Since the onset of war, Sandwith had been in charge of upgrading the British intercept (Y Service) and HF/DF networks. The chief American delegates were the recent winners in the bureaucratic battle for control of OP20G, Joseph Redman and Joseph Wenger, reputedly the Navy's foremost experts in radio communications.

The British, Canadians, and Americans hammered out agreements that did in fact integrate and greatly improve the collection and distribution of raw Axis radio traffic and HF/DF signals. Adding to the British Atlantic HF/DF network, by summer the Americans had in operation four HF/DF stations on the East Coast, equipped with Type DAB receivers. In addition, the Americans established at Sewall, Maine, a "pilot" model of the more sophisticated Type DAJ receiver, which was fully automatic and which produced a bearing on a U-boat transmission nearly instantaneously.

The historian Bradley Smith wrote that in addition to these important advances in electronics, the British chose this forum to describe to the Americans in detail "how the British extracted intelligence from intercepted enemy radio traffic and how they put it into a form that could be used in naval operations." This included fairly informative disclosures about techniques employed at Bletchley Park, the Admiralty's OIC, and in the U-boat Tracking Room.

The historian Harry Hinsley wrote, additionally, that the British finally—and unequivocally—promised to give the U.S. Navy Department a "bombe," in order "to save it the trouble of designing its own machine." However, Hinsley added, the British were slow to make good on this promise and that as a result of the delay, by June American and British relations "were strained."

On the heels of this conference, Rodger Winn flew to Washington to urge Admiral King and his senior assistants to create a U-boat Tracking Room similar to and linked with his own. King already had a top secret "War Room" akin to the Admiralty's OIC but no U-boat Tracking Room, as such. The American version of the OIC, commanded by King's flag secretary and confidant, George C. Dyer, who limited access to a very few, was known as the Combined Operations and Intelligence Center (COIC).

When Winn met with King to make his case in persuasive and lawyerly fashion, he encountered no difficulties. King readily agreed, and his deputies assigned the submarine tracking task to a Navy captain, Kenneth A. Knowles, who had retired with a physical disability but had returned to active duty after the Pearl Harbor attack.

A great many avenues opened up as a result of these exchanges. But some Americans remained exasperated over what appeared to be the continuing British reluctance to provide them with a bombe and to tackle four-rotor Enigma with all-out vigor. Therefore the Americans did not slacken in their secret efforts to design their own version of a bombe. This important work was carried forward by Howard Engstrom, the Yale mathematician and naval reservist. Called to active duty in February with the rank of full lieutenant, Engstrom took command of OP20G's "Research Section," and devoted himself full-time to naval Enigma. Within merely four months, he rose another notch in rank to lieutenant-commander, a small tribute to his genius and his progress on a bombe design.

NINE

B ritish reconnaissance aircraft brought back pictures in February 1942 that suggested the Germans had built a new and effective radar network along the
Channel coast of Occupied France. On the recommendation of an RAF scientist
concerned with intelligence matters, R. V. Jones, British commando forces, under
the direction of Admiral Louis Mountbatten, drew plans to raid one radar site and
capture the gear and the German operators. Mountbatten chose as his objective an
installation on Cape d'Antifer, a 400-foot chalk headland near the village of
Bruneval, about 12 miles north of Le Havre.

In the late afternoon of February 27, a force of 120 British commandos, led by
John D. Frost, boarded twelve Whitley aircraft. Later that evening, in a snowfall,
the commandos parachuted into fields near the radar site. In a brief but eminently
successful operation, which cost only two men killed, Frost and his men got the
gear, captured a German operator, and were evacuated by Royal Navy vessels that
nosed up to an accessible beach nearby. From the booty acquired, the British were
able to deduce a great deal about German radar technology and production. The
great success of the "Bruneval Raid" encouraged plans for larger raids on the
French coastline.

Hitler was enraged by this raid, which made a mockery of his overhyped beach
defenses. He demanded an investigation of the state of all German coastal installations in Occupied France. The review concluded that, owing to the shift of German
ground and air forces to the Soviet Union and *Kriegsmarine* forces to Norway, the
Atlantic U-boat bases in particular were inadequately defended against attack. On

March 26, Admiral Raeder relayed Hitler's "strict orders" that pending Army and air reinforcements, all U-boat commands near the coast were to "pull back" to safer ground.

The U-boat command structure, from Dönitz on down, was dismayed. Dönitz and his staff, and the seven combat flotilla commanders and staffs, were deeply entrenched at Brest, St. Nazaire, Lorient, La Pallice, and Bordeaux. Apart from the massive U-boat pens, the Germans had built elaborate communications facilities and rest camps for crews. To move all this away from the coast was to require a massive effort at the time all energies were directed at the U-boat campaign in the Americas.

As Dönitz viewed Hitler's "strict orders," he and his Kerneval staff had little choice but to return to Paris. "This is a regretted step back where administration is concerned," he logged, "since the direct contact with the front—that is, the personal touch between commanding officer and his operational boats and crews—will not be possible to anything like the same extent from Paris." Accordingly, he directed the staff to explore alternatives—the city of Angers, for one—that would leave him "as far forward as possible."

London and Washington worried constantly that the *Tirpitz,* like the *Bismarck,* might sortie from Norway into the North Atlantic to raid merchant ships and troopship convoys. It was believed the *Tirpitz* was likely to conclude such a sortie at St. Nazaire, where a huge dry dock had been constructed on the Loire River for the giant, 83,423-ton French luxury passenger liner *Normandie.** The British therefore put in motion a scheme to mount a commando raid on St. Nazaire, primarily to destroy the dry dock and discourage a *Tirpitz* sortie, but also to do whatever other mischief it could.

The armada transporting the commando force sailed from Falmouth on the afternoon of March 26, the same day Raeder relayed Hitler's order to relocate U-boat coastal installations. Deceptively flying *Kriegsmarine* flags, the armada consisted of the ex-American four-stack destroyer *Buchanan,* renamed *Campbeltown,* a gunboat, a torpedo boat, and sixteen motor launches, escorted part of the way by two other British destroyers. A total of 353 Royal Navy personnel manned *Campbeltown* and the eighteen small craft, which carried 268 commandos who had trained tirelessly for the mission. The fleet of small craft was to descend upon St. Nazaire in the middle of the night and land the commandos. Stripped of unnecessary gear—and weight—and loaded with three tons of TNT, *Campbeltown* was

---

* Upon the outbreak of the war in 1939, the *Normandie,* which made her first Atlantic crossing in 1935, was "interned" in New York. After Pearl Harbor, she was "seized" by the United States government for conversion to a troop transport, to be christened *Lafayette.* On February 9, 1942, while undergoing conversion by 2,500 workers of Todd Shipyards, Inc., she caught fire. The thirty-six units of the New York fire department (including three fireboats) that responded to the alarm pumped 839,000 gallons of water into the ship, causing it to capsize at the dock. A prodigious salvage effort ensued, but *Normandie* was too far gone. She was sold for scrap in 1946. Sabotage was suspected but never proven.

to wedge herself into the lock of the *Normandie* dry dock. A delayed-action fuse
was to explode the TNT after the commandos had withdrawn in the small craft.

As the armada approached the coast of France early on the morning of March
27, Gerd Kelbling in *U-593* discovered it. Released from the reshuffled *Westwall*
group, Kelbling was returning to France. As he reported the force to Kerneval at
7:20 A.M. ("three destroyers, ten torpedo boats"), the two escorting destroyers,
Atherstone and *Tynedale,* spotted and attacked him, holding him down for many
hours and preventing follow-up reports. Kerneval made the mistake of dismissing
the formation as one probably "returning from a mine-laying expedition off the
French-Biscay coast."

A British submarine positioned off St. Nazaire on the evening of March 27
transmitted beacons to guide the commando flotilla to the mouth of the Loire. As
part of the plan, the RAF bombed St. Nazaire at 11:00 P.M., but that was probably a
mistake inasmuch as it woke up the town and alerted the military defenses. As the
armada proceeded up the Loire at 1:30 A.M., March 28, the Germans detected it
and illuminated it with searchlights. An enormous, confused firefight ensued.
Campbeltown steamed ahead full speed and at 1:34, rammed the lock per plan, and
wedged herself firmly in the dry dock, but the time fuse on the TNT failed.

Soon after the first shots were exchanged, Dönitz was notified. The initial, panicky report gave the impression that an Allied force of "twenty cruisers and destroyers" was assaulting St. Nazaire and that even heavier warships might be
standing off the mouth of the Loire. The stream of follow-up but exaggerated reports indicated that the Allies were mounting a major invasion. Accordingly, forty-
one minutes after the first alarm, Dönitz sent a message to all U-boats at sea that
were east of 29 degrees west longitude: "Make for St. Nazaire at highest speed.
English landings in progress." Five boats that were outbound to the Americas reversed course; the four boats of group *York,* already inbound to France, rang up full
speed.

There were two U-boat combat flotillas based at St. Nazaire: the 7th, commanded by Herbert Sohler, and the 10th, commanded by Günter Kuhnke. When
the senior officer, Sohler, established contact with Dönitz, he reported that all
headquarters offices and the U-boats had been stripped of "secret documents" and
that all crews at the rest camp in La Baule had been evacuated inland to the town
of La Roche Bernard. In accordance with orders issued by Dönitz on March 14,
demolition charges had been set to prevent any U-boat from falling into enemy
hands.

Confused and furious fighting raged in St. Nazaire for several hours, during
which German forces gradually got the upper hand. They sank or severely damaged fourteen of the eighteen British small craft; only four motor launches finally
made it back to England. The Germans killed or captured almost half (171 of 353)
of the Royal Navy personnel and all but five of the 268 commandos. (Of these,
eighty-five naval personnel and fifty-nine commandos survived the war.) But the
raiders achieved their goal: the faulty fuse on the TNT in *Campbeltown* finally detonated at noon—about eight hours late—destroying the lock and killing a number
of Germans who were on board the vessel attempting to defuse the TNT. Some

military and civilian sightseers were also killed. Total German casualties as a result of the raid were sixty-seven killed, sixty-two severely wounded, and seventy-four slightly wounded.

The repercussions of this raid were far-reaching. On the afternoon of March 28, Hitler directed Dönitz to move U-boat headquarters and the submarine crews to "a safe place." At 10:00 A.M. on March 30, Dönitz reactivated his headquarters in a building on Avenue Maréchal Manoury in Paris, linked by teletype to the radio facilities at Kerneval. In response to Hitler's usual demand for an investigation, the Berlin-based Army generals, Alfred Jodl and Wilhelm Keitel, denigrated the performance of the *Kriegsmarine*. Viewing the criticism as a personal insult, Admiral Raeder not only vigorously defended the *Kriegsmarine*'s performance to Hitler, but also demanded an official apology from Hitler's lackey, Keitel, thus sharply widening the growing gap between himself and Hitler's inner circle.

HITLER'S DOUBTS AND PROMISES

The U-boat campaign in American waters was savaging Allied shipping at a record rate and disrupting all plans, and had given German morale a timely lift. Yet in April 1942, some high-ranking Berlin strategists who had Hitler's ear began to view the U-boat war with deep misgivings. The enlarged, high-priority U-boat construction program was absorbing high-grade steel and scarce copper, which was desperately needed by the *Wehrmacht* and *Luftwaffe* for the war against the Soviet Union. Moreover, the Americans had announced the new—and massive— merchant-ship building goals for 1942–1943. Despite the mounting rate of sinkings by U-boats, the dissenting strategists viewed the naval situation as "hopeless" for the long term. That is, Germany could by no means build enough U-boats to make a decisive dent in the announced Allied shipping program.

There was a more pressing point. Notwithstanding the great numbers of sinkings in American waters, enormous amounts of military supplies were still getting through to the British Isles, to the British Eighth Army, and to the Soviet Union via the North and South Atlantic, the Arctic, and Indian Ocean sea routes. The critics argued that if Germany was to gain swift victories in the Soviet Union and the Mediterranean Basin, it was far more important to sink merchant ships in those areas rather than American coastal shipping, which included banana, sugar, and molasses vessels, and others of no military consequence, or vessels transporting raw materials, such as bauxite, which could not be transformed into weaponry soon enough to affect the outcome of the short-term fighting. The critics thus urged that the U-boat force be concentrated against those Allied convoys which were directly supporting the battlefronts of Germany's enemies.

So it was that at the height of the most successful U-boat campaign of the war, admirals Raeder and Dönitz were compelled to justify to Hitler not only the continuance of the large-scale U-boat building program but also the decision to suspend attacks against convoys in war zones in favor of coastal shipping in American waters. Admiral Raeder made the *Kriegsmarine*'s case for the U-boat strategy to

Hitler in four meetings—April 16, May 13 and 14, and June 15—at *Wolfsschanze*. Dönitz attended the May 14 meeting and made the presentation. His chief points:

•   That he did not believe the race between the enemy shipbuilding program and the U-boat sinkings was in any way "hopeless." The announced Allied goal of building 8.2 million new tons of shipping in 1942 was probably propaganda. The experts at the OKM had calculated that the Allies could build no more than about 5 million tons in 1942. Hence Axis forces (submarines, surface ships, aircraft, etc.) need only sink 400,000 to 500,000 tons of shipping per month to keep pace with new construction and "anything above that number" cut "into the basic tonnage of the enemy." All Axis forces were presently sinking ships at the rate of approximately 700,000 tons a month.*

•   That since the United States and Great Britain had pooled all merchant shipping, the merchant fleets had to be regarded as one. It was immaterial *where* a ship was sunk. Therefore the best policy was to sink ships wherever the greatest number could be sunk at the lowest cost in U-boats lost. Germany should not concentrate "in one specific area" if that meant sinking fewer ships, except in unusual cases (Arctic, Mediterranean) where U-boats were required to relieve pressure on the *Wehrmacht*. Allied tonnage sunk anywhere degraded the ability of the enemy to mount a "second front."

•   That U-boat operations in American waters were therefore entirely justified. In the four-month period from January 10 to May 10, U-boats had sunk 303 ships for 2 million tons, including 112 tankers for 927,000 tons. The Americans had begun building an overland oil pipeline from Texas to the Eastern Seaboard (the so-called "Big Inch") but it would not be ready for at least a year, during which time American industry was to remain dependent on coastal tankers. Every tanker sunk "represents a direct setback" to American industrial production. The U-boat force was "attacking the evil at the root."

•   That if and when sinkings in American waters became unprofitable, Dönitz would resume attacks on the North Atlantic and other convoy routes. The expected arrival in June and July of large numbers of boats that had been delayed by Baltic ice and the shortage of labor in the shipyards for final fit-outs, and the use of U-tankers, should make it easier to find convoys and to mount sustained attacks on them. The many war patrols to the Americas by numerous new boats had been beneficial from a training standpoint and had produced yet another generation of capable skippers—such as Albrecht Achilles, Otto von Bülow, Peter Cremer, and others—who could lead the attacks on the convoys.

In conclusion, Dönitz assured Hitler that "the outlook in regard to submarine warfare is promising." The submariners had faith in their equipment and believed in their fighting ability. The most urgent thing to do was to get the delayed sub-

---

* Implying that all Axis forces were not only keeping pace with new construction, but also cutting into the basic tonnage by 200,000 to 300,000 tons per month. The estimate of sinkings was very nearly accurate. According to Admiralty figures, in April 1942, Allied merchant-ship losses to all causes were 132 ships for 674,457 tons. Axis submarines (German, Italian, Japanese) accounted for seventy-four ships for 431,664 tons.

marines out of the Baltic Sea to the Atlantic quickly and "in general to have as many submarines as possible out at sea engaged in operations."

For some months Hitler had been mulling over a monstrous idea to impair Allied shipping: Shoot the merchant crewmen in the lifeboats. That idea first appears in official German records in the minutes of a conference on January 3, 1942, between Hitler and the Japanese Ambassador, Hiroshi Ōshima. "We are fighting for our existence," Hitler told Ōshima, according to the stenographic notes of the meeting, "and our attitude cannot be ruled by any humane feelings." If U-boat crews shot up the Allied lifeboats, Hitler explained, when the word got around, "the Americans would soon have difficulties in enlisting new people" to man the merchant ships.

This murderous idea next appears, officially, in the OKM diary of February 4, 1942, digesting the topics discussed during meetings between Hitler and Admiral Raeder. The OKM diarist phrased the exchange delicately: Hitler, he wrote, "brought up the question of intensifying warfare on supply traffic by abandoning any consideration for the crews of enemy steamers." Admiral Raeder strongly objected to the idea "for obvious reasons," the OKM diarist wrote, including "the effect which such a policy would have on our own crews." The U-boat crews would be reluctant to carry out the policy for humane reasons and also out of fear that the Allies would retaliate and murder survivors of sunken U-boats.

In a sworn affidavit filed in defense of Dönitz at the Nuremberg trials, Admiral Raeder recalled that Hitler raised this idea during the Dönitz presentation in the May 14 meeting. "Hitler asked Dönitz," Raeder testified, "whether any action could be taken against the crews of torpedoed merchant ships to prevent them from returning home [to man other ships]. Admiral Dönitz declined unequivocally any action against the survivors of the ship's crew." Raeder added that he, too, told Hitler that such action against surviving merchant crews "was out of the question."

Dönitz went on to suggest that the goal Hitler had in mind could be realized if only the torpedo technicians could produce a reliable magnetic pistol that would explode the torpedoes beneath the targeted ships. That would not only save torpedoes and reduce risks to the U-boats, but—according to the stenographer's notes— would "also have the great advantage that the crew will not be able to save themselves on account of the quick sinking of the torpedoed ship. This greater loss of men will no doubt cause difficulties in the assignment of crews for the great American construction program."

That statement "satisfied" Hitler, Raeder swore in his affidavit, and thereafter Hitler did not approach him "with such a request." Nor was any such order ever issued, Dönitz testified at Nuremberg. "Firing upon these men [shipwreck survivors] is a matter concerned with the ethics of war and should be rejected under any and all circumstances," Dönitz said.

Yet another idea for impeding the manning of new merchant ships arose in the aftermath of this meeting. Berlin directed that upon sinking a ship, U-boats were to make every effort to capture the captain and chief engineer and bring them back to Germany as POWs. Dönitz relayed these orders to all U-boats on June 5, adding that if, in the judgment of the U-boat skipper, such captures would endanger the boat or impair its fighting ability, they were not to be attempted.

To judge by the stenographer's notes of this May 14 meeting, Hitler was apparently convinced that the Dönitz strategy for waging U-boat warfare was sound. "Victory depends on destroying the greatest amount of Allied tonnage possible," the Führer proclaimed. "Thus all offensive operations of the enemy can be slowed down or even stopped entirely. . . . The submarine war will in the end decide the outcome of the war." He approved Raeder's proposal that submarine production be stepped up from seventeen boats a month "to the very limit." The copper and labor shortages were to be overcome by buying copper on the black market in France and Belgium* and by exempting shipwrights from conscription into the *Wehrmacht.*

Dönitz came away from the meeting believing he had won a sweeping victory, that the U-boat force finally had Hitler's unqualified backing, and that Dönitz had a free hand to deploy the boats as he saw fit. But, in fact, Dönitz had won only a partial victory. Humiliated that Germany could not deploy *Tirpitz,* in part because the *Kriegsmarine* had no aircraft carriers to protect her, Hitler directed that work on the carrier *Graf Zeppelin* was to continue at high priority and, furthermore, that the battle cruiser *Gneisenau,* the heavy cruiser *Seydlitz* (under construction), and two large ocean liners, *Europa* and *Potsdam,* be converted to aircraft carriers. This work was to divert high-grade steel, copper, and shipyard workers from U-boat production lines. Moreover, still believing that the Allies intended to invade Norway at any hour, Hitler insisted that not less than twenty U-boats remain in Norway to thwart the supposed invasion and to attack the Murmansk convoys in cooperation with the *Luftwaffe,* even though the nightless Arctic summer had arrived, robbing the U-boats of cover for surface chases and attacks and for charging batteries, and reducing their effectiveness to near zero.

STRATEGIC VICTORIES AT CORAL SEA AND MIDWAY

During the latter days of April and the month of May, Admiral King and his senior advisers had to deal simultaneously with two urgent naval matters: the huge and vitally important battles with Japanese naval forces in the Pacific and the no less vital war against the U-boat in the Atlantic.

The first and most urgent task in the Pacific was to prevent Japanese amphibious invasion of Port Moresby, New Guinea, thereby diminishing the threat to Australia and the line of communications between that continent and the United States. The second most urgent task was to thwart a Japanese amphibious operation in the

---

 * One week earlier, on May 7, Hitler had appointed his crony and erstwhile architect, Albert Speer, as Minister of Armament and War Production, replacing Fritz Todt, who was killed in a plane crash. Speer, who attended the May 14 meeting with Raeder and Dönitz, also heartily endorsed the step-up in U-boat production and suggested that the necessary copper might be obtained by cannibalizing middle- and low-tension electric transmission lines throughout Europe. As an additional measure, the Germans stripped bells from churches all over Europe.

central Pacific, believed to be an invasion of either Midway Island or Oahu in the Hawaiian chain or possibly Alaska or California.

In accordance with the plan to deal with the threat to Port Moresby, devised by King and Nimitz during their meeting in San Francisco, April 25 to 27, Nimitz deployed the carriers *Lexington* and *Yorktown* and supporting forces to the Coral Sea. On May 7, the Allied forces engaged a superior Japanese force composed of the carriers *Shokaku* and *Zuikaku,* the light carrier *Shoho,* and supporting forces. American carrier aircraft sank *Shoho* while Japanese carrier aircraft sank the modern destroyer *Sims* and damaged the fleet tanker *Neosho.* The next day, May 8, the American aviators severely damaged the carrier *Shokaku,* while the Japanese aviators severely damaged the carrier *Lexington* and hit the *Yorktown. Shokaku* limped back to Japan, but *Lexington* was so badly damaged that she was sunk (by the destroyer *Phelps*), as was the damaged tanker *Neosho* (by the destroyer *Henley*). Both sides lost numerous pilots and aircraft and incurred other heavy casualties.*

During the run-up to the Battle of the Coral Sea, on May 3, a light Japanese force occupied Tulagi in the Solomon Island chain, which the Allies had recently evacuated. Alerted to this new threat to the line of communications to Australia, on the following day, May 4, aircraft from the *Yorktown* hit the Japanese invaders, sinking a destroyer, a minelayer, and one transport. The Americans proclaimed a great victory, but it was nowhere near that. Moreover, the Americans soon learned from radio decrypts that the Japanese objective in the lower Solomons was to build an air base on the much larger adjacent island, Guadalcanal. Since a Japanese air base there would pose a grave threat to the line of communications, it was an operation that could not be allowed to proceed. Thus Admiral King had yet another developing problem to deal with in the South Pacific.

Before and after the Battle of the Coral Sea itself, American codebreakers worked feverishly to positively identify the objectives of an impending and larger Japanese amphibious operation in the central Pacific. From various radio decrypts, intelligence advisers to Nimitz in Hawaii concluded that the first and main objective was an invasion of Midway Island in preparation for an invasion of Hawaii, together with an invasion of the islands of Kiska and Attu in the Aleutian chain, to thwart American air attacks on the Japanese home islands. However, intelligence advisers to Admiral King in Washington insisted that the Japanese objective was "south," probably an invasion of New Caledonia, which the Americans had recently reinforced. When further codebreaking information on May 17 and 18 pointed unequivocally to Midway and the Aleutians, King yielded to Nimitz's intelligence and approved a decision to shift the damaged carrier *Yorktown* from the South Pacific to the central Pacific. After rushed repairs, she was to join the carriers *Hornet* and *Enterprise* and supporting forces to repel the Japanese at Midway.

To replace the carrier *Lexington,* lost in the Coral Sea, on May 21 Admiral

---

* In all, the Japanese lost seventy-seven aircraft and 1,074 men; the Americans lost sixty-six aircraft and 543 men.

King directed Atlantic Fleet commander Ingersoll to send the carrier *Wasp* and a destroyer division (nominally six destroyers) to the Pacific as rapidly as possible. Then attached to the British Home Fleet, *Wasp* had only just flown off a second load of aircraft to Malta and required a week's refit at Norfolk. Three days later, on May 24, King notified the British that *Wasp*, the new battleship *North Carolina*, the "jeep" carrier *Long Island* (to be used to ferry aircraft), one heavy and one light cruiser, and a division of destroyers were to be shifted to the Pacific. However, none of these warships arrived in Hawaii in time for the Battle of Midway.*

Acting on further information from Navy codebreakers, Nimitz was able to deploy his three carriers in a clever ambush off Midway. In a remarkable victory on June 4, aircraft from these American carriers sank four fleet carriers of the Imperial Navy covering force (*Akagi, Kaga, Soryu, Hiryu*) and forced the Japanese to withdraw. The American ambush included a dozen submarines, one of which, *Tambor*, caused a collision between the cruisers *Mikuma* and *Mogami*. The latter limped home but American aircraft found and sank *Mikuma*. Japanese aircraft severely damaged the carrier *Yorktown*. The next day, June 5, one of sixteen Japanese submarines in the attack force, *I-168*, torpedoed and sank *Yorktown* and the destroyer *Hammann*, which was assisting the crippled carrier. Secondary Japanese forces occupied the Aleutian islands Kiska and Attu.

Admiral King's preoccupation with the Pacific, as the British sneeringly put it, resulted in two strategic naval victories of immense consequences within six months of Pearl Harbor. The loss of four fleet carriers and one light carrier, the damage to the fleet carrier *Shokaku*, and the loss of the cream of the Japanese naval air arm was a devastating setback to the Imperial Navy. With the return of the carrier *Saratoga* from repairs in the States and the transfer of the carrier *Wasp* from the Atlantic, Nimitz could deploy four fast carrier task forces, sufficient naval air power to counterbalance and hold at bay the remaining Japanese carrier forces. Hence the Japanese were no longer able to undertake big operations such as an invasion of Midway or Hawaii, which required a strong force of sea-based air. Nor were they able to capitalize on the occupation of Kiska and Attu.

The Japanese did not, however, relax pressures in the Pacific. They intensified efforts in New Guinea with an overland attack on Port Moresby, and in the Solomon Island chain, areas where land-based aircraft could provide the Japanese the requisite air umbrella. One month after the Battle of Midway, on July 6, the Japanese landed two construction battalions (2,571 soldiers) on Guadalcanal to commence work on the air base. Owing to a new—and blinding—increase in the complexity in the latest variation of Japanese naval code JN-25, American codebreakers were unable to forewarn of this new Japanese landing. The first solid information on it came from Australian coast watchers hiding out in the Solomons.

The sudden and unexpected appearance of Japanese construction forces on

---

* *Long Island* and a new destroyer, *Aaron Ward*, reached the Pacific in late May. *Wasp*, *North Carolina*, the cruisers *Quincy* and *San Juan*, and six modern destroyers entered the Pacific via the Panama Canal on June 10. The destroyers were *Lang*, *Stack*, *Sterett*, *Wilson*, and the new *Buchanan* and *Farenholt*.

Guadalcanal came as a shock to the Americans. It forced them to enlarge a planned attack on Tulagi and Florida islands (Watchtower) to include the capture of Guadalcanal and to push the timetable forward to the earliest possible date. Commanded by Admiral Robert L. Ghormley (who had been replaced in London by former Chief of Naval Operations Admiral Stark), on August 7, American and Australian naval forces simultaneously landed elements of the 1st Marine Division on Guadalcanal and Tulagi. Although caught by surprise, the Japanese reacted swiftly and effectively. They counterattacked the Allies with strong air and naval forces and sent a steady stream of infantry to drive the American Marines from Guadalcanal.

Neither Washington nor Tokyo had planned for a decisive battle in the Solomon Island chain. However, the struggle for Guadalcanal was to grow into one, dominating all other Allied and Axis operations in the Pacific for the remainder of 1942. The desperate fighting in the air and on the seas and in the jungles was to result in ghastly casualties on both sides and—ultimately—yet another legendary Pacific victory for the Americans.

PENETRATING GULFS

During the spring of 1942, the massive U-boat pens at the French Atlantic bases were completed and brought to peak efficiency. Owing to the diversion of U-boats to the Mediterranean and the Arctic and to delays in the arrival of new boats assigned to the Atlantic, there were ample berthing spaces and repair crews to accommodate promptly all boats in need of refit. Hence the home base turnaround time of many boats was sharply reduced. This development, plus the sailing of six new boats (three IXs, three VIIs) from Germany to the Atlantic force, enabled Dönitz in April to order the largest U-boat force yet to American waters: thirty-one boats—fourteen IXs and seventeen VIIs.

These thirty-one boats were to be resupplied, where necessary, by two U-tankers. These were Wilamowitz-Möllendorf's *U-459,* which had sailed in March and was still on station in the mid-Atlantic, and the new Type XB minelayer,* *U-116,* commanded by thirty-six-year-old Werner von Schmidt, which, owing to the failure of the SMA (moored) mine, had been temporarily released to Dönitz. However, while *U-116* was en route to the operational area on April 29, a Coastal Command Hudson depth-charged and damaged her near Rockall Bank and she was forced to abort to Lorient for repairs. This mishap delayed *U-116*'s deployment for twenty-two days, disrupting the planned resupply operations for the April boats.

The damage to *U-116* was a direct result of intensified Coastal Command air

---

* The Type XB minelayer was the largest U-boat built by Germany in the war. It was 295 feet long and displaced about 1,700 tons. It could carry sixty-six SMA mines and the mooring gear: eighteen in six silos in the bow compartment and forty-eight in external canisters. For defensive purposes, it was fitted with two stern torpedo tubes and carried five internal reloads. In a resupply role, the XB could be fitted with eight topside torpedo canisters.

patrols in the Bay of Biscay. These radar-equipped aircraft caught and damaged two other new boats sailing from Germany in April: the Type IX *U-172,* and the Type VII *U-590.* The last was hit by a Whitley of Squadron 502, piloted by Edward Cotton. Both were compelled to return to France for repairs, delaying their departures to May, thus reducing the total number of April boats that reached America waters to twenty-nine.

Of these twenty-nine, sixteen were Type VIIs, of which nine had made prior patrols to the Americas. Three were commanded by *Ritterkreuz* holders: Günther Krech in *U-558;* Reinhard Suhren in *U-564;* and Gerhard Bigalk in *U-751.* Twelve of the sixteen were to refuel from the tanker *U-459* while she was still on her maiden voyage or while she was on a hurriedly arranged second voyage in early June.

Dönitz assumed correctly that the easy times in American East Coast waters were coming to an end. The April VIIs were certain to confront intensified—perhaps even lethal—ASW measures, especially from airplanes. It was also likely that the Americans had finally initiated coastal convoying. If so, the VIIs were to find the hunting very difficult. It would not be prudent for U-boats to attack inshore convoys in the shallow waters of the continental shelf at any time, day or night. There were not enough VIIs to mount sustained night pack attacks against offshore convoys, assuming they could be found. Should conditions in coastal waters prove to be unfavorable as believed, Dönitz had plans for some VIIs to refuel at sea and patrol to the less well defended Gulf of Mexico and Caribbean Sea.

Reinhard Suhren in *U-564,* who wore Oak Leaves on his *Ritterkreuz,* was the first of the April VIIs to arrive. After refueling from *U-459,* he briefly overlapped Peter Cremer in *U-333* in Florida waters, arriving in early May. Cruising close to shore in shallow waters from Cape Canaveral to Fort Lauderdale, in merely one week, May 3 to 9, Suhren attacked and claimed five ships sunk (including two big tankers) for 30,000 tons. However, two of these ships, the 9,800-ton British tanker *Eclipse* and the 3,500-ton American freighter *Delisle,* survived the torpedo hits and were towed into ports and repaired, reducing Suhren's confirmed bag for the week to three ships sunk for 20,400 tons, including the 7,000-ton Panamanian tanker *Lubrafol.*

Probing farther south to Miami, on May 14 Suhren sank the neutral 4,000-ton Mexican tanker *Potrero del Llano,* named after Mexico's once-great oil fields near Tampico. Suhren claimed the vessel was sailing blacked out and that there were armed escorts in her vicinity, making her a legitimate target. The Mexicans insisted the vessel had bright spotlights illuminating the Mexican flags painted on her sides. Whatever the truth of the matter, the Mexican government seized upon the incident to declare that as of May 22 a state of war was to exist with Germany. Thereupon, Dönitz advised the Atlantic boats that all Mexican ships were fair game and to beware of ASW measures in Mexican waters.

On that same day, May 14, the United States Navy initiated an organized merchant-ship coastal-convoy system to replace the ragged (but effective) Bucket Brigade, between Key West and Norfolk. The plan was to sail a forty-five-ship convoy, escorted by not less than five warships as well as land-based aircraft, non-stop in each direction every three days. The first convoy, KS 500 (Key West, Southbound) sailed from Norfolk on May 14. Its counterpart, KN 100 (Key West, Northbound) sailed on May 15. The schedules were arranged so that all ships passed Cape Hatteras in daylight with maximum available air cover. Although the value of dimouts and blackouts remained in question, some cities along the southern coastline cooperated by imposing them.

Cruising off the Florida Keys on May 17, with all torpedoes expended, Suhren in *U-564* spotted what was probably a section of KS 500. He tracked "fourteen ships escorted by four destroyers" rounding Key West and going west into the Gulf of Mexico. He broke radio silence to convey this important intelligence to Dönitz, then he set a course for home, overclaiming an impressive six ships for 34,000 tons sunk. However, his confirmed score—four ships for 24,400 tons, plus damage to two others—was the best patrol of the April VIIs.

On the final leg of his patrol in the Bay of Biscay, Suhren confronted a new and formidable hazard. After eighteen months of R&D and bureaucratic delays, RAF Coastal Command had finally (on June 1) put in service the aircraft-mounted Leigh Light, designed to illuminate U-boats during the last mile of the approach, when ASV meter-wavelength radar was blind. As part of intensified ASW air patrols in the Bay of Biscay, five twin-engine Wellingtons of Coastal Command Squadron 172 had been fitted with these lights.

While Suhren was approaching the French coast on the night of June 4, Squadron Leader Jeaff H. Greswell picked up an ASV contact and commenced the first combat approach with a Leigh Light. His target was the Italian submarine *Luigi Torelli*, commanded by Augusto Migliorini, outbound from Bordeaux to the West Indies. Greswell homed on *Torelli* by radar, then switched on the Leigh Light, but owing to a faulty setting in his altimeter, his approach was too high and he saw no sign of a submarine. However, Migliorini, mistaking the Wellington for a German aircraft, fired recognition flares, precisely pinpointing his boat. On a second approach with the Leigh Light, Greswell got *Torelli* squarely in the brilliant beam and straddled her with four shallow-set 300-pound Torpex depth charges from an altitude of fifty feet. The blasts savaged the boat, forcing Migliorini to abort.*

Suhren reached France safely the next day. He found the Kerneval staff in a minor uproar about the attack on *Torelli*. Notwithstanding repeated assurances to the contrary by technical authorities in Berlin and elsewhere, it seemed obvious that the British had managed to miniaturize radar to fit in aircraft. Dönitz demanded that the technical services immediately produce a "radar detector" or FuMB (an abbreviation of the German phrase for "Radar Observation Equipment"). Thanks to prewar R&D by the French firm Metox-Grandin, to which they had earlier gained access, the Germans were able to quickly produce a prototype

---

* To Aviles, Spain, where the boat ran aground. When she resailed, two Sunderlands of RAAF Squadron 10, piloted by Thomas A. Egerton and E. St. C. Yeoman, dropped fifteen depth charges and hounded her into Santander, Spain, where she was "interned." A month later she "escaped" and limped into Bordeaux.

receiver and a small, crude, diamond-shaped, dismountable aerial made of wire and wood that could be set up on the bridge of a U-boat while it was on the surface. Astonishingly, this primitive FuMB (known as the "Biscay Cross") was capable of detecting meter-wavelength radar emissions at up to 18.6 miles and to warn of them by emitting a "whistling" or "humming" noise. Dönitz issued orders to equip all U-boats in the Atlantic force with a FuMB, but the order could not be carried out fully until early September.

The other fifteen VIIs of the April group sailed for the Americas day by day. Inasmuch as the weather in Canadian waters had dramatically improved and Dönitz wished to hold Allied ASW forces there to the greatest extent possible and to disrupt North Atlantic convoy sailings to and from Halifax, Sydney, and St. John's, he directed four of the boats to patrol off Newfoundland and Nova Scotia. The other eleven were to continue south to the United States East Coast and to the Bahama Islands, east of Florida. If the planned refuelings with *U-459* were successful, five of the Type VIIs were to go further yet and explore the distant Caribbean Sea and the Gulf of Mexico.

Three of the four boats assigned to patrol Canadian waters had made prior patrols to the Americas: Heinz-Otto Schultze in *U-432,* Karl Thurmann in *U-553,* and Viktor Vogel in *U-588.* The fourth was the Type VIID minelayer *U-213,* commanded by Amelung von Varendorff, who had made one prior patrol in the defense of Norway. Before attacking any shipping, von Varendorff had first to carry out an unwelcomed special mission: to land an *Abwehr* agent on the coast of New Brunswick.*

Two of the four Canada-bound Type VIIs, Thurmann's *U-553* and Vogel's *U-588,* were diverted for several days in the futile hunt for the big troopship convoy AT 15–NA 8. Released from that duty, both approached Canadian coastal waters behind schedule. On May 6 Thurmann shot at a freighter escorted by a "corvette," but the torpedo failed or missed and the escort drove him off with depth charges. On the following day, an aircraft dropped three close "aerial bombs," which caused considerable damage to the boat. Seeking a "quiet" area to make repairs, Thurmann limped through Cabot Strait into the Gulf of St. Lawrence, a large, shallow, landlocked body of water at the mouth of the St. Lawrence River,† which to then had not been penetrated by U-boats.

The other VII, Viktor Vogel in *U-588,* took up station directly off Halifax, Nova Scotia. On May 9 he attacked and damaged the 7,500-ton American freighter *Greylock.* Harassed by ASW air and surface patrols, Vogel slowly inched south to Cape Sable. Near there on May 10, he sank the 4,000-ton British freighter *Kitty's*

---

* Perhaps because a minelayer was employed, some historians have written incorrectly that *U-213*'s special mission was to lay mines.

† The St. Lawrence River, an outlet of the Great Lakes, is about 750 miles long. By means of an aged system of locks and canals, shallow-draft ships less than 270 feet long could navigate its entire length. During World War II, big oceangoing ships could only go upriver about halfway, to the cities of Quebec and Montreal.

Brook. His attacks temporarily froze the Boston–Halifax–Boston convoys and other fast ships sailing alone.

After completing repairs to *U-553,* Thurmann, on his own initiative, decided to explore the Gulf of St. Lawrence. He crawled slowly northwest toward Anticosti Island, which lies off the Gaspé Peninsula in the broad estuary of the St. Lawrence River. While *U-553* was incautiously cruising the surface on the afternoon of May 10, an American B-17, based at Gander, saw and attacked her, dropping five bombs or depth charges from an altitude of about 2,300 feet. Although these explosions caused severe damage to the boat, Thurmann pressed on toward Anticosti. The American airmen were dilatory in reporting their attack to other Allied ASW forces in the area, so no follow-up air-sea hunt was mounted and the danger *U-553* presented to the river traffic was not immediately appreciated.

In a remarkable and bold thrust, which was to be likened to Prien's penetration of Scapa Flow, Thurmann reached the mouth of the St. Lawrence River by the early hours of May 12. Within the first four hours of daylight, he spotted five big, outbound, oceangoing freighters and shot torpedoes at four. He claimed sinking three ships and a hit for damage on the fourth. Postwar records credited two freighters sunk: the 5,400-ton British *Nicoya* and the 4,700-ton Dutch *Leto.*

The presence of *U-553* in the Gulf of St. Lawrence caused an uproar. Dönitz, the U-boat staff, the Canadian government, and Allied ASW forces were equally thunderstruck. The Allies temporarily froze all gulf and river shipping, extinguished navigation lights, and saturated the gulf with ASW air patrols. With nine torpedoes remaining, Thurmann lay low for a week, making repairs, eluding enemy aircraft and warships, and patiently waiting for the resumption of ship traffic. Finally, on May 21, he gave up and exited the gulf via Cabot Strait. Upon receipt of Thurmann's report, Dönitz replied with congratulations. Praising Thurmann by name, Berlin propagandists crowed over his feat, implying that U-boats were operating with impunity in the Gulf of St. Lawrence.

Meanwhile, the third VII of the group assigned to Canadian waters, von Varendorff in the Type VIID minelayer *U-213,* arrived to land the *Abwehr* agent. Logged aboard *U-213* as *Kriegsmarine* lieutenant "M. A. Langbein," the agent carried forged papers in the name of "Alfred Haskins" of Toronto. His probable mission was to report the sailings of Halifax convoys and other military information. He had a portable radio transmitter-receiver, civilian clothes, and $7,000 in U.S. currency. Entering the Bay of Fundy, von Varendorff landed the agent via rubber dinghy on Melvin's Beach, near the town of St. Martins, New Brunswick, in the early hours of May 14.* Von Varendorff then explored the Bay of Fundy for enemy merchant ships, but found none.

---

* "Langbein-Haskins" was the first German agent to reach the Americas by submarine, but he apparently double-crossed the *Abwehr.* He buried his uniform and the radio near the beach and made his way to Montreal. A month later, on June 19, 1942, he resettled in Ottawa. On November 1, 1944, he turned himself in to Canadian authorities, who put him in an internment camp for the rest of the war. Canadian counterintelligence officers concluded that "Langbein-Haskins" never engaged in espionage. He merely lived well in Ottawa on *Abwehr* money until it ran out.

The fourth and last of the Canada-bound boats, Schultze in *U-432,* reached the Nova Scotia area in mid-May. He cruised south to Cape Sable, where on May 17 Vogel in *U-588* sank the 2,100-ton Norwegian freighter *Skottland* but missed the British freighter *Fort Binger,* which was manned by a Free French crew who aggressively counterattacked Vogel by gun and drove him off. East of Cape Sable that same day, Schultze in *U-432* attacked and sank by gun the 325-ton Boston-based fishing trawler *Foam.* At about this same time, von Varendorff in the VIID minelayer *U-213,* having found no shipping, exited the Bay of Fundy at Cape Sable.

The U-boat staff was puzzled that none of the four boats assigned to Canadian waters had found a major convoy. Believing the Allies may have shifted the routes farther offshore, Kerneval ordered Vogel, von Varendorff, and Schultze to reconnoiter an area about 200 miles southeast of Cape Sable. Leaving the Gulf of St. Lawrence, Thurmann in *U-553* replaced the three boats in the Cape Sable area and explored the Bay of Fundy.

Taking up the assigned stations well to the southeast of Cape Sable, Vogel, Schultze, and von Varendorff found no convoys but encountered numerous ships sailing alone. On May 21 and 23, Vogel in *U-588* sank two by gun and torpedo: the 3,300-ton American freighter *Plow City* and the 4,500-ton British freighter *Margot.** Having expended all his torpedoes to sink four confirmed ships for 14,000 tons, Vogel set a course for France. Nearby, Schultze in *U-432* sank the lone 4,500-ton British freighter *Zurichmoor,* then returned to the Cape Sable area, switching places with Thurmann in *U-553,* who was running low on fuel and food. While 240 miles due south of Cape Sable on June 2, Thurmann in *U-553* sank the 7,000-ton British freighter *Mattawin.* Although he was nearly out of food and had but three torpedoes and little fuel remaining, Thurmann was reluctant to head home. However, on June 11, a Catalina found and attacked *U-553,* dropping two close depth charges which disabled the port diesel and forced Thurmann to abort. On May 26, von Varendorff in the VIID minelayer *U-213* chased a freighter for eight hours to achieve a favorable firing position, but all three torpedoes missed.

Three of the four April boats that were assigned to Canadian waters did not refuel. Von Varendorff in the VIID minelayer *U-213,* which had 50 percent greater fuel capacity than a VIIC (169 tons vs. 113 tons), had no need to replenish. Upon completing his patrol of sixty days, during which he successfully landed the *Abwehr* agent but sank no ships whatsoever and came home rather soon, von Varendorff drew a stern rebuke. Thurmann in *U-553* and Vogel in *U-588* carried out patrols of sixty-seven and fifty days, respectively.

Returning to the Cape Sable area, Heinz-Otto Schultze in *U-432* had a busy time. On May 31 he sank a 1,200-ton Canadian coaster. On June 2 he sank by gun two small American fishing trawlers: the 41-ton *Aeolus* and the 102-ton *Ben and Josephine.* Citing these sinkings and that of the trawler *Foam,* some historians were to condemn Schultze for ruthlessness. But apparently Dönitz and/or the

---

* Gary Gentile wrote that Vogel gave the survivors of both ships rum and cigarettes, but refused a request from *Margot*'s captain to tow the lifeboats to shore.

U-boat staff encouraged such attacks in the belief that fishing trawlers and other small craft reported U-boat sightings by radio.*

While about seventy miles southwest of Cape Sable on June 9, Schultze in *U-432* found a convoy. He reported twelve freighters escorted by "two destroyers, two corvettes, and a blimp." Since no other boats were nearby, Kerneval authorized Schultze to attack alone. Firing a full bow salvo at two big freighters, he claimed sinking one 8,000-tonner and damaging another, but the records confirmed only damage to the 7,000-ton Norwegian vessel *Kronprinsen*. Low on fuel and torpedoes, Schultze set a course for France, refueling from *U-459* on the way. Since his claims and credits for this and prior patrols exceeded 100,000 tons, he was awarded a *Ritterkreuz*.†

DIFFICULT HUNTING ON THE EAST COAST

The eleven other VIIs of the April group headed for the United States East Coast and the Bahama Islands. Inbound, two of the skippers, Hans-Heinrich Giessler in *U-455* and Gerd Kelbling in the new *U-593*, were held in Canadian waters to hunt for the big troopship convoy AT 15-NA 8. Their hunts for this military target were futile, but the diversion took Giessler's *U-455* into the path of the lone 7,000-ton tanker *British Workman*, which he sank by torpedo on May 3 about 200 miles south of Cape Race.

Both boats had expended considerable fuel during the hunt for AT 15-NA 8 and they were unable to reach Cape Hatteras. Both remained in the waters between Nova Scotia and northern New Jersey and New York. Giessler in *U-455* had no further luck in American waters, but homebound in the mid-Atlantic he sank a second British tanker, the 6,900-ton *George H. Jones*. Kelbling in *U-593* hit the Greek freighter *Stavros* for damage and sank the 8,400-ton Panamanian tanker *Persephone* close off the coast of northern New Jersey. She was the only tanker sunk in the Eastern Sea Frontier in the month of May. Neither Giessler nor Kelbling refueled this time. The former was out sixty-two days, the latter fifty-nine days.

Nine VIIs patrolled the waters from New Jersey southward. As expected, these boats confronted greatly intensified ASW measures, including "heavy" air patrols all along the East Coast, mounted by 172 Navy and Coast Guard aircraft, plus the Army Air Forces planes. By the time these boats arrived, the Bucket Brigade convoys were in full operation and, as related, on May 14, the first Key West–Norfolk–Key West convoys sailed. Sixteen destroyers of the Atlantic Fleet‡ spent an

---

  * In May and June 1942, U-boats in American waters sank over a dozen small sailing vessels and fishing trawlers by gun. American submarines in Japanese waters routinely sank fishing trawlers for the same reasons.

  † At the time of the award, his confirmed score—all on *U-432*—was nineteen ships sunk for 68,900 tons, including the three trawlers.

  ‡ *Bristol, Broome, Cole, Dallas, Dickerson, Du Pont, Ellis, Herbert, Lea, Ludlow, MacLeish, McCormick, Roper, Semmes, Simpson, Woolsey.*

aggregate 238 days under control of the Eastern Sea Frontier: 184 days at sea on ASW missions, 54 days in replenishment or refit.

The historian of the Eastern Sea Frontier wrote of the month of May, in part:

> There was an extraordinary change this month in the fortunes of the war beneath the sea. April, when ships had gone down at the rate of almost one per day, was the worst month within the Frontier since the submarine first invaded this coast. As it drew to a close there was no indication and no hope that these severe losses could be appreciably reduced in the foreseeable future. In fact when two vessels went down on the 30th [of April], it was possible to predict that sinkings might well increase. Then, in the first 17 days of May not one ship was lost in the Eastern Sea Frontier.* In the fourteen days that remained [of May] only four vessels were sunk in our waters. . . .†

While inbound to the Cape Hatteras area, three VIIs sank ships near the outer boundary line of the Eastern Sea Frontier:

• Ulrich Gräf, the new and aggressive skipper of the *U-69,* got the 600-ton four-masted American sailing vessel *James E. Newsom* by gun.

• Friedrich-Hermann Praetorius in *U-135* got the 7,100-ton British freighter *Qu'Appelle.* Responding to her SOS, a Canadian aircraft sighted her lifeboats and, two days later, a Canadian minesweeper rescued thirty-four survivors from the boats. They reported thirteen crew had been killed in the sinking.

• Gerhard Feiler in *U-653* got the 6,200-ton British freighter *Peisander,* en route from Australia. A week after the sinking, her five lifeboats reached Nantucket Island.

One VII that reached the Cape Hatteras–Cape Lookout area was lost: the *U-352,* commanded by thirty-one-year-old Hellmut Rathke. He had made one prior patrol in the defense of Norway during which he fired at a "destroyer" but he had not yet hit anything. After he replenished inbound from *U-459,* Rathke boldly closed on Onslow Bay, North Carolina, on May 8. There he found a freighter escorted by a Coast Guard cutter. He fired three torpedoes at the two ships, but all missed or malfunctioned.

Late in the afternoon on the following day, Rathke sighted another Coast Guard cutter sailing alone, thirty miles south of Cape Lookout. She was the 165-footer *Icarus,* southbound from New York to Key West to join the new coastal-convoy organization. Commanded by fifty-two-year-old Maurice D. Jester, who rose from the enlisted ranks, *Icarus* was a taut ship with five months of ASW duty. Believing the Cape Hatteras-Cape Lookout area to be infested with U-boats, *Icarus* was on full alert. As Rathke closed to point-blank range to fire a single torpedo, *Icarus* got a solid sonar contact at 2,000 yards. Rathke shot before *Icarus*

---

* Not counting escort vessels. As related, von Forstner in *U-402* sank the converted yacht *Cythera* off Cape Fear, May 2. On May 11, Günther Krech in the VII *U-558* sank the British ASW trawler *Bedfordshire* off Cape Lookout, with the loss of all thirty-seven crewmen. Six bodies were recovered and four were buried on Ocracoke Island in a plot deeded to the British government.

† *Skottland, Plow City, Margot, Persephone.*

could take action, but the torpedo prematured, or malfunctioned, or hit the ocean bottom, erupting in an explosion that shook *Icarus* from stem to stern.

Jester and the crew of *Icarus* reacted smartly and professionally, firing five shallow-set depth charges from the tracks and Y gun at a likely spot. All five closely straddled *U-352* and exploded with immense force, wrecking the boat and killing the first watch officer, Josef Ernst. Rathke bottomed at 114 feet to play dead, but when *Icarus* dropped five more close, shattering depth charges, he surfaced to abandon ship and scuttle.

When *U-352* broached stern up, *Icarus* raked her with her 3" bow gun and machine guns from close range. This hail of fire killed or wounded many Germans who were leaping into or already in the sea. Homer Hickam wrote that an *Icarus* crewman yelled at his fellow Americans: "For God's sake! Don't shoot them in the water!" Struggling in the sea, shouting to the Americans to stop shooting and to save his wounded men, Rathke used his belt as a tourniquet on a wounded machinist, Gerhard Reussel, whose left leg had been shot off.

Fearing that another U-boat might be nearby, Jester hauled *Icarus* away, requesting instructions from various naval shore commands by radio. Should he rescue the German survivors or leave them in the water? Directed to rescue the survivors, Jester returned to the scene within the hour and fished out thirty-three Germans, including machinist Reussel, who died of his wounds on board *Icarus,* and took them into Charleston, South Carolina. The bodies of thirteen other Germans who were killed inside the boat or in the water were left behind. The thirty-two survivors—the first German submariners to be captured by the Americans—were taken to an internment camp at Fort Bragg, North Carolina. Reussel was buried with military honors in the National Cemetery at Beaufort, South Carolina.

The Navy ordered salvage divers to comb *U-352* to obtain Enigma and other intelligence information, but since *Icarus* had failed to buoy the wreck, the task was difficult. Divers from the Navy salvage tug *Umpqua,* protected from U-boat attack by the British ASW trawlers *Northern Duke, Northern Dawn,* and *Stella Polaris,* finally found *U-352* in 114 feet of water on May 23. They buoyed the wreck, reported on the damage, and took photographs, but for various reasons, salvage operations were not pursued. No divers entered the boat. She yielded no intelligence information.*

Three of this group of VIIs attacked ships on the homeward voyage. On June 1, Dietrich Borchert in *U-566* sank the 9,000-ton British freighter *Westmoreland,* only his second success in two patrols to American waters. Upon reaching France, he left the boat for other duty. When Bermuda learned of *Westmoreland*'s loss, the old (1918) 1,000-ton American minesweeper *Gannet,* serving as a tender for the Navy's Catalina Squadron 74 on Bermuda, and a British ASW yacht, *Sumar,* put out to look for survivors. Gerhard Feiler in *U-653* came upon *Gannet* and

---

* The *U-352* was rediscovered in 1975 by American salvage and sport divers. Although many have dived on her and vividly described her wrecked condition, none has attempted to enter the boat.

Sumar on June 7. He torpedoed *Gannet,* which sank in four minutes.* Praetorius in *U-135* sank the 4,500-ton Norwegian freighter *Pleasantville* well east of South Carolina.

In view of the poor hunting and the strong ASW measures in the Eastern Sea Frontier, Dönitz directed five VIIs of the April group, which had replenished from *U-459,* to patrol far to southward: four to the Caribbean Sea, one to the Gulf of Mexico.

The first of the four VIIs to reach the Caribbean Sea was Dietrich Hoffmann in the new *U-594.* His patrol was a disastrous flop: eight misses on a tanker and a freighter, and a gunner washed overboard and lost during a gun attack on the tanker. Upon receiving Hoffmann's reports, Dönitz canceled a proposed second refueling and ordered him to return directly to France at once. He arrived on June 25, completing a seventy-six-day patrol during which he sank nothing. After a careful review of the patrol, Dönitz sent Hoffmann to other duty and gave command of *U-594* to another officer.

The other three VIIs followed. Patrolling near Trinidad, Ulrich Gräf, the new skipper of *U-69,* sank two ships for 9,400 tons, including the 6,800-ton Norwegian tanker *Lise,* but he was then ordered to carry out a special mission off the Vichy island of Martinique (see below). *Ritterkreuz* holder Günther Krech added luster to his and *U-558*'s reputation by positively sinking five more ships, bringing his total for the patrol to six confirmed ships for 16,400 tons, plus damage to the 7,100-ton American tanker *William Boyce Thompson. Ritterkreuz* holder Gerhard Bigalk in *U-751* sank two medium American freighters *(Nicaro, Isabella)* for 4,555 tons. Homebound, he fired three torpedoes at a big freighter, but two failed and the third missed.

The aggregate returns of the sixteen VIIs that sailed to the Americas in April declined: thirty-three confirmed ships (seven tankers) sunk plus five sailing vessels and fishing trawlers for about 158,200 tons.

As related, the most successful patrol was that of *Ritterkreuz* holder Reinhard Suhren in *U-564,* completed just before the Allies initiated full-scale convoying on the United States East Coast. Including the "neutral" tanker which brought Mexico into the war, Suhren sank four confirmed ships (two tankers) for 24,400 tons and damaged two other ships for 13,200 tons. The second best patrol was that of Karl Thurmann in *U-553,* who, as related, penetrated the Gulf of St. Lawrence on his own initiative and sank there and elsewhere three confirmed ships for 17,000 tons. Three other boats (*U-455, U-588,* and *U-753*) sank about 14,000 tons each, including three tankers.† Two (*U-69, U-135*) sank about 12,000 tons each, including one tanker. Six boats sank under 10,000 tons each, including one tanker, and three boats (*U-213, U-352,* and *U-594*) sank no ships at all. One boat, *U-352,* was lost.

Eleven of these sixteen VIIs refueled. Discounting the lost *U-352,* the other ten

---

*   Fourteen of her crew died in the sinking, but sixty-two others were rescued by Catalinas and by the four-stack destroyer *Hamilton.*

†   For details of *U-753* in the Gulf of Mexico, see pages 580–581.

were able to extend their patrols to an average sixty-nine days and sank an average 2.7 ships per boat per patrol. The five VIIs that did not refuel, including the luckless *U-213* (minelayer), patrolled for an average sixty days and sank an average 2.0 ships per boat per patrol. Discounting the badly handled *U-213*, the four VIIs that did not refuel sank an average 2.5 ships per boat per patrol. Thus it was that the refueling of this group extended the patrols by about nine days, but did not appreciably increase the sinkings. Much still depended on the area of the patrols, aggressiveness of the skippers, skill of the crews, weather, luck, and other factors.

Contrary to the myths that arose in later years, the returns of the five VIIs sent to the Caribbean and Gulf of Mexico were disappointing. At sea an average of seventy days, these boats sank eleven ships for about 38,600 tons in the Caribbean and gulf, an average of 2.2 ships for 7,700 tons sunk per boat per patrol. This return was no better than the VII returns from other waters and it was small compensation for the extreme hardships the crews endured from the terrible tropical heat and humidity and the chronic shortages of food and fresh water.

In the first five months of the campaign in the Americas, Dönitz mounted seventy patrols by Type VIIs. These sank 155 confirmed ships for 778,307 tons, including all trawlers and sailing vessels and ships encountered in the ocean coming and going. Partly reflecting the result of the attacks on convoy Outbound North 67, the nine VIIs that sailed in February achieved the best results.

Month	Boats	Sunk	Tons	Average
December	10	18	85,374	1.8
January	14	24	124,922	1.7
February	9	29	167,864	3.2
March	20	46	241,937	2.3
April	17	38	158,210	2.2

For those staffers who opposed sending VIIs to the Americas, the decline in returns of the April boats was persuasive. The fifteen surviving VIIs that sailed in April had spent 991 days at sea to sink 158,210 tons of confirmed shipping, merely 25 percent of what was thought to be a reasonable return. The critics made the case for operating the VIIs in packs closer to home, especially in summertime, when the climate in southern American waters was so hot and debilitating, and so much more favorable for operations in the North Atlantic.

Dönitz conceded that the return on investment for the VIIs in American waters was marginal and that the patrols were very hard on the crews. And yet he did not want to stop altogether the VII patrols to American waters. Even a few VIIs operating on the Eastern Seaboard would insure that the Allies continued convoying there with the usual shipping delays and would tie down substantial numbers of ships and aircraft on ASW missions. However, he directed that most of the VIIs sent to United States waters in the month of May should first carry out special missions, such as minelaying or landing *Abwehr* agents.

SLAUGHTER IN THE GULF OF MEXICO AND CARIBBEAN SEA

Thirteen of the twenty-nine boats of the April group that reached the Americas were Type IXs, ten of which had made a prior patrol to that area.

The first IX to sail was *U-125,* a Type C commanded by Ulrich Folkers, who had made a disappointing maiden patrol off Cape Hatteras in January. Dönitz assigned him to virgin territory: an area in the Caribbean off southwest Cuba, at the southern approaches to the Yucatan Channel, which separates Cuba and the Yucatan area of Mexico. Outbound from France, Folkers sank by torpedo and gun a lone 5,100-ton American freighter in mid-ocean. Upon reaching his area in early May, he found heavy, unescorted shipping plying between the Panama Canal Zone and the Gulf of Mexico. In the ensuing sixteen days, May 3 to May 18, Folkers sank by torpedo and/or gun eight more ships, including two tankers, the 8,900-ton American *Mercury Sun,* and the 12,000-ton Canadian *Calgarolite,* bringing his total bag to nine confirmed ships for 47,000 tons. Discounting the two "unknowns" Hardegen claimed on his first Drumbeat patrol, it was the most fruitful voyage by any U-boat in American waters to date. Proudly reporting this bonanza and suggesting that other boats should patrol the area, Folkers returned directly to France without refueling, completing the round trip in seventy-one days.

The next two boats to sail were the new extended-range Type IXC/40 sister ships, *U-506* and *U-507.* These and von Mannstein's Type VII *U-753* were to launch the U-boat campaign in the Gulf of Mexico, where it was believed, correctly, ASW measures were weak. Both IXs were to enter the gulf via the Old Bahama Channel (north of Cuba) and the Straits of Florida. Upon reaching the Old Bahama Channel on April 30, Harro Schacht, age thirty-four, in *U-507,* found and sank the lone 2,900-ton American tanker *Federal* by gun. Trailing by several days, on May 3, Erich Würdemann, age twenty-eight, in *U-506,* shot a torpedo to sink the 600-ton Nicaraguan freighter *Sama* in the Florida Straits.

Dönitz had directed both IXs to proceed northwest across the gulf to the mouth of the Mississippi River. It was assumed, correctly, that the area would be swarming with ships. Several surprise sinkings might close the Mississippi to traffic, a worthwhile objective, but not without real danger for these big boats: the water at the delta was muddy and quite shallow and the currents were extremely tricky.

Protection of shipping in the Gulf of Mexico and Yucatan Channel was the responsibility of the newly established Gulf Sea Frontier, commanded by Russell S. Crenshaw, who had set up headquarters in Key West, terminus of the East Coast Bucket Brigade and other convoys.* Like Adolphus Andrews, his counterpart on the East Coast, Crenshaw had only slim resources: two four-stack destroyers (*Noa, Dahlgren*), nine 165-foot and 125-foot Coast Guard cutters, five large converted yachts, and about thirty-five Army, Navy, and Coast Guard aircraft. Astonishingly, two of these aircraft on hurriedly mounted ASW patrols scored near misses on

---

* Unescorted gulf shipping assembled for the escorted trip up the East Coast in an artificially created anchorage near Key West, protected by a field of 3,460 mines. On April 26, the four-stack destroyer *Sturtevant* struck one of the mines and sank, with the loss of fifteen men.

both *U-506* and *U-507*. Würdemann in *U-506* reported heavy damage to one of his two stern tubes. Schacht in *U-507* reported damage to his starboard bow plane and the loss of two tons of fuel oil, apparently from a ruptured tank.

Schacht in *U-507* sank the first ship inside the gulf, the 2,700-ton American freighter *Norlindo*. Hit by a single torpedo, she sank stern first in three minutes. Schacht gave the survivors forty packs of cigarettes, a cake adorned with French writing, crackers, matches, water, and ten gallons of lime pulp made from fresh limes. "Sorry we can't help you [further]," Schacht said in perfect English, according to the survivors, "Hope you get ashore okay."

The next night, May 5, Schacht sank two American tankers by torpedoes. The first was the 5,100-ton *Munger T. Ball,* fully loaded with gasoline, which burst into flames. Thirty-seven of forty-one crewmen perished. The second was the 7,000-ton *Joseph M. Cudahy,* which radioed a report of the *Ball* sinking, adding unwisely and unnecessarily, "Nine miles away." Upon hearing that, Schacht immediately searched for, found, and chased *Cudahy*. His first torpedo missed, but the second hit and she sank. Twenty-seven of thirty-seven crewmen died.

Later that night, the *U-507* crew downloaded torpedoes from the topside canisters. While doing so, the restraining gear broke and a torpedo slid uncontrolled into the bow compartment. On its downward path, it struck and gashed open the arm of a radioman, a severe and excruciatingly painful injury. Schacht reported the injury to Kerneval and the fact that he had no painkillers. Kerneval arranged a rendezvous with Würdemann in *U-506,* who had morphine; however, the boats failed to meet. Kerneval arranged a second rendezvous, which also failed, then a third, likewise fruitless. The sinkings and the numerous radio transmissions to set up the rendezvous attracted swarms of Army, Navy, and Coast Guard aircraft and led to stringent shipping controls in the Gulf Sea Frontier, similar to those in effect in the Eastern Sea Frontier.

Schacht gave up trying to find Würdemann and resumed his course to the Mississippi River. He put the injured crewman in an officer's bunk, dressed his festering wound, and gave him sleeping pills. On May 6, he came upon the 6,800-ton American freighter *Alcoa Puritan,* loaded with bauxite. Schacht missed with one torpedo, attacked with his 4.1" deck gun, then finished off the ship with a torpedo.* On the day after that, he sank the 3,100-ton Honduran freighter *Ontario* by gun. A day later still, May 8, he sank the 2,400-ton Norwegian freighter *Torny* with a single torpedo. Two crew members died; a Navy seaplane rescued the twenty-four survivors.

Both *U-506* and *U-507,* on about May 10, finally closed on the mouth of the Mississippi River. Würdemann in *U-506* mounted the first attack. He shot four torpedoes at the old (1920) 7,000-ton American tanker *Aurora,* sailing in ballast. After the crew abandoned ship, Würdemann surfaced and raked the ship with his 4.1" deck gun. He claimed that *Aurora* sank in flames, but in fact, a Coast Guard vessel towed her into Burrwood, Louisiana, and she ultimately returned to service.

---

* Samuel Eliot Morison wrote that Schacht also shouted apologies and good luck to the fifty survivors. All were rescued by the 125-foot Coast Guard cutter *Boutwell*.

Würdemann and Schacht patrolled off the mouth of the Mississippi River for ten days, May 11 to May 20. In a notable series of torpedo attacks, Würdemann in *U-506* hit seven different American ships, sinking five: the tankers *Gulfpenn,* 8,900 tons (90,000 barrels of fuel oil); *David McKelvy,* 6,800 tons (80,000 barrels of fuel oil); *Gulfoil,* 5,200 tons (petroleum products); *Halo,* 7,000 tons*; and the freighter *Heredia,* 4,700 tons (bananas, coffee). Crew losses were heavy: thirteen of thirty-eight on *Gulfpenn,* seventeen on *McKelvy,* twenty-one on *Gulfoil,* all but three on *Halo,* and thirty-eight of sixty-one on *Heredia.* The damaged ships were the tankers *William C. McTarnahan* and *Sun,* sailing in ballast. Bedeviled by nine torpedo misses, failures, or malfunctions, including two circular runners, Schacht in *U-507* sank two ships: the 10,700-ton American tanker *Virginia* by two torpedoes, and the 4,150-ton Honduran freighter *Amapala* by gunfire, boarding, and scuttling. Twenty-seven of forty-one crew members on *Virginia* perished.

Having expended all torpedoes, *U-506* and *U-507* headed home by way of the Straits of Florida. On the way back, Würdemann in *U-506* sank two British freighters by gun east of Florida, raising his confirmed score to eight ships (four tankers) for about 40,000 tons sunk plus damage to three big tankers. Schacht's total was nine confirmed ships (four tankers) sunk for about 45,000 tons. According to Homer Hickam in his book *Torpedo Junction,* over 200 crewmen in these seventeen lost ships (eight tankers) were killed in the sinkings or later died in the water or in lifeboats or rafts.

As noted earlier, the single VII of the April group assigned to the Gulf of Mexico was the *U-753,* commanded by thirty-four-year-old Alfred Manhardt von Mannstein. He had made one prior patrol in the defense of Norway, cut short when *U-753* was rammed and severely damaged topside by a British "destroyer." The voyage to America was thus *U-753*'s first full-scale patrol.

Von Mannstein operated in the Gulf of Mexico for about two weeks, May 19 to June 1, in the wakes of *U-506* and *U-507.* Inbound to the gulf via the Straits of Florida on May 19, he spotted a convoy off the western tip of Cuba. He boldly swung around to close and shoot submerged, but the boat suddenly rose and a merchant ship rammed her, mangling the deck gun, which the crew later dismounted and stowed below. This mishap thwarted the attack on the convoy, but over the next several days he shot five torpedoes to sink the 7,200-ton American freighter *George Calvert* and attacked a 300-ton British sailing schooner with a cargo of lumber, *E. P. Theriault,* by gun. He boarded her and set scuttling charges, but *Theriault* survived.

Continuing this relentlessly aggressive patrol, von Mannstein had mixed success. An attack on an *Erie*-class gunboat failed: one torpedo missed, and another ran hot in the tube and had to be ejected. Proceeding northwest to the mouth of the Mississippi River, von Mannstein attacked two big tankers, May 25 to 27. He damaged the 6,600-ton Norwegian *Haakon Hauan* and sank her sister ship, the 6,600-

---

* *Halo* was loaded with 63,000 barrels of crude oil. According to Jürgen Rohwer, she had been hit and damaged by two other U-boats earlier in the year: *U-130* and *U-126.*

ton *Hamlet,* expending five torpedoes. On June 1, von Mannstein left via the Florida Straits, having sunk in this first Type VII foray into the Gulf of Mexico two confirmed ships (one tanker) for about 13,800 tons.

While *U-753* was homebound in the Bay of Biscay in the late afternoon of June 23, a Whitley of Coastal Command Squadron 58, piloted by W. Jones, found and depth-charged her. The initial attack was skillful: the explosions knocked out *U-753*'s diesels and rendered her incapable of diving. The British failed to follow up the attack and, although "badly damaged," *U-753* managed to survive. France-based German aircraft and motor launches found *U-753* the next morning and escorted her into La Pallice, where she remained out of action for the next three months.

This calamity, atop the British aircraft attacks on other boats in June, persuaded Dönitz on June 24 to change procedures for crossing the Bay of Biscay. Until then, the orders were fairly loose, leaving tactics up to the skippers. Most preferred to run on the surface day and night to get across this increasingly dangerous area as quickly as possible, relying in daytime on lookouts to spot enemy aircraft early enough to dive to safety, and feeling more or less immune to attack at night. Since the radar-equipped Leigh Light Wellingtons rendered surface travel risky day *or* night, Dönitz decreed specifically that all U-boats were to cross the Bay of Biscay submerged, surfacing only briefly at night to recharge their batteries and to refresh the air in the boat.

This was not a welcome change inasmuch as the boats could barely log more than a hundred miles a day, and this greatly prolonged the crossing and reduced time in the operating areas, but it was intended to be only temporary, pending the arrival of the Metox radar detectors, or FuMBs, and much-improved antiaircraft weaponry, including twin 37mm and 20mm rapid-fire guns. With Metox and these more powerful weapons, Dönitz believed that a U-boat could successfully fight it out with an enemy plane in daytime, hence travel on the surface during the day could be resumed.

Of the three older, shorter-range Type IXBs which set off for the United States East Coast in April, two made promising starts. Werner Winter in *U-103,* who refueled from the U-tanker *U-459,* sank a 6,000-ton British freighter in mid-Atlantic May 5. The same day, Hermann Rasch in *U-106* sank an 8,000-ton Canadian freighter. But after that it was all downhill. Patrolling offshore from Cape Hatteras to Florida, neither boat saw anything for days on end. Similarly, the third IXB, *U-107,* commanded by Harald Gelhaus, who arrived off Cape Hatteras a week later, saw nothing. All three U-boats felt the effect of the new Key West–Norfolk–Key West convoy system.

The absence of East Coast traffic and the great successes of Folkers, Schacht, and Würdemann in the Yucatan Channel and the Gulf of Mexico prompted Dönitz to shift these three Type IXBs to those areas. To do so, it was necessary to arrange for Rasch's *U-106* and Gelhaus's *U-107* to be refueled homebound by *U-459,* which was to make a rapid turnaround in France.

Winter in *U-103* and Rasch in *U-106* led the way. Winter went south through the Windward Passage to replace Folkers in the southern approaches to the Yucatan Channel; Rasch went west through the Straits of Florida to replace Schacht and Würdemann in the Gulf of Mexico. As related, at this same time four Type VIIs entered the Caribbean Sea and von Mannstein in the Type VII *U-753* also patrolled in the Gulf of Mexico off the mouth of the Mississippi River.

Both *U-103* and *U-106* found good hunting. Patrolling south of the Yucatan Channel, May 17 to May 28, Winter in *U-103* sank eight ships for 36,200 tons, bringing his bag on this patrol to nine ships for 42,200 tons. His victims included two American tankers: *Sam Q. Brown,* 6,600 tons, and *New Jersey,* 6,400 tons. Homer Hickam wrote that after sinking the 5,000-ton American freighter *Ogontz,* Winter apologized to her captain ("Sorry . . . but this is war"), personally medicated one survivor, and directed that the lifeboats be stocked with cigarettes and food.

Patrolling north of the Yucatan Channel in the Gulf of Mexico for an equal number of days, May 21 to June 1, Rasch in *U-106* missed a huge whale-factory ship with two torpedoes but sank four ships for 21,200 tons and damaged a 4,600-ton American freighter, bringing his sinkings on this patrol to five ships for 29,000 tons. His victims also included two tankers, the Mexican *Faja de Oro,* 6,100 tons, and the American *Carabulle,* 5,000 tons, sunk by 193 rounds from his 4.1" deck gun and two torpedoes. Twenty-two of forty crew members on *Carabulle* perished. Homebound, both *U-103* and *U-106* refueled as planned from *U-459,* which sailed on her second resupply mission June 6 after three weeks of voyage repairs. Counting past claims and sinkings, Winter qualified for a *Ritterkreuz,* which was awarded while he was still at sea.* Upon his return to France, he left the boat to command Combat Flotilla 1.

Lagging behind his sister ships, Gelhaus in *U-107* went south into the Caribbean via the Windward Passage on May 29. That night he sank a 2,600-ton British freighter, then proceeded to the area south of the Yucatan Channel, replacing Winter in *U-103.* In the ensuing ten days, June 1 to June 10, he sank four freighters for 14,200 tons. Homebound, in the mid-Atlantic, he sank the impressive 10,000-ton Dutch freighter *Jagersfontein,* bringing his bag to six freighters for 27,000 tons. Then he refueled from *U-459,* as planned.

In all, these three Type IXBs, *U-103, U-106,* and *U-107,* sank twenty ships for 98,300 tons on patrols of sixty-nine, seventy-six, and eighty-two days, respectively. These successes were directly attributable to the availability of *U-459* for refueling. Without refueling, none of these shorter-range IXBs could have carried out extended patrols in the Gulf of Mexico or the Yucatan Channel.

Altogether, the six Type IX captains who sailed in April (Folkers, Gelhaus, Rash, Schacht, Winter, Würdemann) sank forty-six ships (fourteen tankers) for 230,000 tons. This was an average of 7.7 ships for 38,333 tons per boat per patrol.

In response to this slaughter, Admiral King named the experienced U-boat

---

* At the time of the award, Winter's confirmed sinkings in three patrols were fifteen ships for 79,302 tons. Under Viktor Schütze and Winter, *U-103* had sunk forty-three confirmed ships for about 228,000 tons, ranking her, at that time, the third most successful U-boat after *U-48* and *U-99.*

hunter James L. Kauffman, who had been Commander of Naval Forces, Iceland, to replace Crenshaw. On June 17 Kauffman shifted the headquarters of the Gulf Sea Frontier from Key West to a more elaborate facility in Miami. At the same time, Hap Arnold directed First Air Force commander Follett Bradley to establish an ASW Gulf Task Force to serve under Kauffman's direction, with headquarters in Miami. Composed initially of twenty B-18 bombers and two squadrons of observation planes, the Gulf Task Force was activated about June 1. It was reinforced by eight B-17 bombers and two observation squadrons from Third Air Force training units in Florida and Louisiana, and by the Civil Air Patrol.

In her study of U-boats in the Gulf of Mexico,* Melanie Wiggins writes that in the wake of this May slaughter of shipping, local officials resorted to stern measures. Convinced of the truth of rumors that the U-boat skippers obtained help from "Axis aliens" living along the coast, American and Mexican authorities rounded up suspects and spirited them away (a story that needs further airing). Notwithstanding the Navy's doubts of its value and the dangers to motorists and truckers, on June 1 American officials dimmed out Galveston and other areas along the coastline.†

This slaughter in the gulf drew vigorous demands for better protection of shipping from oil companies, merchant seamen, and, behind the scenes, the British. Rising in defence of the Navy, Congressman Carl Vinson, Chairman of the House Naval Affairs Committee, declared on June 6 that American ASW forces had "passed growing pains" and were "well established and functioning effectively," and that his committee was fully confident that Axis submarines would be defeated. "Critics should remember," he said, "that the British have had three years [sic] experience in coping with the U-boat problem and that the British Isles [where the problem had been largely overcome] would fit comfortably into the Gulf of Mexico."

Four long-range Type IXs patrolled the southern Caribbean from Trinidad to the Panama Canal. Three of the four were directed to attack shipping off the canal, but when *B-dienst* predicted heavy tanker traffic off Trinidad, that mission was canceled. All four boats patrolled in the eastern Caribbean near Trinidad and the north coast of Venezuela.

The first to sail was Jürgen Wattenberg in the IXC *U-162,* who had been forced to abort his first patrol to the Americas with mechanical defects. At forty-two years of age, Wattenburg (crew of 1921) was the oldest active skipper of an attack boat in the Atlantic U-boat force. Earlier in the war he had served on the "pocket" battleship *Admiral Graf Spee,* but after she was scuttled, he had made his way back to Germany.

---

    * *Torpedoes in the Gulf* (1995).

    † On May 25, Mayor Fiorello La Guardia dimmed out New York City. By that time, there were very few U-boats in the area, operating too far offshore to take advantage of the glow, even if that were possible.

Perhaps eager to avenge the humiliating loss of that ship, Wattenburg conducted a notably aggressive patrol in *U-162*. In a nineteen-day period, April 30 to
May 18, he sank eight confirmed ships by torpedo and gun for 47,000 tons plus a
119-ton American sailing schooner, *Florence M. Douglas*. His sinkings included
four tankers.* One of his victims, the 6,700-ton Brazilian freighter *Parnahyba*,
moved the Brazilian government one step closer to a declaration of war against
Germany. The sailing schooner yielded three live pigs. The Germans ate two but
adopted the third, "Douglas," as a mascot, which they presented to flotilla commander Viktor Schütze when they reached France.

The return trip of *U-162* was also memorable. By the night of June 8, when Wattenburg reached the western fringes of the Bay of Biscay, RAF Coastal Command
ASW patrols were intense. One of these aircraft equipped with meter-wavelength
ASV radar caught *U-162* on the surface. Wattenburg crash-dived. The bombs or
depth charges caught the boat at 80 or 90 feet but did no serious damage. Still, it
was a new and disconcerting experience for the crew, another of the air attacks that
led to Dönitz's specific order of June 24 to cross the Bay of Biscay submerged.

The other three IXs arrived in the Trinidad area about the time Wattenburg in
U-162 was concluding his patrol. Two of the three skippers, Werner Hartenstein in
U-156 and Jürgen von Rosenstiel in *U-502*, had opened the U-boat war in the
Caribbean in February; the other, Adolf-Cornelius Piening in *U-155*, had made one
patrol to Cape Hatteras.

Piening in the IXC *U-155* hunted west of Trinidad toward the island of Los
Testigos, where the shipping was so dense that he and his crew scarcely slept.
Notwithstanding a double miss on a tanker, in seventeen days, May 14 to May 30,
he sank by torpedo seven confirmed ships for 33,000 tons and probably damaged
another. His victims included two tankers: the 8,100-ton British *San Victorio* (ben-
zine and paraffin) and the 7,800-ton Panamanian *Sylvan Arrow*. The loss of life on
San Victorio was brutal: Only one man of fifty-four survived. Intending to close
the coast of Venezuela to raid shipping with his deck gun, Piening was thwarted by
the failure of his gyrocompass. He returned directly to France without refueling, a
round trip of merely fifty-six days.

Werner Hartenstein in *U-156* had even better success in Atlantic waters east of
Trinidad. In a six-day period from May 13, he sank five freighters for 25,600 tons
and damaged the 8,000-ton British tanker *San Eliseo*. However, Hartenstein's rich
harvest was interrupted by a message from Dönitz assigning him to a special mission.

From press reports and other sources, Hitler had formed the incorrect impression that the United States intended to invade and capture the Vichy island of Martinique and the naval vessels there, including the old aircraft carrier *Béarn*. Unable
to persuade the Vichy government to scuttle the warships, and unaware that pressure from Washington already had persuaded the Vichy French to immobilize
them, Hitler directed Raeder to send U-boats to Martinique to thwart an invasion

---

* The American *Esso Houston*, 7,700 tons, and three British, *Athelempress*, 8,900 tons; *British
Colony*, 6,900 tons; *Beth*, 6,900 tons.

and/or to destroy any Vichy warships—*Béarn* in particular—which might attempt to leave the harbor to join the Free French Navy serving with Allied naval forces.

Inasmuch as Hartenstein in *U-156* had earlier sneaked into Fort-de-France (to land an injured officer) and fortuitously had brought along updated charts of Martinique, Dönitz assigned him to lead the mission. He was reinforced by one other boat, *U-69*, a Type VII commanded by Ulrich Gräf, who had earlier refueled from *U-459* and come south to the Caribbean.

Hartenstein and Gräf took up stations off Martinique on May 20. The next day Hartenstein sank a 1,700-ton Dominican freighter and Gräf sank a 1,900-ton Canadian freighter. Upon receiving the sinking reports, Dönitz reminded the skippers tartly that their "main task" was to attack American warships or Vichy warships leaving Fort-de-France. Four days later, May 25, Hartenstein hit the four-stack American destroyer *Blakeley*. The blast blew off sixty feet of her bow, killing six and wounding twenty-one crewmen. Astonishingly, *Blakeley* managed to limp into Fort-de-France. Dönitz denied a request from Hartenstein to penetrate the harbor to finish off the destroyer.*

The hit on *Blakeley* caused uproars in Washington and Vichy. Perhaps as a result, the Vichy French government disclosed to Berlin that its warships at Martinique had been immobilized and posed no threat to either the Allies or the Axis. Even so, Hartenstein and Gräf remained off the island for another week. During that time Hartenstein sank two more ships, including the 6,000-ton Brazilian *Alagrete*, but he paid a heavy price. An American Catalina, apparently equipped with meter-wavelength ASV radar, found and bombed *U-156*. The blast cracked two main ballast tanks and a fuel ballast tank and knocked out all the hydrophone gear. Reporting this mishap, Hartenstein aborted the patrol and complained of the nearly unendurable tropical heat, made all the worse because the constant pressure of American ASW forces had forced him to remain submerged 121 hours out of 168 hours during the previous seven days.

In the meantime, the fourth Type IX in the southern Caribbean, *U-502*, commanded by Jürgen von Rosenstiel, had been patrolling farther westward, near the islands of Curaçao and Aruba, where she had done well on her first Caribbean patrol. This time the hunting was poor. In two weeks von Rosenstiel sank but one ship, the 5,000-ton Brazilian *Goncalves Dias*. In early June, however, when Dönitz shifted *U-502* easterly to the Trinidad area, her successes improved dramatically. In the two-week period, June 2 to June 15, von Rosenstiel sank six confirmed ships for 31,300 tons, bringing his score for the patrol to an impressive eight ships for 41,200 tons. His victims included two American tankers: *M. F. Elliott*, 6,900 tons, and *F. K. Lane*, 6,600 tons.

Upon departing Martinique, Hartenstein in *U-156* teamed up with von Rosenstiel in *U-502* for the return voyage to France. On June 22 Hartenstein, who had conducted a largely stationary patrol, transferred fuel oil to von Rosenstiel, who

---

* An American ship towed *Blakeley* to the nearby island of St. Lucia, where Washington had established air and naval bases. *Blakeley* was fitted with a new bow and returned to service in September 1942.

had roamed considerably. The following day, von Rosenstiel in *U-502* sighted the 4,600-ton British freighter *Willimantic,* sailing alone, but he had neither torpedoes nor deck gun ammunition. Responding to the sighting report, Hartenstein in *U-156* found and sank *Willimantic* by gun and took her captain prisoner. This sinking raised Hartenstein's bag for the patrol to an even more impressive nine freighters and a sailing vessel sunk for 40,000 tons, plus damage to the 8,000-ton British tanker *San Eliseo* and the American destroyer *Blakeley.*

Hartenstein and Rosenstiel reached the western fringes of the Bay of Biscay in early July. The Wellingtons of Coastal Command Squadron 172, fitted with ASV radar and Leigh Lights, had been patrolling the bay for about one month. In the early hours of July 5, a Wellington, commanded by Pilot Officer Wiley B. Howell, an American serving in the RAF, picked up Rosenstiel's *U-502* and straddled her with four shallow-set 250-pound depth charges. Nothing more was ever heard from *U-502.* There were no survivors of this first successful sinking by a Leigh Light Wellington.

In all, the four IXs patrolling the southwest Atlantic and the Caribbean also achieved very good results. They sank thirty-four confirmed ships (eight tankers) for about 164,000 tons, an average of 8.5 ships for 41,000 tons per boat per patrol.

The last three of the thirteen IXs to sail in April drew a special mission. Operating loosely as a group, they were to attack Allied shipping in the area of the Brazilian island of Fernando de Noronha, 250 miles northeast of Natal, at the "bulge" in Brazil. These skippers were *Ritterkreuz holder* Ernst Bauer in *U-126,* Ulrich Heyse in *U-128,* and Albrecht Achilles in *U-161.* All had made prior patrols to the Americas. Each boat carried twenty-three torpedoes: fifteen electrics internally and eight airs in topside canisters.

While en route to this distant area, on May 11, Heyse in the IXC *U-128* came upon a large northbound convoy, Sierra Leone 109, composed of thirty-one ships guarded by only four escorts. The escorts picked up Heyse's contact report by Huff Duff, chased down the bearing, and drove him off and down. Three delivered depth-charge attacks. Two of the escorts, the sloops *Landguard* (ex-American Coast Guard cutter *Shoshone*) and *Hastings,* incurred "major engine defects" from their own depth-charge explosions. As a consequence, *Landguard* had to be taken in tow by a merchant ship, leaving only three escorts to protect the convoy.

The next day, May 12, Heyse brought up Bauer in *U-126* and Achilles in *U-161.* After dark, Heyse in *U-128* attacked, firing four bow torpedoes at two ships. He reported several hits, but only one vessel, the 3,500-ton British freighter *Denmark* (loaded with iron ore) went down. Exceptionally aggressive action by the escorts, including *Landguard,* who slipped her tow, held all three U-boats at bay. Under orders to conserve fuel and torpedoes for the special mission, the three boats did not press the attack on the convoy.

Arriving in the area of Fernando de Noronha, the task force could find no shipping. Therefore in early June Dönitz ordered the pack to rake northwesterly along the coast of South America to Trinidad. Cruising that area over the next thirty days, Bauer in *U-126* exceeded his earlier, spectacular patrol to the Windward Passage by sinking five confirmed ships for 41,500 tons and two sailing ships, plus damage to the 7,100-ton American tanker *Gulfbelle,* which fought back spiritedly with her guns. His sinkings included two Norwegian tankers: *Höegh Giant,* 11,000 tons, and *Leiv Eiriksson,* 10,000 tons. In an adjacent area, east of Trinidad, in the period from June 8 to 28, Heyse in *U-128* sank four more ships for 32,000 tons, and damaged the 5,700-ton American freighter *Steel Engineer.* His victims also included two Norwegian tankers: *South Africa,* 9,200 tons, and *Andrea Brövig,* 10,200 tons.* Achilles in *U-161* found the weather and the hunting poor. Near Trinidad, where he achieved fame on his first patrol, he found a convoy on June 14 but managed to sink only one 8,000-ton freighter, *Scottsburg,* and in return was rammed.†

After makeshift repairs, Achilles went west to the Panama Canal area, where he sank a 35-ton American sailing vessel, *Cheerio,* by gun and torpedoed a 3,300-ton freighter at dockside in Puerto Limon, Costa Rica. However, the freighter was later salvaged. Homebound, he attacked a military convoy and sank a ship loaded with important cargo. Also homebound, Bauer in *U-126* found a "heavily smoking" northbound convoy west of the Bay of Biscay, but Dönitz suspected it was a U-boat "trap" and refused Bauer permission to attack.

All three boats of this special task force refueled in July on the way back to France. Bauer in *U-126* arrived on July 22, having sunk seven confirmed ships (two tankers) for about 42,000 tons. Heyse in *U-128* arrived on July 25, having sunk five confirmed ships (two tankers) for about 36,000 tons. Achilles arrived on August 7, completing a record patrol of 102 days, during which he sank two confirmed freighters for 14,200 tons, and damaged another of 3,300 tons at dockside in Costa Rica.

The returns of the thirteen Type IXs sailing in April to the Gulf of Mexico and the Caribbean shattered all existing records. Including the sailing vessels, they sank ninety-five confirmed ships (twenty-six tankers) for 482,843 tons, an average of 7.3 ships of about 37,141 tons sunk per boat per patrol, which on average was seventy-six days. One Type IX—Rosenstiel's *U-502*—was lost in the Bay of Biscay. The "exchange rate" of these boats was thus ninety-five to one, a kill ratio never again achieved in the war.

Six of the thirteen Type IXs that sailed to the Americas refueled, including the lost *U-502.* These six patrolled for an average eighty-three days. The seven IXs that did not refuel patrolled for an average of seventy days. Thus refueling added an average of about thirteen days of patrolling for the six boats of this group. These six sank an average of 6.3 ships per boat per patrol. The seven boats that did not refuel sank an average of 8.1 ships per boat patrol.

---

* Onetime merchant seaman Heyse stated in a document for submission in defense of Dönitz at Nuremberg that he gave "dry bread and rum" to all the survivors of the Norwegian tanker *South Africa,* assisted survivors of the American freighter *Polybius* into lifeboats, and took aboard the captain of the American freighter *West Ira,* who later sent Heyse a Christmas card recalling his "nice time" on *U-128* during the voyage to France.

† The crew of *Scottsburg* was rescued by another American freighter, the 6,000-ton *Kahuku,* which, however, was sunk two days later by Bauer in *U-126.* Bauer rescued a twice-sunk *Scottsburg* survivor, Archie Gibbs. Four days later, Bauer put Gibbs on board a small Venezuelan vessel, which made port, and Gibbs had an amazing story to tell.

ALLIED OIL PROBLEMS MOUNT

The slaughter inflicted by the twenty-nine U-boats that sailed to the Americas in April was undeniably a spectacular German naval victory: 133 confirmed ships sunk (thirty-three tankers) for 641,100 gross tons and fourteen ships damaged (six tankers) for 81,000 gross tons. The number of the victims sunk or damaged was thus 147 ships (thirty-nine tankers) for 722,000 gross tons.

The great majority of these ships were sunk and damaged in the Gulf of Mexico and the Caribbean Sea or in the approaches to those areas in the western Atlantic. The German victory was made possible by a swift and adroit shift of U-boats from the United States East Coast to those two areas, which were not yet prepared for U-boat warfare. Had the Allies been able to read four-rotor naval Enigma on the U-boat net *Triton* (Shark), almost certainly they would have detected this shift as well as the refueling operations early enough to have taken special precautions and more effective ASW measures. For example, the destruction of the tanker *U-459* doubtless would have disrupted U-boat operations and spared many Allied ships in May and June.

In the five months, January 1 to June 1, 1942, the Germans and Italians sank 129 tankers in the Atlantic, Caribbean, and Gulf of Mexico. Of these, forty-nine were of American registry, thirty-seven were British, nineteen were Norwegian, and twelve were Panamanian. The other twelve were Canadian, Dutch, Venezuelan, Mexican, and Russian.

With the introduction of the Halifax–Boston–Halifax and Norfolk–Key West–Norfolk convoy systems, admirals King and Andrews had reduced tanker losses in the Eastern Sea Frontier to near zero (one loss in May; one in June). The difficult problem areas remained the Caribbean Sea and the Gulf of Mexico. King was not yet able to provide sufficient air and surface escorts to establish convoys between Trinidad and Key West and between the Texas and Louisiana oil ports and Key West.

Per plan, the British and Canadians established two convoy systems in the Caribbean Sea during May:

• A British route running between Aruba-Curaçao and Trinidad. One British group (B-5) of the Mid-Ocean Escort Force (MOEF) shifted from the North Atlantic run to the Caribbean to provide surface escort, reducing the MOEF from twelve to eleven groups: six British, four Canadian, and one American.* American aircraft provided additional cover; the British ordered Coastal Command Squadron 53 (twenty Hudsons) to Trinidad. As related, from Trinidad British tankers sailed to Freetown, Sierra Leone, unescorted, thence in convoy to the British Isles.

• A Canadian route running between Trinidad and Halifax via Bermuda.

---

* This last American MOEF, A-3, was usually composed of two of the five Atlantic-based *Treasury*-class Coast Guard cutters (*Campbell, Ingham, Spencer, Bibb,* or *Duane*) and up to six Canadian corvettes.

Four (later six) Canadian corvettes shifted from the MOEF to provide surface escort. American aircraft on Trinidad and Bermuda furnished additional cover. Canadian warships of the Western Local Escort Force (WLEF) escorted the tankers on the trip from Halifax to Portland, Maine, the Atlantic terminus of a pipeline to refineries in Montreal, which had come into operation in November 1941.

One reason that King was unable to establish American convoy routes in the Caribbean and Gulf of Mexico in May was the failure of President Roosevelt's much-touted 110-foot SC building program ("Sixty Ships in Sixty Days") to live up to its billing. By May 1, this program had encountered many difficulties and was embarrassingly behind schedule. So was the 175-foot PC building program; from January 1 to May 1, only a dozen PCs were completed and half of these were still in workup.* As one consequence, on May 21, Admiral King asked Admiral Pound for the loan of "fifteen or twenty corvettes" from the British "Home Station" so that he could initiate American convoys in the Gulf of Mexico and Caribbean. Pound replied that the British had no corvettes on the "Home Station"; however, he was willing to reduce MOEF groups from eleven to ten to meet this request, provided the Admiralty could be assured that American and Canadian escort groups "worked as hard" as British groups. Believing that a further reduction in MOEF groups would almost certainly invite a renewal of intense U-boat attacks on the North Atlantic run, King let the matter rest, but not happily.

In the first week of June, as the great Battle of Midway loomed, King convened yet another Convoy Conference in Washington to deal with the Caribbean and Gulf of Mexico shipping crisis. The conferees decided that a proposed convoy system, Guantánamo Bay–New York–Guantánamo Bay,† be postponed in favor of a temporary Key West–Trinidad–Key West system to be initiated on July 1. In addition, a temporary Key West–Panama–Key West system and a Gulf of Mexico system were to follow as soon as possible. The British agreed to retain the British MOEF group B-5 in the Caribbean to facilitate the start-up of these convoys.

At this time King renewed the Navy's long-standing request for destroyer escorts (DEs). On June 15, he wrote Roosevelt that "We need modified DEs [i.e., the American, not the British version] at the earliest possible moment. If we cannot get them soon," King continued, "it will be necessary to put some important [shipping] routes 'out of bounds' in order to prevent prohibitive losses." However, at that time Roosevelt believed that the emergency invasion of France (Sledgehammer) in late summer of 1942 was still a strong possibility and the construction of landing craft of various types remained priority number one for several more months.

In addition to this frustrating situation, King also had to wage continuous bureaucratic warfare with the Army and Army Air Forces over methods of employing land-based aircraft for ASW purposes.

In compliance with the agreement of March 26 between the Army and Navy,

---

*   See Appendix 14.
†   Guantánamo Bay is an American naval base and anchorage on the eastern extremity of Cuba, facing the Windward Passage.

the Army Air Forces had parceled out units of the 1st Bomber Command to the Eastern and Gulf Sea Frontiers and had placed its Antilles Air Task Force under control of the Caribbean Sea Frontier. The several sea frontier commanders, Andrews, Kauffman, and Hoover, had assigned these land-based Army aircraft to two principal tasks: air escort for convoys and/or important ships sailing alone, and search patrols in likely U-boat operating areas.

Stimson and Marshall of the Army and Hap Arnold of the Army Air Forces were not in agreement with the Navy's disposition and utilization of its land-based aircraft. As Arnold's airmen saw it, the units of the 1st Bomber Command had been "chopped up" and meted out to the various sea frontiers for permanent duty. Aircraft assigned to one sea frontier were not allowed to cross boundaries into another sea frontier. The rotation of aircraft and crews from ASW patrols to training in navigation and high-level bombing, and vice versa, had not worked well. The aircrews hated area and convoy patrols. It was dull, *defensive,* and very difficult work, even with meter-wavelength ASV radar, and the rewards were few.

In five months of ASW operations, Hap Arnold and the air staff had settled on a firm doctrine to counter U-boats. Rather than decentralizing and delegating control of air units to the various sea frontiers as King insisted, Arnold and the airmen urged creation of a centralized single command in control of highly mobile air units which, in theory, could be shifted rapidly from frontier to frontier as the situation required. In place of *defensive* patrolling and escorting, the centralized command was to devote its resources principally to *offensive* ASW operations, pouncing upon a reported U-boat or group of U-boats with well-trained and equipped "hunter-killer" air units, capable of mounting persistent and prolonged chases.

In furtherance of this doctrine, on May 20 the War Department directed Hap Arnold to reorganize the 1st Bomber Command. "The reorganization should be of a character," the directive specified, "that will fulfill the special requirements of antisubmarine and Allied air operations, in consonance with the Army responsibility in operating in support of, or in lieu of naval forces for protection of shipping." Arnold was to provide 1st Bomber Command with every available twin-engine B-18 (medium) bomber in the United States and to equip these with centimetric-wavelength ASV radar as fast as the sets became available and with proper depth-charge and bomb racks for ASW. As the planes were so equipped, they were to be organized into "Submarine Destroyer Squadrons," to operate from a network of new bases on the East and Gulf Coasts, employing tactics recommended by the ASW R&D group at Langley Field, and linked by first-class communication.

When Secretary of War Stimson informed Secretary of the Navy Knox and Admiral King of the Army Air Forces doctrine and reorganization plans for the 1st Bomber Command, the navalists were lukewarm and cautious. In a formal response that left Stimson almost incredulous, King welcomed the assignment of 1st Bomber Command exclusively to an ASW role but disapproved the idea of a centralized ASW command, even if the commander was to be an admiral. He recommended against any hurried and radical command-and-control changes that might interfere with ongoing operations.

• • •

The loss of the 129 Allied tankers deeply dismayed and disturbed the British. It appeared that British petroleum stockpiles—or oil reserves—might fall to an unacceptable level. The situation had been worsened by the need to transfer about fifty British tankers to the Indian Ocean to support British operations there and in the Mediterranean Basin, and by the decision to route British-bound tankers the longer way from Trinidad east to Freetown, thence north in the slow Sierra Leone convoys.

To prevent a dangerous depletion of oil reserves, on May 2 the British petitioned the Americans for the "loan" (i.e., gift) of the equivalent of seventy tankers of 10,000 deadweight tons, a total of 700,000 deadweight tons. President Roosevelt "dramatically and almost unexpectedly" (as London put it) honored this request, despite America's own tanker losses and the shortage of such vessels in the Pacific. The oil czar, Harold Ickes, notified the British on May 14 that the request (known as "Red Gap") was to be met in the "next four weeks." It was not only met, but exceeded substantially: a total of 854,000 deadweight tons, 170,000 for Canada and 684,000 for the United Kingdom.

This second generous gift of oil tankers to Britain was made possible by the following factors:

• The dramatic rise in deliveries of oil from Texas to the northeast United States by railroad tank cars. In January 1942, the oil industry delivered about 100,000 barrels a day to that area by rail. By June 1942, rail deliveries had risen to about 726,000 barrels a day.

• The start-up of the Plantation Pipeline. Running from Baton Rouge via Bremen, Georgia, to Greensboro, North Carolina, this line delivered about 50,000 barrels a day. From Greensboro, the oil moved further northeast by rail and barge. By June 1942, this pipeline, and those in the upper Midwest, delivered about 125,000 barrels of oil per day to the Northeast.*

• The initiation of gasoline rationing in the northeast United States on May 15, 1942.

• Far more efficient use of all means of conveying oil to the Northeast in 1942.

• Production of new tankers by Jerry Land's Maritime Commission.

• The astonishingly rapid reconversion of many oil-burning industrial plants to coal-burning or to natural gas.

Nor was that all. To prevent a dangerous fall in oil reserves, on August 1, London again petitioned Washington for tanker assistance. This time (the "Blue Gap") the British requested the equivalent of fifty-four tankers of 10,000 deadweight tons, a total of 540,000 more deadweight tons. President Roosevelt promptly met this request as well. Within thirty days—by September 1—oil czar Ickes had allocated to the British the equivalent of forty more tankers, or a total of 400,000 dead-

---

* The total "overland" deliveries of oil rose nearly fivefold from 203,000 barrels a day in January 1942 to 956,000 barrels a day in June 1942. In the same period, deliveries by ocean tankers fell sixfold, from 1.3 million barrels a day to 226,000 barrels a day.

weight tons. The rest of the British request was fulfilled in the months of October and November.

The total tanker assistance by the Americans to the British in 1942 (Red and Blue Gaps) was thus more than 124 "notional tankers" of 10,000 deadweight tons, or 1.24 million deadweight tons. In response to the first assist (Red Gap) Churchill cabled Roosevelt on May 27:

> I must express my gratitude for your allocation of 70 tankers to build up United Kingdom stocks of oil. Without this help our stocks would have fallen to a danger-ous level by the end of the year. This action is the more generous considering recent heavy American tanker losses and the sacrifices involved in releasing so many ships.

THE ARGONAUT CONFERENCE

The Allied shipping situation, which governed all plans, together with the need to clarify and coordinate global strategy, war production programs, and other matters, persuaded Churchill to suggest a second meeting with Roosevelt in Washington. Roosevelt approved the conference, designated Argonaut, and not a minute too soon.

By that time—June 1942—Hitler's vast mechanized armies were surging out of the Ukraine toward the Caucasus Mountains and the rich oil fields at Baku on the Caspian Sea and southeast toward Stalingrad on the Volga River. Anticipating a renewed German attack on Moscow, Stalin had concentrated his forces in the cen-ter. As a consequence Red armies on the south and southeastern fronts were hard-pressed to resist the German advance. Personally directing this massive offensive, Hitler moved his command post to a site in the Ukraine.

German successes in the Mediterranean Basin provided additional impetus for this third round of Roosevelt-Churchill talks. Near Tobruk, on June 12–13, Erwin Rommel's *Afrika Korps* delivered the British Eighth Army what appeared to be a decisive blow, setting the stage for the capture of Tobruk and possibly the whole of Egypt. At about the same time, June 13–16, the *Luftwaffe*—and some Italian naval units—decisively repulsed an all-out British attempt to reinforce Malta by simulta-neously sailing heavily escorted convoys east from Gibraltar and west from Alexandria. Only two out of the seventeen supply ships in the two convoys got through; the rest were sunk or turned back. In the aftermath of these British setbacks on land and sea, the Royal Navy abandoned its major base at Alexan-dria, withdrawing eastward to Haifa, Palestine, and Beirut, Lebanon.

Worse yet was a disturbing forecast from Rodger Winn in the Admiralty's U-boat Tracking Room. On June 1, Winn estimated that the Germans had built 355 U-boats to then, of which only seventy-five were positively known to have been sunk. That left a net force of about 280 to 285 commissioned U-boats on June 1.*

---

* Those at the fronts deployed, by Winn's guesstimates, as follows: 125 in the Atlantic force, 35 in the Mediterranean force, 15 in the Arctic force, the rest in Germany. The actual deployment was 86 in the Atlantic force, 21 in the Mediterranean, and 21 in the Arctic.

Furthermore, Winn estimated, the Germans were building new U-boats at the rate of "15–25 per month." If the forecast proved accurate, it meant the net force was to grow to at least 400 U-boats by January 1, 1943.

Many responsible American officials believed that disturbing forecast to be greatly understated, among them Adolphus Andrews, commander of the Eastern Sea Frontier. Analyzing the Winn paper, his diarist wrote in June that the number of surviving U-boats might be not 280 or 285 but as many as 325, of which not 125 but as many as 140 were assigned to the Atlantic force. Doubtless reflecting the views of Andrews, the diarist went on to predict:

> At the present rate of building the Germans will have over 500 submarines by January 1, 1943. It is probable that most of the new construction will ultimately be used against us in the Atlantic. When it is remembered that in the first six months of the war [i.e., war with the United States] an average of 100 submarines available to operate in the Atlantic have caused very large losses, doubling or tripling of this number presents a problem of great seriousness, particularly when it is also remembered that sinkings of U-boats [by the Allies] have been so small as to be almost negligible during the same period. U-boat crews which were green in March are now hardened veterans [and] will form the working nucleus of the larger fleet to be at sea six months from now.
>
> The solution of this problem lies primarily in developing the means to *destroy* submarines and not so much in their location and detection (where most of our research endeavor has been placed to date). Though attack, capture and holding of the Bay of Biscay coast would be a dangerous and costly operation, it may be more costly to permit the enemy to use and expand activities from these bases.

Amid great secrecy, Churchill left the British Isles June 17 in a Boeing Flying Clipper. Twenty-six and a half hours later, the huge flying boat landed on the Potomac River in Washington. There Churchill transferred to a smaller aircraft and flew to the President's home in Hyde Park, New York, where Roosevelt, Churchill, and Harry Hopkins commenced strategy talks. Churchill stressed these points:

• The "heavy sinkings" of merchant ships by U-boats in American waters constituted the "greatest and most immediate danger" to the Allies. He urged Roosevelt to do everything possible to hasten the extension of the convoy network into the Gulf of Mexico and the Caribbean.

• If mounted in early September 1942, as planned, Sledgehammer was "certain to lead to disaster." No responsible British military authority favored it.

• Rather than Sledgehammer, the Allies should reconsider Gymnast, the postponed Allied invasion of French Northwest Africa, and Jupiter, an Allied occupation of extreme northern Norway to provide land-based flank protection for Murmansk convoys.

• British scientists had made substantial (paper) progress on an atomic bomb, disguised in the British Isles for security reasons as R&D on "Tube Alloys." The British and Americans should "at once pool all our information, work together on equal terms, and share the results."

In Washington at this time, June 19, the normally cool and reserved Army Chief of Staff, George Marshall, blasted King with a memo that has served King's critics well. The intent and timing of this memo, the content of which King knew as well as or better than Marshall, is not at all clear. Listing the heavy Allied shipping losses in four categories, Marshall wrote:

> The losses by submarines off our Atlantic seaboard and in the Caribbean now threaten our entire war effort. . . . We are all aware of the limited number of escort craft available, but has every conceivable improvised means been brought to bear on this situation? I am fearful that another month or two of this [loss rate] will so cripple our means of transport that we will be unable to bring sufficient men and planes to bear against the enemy in critical theaters to exercise a determining influence in the war.

Marshall's memo drew from King on June 21 a remarkably calm and lengthy review of the steps already taken to combat the U-boat, together with King's views on what was required for the future. "Though we are still suffering heavy losses outside the east convoy zone," King wrote, "the situation is not hopeless." He stressed these points:

• The U-boat threat could only be eliminated completely by "wiping out the German building yards and bases" with heavy bomber attacks. This was a matter which King had been "pressing with the British, so far with only moderate success."

• Meanwhile, if all shipping could be brought under defensive escort and air cover, "our losses will be reduced to an acceptable figure." King went on to emphasize his unwavering view that "escort is not just *one* way of handling the submarine menace; it is the *only* way that gives any promise of success."* Hence, "we must get every ship that sails the seas under constant close protection."

• Alluding to the Army Air Forces' doctrine of offensive "hunter-killer" air patrols to the exclusion of defensive convoy escort, King again threw cold water on that approach. "The so-called patrol and hunting operations have time and again proved futile," he wrote. The only efficient way to kill U-boats at sea was to attack "continuously and relentlessly" those U-boats that had been drawn to the convoys. However, this was a doctrine that required enormous numbers of radar-equipped, well-trained surface escorts and land- and carrier-based aircraft, not yet in sight, let alone in hand.

King concluded his memo by asking Marshall for assistance in five categories:

• Build up, "as soon as practicable," a force of about 1,000 radar-equipped Army aircraft to patrol the projected 7,000 miles of convoy lanes in the Eastern, Gulf, Caribbean, and Panama Sea Frontiers. This airpower was not to be "a temporary measure pending augmentation" of naval surface forces but rather "a permanent arrangement" to "protect our shipping properly."

• Reduce requests for "special convoys" to rush Army troops to "the Caribbean and other local danger zones" until such time as surface escorts were

---

* King's italics.

plentiful. The protection provided for "special convoys" diminished the protection available for "shipping in general."

• Reduce unescorted cargo-ship movements, and insist that such ships travel in established convoys.

• Reduce the growing requirements for the protection of important coastal structures, such as oil refineries, from U-boat gun bombardments, which were "not formidable," only "occasional," and easily thwarted.

• Examine every "new project with respect to its effect on our antisubmarine effort." Any such military proposal or operation that "retards the output of antisubmarine vessels or involves the diversion of vessels engaged in protection of merchant shipping will unduly aggravate the present bad situation."

President Roosevelt, Churchill, and Hopkins left Hyde Park for Washington via presidential train on the evening of June 20. Upon arrival at the White House the next day, they confronted shocking news: Some 33,000 seasoned British and Commonwealth troops had surrendered Tobruk to an Axis force of about half that number. Churchill wrote later: "This was one of the heaviest blows I can recall during the war."

The American and British delegations that assembled for the Argonaut conference in Washington met off and on from June 21 to June 27. The shipping crisis and the military setback in North Africa dominated all else.

Under relentless pressure from Churchill and his advisers, as well as from Stimson, Marshall, and others in Washington, President Roosevelt again chastised Admiral King for the delays in initiating convoys. Reviewing the heavy losses of unescorted shipping in North American waters for the period May 17 to June 27, Roosevelt wrote King privately:

> One hundred and eighteen ships sailing independently were lost as against twenty under escort. I realize the problem of making up escorts for convoys but about three months have elapsed since we undertook it. I also realize that strict observance of convoy rules will slow up voyages of many ships but, frankly, I think it has taken an unconscionable time to get things going, and further, I do not think that we are utilizing a large number of escort vessels which could be used, especially in the Summer time. We must speed things up and we must use the available tools even though they are not just what we would like to have.

Apart from ignoring the delays in his emergency SC program ("Sixty Ships in Sixty Days") and the PC program, and the low priority granted to destroyer escort construction, this memo reflected Roosevelt's wrongheaded notion that small, cheap, mass-produced vessels such as SCs, private fishing trawlers, and yachts could do the convoy escort job in American waters. It drew from King a prompt and remarkably restrained reply, which stressed tactfully the impracticality of Roosevelt's obsession with small-boat escorts.

"I am in entire accord with your view as to the advantages of escorted convoys," King wrote Roosevelt. "I have established convoy systems, beginning with the most dangerous areas, as acquisition of escort vessels permitted. I have used vessels of every type and size that can keep up with the ships they guard. I have accepted the smallest escorts that give promise of a reasonable degree of protection."

After listing the various convoy systems in place, King wrote that "these convoys are a step in the right direction" but that the Allies "are still at a disadvantage":

• Escorts are unduly weak, consisting of too large a proportion of small craft with little fighting power.

• Only medium-speed (nominally 10-knot) convoys are at present possible. Fifteen-knot and faster ships normally proceed independently. Very slow ships are, where possible, moved from port to port in daylight with a token escort of small craft.

• There are no regular convoys at present to Gulf of Mexico ports, but it is expected that 83-foot Coast Guard cutters will become available in the near future for this service.

• Small craft now used in the Caribbean frequently cannot keep up with convoys against the trade winds.

• A dangerous concentration of unprotected shipping exists in the open sea beyond Trinidad.

• The smaller craft now extensively used in escort service will not stand winter weather in the North Atlantic.

King concluded:

> My goal—and I believe yours also—is to get every ship under escort. For this purpose we (the United States and Great Britain) need a very large number— roughly 1,000—sea-going escort vessels of DE [destroyer escort] or corvette type. I am doing my best to get them quickly.

The military setback in North Africa was of great concern to the delegates at the Argonaut conference. To prevent a rout of the British Eighth Army, the loss of Egypt and the Suez Canal, and a possible linkup of German forces in the Middle East, the Americans offered the following emergency forces:

• The American 2nd Armored Division, commanded by George S. Patton, Jr., which was training in a California desert. In response to a summons from Marshall, Patton arrived in Washington on June 22 to draw plans for the movement. After several days of study, Patton recommended that it would be more appropriate to send *two* American divisions to North Africa. In any case, the scheme died aborning owing to the lack of shipping and other factors.

• Three hundred new American Sherman tanks, right off the assembly line, as well as 100 new 105mm self-propelled antitank guns. The tanks, less engines, were loaded into fast cargo ships. The 300 tank engines were loaded into a single ship, the 6,200-ton American *Fairport*. This special fast military convoy, AS 4, sailed hurriedly from New York on July 13, escorted by two cruisers and seven destroyers.

As related, while homebound, a Type IX of the April group, *U-161,* commanded by Albrecht Achilles, came upon this important special convoy on July 16. Achilles boldly set up on and shot at two of the nine cargo ships. As Churchill recalled in his war memoir, the torpedoes hit the *Fairport,* which sank with all the tank engines. Two modern destroyers, *Kearny* and *Wilkes,* jumped on *U-161* and depth-charged and hunted her for nine hours. They claimed a kill, but it was not so. Achilles reported that the *U-161* incurred "considerable damage," but neither he nor Dönitz was aware of the vital cargo in the holds of the *Fairport.*

Upon learning of the loss of the *Fairport,* Churchill wrote in his memoir, Roosevelt directed immediately that 300 more engines for the Shermans be loaded and sent to North Africa. This "fast ship" actually overtook the convoy. The first ships of the convoy, Churchill continued, reached Port Said on September 2 with 193 Shermans and twenty-eight 105mm self-propelled antitank guns. The rest of the ships arrived September 5. The actual number of weapons delivered to Port Said was 317 Sherman tanks and ninety-four 105mm antitank guns.

• Six American Army Air Forces groups: three fighter, one medium bomber, and one heavy bomber (B-24s). One fighter group, the 57th, composed of seventy P-40s, was rushed overseas on the aircraft carrier *Ranger.* Departing the States on July 1, she was escorted by Task Force 22: the heavy cruiser *Augusta,* the brand-new light cruiser *Juneau,* and six destroyers. As before, *Ranger* launched these planes while at sea off the Gold Coast (on July 19). They flew to Accra, Ghana, thence to Egypt.

The rest of these air groups plus 4,000 Army Air Forces ground personnel began moving to North Africa by ship or other means in July. In addition, Roosevelt diverted to North Africa forty A-20 medium bombers, which had been en route to the Soviet Union, plus a special group of twenty-five B-24s en route to China* and transferred the twenty-four heavy bombers of the Tenth Air Force from India to Egypt.

Churchill boarded a Boeing Flying Clipper at Baltimore on June 25 for the return trip to the British Isles. Fortunately for Britain, Erwin Rommel's *Afrika Korps* ran low on gasoline, ammunition, and other supplies, and could not advance into Egypt beyond El Alamein. In subsequent weeks, Churchill swept a broom through the top echelons of his Middle East forces, appointing Harold Alexander as Commander in Chief, and Bernard Law Montgomery as commanding general of the Eighth Army. These new generals were to benefit spectacularly from the arrival in North Africa of the American Sherman tanks, antitank guns, and airpower, and by new breaks into German Army Enigma.

Notwithstanding the Argonaut talks, American and British global war planners were still at sixes and sevens. In view of the German advances in the Soviet Union, Marshall still wanted to carry out Sledgehammer in 1942. Contrarily, the British

---

* This group, codenamed Halpro, bombed the Ploesti oil fields, becoming the first Army Air Forces planes to strike a strategic target in Europe.

still opposed Sledgehammer and because of the threat Rommel posed to Egypt and the Middle East, urged Gymnast (renamed Torch), the invasion of Vichy French Algeria and Morocco.

To resolve this impasse, Roosevelt, who favored Torch, sent King and Marshall, who did not, to London to confer with Churchill, Harry Hopkins, and Dwight Eisenhower, who had only just arrived to command all American forces in Europe. King and Marshall departed by air on July 16 and arrived in London the next day. The upshot of these talks was that at British insistence, Sledgehammer was finally abandoned and Torch took its place. It was to be staged when the shipping situation permitted, hopefully in October.

GROUP *HECHT*

The arrival in France of four new Type IXs and exceptionally efficient refit operations at the French bases enabled Dönitz to order twenty-one boats to American waters in May: twelve Type VIIs and nine Type IXs. Notwithstanding increasing risks and declining returns, all the Type VIIs and one older, short-range IXB, *U-124,* were directed to patrol the United States East Coast waters. The eight other longer-range IXs were to be evenly divided between the Gulf of Mexico and the Caribbean. The May boats were to be supported by the tanker *U-459* and by the big XB minelayer, *U-116,* which resailed May 16 after twelve days in port for battle-damage repairs.

By this time codebreakers at *B-dienst* had developed what the OKM diarist characterized as "excellent" information on the routes and sailing dates of North Atlantic convoys. Noting that the Type IXB *U-124* and six Type VIIs were to sail for the Americas at about the same time in early May,* Dönitz ordered them to form a group and rake the North Atlantic convoy routes as they proceeded westward. If they found and attacked a convoy, several purposes could be served. The battle would toughen green U-boat crews, ferret out new Allied detection gear and weaponry, and—hopefully—discourage further transfer of ASW forces from the North Atlantic run to the Caribbean. Should a battle develop, the big XB minelayer *U-116* was to sail in exclusive support of the group. After replenishment from *U-116,* the boats were to proceed to American waters.

Designated group *Hecht,* the seven boats sailed from French bases May 3 to May 7. Two were commanded by young *Ritterkreuz* holders: Otto Ites in the Type VII *U-94,* and Johann Mohr in the Type IXB *U-124.* Of the other five boats, three were experienced and two were green. Already at sea, vainly seeking her blockade runner, the famous *U-96,* commanded by a new skipper, Hans-Jürgen Hellriegel, age twenty-four, onetime first watch officer to Engelbert Endrass, joined group *Hecht* west of the Bay of Biscay, making a total of eight U-boats.

Some of the *Hecht* boats were fitted with a new defensive device designed to

---

* Plus *U-96,* which had sailed in late April to a nearby area to escort the blockade runner *Portland* into France, but could not find her.

confuse enemy sonar. Known as *Bolde* (probably derived from *kobold,* German for goblin or deceiving spirit), it was a perforated or degradable canister filled with calcium hydride that was fired from an internal tube called a *Pillenwerfer* (pill thrower) and floated at a depth of about 100 feet. When saltwater mixed with the calcium hydride, it generated a great mass of hydrogen bubbles for about six minutes. The bubbles reflected sonar pulses, giving off an echo that, to an inexperienced sonar operator, sounded like a submarine hull. The hope was that by laying a trail of *Boldes* between it and a pursuing enemy, a U-boat might elude sonar.*

Acting on the "excellent" intelligence on Allied convoys generated by *B-dienst,* group *Hecht* raked westward along specific sea-lanes. In the early hours of May 11, one of the experienced boats, *U-569,* commanded by Hans Peter Hinsch, made contact with a convoy, Outbound North (Slow) 92, in mid-Atlantic. It was escorted by the American escort group A-3. The group was composed of the big *Treasury*-class Coast Guard cutter *Spencer,* the modern (1940) American destroyer *Gleaves,* and four Canadian corvettes, one of which, *Bittersweet,* was equipped with Type 271 centimetric-wavelength radar. A rescue ship, *Bury,* trailing the convoy, was fitted with Huff Duff.

Hinsch in *U-569* got off a contact report which brought up the two *Ritterkreuz* holders, Ites in *U-94* and Mohr in *U-124.* The rescue ship *Bury* DFed Hinsch's transmissions, but the American escort commander, John B. Heffernan (in *Gleaves*), failed to appreciate the full extent of the impending danger. That night Mohr easily penetrated the thin, unalert screen. In two separate, close attacks, he fired seven torpedoes at overlapping columns of ships. He claimed sinking five vessels for 19,000 tons and damage to one; postwar records credited him with sinking four freighters (three British, one Greek) for 21,800 tons. Coming in behind Mohr, Otto Ites sank one confirmed freighter for 5,600 tons, from which he captured the captain. The shadower, Hinsch in *U-569,* claimed one ship sunk but it could not be confirmed.

During the next day, May 12, six of the eight boats of group *Hecht* made contact with the convoy. The three new arrivals were commanded by green skippers on first patrols: Hellriegel in the veteran *U-96,* Horst Dieterichs, age thirty, in the new *U-406,* and Heinrich Müller-Edzards, age thirty-two, in the new *U-590.* Only one of the six boats had any luck. *Ritterkreuz* holder Otto Ites sank two more freighters for 8,900 tons. He approached the lifeboats of one sinking ship, the Swedish *Tolken,* to capture her captain, but gunners still on board the ship drove *U-94* off and under. Foul weather and poor visibility thwarted further attacks. Assessing the damage—seven confirmed ships sunk—the staff at Western Approaches severely criticized the performance of the American and Canadian escorts. The Canadian naval historian Marc Milner wrote in his book *North Atlantic Run* that as a result, the American escort commander, Heffernan, "was quietly moved to another command."

The easy success of *Hecht* against this unalert convoy and the miserable hunting off the United States East Coast in May persuaded Dönitz to change the plan.

---

* The Allies developed a similar device, known as a Submarine Bubble Target (SBT).

The XB minelayer *U-116* replenished the eight boats of *Hecht* with fuel, food, and torpedoes, but only two of the seven Type VIIs were authorized to proceed to America: Otto von Bülow's *U-404* and Ernst-August Rehwinkel's *U-578.* The other six boats of *Hecht,* commanded by three veteran and three green skippers, were to remain in the North Atlantic to exploit the information on Allied convoys coming from *B-dienst.*

The information from *B-dienst* was plentiful, but bad weather bedeviled *Hecht.* Nearly a month passed before the boats locked firmly onto another convoy. This was Outbound North (Slow) 100, escorted by the well-trained and experienced Canadian group C-1, which, however, had sailed minus one destroyer and one corvette (both in refit), leaving only five ships: the veteran Canadian destroyer *Assiniboine* and four corvettes, two British and two Free French. All five escorts were equipped with radar (four with Type 271) and the convoy rescue ship, *Gothland,* was fitted with Huff Duff. Additional protection was provided by the fighter-catapult ship, *Empire Ocean,* carrying a Hurricane fighter.

Mohr in *U-124* found and reported this convoy on June 8. After Hinsch in *U-569* made contact and took over as shadower, Mohr closed to attack, but the feisty, battlewise, radar-equipped corvettes blocked his approach. Undeterred, Mohr coolly shifted his attack to the escorts, firing two stern tubes at one "destroyer" and two bow tubes at another "destroyer." The stern torpedoes missed, but the bow torpedoes hit the British-built, Free French–manned corvette *Mimose,* which disintegrated in a ball of flames. The other four escorts counterattacked *U-124* and drove her off, thwarting Mohr's attack on the convoy itself. At first light the next day, *Assiniboine* found four survivors of *Mimose,* but no more.

By the afternoon of June 9, all six boats of group *Hecht* were in contact with the convoy, but new problems arose. The three new skippers (Hellriegel, Dieterichs, Müller-Edzards) reported defective engines, probably the result of the hard chase in heavy seas. Dönitz therefore ordered those three boats to withdraw, leaving only Ites in *U-94,* Mohr in *U-124,* and Hinsch in *U-569* to mount the second attack. Leading the assault that night, Ites sank two British freighters for 11,600 tons and Mohr sank one 4,100-ton British freighter. Later, Hinsch hit and stopped a straggler, the 4,500-ton British freighter, *Pontypridd.* Then he and Ites put her under with finishing shots, to share credit. Impenetrable fog saved the convoy from further attacks.

Numerous eastbound convoys eluded group *Hecht* in June. These included troopship convoy AT 16 from New York, combined with NA 10 from Halifax. This formation consisted in total of six troopships escorted by Task Force 35: the battleship *New York* and nine American destroyers. Three of the destroyers in this formation (*Eberle, Ericsson, Roe*) peeled off in Halifax on June 16 and escorted the four troopships of convoy NA 11 from there.

Following the battle with Outbound North (Slow) 100, the six boats of *Hecht* reversed course and combed convoy routes on the return to France, handicapped by Ites in *U-94,* who also developed engine problems. Ironically, on June 16, Ites found a big convoy, Outbound North (Slow) 102. Composed of sixty-three merchant ships, it was escorted by the American group A 3, which had a new commander, Paul R. Heineman. In view of the known presence of *Hecht,* A-3 had been beefed up to nine veteran, very alert ships: three big *Treasury*-class Coast Guard cutters, *Campbell, Duane,* and *Ingham,* the four-stack destroyer *Leary,* the Canadian destroyer *Restigouche,* and four Canadian corvettes. Most of the ships had radar; *Restigouche* had Huff Duff.

All six U-boats attempted to mount a loosely coordinated attack on convoy Outbound North (Slow) 102, but it failed. *Restigouche* DFed the assembly and subsequent chatter and alerted the escorts. The green skipper, Horst Dieterichs in *U-406,* fired a full salvo of five torpedoes at two "destroyers," but all missed and the "destroyers" ran him off. Other escorts blocked the approaches of Mohr in *U-124.* Still others caught and depth-charged Ites in *U-94* and Müller-Edzards in *U-590* for seven and nine hours, respectively. Lucky to have survived these merciless poundings, both boats limped to France with heavy damage, where they remained for forty-one and forty-seven days, respectively, under repair and training.

Mohr reported that the convoy had escaped in fog and that further pursuit was "hopeless." However, by chance, at dawn on June 18 he happened upon it again and unhesitatingly and audaciously mounted a lone surface attack in broad daylight, firing four bow torpedoes at three big freighters from long range. He claimed two sinkings and damage to the third ship, but postwar records credited only the sinking of the 5,600-ton American freighter *Seattle Spirit.* Ringing up on full speed, Mohr eluded the escorts and set a course for Lorient.

The six boats of group *Hecht* returned to France in the last week of June, during the height of Kerneval's intense investigation into the possibility that the Allies had miniaturized radar for aircraft and surface-ship use. Calling up Mohr on a new radio-telephone which scrambled his end of the conversations, Dönitz asked if Mohr had detected any sign that the Allies had shipboard radar. Mohr reported that he had been forced to take evasive action seven times during his patrol but had been directly run down and attacked by the escorts only once. He therefore concluded that the Allies had *not* yet installed radar on the escorts(!).

Including the *U-96,* which had sailed earlier, the six *Hecht* boats patrolled for an average of fifty-seven days. They attacked three Outbound North (Slow) convoys, 92, 100, and 102, sinking thirteen ships (including the corvette *Mimose*) for about 62,500 tons. The *Ritterkreuz* holders, Otto Ites in *U-94* and Johann Mohr in *U-124,* accounted for 92 percent of the sinkings. Mohr got seven ships for 32,500 tons; Ites got five ships for 25,500 tons. In addition, Ites and Hinsch in *U-569* shared credit for one 4,500-ton freighter. The three new skippers, Hellriegel, Dieterichs, and Müller-Edzards, sank no ships.

Although the young *Ritterkreuz* holders Ites and Mohr had done well as usual, group *Hecht* as a whole had to be deemed a keen disappointment. The return on investment, including twenty-five days of exclusive support from *U-116,* was poor. Moreover, the numerous convoy chases were hard on the boats; refits and battle damage repairs averaged forty-three days.* On analysis, it was seen that sinkings by the *Hecht* boats diminished dramatically when they confronted large, skilled es-

---

* Excluding Mohr's *U-124,* which was due for a long overhaul. While the boat was shifting pens during this refit, Allied aircraft bombed and damaged her, delaying her return to combat to mid-November.

cort groups, as they did in the last convoy, Outbound North (Slow) 102. As in earlier times, foul weather and the fog on the Grand Banks of Newfoundland had spoiled much of the hunting.

MINES, AGENTS, AND MISHAPS

The diversion of five Type VIIs to group *Hecht* reduced the number of VIIs of the May group to reach United States waters to eight. Five of the eight had first to carry out special missions: three were to lay minefields at New York and the Chesapeake and Delaware bays, and two were to land *Abwehr* agents in New York and Florida.

The three boats assigned to lay mines sailed from France on May 19. While en route to America, Joachim Berger in *U-87* was directed to mine Boston rather than New York because the ships repatriating German and Italian diplomats (*Gripsholm,* for one) had not yet sailed from New York.

Horst Degen in *U-701* arrived off the mouth of Chesapeake Bay after dark on June 12. It was the time of the new moon and pitch black. To facilitate the heavy traffic in and out of Chesapeake Bay, the Cape Henry and Cape Charles lights were burning. The lights enabled Degen to fix his position and to navigate directly to the main channel. Working quietly on electric motors close to an unalert patrol boat, at about 1:30 A.M., June 13, Degen laid the fifteen delayed-action TMB mines in thirty-six feet of water in about thirty minutes. He then ran out to deep water, submerged, and loaded his five empty tubes with torpedoes and later downloaded two air torpedoes from topside canisters.

In the late afternoon of June 15, a coastal convoy from Key West, KN 109, composed of twelve ships and six escorts, arrived off the entrance to Chesapeake Bay. At about that same time Degen's mines, delayed for sixty hours, activated. As the convoy stood into Norfolk, it passed directly over Degen's field. The mines severely damaged two big, loaded American tankers, *R. C. Tuttle* and *Esso Augusta,* and destroyed the 500-ton British ASW trawler *Kingston Ceylonite,* which was escorting the freighter *Delisle,* damaged earlier in Florida waters by Suhren in *U-564.* Seventeen of the thirty-two-man British crew on the trawler perished. Believing at first these ships had been torpedoed, the convoy escort, including the four-stack destroyer *Bainbridge* and the 165-foot Coast Guard cutters *Dione* and *Calypso,* ran about madly throwing off depth charges. One of *Bainbridge*'s missiles detonated another German mine, which damaged her, but only slightly. Two days later, June 17, another of the mines blew up the outbound 7,100-ton American freighter *Santore,* which could not be salvaged. Upon hearing (incorrectly) from *B-dienst* that these mines had sunk four merchant ships and a destroyer, Dönitz radioed Degen a "well done," and ordered him to patrol the dangerous waters off Cape Hatteras.

Paul-Karl Loeser in *U-373* laid his minefield off Cape May, New Jersey, in the mouth of Delaware Bay, on the night of June 11. Apparently the field was mislaid or the mines malfunctioned. One mine sank the 400-ton American tugboat, *John R. Williams,* on June 24, but no others caused any damage. After planting the field,

Loeser proceeded to the Cape Hatteras area to reinforce Degen in *U-701*. He reported a double miss on a 4,000-ton freighter on June 14, and a single hit for damage on a 5,000-ton British freighter on June 15. Since he did not have enough torpedoes left to justify a refueling, he sailed at slow speed for France, arriving after fifty-one days at sea.

Joachim Berger in *U-87* laid his mines off Boston, but the field produced no results whatsoever. After reloading his tubes with torpedoes, he patrolled north from Boston toward Halifax. Late on June 15, in foul weather, he intercepted convoy Halifax-Boston 25, comprised of six ships and five escorts. Berger sank two big ships from the convoy: the 8,400-ton British freighter *Port Nicholson,* and the 5,900-ton American passenger-cargo vessel *Cherokee,* which had taken on military passengers at Iceland for a voyage to the States. Eighty-six of the 169 men on board perished in the *Cherokee* sinking, one of the very few times in World War II that a U-boat sank a ship carrying Allied troops.

Berger cruised farther north to Halifax. On June 22 a Hudson of Canadian Air Force Squadron 11 found and attacked the boat, but missed. The next day the squadron leader, W. C. Van Camp, saturated the area with five aircraft. At dawn, one of the Hudsons came out of the sun and fog and caught *U-87* on the surface and dropped three close depth charges near her stern. The explosions knocked the port diesel engine off its mounts, wrecked the stern tube (and its torpedo), and damaged part of the aft main-storage battery. For the second time in as many patrols to Canadian waters, Berger was forced to abort with battle damage and limped home, lucky to have survived.

The *U-87, U-373,* and *U-701* planted forty-five TMB mines. Only those of Degen's *U-701* off Norfolk did any significant damage: a 7,100-ton freighter and a British ASW trawler sunk, two big tankers totaling 22,900 tons damaged (but salvaged). Nonetheless Dönitz directed the staff to prepare for other mining missions in the Americas.

The two VIIs designated to land the *Abwehr* agents in the United States were the *U-202,* commanded by thirty-eight-year-old Hans-Heinz Linder, and the *U-584,* commanded by Joachim Deecke, age twenty-nine, classmates from the crew of 1933. Linder had made several patrols in the North Atlantic, including one to the United States in March. Deecke had made several patrols, all in Arctic waters. After a complete overhaul in Germany, he arrived in France on May 16 for Atlantic duty. Each boat was to carry four agents. Linder in *U-202* was to land his four on Long Island; Deecke in *U-584* was to land his four in north Florida.

The eight agents had been schooled in sabotage. Each team brought along four crates of explosives that were to be used to blow up aircraft and tank factories and shipyards. To facilitate concealment and travel, the agents had been given about $154,000 in American money. Several of the agents had lived in the United States. Some had fathers, mothers, wives, and other relatives and close friends living there. The two team leaders were to meet in Cincinnati on July 4 to plan and coordinate the sabotage.

Linder in *U-202* arrived off the eastern end of Long Island near Amagansett on the evening of June 12 in heavy mist and fog. Inching perilously close to the beach in shallow water, the crew launched an inflatable rubber boat, manned by two seamen and tethered by a line to *U-202*. The four agents* loaded the four crates of explosives and a seabag into the boat, then climbed aboard. As Linder's deck crew played out the tether, the boat drifted through crashing surf to the beach. The four agents unloaded the four boxes and the seabag. Upon feeling tugs on the rope, Linder's deck crew pulled the boat and the two seamen back to *U-202*.

During the wait, *U-202* had grounded on a sand bar. Linder had gone ahead and astern with full power on the diesels and sallied ship, but *U-202* would not budge. As dawn approached, the men topside could hear cocks crowing and automobile horns. Believing the boat was doomed, Linder prepared to destroy secret papers and scuttle, but fortunately for the Germans, the heavy mist lingered. When the tide flooded, Linder lightened ship by dumping several fuel tanks and was able to work *U-202* free and run to deep water. Upon reporting his special mission carried out, he was ordered to patrol the Cape Hatteras area.

On the beach, the four would-be saboteurs changed into civilian clothes and buried the four boxes of explosives and the seabag. As they were so engaged, a twenty-one-year-old Coast Guard beach patrolman, John C. Cullen, hearing German voices, emerged from the mist to confront them. The leader of the team, Georg Dasch, asserted that they were shipwrecked fishermen and offered Cullen $300 to "forget" that he had found them on the beach. Outnumbered and unarmed, Cullen pretended to go along with the bribe. He accepted the money (actually only $240), but he returned immediately to his headquarters to spread the alarm. Meanwhile, the four agents split up and walked to Amagansett to catch trains into New York City, where they were to rendezvous later that day at a restaurant.

Dasch wrote subsequently that he despised Hitler and the Nazis and for that reason he decided to defect and to betray the scheme at the first opportunity. He confided his decision to his teammate Ernest Burger, who agreed to join in the betrayal. On about June 17 or 18, Dasch took a train to Washington, D.C., to reveal the full scheme to FBI director J. Edgar Hoover. Burger remained in a New York hotel to keep a close eye on the other two agents of the team.

Meanwhile, late on June 16, Joachim Deecke in *U-584* closed the north Florida coast with the other four agents.† In the early hours of the following morning Deecke put them and their four crates of explosives ashore by inflatable rubber boat at Ponte Vedra Beach, seven miles south of Jacksonville. Deecke withdrew *U-584* with no difficulties and upon reporting his mission accomplished, he, too, was ordered to patrol the Cape Hatteras area. The four agents buried the explosives, changed into civilian clothes, and took a bus to Jacksonville, where they split up into two groups and went on to various locations in the Midwest.

In Washington, on June 18, Dasch made contact with the FBI. The Bureau sent a senior agent, D. L. Traynor, to the Mayflower Hotel to see Dasch, who revealed

---

* Georg J. Dasch (leader), Heinrich H. Heinck, Richard Quirin, and Ernest P. Burger. Only the last traveled under his real name.

† Edward J. Kerling (leader), Herbert Haupt, Werner Thiel, and Hermann Neubauer. Only Haupt traveled under his real name.

all about his own group and the other group that landed in Florida. Within twenty-four hours, the FBI had rounded up the other three agents of Dasch's team, Burger, Heinck, and Quirin, and, based on information from Dasch, were soon hot on the trail of the team that landed in Florida. On June 23, FBI agents arrested the other team leader, Kerling, and his teammate, Thiel. By June 27, the last two agents, Haupt and Neubauer, were in custody.

Concealing Dasch's defection, FBI director Hoover immediately announced the capture of the eight agents and the arrest of fourteen relatives or friends. The agents and ten relatives or friends were tried in Washington, New York, and Chicago, July to October, 1942. Six of the eight agents who came by U-boat were found guilty of wartime espionage and electrocuted in a jail in Washington, D.C., on August 8. Dasch and his codefector Burger were sentenced to life and thirty years imprisonment, respectively. In 1948, President Harry S Truman commuted their sentences to the five years, eight months already served and returned them to Germany, where in 1959 Dasch published a book about the mission and his reasons for betraying his cohorts. The ten relatives or friends were also found guilty. In the postwar years Truman commuted their sentences as well.

Upon detachment from group *Hecht* early in its operations, von Bülow in *U-404* and Rehwinkel in *U-578* proceeded independently to the East Coast of the United States. Both boats had made prior and successful patrols to the Americas.

Inbound to his area, von Bülow in *U-404* sank three ships for 12,300 tons. The first two were 5,500-ton American freighters. He got the first with torpedoes and stopped the second, *West Notus,* with one round from his deck gun. After the crew took to the lifeboats, von Bülow sent a party to scuttle the ship. While his party was so engaged, he rounded up some stray survivors, put them in a sound lifeboat, and gave some of the men medical assistance and others bottles of Perrier water. His third victim was the 1,300-ton Swedish neutral *Anna.* When von Bülow missed her with a single torpedo, he surfaced and sank her with his gun. Her loss drew a diplomatic protest from Stockholm, but von Bülow insisted that the ship was sailing blacked out and zigzagging, and so he was not blamed. After that, Kerneval directed von Bülow to patrol the Cape Hatteras area.

While still well offshore, Rehwinkel in *U-578* sank two big freighters for about 13,000 tons. The first was a 6,300-ton Dutchman, *Polyphemus,* sailing in company with another big ship, which Rehwinkel chased doggedly but lost. The second was the 6,800-ton Norwegian *Berganger,* loaded with coffee, which Rehwinkel stopped with a single torpedo. When he surfaced to put the ship under with his deck gun, the Norwegian shot back accurately, forcing *U-578* to submerge and shoot two more torpedoes to sink the ship. Still well offshore, on June 10, Rehwinkel encountered a big freighter at which he fired his last six torpedoes, but none hit. He remained in the offshore area another week, then headed home.

After planting his mines at the mouth of the Chesapeake Bay, Horst Degen in *U-701* patrolled the waters off Cape Hatteras, as directed. On June 16 and 17 he reported scant traffic, heavy ASW aircraft and surface-ship patrols, and a double miss on a freighter, leaving him with six torpedoes. The aircraft had dropped "many well-aimed bombs," one of which had damaged his main periscope. One of three "destroyers" he spotted in formation had peeled off and attacked *U-701* with depth charges. Degen did not say so, but his air-cleaning machinery was not working properly and his men were nauseous half the time and suffering from the heat inside the boat. Hence, every afternoon at about 1:00 or 2:00, Degen surfaced for about ten minutes, started the diesels, and sucked fresh air into the boat through the conning-tower hatch.

In the early dark hours of June 19, *U-701* encountered a small (165-ton) Navy trawler, *YP-389.* She had just come out from Morehead City, North Carolina, to patrol the outer edge of a newly laid Cape Hatteras defensive minefield to warn friendly ships not to get too close. Degen boldly attacked the trawler with his deck gun. The *YP-389* was armed with a 3" bow gun, but it was out of commission, so she could not shoot back. Degen put *YP-389* under and sailed away. Six of the crew died, but eighteen were rescued the next day by Coast Guard cutters. Gary Gentile wrote that a Navy court of inquiry recommended that *YP-389*'s captain be court-martialed for "failure to seek encounter with the enemy" and "culpable inefficiency."

In due course, four other VIIs of the small May group proceeded to Cape Hatteras: the *U-202* and *U-584,* which had landed the agent teams in New York and Florida; *U-332,* commanded by Johannes Liebe, which had sailed independently from France; and von Bülow in *U-404.* Soon after Liebe in *U-332* arrived, an ASW aircraft caught and bombed him and forced him to abort. During his long, slow voyage home, Liebe refueled from one of two new U-tankers* and sank by torpedo and gun two lone freighters for 10,600 tons. The first was the 6,000-ton American vessel *Raphael Semmes.* Liebe reported that he fished ten injured survivors from the water, medicated their wounds, then released them to the lifeboats. The second was the 4,600-ton Portuguese neutral *Leonidas M.,* sunk against firm but belated orders from Kerneval. Liebe captured her captain and engineer and took them to France.

The other four VIIs at or converging on the Cape Hatteras-Cape Lookout area had a busy time during the last ten days of June.

• En route to the area, Linder in *U-202,* who had landed the agent team on Long Island, sank the neutral 4,900-ton Argentine freighter *Rio Tercero* on June 22. He picked up her captain, who angrily protested the sinking, claiming there were thirteen Argentine flags displayed on the sides and superstructure. Linder attempted to placate the captain with some brandy and a pair of shoes, but the sudden appearance of ASW aircraft forced him to break off discussions, release the captain, and dive. Linder had no luck at Cape Hatteras but well offshore on the last day of the month, he sank the 5,900-ton American vessel, *City of Birmingham,* crowded with 381 passengers and crew. Although the ship went down in four minutes, only nine persons perished. Ships sailing in company or nearby rescued the

---

* *U-461,* commanded by Wolf Stiebler, age thirty-four, which sailed from France June 21. The other was *U-460,* commanded by Friedrich Schäfer, age forty-nine, which sailed from France on June 7.

372 survivors. Homebound, Linder refueled from the new tanker *U-460*, then intercepted convoy Outbound South 34 near the Azores, and brought up several other boats, which profited.

• Deecke in *U-584* had a frustrating time, attributed by some to the shock of shifting from Arctic waters to near-tropical American waters. On June 22, he found two big tankers. A diesel-engine breakdown thwarted an attack on the first, but he shot six torpedoes at the second. Three torpedoes were duds and three missed, and the ship got away, he reported. Off Hatteras on June 27, he found a convoy and fired two torpedoes at an escorting "destroyer," but both missed. After refueling from *U-460* for the trip home, he sighted a huge, 18,000-ton tanker and chased, but she was too fast for *U-584*. After fifty-nine days at sea, Deecke arrived in France. He had landed the agent team in Florida but he had sunk no ships.

• Coming up to the Hatteras area from Georgia, in the early hours of June 24, von Bülow in *U-404*, who had refueled from the XB (minelayer) *U-116*, sank a 3,300-ton Yugoslavian freighter with three torpedoes. Later that day, he found an eleven-ship northbound convoy off Hatteras, escorted by the 165-foot Coast Guard cutter *Dione*, a British ASW trawler, and several smaller vessels. After sunset, von Bülow boldly ran in and sank two medium freighters from the convoy, *Nordal* and *Manuela*, but the cutter *Dione* and ASW aircraft foiled a second attack. Homebound on June 29, he encountered and sank the 6,800-ton Norwegian freighter *Moldanger*, sailing alone. Nine of the thirty crewmen who were rescued spent forty-eight harrowing days on a life raft. Von Bülow claimed sinking seven freighters for 42,172 tons, making his the most successful of all the VII patrols to the Americas in tonnage sunk, but postwar analysis reduced the claim to seven freighters for 31,061 tons, which almost exactly tied the record patrol of Hans Oestermann in *U-754* to Hatteras in April.

• Horst Degen in *U-701* doggedly patrolled off Hatteras, surfacing briefly in early afternoon to suck foul air out of the boat. German sources credit Degen with damage to the big Norwegian freighter *Tamesis* on June 25, but other sources suggest that ship hit one of the American defensive mines. In any case, *Tamesis* was salvaged. On June 27, Degen intercepted a thirty-one-ship southbound convoy and shot two torpedoes at a 7,000-ton tanker, *British Freedom*. One torpedo hit, but the tanker was sailing in ballast and was salvaged. One of the escorts, a converted yacht, *St. Augustine*, dropped thirteen depth charges and forced Degen off. At noon the next day, Degen came upon the big, fully loaded 14,000-ton American tanker *William A. Rockefeller*, escorted by a Coast Guard aircraft. He stopped the tanker with a single torpedo. Seeing the shadow of *U-701*, the aircraft counterattacked with two depth charges and vectored in an 83-foot Coast Guard cutter, *Number 470*. The cutter threw over seven depth charges, which prevented another daylight attack and then rescued the crewmen. Degen returned to the scene after dark and put another torpedo into the tanker. That one sent her to the bottom, the only tanker sunk by a U-boat in the Eastern Sea Frontier in June.

To then, Degen had conducted an exceptional patrol. His mines had sunk the British ASW trawler *Kingston Ceylonite* and the 7,100-ton American freighter *Santore*, damaged two American tankers, the 11,600-ton *Robert C. Tuttle* and the

11,200-ton *Esso Augusta,* and slightly damaged the four-stack destroyer *Bainbridge.* By torpedo and gun he had sunk the tanker *William A. Rockefeller* and the trawler *YP-389,* and damaged the 7,000-ton tanker *British Freedom* and possibly the 7,300-ton Norwegian freighter *Tamesis.* In all: possibly nine ships for about 60,000 tons sunk or damaged, the best VII patrol of all.

The other two VIIs of the May group that had laid mines, *U-87* and *U-373,* were within sight of Lorient by July 7. Strangely, Degen in *U-701,* who had sailed the same day as they and had not yet refueled, was still off Cape Hatteras, seeking one more ship to sink with his remaining two or three torpedoes, even though he had found no traffic for nine straight days and nights. The heat and foul air inside the boat were nearly unbearable and he faced a tedious three-week voyage home.

Shortly after 1:00 P.M. that day, Degen cautiously surfaced to freshen the air in the boat. He and his first watch officer, Konrad Junker, a junior officer, and the senior quartermaster, Günther Kunert, went to the bridge to serve as lookouts, each man responsible for covering one quarter (90 degrees) of the horizon. Seeing no aircraft or ships, Degen sucked fresh air into the boat for a while, then gave orders to dive. As Junker was preparing to go below, he suddenly shouted: "Aircraft! Port quarter." Momentarily stunned, Degen turned angrily on Junker: "You saw it too late!"

The plane was one of thirteen Hudsons of the Army Air Forces' 396th Medium Bombardment Squadron. Formerly based in California on ASW duty, the outfit had recently moved to the Marine Corps air station at Cherry Point, North Carolina. The squadron flew six five-hour ASW missions during daylight hours, patrolling offshore between Cape Hatteras and Charleston, South Carolina. The plane was piloted by twenty-four-year-old Harry J. Kane, assisted by four aircrew. At 2:12 P.M. that day, while flying at 1,500 feet in broken clouds, Kane himself spotted *U-701* about seven miles off his left wingtip. Reflexively, he turned directly toward the U-boat on a descending flight path and alerted his crew, which made ready three 325-pound Mark XVII depth charges, fitted with newly issued fuses set to detonate at twenty-five feet.

Although Degen had dived *U-701,* it was too late to get "deep." Kane passed over the boat's swirl at an altitude of fifty feet and dropped all three depth charges. The first charge fell twenty-five feet short of the boat but the next two hit close to or on *U-701*'s stern. The explosions wrecked and flooded all of the boat aft of the conning tower. Within two minutes the control room filled with salt water almost to the overhead. Unable to blow the ballast tanks, Degen immediately led an escape party through the conning-tower hatch. Eighteen men got out that way, rising in the giant air bubbles. Unknown to Degen, when the boat hit bottom, eighteen others escaped through the bow torpedo-room loading hatch. The Germans estimated that about seven of the total crew of forty-three died in the sinking or the escape procedure.

Kane circled overhead, watching the two separate groups of survivors pop to the surface. He dropped four life vests and a rubber lifeboat to the Germans and marked the location with a smoke bomb. He then notified all agencies concerned by radio and attempted to guide an 83-foot Coast Guard cutter, *Number 472,* by radio and signal lamp to the site of the sinking. However, by that time the smoke bomb had exhausted itself and the swift current of the Gulf Stream had swept the two separate groups of survivors well to the north, and the cutter found nothing. By 4:30 P.M., Kane was low on fuel and had to leave.

American aircraft, patrol boats, and a blimp scoured the seas for the survivors on the following day, July 9, but found nothing. Huddled together in two groups— each unknown to the other—the Germans began to die one by one from shock and exposure or madness from drinking saltwater. Degen's rapidly dwindling group clung to a makeshift "raft," consisting of three escape lungs and three life preservers (two of the preservers from the Hudson) lashed together. The men scavenged a lemon and a coconut that drifted by.

About noon the next day, July 10, a Navy blimp, K-8, piloted by George S. Middleton, found seven survivors of *U-701* in two groups about 110 miles offshore. The blimp crew lowered a life raft, blankets, water, food, and a first-aid kit, then radioed for a seaplane. A Coast Guard pilot, Richard L. Burke, homed on the blimp and landed near the seven survivors, who had been in the water forty-nine hours. Among the living were Degen and his senior quartermaster, Kunert, and three men who had escaped from the bow compartment. Burke flew the survivors to Norfolk, where they were hospitalized and then turned over to ONI and FBI officials. Later in the day, the 83-foot Coast Guard cutter *Number 480* recovered five German bodies. No sign of the other thirty-one men of *U-701* was ever found.*

The ONI interrogators wrote that the seven survivors of *U-701* were grateful for their rescue and appeared to be cooperative. They revealed much of interest, including the important news that U-tankers had come into service in the North Atlantic. However, the survivors artfully concealed knowledge of their own and *U-87*'s and *U-373*'s mining missions and the landing of *Abwehr* agents by *U-202* and *U-584*. After the ONI had milked the survivors dry—or so it was assumed— Degen and Kunert were incarcerated in an officers' POW camp in Arizona and the five enlisted men at camps elsewhere. The news about the U-tankers was slow to reach the operating forces; the British continued to doubt that it was true.

In all, the eight VIIs of the May group that reached American waters sank twenty ships for about 102,000 tons, including three trawlers for 1,000 tons. This was an average of 2.5 ships for 12,750 tons sunk per boat per patrol. One boat, von Bülow's *U-404*, accounted for nearly one-third of all the sinkings and the tonnage. Excluding the lost *U-701*, the boats were at sea for an average of sixty days. The minefields planted by *U-87, U-373,* and *U-701* caused the Americans no little consternation, but the forty-five mines, which displaced fifteen torpedoes in the boats,

---

* Owing to imprecise or erroneous position reports from the Hudson and others, the Navy could not find *U-701* for salvage purposes. In 1989, sport divers found her on the bottom, lying on her starboard side. The divers confirmed severe damage to the stern. They contacted Degen and assured him the remains of the crew would not be disturbed.

actually sank only two trawlers and one freighter for a total of about 8,000 tons. The fifteen displaced torpedoes might have achieved much more.

Fortunately for the Allies, the Germans were unaware of a major shipping accident that might have yielded more sinkings yet. On the night of June 28, the 350-foot merchant ship *Stephen R. Jones,* en route from Norfolk to Boston with 6,300 tons of coal, ran aground in the Cape Cod Canal, then capsized and broke in half. This mishap blocked the canal, forcing all north and southbound ship traffic in that area to go "outside" around Cape Cod. Owing to the destruction of the ship and to strong currents in the canal, it took about four weeks to clear away all the wreckage, repair damage, and reopen the canal. Had the Germans known about this mishap, Dönitz could have concentrated the U-boats off Cape Cod, probably with good results and without great risk, inasmuch as a large pool of deep water (650–700 feet) lies fifteen miles off the cape.

This temporary closing of the Cape Cod Canal lent impetus to a proposed plan to transfer the assembling and sailing of Halifax and Slow convoys from Canadian ports to New York.

MORE RECORD PATROLS BY THE TYPE IXs

Eight Type IXs, including three new arrivals from Germany, sailed to the Americas in May. Four had made prior patrols to the Americas but one of them, *U-129,* had a new skipper, replacing *Ritterkreuz holder* Nikolaus Clausen. The other veteran, *U-68,* had made three prior patrols to Freetown and the South Atlantic.

Dönitz intended that the first two IXs to sail in May, *U-158* and *U-504*—both experienced boats—were to patrol off the mouth of the Mississippi River. However, there was a mixup in the issuance of the orders. As a result, Erich Rostin in *U-158* patrolled the north end of the Yucatan Channel and Fritz Poske in *U-504* patrolled the south end of the Yucatan Channel, and the mouth of the Mississippi River was left unthreatened temporarily.

South of the Yucatan Channel, the very senior (crew of 1923) thirty-seven-year-old Fritz Poske in *U-504* sank a small British freighter on May 29. Then, it seemed, all traffic ceased and eleven frustrating days passed before it resumed. After that, in the week from June 8 to June 14, Poske sank five more freighters, bringing his total to six for about 20,000 tons. He then returned to France without refueling, completing a voyage of sixty-seven days.

While en route to his assigned area north of the Yucatan Channel, Erich Rostin in *U-158* sank three ships: two in the mid-Atlantic (one the 8,100-ton British tanker *Darina*) and one south of Cuba. After passing north through the Yucatan Channel into the Gulf of Mexico, between June 4 and June 7, Rostin sank three more freighters. When the mixup in orders was discovered, Rostin was directed to patrol the mouth of the Mississippi River, to which, belatedly, *U-67, U-129,* and the new *U-157* were also headed. Arriving first, Rostin in *U-158* sank two big tankers, the 13,500-ton Panamanian *Sheherazade* and the aged (1918) 8,200-ton American *Cities Service Toledo* (83,000 barrels of crude oil) on June 11 and 12.

On his course to the Mississippi River via the Old Bahama Channel and the Straits of Florida, Wolf Henne, age thirty-six, in the new *U-157* found and sank a 6,400-ton American tanker, *Hagan,* which was loaded with molasses. Upon learning of this loss, the commander of the Gulf Sea Frontier, James Kauffman, directed all available forces to "hunt this submarine to exhaustion and destroy it."

An Army Air Forces B-18 picked up *U-157* on ASV radar at first light on June 11. Closing to two miles, the aircrew saw *U-157* on the surface and attacked, passing over the boat at 900 feet, but the attack failed when the bomb-bay doors malfunctioned. Making a diving turn, the B-18 came in a second time at 300 feet, but by then *U-157* was nearly under. The plane dropped four Mark XVII depth charges set for twenty-five feet. All charges detonated, but the outcome was unknown. An hour and a half later a Pan American Airways commercial airliner saw the U-boat on the surface. But still later that morning, three other Army aircraft could not find her.

An armada of ASW vessels sailed from the schools in Key West and Miami. The Key West group, composed of nine ships, included the four-stack destroyers *Dahlgren* and *Noa,* and the 165-foot Coast Guard cutters *Thetis* and *Triton.* The Miami group was composed of five PCs, reinforced by the four-stack destroyer *Greer,* which joined it on June 12. All fifteen vessels converged in the Florida Straits between Key West and Havana.

The American air and sea forces hunted *U-157* relentlessly for forty-eight hours, June 11 to June 13. On the night of June 12–13, radar-equipped Army Air Forces B-18s reestablished contact with the U-boat. At dawn on June 13, Kauffman directed the Key West group to the site and recalled the Miami group. At about 4:00 P.M., the 165-foot Coast Guard cutter *Thetis* got a "strong" sonar contact. Her captain, Nelson C. McCormick, who had earlier commanded a sister ship, *Dione,* off Cape Hatteras, carried out an immediate and skillful attack, dropping ten depth charges in two runs, which brought up huge air bubbles and oil. The destroyer *Noa,* the 165-foot Coast Guard cutter *Triton,* and three other vessels converged on *Thetis* and dropped twenty-two more depth charges at the oil slick.

These attacks without doubt destroyed *U-157,* with the loss of all hands. *Thetis* and the other vessels found not only great quantities of oil but also two pairs of trousers, a small tube of oil made in Germany, and pieces of deck grating and other wood. The Army Air Forces rightfully claimed part credit for the kill, as did *Noa* and *Triton* and several other vessels, but Kauffman gave sole credit to McCormick in *Thetis.* Dönitz was unaware of the loss for a number of days.

The other two IXs en route to the mouth of the Mississippi River, *U-67* and *U-129,* were several days behind *U-157* and had no hint of her loss either. Passing through the Florida Straits on June 16, Günther Müller-Stöckheim in *U-67* sank a 2,200-ton Nicaraguan freighter very close to the site of the *U-157* loss. Two nights later, on June 18, the new skipper of *U-129,* Hans-Ludwig Witt, age thirty-two, who had put down two big freighters in the mid-Atlantic, sank a 3,500-ton American freighter in the west end of the Old Bahama Channel. The following day Witt encountered—and reported—two convoys in the Straits of Florida. However, as there were no other U-boats nearby to help Witt, who was a green skipper, Dönitz forbade him to attack or even shadow these convoys.

Still unaware that *U-157* was lost, Kerneval suddenly realized that its revised orders had directed four boats to the mouth of the Mississippi River. To relieve this dangerous congestion, Kerneval directed Witt's *U-129* and Rostin's *U-158* to patrol the coast of Mexico—Germany's newest enemy—from the Yucatan Channel to Tampico, Mexico's principal oil port. Only Müller-Stöckheim's *U-67* and Henne's (lost) *U-157* were to patrol the mouth of the Mississippi River.

Both Rostin and Witt found good hunting in Mexican waters. In the week June 17 to June 23, Rostin in *U-158* sank four more ships, including the Norwegian tanker *Moira,* 1,600 tons, bringing his total for this patrol to an astonishing twelve confirmed ships (four tankers) for 61,200 tons. This was the best patrol by any boat to the Americas and it earned Rostin a *Ritterkreuz,* awarded by radio on June 28.* The new skipper, Witt, in *U-129* sank five more ships, including two Mexican tankers: the 7,000-ton *Tuxpan* and the 2,000-ton *Las Choapas.*

Homebound, all torpedoes expended, Rostin in *U-158* encountered the 4,000-ton Latvian freighter *Everalda* in the open ocean midway between North Carolina and the island of Bermuda. He stopped the ship with his deck gun, took the captain and "one Spaniard" prisoner, and sent a party on board to capture her secret papers and scuttle her. This sinking, which Rostin reported by radio, raised his confirmed score for this patrol to a record thirteen ships for 65,108 tons.†

Rostin's report of this latest sinking and the capture of two prisoners and secret documents went to Kerneval at about noon, June 30. Several British DF installations, including one on the island of Bermuda merely 130 miles to the southeast, picked up Rostin's transmissions and plotted a fix. Bermuda then relayed the U-boat's position to an aircraft of the American Navy's Bermuda-based Patrol Squadron 74, equipped with Mariner flying boats. A Mariner pilot, Richard E. Schreder, turned immediately toward the estimated position of the U-boat. After a run of merely fifty miles, he found *U-158* cruising on the surface. He could see "about fifteen men" lounging on deck, sunning themselves, an inexplicably careless lapse so close to Bermuda. Schreder attacked, dropping two demolition bombs that missed, and two Mark XVII depth charges with shallow settings. One of the latter hit the boat's bridge and wedged in the superstructure, the aircrew reported. When Rostin dived to escape, it apparently detonated, fatally damaging *U-158,* which sank with no survivors.

Unaware of the loss, when *U-158* did not appear for resupply from a U-tanker northeast of Bermuda, Dönitz assumed Rostin had had an engine and/or a radio

---

  * At the time of the award, Rostin's claimed sinkings were nineteen ships for about 112,000 tons. His confirmed sinkings were sixteen ships for about 90,400 tons.

  † In his two patrols to the Americas, Erich Rostin, virtually unknown in Germany, sank seventeen confirmed ships for 94,342 tons. In his two patrols to the Americas, Reinhard Hardegen in *U-123,* a national hero, sank fifteen confirmed ships for 81,661 tons, plus the two ships that were salvaged. Rostin's two-patrol record was not exceeded by any other boat.

failure. Hoping for the best, he directed the U-tanker to stand by at the rendezvous during certain hours for a full week. All other boats were to keep an eye out for *U-158.* When the facts were learned after the war, it was to be remarked that Rostin had enjoyed his *Ritterkreuz* for only two days.

Müller-Stöckheim in *U-67* arrived off the mouth of the Mississippi River on June 19. Inasmuch as Henne in *U-157* had been sunk off Key West and *U-129* and *U-158* had been sent to patrol the Mexican coastline, Müller-Stöckheim had this rich territory all to himself for a time. Ranging the Gulf Coast from Florida to Texas, in the three weeks from June 20 to July 13, Müller-Stöckheim attacked six tankers. He sank four and damaged two* and also sank a 2,200-ton freighter, making his confirmed sinkings for the patrol six ships for 30,000 tons. After a protracted voyage home on one engine, and a refueling, he reached France on August 8, having been at sea eighty-one days.

Returning from the Mexican coast, the new skipper Witt in *U-129* patrolled the Yucatan Channel, going south to Honduras then back north to the Gulf of Mexico. He sank three more ships, including the 6,300-ton Russian tanker *Tuapse.* On July 21 he finally commenced the long slow journey home on one engine. His claimed and confirmed sinkings for his first patrol as skipper were impressive indeed: eleven ships (three tankers) for about 41,500 tons. He was out for ninety-four days.

Three IXs of the May group patrolled to the Panama Canal area: Karl-Friedrich Merten in *U-68,* Helmut Witte in the new *U-159,* and Carl Emmermann in the new *U-172.* Upon sailing, Merten in *U-68* received orders to help escort the blockade runner *Müensterland* into Bordeaux. He made contact with the vessel and another escort, *U-437,* in the southwestern reaches of the Bay of Biscay on May 15, but Allied aircraft spoiled the rendezvous. Merten was forced to sneak into El Ferrol, Spain, to repair an exhaust valve; *Müensterland* went on to Bordeaux alone, *U-437* to St. Nazaire. Moored alongside the "interned" German vessel *Max Albrecht,* Merten completed repairs, topped off his fuel tanks, and resailed *U-68* after a few hours.

While en route to the Caribbean, both of these new IXs encountered Allied ships in mid-ocean, sailing alone. Witte in *U-159* claimed sinking five for 26,200 tons, but only three for 14,600 tons were confirmed, including the 2,600-ton British tanker *Montenol.* Emmermann in *U-172* sank three for 17,900 tons, including the 9,000-ton British tanker *Athelknight.* These two boats—and Merten in *U-68*—reached the Trinidad area during the first week in June. On June 5 and 6 Merten sank two big tankers, the 6,700-ton American *L. J. Drake* and the 13,000-ton Panamanian *C. O. Stillman.*

---

* The tankers sunk were three Americans—*Raleigh Warner,* 3,700 tons; *Benjamin Brewster,* 6,000 tons; and *R. W. Gallagher,* 8,000 tons—and one British, *Empire Mica,* 8,000 tons. The tankers damaged were the Norwegian *Nortind,* 8,200 tons, and the American *Paul H. Harwood,* 6,600 tons.

The three boats proceeded west to Panama. On the way, Witte in *U-159* attacked by gun two sailing ships, the Brazilian *Paracury* and the 150-ton Honduran *Sally.* He left both with decks awash and, he thought, doomed, but the crew of the 265-ton *Paracury* reboarded and saved her. Near Curaçao and Aruba, on June 7, Witte sank a 3,400-ton American freighter. Not far away, on June 8, Emmermann in *U-172* sank a 1,700-ton American freighter.

The three boats were deployed along the sea-lanes leading to Panama by June 10. That day the most important American warship formation to reach Panama in months must have passed close to all three: the carrier *Wasp,* the new battleship *North Carolina,* the cruisers *Quincy* and *San Juan,* and seven destroyers. These warships were bound for the Pacific to reinforce Operation Watchtower—the proposed Allied capture of Guadalcanal, Tulagi, and Florida islands in the Solomon Island chain.

That night Merten in *U-68* spotted two big heavily laden freighters inbound to Panama. He eased in close and fired five torpedoes. Two missed but two hit the 5,000-ton British freighter *Ardenvohr,* which sank quickly, and one hit the 8,600-ton British freighter *Surrey,* which sank slowly. Noting that the crew of *Surrey* had hauled away the lifeboats in great haste, Merten's curiosity was aroused. He fished out and queried a lone survivor who had been left behind. He informed Merten that *Surrey,* which finally sank beneath the waves, was loaded with 5,000 tons of dynamite!

As if on cue, the dynamite somehow exploded. The force of the blast lifted *U-68* completely out of the water and slammed her down so hard that Merten thought the boat had been torpedoed. The crash temporarily knocked out the two diesels and the gyro compass, and smashed gauges and crockery throughout the boat.

While Merten was below surveying the damage, the bridge reported yet another ship. After the engineer got the diesels back on the line, Merten commenced a long stern chase. When he saw that he could not overtake the vessel before daylight, he shot one torpedo from extreme range. It hit, sinking the 5,900-ton British freighter *Port Montreal,* also bound for the Pacific with war matériel. Upon receiving Merten's sinking report to then—five ships (three tankers) for 40,000 tons—Dönitz awarded him a *Ritterkreuz.**

Over the next two days, June 11 to 13, Witte in *U-159* went into action very close to Panama. He attacked and claimed sinking four freighters for 28,700 tons. Three of the four for 18,600 tons (one British, two American) were later confirmed, but there was no record of the other. Counting earlier overclaims in this patrol, Witte reported that he had sunk nine ships for about 53,000 tons. His confirmed score to this point was six ships for 43,300 tons. Having exhausted his torpedo supply, Witte withdrew easterly to the Aruba-Curaçao area, as did Merten in *U-68.*

The assaults by Merten and Witte—six ships sunk in three days—humiliated the Panama Sea Frontier. In response, the naval commander, Clifford van Hook, organized a "killer group," composed of two destroyers (the modern *Edison* and the four-stack *Barry*), sundry smaller craft, and Catalinas. The Army Air Forces

---

* At the time of the award, Merten's confirmed score was sixteen ships for 102,234 tons.

beefed up land-based ASW units. While these forces were in play, June 14 to June 18, Carl Emmermann in *U-172* sank four ships for 12,800 tons immediately off Panama, including, by gun, the 125-ton British sailing schooner *Dutch Princess* and the 2,000-ton American tanker *Motorex*. Intensified air patrols, improved control of shipping, and a spell of bad weather spoiled Emmermann's hunting, restricting him to a second gun attack on a sailing schooner, the 35-ton Colombian vessel *Resolute*.*

While patrolling near Aruba and Curaçao, Merten in *U-68* and Witte in *U-159* sank two more ships each. Both of Merten's victims were tankers. One was the 2,500-ton Panamanian *Arriaga;* awkwardly, the other was the 9,200-ton Vichy French *Frimaire,* under Portuguese charter, for which the OKM had specifically requested safe passage. When officers at the OKM learned the *Frimaire* had been sunk, they were furious, but Dönitz defended Merten—his most recent *Ritterkreuz* winner—who insisted the ship had no Vichy or Portuguese markings. The two sinkings raised Merten's confirmed score for the patrol to seven ships (four tankers) for about 51,000 tons. Witte's two victims were small freighters, both sunk by deck gun.

Homebound, Witte in *U-159* and Emmermann in *U-172* each sank another ship. Lacking torpedoes, Witte stopped the 9,600-ton American tanker *E. J. Sadler* with his bridge-mounted antiaircraft guns, then put a party on board to scuttle. The sinking of *Sadler* raised Witte's confirmed score to ten ships (two tankers) for about 50,000 tons. Emmermann stopped the 8,400-ton American freighter *Santa Rita* with his last torpedo and likewise put a party on board to scuttle. He also took the captain prisoner and directed the demolition party to ransack the ship for anything useful. They returned with extremely valuable charts and documents that revealed Allied shipping routes and the location of the minefields in Cape Town, South Africa, and at some other ports. The sinking of *Santa Rita* raised Emmermann's confirmed score to ten ships (two tankers) for 40,800 tons, counting the two sailing schooners.

While Witte in *U-159* was inbound in the Bay of Biscay, on the night of July 11–12, a Wellington of Coastal Command's 172 Squadron, fitted with ASV radar and a Leigh Light, found the boat and attacked. Witte ordered his bridge gunners to shoot out the light, but they were blinded by its glare. The aircraft dropped four 250-pound depth charges that shook the boat severely and caused a great deal of minor damage, but nothing fatal. The pilot was the American serving in the RAF, Wiley B. Howell, who seven nights earlier had hit and sunk Jürgen von Rosenstiel's Type IX *U-502* with the loss of all hands.

In all, eight Type IXs sailed to the Americas in May. One, Wolf Henne in the new *U-157,* who sank one ship, had been lost attempting to enter the Gulf of Mexico.

---

* Naval historian Samuel Eliot Morison wrote: "The U-boat machine-gunned women and children passengers at point blank range." If true, it was doubtless unintentional, one of several unfortunate instances when lifeboats or survivors may have drifted into the gunfire. The episode was not introduced as evidence at Dönitz's trial at Nuremberg.

The other seven, including two new boats, Witte in *U-159* and Emmermann in *U-172*, turned in record-breaking returns. Not counting the three sailing ships sunk by Witte and Emmermann, these eight IXs sank sixty-one ships for 304,000 tons: an average of 7.6 ships for 38,000 tons per boat per patrol. Counting the truncated voyages of the two lost boats, *U-157*, sunk in the Florida Straits, and *U-158*, sunk near Bermuda, the May IXs spent 517 days at sea.

The outstanding returns of the IXs that sailed in May to the Caribbean and Gulf of Mexico helped offset the diminishing returns of the Type VIIs on the United States East Coast, most of which had carried out special missions. The combined total sinkings of the May boats (including the sailing schooners, trawlers, and the other vessels sunk by gun and mines) was eighty-four ships of 407,000 tons. This was an overall average of 5.25 ships of 25,437 tons per boat per patrol. In return, three U-boats were lost: the IXs *U-157* and *U-158* and the VII *U-701*.

TEN

THE SHIFTING CHARACTER OF THE U-BOAT WAR

The massive German offensive in the Ukraine dominated all else in the summer of 1942. German forces had reached Rostov and Stalingrad by mid-July and were driving south to the Caucasus Mountains. Allied war planners in Washington and London assumed—quite wrongly—that the military forces of the Soviet Union could not hold out much longer. To help relieve pressures on the Red armies, they rushed preparation for Torch, the invasion of French Northwest Africa, which had replaced Sledgehammer as the emergency "second front" in 1942.

Over continuing objections from London, the Americans pressed for more and bigger Murmansk convoys to clear out the logjam of merchant ships loaded with war matériel for the Soviet Union. Reluctantly, the Admiralty had sailed convoy PQ 16 and its reverse, opposite-sailing sister convoy QP 12, on May 21. Capitalizing on the increasing hours of daylight in the Arctic, German dive bombers and torpedo planes based in northern Norway had sunk six out of thirty-five merchant ships from PQ 16 but none from QP 12. Hampered by the increasing hours of daylight, the Arctic U-boats had sunk one freighter from PQ 16, the 6,200-ton American *Syros*.

Under heavy pressure from Washington, the Admiralty sailed PQ 17 and its reverse, QP 13, on June 27. PQ 17 was the largest Murmansk convoy yet. The grim saga of this convoy will be related in due course. Suffice to say for now that it was a disaster, the worst convoy debacle of the war, and that the British refused to sail PQ 18 until all conditions in the Arctic were more favorable for the Allies. Partly as a result of this decision, on July 14, the battleship *Washington* and four destroyers* left the Home Fleet and returned to the States.

On the other side of the globe, preparations for Watchtower, the invasion of Guadalcanal, proceeded apace but on a shoestring. Hampered by a shortage of everything, the amphibious forces suffered yet another setback when, on August 4, the modern (1935) American destroyer *Tucker* struck a mine and sank off the island of Espiritu Santo in the New Hebrides.

Watchtower finally took place August 7. The carriers *Enterprise, Saratoga, Wasp* and the battleship *North Carolina,* recently transferred from the Atlantic Fleet to the Pacific Fleet, as well as numerous heavy and light cruisers backed up the landing forces. Thirty American destroyers, including seven recently transferred from the Atlantic Fleet to the Pacific Fleet, provided escorts and screens for the naval forces. America's first "jeep" carrier, *Long Island,* also fresh from the Atlantic Fleet, ferried fighter aircraft to a position near the island and flew them off. Japanese aircraft badly mauled the American destroyer *Mugford* on D day, and the American destroyer *Jarvis* on the day following.

On the second night of this operation, August 8–9, a Japanese force of seven cruisers (five heavy, two light) and one destroyer rushed from Rabaul to attack the Allied invaders. This engagement, a tragedy of errors known as the Battle of Savo Island, resulted in a devastating setback to the Allied naval forces. The Japanese sank four heavy cruisers (*Astoria, Canberra, Quincy, Vincennes*), damaged the destroyer *Jarvis,* and badly wrecked the heavy cruiser *Chicago,* which limped back to California for months of repairs.

The loss of these warships endangered the Allied troops who had landed on Guadalcanal, established a foothold, and captured the Japanese landing strip, renamed Henderson Field. As a consequence, Admiral King directed Ingersoll to recall from the British Home Fleet all other American warships, including the heavy cruisers *Wichita* and *Tuscaloosa* and the remaining two American destroyers, *Emmons* and *Rodman.* King then sent the new battleships *Washington* and *South Dakota* to the Pacific with an escort of six recently commissioned destroyers.†

In subsequent days, Allied and Japanese warships clashed again and again in the Solomon Island chain, resulting in further heavy Allied losses. On August 22, Japanese surface forces sank the destroyer *Blue.* Two days later aircraft from *Saratoga* sank the Japanese "jeep" carrier *Ryujo,* but Japanese aircraft hit and badly mangled the fleet carrier *Enterprise,* which limped to Pearl Harbor for repairs. On August 31, a Japanese submarine, *I-123,* hit and badly damaged the carrier *Saratoga,* her second unfortunate encounter with an enemy submarine in 1942. Two weeks later, on September 15, the Japanese submarine *I-19* hit and so badly damaged the carrier *Wasp* that she had to be sunk by the destroyer *Lansdowne,* leaving only one battle-ready Allied carrier in the Pacific, *Hornet.* That same day,

---

*   *Mayrant, Rhind, Rowan, Wainwright.*
†   *Barton, Duncan, Lansdowne, Lardner, McCalla, Meade.* The last was commissioned June 22.

the Japanese submarine *I-15* hit and badly damaged the battleship *North Carolina* and the modern destroyer *O'Brien. North Carolina* limped to Pearl Harbor for extended repairs, but while en route to San Francisco for repairs, *O'Brien* came apart and sank on October 19. The destroyer *Lang,* steaming in company, rescued the crew.

All the while, warships of the shrinking Atlantic Fleet faithfully escorted troop convoys (ATs and NAs) from New York and Halifax to the British Isles and vice versa (TAs). The old battleships *Arkansas, New York,* and *Texas,* the light cruisers *Brooklyn* and *Philadelphia,* and destroyers provided the surface escort. Allied aircraft on the Eastern Seaboard and in Nova Scotia, Newfoundland, Iceland, and the British Isles provided air escort. No U-boat attacked any of these troopship convoys and only two incidents marred an otherwise perfect record:

• In the evening of August 22 in heavy fog off Halifax, the modern (1940) destroyer *Buck,* the flagship of John B. Heffernan, commander of a group of thirteen destroyers escorting troop convoy AT 20 (ten merchant ships plus *New York* and *Philadelphia*), collided with the transport *Awatea.* Seven men on *Buck* perished. Ordered to assist these damaged vessels, the modern (1941) destroyer *Ingraham* collided with a Navy tanker, *Chemung,* and sank so swiftly that only eleven men were saved. The damaged tanker *Chemung* took the severely damaged destroyer *Buck* in tow until the Navy tug *Cherokee* arrived at the scene. The badly damaged transport *Awatea,* escorted by the destroyer *Bristol,* turned back and put into Boston, as did *Chemung* and *Buck.* As a consequence of these accidents, convoy AT 20, which proceeded to the British Isles, was reduced by five ships. *Ingraham* was the fifth destroyer of the Atlantic Fleet to be lost in less than a year.

• On September 3, while inbound to New York in convoy TA 18, the big American liner *Manhattan,* converted to troopship *Wakefield,* caught fire. The convoy escort (*Arkansas, Brooklyn,* and nine American destroyers) and numerous vessels that put out from Halifax removed about 1,500 passengers and crew from *Wakefield* and took them on to New York. Two tugboats towed *Wakefield* into Halifax, escorted by the *Treasury*-class Coast Guard cutter *Campbell.* Rebuilt in the States, *Wakefield* returned to service in 1944.

While these operations were in progress during the summer of 1942, the U-boat campaign in the Atlantic gradually changed in tempo, emphasis, and character. Two important factors led to the change.

First was a significant growth in the number of attack boats in the Atlantic U-boat force. This occurred because of the unusually low combat loss rate over the summer months, the completion of the buildup of the Arctic–Norway U-boat force to Hitler's mandated level, a decision to limit the buildup of the Mediterranean U-boat force, and the arrival of a flood of new boats that had been delayed in the Baltic by the heavy winter-ice conditions.*

---

* Even so, on June 21 Dönitz complained to Berlin that of 138 U-boats recently commissioned, sixty-three were still in the Baltic four months after commissioning. Moreover, accidents in the Baltic

The growth of the Atlantic U-boat force was significant, yet far less so than is usually depicted. Taking into account gains and losses, the force levels on the first of the month were as follows:

	June	July	August	September
Type VII	51	57	61	77 (+26)
Type IX	35	37	41	47 (+12)
Totals:	86*	94	102	124 (+38)

The second factor was the sudden buildup of the Atlantic U-tanker force. In addition to the three aforementioned Type XIV tankers (*U-459, U-460, U-461*), the new *U-462, U-463,* and *U-464* set sail for the Atlantic in the summer. One of these, *U-464,* was lost as she entered the Atlantic (page 657), but the other five Type XIVs survived. In addition, pending the correction of defects in the SMA mines, the big minelayer *U-116* continued in service as a provisional U-tanker.

These six U-tankers plus the net gain of twenty-six Type VIIs over the summer offered the possibility of renewing the U-boat wolf pack war against the important North Atlantic convoy run in the distant Greenland "air gap" on a much firmer basis. The fresh VIIs outbound from Germany or France could attack en masse Outbound North and Outbound North (Slow) convoys proceeding westward toward Canada into ever-decreasing ASW measures, refuel from a U-tanker, then, provided they still had torpedoes, attack the Halifax and Slow Convoys proceeding eastward to the British Isles while they were still in the "air gap."

The biggest weakness in this scheme was that an extremely high percentage of the U-boats so assigned were to be new ones fresh from Germany. Since these green boats were to confront the most well-organized and experienced ASW air and surface forces in the Allied navies, U-boat losses were bound to rise sharply.

The possibility of renewing the convoy war on the North Atlantic run arose, coincidentally, with the increase in effectiveness of Allied ASW measures in the Americas, including convoying in the Eastern, Gulf, and Caribbean Sea Frontiers. The resulting decrease in successes by the Type VIIs in those waters strengthened the hands of those in Berlin who had objected to sending VIIs to the Americas in the first place. Although Dönitz had plans to mount some wolf pack, or group, attacks on Allied convoys in the Caribbean by some veteran VIIs supported by U-tankers, he fully recognized the difficulties this entailed, including the debilitating impact of the tropical climate on the VII crews, and was more than willing to curtail and cancel those plans in favor of a shift of those veteran VIIs to the North Atlantic run to renew the U-boat war in those latitudes.

---

continued. The VII *U-596* had a battery explosion that delayed her sailing from June to August. The VII *U-606* had a bad engine-room fire. The VII *U-444* rammed and sank the VII *U-612* on August 6. The *U-612* was salvaged but restricted to service as a school boat. Repeatedly set back by mechanical problems—some attributed to sabotage—it took the IX *U-164* nearly eight months to get out of the Baltic.

* Includes all attack boats of the Atlantic force undergoing battle-damage repairs, such as *U-123, U-124, U-333, U-563, U-753.*

The arrival of the new U-tankers was also a timely boon for the Type IXs. The U-tankers enabled the IXs assigned to the waters of the Gulf of Mexico and Caribbean to extend patrols in the hunting areas and to reach the approaches to the Panama Canal and Brazil without being obsessively concerned about running out of fuel on the way home. In addition, the U-tankers enabled Dönitz to again assign IXs to patrol the distant Freetown area and beyond to interdict ship traffic in West African waters, including tankers coming from Trinidad under the new and temporary routing arrangement.

The gradual shift of patrol areas by the VIIs and IXs in the summer of 1942 developed as follows:

TYPE VIIs

	June	July	August	Totals
Americas	13*	11	3	27
North Atlantic	4	15	29	48
Central Atlantic	4	2	8	14
Totals:	21	28	40	89

TYPE IXs

	June	July	August	Totals
Americas	10†	7	8	25
North Atlantic	0	3‡	0	3
Central Atlantic	0	6	7	13
Totals:	10	16	15	41

Hitler very nearly upset all plans for deployment of U-boats over the summer. He suddenly proposed that Germany launch war against blatantly pro-American Brazil, which had provided the Americans with numerous air and naval bases, with a surprise attack by "ten or fifteen" boats operating against her major seaports. Dönitz was intrigued, but in order to mount this surprise attack, it would have been necessary to cancel almost all other deployment plans, including the U-boat campaign in North American waters. He therefore urged that the attack on Brazil be delayed until he had more attack boats and a U-tanker to support them.

Berlin overrode Dönitz. On June 15, Hitler directed Admiral Raeder to execute the mission in early August, and five days later the OKM issued an order to Dönitz to proceed. Dönitz in turn reluctantly designated ten U-boats for the task, supported by the provisional tanker *U-116,* and issued the skippers secret orders.

---

  *   Sixteen sailed but the VIICs *U-71* and *U-552,* which attacked a convoy en route, returned to France for replenishment and/or battle-damage repairs, and the VIID minelayer *U-214* was damaged by a British aircraft in the Bay of Biscay and forced to abort.

  †   Eleven sailed; one, *U-105,* was damaged by a British aircraft in the Bay of Biscay and forced to abort.

  ‡   Originally bound for the Americas via the North Atlantic, *U-43, U-174,* and *U-176* became involved in convoy chases and remained in that area.

However, when Hitler's foreign minister, Joachim von Ribbentrop, got wind of the plan, he objected to it vigorously on the grounds that it might alienate the pro-German governments in Argentina and Chile. On June 26, Hitler canceled the scheme.

At about this same time, Hitler became convinced that the Allies intended to seize the Portuguese Azores and Madeira islands. At a meeting with Admiral Raeder on June 15, according to the notes of the conference, Hitler proposed "that an operational group of submarines be held in readiness for the purpose of quick interference in case the enemy should suddenly strike. . . ." Raeder demurred, stating that "we cannot afford to divert a considerable number of submarines for such a purpose alone." However, Raeder went on, it might be possible to form such a group "within the framework of our present submarine warfare." That is, to promptly assemble a pack from the streams of U-boats going to and from the Americas and West Africa. This solution satisfied Hitler.

JUNE PATROLS TO THE AMERICAS

Dönitz scheduled thirty-five patrols to all Atlantic areas in June: twenty-four Type VIIs and eleven Type IXs. Twenty-seven boats were to continue the campaign in American waters. The other eight—all VIIs—were to sail late in the month to cadre new packs in the eastern and south Atlantic.

The June boats were to be supported by four U-tankers: von Wilamowitz-Möllendorf's Type XIV *U-459* and Werner Schmidt's Type XB minelayer *U-116,* making second voyages; and the two new Type XIVs *U-460* and *U-461.*

Two of the Type VIIs sailing to the Americas in June were hit and disabled by Coastal Command aircraft in the Bay of Biscay:

• On June 5, a Sunderland of the Royal Australian Air Force Squadron 10, based in southern England and piloted by S.R.C. Wood, straddled the veteran *U-71,* commanded by Walter Flachsenberg, with eight shallow-set Torpex depth charges, then raked it with 2,000 rounds of machine-gun fire, killing one of the crew. A Focke-Wulf Condor on patrol in the area attacked the Sunderland, wounding two airmen. German PT boats raced out to escort *U-71* into La Pallice. Repaired quickly, the boat resailed a week later, on June 11.

• On June 15, an Allied aircraft attacked the *U-214,* commanded by Günther Reeder, age twenty-six. She was another Type VIID minelayer, temporarily assigned to torpedo operations, that had sailed from Germany in May. Although the boat incurred "heavy" damage, the OKM diarist recorded, she managed to limp back to France on June 17. Repairs delayed her sailing to the first week in August.

The attacks on these outbound as well as the inbound boats in the Bay of Biscay infuriated Dönitz. He complained bitterly in his diary that owing to the unavailability of German aircraft, the Bay of Biscay had become a "playground" for British aircraft. It was "sad and very depressing" for the U-boat crews to realize that Germany had provided "no forces whatever" to protect U-boats in the Bay of Biscay or to escort damaged boats into port, leaving them vulnerable to repeated

British aircraft attacks and forcing them to creep in and out of the bay mostly sub-merged.

Dönitz iterated long-standing requests through official channels for aircraft protection. When these again failed to get results, on July 2 he flew to confer face-to-face with *Luftwaffe* chief Hermann Göring at his headquarters in East Prussia. Göring explained that up to now the *Luftwaffe* had sent every available aircraft to the Soviet Union or to the Mediterranean Basin. Nonetheless, he conceded the necessity for U-boat protection in the Bay of Biscay and personally ordered that twenty-four more JU-88s be assigned to the *Luftwaffe* Atlantic command.

As the other VIIs prepared to embark for the Americas, reliable Axis agents in Tangier reported the sailing of Homebound Gibraltar 84. Following the disastrous loss of *Ritterkreuz holder* Engelbert Endrass in *U-567* and four other boats to the heavily escorted convoy Homebound Gibraltar 76 in December 1941, Dönitz had prohibited attacks on inbound or outbound Gibraltar convoys. However, believing that after a layoff of six months, a sudden pack attack might find the escorts thinned out and unalert, Dönitz directed that nine of the most experienced Type VIIs bound to the Americas were to divert to attack convoy Homebound Gibraltar 84, then refuel from a U-tanker and proceed westward. A successful attack would satisfy those at the OKM and elsewhere who insisted that the Type VIIs be utilized to interdict shipping closer to the battlefields.

This very special pack was named *Endrass* to honor his memory and to avenge his loss to a Gibraltar convoy. Five of the nine boats, including *U-552,* commanded by the reigning "ace," Erich Topp, and Flachsenberg's resailing *U-71,* were among the most experienced boats in the Atlantic force. Two were transfers from the Arctic command: Ernst Vogelsang in *U-132,* who had sunk the *Treasury*-class Coast Guard cutter *Alexander Hamilton* off Iceland in January and in so doing had incurred severe battle damage, and Rudolf Schendel in *U-134,* who had only just arrived in the Atlantic. Two other boats were green: Dietrich Lohmann, age thirty-two, in the new *U-89,* fresh from Germany, and Werner-Karl Schulz, age thirty-one, in the new *U-437,* who had escorted the blockade runner *Münsterland* into France but had yet to make a full war patrol.

The convoy sailed from Gibraltar on June 9. Composed of twenty merchant ships, it was escorted by Johnny Walker's famous Escort Group 36, which had been reduced temporarily to four vessels: Walker's sloop *Stork* and three corvettes. The convoy included one fighter-catapult ship, *Empire Morn,* equipped with one Hurricane to counterattack German aircraft. A rescue vessel, *Copeland,* fitted with Huff Duff, brought up the rear. On June 11, three escorted merchant ships from Lisbon joined the convoy, but those escorts proceeded to other assignments.

Attentive Focke-Wulf Condors tailed the three ships from Lisbon and reported the linkup with convoy Homebound Gibraltar 84. Responding to these accurate signals on the afternoon of June 14, Erich Topp in *U-552* made contact with the convoy and brought up other Condors and three U-boats of group *Endrass:* Vogelsang in *U-132* and the two green skippers, Lohmann in *U-89* and Schulz in *U-437*.

The rescue ship *Copeland* DFed Topp's signals and alerted Johnny Walker in *Stork,* who went to battle stations promptly and directed *Empire Morn* to launch its Hurricane to drive off the German planes. The Hurricane carried out its mission, then ditched alongside *Stork,* which recovered the pilot. Meanwhile *Stork* and the corvette *Gardenia* had found Vogelsang in *U-132* astern of the convoy. In a relentless, well-conducted series of attacks, *Stork* and *Gardenia* dropped 110 depth charges near *U-132,* severely damaging the boat and forcing it to fall out and back. At about that same time the corvettes *Marigold* and *Convolvulus* found and attacked Lohmann in *U-89* and Schulz in *U-437,* forcing them off as well. Lohmann later reported he was hunted and depth-charged for thirty-one hours.

That night, while Walker's four escorts were chasing other boats, Topp in *U-552* moved in to attack. He shot a full salvo of five torpedoes (four bow, one stern) from about 3,000 yards. Two torpedoes missed or malfunctioned, but the other three hit and sank three different ships: two British freighters, *Etrib* and *Pelayo,* for 3,300 tons, and the 7,400-ton Norwegian tanker *Slemdal.* In the ensuing chaos Topp hauled off, reloaded his tubes, and eased back for a second attack. Again he fired a full salvo of five torpedoes. Again two missed or malfunctioned, Topp reported, and the other three hit. But he was mistaken; only two of the five hit and detonated, sinking two more British freighters for 5,200 tons: *City of Oxford* and *Thurso.*

During the next day, June 15, five or more boats of group *Endrass* made contact with the convoy. Still hanging on, Topp loaded his last two torpedoes in his bow tubes for a daylight submerged attack, but he could not get around Walker's aggressive escorts to shoot. One escort caught Topp and dropped eight depth charges close to the boat, cracking a fuel-ballast tank and causing other serious damage. Another escort caught Walter Flachsenberg in *U-71.* The depth charges forced Flachsenberg to abort with battle damage for the second time in June. Only one other of the nine group *Endrass* boats was able to mount an attack: Günther Heydemann in *U-575.* He fired a full bow salvo at overlapping targets, but all four torpedoes missed or malfunctioned.

Commencing June 16, the British powerfully reinforced convoy Homebound Gibraltar 84 with surface ships and long-range aircraft. The destroyer *Wild Swan* and two frigates, *Spey* and *Rother,* joined temporarily, until the arrival of Lancaster and B-24 Liberator heavy bombers and Catalina flying boats from southern England. On June 17 Dönitz sent a flight of a dozen of the newly acquired JU-88s to assist the U-boats, but the German pilots mistook a fleet of Spanish fishing trawlers, amidst which the destroyer *Wild Swan* was cruising, for the convoy. *Wild Swan* claimed four JU-88 kills before the dive bombers sank her and four trawlers. The destroyer *Vansittart* rescued 133 survivors of *Wild Swan* and eleven Spanish fishermen.

As Homebound Gibraltar 84 inched closer to the British Isles, Coastal Command added medium-range Hudsons to the air coverage. Altogether thirty-six different aircraft flew out from England to Walker's assistance. In the face of this air saturation, Dönitz canceled the operations of group *Endrass.* Flachsenberg in *U-71* and Topp in *U-552* returned to France for battle repairs and replenishment. Upon arrival, Flachsenberg left the boat for other duties. Although *U-132* was badly damaged, Vogelsang, who had been worked over badly in two successive Atlantic outings, resisted orders to return to France.

Johnny Walker had lost five of twenty-three ships in his convoy, yet he was commended for thwarting with very slim forces what might easily have become a massacre. For Dönitz, the outcome was a sharp disappointment. Of the nine skippers in group *Endrass,* only one, Erich Topp, had inflicted any real damage on the enemy: five confirmed ships sunk for 15,858 tons. Dönitz blamed the lack of success on the unexpected appearance of the very-long-range land-based aircraft (Lancasters and Liberators) and the failure of the JU-88s to counter them. However, shipboard Type 271 radar and Huff Duff (about which Dönitz knew nothing), aircraft radar, and shallow-set Torpex depth charges were also important ASW measures working against the Germans.

As planned, the seven remaining Type VIIs of group *Endrass* refueled from the U-tankers and proceeded to American waters. Six other Type VIIs sailed independently to the Americas in June, for a total of thirteen. The independents included one *Ritterkreuz* holder, Rolf Mützelburg in *U-203.*

Kerneval directed two of the thirteen VIIs en route to the Americas to begin their patrols in Canadian waters. Ernst Vogelsang in *U-132* was to emulate Thurmann in *U-553* and penetrate the Gulf of St. Lawrence. The green skipper, Fritz Hoeckner, age twenty-nine, in the new Type VIID minelayer *U-215* was to patrol near Cape Sable. Both boats reached Canadian waters on about July 1.

At this time convoys AT 17A–AT 17B sailed from New York and Halifax. Composed of nine troopships, the combined convoys were escorted by Task Force 37 (the battleship *Texas,* the cruiser *Philadelphia,* and fourteen American destroyers), which sailed all the way across to the British Isles. Four of the destroyers went on to Scapa Flow to replace other American ships leaving the British Home Fleet: *Emmons, Hambleton, Macomb,* and *Rodman.*

Neither *U-132* nor *U-215* had any contact with troopship convoy AT 17A–AT 17B, but Hoeckner in *U-215* drew first blood, a fatal encounter for the boat and crew, as it turned out. On July 3, his twenty-fifth day at sea, while south of Cape Sable, he found the thinly escorted Boston-Halifax convoy BX 2. He attacked and sank the 7,200-ton American Liberty ship *Alexander Macomb,* but one of the escorts fixed and counterattacked *U-215* with depth charges. The Allies gave credit for the kill to the British ASW trawler *Le Tigre.* There were no survivors from *U-215.*

Vogelsang in *U-132* ran right through the Cabot Strait into the Gulf of St. Lawrence on July 1. Crossing the gulf on a northwest course, he rounded the Gaspé Peninsula and boldly entered the mouth of the St. Lawrence River at Cap-Chat. There he waited for a Quebec-Sydney convoy. In the early hours of July 6, he found one (Number 15) in bright moonlight and fired a full salvo of five torpedoes. Three missed or malfunctioned, but the other two hit and sank two freighters for about 6,000 tons. After a fast reload, Vogelsang mounted a second attack and sank another freighter for 4,300 tons. One of the Canadian escorts, the minesweeper *Drummondville,* counterattacked *U-132,* drove her under, and pummeled her with close depth charges, but inexplicably failed to persist in the attack. As a result, Vogelsang escaped downriver into the gulf and got away to make urgent repairs. His bold attack on Quebec's "doorstep" caused yet another outburst of indignation within the Canadian government, but the losses were withheld from the public.

Vogelsang patrolled the Gulf of St. Lawrence for two more weeks, but it was tough going. During the day the skies were dense with Allied aircraft, many on training flights. At night fog rolled in and obscured visibility. Finally, on the afternoon of July 20, while submerged off Cap-de-la-Madeleine in the St. Lawrence estuary, Vogelsang found another Quebec-Sydney convoy (Number 19). He fired a two-torpedo fan at the 4,400-ton British freighter *Frederika Lensen.* One missed or malfunctioned but the other hit. Frantic efforts to salvage the ship failed; she broke amidships and foundered. Allied air and surface forces again botched the counterattack and Vogelsang ran back through the Cabot Strait to open seas. His successes in the St. Lawrence River and the gulf (four ships) were twice those of Thurmann in *U-553* (two ships), and they encouraged Dönitz to plan other forays to the area, regardless of the risks.

Five VIIs patrolled the United States East Coast from Cape Cod to Cape Lookout. On the way, two skippers, Kurt Diggins, age twenty-eight, in the new *U-458* and the veteran Hans Oestermann in *U-754* sank freighters in mid-ocean. However, all five VIIs reported a dearth of traffic (now sailing in convoy) and heavy ASW measures.

Patrolling off Cape Lookout in the early hours of July 11, the veteran Hans-Dieter Heinicke in *U-576* found a northbound convoy. When he reported it to Kerneval, he was told to attack and to bring up any other boats in the area. A likely helping hand was the veteran Siegfried von Forstner in *U-402,* who was just then closing on Cape Hatteras. Heinicke trailed the convoy north toward Cape Hatteras, but he later reported he had lost contact before he could shoot and therefore he could not vector in any other boats. Von Forstner in *U-402* and Heinicke in *U-576* took up independent stations off Cape Hatteras.

Over the next forty-eight hours, July 12 to 14, four aircraft patrolling Cape Hatteras reported attacks on U-boats. On July 12 a Coast Guard plane, piloted by E. B. Ing, straddled a U-boat with two 325-pound depth charges from an altitude of 200 feet. The next day an Army Air Forces B-17 Flying Fortress, piloted by A. H. Tuttle, also flying at 200 feet, straddled a U-boat with six depth charges. On July 14 two Navy aircraft, piloted by William R. Jemison and George L. Schein, dropped four shallow-set Mark XVII depth charges on a U-boat from low altitude. All four aircraft reported probable or certain kills or heavy damage.

So far it has not been possible to ascertain which planes hit which U-boats. On July 13, Heinicke in *U-576* reported to Kerneval that he had incurred damage from aircraft bombs and was "attempting repairs." The next day, July 14, Heinicke reported he could not make repairs and that he was aborting the patrol. Also on July 14, von Forstner in *U-402* reported he had been heavily bombed and depth-charged and that as a result he had had a battery explosion. In response, Kerneval ordered von Forstner to make repairs in an area 360 miles due east of Hatteras, beyond range of most ASW aircraft.

In the late afternoon of July 15, Heinicke in *U-576,* perhaps limping homeward, came upon another convoy off Cape Hatteras. Merely a few hours out from Norfolk, it was the southbound KS 520, comprised of nineteen merchant ships. The convoy was escorted by seven surface craft, including the American four-stack destroyers *Ellis* and *McCormick,* and the on-loan British corvette *Spry** (equipped with Type 271 centimetric-wavelength radar and the first Hedgehog to be developed by the British), the 165-foot Coast Guard cutter *Triton,* a blimp, and several aircraft. Perhaps brooding over his failure to attack the convoy he had found earlier off Cape Lookout, Heinicke elected to attack this one, even though his boat was seriously damaged and unstable.

Heinicke set up on three ships and probably fired a full bow salvo. His torpedoes sank the 2,100-ton Nicaraguan freighter *Bluefields* and damaged two big American ships: the 8,300-ton freighter *Chilore* and the 11,100-ton tanker *J. A. Mowinckel.* The two damaged ships ran due west to beach, but in so doing they plowed into the Hatteras defensive minefield. *Chilore* was wrecked beyond repair, but *Mowinckel* was salvaged and eventually returned to service. The Navy tug *Keshena,* attempting to rescue *Chilore,* also hit a mine and sank.

Upon firing the torpedoes, *U-576* destabilized and broached close astern of the American merchant ship *Unicoi.* Her Armed Guard crew, commanded by M. K. Ames, on full alert at the 5" stern gun, opened fire on *U-576* and claimed a solid hit on the conning tower. At about the same time, two Navy aircraft of Patrol Squadron 9, piloted by Frank C. Lewis and Charles D. Webb, straddled *U-576* with two Mark XVII depth charges set for fifty feet. The boat sank in deep water with no survivors.

There were four other VIIs then in the vicinity of or closing on Cape Hatteras: Dietrich Lohmann in the new *U-89,* Siegfried von Forstner in the damaged *U-402,* Kurt Diggins in the new *U-458,* and Hans Oestermann in *U-754.* Believing (incorrectly) that the Type VIID minelayer *U-215* and (correctly) that Degen's *U-701* had been sunk at Hatteras, and that *U-402* and *U-576* had been badly damaged at Hatteras (but unaware of *U-576*'s loss), Dönitz concluded that the meager successes did not justify the risks and losses. Therefore, on July 19, he directed the damaged *U-402* to abort to France and the *U-89, U-458,* and *U-754* to shift from American to Canadian waters, southeast of Halifax, joining Vogelsang in *U-132,* then exiting the Gulf of St. Lawrence.

The withdrawal of these four VIIs from the United States East Coast marked the end of the intense six-month U-boat campaign in those waters.

---

* At Argentia, on May 29, *Spry* had caught fire while alongside the valuable new destroyer tender *Prairie.* The fire spread to *Prairie,* causing "extensive damage," which compelled *Prairie* to return to Boston for months of repairs.

The four VIIs that gathered in Canadian waters had mixed success. Off Halifax, Vogelsang in *U-132* sank the 6,700-ton British freighter *Pacific Pioneer,* bringing his total for the patrol to five ships for 21,400 tons, and earning him high praise. Diggins in *U-458* sank the 4,900-ton British tanker *Arletta.* Oestermann in *U-754* sank the 260-ton American trawler *Ebb* by gun, killing five fishermen and wounding seven. Lohmann in *U-89* found a convoy south of Cape Sable and set up on a fat tanker, but an escort "ruined" his attack. He shot two torpedoes at the escort, a "destroyer," but they missed or malfunctioned. Several days later he sank the 54-ton Canadian fishing trawler *Lucille M* by gun. Her eleven survivors reported that Lohmann expressed regret over the sinking, but said he "was under orders and had to obey." That trawler was the only vessel Lohmann sank on his 77-day patrol to America.

The Canadian military historian, W.A.B. Douglas, has established that within a period of one week, July 30 to August 5, Hudsons of Canadian squadrons 11 and 113, capitalizing on a new land-based Huff Duff network, found and hit all four of these boats. Pilots W. Graham and N. E. Small attacked *U-89* on July 30 and August 5, respectively. Small also attacked *U-754* and *U-458* on July 31 and August 2, respectively. Pilot G. T. Sayre attacked *U-132* on July 31.

Small's hit on Oestermann in *U-754* on July 31 was a fatal blow. Flying at 3,000 feet in good weather, he saw *U-754* running on the surface three miles distant. As Small dived to attack, Oestermann's bridge watch belatedly caught sight of the Hudson and scrambled for the conning-tower hatch, but it was too late to get deep. Small dropped four depth charges that fell close, then circled the area for almost an hour. Presently, *U-754*'s conning tower reappeared and Small machine-gunned it. A still-unexplained "heavy explosion" broke the surface of the water. Later, some ships found a large oil slick and debris. The *U-754* sank with the loss of all hands in 360 feet of water, the first U-boat to fall victim to a Canadian aircraft.

While homebound on August 16 in the Bay of Biscay, Lohmann in *U-89* was hit for the third time by Allied aircraft. The attacker was a B-24 Liberator of British Squadron 120, piloted by Squadron Leader Terence M. Bulloch. The depth charges fell wide and did not cause fatal damage. Although this attack failed, Bulloch went on to become the leading U-boat killer in the RAF. One of his copilots, Bryan W. Turnbull, a New Zealander, also became a noted U-boat killer.

The other six VIIs that sailed to the Americas in June patrolled independently in southern areas from Florida to Trinidad. The July heat and humidity were nearly unbearable, ruining much of the food and drinking water. The men were felled by painful boils and rashes. Steadily improving Allied ASW and the initiation of convoying in the Gulf of Mexico and then the Caribbean Sea frustrated the hunters.

• Horst Uphoff in the veteran *U-84,* who sank a 6,600-ton Norwegian freighter while he was inbound to American waters, patrolled the Straits of Florida, opposite Havana. On July 7 he reported "strong" air and surface ASW forces day and night in the straits and speculated (correctly) that the aircraft patrolling at night were equipped with ASV radar. Urging him on, Kerneval scolded: "There is no confirmation of radar" in use anywhere on the United States coastline(!). In a spirited effort, from July 13 to July 26, Uphoff sank a 6,000-ton American freighter and a 1,600-ton Honduran freighter, damaged the 7,200-ton American freighter *William Cullen Bryant,* and missed another freighter with his last two torpedoes.

• While approaching the north Florida coast on July 5, Rudolf Schendel in *U-134,* the recent transfer from the Arctic, met a Swedish neutral, *Venezia.* When he queried Kerneval for instructions, he was told to sink her. He fired a salvo of two torpedoes, but both missed and the ship got away. When he reported no traffic off Georgia or Florida, Kerneval ordered him to patrol the mouth of the Mississippi River, going there via the Straits of Florida. Harassed by "heavy" aircraft ASW patrols, Schendel prowled the Gulf Coast for a full week, July 19 to July 26, but he again saw no ships. After withdrawing from the gulf through the Straits of Florida on July 27, he came upon a convoy in the Old Bahama Channel, but air escorts forced him off, thwarting an attack. A week later, while patrolling the Windward Passage, Schendel reported sinking an American "destroyer," but it was not confirmed. Perhaps overcome by the severity of the climate, on August 6, Schendel reported himself too ill to continue and *U-134* returned to France, having sunk no ships during her eighty-four-day patrol.

• The old hand Helmut Möhlmann in *U-571* also patrolled the Straits of Florida, overlapping part of the time with Uphoff in *U-84.* On July 7 he found a convoy and sank the 8,100-ton British freighter *Umtata.* The next night Möhlmann stopped the 9,800-ton American tanker *J. A. Moffett, Jr.* with two torpedoes, then demolished her with twenty rounds from his deck gun. Salvage vessels towed *Moffett* to port but she was beyond saving. The very next night, July 9, Möhlmann sank a 1,100-ton Honduran freighter. Six days later he shot a full bow salvo at what he claimed to be a zigzagging freighter of 15,000 tons, but which turned out to be the 11,400-ton American tanker *Pennsylvania Sun.* She also made it to port and eventually returned to service. Homebound on July 20, Möhlmann encountered a huge "two funnel" ocean liner, but it was moving too fast to pursue.

• Werner-Karl Schulz in the *U-437,* embarked on his first full combat patrol, was directed to begin his hunt in the area south of the Yucatan Channel to Panama. Going via the Windward Passage and the south coast of Cuba, Schulz found no traffic. After a frustrating and useless week, Kerneval ordered Schulz to retrace his course and patrol the Windward Passage and surrounding areas. On July 17 he found a convoy but his attack was foiled by air and surface escorts. Finally he was able to shoot two torpedoes at two different large freighters from extreme range. He claimed hits on both vessels, but they could not be confirmed. On July 20 Schulz found a big "ocean liner" at which he fired three torpedoes. He claimed two hits but this success could not be confirmed either, and a Catalina thwarted a second attack. Later that same day Schulz fired four single torpedoes at a formation of ships in convoy, but all malfunctioned or missed, making a total of nine futile shots. Like Schendel in *U-134,* Schulz returned to France without having sunk a single ship.

• Sailing independently from France in the veteran *U-203,* the *Ritterkreuz* holder Rolf Mützelburg, who had patrolled off Cape Hatteras in April, set off for the Trinidad area. On the way there, on June 26 and 28, he sank by torpedo and gun three freighters totalling 16,000 tons. Near Trinidad on July 7 and 11, he sank a 7,000-ton British freighter by torpedo and the 10,000-ton Panamanian tanker *Stanvac Palembang* by torpedo and gun. Having exhausted his torpedoes and gun ammunition to sink five confirmed ships (one tanker) for 33,000 tons, Mützelburg set a course for France.

In tonnage sunk, Mützelburg's was the third best Type VII patrol to America after Erich Topp in *U-552* (40,000 tons) and Walter Flachsenberg in *U-71* (39,000 tons). Furthermore, these sinkings raised Mützelburg's total claims to 200,000 tons, qualifying him for Oak Leaves to his *Ritterkreuz.* Dönitz bestowed this honor on Mützelburg by radio on July 15.* As was the custom, Hitler was to later present Mützelburg the Oak Leaves. Although he could have had almost any job he wanted, he elected to remain skipper of *U-203.*

• Günther Heydemann in the veteran *U-575* also patrolled the eastern Caribbean near Trinidad. As a member of group *Endrass* he had shot four torpedoes (for no hits) in the battle with convoy Homebound Gibraltar 84, so he had to husband his weapons. He entered his area via Mona Passage, separating the Dominican Republic and Puerto Rico, and there sank a 2,700-ton American freighter by torpedo. Near Trinidad, on July 9, he sank a 5,300-ton British freighter by torpedo and gun. That success and a sinking by Mützelburg in *U-203* on the same day apparently froze traffic in the eastern Caribbean temporarily. Heydemann saw nothing for the next nine days. The tedium was finally relieved on July 17 when *U-575* came upon a group of five freighters, but Heydemann botched the attack, wasting two more precious torpedoes. The next day, July 18, he fired his last torpedoes to damage the 13,000-ton British tanker *San Gaspar,* and sank two British sailing ships by gun off Caracas, Venezuela.

The returns from the thirteen VIIs that reached the Americas in June were only so-so: twenty-seven ships for 124,000 tons, an average of two ships for 9,500 tons per boat per patrol. Two skippers, Vogelsang in *U-132* off Canada and Mützelburg in *U-203* off Trinidad, accounted for about one-third of the total: ten ships for 54,000 tons. Three of these thirteen VIIs sank no ships. Three were lost: Hoeckner's Type VIID minelayer *U-215* and Oestermann's *U-754* in Canadian waters and Heinicke's *U-576* off Cape Hatteras. Another boat, von Forstner's *U-402,* was badly damaged and nearly lost.

SHARPLY DIMINISHING RETURNS FROM THE TYPE IXS

Eleven Type IXs sailed for the Americas in June. One of the first was the veteran IXB *U-105,* commanded by Heinrich Schuch. On the morning of June 11, a radar-

---

* At the time of the award, Mützelburg's confirmed score was twenty ships for about 83,000 tons. At that time, only two other skippers of the Atlantic U-boat force wore the Oak Leaves: Erich Topp in *U-552* and Reinhard Suhren in *U-564.*

equipped Sunderland of Australian Squadron 10, piloted by Eric B. Martin, caught the boat on the surface about 150 miles west of Cape Finisterre. Martin dropped six shallow-set Torpex depth charges and two 250-pound ASW bombs. The attack severely damaged *U-105*, killing or wounding about ten men. Dönitz diverted four inbound and outbound boats to assist *U-105*, but none could find her. She limped unassisted into El Ferrol, Spain, and after makeshift repairs, the boat resailed on June 28 with a German aircraft escort and reached France. Repairs kept her out of action until late November. Pilot Martin and his copilot, Jaques Hazard, a Frenchman, as well as his navigator, A. Meaker, were killed in action during the next several weeks.

Of the ten Type IXs that reached American waters, six were new. The presence of the U-tankers enabled four of these to sail directly from Kiel to the Americas without stopping in France to replenish. The oldest and most experienced of the four veteran boats, *U-66*, had a new skipper, replacing the *Ritterkreuz* holder Richard Zapp. Two boats—the new *U-166* and *U-66*—had to carry out hated mining missions.

Three IXs sailed during the first half of the month: Wilfried Reichmann's new *U-153*, Walther Kölle's *U-154*, and Axel-Olaf Loewe's *U-505*. Kölle in *U-154* had aborted one patrol to the Americas and completed another, sinking five confirmed ships. Loewe in *U-505* had made one prior patrol, a long one to Freetown, sinking four ships. Kölle in *U-154* was to patrol the Gulf of Mexico; Reichmann in *U-153* and Loewe in *U-505* were to patrol the western Caribbean near Panama.

While still in the Atlantic approaching the Caribbean, all three boats encountered heavy unescorted traffic northwest of Anegada. The green skipper, Wilfried Reichmann in *U-153*, came upon four freighters in four days. An engine failure foiled the attack on the first, but he sank the other three (two American, one British) for 16,200 tons from June 25 to June 29. Nearby, Walther Kölle in the sister ship *U-154* claimed sinking a ship of 3,200 tons on June 28, but that claim could not be confirmed. Also nearby, Axel-Olaf Loewe in *U-505* on June 28 and 29 sank two freighters for 12,600 tons, the first after an arduous seven-hour stern chase. The second was the 7,200-ton Liberty ship *Thomas McKean*, on her maiden voyage to the war zone. Loewe closed the lifeboats of *McKean* to ask if the survivors needed provisions or water and gave them a course to the nearest land.

These three IXs entered the Caribbean via the Windward and Mona passages in early July. Leading the others by several days, Kölle in *U-154* sailed south of Cuba, then north through the Yucatan Channel into the Gulf of Mexico. In the Yucatan Channel on July 6, he sank the 65-ton Panamanian trawler *Lalita* by gun. While patrolling off Alabama and the west coast of Florida, Kölle shot a two-torpedo fan at a freighter but missed and, during an emergency dive, lost a man overboard, a demoralizing episode. On July 19, he reported a leak in a fuel-oil ballast tank that left a telltale trace in the water and could not be fixed. Kerneval first refused and then approved Kölle's request to abort. When Kölle arrived in France after an 81-day patrol, having sunk only the 65-ton trawler, he went to other duty and Dönitz gave command of the *U-154* to Heinrich Schuch, whose IXB *U-105* had been bombed and disabled.

Entering the Caribbean via the Mona Passage, Reichmann in *U-153* and Loewe in *U-505* sailed westerly to Panama, passing north of Aruba and Curaçao. On July 5 and 6, Army Air Forces crews of the 59th Bombardment Squadron, in three different radar-equipped B-18s, reported attacks on U-boats. Each dropped four shallow-set Mark XVII depth charges. Inasmuch as Loewe in *U-505* did not log an air attack at this time, the three B-18s probably attacked Reichmann in *U-153*. The airmen reported "damage" but did not claim a sinking. The extent of "damage" to *U-153,* if any, is not known.

While sixty miles off Almirante, on the evening of July 11, a small seaport in northern Panama, Reichmann in *U-153* encountered the 560-ton American Navy net tender *Mimosa* (YN-21), which mounted a 3" gun. *Mimosa* excitedly reported to the Panama Sea Frontier that a U-boat had attacked her, firing three torpedoes, indicating that the green Reichmann mistook her for a larger warship. The first missed the bow; the other two ran under the shallow keel. *Mimosa* boldly shot two rounds from her 3" gun at the U-boat.

The commander of the Panama Sea Frontier, Clifford van Hook, issued orders to hunt this U-boat to destruction. A radar-equipped Catalina of Patrol Squadron 3 reached the scene shortly after midnight and the nearby *PC-458* (also known as U.S.S. *Evelyn R.*), mounting sonar, a 3" gun, and twelve depth charges, joined in the hunt. At about 4:00 A.M., the Catalina got a radar contact at four miles and dropped two brilliant parachute flares. These illuminated a surfaced U-boat, which the Catalina attacked, dropping four Mark XVII depth charges, two set for 25 feet and two for 50 feet. The crew reported a perfect "straddle." However, when daylight came, there was no sign of a disabled U-boat or debris. Nonetheless, van Hook directed *PC-458* to work the area with sonar and saturated the skies with Army and Navy aircraft (B-18s, Catalinas, P-39 fighters, etc.).

The aircraft and the PC hunted the U-boat all-out for twenty-four hours. Finally, at about 10:00 A.M. on July 13, a Catalina reported "a moving oil slick" and directed *PC-458* to the spot. After gaining sonar contact, the PC let go ten depth charges set for 150 to 300 feet. Meanwhile, the circling aircraft dropped eight bombs and twenty-four depth charges, a total of forty-two missiles. Other than the oil slick, no sign of a U-boat appeared. Toward evening, the new (1942) American destroyer *Lansdowne,* commanded by William R. Smedberg III, relieved the PC. *Lansdowne* promptly got sonar contact and dropped four 600-pound depth charges. Nothing further was ever heard from *U-153*. In a controversial decision, Washington gave equal credit for the kill to the *Lansdowne* and to the B-18s of Army Air Forces Squadron 59, which had supposedly bombed her off Aruba on July 5 and 6.

Not many miles away, Loewe in *U-505* patrolled off Panama. A crewman wrote: "For sixteen days we moved slowly back and forth off Colon. Not a thing in sight; the sea was empty. Finally, in disgust, Loewe took the boat south [closer] to the coast. . . . Here on 21 July we underwent our first ordeal, a plane almost caught us on the surface and dropped two bombs before we had even fifty meters of water over us. *U-505* suffered no damage, however, and no further attack came." The next day, July 22, *U-505* sank by gun the 110-ton Colombian sailing ship *Roamar.*

After that, Loewe became "ill" and was relieved by his first watch officer, Herbert Nollau, who returned the boat to France. Loewe was sent to other duty.

These three Type IX patrols, mounted at such expense in resources, were unmitigated disasters. Within the Gulf of Mexico and the Caribbean, the three boats, meeting strong air patrols and convoying, sank only two sailing ships for 175 tons. One green boat, *U-153,* had been lost; the other two appear to have been badly mismanaged.

Another new Type IX, *U-166,* commanded by Hans-Günter Kuhlmann, age twenty-eight, former merchant marine officer and first watch officer to Werner Hartmann on *U-37,* was assigned to lay TMB (magnetic) mines at the mouth of the Mississippi River. The *U-166* was Kuhlmann's second command. His first, the new Type VII *U-580,* had been rammed and sunk by a target ship in Baltic exercises in November 1941. His crew was saved and assigned to *U-166.* Launched November 3, 1941, the *U-166* had been rushed to completion and commissioned on March 23. After merely two months and nine days of workup in the Baltic, *U-166* sailed for France. She arrived June 10 and sailed on to the Americas one week later with six torpedoes in her bow and stern tubes, nine mines stowed on the deck plates in the bow compartment, and thirteen other torpedoes stowed internally and externally.

Approaching the Gulf of Mexico via the Old Bahama Channel and the Straits of Florida, Kuhlmann found plenty of action. On July 10, he attacked a small convoy (two freighters, two escorts) but all six torpedoes missed or malfunctioned, perhaps as a result of the rushed training in the Baltic. The next day, July 11, he sank by gun the 84-ton Dominican sailing vessel *Carmen.* Near the north end of the Windward Passage on July 13, he encountered a large, heavily escorted convoy of eleven ships, from which he torpedoed and sank a 2,300-ton American freighter. Passing through the Straits of Florida on July 16, he sank by gun the 16-ton American trawler *Gertrude.*

Kuhlmann reported that he planted his nine mines on the night of July 24–25 at the mouth of the Mississippi River, about 650 yards off the jetty heads. The mines had delayed-action fuses to enable Kuhlmann to clear the area. Something went wrong; none of the mines ever detonated. But on July 30, Kuhlmann sank by torpedo the armed and escorted 5,200-ton American cargo-passenger vessel *Robert E. Lee,* jammed with men, women, and children en route from Trinidad to New Orleans. Although this ship sank in fifteen minutes, only seventeen of the 407 persons on board perished. The escort *PC-566,* the SC *519,* and a tugboat rescued the other 390 from twenty-two lifeboats and rafts.

Coast Guard seaplanes based in Houma, Louisiana, routinely patrolled the mouth of the Mississippi River. At 1:40 on the afternoon of August 1, pilot Henry C. White, flying at 1,500 feet, saw a U-boat on the surface. White dived immediately to attack, and at 250 feet he dropped his single Mark XVII depth charge, set to detonate at 25 feet. Craning out the window, his radioman, George H. Boggs, Jr., reported what appeared to be a direct hit on the starboard side. In due course, two Army observation aircraft and White's relief arrived and he flew back to Houma.

The Gulf Sea Frontier credited White with "probable damage" to a U-boat, but in fact White had sunk *U-166* in about 120 feet of water with the loss of all hands. Since the kill was not recognized at the time, no effort to salvage the boat was made. It was the only U-boat sunk by Coast Guard aircraft in the war. For this feat, White was belatedly awarded the Distinguished Flying Cross.*

The four new IXs that sailed from Kiel directly to the Americas in June all had miserable patrols.

The first to leave were *U-171* and *U-173*. The *U-171* was commanded by Günther Pfeffer, age twenty-seven, who had been first watch officer to *Ritterkreuz holder* Heinrich Bleichrodt in *U-67* during that boat's assignment to R&D. The *U-173* was commanded by Heinz-Ehler Beucke, age thirty-eight, a senior officer from the crew of 1922. As planned, on July 6 both boats refueled from the new tanker *U-460*, commanded by Friedrich Schäfer, which was positioned north of Bermuda. Kerneval then assigned the boats to patrol the western end of the Gulf of Mexico, going via the Windward Passage to the waters south of Cuba, thence north through the Yucatan Channel. Gaining a few days on *U-173*, Pfeffer in *U-171* passed through the Yucatan Channel into the Gulf of Mexico on July 22. He continued northwest to the area near Galveston, Texas, where he sank a 4,400-ton Mexican freighter. He then cruised easterly to the mouth of the Mississippi River, where Kuhlmann in *U-166*, having laid his mines, was stalking ships with torpedoes. On July 29, Pfeffer reported a double miss on the tanker *Esso Richmond*. On July 31, he found an eleven-ship convoy hugging the shore, but a Coast Guard aircraft drove him off with a depth charge.

Pfeffer in *U-171* patrolled the area from the Mississippi River west to the Mexican coastline for a full month, August 4 to September 4. Harassed by "strong" air patrols and frustrated by coast-hugging convoys, he was able to sink two tankers in that period: the 6,800-ton American *R. M. Parker, Jr.* on August 13, and the 6,500-ton Mexican *Amatlán* on September 4. He then set sail for France, going by way of the Yucatan Channel to the Caribbean and the Mona Passage to the Atlantic. On September 24 he refueled a second time from a tanker, the new *U-461*, commanded by Wolf Stiebler.

Approaching Lorient on the afternoon of October 9 at the end of this 115-day patrol, Pfeffer in *U-171* was directed to rendezvous with an escort at 4:00 P.M. He arrived two hours early, strayed slightly off course, and struck a British mine. The *U-171* sank like a stone. The escort arrived and rescued thirty men, including Pfeffer and all of his officers, but twenty-two of the crew were killed in the sinking.

---

* The *U-166* burst into the news in April 1971, when a Florida salvor asserted that she had somehow drifted across the gulf to the Tampa area and that there was danger that the 200 tons of mercury she carried for ballast trim would leak out and kill the marine life. It was all nonsense. *U-166* could not rise and "drift" from her grave and she carried no mercury for ballast trim. Although *U-166* sank in shallow water, sport divers have not been able to find her. Very likely she is buried in silt deposited by the Mississippi River.

•   •   •

Trailing *U-171* by a few days, Beucke in *U-173* went through the Windward Passage into the Caribbean on July 19. While passing westbound close to the Cayman Islands, Beucke was caught and bombed by an Allied aircraft. Reporting this mishap to Kerneval, he stated that both periscopes were out of commission and that "repairs were improbable." He requested and gained permission to withdraw to open ocean—beyond range of Caribbean-based ASW aircraft—to attempt periscope repairs. However, the crew was unable to do the job.

Kerneval canceled *U-173*'s assignment to the Gulf of Mexico and directed Beucke to patrol in the open ocean south to Dutch Guiana (Surinam). Beucke complied with these orders or with minor alterations to them for a full month. In that time he reported only two ships, one on August 8 and one on August 17. He shot two torpedoes at the first ship but missed. He could not gain shooting position for the second.

Then came a second calamity. On August 27, another ASW aircraft caught and bombed *U-173*. Beucke reported that the explosion knocked out five of his six torpedo tubes and smashed four topside canisters and the G7a air torpedoes they contained. Both periscopes were still out; the boat could not dive deep.

Upon receiving this message, Kerneval ordered Beucke to bring *U-173* home to France. On the way, he chased a fast 20,000-ton ocean liner, but lost the race. He refueled for the second time from another tanker, the new *U-462,* commanded by Bruno Vowe, age thirty-eight. He arrived in France on September 20, completing a 98-day patrol, during which he had sunk no ships. He left the boat for other duty.

The second two IXs to sail from Kiel direct to the Americas were the longer-range Type IXC/40s, *U-508,* commanded by Georg Staats, age twenty-six, and *U-509,* commanded by Karl-Heinz Wolff, age thirty-two. The *U-508* was Staats's second command. His first, the Type VIIC *U-80,* had had a battery explosion in the Baltic and had been relegated to a school boat. The *U-508* and *U-509* refueled from Friedrich Schäfer's tanker *U-460.* They were then directed to patrol the Straits of Florida.

Wolff in *U-509* headed for his patrol area in a roundabout way, via the Mona Passage and the Yucatan Channel. Upon reaching the channel on August 2, he was depth-charged by ASW aircraft and notified Kerneval that it was necessary for *U-509* to withdraw for repairs. The next day he reported that it was "impossible to disperse oil trace." Slowly retracing his steps, Wolff retired through the Yucatan Channel to the Caribbean, thence to open ocean east of Trinidad. Like *U-173,* *U-509* was bombed a second time. On August 25 Wolff reported that he was "ill" and that he was returning to France. When he arrived on September 12, having sunk nothing whatsoever, he left the boat for other duty.

Inbound to the Straits of Florida via the old Bahama Channel, Staats in *U-508* encountered a "battleship" escorted by three "destroyers" with a tanker and a fast freighter. The "destroyers" thwarted his attack on the "battleship." He fired three torpedoes at the tanker and four at the freighter, but all seven missiles missed or malfunctioned. He then patrolled the Straits of Florida close to Havana and the north coast of Cuba.

In the two-week period from August 5 to 18, Staats scarcely slept. On August 5 and 6, he found separate convoys, heavily escorted by aircraft. He attacked the second of these, claiming one certain and one probable hit, but the hits could not be confirmed. Aircraft attacking with bombs and depth charges forced him off before he could mount a second attack. On August 12 he charged into another convoy, escorted by three "destroyers" and two Catalinas. Two of four torpedoes missed or malfunctioned, but the other two hit, sinking two small Cuban coasters for 2,700 tons. While evading the "destroyers," Staats reported, he employed sonar-deceiving *Bolde* (bubble targets or noisemakers) with "good" results. On August 17, he expended his last torpedoes on yet another convoy, claiming two hits but these could not be confirmed either. Homebound to France, Staats met the outbound Type IXC *U-163* from which he obtained fuel in exchange for drinking water.

These four new IXs sailing direct from Kiel turned in the worst Type IX performances of the war to then: five confirmed ships sunk for 20,300 tons. This was an average of about 1.25 ships for 4,000 tons per boat per patrol. Beucke in *U-173* and Wolff in *U-509* sank no ships whatsoever. Pfeffer in *U-171* lost his boat and twenty-two men.*

The other two IXs of the June group, *U-66* and *U-160,* patrolled near Trinidad.

Georg Lassen in *U-160,* who had made one prior patrol to the Cape Hatteras-Cape Lookout area, sinking five ships for about 37,000 tons, reached Trinidad about July 11. Patrolling the main shipping route in the narrow passage between the islands of Trinidad and Tobago, Lassen encountered "heavy" ASW air patrols. He got off to a wobbly start, missing two big freighters with a two-torpedo fan, but he soon compensated. In the period from July 16 to 21, he sank three ships: a 5,500-ton freighter and two tankers, the 7,000-ton Panamanian *Beaconlight* and the 8,100-ton British *Donovania.* Moving around to the east of Trinidad, in the ten days from July 25 to August 4, he sank three more freighters for 8,700 tons and savaged the 6,200-ton Norwegian tanker *Havsten* with torpedoes and gunfire. Total confirmed sinkings: six ships (two tankers) for about 29,000 tons. Claiming seven ships, including *Havsten,* sunk for 61,568 tons, Lassen qualified for a *Ritterkreuz,* which was awarded by radio while he was en route to France.†

The new skipper of the veteran *U-66* was Friedrich Markworth, age twenty-seven, who had been first watch officer on Werner Winter's *U-103* during two highly successful patrols to the Americas. One important task he had to carry out was to lay six TMB (magnetic) mines in the port of Castries, on the island of St.

---

* Pfeffer and some crew returned to Germany to man a new boat.

† At the time of the award, Lassen's confirmed score was eleven ships for 66,000 tons sunk, plus damage to two tankers. The first tanker, *Bidwell,* was salvaged. The second, *Havsten,* was abandoned. Two days later the Italian submarine *Tazzoli* found *Havsten* and sank her with two torpedoes.

Lucia, where the Americans had established a naval base to keep watch on adjacent Vichy Martinique.

In addition to the six mines, *U-66* carried nineteen torpedoes, thirteen internally and six in topside canisters. In case he should encounter shipping en route to the Caribbean, Markworth sailed with all six torpedo tubes loaded and the six mines stored above the floor plates in the bow compartment. As it happened, on July 9, during the voyage out, Markworth did encounter a ship, the 6,400-ton Yugoslavian freighter *Triglav,* which he sank with two torpedoes. He then loaded each of those empty tubes with three TMB mines.

Markworth stood off the port of Castries submerged at about noon on July 20. When the net boom opened to permit entry of a small craft, he boldly took *U-66* inside. Cruising at periscope depth, he quickly laid the six mines. He then *backed out* as the net boom was closing. Equipped with delayed-action fuses, the mines activated later. Nine days after they were sown, on July 29, a small, fast-moving launch triggered one mine. No one was hurt, but local authorities immediately closed the port to shipping and sent for a minesweeper. On August 2, two fast British motor launches from Trinidad triggered three more mines, but neither boat was damaged. Minesweepers cleared the other two mines and Castries reopened to traffic on about August 9.

Markworth's mines caused no harm—other than frayed nerves—but he went on to conduct a notable first patrol. He sank three more freighters near Trinidad between July 26 and August 6. Then came a frustrating lull of three weeks during which he saw nothing. Doggedly patrolling east of Trinidad in the open Atlantic, on August 28 he apparently discovered a new shipping lane between Trinidad and Cape Town, South Africa. In three days he sank four more ships: three freighters laden with war matériel for the British forces in Egypt, and the 8,600-ton British tanker *Winamac.* Homebound on September 9, he sank the 6,400-ton Swede *Peiping,* en route from Buenos Aires to New York, bringing his total for the patrol to nine ships sunk for about 49,000 tons. The celebration was muted by the death of a crewman, who was buried at sea on September 13.

Per plan, *U-66* rendezvoused with Schäfer's tanker *U-460.* Markworth requested a routine refueling of 25 cubic meters, and Schäfer obliged—or so both skippers believed. But Schäfer's crew made a mistake and delivered 16 cubic meters of oil and 9 cubic meters of seawater to *U-66.* When the mistake was later discovered, Markworth was forced to sneak into El Ferrol, Spain, and refuel a second time from the "interned" German tanker *Max Albrecht,* to which he transferred a sailor who was seriously ill. The boat finally arrived in France on September 29, after ninety-six days at sea. The sailor who was left in Spain recovered and returned to France in time for the boat's next patrol.

The returns of the ten Type IXs that sailed to the Americas in June were disappointing: thirty-one ships for about 135,000 tons, including four trawlers or sailing ships. This was an average of 3.1 ships of 13,500 tons per boat per patrol, a drastic drop from the results of the IXs that sailed in May. Two boats, Markworth in *U-66* and Lassen in *U-160,* sank well over half the total: fifteen ships for 78,200 tons. Two boats, Beucke's *U-173* and Wolff's *U-509,* sank no ships at all. Three Type

IXs were lost: Reichmann's *U-153* and Kuhlmann's *U-166* in American waters to American forces, and *U-171* to a British mine off Lorient.

In view of the so-so returns of the VIIs, the combined results of the twenty-three boats that reached the Americas in June were likewise disappointing: fifty-eight ships (including all the trawlers and sailing vessels) sunk for about 259,000 tons. This was an average of about 2.5 ships for about 11,260 tons sunk per boat per patrol. Altogether, six boats (three VIIs and three IXs) of this group had been lost (five with all hands), a casualty rate of 26 percent. Clearly the U-boat campaign in American waters was returning less and less for greater and greater risk and losses, but Dönitz was not yet ready to give up that campaign.

THE ARCTIC: CONVOY PQ 17

Throughout the spring and summer of 1942, Hitler remained convinced that the Allies intended to invade Norway. In compliance with his specific orders, big ships of the *Kriegsmarine* were kept on alert in that region to repel invaders: *Tirpitz*, the heavy cruiser *Hipper*, and the "pocket" battleships *Admiral Scheer* and *Lützow* (ex-*Deutschland*), the latter back in action after a year of repairs and workup. None was to sail until Hitler gave a direct order.

Also in compliance with Hitler's specific orders, a force of twenty to twenty-five U-boats were based in Norway. The primary task of this force was to help repel Allied invaders. Secondarily they patrolled Arctic waters to attack PQ and QP convoys en route to and from Murmansk, respectively. On any given day about half the force was at sea hunting convoys, the other half in ports undergoing voyage or battle-damage repairs or on anti-invasion alert.

The U-boats operated under numerous handicaps. In contrast to the Atlantic and Mediterranean areas, there was no single U-boat commander or headquarters in Norway at this time. Command of and responsibility for the Norway U-boat forces shifted between the admiral commanding Group North (in Kiel), the admiral commanding Norway, and the admiral commanding Arctic waters, A. D. Hubert Schmundt, in Narvik. The newly assigned U-boat specialists and *Ritterkreuz* holders Jürgen Oesten and Herbert Schultze could advise the admirals on U-boat operations, but they were not empowered to issue direct orders. There were as yet no U-boat flotillas or staffs to provide shore-based backup.* Since base facilities were primitive, U-boats requiring extensive battle-damage repairs or overhauls had to return to Germany. Coordination and communications between the *Kriegsmarine* and *Luftwaffe* in Norway left much to be desired.

Inasmuch as British codebreakers were reading *Luftwaffe* Red Enigma as well as the three-rotor naval Enigma employed by the admiral commanding Norway, the Admiralty was the beneficiary of superb intelligence on German plans and operations in Norway and the Arctic. The British closely watched the movements of

---

* Combat Flotilla 11, commanded by Hans Cohausz, onetime skipper of *U-A,* was formally established in Bergen on June 6, but weeks elapsed before it was fully staffed and operational.

the big ships, the dispositions of the U-boats, and the *Luftwaffe* buildup in northern Norway. The Enigma intelligence enabled the British to anticipate attacks on PQ and the opposite-sailing QP sister convoys, but owing to the lack of maneuvering room in the Barents Sea and saturation *Luftwaffe* aerial reconnaissance, they were rarely able to escape detection or to divert convoys around known U-boat patrol lines.

In the midst of the battle with PQ 16, Hitler suddenly became convinced that an Allied invasion of Norway might come at any hour. Accordingly he flashed alerts to his military commanders in Norway and on May 27, for the second time in 1942, directed that *all* Type VII U-boats outbound from Germany to the Atlantic be diverted to the defense of Norway. The OKM calculated that if this order stood, eight new Type VIIs could reach Norway by June 10. Further diversions of new Type VIIs to Norway in June and July, the OKM diarist noted, could raise the total number of U-boats diverted to that area to "forty or fifty," a terrible blow to the Atlantic U-boat force.

Hitler's order provoked another heated debate over deployment of U-boats to Arctic waters. Dönitz again forcefully stated his view that no boats whatever should be deployed there. The U-boat force had not been able to prevent the British invasion of Norway in April 1940; the returns from U-boat operations against PQ and QP convoys did not come close to justifying the effort expended. To then, all the Norway-based U-boats had sunk only eight confirmed merchant ships plus the destroyer *Matabele* from the several hundred that had sailed in sixteen PQ convoys to Murmansk, and only one merchant ship from the twelve homebound QP convoys. Three U-boats had been lost with all hands (*U-655, U-585,* and *U-702*), a high price to pay for nine merchant ships and a destroyer. Several other U-boats had incurred heavy battle damage.

Admiral Raeder and the OKM again calmed Hitler's fear of an invasion and persuaded him to rescind the order diverting all new Type VIIs to Norway. But Raeder did not agree with Dönitz that all U-boats should be withdrawn from the Arctic. Notwithstanding the disappointing level of sinkings and the increased risk posed by the absence of darkness in the summer months, Raeder believed the *Kriegsmarine* should be in position to deploy "about eight" U-boats against each and every PQ convoy. These were to find and shadow the convoys for the benefit of the *Luftwaffe,* lie in wait on patrol lines to intercept the ships, polish off cripples left behind by the airmen, and rescue Germans who had to ditch in damaged aircraft.

Raeder and the OKM calculated that to send "about eight" U-boats against every PQ convoy, a total force of twenty-three boats would be required. Inasmuch as three boats had been lost and by prior agreement three Norway-based boats had been transferred to the Atlantic force in May (*U-134, U-454,* and *U-584*), it was necessary to divert six more Type VIIs to Norway* in order to maintain the force at twenty-three boats. Dönitz again protested the diversions, but to no avail. Admiral Raeder replied

---

*   *U-88, U-255, U-355, U-408, U-457, U-601.*

that in view of the importance of stopping the flow of war matériel to the Soviet Union, a force level of twenty-three boats in Norway was not unreasonable.

There was another factor of importance. To stress the Allied military assistance to the Soviet Union and uphold morale in Moscow and in the ranks of the besieged Red armies, President Roosevelt directed that Murmansk convoys receive maximum publicity. Thus these convoys for a time became much more prominent than others. To have permitted these high-profile convoys to pass to Murmansk unchallenged would have been a setback, psychological and otherwise, for the Germans.

Encouraged by the wild *Luftwaffe* overclaims of damage to PQ 16, Admiral Raeder and the OKM conceived an elaborate plan, *Rosselsprung* (Knight's Move), to utterly destroy PQ 17 and thereby force the Allies to close down the Murmansk run. A pack of U-boats, *Eisteufel* (Ice Devil), was to form a patrol line across the path of the oncoming convoy northeast of Jan Mayen Island. The four big surface ships, *Tirpitz, Admiral Scheer, Lützow,* and *Hipper,* with destroyer screens, were to stage northward through Narvik and Altenfiord. If the circumstances proved to be favorable for the big surface ships—and if Hitler authorized their sailing—they were to converge on the convoy at about the same time the U-boat pack and the *Luftwaffe* got there.

The Germans did not know when PQ 17 was to leave Iceland. To detect the departure as early as possible, Hubert Schmundt in Narvik, temporarily commanding the U-boat force, sent three boats to patrol the north end of the Denmark Strait in early June. These were Heinrich Timm in *U-251,* Friedrich-Karl Marks in *U-376,* and Reinhard von Hymmen in the newly arrived *U-408.* Marks in *U-376* spotted a "cruiser," but by the time he got permission to attack it, the warship was gone. On Schmundt's order, Marks reconnoitered the boundary of the ice pack to make certain PQ 17 had not found an open passage to the north of Jan Mayen Island. It had not.

The British reluctantly sailed PQ 17 to Murmansk and its reverse, QP 13, from Murmansk, on June 27. The largest convoy to Murmansk yet, PQ 17, numbered forty ships: thirty-five big, heavily laden freighters (one of them, *Empire Tide,* with a catapult), three rescue vessels, and two tankers for refueling escorts. The convoy was guarded by sixty-two Allied warships: twenty-one British close escorts;* seven Allied warships in a cruiser covering force;† nineteen Allied warships in a distant covering force;‡ and fifteen Allied submarines placed ahead.§

---

*   Six destroyers, four corvettes, two submarines, three minesweepers, two antiaircraft gun ships, and four ASW trawlers.

†   Two British heavy cruisers, *London* and *Norfolk;* two American heavy cruisers, *Tuscaloosa* and *Wichita;* the British destroyer *Somali;* and two modern American destroyers, *Rowan* and *Wainwright.*

‡   The British carrier *Victorious,* the battleship *Duke of York,* heavy cruisers *Nigeria* and *Cumberland,* and twelve destroyers; the American battleship *Washington;* and two modern American destroyers, *Mayrant* and *Rhind.*

§   The British submarines *Sahib, Seawolf, Sturgeon, Tribune, Trident, Unrivalled, Unshaken,* and *Ursula;* the Free French *Minerve;* and six Soviet submarines.

None of the three U-boats on lookout in the Denmark Strait detected the sailing of PQ 17 or any of its massive escort. Almost immediately after sailing, the convoy "lost" three of its forty ships. The American freighter *Richard Bland* grounded on rocks and was forced to abort. The American freighter *Exford* and the 3,300-ton British tanker *Grey Ranger* ran into floating ice and incurred damage. *Exford* aborted to Iceland. Owing to her damage, *Grey Ranger,* which was to refuel escorts, would go only part way, then rendezvous with and refuel the escorts of QP 13. The 8,400-ton tanker *Aldersdale* would go all the way to Murmansk, refueling PQ 17 escorts.

Schmundt established the U-boat patrol line *Eisteufel* (Ice Devils) across the expected path of PQ 17 near Jan Mayen Island. As U-boats arrived, Schmundt added to the line until it consisted of six boats. On July 1, one of these skippers, Max-Martin Teichert in *U-456,* found PQ 17 and flashed the alarm, but the four-stack destroyer *Leamington* drove him off. Two other boats, von Hymmen in *U-408* of the Denmark Strait patrol, low on fuel, and a new boat from Germany, *U-255,* commanded by Reinhardt Reche, age twenty-seven, came up in the fog patches to confirm Teichert's sighting. From Narvik, Schmundt directed these three boats, plus Heinz Bielfeld in *U-703,* to shadow and to make beacons for the benefit of all German forces.

On the following day, July 2, the U-boat shadowers and the Ice Devils merged at about the same time that PQ 17 and QP 13 passed, sailing in opposite directions. One of the Ice Devils, Heino Bohmann in *U-88,* spotted and reported QP 13. It consisted of thirty-five ships and fifteen escorts, but the German aim was to sink ships laden with armaments for the Soviet Union, not the returning empty ships. Schmundt therefore specifically ordered Bohmann—and all other U-boat skippers—to ignore the Iceland-bound QP 13 and concentrate on the Murmansk-bound PQ 17.*

Although Hitler had yet to authorize attacks by the big surface ships, upon discovery of the convoys, the German admirals deployed them northward to the most favorable jumping-off position in Altenfiord near the North Cape of Norway. During these movements, the newly-arrived "pocket" battleship *Lützow* and three destroyers ran onto rocks in the fog and incurred such heavy damage that they had to be withdrawn from the operation. That humiliating accident left only the super-battleship *Tirpitz,* the "pocket" battleship *Admiral Scheer,* the heavy cruiser *Hipper,* and their screens (seven destroyers, two torpedo boats) to mount the surface-ship attack on PQ 17. Hitler finally authorized them to sail, but only if there was no risk of a loss to Allied carrier-based aircraft or submarines, which would embarrass Germany and jeopardize the defense of Norway. These restrictions led the German admirals in charge of surface-ship operations to proceed with utmost caution.

During that day and the next, July 3, all eleven U-boats in the area closed on convoy PQ 17 or took up positions along its track. As Schmundt wrote later, "con-

---

* After entering the Denmark Strait unmolested by the Germans, a section of QP 13 accidentally ran into an Allied defensive minefield. The British minesweeper *Niger* and five big ships totaling about 31,000 tons hit mines, blew up, and sank. One of the lost ships, the Soviet cargo-passenger vessel *Rodina,* was transporting the wives and families of Soviet diplomats to England.

ditions for U-boat warfare were the most unfavorable imaginable." Dense fog patches lay over a sea of mushy, crushed ice. The fog hid the U-boats, but from time to time the convoy ran out of it without warning, leaving the U-boats naked in bright sunlight and in full view of the ships and escorts. In the open areas, the seas were flat, glassy calm, making it dangerous to use periscopes for submerged attacks. Reinhardt Reche in the new *U-255* got close enough submerged to shoot a two-torpedo fan at a "destroyer," but both torpedoes missed. Escorts counterattacked and dropped forty depth charges near *U-255* but none was close enough to do real harm. At least six other boats attempted attacks, but the veteran escorts beat them off, and one by one the U-boats fell behind and lost contact. German aircraft, homing on U-boat beacons, assumed the shadower role. Contemptuous of the difficulties the U-boats faced or the inexperience of the crews, German admirals conducting the action were furious at the failure of the U-boats to get close and attack.

Luftwaffe dive bombers and torpedo planes attacked PQ 17 and elements of the cruiser support force that had closed up to protect it on July 4. The escorts threw up dense walls of ack-ack but the aircraft, staging from bases in northern Norway, had sufficient fuel to mount several attacks. Even so, they achieved little. In the early morning, a torpedo bomber hit and savaged the 7,200-ton American freighter *Christopher Newport.* After her crew abandoned ship, two British escorts tried to put the hulk under, but both attempts failed. Later in the day, Karl Brandenburg in the new *U-457* found the ravaged, abandoned hulk and sank it with a torpedo.

During this action, Brandenburg got a periscope glimpse of some elements of the cruiser force. In his report, he stated that he had seen heavy units with the convoy, including a "battleship." On the basis of this incorrect report, Admiral Raeder, assuming these heavy units to be the distant covering force, which included an aircraft carrier, and mindful of Hitler's restriction, refused to authorize the sailing of *Tirpitz* until the supposed carrier had been sunk. Since the U-boats had the best chance of sinking the carrier, Schmundt directed Brandenburg in *U-457* to ignore PQ 17 and to shadow the "battleship" (and presumably the carrier) and to bring up other boats. Inasmuch as three of the eleven boats that had sailed in early June to serve as lookouts in the Denmark Strait had to refuel in Narvik or Kirkenes, and two boats had to shadow the convoy in behalf of the *Luftwaffe,* only five other boats were available to join Brandenburg in *U-457* to hunt down the "battleship." So that there could be no mistake or confusion, Schmundt advised all U-boats that their "main targets" were the Allied heavy units.

Later on July 4, large flights of *Luftwaffe* aircraft attacked PQ 17 twice. A group of dive bombers and torpedo planes in the second attack hit three ships: the 4,800-ton British freighter *Navarino,* the 7,200-ton American freighter *William Hooper,* and the Soviet tanker *Azerbaijan.* After taking off the crew, British escorts sank *Navarino.* Hilmar Siemon in *U-334* happened upon the abandoned hulk of *William Hooper* and put her under with torpedoes. *Azerbaijan* made temporary repairs and sailed on.

In London, First Sea Lord Dudley Pound fretted. He knew from various intelligence sources, including Enigma, that *Tirpitz* and the other big German ships had staged to northern Norway, doubtless to attack PQ 17. However, he was unaware of the restriction Hitler had placed on the sailing of the German surface forces or of the accident to *Lützow*. Contrary to all advice, he wrongly assumed that *Tirpitz* and the other big ships had sailed late on July 4 to attack the Allied forces. Pound calculated that the Germans could reach PQ 17 and the covering cruiser force by the afternoon of July 5. Combined with the power of the U-boats and *Luftwaffe*, the German surface ships might sink the whole of PQ 17 and the cruiser force as well. To avoid this possible catastrophe, Pound issued fateful—and controversial—orders for the convoy to "scatter" and for the cruiser force to reverse course and withdraw to the southwest. Although no orders had been issued to them, the six destroyers in the close escort joined the withdrawing cruiser force. Like the merchant ships, the remaining fifteen close escorts scattered in all directions.

The U-boats were first to report and benefit from the scatter. Teichert in *U-456* and Brandenburg in *U-457* signaled that the cruiser force (wrongly believed to be the battleship-carrier covering force) had reversed course at very high speed. Unable to pursue at that speed, they and other skippers requested permission to attack the many unescorted merchant ships all around them. Schmundt authorized this shift in targets and amid the repeated *Luftwaffe* attacks, the U-boats had a field day.

• Heinz Bielfeld in *U-703* sank the 6,600-ton British freighter *Empire Byron*, which had been damaged by the *Luftwaffe*, and the 5,500-ton British freighter *River Afton*. Bielfeld captured a British Army officer from *Empire Byron* and the captain of *River Afton*, and gave the survivors in lifeboats food and water.

• Heino Bohmann in *U-88* sank the 5,100-ton American freighter *Carlton* and the 7,200-ton American freighter *Daniel Morgan*, which had been damaged by the *Luftwaffe*.

• Hilmar Siemon in *U-334* sank the 7,200-ton British freighter *Earlston*, which had been damaged by German aircraft, and captured her captain.

• Max-Martin Teichert in *U-456* sank the 7,000-ton American freighter *Honomu* and captured her captain.

Also enjoying a field day, the German airmen had difficulty distinguishing friend from foe. One dive bomber hit Siemon in *U-334*. Another hit Brandenburg in *U-457*. The two bombs that fell near *U-334* caused such heavy damage that Siemon was forced to abort. At Siemon's request, Schmundt directed Teichert in *U-456* to escort *U-334* into Kirkenes. At about the same time, Heinrich Göllnitz in *U-657*, who had sunk no ships, aborted owing to a leak in an external fuel-oil tank that was leaving an oil trace. These three withdrawals reduced the U-boat force to five, but the three boats that refueled in Narvik and Kirkenes (*U-251*, *U-376*, *U-408*) resailed immediately, again raising the Arctic force to eight U-boats.

Upon learning that the Allied covering force, the cruiser force, and the destroyers of the close escort had fled and that the convoy had scattered, Admiral Raeder persuaded Hitler that *Tirpitz, Admiral Scheer,* and *Hipper* could sail without undue risk. Thereupon the Führer approved *Rosselsprung* (Knight's Move). Raeder relayed the approval to the forces at sea, stressing that every precaution must be taken to prevent the loss or severe damage to any of the three big ships, especially *Tirpitz*.

Escorted by seven destroyers and two motor torpedo boats, the three big German ships sailed from Altenfiord at 3:00 P.M., July 5. As the force emerged from protected waters to open sea, the Soviet submarine *K-21* saw it and attacked *Tirpitz,* claiming two hits, which were, however, not confirmed. An hour later, a Coastal Command Catalina also saw and reported the force. Two hours after that the British submarine *Unshaken,* commanded by H. P. Westmacott, saw and radioed an exact description of the force.

Hearing of these Allied sightings from *B-dienst,* Admiral Raeder deemed the sortie to be too risky and on his own authority he canceled *Rosselsprung,* merely six and a half hours after it commenced. For the second time, *Tirpitz* returned to port without having achieved anything with her massive armament. However, her mere presence in the area had persuaded Admiral Pound to scatter PQ 17, leaving all its surviving ships and close escorts vulnerable to aircraft and U-boat attack.

Over the next ten days, German aircraft and U-boats scoured the Barents Sea in search of ships from the scattered convoy. One German aircraft sank one more freighter, the 5,400-ton American *Pan Atlantic;* other aircraft damaged a half dozen other ships. Reinhardt Reche in *U-255* was the most successful of the U-boat skippers. He sank three American freighters for about 18,400 tons, plus the 7,200-ton Dutchman *Paulus Potter,* which had been hit by the *Luftwaffe* and abandoned in such haste that "secret papers" had been left behind.* Günter La Baume in *U-355* sank one British freighter for 5,100 tons. Three other boats sank one ship each that had been damaged by the *Luftwaffe:* Heinrich Timm in *U-251,* Friedrich-Karl Marks in *U-376,* and Karl Brandenburg in *U-457,* who barely avoided an attack by a Soviet submarine.

When the final sinking reports reached Berlin, the German high command was exultant. It believed that for the first time in the war an entire Allied convoy had been wiped out. The *Luftwaffe* claimed sinking twenty ships for 131,000 tons. The U-boats claimed sinking sixteen ships for 113,963 tons, a combined total of thirty-six ships for 245,000 tons. In reality, fourteen of the thirty-eight merchant and rescue ships that confronted the German air and U-boat attacks survived to reach Soviet ports and none of the warships was lost. In part the huge overclaims resulted from aircraft and submarines "sinking" the same ships. The results, as calculated by Jürgen Rohwer and other students of the battle:

Ships sunk by aircraft alone:	8 for 40,425 tons †
Ships sunk by U-boats alone:	7 for 41,041 tons ‡
Ships sunk by aircraft and U-boats:	9 for 61,255 tons
Totals:	24 for 142,721 tons§

---

* A boarding party from *U-255* recovered the papers, which included exact details on the composition of PQ 17, as well as "new signal codebooks for convoys" and "other welcome papers."

† Hermann Göring awarded three *Ritterkreuzes* to airmen who engaged in the battle with PQ 17.

‡ The eleven U-boats deployed against PQ 17 shot a total of seventy-two torpedoes, of which twenty-seven were believed to have hit and exploded. Nine of the eleven boats were credited with sinkings. Reinhardt von Hymmen in *U-408* and Heinrich Göllnitz in *U-657* (who aborted with an oil leak) sank no ships.

§ Twenty-two of the twenty-four confirmed ships sunk were big freighters, heavily laden with war matériel. Fourteen of the twenty-four were American ships. The lost cargo included 3,350 trucks

Until the battle of PQ 17 there was a possibility that Dönitz might persuade Berlin to release some or all of the twenty-three Type VII boats in Norway and the Arctic for duty in the Atlantic. In view of the inflated—and credited—U-boat sinking claims and the convoy detection and shadow service U-boats provided for the *Luftwaffe,* any prospect of transfers evaporated.

The destruction of PQ 17 led the British to suspend the Murmansk run until the Arctic days had some hours of darkness and steps could be taken to greatly improve the defense of the merchant ships. These steps included the establishment of RAF Hampden and Catalina squadrons on airfields near Murmansk and an Allied refueling facility for escorts and warships on the island of Spitzbergen, the adaptation of the Royal Navy's American-built "jeep" carrier *Avenger* for temporary Arctic service,* the fitting of merchant ships with more flak guns and tethered blimps, and the return of numerous Home Fleet warships temporarily assigned to the Mediterranean and elsewhere. Notwithstanding the intense political pressures from Washington and Moscow, London held firm and no PQ or QP convoys set sail in July or August.

THE MEDITERRANEAN: SUPPORTING ROMMEL

The twenty Type VII U-boats based in the Mediterranean on April 1, 1942, to support Erwin Rommel's *Afrika Korps* continued to operate under extremely difficult conditions. The patrols were still brief but nerve-shattering and risky. Some skippers cracked from the strain. Others rotated back to Germany to command larger U-boats under construction. Notwithstanding pressures from Berlin and Rome and the new Mediterranean U-boat commander, Leo Kreisch, the Italian-run shore facilities at La Spezia, Pola, and Salamis remained slow and slovenly. When on April 1, an Allied aircraft hit Helmut Rosenbaum in *U-73* with four bombs or depth charges, repairs at La Spezia required four full months.

The Mediterranean U-boats had been organized into Combat Flotilla 29 for administrative purposes in early 1942. The flotilla commander during the first six months was the fifty-eight-year-old Franz Becker. In June 1942, he was relieved by *Ritterkreuz* holder Fritz Frauenheim, who had won fame in the Atlantic while commanding *U-101.* He was to hold that post a full year.

Six boats patrolled the eastern Mediterranean in April 1942. Off Mersa Matruh on April 7, Egon-Reiner von Schlippenbach in *U-453* hit by mistake the 9,700-ton

---

and vehicles, 430 tanks, 210 aircraft, and about 100,000 tons of other war supplies. About 153 merchant marine officers and men (107 Americans) died in the sinkings or in lifeboats; about 1,300 others (581 Americans) survived. The ships that reached Soviet ports delivered 896 vehicles, 164 tanks, 87 aircraft, and about 57,000 tons of other military cargo. In mounting 202 dive-bomber and torpedo sorties, the *Luftwaffe* lost only five aircraft and a few men. The U-boat force incurred no losses.

* The first four American-built "jeep" carriers for the Royal Navy had been delayed. As related, during workup in the Caribbean, *Archer* collided with and sank the Peruvian freighter *Brazos,* damaging herself so badly that she had to be towed to the Charleston naval base for repairs. All four had severe teething problems with their newly designed high-performance diesel engines.

British hospital ship *Somersetshire* with three torpedoes. Fortunately for all concerned, she survived the hits and limped into Alexandria. Hitler personally approved the OKM's plan to keep the error secret like the *Athenia* affair and to deny any Allied charges of atrocities. Von Schlippenbach altered his log accordingly. In nearly the same spot, on April 23 a new skipper in *U-565,* Wilhelm Franken, age twenty-seven, claimed sinking two freighters for 9,500 tons, but postwar records confirmed only one, a 1,400-ton British coaster.

Four of the six boats sailing to the eastern Mediterranean were assigned to lay TMB (magnetic) mines during the period from April 13 to April 15.

•   The *U-81,* commanded by Fritz Guggenberger, who had won a *Ritterkreuz* for sinking the aircraft carrier *Ark Royal,* planted a field at Haifa, Palestine. No confirmed sinkings were attributed to this field. After planting the mines, Guggenberger cruised north toward Beirut, where he sank two ships by torpedo: the 1,150-ton Vichy French trawler *Viking* and the 6,000-ton British tanker *Caspia.* Returning to Palestinian waters from April 16 to April 26, Guggenberger sank seven sailing ships by gun and one by ramming, and bombarded an electric power station in Tel Aviv.

•   The *U-331,* commanded by Hans-Dietrich von Tiesenhausen, who had won a *Ritterkreuz* for sinking the battleship *Barham,* planted a field at Beirut. Von Tiesenhausen then entered the harbor on the surface in darkness and fired a torpedo at a 3,000-ton Norwegian freighter moored at a pier. He thought he damaged that ship, but she was shielded by barges that absorbed the explosion. The next day he fired a torpedo at a 4,000-ton freighter, but the torpedo failed to explode. In the several days following, von Tiesenhausen sank three sailing vessels and destroyed the electric power station in Beirut by gun. As far as could be determined, his minefield did not sink or damage any Allied vessels.

•   The *U-561,* commanded by Robert Bartels, planted a field at Port Said, the Mediterranean entry to the Suez Canal. A month later, on May 15, these mines sank two freighters for 11,754 tons and damaged a third for 4,000 tons. In view of these successes, Bartels was directed to lay another field at Port Said on June 18 and yet another on July 10. However, the second and third fields produced no recorded results. After that, Bartels left *U-561* and returned to Germany to commission one of the large U-boats.

•   The *U-562,* commanded by Horst Hamm, planted a field at Famagusta, a seaport on the east coast of Cyprus. About two weeks later, on April 29, these mines sank a 156-ton sailing ship and an 81-ton tugboat, but nothing of military value. After laying the field, Hamm took *U-562* to Turkish waters. The British asserted later that he violated international law by entering a Turkish harbor, where he found a British ship taking on cargo, then followed her to sea and attempted to sink her. However, the attack failed.

Three U-boats patrolled the western Mediterranean in late April to interdict the powerful Allied naval forces, including the American carrier *Wasp,* attempting to get aircraft and supplies to Malta. None found any warships to attack. Two of the three boats were lost:

•   On May 1, a Hudson of British Squadron 233, flying at 1700 feet and piloted by Sergeant Brent, sighted the *U-573,* commanded by Heinrich Heinsohn.

The plane dived and dropped three 250-pound depth charges set for 25 feet. One failed to detonate but the other two exploded close, savaging *U-573.* Soon the circling Hudson's crew saw about ten men on the bridge raise their hands in surrender. In response, the Hudson's crew passed up an opportunity for a machine-gun strafing attack, for which it was later severely reprimanded.*

Running low on fuel, the Hudson was forced to break off and return to base. Although *U-573* could not dive, Heinsohn eluded all other Allied aircraft and ships and limped into Cartagena, Spain, assisted the last few miles by two Spanish Navy tugs. Technically "interned," Heinsohn reported to Berlin that repairs to *U-573* were to take three months and that Spanish authorities agreed to "cooperate." However, Berlin decided against repairs and gave the boat to Spain, which repaired it and rechristened it *G-7.* Heinsohn and his crew eventually returned to Germany for reassignment.

• In the same area on the following day, May 2, a Sunderland of British Squadron 202, piloted by R. Y. Powell, caught *U-74,* commanded by Karl Friedrich, who had recently replaced the *Ritterkreuz holder* Eitel-Friedrich Kentrat. In contrast to the Hudson's casual attack on *U-573,* the Sunderland doggedly held contact with *U-74* and brought in the British destroyers *Wishart* and *Wrestler.* The combined air and sea attack destroyed *U-74* with no survivors.

The loss of *U-74* and *U-573* reduced the Mediterranean force to eighteen boats, including those such as *U-73* undergoing prolonged battle-damage repairs. Excluding small craft, the entire Mediterranean U-boat force sank but three merchant ships for 8,500 tons—and no warships—in April. Perhaps because of the continuing poor returns and the high risks, there was no great rush to replace the lost boats.

When Erwin Rommel resumed the long-delayed offensive from Gazala (Libya) toward Egypt on May 27, the U-boat force commander, Leo Kreisch, deployed nine boats to assist Axis ground forces. Eight of the boats patrolled close to the African coast from Gazala to Mersa Matruh to attack Allied vessels attempting to supply or evacuate the reeling British Eighth Army. The other, *U-83,* commanded by Hans-Werner Kraus, was to land an Axis commando force in the Gulf of Bomba. While closing the coast, Kraus shot at an escorted steamer. He claimed he missed his target and hit and sank the "corvette" escort, but the claim could not be confirmed. Owing to "technical problems" the commando operation was aborted, but Kraus continued his patrol.

Two boats were lost in the early stages of Rommel's offensive, reducing the Mediterranean force to sixteen.

• On the morning of May 27, a British Blenheim bomber spotted a U-boat sixty miles off the coast of Bardia, midway between Tobruk and Mersa Matruh. This was *U-568,* commanded by twenty-eight-year-old Joachim Preuss, who had hit and damaged the American destroyer *Kearny* the previous October. The

---

* The correct procedure in such cases, Coastal Command headquarters stated, was to continue offensive action by all weapons, in order to keep the U-boat crew below and prevent scuttling until a surface ship arrived.

Blenheim dropped a number of close bombs, one of which ruptured a fuel tank and caused a leak. In response to the plane's signal, the commander of a nearby convoy escort detached two destroyers, *Hurworth* and *Hero,* to carry on the hunt. The ships gained sonar contacts and in eight attacks over two hours *Hurworth* fired fifty depth charges at *U-568,* and in three attacks *Hero* fired twenty.

Since *Hurworth* was out of depth charges and *Hero* had only twenty left, the convoy-escort commander detached a third destroyer, *Eridge,* which arrived at 6:00 P.M. with thirty-five depth charges and took over the hunt. *Hero* carried out four more attacks, expending all of her depth charges. *Eridge* carried out six attacks, expending all but five of her depth charges. While *Hero* and *Eridge* held sonar contact and stalked, *Hurworth* broke off to run into Tobruk to get yet more depth charges.

After about twelve hours of brutal punishment, Preuss had no choice but to surface and attempt to shake the destroyers in the darkness. At about midnight on May 27–28, he came up merely 1,250 yards ahead of *Eridge.* Although *Eridge* and *Hero* had Type 286 radar, neither set picked up *U-568,* but the lookouts did, and both destroyers opened fire with main batteries, drawing *Hurworth* back to the scene. Preuss dived and eluded immediate destruction but when he surfaced again at 4:00 A.M., close to the three destroyers, they saw him and again opened fire. Guns blazing, *Eridge* ran in and dropped three of her five remaining depth charges, set for fifty feet. By that time Preuss and his crew had scuttled ship and were jumping into the water, begging to be rescued. *Hurworth* and *Eridge* sent boarding parties to capture secret papers, but they arrived too late, and *U-568* sank beneath their feet. The whaleboats picked up Preuss and forty-six other Germans, apparently the entire crew.

• On the morning of June 2, a Swordfish of British Fleet Air Arm Squadron 815, piloted by G. H. Bates, found and attacked another U-boat off Bardia, but much closer to the shore. This was *U-652,* commanded by Georg-Werner Fraatz, who had engaged the American destroyer *Greer* the previous September. The Swordfish attacks utterly disabled—but did not sink—*U-652.* When Fraatz radioed his situation and asked for help, Guggenberger in *U-81,* who was nearby searching for some German airmen who had ditched, responded within two hours. Fraatz and Guggenberger attempted to tow *U-652* to Salamis but failed. After the crewmen of *U-652* transferred to *U-81,* Fraatz sank his wrecked boat with one of Guggenberger's stern torpedoes. Fraatz and his crew debarked at Salamis and later returned to Germany to commission one of the big U-boats.

The other boats patrolling off North Africa in June in support of Rommel had mixed success. Franz-Georg Reschke in *U-205* sank the 5,450-ton British light cruiser *Hermione,* which was attempting to reach Malta. This success earned Reschke high praise from Berlin propagandists, but not, as expected, a *Ritterkreuz.* Wilhelm Dommes in *U-431* sank a 4,200-ton tanker, a 2,000-ton coaster, and possibly a 300-ton landing craft, and rescued nine downed German airmen. Heinrich Schonder in *U-77* sank the 1,000-ton British *Hunt*-class destroyer *Grove.* Hans-Dietrich von Tiesenhausen in *U-331* and Egon-Reiner von Schlippenbach in *U-453* attacked a convoy, claiming damage to three ships.

After aborting the commando raid, Hans-Werner Kraus in *U-83* patrolled off

Palestine and Lebanon. In a furiously aggressive seven-day period, June 7 to 13, Kraus claimed sinking three small freighters and four sailing ships, and damage to a 6,000-ton freighter. While returning to Salamis on June 19, Kraus received word that he had been awarded a *Ritterkreuz*. A crewman remembered that *U-83* entered Salamis flying twenty pennants representing total ships claimed sunk and sporting a big *Ritterkreuz* on the conning tower with the figure "20" beneath it. Wilhelm Dommes in *U-431* entered Salamis at the same time, flying seven pennants, representing the total ships he claimed sunk. The crewmen remembered that the simultaneous entry of *U-83* and *U-431* into Salamis had been staged and filmed by propagandists and shown as a newsreel in German movie theaters.*

Several other U-boats had success in the Palestine-Lebanon area in June. Heinz-Joachim Neumann in *U-372* sank the valuable 14,650-ton submarine tender *Medway,* mother ship of the British 1st Submarine Flotilla, while she was shifting from Alexandria, Egypt, to a safer berth in Beirut, Lebanon. Escorted by a light cruiser and seven destroyers(!), *Medway* had embarked 1,135 men. Because of smart seamanship during the rescue, only thirty men were lost. Hans-Otto Heidtmann in *U-559* sank a 4,700-ton tanker and damaged another of 6,000 tons, also earning a "well done" from Berlin propagandists. The *U-97,* commanded by a new skipper, Friedrich Bürgel, age twenty-five, sank three coasters for about 4,000 tons off Haifa.

In his drive east toward Egypt, Rommel again bypassed the British citadel of Tobruk. This time the Germans assumed the British would attempt a "Dunkirk"— an evacuation by sea. To thwart that possibility, the Germans rushed three U-boats to the area to establish a blockade, but it was unnecessary. As related, on June 21, the garrison in Tobruk surrendered to Axis forces.

During this phase of the fighting in the Mediterranean, British air and naval forces eliminated four more Italian submarines. A Catalina of British Squadron 202, piloted by Australian R. M. Corrie, sank *Veniero* on June 7. The British submarine *Ultimatum,* commanded by Peter R. H. Harrison, which had sunk *Millo* in March, sank *Zaffiro* on June 24. The corvette *Hyacinth* drove *Perla* to the surface with depth charges and captured the boat and twenty-five survivors.† Two South African trawlers, *Protea* and *Southern Maid,* assisted by a British aircraft, sank *Ondina* on July 11.

---

* The award of the *Ritterkreuz* to Kraus was apparently part of a propaganda scheme to give recognition to German submariners in the Mediterranean. At the time of the award, Kraus's claimed sinkings on *U-83* totaled twelve ships for 35,000 tons, including the seven small ships off Palestine. Up to then, he had sunk only one confirmed ship of any size: the 2,000-ton Portuguese freighter *Corte Real,* which he stopped in the Atlantic by gun, searched, and deemed to be carrying contraband, then sank with a single torpedo.

† *Perla* yielded some intelligence papers of value but apparently nothing helpful to Allied codebreakers. They were still reading the Italian naval code C-38m but had not broken any German naval codes employed in the Mediterranean area. In August, shortly after *Perla*'s capture, Allied codebreakers turned to the German naval Enigma network *Süd* (Porpoise), used by German naval commanders and surface ships in the Mediterranean, Balkans, and Black Sea. It proved to be a "relatively uncomplicated prewar machine," which "could be decrypted with no special difficulty," but it provided no cribs for breaking the four-rotor Enigma in use on the Triton (Shark) net in the Atlantic or tactical information of value.

• • •

When Erwin Rommel's *Afrika Korps* ran out of supplies and bogged down at El Alamein in early July, the British redoubled their efforts to get aircraft and supplies to Malta. These efforts culminated with the dispatch from England of a convoy, Pedestal, comprised of fourteen big, fast merchant ships, massively escorted by British warships, including the battleship *Nelson* and carrier *Victorious,* temporarily detached from the Home Fleet.

Alerted by intelligence sources, the Axis prepared a hot reception for Pedestal. The Axis naval forces included an Italian cruiser squadron, about eighteen Italian submarines and twelve PT boats, and three German U-boats: the *U-73,* commanded by Helmut Rosenbaum (returning to action after four months of battle-damage repairs), the *U-205,* commanded by Franz-Georg Reschke, and the *U-331,* commanded by *Ritterkreuz holder* Hans-Dietrich von Tiesenhausen. However, on August 9, an Allied aircraft hit *U-331,* wounding two men and forcing her to abort to La Spezia for repairs.

Convoy Pedestal passed by Gibraltar into the Mediterranean in a dense fog the evening of August 10. On the following day, Axis air forces found, reported, and attacked the huge formation, which included two battleships, four aircraft carriers, seven cruisers, and thirty-two destroyers. The Italian submarine *Uarsciek* was the first of the Axis naval units to attack, firing three torpedoes at the carrier *Furious,* which was to go only part way to launch Spitfires for Malta. The Italian skipper reported two solid hits, but these could not be confirmed in British records. Unaware of her close call, *Furious* launched her thirty-seven Spitfires, then prepared to reverse course for Gibraltar.

Helmut Rosenbaum in *U-73* lay submerged not far away. In the early afternoon of that same day, August 11, the whole huge formation came right toward him. He had an easy shot at four of the fourteen merchant ships in the convoy, but his orders were to attack major warships first. As the formation bore down upon him, he got a quick periscope glimpse of the old 22,600-ton aircraft carrier *Eagle,* screened by seven destroyers. Coolly slipping between the escorts, Rosenbaum closed to 500 yards and fired four bow torpedoes. All hit. *Eagle* sank in eight or ten minutes, with the loss of about 260 of her 1,160-man crew and all sixteen of her aircraft. The destroyers *Laforey, Lookout,* and *Malcolm* and the fleet tug *Growler* rescued most of *Eagle's* survivors, while the other destroyers hunted vainly for *Eagle's* killer. Rosenbaum took *U-73* very deep and lay doggo, unharmed by a rain of poorly aimed depth charges.

Later that afternoon Rosenbaum surfaced and got off a contact report that concluded: "Hit *Eagle* four torpedoes 500 yards. Sinking noises clearly heard. Depth-charged. No damage." Congratulatory messages poured in from Berlin, Rome, and elsewhere. Admiral Raeder directed that Rosenbaum be immediately awarded a *Ritterkreuz.** When *U-73* returned to La Spezia, he was promoted and sent to com-

---

* At the time of the award, Rosenbaum had sunk six confirmed ships for 52,000 tons, including *Eagle,* the third carrier after *Courageous* and *Ark Royal* to be sunk by U-boats.

mand the German U-boat force in the Black Sea.* His first watch officer on this patrol, Horst Deckert, age twenty-three, the son of German-American parents who lived in Chicago, was promoted to command *U-73*.

After *Furious* reversed course for Gibraltar, she was screened by a half-dozen destroyers, many of them crowded with *Eagle* survivors. One of the screen was *Wolverine*—famous for supposedly sinking Günther Prien in *U-47*—commanded by a new skipper, twenty-nine-year-old Peter Gretton. That night *Wolverine* picked up an unidentified submarine on her radar at close range. Unhesitatingly Gretton rang up flank speed and rammed the target at 26 knots. It proved to be the medium-size Italian submarine *Dagabur,* which sank instantly with the loss of all hands. The "terrific" impact of the collision severely damaged the aged *Wolverine,* which limped into Gibraltar, where in due course she got a temporary bow and went onward to England. There Gretton was decorated and promoted to command Escort Group B-7 on the North Atlantic run.

Convoy Pedestal pressed onward toward Malta, entering the perilous narrows separating Tunisia and Sardinia and Tunisia and Sicily. Per plan, the valuable battleships and carriers of the covering force prepared to reverse course and return to Gibraltar, leaving only the less valuable cruisers and destroyers to protect the merchant ships. However, before this dispersal could be executed, Axis air and naval forces inflicted severe damage on the British formations. Aircraft hit the destroyer *Foresight* and the new carrier *Indomitable,* so badly damaging *Foresight* that she had to be sunk. In a memorable salvo, the Italian submarine *Axum,* commanded by Renato Perrini, hit the 4,200-ton light cruiser *Cairo,* the 8,000-ton heavy cruiser *Nigeria,* and the 9,500-ton American tanker *Ohio,* in British charter. Hopelessly damaged, *Cairo,* too, had to be sunk. The Italian submarine *Dessie,* commanded by Renato Scandola, sank the 7,500-ton British freighter *Deucalion* (possibly damaged by aircraft) and perhaps damaged the 12,800-ton British freighter *Brisbane Star* (possibly damaged by aircraft). The Italian submarine *Alagi,* commanded by Sergio Puccini, sank the 7,300-ton British freighter *Clan Ferguson* and damaged the 8,000-ton heavy cruiser *Kenya.* The Italian submarine *Bronzo,* commanded by Cesare Buldrini, damaged the 12,700-ton British freighter *Empire Hope* (possibly damaged by aircraft), which had to be sunk by an escort.

The medium-size Italian submarine *Cobalto,* on her maiden patrol, twice achieved a near-perfect position to sink the carrier *Indomitable.* However, before she could shoot, the screening destroyers *Pathfinder* and *Ithuriel* independently spotted *Cobalto* and thwarted both attacks. Upon sighting *Cobalto's* periscope, *Ithuriel* closed and dropped five depth charges set for 50 feet, which brought the submarine to the surface. Firing her 4.7" batteries and other weapons, *Ithuriel* ran in and rammed *Cobalto* a glancing blow abaft her conning tower. While the Italian submariners were jumping into the water, *Ithuriel* put her stem against the conning

---

* The ducks *U-9, U-18, U-19, U-20, U-23,* and *U-24* had been decommissioned and disassembled and laboriously shipped by rail and barge to Galati, Romania, on the Black Sea, where they were reassembled and recommissioned for the purpose of attacking Soviet naval units in the Black Sea and Sea of Azov.

tower and a boarding party scampered down a ladder onto *Cobalto*. The leader of the boarding party hurried inside the submarine to grab cryptographic materials, but *Cobalto* sank immediately. *Ithuriel* recovered all members of her boarding party as well as forty-two Italian prisoners.

As Pedestal pressed eastward to Cape Bon, the two battleships, two remaining carriers, and screens reversed course for Gibraltar, per plan. Thereafter, in the early hours of August 13, a dozen large and small Axis motor torpedo boats tore into the convoy. These hit and stopped the heavy cruiser *Manchester,* which the British scuttled the next day, and sank four or five of the big merchant ships. At dawn Axis aircraft resumed the assault, hitting other stragglers.

The Italian Navy had planned to strike the convoy with a cruiser squadron, but when Axis air forces failed to provide adequate air cover, the strike was canceled. Some of these retiring Italian warships steamed right into the crosshairs of the British submarine *Unbroken,* commanded by Alastair Mars, patrolling north of Sicily. Mars had only four torpedoes left, but these, fired in a single salvo, hit and severely damaged the 10,000-ton heavy cruiser *Bolzano* and the 7,000-ton light cruiser *Muzio Attendolo*. Destroyers counterattacked, dropping 105 depth charges, but *Unbeaten* escaped and put into Malta. Neither Italian cruiser was repaired in time to see further action in the war.

Only five of the fourteen merchant ships of the Pedestal convoy reached Malta. British propagandists asserted that since the thirty-seven Spitfires and 32,000 tons of cargo brought in by Pedestal had "saved" Malta, whose forces decisively interdicted the flow of supplies to Rommel in the ensuing weeks, it had been worth the terrible cost in lost and damaged ships. However, postwar British naval studies contend that Allied air and naval forces basing on Malta played only a small and indecisive role in checking Rommel.

During the terrible ordeal of convoy Pedestal, the British sailed a "decoy convoy" (Drover) from Alexandria westward toward Malta. Its mission was to draw Axis forces away from Pedestal. Anticipating this convoy, but unaware that it was a decoy, the Germans deployed a half dozen U-boats into the eastern Mediterranean. British aircraft escorting this "decoy convoy" and other convoys plying between Port Said, Haifa, and Beirut during August made U-boat operations more hazardous than usual.

Very late on the evening of August 3, a radar-equipped Wellington of British Squadron 221, supporting convoy Drover off Tel Aviv, Palestine, got a contact on a U-boat. This was the *U-372,* commanded by Heinz-Joachim Neumann, who had sunk the big and important submarine tender *Medway* on his prior patrol. When he came upon this convoy, he was on the way to put an agent ashore near Beirut, then conduct antiship operations.

The Wellington pilot, Sergeant Gay, dropped flares near *U-372* and requested assistance from the convoy escorts. Two big destroyers, *Sikh* and *Zulu,* peeled out. *Sikh* promptly got a good sonar contact and carried out six dogged depth-charge attacks while *Zulu* carried out one. Neumann got away but when he later surfaced, a lookout in *Sikh*'s crow's nest saw the boat, and the two destroyers opened fire with their 4.7" main batteries, forcing Neumann under again. Assisted by aircraft, the destroyers each carried out three more depth-charge attacks. Two other destroyers, *Croome* and *Tetcott,* arrived about noon with full loads of depth charges and each carried out three attacks. Finally, at 1:30 P.M., the battered and wrecked *U-372* rose to the surface and scuttled. The destroyers captured Neumann and forty-five other Germans, including the unlanded agent.

In the days following, British aircraft caught three other U-boats. North of Alexandria on August 4, Friedrich Bürgel in *U-97* was severely damaged. The boat limped back to Salamis, where battle-damage repairs took months. On August 17, the new *Ritterkreuz* holder, Hans-Werner Kraus in *U-83,* sank the 5,900-ton Canadian liner *Princess Marguerite* (misidentified as a 12,500-ton auxiliary cruiser), but British aircraft counterattacked and heavily damaged and disabled *U-83*. In response to calls for help from Kraus, Axis aircraft, surface ships, and submarines rescued *U-83,* but she, too, was out of action at Salamis for many months and Kraus also returned to Germany to commission one of the big U-boats. On August 22, a British aircraft inflicted heavy damage on Wilhelm Franken in *U-565*. He, too, reached Salamis, but he was also out of action for a long time.*

Only one of the half dozen German U-boats patrolling the eastern Mediterranean in late July and August turned in a noteworthy cruise. Emulating Kraus's patrol in June, Heinrich Schonder in *U-77* sank ten sailing ships by gun off the coast of Palestine, Lebanon, and Cyprus in the two-week period from July 30 to August 13. Like Kraus, Schonder won a *Ritterkreuz,* awarded August 19.† Like Kraus and some of the other skippers, Schonder returned to Germany to commission one of the large U-boats.

The aggregate returns from the Mediterranean U-boats remained thin. In the five-month period from April 1 to August 31, inclusive, the twenty U-boats of the force sank four major warships (carrier *Eagle,* submarine tender *Medway,* light cruiser *Hermione, Hunt-*class destroyer *Grove*) for 43,750 tons and thirteen merchant ships for 45,630 tons, a total of seventeen ships for about 90,000 tons. Italian submarines put away the British light cruiser *Cairo* and, by mistake, the Italian destroyer *Admiral Usodimare.* In the same period, five U-boats had been lost, reducing the Mediterranean force to fifteen boats, and several, such as *U-83, U-97,* and *U-565,* had been badly damaged. The exchange rate was thus 1.3 ships sunk for each U-boat, ordinarily an unacceptable ratio but tolerated in this case because the U-boats supported Rommel.

By September 1, 1942, thirteen U-boats had been lost inside the Mediterranean. The British had captured 219 German survivors from eight of the boats,

---

   * At this time, British forces in the Mediterranean sank yet another Italian submarine, *Scirè*. While she was attempting to sneak into Haifa to launch three Chariots (or "human torpedoes") on August 10, the ASW trawler *Islay* destroyed her.

   † Schonder's award also appears to be part of the effort to give Mediterranean U-boats greater recognition. At the time of the award (the third *Ritterkreuz* won by Mediterranean skippers within two months), Schonder's confirmed sinkings on the duck *U-58* and the *U-77* were nine ships for about 35,000 tons (including the *Hunt-*class destroyer *Grove*) plus the ten sailing ships.

but the other 500 or so submariners were killed or missing. Notwithstanding this brutal casualty rate, Hitler decreed that the U-boats were to continue to support Erwin Rommel. The OKM therefore directed Dönitz to plan further transfers of Type VIIs from the Atlantic force to the Mediterranean force.

RETURN TO THE NORTH ATLANTIC RUN

The arrival of thirteen new Type VIIs in the Atlantic force in July and the decision to limit Type VII sailings to the Americas enabled Dönitz to resume group, or wolf pack, attacks against cargo convoys on the North Atlantic run. The first group, *Wolf*, was composed of ten VIICs that sailed in late June and early July. It was to establish a patrol line in the distant "air gap" between Iceland and Greenland.

As in the anticonvoy campaign during the summer and fall of 1941 in this area, the boats of group *Wolf* were to be individually relieved at sea by other boats as required, in order to maintain a continuous U-boat presence. When the arriving replacements and reinforcements outnumbered the original cadre, the pack was to be renamed. When the number of boats in the North Atlantic rose sufficiently high to permit it, additional groups were to be formed to operate simultaneously.

Group *Wolf* was an odd mixture of old and new skippers and boats. Seven boats came from Germany, three from France. The boats from Germany included five new VIIs, one older VII, *U-454*, transferring from the Arctic, and the aged Type IX *U-43*, returning from a long overhaul. Six of the ten skippers, including Hardo Rodler von Roithberg, age twenty-four, in the veteran *U-71*, sailing from France, and Hans-Joachim Schwantke, age twenty-three, in the veteran *U-43*, were making first patrols as captain. Two of the ten skippers were *Ritterkreuz* holders: Erich Topp in *U-552* from France and Ernst Mengersen, who won his medal on the retired *U-101*, returning from Germany to the Atlantic in a new VII, *U-607*, his fourth U-boat command in the war.

The three boats sailing from French bases had to elude the intensified round-the-clock Coastal Command aircraft patrols. Topp in *U-552* and von Roithberg in *U-71* got through unscathed but Walter Schug in *U-86* did not. On the night of July 5, when a Coastal Command Wellington bombed and sank the inbound *U-502*, another aircraft, as yet unidentified, caught and bombed *U-86*. Schug reported to Kerneval that the close depth-charge blasts had knocked out four of his five torpedo tubes and damaged the fifth. His crew repaired some of the damage—avoiding an abort—but *U-86* was not fully combat-ready on this patrol.

En route to the patrol line, one of the five new boats sailing from Germany, *U-90*, commanded by Hans-Jürgen Oldörp, age thirty-one, reported a fast eastbound convoy on July 9. Dönitz ordered three other new boats sailing from Germany to home on *U-90*, but owing to *U-379*'s lack of training, he restricted Paul-Hugo Kettner from attacking except under the most favorable circumstances. Harassed by surface escorts and Iceland-based ASW aircraft, Oldörp in *U-90* doggedly shadowed for almost 200 miles before Dönitz canceled the operation.

By July 13, nine of the ten group *Wolf* boats had formed a patrol line running southeasterly from Greenland. That day, von Roithberg in *U-71* found and reported another eastbound convoy. Horst Kessler, age twenty-seven, in the new boat *U-704,* requested beacon signals. Erich Topp in *U-552* encountered—and reported—two "destroyers," which may have been convoy escorts. However, the convoy maneuvered radically and escaped into fog so dense that Dönitz was again compelled to cancel operations. He soon ordered a new patrol line to intercept yet another eastbound convoy reported by *B-dienst.* But heavy fog persisted for a full week, utterly frustrating group *Wolf.*

Finally, on the evening of July 24, Erich Topp in *U-552* found and held on doggedly to a convoy. It was the westbound Outbound North 113, composed of thirty-three empty ships escorted by six warships: the four-stack destroyers *Burnham* of the Royal Navy and *St. Croix* of the Royal Canadian Navy, and four British corvettes. Upon picking up the U-boat shadow signals on Huff Duff, the *Burnham* and *St. Croix* raced ahead of the convoy and found two U-boats on the surface. *Burnham* chased one boat, the *St. Croix* the other. *St. Croix*'s quarry was Oldörp's *U-90,* twenty-six days out from Kiel on her maiden voyage. Commanded by A. H. Dobson, *St. Croix* drove *U-90* under and blasted her with three well-conducted depth-charge attacks. Running in for a fourth attack, *St. Croix* heard an unusually loud underwater explosion, then saw debris rising to the surface. That was all that could be found of *U-90,* which went down with all hands, the second confirmed U-boat to be sunk by Canadian surface forces.

While the two destroyers were off hunting U-boats, Topp in *U-552* eased in to attack, bedeviled by a diesel-engine failure that reduced his maximum speed to 9 or 10 knots. He shot at and hit two British ships: the 8,100-ton tanker *British Merit* and the 5,100-ton freighter *Broompark.* Sailing in ballast, the damaged tanker reached port to be salvaged, but *Broompark,* badly wrecked, sank under tow. Gunfire from the freighter *Salsten* and perhaps from one or more of the four corvettes drove Topp off and under, foiling his second attack. No other U-boat could get close enough to shoot.

Despite the fog and his diesel-engine problems, Topp managed to hang on and to shadow Outbound North 113. During July 25, his beacons brought up the group *Wolf* boats for the second time. Using radar and Huff Duff to advantage, the six escorts held off most of the boats, pounding the aged Type IX *U-43* with a heavy depth-charge attack. This time only the *Ritterkreuz holder* Ernst Mengersen in the new *U-607* got in to shoot. He hit and damaged the 7,000-ton British freighter *Empire Rainbow.* A day or so later, Horst Kessler in the new *U-704* encountered this same ship and finished her off with a torpedo. All other vessels of the convoy, save one, slipped into the fog off the Newfoundland Bank and reached port safely.*

The *U-90* was the tenth boat of the Atlantic force to be lost since June 1. Dönitz well knew that the resumption of U-boat warfare against North Atlantic convoys would result in still greater losses. Believing that he should soften this coming blow to the German public, on July 27 he announced that the campaign in

---

* As related earlier, after he left the Gulf of St. Lawrence, Vogelsang in *U-132* sank the 6,700-ton freighter *Pacific Pioneer* of this convoy.

the Americas had been more difficult than portrayed in the media and that yet "harder times" lay ahead. Upon hearing this unusual public address, Rodger Winn in the Admiralty's U-boat Tracking Room speculated correctly that it signaled a resumption of full-scale U-boat war against the North Atlantic convoy run.

As if to give emphasis to Dönitz's statement, another U-boat was lost in that area. She was the new Type VIIC *U-335,* commanded by Hans-Hermann Pelkner.

Having sailed from Kiel on July 31, Pelkner, age thirty-three, was north of the Shetlands on August 3. His assignment was to probe west along likely North Atlantic convoy routes and to join whatever group was in operation. Another new boat, *U-174,* a Type IXC bound for the Americas, sailed close by with the same orders.

The Admiralty has not attributed the killing of *U-335* to Enigma intelligence, but it seems likely that this was the case. Perhaps British codebreakers obtained information on her departure and that of *U-174* from *Werft* dockyard codes or from the three-rotor Enigma traffic of the admiral commanding Norway. Whatever the case, on August 1, the Admiralty informed the new British submarine *Saracen,* which was in workup north of the Shetlands, to be on the lookout for two U-boats that might pass through her area during the next two days. *Saracen,* commanded by Michael G. R. Lumby, went on full alert.

Late in the afternoon of August 3, while running submerged, the periscope watch of *Saracen* picked up *U-335* at 3,000 yards. Three minutes later, Lumby commenced firing all six bow tubes at seven-second intervals. One or more torpedoes hit and *U-335* blew sky-high. Upon surfacing to collect debris for proof of a kill, Lumby found one German body and two survivors. When he attempted to fish them out, one refused to be rescued and deliberately drowned himself, Lumby reported. The other, Rudolf Jahnke, a signalman who was thrown from *U-335*'s bridge when the torpedo struck, willingly came on board. *Saracen* reloaded her tubes and remained on alert, hoping to find and kill the other boat, but she had no further luck.

On July 29 and 30 in the mid-Atlantic, the nine surviving boats of group *Wolf* refueled from the tanker *U-461,* commanded by the aptly named Wolf Stiebler. It was then discovered that *U-90* was missing. At the same time, Walter Schug in *U-86* conceded that the bomb damage he incurred crossing the Bay of Biscay had rendered his boat incapable of hard convoy warfare. He was therefore detached from group *Wolf* and ordered to patrol for single ships in the waters of the western Atlantic. When he eventually returned to France, he reported he had sunk only one 342-ton American sailing vessel, *Wawaloam,* by gun.

While group *Wolf* was refueling, on July 29 and 30, a newly sailed Type VII, *U-210,* commanded by Rudolf Lemcke, age twenty-eight, discovered another westbound convoy. This was Outbound North 115, composed of forty-one empty merchant ships, escorted by the all-Canadian group C-3, comprised of the destroyers *Saguenay* and *Skeena* and four corvettes. Acting on Lemcke's contact reports, Kerneval hurriedly formed a temporary six-boat group—named *Pirat*—from the stream of nearby boats bound for the Americas along the northern routes. Pending contact by the other boats, Lemcke was prohibited from attacking, an infuriating restriction, softened somewhat by news from Kerneval that his wife had just given birth to twins and that all was well at home.

The Canadian escorts were handicapped by the lack of modern equipment, such as Type 271 centimetric-wavelength radar and Huff Duff. Nonetheless, as the six boats of group *Pirat* assembled to attack, the Canadians picked up their radio transmissions and the veteran escort commander, D. C. Wallace in *Saguenay*, responded with exceptionally aggressive maneuvers. As a consequence, not one of the boats of group *Pirat* could get into position to shoot. Moreover, on the night of July 31, two of the veteran Canadian escorts, the destroyer *Skeena*, commanded by K. L. Dyer, and the corvette *Wetaskiwin*, commanded by Guy S. Windeyer, trapped the experienced Type VIIC *U-588*, commanded by Viktor Vogel, and sank her by depth charges with the loss of all hands. She was the second U-boat after *U-90* to fall to Canadian surface escorts in the North Atlantic within a week.

The aggressive maneuvering by the Canadian escorts burned fuel oil at a great rate. Therefore the destroyers *Saguenay* and *Skeena* were compelled to leave the convoy and go directly to St. John's, Newfoundland. To make matters worse, the corvette *Wetaskiwin* separated from the convoy, became lost in the fog, and also went directly to St. John's. These departures temporarily reduced the escort to merely three corvettes, but two other destroyers, the British *Witch* and the Canadian four-stack *Hamilton,* and another corvette, *Agassiz,* put out from Newfoundland to reinforce the group.

Although convoy Outbound North 115 was sailing into the protective fog of the Newfoundland Bank and ever closer to radar-equipped land-based ASW aircraft, Dönitz directed the eight remaining boats of group *Wolf* to reinforce the six of group *Pirat* and attack as they completed refueling. The first of the *Wolf* boats to find the convoy was Erich Topp in *U-552*. He gave the alarm and shadowed, bringing up boats of both groups. In the confused, fogbound attacks which ensued on the night of August 2–3, Topp claimed sinking two 8,000-ton freighters, but postwar analysis reduced his confirmed score to damage to the 10,600-ton British tanker *G. S. Walden,* which was salvaged, and the sinking of the 7,200-ton freighter *Belgian Soldier.* Another *Wolf* boat, *U-607,* commanded by *Ritterkreuz holder* Ernst Mengersen, shared credit for sinking *Belgian Soldier.* Only one of the *Pirat* skippers, the veteran Karl Thurmann in *U-553,* sank a ship: the 9,400-ton British freighter *Loch Katrine.*

The British destroyer *Witch* and the five Canadian warships of the reorganized escort group put up a feisty defense. In the fog, the corvette *Sackville,* commanded by Alan H. Easton, came upon Topp in *U-552*, opened fire, and nearly rammed the U-boat. *Sackville*'s shells holed *U-552*'s main-engine air induction and exhaust pipes and damaged her rear periscope, forcing Topp to abort.* Hans-Joachim Schwantke, the new skipper of the aged *U-43,* reported that as a result of close and

---

* This action and others in convoy Outbound North 115 are vividly described in Easton's war memoir, *Fifty North* (1963).

persistent depth charges, both air compressors were broken and two bow torpedo-tube outer doors were jammed half open, and he, too, had to abort. Thurmann in *U-553* reported that an escort pursued and depth-charged him for five hours, but he escaped with slight damage. After taking on all the fuel oil Topp in *U-552* could spare, Thurmann in *U-553* proceeded to the Caribbean, as did four other boats that were temporarily diverted to group *Pirat.*

The aborts of Topp and Schwantke so reduced the original *Wolf* group that it was disbanded. The six remaining boats, all of which had refueled and had plenty of torpedoes, were used to cadre a new group.

The results of group *Wolf* and its temporary offspring, group *Pirat,* were not impressive. In a full month of operations—early July to early August—the ten boats of *Wolf* had firmly locked on to only two convoys, both westbound: Outbound North 113 and Outbound North 115. As in the case of the earlier small group, *Hecht,* only the *Ritterkreuz* holders (Topp and Mengersen) managed to penetrate the escort screens and carry out effective attacks. These attacks, however, had produced meager returns: three empty freighters sunk for about 20,000 tons, and two empty tankers damaged for about 19,000 tons. One boat of the *Wolf* group, *U-90,* had been lost and three, *U-43, U-86,* and *U-552,* had incurred heavy battle damage. In the short-lived group *Pirat,* Karl Thurmann in *U-533* had sunk one ship for 9,400 tons, but one boat, Viktor Vogel's *U-588,* had been lost.

While Topp in *U-552* was crossing the Bay of Biscay on August 10 inbound to Lorient, a Coastal Command aircraft caught and bombed him. Fortunately for the Germans, the damage was slight and Topp reached port on August 13 without further incident. Inasmuch as his total claims had then reached 250,000 tons or more, Topp qualified for the addition of Crossed Swords to his *Ritterkreuz,** the second submariner after Otto Kretschmer to earn that high distinction. Upon receiving the award from Hitler in person, Topp left *U-552* to command the 27th Flotilla in the Training Command and did not return to combat.

A new group, *Steinbrink,* composed initially of eight boats (six left over from group *Wolf* and two newly arrived), formed in the "air gap" southeast of Greenland. On August 5, one of the latter, Gerd Kelbling's experienced *U-593* from France, found and shadowed an eastbound convoy.

This was Slow Convoy 94. Composed of thirty-three heavily laden merchant ships, it was escorted by Canadian group C-1. There were seven warships in the escort group: the (ex-British) Canadian destroyer *Assiniboine,* and three Canadian and three British corvettes. Although nominally Canadian, the group was commanded by a British officer, A. Ayer, in the British corvette *Primrose.* None of the escorts had Huff Duff. Only one vessel, the British corvette *Nasturtium,* had Type 271 centimetric-wavelength radar.

---

* At the time of the award, Topp's confirmed score on the duck *U-57* and *U-552* was 34 ships sunk for about 185,000 tons, including the destroyer *Reuben James.* In ships and tonnage sunk, he stood fourth among all skippers in the war.

After other boats reported contact on the convoy, Kelbling in *U-593* attacked an element of the formation that had separated from the main body. He claimed hits on two freighters, but in fact he had hit only one, the 3,600-ton Dutchman, *Spar,* which sank. The corvettes *Nasturtium* and *Orillia* counterattacked with depth charges, which exploded near Kelbling in *U-593* and a new arrival from Germany, Jürgen Quaet-Faslem, age twenty-nine, in *U-595.* The boats hung on, bringing up others, but none was able to attack.

Later the following afternoon, August 6, the Canadian destroyer *Assiniboine,* commanded by John H. Stubbs, got a contact on her Type 286 meter-wavelength radar at about 2,000 yards. Moments later lookouts saw a U-boat stopped dead on the surface. *Assiniboine* fired one round from her 4.7" main battery, set up a salvo of shallow-set depth charges, and went ahead full speed to ram. Her target was the new *U-210,* commanded by Rudolf Lemcke, who had earlier found Outbound North 113, but had not yet fired a torpedo. Astonishingly, the single round from *Assiniboine*'s gun hit *U-210* in a fuel ballast tank, impairing her ability to dive. Lemcke rang up maximum speed and ran for a patch of fog.

John Stubbs in *Assiniboine* was not to be denied that day. Tracking *U-210* through fog patches by radar, he closed and fired several more rounds from his main battery. Maneuvering wildly to get so close to the destroyer that she could not depress her main guns, Lemcke's men shot back at point-blank range with bridge guns. The German fire killed one man, wounded thirteen others, and set the destroyer's bridge on fire. However, three or four 4.7" rounds from *Assiniboine* hit *U-210,* one at the bridge. It blew Lemcke to pieces, killed five other men, and smashed the bridge and conning tower.

Although wounded in the chest, *U-210*'s first watch officer, twenty-two-year-old Günther Göhlich, crew of 1938, assumed command of the wrecked boat. In desperation he fired a torpedo at *Assiniboine* but missed. Meanwhile, belowdecks, the chief engineer, Heinz Sorber, dived the boat. But it was too late. *Assiniboine* rammed *U-210* twice and dropped shallow-set depth charges, which savaged the boat. When it was clear that the game was lost, Göhlich ordered the crew to scuttle and abandon ship. After opening the vents of one ballast tank, Göhlich and Sorber and thirty-five others clambered topside through the torpedo-loading hatch and jumped into the sea. Following correct procedure, a radio operator threw two Enigma boxes overboard. Thirty-eight minutes after *Assiniboine* first got radar contact, *U-210* upended and sank.

In the meantime, the British corvette *Dianthus* appeared out of the fog and assisted *Assiniboine* in fishing the Germans from the sea. *Dianthus* picked up twenty-seven men, *Assiniboine* ten. During the search, *Assiniboine*'s commander realized that his own ship was too badly damaged to continue the voyage to the British Isles, so he took six Germans from *Dianthus* and turned about for Canada. Keeping the other twenty-one Germans, *Dianthus* proceeded with the convoy toward the British Isles. Repairs to *Assiniboine* kept her out of action until January 1943. In due course, Stubbs's sixteen Germans, including Göhlich and Sorber, were turned over to American naval authorities.

The oft-maligned Canadians had reason to be proud. The *U-210* was the fourth confirmed U-boat to be sunk by Canadian air or surface ships within a period of two weeks.

Slow Convoy 94 wallowed onward to the British Isles. Group *Steinbrink,* reinforced by a half dozen westbound boats, including two Americas-bound Type IXCs, *U-174* and *U-176,* pursued. On the morning of August 8, three new Type VIIs, *U-607, U-660,* and *U-704,* closed the formation and each shot three torpedoes. All malfunctioned or missed. In the afternoon of the same day, two other boats, the new Type VII *U-379,* commanded by Paul-Hugo Kettner, age thirty, and the new Type IXC *U-176,* commanded by Reiner Dierksen, age thirty-four, boldly submerged ahead of the convoy and attacked by periscope in broad daylight.

The unexpected daylight attacks caused utter chaos. Kettner in *U-379* hit and sank two freighters for 8,900 tons, one American, one British. Dierksen in *U-176* fired six torpedoes and sank three freighters for 16,700 tons, two British, one Greek. In sheer panic, the crews of three other freighters abandoned ship. Prodded by the escort commander, two crews soon reboarded, but the third, from the 3,700-ton British freighter *Radchurch,* refused. Dierksen in *U-176* found this abandoned ship and sank it as well.

Later that afternoon, a masthead lookout on the British corvette *Dianthus,* commanded by C. E. Bridgeman, spotted two U-boats about six miles away. Bridgeman immediately fired twelve rounds from his main 4" battery, but none hit and the U-boats dived. Combing the area for several hours, *Dianthus* finally regained contact with *U-379* and fired off eight star shells. Kettner dived instantly, but his evasion was inept and *Dianthus* blew him back to the surface with five well-aimed depth charges.

When *U-379* popped up, *Dianthus* fixed the boat in her searchlight, dropped five more depth charges, and slewed about to ram, with all guns blazing. Firing snowflakes to illuminate the scene, *Dianthus* crashed into the forward deck of *U-379,* rode over the U-boat, and dropped five more shallow-set depth charges. These explosions forced Kettner to scuttle and abandon ship. As Kettner and the crew were leaping into the sea, Bridgeman pumped another seven rounds of 4" shells into the *U-379,* raked her with machine-gun fire, and rammed her three more times. After midnight on August 9, the U-boat finally upended and sank. Bridgeman brought one of the twenty-one prisoners of *U-210* to his bridge to help in fishing out the crew of *U-379,* but only five survivors were found, all enlisted men. Worried about his own considerable bow damage and fearful of a U-boat attack, Bridgeman soon suspended the search. He tossed over a life raft for any other Germans, but none of them survived.

During the next day, August 9, Western Approaches reinforced the escort of Slow Convoy 94. A B-24 Liberator bomber and a Catalina flew out from Iceland to circle overhead. Two destroyers, the British *Broke,* equipped with Huff Duff, and the Polish *Blyskawica,* joined. The skipper of *Broke,* A.F.C. Layard, who was senior officer present, assumed command of the escort.

That day a dozen U-boats were in close contact with the convoy. Three skippers, all on maiden patrols, attacked the formation. Ulrich Thilo, age thirty-nine, in the Type IXC *U-174,* shot three torpedoes into the center of the formation, but inexplicably, not one hit a ship. Hans Gilardone, age thirty, in the VII *U-254,* who had sunk a 1,200-ton freighter on his way out from Germany, also fired three torpedoes into the middle of the formation and missed. Odo Loewe, age twenty-seven, in the VII *U-256,* who missed a "destroyer" with four torpedoes while outbound from Germany, fired three more at a "destroyer" and missed again.

By August 10 more than a dozen U-boats were still trailing Slow Convoy 94. Three skippers in new Type VIIs submerged ahead and attacked the convoy by periscope in broad daylight. The first was Eberhard Bopst, age twenty-eight, in *U-597.* His torpedoes missed or malfunctioned and he got no hits. The other two were Rudolf Franzius, age thirty-one, in *U-438* and Götz Baur, age twenty-five, in *U-660.* Both skippers simultaneously hit and sank the 4,400-ton Greek freighter *Condylis,* to share credit. Baur sank two British freighters for 10,000 tons and damaged another, the 6,000-ton *Oregon.* Coming upon the damaged *Oregon,* Franzius in *U-438* put her under with a finishing shot, to share credit. Confirmed results of these attacks: four freighters for 20,500 tons sunk.

Beginning August 11, Western Approaches saturated the air in the area of Slow Convoy 94 and beefed up the surface escort with the onetime Coast Guard cutter *Sennen* and four fleet destroyers. The aircraft (Liberators, Catalinas, and a B-17 Flying Fortress) drove off the U-boats and forced Dönitz to cancel the operation. Five skippers reported "major" depth-charge damage from aircraft or surface ships or other defects that forced them to abort: von Roithberg in *U-71* (yet again!), Kelbling in *U-593,* Quaet-Faslem in *U-595,* Bopst in *U-597,* and Kessler in *U-704.* They were joined on the homeward voyage by two boats that had only one remaining torpedo each: Hans Gilardone in *U-254* and the *Ritterkreuz holder* Ernst Mengersen in *U-607.*

Berlin propagandists bragged that the U-boat attack on Slow Convoy 94 resulted in the sinking of "more than 84,000 tons" of shipping. The confirmed bag, run up by five green skippers, was eleven ships sunk for 53,421 tons. A dozen other skippers got in close and some shot torpedoes, but none sank anything. Two new U-boats, Lemcke's *U-210* and Kettner's *U-379,* were sunk by the escorts; another, Pelkner's *U-335,* was lost to the enemy en route to join in the battle. The "exchange" rate in this battle was thus an intolerable 3.7 ships sunk for one U-boat.

A new group, *Loss,* came into being August 12. It was composed of seven boats from group *Steinbrink,* including the two Type IXCs, *U-174* and *U-176,* which had canceled patrols to the Americas, and three newly sailed boats from Germany. Based on information developed by *B-dienst,* Dönitz deployed group *Loss* on a line 500 miles due south of Iceland to intercept convoy Outbound North 120.

As the group was moving into position, one of the boats, the new *U-705,* commanded by Karl-Horst Horn, age twenty-five, found a convoy. It was not the one expected but rather the eastbound Slow Convoy 95. It was guarded by the one remaining American MOEF escort group in the North Atlantic, A-3, commanded by Paul Heineman. It consisted of the big *Treasury*-class Coast Guard cutter *Spencer,* the four-stack American destroyer *Schenck,* and four Canadian and two British corvettes.

The surprise appearance of Slow Convoy 95 confused the Germans. Nonetheless, Kerneval added three nearby new boats to group *Loss,* bringing the total to thirteen. But only three got into a favorable position in time to shoot. Horn in *U-705* sank the 3,300-ton American freighter *Balladier.* Herbert-Viktor Schütze, age twenty-five, in the new *U-605* shot at a freighter but missed. Odo Loewe in *U-256* also missed a freighter. An escort caught and shelled *U-256,* but she got away. Still confused, Kerneval canceled the operations against the heavily laden eastbound ships of Slow Convoy 95 in favor of a renewed search for the empty westbound ships of Outbound North 120.

Three veteran boats sailed from France to join group *Loss.* These were the *U-135,* commanded by Friedrich-Hermann Praetorius; the *U-373,* commanded by Paul-Karl Loeser; and the *U-578,* commanded by Ernst-August Rehwinkel, the latter famous for having sunk the American destroyer *Jacob Jones* off New Jersey. Coastal Command aircraft caught and attacked all three boats in the Bay of Biscay on August 10 and 11. The plane that attacked *U-135* killed two men by machine-gun fire. A Sunderland bombed Loeser in *U-373,* but he dived deep and escaped. The attack on Rehwinkel in *U-578,* carried out by a Wellington of the Czech-manned Squadron 311, piloted by Josef Nýlvt, was fatal. The *U-578* went down with the loss of all hands. Nýlvt was killed in action a month later.

Believing the Allies were routing convoys farther north, Dönitz shifted group *Loss* in that direction. Praetorius in *U-135* was not informed of the movement, and as a result, when he took up the southernmost position on the line, he was about 100 miles out of position. By happenstance, this error placed Praetorius directly in the path of convoy Outbound North (Slow) 122, which, exactly contrary to the German guesstimates, had been routed farther south than usual.

Due to an encoding error, Kerneval could not read Praetorius's initial contact report. Three hours later, when he sent another, correctly encoded, Dönitz was puzzled and delayed any deployment for several more hours until the picture clarified. After receiving Praetorius's third contact report, Dönitz finally conceded that it must be Outbound North (Slow) 122, routed to a southerly course rather than a northerly one. He radioed all boats to converge on *U-135* and to attack.

Convoy Outbound North (Slow) 122 was escorted by group B-6, nominally British. Commanded by J. V. Waterhouse, it was comprised of the British destroyer *Viscount,* equipped with Type 271 centimetric radar, Huff Duff, and a Hedgehog, and four corvettes manned by Norwegian crews and fitted with Type 271 radar. A rescue ship, *Stockport,* also equipped with Huff Duff, brought up the rear.

By August 24, nine U-boats of group *Loss* had made contact with the convoy, but it sailed into fog cover and only three boats could attack: Reiner Dierksen in the Type IXC *U-176,* Rudolf Franzius in *U-438,* and Herbert-Viktor Schütze in *U-605.* Dierksen and Franzius hit and sank the same ship, the 7,500-ton British freighter *Empire Breeze,* to share credit. In addition, Franzius sank the 1,600-ton Norwegian freighter *Trolla.* Schütze sank two other British freighters for 8,200 tons. Total: four ships sunk for 17,300 tons.

Making good use of radar and Huff Duff in the fog, *Viscount* and the other escorts skillfully thwarted other attacks and counterattacked. *Viscount* carried out a Hedgehog attack—perhaps the first of the war—that resulted in a "tremendous rippling explosion" believed to be a kill, but it could not be confirmed. Six U-boats reported serious damage:

- Schütze in *U-605:* one escort holed his conning tower so badly he was forced to abort.
- Franzius in *U-438:* one escort drove him under and pounded him with depth charges, inflicting so much damage that he was forced to abort as well.
- Thilo in the new Type IXC *U-174:* an escort hit him with gunfire "at close range," drove him under, and chased him for five hours with "well placed" depth charges, inflicting "considerable" damage.
- Horn in *U-705:* an escort hit him with gunfire, inflicting "several casualties," forcing him to abort.
- Loewe in *U-256:* incurred such heavy damage from depth charges that he, too, was forced to abort.
- Praetorius in *U-135:* "heavy damage" from depth charges.

While inbound to France in the Bay of Biscay on August 31, Odo Loewe in the damaged *U-256* was attacked and further damaged by two Coastal Command Whitleys piloted by Edward B. Brooks and E. O. Tandy. Fortunately for Loewe and his men, Rudolf Franzius in the damaged *U-438* was close by. Franzius radioed Kerneval for assistance and took aboard thirty men from *U-256,* leaving only a salvage crew. Kerneval rushed air cover and motor torpedo boats to the scene and the latter towed the wrecked *U-256* into Lorient. The boat was found to be so badly damaged that she was withdrawn from combatant status, and Loewe and most of his crew were transferred to another boat.

Two Whitleys of Bomber Command Squadron 77, on loan to Coastal Command, found and attacked U-boats in the Bay of Biscay on September 3. One Whitley, piloted by A. A. MacInnes, hit Karl-Horst Horn in *U-705,* who was aborting with damage and wounded. MacInnes sank *U-705* by depth charges with the loss of all hands. The other Whitley, piloted by T. S. Lea, hit Götz Baur in *U-660,* but he escaped with slight damage. The Admiralty gave wartime credit to Lea for sinking *U-705,* but upon later investigation credited MacInnes.

In view of the growing number of Type VII U-boats operating against convoys, Kerneval welcomed the sailing from Kiel on August 8 of the sixth of the Type XIV U-tankers, the *U-464,* commanded by Otto Harms, age thirty-three. However, en route to the Atlantic, the boat developed an oil trace and Harms had to put into Bergen for repairs, delaying his final departure to August 16.

Four days later the *U-464* reached a position about 160 miles east-southeast of Iceland. Although those waters were teeming with Allied warships plying between Iceland and the British Isles and with aircraft on local ASW patrol or convoy escort,* Harms was dangerously lolling on the surface at dawn when an American

---

* At that time there were forty-eight ASW aircraft based on Iceland: twenty-nine British, ten American, and nine Norwegian.

Catalina of the Navy's Patrol Squadron 73, which was assigned to provide air cover for a small convoy, appeared out of the low and dirty clouds overhead.*

Inasmuch as the U-tanker was merely four miles from the convoy and visibility was very poor, the pilot, Robert B. Hopgood, thought at first that it might be one of the convoy's destroyers. Accordingly, he flew low and shot off a recognition flare to establish his identity and to prevent friendly fire. Caught flat-footed in the clumsy, painfully slow-diving *U-464,* Harms could do nothing but bluff. Hoping to be taken for an Icelandic fishing vessel or Allied warship, he responded to the recognition flare by releasing one himself. It burned yellow-white, and bore not the slightest resemblance to the proper signal. Attempting to carry the deception a step further, Harms directed the men on his bridge to wave at the plane in a friendly fashion.

Hopgood realized by then that the vessel beneath him was a U-boat. With great presence of mind he attacked instantly, dropping five of his six Mark XVII depth charges, set for twenty-five feet. Two missiles straddled the conning tower and the explosions appeared to lift the boat clear out of the water. Per the ASW doctrine then in force, Hopgood notified all authorities concerned by radio. He then climbed, circled, and came in for a strafing run, raking the boat with 30- and 50-caliber machine-gun fire. The *U-464* responded with superior and "accurate" fire from her two 37mm flak guns, mounted on platforms fore and aft of the bridge, and from a 20mm gun on the bridge. This fire held the Catalina at a distance and, as a result, Hopgood lost sight of the *U-464.*

But the blast of the depth charges had badly damaged *U-464.* Unable to dive or to escape on the surface, Harms concluded that other Allied aircraft and ships would arrive soon and that he had no choice but to scuttle. Fortunately for the Germans, an Icelandic fishing trawler, *Skaftfellingor,* appeared out of the fog and drizzle. Harms maneuvered *U-464* close to the trawler and demanded rescue. While the German gunners held the trawler in their sights, part of the *U-464* crew jumped into the sea, climbed on the Icelander, and "captured" it. After that, Harms raised a German flag on *U-464* and scuttled. He and the rest of the Germans got on board the trawler, perhaps hopeful of escaping in the foul weather to Norway.

In the meantime, the Catalina pilot Hopgood found the heavily escorted convoy to which he had been assigned. By signal lamp he informed the British escort commander of his attack and requested help. The British were skeptical and reluctant to rob the convoy of protection, but finally released two of the four destroyers, the ex-American four-stacks *Castleton* and *Newark.* Hopgood guided the destroyers back to the site of his attack, arriving in time to see the Germans shift to the trawler and scuttle *U-464. Castleton* fired one warning round over the trawler, then closed to capture the Germans, who offered no resistance. *Castleton* took aboard fifty-two Germans, including one surgeon who, in accordance with international law, was treated as a noncombatant. Harms reported that in the Catalina's initial attack, two of his men were hurled overboard and not recovered. The U.S. Navy awarded Hopgood a Navy Cross.

---

* The convoy was Reykjavik–United Kingdom 36, consisting of two cruisers and four destroyers escorting four large and important merchant ships.

Earlier German U-boat prisoners had disclosed to British interrogators that U-tankers were operating in the Atlantic, but the British had dismissed these revelations as fanciful. Prisoners from Kettner's *U-379,* who were recovered on August 8, and those from *U-464,* recovered August 20, talked freely of U-tanker operations. Even so, the British continued to doubt. "There may be some truth in the story," the British Anti-Submarine Report for August 1942 smugly proclaimed, "but at present, it must be treated with reserve."

By the closing days of August, there were enough U-boats in the North Atlantic to form two groups. These were the old *Loss* and the new *Vorwärts,* created from a stillborn group, *Stier,* and other boats sailing in August. Some boats of *Loss* refueled from the U-tanker *U-462,* commanded by Bruno Vowe, others from the Type IXC *U-176,* whose cruise to the Americas had been canceled.

Independently of these groups, Klaus Rudloff, age twenty-six, in the new *U-609* patrolled during August off Reykjavik. He saw numerous warships (and twice shot at "destroyers") but sank nothing. Late in August, Kerneval shifted the boat southerly into the convoy lanes to join group *Vorwärts.* While complying with these orders on August 31, Rudloff came upon the eastbound Slow Convoy 97. In response to his alert, Kerneval directed group *Vorwärts,* composed of more than a dozen boats—all green—to attack.

British operations research scientists had concluded from mathematical models that if North Atlantic convoys were nearly doubled in size, from about thirty to sixty ships, it would about halve the number of convoys available for U-boats to attack and thereby lessen ship losses by about 56 percent. Authorities at Western Approaches greeted this recommendation with no little skepticism, but nonetheless agreed to try it out and sailed Slow Convoy 97 with fifty-eight ships. It was escorted by Canadian group C-2, composed of two British four-stack destroyers, *Broadway* and *Burnham,* and four Canadian corvettes. The destroyers were fitted with Type 271 radar; a rescue ship carried Huff Duff.

Nine U-boats made contact with Slow Convoy 97. Four boats attacked, Klaus Rudloff in *U-609* twice. In the first, he sank two freighters for 10,300 tons. In the second, he shot his last two torpedoes, singly, claiming one "possible" hit, but it could not be confirmed. Heinz Walkerling, age twenty-seven, in the new *U-91* fired four torpedoes into the formation but all missed. Klaus Harney, age twenty-five, in the new *U-756,* merely seventeen days out from Kiel, and Horst Höltring, age twenty-nine, in the new *U-604,* shot but also missed.

Beginning September 1, long-range American and British aircraft (Catalinas and Sunderlands) gave Slow Convoy 97 close cover. Walkerling in *U-91* reported that the aircraft forced him under "once or twice every hour." Therefore it was impossible to haul around the convoy to get into a favorable shooting position ahead. Hans-Ferdinand Massmann, age twenty-five, in the new *U-409,* fourteen days out from Kiel, reported that aircraft bombs had smashed both of his periscopes, forcing him to abort. In these attacks the British airmen claimed sinking at least one U-boat. Later, when it was learned that Klaus Harney's *U-756* was lost at this time,

September 3, with all hands, the Admiralty credited "British aircraft" with the kill. Upon further study after the war, Admiralty historians withdrew the credit and gave it to the Canadian corvette *Morden.* The *U-756* was the fifth U-boat to be sunk by Canadian air and surface forces within a period of six weeks, a notable achievement but one that was not realized at the time.

The prediction by Dönitz on July 27 that the U-boat war was to turn "hard" was timely and correct. In the six-week period, July 24 to September 3, Allied air and surface escorts and submarines in the North Atlantic area sank nine U-boats (eight Type VIIs and one Type XIV U-tanker) and wrecked another VII, *U-256,* almost beyond repair. About 400 German submariners had been lost in the sinkings, ninety-four of them captured. Thirteen boats had been forced to abort with battle damage and casualties.

A close analysis of the renewed anticonvoy operations in the North Atlantic by the forty-eight attack U-boats sailing in July and August is revealing. Altogether thirty-eight of these patrols (80 percent) were carried out by new boats or new skippers. All the boats sank forty-four ships, an average of .91 ships per boat per patrol. Twenty-three boats, or nearly half of all those putting out, sank no ships.

	Patrols	New C.O.		Ships Sunk	Per Boat	Boats Lost		None sunk	
July	18	15	(83%) *	18.5	1.03	3	(17%)	9	(50%)
August	30	23	(77%) †	25.5	0.85	5	(17%)	14	(47%)
Totals:	48	38	(80%)	44.0	0.92	8	(17%)	23	(48%)

The most striking fact in this analysis is that nearly half of all the U-boats sank no ships at all and as a result, the average of the VII sinkings fell below one ship per boat per patrol. In part this was attributable to the very high percentage of hurriedly trained and inexperienced crews and skippers, but other factors contributed. Most have been identified earlier. All bear repeating:

• The Type VII U-boat that made up the preponderance of the Atlantic force was less than suitable for anticonvoy operations in the distant Greenland "air gap" owing to its limited range and torpedo capacity. It required supporting U-tankers to effectively carry on such operations. Although the U-tanker force had increased in strength, there were still not enough U-tankers‡ and, besides that, the need to refuel the VIIs resulted in a weak link in the operational chain.

• Two-hundred-mile "patrol lines" of twelve or more boats were useful for detecting some convoys but were disadvantageous in massing for a group attack. The boats most distant from the convoy were often unable to close up in time, especially in heavy seas or where Allied aircraft made surface travel hazardous. Therefore most successful "pack attacks" were still carried out on the first night by the few boats closest to the convoy.

---

* Includes two veteran boats with new skippers.

† Includes one veteran boat with a new skipper.

‡ A U-tanker could refuel only about thirteen U-boats per voyage. Therefore, about one tanker was needed for efficient operation of each attack group.

- All anticonvoy operations were dependent on accurate navigation. The boat first making contact had to know where it was in order to notify U-boat Control and to bring up the other boats. They too had to know where they were in order to set a correct course to the gathering point. Lacking any kind of electronic aids, all the boats had to navigate by dead reckoning and by sextant readings on the stars, the sun, and the planets. Owing to weather conditions, sextant readings were often unobtainable for days at a time.

- If the contact keeper or shadower attempted to bring up the other boats of the patrol line by radio-beacon signals, as was usually the case, shore stations and/or convoy escorts usually detected the initial contact report and homing beacon by DF and/or Huff Duff. Thereupon one or more escorts of the convoy could "run down the bearing" and, assisted by radar, find and sink the shadower or drive it under with gunfire and depth charges while the convoy made a radical turn to port or starboard to elude the other U-boats attempting to gather for a mass attack.

- U-boats had no radar of any kind, only the Metox radar detector, which was useful in crossing the Bay of Biscay but too clumsy to use in a convoy battle. Hence at night or in the foggy weather often encountered in the Greenland "air gap" and on the Newfoundland Bank, radar-equipped aircraft and surface ships held a great advantage over U-boats in that they could "see" electronically in the dark or fog and therefore could pounce on a surfaced U-boat suddenly and with complete surprise.

- U-boat Control tightly directed most pack attacks by long-distance radio transmissions. Owing to atmospheric disturbances, especially in the Greenland "air gap" area, often these messages were not received or were received in garbled and undecipherable condition. In such cases, the U-boats involved in the operations had to wait for or ask for retransmissions, incurring considerable delays or the risk of being DFed.

Thus a sustained U-boat "pack attack," so promising in theory, in actuality was still extremely difficult to mount. This was especially true if the U-boats were green and the escorting forces were experienced. Allied surface ships and aircraft, "signals intelligence" (codebreaking, traffic analysis, etc.), and electronic devices (radar, Huff Duff) about which the Germans were largely unaware, had already drastically reduced the U-boat threat to convoys.

Histories of the Battle of the Atlantic which imply that as more and more U-boats joined the Atlantic force in the summer and fall of 1942, the threat to North Atlantic convoys increased to a precarious level, are not correct. As will be seen, the number of U-boats that failed to sink any ships at all per patrol rose steadily and, for the Germans, ominously, from half of those sailing to the North Atlantic in July and August 1942, to well beyond that figure in the spring of 1943. Hundreds of convoys on the North Atlantic run—thousands and thousands of ships—crossed the North Atlantic in 1942 unharmed.

RETURN TO THE MIDDLE AND SOUTH ATLANTIC

At the time Dönitz launched group *Wolf* against the North Atlantic convoys, he deployed a smaller group, *Hai* (Shark), to reopen the U-boat war in the middle and South Atlantic.

Group *Hai* was composed of four veteran boats sailing from France in June, plus the veteran *U-752*, sailing in early July. All were Type VIICs, which were better suited for attacking convoys than the Type IXs. They were to patrol to Freetown, supported by the Type XB minelayer *U-116*, temporarily serving in the Atlantic force as a supply boat. She could provide fuel oil, lubricating oil, fresh water, and food, but not torpedoes.

The ablest and most experienced skipper in group *Hai* was the *Ritterkreuz* holder Adalbert Schnee in *U-201*. He did not disappoint. Southbound on July 6, he found and sank the impressive 14,500-ton British freighter *Avila Star*. Four days later he discovered convoy Outbound South 33, west of the Madeira Islands. Schnee shadowed and brought up all of group *Hai*, save the *U-752*, which had sailed last.

A hard convoy battle raged over the next seventy-two hours. Schnee in *U-201* sank four British ships for 26,000 tons: three freighters and the 7,000-ton tanker *British Yeoman*. Werner Schulte in *U-582* sank two big British freighters for 16,400 tons. Werner von Schmidt in the provisional tanker *U-116* (which had two stern torpedo tubes) sank the 4,300-ton British freighter *Shaftesbury* and captured her captain. The irrepressibly aggressive Heinrich Zimmermann in *U-136* (who had sunk two corvettes, *Arbutus* and *Spikenard*, within a week in February) attacked but was trapped by three escorts: the Free French destroyer *Leopard*, the British frigate *Spey*, and the British sloop *Pelican*, all of which adroitly capitalized on radar and Huff Duff. Pounded by gunfire and depth charges, the *U-136* went down with the loss of all hands. The cautious Heinz Hirsacker in *U-572* made contact with the convoy but did not attack.

Adalbert Schnee's report electrified Kerneval. Including the *Avila Star*, he had sunk by torpedo and gun five ships for 40,500 tons in a mere nineteen days. Counting past claims and overclaims, Schnee's score exceeded 200,000 tons and therefore he qualified for the award of Oak Leaves to his *Ritterkreuz*. As with Rolf Mützelburg in *U-203*, the award was radioed to Schnee* and plans were set in motion for Hitler to present the medals to Schnee and Mützelburg at the same time.

After the attack on Outbound South 33, Schnee was left with one torpedo and a few rounds of deck-gun ammunition. He therefore asked Kerneval if he could be detached from group *Hai* and remain in his present position. But Kerneval denied the request, emphasizing that *U-201* could serve well in a reconnaissance role. Schnee complied unhappily. Off Freetown, he found no traffic whatsoever. After he had expended his last torpedo to sink what he claimed to be a corvette—in actuality the 500-ton British ASW trawler *Laertes*—he was permitted to return to

---

    * At the time of the award, Schnee's claims on the duck *U-60* and the *U-201* totaled 29 ships for about 210,000 tons. His confirmed score was 22 ships for about 92,000 tons.

France, where Hitler awarded him and Mützelburg the Oak Leaves in a joint ceremony. Promoted to a newly created job, First Staff Officer (Operations) to Dönitz, Schnee turned the *U-201* over to a new skipper and did not return to combat.

Patrolling off Freetown or to seaward, the remaining three VIIs of group *Hai* had mixed success. The aggressive Karl-Ernst Schroeter in *U-752,* who had made prior patrols in Arctic, North Atlantic, and American waters, sank four freighters (one American, one British, one Norwegian, one Dutch) for 21,700 tons. Werner Schulte in *U-582* sank two more ships (both American) for 14,300 tons, bringing his score to four ships for 30,600 tons, and captured the captain and engineer of one of them, *Stella Lykes.* Heinz Hirsacker in *U-572* turned in another disappointing patrol: one Dutch freighter for 5,300 tons sunk.

Although the loss of the comer Heinrich Zimmermann in *U-136* was keenly felt, and Hirsacker again failed, group *Hai* was deemed a success. Altogether the four surviving VIIs and Werner von Schmidt's *U-116* (minelayer) sank sixteen ships for about 103,000 tons. Notwithstanding the terrible heat—Schnee reported temperatures of 120 degrees inside *U-201*—the good results of *Hai* and the availability of U-tankers persuaded Dönitz to send additional boats to the Azores and West Africa.

Seven boats sailed to West African waters in July: six Type IXs and the Type VIID minelayer *U-213.* In due course, these and other boats were to be supported by three of the five tankers, *U-459, U-460,* and *U-462.* While outbound from Lorient on July 27, a Coastal Command Wellington of the Czech Squadron 311, piloted by J. Stransky, attacked *U-106,* commanded by Hermann Rasch. Rasch boldly fought back with his bridge flak guns. In this battle, one officer was killed and Rasch was wounded, forcing him to abort. The boat did not sail again until late September.

A week out from Lorient on July 31, the VIID minelayer *U-213* commanded by Amelung von Varendorff found a convoy near the Azores. Von Varendorff reported the contact to Kerneval and then attacked, but the result was fatal. The British sloops *Erne, Rochester,* and *Sandwich,* all fitted with Huff Duff, caught and sank *U-213* with the loss of all hands.

Two Type IXs sailed south in loose company: Ernst Kals in the *U-130* and Harro Schacht in *U-507.* On July 14 Kals in *U-130* came upon a northbound convoy, Sierra Leone 115. It was escorted by four warships, one of which, *Lulworth,* was an ex-Coast Guard cutter. Schacht in *U-507* and Primo Longobardo in the Italian submarine *Pietro Calvi* heard Kals's alert and closed on the convoy.

The *Lulworth* picked up "strong" Huff Duff signals and ran out the bearing. She came upon Longobardo in *Calvi* and Kals in *U-130* having a tête-à-tête. When the submarines saw *Lulworth,* they crash-dived. An hour and a half later, *Lulworth* got *Calvi* on sonar and carried out three depth-charge attacks that severely damaged the Italian and forced her to the surface. *Calvi* had two 4.7" deck guns versus *Lulworth*'s two 3" guns, but the depth charges had knocked out both of *Calvi*'s guns. Longobardo fired his stern tubes, but *Lulworth* evaded, responding with her 3" and smaller weapons. Her accurate fire hit *Calvi*'s bridge, killing Longobardo and his second-in-command, whereupon *Lulworth* came about to ram. *Calvi* evaded wildly, but on the third try *Lulworth* hit the Italian boat in her stern, smashing her propellers and forcing her to surrender.

Meanwhile, in response to *Lulworth*'s alarm, two sloops, *Bideford* and *Londonderry*, rushed to the scene. By that time *Lulworth* had put a boarding party on *Calvi*, but the British were hampered by a fire in the conning tower, flooding, and the rush of the Italians to get topside and jump into the sea. Creeping into the scene, Kals in *U-130* attempted to attack *Lulworth*, but the latter heard the U-boat on sonar and let fly more depth charges, driving Kals off. The explosions probably killed some Italians in the water and further damaged *Calvi*, which suddenly upended and sank. The *Lulworth* boarding party had reached the interior of the boat but found only a "chart and rough log." Its leader was trapped in the sudden sinking and killed. The British vessels rescued thirty-five of seventy-eight crew members from *Calvi*.

Kals hauled out to report what he had done to help *Calvi* and to request instructions. *Calvi*'s loss and the inability of Kals to get around the escorts led Kerneval to believe the convoy to be far more strongly protected than was the case. Accordingly, Kerneval directed Kals in *U-130* and Schacht in *U-507* to break off operations and proceed to the Freetown area, where they were to refuel from von Schmidt's Type XB minelayer *U-116*, which had earlier supported group *Hai*.

It was a long, slow, hot journey to the south. En route Kals in *U-130* sank two big ships by torpedo and gun: the 10,100-ton Norwegian tanker *Tankexpress* and the 7,200-ton British freighter *Elmwood*. As planned, Kals and Schacht refueled from *U-116* on July 28. Two days later, Kals sank the 8,400-ton British freighter *Danmark*, bringing his score to 25,700 tons. Schacht in *U-507*, who had made a sensational patrol to the Gulf of Mexico in May, found no targets.

Kals in *U-130* remained off Freetown for the entire month of August. In that time he sank by torpedo and gun four more ships for 25,900 tons, including two more Norwegian tankers: *Malmanger*, 7,100 tons, and *Mirlo*, 7,500 tons. These successes brought his confirmed score to seven ships (three tankers) for 51,528 tons. Counting sinkings in three prior patrols, Kals qualified for a *Ritterkreuz*,* awarded by radio while he was homebound.

Finding no action off Freetown, Schacht in *U-507* requested authority to cross the Atlantic to Brazilian waters. Although von Ribbentrop had killed the earlier scheme to launch open warfare with Brazil by a sudden strike of about ten U-boats, Berlin did not object to a one-boat foray, provided that Schacht scrupulously avoided attacks on Argentine and Chilean ships.

Schacht reached the coast of Brazil on August 16. That day and the next he attacked six Brazilian freighters, ranging in size from 4,900 tons to 1,100 tons. One torpedo prematured, but the others hit solidly to sink five ships for 14,800 tons. He climaxed the foray on August 19 with a gun attack on the 90-ton sailing vessel *Jacyra*. He then expended five torpedoes on August 22 to sink a 3,200-ton Swedish freighter. Total sunk: seven ships for 18,100 tons.

In direct reaction to these sinkings, Brazil declared war on Germany on August

---

* At the time of the award, Kals's confirmed score was eighteen ships for about 116,500 tons.

22. Scarcely noticed at the time, the declaration merely formalized what had been for several months a state of war. Dönitz planned follow-up U-boat forays to Brazil, but the German Foreign Ministry, still fearful of antagonizing Argentina and Chile, did not view them with enthusiasm.

Two Type IXs working in loose cooperation sailed beyond Freetown to the African Gold Coast, or British Ghana and Nigeria. These were Ulrich Folkers in the IXC *U-125,* who refueled from *U-462,* and Erich Würdemann in the Type IXC/40 *U-506.* Würdemann had fair luck to September 5, sinking three ships for 16,400 tons. Folkers in *U-125* could not have had worse luck. To the same date he had sunk but one 815-ton British coaster.

The other IX of the July group was the older Model B, *U-109,* commanded by *Ritterkreuz* holder Heinrich Bleichrodt. Patrolling off Freetown in August, he sank two tankers for 11,800 tons, the 6,000-ton Norwegian *Arthur W. Sewall* and the 5,700-ton British *Vimeira,* from which Bleichrodt captured the captain. Then followed two barren and frustrating weeks at the end of which, on August 25, Bleichrodt also asked permission to go to Brazil, but Kerneval denied the request. Resupplied by the tanker *U-460,* Bleichrodt had better luck in September, sinking three big British freighters for about 24,000 tons, from the last of which, *Peterton,* Bleichrodt recovered valuable "secret papers" describing the Allied sailing routes in those waters. These sinkings raised Bleichrodt's total to five ships (two tankers) for about 35,600 tons. While homebound on September 23, Bleichrodt got word that he had been awarded Oak Leaves to his *Ritterkreuz.**

In the first half of August, eight attack boats sailed from French bases to West African waters: another IXB, *U-107,* and seven Type VIIs. These boats were also to be supported by the three tankers (*U-459, U-460,* and *U-462*) as well as by the former Dutch submarine *U-D5,* outfitted as a torpedo-supply boat.

The *U-107,* commanded by Harald Gelhaus, sailed on August 15. After crossing the Bay of Biscay, he reported to Kerneval that his Metox radar-detector gear worked well, enabling him to avoid attacks by six separate aircraft(!).

As these U-boats were putting out, on August 19 the British carried out a third hit-and-run "raid" on Occupied France, a very large one. About 5,000 Canadian and about 1,000 other Allied troops, massively supported by the RAF, stormed ashore at the channel port of Dieppe. The Germans decisively repulsed the raiders and inflicted a humiliating defeat. Canadian forces incurred 3,363 casualties; other Allied ground forces, 247. The Germans captured about 2,200 men. The Royal Navy, which incurred 550 casualties, lost the destroyer *Berkeley* and numerous landing craft. Although the raid was less than a model of perfection, the huge Allied casualties that resulted further strengthened the British resolve not to mount the main invasion, Roundup, until such time that the Allies could be certain of a reasonable chance of success.

Upon learning that an Allied raid was in progress at Dieppe, Kerneval diverted

---

* At the time of the award, his confirmed score on *U-48* and *U-109* was twenty-six and a half ships for 150,000 tons.

Gelhaus in the outgoing *U-107* (as well as *U-69* and *U-432*) to attack the enemy naval forces in the English Channel, but the Allies withdrew from the Dieppe area before *U-107* got there. When this became apparent, Kerneval directed Gelhaus to turn about and sail to southern waters, orders to follow.

The seven Type VIIs formed a new group, *Blücher,* replacing *Hai.* These boats included the *Ritterkreuz* holder Peter Cremer in *U-333,* who had barely survived a patrol to Florida in May, and the resailing Type VIID minelayer *U-214,* which had been crippled by a Coastal Command aircraft in June.

Close by the Portuguese Azores on August 16, Gerhard Feiler in the veteran *U-653* of group *Blücher* found a northbound convoy, Sierra Leone 118. It consisted of thirty-three merchant ships, escorted by the armed merchant cruiser *Cheshire* and four other British warships, including the ex-Coast Guard cutter *Gorleston.* She and two other escorts, the sloops *Folkestone* and *Wellington,* had Huff Duff.

As the other six boats of group *Blücher* homed in on Feiler's beacons, the escorts got bearings by radar and Huff Duff. Running down a Huff Duff contact, *Folkestone* found Cremer in *U-333,* who was making a radio report, forced him under, and attacked with depth charges six separate times. These attacks, Cremer wrote, were "really close" and they shook the boat "to the breaking point." The explosions bent his starboard propeller shaft upward, causing internal sparks and a loud and unnerving "screech" in the starboard clutch. The damage forced Cremer to abort.

The *U-566,* commanded by a new skipper, Gerhard Remus, age twenty-six, chose to open the battle with a daylight submerged attack. Remus fired three torpedoes at two ships and claimed he sank both for 11,700 tons. In reality, only the 6,600-ton Norwegian freighter *Triton* went down. The escorts pounced on Remus with depth charges, but he evaded, surfaced after dark, and continued stalking the main body.

By the morning of August 18, the convoy had reached a point about 600 miles south of England. This placed it within range of the B-24 Liberators of Coastal Command Squadron 120. The squadron leader, Terence Bulloch, flew the first mission. Cremer in *U-333,* who was aborting, and Remus in *U-566,* who was attempting to haul ahead of the convoy, both reported attacks by "land-based" bombers, but the damage to both boats was only "slight."

In the afternoon of August 18, Günther Reeder in the VIID minelayer *U-214* got in to carry out a submerged daylight attack. He fired a full bow salvo of four torpedoes into the formation, claiming four ships sunk for 20,000 tons. In actuality, he sank two big freighters for 13,800 tons and damaged the 10,100-ton armed merchant cruiser *Cheshire,* which was saved and towed to port. Reeder reported that "land-based" aircraft prevented him from hauling ahead for a second attack.

One of the Liberators, piloted by Squadron Leader Bulloch, attacked Feiler in *U-653* with six depth charges and two bombs. The close blasts knocked a crewman overboard and drove the boat under with "severe" damage, the second U-boat (after *U-89*) Bulloch had seriously damaged in as many days. Upon receiving Feiler's report later in the evening, Kerneval ordered him to give all the fuel he could spare to the Type VIIs *U-406* and *U-566* and then to abort. He limped into Brest on August 31. The boat was out of action for two months.

Müller-Edzards in *U-590* got contact on the convoy, but the escorts drove him under and put his radio out of commission. Another boat relayed his request to Kerneval for authority to abort. Kerneval directed Müller-Edzards to stay put and if at all possible, to attack, but nothing came of these orders. Unable to communicate or repair the radio, Müller-Edzards aborted, arriving in St. Nazaire on August 23. After hurried repairs, he resailed four days later.

Coastal Command Liberators, Sunderlands, and Catalinas were providing Sierra Leone 118 with nearly continuous air coverage by August 19. Nonetheless, in the late afternoon Horst Dieterichs in *U-406,* who had temporarily lost his starboard diesel, got ahead, submerged, and attacked by periscope. He hit and sank the 7,500-ton British freighter *City of Manila,* but in return the escorts hunted and attacked the boat relentlessly, inflicting heavy damage and casualties. Reluctant to abort, Dieterichs broke off the chase and hauled out to the west to make repairs. In the process, he discovered his lubricating oil was contaminated.

In view of the heavy air coverage, Dönitz canceled operations against Sierra Leone 118 on August 20. For the Germans the results of the action were only so-so. Three of the seven boats of group *Blücher* had attacked and sunk four ships for 28,000 tons and damaged the armed merchant cruiser *Cheshire.* In return, the air and surface escorts had forced three boats to abort: Cremer's *U-333,* Feiler's *U-653,* and Müller-Edzards's *U-590.* A fourth boat, *U-594,* commanded by a new skipper, Friedrich Mumm, age twenty-seven, who had lost both air compressors during a depth-charge attack, was directed to obtain spare parts from a U-tanker.

Allied ASW forces had gutted group *Blücher.* Kerneval therefore directed Gelhaus in the IXB *U-107* to join the three surviving Type VII boats, *U-214, U-406,* and *U-566.* As these orders were being carried out on August 25, Günther Reeder in the VIID minelayer *U-214* reported contact with another northbound convoy midway between the Canaries and the Azores.

The new convoy was Sierra Leone 119. Reeder shadowed, bringing up other boats, but the escorts, acting on Huff Duff contacts, drove *U-214* off and under. Gerhard Remus in *U-566* and Gelhaus in *U-107* got contact next. Remus carried out a submerged daylight attack, sinking two big freighters for 14,000 tons. In response, escorts counterattacked and one of them rammed *U-566,* demolishing her bridge and raking back her periscopes. After burning away the worst of the ragged steel with welding torches, Remus limped to France. Repairs to the boat delayed her return to combat until late October.

Air and surface escorts thwarted attacks on the convoy Sierra Leone 119 by the other boats of group *Blücher.* Reeder in *U-214* reported that "radar-equipped aircraft" had held him down for "a whole night" and as a result, he fell farther and farther behind and could never gain a firing position. Gelhaus in *U-107* reported that the surface escorts drove him under and depth-charged him for a full eight hours. He cleared the area with "a loud knocking noise," which, however, his crew was able to fix. Driven off by aircraft, Horst Dieterichs in *U-406* attempted a daylight submerged attack, but it failed.

The surviving *Blücher* boats, *U-107*, *U-214*, and *U-406*, doggedly shadowed the convoy northward but to no purpose. In view of the heavy air cover, Dönitz canceled operations against Sierra Leone 119. For the second time, Kerneval reorganized group *Blücher* for operations off Freetown. The new group was to consist of *Ritterkreuz* holder Peter Cremer in the resailing *U-333*, Müller-Edzards in the rejoining *U-590*, Joachim Berger in the veteran VIIB *U-87*, plus *U-107*, *U-214*, and *U-406*. Pending the sailing or resailing of the three boats from France, Kerneval parked *U-107* and *U-214* in a waiting area off Lisbon. While there on September 3, Gelhaus in *U-107* sank two British freighters for 8,600 tons.

The return of U-boats to South Atlantic waters in the summer of 1942 was not only timely but also profitable. The five boats of group *Hai* sank sixteen ships for 103,000 tons. The seven Type VIIs and IXs sailing independently in July sank thirty ships for 158,700 tons. The seven Type VIIs and IXs assigned to group *Blücher* sank eight ships for about 48,000 tons to September 3. Total: fifty-four ships for about 309,600 tons. Two Type VIIs, the *U-136* and the Type VIID minelayer *U-213*, had been lost with all hands. The exchange rate was thus twenty-seven ships sunk for each U-boat, much higher than the rate in the North Atlantic. In view of the good returns, Dönitz ordered an increase in patrols to South Atlantic and West African waters for the fall of 1942.

FURTHER PATROLS TO THE AMERICAS

The renewal of the U-boat campaign on the North, middle, and South Atlantic convoy routes in July and August absorbed the majority of the U-boats. Even so, Dönitz was reluctant to abruptly discontinue the campaign in the Americas. Apart from the sinkings to be had, a continued U-boat presence in American waters would insure expansions of the convoy network with all its inherent delays, tie down ASW forces, and forestall a shift of them to other areas. Hence twenty-eight more boats sailed to the Americas: ten Type VIIs and seven Type IXs in July, and three Type VIIs and eight Type IXs in August.

Of the ten Type VIIs sailing in July, six were veteran boats from France, the other four new boats from Germany. Two of the six from France were captained by *Ritterkreuz* holders: Reinhard Suhren in *U-564* and Gerhard Bigalk in *U-751*. Eight of the ten were to patrol the Caribbean area. The other two, Bigalk's *U-751* and the *U-98*, commanded by Wilhelm Schulze, were to lay TMB (magnetic) minefields at Charleston, South Carolina, and Jacksonville, Florida, respectively.

Bigalk in *U-751*, who had won his *Ritterkreuz* for sinking the "jeep" carrier *Audacity* during the December 1941 battle with convoy Homebound Gibraltar 76, sailed from St. Nazaire. Three days later, on July 17, a Whitley of Coastal Command Squadron 502, piloted by A.R.A. Hunt, spotted the boat on the surface. Attacking from an altitude of fifty feet, the Whitley dropped six 250-pound Mark VII depth charges with Torpex warheads set for 25 feet. The close straddle literally lifted *U-751* out of the water, the airmen reported. Nonetheless, the Whitley mounted a second attack with ASW bombs and machine guns.

The *U-751* survived these attacks and contrary to doctrine, Bigalk dived. A couple of hours later when he returned to the surface, a big British four-engine Lancaster of Bomber Command Squadron 61, on loan to Coastal Command and piloted by Peter R. Casement, was orbiting overhead. As the Lancaster ran in to attack, the *U-751* "fired back with all her guns." The Lancaster dropped ten close Mark VIII depth charges, then a string of ASW bombs. The bow of the U-boat rose vertically and she slid stern first beneath the sea. The crew spilled into the water, some of them shaking fists in defiance, the British aircrew reported. The British made no attempt to rescue the Germans. None survived.*

Wilhelm Schulze in *U-98* laid his dozen mines off Jacksonville on August 9. Something must have gone wrong because the field produced no sinkings. Remaining well offshore, Schulze cruised north to the Cape Hatteras area to patrol in deep water. On the night of August 22, in bright moonlight, he found a convoy off Cape Lookout, but the air and surface escorts thwarted his attack. Upon the return of *U-98* to France, it was noted that Schulze had made two long and arduous patrols to American waters without a single sinking, and he left the boat for other duties.

On the day British aircraft sank Bigalk in *U-751*, July 17, a homebound boat, Hans-Heinz Linder in *U-202*, found a convoy, Outbound South 34, close to the site of that sinking. Linder shadowed—and reported—until he was forced off by the escorts. His signals brought in two Type VIIs outbound to the Americas, *Ritterkreuz* holder Reinhard Suhren in *U-564* and Ludwig Forster in *U-654*, as well as two Type IXs, one outbound and one homebound.†

Owing to a shortage of fuel, Linder in *U-202* had to break off and continue to France, but by then Suhren had gained and held contact. After Forster in *U-654* reported that he was also in contact, Suhren attacked, firing four bow torpedoes at four different ships. He claimed four hits on four ships: two ships for 10,000 tons sunk and two for 13,000 tons damaged. A postwar analysis credited the two sinkings for 11,100 tons but not the damage. The outbound Type IXB *U-108*, commanded by *Ritterkreuz* holder Klaus Scholtz, shot a full salvo of six torpedoes (four bow, two stern) at three ships, but all six missed or malfunctioned. No other boat could get in to attack, and the rest of the convoy escaped.

Suhren in *U-564* and Forster in *U-654* continued southwest to the Caribbean. On July 22, Suhren came upon a heart-stopping sight one thousand miles due west of Gibraltar: two westbound "British battleships," escorted by three "destroyers." Suhren shadowed and reported but he could not gain a shooting position. His reports brought up Forster in *U-654* and Rolf Mützelburg in *U-203*, homebound from his notable patrol in the Caribbean, but neither boat could overtake the vessels. Suhren and Mützelburg met at sea the following day so that outbound Suhren could transfer a sick crewman to homebound *U-203*. Doubtless Suhren, who wore

---

* The assertion in some American records that *U-751* planted a minefield at Charleston is obviously in error.

† The convergence of six U-boats (two IXs, four VIIs) in the area near Outbound South 34 suggests that Dönitz had prior knowledge of its position and that Bigalk in *U-751*, who carried torpedoes as well as mines, was part of a special operation against this convoy. However, no records have come to light to confirm this possibility.

Oak Leaves on his *Ritterkreuz,* extended congratulations to Mützelburg, who had attained the same honor a week before.

Still traveling in company on August 3, Suhren in *U-564* and Forster in *U-654* met the new U-tanker *U-463,* commanded by Leo Wolfbauer. The VIIs topped off fuel tanks, but Suhren needed torpedoes. Upon learning that the luckless Type IX *U-154,* which was homebound from the Caribbean, had a full load, Suhren arranged via Kerneval to meet *U-154* and take on some of her torpedoes.* Afterward the two VIIs proceeded to and entered the Caribbean Sea, Suhren to the area west of Trinidad, Forster farther west to Panama.

By that time almost all Allied shipping in the Caribbean Sea had been organized into convoys, running between Key West, Trinidad, Aruba, Curaçao, and Guantánamo Bay. Most of the air and surface escorts for these convoys were American, but the British and Canadians had each contributed one surface escort group, and the British a squadron of twenty Hudsons from Coastal Command based on Trinidad.

Aware of the expanded convoy networks in the Caribbean, Dönitz encouraged his VII skippers to work together informally, if at all possible. Upon finding a convoy, a skipper was to broadcast a contact report, then attack. If other VIIs were nearby, they were to converge on the contact at high speed, mindful that in the Caribbean there was not much sea room for a prolonged convoy chase, that the number of Allied ASW aircraft was seemingly increasing day-by-day and therefore air attacks were likely, and that radio traffic between U-boats should be kept to a minimum.

When Jürgen Wattenberg in the Type IX *U-162* reported a convoy just west of Trinidad on August 19, Suhren in *U-564* unhesitatingly raced to the scene, made contact, and attacked. Notwithstanding "two pistol failures," he claimed he sank a tanker and a freighter for 15,000 tons and damaged two for 13,000 tons, but only the two sinkings for about 13,000 tons could be confirmed, including the 7,000-ton tanker *British Consul.* Shifting to the area east of Trinidad, in the Atlantic Ocean, for the next ten days, Suhren saw nothing worth a torpedo. However, on August 30, when he closed on Trinidad, he found and sank by torpedo and gun the 8,200-ton Norwegian tanker *Vardaas.*

Having exhausted all torpedoes, Suhren headed for France. He reported five ships (two tankers) sunk for 35,000 tons—an estimate close to the actuality—and four others for 26,000 damaged. The staff at Kerneval misinterpreted his report, logging that Suhren had *sunk* a total of nine ships for 60,000 tons. Or perhaps the misinterpretation was deliberate to justify yet another honor: the addition of Swords to Suhren's *Ritterkreuz* on September 1.† Upon returning to France, Suhren left the boat. Later he took over a newly created and exalted post in Norway, Commander of U-boats, North.

---

* A hard, hazardous task, accomplished by floating buoyed torpedoes from one boat to the other.

† After Kretschmer and Topp, Suhren was the third skipper to earn Swords to his *Ritterkreuz.* Uniquely, he had won his *Ritterkreuz* while serving as first watch officer of the record-breaking *U-48* under Herbert Schultze, Hans Rösing, and Heinrich Bleichrodt. As captain of the *U-564* for five patrols, Suhren had sunk 18 ships for about 95,000 tons.

Ludwig Forster in the VII *U-654* patrolled off Panama for ten days, August 12 to 21. During that time he saw only one vessel, a fast-moving motor torpedo boat. Upon receiving his interim report, Kerneval shifted the boat to the area directly south of Guantánamo Bay in the Windward Passage. The next day, August 22, a radar-equipped Army Air Forces B-18 of the 45th Bombardment Squadron caught *U-654* running on the surface. Attacking swiftly and skillfully, the pilot, P. A. Koening, dropped four shallow-set Torpex depth charges, which straddled the boat. Moments later oil and debris floated to the surface, the last sign of *U-654*. There were no survivors.

The other six VIIs that sailed to American waters in July went to the Caribbean via the North Atlantic routes. Kerneval directed several of these temporarily to attack convoys and refuel. As related, one veteran boat, Karl Thurmann's *U-553*, sank the 9,400-ton British freighter *Loch Katrine* from convoy Outbound North 115. During a refueling on August 5, a crewman on the new boat *U-598*, commanded by Gottfried Holtorf, washed overboard and drowned.

Four of the six boats patrolled close to the Windward Passage, on the lookout for Key West–Guantánamo Bay and Key West–Trinidad convoys, which they hoped to attack in loosely coordinated actions. On August 12, the new VII *U-658*, commanded by Hans Senkel, age thirty-two, found one, Key West–Trinidad 13. His alert brought in the other three VIIs, which found, in addition, the northbound Trinidad–Key West 12. In the attacks that ensued, Senkel claimed sinking a tanker and freighter for 21,000 tons and a hit on a 6,000-ton freighter, but only one minor sinking, a 1,311-ton Dutch freighter, was confirmed. Gottfried Holtorf in the new *U-598* sank two British ships, a 2,300-ton freighter and the 7,000-ton tanker *Empire Corporal,* and damaged the 6,200-ton British tanker *Standella.* Karl Thurmann in *U-553* sank two freighters for 10,000 tons and so badly damaged a third, the 7,000-ton British *Empire Bede,* that she had to be sunk by the British corvette *Pimpernel.* The new *U-600,* commanded by Bernard Zurmühlen, which had earlier sunk a 130-ton British sailing ship but missed a "destroyer" with a salvo of three torpedoes, sank two freighters for 9,600 tons. Total for the four boats: eight confirmed freighters for 37,200 tons sunk, one tanker damaged.

The overlapping battles with these two opposite-sailing convoys were fierce. The boats reported "strong" air and surface escorts. Zurmühlen in *U-600* stated that the Allied aircraft were able to locate his boat with great precision at night, indicating they were equipped with ASV radar. Moreover, he said, the surface escorts had "very good sonar" and their depth charges were uncomfortably "accurate." As a result, the *U-600* had incurred "considerable" damage that the crew could not repair, and Zurmühlen was forced to abort. Holtorf in *U-598* likewise reported heavy depth-charge damage that forced him to abort. Hans Senkel in *U-658* said he had been hounded by a "Q-ship" and that owing to a shortage of fuel, it was necessary to commence his return immediately.

Thus three of the four boats at the Windward Passage left for France. Shortly after clearing the Caribbean, Zurmühlen in *U-600* ran across a big, fast freighter but in spite of "faultless data," he missed with two torpedoes. En route home, he and Senkel in *U-658* and Holtorf in *U-598* refueled from Leo Wolfbauer's tanker *U-463*. While entering the channel leading into La Pallice, *U-600* triggered a British mine. The boat survived, but two months were required to repair both this battle damage and that incurred in the Caribbean. Holtorf's *U-598* remained in port for 105 days, undergoing battle-damage repairs.

Karl Thurmann in *U-553* patrolled the Caribbean for another ten days but found no more targets. Having refueled on the way to American waters and exercised strict fuel discipline, he did not require a refill to get home. His claims, including the big freighter sunk in the North Atlantic, totaled five ships for 32,000 tons, plus a 6,000-ton tanker damaged. Counting overclaims, Thurmann qualified for a *Ritterkreuz*, which was awarded on August 24, while he was still in the Caribbean. Berlin propagandists cheered the award, crediting Thurmann with sinking eighteen ships for 106,000 tons plus damage to twenty others.* When Thurmann reached France, *U-553* underwent a four-month overhaul and did not resail until January 1943.

After refueling from a U-tanker, the new *U-217*, a Type VIID (minelayer), patrolled off Aruba and Curaçao. On the night of August 18, her commander, Kurt Reichenbach-Klinke, age twenty-five, poked his bow into the harbor at Willemstad, Curaçao, and shot three torpedoes at the tanker *Esso Concord*, moored to a pier. He claimed a sinking but it could not be confirmed. The next day he attacked and sank with his gun the 75-ton British sailing vessel *Seagull D*, which he claimed was transporting "fifty soldiers." While *U-217* was engaged in this action, an Army Air Forces B-18 found and attacked the boat with depth charges and bombs, inflicting so much damage that Reichenbach-Klinke was compelled to withdraw to a distant area to make repairs. Reporting that "several" of his crew had been felled by heat strokes, Reichenbach-Klinke returned to France on October 16, completing a miserable patrol of ninety-five days, during which he sank no ships other than the sailboat.

The last of the July boats to enter the Caribbean was Günther Krech in the VII *U-558*. Mere hours behind him came *Ritterkreuz holder* Otto Ites in the VII *U-94*, who sailed from France on August 2. Both boats refueled from Bruno Vowe's tanker, *U-462*, on August 20, each filling their tanks to the brim. The boats then proceeded to the Windward Passage to hunt for convoys. On August 24, Krech in *U-558* slipped through the passage and sank a 2,000-ton British freighter on the south side, a romper from convoy Trinidad–Key West 15. He broke radio silence to report that while in the passage he was bombed and depth-charged by an enemy ASW group composed of aircraft and destroyers working in cooperation. Kerneval directed Krech to leave the area and patrol westward along the south coast of Cuba to the Yucatan Channel.

Ites in *U-94* combed the southern approaches to the Windward Passage, hunting convoys. On August 27 he found one and flashed an alarm. It was the main body of the heavily escorted northbound convoy Trinidad–Key West 15, consisting

---

*   At the time of the award, Thurmann's confirmed score was fourteen ships for 80,237 tons.

of twenty-one merchant ships and nine escorts of mixed nationality. There were no other Type VIIs near enough to attack, but a Type IXC/40 of the July group, *U-511,* commanded by Friedrich Steinhoff, responded.

That evening a radar-equipped Catalina of Patrol Squadron 92, based at the American naval installation at Guantánamo Bay, Cuba—facing the Windward Passage—joined the convoy to provide air escort. It was a beautiful tropical night, illuminated by a bright, full moon. At about 3:00 A.M., August 28, the airmen picked up *U-94* on radar and then saw her on the surface astern of the convoy. The pilot, Gordon R. Fiss, attacked from an altitude of about seventy-five feet, dropping four new, experimental, 625-pound Mark XXIX depth charges,* set to detonate at fifty feet. Ites saw the plane coming and dived, but it was too late to get deep. The heavy, close explosions blew *U-94* back to the surface and damaged her propulsion system, cutting her maximum speed to about 11 knots, not enough to evade even the slowest escorts, so Ites dived again.

Airman Fiss flew to one of the escorts, the Canadian corvette *Oakville,* commanded by Clarence A. King, and flashed an alert by signal lamp. King rang up full speed and upon reaching the site where Fiss had dropped flares, threw over five depth charges set for 100 feet. After the water calmed, King's men got *U-94* on sonar and then by moonlight saw the boat dead ahead on the surface. King unhesitatingly turned *Oakville* to ram, machine guns and cannons blazing. *Oakville* struck *U-94* a glancing blow, skewing the U-boat around wildly. Hauling off so that he could bring his 4" gun to bear, King got off four rounds, one of which blew away *U-94*'s deck gun. Then King rammed *U-94* a second time, simultaneously throwing over one depth charge set to explode directly beneath the U-boat.

Incapable of diving or firing back or outrunning *Oakville,* Ites gave orders to abandon and scuttle. He and his men swarmed topside into the hurricane of machine-gun and cannon fire from *Oakville,* which killed or fatally wounded about a dozen Germans. Hit twice in the leg, Ites leaped into the water as King swung *Oakville* around to ram *U-94* for the third time. *Oakville* hit the U-boat hard and square abaft the conning tower, tearing gaping holes in her own bottom. At the moment of collision, a "boarding party" consisting solely of one of *Oakville*'s officers, H.E.T. Lawrence, and a petty officer, A. J. Powell, courageously jumped onto the bow of *U-94* with pistols drawn to thwart the scuttling and to capture Enigma documents and/or perhaps even the entire U-boat. At nearly that same moment, the wounded Ites and another severely wounded German swam up to *Oakville* and were hauled aboard.

Complying with standard procedure, the boarders, Lawrence and Powell, rushed the conning tower with pistols to hold the Germans below and thereby thwart the scuttling. The Canadians shot two Germans in the conning tower who ignored their orders. The "extremely frightened" Germans who were still below "set up a terrific clamor," Lawrence reported, so much so that he allowed them to come topside. While Powell held these Germans in loose captivity with his pistol,

---

* The weapon, which was not adopted, had a 464-pound TNT warhead. The majority of airmen preferred to carry a greater load of the smaller, lighter, Mark XVII depth charge with a Torpex warhead.

Lawrence rushed below to the pitch-dark control room, which was rapidly flooding and smelled of "gas." In a hurried search by his own dimming flashlight, Lawrence could find no "secret papers" of any kind. As *U-94* upended and sank, stern first, he grabbed four pairs of binoculars and rushed topside. Boats from *Oakville* and from another escort, the American four-stack destroyer *Lea,* fished the two Canadians and twenty-four Germans from the water.

While *Oakville* and *Lea*—and the Catalina—were so distracted, Friedrich Steinhoff in the Type IXC/40 *U-511* moved in and attacked the convoy. He fired a full salvo at three different tankers. Astonishingly, in these first shots as skipper, Steinhoff hit all three. He sank the 13,000-ton British *San Fabian* and the 9,000-ton Dutch *Rotterdam,* and damaged the 8,800-ton American *Esso Aruba,* which limped into Guantánamo Bay under her own steam. One of three American SCs in the escort rescued the fifty-nine survivors of the two sunken tankers.

The Americans took custody of the twenty-six German survivors of *U-94* at Guantánamo Bay. They were smugly satisfied to discover that in Ites they had captured a *Ritterkreuz* holder, or "star." Over the next several weeks American intelligence officers grilled Ites and his men, who appeared to cooperate and talk freely but who actually revealed very little of value. When the Americans queried Ites about the Enigma machine on *U-94,* he was disarmingly casual. The machines were not secret, he said. Before the war they had been sold on the open market but they were "useless if the settings were not known." Had he known the Allies wanted an Enigma, Ites went on cavalierly, he would have "brought mine along for you."

There was an unpleasant aftermath to the *U-94* sinking. The commandant of the Guantánamo naval base, George L. Weyler, attempted to enlarge the American contribution and diminish that of the Canadians by insisting that the destroyer *Lea* had "opened fire" on *U-94* and therefore had earned part credit for her destruction. Furthermore, Weyler's official report of the action to higher American authorities contained veiled criticisms of the Canadians. Based on the reports of the American crews of the Catalina and *Lea, Oakville*'s skipper, Clarence King, was able to demolish Weyler's case and refute his tactless report. Official credit for the kill was divided equally between Catalina pilot Fiss and his aircrew, and skipper King and the *Oakville* crew. The *U-94* was the sixth U-boat to be killed all or in part by Canadian forces within six weeks, a remarkable achievement, but one that was not realized at the time.

Dönitz deduced promptly that Ludwig Forster in *U-654* and Otto Ites in *U-94* had been sunk, most likely, he believed, by enemy air. The loss of the much-admired twenty-four-year-old *Ritterkreuz* holder Ites—who had discovered the cause of the deep-running torpedoes in January—was keenly felt throughout the U-boat arm. His loss may have influenced Dönitz's decision to send no more Type VIIs to the Caribbean to attack convoys. The area was too confined, the convoys too heavily guarded by Allied ASW forces. Thus *U-94* became the last of the Type VIIs to draw an assignment inside the Caribbean or the Gulf of Mexico.

Unaware of these actions, Günther Krech in *U-558,* the only Type VII to make two patrols inside the Caribbean, cruised westward along the south coast of Cuba to the southern approaches to the Yucatan Channel. He remained in that once-rich area for ten days without seeing anything worth a torpedo. Then he cruised south to Panama and eastward to Aruba, Curaçao, and Trinidad. Finally, on September 13, he ran into a convoy sailing from Trinidad via Aruba to Guantánamo. In two successive attacks, Krech claimed numerous hits that sank a tanker and freighter for 15,000 tons and damaged a tanker and freighter for 12,000 tons. Postwar analysis credited three big ships sunk: two freighters for 15,200 tons and the 6,700-ton Norwegian tanker *Vilja*. Three days later in the waters west of Trinidad, he sank a 2,600-ton American freighter, bringing his confirmed sinkings for this patrol to five ships for 26,400 tons. These sinkings qualified Krech for a *Ritterkreuz*, which was awarded on September 17* as he pointed *U-558*'s prow eastward. Upon reaching France, the boat underwent a three-month overhaul and did not resail until January 1943.

Besides Ites in *U-94*, only two other Type VIIs sailed to American waters in August. Both were veteran boats: Ulrich Gräf in *U-69* and Hans-Heinrich Giessler in *U-455*. Both were assigned to lay TMB (magnetic) mines: Gräf in *U-69* to reseed the entrance to Chesapeake Bay where Degen in *U-701* had planted a field; Giessler to foul Charleston, South Carolina, in place of Bigalk in *U-751*, who was lost before he got out of the Bay of Biscay. Both boats carried torpedoes as well.

MORE POOR RETURNS FROM THE TYPE IXs

Eighteen Type IXs sailed to the Americas in late summer, ten in July and eight in August. As related, three of the July group that went by northern routes† ran into convoys or joined organized packs and remained in the North Atlantic. Of the fifteen Type IXs that reached American waters, twelve were on maiden patrols.

In the July group of seven, four patrolled east and southeast of Trinidad, where traffic to and from Freetown, Cape Town, and North and South America converged. The other three boats patrolled inside the Caribbean Sea. All seven encountered "heavy" air patrols.

The old hand Adolf-Cornelius Piening in *U-155* crossed the Atlantic via the southern route in company with Karl Neitzel, age forty-one, in the new *U-510*. In late July they refueled from the new tanker, *U-463*, commanded by Leo Wolfbauer. After that the boats separated, Piening in *U-155* to patrol east of Trinidad and south to Dutch Guiana (Surinam), and Neitzel in *U-510* to patrol through the Windward Passage along the south coast of Cuba to the southern approaches of the Yucatan Channel.

Piening turned in another notable performance. In a two-week period, July 28 to August 10, he sank by torpedo and gun ten ships for 44,000 tons. These included the 8,100-ton British tanker *San Emiliano* and two 400-ton Dutch coasters. He captured several officers from two of the ships, the Norwegian *Bill* and the British

---

* At the time of the award, Krech's confirmed score was fifteen ships for 104,593 tons, including two British warships: the corvette *Gladiolus* and the ASW trawler *Bedfordshire*.

† *U-43, U-174,* and *U-176.*

Empire Arnold. Counting the sinkings and claims in his two prior patrols to American waters, Piening qualified for a *Ritterkreuz,* which was awarded while he was still in the operational area.*

After that, the patrol turned sour. While cruising off the coast of French Guiana near the infamous Devil's Island, Brazil-based Allied aircraft harassed *U-155.* On August 18, an attack by a patrol plane killed one crewman and nearly sank the boat with depth charges, bombs, and machine-gun fire. Piening escaped, but the explosions severely damaged his batteries and restricted his ability to dive. Upon receiving this report, Kerneval told Piening to stand by where he was until another boat could provide him assistance.

En route to the Caribbean via the Windward Passage on August 2, Karl Neitzel in the new *U-510* sighted a lighted ship, which appeared to be a neutral. Per standing orders, Neitzel radioed Kerneval for authority to shoot. The staff ruled that if the ship was not Argentine, Swiss, or Portuguese, he should sink it. He did and learned from the captain, whom he captured, that she was the 5,300-ton Uruguayan neutral *Maldonaldo,* en route to New York with corned beef. The sinking infuriated the Uruguayans and edged that little country closer to a declaration of war.

Two days later Neitzel's hydrophones (passive sonar) failed. In view of the intensified ASW measures in the Caribbean and the inexperience of the boat, Kerneval canceled its Caribbean foray and redirected it to the supposedly safer open waters of the Atlantic, east of the Windward Islands. On August 10 Neitzel found and attacked the 8,000-ton British tanker *Alexia,* which mounted a spirited gun defense. Neitzel claimed she was a 14,000-tonner and that he had sunk her, but she was only damaged and later reached port.

Cruising south toward the northeast coast of South America, Neitzel suddenly encountered heavy ship traffic east of Trinidad. On August 18 he shot four torpedoes at a big fast freighter, but missed. The next day he sank a 5,000-ton British freighter, which he claimed to be 11,600 tons. That sinking drew a counterattack from Allied aircraft, one of which damaged *U-510.* Upon learning that Neitzel's boat had also incurred damage, Kerneval directed him to rendezvous with Piening in the damaged *U-155,* who was marking time near Devil's Island. Neitzel gave Piening some bridging cables for his batteries, but this was not sufficient. Kerneval therefore ordered both boats to return to France in company. An outbound boat was to give *U-155* the necessary spare parts to repair the battery.

The *Ritterkreuz* holder Klaus Scholtz in the Type IXB *U-108* traveled by the southern route directly to the area east of Trinidad. As related earlier, he was one of five inbound and outbound boats that responded on July 17 to the discovery of convoy Outbound South 34 by Linder in the inbound *U-202.* As also related, Scholtz had joined Suhren in *U-564* in an attack on the convoy, and had fired a full salvo of six torpedoes (four bow, two stern) into the formation, all of which missed.

---

* At the time of the award, Piening's confirmed score was 20 ships (four big tankers) for 94,635 tons.

When Scholtz in *U-108* reached the area east of Trinidad, he had to strictly husband fuel and torpedoes. Nonetheless, he turned in another noteworthy performance. On August 3 he sank the 6,200-ton British tanker *Tricula.* A week later, he chased a "big" ocean liner in vain, but sank the 2,700-ton Norwegian freighter *Brines.* Off French Guiana in the three-day period from August 15 to August 17, he found several tankers sailing alone and sank one of them, the 8,600-ton American *Louisiana.* In retaliation, aircraft attacked *U-108* with bombs and depth charges, but the boat survived. Damaged and low on fuel, Scholtz headed home. His claims and overclaims qualified him for Oak Leaves to his *Ritterkreuz,* awarded on September 10 when the boat arrived in France. Subsequently, Scholtz left the boat to command Combat Flotilla 12 at Bordeaux.*

The relentlessly aggressive forty-two-year-old Jürgen Wattenberg, former navigator of the *Graf Spee,* departed France for his third patrol in *U-162* on July 7. Mechanical defects had compelled him to abort his first patrol to the Americas. On his second, east of Trinidad, he had sunk nine confirmed ships for 47,000 tons, including three tankers. Determined to duplicate or exceed his second patrol and win a *Ritterkreuz,* Wattenberg opted for those same waters east of Trinidad. On the way, he, too, had responded to *U-202*'s alert on convoy Outbound South 34, expending considerable fuel to no purpose, but no torpedoes.

Wattenberg arrived in the waters off Trinidad in early August. Harassed by ASW aircraft, he had no success for two weeks. As related, on August 18, he found a Trinidad–Aruba–Key West convoy, gave the alarm, tracked, and brought in Reinhard Suhren in the VII *U-564.* In this loosely coordinated convoy attack, Wattenberg sank a 5,700-ton American freighter. He continued tracking the convoy for several days, but was unable to make another attack and returned to waters east of Trinidad. There, in a one-week period, from August 24 to August 30, he sank two more big freighters and the 8,300-ton Norwegian tanker *Thelma,* bringing his score for the patrol to four confirmed ships sunk for 30,500 tons.

Late in the afternoon of September 3, when *U-162* was about forty miles south of Barbados, Wattenberg spotted what he believed to be a single destroyer. He gave the order to attack submerged, but when he closed to shooting range, he saw there were not one but *three* destroyers! These were British warships en route to Trinidad to escort a convoy northward. Bravely or foolishly, Wattenberg continued the attack, firing a bow torpedo at the center ship, *Pathfinder.* However, the torpedo malfunctioned, broached, and headed directly for the left ship, *Quentin,* which maneuvered wildly to evade and did so, but just barely.

The three destroyers ran in and pounded *U-162* with depth charges. *Pathfinder* dropped ten, *Quentin* six, and the other ship, *Vimy,* fourteen. The charges damaged *U-162* severely but Wattenberg held her in control and lay doggo. Believing that

---

* At the time of the award, Scholtz's confirmed score was 26 ships for 130,677 tons, including the *Brines,* which is not included in most German sources. His transfer to shore duty left two skippers who wore Oak Leaves in command of Atlantic U-boats: Bleichrodt in *U-109* and Mützelburg in *U-203.*

the U-boat would eventually surface and try to escape to the east, the senior British commander told *Vimy,* which had Type 271 centimetric radar, to stay put, while *Quentin* and *Pathfinder,* which had meter-wavelength Type 286 radar, searched easterly. Not long after *Quentin* and *Pathfinder* departed, *U-162* surfaced. *Vimy* immediately got her on radar at 2,800 yards.

Vimy recalled *Quentin* and *Pathfinder* and ran in at full speed to ram, firing her main battery. The second round hit *U-162* and burst inside the pressure hull. Hopelessly outnumbered and outgunned, Wattenberg ordered his men to scuttle and abandon ship. As his men jumped overboard, he fired two red flares to mark the spot. Blinded by the flares and suspecting a ruse, *Vimy* attempted to abort the ramming, but her left screw crunched into *U-162*'s aft section, temporarily disabling the destroyer. As the ships entangled, *Vimy* threw over another shallow-set depth charge, which hastened *U-162*'s demise and injured many Germans in the water. The three destroyers rescued Wattenberg and forty-eight of his men and took them to Trinidad. Two Germans died in the sinking.

The British turned over Wattenberg and his men to American intelligence officers in Trinidad. They found these Germans to be "extremely security-conscious" and as a result, they learned "little of intelligence value." In due course the Americans were to discover that Wattenberg was an unyielding foe and troublemaking prisoner, who eventually conceived an elaborate scheme that enabled him and several other U-boat skippers to escape from an Arizona POW camp.

Three Type IXs of the July group which patrolled inside the Caribbean were new. Prior to her patrol, *U-511,* a Type IXC/40, commanded by Friedrich Steinhoff, age thirty-three, had been diverted to the *Wehrmacht*'s experimental rocket station at Peenemünde, where German scientists and engineers were developing the V-1 cruise and V-2 ballistic missiles. The German rocket experts had developed a small ballistic missile designed to be fired from a submerged submarine. The *U-511* had served briefly as a test platform, but the submarine-launched missile was not fully developed, nor was it to be by war's end.

The *U-511* and the new *U-164,* commanded by Otto Fechner, age thirty-six, sailed for the Caribbean by way of the North Atlantic routes. On July 29, both boats were drawn into the chase of convoy Outbound North 115, but *U-164* had a diesel-engine failure and was forced to fall out, and *U-511* became lost in fog. Following this fruitless diversion, the boats refueled from Leo Wolfbauer's tanker *U-463* and proceeded to the Caribbean.

Fechner in *U-164* entered the Caribbean via the Mona Passage. Proceeding to the area near Aruba and Curaçao, he encountered "heavy" air patrols but very few ships. When Otto Ites in the Type VII *U-94* reported the convoy Trinidad–Key West 15 south of the Windward Passage on August 25, Fechner in *U-164* made contact and sank a 3,800-ton Dutch freighter. Remaining inside the Caribbean near Jamaica and the south coast of Cuba, he sank one other small freighter of 1,700 tons, then left the Caribbean in frustration to cruise the Atlantic east of Trinidad. There an ASW aircraft bombed him and ruptured a fuel tank, forcing him to return to France. In an arduous patrol of eighty-two days, he sank two ships for 5,500 tons.

Steinhoff in *U-511* entered the Caribbean through the Windward Passage. On August 20 he found a convoy south of the passage, but a radar-equipped Catalina drove the boat under and held it there for hours. As related, when Otto Ites in *U-94* found the main body of convoy Trinidad–Key West 15 in the same waters on August 27, Steinhoff responded, and while the convoy escorts and Catalina sank *U-94*, Steinhoff attacked the convoy and sank two tankers for 22,000 tons and damaged another of 7,800 tons, which limped into Guantánamo Bay. He cruised these heavily patrolled waters until September 8 but had no further luck.

The third and last Type IX of the July group to enter the Caribbean was the new *U-163*, commanded by Kurt-Eduard Engelmann, age thirty-nine. He was assigned to replace Neitzel in *U-510*, who had aborted his patrol to the Yucatan Channel, going via the Windward Passage and the south coast of Cuba. While approaching the Windward Passage on the night of August 12–13, Engelmann reported, he was attacked by Catalinas. When Karl Thurmann in *U-553* found convoy Trinidad–Key West 13 on August 17, Engelmann responded, but he could not get around the escort to shoot, he said. Three days later he reported that his evaporators were out of commission, that he had very little drinking water, and that he was therefore forced to abort the patrol. He returned to France after fifty-eight days at sea, having sunk no ships of any kind.

Altogether the seven Type IXs that sailed to the Americas in July sank twenty-three ships (four tankers) for about 130,000 tons. This was a disappointing average of about 3.3 ships of about 18,500 tons sunk per boat per patrol, similar to the diminished returns of the Type IXs that sailed to the Americas in June. One Type IX, Wattenberg's *U-162*, was lost.

WITHDRAWAL FROM THE CARIBBEAN

Eight Type IXs sailed to the Americas in August. In view of the intense Allied ASW air patrols and the extension of the convoy network to all sectors of the Gulf of Mexico and the Caribbean, none was directed to those waters. Three IXs carried out a special mission in Canadian waters; the other five patrolled the target-rich area east of Trinidad in the Atlantic.

German codebreakers in *B-dienst* provided Dönitz with a great flow of information on North Atlantic convoys. Nonetheless, the U-boats in that sector had difficulty in locating the eastbound Halifax and Slow Convoys. Believing that these convoys might be departing Canada via Belle Isle Strait and going far to the north, Dönitz assigned three Type IXs of the August group to reconnoiter the strait and the seas to the north of its mouth.*

The three boats sailed from Kiel on August 7 and 8 and arrived off the mouth of Belle Isle Strait about three weeks later. On August 27–28, two of the boats, *U-517* and *U-165*, found a small military convoy en route from Sydney, Nova Scotia, to Greenland via Belle Isle Strait. It consisted of a half dozen ships sailing in

---

* Originally this task had been assigned to three Type VIIs of the July group, but they became involved in convoy battles and were eventually redirected to the Caribbean.

two sections. The first section was made up of the 5,600-ton American passenger-cargo vessel *Chatham,* with 562 troops and crew on board, escorted by the 240-foot Coast Guard cutter *Mojave.* The second section, comprising several other ships, was escorted by two 165-foot Coast Guard cutters, *Algonquin* and *Mohawk.*

Both U-boats closed and attacked. Paul Hartwig in *U-517* sank the *Chatham,* which fortunately went down slowly. Her escort, *Mojave,* rescued 293 men. Later, the American four-stack destroyer *Bernadou* and the Canadian corvette *Trail* rescued another 256 men.* Eberhard Hoffmann in the *U-165* hit and damaged two ships in the second section, the old (1921) 7,300-ton U.S. Navy tanker *Laramie* and the 3,300-ton freighter *Arlyn.* The *Laramie* was loaded with 361,000 gallons of aviation gas, 55,000 gallons of oil, and general cargo, which included depth charges. The torpedo hit killed four men and blew a huge hole in her port bow, but her captain, Peter M. Moncy, skillfully and bravely saved the ship and returned it to Sydney, escorted by the *Mohawk.*† Hartwig in *U-517* put a finishing shot into *Arlyn.*

After clearing with Kerneval, Hoffmann and Hartwig boldly took their big IXs south down the shallow, fifteen-mile-wide Belle Isle Strait. Hartwig in *U-517* poked his nose into a supposed convoy-assembly area, Forteau Bay, but it was empty. While still in the strait in darkness on September 3, he met two small convoys passing on opposite courses and sank the 1,800-ton Canadian laker *Donald Stewart.* Three Canadian corvettes and a minesweeper pounced on *U-517,* but the attacks failed or were not persistent and Hartwig, who had greater speed, easily escaped on the surface into the wide, fogbound waters of the Gulf of St. Lawrence.

Hoffmann in *U-165* entered the Gulf of St. Lawrence first. He cruised south to the east coast of Cape Breton Island, where he botched an attack on a 1,900-ton Canadian coaster. He then sailed northwest to the tip of the Gaspé Peninsula, rounded it, and proceeded west up the St. Lawrence River to a point opposite Matane. There he met convoy Quebec-Sydney 33, comprised of eight big ships, escorted by a corvette, a minesweeper, two motor torpedo boats, and the armed yacht *Raccoon.* In a dogged series of attacks over the next twenty-four hours, Hoffmann claimed hits on three ships for 19,000 tons. Postwar records confirmed two sinkings: the 4,700-ton Greek freighter *Aeas* and the 358-ton *Raccoon.*

Responding to Hoffmann's signals and beacons, Hartwig in *U-517* sailed across the gulf to intercept the same convoy as it rounded the Gaspé Peninsula southbound. Late on the afternoon of September 7, Hartwig attacked and sank three ships: Greek freighters of 5,700 and 3,300 tons, and a 1,700-ton Canadian coaster. The four surviving escorts, reinforced by another minesweeper, were apparently too dumbstruck (or ill-trained) to mount an effective counterattack. A Hudson of the British 113 Squadron caught Hartwig on the surface and claimed a "probable" kill, but the pilot botched the attack and *U-517* sailed on untouched.

---

* *Chatham* was the second American "troopship" to be lost in the war after the *Cherokee.* Thirteen men died in the sinking.

† Notwithstanding Admiral King's reluctance to give medals for saving one's ship, Moncy was awarded a Navy Cross.

These eight sinkings plus severe damage to the tanker *Laramie* within a period of twelve days caused yet another uproar in the Canadian government. Rolf Rüggeberg in the third boat, *U-513,* who remained "outside" in the Atlantic, added greatly to the uproar with a daring feat. Taking advantage of foul weather during the night of September 4, he edged *U-513* into Conception Bay (on the north tip of the Avalon Peninsula) on the surface, submerged in a convoy-assembly area, Wabana Roads, and the next day sank two big loaded freighters at anchor: the 5,400-ton British *Saganaug* and the 7,300-ton Canadian *Lord Strathcona.* In the ensuing chaos a fleeing freighter unknowingly rammed *U-513,* severely damaging her conning tower and putting a damper on Ruggeberg's dare-deviltry.

Notwithstanding the mounting uproar and the ASW response, the three IXs continued the hunt. Hartwig in *U-517* sank the Canadian corvette *Charlottetown* and two more freighters for 4,900 tons, raising his score to nine confirmed ships for 27,283 tons sunk. Hoffmann in *U-165* sank another 3,700-ton freighter and damaged two more, raising his score to three ships sunk for 8,754 tons and four damaged for 21,751 tons. Rüggeberg in *U-513,* who remained in the Atlantic off Conception Bay and St. John's, made only one other attack, during which he hit and damaged the 7,200-ton American-built British Liberty ship *Ocean Vagabond.*

Berlin and Kerneval were jubilant at the outcome of this foray in Canadian waters and praised Hartwig and Hoffmann highly. To Hartwig's claim of 44,000 tons sunk, Dönitz arbitrarily added 8,000 tons for a ship Hartwig shot at on September 15 but did not claim. This gave Hartwig a propaganda total of ten ships for 52,000 tons, with which Berlin happily bludgeoned the Canadians. But there was a third act. Approaching Lorient on September 29, Hoffmann in *U-165* struck a British mine and the boat blew up and sank with the loss of all hands.

The easy success of Hartwig and Hoffmann inside the Gulf of St. Lawrence— and the highly favorable propaganda they generated—persuaded Dönitz to continue what came to be known in Canadian history as "the Battle of the St. Lawrence." Several of the IXs sailing from Germany or France in September were assigned to proceed independently to the gulf.

In the meantime, the two Type VIIs that had been ordered to plant TMB (magnetic) minefields in United States waters were pressed into the battle in Canada. After planting his field off the entrance to the Chesapeake Bay on September 10, Ulrich Gräf in *U-69* headed for the Cabot Strait. After planting his field off Charleston, South Carolina, Hans-Heinrich Giessler in *U-455* went north to patrol off St. John's, Newfoundland, replacing Rüggeberg in *U-513.**

Upon entering the Gulf of St. Lawrence, Gräf in *U-69* proceeded directly to the mouth of the St. Lawrence River. He then cruised upriver to Matane and beyond, penetrating deeper than any other U-boat skipper, including the pioneer Vogelsang. On October 10, Gräf met a convoy of seven ships and three escorts headed up-

---

* The 7,300-ton tanker *Petrofuel* detonated a mine in Gräf's field off the mouth of the Chesapeake but was not damaged. Neither minefield produced any sinkings. Both fields were discovered and swept by the Americans.

stream to Quebec City, 173 miles distant. Coolly Gräf set up on and sank the 2,400-ton Canadian freighter *Carolus,* then ran downstream before Allied ASW forces could collect their wits.

Returning to safer waters at the Cabot Strait, on October 14 Gräf found and sank a 2,200-ton Canadian railway ferry, *Caribou,* escorted by the minesweeper *Grandmère.* There were 237 persons on board *Caribou,* including 118 military personnel. Spotting *U-69, Grandmère* attempted to ram, but missed. She then dropped eighteen depth charges. Reinforced by other air and surface escorts at dawn, which held Gräf on the bottom for sixteen hours, *Grandmère* rescued 103 of the 237 persons on *Caribou.* The other 136, including many women and children, died in the blast or in the water.

Having gone upriver farther and killed more civilians than any other U-boat skipper, Gräf, too, caused an enormous uproar in Ottawa. Homebound on October 20, he attacked a convoy near Argentia and hit the 7,800-ton British freighter *Rose Castle,* but the torpedo malfunctioned, sparing the ship. Upon his return to France, Gräf received a "well done."

Giessler in *U-455* arrived off St. John's, Newfoundland, on about October 1 and patrolled foggy waters close to shore for nearly two weeks. He saw only two ships, both beyond reach. On October 14 he reported his gyro compass had failed and that he was aborting. When he arrived in France after sixty-eight days at sea— and no sinkings—it was noted that in four patrols Giessler had sunk only two ships (both tankers) for 13,900 tons, and he left the boat for other duty.

The five Type IXs of the August group that were assigned to patrol the area east of Trinidad sailed from Kiel on August 12 to August 15. Three of the boats, *U-175, U-512,* and *U-514,* commissioned in November and December 1941, had been icebound in the Baltic for three or four months. Another, *U-515,* commissioned in February 1942, had also been delayed by ice. The last, *U-516,* commissioned on March 10, 1942, was not seriously delayed by the ice but her workups and final fitting out took five full months.

The *U-512* was commanded by Wolfgang Schultze, age thirty-one, one of two sons of a *Kriegsmarine* admiral. According to his peers, he was a vain, temperamental, spoiled brat who drank heavily, even on board ship. During the boat's belated Baltic workup, Schultze rammed and capsized a small freighter (*Morgenrot*) and was himself rammed by another U-boat. These and other mishaps further delayed *U-512* and gave the impression that Schultze was not only reckless but incompetent.

En route to Trinidad Schultze met Bruno Vowe's tanker, *U-462,* and replenished. Thereafter, on about September 8, he encountered a big, lone, fast freighter which he estimated at 12,000 tons. In two separate surface attacks he fired four bow torpedoes. None hit or exploded, leading Schultze to conclude, probably wrongly, that the freighter had streamed antitorpedo nets. Four days later he came upon the fully loaded 10,900-ton American tanker *Patrick J. Hurley.* He fired two torpedoes at her but both missed. He then attacked with his 4.1" deck gun, his new

37mm flak gun, and other weapons. The *Hurley* crew returned a few rounds from her stern gun but quickly conceded the contest and abandoned ship, allowing *Hurley* to sink in a ball of fire.

A few days later, on September 19, Schultze spotted a lone freighter about fifty miles east of Martinique. She was the 3,700-ton Spanish neutral *Monte Gorbea,* sailing under her own colors. Brashly assuming she was a British ship in disguise—or so he told Dönitz—Schultze torpedoed and sank her. When *B-dienst* picked up her distress calls and informed the OKM, Berlin was furious. Admiral Raeder issued orders through Dönitz that when Schultze returned to France he was to be court-martialed. Dönitz informed "all boats" of the error and impending court-martial and passed along a stern reminder from Raeder that all skippers were to "comply exactly" with orders concerning the safe treatment of neutrals.

In the meantime, two other IXs of this group arrived east of Trinidad: *U-514,* commanded by Hans-Jürgen Auffermann, and *U-515,* commanded by Werner Henke. A onetime naval pilot, the twenty-seven-year-old Auffermann had served as first watch officer on *U-69* on her pioneering patrol to Freetown for which Jost Metzler had won a *Ritterkreuz.* A longtime prewar merchant marine sailor, the thirty-four-year-old Henke had served as second and first watch officer on the *U-124* when Georg-Wilhelm Schulz won his *Ritterkreuz.*

Patrolling the Windward Islands on September 11, Auffermann in *U-514* scouted the most easterly of the islands, Barbados. Its capital, Bridgetown, was situated in a spacious harbor, Carlisle Bay, which had recently been sealed by an antisubmarine net, supported by a floating boom. Spotting two freighters moored at the Bridgetown waterfront, Auffermann fired a series of torpedoes, which broke through the net and hit one of the ships, the 5,500-ton Canadian *Cornwallis.* He claimed sinking *Cornwallis* and another ship of 4,500 tons, but the second could not be confirmed. The torpedo blasts stupefied the citizens of peaceful Bridgetown, who rushed to the waterfront to see *Cornwallis* settle heavily in the mud. Later the ship was patched up and returned to service, only to be sunk later in the war by another U-boat.

Patrolling the area directly east of Trinidad in a ten-day period from September 12 to September 23, Henke in *U-515* turned in a spectacular first patrol. He sank by gun or torpedo eight confirmed ships for 42,000 tons and damaged two others for 10,700 tons. Among his victims was the British freighter *Ocean Vanguard,* which, in the fall of 1941, had been the first of the sixty American-built Liberty-type cargo vessels to enter British service, and two tankers: the 10,000-ton Panamanian *Stanvac Melbourne* and the 4,700-ton Dutch *Woensdrecht.* This nearly perfect performance was marred by a single setback. On September 15, while attacking the 5,600-ton American freighter *Mae,* Henke's deck gun misfired and killed one of his men. Overcredited with sinking ten ships for 54,000 tons, Henke returned speedily to France, where he and his men were showered with praise and medals.

The last ship Henke torpedoed was the 6,000-ton American freighter *Antinous.* After her crew had abandoned ship in lifeboats, Schultze in *U-512* came upon the hulk on September 24 and sank it with a single torpedo. This raised Schultze's total bag to three ships for 20,600 tons, including the Spanish neutral, for which he was to face a court-martial.

By then a third IXC/40 had arrived on the scene: the *U-516,* commanded by Gerhard Wiebe, age thirty-five. Wiebe had had a lively voyage to the Americas. South of Iceland on August 27, he had encountered the fast 9,700-ton British freighter *Port Jackson,* sailing alone. He had fired a full bow salvo at her, but all four torpedoes had missed. He had then opened fire with his deck gun, scoring two hits, but the ship had escaped in the fog. Acting on a sighting by another U-boat, on August 31 in the mid-Atlantic Wiebe had found the fast, 11,000-ton American tanker *Jack Carnes,* sailing in ballast. He had chased the ship for 270 miles (eighteen hours at 15 knots) and had finally sunk her with seven torpedoes. On September 6 he had met the aborting *U-163* and received six torpedoes from her. Approaching the area east of Trinidad on September 19, Wiebe had sunk by torpedo the 6,200-ton American freighter *Wichita.*

In the latter days of September, Schultze in *U-512* and Wiebe in *U-516,* working in loose cooperation, cruised southward off the coast of French Guiana. On September 28, Wiebe came upon the 1,200-ton Brazilian coaster *Antonico.* Since he was short of torpedoes, he sank her with his deck gun in an action that lasted only twenty minutes, he reported.* Two days later he sank by torpedo and gun the 5,300-ton British freighter *Alipore.*

Schultze in *U-512* was close by but he found no targets. Although Allied aircraft had earlier attacked the boat and "slightly" wounded Schultze, he incautiously elected to remain on the surface in daylight. Near Devil's Island on the morning of October 2, a radar-equipped Army Air Forces B-18 of Squadron 99, based at Trinidad, caught *U-512* so disposed. The pilot ran in at an altitude of fifty feet and straddled the U-boat with two standard Mark XVII and two monster Mark XXIX experimental depth charges. The explosions smashed *U-512* and drove her to the bottom in 138 feet of water. Apparently most of the compartments flooded instantly and drowned two-thirds of the crew, including Schultze.

The bow torpedo compartment sustained heavy damage but flooded gradually. Sixteen men were trapped there. Had they all had escape lungs they might have survived, but owing to improper stowage, the lungs had become wet with condensation and all but four had been taken to the engine room to dry out. As water and chlorine gas (saltwater mixing with electric-torpedo batteries) filled the compartment, four men strapped on the escape lungs. Others began to collapse from gas, rising air pressure, shock, and panic.

Two men, one wearing a lung, one not, attempted to organize an escape through the angled torpedo-loading hatch. They removed the hatch brace, undogged the hatch, and let seawater flow into the compartment until the pressure

---

* The survivors of *Antonico* asserted that Wiebe shot at them in the lifeboats, killing six and wounding ten men. These charges were brought against Dönitz at his Nuremberg trial but to small effect. Dönitz responded that the survivors had doubtless drifted into gunfire aimed at the ship and that had Wiebe intended to wipe out the survivors, as charged, he would not have departed the scene in a mere twenty minutes.

equalized and they could push the hatch fully open. They then swam out of the boat, but only the man with the escape lung reached the surface alive. He waved frantically to the plane circling overhead, and the aircrew dropped him a life belt and an inflatable raft. This lone survivor of *U-512* drifted in the raft for ten days, until on October 12 the American four-stack destroyer *Ellis* fished him from the sea. No sign of the other forty-eight men on *U-512* was ever found.

The other two boats in this area, Auffermann's *U-514* and Wiebe's *U-516,* found the hunting less and less rewarding. In pursuit of targets, Auffermann sailed south to the Equator. In the estuary of the Amazon River on September 28, he sank two Brazilian freighters for 8,200 tons. Returning northward via the waters off French Guiana on October 12, he sank a 5,700-ton American freighter not far from the area where *U-512* had met her end. Wiebe in *U-516* found no more targets off South America, but on the way home he sank a 5,800-ton British ship on October 23. Including a 167-ton sailing ship sunk by gun, Auffermann's confirmed score in *U-514* on this ninety-day patrol was five ships for 17,354 tons, plus heavy damage to the freighter *Cornwallis* in Barbados. Wiebe's confirmed score on this ninety-five-day patrol, including the tanker *Jack Carnes,* was five ships for 28,400 tons sunk, plus damage to the 9,700-ton British freighter *Port Jackson.*

The last of the five IXs of the August group to patrol this area was Heinrich Bruns in *U-175.* Cruising the shallow waters off British Guiana, Bruns had very good luck. In a mere eighteen days, from September 18 to October 5, he sank by gun and torpedo nine confirmed freighters for 33,400 tons. He returned *U-175* to France after seventy-four days at sea.

Altogether the five new Type IXs that patrolled east of Trinidad and south to French, Dutch, and British Guiana and the northern border of Brazil sank thirty confirmed ships for 143,000 tons. Henke in *U-515* and Bruns in *U-175* accounted for over half the total: seventeen ships for about 75,500 tons. One of the five IXs, *U-512,* was lost, taking down forty-eight of her forty-nine-man crew.

ASSESSMENTS

The withdrawal of Type VIIs from independent patrols to American waters in August of 1942 was another major turning point in the Battle of the Atlantic. That and a sharp decline in Type IX patrols signaled the beginning of the end of the all-out U-boat war against the Americas and provides a convenient milestone to sum up and assess that campaign.

Any such assessment must begin by restating the distortions in existing accounts. Admiral King and the American naval staff emerge in most of these as fools or knaves or worse, the U.S. Army leaders and the British as brilliant and infallible warlords. To see the U-boat campaign in American waters in a proper light, these important reminders and correctives are required.

First, it must be remembered that the historically majestic British Royal Navy was in a state of serious decline, and the American Navy was in vigorous ascendancy. As historian James R. Leutze has shown,* British navalists did not gladly admit of this role reversal and were quite unwilling to surrender naval supremacy to their untutored, uncouth country cousins. This jealousy, very much prevalent in 1942, colored the views of British navalists regarding the effectiveness of the American and Canadian navies and leaders, and, subsequently, British naval historians, who have uncritically accepted contemporary, biased British reports on the North American cousins as gospel.

Besides that, it must be remembered that notwithstanding the public displays of amity, the American and British war planners were in serious disagreement over strategy for most of 1942. The Americans were eager to mount Sledgehammer, the invasion of Occupied France, and to come to grips directly with German power on the ground. Contrarily, the British opposed Sledgehammer in favor of a number of low-intensity operations on the "periphery" and what was predicted to be a morale-crushing, war-winning strategic bombing campaign against German industry and cities.

American and British navalists held divergent views over the strategic role of Allied sea power in the Atlantic theater. As was done by Americans in World War I, Admiral King assigned highest priority to the safe delivery of soldiers and other military personnel to overseas destinations, particularly those American forces embarked originally for the British Isles to carry out Sledgehammer. The British laid nearly equal stress on the importance of protecting "trade" or merchant shipping engaged in transporting food, oil, and tools of war to the British Isles, which were deemed vital for her survival and her ability to wage the kind of war the British War Cabinet preferred.

British historians and popular writers seldom acknowledge there was ever a divergence of strategic views over the use of maritime assets in 1942 or that the protection of troop transports was seen by the Americans as the most vital task of all. They mainly write that the Americans were incredibly stupid in the protection of merchant shipping, "refusing" as they did to initiate convoying in American waters until May, and, as a consequence, suffered a devastating naval defeat. The recent suggestions by American naval historians Dean C. Allard and Robert W. Love, Jr., that the transporting of American troops from the United States across the Atlantic to the British Isles in the first eight months of 1942 with no losses† was a significant naval victory by and of itself, has largely gone unremarked by British historians.

Another aspect of the Allied naval disputations in this period that the critics of Admiral King seldom acknowledge is that the American Navy had to cope with a "two-ocean war." In order to protect the line of communications to Australia and prevent an invasion of that continent, as set forth in Anglo-American strategic

---

    *   *Bargaining for Supremacy* (1977).

    †   Among other forces, four Army divisions: 1st, 5th, and 34th Infantry and 1st Armored. The number of American military personnel disembarked in the British Isles in this period was roughly 157,000. (See tables in Behrens, p. 283, and Bykofsky and Larson, p. 102.) The thirteen men lost on the troopship *Chatham* were outbound from Nova Scotia to Greenland.

agreements, the Americans had to send tens of thousands of soldiers and airmen to Hawaii, New Caledonia, the Fiji Islands, and Australia.* These troopship convoys, most crossing vast stretches of the Pacific Ocean, had to be protected as stoutly as the Atlantic troopship convoys. It was therefore not possible (as urged by the British Admiralty) to withdraw American destroyers from the Pacific to serve as escorts for cargo convoys in the Atlantic.

When the shortage of destroyers and other suitable vessels forced King to choose between escorting American and British troopships and escorting cargo vessels and tankers, he chose to protect the troops.

A third important factor to remember in order to see the U-boat campaign in American waters in a proper light is that the American Army and Navy were in serious disagreement over ways of coping with the U-boat threat throughout 1942. The Army believed that special units of radar-equipped, four-engine, land-based aircraft, such as the B-24 Liberators, should be employed to hunt down U-boats "offensively," a so-called hunter-killer strategy. Contrarily, the Navy deemed hunter-killer operations to be futile and urged that such aircraft be employed "defensively" for the protection of convoys, to which U-boats were certain to be drawn like bees to honey, and "offensively" only against submarine-building yards, forward bases, and known "choke points" such as the Bay of Biscay.

Because of this divergence of views and because the Army Air Forces were opposed for political, doctrinal, and other reasons to rescinding a prewar agreement that gave it exclusive control of land-based aircraft, in 1942 the Navy was barred from organizing its own land-based aircraft units for convoy escort. Instead, the Navy had to beg and borrow Army Air Forces units, whose personnel were not trained in convoy escort or ASW and, in any case, detested this "defensive" assignment as opposed to the glamorous "offensive" strategic bombing of the German heartland. It is not surprising, therefore, that in the eight months of the U-boat campaign in American waters the Army Air Forces units failed abysmally, sinking only one U-boat (*U-701*) unassisted by surface ships or other forces.

In the existing accounts of the U-boat campaign in the Americas, this absurd and wasteful interservice battle over control of airpower is almost never depicted adequately. That President Roosevelt allowed it to persist throughout 1942 and half of 1943 is one of the great military misfortunes of World War II. Be that as it may, the situation demands the fullest exposition in discussing this phase of the U-boat war.

A fourth factor to recall is that the Allies "lost" naval Enigma on the U-boat Triton (Shark) net in early 1942. The official British intelligence historian has dismissed this setback as of small consequence in the U-boat campaign in the Americas, but in fact, it was of vital importance. Had U-boat naval Enigma not been lost, the Americans would have discovered at once that this new campaign was an all-out German assault, employing all available Atlantic submarines, including medium-range Type VIIs and new U-tankers. Informed of these facts and other tactical data, such as the fact that the U-boats were not to operate in coordinated

---

* Among other forces, six American Army divisions: Americal, 27th, 32nd, 37th, 40th, and 41st Infantry, and the Marine Corps 1st Division.

groups or "wolf packs," the American military high command doubtless would have reacted differently, perhaps even to the extent of authorizing unescorted oil and cargo convoys.

A fifth factor to remember is that in early 1942 just as the campaign in the Americas was being launched, the Germans discovered the last major defect in their submarine torpedoes. This was the leak in the balance chamber that caused them to run much deeper than set. The steps taken to correct this defect greatly improved torpedo performance and the percentage of hits in American waters.

A sixth factor to keep in mind is that in 1940–1941, the Americans loaned to the British and Canadians fifty four-stack destroyers and ten *Lake*-class Coast Guard cutters. Had these sixty big warships remained in U.S. Navy control, they would have been sufficient to establish convoy networks immediately on the East Coast and in the Gulf of Mexico and the Caribbean, preventing the loss of scores of ships and hundreds of merchant seamen.

Having set forth those important reminders, the assessment of the U-boat campaign in the Americas may now proceed in a fairer prospective. To assist in this assessment, it is necessary to examine another set of numbers. These are derived from U-boat sailings to American waters from December 18, 1941, through August 31, 1942.*

• The Germans mounted 184 war patrols: 80 by Type IXs and 104 by Type VIIs. This was an average of about twenty sailings per month, a much heavier commitment of force than usually depicted.

• These boats sank 609 ships for 3.1 million gross tons, including all trawlers, small auxiliaries, and sailing vessels as well as ships sunk en route to and from the Americas. This was an average of about sixty-eight vessels a month for about 350,000 tons.

The ships sunk in the campaign in the Americas in this period constitute about one-quarter of all Allied shipping sunk by German U-boats in World War II. Thus, the campaign was the single most important of the war in terms of sinkings achieved in a relatively brief time period for effort expended—the high-water mark of the U-boat war. Only about six of the 184 patrols to American waters in this period resulted in no sinkings or damage to Allied shipping. Moreover, German losses were relatively modest: twenty-two U-boats (ten IXs and twelve VIIs). Of the approximately 1,000 submariners manning these boats, only about 200 survived, 114 of these as POWs.†

One of the ironies of this most successful campaign was that the Type IX boats, which Dönitz had so ardently opposed, achieved by far the greatest successes. Fortuitously for the Germans, thirty-four new Type IXs, long in production, workup, and retrofit, became available to the Atlantic force in the first eight months of 1942. The eighty patrols by the Type IXs accounted for 384 of the vessels sunk (63 percent of the total) for about 2.0 million gross tons (65 percent). The 104 patrols

---

* See Appendix 4 and Plate 12.
† From *U-94, U-162, U-352, U-512,* and *U-701.*

PLATE 12

SUMMARY OF SINKINGS BY U-BOATS PATROLLING TO AMERICAN WATERS

DECEMBER 1941–AUGUST 1942

DECEMBER BOATS	SHIPS SUNK	TONS	AVERAGES	
5 IXs	23	150,505	4.6	30,101
10 VIIs	18	85,374	1.8	8,537
JANUARY BOATS				
12 IXs	47	276,044	3.9	23,003
14 VIIs	24	124,922	1.7	8,923
FEBRUARY BOATS				
9 IXs	28	176,630	3.1	19,625
9 VIIs	29	167,864	3.2	18,651
MARCH BOATS				
6 IXs	29	164,109	4.8	27,351
20 VIIs	46	241,937	2.3	12,097
APRIL BOATS				
14 IXs	95	482,843	6.7	34,488
17 VIIs	38	158,210	2.2	9,159
MAY BOATS				
9 IXs	64	304,510	8.0	38,064
8 VIIs	20	102,082	2.5	12,760
JUNE BOATS				
10 IXs	31	135,100	3.1	13,510
13 VIIs	27	123,904	2.0	9,531
JULY BOATS				
7 IXs	23	129,648	3.3	18,521
10 VIIs	22	109,240	2.2	10,924
AUGUST BOATS				
8 IXs	44	191,696	5.5	23,962
3 VIIs	2	4,597	0.6	1,532
SUBTOTALS:				
80 IX patrols	384	2,011,085	4.8	25,138
104 VII patrols	225	1,111,371	2.2	10,686
GRAND TOTAL:				
184 patrols	609	3,122,456	3.3	16,969

Losses: 10 IXs and 12 VIIs = 22 U-boats.
"Exchange Rate" = 27.7 ships sunk per each U-boat lost.

by the Type VIIs accounted for the other 225 vessels (37 percent) for about 1.1 million gross tons (35 percent). Overall, the Type IXs averaged 4.8 vessels sunk for 25,100 gross tons per boat per patrol compared with an average 2.2 vessels sunk for 10,686 gross tons per boat per patrol by the Type VIIs. By this reckoning, had Dönitz had his way and there had been far fewer Type IXs, and had the eighty Type IX patrols been carried out by Type VIIs, the total sinkings in the campaign would have been considerably less: perhaps 400 ships for about 2.0 million tons, rather than 609 ships for 3.1 million tons.

A striking feature of this campaign in the Americas was the very large number of Allied tankers that fell victim to the Germans in the first eight months of 1942.* Losses by area:

U.S. Eastern Seaboard	43
Gulf of Mexico	22
Caribbean/Latin America	72†
Canada	6
Total	143

When these tanker losses are added to the tankers sunk by Axis submarines en route to and from the Americas and patrolling to other areas, such as Freetown, Sierra Leone, and the Azores, during the first eight months of 1942, the total of tanker losses in this period rises to 188.

This was indisputably a blow to the Allies. The losses restricted a number of Allied military operations and were the cause of much friction between the U.S. Army and Navy and between London and Washington. But contrary to some accounts, it was not a crippling blow. The American, British, and Canadian shipyards produced ninety-two bigger and better tankers for about 925,000 tons in 1942, replacing half the number of tankers lost but nearly two-thirds of the tonnage lost. In 1943, American shipyards alone produced another 214 tankers for about 2.1 million gross tons, while tanker losses to U-boats fell dramatically to forty-eight for 373,000 tons.

The Americans compensated for the drop in the oil flow caused by the tanker losses and convoying in 1942 through a drastic reduction in their dependence on oceangoing tankers and by the use of alternative oil-delivery systems. This shift can be seen in the following chart of the oil flow from Texas and Louisiana to the northeast United States, measured in barrels per day:

Delivery System	Jan. 1942	Dec. 1942
Railroad tank cars	98,500	740,063
Pipelines	62,500	158,180
Barges, lake vessels	42,500	64,380
Oceangoing tankers	1,268,500	111,759
Totals	1,472,000	1,074,382

The deficit in this flow of oil was overcome in 1942 by gasoline rationing on the Eastern Seaboard and the conversion of factories from oil to coal and to natural gas, as well as a depletion of oil stockpiles in that area.

---

* See Appendix 17.

† Includes one tanker sunk by *U-512* and two by *U-515* in early September.

The decreased dependence on oceangoing tankers for oil delivery to the northeastern United States and the output of new tankers in 1942 enabled the Americans to again "loan" the British tankers. In response to requests from London (the so-called Red Gap and Blue Gap), Washington made available in 1942 the equivalent of about 100 tankers. This emergency diversion of ships, together with stricter gasoline rationing in the British Isles and a depletion of British stockpiles, averted the oft-predicted oil crisis there in the first eight months of 1942. However, convoying in the Americas and the rerouting of tankers inbound to the British Isles via Freetown, together with intensified British military operations in North Africa, the Middle East, and the Indian Ocean area, strained British oil resources to the absolute limit.

Over and above the tankers, the U-boats engaged in the campaign in the Americas sank 440 Allied cargo ships, trawlers, auxiliaries, and sailing vessels for about 1.7 million gross tons. This was another tough blow, but contrary to many accounts, it was not a crippling one either. The losses were made good quickly by new ship construction. In 1942, American, British, and Canadian shipyards produced about 7.1 million gross tons, or about a million more gross tons than were lost to U-boats (6.1 million).* In particular, American shipyards performed truly astonishing feats during this period. These can best be shown by yet another set of figures that compare worldwide Allied shipping losses to all Axis submarines with new construction in American yards in the summer of 1942 (see below).

In summary, while it is undeniably true that the sinking of 609 ships for 3.1 million gross tons in the North American campaign was a notable German naval achievement, it did not by any means dent decisively the Allied merchant-ship pool of about 30 million gross tons. As related, most of the merchant-ship losses were made good quickly by new construction and, owing to the shifts in oil delivery systems in the United States and to rationing, no crippling oil crises developed in the Americas or British Isles in 1942—only a number of frustrating, temporary spot shortages requiring emergency measures.

	Sunk†	G.R Tons	Built‡	G.R. Tons
May	125	607,247	57	416,000
June	144	700,235	67	504,000
July	96	476,065	71	524,000
August	108	544,410	68	499,000
September	98	485,413	94	691,000
Totals	571	2,813,370	357	2,634,000

---

* The 43,000 shipbuilders in the British Isles produced a total of about 1.3 million tons of new merchant ships in 1942; the Canadians about half a million.

† Admiralty figures, by Axis submarines in all waters.

‡ In American yards only. Note that new ships averaged 7,300 tons; older ships in the "sunk" column, 4,900 tons. Hence not as many new ships were required to equal or surpass the gross registered tonnage of ships sunk.

PLATE 13

PRINCIPAL NORTH ATLANTIC CARGO CONVOYS INBOUND TO THE BRITISH ISLES

JANUARY 1, 1942–AUGUST 31, 1942

Numbers of Ships Arriving and Losses to Enemy Action[1]

MONTH	HALIFAX, N.S.	SYDNEY, N.S.	FREETOWN, S.L.	TOTALS
January	175 (1)	122 (1)[2]	88 (1)	385 (3)
February	311 (3)	——	66	377 (3)
March	257 (1)	——	124	381 (1)
April	313	——	96	409
May	346	——	121 (1)	467 (1)
June	114	138	143	395
July	154	198	103	455
August	144	139 (15)	101 (7)	384 (22)
Totals:	1,814 (5)	597 (16)	842 (9)	3,253 (30)[3]

1. Source: *British Monthly Anti-Submarine Reports,* Jan. 1942 to Aug. 1942, and Rohwer, *Axis Submarine Successes.*

2. With the sailing of Slow Convoy 64, 1/9/42, Sydney closed for the winter and Slow Convoys 65 to 84 sailed from Halifax. Sydney reopened on 5/29/42 with the sailing of Slow Convoy 85.

3. In addition, three escorts were lost, the ex-American British destroyer *Belmont,* the British sloop *Culver,* and Canadian corvette *Spikenard.* U-boats hit and damaged another escort, the British auxiliary merchant cruiser *Cheshire.* U-boats sank forty-seven of the 2,285 vessels in westbound convoys (ON, ONS) during this period, including three corvettes: the Free French *Alysee* and *Mimose,* and the British *Arbutus.*

Another striking feature of this campaign was the relatively small effect it had on the vital lifeline transporting cargo from North America to the British Isles (see Plate 13). In the first eight months of 1941, 2,867 loaded ships in Halifax and Slow convoys had arrived in the United Kingdom. By comparison, in the first eight months of 1942, 2,411 loaded ships in Halifax and Slow convoys arrived in the United Kingdom. The difference—456 fewer ships in 1942—was due not so much to U-boat sinkings in American waters as to three other factors:

• The diversion of about 200 loaded cargo ships to northern Russia in convoys PQ 7 through PQ 17. Of this total, 42 ships sailed in convoys PQ 7 through PQ 11, about 160 ships in convoys PQ 12 (departing March 1) through PQ 17.

• The "opening out" of Halifax convoy sailings from every six days to every seven days, in part to compensate for the diversion of American destroyers in the MOEF to the escort of troopship convoys. This step reduced the number of Halifax convoy sailings per year by about nine, from about sixty-one per year to about fifty-two. Assuming a rock-bottom average of forty ships per Halifax convoy, that amounted to a reduction of about 360 ship arrivals per year in Halifax convoys, or about 240 ships in the first eight months of 1942.

PLATE 14

COMPARISON OF IMPORTS TO THE UNITED KINGDOM
IN 1941 AND 1942[1]

(Thousands of Tons)

	FOOD		SUPPLY		OIL, ETC.		TOTALS	
	1941	1942	1941	1942	1941	1942	1941	1942
January	1,094	984	1,319	1,022	541	1,037	2,954	3,043
February	915	956	1,237	911	842	1,139	2,994	3,006
March	1,123	1,015	1,264	927	953	724	3,340	2,666
April	1,038	1,099	1,322	1,001	877	896	3,237	2,996
May	1,331	1,162	1,437	1,052	1,186	623	3,954	2,837
June	1,557	1,047	1,219	1,044	1,208	774	3,984	2,865
July	1,544	958	1,104	1,208	1,227	988	3,875	3,154
August	1,360	674	1,352	1,245	1,416	916	4,128	2,835
Totals:	9,962	7,895	10,254	8,410	8,250	7,097	28,466	23,402

1. Source: Hancock, *Statistical Digest* (1975), p. 184. Note that the figures shown here are for eight months, not twelve. Category "Supply" includes munitions and miscellaneous.

• The rerouting of many loaded tankers en route from the Caribbean to the United Kingdom via Freetown, thence homeward in slow Sierra Leone convoys.

These three measures plus losses to U-boats resulted in yet another sharp drop in total imports to the United Kingdom in the first eight months of 1942: from 28,466, 000 tons in 1941 to 23,402,000 in 1942 (see Plate 14). This was a decline in basic imports of about 5 million tons, and it led to very real hardships in the British Isles—food, heating fuel, and gasoline shortages, among others—and to serious second thoughts about diverting so much shipping to provide aid to the Soviet Union and about embarking on further military campaigns such as Torch; it led as well to renewed demands on Washington for a larger share of the shipping allocations.

On one hand, it would not be correct to suggest that the U-boat campaign in American waters was of small consequence. It hurt the Allies badly in several ways and caused death and terror in the ranks of the American and British merchant marines. On the other hand, it must be deemed an unrealized victory in the sense that it did not achieve the decisive strategic results that Dönitz sought. Men and matériel and new ships of all types continued to flow from the United States to the far corners of the globe in prodigious quantities.

The principal achievement of the U-boat campaign in American waters was to force the Allies to commit vast resources to extending the convoy network to the Eastern Seaboard, the Gulf of Mexico, the Caribbean Sea, and Latin America. Even though the U-boat menace in these areas diminished rather quickly and soon evaporated in the face of improved ASW, this new and complex network, called the "Interlocking Convoy System," remained in place to the end of the war. Even allowing for exaggeration in Churchill's estimate that convoying by itself reduced British imports by "one-third," doubtless convoying in North and South American waters, however efficient, substantially retarded the flow of raw materials and goods by ship to the end of hostilities.

This concludes our study of the first two phases of the German U-boat campaign—the nearly separate wars against the British Empire and the Americas, taking the story to September 1, 1942. The U-boat campaign against Allied shipping continued for thirty-two more months—in fact, to May 8, 1945, the very last day of the war in Europe. This third and final phase of the campaign will be described and assessed in Volume II of this study.

APPENDIX 1

(Note: Ships in the appendices are not italicized or listed in the index.)

OCEANGOING U-BOATS ASSIGNED TO COMBAT

THE FIRST THREE YEARS: AUGUST 1939 – AUGUST 1942

BOAT	TYPE	SKIPPER	CREW	D.O.B.	LOST/ RETIRED
IN SERVICE 9/1/39:					
U-26	I	Klaus Ewerth	1925	3/07	
		Heinz Scheringer	1927	8/07	7/1/40
U-27	VII	Johannes Franz	1926	5/07	9/20/39
U-28	VII	Günter Kuhnke	1931	9/12	11/15/40 R
U-29	VII	Otto Schuhart	1929	4/09	12/15/40 R
U-30	VII	Fritz-Julius Lemp	1931	2/13	8/15/40 R
U-33	VII	Hans-Wilhelm von Dresky	1933	1/08	2/12/40
U-34	VII	Wilhelm Rollmann	1926	8/07	8/15/40 R
U-36	VII	Wilhelm Frölich	1929	3/10	12/4/39
U-37	IX	Heinrich Schuch	1925	8/06	
		Werner Hartmann	1921	12/02	
		Victor Oehrn	1927	10/07	
		Nikolaus Clausen	1929	6/11	4/15/41 R
U-38	IX	Heinrich Liebe	1933	1/08	
		Heinrich Schuch	1925	8/06	11/21/41 R
U-39	IX	Gerhard Glattes	1927	2/09	9/14/39
U-40	IX	Werner von Schmidt	1926	4/06	
		Wolfgang Barten	1931	8/09	10/13/39
U-41	IX	Gustav-Adolf Mugler	1931	10/12	2/5/40
U-45	VIIB	Alexander Gelhaar	1927	11/08	10/14/39
U-46	VIIB	Herbert Sohler	1928	7/08	
		Engelbert Endrass	1935	3/11	8/1/41 R
U-47	VIIB	Günther Prien	1933	1/08	3/18/41
U-48	VIIB	Herbert Schultze	1930	7/09	
		Hans-Rudolf Rösing	1924	9/05	
		Heinrich Bleichrodt	1931	10/09	
		Herbert Schultze	1930	7/09	7/1/41 R
U-52	VIIB	Wolfgang Barten	1931	8/09	
		Otto Salmann	1932	7/08	5/1/41 R
U-53	VIIB	Ernst-Günther Heinicke	1927	9/08	
		Harald Grosse	1925	11/06	2/24/40

R = Retired to Training Command.
AMER = First patrol in the Americas.
ARC = First patrol in the Arctic area.

BOAT	TYPE	SKIPPER	CREW	D.O.B.	LOST/ RETIRED
SEPTEMBER 1939:					
U-31	VII	Johannes Habekost	1933	2/07	3/11/40 [1]
		Wilfried Prellberg	1933	10/13	11/2/40
U-32	VII	Paul Büchel	1925	8/07	
		Hans Jenisch	1929	10/13	10/30/40
U-35	VII	Werner Lott	1926	12/07	11/29/39
OCTOBER 1939:					
U-25	I	Viktor Schütze	1925	6/06	
		Heinz Beduhn	1925	8/07	8/1/40
U-42	IX	Rolf Dau	1926	4/06	10/13/39
NOVEMBER 1939:					
U-43	IX	Wilhelm Ambrosius	1926	6/03	
		Wolfgang Lüth	1933	10/13	
U-49	VIIB	Curt von Gossler	1932	9/05	4/15/40
DECEMBER 1939:					
None					
JANUARY 1940:					
U-44	IX	Ludwig Mathes	1928	11/08	3/13/40
U-51	VIIB	Dietrich Knorr	1931	2/12	8/20/40
U-55	VIIB	Werner Heidel	1933	6/09	1/30/40
FEBRUARY 1940:					
U-50	VIIB	Max-Hermann Bauer	1930	7/12	4/10/40
U-54	VIIB	Günter Kutschmann	1929	1/11	2/13/40
MARCH 1940:					
None					
APRIL 1940:					
U-64	IXB	Georg-Wilhelm Schulz	1932	3/06	4/13/40
U-65	IXB	Hans-Gerrit von Stock-			
		hausen	1926	8/07	
		Joachim Hoppe	1933	3/15	4/28/41
U-A		Hans Cohausz	1926	11/07	
		Hans Eckermann	1925	5/05	
U-101	VIIB	Fritz Frauenheim	1930	3/12	
		Ernst Mengersen	1933	6/12	11/15/41 R
MAY 1940:					
U-122	IXB	Hans Günther Looff	1925	2/06	7/7/40
JUNE 1940:					
U-99	VIIB	Otto Kretschmer	1930	5/12	3/17/41
U-102	VIIB	Harro von Kloth-			
		Heydenfeldt	1931	4/11	7/1/40
JULY 1940:					
None					
AUGUST 1940:					
U-100	VIIB	Joachim Schepke	1930	3/12	3/17/41
U-124	IXB	Georg-Wilhelm Schulz	1932	3/06	
		Johann Mohr	1934	6/16	

BOAT	TYPE	SKIPPER	CREW	D.O.B.	LOST/ RETIRED
SEPTEMBER 1940:					
U-103	IXB	Viktor Schütze	1925	6/06	
		Werner Winter	1930	3/12	
U-123	IXB	Karl-Heinz Moehle	1930	7/10	
		Reinhard Hardegen	1933	3/13	
OCTOBER 1940:					
U-93	VIIC	Claus Korth	1932	10/11	
		Horst Elfe	1936	4/17	1/15/42
NOVEMBER 1940:					
U-94	VIIC	Herbert Kuppisch	1933	12/09	
		Otto Ites	1936	2/18	8/28/42
U-95	VIIC	Gerd Schreiber	1931	4/12	11/28/41
U-104	IXB	Harald Jürst	1932	3/13	11/28/40
DECEMBER 1940:					
U-96	VIIC	Heinrich Lehmann-Willenbrock	1931	12/11	
		Hans-Jürgen Hellriegel	1936	6/17	
U-105	IXB	Georg Schewe	1930	11/09	
JANUARY 1941:					
U-106	IXB	Jürgen Oesten	1933	10/13	
		Hermann Rasch	1934	8/14	
U-107	IXB	Günther Hessler	1927	6/09	
		Harald Gelhaus	1935	7/15	
FEBRUARY 1941:					
U-69	VIIC	Jost Metzler	1932	2/09	
		Wilhelm Zahn	1930	7/10	
U-70	VIIC	Joachim Matz	1932	10/13	3/7/41
U-73	VIIB	Helmut Rosenbaum	1932	5/13	
U-97	VIIC	Udo Heilmann	1933	3/13	
U-108	IXB	Klaus Scholtz	1927	3/08	
U-552	VIIC	Erich Topp	1934	7/14	
MARCH 1941:					
U-74	VIIB	Eitel-Friedrich Kentrat	1928	9/06	5/2/42
U-76	VIIB	Friedrich von Hippel	1934	1/15	4/5/41
U-98	VIIC	Robert Gysae	1931	1/11	
U-110	IXB	Fritz-Julius Lemp	1931	2/13	5/9/41
U-551	VIIC	Karl Schrott	1932	3/11	3/23/41
APRIL 1941:					
U-75	VIIB	Helmuth Ringelmann	1931	4/12	12/28/41
U-201	VIIC	Adalbert Schnee	1934	12/13	
U-553	VIIC	Karl Thurmann	1928	9/09	
MAY 1941:					
U-66	IXC	Richard Zapp	1926	4/04	
U-77	VIIC	Heinrich Schonder	1935	7/10	
U-109	IXB	Hans-Georg Fischer	1926	2/08	
		Heinrich Bleichrodt	1931	10/09	
U-111	IXB	Wilhelm Kleinschmidt	1933	1/07	10/4/41
U-204	VIIC	Walter Kell	1933	12/13	10/19/41
U-556	VIIC	Herbert Wohlfarth	1933	6/15	6/27/41
U-557	VIIC	Ottokar Paulshen	1934	10/15	12/16/41

BOAT	TYPE		SKIPPER	CREW	D.O.B.	LOST/RETIRED
JUNE 1941:						
U-68	IXC		Karl-Friedrich Merten	1926	8/05	
U-71	VIIC		Walter Flachsenberg	1928	10/08	
			Hardo Rodler von Roithberg	1937	2/18	
U-79	VIIC		Wolfgang Kaufmann	1933	6/12	12/23/41
U-202	VIIC		Hans-Heinz Linder	1933	2/13	
U-203	VIIC		Rolf Mützelburg	1932	6/13	
U-371	VIIC		Heinrich Driver	1933	7/12	
U-558	VIIC		Günther Krech	1933	9/14	
U-559	VIIC		Hans Heidtmann	1934	8/14	
U-561	VIIC		Robert Bartels	1935	4/11	
U-562	VIIC		Herwig Collmann	1935	9/15	
			Horst Hamm	1935	3/16	
U-564	VIIC		Reinhard Suhren	1935	4/16	
U-651	VIIC		Peter Lohmeyer	1932	1/11	6/29/41
U-751	VIIC		Gerhard Bigalk	1933	11/08	7/17/42
JULY 1941:						
U-81	VIIC	ARC	Fritz Guggenberger	1934	3/15	
U-83	VIIB		Hans-Werner Kraus	1934	7/15	
U-125	IXC		Günther Kuhnke	1931	9/12	
U-126	IXC		Ernst Bauer	1933	2/14	
U-205	VIIC		Franz-Georg Reschke	1929	5/08	
U-331	VIIC		Hans-Dietrich von Tiesenhausen	1934	2/13	
U-372	VIIC		Heinz-Joachim Neumann	1930	4/09	8/4/42
U-401	VIIC		Gero Zimmermann	1929	6/10	8/3/41
U-431	VIIC		Wilhelm Dommes	1931	4/07	
U-451	VIIC	ARC	Eberhard Hoffmann	1933	10/12	12/21/41
U-563	VIIC		Klaus Bargsten	1935	10/11	
U-565	VIIC		Johann Jebsen	1935	4/16	
U-571	VIIC		Helmut Möhlmann	1933	6/13	
U-652	VIIC	ARC	Georg-Werner Fraatz	1935	3/17	6/2/42
AUGUST 1941:						
U-82	VIIC		Siegfried Rollmann	1934	9/14	2/6/42
U-84	VIIB		Horst Uphoff	1935	10/16	
U-85	VIIB		Eberhard Greger	1935	9/15	4/14/42
U-129	IXC		Nikolaus Clausen	1929	6/11	
U-206	VIIC		Herbert Opitz	1934	3/15	11/29/41
U-207	VIIC		Fritz Meyer	1934	2/16	9/11/41
U-432	VIIC		Heinz-Otto Schultze	1934	9/15	
U-433	VIIC		Hans Ey	19??	6/16	11/16/41
U-452	VIIC		Jürgen March	1933	3/14	8/25/41
U-501	IXC/40		Hugo Förster	1924	1/05	9/10/41
U-566	VIIC	ARC	Dietrich Borchert	1934	2/09	
U-567	VIIC		Theodor Fahr	1930	11/09	
			Engelbert Endrass	1935	3/11	12/21/41
U-568	VIIC		Joachim Preuss	1933	5/14	5/28/42
U-569	VIIC		Hans-Peter Hinsch	1934	7/14	
U-570	VIIC		Hans-Joachim Rahmlow	1928	10/09	8/27/41[2]
U-752	VIIC	ARC	Karl-Ernst Schroeter	1934	12/12	
SEPTEMBER 1941:						
U-67	IXC		Günther Müller-Stöckheim	1934	12/13	
U-132	VIIC	ARC	Ernst Vogelsang	1931	8/11	

BOAT	TYPE		SKIPPER	CREW	D.O.B.	LOST/ RETIRED
U-208	VIIC		Alfred Schlieper	1934	1/15	12/7/41
U-373	VIIC		Paul-Karl Loeser	1935	4/15	
U-374	VIIC		Unno von Fischel	1934	11/1	1/12/42
U-502	IXC/40		Jürgen von Rosenstiel	1933	11/12	7/5/42
U-572	VIIC		Heinz Hirsacker	1934	8/14	
U-573	VIIC		Heinrich Heinsohn	1933	2/10	4/29/42
U-575	VIIC		Günther Heydemann	1933	1/14	
U-576	VIIC	ARC	Hans-Dieter Heinicke	1933	5/13	7/15/42
OCTOBER 1941:						
U-133	VIIC		Hermann Hesse	1935	3/09	
			Eberhard Mohr	1935	11/15	3/14/42
U-332	VIIC		Johannes Liebe	1933	7/13	
U-402	VIIC		Siegfried von Forstner	1930	9/10	
U-577	VIIC		Herbert Schauenburg	1931	5/12	1/9/42
U-578	VIIC	ARC	August Rehwinkel	19??	10/01	8/9/42
NOVEMBER 1941:						
U-127	IXC		Bruno Hansmann	1933	12/07	12/15/41
U-131	IXC		Arend Baumann	1922	3/03	12/17/41
U-134	VIIC	ARC	Rudolf Schendel	1932	1/14	
U-375	VIIC		Jürgen Könenkamp	1932	8/13	
U-434	VIIC		Wolfgang Heyda	1932	11/13	12/18/41
U-453	VIIC		Egon-Reiner von Schlippenbach	1934	4/14	
U-454	VIIC	ARC	Burkhard Hackländer	1933	12/14	
U-574	VIIC		Dietrich Gengelbach	1934	10/14	12/19/41
U-584	VIIC	ARC	Joachim Deecke	1933	6/12	
DECEMBER 1941:						
U-86	VIIB		Walter Schug	1934	10/10	
U-87	VIIB	AMER	Joachim Berger	1934	6/13	
U-128	IXC		Ulrich Heyse	1933	9/06	
U-130	IXC		Ernst Kals	1924	8/05	
U-135	VIIC	AMER	Friedrich-Hermann Praetorius	1935	2/04	
U-156	IXC		Werner Hartenstein	1928	2/08	
U-333	VIIC	AMER	Peter Erich Cremer	1932	3/11	
U-581	VIIC		Werner Pfeifer	1933	5/12	2/2/42
U-582	VIIC		Werner Schulte	1937	11/12	
U-585	VIIC	ARC	Bernhard Lohse	1932	4/13	3/30/42
U-653	VIIC		Gerhard Feiler	1934	9/09	
U-654	VIIC		Ludwig Forster	1936	10/15	8/22/42
U-701	VIIC	AMER	Horst Degen	1933	7/13	7/2/42
U-753	VIIC		Alfred Manhardt von Mannstein	1925	3/08	
U-754	VIIC	AMER	Hans Oestermann	1933	5/13	7/31/42
JANUARY 1942:						
U-136	VIIC		Heinrich Zimmermann	1933	1/07	7/11/42
U-161	IXC		Albrecht Achilles	1934	1/14	
U-213	VIID		Amelung von Varendorff	1935	12/13	7/31/42
U-352	VIIC		Helmut Rathke	1930	12/10	5/9/42
U-404	VIIC		Otto von Bülow	1930	10/11	
U-435	VIIC	ARC	Siegfried Strelow	1931	4/11	
U-455	VIIC		Hans-Heinrich Giessler	1931	1/11	
			Hans Martin Scheibe	1936	4/18	

BOAT	TYPE		SKIPPER	CREW	D.O.B.	LOST/RETIRED
U-456	VIIC	ARC	Max-Martin Teichert	1934	1/15	
U-504	IXC/40		Fritz Poske	1923	10/04	
U-505	IXC/40		Axel-Olaf Loewe	1928	1/09	
			Peter Zschech	1936	10/18	
U-586	VIIC	ARC[3]	Dietrich von der Esch	1934	1/15	
U-587	VIIC		Ulrich Borcherdt	1934	9/09	3/27/42
U-588	VIIC		Viktor Vogel	1932	11/12	7/31/42
U-591	VIIC	ARC[4]	Hans-Jürgen Zetzsche	1934	10/15	
U-656	VIIC		Ernst Kröning	1925	1/05	3/1/42

FEBRUARY 1942:

BOAT	TYPE		SKIPPER	CREW	D.O.B.	LOST/RETIRED
U-154	IXC		Walther Kölle	1926	9/07	
U-155	IXC	AMER	Adolf-Cornelius Piening	1930	9/10	
U-158	IXC	AMER	Erich Rostin	1933	10/07	6/30/42
U-160	IXC	AMER	Georg Lassen	1935	5/15	
U-162	IXC	AMER	Jürgen Wattenberg	1921	12/00	
U-209	VIIC	ARC	Heinrich Brodda	1921	5/03	
U-377	VIIC	ARC	Otto Köhler	1931	11/09	
U-403	VIIC	ARC	Heinz-Ehlert Clausen	1932	7/09	
U-405	VIIC	ARC	Rolf-Heinrich Hopmann	1926	3/06	
U-436	VIIC	ARC	Günther Seibicke	1932	8/11	
U-503	IXC/40		Otto Gericke	1933	12/08	3/15/42
U-589	VIIC	ARC	Hans-Joachim Horrer	1933	2/08	
U-592	VIIC	ARC	Karl Borm	1933	8/11	

MARCH 1942:

BOAT	TYPE		SKIPPER	CREW	D.O.B.	LOST/RETIRED
U-252	VIIC		Kai Lerchen	1933	4/11	4/14/42
U-334	VIIC	ARC	Hilmar Siemon	1934	3/15	
U-376	VIIC	ARC	Friedrich-Karl Marks	1934	6/14	
U-378	VIIC	ARC	Alfred Hoschatt	1927	2/09	
U-459	XIV	AMER	Georg von Wilamowitz-Möllendorf	1914	11/1893	
U-506	IXC/40		Erich Würdemann	1933	1/14	
U-507	IXC/40		Harro Schacht	1926	12/07	
U-593	VIIC		Gerd Kelbling	1934	6/15	
U-594	VIIC		Dietrich Hoffmann	1932	6/12	
			Friedrich Mumm	1936	1/15	
U-655	VIIC	ARC	Adolph Dumrese	1929	11/09	3/24/42
U-657	VIIC	ARC	Heinrich Göllnitz	1935	8/09	
U-702	VIIC	ARC	Wolf-Rüdiger von Rabenau	1933	1/08	4/4/42
U-703	VIIC	ARC	Heinz Bielfeld	1934	8/16	

APRIL 1942:

BOAT	TYPE		SKIPPER	CREW	D.O.B.	LOST/RETIRED
U-116	XB	AMER	Werner von Schmidt	1926	4/06	
U-157	IXC		Wolf Henne	1924	8/05	6/13/42
U-159	IXC		Helmut Witte	1934	4/15	
U-172	IXC		Carl Emmermann	1934	3/15	
U-251	VIIC	ARC	Heinrich Timm	1933	4/10	
U-406	VIIC		Horst Dieterichs	1934	3/12	
U-437	VIIC		Werner-Karl Schulz	1928	10/10	
U-590	VIIC		Heinrich Müller-Edzards	1933	3/10	

MAY 1942:

BOAT	TYPE		SKIPPER	CREW	D.O.B.	LOST/RETIRED
U-88	VIIC	ARC	Heino Bohmann	1934	3/14	
U-89	VIIC	AMER	Dietrich Lohmann	1930	10/09	
U-153	IXC		Wilfried Reichmann	1924	9/05	7/13/42

BOAT	TYPE		SKIPPER	CREW	D.O.B.	LOST/ RETIRED
U-166	IXC		Hans-Günter Kuhlmann	1937	11/13	8/1/42
U-214	VIID		Günther Reeder	1935	11/15	
U-408	VIIC	ARC	Reinhard von Hymmen	1933	11/14	

JUNE 1942:

BOAT	TYPE		SKIPPER	CREW	D.O.B.	LOST/ RETIRED
U-90	VIIC		Hans-Jürgen Oldörp	1935	6/11	7/24/42
U-171	IXC	AMER	Günther Pfeffer	1934	10/14	
U-173	IXC	AMER	Heinz-Ehler Beucke	1922	1/04	
			Hans-Adolph Schweichel	1936	5/15	
U-215	VIID		Fritz Hoeckner	1933	12/12	7/3/42
U-255	VIIC	ARC	Reinhart Reche	1934	12/14	
U-355	VIIC	ARC	Günter La Baume	1929	4/11	
U-379	VIIC		Paul-Hugo Kettner	1933	7/12	8/8/42
U-457	VIIC	ARC	Karl Brandenburg	1924	7/06	
U-458	VIIC	AMER	Kurt Diggens	1934	10/13	
U-460	XIV		Friedrich Schäfer	19??	2/1893	
			Ebe Schnoor	19??	6/1895	
U-461	XIV		Wolf-Harro Stiebler	1932	8/07	
U-508	IXC/40	AMER	Georg Staats	1935	3/16	
U-509	IXC/40	AMER	Karl-Heinz Wolff	1928	10/09	
U-597	VIIC		Eberhard Bopst	1933	12/13	
U-704	VIIC		Horst Kessler	1934	8/14	

JULY 1942:

BOAT	TYPE		SKIPPER	CREW	D.O.B.	LOST/ RETIRED
U-163	IXC	AMER	Kurt-Eduard Engelmann	1923	4/03	
U-164	IXC	AMER	Otto Fechner	1924	11/05	
U-174	IXC		Ulrich Thilo	1922	1/03	
U-176	IXC		Reiner Dierksen	1933	3/08	
U-210	VIIC		Rudolf Lemcke	1933	5/14	8/6/42
U-217	VIID	AMER	Kurt Reichenbach-Klinke	1935	2/17	
U-254	VIIC		Hans Gilardone	1932	7/12	
U-256	VIIC		Odo Loewe	1934	9/14	
U-335	VIIC		Hans-Hermann Pelkner	1935	4/09	8/3/42
U-462	XIV		Bruno Vowe	1923	7/04	
U-463	XIV		Leo Wolfbauer	1913	7/1895	
U-510	IXC/40	AMER	Karl Neitzel	1923	1/01	
U-511	IXC/40	AMER	Friedrich Steinhoff	1935	7/09	
U-595	VIIC		Jürgen Quaet-Faslem	1934	5/13	
U-598	VIIC	AMER	Gottfried Holtorf	1935	5/12	
U-600	VIIC	AMER	Bernhard Zurmühlen	1934	3/09	
U-601	VIIC	ARC	Peter-Ottmar Grau	1934	5/14	
U-605	VIIC		Herbert-Viktor Schütze	1935	2/17	
U-607	VIIC		Ernst Mengersen	1933	6/12	
U-609	VIIC		Klaus Rudloff	1935	1/16	
U-658	VIIC	AMER	Hans Senkel	1933	1/10	
U-660	VIIC		Götz Baur	1935	8/17	

AUGUST 1942:

BOAT	TYPE		SKIPPER	CREW	D.O.B.	LOST/ RETIRED
U-91	VIIC		Heinz Walkerling	1935	5/15	
U-92	VIIC		Adolf Oelrich	1935	3/16	
U-165	IXC	AMER	Eberhard Hoffmann	1925	5/07	
U-175	IXC	AMER	Heinrich Bruns	1931	4/12	
U-179	IXD2		Ernst Sobe	1924	9/04	
U-211	VIIC		Karl Hause	1935	7/16	
U-216	VIID		Karl-Otto Schultz	1934	11/1	
U-218	VIID		Richard Becker	1934	2/11	
U-259	VIIC		Klaus Köpke	1935	1/15	

BOAT	TYPE		SKIPPER	CREW	D.O.B.	LOST/ RETIRED
U-380	VIIC		Josef Röther	1927	10/0	
U-407	VIIC		Ulrich-Ernst Brüller	1936	9/17	
U-409	VIIC		Hans-Ferdinand Massmann	1936	6/17	
U-410	VIIC		Kurt Sturm	1925	1/06	
U-411	VIIC		Gerhard Litterscheid	1935	6/14	
U-438	VIIC		Rudolf Franzius	1932	6/11	
U-464	XIV		Otto Harms	1933	4/09	8/20/42
U-512	IXC/40	AMER	Wolfgang Schultze	1930	10/10	
U-513	IXC/40	AMER	Rolf Rüggeberg	1926	3/07	
U-514	IXC/40	AMER	Hans-Jürgen Auffermann	1934	10/14	
U-515	IXC/40	AMER	Werner Henke	1934	5/08	
U-516	IXC/40	AMER	Gerhard Wiebe	1925	1/07	
U-517	IXC/40	AMER	Paul Hartwig	1935	9/15	
U-596	VIIC		Günter Jahn	1931	9/10	
U-599	VIIC		Wolfgang Breithaupt	1932	9/13	
U-604	VIIC		Horst Höltring	1933	6/13	
U-608	VIIC		Rolf Struckmeier	19??	NA	
U-617	VIIC		Albrecht Brandi	1935	6/14	
U-659	VIIC		Hans Stock	1935	8/15	
U-705	VIIC		Karl-Horst Horn	1935	12/16	
U-755	VIIC		Walter Göing	1934	8/14	
U-756	VIIC		Klaus Harney	1934	3/17	

SUMMARY TO 9/1/42

U-boats deployed:	275
U-boats lost:	94
U-boats retired:	10
Net balance:	171
Manpower lost:	4,230 (est.)[5]
(captured) :	1,365

---

1. Sunk in home waters, salvaged, sunk again 11/2/40.
2. Captured.
3. After one Atlantic patrol.
4. After one Atlantic patrol.
5. 94 boats times 45 crew members.

APPENDIX 2

U-BOAT PATROLS TO THE NORTH ATLANTIC

AUGUST 1939 – AUGUST 1942

BOAT	TYPE	SKIPPER	SAILED	RETURNED	SHIPS SUNK	TONS
AUGUST 1939:						
U-28	VII	Günter Kuhnke*	8/19	9/29	1	4,955
U-29	VII	Otto Schuhart*	8/19	9/26	4	41,905 [1]
U-33	VII	Hans-Wilhelm von Dresky*	8/19	9/27	3	5,814
U-34	VII	Wilhelm Rollmann*	8/19	9/26	3	13,891 [2]
U-37	IX	Heinrich Schuch*	8/19	9/15		None
U-38	IX	Heinrich Liebe*	8/19	9/17	2	16,698
U-39	IX	Gerhard Glattes*	8/19	Lost 9/14		None
U-40	IX	Werner von Schmidt*	8/19	9/17		None
U-41	IX	Gustav-Adolf Mugler*	8/19	9/17	2	2,172 [3]
U-45	VIIB	Alexander Gelhaar*	8/19	9/15		None
U-46	VIIB	Herbert Sohler*	8/19	9/15		None
U-47	VIIB	Günther Prien*	8/19	9/15	3	8,270
U-48	VIIB	Herbert Schultze*	8/19	9/17	3	14,777
U-52	VIIB	Wolfgang Barten*	8/19	9/17		None
U-30	VII	Fritz-Julius Lemp*	8/22	9/27	3	23,206 [4]
U-27	VII	Johannes Franz*	8/23	Lost 9/20	2	624
U-26	I	Klaus Ewerth*	8/29	9/26	3	17,414+M
U-53	VIIB	Ernst-Gunther Heinicke*	8/29	9/30	2	14,018
U-36	VII	Wilhelm Fröhlich*	8/31	9/29	2	2,813 [5]
SEPTEMBER 1939:						
U-32	VII	Paul Büchel*	9/5	9/30	2	5,738+M [6]
U-31	VII	Johannes Habekost*	9/8	10/2	2	8,706
U-35	VII	Werner Lott*	9/8	10/12	4	7,850+
OCTOBER 1939:						
U-42	IX	Rolf Dau*	10/2	Lost 10/13		None
U-48	VIIB	Herbert Shultze	10/4	10/25	5	37,153
U-37	IX	Werner Hartmann* (C.O.)	10/5	11/8	8	35,306
U-45	VIIB	Alexander Gelhaar	10/5	Lost 10/14	2	19,313
U-46	VIIB	Herbert Sohler	10/7	11/16	1	7,028
U-47	VIIB	Günther Prien	10/7	10/17	1	29,150 [7]
U-40	IX	Wolfgang Barten* (C.O.)	10/10	Lost 10/13		None

   * = First patrol of boat or skipper (C.O.).
   + = Damaged ships or shared credit.
   M = Mine mission.
Abort = Forced by battle damage, mechanical failure, etc., to return.

BOAT	TYPE	SKIPPER	SAILED	RETURNED	SHIPS SUNK	TONS
U-34	VII	Wilhelm Rollmann	10/17	11/12	5	19,722[8]
U-25	I	Victor Schütze*	10/18	11/4	1	5,874 Abort
U-31	VII	Johannes Habekost	10/21	10/31	2	160 M[9]
U-53	VIIB	Ernst-Gunther Heinicke	10/21	11/29		None
U-26	I	Klaus Ewerth	10/22	12/5		None/M
U-33	VII	Hans-Wilhelm von Dresky	10/29	11/28	8	17,023+M[10]

NOVEMBER 1939:

BOAT	TYPE	SKIPPER	SAILED	RETURNED	SHIPS SUNK	TONS
U-43	IX	Wilhelm Ambrosius*	11/6	12/14	4	16,030
U-41	IX	Gustav-Adolf Mugler	11/7	12/7	4	12,914
U-28	VII	Günter Kuhnke	11/8	12/18	3	19,854 M[11]
U-49	VIIB	Curt von Gossler*	11/9	11/29	Abort	None
U-29	VII	Otto Schuhart	11/14	12/16		None/M
U-38	IX	Heinrich Liebe	11/14	12/16	3	13,269
U-47	VIIB	Günther Prien	11/16	12/17	3	23,168
U-31	VII	Johannes Habekost	11/18	12/9	6	12,338
U-35	VII	Werner Lott	11/18	Lost 11/29		None
U-48	VIIB	Herbert Schultze	11/21	12/21	4	25,618

DECEMBER 1939:

BOAT	TYPE	SKIPPER	SAILED	RETURNED	SHIPS SUNK	TONS
U-36	VII	Wilhelm Fröhlich	12/3	Lost 12/4[12]		None
U-30	VII	Fritz-Julius Lemp	12/9	12/14	Abort	None/M
U-46	VIIB	Herbert Sohler	12/19	1/10	1	924
U-30	VII	Fritz-Julius Lemp	12/23	1/17	5	22,797+M[13]
U-32	VII	Paul Büchel	12/29	1/22	1	959 M

JANUARY 1940:

BOAT	TYPE	SKIPPER	SAILED	RETURNED	SHIPS SUNK	TONS
U-44	IX	Ludwig Mathes*	1/6	2/9	8	29,688
U-34	VII	Wilhelm Rollmann	1/11	2/6	2	13,432 M[14]
U-25	I	Victor Schütze	1/13	2/19	6	27,335 Abort
U-31	VII	Johannes Habekost	1/17	2/3		None/M
U-55	VIIB	Werner Heidel*	1/17	Lost 1/30	4	12,937
U-51	VIIB	Dietrich Knorr*	1/18	2/7	2	3,143 Abort
U-41	IX	Gustav-Adolf Mugler	1/27	Lost 2/5	1	9,874
U-48	VIIB	Herbert Schultze	1/31	2/24	4	31,526 M

FEBRUARY 1940:

BOAT	TYPE	SKIPPER	SAILED	RETURNED	SHIPS SUNK	TONS
U-26	I	Heinz Scheringer* (C.O.)	2/1	3/1	3	10,580
U-37	IX	Werner Hartmann	2/1	2/27	8	24,539[15]
U-33	VII	Hans-Wilhelm von Dresky	2/7	Lost 2/12		None/M
U-50	VIIB	Max-Hermann Bauer*	2/8	3/2	4	16,089 Abort
U-53	VIIB	Harald Grosse* (C.O.)	2/8	Lost 2/24	5	13,298+
U-29	VII	Otto Schuhart	2/11	3/12	3	11,399 M[16]
U-54	VIIB	Günter Kutschmann*	2/12	Lost 2/13		None
U-28	VII	Günter Kuhnke	2/18	3/25	2	11,215 M
U-32	VII	Hans Jenisch* (C.O.)	2/26	3/25	2	7,886 M[17]
U-38	IX	Heinrich Liebe	2/29	4/6	5	14,309

MARCH 1940: (Invasion of Norway)

BOAT	TYPE	SKIPPER	SAILED	RETURNED	SHIPS SUNK	TONS
U-52	VIIB	Otto Salmann* (C.O.)	3/2	4/4		None
U-31	VII	Johannes Habekost	3/11	Lost 3/11[18]		None
U-30	VII	Fritz-Julius Lemp	3/11	3/29		None
U-34	VII	Wilhelm Rollmann	3/11	3/29		None
U-46	VIIB	Herbert Sohler	3/11	4/23		None
U-47	VIIB	Günther Prien	3/11	3/29	1	1,146

BOAT	TYPE	SKIPPER	SAILED	RETURNED	SHIPS SUNK	TONS
U-49	VIIB	Curt von Gossler	3/11	3/29		None
U-51	VIIB	Dietrich Knorr	3/11	4/26		None
U-44	IX	Ludwig Mathes	3/12	Lost 3/13		None
U-43	IX	Wilhelm Ambrosius	3/14	4/6		None

APRIL 1940: (Norway Operations)

BOAT	TYPE	SKIPPER	SAILED	RETURNED	SHIPS SUNK	TONS
U-37	IX	Werner Hartmann	4/1	4/18 [19]	3	18,715
U-25	I	Victor Schütze	4/3	5/6		None
U-30	VII	Fritz-Julius Lemp	4/3	5/4		None
U-34	VII	Wilhelm Rollmann	4/3	4/30	1	495
U-47	VIIB	Günther Prien	4/3	4/18		None
U-49	VIIB	Curt von Gossler	4/3	Lost 4/15		None
U-48	VIIB	Herbert Schultze	4/4	4/20		None
U-50	VIIB	Max-Hermann Bauer	4/5	Lost 4/10		None
U-64	IXB	Wilhelm Georg Schulz*	4/6	Lost 4/13 [20]		None
U-52	VIIB	Otto Salmann	4/7	4/30		None
U-38	IX	Heinrich Liebe	4/7	4/27		None
U-65	IXB	Hans-Gerrit von Stockhausen*	4/8	5/13		None
U-43	IX	Wilhelm Ambrosius	4/12	4/23		None/Supply
U-26	I	Heinz Scheringer	4/15	4/25	1	5,159 [21]
U-29	VII	Otto Schuhart	4/18	5/4		None/Supply
U-47	VIIB	Günther Prien	4/18	4/26		None
U-32	VII	Hans Jenisch	4/27	5/12		None/Supply
U-A	Turk	Hans Cohausz*	4/27	5/9		None/Supply
U-101	VIIB	Fritz Frauenheim*	4/29	5/9		None/Supply

MAY 1940: ("Happy Time")

BOAT	TYPE	SKIPPER	SAILED	RETURNED	SHIPS SUNK	TONS
U-43	IX	Wilhelm Ambrosius	5/13	7/22	4	29,456
U-37	IX	Viktor Oehrn* (C.O.)	5/15	6/9	10	41,207+
U-122	IXB	Hans-Günther Looff*	5/17	5/24		None/Supply
U-28	VII	Günter Kuhnke	5/20	6/1	Abort	None
U-101	VIIB	Fritz Frauenheim	5/21	6/25	7	42,022
U-26	I	Heinz Scheringer	5/23	6/5		None/Supply
U-48	VIIB	Hans-Rudolf Rösing* (C.O.)	5/26	5/30	Abort	None
U-29	VII	Otto Schuhart	5/27	7/9	4	25,061 [22]

JUNE 1940:

BOAT	TYPE	SKIPPER	SAILED	RETURNED	SHIPS SUNK	TONS
U-46	VIIB	Engelbert Endrass* (C.O.)	6/1	6/30	5	35,347+ [23]
U-32	VII	Hans Jenisch	6/3	6/30	5	16,098
U-48	VIIB	Hans-Rudolf Rösing	6/3	6/29	7	31,533
U-47	VIIB	Günther Prien	6/4	7/6	8	51,483
U-38	IX	Heinrich Liebe	6/6	7/2	6	30,353 [24]
U-A	Turk	Hans Cohausz	6/7	8/28	7	40,706 [25]
U-51	VIIB	Dietrich Knorr	6/7	7/5	3	22,168
U-25	I	Heinz Beduhn* (C.O.)	6/8	6/29	1	17,046 [26]
U-28	VII	Günter Kuhnke	6/8	7/6	3	10,303
U-30	VII	Fritz-Julius Lemp	6/8	7/7	6	26,329 [27]
U-52	VIIB	Otto Salmann	6/8	7/21	4	13,542
U-65	IXB	Hans-Gerrit von Stockhausen	6/14	7/7	2	29,301
U-122	IXB	Hans-Günther Loof	6/14	Lost 7/7	1	5,911
U-99	VIIB	Otto Kretschmer*	6/19	6/24	Abort	None
U-26	I	Heinz Scheringer	6/20	Lost 7/1	1	6,701+
U-34	VII	Wilhelm Rollmann	6/22	7/18	8	22,434 [28]

BOAT	TYPE	SKIPPER	SAILED	RETURNED	SHIPS SUNK	TONS
U-102	VIIB	Harro von Klot-Heydenfeldt*	6/22	Lost 6/30	1	5,219
U-99	VIIB	Otto Kretschmer	6/27	7/21	6	20,755[29]

JULY 1940:

BOAT	TYPE	SKIPPER	SAILED	RETURNED	SHIPS SUNK	TONS
U-30	VII	Fritz-Julius Lemp	7/13	7/24	1	712 Abort
U-34	VII	Wilhelm Rollmann	7/23	8/3	5	29,990[30]
U-99	VIIB	Otto Kretschmer	7/25	8/5	4	32,345+
U-52	VIIB	Otto Salmann	7/27	8/12	3	17,102

AUGUST 1940:

BOAT	TYPE	SKIPPER	SAILED	RETURNED	SHIPS SUNK	TONS
U-25	I	Heinz Beduhn	8/1	Lost 8/3		None
U-37	IX	Viktor Oehrn	8/1	8/12	1	9,130 Abort
U-38	IX	Heinrich Liebe	8/1	9/3	2	12,493
U-46	VIIB	Engelbert Endrass	8/1	9/8	5	33,425+[31]
U-30	VII	Fritz-Julius Lemp	8/6	8/27	2	12,407
U-48	VIIB	Hans-Rudolf Rösing	8/7	8/29	5	29,169
U-65	IXB	Hans-Gerrit von Stockhausen	8/8	8/22	Abort	None[32]
U-51	VIIB	Dietrich Knorr	8/9	Lost 8/20	1	5,709
U-100	VIIB	Joachim Schepke	8/9	9/1	6	25,812+
U-101	VIIB	Fritz Frauenheim	8/9	9/4	3	12,311 Abort
U-28	VII	Günter Kuhnke	8/11	9/17	4	9,945+
U-32	VII	Hans Jenisch	8/15	9/8	3	13,093+[33]
U-37	IX	Viktor Oehrn	8/16	8/30	7	24,409[34]
U-124	IXB	Wilhelm Georg Schulz*	8/19	9/14	2	10,563
U-47	VIIB	Günther Prien	8/27	9/26	6.5	37,585[35]
U-65	IXB	Hans-Gerritt von Stockhausen	8/29	9/26	2	10,192

SEPTEMBER 1940:

BOAT	TYPE	SKIPPER	SAILED	RETURNED	SHIPS SUNK	TONS
U-29	VII	Otto Schuhart	9/2	10/1	1	6,223 Abort
U-99	VIIB	Otto Kretschmer	9/3	9/25	6.5	28,949[36]
U-48	VIIB	Heinrich Bleichrodt* (C.O.)	9/7	9/29	8	36,198+[37]
U-43	IX	Wilhem Ambrosius	9/9	10/18	1	5,802
U-100	VIIB	Joachim Schepke	9/11	9/29	7	50,340
U-31	VII	Wilfried Prellberg* (C.O.)	9/15	10/8	2	4,400 Abort
U-46	VIIB	Engelbert Endrass	9/15	9/29	2	3,920 Abort
U-32	VII	Hans Jenisch	9/18	10/6	7.5	39,213[38]
U-123	IXB	Karl-Heinz Moehle*	9/19	10/21	3.5	15,959
U-103	IXB	Viktor Schütze*	9/21	10/19	5.5	22,127[39]
U-37	IX	Viktor Oehrn	9/24	10/21	5.5	26,669
U-38	IX	Heinrich Liebe	9/25	10/24	4	30,345+

OCTOBER 1940:

BOAT	TYPE	SKIPPER	SAILED	RETURNED	SHIPS SUNK	TONS
U-93	VIIC	Claus Korth*	10/5	10/25	3	13,214[40]
U-48	VIIB	Heinrich Bleichrodt	10/5	10/25	6.5	40,094+[41]
U-101	VIIB	Fritz Frauenheim	10/5	10/24	4	14,616+
U-124	IXB	Wilhelm Georg Schulz	10/5	11/13	5	20,061
U-28	VII	Günter Kuhnke	10/11	11/15	.5	2,694[42]
U-100	VIIB	Joachim Schepke	10/11	10/23	3.5	20,959+[43]
U-46	VIIB	Engelbert Endrass	10/13	10/26	5	22,966
U-99	VIIB	Otto Kretschmer	10/13	10/21	6.5	28,949[44]
U-47	VIIB	Günther Prien	10/14	10/23	4.5	25,055+
U-31	VII	Wilfried Prellberg	10/21	Lost 11/2	.5	2,694
U-32	VII	Hans Jenisch	10/23	Lost 10/30	1	42,348[45]
U-99	VIIB	Otto Kretschmer	10/30	11/9	4	42,407

BOAT	TYPE	SKIPPER	SAILED	RETURNED	SHIPS SUNK	TONS
NOVEMBER 1940:						
U-29	VII	Otto Schuhart	11/3	11/30		None
U-47	VIIB	Günther Prien	11/3	12/6	1.3	10,347[46]
U-93	VIIC	Claus Korth	11/7	12/15		None
U-100	VIIB	Joachim Schepke	11/7	11/27	7	24,601
U-103	IXB	Viktor Schütze	11/9	12/12	7	38,465
U-104	IXB	Harald Jürst*	11/12	Lost 11/21	1	8,240+
U-123	IXB	Karl-Heinz Moehle	11/14	11/28	6	27,895
U-52	VIIB	Otto Salmann	11/17	12/28	2	7,034
U-43	IX	Wolfgang Lüth* (C.O.)	11/17	12/16	3	21,262+
U-94	VIIC	Herbert Kuppisch*	11/20	12/31	2	12,031
U-95	VIIC	Gerd Schreiber*	11/20	12/6	1.3	7,444
U-101	VIIB	Ernst Mengersen* (C.O.)	11/24	12/7	5.5	28,505+
U-99	VIIB	Otto Kretschmer	11/27	12/12	3.3	28,707
DECEMBER 1940:						
U-100	VIIB	Joachim Schepke	12/3	1/1	3	17,166
U-96	VIIC	Heinrich Lehmann-				
		Willenbrock*	12/4	12/29	5	37,037+
U-95	VIIC	Gerd Schreiber	12/16	1/14	1	12,823
U-124	IXB	Wilhelm Georg Schulz	12/16	1/22	1	5,965
U-38	IX	Heinrich Liebe	12/18	1/22	1.5	6,250[47]
U-105	IXB	George Schewe*	12/24	1/31	2	11,359
JANUARY 1941:						
U-106	IXB	Jürgen Oesten*	1/4	2/6	2	13,640
U-94	VIIC	Herbert Kuppisch	1/9	2/19	3	12,653
U-96	VIIC	Heinrich Lehmann-				
		Willenbrock	1/9	1/22	2	29,053[48]
U-93	VIIC	Claus Korth	1/11	2/13	4	23,943
U-123	IXB	Karl-Heinz Moehle	1/16	2/28	4	22,186
U-103	IXB	Viktor Schütze	1/21	2/25	3.5	28,206[49]
U-52	VIIB	Otto Salmann	1/22	2/25	2	4,662
U-101	VIIB	Ernst Mengersen	1/23	2/19	2	10,699
U-48	VIIB	Herbert				
		Schultze* (again C.O.)	1/25	2/27	2	8,640
U-107	IXB	Günther Hessler*	1/25	3/3	4	32,163
FEBRUARY 1941:						
U-96	VIIC	Heinrich Lehmann-				
		Willenbrock	2/1	2/28	6.5	44,232
U-37	IX	Nikolaus Clausen* (C.O.)	2/2	2/18	3	4,781 Abort
U-73	VIIB	Helmut Rosenbaum*	2/8	3/3	1	4,260
U-69	VIIC	Jost Metzler*	2/13	3/3	3	18,576
U-95	VIIC	Gerd Schreiber	2/16	3/19	5	24,900
U-108	IXB	Klaus Scholtz*	2/16	3/12	2	8,078
U-46	VIIB	Engelbert Endrass	2/17	3/4	Abort	None
U-97	VIIC	Udo Heilmann*	2/19	3/7	3	16,764+
U-47	VIIB	Gunther Prien	2/20	Lost 3/?	4.5	26,629+[50]
U-552	VIIC	Erich Topp*	2/22	3/16	2	12,749
U-99	VIIB	Otto Kretschmer	2/22	Lost 3/17	6.5	51,392+
U-70	VIIC	Joachim Matz*	2/23	Lost 3/7	1	820+
U-37	IX	Nikolaus Clausen	2/27	??	1	3,050+Retired
U-46	VIIB	Engelbert Endrass	2/27	4/10	4	21,742
MARCH 1941:						
U-74	VIIB	Eitel-Friedrich Kentrat*	3/5	4/11	1	5,724+
U-98	VIIC	Robert Gysae*	3/13	4/14	4	15,588

BOAT	TYPE	SKIPPER	SAILED	RETURNED	SHIPS SUNK	TONS
U-100	VIIB	Joachim Schepke	3/13	Lost 3/17		None
U-110	IXB	Fritz-Julius Lemp*	3/13	3/29	Abort	None+
U-46	VIIB	Engelbert Endrass	3/15	4/10	4	21,778
U-48	VIIB	Herbert Schultze	3/17	4/8	5	27,256
U-69	VIIC	Jost Metzler	3/18	4/11	1	3,759
U-551	VIIC	Karl Schrott*	3/18	Lost 3/23		None
U-97	VIIC	Udo Heilmann	3/20	4/10	3	20,510
U-73	VIIB	Helmut Rosenbaum	3/25	4/24	4	25,148
U-52	VIIB	Otto Salmann	3/27	3/30	Abort	None
U-101	VIIB	Ernst Mengersen	3/27	5/5	Abort[51]	None
U-76	VIIB	Friedrich von Hippel*	3/29	Lost 4/5	2	7,290
U-94	VIIC	Herbert Kuppisch	3/29	4/18	2	10,994

APRIL 1941:

BOAT	TYPE	SKIPPER	SAILED	RETURNED	SHIPS SUNK	TONS
U-52	VIIB	Otto Salmann	4/3	5/3	2	13,993
U-108	IXB	Klaus Scholtz	4/3	5/4	1	16,144[52]
U-552	VIIC	Erich Topp	4/7	5/6	3	15,970+
U-123	IXB	Karl-Heinz Moehle	4/10	5/11	1	6,991
U-75	VIIB	Helmuth Ringelmann*	4/10	5/13	1	10,146
U-65	IXB	Joachim Hoppe* (C.O.)	4/12	Lost 4/28	1	8,897
U-95	VIIC	Gerd Schrieber	4/12	5/13	1	4,873
U-96	VIIC	Heinrich Lehmann-Willenbrock	4/12	5/22	4	30,227
U-553	VIIC	Karl Thurmann*	4/14	5/5	Abort	None
U-110	IXB	Fritz-Julius Lemp	4/15	Lost 5/9	3	10,056
U-201	VIIC	Adalbert Schnee*	4/29	5/18	1.5	9,897+[53]

MAY 1941:

BOAT	TYPE	SKIPPER	SAILED	RETURNED	SHIPS SUNK	TONS
U-94	VIIC	Herbert Kuppisch	5/1	6/6	5	31,940
U-97	VIIC	Udo Heilmann	5/2	5/30	3	17,852
U-556	VIIC	Herbert Wohlfarth*	5/2	5/30	4	23,391+
U-93	VIIC	Claus Korth	5/3	6/9	1	6,325
U-98	VIIC	Robert Gysae	5/5	5/29	2	15,905+
U-111	IXB	Wilhelm Kleinschmidt*	5/5	7/7	3	15,978
U-74	VIIB	Eitel-Friedrich Kentrat	5/8	5/30	Abort	None
U-43	IX	Wolfgang Lüth	5/11	7/1	3	8,017
U-109	IXB	Hans-Georg Fischer*	5/12	5/29	1	7,402 Abort
U-557	VIIC	Ottokar Paulshen*	5/13	7/11	1	7,296
U-66	IXC	Richard Zapp	5/13	6/12	Abort	None
U-46	VIIB	Engelbert Endrass	5/16	6/13	3	17,100
U-73	VIIB	Helmut Rosenbaum	5/20	6/25		None
U-48	VIIB	Herbert Schultze	5/21	6/22	5	38,462 Retired
U-204	VIIC	Walter Kell*	5/24	6/28	2	7,902
U-101	VIIB	Ernst Mengersen	5/28	7/4	2	13,157
U-108	IXB	Klaus Scholtz	5/28	7/7	7	26,895
U-75	VIIB	Helmuth Ringelmann	5/29	7/3	1	4,801
U-77	VIIC	Heinrich Schonder*	5/29	7/7	3	11,755

JUNE 1941:

BOAT	TYPE	SKIPPER	SAILED	RETURNED	SHIPS SUNK	TONS
U-558	VIIC	Günther Krech*	6/1	7/9		None
U-203	VIIC	Rolf Mützelburg*	6/2	6/29	3	11,325
U-552	VIIC	Erich Topp	6/3	7/2	3	24,401
U-751	VIIC	Gerhard Bigalk*	6/3	7/5	1	5,370
U-371	VIIC	Heinrich Driver*	6/5	7/1	1	4,765+
U-559	VIIC	Hans Heidtmann*	6/5	7/5	Abort	None
U-651	VIIC	Peter Lohmeyer*	6/7	Lost 6/29	2	11,639
U-553	VIIC	Karl Thurmann	6/7	7/19	2	7,945

BOAT	TYPE	SKIPPER	SAILED	RETURNED	SHIPS SUNK	TONS
U-79	VIIC	Wolfgang Kaufmann*	6/8	7/5	1	1,524+
U-201	VIIC	Adalbert Schnee	6/8	7/19		None
U-71	VIIC	Walter Flachsenberg*	6/14	7/2	Abort	None
U-202	VIIC	Hans-Heinz Linder*	6/17	7/23		None
U-564	VIIC	Reinhard Suhren*	6/17	7/27	3	18,678+
U-562	VIIC	Herwig Collmann*	6/19	7/30	Abort	None
U-556	VIIC	Herbert Wohlfarth	6/19	Lost 6/27		None
U-96	VIIC	Heinrich Lehmann-Willenbrock	6/19	7/9	1	5,954 Abort
U-98	VIIC	Robert Gysae	6/23	7/23	2	10,842
U-561	VIIC	Robert Bartels	6/25	8/1	1	1,884+ Abort
U-95	VIIC	Gerd Schreiber	6/30	7/31		None+
U-68	IXC	Karl-Friedrich Merten	6/30	8/1		None

JULY 1941:

BOAT	TYPE	SKIPPER	SAILED	RETURNED	SHIPS SUNK	TONS
U-97	VIIC	Udo Heilmann	7/2	8/8		None
U-331	VIIC	Hans-Dietrich von Tiesenhausen*	7/2	8/19	Abort	None
U-74	VIIB	Eitel-Friedrich Kentrat	7/4	8/12	1	5,415
U-126	IXC	Ernst Bauer*	7/5	8/26	4	5,400+
U-565	VIIC	Johann Jebsen*	7/8	8/6	Abort	None
U-372	VIIC	Heinz-Joachim Neumann*	7/9	8/13	2	8,341
U-401	VIIC	Gero Zimmermann*	7/9	Lost 8/3		None
U-431	VIIC	Wilhelm Dommes*	7/10	8/11	Abort	None
U-203	VIIC	Rolf Mützelburg	7/10	7/31	3	4,305+ Abort
U-125	IXC	Günter Kuhnke*	7/15	7/28	Abort	None
U-79	VIIC	Wolfgang Kaufmann	7/21	8/16	1	2,475
U-204	VIIC	Walter Kell	7/21	8/21	2	5,982 [54]
U-371	VIIC	Heinrich Driver	7/23	8/18	2	13,984
U-205	VIIC	Franz-Georg Reschke*	7/24	8/26	None/Escort	
U-559	VIIC	Hans Heidtmann	7/26	8/21	1	3,255+
U-46	VIIB	Engelbert Endrass	7/26	9/14	None/Retired	
U-83	VIIB	Hans-Werner Kraus*	7/26	9/8		None
U-73	VIIB	Helmut Rosenbaum	7/29	8/1	Abort	None
U-75	VIIB	Helmuth Ringelmann	7/29	8/26	1	4,512 Escort
U-563	VIIC	Klaus Bargsten*	7/31	9/10		None

AUGUST 1941:

BOAT	TYPE	SKIPPER	SAILED	RETURNED	SHIPS SUNK	TONS
U-71	VIIC	Walter Flachsenberg	8/2	9/7		None
U-77	VIIC	Heinrich Schonder	8/2	9/10		None
U-96	VIIC	Heinrich Lehmann-Willenbrock	8/2	9/12	1	5,954
U-751	VIIC	Gerhard Bigalk	8/2	9/8		None
U-43	IX	Wolfgang Lüth	8/2	9/23		None
U-105	IXB	Georg Schewe	8/3	9/20	1	1,549 Abort
U-568	VIIC	Joachim Preuss*	8/3	9/10	1	925 [55]
U-129	IXC	Nikolaus Clausen*	8/3	8/29	Abort [56]	None
U-206	VIIC	Herbert Opitz*	8/5	9/10	Abort [57]	None
U-567	VIIC	Theodor Fahr*	8/5	9/12	1	3,485
U-38	IX	Heinrich Schuch* (C.O.)	8/6	9/13	1	1,700
U-501	IXC/40	Hugo Förster*	8/7	Lost 9/10	1	2,000
U-553	VIIC	Karl Thurmann	8/7	9/16	3	12,532
U-73	VIIB	Helmut Rosenbaum	8/7	9/17	Abort	None
U-101	VIIB	Ernst Mengersen	8/7	9/2	Abort	None
U-84	VIIB	Horst Uphoff*	8/8	9/22		None
U-569	VIIC	Hans-Peter Hinsch*	8/11	9/21	Abort	None

BOAT	TYPE	SKIPPER	SAILED	RETURNED	SHIPS SUNK	TONS
U-82	VIIC	Siegfried Rollmann*	8/11	9/18	4	24,362+
U-202	VIIC	Hans-Heinz Linder	8/11	9/17	2	2,210
U-106	IXB	Jürgen Oesten	8/12	9/11	None/Escort	
U-452	VIIC	Jürgen March*	8/13	Lost 8/25		None
U-201	VIIC	Adalbert Schnee	8/14	8/27	4	7,825
U-564	VIIC	Reinhard Suhren	8/16	8/27	5	8,458+[58]
U-552	VIIC	Erich Topp	8/17	8/26	1	2,129 Abort
U-557	VIIC	Ottokar Paulshen	8/18	9/19	4	20,407
U-69	VIIC	Jost Metzler	8/20	8/27	Abort[59]	None
U-561	VIIC	Robert Bartels	8/20	9/20	Abort	None
U-652	VIIC	Georg-Werner Fraatz	8/21	9/18	1	3,410+
U-207	VIIC	Fritz Meyer*	8/24	Lost 9/11	3	10,970
U-570	VIIC	Hans-Joachim Rahmlow*	8/24	Captured 8/27		None
U-95	VIIC	Gerd Schreiber	8/26	9/20	Abort	None
U-432	VIIC	Heinz-Otto Schultze*	8/26	9/19	4	15,138
U-433	VIIC	Hans Ey*	8/26	9/25		None
U-558	VIIC	Günther Krech	8/26	9/16	1	10,298 Abort[60]
U-562	VIIC	Herwig Collmann	8/26	9/2	Abort	None
U-81	VIIC	Fritz Guggenberger	8/27	9/19	1	3,232+
U-85	VIIB	Eberhard Greger*	8/27	9/18	1	4,748 Abort
U-98	VIIC	Robert Gysae	8/31	9/26	1	4,392

SEPTEMBER 1941:

BOAT	TYPE	SKIPPER	SAILED	RETURNED	SHIPS SUNK	TONS
U-69	VIIC	Wilhelm Zahn* (C.O.)	9/1	10/1		None
U-565	VIIC	Johann Jebsen	9/1	10/7		None
U-572	VIIC	Heinz Hirsacker*	9/1	10/2		None
U-94	VIIC	Otto Ites* (C.O.)	9/2	10/9	4	29,319[61]
U-373	VIIC	Paul-Karl Loeser*	9/2	10/2		None
U-552	VIIC	Erich Topp	9/2	10/5	3	19,187
U-575	VIIC	Günther Heydemann*	9/2	10/9	1	4,652
U-79	VIIC	Wolfgang Kaufmann	9/4	9/18	Abort	None
U-74	VIIB	Eitel-Friedrich Kentrat	9/8	9/26	2	7,891[62]
U-372	VIIC	Heinz-Joachim Neumann	9/10	10/13	1	3,410
U-562	VIIC	Horst Hamm* (C.O.)	9/11	10/15	2	9,053
U-431	VIIC	Wilhelm Dommes	9/13	10/12	1	3,198
U-124	IXB	Johann Mohr* (C.O.)	9/16	10/1	6	11,659
U-371	VIIC	Heinrich Driver	9/16	Into Mediterranean 9/27		
U-564	VIIC	Reinhard Suhren	9/16	11/1		None
U-201	VIIC	Adalbert Schnee	9/18	9/30	6	15,193+
U-97	VIIC	Udo Heilmann	9/20	Into Mediterranean 9/27		
U-203	VIIC	Rolf Mützelburg	9/20	9/30	3	7,658
U-204	VIIC	Walter Kell	9/20	10/9	2	9,902 Escort
U-559	VIIC	Hans Heidtmann	9/20	Into Mediterranean 9/26		
U-205	VIIC	Franz-Georg Reschke	9/23	10/2	Abort	None
U-331	VIIC	Hans Dietrich von Tiesenhausen	9/24	Into Mediterranean 9/30		
U-573	VIIC	Heinrich Heinsohn*	9/26	11/15		None
U-75	VIIB	Helmuth Ringelmann	9/27	Into Mediterranean 10/3		
U-79	VIIC	Wolfgang Kaufmann	9/27	Into Mediterranean 10/5		
U-83	VIIB	Hans-Werner Kraus	9/27	11/1	1	2,044+
U-129	IXC	Nikolaus Clausen	9/27	10/8	None/Rescue	
U-71	VIIC	Walter Flachsenberg	9/29	10/31		None
U-208	VIIC	Alfred Schlieper*	9/29	11/12		None
U-374	VIIC	Unno von Fischel*	9/29	11/11	1	5,120

BOAT	TYPE	SKIPPER	SAILED	RETURNED	SHIPS SUNK	TONS
U-502	IXC/40	Jürgen von Rosenstiel*	9/29	11/9	Abort	None+
U-206	VIIC	Herbert Opitz	9/30	10/28	2	4,006 [63]

OCTOBER 1941:

BOAT	TYPE	SKIPPER	SAILED	RETURNED	SHIPS SUNK	TONS
U-563	VIIC	Klaus Bargsten	10/4	11/1	2	3,312 [64]
U-109	IXB	Heinrich Bleichrodt* (C.O.)	10/5	11/18	None/Escort	
U-553	VIIC	Karl Thurmann	10/6	10/22	3	12,532
U-568	VIIC	Joachim Preuss	10/9	11/7	1	6,023+ [65]
U-73	VIIB	Helmut Rosenbaum	10/11	11/11		None
U-77	VIIC	Heinrich Schonder	10/11	11/13	Abort	None
U-101	VIIB	Ernst Mengersen	10/11	11/7	1	1,190 [66] Retired
U-432	VIIC	Heinz-Otto Schultze	10/11	11/2	4	19,818+
U-558	VIIC	Günther Krech	10/11	10/25	4	21,318 [67]
U-751	VIIC	Gerhard Bigalk	10/11	11/8		None
U-569	VIIC	Hans-Peter Hinsch	10/12	11/12	1	3,349
U-38	IX	Heinrich Schuch	10/14	10/31	Abort	None/Retired
U-82	VIIC	Siegfried Rollmann	10/14	11/19	2	9,317
U-123	IXB	Reinhard Hardegen	10/14	11/22		None+ [68]
U-84	VIIB	Horst Uphoff	10/16	11/18		None
U-85	VIIB	Eberhard Greger	10/16	11/27		None
U-202	VIIC	Hans-Heinz Linder	10/16	11/13	2	6,608
U-93	VIIC	Horst Elfe* (C.O.)	10/18	11/21		None
U-203	VIIC	Rolf Mützelburg	10/18	11/12	2	10,456
U-571	VIIC	Helmut Möhlmann	10/18	11/26		None
U-577	VIIC	Herbert Schauenburg*	10/19	11/26		None
U-106	IXB	Hermann Rasch* (C.O.)	10/21	11/22		None+
U-74	VIIB	Eitel-Friedrich Kentrat	10/22	11/12	1	8,531
U-133	VIIC	Hermann Hesse*	10/22	11/26		None
U-552	VIIC	Erich Topp	10/25	11/26	1	1,190 [69]
U-567	VIIC	Engelbert Endrass* (C.O.)	10/25	11/26		None
U-402	VIIC	Siegfried von Forstner*	10/26	12/9		None
U-96	VIIC	Heinrich Lehmann-Willenbrock	10/27	12/6	1	5,998
					Abort Mediterranean attempt	
U-98	VIIC	Robert Gysae	10/29	11/29		None
U-201	VIIC	Adalbert Schnee	10/29	12/9		None
U-69	VIIC	Wilhelm Zahn	10/30	12/8	Abort	None
U-332	VIIC	Johannes Liebe*	10/30	12/16	Abort Mediterranean attempt	
U-373	VIIC	Paul-Karl Loeser	10/30	11/21	Abort	None
U-572	VIIC	Heinz Hirsacker	10/30	11/29		None

NOVEMBER 1941:

BOAT	TYPE	SKIPPER	SAILED	RETURNED	SHIPS SUNK	TONS
U-561	VIIC	Robert Bartels	11/1	11/26	2	8,531
U-433	VIIC	Hans Ey	11/1	Into Mediterranean 11/17		
U-652	VIIC	Georg-Werner Fraatz	11/1	Into Mediterranean 11/29		
U-434	VIIC	Wolfgang Heyda*	11/2	Lost 12/18		None
U-205	VIIC	Franz-Georg Reschke	11/3	Into Mediterranean 11/11		
U-81	VIIC	Fritz Guggenberger	11/5	Into Mediterranean 11/12		
U-105	IXB	Georg Schewe	11/8	12/13		None
U-565	VIIC	Johann Jebsen	11/8	Into Mediterranean 11/16		
U-574	VIIC	Dietrich Gengelbach*	11/8	Lost 12/19	1	1,190 [70]
U-575	VIIC	Günther Heydemann	11/9	12/17	Abort Mediterranean attempt	
U-43	IX	Wolfgang Lüth	11/10	12/16	3	22,337 [71]
U-375	VIIC	Jürgen Könenkamp*	11/12	Into Mediterranean 12/9		
U-453	VIIC	Egon-Reiner von Schilippenbach*	11/12	Into Mediterranean 12/9		

BOAT	TYPE	SKIPPER	SAILED	RETURNED	SHIPS SUNK	TONS
U-372	VIIC	Heinz-Joachim Neumann	11/13	Into Mediterranean 12/8		
U-654	VIIC	Hans-Joachim Hesse*	11/16	11/20	Abort	None[72]
U-431	VIIC	Wilhelm Dommes	11/16	Into Mediterranean 11/24		
U-95	VIIC	Gerd Schreiber	11/19	Into Mediterranean 11/27		
U-557	VIIC	Ottokar Paulshen	11/19	Into Mediterranean 11/26		
U-562	VIIC	Horst Hamm	11/20	Into Mediterranean 11/27		
U-558	VIIC	Günther Krech	11/24	12/7	Abort Mediterranean attempt	
U-451	VIIC	Eberhard Hoffmann	11/25	12/12		None
U-67	IXC	Günther Müller-Stöckheim	11/26	12/26		None
U-131	IXC	Arend Baumann*	11/27	Lost 12/17	1	4,016
U-127	IXC	Bruno Hansmann*	11/29	Lost 12/15		None
U-563	VIIC	Klaus Bargsten	11/29	12/2	Abort Mediterranean attempt	
U-71	VIIC	Walter Flachsenberg	11/29	12/5	Abort Mediterranean attempt	
U-206	VIIC	Herbert Opitz	11/29	Lost 11/29		None

DECEMBER 1941: (For Patrols to the Americas, See Appendix 4)

BOAT	TYPE	SKIPPER	SAILED	RETURNED	SHIPS SUNK	TONS
U-130	IXC	Ernst Kals*	12/1	12/16	3	14,971
U-566	VIIC	Dietrich Borchert	12/3	12/23		None
U-208	VIIC	Alfred Schlieper	12/3	Lost 12/11		None
U-568	VIIC	Joachim Preuss	12/4	Into Mediterranean 12/10		
U-374	VIIC	Unno von Fischel	12/6	Into Mediterranean 12/10		
U-74	VIIB	Eitel-Friedrich Kentrat	12/9	Into Mediterranean 12/15		
U-108	IXB	Klaus Scholtz	12/9	12/25	2	7,620
U-77	VIIC	Heinrich Schonder	12/10	Into Mediterranean 12/16		
U-86	VIIC	Walter Schug*	12/10	12/22		None
U-107	IXB	Harald Gelhaus* (C.O.)	12/10	12/26		None
U-128	IXC	Ulrich Heyse*	12/10	12/24		None
U-432	VIIC	Heinz-Otto Schultze	12/10	12/23	Abort	None
U-569	VIIC	Hans-Peter Hinsch	12/10	12/23	Abort Mediterranean attempt	
U-83	VIIB	Hans-Werner Kraus	12/11	Into Mediterranean 12/18		
U-573	VIIC	Heinrich Heinsohn	12/11	Into Mediterranean 12/18		
U-576	VIIC	Hans-Dieter Heinicke	12/11	12/23		None
U-202	VIIC	Hans-Heinz Linder	12/13	12/27	Abort Mediterranean attempt	
U-581	VIIC	Werner Pfeifer*	12/13	12/24		None
U-451	VIIC	Eberhard Hoffmann	12/15	Lost 12/21		None
U-654	VIIC	Ludwig Forster (C.O.)	12/15	12/25	Abort	None
U-133	VIIC	Hermann Hesse	12/16	Into Mediterranean 12/21		
U-653	VIIC	Gerhard Feiler*	12/16	1/13		None
U-577	VIIC	Herbert Schauenburg	12/16	Into Mediterranean 12/23		
U-71	VIIC	Walter Flachsenberg	12/18	1/21		None
U-567	VIIC	Engelbert Endrass	12/18	Lost 12/21	1	3,324
U-751	VIIC	Gerhard Bigalk	12/18	12/26	1	10,000[73]
U-582	VIIC	Werner Schulte*	12/20	2/7	1	5,189
U-571	VIIC	Helmut Möhlmann	12/21	1/27		None
U-93	VIIC	Horst Elfe	12/23	Lost 1/15		None
U-156	IXC	Werner Hartenstein*	12/24	1/10	Abort	None
U-753	VIIC	Alfred Manhardt von Mannstein*	12/24	12/30		None
U-373	VIIC	Paul-Karl Loeser	12/25	1/15	None/Escort	
U-43	IX	Wolfgang Lüth	12/30	1/22	None/to Germany	

JANUARY 1942:

BOAT	TYPE	SKIPPER	SAILED	RETURNED	SHIPS SUNK	TONS
U-161	IXC	Albrecht Achilles*	1/3	1/15		None
U-561	VIIC	Robert Bartels	1/3	Into Mediterranean 1/15		
U-73	VIIC	Helmut Rosenbaum	1/4	Into Mediterranean 1/14		

BOAT	TYPE	SKIPPER	SAILED	RETURNED	SHIPS SUNK	TONS
U-504	IXC/40	Friedrich Poske*	1/6	1/20		None
U-572	VIIC	Heinz Hirsacker	1/7	2/10	Abort Mediterranean attempt	
U-587	VIIC	Ulrich Borcherdt*	1/8	1/30		None
U-588	VIIC	Viktor Vogel*	1/8	1/30		None
U-402	VIIC	Siegfried von Forstner	1/11	2/11		None+
U-581	VIIC	Werner Pfeifer	1/11	Lost 2/2	1	364
U-586	VIIC	Dietrich von der Esch*	1/12	2/12		None+[74]
U-94	VIIC	Otto Ites	1/12	1/30	Abort	None
U-575	VIIC	Günther Heydemann	1/13	2/26	None/Escort	
U-132	VIIC	Ernst Vogelsang	1/15	2/8	1	2,216[75] Abort
U-455	VIIC	Hans-Heinrich Giessler*	1/15	2/28		None
U-591	VIIC	Hans-Jürgen Zetsche*	1/15	2/20	1	4,028[76]
U-352	VIIC	Hellmut Rathke	1/15	2/26		None
U-656	VIIC	Ernst Kröning	1/15	1/28		None
U-578	VIIC	August Rehwinkel	1/15	1/26		None
U-753	VIIC	Alfred Manhardt von Mannstein	1/17	2/1	Abort	None
U-404	VIIC	Otto von Bülow*	1/17	2/1		None
U-505	IXC/40	Axel-Olaf Loewe*	1/19	2/3		None
U-136	VIIC	Heinrich Zimmermann*	1/22	3/1	3	8,739[77]
U-213	VIID	Amelung von Varendorff*	1/24	3/19	None/M	
U-332	VIIC	Johannes Liebe	1/27	2/8	Abort	None[78]

FEBRUARY 1942: (Defense of Norway)

BOAT	TYPE	SKIPPER	SAILED	RETURNED	SHIPS SUNK	TONS
U-752	VIIC	Karl-Ernst Schroeter	2/4	3/13		None
U-154	IXC	Walther Kölle*	2/7	3/1		None
U-503	IXC/40	Otto Gericke*	2/15	2/22		None
U-135	VIIC	Friedrich-Hermann Praetorius	2/22	4/3		None
U-87	VIIB	Joachim Berger	2/22	3/27		None
U-553	VIIC	Karl Thurmann	2/24	4/1		None
U-569	VIIC	Hans-Peter Hinsch	2/26	4/2	1	984
U-701	VIIC	Horst Degen	2/26	4/1	3	1,253+
U-753	VIIC	Alfred Manhardt von Mannstein	2/26	3/26		None

MARCH 1942:

BOAT	TYPE	SKIPPER	SAILED	RETURNED	SHIPS SUNK	TONS
U-506	IXC/40	Erich Würdemann*	3/2	3/25		None
U-593	VIIC	Gerd Kelbling*	3/2	3/28		None
U-507	IXC/40	Harro Schacht*	3/7	3/25		None
U-594	VIIC	Dietrich Hoffmann*	3/14	3/30		None
U-455	VIIC	Hans-Heinrich Giessler	3/21	3/30		None
U-252	VIIC	Kai Lerchen*	3/26	Lost 4/14		None[79]

APRIL 1942:

BOAT	TYPE	SKIPPER	SAILED	RETURNED	SHIPS SUNK	TONS
U-437	VIIC	Werner-Karl Schulz*	4/4	4/16		None
U-172	IXC	Carl Emmermann*	4/22	5/3		None
U-159	IXC	Helmut Witte*	4/22	5/3		None
U-96	VIIC	Hans-Jürgen Hellriegel* (C.O.)	4/23	7/1		None
U-437	VIIC	Werner-Karl Schulz	4/29	5/18	None/Escort[80]	
U-157	IXC	Wolf Henne*	4/30	5/10		None

MAY 1942:

Group Hecht:[81]

BOAT	TYPE	SKIPPER	SAILED	RETURNED	SHIPS SUNK	TONS
U-590	VIIC	Heinrich Müller-Edzards*	5/3	6/26		None

BOAT	TYPE	SKIPPER	SAILED	RETURNED	SHIPS SUNK	TONS
U-124	IXB	Johann Mohr	5/4	6/26	7	32,429 [82]
U-569	VIIC	Hans-Peter Hinsch	5/4	6/28	1	4,458+
U-406	VIIC	Horst Dieterichs*	5/5	7/1		None
U-94	VIIC	Otto Ites	5/14	6/23	5	25,502+
U-153	IXC	Wilfried Reichmann*	5/18	5/30		None
U-166	IXC	Hans-Günther				
		Kuhlmann*	5/30	6/10		None

JUNE 1942:

BOAT	TYPE	SKIPPER	SAILED	RETURNED	SHIPS SUNK	TONS
U-71	VIIC	Walter Flachsenberg	6/4	6/5	Abort	None
U-459	XIV	Georg von Wilamowitz-				
		Möllendorf	6/6	7/19		None/Supply
U-460	XIV	Friedrich Schäfer*	6/7	7/31		None/Supply
U-552	VIIC	Erich Topp	6/9	6/19	5	15,858
U-71	VIIC	Walter Flachsenberg	6/11	6/20	Abort	None
U-461	XIV	Wolf Stiebler*	6/21	8/16		None/Supply
U-379	VIIC	Paul-Hugo Kettner*	6/25	Lost 8/8	2	8,904
U-597	VIIC	Eberhard Bopst*	6/27	8/16		None
U-90	VIIC	Hans-Jürgen Oldörp*	6/30	Lost 7/24		None
U-704	VIIC	Horst Kessler*	6/30	8/16		None

JULY 1942:

BOAT	TYPE	SKIPPER	SAILED	RETURNED	SHIPS SUNK	TONS
U-86	VIIB	Walter Schug	7/2	9/18	1	342
U-71	VIIC	Hardo Rodler von				
		Roithberg* (C.O.)	7/4	8/15		None
U-552	VIIC	Erich Topp	7/4	8/13	1.5	8,719+ Abort
U-454	VIIC	Burkhard Hackländer	7/4	8/17		None
U-43	IX	Hans-Joachim				
		Schwantke* (C.O.)	7/4	8/15		None/Abort
U-607	VIIC	Ernst Mengersen*	7/9	8/16	1.5 [83]	13,884
U-463	XIV	Leo Wolfbauer*	7/11	9/3		None/Supply
U-254	VIIC	Hans Gilardone*	7/14	8/19	1	1,218
U-588	VIIC	Viktor Vogel	7/14	Lost 7/31		None
U-609	VIIC	Klaus Rudloff*	7/16	9/10	2	10,288
U-210	VIIC	Rudolf Lemcke*	7/18	Lost 8/6		None
U-176	IXC	Reiner Dierksen*	7/21	10/2	5.5 [84]	31,886
U-593	VIIC	Gerd Kelbling	7/22	8/19	1	3,616
U-462	XIV	Bruno Vowe*	7/23	9/21		None/Supply
U-595	VIIC	Jürgen Quaet-Faslem*	7/23	8/18		None
U-660	VIIC	Götz Baur*	7/25	9/5	3	15,286 [85]
U-256	VIIC	Odo Loewe*	7/28	9/3	Abort	None
U-605	VIIC	Herbert-Viktor Schütze*	7/28	9/4	3	8,409 Abort
U-174	IXC	Ulrich Thilo*	7/30	9/6		None
U-335	VIIC	Hans-Hermann Pelkner*	7/31	Lost 8/3		None

AUGUST 1942:

BOAT	TYPE	SKIPPER	SAILED	RETURNED	SHIPS SUNK	TONS
U-705	VIIC	Karl-Horst Horn*	8/1	Lost 9/3	1	3,279+
U-438	VIIC	Rudolf Franzius*	8/1	9/3	2+ [86]	10,546 Abort
U-464	XIV	Otto Harms*	8/4	Lost 8/20		None/Supply
U-569	VIIC	Hans-Peter Hinsch	8/4	10/8		None
U-604	VIIC	Horst Höltring*	8/4	9/8	1	7,906
U-755	VIIC	Walter Göing*	8/4	10/5	1	1,827
U-373	VIIC	Paul-Karl Loeser	8/6	10/4		None
U-578	VIIC	Ernst-August				
		Rehwinkel	8/6	Lost 8/10		None
U-135	VIIC	Friedrich-Hermann				
		Praetorius	8/8	10/3	None	Abort

BOAT	TYPE	SKIPPER	SAILED	RETURNED	SHIPS SUNK	TONS
U-596	VIIC	Gunter Jahn*	8/8	10/3	2	10,642
U-92	VIIC	Adolf Oelrich*	8/12	9/25		None
U-432	VIIC	Heinz-Otto Schultze	8/15	10/4	1	5,868
U-91	VIIC	Heinz Walkerling*	8/15	10/6	1	1,375 [87]
U-407	VIIC	Ernst-Ulrich Brüller*	8/15	10/9		None
U-659	VIIC	Hans Stock*	8/15	9/16	Abort	None+
U-756	VIIC	Klaus Harney*	8/15	Lost 9/1		None
U-409	VIIC	Hans-Ferdinand Massmann*	8/18	9/9		None
U-411	VIIC	Gerhard Litterscheid*	8/18	9/30		None
U-608	VIIC	Rolf Struckmeier*	8/20	9/24		10,323 +[88] Abort
U-380	VIIC	Josef Röther*	8/22	10/7	1	2,994
U-404	VIIC	Otto von Bülow	8/23	10/13	1	1,120 +[89]
U-96	VIIC	Hans-Jürgen Hellriegel	8/24	10/5	4	15,959+
U-584	VIIC	Joachim Deecke	8/24	10/10	2	12,913
U-218	VIID	Richard Becker*	8/25	9/29	Abort	None+
U-211	VIIC	Karl Hause*	8/26	10/6	1	21,560 +[90]
U-410	VIIC	Kurt Sturm*	8/27	10/28		None
U-599	VIIC	Wolfgang Breithaupt*	8/27	Lost 10/24		None
U-216	VIID	Karl-Otto Schultz*	8/29	Lost 10/20	1	4,989
U-259	VIIC	Klaus Köpke*	8/29	10/5		None
U-617	VIIC	Albrecht Brandi*	8/29	10/7	4	15,079+

1. Includes 18,600-ton fleet carrier Courageous.
2. Includes the 2,534-ton Hanonia, taken as a prize.
3. Both captured as prizes.
4. Includes 13,600-ton liner Athenia.
5. Held in North Sea.
6. Damaged two others with minefield.
7. Sank the British battleship Royal Oak in Scapa Flow.
8. Includes a 3,176-ton prize.
9. Also damaged the British battleship Nelson 12/4/39.
10. Includes two ships for 11,929 tons sunk by mines.
11. Includes a 9,577-ton ship sunk by mines.
12. Sunk in North Sea.
13. Damaged the 31,100-ton British battleship Barham.
14. Includes 7,807-ton ship sunk by mines.
15. Landed two agents in Ireland.
16. Includes one 710-ton ship sunk by mines.
17. Includes one 5,068-ton ship sunk by mines.
18. Sunk near Wilhelmshaven, but salvaged.
19. Escorted Atlantis.
20. Escorted Orion; sunk in Narvik harbor.
21. While on supply mission to Norway.
22. Refueled in Spain 6/24 and returned to Germany.
23. Includes 20,277-ton auxiliary cruiser Carinthia.
24. Landed agent in Ireland.
25. Prolonged cruise to West Africa.
26. Rammed and aborted.
27. Refueled in Spain 6/26 and was first U-boat to enter Lorient in Occupied France on 7/7. Resailed from there 8/6.
28. Includes British destroyer Whirlwind.

29. Includes Estonian prize Merisaar, 2,136 tons, subsequently sunk by the Luftwaffe.
30. Includes British submarine Spearfish.
31. Includes 15,000-ton auxiliary cruiser Dunvegan Castle.
32. Aborted landing of two agents in Ireland and put into Brest.
33. Damaged British light cruiser Fiji.
34. Includes British sloop Penzance.
35. Shared credit for 5,156-ton Elmbank with U-99.
36. Includes 1,074-ton Luimneach, erroneously credited to U-46.
37. Includes British sloop Dundee and 11,000-ton liner City of Benares.
38. Shared credit for Corrientes, 6,863 tons, with U-37.
39. Shared credit for Graigwen, 3,697 tons, with U-123.
40. First VIIC in combat.
41. Shared credit for Shirak, 6,023 tons, with U-47.
42. Shared credit for Matina, 5,389 tons, with U-31.
43. Hit Shekatika, 5,458 tons, with one torpedo; sinking credited to U-123.
44. Shared credit for Clintonia, 3,106 tons, with U-123.
45. Liner Empress of Britain, damaged by Luftwaffe.
46. Shared one-third credit for Conch, 8,376 tons, with U-95 and U-99.
47. Shared credit for Ardanbhan, 4,980 tons, with Tazzoli.
48. Two 15,000-ton British freighters, Almeda Star and Oropesa.
49. Shared credit with U-96 for 10,516-ton British tanker A. F. Corwin.
50. Prien and Kretschmer shared credit for the 20,638-ton British whale factory-cum-tanker Terje Viken.
51. Diesel exhaust failed, filling the boat with carbon monoxide. Three crew died; four others fell desperately ill.
52. In a special mission to Denmark Strait, sank armed merchant cruiser Rajaputana.
53. May also have sunk French steamer Kervegen, 2,018 tons.
54. Includes the ex-American four-stack British destroyer Bath.
55. British corvette Picotee.
56. Suspected outbreak of diphtheria.
57. Rescued six British airmen and took them to France.
58. Includes British corvette Zinnia.
59. Aborted owing to illness of skipper.
60. Aborted owing to illness of a midshipman.
61. Patrol terminated in the Baltic for complete yard overhaul and upgrading.
62. Includes Canadian corvette Levis.
63. Includes the British corvette Fleur de Lys.
64. Includes British destroyer Cossack.
65. Damaged American destroyer Kearny.
66. Fatally damaged the ex-American four-stack British destroyer Broadwater.
67. Includes British corvette Gladiolus.
68. Damaged 14,000-ton British armed merchant cruiser Aurania.
69. The American destroyer Reuben James.
70. Ex-American four-stack British destroyer Stanley.
71. Including 11,900-ton American tanker Astral.
72. Aborted to Norway with crew illness; resailed in December with a new skipper.
73. The British "jeep" carrier Audacity.
74. After one Atlantic patrol, resumed assignment to the Arctic.
75. American Coast Guard cutter Alexander Hamilton.
76. After one Atlantic patrol, resumed assignment to the Arctic.
77. Includes British corvette Arbutus and the Canadian corvette Spikenard.
78. Searched for survivors of Spreewald.
79. Landed agent in Iceland.

80. After a brief transit patrol from Kiel to France, escorted blockade runner Münsterland into France.
81. Plus U-404 and U-578, which went on to the Americas and U-96.
82. Includes Free French corvette Mimose.
83. Shared one-half credit with U-552 for sinking 7,167-ton Belgian Soldier.
84. Shared one-half credit with U-438 for sinking 7,457-ton Empire Breeze.
85. Baur sank two freighters alone and shared one-half credit with Franzius in U-438 for two more.
86. Shared one-half credit with U-660 for the sinkings of two freighters in Slow Convoy 94, and with U-176 for sinking 7,457-ton Empire Breeze.
87. The Canadian destroyer Ottawa.
88. Shared one-half credit with U-211 for sinking the 13,797-ton Hektoria and the 6,849-ton Empire Moonbeam.
89. The British destroyer Veteran.
90. Sank 11,237-ton Esso Williamsburg and shared one-half credits with U-608 for Hektoria and Empire Moonbeam.

APPENDIX 3

U-BOAT PATROLS TO THE SOUTH ATLANTIC

OCTOBER 1940 – AUGUST 1942

BOAT	TYPE	SKIPPER	SAILED	RETURNED	SHIPS SUNK	TONS
OCTOBER 1940:						
U-65	IXB	Hans-Gerrit von Stockhausen	10/15	1/10	8	47,785 +
NOVEMBER 1940:						
U-37	IX	Nikolaus Clausen* (C.O.)	11/28	1/7	7	11,201
DECEMBER 1940:						
None						
JANUARY 1941:						
None						
FEBRUARY 1941:						
U-105	IXB	Georg Schewe	2/22	6/13	12	70,450
U-124	IXB	Wilhelm Schulz	2/23	5/1	11	52,397
U-A	Turk	Hans Eckermann* (C.O.)	2/27	3/18	Abort	None +
U-106	IXB	Jürgen Oesten	2/28	6/18	7	42,218 +[1]
MARCH 1941:						
U-107	IXB	Günter Hessler	3/29	7/2	14	86,699
APRIL 1941:						
U-38	IX	Heinrich Liebe	4/9	6/24	8	47,279
U-103	IXB	Viktor Schütze	4/11	7/12	13	65,172
U-A	Turk	Hans Eckermann	4/14	4/26	Abort	None
MAY 1941:						
U-69	VIIC	Jost Metzler	5/5	7/8	6	28,423 +M
U-A	Turk	Hans Eckermann	5/16	7/30		None
JUNE 1941:						
U-123	IXB	Reinhard Hardegen* (C.O.)	6/16	8/26	5	21,507
U-66	IXC	Richard Zapp	6/23	8/5	4	19,078

* = First patrol of boat or skipper (C.O.).
+ = Damaged ships or shared credit.
M = Mine mission.
Abort = Forced by battle damage, mechanical failure, etc., to return.

BOAT	TYPE	SKIPPER	SAILED	RETURNED	SHIPS SUNK	TONS
JULY 1941:						
U-124	IXB	Wilhelm Schulz	7/12	8/26	Abort	None
U-93	VIIC	Claus Korth	7/12	8/21	Abort	None
U-94	VIIC	Herbert Kuppisch	7/12	8/16	Abort	None
U-109	IXB	Heinrich Bleichrodt* (C.O.)	7/28	8/17	Abort	None
AUGUST 1941:						
U-108	IXB	Klaus Scholtz	8/12	10/21		None
U-125	IXC	Günter Kuhnke	8/12	11/5		None
U-111	IXB	Wilhelm Kleinschmidt	8/14	Lost 10/4	2	14,193
U-107	IXB	Günter Hessler	8/30	11/11	3	13,641
SEPTEMBER 1941:						
U-66	IXC	Richard Zapp	9/2	11/9	1	7,015
U-68	IXC	Karl-Friedrich Merten	9/8	12/8	4	23,697
U-67	IXC	Günther Müller-Stöckheim	9/14	10/16	1	3,753 Abort[2]
U-103	IXB	Werner Winter	9/13	11/9	2	10,594
U-126	IXC	Ernst Bauer	9/24	12/13	4	23,866
U-129	IXC	Nikolaus Clausen	9/29	10/31		None/Rescue
OCTOBER 1941:						
U-A	Turk	Hans Eckermann	10/23	12/24		None
U-129	IXC	Nikolaus Clausen	10/27	12/27		None
U-124	IXB	Johann Mohr	10/30	12/27	2	11,125[3]
NOVEMBER 1941:						
None						
DECEMBER 1941:						
None						
JANUARY 1942:						
None						
FEBRUARY 1942:						
U-68	IXC	Karl-Friedrich Merten	2/11	4/13	7	39,350
U-505	IXC/40	Axel-Olaf Loewe	2/11	5/7	4	25,041
MARCH 1942:						
None						
APRIL 1942:						
None						
MAY 1942:						
None						
JUNE 1942:						
U-582	VIIC	Werner Schulte	6/27	8/12	4	30,644
U-201	VIIC	Adalbert Schnee	6/27	8/8	6	41,036
U-116	XB	Werner von Schmidt	6/27	8/23	1	4,284 + Supply
U-572	VIIC	Heinz Hirsacker	6/30	9/3	1	5,281
U-136	VIIC	Heinrich Zimmermann	6/30	Lost 7/11		None
JULY 1942:						
U-752	VIIC	Karl-Ernst Schroeter	7/2	9/4	4	21,651

BOAT	TYPE	SKIPPER	SAILED	RETURNED	SHIPS SUNK	TONS
U-130	IXC	Ernst Kals	7/4	9/12	7	51,528
U-507	IXC/40	Harro Schacht	7/4	10/12	7	18,132 [4]
U-109	IXB	Heinrich Bleichrodt	7/18	10/6	5	35,601
U-213	VIID	Amelung von Varendorff	7/19	Lost 7/31		None
U-106	IXB	Hermann Rasch	7/25	7/31	Abort	None
U-125	IXC	Ulrich Folkers	7/27	11/6	6	25,415
U-506	IXC/40	Erich Würdemann	7/28	11/7	5	28,023 [5]

AUGUST 1942:

BOAT	TYPE	SKIPPER	SAILED	RETURNED	SHIPS SUNK	TONS
U-333	VIIC	Peter Cremer	8/1	8/24	Abort	None
U-594	VIIC	Friedrich Mumm* (C.O.)	8/4	9/28	1	6,074
U-653	VIIC	Gerhard Feiler	8/5	8/31	Abort	None
U-566	VIIC	Gerhard Remus* (C.O.)	8/6	9/5	2	12,268 + Abort
U-214	VIID	Günther Reeder	8/9	10/9	2	13,840 +
U-406	VIIC	Horst Dieterichs	8/9	10/8	1	7,452
U-107	IXB	Harald Gelhaus	8/15	11/18	3	23,508
U-179	IXD2	Ernst Sobe*	8/15	Lost 10/8	1	6,558
U-172	IXC	Carl Emmermann	8/19	12/27	8	60,048 [6]
U-459	XIV	Georg von Wilamowitz-Möllendorf	8/19	11/5		None/Supply
U-504	IXC/40	Friedrich Poske	8/19	12/11	6	36,156
U-68	IXC	Karl-Friedrich Merten	8/20	12/6	9	56,230
U-156	IXC	Werner Hartenstein	8/20	11/16	3	30,381 [7]
U-159	IXC	Helmut Witte	8/24	1/5/43	11	63,730
U-590	VIIC	Heinrich Müller-Edzards	8/27	11/24		None
U-D5	Dutch	Bruno Mahn*	8/27	11/12	1	7,628
U-87	VIIB	Joachim Berger	8/31	11/20	1	7,392

---

1. Damaged British battleship Malaya.
2. Rammed by British submarine Clyde.
3. Includes British cruiser Dunedin.
4. Patrolled Brazilian waters, then participated in the rescue of Laconia survivors.
5. Participated in the rescue of Laconia survivors.
6. Including the 23,456-ton liner Orcades.
7. Including the 19,695-ton liner Laconia.

APPENDIX 4

U-BOAT PATROLS TO THE AMERICAS

DECEMBER 1941 – AUGUST 1942

BOAT	TYPE	SKIPPER	SAILED	RETURNED	SHIPS SUNK	TONS
DECEMBER 1941:						
Type IXs (6):						
U-502	C/40	Jürgen von Rosenstiel	12/18	12/22	Abort	None
U-125	C	Ulrich Folkers* (C.O.)	12/18	2/23	1	5,666
U-123	B	Reinhard Hardegen	12/23	2/9	7	46,744
U-66	C	Richard Zapp	12/25	2/10	5	33,456
U-109	B	Heinrich Bleichrodt	12/27	2/23	4	27,651
U-130	C	Ernst Kals	12/27	2/25	6	36,988
			Totals:		23	150,505
Type VIIs (10):						
U-84	B	Horst Uphoff	12/21	2/7		None
U-135	C	Friedrich-Hermann Praetorius*	12/24	1/31	1	9,626
U-552	C	Erich Topp	12/25	1/27	2	6,722
U-203	C	Rolf Mützelburg	12/26	1/29	2	1,977+
U-86	B	Walter Schug	12/27	2/15	1	4,271+
U-87	B	Joachim Berger*	12/27	1/29	2	16,324 Abort
U-333	C	Peter Cremer*	12/27	2/9	3	14,045[1]
U-701	C	Horst Degen*	12/27	2/9	1	3,657
U-754	C	Hans Oestermann*	12/30	2/9	4	11,386
U-553	C	Karl Thurmann	12/31	2/3	2	17,366
			Totals:		18	85,374
			Grand Total:		41	235,979
JANUARY 1942:						
Type IXs (12):						
U-103	B	Werner Winter	1/3	3/1	4	26,539
U-106	B	Hermann Rasch	1/3	2/22	5	42,139
U-107	B	Harald Gelhaus	1/7	3/7	2	10,850+
U-128	C	Ulrich Heyse	1/8	3/23	3	30,803
U-108	B	Klaus Scholtz	1/12	3/4	5	20,082

* = First patrol of boat or skipper (C.O.).
+ = Damaged ships or shared credit.
M = Mine mission.
Abort = Forced by battle damage, mechanical failure, etc., to return.

BOAT	TYPE	SKIPPER	SAILED	RETURNED	SHIPS SUNK	TONS
U-67	C	Günther Müller-Stockheim	1/19	3/30	2	17,469+
U-156	C	Werner Hartenstein	1/19	3/17	5	22,723+
U-502	C/40	Jürgen von Rosenstiel	1/19	3/16	5	25,232+
U-161	C	Albrecht Achilles	1/24	4/2	5	28,033+[2]
U-504	C/40	Fritz Poske	1/26	4/1	4	26,561
U-129	C	Nikolaus Clausen	1/26	4/5	7	25,613
U-105	B	Heinrich Schuch* (C.O.)	1/26	2/18	Abort	None[3]
				Totals:	47	276,044

Type VIIs (14):

BOAT	TYPE	SKIPPER	SAILED	RETURNED	SHIPS SUNK	TONS
U-654	C	Ludwig Forster*	1/3	2/19	1	900[4]
U-582	C	Werner Schulte*	1/4	2/7	1	5,189
U-85	C	Eberhard Greger	1/10	2/23	1	5,408
U-82	C	Siegfried Rollmann	1/11	Lost 2/6	3	19,307[5]
U-575	C	Günther Heydemann	1/14	2/26		None[6]
U-751	C	Gerhard Bigalk	1/14	2/23	2	11,487+
U-566	C	Dietrich Borchert*	1/15	3/9	1	4,181
U-98	C	Robert Gysae	1/18	2/27	1	5,298
U-564	C	Reinhard Suhren	1/18	3/6	1	11,410+
U-576	C	Hans-Dieter Heinicke	1/20	2/28	1	6,946
U-432	C	Heinz-Otto Schultze	1/21	3/16	6	27,820
U-96	C	Heinrich Lehmann-Willenbrock	1/31	3/23	5	25,464
U-653	C	Gerhard Feiler*	1/31	3/30	1	1,582
U-69	C	Wilhelm Zahn	1/31	3/17		None
				Totals:	24	124,922
				Grand Total:	71	400,966

FEBRUARY 1942:

Type IXs (9):

BOAT	TYPE	SKIPPER	SAILED	RETURNED	SHIPS SUNK	TONS
U-126	C	Ernst Bauer	2/2	3/29	7	32,955+
U-158	C	Erich Rostin*	2/2	3/31	4	29,234+
U-154	C	Walther Kölle	2/7	3/1	Abort	None
U-155	C	Adolf-Cornelius Piening*	2/7	3/27	3	17,657
U-162	C	Jürgen Wattenberg*	2/7	3/18	Abort	None
U-124	B	Johann Mohr	2/21	4/10	7	42,048+
U-160	C	Georg Lassen*	2/24	4/28	5	36,731
U-105	B	Heinrich Schuch	2/25	4/15	2	18,005
U-503	C/40	Otto Gericke	2/28	Lost 3/15		None
				Totals:	28	176,630

Type VIIs (9):

BOAT	TYPE	SKIPPER	SAILED	RETURNED	SHIPS SUNK	TONS
U-578	C	Ernst-August Rehwinkel	2/3	3/25	3	11,630[7]
U-656	C	Ernst Kröning	2/4	Lost 3/1		None
U-558	C	Günther Krech	2/10	3/11	5	36,935[8]
U-587	C	Ulrich Borcherdt	2/12	Lost 3/27	2	6,619+
U-588	C	Viktor Vogel	2/12	3/27	2	11,566+
U-94	C	Otto Ites	2/12	4/2	4	14,442+
U-404	C	Otto von Bülow	2/14	4/3	4	22,653
U-332	C	Johannes Liebe	2/17	4/10	4	25,125
U-71	C	Walter Flachsenberg	2/23	4/20	5	38,894
				Totals:	29	167,864
				Grand Total:	57	344,494

BOAT	TYPE	SKIPPER	SAILED	RETURNED	SHIPS SUNK	TONS

MARCH 1942:

Type IXs (6):

BOAT	TYPE	SKIPPER	SAILED	RETURNED	SHIPS SUNK	TONS
U-123	B	Reinhard Hardegen	3/2	5/2	8	34,917+[9]
U-154	C	Walther Kölle	3/11	5/9	5	28,715
U-66	C	Richard Zapp	3/21	5/27	6	43,946+
U-130	C	Ernst Kals	3/24	6/16	2	13,092
U-109	B	Heinrich Bleichrodt	3/25	6/3	3	12,099
U-108	B	Klaus Scholtz	3/25	6/3	5	31,340
			Totals:		29	164,109

Resupply Operations:

BOAT	TYPE	SKIPPER	SAILED	RETURNED	SHIPS SUNK	TONS
U-A	Turk	Hans Cohausz* (Again C.O.)	3/14	4/24	None/Supply	
U-459	XIV	Georg von Wilamowitz-Möllendorf*	3/21	5/15	None/Supply	

Type VIIs (20):

BOAT	TYPE	SKIPPER	SAILED	RETURNED	SHIPS SUNK	TONS
U-373	C	Paul-Karl Loeser	3/1	4/17	2	9,867
U-202	C	Hans-Heinz Linder	3/1	4/26	1	5,249+
U-552	C	Erich Topp	3/7	4/27	6	39,475+[10]
U-754	C	Hans Oestermann	3/7	4/25	7	31,578+
U-571	C	Helmut Möhlmann	3/10	5/7	3	24,319
U-203	C	Rolf Mützelberg	3/12	4/30	2	14,232+
U-572	C	Heinz Hirsacker	3/14	5/13	2	9,532+
U-84	B	Horst Uphoff	3/17	5/14	2	8,240
U-582	C	Werner Schulte	3/19	5/24	None/Escort	
U-654	C	Ludwig Forster	3/21	5/29	3	17,755
U-85	B	Eberhard Greger	3/21	Lost 4/14	1	4,904
U-201	C	Adalbert Schnee	3/24	5/11	3	15,313
U-575	C	Günther Heydemann	3/24	5/13	1	6,887
U-136	C	Heinrich Zimmermann	3/24	5/20	3	12,707
U-86	B	Walter Schug	3/25	5/26	None	
U-402	C	Siegfried von Forstner	3/26	5/20	3	11,135
U-752	C	Karl-Ernst Schroeter	3/28	5/22	2	10,707
U-576	C	Hans-Dieter Heinicke	3/29	5/16	2	6,441
U-333	C	Peter Cremer	3/30	5/26	3	13,596+
U-98	C	Wilhelm Schulze* (C.O.)	3/31	6/6	None	
			Totals:		46	241,937
			Grand Total:		75	406,046

APRIL 1942:

Type IXs (14):

BOAT	TYPE	SKIPPER	SAILED	RETURNED	SHIPS SUNK	TONS
U-125	C	Ulrich Folkers	4/4	6/13	9	47,055
U-507	C/40	Harro Schacht	4/4	6/4	9	44,782
U-506	C/40	Erich Würdemann*	4/6	6/15	8	39,906+
U-162	C	Jürgen Wattenberg	4/7	6/10	9	47,181
U-103	B	Werner Winter	4/15	6/22	9	42,169
U-106	B	Hermann Rasch	4/15	6/29	5	29,154+
U-155	C	Adolf-Cornelius Piening	4/20	6/14	7	33,086
U-107	B	Harald Gelhaus	4/21	7/11	6	26,983
U-156	C	Werner Hartenstein	4/22	7/7	10	39,785+[11]
U-172	C	Carl Emmermann	4/22	5/3	Abort	None
U-502	C/40	Jürgen von Rosenstiel	4/22	Lost 7/5	8	41,213
U-126	C	Ernst Bauer	4/25	7/25	7	41,708+

BOAT	TYPE	SKIPPER	SAILED	RETURNED	SHIPS SUNK	TONS
U-128	C	Ulrich Heyse	4/25	7/22	5	35,620
U-161	C	Albrecht Achilles	4/28	8/7	3	14,201+
			Totals:		95	482,843

Resupply Operations:

U-116	XB	Werner von Schmidt*	4/25	5/5	Abort	None/ Supply

Type VIIs (17):

BOAT	TYPE	SKIPPER	SAILED	RETURNED	SHIPS SUNK	TONS
U-590	C	Heinrich Müller-Edzards*	4/4	4/17	Abort	None
U-564	C	Reinhard Suhren	4/4	6/5	4	24,390+
U-594	C	Dietrich Hoffmann*	4/11	6/25		None
U-558	C	Günther Krech	4/12	6/21	6	16,380
U-69	C	Ulrich Gräf* (C.O.)	4/12	6/25	4	11,976
U-751	C	Gerhard Bigalk	4/15	6/15	2	4,555
U-455	C	Hans-Heinrich Giessler	4/16	6/16	2	13,908
U-352	C	Hellmut Rathke	4/17	Lost 5/9		None
U-566	C	Dietrich Borchert	4/18	6/30	1	8,967
U-553	C	Karl Thurmann	4/19	6/24	3	16,995
U-588	C	Viktor Vogel	4/19	6/7	4	13,975+
U-593	C	Gerd Kelbling	4/20	6/17	1	8,426+
U-753	C	Alfred Manhardt v. Mannstein	4/22	6/25	2	13,769+
U-213	D	Amelung von Varendorff	4/23	6/21		None [12]
U-653	C	Gerhard Feiler	4/25	7/6	2	7,065 [13]
U-135	C	Friedrich-Hermann Praetorius	4/26	7/5	2	11,676
U-432	C	Heinz-Otto Schultze	4/30	7/2	5	6,128+
			Totals:		38	158,210
			Grand Total:		133	641,053

MAY 1942:

Type IXs (8):

BOAT	TYPE	SKIPPER	SAILED	RETURNED	SHIPS SUNK	TONS
U-504	C/40	Fritz Poske	5/2	7/7	6	19,418
U-158	C	Erich Rostin	5/4	Lost 6/30	13	65,108
U-172	C	Carl Emmermann	5/11	7/21	10	40,745
U-68	C	Karl-Friedrich Merten	5/14	7/9	7	50,898
U-159	C	Helmut Witte	5/14	7/13	10	50,354
U-157	C	Wolf Henne	5/18	Lost 6/13	1	6,401
U-67	C	Günther Müller-Stockheim	5/20	8/8	6	30,015+
U-129	C	Hans-Ludwig Witt* (C.O.)	5/20	8/21	11	41,571
			Totals:		64	304,510

Resupply Operations:

U-116	XB	Werner von Schmidt	5/16	6/9	None/Supply/ group Hecht	

Type VIIs (8):

BOAT	TYPE	SKIPPER	SAILED	RETURNED	SHIPS SUNK	TONS
U-404	C	Otto von Bülow	5/6	7/14	7	31,061 H
U-578	C	Ernst-August Rehwinkel	5/7	7/3	2	13,095 H
U-373	C	Paul-Karl Loeser	5/19	7/8	1	396 M
U-87	B	Joachim Berger	5/19	7/8	2	14,298 M
U-701	C	Horst Degen	5/19	Lost 7/7	4	21,769+M [14]
U-332	C	Johannes Liebe	5/24	8/1	2	10,738
U-584	C	Joachim Deeke	5/25	7/22		None [15]

BOAT	TYPE	SKIPPER	SAILED	RETURNED	SHIPS SUNK	TONS
U-202	C	Hans-Heinz Linder	5/27	7/25	2	10,725 [16]
				Totals:	20	102,082
				Grand Total:	84	406,592

H = ex-group Hecht

JUNE 1942:

Type IX (11):

BOAT	TYPE	SKIPPER	SAILED	RETURNED	SHIPS SUNK	TONS
U-105	B	Heinrich Schuch	6/?	6/28	Abort	None
U-154	C	Walther Kölle	6/4	8/23	1	65
U-153	C	Wilfried Reichmann	6/6	Lost 7/13	3	16,166
U-505	C/40	Axel-Olaf Loewe	6/7	8/25	3	12,748
U-173	C	Heinz-Ehler Beucke*	6/15	9/20		None
U-166	C	Hans-Günther Kuhlmann	6/17	Lost 8/1	4	7,593 M
U-171	C	Günther Pfeffer*	6/17	Lost 10/9	3	17,641
U-160	C	Georg Lassen	6/20	8/24	6	29,281 +
U-508	C/40	Georg Staats*	6/25	9/15	2	2,710
U-509	C/40	Karl-Heinz Wolff*	6/25	9/12		None
U-66	C	Friedrich Markworth* (C.O.)	6/26	9/29	9	48,896 M
				Totals:	31	135,100

Type VII (13):

BOAT	TYPE	SKIPPER	SAILED	RETURNED	SHIPS SUNK	TONS
U-203	C	Rolf Mützelburg	6/3	7/29	5	32,985
U-437	C	Werner-Karl Schulz	6/6	8/12		None/E
U-89	C	Dietrich Lohmann*	6/6	8/21	1	54 E
U-215	D	Fritz Hoeckner*	6/9	Lost 7/3	1	7,191
U-132	C	Ernst Vogelsang	6/10	8/16	5	21,350 E
U-575	C	Günther Heydemann	6/10	8/7	4	8,274 E
U-84	B	Horst Uphoff	6/10	8/13	3	14,206 +E
U-571	C	Helmut Möhlmann	6/11	8/7	2	9,192 +E
U-134	C	Rudolf Schendel	6/11	9/1		None/E
U-214	D	Günther Reeder*	6/13	6/17	Abort	None
U-576	C	Hans-Dieter Heinicke	6/16	Lost 7/15	2	10,373
U-402	C	Siegfried von Forstner	6/16	8/5	Abort	None
U-754	C	Hans Oestermann	6/19	Lost 7/31	2	12,695
U-458	C	Kurt Diggins*	6/21	8/26	2	7,584
				Totals:	27	123,904
				Grand Total:	58	259,004

E = ex-group Endrass

JULY 1942:

Type IX (7):

BOAT	TYPE	SKIPPER	SAILED	RETURNED	SHIPS SUNK	TONS
U-510	C/40	Karl Neitzel*	7/7	9/13	2	10,256
U-162	C	Jürgen Wattenberg	7/7	Lost 9/3	4	30,481
U-155	C	Adolf-Cornelius Piening	7/9	9/15	10	43,892
U-108	B	Klaus Scholtz	7/13	9/10	3	17,495
U-511	C/40	Friedrich Steinhoff*	7/16	9/29	2	21,999
U-164	C	Otto Fechner*	7/18	10/7	2	5,525
U-163	C	Kurt-Eduard Engelmann*	7/21	9/16	Abort	None
				Totals:	23	129,648

Type VIIs (10):

BOAT	TYPE	SKIPPER	SAILED	RETURNED	SHIPS SUNK	TONS
U-658	C	Hans Senkel*	7/7	9/12	3	12,146
U-598	C	Gottfried Holtorf*	7/7	9/13	2	9,295 Abort

BOAT	TYPE	SKIPPER	SAILED	RETURNED	SHIPS SUNK	TONS
U-564	C	Reinhard Suhren	7/9	9/18	5	32,181
U-654	C	Ludwig Forster	7/9	Lost 8/22		None
U-217	D	Kurt Reichenbach-Klinke*	7/14	10/16	1	75
U-751	C	Gerhard Bigalk	7/14	Lost 7/17		None/M
U-600	C	Bernhard Zurmühlen*	7/14	9/12	3	9,682 Abort
U-98	C	Wilhelm Schulze	7/14	9/16		None/M
U-553	C	Karl Thurmann	7/19	9/17	3	19,440+
U-558	C	Günther Krech	7/29	9/17	5	26,421
				Totals:	22	109,240
				Grand Total:	45	238,888

AUGUST 1942:

Type IXs (8):

BOAT	TYPE	SKIPPER	SAILED	RETURNED	SHIPS SUNK	TONS
U-165	C	Eberhard Hoffmann*	8/7	Lost 9/27	3	8,754
U-513	C/40	Rolf Rüggeberg*	8/7	10/22	2	12,789
U-517	C/40	Paul Hartwig*	8/8	10/19	9	27,283 [17]
U-514	C/40	Hans-Jürgen Auffermann*	8/12	11/9	5	17,354
U-515	C/40	Werner Henke*	8/12	10/14	8	42,114
U-516	C/40	Gerhard Wiebe*	8/12	11/14	5	29,357
U-175	C	Heinrich Bruns*	8/15	10/27	9	33,426
U-512	C/40	Wolfgang Schultze*	8/15	Lost 10/2	3	20,619
				Totals:	44	191,696

Type VII (3):

BOAT	TYPE	SKIPPER	SAILED	RETURNED	SHIPS SUNK	TONS
U-94	C	Otto Ites	8/2	Lost 8/28		None
U-69	C	Ulrich Gräf	8/16	11/5	2	4,597 M
U-455	C	Hans-Heinrich Giessler	8/22	10/28		None/M
				Totals:	2	4,597
				Grand Total:	46	196,293

Note: See Plate 12 for a summary of successes and losses.

---

1. Not counting the 5,100-ton German blockade-runner Spreewald, sunk by error.
2. Including 1,100-ton Coast Guard tender Acacia.
3. Sank British sloop Culver, rescued survivors of Spreewald, and returned to France.
4. Free French corvette, Alysse.
5. Including ex-American four-stack British destroyer Belmont.
6. Delayed by a diversion to hunt for Spreewald survivors.
7. Including American destroyer Jacob Jones.
8. All from convoy Outbound North 67.
9. Not counting tankers Esso Baton Rouge and Oklahoma, sunk but raised and returned to service.
10. Damage included the 6,300-ton Dutch tanker Ocana, later sunk by British warships.
11. Plus damage to American destroyer Blakeley.
12. Landed agent near St. John's, Newfoundland, 5/16.
13. Includes 840-ton American seaplane tender Gannet.
14. Plus slight damage to American destroyer Bainbridge.
15. Landed four agents at Ponte Vedra, Florida, 6/17.
16. Landed four agents on Long Island, New York, 6/13.
17. Includes Canadian corvette Charlottetown.

APPENDIX 5

U-BOATS ASSIGNED TO THE ARCTIC AREA

JULY 1941 – AUGUST 1942

BOAT	TYPE	SKIPPER	ARRIVED	DEPARTED/LOST	
U-81	VIIC	Fritz Guggenberger	7/41	9/41	
U-451	VIIC	Eberhard Hoffmann	7/41	9/41	
U-571	VIIC	Helmut Möhlmann	7/41	9/41	
U-652	VIIC	Georg-Werner Fraatz	7/41	9/41	
U-566	VIIC	Dietrich Borchert	8/41	12/41	
U-752	VIIC	Karl-Ernst Schroeter	8/41	12/41	
U-132	VIIC	Ernst Vogelsang	9/41	12/41	
U-576	VIIC	Hans-Dieter Heinicke	10/41	12/41	
U-134	VIIC	Rudolf Schendel	11/41	5/42	
U-578	VIIC	Ernst-August Rehwinkel	11/41	12/41	
U-584	VIIC	Joachim Deecke	12/41	5/42	
U-454	VIIC	Burkhard Hackländer	12/41[1]	5/42	
U-585	VIIC	Bernhard Lohse	12/41	3/30/42	Lost
U-435	VIIC	Siegfried Strelow	1/42	[11/42]*	
U-456	VIIC	Max-Martin Teichert	1/42	[12/42]	
U-209	VIIC	Heinrich Brodda	2/42	[2/43]	
U-377	VIIC	Otto Köhler	2/42	[2/43]	
U-403	VIIC	Heinz-Ehlert Clausen	2/42	[12/42]	
U-405	VIIC	Rolf-Heinrich Hopmann	2/42	[12/42]	
U-436	VIIC	Günther Seibicke	2/42	[10/42]	
U-589	VIIC	Hans-Joachim Horrer	2/42	[9/14/42 Lost]	
U-592	VIIC	Karl Borm	2/42	[2/43]	
U-334	VIIC	Hilmar Siemon	3/42	[6/14/43 Lost]	
U-376	VIIC	Friedrich-Karl Marks	3/42	[2/43]	
U-378	VIIC	Alfred Hoschatt	3/42		
		Erich Mäder	10/42	[4/43]	
U-586	VIIC	Dietrich von der Esch	3/42[2]	[9/43]	
U-591	VIIC	Hans-Jürgen Zetzsche	3/42[3]	[12/42]	
U-655	VIIC	Adolf Dumrese	3/42	[3/24/42 Lost]	
U-657	VIIC	Heinrich Göllnitz	3/42	[5/43]	

* Dates in brackets denote U-boats departed or lost beyond the scope of this volume.

BOOT	TYPE	SKIPPER	ARRIVED	DEPARTED/LOST
U-702	VIIC	Wolf-Rüdiger von Rabenau	3/42	4/?/42 Lost
U-703	VIIC	Heinz Bielfeld	3/42	
		Joachim Brünner	5/43	[9/30/44 Lost]
U-251	VIIC	Heinrich Timm	4/42	[7/43]
U-88	VIIC	Heino Bohmann	5/42	[9/12/42 Lost]
U-408	VIIC	Reinhard von Hymmen	5/42	[11/5/42 Lost]
U-255	VIIC	Reinhart Reche	6/42	[11/43]
U-355	VIIC	Günter La Baume	6/42	[4/1/44 Lost]
U-457	VIIC	Karl Brandenburg	6/42	[9/16/42 Lost]
U-601	VIIC	Peter-Ottmar Grau	7/42	
		Otto Hansen	[11/43]	[2/25/44 Lost]

1. Sank British destroyer Matabele 1/17/42.
2. After one patrol in the Atlantic.
3. After one patrol in the Atlantic.

APPENDIX 6

U-BOATS TRANSFERRED TO THE MEDITERRANEAN SEA

SEPTEMBER 1941 – AUGUST 1942

BOAT	TYPE	SKIPPER	ARRIVED	LOST
U-371	VIIC	Heinrich Driver	9/21/41	
		Heinz-Joachim Neumann	4/21/42	
		Waldemar Mehl	5/24/42	
U-559	VIIC	Hans-Otto Heidtmann	9/26/41 [1]	
U-97	VIIC	Udo Heilmann	9/27/41	
		Friedrich Bürgel	5/16/42	
U-331	VIIC	Hans-Dietrich von Tiesenhausen	9/30/41 [2]	
U-75	VIIB	Helmuth Ringelmann	10/3/41	12/28/41
U-79	VIIC	Wolfgang Kaufmann	10/5/41	12/23/41
U-205	VIIC	Franz-Georg Reschke	11/11/41 [3]	
U-81	VIIC	Fritz Guggenberger	11/12/41 [4]	
U-433	VIIC	Hans Ey	11/16/41	11/16/41
U-565	VIIC	Johann Jebsen	11/16/41 [5]	
		Wilhelm Franken	3/18/42	
U-431	VIIC	Wilhelm Dommes	11/24/41	
U-557	VIIC	Ottokar Paulshen	11/26/41 [6]	12/16/41
U-562	VIIC	Horst Hamm	11/27/41	
U-95	VIIC	Gerd Schreiber	11/28/41	11/28/41
U-652	VIIC	Georg-Werner Fraatz	11/29/41 [7]	6/2/42
U-372	VIIC	Heinz-Joachim Neumann	12/8/41	8/4/42
U-375	VIIC	Jürgen Könenkamp	12/9/41	
U-453	VIIC	Egon-Reiner von Schlippenbach	12/9/41	
U-568	VIIC	Joachim Preuss	12/10/41 [8]	5/28/42
U-74	VIIB	Eitel-Friedrich Kentrat	12/15/41	
		Karl Friedrich	3/25/42	5/2/42
U-77	VIIC	Heinrich Schonder	12/16/41 [9]	
		Otto Hartmann	8/30/42	
U-83	VIIB	Hans-Werner Kraus	12/18/41	
U-573	VIIC	Heinrich Heinsohn	12/18/41	4/29/42 Int.[10]
U-133	VIIC	Hermann Hesse	12/21/41 [11]	
		Eberhard Mohr	2/??/42	3/14/42
U-577	VIIC	Herbert Schauenburg	12/23/41	1/9/42
U-374	VIIC	Unno von Fischel	12/30/41	1/12/42
U-73	VIIB	Helmut Rosenbaum	1/14/42 [12]	
U-561	VIIC	Robert Bartels	1/15/42	

SUMMARY TO 9/1/42

Boats into the Mediterranean: 28
Boats lost: 13 (46 percent)
Net force: 15

Manpower loss: 585 [13]
Captured: 167

---

1. Sank Australian sloop Parramatta 11/27/41.
2. Sank British battleship Barham 11/25/41.
3. Sank British light cruiser Hermione 6/16/42.
4. Sank British aircraft carrier Ark Royal 11/13/41.
5. Sank British light cruiser Naiad 3/11/42.
6. Sank British light cruiser Galatea 12/14/41.
7. Sank British Hunt-class destroyer Heythrop 3/20/42 and British destroyer Jaguar 3/26/42.
8. Sank British corvette Salvia 12/24/41.
9. Sank British Hunt-class destroyer Grove 6/12/42.
10. Interned in Spain.
11. Sank British destroyer Gurkha II 1/17/42.
12. Sank British carrier Eagle 8/11/42.
13. 12 boats times 45 crew members. The manpower loss shown here is also included in Appendix 1. The crew of U-573, which beached in Spain, was interned and then repatriated.

APPENDIX 7

SINKINGS BY TYPE II U-BOATS (DUCKS)

SEPTEMBER 1939 – NOVEMBER 1941

BOAT	TYPE	SKIPPER	SHIPS	TONNAGE
U-3	IIA	Joachim Schepke	2	2,348
U-4	IIA	Harro von Klot-Heydenfeldt	3	5,133
		Hans Peter Hinsch	1	1,090 [1]
U-7	IIB	Werner Heidel	3	5,892
U-9	IIB	Wolfgang Lüth	8	17,221 [2]
U-10	IIB	Joachim Preuss	2	6,356
U-13	IIB	Karl Daublebsky von Eichhain	3	15,967
		Heinz Scheringer	1	1,421
		Max Schulte	3	8,594
U-14	IIB	Herbert Wohlfarth	9	12,362
U-15	IIB	Heinz Buchholz	2	4,274
		Peter Frahm	1	358
U-16	IIB	Hannes Weingärtner	1	3,378
		Horst Wellner	1	57
U-17	IIB	Udo Behrens	2	1,615
U-18	IIB	Max-Hermann Bauer	1	345
		Ernst Mengersen	1	1,000
U-19	IIB	Hans Meckel	3	12,344
		Wilhelm Müller-Warnecke	1	6,371
		Joachim Schepke	9	15,715
U-20	IIB	Carl-Heinz Moehle	4	10,792
		Harro von Klot-Heydenfeldt	6	16,399+ [3]
U-21	IIB	Fritz Frauenheim	5	6,974
		Wolf Stiebler	2	4,900
U-22	IIB	Karl-Heinrich Jenisch	7	8,422 [4]
U-23	IIB	Otto Kretschmer	6.5	19,896 [5]
U-24	IIB	Harald Jeppener-Haltenhoff	1	961
U-56	IIC	Wilhelm Zahn	2	3,452
		Otto Harms	2	22,331 [6]
U-57	IIC	Claus Korth	8.5	41,383 [7]
		Erich Topp	6	36,861
U-58	IIC	Herbert Kuppisch	4	13,642
		Heinrich Schonder	4	16,315
U-59	IIC	Harald Jürst	13	12,137
		Joachim Matz	5	19,534
U-60	IIC	Georg Schewe	1	4,373
		Adalbert Schnee	2	3,188
U-61	IIC	Jürgen Oesten	6	20,754
U-62	IIC	Hans-Bernard Michalowski	3	6,142 [8]
U-63	IIC	Günther Lorentz	1	3,840

BOAT	TYPE	SKIPPER	SHIPS	TONNAGE
U-137	IID	Herbert Wohlfarth	7	25,444
U-138	IID	Wolfgang Lüth	5	39,971
		Franz Gramitzky	1	8,593
U-140	IID	Hans-Peter Hinsch	3	13,207
		Hans-Jürgen Hellriegel	1	206
U-141	IID	Philipp Schüler	2	6,383
U-143	IID	Harald Gelhaus	1	1,418
U-144	IID	Gert von Mittelstaedt	1	161
U-146	IID	Otto Ites	1	3,496
U-147	IID	Reinhard Hardegen	1	4,811
		Eberhard Wetjen	2	3,753
U-149	IID	Horst Höltring	1	206
		Totals:	172	501,787

1. British submarine Thistle.
2. Includes French submarine Doris.
3. Damaged the British heavy cruiser Belfast.
4. Includes British destroyer Exmouth.
5. Includes British destroyer Daring; shared credit for 5,000-ton Loch Maddy.
6. Includes 17,000-ton British auxiliary cruiser Transylvania.
7. Shared credit for Loch Maddy.
8. Includes British destroyer Grafton.

APPENDIX 8

ITALIAN SUBMARINES BASED IN THE ATLANTIC[1]

(Angelo Parona, Commanding)

NAME	ARR. BORDEAUX	SANK/TONS		FATE
Malaspina	9/4/40	3	16,384	Lost 11/41
Barbarigo	9/8/40	7	39,300	Lost 6/43–8/43
Dandolo	9/10/40	2	6,554	To Italy 7/41
Marconi	9/28/40	7	18,887	Lost 10/41–12/41
Finzi	9/29/40	5	30,760	Seized 9/43[2]
Bagnolini	9/30/40	2	6,962	Seized 9/43
Emo	10/3/40	2	10,958	To Italy 9/41
Tarantini	10/5/40		None	Lost 12/15/40
Torelli	10/5/40	7	42,871	Seized 9/43
Faa'di Bruno	10/5/40		None	Lost 10/40–1/41
Otaria	10/6/40	1	4,662	To Italy 9/41
Baracca	10/6/40	3	8,989	Lost 9/8/41
Giuliani	10/6/40	3	16,103	Seized 9/43
Glauco	10/22/40		None	Lost 6/27/41
Calvi	10/23/40	6	34,193	Lost 7/15/42
Tazzoli	10/24/40	18	96,650[3]	Lost 5/43-8/43
Argo	10/24/40	1	5,066	To Italy 10/41
Da Vinci	10/31/40	13	90,415[4]	Lost 5/23/43
Veniero	11/2/40	2	4,987	To Italy 8/41
Nani	11/4/40	2	1,939	Lost 1/41–2/41
Cappellini	11/5/40	5	31,648	Seized 9/43
Morosini	11/28/40	6	40,927	Lost 8/42–9/42
Marcello	12/2/40	1	1,550	Lost 2/41–4/41
Bianchi	12/18/40	3	14,705	Lost 7/5/41
Brin	12/18/40	2	7,241	To Italy 9/41
Velella	12/25/40		None	To Italy 8/41
Mocenigo	12/26/40	1	1,253	To Italy 8/41
Guglielmotti	5/6/41		None	To Italy 10/41
Archimede	5/7/41	2	25,629[5]	Lost 5/15/43
Ferraris	5/9/41		None	Lost 10/25/41
Perla	5/20/41		None	To Italy 10/41
Cagni	2/20/43	2	5,840	Surrendered 9/43[6]
Totals:		106	564,473	

Total submarines deployed: 32

Total submarines lost: 16 (50%)

Returned to Mediterranean: 10

Seized, surrendered: 6

---

1. Sources: Alberto Santoni in Howarth and Law; Röhwer, *Axis Submarine Successes.*
2. "Seized" = by Germans or Japanese.
3. The second most successful Italian submarine in Allied tonnage sunk. Sixteen confirmed ships for 86,535 tons were sunk by Carlo Fecia di Cossato, who won a German *Ritterkreuz.*
4. Counting four ships for 29,828 tons sunk in the Mediterranean in April 1943, Tazzoli, with a total bag of 17 confirmed ships for 120,243 tons, was the most successful of the Italian submarines and, indeed, the most successful non-German submarine of World War II in tonnage sunk. Ten of the 17 ships for 108,656 tons were sunk by Gianfranco Gazzana Priaroggia, who also won a German *Ritterkreuz.* His successes included the 21,500-ton liner Empress of Canada.
5. Including 20,000-ton liner Oronsay.
6. To Allied force at Durban.

APPENDIX 9

THE BRITISH DESTROYER SITUATION

1939 – 1941

The British built hundreds of destroyers in World War I, but most of them were unfit or gone by the mid-1920s. In 1927, the Admiralty commenced a "modern" destroyer-building program. For that year and through 1935, the Admiralty ordered nine destroyers a year except in 1929 (the year of the economic crash), when it ordered only five. These ships were 312 feet in length and displaced about 1,400 tons. Except as noted in parentheses, the names of the ships began with the letter assigned to the annual order (e.g., Acasta in the "A" order of 1927).

YEAR	CLASS	NUMBER	LAUNCHED	
1927	A	9	1929	(Codrington)
1928	B	9	1930	(Keith)
1929	C	5 [1]	1931	(Kempenfelt)
1930	D	9	1932	
1931	E	9	1933	
1932	F	9	1934	
1933	G	9	1935	
1934	H	9	1936	
1935	I	9	1937	

In the mid-1930s when Germany, Italy, and Japan laid down larger, heavier-gunned fleet destroyers, the Admiralty followed suit with the Tribal class (Afridi, Cossack, etc.). These ships, mounting eight 4.7" guns in four turrets, were 355 feet in length and displaced about 1,900 tons. The Admiralty ordered sixteen of this type for delivery by 1937.

Meanwhile, the annual destroyer orders continued. The Admiralty reduced the number of ships purchased from nine to eight, but they were larger than their predecessors: 339 feet in length, displacing about 1,700 tons. These were the last "modern" destroyers to enter service before the war.

1936	J	8	1938	
1937	K	8	1939 [2]	

As can be seen from the foregoing lists, by the time World War II commenced, the Admiralty had built a grand total of 109 "modern" destroyers. However, the British transferred the five ships of the 1929 class to the embryonic Canadian Navy in 1937–39,[3] leaving the Royal Navy a force of 104 "modern" destroyers. The Admiralty converted thirteen of these (9 Es, 4 Is) to fast minelayers, leaving 91 for regular service.

Upon the outbreak of war, two further annual orders were under construction, as well as eight vessels intended originally for Brazil and Turkey that were retained, six with the H class and two with the I class.

ex-Brazil	H (add)	6	1940	
ex-Turkey	I (add)	2	1942	
1938	L	8	1940–1941	(Gurkha II)
1939	M	8	1941–1942	(Orkan)

In addition to the fleet of "modern" destroyers, the Royal Navy had in commission about sixty smaller World War I–vintage destroyers. Thus, when World War II began, the Royal Navy had a total destroyer force of about 165 vessels.[4]

When Winston Churchill assumed the post of First Lord of the Admiralty in September 1939, he was immensely displeased with the destroyer situation in the Royal Navy. He declared that British destroyers had become too big, too complex, and too expensive, and took too long to build. For urgently needed convoy escort, he insisted that the Admiralty order, in addition to the regular fleet destroyers, fifty smaller, less complex destroyers that could be built in one-third the time of the regular ones. His insistence resulted in a crash program to build the Hunt-class "escort destroyer," a ship 264 feet in length with a displacement of about 1,000 tons, armed with four (later six) 4" guns in twin mountings.

Remarkably, British shipyards launched twenty-eight Hunts by the end of December 1940. Had the U-boat war been confined more or less to the home waters of the British Isles and to the Mediterranean (as in World War I), these little ships might well have made a big difference as convoy escorts. However, by the time the Hunts entered service in 1941, the main arena of the U-boat war had spread to the wider reaches of the Atlantic, beyond the useful range of these short-legged vessels. Besides that (and severe teething problems) the Hunts were not suitable for operations in the extremely rough waters of the North Atlantic. Altogether in the war, the Admiralty built eighty-six Hunts, which were useful mainly in the Mediterranean.

As the war progressed the Admiralty mass-produced 120 more fleet destroyers, more or less standardized at a length of 339 feet. In addition, it built sixteen Battle-class destroyers that, like the Tribal class, were big, complex vessels, 355 feet in length.

British destroyer losses in the period from, 1939 to the end of 1941 were heavy: a total of fifty-six vessels. Forty-six of these were "modern." The cause of loss other than enemy air attack is noted in parentheses.

NAME	DATE LOST	TONS	DATE COMM.	AREA
1939 (3) (ALL MODERN)				
Blanche	11/13/39	1,400	1931	R.Thames (Mine)
Gipsy	11/21/39	1,300	1936	Harwich (Mine)
Duchess	12/12/39	1,400	1933	Scotland (Accident)
1940 (34) (26 MODERN)				
Greenville	1/19/40	1,500	1936	North Sea (Mine)
Exmouth	1/21/40	1,500	1934	North Sea (U-22)
Daring	2/18/40	1,400	1932	North Sea (U-23)
Glowworm	4/8/40	1,400	1936	Norway
Gurkha I (T for Tribal)	4/9/40	1,900	1938	Norway
Hunter	4/10/40	1,400	1936	Norway
Hardy	4/10/40	1,500	1936	Norway
Afridi (T)	5/3/40	1,900	1938	Norway
Valentine	5/15/40	1,000	1917	R. Scheldt
Whitley	5/19/40	1,100	1918	Ostend[5]
Wessex	5/24/40	1,100	1918	Calais
Grafton	5/29/40	1,300	1936	Dunkirk (U-62)
Grenade	5/29/40	1,300	1936	Dunkirk
Wakeful	5/29/40	1,100	1917	Dunkirk
Basilisk	June	1,400	1931	Dunkirk
Keith	June	1,400	1931	Dunkirk
Havant	June	1,400	1939	Dunkirk
Acasta	June	1,400	1930	Norway
Ardent	June	1,400	1930	Norway[6]
Khartoum	6/23/40	1,700	1939	Yemen (Accident)
Whirlwind	7/5/40	1,100	1918	N. Atlantic (U-34)
Escort (Minelayer)	7/11/40	1,400	1934	Med. (Marconi)
Imogen	7/16/40	1,400	1937	N. Atlantic (Accident)
Brazen	7/20/40	1,400	1931	Dover
Codrington	7/27/40	1,600	1930	Dover

NAME	DATE LOST	TONS	DATE COMM.	AREA
Wren	7/27/40	1,100	1923	Aldeburgh
Delight	7/29/40	1,400	1933	Portland
Hostile	8/23/40	1,400	1933	Med. (Mine)
Esk (Minelayer)	9/1/40	1,400	1934	North Sea (Mine)
Ivanhoe (Minelayer)	9/1/40	1,400	1937	North Sea (Mine)
Venetia	10/19/40	1,100	1917	R. Thames (Mine)
Sturdy	10/30/40	900	1919	Scotland (Accident)
Acheron	12/22/40	1,400	1931	Isle of Wight (Mine)
Hyperion	12/22/40	1,400	1936	Med. (Mine)
1941 (22) (17 MODERN)				
Gallant	1/20/41	1,400	1936	Med. (Mine)
Dainty	2/24/41	1,400	1932	Med.
Exmoor (Hunt Class)	2/25/41	1,000	1940	Lowestoft
Mohawk (T)	4/16/41	1,900	1938	Med.[Tunisia]
Diamond	4/27/41	1,400	1932	Med.[Greece]
Wryneck	4/27/41	1,100	1918	Med.[Greece]
Jersey	5/2/41	1,800	1939	Med.[Malta] (Mine)
Juno	5/21/41	1,800	1939	Med.[Crete]
Greyhound	5/22/41	1,400	1936	Med.[Crete]
Kashmir	5/22/41	1,800	1939	Med.[Crete]
Kelly	5/23/41	1,800	1939	Med.[Crete]
Mashona (T)	5/28/41	1,900	1939	N. Atlantic
Hereward	5/29/41	1,400	1936	Med.[Crete]
Imperial	5/29/41	1,400	1937	Med.[Crete][7]
Waterhen	6/29/41	1,100	1918	Med.[Egypt]
Defender	7/11/41	1,400	1932	Med.[Egypt]
Fearless	7/23/41	1,400	1934	Med. Convoy
Bath (ex-U.S.N.)	8/19/41	1,000	1919	N. Atlantic (U-204)
Broadwater (ex-U.S.N.)	10/18/41	1,200	1920	N. Atlantic (U-101)
Cossack (T)	10/27/41	1,900	1938	N. Atlantic (U-563)
Kandahar	12/19/41	1,800	1939	Med. [Libya] (M)
Stanley (ex-U.S.N.)	12/19/41	1,200	1919	N. Atlantic (U-574)

Owing to these losses and to the unsuitability of the Hunts for operations in the North Atlantic, in the summer of 1940 Prime Minister Churchill requested that President Roosevelt "lend" the British fifty (or more, if possible) destroyers for convoy escort. This resulted in the famous 1940 "Destroyer Deal" in which the United States transferred to the British and Canadian navies fifty 314-foot, 1,200-ton World War I—vintage "four stack" destroyers. The British renamed these ships after towns common to the United States and Britain, hence they became Town-class vessels. In a second, less well known loan in early 1941, Roosevelt transferred to Britain ten relatively modern (1928–1932) 250-foot, 1,700-ton very-long-range Coast Guard cutters, which the British classified as sloops. The loans in more detail:

AMERICAN NAME	BRITISH NAME	TRANSFERRED	OPERATIONAL
U.S. Navy Destroyers (50):			
Aaron Ward	Castleton	9/9/40	10/9/40
Abbot	Charleston	9/23/40	1/6/41
A. P. Upshur	Clare	9/9/40	10/14/41
Aulick	Burnham	10/8/40	11/12/40
Bailey	Reading	11/26/40	3/8/41
Bancroft	St. Francis	9/24/40	Canada
Branch	Beverley	10/8/40	11/19/40
Buchanan	Campbeltown	9/9/40	11/24/40
Claxton	Salisbury	12/5/40	3/3/41
Conner	Leeds	9/23/40	3/2/41

AMERICAN NAME	BRITISH NAME	TRANSFERRED	OPERATIONAL
Conway (ex-Craven)	Lewes	9/9/40	2/1/42
Cowell	Brighton	9/23/40	1/17/41*
Crowinshield	Chelsea	9/9/40	10/12/40*
Doran (ex-Bagley)	St. Marys	9/23/40	11/1/40
Edwards	Buxton	10/8/40	3/3/41
Evans	Mansfield	10/23/40	Norwegian manned
Fairfax	Richmond	11/26/40	3/16/41*
Foote	Roxborough	9/23/40	3/18/41*
Hale	Caldwell	9/9/40	10/23/40
Haraden	Columbia	9/9/40	Canada
Herndon	Churchill	9/9/40	1/14/41*
Hopewell	Bath	9/23/40	Norwegian manned
Hunt	Broadway	10/8/40	11/19/40
Kalk	Hamilton	9/9/40	Canada
Laub	Burwell	10/8/40	2/24/41
Maddox	Georgetown	9/23/40	12/17/40*
Mason	Broadwater	9/9/40	1/31/41
MacKenzie	Annapolis	9/29/40	Canada
McCalla	Stanley	9/9/40	9/1/41
McCook	St. Croix	9/24/40	Canada
McLanahan	Bradford	10/8/40	10/1/41
Meade	Ramsey	11/26/40	1/29/41
Philip	Lancaster	10/23/40	1/11/41
Ringgold	Newark	11/26/40	8/15/41
Robinson	Newmarket	11/26/40	4/24/41
Rodgers	Sherwood	10/23/40	4/8/41
Satterlee	Belmont	10/8/40	8/20/41
Sigourney	Newport	11/26/40	9/24/41
Shubrick	Ripley	11/26/40	3/3/41
Stockton	Ludlow	10/23/40	3/1/41
Swansey	Rockingham	11/26/40	2/22/41
Thatcher	Niagara	9/26/40	Canada
Thomas	St. Albans	9/23/40	11/1/40*
Tillman	Wells	12/5/40	410/41
Twiggs	Leamington	10/23/40	1/5/41*
W. C. Wood	Chesterfield	9/9/40	2/27/41
Welles	Cameron	9/9/40	Never
Wickes	Montgomery	10/25/40	1/12/41
Williams	St. Clair	9/24/40	Canada
Yarnall	Lincoln	10/23/40	Norwegian manned*

U.S. Coast Guard Cutters (10):

Cayuga	Totland	5/12/41	Same
Champlain	Sennen	5/12/41	Same
Chelan	Lulworth	5/2/41	Same
Itasca	Gorleston	5/30/41	Same
Mendota	Culver	4/30/41	Same
Pontchartrain	Hartland	4/30/41	Same
Saranac	Banff	4/30/41	Same
Sebago	Walney	5/12/41	Same
Shoshone	Languard	5/20/41	Same
Tahoe	Fishguard	4/30/41	Same

* = Transferred from the UK to the USSR in 1944.

1. Two other, similar vessels were built by Thornycroft for the Royal Canadian Navy: Saguenay and Skeena, both commissioned in 1931.
2. Two of these, Khartoum and Kipling, were completed shortly after the outbreak of war in November 1939 and January 1940, respectively.
3. These became St. Laurent, Fraser, Ottawa I, Restigouche and Assiniboine.
4. Another fifteen destroyers in the Royal Navy of the World War I V and W class had been converted to be convoy "escort destroyers."
5. Whitley and Wessex were sunk while attempting to reinforce or rescue elements of the British Expeditionary Force (B.E.F.). Counting them, the British lost eight destroyers in the evacuation of the B.E.F.; the French lost three. Nineteen other British destroyers were damaged in those operations. On June 5, an American naval attaché in London estimated that out of ninety-four destroyers in British home waters, only forty-three were combat-ready.
6. Eight other British destroyers were "seriously damaged" during operations in Norway.
7. Seven other British destroyers were badly damaged during the evacuation of Crete.

APPENDIX 10

THE CANADIAN DESTROYER SITUATION

1939 – 1945

When World War II commenced, the embryonic Royal Canadian Navy had six fairly modern (1931–1939) British-built destroyers in commission, as noted below. Soon after the declaration of war, the Admiralty transferred to the Canadian Navy another British-built destroyer (Assiniboine). A year later, as part of the famous Anglo-American "Destroyer Deal," Canada acquired seven ex-American four-stack destroyers. At about the same time, the Admiralty transferred another destroyer, Margaree, to the Canadian Navy, in effect replacing the prewar Canadian destroyer Fraser, which was rammed and sunk accidentally by the British anti-aircraft cruiser Calcutta. Ironically, a British merchant ship, Port Fairy, rammed and sank Margaree on her first war mission under Canadian command. In subsequent war years, the Admiralty transferred eleven other destroyers to Canada, making a total of twenty-seven destroyers to be commissioned in the Canadian Navy during the war, plus the ex-American four-stack Buxton, a static training ship. Four British-designed Tribal-class destroyers built in Canada were not completed before the end of the war. The Canadian destroyers:

NAME	COMMISSIONED	SOURCE
Algonquin	12/22/43	UK (ex-Valentine)
Annapolis	3/29/41	USA (ex-MacKenzie)
Assiniboine	9/10/39	UK (ex-Kempenfelt)
Athabaskan	2/2/43	UK Tribal-class
Chaudiere	10/16/43	UK (ex-Hero)
Columbia	9/20/40	USA (ex-Haraden)
Fraser	2/17/37	UK (ex-Crescent)
Gatineau	11/23/43	UK (ex-Express)
Haida	8/30/43	UK Tribal-class
Hamilton	6/25/41	USA (ex-Kalk)
Huron	7/19/43	UK Tribal
Iroquois	10/1/42	UK Tribal
Kootenay	4/12/43	UK (ex-Decoy)
Margaree	9/6/40	UK (ex-Diana)
Niagara	9/24/40	USA (ex-Thatcher)
Ottawa I	6/15/38	UK (ex-Crusader)
Ottawa II	3/20/43	UK (ex-Griffin)
Qu'appelle	2/8/44	UK (cx-Foxhound)
Restigouche	6/15/38	UK (ex-Comet)
Saguenay	5/22/31	UK Direct purchase
Saskatchewan	5/31/43	UK (ex-Fortune)
St. Clair	9/24/40	USA (ex-Williams)
St. Croix	9/25/40	USA (ex-McCook)
St. Francis	9/24/40	USA (ex-Bancroft)
St. Laurent	2/17/37	UK (ex-Cygnet)
Sioux	2/21/44	UK (ex-Vixen)
Skeena	6/9/31	UK Direct purchase

APPENDIX 11

EXCHANGE OF OCEAN-ESCORT VESSELS OTHER THAN DESTROYERS BETWEEN THE
ROYAL NAVY AND THE ROYAL CANADIAN NAVY

1942 – 1944

FROM THE ROYAL NAVY TO THE ROYAL CANADIAN NAVY:

Modified Flower-Class Corvettes (4)

SHIP	COMMISSIONED IN RCN
Forest Hill	12/1/43
Giffard	11/10/43
Longbranch	1/5/44
Mimico	2/8/44

Castle-Class Corvettes (12)

Arnprior	6/8/44
Bowmanville	9/28/44
Copper Cliff	7/25/44
Hespeler	2/28/44
Humberstone	9/6/44
Huntsville	6/6/44
Kincardine	9/16/44
Leaside	8/21/44
Orangeville	4/24/44
Petrolia	6/29/44
St. Thomas	5/4/44
Tillsonburg	6/29/44

River- and Loch-Class Frigates (10)

Annan	6/13/44
Ettrick	1/29/44
Loch Achanalt	7/31/44
Loch Alvie	8/10/44
Loch Morlich	7/17/44
Meon	2/7/44
Monnow	3/8/44
Nene	4/6/44
Ribble	7/24/44
Teme	2/28/44

APPENDIX 11

FROM THE ROYAL CANADIAN NAVY TO THE ROYAL NAVY[1]:

Modified Flower-Class Corvettes (7)

SHIP	EX-U.S.N.	LAUNCHED
Dittany	Beacon	10/13/42
Honesty	Caprice	9/28/42
Linaria	Clash	11/18/42
Rosebay	Splendor	2/11/43
Smilax	Tact	12/24/42
Statice	Vim	4/10/43
Willowherb	Vitality	3/24/43

River-Class Frigates (8)

Barle	PG 103	9/26/42
Cuckmere	PG 104	10/24/42
Evenlode	PG 105	8/22/42
Findhorn	PG 106	12/5/42
Inver	PG 107	12/5/42
Lossie	PG 108	4/30/43
Parret	PG 109	4/30/43
Shiel	PG 110	5/26/43

---

1. All vessels were originally intended for the U.S.N.

APPENDIX 12

THE AMERICAN DESTROYER SITUATION

JANUARY 1942 – SEPTEMBER 1942

Before, during, and just after World War I, the American Navy commissioned about 300 new four-stack destroyers. Many of these were scrapped or laid up in order to comply with ship limitations in various naval treaties in the 1920s and 1930s. Commencing in 1934 with Farragut (DD 348), the Navy began commissioning a fleet of modern destroyers that by 12/31/41 numbered about 100 vessels.

After the United States entered the war on December 8, 1941, the British formed the impression that Admiral King stripped the Atlantic Fleet of most destroyers capable of antisubmarine warfare or convoy escort in the first nine months of 1942 to fight the Japanese in the Pacific. This impression has gradually assumed the status of "fact," but it is not true.[1]

When the Japanese struck Pearl Harbor, there were ninety-two commissioned American destroyers in the Atlantic theater. In the nine months to September 1, 1942, nineteen of these (21 percent) were sent to the Pacific, along with nine capital ships: carriers Hornet, Wasp, and Yorktown; battleships Idaho, Mississippi, New Mexico, North Carolina, South Dakota, and Washington.

In the same nine months, the Navy commissioned a total of forty-six new destroyers, forty on the East Coast and six on the West Coast. Fourteen of those commissioned on the East Coast and all (six) commissioned on the West Coast were sent to the Pacific theater, a total of twenty. The other twenty-six were sent to the Atlantic Fleet, raising the number of destroyers assigned to the Atlantic theater in this period to ninety-nine, but four destroyers were lost (Ingraham, Jacob Jones, Sturtevant, Truxton), leaving a net force of ninety-five destroyers in the Atlantic theater on September 1, 1942. That was three more than the count on December 7, 1941, virtually no change.

When the Japanese struck Pearl Harbor, there were eighty-five commissioned American destroyers in the Pacific and Far East: fifty assigned to the Pacific Fleet, thirteen to the Asiatic Fleet, and twenty-two to the 11th, 12th, 13th, 14th, and 15th Naval Districts. In the nine months to September 1, 1942, thirty-nine destroyers were added, raising the total number assigned to the Pacific in this period to 124, but ten were lost, leaving a net force of 114 destroyers on September 1, 1942, in the Pacific theater, compared to ninety-five in the Atlantic theater.

From this data it is clear that Admiral King did not strip the Atlantic Fleet of most destroyers capable of antisubmarine warfare or convoy escort in the first nine months of 1942. The size of the Atlantic Fleet destroyer force remained fairly constant. Details:

Destroyers in the Atlantic on 12/7/41 (92)[2]

SHIP	HULL #	COMM.	TRANSFERS	COMMENT
Anderson	411	1939	Pacific 1/42	with Mississippi/New Mexico
Babbitt	128	1919		
Badger	126	1919		
Bainbridge	246	1921		
Barney	149	1919		
Barry	248	1920		
Benson	421	1940		
Bernadou	153	1918		
Biddle	151	1919		
Blakeley	150	1919		Torpedo damage 5/25/42
Borie	215	1920		
Breckinridge	148	1919		
Bristol	450	1941		
Broome	210	1919		
Buck	420	1940		Collision damage 8/22/42
Charles F. Hughes	428	1940		
Cole	155	1919		
Dahlgren	187	1920		
Dallas	199	1919		
Davis	395	1938		
Decatur	341	1922		
Dickerson	157	1919		
Du Pont	152	1918		
Eberle	430	1940		
Edison	439	1941		
Ellis	154	1919		
Ellyson	454	1941		Collision damage 5/17/42
Emmons	457	1941		
Ericsson	440	1941		
Gleaves	423	1940		
Goff	247	1921		
Grayson	435	1941	Pacific 3/42	with Hornet
Greer	145	1918		
Gwin	433	1941	Pacific 3/42	with Hornet
Hammann	412	1939	Pacific 1/42	with Mississippi/New Mexico
Herbert	160	1919		
Hilary P. Jones	427	1940		
Hughes	410	1939	Pacific 12/41	with Yorktown
Ingraham	444	1941		Lost 8/22/42 (collision)
J. Fred Talbot	156	1919		
Jacob Jones	130	1919		Lost 2/28/42 (U-boat)
Jouett	396	1939		
Kearny	432	1940		
Lang	339	1939	Pacific 6/42	with Wasp/North Carolina
Lansdale	426	1940		
Lea	118	1918		
Leary	158	1919		
Livermore	429	1940		
Ludlow	438	1941		
MacLeish	220	1920		
Madison	425	1940		
Mayo	422	1940		
Mayrant	402	1939		
McCormick	223	1920		
McDougal	358	1936		

Meredith	434	1941	Pacific 3/42	with Hornet
Moffett	362	1936		
Monssen	436	1941	Pacific 3/42	with Hornet
Morris	417	1940	Pacific 1/42	with Mississippi/New Mexico
Mustin	413	1939	Pacific 1/42	with Idaho
Niblack	424	1940		
Nicholson	442	1941		
Noa	343	1921		
O'Brien	415	1940	Pacific 1/42	with Idaho
Overton	239	1920		
Plunkett	431	1940		
Rhind	404	1939		
Roe	418	1940		
Roper	147	1919		
Rowan	405	1935		
Russell	414	1939	Pacific 12/41	with Yorktown
Sampson	394	1938	Pacific 1/42	with Warrington[3]
Schenck	159	1919		
Simpson	221	1920		
Sims	409	1939	Pacific 12/41	with Yorktown
Somers	381	1937		
Stack	406	1939	Pacific 6/42	with Wasp/North Carolina
Sterett	407	1939	Pacific 6/42	with Wasp/North Carolina
Sturtevant	240	1920		Lost 4/26 (American mine)
Swanson	443	1941		
Tarbell	142	1918		
Tattinall	125	1919		
Trippe	403	1939		
Truxtun	229	1921		Lost 2/18 (storm)
Upshur	144	1918		
Wainwright	419	1940		
Walke	416	1940	Pacific 12/41	with Yorktown
Warrington	383	1938	Pacific 1/42	with Sampson
Wilkes	441	1941		Damage 2/18 (storm)
Wilson	408	1939	Pacific 6/42	with Wasp/North Carolina
Winslow	359	1937		
Woolsey	437	1941		

Transferred to the Pacific:	19
Lost (various causes):	4
Net decrease to 9/1/42:	23

New Destroyers Commissioned (46)

12/7/41 – 9/1/42

SHIP	HULL #	COMM.	TRANSFERS	COMMENTS
Corry	463	12/41		
Hambleton	455	12/41		Collision damage 5/17
Rodman	456	1/42		
Macomb	458	1/42		
Forrest	461	1/42		
Fitch	462	2/42		
Hobson	464	2/42		
Laffey	459	3/42	Pacific built	
Aaron Ward	483	3/42	Pacific 5/42	

Buchanan	484	3/42	Pacific 6/42	with Wasp/North Carolina
Woodworth	460	4/42	Pacific built	
Duncan	485	4/42	Pacific 8/42	with South Dakota
Lansdowne	486	4/42	Pacific 8/42	with South Dakota
Farenholt	491	4/42	Pacific 6/42	with Wasp/North Carolina
Bancroft	598	4/42	Pacific 8/42	
Lardner	487	5/42	Pacific 8/42	with South Dakota
McCalla	488	5/42	Pacific 8/42	
Bailey	492	5/42	Pacific 8/42	
Barton	599	5/42	Pacific 8/42	with Washington
Beatty	640	5/42		
Fletcher	445	6/42	Pacific 9/42	
Nicholas	449	6/42	Pacific 8/42	with Washington
O'Bannon	450	6/42	Pacific 9/42	
Mervine	489	6/42		
Meade	602	6/42	Pacific 8/42	with Washington
Caldwell	605	6/42	Pacific built	
Cowie	632	6/42		
Knight	633	6/42		
Tillmann	641	6/42		
Radford	446	7/42	Pacific 12/5/42	
Jenkins	447	7/42		
Chevalier	451	7/42	Pacific 1/43	
Quick	490	7/42		
Murphy	603	7/42		
Coghlan	606	7/42	Pacific built	
Frazier	607	7/42	Pacific built	
LaVallette	448	8/42	Pacific 12/42	
Saufley	465	8/42	Pacific 9/9/42	
Strong	467	8/42	Pacific 12/27/42	
Taylor	468	8/42	Pacific 12/17/42	
Boyle	600	8/42		
Parker	604	8/42		
Gansevoort	608	8/42	Pacific built	
Doran	634	8/42		
Butler	636	8/42		
Champlin	601	9/42		

Atlantic built and by 9/1/42 transferred to the Pacific:	14
Pacific built and remained:	6
Total:	20
Atlantic built and remained through 9/1/42:	26

---

1. See, for example, this statement by the Canadian historian W.D.G. Lund in Boutilier (p. 144): "When the United States entered the war, all of the American destroyers were withdrawn immediately for service in other theatres, and by February 1942, there were only two United States Coast Guard cutters available for duty as convoy escorts." Evidently based on an erroneous statement in the *Administrative History of the U.S. Atlantic Fleet* (No. 138, Vol. 1, p. 261), the American historian Michael Gannon, in his *Operation Drumbeat* (p. 177), wrote that "two squadrons of the newest, long-legged destroyers had been removed to the Pacific Theater in late December." Since a full-strength destroyer squadron numbered twelve vessels, the inference is that twenty-four destroyers were transferred from the Atlantic to the Pacific in December 1941, whereas the correct figure was four vessels.

2. This list does not include 33 old destroyers that had been converted to fast transports (APD), destroyer minesweepers (DMS), destroyer minelayers (DM), and to miscellaneous auxiliaries (AG). On 12/7/41, there were six APDs in the Atlantic Fleet (Colhoun, Gregory, Little, Manley, McKean, Stringham), all of which were sent to the Pacific by 9/1/42. There were five DMSs in the Atlantic Fleet (Hamilton, Hogan, Howard, Palmer, Stansbury), which remained in the Atlantic Fleet at least through the invasion of North Africa (Torch). There was one AG (Semmes) in the Atlantic force. In addition, there were 13 destroyer-minesweepers and eight destroyer-minelayers in the Pacific on 12/7/41. Although none of these vessels was suitable for antisubmarine warfare, it is possible that some historians have mistakenly counted them as such.

3. Delayed with Warrington to escort H.M.S. Duke of York back to UK, but that mission was canceled.

APPENDIX 13

AMERICAN DESTROYER ESCORT- AND FRIGATE-BUILDING PROGRAMS

The United States Maritime Commission built 671 large oceangoing vessels intended as convoy escorts in World War II. These were designated "destroyer escorts" and "frigates." As indicated below, during the war the Americans transferred a total of ninety-nine of these vessels to Great Britain's Royal Navy (seventy-eight destroyer escorts and twenty-one frigates); six destroyer escorts to the Free French naval forces, operating under British control; and eight destroyer escorts to Brazil.

The American destroyer escorts (DEs) were produced in six "classes" or types, five of them quite similar. The frigates (PFs) derived from the British River-class frigate were all of one class, the twin-screw City. In detail:

TYPE	NO. BUILT	NO. TRANSFERRED	DISPL.	LENGTH	MAX. SPEED
Evarts	97	32 to UK[1]	1,150	289	21
Edsall	85[2]		1,200	306	21
Cannon	71	14 to FF, BZ	1,240	306	21
Buckley	154[3]	46 to UK[4]	1,400	306	24
Rudderow	72[5]		1,450	306	24
J. C. Butler	94		1,350	306	24
City (PF)	98[6]	21 to UK[7]	1,430	304	20
Totals:	671	113 (99 to UK)			

Owing to President Roosevelt's decision to give higher priority to the construction of landing craft and merchant ships in 1942, the destroyer escort and frigate programs lagged seriously. The first destroyer escort, Baynton, which went to the Royal Navy, was not commissioned until January 20, 1943. Commencing in about April 1943, the rest of the DEs came along at a rate of about twenty per month from shipyards in California, Massachusetts, New Jersey, Pennsylvania, Texas, and Virginia. The frigates for the U.S. Navy came along in 1943 and 1944 from shipyards in California, Ohio, and Wisconsin. The twenty-one frigates for the Royal Navy were built in Providence, Rhode Island.

---

1. Designated R.N. Captain Class.
2. Twenty-eight were manned by Coast Guard crews.
3. Six were converted to U.S.N. fast transports (APDs).
4. Also designated R.N. Captain Class.
5. Thirty-three were converted to U.S.N. APDs.
6. Two, Asheville and Natchez, were built in Montreal, Canada (on a reverse Lend-Lease plan), for the U.S.N. and were delivered in 1942. The remaining seventy-five were manned by Coast Guard crews.
7. Designated R.N. Colony class.

APPENDIX 14

AMERICAN PATROL CRAFT-BUILDING PROGRAM IN WORLD WAR II

JANUARY 1, 1942 – JULY 1, 1942

The United States Maritime Commission built 417 patrol craft in World War II. These consisted of 354 175-foot PCs and sixty-three 180-foot PCEs. The Americans transferred forty-four PCs to other navies and fifteen PCEs to the Royal Navy, which designated the ships Kil class. As shown below, thirty-one PCs were completed in the first half of 1942, but owing to delays in fitting out and workup and diversions to schools, on July 1, 1942, the Eastern Sea Frontier had only seven PCs available for convoy escort.

PC HULL NUMBER	COMPLETED
451	Prewar
452	Prewar
457	Prewar
461	3/19/42
462	4/15/42
463	4/28/42
464	5/15/42
465	5/25/42
466	6/3/42
477	3/30/42
478	4/1/42
479	4/30/42
483	3/12/42
484	4/3/42
485	4/23/42
486	5/15/42
487	6/2/42
490	5/12/42
491	4/13/42
492	4/5/42
493	5/28/42
494	5/23/42
495	4/23/42
560	6/17/42
563	6/17/42
565	5/25/42
566	6/15/42
567	6/27/42
569	5/9/42
570	4/18/42
571	6/19/42
572	5/26/42
573	6/13/42
588	6/22/42

APPENDIX 15

OCEAN-ESCORT VESSELS LENT BY THE ROYAL NAVY TO THE U.S. NAVY

1942 – 1943 [1]

From the Royal Navy active list: 10 Flower-class single-screw corvettes (PEs), redesignated USN gunboats (PGs).

R.N. NAME	U.S.N. NAME	HULL #		TRANSFERRED
Veronica	Temptress	PG 62		3/21/42
Heliotrope	Surprise	PG 63		3/24/42
Hibiscus	Spry	PG 64		5/2/42 [2]
Arabis	Saucy	PG 65		4/30/42
Periwinkle	Restless	PG 66		4/30/42
Calendula	Ready	PG 67		3/12/42
Begonia	Impulse	PG 68		3/16/42
Larkspur	Fury	PG 69		3/17/42
Heartease	Courage	PG 70		3/18/42
Candytoft	Tenacity	PG 71		6/11/42

From Canadian shipyards: two R.N. River-class frigates (PF) and eight modified (twin-screw) Flower-class corvettes (PE), redesignated U.S.N. gunboats (PG).

Adur	Asheville	PF 1		12/1/42
Annan	Natchez	PF 2		12/16/42
Comfrey	Action	PG 86		11/22/42
Cornel	Alacrity	PG 87		12/10/42
Flax	Brisk	PG 89		12/6/42
Mandrake	Haste	PG 92	(U.S.C.G.)	4/6/43
Milfoil	Intensity	PG 93	(U.S.C.G.)	3/31/43
Musk	Might	PG 94		12/22/42
Nepeta	Pert	PG 95	(U.S.C.G.)	7/23/43
Privet	Prudent	PG 96	(U.S.C.G.)	8/16/43

---

1. Not including twenty-four coal-burning trawlers (APCs) in 1942. All vessels listed herein were returned to Great Britain after the war.
2. At Argentia, Newfoundland, on May 29, 1942, Spry caught fire and incurred severe damage. The fire spread to the Task Force 24 headquarters ship, the 16,500-ton destroyer tender Prairie, which also incurred "extensive" damage and was under repair for three months.

APPENDIX 16

EMPLOYMENT OF ATLANTIC FLEET DESTROYERS AS ESCORTS FOR TROOPSHIP[1] AND SPECIAL-CARGO CONVOYS AND FOR OTHER TASKS

November 1941– September 1942

The American destroyers of the Atlantic Fleet worked exhaustively in 1942 on special tasks. Chief among these was the escort of troopships transporting Allied forces overseas and cargo ships with high-priority combat gear, such as tanks and aircraft for the British in North Africa and elsewhere, and for the Soviet Union. In operations solely under American control, only one—repeat one—cargo ship was lost to enemy action and no—repeat no—troopships. These convoys and tasks in detail:

1. **WS 12X**   Halifax to Cape Town, Bombay, Singapore, etc. Six American troopships (with 20,000-plus British troops embarked). Sailed 11/10/41; arrived Cape Town 12/9/41. Escort (Task Group 14.4): Ranger, Quincy, Vincennes, Cimarron (tanker), and eight American destroyers: Mayrant, McDougal, Moffett. Rhind, Rowan, Trippe, Wainwright, Winslow.

2. **TC 16**   New York to Iceland and UK three troopships (2 aborted; net, 1 ship). Sailed 12/12/41; arrived 12/23/41. Escort (Task Force 19): Arkansas, Nashville and six American destroyers: Eberle, Ericsson, Hamilton, Ingraham, Livermore, Ludlow. Three British troopships joined from Halifax, making four ships total.

3. **TF 17**   Transfer from Atlantic Fleet to Pacific Fleet of carrier Yorktown, light cruisers Richmond and Trenton, and four modern (1939–1940) destroyers: Hughes, Russell, Sims, Walke. Yorktown sailed from Norfolk 12/16; left Panama Canal Zone 12/22.

4. **TFs**   Transfer from Atlantic Fleet to Pacific Fleet of the three older battleships Idaho, Mississippi, and New Mexico, and five modern (1939–1940) destroyers: Anderson, Hammann, Morris, Mustin, O'Brien. Shifts completed in January 1942.

5. **TG**   Transfer from Atlantic Fleet to Pacific Fleet of two more modern (1938) destroyers, Sampson and Warrington. Sailed from Newport 1/12; arrived Panama 1/17.

6. **AT 10**   New York to Iceland and Northern Ireland. Four troopships. Sailed 1/15/42, arrived Iceland 1/25; arrived Northern Ireland 1/27. Escort (Task Force 15): Texas, Quincy, Wasp and 13 American destroyers: Eberle, Grayson, Gwin, Livermore, Mayrant, Meredith, Monssen, Roe, Rowan, Stack, Sterett, Trippe, Wainwright.

7. **NA 1**   Halifax to UK. Two troopships. Sailed 1/10/42; arrived 1/18. Escort: three ex-American four-stack Canadian or British destroyers: Beverley, Hamilton, Rockingham.

8. **BT 200**   New York to Pacific. Eight troopships. Sailed 1/21; arrived Panama 1/31. Escort (Task Force 16): Vincennes; 14 American destroyers, destroyer transports, or destroyer minesweepers: Colhoun, C. F. Hughes, Gregory, Hamilton, H. P. Jones, Howard, Ingraham, Lansdale, Little, Ludlow, Manley, McKean, Palmer, Stringham. Hamilton collided with a merchant ship and aborted.

9. **BC 100**   Charleston, South Carolina, to Pacific. Six troopships. Sailed 1/23, joined convoy BT 200. Escort: see BT 200.

10. NA 2   Halifax to UK. Two troopships. Sailed 1/31, arrived 2/7. Escort: two British destroyers, ex-American four-stack Belmont and Firedrake. U-82 sank Belmont 1/31 in the western Atlantic.

11. NA 3   Halifax to UK. Two troopships. Sailed 2/11; arrived 2/19. Escort: two British destroyers, ex-American four-stack Montgomery and Garland.

12. AT 12   New York to Northern Ireland. Fifteen troopships. Sailed 2/19; arrived 3/4. Escort (Task Force 32): New York, Philadelphia, ten American destroyers: C. F. Hughes, H. P. Jones, Ingraham, Lansdale, Ludlow, Mayrant, Roe, Rowan, Trippe, Wainwright. From MOMP, six British destroyers: two ex-American four-stacks, Leamington and Newport, and Badsworth, Keppel, Lamerton, Watchman.

13. NA 4   Halifax to UK. Two troopships. Sailed 3/1, arrived 3/8. Escort: two ex-American four-stack British destroyers, Beverley, Rockingham.

14. BT 201 New York to Pacific. Seven troopships. Sailed 3/4; arrived Panama 3/12. Escort (Task Force 18): Nashville, Vincennes, Hornet. Nine American destroyers or destroyer transports: Dickerson, Ellyson, Grayson, Gwin, Manley, Meredith, Monssen, Stansbury, Sturtevant. Four modern destroyers, Grayson, Gwin, Meredith, and Monssen, transferred to the Pacific with Hornet.

15. AS 1   Special Supply. Charleston, S.C., to Ascension Island. Three ships. Sailed 3/14; arrived Ascension 3/31. Escort: Cincinnati, Memphis, and five American destroyers: Ellis, Greer, Jouett, Somers, and Winslow.

16. NA 5   Halifax to UK. Two troopships. Sailed 3/14; arrived 3/22. Escort: two new American destroyers, Nicholson and Swanson.

17. AS 2   Special Supply. Charleston, S.C., to Africa. Four ships and the "jeep" carrier H.M.S. Archer (in transit). Sailed 3/19; arrived Freetown 4/3. Escort: cruiser H.M.S. Devonshire and three American destroyers: Cole, Du Pont, Upshur.

18. NA 6   Halifax to UK. Two troopships. Sailed 3/21, arrived 3/28. Escort: ex-American four-stack Canadian destroyer St. Clair, British destroyer Witherington, and ex-American four-stack British destroyers Chesterfield and Churchill from WOMP.

19. TF 39   Portland, Maine, to Scapa Flow. Sailed 3/25; arrived 4/4. Renamed Task Force 99: Wasp, Washington, Wichita, Tuscaloosa, and six destroyers: Lang, Madison, Plunkett, Sterett, Wainwright, Wilson.

20. AT 14   New York to Argentia and Iceland. Five troopships. Sailed 4/7, arrived 4/18. Escort (Task Force 37): Philadelphia and ten American destroyers: Bernadou, Blue, Cole, Du Pont, Eberle, Ellis, Ericsson, Kearny, Lea, Livermore.

21. NA 7   Halifax to UK. Two troopships. Sailed 4/10, arrived 4/18. Joined convoy AT 14. Escort: see AT 14.

22. BT 202 New York and Norfolk to Pacific. Seventeen troopships. Sailed 4/10, arrived Panama 4/17. Escort (Task Force 38): Texas; Brooklyn and 11 American destroyers: C. F. Hughes, Dickerson, Ellyson, H. P. Jones, Ingraham, Lansdale, Mayrant, Rhind, Roe, Rowan, Trippe.

23. TF   To Argentia, commencing April 23 to counter a sortie of Tirpitz et al., New battleship North Carolina (later, new South Dakota), carrier Ranger (later Wasp), two heavy cruisers, a light cruiser, and "four or five destroyers."

24. TF   UK to Mediterranean, aircraft-ferry mission. Sailed 4/14. The carrier Wasp, two American destroyers, Lang and Madison, and four British destroyers. Flew off 47 Spitfires for Malta. Return: 4/26.

25. TF 36   Newport, R.I., to Accra, Ghana; aircraft-ferry mission. Sailed 4/22, arrived Accra 5/10 and flew off 68 P-40 aircraft. The carrier Ranger, Augusta, and five destroyers: Ellyson, Emmons, Hambleton, Macomb, Rodman. Ellyson and Hambleton incurred damage in a collision 5/17. TF returned to the States on 5/28; Ranger to Argentia temporarily.

26. TF 99   Scapa Flow to help Home Fleet escort Murmansk convoys PQ 15 and QP 11. Sailed 4/28. Washington, Wichita, Tuscaloosa, and four destroyers: Madison, Plunkett, Wain-

wright, Wilson. Returned to Scapa Flow 5/7. Madison and Plunkett returned to the States.

27. AT 15   New York to Argentia, Iceland, and, UK. Thirteen troopships. Sailed 4/30, arrived 5/12. Escort (Task Force 38): New York, Brooklyn, "jeep" carrier H.M.S. Avenger (in transit) and fourteen American destroyers: Buck, C. F. Hughes, H. P. Jones, Eberle, Edison, Ericsson, Ingraham, Lansdale, Mayrant, Nicholson, Rhind, Rowan, Swanson, Trippe. To Scapa Flow: Mayrant, Rhind, Rowan.

28. NA 8   Halifax to UK. Four troopships. Sailed 5/3, joined AT 15. Escort: see AT 15.

29. TF   UK to Mediterranean; aircraft-ferry mission. Sailed 5/5. Wasp, two American destroyers, Lang, Sterett, and two British destroyers. Flew off 47 Spitfires for Malta. Returned to Scapa Flow 5/15.

30. TF 99   Scapa Flow to help Home Fleet escort Murmansk convoys PQ 16 and PQ 12. Sailed 5/16. Washington, Tuscaloosa, and four destroyers: Mayrant, Rhind, Rowan, Wainwright. Returned to Scapa Flow 5/26.

31. NA 9   Halifax to UK. One troopship. Sailed 5/18, arrived 5/25. Escort: two new American destroyers, Buck and Bristol.

32. TF 38   Transfer of Wasp and three destroyers, Lang, Sterett, and Wilson, from Scapa Flow to the States on 5/18. Joined New York, Brooklyn, etc., of AT 15, returning from Iceland.

33. AS 3   Special Supply. Charleston, S.C., to Africa. Four ships. Sailed 5/28, arrived Freetown 6/13. Joined WS 19P. Escort (Task Force 34): Texas and four American destroyers: Bernadou, Cole, Dallas, Ludlow. Dallas aborted with engine problems.

34. AT 16   New York to UK. Four troopships. Sailed 5/31, arrived 6/9. Escort (Task Force 35): New York and eight American destroyers: Benson, Eberle, Ericsson, Gleaves, Kearny, Livermore, Mayo, Niblack.

35. NA 10   Halifax to UK. Two troopships. Sailed 6/3, joined AT 16. Escort: see AT 16.

36. TFs   Transfer from Atlantic Fleet to Pacific Fleet of new battleship North Carolina, carrier Wasp, "jeep" carrier Long Island, cruisers Quincy and San Juan, and seven destroyers: Buchanan, Farenholt, Lang, Monssen, Stack, Sterett, Wilson. Cleared the Panama Canal by 6/10/42.

37. NA 11   Halifax to UK. Four troopships. Sailed 6/16, arrived 6/23. Escort: three American destroyers: Eberle, Ericsson, Roe.

38. AT 17A   New York to Iceland and UK. Seven troopships. Sailed 7/1, arrived 7/13. Escort (Task Force 37): Texas, Philadelphia, and 14 American destroyers: Buck, Bristol, Edison, Emmons, Hambleton, Ingraham, Ludlow, Macomb, Nicholson, Rodman, Swanson, Trippe, Wilkes, Woolsey. To Scapa Flow: Emmons, Hambleton, Macomb, Rodman.

39. AT 17B   Halifax to UK. Two troopships. Sailed 7/5, joined AT 17A. Escort: see AT 17A.

40. TF 99   Scapa Flow to help Home Fleet escort Murmansk convoys PQ 17 and QP 13. Sailed 7/1. Washington, Tuscaloosa, Wichita, and four destroyers: Mayrant, Rhind, Rowan, Wainwright. Returned to Scapa Flow 7/10. Washington and these four destroyers returned to the States, leaving Tuscaloosa and four destroyers at Scapa Flow: Emmons, Hambleton, Macomb, Rodman.

41. TF 22   Newport, R.I., to Accra, Ghana; aircraft-ferry mission. Sailed 7/1. Arrived Accra 7/19 and flew off 72 P-40 aircraft. Ranger, Augusta, Juneau and six destroyers: Corry, Hobson, Fitch, Forrest, Livermore, Kearny. Returned to Norfolk 8/5.

42. AS 4   Special Supply. New York to Africa. Nine ships. Sailed 7/13, joined WS 21P. Escort: Omaha, Juneau, and seven American destroyers: Davis, Gleaves, Kearny, Livermore, Mayo, Somers, Wilkes. U-161 sank one merchant ship, Fairport, loaded with tank engines.

43. AS 5   Special Supply. New York to Africa. One troopship (Pasteur). Sailed 7/16, arrived 7/24. Escort (24 hours): American destroyer transport Stansbury.

44. AS 6   Special Supply. Charleston, S.C. to Ascension Island. Three ships. Sailed 7/26, arrived 8/14. Escort: Cincinatti, Winslow, and two American destroyers: Dallas, Ellis.

45. AT 18   New York to Iceland and UK. Thirteen troopships. Sailed 8/6, arrived 8/18. Escort (Task Force 38): Arkansas, Brooklyn, and 17 American destroyers: Benson, Eberle, Ericsson, Gleaves, C. F. Hughes, H. P. Jones, Kearny, Lansdale, Livermore, Madison, Mayo, Mayrant, Niblack, Nicholson, Plunkett, Rhind, Roper.

46. NA 14   Halifax to UK. Two troopships. Sailed 8/9, joined AT 18. Escort: see AT 18.[2]

47. TFs   Transfer from the Atlantic Fleet to the Pacific Fleet of new battleships South Dakota and Washington and six new destroyers: Barton, Duncan, Lansdowne, Lardner, Meade, Nicholas. Shift completed in 8/42.

48. AT 20   New York to Iceland and UK. Seven troopships. Sailed 8/19, arrived 8/31. Escort (Task Force 37): New York, Philadelphia, and 13 American destroyers: Buck, Bristol, Cole, Eberle, Edison, Ericsson, Ingraham, Ludlow, Nicholson, Roe, Swanson, Wilkes, Woolsey. Buck and Ingraham involved in separate collisions with merchant ships. Buck aborted; Ingraham sank.[3]

49. NA 15   Halifax to UK. Two troopships. Sailed 8/22, joined AT 20. Escort: see AT 20.

50. TF   Wichita, Hambleton, and Macomb transferred from Scapa Flow and Iceland to New York, 8/16 to 8/22.

51. TF   Scapa Flow to Kola Inlet to deliver special cargo and return stranded merchant marine crews. Sailed from Iceland 8/19. Tuscaloosa; two American destroyers, Emmons and Rodman; and three British destroyers. The American warships returned to the States in early September.

52. AT 23   New York to UK. Nine troopships. Sailed 9/26, arrived 10/7. Escort (Task Force 38): Arkansas and nine American destroyers: Benson, Gleaves, C. F. Hughes, H. P. Jones, Lansdale, Madison, Mayo, Niblack, Plunkett.

53. NA 16   Halifax to UK. Four troopships. Sailed 9/29, joined AT 23. Escort: see AT 23.

Commencing in October 1942, American troops embarked for the British Isles sailed the North Atlantic run on big liners, such as the Queen Mary, Queen Elizabeth, etc. A total of forty American destroyers worked up and participated in Torch, the Allied invasion of North Africa, on 11/8/42. From Torch onward, American troops embarked for North Africa sailed in heavily escorted troopship convoys on the "Southern Route," designated United States–Gibraltar (UG) and/or United States–Gibraltar Fast (UGF) and Slow (UGS).

---

1. Does not include large ocean liners, such as the Queen Elizabeth, Queen Mary, etc., sailing unescorted, or British-escorted troopship convoys in the eastern Atlantic, usually designated "Winston Special," or WS. The escorts listed sailed either part or all of the voyage or returned with aborting ships. Convoys returning to the Americas (TA, AN, etc.) are not shown either.

2. Convoy NA 13 did not employ American escorts. Details: Halifax to UK. Two troopships. Sailed 7/21, arrived 7/29. Escort: one ex-American four-stack Canadian destroyer, Annapolis, and three British destroyers, Amazon, Boadicea, Vanoc.

3. Convoy AT 19 consisted of the Queen Mary from Cape Town to the Clyde, 7/7 to 8/8. Convoy AT 21 consisted of the Queen Elizabeth, New York to the Clyde, 8/30 to 9/5. Convoy AT 22 consisted of the Queen Mary, New York to the Clyde, 9/5 to 9/11.

APPENDIX 17

ALLIED TANKER LOSSES TO AXIS SUBMARINES
IN THE ATLANTIC OCEAN AREA

SEPTEMBER 1939 – DECEMBER 1942

Throughout the war, a prime target of German U-boats was the combined Allied tanker fleet, which was engaged in the vital task of transporting crude oil and petroleum products to the United States East Coast, to Canada, and to the British Isles.

At the beginning of the war, September 1939, the individual tanker fleets of the non-Axis nations were of substantial size:

NATION(S)	TANKERS	TONNAGE (G.R.T.)
British Empire	453	3,200,000
Norway	268	2,107,000
Holland	107	539,000
France & other		
European countries	133	876,000
U.S.A. & Panama	430	3,224,000
Other American	54	216,000
Totals:[1]	1,445	10,162,000

In the period from 9/1/39 to 12/31/42, British and American shipyards completed 176 new tankers for 1,754,000 gross registered tons.

YEAR	U.S.A.		BRITISH EMPIRE	
	SHIPS	G.R.T.	SHIPS	G.R.T.
1939	11	120,000		
1940	16	149,000	3	31,000
1941	27	258,000	27	271,000
1942	61	613,000	31	312,000
Totals:[2]	115	1,140,000	61	614,000

In the first twenty-eight months of the war—up to the Japanese attack on Pearl Harbor—Axis submarines sank 117 tankers for 936,777 gross registered tons. During this period (as shown) shipyards in the British Empire and the United States completed eighty-four new tankers for about 829,000 G.R.T. Thus the loss of non-Axis tanker tonnage to Axis submarines in the Atlantic area in this period was nearly matched by Allied new tanker construction. Although London feared—and often predicted—dire oil shortages in the British Isles during this period, none ever really occurred. Hardships and inconveniences, such as civilian gasoline and fuel-oil rationing, resulted not solely from actual tanker losses, but rather from the drastic slowdown of oil imports due to convoying and, of course, to the diversion of oil imports to war-making purposes. Losses in detail:

ALLIED TANKER LOSSES IN THE ATLANTIC AREA

9/1/39 to 12/31/41

DATE	SHIP	REGISTRY	G.R.TONS	AREA/CONVOY	U-BOAT
1939 (12)					
9/8	Regent Tiger	British	10,176	E. Atlan.	U-29
9/8	Kennebec	British	5,548	E. Atlan.	U-34
9/11	Inverliffey	British	9,456	E. Atlan.	U-38
9/14	British Influence	British	8,431	E. Atlan.	U-29
9/15	Cheyenne	British	8,825	E. Atlan.	U-53
10/12	Emile Miguet	France	14,115	E. Atlan.	U-48
10/17	Deodata	Norway	3,295	E. Atlan.	U-19(M)[3]
11/12	Arne Kjöde	Norway	11,019	E. Atlan.	U-41
11/17	Sliedrecht	Dutch	5,133	E. Atlan.	U-28
11/26	G. E. Reuter	Swede	6,336	E. Atlan.	U-48
12/6	Britta	Norway	6,214	E. Atlan.	U-47
12/9	San Alberto	British	7,397	E. Atlan.	U-48
1940 (53)					
1/10	El Oso	British	7,267	HX 14B	U-30(M)
1/12	Danmark	Danish	10,517	North Sea	U-23
1/16	Inverdargle	British	9,456	E. Atlan.	U-33(M)
1/20	Caroni River	British	7,807	E. Atlan.	U-34(M)
1/30	Vaclite	British	5,026	E. Atlan.	U-55
2/2	Creofield	British	838	North Sea	U-59
2/13	C. Maersk	Danish	5,177	E. Atlan.	U-25
2/14	Gretafield	British	10,191	North Sea	U-57
2/15	Den Haag	Dutch	8,971	E. Atlan.	U-48
2/22	Br. Endeavor	British	4,580	Gib.	U-50
2/25	Daghestan	British	5,742	North Sea	U-57
4/10	Sveaborg	Swede	9,076	E. Atlan.	U-37
5/1	San Tiburcio	British	5,995	North Sea	U-9 (M)
5/29	Telena	British	7,406	Gib.	U-37
6/15	Italia	Norway	9,973	HX 48	U-38
6/20	Moerdrecht	Dutch	7,493	HX 49	U-48
6/21	Yarraville	British	8,627	Gib.	U-43
6/21	San Fernando	British	13,056	HX 49	U-47
6/22	Eli Knudsen	Norway	9,026	HX 49	U-32
6/25	Saranac	British	12,049	E. Atlan.	U-51
6/27	Leticia	Dutch	2,580	E. Atlan.	U-47
7/2	Athellaird	British	8,999	Biscay	U-29
7/7	Lucretia	Dutch	2,584	E. Atlan.	U-34
7/14	Sarita	Norway	5,824	Freetown	U-A
7/16	Scottish Minstrel	British	6,998	HX 55	U-61
7/27	Thiara	British	10,364	E. Atlan.	U-34
8/12	British Fame	British	8,406	OB 193	Malaspina
8/15	Sylvafield	British	5,709	HX 62	U-51
8/24	La Brea	British	6,665	HX 65	U-48
8/25	Athelcrest	British	6,825	HX 65A	U-48
8/25	Pecten	British	7,468	HX 65	U-57
9/20	New Sevilla	British	13,801	OB 216	U-138
9/21	Invershannon	British	9,154	HX 72	U-99
9/21	Torinia	British	10,364	HX 72	U-100
9/22	Frederick S. Fales	British	10,525	HX 72	U-100
9/26	Stratford	British	4,753	E. Atlan.	U-137
10/6	Nina Borthen	Norway	6,123	Atlantic	U-103
10/6	British General	British	6,989	Atlantic	U-37
10/12	Davanger	Norway	7,102	HX 77	U-48

10/17	Languedoc	British	9,512	SC 7	U-48
10/19	Shirak	British	6,023	HX 79	U-48
10/20	Caprella	British	8,230	HX 79	U-100
10/20	Sitala	British	6,218	HX 79	U-100
10/20	Janus	Swede	9,965	HX 79	U-46
11/5	Scottish Maiden	British	6,993	HX 83	U-99
11/15	Havbör	Norway	7,614	Freetown	U-65
11/18	Congonian	British	5,056	Freetown	U-65
12/1	Appalachee	British	8,826	HX 90	U-101
12/2	Conch	British	8,376	HX 90	U-95, U-47, U-99
12/2	Victor Ross	British	12,247	OB 251	U-43
12/19	Rhone	Vichy Fr.	2,785	Gib.	U-37
12/21	C. Pratt	Panama	8,982	Freetown	U-65
12/24	British Premier	British	5,872	Freetown	U-65

1941 (52)

1/29	W. B. Walker	British	10,468	SC 19	U-93
2/13	A. F. Corwin	British	10,516	HX 106	U-96, U-103
2/13	Clea	British	8,074	HX 106	U-96
2/17	E. R. Brown	British	10,455	HX 107	U-103
2/22	Scottish Standard	British	6,999	OB 287	U-96
2/24	British Gunner	British	6,894	OB 289	U-97
3/1	Cadillac	British	12,062	HX 109	U-552
3/7	Terje Viken	British	20,638	OB 293	U-99
3/7	Athelbeach	British	6,568	OB 293	U-99
3/16	Ferm	Norway	6,593	HX 112	U-99
3/16	Beduin	Norway	8,136	HX 112	U-99
3/16	Venetia	British	5,728	HX 112	U-99
3/23	Chama	British	8,077	E.Atlan.	U-97
3/31	Castor	Swede	8,714	Atlantic	U-46
4/2	British Reliance	British	7,000	SC 26	U-46
4/3	British Viscount	British	6,895	SC 26	U-73
4/4	Conus	British	8,132	Atlantic	U-97
4/6	Lincoln Ellsworth	Norway	5,580	Atlantic	U-94
4/9	Duffield	British	8,516	Azores	U-107
4/28	Oilfield	British	8,516	HX 121	U-96
4/28	Caledonia	Norway	9,892	HX 121	U-96
5/2	Capulet	British	8,190	HX 121	U-552, U-201
5/6	Sangro	prize, ex-Ital.	6,466	E. Atlan.	U-97
5/9	Alfred Olsen	Norway	8,817	Freetown	Tazzoli
5/17	Marisa	Dutch	8,029	Freetown	U-107
5/20	British Security	British	8,470	HX 126	U-556
5/20	J. P. Pedersen	Norway	6,128	HX 126	U-94
5/21	Elusa	Dutch	6,235	HX 126	U-93
5/22	British Grenadier	British	6,857	Freetown	U-103
5/30	Cairndale	British	8,129	Gib.	Marconi
6/3	Inversuir	British	9,456	Atlantic	U-48
6/5	Wellfield	British	6,054	Atlantic	U-48
6/8	Ensis	British	6,207	Atlantic	U-46
6/8	Pendrecht	Dutch	10,746	OB 328	U-48
6/12	Ranella	Dutch	5,590	OG 64	U-553
6/28	Auris	British	8,030	Gib.	DaVinci
7/21	Ida Knudsen	Norway	8,913	Gib.	Torelli
7/26	Horn Shell	British	8,272	Azores	Barbarigo
8/19	Sildra	Norway	7,313	Freetown	Tazzoli

9/11	Bulysses	British	7,519	SC 42	U-82
9/20	T. J. Williams	British	8,212	SC 44	U-552
9/20	Barbro	Norway	6,325	SC 44	U-552
9/26	I. C. White	Panama	7,052	Brazil	U-66
10/1	San Florentino	British	12,842	ON 19	U-94
10/17	W. C. Teagle	British	9,552	SC 48	U-558
10/17	Erviken	Norway	6,595	SC 48	U-558
10/17	Barfonn	Norway	9,739	SC 48	U-432
10/19	Inverlee	British	9,158	Gib.	U-204
10/20	British Mariner	British	6,996	Freetown	U-126
10/22	Darkdale	British	8,145	St. Helena	U-68
12/2	Astral	USA	11,900	Azores	U-43
12/31	Cardita	British	8,237	E. Atlan.	U-87

TOTAL SHIPS LOST		GROSS TONS LOST
British Empire	76	628,110
Norway	20	150,221
Dutch	9	57,361
Other Non-Axis[4]	12	101,085
Totals:	117	936,777

Many historians and popular writers assert that in 1942, when the Germans launched Drumbeat, the U-boat attack on shipping in American waters, Allied tanker losses "on the United States East Coast" were simply horrific. Furthermore, some British historians stress that most of these tankers were of British registry or of Norwegian and Dutch registry under British charter. Neither statement is true.

In the first six months of 1942, the Germans sank forty-three Allied tankers in United States East Coast waters. Of these, thirty-two (about 75 percent) were of United States or Panamanian registry. Only nine were of British, Norwegian, or Dutch registry. No Allied tankers whatsoever were sunk by U-boats in East Coast waters in the second half of 1942.

In detail:

ALLIED TANKER LOSSES ON THE U.S. EASTERN SEABOARD (43)

1/1/42 TO 12/31/42

DATE	SHIP	REGISTRY	G.R.TONS	AREA	U-BOAT
1/14	Norness	Panama	9,577	New York	U-123
1/15	Coimbra	British	6,768	New York	U-123
1/18	Allan Jackson	USA	6,635	Hatteras	U-66
1/21	Alexander Höegh	Norway	8,248	Maine	U-130
1/22	Olympic	Panama	5,335	Hatteras	U-130
1/24	Empire Gem	British	8,139	Hatteras	U-66
1/25	Varanger	Norway	9,305	New Jersey	U-130
1/27	Francis E. Powell	USA	7,096	Maryland	U-130
1/30	Rochester	USA	6,836	Virginia	U-106
2/2	W. L. Steed	USA	6,182	Maryland	U-103
2/5	Indian Arrow	USA	8,327	Maryland	U-103
2/5	China Arrow	USA	8,403	Maryland	U-103
2/19	Pan Massachusetts	USA	8,202	Florida	U-128
2/22	Republic	USA	5,287	Florida	U-504
2/22	Cities Ser. Empire	USA	8,103	Florida	U-128
2/23	W. D. Anderson	USA	10,227	Florida	U-504
2/26	Mamura	Dutch	8,245	Florida	U-504
2/28	R. P. Resor	USA	7,451	New Jersey	U-578

3/10	Gulftrade	USA	6,676	New Jersey	U-588
3/13	John D. Gill	USA	11,641	N. Carolina	U-158
3/15	Ario	USA	6,952	N. Carolina	U-158
3/16	Australia	USA	11,628	Hatteras	U-332
3/17	San Demetrio	British	8,073	Virginia	U-404
3/17	Ranja	Norway	6,355	Georgia	U-71
3/18	E. M. Clark	USA	9,647	Hatteras	U-124
3/19	Papoose	USA	5,939	N. Carolina	U-124
3/19	W. E. Hutton	USA	7,076	N. Carolina	U-124
3/21	Esso Nashville	USA	7,934	N. Carolina	U-124[5]
3/23	Naeco	USA	5,373	N. Carolina	U-124
3/26	Dixie Arrow	USA	8,046	Hatteras	U-71
4/1	Tiger	USA	5,992	Hatteras	U-754
4/5	Byron T. Benson	USA	7,953	Hatteras	U-552
4/7	British Splendour	British	7,138	Hatteras	U-552
4/9	Atlas	USA	7,137	N. Carolina	U-552
4/10	Tamaulipas	USA	6,943	N. Carolina	U-552
4/10	San Delfino	British	8,072	Hatteras	U-203
4/11	Gulfamerica	USA	8,081	Florida	U-123
4/30	Ashkabad	USSR	5,284	N. Carolina	U-402
5/6	Halsey	USA	7,088	Florida	U-333
5/9	Lubrafol	Panama	7,138	Florida	U-564
5/14	Potrero del Llano	Mexico	4,000	Florida	U-564
5/25	Persephone	Panama	8,426	New Jersey	U-593
6/28	William Rockefeller	USA	14,054	Hatteras	U-701

TOTAL SHIPS LOST		GROSS TONS LOST
USA	28[6]	220,909
British	5	38,190
Norway	3	23,908
Panama	4	30,476
Dutch	1	8,245
Other Allied	2[7]	9,284
Totals:	43	331,012

This was not by any means the whole story of Allied tanker losses in 1942. Axis submarines sank more than twice as many tankers in the Gulf of Mexico, the Caribbean Sea, and in the western Atlantic near Trinidad: 99 vessels for 742,571 tons. In detail:

ALLIED TANKER LOSSES IN THE GULF OF MEXICO, CARIBBEAN SEA, AND TRINIDAD AREAS (99)

1/1/42 TO 12/31/42

DATE	SHIP	REGISTRY	G.R. TONS	AREA	U-BOAT
2/16	Oranjestad	British	2,396	Aruba	U-156
2/16	Tia Juana	British	2,395	Aruba	U-502
2/16	Monagas	Venezuela	2,650	Aruba	U-502
2/16	San Nicolas	British	2,391	Aruba	U-502
2/21	J. N. Pew	USA	9,033	Aruba	U-67
2/21	Circe Shell	British	8,207	Trinidad	U-161
2/22	Kongsgaard	Norway	9,467	Aruba	U-502
2/23	Thalia	Panama	8,329	Aruba	U-502
2/25	La Carriere	British	5,685	P. Rico	U-156
2/25	Esso Copenhagen	Panama	9,245	W. Atlan.	Torelli

2/28	Oregon	USA	7,017	W. Atlan.	U-156
3/5	O. A. Knudsen	Norway	11,007	Bahamas	U-128
3/6	Melpomene	British	7,011	W. Atlan.	Finzi
3/7	Uniwaleco	Canada	9,755	Trinidad	U-161
3/9	Hanseat	Panama	8,241	Wind. Psg.	U-126
3/10	Charles Racine	Norway	9,957	W. Atlan.	Finzi
3/14	Penelope	Panama	8,436	P. Rico	U-67
3/15	Athelqueen	British	8,780	W. Atlan.	Tazzoli
3/16	Oscilla	Dutch	6,341	W. Atlan.	Morosini
3/23	Peder Bogen	British	9,741	W. Atlan.	Morosini
3/31	T. C. McCobb	USA	7,452	W. Atlan.	Calvi
4/4	Comol Rico	USA	5,034	W. Atlan.	U-154
4/5	Catahoula	USA	5,053	W. Atlan.	U-154
4/8	Eugene V. R. Thayer	USA	7,138	Brazil	Calvi
4/12	Ben Brush	Panama	7,691	Brazil	Calvi
4/13	Empire Amethyst	British	8,032	Aruba	U-154
4/16	Amsterdam	Dutch	7,329	Trinidad	U-66
4/17	H. von Riedemann	Panama	11,020	Trinidad	U-66
4/29	Harry G. Seidel	Panama	10,354	Trinidad	U-66
4/30	Athelempress	British	8,941	W. Atlan.	U-162
4/30	Federal	USA	2,881	Wind. Psg.	U-507
5/2	Sandar	Norway	7,624	Trinidad	U-66
5/5	Munger T. Ball	USA	5,104	Gulf Mex.	U-507
5/5	Joseph M. Cudahy	USA	6,950	Gulf Mex.	U-507
5/9	Calgarolite	Canada	11,941	Cayman	U-125
5/12	Lise	Norway	6,826	Aruba	U-69
5/12	Virginia	USA	10,731	Gulf Mex.	U-507
5/13	Esso Houston	USA	7,699	W. Atlan.	U-162
5/13	Gulfpenn	USA	8,862	Gulf Mex.	U-506
5/14	British Colony	British	6,917	W. Atlan.	U-162
5/14	David McKelvy	USA	6,821	Gulf Mex.	U-506
5/17	San Victorio	British	8,136	Trinidad	U-155
5/17	Gulfoil	USA	5,189	Gulf Mex.	U-506
5/18	Beth	British	6,852	W. Atlan.	U-162
5/18	Mercury Sun	USA	8,893	Wind. Psg.	U-125
5/20	Halo	USA	6,986	Gulf Mex.	U-506
5/20	Sylvan Arrow	Panama	7,797	Trinidad	U-155
5/21	Faja de Oro	Mexico	6,067	Gulf Mex.	U-106
5/23	Sam Q. Brown	USA	6,625	Yucatan	U-103
5/26	Carabulle	USA	5,030	Gulf Mex.	U-106
5/27	Hamlet	Norway	6,578	Gulf Mex.	U-753
5/28	New Jersey	USA	6,414	Cayman	U-103
6/3	Höegh Giant	Norway	10,990	Lat. Amer.	U-126
6/3	M. F. Elliott	USA	6,940	Trinidad	U-502
6/5	L. J. Drake	USA	6,693	P. Rico	U-68
6/6	C. O. Stillman	Panama	13,006	P. Rico	U-68
6/8	South Africa	Norway	9,234	W. Atlan.	U-128
6/9	Franklin K. Lane	USA	6,589	Trinidad	U-502
6/11	Hagan	USA	6,401	Wind. Psg.	U-157
6/11	Sheherazade	Panama	13,467	Gulf Mex.	U-158
6/12	Cities Serv. Toledo	USA	8,192	Gulf Mex.	U-158
6/15	Frimaire	Portugal	9,242	Aruba	U-68
6/17	Moira	Norway	1,560	Gulf Mex.	U-158
6/18	Motorex	USA	1,958	Panama	U-172
6/22	E. J. Sadler	USA	9,639	P. Rico	U-159
6/23	Rawleigh Warner	USA	3,664	Gulf Mex.	U-67
6/23	Andrea Brövig	Norway	10,173	Trinidad	U-128
6/23	Arriaga	Panama	2,469	Aruba	U-68
6/27	Tuxpan	Mexico	7,008	Gulf Mex.	U-129
6/27	Leiv Eiriksson	Norway	9,952	Trinidad	U-126

6/27	Las Choapas	Mexico	2,005	Gulf Mex.	U-129
6/29	Empire Mica	British	8,032	Gulf Mex.	U-67
7/4	Tuapse	USSR	6,320	Yucatan	U-129
7/8	J. A. Moffett, Jr.	USA	9,788	Gulf Mex.	U-571
7/10	Benjamin Brewster	USA	5,950	Gulf Mex.	U-67
7/11	Stanvac Palembang	Panama	10,013	Trinidad	U-203
7/13	R. W. Gallagher	USA	7,989	Gulf Mex.	U-67
7/16	Beaconlight	Panama	6,926	Trinidad	U-160
7/21	Donovania	British	8,149	Trinidad	U-160
8/3	Tricula	British	6,221	W. Atlan.	U-108
8/6	Havsten	Norway	6,161	W. Atlan.	Tazzoli[8]
8/9	San Emiliano	British	8,071	Lat. Am.	U-155
8/13	R. M. Parker, Jr.	USA	6,779	Gulf Mex.	U-171
8/14	Empire Corporal	British	6,972	Wind. Psg.	U-598
8/17	Louisiana	USA	8,587	Lat. Am.	U-108
8/19	British Consul	British	6,940	Trinidad	U-564
8/26	Thelma	Norway	8,297	Atlantic	U-162
8/27	San Fabian	British	13,031	Wind. Psg.	U-511
8/27	Rotterdam	Dutch	8,968	Wind. Psg.	U-511
8/30	Vardaas	Norway	8,176	W. Atlan.	U-564
8/31	Winamac	British	8,621	W. Atlan.	U-66
9/4	Amatlan	Mexican	6,511	Gulf Mex.	U-171
9/12	Stanvac Melbourne	Panama	10,013	Trinidad	U-515
9/12	Woensdrecht	Dutch	4,668	Trinidad	U-515
9/13	Vilja	Norway	6,672	Trinidad	U-558
11/3	Thorshavet	British	11,015	Trinidad	U-160
11/3	Leda	Panama	8,546	Trinidad	U-160
11/5	Meton	USA	7,027	Trinidad	U-129
11/5	Astrell	Norway	7,595	Trinidad	U-129

TOTAL SHIPS LOST		GROSS TONS LOST
USA	33	225,108
British	22	162,536
Norway	16	130,269
Panama	15	135,553
Dutch	4	27,306
Other	9[9]	61,499
Totals:	99	742,271

From the foregoing two lists, it can be seen that the total loss of Allied tankers to Axis submarines in "American waters" in 1942 was 142 ships for 1,073,283 gross registered tons. The total tanker losses in these areas by registry:

SHIPS		GROSS TONS
USA	61	446,017
British	27	200,726
Norway	19	154,177
Panama	19	166,029
Dutch	5	35,551
Other	11	70,783
Totals:	142	1,073,283

From this tabulation it can be seen that British tanker losses in "American waters" in 1942 were not nearly so heavy as often depicted in British accounts. Altogether Axis submarines sank twenty-seven British-registered tankers, fewer than the loss of British-registered tankers to Axis submarines in 1940 (36) and 1941 (33). Axis submarines also sank twenty-four Norwegian and Dutch tankers, presumed to be under British charter, bringing the total loss of "British-controlled" tankers in "American waters" in 1942 to fifty-one. American and Panamanian losses totaled eighty vessels.

To complete this analysis it is necessary to take into account Allied tankers sunk in 1942 by Axis submarines in areas of the Atlantic other than "American waters." These losses reflect the resumption of U-boat attacks on the North Atlantic convoys in the late summer and the fall of 1942, some of which are described in the text of Volume II. In this third and last category, Axis submarines sank another 71 tankers for 594,222 gross registered tons.

The losses in this category in detail:

ALLIED TANKER LOSSES IN OTHER WATERS (71)

1/1/42 TO 12/31/42

DATE	SHIP	REGISTRY	G.R. TONS	AREA/ CONVOY	U-BOAT
1/15	Diala	British	8,106	ON 52	U-553
1/17	Nyholt	Norway	8,087	ON 52	U-87
1/22	Inneröy	Norway	8,260	W. Atlan.	U-553
1/22	Athelcrown	British	11,990	W. Atlan.	U-82
1/23	Leiesten	Norway	6,118	ON 56	U-82
1/26	Pan Norway	Norway	9,231	Atlantic	U-123
1/31	San Arcadio	British	7,419	W. Atlan.	U-107
2/5	Montrolite	Canada	11,309	W. Atlan.	U-109
2/11	Victolite	Canada	11,410	W. Atlan.	U-564
2/22	Kars	British	8,888	W. Atlan.	U-96
2/22	Adellen	British	7,984	ON 67	U-155
2/24	Inverarder	British	5,578	ON 67	U-558
2/24	Empire Celt	British	8,032	ON 67	U-162, U-158
2/24	Anadara	British	8,009	ON 67	U-558
2/24	Finnanger	British	9,551	ON 67	U-558
2/24	Eidanger	Norway	9,432	ON 67	U-558
3/6	Sydhav	Norway	7,587	Freetown	U-505
3/14	British Resource	British	7,209	W. Atlan.	U-124
3/22	Muskogee	USA	7,034	W. Atlan.	U-123
3/23	British Prudence	British	8,620	W. Atlan.	U-754
3/24	Empire Steel	British	8,138	W. Atlan.	U-123
3/25	Ocana	Dutch	6,256	W. Atlan.	U-552
3/25	Narragansett	British	10,389	W. Atlan.	U-105
3/27	Svenör	Norway	7,616	W. Atlan.	U-105
3/31	San Gerardo	British	12,915	W. Atlan.	U-71
4/6	Koll	Norway	10,044	W. Atlan.	U-571
4/6	Kollskegg	Norway	9,858	W. Atlan.	U-754
4/12	Esso Boston	USA	7,699	Atlantic	U-130
4/29	Mobiloil	USA	9,925	W. Atlan.	U-108
5/3	British Workman	British	6,994	Canada	U-455
5/20	Darina	British	8,113	ON 93	U-158
5/20	Norland	Norway	8,134	ON 93	U-108
5/21	Montenol	British	2,646	Azores	U-159
5/27	Athelknight	British	8,940	W. Atlan.	U-172
5/31	Dinsdale	British	8,214	S. Atlan.	Cappellini
6/11	George H. Jones	British	6,914	W. Biscay	U-455
6/15	Slemdal	Norway	7,374	W. Biscay	U-552
7/15	British Yeoman	British	6,990	Gib.	U-201
7/25	Tankexpress	Norway	10,095	Freetown	U-130
8/5	Arletta	British	4,870	Canada	U-458
8/7	Arthur W. Sewall	Norway	6,030	Freetown	U-109
8/9	Malmanger	Norway	7,078	Freetown	U-130
8/11	Mirlo	Norway	7,455	Freetown	U-130

8/11	Vimeira	British	5,728	Freetown	U-109
8/31	Jack Carnes	USA	10,907	Azores	U-516
9/10	Sveve	Norway	6,313	ON 127	U-96
9/10	Empire Oil	British	8,029	ON 127	U-659,U-584
9/12	Hektoria	British	13,797	ON 127	U-211,U-608
9/12	Daghild	Norway	9,272	ON 127	U-404,U-608
9/12	P. J. Hurley	USA	10,865	Atlantic	U-512
9/23	Athelsultan	British	8,882	SC 100	U-617
9/23	Esso Williamsburg	USA	11,237	Atlantic	U-211
10/3	R. H. Colley	USA	11,651	HX 209	U-254
10/14	Southern Empress	British	12,398	SC 104	U-221
10/22	Donax	British	8,036	ON 139	U-443
10/27	Anglo Maersk	British	7,705	SL 125	U-604
10/27	Sourabaya	British	10,107	HX 212	U-436
10/27	Gurney E.Newlin	USA	8,225	HX 212	U-436,U-606
10/27	Kosmos II	Norway	16,966	HX 212	U-606,U-624
10/29	Pan New York	USA	7,701	HX 212	U-624
10/29	Bullmouth	British	7,519	Azores	U-409, U-659
11/3	Hahira	USA	6,855	SC 107	U-521
11/4	Hobbema	Dutch	5,507	SC 107	U-129
11/10	Cerinthus	British	3,878	Freetown	U-128
11/18	President Sergent	British	5,344	ONS 144	U-624
11/23	Caddo	USA	10,172	Atlantic	U-518
11/28	Brilliant	USA	9,132	SC 109	U-43
12/8	Empire Spencer	British	8,194	HX 217	U-524
12/16	Bello	Norway	6,125	ON 153	U-610
12/20	Otina	British	6,217	ON 153	U-621
12/29	Pres. Francqui	Belgian	4,919	ONS 154	U-225,U-336

TOTAL SHIPS LOST		GROSS TONS LOST
USA	12	111,403
British	35	282,343
Norway	19	161,075
Dutch	2	11,763
Other	3 [10]	27,638
Totals:	71	594,222

When the foregoing three tabulations of Allied tanker losses to Axis submarines in 1942 are combined, the result is a total of 213 vessels of 1,667,505 gross registered tons. The loss of United States–registered tankers actually exceeded those of the British in 1942 by eleven vessels. Viz.:

SHIPS		GROSS TONS
USA	73	557,420
Panama	19	166,029
British	62	483,069
Norway	38	315,252
Dutch	7	47,314
Other	14	98,421
Totals:	213	1,667,505

During this period, 1942, Allied shipyards (as shown) completed ninety-two tankers [11] for 925,000 tons. Thus in 1942, tanker losses to Axis submarines exceeded new tanker completions by 121 ships for 742,505 gross tons. This deficit left the combined Allied tanker fleet on January 1, 1943, at 1,291 ships for 9,311,718 tons, a net loss to Axis submarines of 154 tankers for 850,282 gross registered tons since the beginning of the war, or about 10 percent of the fleet.

This deficit was more than offset by the spectacular tanker gains over losses in 1943. That year, American and British shipyards completed 245 new tankers for 2,031,000 gross registered tons. Meanwhile, in 1943, Axis submarines sank only forty-eight Allied tankers for 373,138 gross tons. Hence, the net gain over all losses was forty-three tankers for 805,304 gross registered tons. On January 1, 1944, the combined Allied tanker fleet numbered about 1,488 vessels for about 10,969,580 gross tons, slightly more than in September 1939.

From this analysis it can be seen that while the U-boat campaign against the combined Allied tanker fleet caused great hardships and inconveniences, it failed to achieve a decisive strategic success. The only really serious Allied setback occurred in 1942, but this was quickly overcome in 1943. To recapitulate, the numbers at a glance:

	SHIPS	GROSS TONS
Non-Axis tanker fleet 9/39:	1,445	10,162,000
New construction 9/39 to 12/42:	176	1,754,000
Total vessels 9/39 to 12/42:	1,621	11,916,000
Losses 9/39 to 12/41:	(117)	(936,777)
Losses 1/42 to 12/42:	(213)	(1,667,505)
Total losses 9/39 to 12/42:	(330)	(2,604,282)
Non-Axis tanker fleet 1/43:	1,291	9,311,718
New construction 1/43 to 1/44:	245	2,031,000
Losses 1/43 to 1/44:	(48)	(373,138)
Non-Axis tanker fleet 1/44:	1,488	10,969,580

1. Appendix IV, "Tanker Statistics," p. 243 in Payton-Smith, *Oil.*

2. Fischer, *Statistical Summary,* pp. 40-43; Hancock, *Statistical Digest,* p. 135.

3. (M) = losses to mines planted by U-boats.

4. Four Swedes, two Danes, two Panamanians, one Vichy French (in error), one Free French, one American (Astral), one prize.

5. When torpedoed, the ship broke in half. The Navy and Coast Guard salvaged the stern, fitted on a new bow, and returned the ship to service.

6. In addition, the 9,300-ton F. W. Abrams hit an American mine on 6/11 at Cape Lookout and sank.

7. One Russian, one Mexican.

8. After damage by U-160.

9. Four Mexican, two Canadian, one Venezuelan, one USSR, one Portuguese (neutral).

10. Two Canadian, one Belgian.

11. Sixty-one in American yards, thirty-one in British yards.

APPENDIX 18

ALLIED AND NEUTRAL SHIPS AND TONNAGE SUNK BY GERMAN AND ITALIAN SUBMARINES IN WORLD WAR II

SEPTEMBER 3, 1939–AUGUST 31, 1942[1]

	1939		1940		1941		1942	
January			(53)	163,029	(23)	129,711	(56)	301,224
Febuary			(50)	182,369	(47)	254,118	(72)	429,255
March			(26)	69,826	(41)	236,549	(93)	507,514
April			(6)	30,927	(41)	239,719	(81)	418,161
May			(14)	61,635	(63)	362,268	(129)	616,835
June			(66)	375,069	(66)	325,817	(136)	636,926
July			(41)	201,975	(26)	112,624	(96)	467,051
August			(56)	288,180	(27)	85,603	(117)	587,245
September	(48)	178,621	(60)	288,585	(57)	212,237		
October	(33)	156,156	(66)	363,267	(28)	170,786		
November	(27)	72,721	(36)	181,695	(15)	76,056		
December	(39)	101,823	(46)	256,310	(23)	93,226		
Totals:	(147)	509,321	(520)	2,462,867	(457)	2,298,714	(780)	3,964,211

Total 1939–1941:	(1,124)	5,270,902
Total 1942 (8 months):	(780)	3,964,211
Grand Totals:	(1,904)	9,235,113

---

1. Source: Tarrant (1989). Number of ships lost in parentheses; tonnage is GRT. Note: Losses include ships in convoy or alone and those that fell victim to submarine-laid mines. Comparable Admiralty loss figures to Axis submarines do not include victims of submarine-laid mines.

ACKNOWLEDGMENTS
AND SOURCES

This history is based on nine years of continuous research in archives and published works. For the German side, it relies heavily on the daily war diaries of German naval headquarters in Berlin and U-boat headquarters at various locations, and on the war diaries (or patrol reports) of individual U-boats. For the Allied side, it relies heavily on after-action reports from convoys and from warships and aircraft that tangled with U-boats, and on interrogation reports of captured German and Italian submariners.

The war diaries of the various U-boat commands, amounting to thousands of pages (most translated into English), are immensely detailed. They include sailing and return dates and daily positions (known and assumed) of all U-boats on patrol; names, composition, and action of groups ("wolf packs"); sightings, chases, and sinking of Allied ships; battle damage or mechanical breakdowns incurred; information regarding offensive and defensive weapons; and assessments of strategy and tactics by Karl Dönitz or others. Using these diaries and confirmed Allied ship losses to U-boats as compiled by others, intelligence derived from the German naval Enigma, and data from other sources, including individual U-boat war diaries, it has been possible to recreate almost all significant features of the patrols of virtually all the U-boats.

The published sources vary widely in authenticity, reliability, and literary quality. Those of greatest merit include the official and semiofficial Allied war histories, and all the writings of the esteemed German professor Jürgen Rowher, as well as Günther Hessler and Karl Dönitz. Also of special note are the works of British authors Geoffrey Patrick Jones and Norman L. R. Franks, who have diligently probed official British archives to record specific U-boat kills by British air and naval forces. For equally competent and reliable research of this type, the American authors Philip Lundeberg, William T. Y'Blood, and Max Schoenfeld and the Canadians W.A.B. Douglas, Michael L. Hadley, and Marc Milner should not go unmentioned.

Herr Horst Bredow, director of the impressive *Stiftung Traditionsarchive Unterseeboote* in Cuxhaven, Germany, provided much general help and background and specific documents of great value. One is an updated list (in booklet form) of all German U-boats built in World War II. The data for each boat include type, place of construction, dates of launching, commissioning, and assignment to battlefront flotilla (or schools, etc.), skippers and dates they commanded, and final fate of boat and crew. The other document is a compilation of Allied warships and merchant ships that were sunk by each U-boat, broken down by skippers of those individual U-boats.

Many other persons assisted us in our research, and we are deeply grateful. We would especially like to thank Marcia Carr, Joan's brother, Charles H. ("Ham") Rutledge, and Frederic Sherman. Marcia, the chief librarian of the Washington Island Library, obtained for us literally hundreds of books and periodicals (some of them quite obscure) through the Wisconsin Interlibrary Loan system. Ham Rutledge, a professional computer expert, created a special program to compile the index and nursed Joan through countless PC complications and challenges. Purely as a favor, our dear friend Fred, a retired newspaper editor, copyedited the entire manuscript.

The massive research collected in the preparation of this work, including thousands of pages of documents and microfilm and microfiche, has been deposited with our other papers at the American Heritage Center, University of Wyoming, in Laramie. We invite serious researchers to make use of this collection.

BIBLIOGRAPHY

The bibliography for *Hitler's U-boat War*, containing over one thousand entries, will be published in Volume II in the fall of 1997. In the meantime, it may be viewed on or downloaded from the following Random House website:

http://www.randomhouse.com/uboat/biblio.html

INDEX

This index has three parts: Ships, U-boats, and General. It was compiled by my wife, Joan Blair, and her brother, C. Hamilton Rutledge, who created the software. For technical details consult Hamilton's home page on the Internet:

http://ourworld.compuserv.com/homepages/hamrut

Please note that ships listed in the appendices are *not* indexed.

SHIPS

U-BOATS

GENERAL

ABOUT THE AUTHOR

CLAY BLAIR served in combat on a submarine in the Pacific, attended Tulane and Columbia universities, and became the national security correspondent for *Time, Life,* and the *Saturday Evening Post* magazines in Washington, then editor in chief of the *Saturday Evening Post.* He has published hundreds of magazine articles and twenty-four books. These include biographies of Admiral H. G. Rickover; Generals Douglas MacArthur, Omar N. Bradley, and Matthew B. Ridgeway; and John F. Kennedy; and, most recently, a definitive account of the conflict in Korea, *The Forgotten War.* He lives with his wife on Washington Island, Wisconsin.

ABOUT THE TYPE

This book was set in Times Roman, designed by Stanley Morison specifically for *The Times* of London. The typeface was introduced in the newspaper in 1932. Times Roman has had its greatest success in the United States as a book and commercial typeface, rather than one used in newspapers.